Landmark Debates in Congress

Landmark Debates in Congress

From the Declaration of Independence to the
War in Iraq

Stephen W. Stathis

CQ PRESS

A Division of SAGE
Washington, D.C.

CQ Press
2300 N Street, NW, Suite 800
Washington, DC 20037

Phone: 202-729-1900; toll-free, 1-866-4CQ-PRESS (1-866-427-7737)

Web: www.cqpress.com

Cover design: Auburn Associates, Inc.
Cover photos: The Granger Collection, New York (top); AP Images: Sen. John W. Warner (bottom left) and Sen. Carl Levin (bottom right)
Composition: Auburn Associates, Inc.

∞ The paper used in this publication exceeds the requirements of the American National Standard for Information Sciences—Permanence of Paper for Printed Library Materials, ANSI Z39.48-1992.

Printed and bound in the United States of America

12 11 10 09 08   1 2 3 4 5

Library of Congress Cataloging-in-Publication Data

Stathis, Stephen W.
    Landmark debates in Congress : from the Declaration of independence to the war in Iraq / Stephen W. Stathis.
        p. cm.
    Includes bibliographical references and index.
    ISBN 978-0-87289-976-6 (hardback : alk. paper) 1. United States—Politics and government. 2. United States—Politics and government—Sources. 3. Speeches, addresses, etc., American. 4. Speeches, addresses, etc., American—History and criticism. 5. United States. Congress—History 6. Parliamentary practice—United States—History. 7. Legislation—United States—History. I. Title.

    JK31.S73 2008
    328.73′02—dc22

                                                                      2008041380

To Douglas D. Alder, Stanford Cazier, Milton R. Merrill, and William R. Tansill,
teachers extraordinaire

Contents

Contents

Contents

Preface

Landmark Debates in Congress presents and analyzes pivotal congressional debates that reflect the mood of the country as it evolved from thirteen colonies with a population of 2.5 million in 1776 to a nation of more than 300 million in fifty states in 2008. This rhetorical collection does not, in every instance, represent the finest in public speaking, logic, purpose, or commitment, nor does it always show Congress at a deliberative pinnacle.

Some of the selections rightly could be considered prejudiced, partisan, self-serving, parochial, and occasionally verging on the absurd. Others provide lively, political exchanges that momentarily captured national attention and interest before largely fading from public memory. Of course, there are also those that represent the finest in political persuasion and imagination. As a body, these exchanges exemplify the essence of the American democratic struggle, starting in Philadelphia more than two centuries ago, to frame a government that would provide a forum where all can be heard.

Selections are not included for some momentous issues—such as the Louisiana Purchase, contentious Supreme Court nomination of Louis Brandeis, and the first Gulf War—because essentially there was no memorable congressional debate accompanying their consideration.

A number of the topics considered in this volume—including the House Gag Rule, McCarthyism, and Medicare and Medicaid—span several Congresses. These exchanges seemingly support a commonly held belief that national legislators move slowly and indecisively, but the lesson to be drawn from these debates, and many of the others included in this compilation, is that reaching a consensus is often extremely challenging given the divergent membership of the House and the Senate and the disparate constituencies they represent.

What we learn from the words of debates recorded in the *Annals of Congress,* the *Congressional Globe,* the *Congressional Record,* and other congressional sources is that opinions are always in abundance. Realistically, a significant portion of the views expressed may have been shared by particular segments of the American population while not representative of the nation as a whole. The opinions illuminate the challenge facing each member of Congress who sincerely seeks to repre-

sent his or her constituency, and his or her own conscience. The pages that follow are filled with arguments that may have touched the souls of those who heard them, but did not sway their opinions or votes.

The speeches included in this collection could not be reproduced in their entirety or *Landmark Debates in Congress* would be a much larger work. Four asterisks, denoted in the design as four stars, indicate breaks in the debates that encompass more than a sentence or two; these may reflect omitted paragraphs or entire sections of speeches. With such a wealth of information to choose from, selecting the passages to include was challenging.

Landmark Debates in Congress was conceived as a window into how Congress, seemingly constituting a cross-section of society, has wrestled with some of the most thorny questions facing American democracy. Often neither the attending debate nor the resulting decision ultimately received the acclaim of the people. Several debates, particularly those touching on civil rights, civil liberties, and congressional-executive relations, illustrate obvious concerns about why the nation's legislators often have to return to issues they seemingly resolved earlier.

An amazing volume of literature, as the accompanying bibliographical selections exemplify, has been devoted to capturing the ebbs and flows of American democracy as it has been shaped and molded by Congress. Much of the literature examined in writing *Landmark Debates in Congress* offers thoughtful and far-reaching insights into the thinking of the time. Without these splendid works, preparing this volume would have been a far more challenging. The exceptional contributions of those who have devoted their professional careers to helping us better understand the weighty issues considered in this volume should not be overlooked.

Landmark Debates in Congress also benefited enormously from the insightful and thoughtful suggestions of a significant number of colleagues at the Library of Congress and the Congressional Research Service. The historical perspectives of Richard Beth, Louis Fisher, Jane Gravelle, Michael Koempel, Barbara Miles, Dick Nanto, Thomas Neale, Walter Oleszek, Harold Relyea, Paul Rundquist, and Denis Steven Rutkus were especially helpful. Particular appreciation is extended to the John W. Kluge Center at the Library of Congress, under the directorship of Carolyn T. Brown, who selected me to be the Library Kluge Staff fellow for fiscal year 2007. Although my year at the Kluge Center was spent working on a history of Congress, the foundation laid for that work proved indispensable in completing this volume.

It is with sincere appreciation that I acknowledge the enthusiastic encouragement of CQ Press acquisitions editor Doug Goldenberg-Hart, development editor Nancy Matuszak, copy editor Larry Baker, and production editor Belinda Josey, without whom this volume would not have been brought to completion.

Deep expressions of gratitude are due to my wife, Barbara Stathis, and our daughter, Jennifer Mathis, both of whom read and proofed the text in its entirety, and offered numerous beneficial editorial suggestions. Their love, support, and patience cannot adequately be expressed in words.

Looking back on my nearly four decades as a historian rekindles fond memories of many who set aside their own pursuits to graciously and generously share their wisdom with me. Foremost among those mentors have been Douglas D. Alder, Stanford Cazier, Milton R. Merrill, and William R. Tansill. They breathed into their students a thirst for understanding history and politics that could never possibly be quenched. They enthusiastically sought to develop a heightened level of confidence and curiosity within others that befits the dedication of this volume in their honor.

Stephen W. Stathis

Introduction

Presenting a collection of landmark congressional debates spanning the entirety of the American experience is particularly relevant given the frequent, but mistaken, expression by scholars and the media that debate in our national legislature is no longer substantive or important. Debate is a critical ingredient of our deliberative democracy. Although the term *deliberation* has recently been used in various ways, here it implies a collective decision-making process. It is difficult to conceive of such a process as being collective except by basing it on a continual exchange of ideas. The popular American concept of such deliberation is that this give-and-take should, during its final stages, take place on the House and Senate floors. In practice, however, many of these discussions occur off the floor, in less formal encounters in committees, corridors, and offices.

This does not mean, however, that congressional floor debates are irrelevant to the deliberative process. As long as the considerations that underlie the actual decisions are argued, articulated, and expressed during floor debate, they illuminate the actual deliberative process, even if they no longer constitute it. Under conditions where floor debate is at the heart of the deliberative process, one may expect debate to exhibit more often the heights of oratorical device. When floor debate reflects the deliberative process, rather than embodying it, oratorical style may not be as inspiring, but it still serves to enlighten the audience about the real rationale of the decision undertaken.

Landmark Debates in Congress documents more than fifty of the nation's most pivotal congressional debates. These debates were selected because of their historical significance, lucid delineation of important national issues, significant insights on particular questions and periods, argumentative force and rhetorical brilliance, and originality. The topics addressed are as varied as the nation itself. While some debates characterized as landmark have become obscured or been forgotten, at the time of their delivery, the speakers were responding to a perceived need for action or restraint. Their rhetoric represented a significant departure from previous policy, a creative response to an emergency, or a solution to a longstanding national concern. The fact that such issues are debated in the United States dramatizes one of the most important characteristics of the nation's democracy — domestic as well as foreign policy issues are thrashed out in public, laws are enacted, and decisions are reached with the nation watching.

DELIBERATIVE INTENT

Half a century ago, historian Lynn Montross, in *The Reluctant Rebels,* characterized the Continental Congress as "perhaps the only parliament on earth to make a practice of deliberating before breakfast. From six in the morning until ten at night the delegates kept their noses to the grindstone." While they "were debating independence, planning confederation, publishing memorable state papers, conferring on strategy and seeking foreign alliances," they were also minutely involved in a military effort that ultimately resulted in victory against the British at Yorktown, Virginia.[1] They thought seriously and deeply about the problems of government, and they understood that society is complex and that answers to important questions are rarely simple or easy.

During a 1775 debate in the British House of Lords on the conflict between the United States and Great Britain, William Pitt, the earl of Chatham, eloquently captured the Continental Congress members' commitment to being a truly deliberative body. In his famous tribute, Pitt said that he had "studied and admired the master states of the world" and "that for solidity of reason, force of sagacity, and wisdom of conclusion ... no nation, or body of men, can stand in preference to the general congress at Philadelphia."[2] The prophetic character of Pitt's observation was borne out in the debates that produced the four greatest documents of this revolutionary assembly — the Articles of Association (1774), the Declaration of Independence (1776), the Articles of Confederation (1777–1781), and the Northwest Ordinance (1787).

The same deliberative tenacity was exhibited during the summer of 1787, when the delegates to the Constitutional Convention met for sixteen-and-a-half weeks in Philadelphia to mold and shape for a democratic government a charter that has endured more than two centuries. Their success required astuteness and a tolerant willingness to find workable compromises among conflicting views. The Framers, political scientist Clinton Rossiter has observed, "were heroes who stayed within the limits of the political, social, economic, and cultural circumstances of their time, heroes who seemed to know instinctively just how far to push their luck in choosing among alternatives that were to be found with these limits." They also remained alert to the spectrum of possibilities and restraints of their positions and the time. "[T]hey made ... virtually no decision that did not run with the grain of American development."[3]

When a copy of the new Constitution reached ambassador John Adams in London, the future president captured the importance of the moment with the following words: "the deliberate union of so great and various a people in such a place is, without partiality or prejudice, if not the greatest exertion of human understanding, the greatest single effort of national deliberation that the world has ever seen."[4]

At the outset, success may have seemed improbable. Men with widely divergent views on how to correct the inadequacies of the Articles of Confederation and to preserve the Union waged the great debates of 1787. If they were to have any hope of achieving this goal, the delegates recognized, very early in their deliberations, a need to be able to speak openly; they thus agreed to bar non-delegates from their meetings, to keep all discussions confidential, and to maintain no record of the proceedings. Fortunately, James Madison violated this last injunction and kept careful notes of the debates, which, after his death, were published by congressional authority. Most important, the delegates took steps to assure that the procedures for their meetings would promote meaningful and productive thinking, rather than contentious arguments.

After all but three of the delegates present on Monday, September 17, 1787, affixed their signatures to an engrossed copy of the Constitution, it still had to be submitted to state conventions for ratification. Among the most significant of the state debates was the one in New York. Alexander Hamilton, James Madison, and John Jay, in an effort to rally support for New York's ratification of the Constitution, wrote eighty-six essays under the pseudonym "Publius." *The Federalist* is today regarded as the single most authoritative source on the political thought of the supporters of the Constitution. *The Federalist* tells readers that the framers believed democracy would be successful if lawmaking reflected "the cool and deliberate sense of the community." During the ratification struggle, Publius maintained that government must moderate, restrain, or even block unwise or unjust popular demands, and that "it is the duty of the persons whom [the people] have appointed to be the guardians of [their] interests, to withstand the temporary delusion, in order to give them time and opportunity for more cool and sedate reflection."[5]

By this means, the government could "suspend the blow meditated by the people against themselves, until reason, justice, and truth can regain their authority over the public mind," and "refine and enlarge the public views." Publius reasoned that the more often a "measure is brought under examination, the greater the diversity in the situations of those who are to examine it, the less must be the danger of those errors which flow from want of due deliberation."[6]

The challenge confronting the framers was to devise a democratic system that would encourage fair consideration of the diverse interests of the entire nation. In *The Federalist,* these interests were variously described as "the public good," "the good of the whole," "the public weal," "great and national objects," "the great and aggregate interests," "the national prosperity and happiness," "the great interests of the nation," "the common interest," "the common good of the society," and "the comprehensive interests of [the] country." The framers recognized that genuine deliberation would often be slow, frustrating, and contentious. Their design for deliberative democracy was a response to the governmental inadequacies and what some perceived to be the democratic excesses of the 1780s, which had prompted the Constitutional Convention.[7]

The democracy fashioned at the Constitutional Convention was founded on the belief that the sense of the nation would emerge through its elected representatives who typically were more knowledgeable and experienced in public affairs and more interested in being involved in politics. In exchange, deliberative democracy demands "that the representatives of the people share the basic values and goals of their constituents; their own deliberations about public policy must be firmly rooted in popular interests and inclinations."[8]

Following the ratification of the Constitution, George Washington was unanimously elected the new nation's first president, and the new government was launched. Many problems, however, remained to be solved, and the debate over those issues began in earnest when the First Congress convened in 1789. That process has continued unabated for more than two centuries as new and different concerns continue to emerge and old questions reappear in different forms. As a means of ensuring that free and open debate would continue, the framers stipulated in the Constitution that senators and representatives "shall not be questioned in any other Place...for any Speech or Debate in either House."[9] Neither house has since placed restraints on the content of congressional speeches other than to institute rules that prohibit remarks that reflect personally on other members. Violations of decorum, however, have included offensive epithets, hecklers in the galleries, and, on occasion, freestyle brawls, particularly during much of the nineteenth century.

The institutional structure of government designed by the framers established a constitutional framework of checks and balances, separation of powers, and bicameralism. These three factors, they felt, would make legislative action more deliberative, and deliberation, over time, would come to be regarded as one of the fundamental ingredients of America's constitutional system.

PURPOSE OF DEBATE

From the outset, members of Congress have faced three seemingly conflicting goals. They have been expected to: (1) represent the views of their local constituencies while simultaneously developing national policies, (2) protect the rights of the minority while fostering majority rule in resolving conflicts, and (3) reach decisions that address the needs of the country only after flexible, wise, and careful deliberation.[10]

The delegates to the Continental Congress, as well as the framers of the Constitution, firmly established the practice of legislators deliberating and debating with each other over how best to resolve the various challenges facing the nation. Benjamin Franklin, who helped write both the Declaration of Independence and the Constitution, told the delegates at the Constitutional Convention that they were there "to *consult*, not to *contend*, with each other, and Declaration of a fix'd opinion, and of determined Resolutions never to change it, neither enlighten nor convince us."[11] Much later, Rep. James A. Garfield (R-Ohio) would characterize Congress as "the forum where the opposing forces of political philosophy meet to measure their strength" and register national will.[12]

For more than two centuries, Congress has continued to be a stage where the great issues of the day are considered and debated. "For, while the right to talk may be the beginning of freedom," Walter Lippman once observed, "the necessity of listening is what makes the right important."[13] Congress has been the stage for some of the nation's most celebrated oratory. It has also served as the platform for less gracious speeches that have emphasized the shortcomings of its members and those of the American people.

Frequently, the results of these debates were compromises that a dedicated minority was able to achieve by effectively tempering the original goal of the majority. One of the most dramatic and historically important of these moments was the failure of an overwhelming and determined radical majority in Congress to impeach President Andrew Johnson and remove him from office in 1868.

The decisions developed from congressional debates have implications that are framed by rules and procedures that attempt to balance the arguments for those in favor and those against a particular position. Although congressional debates do not always represent significant differences between the parties, media accounts tend to portray them in those terms. Such thinking is reinforced by the physical layout of the House and Senate chambers where the majority sits on one side and the minority on the other.[14]

CONGRESSIONAL DEBATE PRIOR TO THE CIVIL WAR

During the high point in its oratory, which lasted until the Civil War, Congress boasted a constellation of exceptional speakers, including such notables as John Quincy Adams, Fisher Ames, Thomas Hart Benton, John C. Calhoun, Henry Clay, Stephen A. Douglas, Robert Y. Hayne, James Madison, John Randolph, William H. Seward, Charles Sumner, and Daniel Webster. Initially, the House primarily functioned as the forum for debate on major issues of national importance. During Congress's first three decades, skilled extemporaneous speakers in the House dominated congressional oratory. Not until the Senate, which kept its doors closed until 1795, modified its rules to allow for more spontaneous exchanges, did senators begin to regularly command attention.

The oratorical shift began with the debate over the Compromise of 1820. Over the next forty years, the Senate "produced the most concentrated outpouring of political eloquence in the nation's history." The "leading actors in these debates … saw their speeches not just as instruments of political action but as artistic creations in the tradition of the great orations of antiquity." Senate speeches were often reprinted in newspapers and magazines. Once reprinted, they generated great discussion in the press on both their subject matter and rhetorical style.[15]

Prior to the Civil War, a number of great political and governmental questions occupied the thoughts of the nation. It was a "time of making and revising state constitutions, of differing interpretations of the federal Constitution, and of extension of the franchise to many who had not participated in the democratic process." The fundamental differences between the South's agrarian economy and the North's emerging industrialism heightened conflicts over already difficult issues, including trade tariffs, territorial expansion in the West, and slavery. The result was a series of "'great debates' in Congress," designed "to intensify and give felicitous expression to feelings already held, rather than to advance new arguments, change opinions, or solve problems." They focused on great constitutional questions that demanded "utilitarian, purposive, practical" oratory.[16]

These great speeches, historian Daniel Boorstin has observed, "seemed almost to displace legislation as the main form of political action." They "possessed a popular power, a historical significance, and a symbolic meaning difficult for us to understand."[17]

The power of those delivering great speeches flowed not only from their ability to captivate an audience, an anonymous author wrote in 1874, "but also in having a receptive, impressionable people to listen to them. Naturally, there must have been that sympathetic relation between the listener and the speaker which enabled the one to work up the other to a white heat, as a blacksmith does his iron, to be made malleable and shaped according to his will." The author speculated that this impressionableness arose from the nation's youth. As the nation grew older, the hold of the orator on the people grew weaker. The prevailing feeling of the period "was like a dry, thirsting, August prairie, requiring only the fire of the orator to set it in a blaze."[18]

THE NATION'S PRIORITIES CHANGE

The material prosperity that followed the Civil War changed that feeling. No longer was the nation "a tinder to set ablaze by the speech of orators." Nor was the country in its early, impressionable years. Soon patriotic exhortation "degenerated into the diffusive ardent harangue of the stump. Everything that sound[ed] like an appeal to conscience or patriotism [was] rejected as buncombe: for there [was] little of one or the other in public life and such rejection [was] logical." [19]

As the nation continued its transformation, new issues became important and priorities shifted. National attention focused on developing the continent, from exploiting its natural resources and building up its industry to constructing railroads and establishing business empires. These opportunities generated great enterprise, invention, and fortune. Against this backdrop, the importance and stature of public officials diminished as did the nature and quality of their utterances. Although vital issues accompanied the industrialization and urbanization of the United States, members of Congress as well as other politicians avoided unpleasant social issues as the nation's principal preoccupation became the accumulation of wealth. [20]

Writing in 1910, House minority leader Champ Clark (D-Mo.) reasoned, however, that there had been a decline in oratory among lawyers and the clergy, not just on Capitol Hill. Clark believed the ebbing of oratory was "chiefly due to the general diffusion of knowledge. As a rule the more information a man has the less emotional he is, and the orator's appeal was to the emotions far more than to the understanding." He attributed the "principal causes of the decadence of oratory" to "the telegraph, the printing press, the telephone, the steam-engine, and the electric car." People, he proffered, had become too busy and preferred straightforward information to oratory. [21]

Others contend that since President Theodore Roosevelt transformed the White House into a "bully pulpit" early in the twentieth century, the country has looked to the White House instead of Capitol Hill for solace in times of national crisis. Unlike the pre–Civil War years when congressional debates often captured the nation's attention, the news now emanating from Capitol Hill most often focuses on corruption, scandals, or veiled efforts to gain power quickly. [22]

CONGRESS UNDERGOES INTERNAL CHANGES

Congressional oratory changed over time for all of these reasons, but also because the House and Senate gradually began to develop widely differing views on extended debate. In the late 1850s, both the House and Senate moved to larger, less intimate, chambers to accommodate rapidly increasing memberships that resulted from the dramatic growth of the nation. Between 1790 and 1860, the census recorded an increase of 27.6 million people (3.9 million to 31.5 million), and Congress admitted twenty new states to the Union. Over the same period, the number of Senate seats more than doubled 26–66 and the number of House seats nearly quadrupled, 64–237. By 1900, there were 88 senators and 357 representatives. This growth in membership was accompanied by an astronomical increase in bills being introduced (from 144 bills in the 1st Congress to 20,893 in the 56th), and a marked upturn in the number of complex issues being considered. [23] The sheer volume of work gradually moved Congress in the direction of precluding extended debate on most bills. Faced with the dilemma of how to deal with an ever increasing workload within a limited timeframe, the two chambers over time embraced disparate views regarding extended debate.

The House developed a complex system of parliamentary devices designed to ensure that the chamber's majority would not be impeded in working its will. Ultimately, the growth in membership led to the adoption of a rule limiting debate on amendments as well as member's use of parliamentary maneuvers that would delay or postpone floor action. Although the Senate experienced the same increase in time pressures, it was unable to develop a similar set of parliamentary devices for limiting delaying tactics because of its rules. Unlike those of the House, Senate rules remain permanently in effect unless the chamber affirmatively acts to change them. Beginning in the latter part of the nineteenth century, the Senate became increasingly susceptible to delaying tactics, and filibusters became more frequent and disruptive. [24] In 1917, the Senate adopted the cloture rule to make it possible to cut off debate, but debate actually remained relatively unfettered because a two-thirds vote was required to invoke cloture. (Since 1975, a three-fifths vote, or 60 senators, has been required.)

The persuasiveness of members suffered, as Congress — particularly the House — became more and more "rigidly curtailed by stringent rules, time" and lack of patience. The "vigorous and persuasive forceful exchange of ideas and opinions" that had earlier characterized congressional proceedings became gradually a "unique blend of formal argumentation and group discussion." [25]

Also, the stage for congressional deliberation slowly shifted from the House and Senate chambers to the committee or subcommittee rooms. There, information was gathered and alternatives examined, and legislation was drafted and refined. The shape of legislation was less frequently determined by speech-making either on the House or Senate floors because it most often had already been formulated, debated, and finalized in committee. When votes were changed, it was most often the consequence of debate on amendments that alter, modify, or transform a bill, resolution, or action, and make it more acceptable and palatable. [26]

At least Bruce Hopkins has gone so far as to credit development of the committee system as the "cardinal arbiter of controversy," thereby leading to the decline in floor debate.[27]

Building upon that theme, other writers have given special attention to the increasingly important role committee hearings have assumed since 1900. For more than a century, committee hearings were the exception rather than the rule. In the twentieth century, however, committees did not generally report a major bill without a hearing. Committee hearings have become indispensable in an attempt to secure passage of legislation. They often laid the foundation for subsequent committee decisions, floor action, and conclusions reached following enactment. Also, over the years, there has been increased reliance on party caucuses to ensure that recalcitrant members are in agreement with the party position. [28]

Radio and television's effect on the changing nature of the debates on Capitol Hill is of much more recent vintage. The first resolution calling for the radio transmission of congressional debate occurred in 1922; twenty-six years later, television was allowed to cover investigating committee hearings. Early in the 1950s, large viewing audiences watched televised hearings of two investigations: one on organized crime, led by Sen. Estes Kefauver (D-Tenn.), and another on alleged communist infiltration of the U.S. armed services, led by Sen. Joseph R. McCarthy (R-Wis.). More than two decades passed before televised hearings again so thoroughly captured the attention of Americans: these were the Senate hearings during the summer of 1973 on the Watergate scandal and House impeachment proceedings against President Richard M. Nixon in July 1974. More recently, the 1987 Iran-Contra hearings and the confirmation hearings of Supreme Court nominees Robert Bork (1987) and Clarence Thomas (1991) attracted extended television coverage.

The House, however, did not allow its floor proceedings to be broadcast by radio until 1978 or by television until the following year. The Senate allowed both starting in 1986. The presence of the electronic media has not appreciably changed chamber proceedings. Television has, however, increased the public's exposure to the legislative process as well as the broad spectrum of issues and perspectives Congress considers.[29] Also, the content of debate has become more closely adapted to the presence of the national citizen audience through such devices as party-orchestrated "messages" and "talking points."

According to Sen. Robert C. Byrd (D-W.Va.), radio and television have "made possible a more intimate style of speaking, using a softer voice, more formal mannerism, and less emphatic gestures than were appropriate in addressing large groups, as the speaker became a 'guest' in the family living room." Before there were live broadcasts from the House and Senate floors, members used the broadcasting media "in campaigns and public forums" elsewhere, but legislative speeches were "aimed at readers of the *Congressional Record*

and at reporters" in the galleries, who might transmit them to their news organizations.[30]

Regardless of where congressional decision making takes place, a majority must ultimately approve most decisions on the House and Senate floors. There, each member has an equal vote and one last opportunity to discuss the merits of legislation before it is passed. House rules emphasize debate, where members with opposing views express their perspectives and opinions. Senate procedure places far greater emphasis on a less structured approach that examines the various options identified, developed, and discussed. While the House and Senate are very different legislative institutions, House and Senate floor proceedings continue to be "important arenas of policymaking."[31]

WHY CONGRESS STILL DEBATES

Historian Henry Steele Commager suggested that perhaps the most important questions about public debates, such as those conducted on Capitol Hill, are as follows: What is the virtue of a public debate? "What purposes are served, what interests are advanced, what conclusions are reached by such debates? Have our great congressional debates actually contributed anything to the solution of the problems being discussed? Have they done more than provide the public with entertainment and the debaters with publicity?" Commager notes that every important issue since the nation's founding has been "fought out in Congress." While it is certainly "not clear that in every instance the conclusions reached were the right ones," the value of the debates lies in their being part of the democratic process. "First, such debate serves to clarify issues. Second, it serves to educate public opinion. Third, it makes possible that reconciliation of conflicting groups and policies, that compromise, without which democracy cannot work."[32]

The principal dissatisfaction with Congress, another author has pointed out, "stems from the belief that Congress is *not* the truly deliberative institution it was designed to be and that effective modern democracy requires." That dissatisfaction, however,

> is rarely, if ever, articulated in this way. Instead we complain that Congress functions too slowly or too fast, that it gives too much power to committee chairmen or too little, that it is understaffed or overstaffed, that it is too responsive to outside interests or not sufficiently attentive to their needs, that it has delegated away its constitutional responsibilities or oversteps its bounds by interfering with the functions properly belonging to the executive branch.[33]

Congress is far more deliberative than most people realize. The mistake most observers make is in relying on floor debates as a key consideration. Congressional deliberation actually begins with the drafting of legislation by a small group of individuals seeking to address a perceived problem. Next, congressional hearings are held, where the important questions relating to the controversy are aired and witnesses often provide detailed explanations and clarifications of the issues to be considered. While a committee goes about its work, other like-minded members join together to deliberate over how best to present their position, and individual members who become substantive experts on a particular set of issues begin to use their knowledge as a means for gaining power and influence over the debate. As this process unfolds, "something like genuine debate evolves on most controversial proposals." Although the number of senators and representatives has remained fixed for nearly half a century, members willing to speak out on issues has significantly increased.[34]

The "notion that [congressional] oratory has declined since the days of Webster, Calhoun, and Clay, is erroneous," or at least it was in the mind of Sen. Henry Cabot Lodge Sr. (R-Mass.) when he wrote about debate standards in 1897. According to Lodge, those men, "particularly Webster, were exceptional rather than representative." Lodge surmised that the average quality of oratory in congressional debates while he was in the Senate was, in fact, "probably higher than ever before," but far too few people bother to follow them.[35]

Often forgotten is that the speeches of Webster, Clay, and Calhoun were actually delivered to a small group of fellow legislators and a few others within the sound of their voices. Former representative and senator Henry L. Dawes (R-Mass.) reminded readers of *The Forum* in 1894 that the public was kept waiting for long periods of time "before it could read and weigh" the "great arguments, the fame of which, as described by those who had listened to it, had spread far and wide." Only their extraordinary character preserved them for the country and coming generations. The stenographer, the telegraph, the daily press, radio, and television have brought the nation and the world onto the floor of the House and Senate, "to be moved by [a member's] words or to cast them out if unworthy." Members now not only need to be concerned about the impression they might have on the few in their chamber, but must also consider the effect of their remarks "upon those beyond the narrow circle of actual vision who will at their leisure critically weigh each word."[36]

While history clearly shows that there has been a decline in vigorous debate and eloquent speeches on the floor of the House and Senate, it does not support a contention that monumental issues are not still being debated by Congress. That is the story told by *Landmark Debates in Congress*. Those who proclaim the demise of congressional debate ignore a rich history of congressional rhetoric that continues today, as it has since 1774. While neither the House nor Senate chambers may again experience the oratorical power of earlier periods on a regular basis, the issues being debated still warrant attention and reflection.

To dismiss congressional debates since the Civil War is to disregard as inconsequential the monumental forensics that preceded such prominent enactments as the Seventeenth Amendment (popular election of senators), the Federal Reserve Act, Prohibition (Eighteenth and Twenty-First Amendments, 1917 and 1933), Women's Suffrage (1919), the Smoot-Hawley Tariff (1930), the Fair Labor Standards Act (1938), and the Lend-Lease Act (1941).

How much less would citizens understand about their legislative process if they did not take time to ponder the stirring oratory accompanying the House revolt against Speaker Joseph G. Cannon (R-Ill., 1910), the rejection of the Treaty of Paris and League of Nations (1919–1920), the Senate's refusal to confirm Supreme Court nominee John J. Parker (1930), or its defeat of President Franklin D. Roosevelt's court-packing plan (1937)?

Or should the congressional rhetoric of the Cold War, which prompted renewed public interest in the activities of Congress, be ignored? Most prominent among those exchanges were the actions of Sen. Joseph R. McCarthy. Subsequent decades produced historic discussions relating to the Civil Rights Acts of 1957 and 1964, the Voting Rights Act of 1965, Watergate (1972–1974), the War Powers Resolution (1973), the Panama Canal Treaties (1978), the Supreme Court nomination of Robert Bork (1987), the North American Free Trade Agreement (1993), and the Iraq War Resolution (2002), all of which the media reported in detail and the American people followed with great interest.

While some may argue that other debates should have been included and chosen selections omitted, the legislative exchanges comprising *Landmark Debates in Congress* were determined to be those oratorical moments most representative of the insightful give and take that the framers envisioned. The debates vividly illuminate the extremely important role Congress has assumed in shaping the political and historical fabric of the American republic. For good or bad, the selections provide graphic snapshots of where the United States has been as a nation, the issues that have stirred the souls of its people, and the political positions that have been challenged along the way. It is not a story about being in harmony or agreement. Rather, the lessons learned from recapturing their essence is that the more one studies history, the less one can deny it.

Notes

1. Lynn Montross, *The Reluctant Rebels: The Story of the Continental Congress, 1774–1789* (New York: Harper, 1950), 9.

2. *Celebrated Speeches of Chatham, Burke, and Erskine* (Philadelphia: E. C. & J. Biddle, 1852), 32.

3. Clinton Rossiter, *1787: The Grand Convention* (New York: Macmillan, 1966), 19.

4. At the time, Adams who was finishing the third volume of his *Defense of the Constitutions of the United States of America;* he praised the draft of the Constitutional Convention's Constitution. Charles Francis Adams, ed., *The Works of John Adams, Second President of the United States,* 10 vols. (Boston: Charles C. Little and James Brown, 1850–1865): VI:219–220.

5. Alexander Hamilton, James Madison, and John Jay, *The Federalist,* ed. Benjamin Fletcher Wright (Cambridge, Mass.: Belknap Press of the Harvard University Press, 1966), no. 63, 415; no. 71, 459. Unless otherwise noted, all references to *The Federalist* are to the Wright edition.

6. *The Federalist,* no. 10, 134; no. 63, 415; and no. 73, 470.

7. Joseph M. Bessette, *The Mild Voice of Reason: Deliberative Democracy and American National Government* (Chicago: University of Chicago Press, 1994), 27.

8. Ibid, 1–2.

9. Constitution of the United States, Article I, Section 5, Clause 4.

10. George E. Connor and Bruce I. Oppenheimer, "Deliberation: An Untimed Value in a Timed Game," in *Congress Reconsidered,* 5th ed., eds. Lawrence C. Dodd and Bruce I. Oppenheimer (Washington, D.C.: CQ Press, 1993), 315.

11. Albert Henry Smyth, ed. *The Writings of Benjamin Franklin,* 10 vols. (New York: Macmillan, 1905–1907), 9:595–596.

12. James A. Garfield, "A Century of Congress," *The Atlantic* 40 (July 1877), 60.

13. Walter Lippman, "The Indispensable Opposition," *The Atlantic Monthly* 164 (August 1939), 188.

14. Theodore F. Sheckels, *When Congress Debates: A Bakhtinian Paradigm* (Westport, Conn.: Praeger, 2000), 1, 5–6.

15. Stephen E. Lucas, "Debate and Oratory," in *The Encyclopedia of the United States Congress,* 10 vols., eds. Donald C. Bacon, Roger H. Davidson, and Morton Keller (New York: Simon and Schuster, 1995), 2: 609–610. See also Robert C. Byrd, *The Senate, 1789–1989,* 4 vols. (Washington, D.C.: GPO, 1988–1993), vol. 3, *Classic Speeches, 1830–1993,* xv–xix.

16. Barnet Baskerville, *The People's Voice: The Orator in American Society* (Louisville: University Press of Kentucky, 1979), 49–51.

17. Daniel J. Boorstin, *The Americans: The National Experience* (New York: Random House, 1965), 308, 311.

18. "Speech-Making in Congress," *Scribner's Magazine* 7 (January 1874), 294.

19. Ibid.

20. Baskerville, *The People's Voice: The Orator in American Society,* 88, 90.

21. Champ Clark, "Is Congressional Oratory a Lost Art?" *The Century Magazine* 81 (December 1910), 308.

22. Lucas, "Debate and Oratory," 613; and Baskerville, *The People's Voice: The Orator in American Society,* 210.

23. *Historical Statistics of the United States: Colonial Times to 1970,* 2 vols. (Washington, D.C.: U.S. Bureau of Census, 1975), II: 1081–1082; and Bacon, *The Encyclopedia of the United States Congress,* 2:382–383.

24. Bertram Myron Gross, *The Legislative Struggle: A Study in Social Combat* (New York: McGraw-Hill, 1953), 374–375.

25. Bruce Hopkins, "The Decline of the Congressional Art," *American Bar Association Journal* 53 (May 1967), 481.

26. George B. Galloway, *The Legislative Process in Congress* (New York: Crowell, 1953), 558; Hopkins, "The Decline of the Congressional Art," 480, 482; and Jerrold Zwirn, "Congressional Debate," *Government Publications Quarterly* 8 (1981), 175.

27. Hopkins, "The Decline of the Congressional Art," 480.

28. Gross, *The Legislative Struggle: A Study in Social Combat,* 285; Lauros G. McConachie, *Congressional Committees* (New York: Crowell, 1898), 63.

29. Ronald Garay, "Broadcasting of Congressional Proceedings," in Bacon, *The Encyclopedia of the United States Congress,* 1:203. See also Ronald Garay, *Congressional Television: A Legislative History* (Westport, Conn.: Greenwood Press, 1984).

30. Byrd, *Classic Speeches, 1830–1993,* xx.

31. Steven S. Smith, *Call to Order: Floor Politics in the House and Senate* (Washington, D.C.: Brookings Institution, 1989), 250.

32. Henry Steele Commager, "Congressional Debate and the Course of Events," *Scholastic* 38 (March 17, 1941), 10, 16.

33. Joseph M. Bessette, "Is Congress a Deliberative Body?" in *The United States Congress: Proceedings of the Thomas P. O'Neill, Jr., Symposium on the U.S. Congress, Boston College, January 30–31, 1981,* ed. Dennis Hale (Boston: Boston College, 1982), 4–5.

34. Ibid., 6–9.

35. "The Standard of Congressional Oratory," *Werner's Magazine,* 19 (March 1897), 251.

36. Henry L. Dawes, "Has Oratory Declined," *The Forum* 18 (October 1894), 156–157.

Declaration of Indepedence

✳ June–July 1776 ✳

When the delegates to the First Continental Congress met at Carpenter's Hall in Philadelphia on September 5, 1774, the purpose of the assemblage was neither revolution nor independence. Most delegates had been instructed to focus on the redress of specific grievances against the policies and programs of King George III and the British Parliament. For more than a decade, American colonists had struggled to overturn the programs and policies designed to reduce the British war debt, cover expenses of an expanding expire, and "rationalize" the historically loose ad hoc relationship between Great Britain and its North American colonies. Most thought that they could quickly "reestablish satisfactory, if not harmonious relations with England," and "their earlier experiences of successful conflict resolution within the imperial structure would be repeated."[1]

The emergency prompting the Philadelphia assemblage, the Intolerable Acts of 1774, accentuated the differences between Britain and the colonies and rallied the other twelve colonies to the plight of Massachusetts. Four of the acts were designed to punish Boston for leading colonial resistance against the 1773 Tea Act, approved to shore up the faltering East India Company. The fifth, the Quebec Act, provided a civil government to Canada and expanded Quebec south of the Great Lakes into the territory between the Ohio and Mississippi rivers. This meant, the colonists concluded, that Britain intended to prohibit further westward settlement.

Congress responded on October 14, 1774, by adopting a Declaration of Rights and Resolves, which articulated the fundamental rights of the colonies, which were held to be "life, liberty, property" and participation in provincial legislatures. Subsequently, it adopted a rigid policy of nonimportation, nonconsumption, and nonexportation with Britain until the grievances identified were redressed. Before Congress again assembled, armed conflict erupted in April 1775 between Massachusetts militia and British troops — first at Lexington and Concord, and then Boston. The first military engagements of the American Revolution were sparked by the discovery of a British plan to seize the military supplies of the Massachusetts Provincial Congress stored at Concord.

Prior to these initial clashes, the American colonies had already begun to assume many of the duties of self-government, expelling their royal governors and other colonial officials, establishing new legislation (usually in the form of provisional conventions), and adopting new constitutions in the place of their colonial charters. Following Lexington, Concord, and Boston, Congress made another attempt to settle its grievances with King George, in the conciliatory Olive Branch Petition. While asserting a desire for reconciliation that would restore harmony and end further hostilities, Congress also adopted a Declaration Setting Forth the Causes and Necessities for Taking Up Arms. In August 1775, after London proclaimed a state of rebellion in America, Congress turned its attention to creating a Navy and Marine Corps. A concerned Congress watched as Americans suffered defeats at Quebec City; Norfolk, Virginia; and Falmouth (Portland), Maine, and struggled with the reality that many Americans remained uncommitted to either war or independence at year's end.

With the publication of *Common Sense,* by radical pamphleteer Thomas Paine, in January 1776, enthusiasm for independence among the American colonies grew rapidly. Paine "proclaimed with the clear and rousing tones of a bugle that 'the period of debate is over.'" For Paine, reconciliation was only "an agreeable dream" whose time had "passed away," and the future interest of the colonies demanded independence. Within a year, the circulation of *Common Sense,* the first effective presentation of the American cause, reached an estimated 100,000, and sentiment for independence increased as colonial assemblies began to openly discuss the question. Then on May 15, Virginia authorized its delegation in the Continental Congress in Philadelphia to propose that the colonies declare themselves "free and independent States, absolved from all allegiance to, or dependence upon, the crown or parliament of Great Britain."[2]

On June 7, in adherence with the Virginia instructions, Richard Henry Lee of Virginia offered a resolution in Congress that the "United Colonies are, and of right ought to be, free and independent states, that they are absolved from all allegiance to the British Crown: and that all political connexion between them and the state of Great Britain is, and ought to be, totally dissolved." John Adams of Massachusetts seconded the resolution. Some three months of debate by the

Benjamin Franklin, left, reads a draft of the Declaration of Independence with John Adams and Thomas Jefferson, at right. The First Continental Congress intended to address grievances against King George III and the British Parliament, but the result was revolution.
Source: Library of Congress.

Continental Congress followed this action. On June 8, James Wilson of Pennsylvania, Robert R. Livingston of New York, John Dickinson of Pennsylvania, Edward Rutledge of South Carolina, and others questioned the wisdom of declaring independence at that time. They felt the states were not ready for independence and that to take such a step without the support of the people would be unsuccessful. Those speaking in favor of the motion included Adams, Lee, and George Wythe of Virginia. They contended that necessity demanded independence, severing ties with Great Britain would improve the chances for commercial treaties and foreign loans, independence was key to the coming summer military campaign, and the people favored independence.[3]

On June 10, Congress voted seven colonies to five to postpone the discussion for three weeks and appoint a committee to draft a declaration of independence. The following day, a five-member committee, consisting of Adams, Livingston, Thomas Jefferson of Virginia, Benjamin Franklin of Pennsylvania, and Roger Sherman of Connecticut were appointed for that purpose. On June 28, the committee presented to Congress a draft declaration, largely prepared by Jefferson.

During the first two days of July, Congress resumed its consideration of Lee's resolution. Dickinson attempted to delay the impending decision with a lengthy, eloquent speech. Adams followed him with a notable oration, prompting Richard Stockton of New Jersey to characterize the future president as "the Atlas of American independence."[4]

Finally, on July 2, Congress voted to sever ties with Great Britain with the unanimous adoption of Lee's resolution (only New York abstained). Next, Congress turned its attention to editing Jefferson's draft declaration. Although much of his work was retained, some forty additions were made and extensive cuts reduced the work's length by one-quarter. Congress completed the revised document on the evening of July 4 and instructed that copies of the Declaration be printed and sent to the states and to the commanding officers of the continental troops. At noon on July 8, a large crowd gathered outside the Pennsylvania State House in Philadelphia to hear the first public reading of the Declaration. In the ceremony that followed, people cheered, bells were rung, and soldiers paraded on the square. That evening, the king's coat of arms was burned amidst a crowd of spectators. The following evening, the Declaration was proclaimed before the Continental Army in New York, and George Washington reported to Congress that "the measure seemed to have their most hearty assent; the Expressions and behaviour both of Officers and Men testifying their warmest approbation of it."[5]

It was not until July 19 that Congress ordered the Declaration to be engrossed on parchment and the title changed to "The Unanimous Declaration of the Thirteen United States of America." On August 2, fifty delegates to the Continental Congress signed the engrossed Declaration. Five more delegates added their signatures to the historic document later that year, and one more signed in 1777.[6]

The Declaration of Independence, as Douglas Freeman Hawke aptly observed, provided the "theoretical basis for the Americans to separate from Great Britain" based upon truths held "to be self-evident, that all men are created equal, that they are endowed by their Creator with certain unalienable Rights, that among these, are Life, Liberty, and the pursuit of Happiness." The Declaration presented a "history of repeated injuries and usurpations" by the king of England, and "all having in direct object the establishment of an absolute Tyranny over" the colonies renounced formally all ties with Great Britain. The signers pledged "with a firm reliance on the protection of divine Providence" to commit their "Lives," "Fortunes," and "sacred Honor" to the support of the Declaration.[7]

Embodied in the "fire-tested text" of the Declaration of Independence, historian Julian P. Boyd wrote, "are the phrases as well as the ideas that stirred the American mind and spirit of that and subsequent generations. It is the embodiment of what Americans were saying in countless sermons, pamphlets, letters, and conversations — even in their last will and testaments." Boyd praises not only Thomas Jefferson "who, at thirty-three, was already committed to 'eternal hostility against every form of tyranny over the mind of man,' but also to a whole generation of men who dared to embrace the stern right of revolution and to proclaim to their world and posterity the high reasons for their daring."[8]

John Hancock, president of the Continental Congress, described the Declaration as "the Ground & Foundation of a future government." James Madison, the Father of the Constitution, called it "the fundamental Act of Union of these States."[9]

JOHN DICKINSON'S NOTES FOR A SPEECH IN CONGRESS

JULY 1, 1776

Arguments against the Independence of these Colonies — In Congress.

The Consequences involved in the Motion now lying before You are of such Magnitude, that I tremble under the oppressive Honor of sharing in its Determination. I feel Myself unequal to the Burthen assigned Me. I believe, I had almost said, I rejoice, that the Time is approaching, when I shall be relieved from its Weight. While the Trust remains with Me, I must discharge the Duties of it, as well as I can — and I hope I shall be the more favorably heard, as I am convinced, that I shall hold such Language, as will sacrifice any private Emolument to general Interests. My Conduct, this Day, I expect will give the finishing Blow to my once too great, and Integrity considered, now too diminish'd Popularity. It will be my Lott to [Prove?] that I had rather vote away the Enjoyment of [...] than the Blood and Happiness of my Countrymen — too fortunate, amidst their Calamities, if I prove a Truth known in Heaven, that I had rather they should hate Me, than that I should hurt them. I might indeed, practise an artful, an advantageous Reserve upon this Occasion. But thinking as I do on the subject of Debate, Silence would be guilt. I despise its Arts — I detest its Advantages. I must speak, tho I should lose my Life, tho I should lose the Affections of my C[ountrymen]. Happy at present, however, I shall esteem Myself, if I can so rise to the Height of this great argument, as to offer to this Honorable Assembly in a fully clear Manner, those Reasons that have so invariably fixed my own Opinion.

It was a Custom in a wise and virtuous State, to preface Propositions in Council, with a prayer, that they might redound to the public Benefit. I beg Leave to imitate the laudable Example. And I do most humbly implore Almighty God, with whom dwells Wisdom itself, so to enlighten the Members of this House, that their Decision may be such as will best promote the Liberty, Safety and Prosperity of these Colonies — and for Myself, that his Divine Goodness may be graciously pleased to enable Me, to speak the Precepts of sound Policy on the important Question that now engages our Attention.

Sir, Gentlemen of very distinguished Abilities and Knowledge differ widely in their Sentiments upon the Point now agitated. They all agree, that the utmost Prudence is required in forming our Decision — But immediately disagree in their Notions of that Prudence, Some cautiously insisting, that We ought to obtain That previous Information which We are likely quickly to obtain, and to make those previous Establishments that are acknowledged to be necessary — Others strenuously asserting, that tho regularly such Information & Establishment ought to precede the Measure proposed, yet, confiding in our Fortune more boldly than Caesar himself, We ought to brave the Storm in a Skiff made of Paper.

In all such Cases, where every Argument is adorn'd with an Eloquence that may please and yet mislead, it seems to me [the proper method of?] discovering the right Path, to enquire, which of the parties is probably the most warm'd by Passion. Other Circumstances being equal or nearly equal, that Consideration would have Influence with Me. I fear the Virtue of Americans. Resentment of the Injuries offered to their Country, may irritate them to Counsels & to Actions that may be detrimental to the Cause they would dye to advance.

What Advantages? 2. 1. Animate People. 2. Convince foreign Powers of our Strength Unanimity, & aid in consequence thereof.

As to 1st — Unnecessary, Life, Liberty Be Property sufficient Motive. General Spirit of America.

As to 2d — Foreign Powers will not rely on Words.

The Event of the Campaign will be the best Evidence. This properly the first Campaign. Who has received Intelligence that such a Proof of our Strength & daring Spirit will be agreeable to France? What must she expect from a People that begin their Empire in so high a stile, when on the Point of being invaded by the whole Power of G. B. aided by [formi-

---

I fear the Virtue of Americans. Resentment of the Injuries offered to their Country, may irritate them to Counsels & to Actions that may be detrimental to the Cause they would dye to advance. — John Dickinson, 1776

---

dable foreign?] aid — unconnected with foreign Power? She & Spain must perceive the imminent Danger of their Colonies lying at our Doors. Their Seat of Empire in another world. Masserano. Intelligence from Cadiz.

More respectful to act in Conformity to the views of France. Take advantage of their Pride, Give them Reason to believe that We confide in them, desire to act in conjunction with their Policies and Interests. Know how they will regard this.... Stranger in the States of the world. People fond of what they have attained in producing. Regard it as a Child — A Cement of affection. Allow them the glory of appearing the vindicators of Liberty. It will please them.

It is treating them with Contempt to act otherwise. Especially after the application made to France which by this time has reach'd them. Bermuda 5 May. Abilities of the person sent. What will they think, if now so quickly after without waiting for their Determination — Totally slighting their sentiments on such a prodigous […] — We haughtily pursue our own Measures? May they not say to Us, Gentlemen You falsely pretended to consult Us, & disrespectfully proceeded without waiting our Resolution. You must abide the Consequences. We are not ready for a Rupture. You should have negotiated till We were. We will not be hurried your Impetuosity. We know it is our Interest to support You. But we shall be in no haste about it. Try your own strength & Resources in which you have such Confidence. We know now you dare not look back. Reconciliation is impossible without declaring Yourselves the most rash & at the same Time the most contemptible Thrasos that ever existed on Earth. Suppose on this Event G. B. should offer Canada to France & Florida to Spain with an Extension of the old Limits. Would not France & Spain accept them? Gentlemen say the Trade of all America is more valuable to France than Canada. I grant it but suppose she may get both. If she is politic, & none doubts that, I averr she has the easiest Game to play for attaining both, that ever presented itself to a Nation.

When We have bound ourselves to an eternal Quarrel with G. B. by a Declaration of Independence, France has nothing to do but to hold back & intimidate G. B. till Canada is put into her Hands, then to intimidate Us into a most disadvantageous Grant of our Trade. It is my firm opinion these Events will take Place — & arise naturally from our declaring Independance.

As to Aid from foreign Powers. Our Declaration can procure Us none this Campaign tho made today. It is impossible.

Now consider if all the advantages expected from foreign Powers cannot be attained in a more unexceptionable manner. Is there no way of giving Notice of a Nation's Resolutions than by proclaiming it to all the world? Let Us in the most solemn Manner inform the House of Bourbon, at least France, that we wait only for her Determination to declare an Independance. We must not talk generally of foreign Powers but of those We expect to favor Us. Let Us assure Spain that we never will give any assistance to her Colonies. Let France become Guarantee. Form arrangements of this Kind.

Besides, first Establish our governments & take the Regular Form of a State. These preventive Measures will shew Deliberation, wisdom, Caution & Unanimity.

Our Interest to keep G. B. in Opinion that We mean Reunion as long as possible. Disadvantage to administration from Opposition. Her Union from our Declaration. Wealth of London &c pour'd into Treasury. The whole Nation ardent against us. We oblige her to persevere. Her Spirit. See last petition of London. Suppose We shall ruin her. France must rise on her Ruins. Her Ambition. Her Religion. Our Danger from thence. We shall weep at our victories. Overwhelm'd with Debt. Compute that Debt 6 Millions of Pa. Money a Year.

The War will be carried on with more Severity. Burning Towns. Letting Loose Indians on our Frontiers. Not yet done. Boston might have been burnt. What advantages to be expected from a Declaration? 1. Animating our Troops. Answer, Unnecessary. 2. Union of Colonies. Answer, Also unnecessary. It may weaken that Union — when the People find themselves engaged in a [war] rendered more cruel by such a Declaration without prospect of End to their Calamities by a Continuation of the War. People changeable. In Bitterness of Soul they may complain against our Rashness & ask why We did not apply first to foreign Powers. Why We did not settle all Differences among ourselves. Take Care to secure unsettled Lands for easing their Burthens instead of leaving them to particular Colonies. Why not wait till better prepar'd. Till We had made an Experiment of our Strength. This [probably?] the first Campaign.

3. Proof of our strength & Spirit. France & Spain may be alarm'd &: provoked. Masserano. Insult to France. Not the least Evidence of her granting Us favorable Terms. Her probable Conditions. The Glory of recovering Canada. She will get that & then dictate Terms to Us.

A *Partition* of these Colonies will take Place if G. B. cant conquer Us. Destroying a House before We have got another. In Winter with a small Family. Then asking a Neighbor to take us in. He unprepared.

4th. The Spirit of the Colonies calls for such a Declaration. Answer, not to be relied on. Not only Treaties with foreign powers but among Ourselves should precede this Declaration. We should know on what Grounds We are to stand with Regard to one another.

Declaration of Virginia about Colonies in *their Limits*.

The Committee on Confederation dispute almost every Article — some of Us totally despair of any reasonable Terms of Confederation.

We cannot look back. Men generally sell their Goods to most Advantage when they have several Chapmen. We have but two to rely on. We exclude one by this Declaration without knowing What the other will give.

G. B. after one or more unsuccessful Campaigns may be enduc'd to offer Us such a share of Commerce as would satisfy Us — to appoint Councillors during good Behaviour — to withdraw her armies — in short to redress all the Grievances complained of in our first petition — to protect our Commerce — Establish our Militias. Let Us know, if We can get Terms from France that will be more beneficial than these. If We can, let Us declare Independance. If We cannot, let Us at least withhold that Declaration, till We obtain Terms that are tolerable.

We have many Points of the utmost moment to settle with France — Canada, Acadia, Cape Breton. What will Content her? Trade, or Territory? What Conditions of Trade? Barbary Pirates. Spain. Portugal. Will she demand an Exclusive Trade as a Compensation or grant Us protection against piratical States only for a share of our Commerce?

When our Enemies are pressing us so vigorously, When We are in so wretched a State of preparation, When the Sentiments & Designs of our expected Friends are so unknown to Us, I am alarm'd at this Declaration being so vehemently prest. A worthy Gentleman told Us, that people in this House have had different Views for more than a 12 month. Amazing after, what they have so repeatedly declared in this House & private Conversations — that they meant only Reconciliation. But since they can conceal their Views so dextrously, I should be glad to read a little more in. the Doomsday Book of America — Not all — that like the Book of Fate might be too dreadful. Title page — Binding. I should be glad to know whether in 20 or 30 Years this Commonwealth of Colonies may not be thought too unwieldy — & Hudson's River be a proper Boundary for a separate Commonwealth to the Northward. I have a strong Impression on my Mind that this will take place.

Sources: This document was identified and dated by John H. Powell in 1941, and no documents have since been discovered that challenge his assessment. "Speech of John Dickinson Opposing the Declaration of Independence, 1 July, 1776," *Pennsylvania Magazine of History and Biography* 65 (Oct. 1941), 458–481. This version of the document, together with notes, is found in Paul H. Smith, Gerard W. Gawalt, Rosemary Fry Plakas, and Eugene R. Sheridan, eds. *Letters of Delegates to Congress, 1774–1789*, 26 vols. (Washington, D.C.: Library of Congress, 1976–2000), 4:351–357.

JOHN ADAMS'S UNRECORDED SPEECH IN FAVOR OF THE DECLARATION OF INDEPENDENCE

1776

John Adams did not write out his speech in favor of the Declaration of Independence, and none of the delegates to the Continental Congress took notes on his remarks. It is possible, however, to reconstruct at least the essence of his thoughts through his recollection of the moment as recorded in his autobiography and the impression of others who were there.

Certainly the most often quoted remembrance of Adams's leading role in the adoption of the Declaration of Independence is that of Thomas Jefferson. In 1824, he recalled in a conversation with Daniel Webster that Adams's passionate but reasoned speech was so powerful in "thought & expression" that it "moved us from our seats." Adams was, Jefferson said, "our Colossus on the floor." [10]

Of the historic moment, John Adams, in his autobiography, wrote the following.

★ ★ ★ ★

The subject had been in contemplation for more than a year and frequent discussions had been had concerning it. At one time and another, all the arguments for it and against it had been exhausted, and were become familiar. I expected no more would be said in public, but that the question would be put and decided. Mr. Dickinson, however, was determined to bear his testimony against it with more formality. He had prepared himself apparently with great labor and ardent zeal, and in a speech of great length, and with all his eloquence, he combined together all that had before been written in pamphlets and newspapers, and all that had from time to time been said in Congress by himself and others. He conducted the debate not only with great ingenuity and eloquence, but with equal politeness and candor, and was answered in the same spirit.

No member rose to answer him, and after waiting some time, in hopes that some one less obnoxious than myself, who was still had been all along for a year before, and still was, represented and believed to be the author of all the mischief, would move, I determined to speak.

It has been said, by some of our historians, that I began by an invocation to the god of eloquence. This is a misrepresentation. Nothing so puerile as this fell from me. I began, by saying that this was the first time of my life that I had ever wished for the talents and eloquence of the ancient orators of Greece and Rome, for I was very sure that none of them ever had before him a question of more importance to his country and to the world. They would probably, upon less occasions than this, have begun by solemn invocations to their divinities for assistance, but the question before me appeared so simple, that I had confidence enough in the plain understanding and common sense that had been given me, to believe that I could answer, to the satisfaction of the House, all the arguments which had been produced, notwithstanding the abilities which had been displayed and the eloquence with which they had been enforced. Mr. Dickinson, some years afterwards, published his speech. I had made no preparation beforehand, and never committed any minutes of mine to writing. But if I had a copy of Mr. Dickinson's before me, I would now, after nine and twenty years have elapsed, endeavor to recollect mine.

Before the final question was put, the new delegates from New Jersey came in, and Mr. Stockton, Dr. Witherspoon, and Mr. Hopkinson, very respectable characters expressed a great desire to hear the arguments. All was silence; no one would speak; all Eyes were turned upon me. Mr Edward Rutledge came to me and said, laughing, "Nobody will speak but you, upon this subject." You have all the topics so ready, that you must satisfy the gentlemen from New Jersey." I answered him, laughing, that it had much the air of exhibiting like an actor or gladiator, for the entertainment of the audience, that I was ashamed to repeat what I had said twenty times before, and I thought nothing new could be advanced by me. The New Jersey gentlemen, however, still insisting on hearing at least a recapitulation of the arguments, and no other gentleman being willing to speak, I summed up the reasons, objections, and answers, in as concise a manner as I could, till at length the Jersey gentlemen said they were fully satisfied and ready

for the question, which was then put, and determined in the affirmative.

Mr. Jay, Mr. Duane, and Mr. William Livingston of New Jersey were not present. But they all acquiesced in the declaration and steadily supported it ever afterwards.

Source: Charles Francis Adams, ed., *The Works of John Adams, Second President of the United States,* 10 vols. (Boston: Little, Brown, 1851–1865), 3:54–59.

★ ★ ★ ★

The son of Richard Stockton, a delegate from New Jersey, wrote a letter to John Adams in 1821, in which he described to the former president his father's reaction to Adams's speech in support of the Declaration of Independence:

"I well remember that on my father's first return home from Congress, in the summer of 1776, after the fourth of July, he was immediately surrounded by his anxious political friends, who were eager for minute information in respect of the great event which had just taken place. Being then a boy of some observation, and of very retentive memory. I remember these words addressed to his Friends. 'The Man to whom the country is most indebted for the great measure of Independence is Mr. John Adams, of Boston. I call him the Atlas of American independence. He it was who sustained the debate, and by the force of his reasoning demonstrated not only the justice but the expediency of the measure.' This I have often spoken of to others and distinctly remember the very language which he used."

Source: Letter is referred to in Charles Francis Adams, ed., *The Works of John Adams, Second President of the United States,* 10 vols. (Boston: Little, Brown, 1851–1865), 3:56.

★ ★ ★ ★

No man better merited, than Mr. John Adams to hold a most conspicuous place in the design [of the Declaration of Independence]. He was the pillar of it's support on the floor of Congress, it's ablest advocate and defender against the multifarious assaults it encountered. — Thomas Jefferson on John Adams

Thomas Jefferson, in a February 19, 1813, letter to William P. Gardner, wrote: "No man better merited, than Mr. John Adams to hold a most conspicuous place in the design [of the Declaration of Independence]. He was the pillar of it's support on the floor of Congress, it's ablest advocate and defender against the multifarious assaults it encountered. For many excellent persons opposed it on doubts whether we were provided sufficiently with the means of supporting it, whether the minds of our constituents were yet prepared to receive it &c. who, after it was decided, united zealously in the measures called for."

Source: Thomas Jefferson to William P. Gardner, February 19, 1813, in Paul Leicester Ford, ed., *The Writings of Thomas Jefferson,* 10 vols. (New York: G. P. Putnam's Sons, 1898), 9:377–378.

Notes

1. Calvin Jillson and Rick K. Wilson, *Congressional Dynamics: Structure, Coordination, and Choice in the First American Congress, 1774–1789* (Stanford, CA: Stanford University Press, 1994), 17.

2. Julian P. Boyd, *The Declaration of Independence* (Washington, D.C.: Library of Congress, 1943), 13; Bruce Kuklick, ed., *Political Writings: Thomas Paine* (Cambridge, UK: Cambridge University Press), x, 17; Hugh Blair Grigsby, *The Virginia Convention of 1776* (Richmond, Va.: J. W. Randolph, 1855), 17.

3. Worthington Chauncey Ford and Roscoe R. Hill, eds., *Journals of the Continental Congress, 1774–1789* (Washington, D.C.: GPO, 1904–1937), 5:425–426; "Thomas Jefferson's Notes of Proceedings in Congress," in Paul H. Smith, Gerard W. Gawalt, Rosemary Fry Plakas, and Eugene R. Sheridan, eds., *Letters of Delegates to Congress, 1774–1789*, 26 vols. (Washington, D.C.: Library of Congress, 1976–2000), 4:160–164.

4. Ford and Hill, *Journals of the Continental Congress, 1774–1789,* 5:431, 489–502; "John Dickinson's Notes for a Speech in Congress," in Smith, *Letters of Delegates to Congress, 1774–1789,* 4:351–357; John H. Hazelton, *The Declaration of Independence: Its History* (New York: Dodd, Mead, 1906), 118, 156–168.

5. Ford and Hill, *Journals of the Continental Congress, 1774–1789,* 5:507; "Thomas Jefferson's Notes of Proceedings in Congress," in Smith et al., *Letters of Delegates to Congress, 1774–1789,* 4:359; Edmund Cody Burnett, *The Continental Congress* (New York: Macmillan, 1941), 182–189; David Freeman Hawke, "Declaration of Independence," in *Dictionary of American History,* 8 vols. (New York: Charles Scribner's Sons, 1976–1978), 2:305; Hazelton, *The Declaration of Independence,* 242–244; John C. Fitzpatrick, ed., *The Writings of George Washington,* 39 vols. (Washington, D.C.: GPO, 1931–1944), 5:247.

6. Ford and Hill, *Journals of the Continental Congress, 1774–1789,* 5: 590–591; Smith et al., *Letters of Delegates to Congress, 1774–1789,* 4: 491–502, 506–507, 510–516, 590–591, 626; Hazelton, *The Declaration of Independence,* 156–162; Boyd, *The Declaration of Independence,* 35; Hawke, "Declaration of Independence," 2:305–306; Robert G. Ferris and Richard E. Morris, *The Signers of the Declaration of Independence* (Flagstaff, Ariz.: Interpretive Publications, 2001), 23.

7. Hawke, "Declaration of Independence," 304; Ford and Hill, *Journals of the Continental Congress,* 5:510–515.

8. Boyd, *The Declaration of Independence,* 35–36.

9. John Hancock to Certain States, July 6, 1776, in Smith et al., *Letters of Delegates to Congress, 1774–1789,* 4:396; James Madison to Thomas Jefferson, February 8, 1825, in Gaillard Hunt, ed., *The Writings of James Madison,* 9 vols. (New York: G.P. Putnam's Sons, 1900–1910), 9:221.

10. "Notes of Mr. Jefferson's Conversation 1824 at *Monticello,*" in Charles M. Wiltse, ed., *The Papers of Daniel Webster: Correspondence,* 14 vols. (Hanover, NH: Published for Dartmouth College by the University Press of New England, 1974–1989), 1:375.

Articles of Confederation
✷ June 1776–November 1777 ✷

Even before the delegates to the Continental Congress voted for independence, some of them recognized the need for the thirteen American colonies to combine their efforts against the British through a central government. Within three months after the first shots of the Revolutionary War were fired at Lexington and Concord, Massachusetts, Benjamin Franklin of Pennsylvania proposed a constitution that he called the "Articles of Confederation and Perpetual Union." Franklin's plan of July 1775 was tabled because a majority of the delegates still sought a favorable reconciliation with England. Richard Henry Lee of Virginia revived the idea of a confederation on June 7, 1776, when he offered a resolution for independence and that "a plan of confederation be prepared and transmitted to the respective colonies for their consideration and approbation." On June 12, Congress appointed a committee consisting of one member from each state to prepare "the form of confederation that might be entered into by these colonies." Ironically, John Dickinson of Pennsylvania, whom the committee entrusted to prepare the draft, had earlier led the fight to thwart consideration of Franklin's proposal but now favored confederation. Exactly one month later, the committee reported a series of "Articles of Confederation and Perpetual Union" that not only borrowed Franklin's title but many of his phrases as well.[1]

At the time, Congress was deeply engaged in war problems. As a consequence, it only intermittently debated the difficult and complex issues raised by the Articles over the next fourteen months before they were finally adopted on November 15, 1777. Ratification of the Articles was delayed until March 1781, as Congress debated proposed modifications recommended by the states. Several smaller states successfully sought to insert a provision making western lands a common possession of all states.[2]

The Articles, which served as the first Constitution of the United States, established the framework for the U.S. government from 1781 to 1789. The new government created by the Articles, however, lacked sufficient authority to solve many of the problems accompanying the American Revolution because it was based on "firm league of friendship" that allowed each state to retain much of "its sovereignty, freedom and independence." Congress, the single organ of government established under the Articles, was restricted from making treaties that prohibited imports and exports, or from prohibiting a state from imposing retaliatory taxes. The responsibility for raising land forces and taxes (which were to be based on land values with improvements) was also delegated to the States.[3]

It would be incorrect to assume, however, that the Articles were the "result of either ignorance or inexperience. On the contrary, they were the natural outcome of the revolutionary movement within the American colonies." The revolutionary movement in America was based on the "idea of the supremacy of the local legislatures, coupled with the social and psychological forces which led men to look upon 'state sovereignty' as necessary to the attainment of the goals of an internal revolution." Consistently, those who led the colonial opposition to Great Britain "denied the authority of any government superior to the legislatures of the several colonies," and viewed a centralized government as a threat to the "state sovereignty" necessary to achieve their revolutionary goals. In actuality, the Articles were "a constitutional expression of the philosophy of the Declaration of Independence." In eighteenth century America, decentralization "meant local self-government, and local self-government meant a form of agrarian democracy." It was a society where the great majority of the American people were small farmers who owned their own land, and mostly voters who insisted that only the propertied should "control the politics of their individual states."[4]

As originally drafted, the Articles provided for a strong central government. Supporters of the original document — John Dickinson, James Wilson, and Benjamin Franklin of Pennsylvania, and John Adams of Massachusetts — argued that the states should no longer retain their separate individuality. By the time the Articles were sent to the states for their ratification, however, advocates of states' rights who feared centralization had significantly weakened the original draft. The final document granted to the central government only expressly delegated powers. They "were designed to prevent the central government from infringing upon the rights of the states," Merrill Jensen concludes in *The Articles of Confederation*. The "Constitution of 1787 was designed as a check upon the power of the states and the democracy that found expression within their bounds." The Articles were grounded on two premises: that the states should be "psychological and legally independent" and "democracy was possible only within fairly small political units whose electorate had a direct check upon the officers of government."[5]

"No issue," Jensen later wrote in *The New Nation,* "was more fought over than that of the nature of the central government to be created by the thirteen states." The first constitution lasted just eight years," but the importance of the document "transcends its duration as a framework of government."[6] As Leonard W. Levy aptly observed, the Articles were the "first written constitution that establish a federal system of government in which the sovereign powers were distributed between the central and local governments." At the time, "Americans believed that sovereignty was divisible and divided it." The "Articles had many defects, the greatest of which was that the United States acted on the states rather than the people and had no way of making states or anyone but soldiers obey." The Articles were, however, "a necessary stage in the evolution of the Constitution of 1787 and contained many provisions that were carried over into that document."[7] Also, they preserved the Union until a more effective system could be established, and afforded the state delegates invaluable experience in establishing an operational and diplomatic framework for government.

Although many of the proceedings of the Continental Congress were not recorded, Thomas Jefferson did take notes of the debate on the Articles of Confederation in July and August 1776. The following excerpt of Jefferson's notes focus on two of the three provisions in the original draft that prompted the most discussion: apportionment of common expenses according to total population (including slaves) and equal representation of all states in Congress. The issue of whether to grant Congress broad powers over Western lands and boundaries was debated later.

THOMAS JEFFERSON'S NOTES OF PROCEEDINGS IN CONGRESS

JULY 12–AUGUST 1, 1776

On Friday July 12 the Committee appointed to draw the articles of confederation reported them and on the 22d the house resolved themselves into a committee to take them into consideration. On the 30th and 31st of that month & 1st of the ensuing, those articles were debated which determined the (*manner of voting in Congress, & that of fixing*) the proportion or quota(s) of money which each state should furnish to the common treasury, and the manner of voting in Congress. The first of these articles was expressed in the original draught in these words. '*Art.* XI. All charges of war & all other expenses that shall be incurred for the common defence, or general welfare, and allowed by the United states assembled, shall be defrayed out of a common treasury, which shall be supplied by the several colonies in proportion to the number of inhabitants of every age, sex & quality, except Indians not paying taxes, in each colony, a true account of which, distinguishing the white inhabitants, shall be triennially taken & transmitted to the assembly of the United states.'

Mr. Chase moved that the quotas should be fixed, not by the number of inhabitants of every condition, but by that of the 'white inhabitants.' He admitted that taxation should be alwais in proportion to property; that this was in theory the true rule, but that from a variety of difficulties it was a rule which could never be adopted in practice. The value of the property in every state could never be estimated justly & equally. Some other measure for the wealth of the state must therefore be devised, some (*measure of wealth must be*) standard referred to which would be more simple. He considered the number of inhabitants as a tolerably good criterion of property, and that this might alwais be obtained. (*yet numbers simply would not*) he therefore thought it the best mode which we could adopt, with (*some*) one exception(*s*) only. He observed that negroes are property, and as such cannot be distinguished from the lands or personalties held in those states where there are few slaves. That the surplus of profit which a Northern farmer is able to lay by, he invests in (*lands*) cattle, horses &c. whereas a Southern farmer lays out that same surplus in slaves. There is no more reason therefore for taxing the Southern states on the farmer's heads & on his slave's head, than the Northern ones on their farmer's heads & the heads of their cattle. That the method proposed would therefore tax the Southern states according to their numbers & their wealth conjunctly, while the Northern would be taxed on numbers only: that Negroes in fact should not be considered as members of the state more than cattle & that they have no more interest in it.

Mr. John Adams observed that the numbers of people were taken by this article as an index of the wealth of the state & not as subjects of taxation. That as to this matter it was of no consequence by what name you called your people, whether by that of freemen or of slaves. That in some coun-

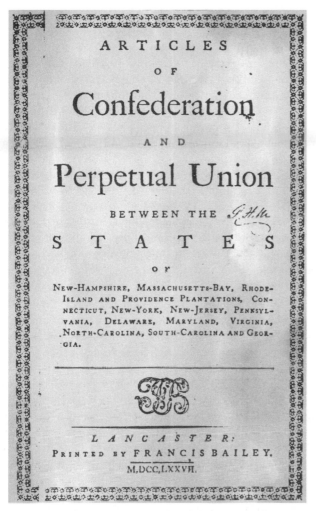

Title page of the first printing of the Articles of Confederation, in 1777. When debating the Articles, members of the Continental Congress grappled over the strength of the central government and that of the states, among other issues.

Source: The Granger Collection, New York.

pay taxes? That the condition of the labouring poor in most countries, that of the fishermen particularly of the Northern states is as abject as that of slaves. It is the number of labourers which produce the surplus for taxation, and numbers therefore indiscriminately are the fair index of wealth. That it is the use of the word 'property' here, & it's application to some of the people of the state, which produces the fallacy. How does the Southern farmer procure slaves? Either by importation or by purchase from his neighbor. If he imports a slave, he adds one to the number of labourers in his country, and proportionably to it's profits & abilities to pay taxes. If he buys from his neighbor, it is only a transfer of a labourer from one farm to another, which does not change the annual produce of the state, & therefore should not change it's tax. That if a Northern farmer works ten labourers on his farm, he can, it is true, invest the surplus of ten men's labour in cattle: but so may the Southern farmer working ten slaves. That a state of 100,000 freemen can maintain no more cattle than one of 100,000 slaves. Therefore they have no more of that kind of property. That a slave may indeed from the custom of speech be more properly called the wealth of his master, than the free labourer might be called the wealth of his employer: but as to the state both were equally it's wealth, and should therefore equally add to the quota of its tax.

Mr. Harrison proposed a compromise, that two slaves should be counted as one freeman. He affirmed that slaves did not do so much work as freemen, and doubted if two effected more than one. That this was proved by the price of labor, the hire of a labourer in the Southern colonies being from 8 to £12, while in the Northern it was generally £24.

Mr. Wilson said that if this amendment should take place the Southern colonies would have all the benefit of slaves, whilst the Northern ones would bear the burthen. That slaves increase the profits of a state, which the Southern states mean to take to themselves; that they also increase the burthen of defence, which would of course fall so much the heavier on the Northern. That slaves occupy the places of freemen and eat their food. Dismiss your slaves & freemen will take their places. It is our duty to lay every discouragement on the importation of slaves; but this amendment would give the *jus trium liberorum* to him who would import slaves. That other kinds of property were pretty equally distributed thro' all the colonies: there were as many cattle, horses, & sheep in the North as the South, & South as the North: but not so as to slaves. That experience has shewn, that those colonies have been alwais able to pay most which have the most (males) inhabitants, whether they be black or white. And the practice of the Southern colonies has alwais been to make every farmer pay poll taxes upon all his labourers whether they be black or white. He acknoleges indeed that freemen work the most; but they consume the most also. They do not produce a greater surplus for taxation. The slave is neither fed nor clothed so expensively as a freeman. Again white women are

tries the labouring poor were called freemen, in others they were called slaves; but that the difference as to the state was imaginary only. What matters it whether a landlord employing ten labourers in his farm, gives them annually as much money as will buy them the necessaries of life, or gives them those necessaries at short hand. The ten labourers add as much wealth annually to the state, increase it's exports as much in the one case as the other. Certainly 500 freemen produce no more profits, no greater surplus for the paiment of taxes than 500 slaves. Therefore the state in which are the labourers called freemen should be taxed no more than that in which are those called slaves. Suppose by any extraordinary operation of nature or of law one half the labourers of a state could in the course of one night be transformed into slaves: would the state be made the poorer or the less able to exempted from labour generally, which negro women are not. In this then the Southern states have an advantage as the article now stands. It has sometimes been said that slavery is necessary because the commodities they raise would be too dear for market if cultivated by freemen; but now it is said that the labor of the slave is the dearest.

Mr. Payne urged the original resolution of Congress, to proportion the quotas of the states to the number of souls.

Dr. Witherspoon was of opinion that the value of lands & houses was the best estimate of the wealth of a nation, and that it was practicable to obtain such a valuation. This is the true barometer of wealth. The one now proposed is imperfect in itself, and unequal between the states. It has been objected that negroes eat the food of freemen & therefore should be taxed. Horses also eat the food of freemen; therefore they also should be taxed. It has been said too that in carrying slaves into the estimate of the taxes the state is to pay, we do no more than those states themselves do, who alwais take slaves into the estimate of the taxes the individual is to pay. But the cases are not parallel. In the Southern colonies slaves pervade the whole colony; but they do not pervade the whole continent. That as to the original resolution of Congress to proportion the quotas according to the souls, it was temporary only, & related to the monies heretofore emitted: whereas we are now entering into a new compact and therefore stand on original ground.

Aug. 1. The question being put the amendment proposed was rejected by the votes of N. Hampshire, Massachusets, Rhode Island, Connecticut, N. York, N. Jersey, & Pennsylvania, against those of Delaware, Maryland, Virginia, North & South Carolina. Georgia was divided.

The other article was in these words. "Art. XVII. In determining questions each colony shall have one vote."

July 30. 31. Aug. 1. Present 41 members. Mr. Chase observed that this article was the most likely to divide us of anyone proposed in the draught then under consideration. That the larger colonies had threatened they would not confederate at all if their weight in congress should not be equal to the numbers of people they added to the confederacy; while the smaller ones declared against an union if they did not retain an equal vote for the protection of their rights. That it was of the utmost consequence to bring the parties together, as should we sever from each other, either no foreign power will ally with us at all, or the different states will form different alliances, and thus increase the horrors of those scenes of civil war and bloodshed which in such a state of separation & independence would render us a miserable people. That our importance, our interests, our peace required that we should confederate, and that mutual sacrifices should be made to effect a compromise of this difficult question. He was of opinion the smaller colonies would lose their rights, if they were not in some instances allowed an equal vote; and therefore that a discrimination should take place among the ques-

tions which would come before Congress. (*He therefore proposed*) that the smaller states should be secured in all questions concerning life or liberty & the greater ones in all respecting property. He therefore proposed that in votes relating to money, the voice of each colony should be proportioned to the number of it's inhabitants.

Dr. Franklin (*seconded the proposition*) thought that the votes should be so proportioned in all cases. He took notice that the Delaware counties had bound up their Delegates to disagree to this article. He thought it a very extraordinary language to be held by any state, that they would not confederate with us unless we would let them dispose of our money. Certainly if we vote equally we ought to pay equally: but the smaller states will hardly purchase the privilege at this price. That had he lived in a state where the representation, originally equal, had become unequal by time & accident he might have submitted rather than disturb government: but that we should be very wrong to set out in this practice when it is in our power to establish what is right. That at the time of the Union between England and Scotland the latter had made the objection which the smaller states now do. But experience had proved that no unfairness had ever been shewn them. That their advocates had prognosticated that it would again happen as in times of old that the whale would swallow Jonas, but he thought the prediction reversed in event and that Jonas had swallowed the whale, for the Scotch had in fact got possession of the government and gave laws to the English. He reprobated the original agreement of Congress to vote by colonies, and therefore was for their voting in all cases according to the number of taxables (*so far going beyond Mr. Chase's proposition*).

Dr. Witherspoon opposed every alteration of the article. All men admit that a confederacy is necessary. Should the idea get abroad that there is likely to be no union among us, it will damp the minds of the people, diminish the glory of our struggle, & lessen it's importance, because it will open to our view future prospects of war & dissension among ourselves. If an equal vote be refused, the smaller states will become vassals to the larger; & all experience has shewn that the vassals & subjects of free states are the most enslaved. He instanced the Helots of Sparta & the provinces of Rome. He observed that foreign powers discovering this blemish would make it a handle for disengaging the smaller states from so unequal a confederacy. That the colonies should in fact be considered as individuals; and that as such in all disputes they should have an equal vote. That they are now collected as individuals making a bargain with each other, & of course had a right to vote as individuals. That in the East India company they voted by persons, & not by their proportion of stock. That the Belgic confederacy voted by provinces. That in questions of war the smaller states were as much interested as the larger, & therefore should vote equally; and indeed that the larger states were more likely to bring war on the confederacy, in proportion as their frontier was more extensive. He admitted that equality of representation was an excellent principle, but then it must be of things which are co-ordinate; that is, of things similar & of the same nature: that nothing relating to individuals could ever come before Congress; nothing but what would respect colonies. He distinguished between an incorporating & a federal union. The union of England was an incorporating one; yet Scotland had suffered by that union: for that it's inhabitants were drawn from it by the hopes of places & employments. Nor was it an instance of equality of representation; because while Scotland was allowed nearly a thirteenth of representation, they were to pay only one fortieth of the land tax. He expressed his hopes that in the present enlightened state of men's minds we might expect a lasting confederacy, if it was founded on fair principles.

John Adams advocated the voting in proportion to numbers. He said that we stand here as the representatives of the people. That in some states the people are many, in others they are few; that therefore their vote here should be proportioned to the numbers from whom it comes. Reason, justice, & equity never had weight enough on the face of the earth to govern the councils of men. It is interest alone which does it, and it is interest alone which can be trusted. That therefore the interests within doors should be the mathematical representatives of the interests without doors. That the individuality of the colonies is a mere sound. Does the individuality of a colony increase it's wealth or numbers? If it does; pay equally. If it does not add weight in the scale of the confederacy; it cannot add to their rights, nor weight in arguments. A has £50. B £500. C. £1000 in partnership. Is it just they should equally dispose of the monies of the partnership? It has been said we are independant individuals making a bargain together. The question is not what we are now, but what we ought to be when our bargain shall be made. The confederacy is to make us one individual only; it is to form us, like separate parcels of metal, into one common mass. We shall no longer retain our separate individuality, but become a single individual as to all questions submitted to the Confederacy. Therefore all those reasons which prove the justice & expediency of equal representation in other assemblies, hold good here. It has been objected that a proportional vote will endanger the smaller states. We answer that an equal vote will endanger the larger. Virginia, Pennsylvania, & Massachusets are the three greater colonies. Consider their distance, their difference of produce, of interests, of manners, & it is apparent they can never have an interest or inclination to combine for the oppression of the smaller. That the smaller will naturally divide on all questions with the larger. Rhode Isld. from it's relation, similarity & intercourse will generally pursue the same objects with Massachusets; Jersey, Delaware & Maryland with Pennsylvania.

Dr. Rush took notice that the decay of the liberties of the Dutch republic proceeded from three causes. (1) The perfect unanimity requisite on all occasions. (2) Their obligation to consult their constituents. (3) Their voting by provinces. This last destroyed the equality of representation, and the liberties of Great Britain also are sinking from the same defect. That a part of our rights is deposited in the hands of our legislatures. There it was admitted there should be an equality of representation. Another part of our rights is deposited in the hands of Congress: why is it not equally necessary there should be an equal representation there? Were it possible to collect the whole body of the people together, they would determine the questions submitted to them by their majority. Why should not the same majority decide when voting here by their representatives? The larger colonies are so providentially divided in situation as to render every fear of their combining visionary. Their interests are different, & their circumstances dissimilar. It is more probable they will become rivals & leave it in the power of the smaller states to give preponderance to any scale they please. The voting by the number of free inhabitants will have one excellent effect, that of inducing, the colonies to discourage slavery & to encourage the increase of their free inhabitants.

Mr. Hopkins observed there were four larger, four smaller & four middlesized colonies. That the four largest would contain more than half the inhabitants of the Confederating states, & therefore would govern the others as they should please. That history affords no instance of such a thing as equal representation. The Germanic body votes by states. The Helvetic body does the same; & so does the Belgic confederacy. That too little is known of the antient confederations to say what was their practice.

Shall two millions of people put it in the power of one million to govern them as they please? It is pretended too that the smaller colonies will be in danger from the greater. Speak in honest language & say the minority will be in danger from the majority. — Thomas Jefferson

---

Mr. Wilson thought that taxation should be in proportion to wealth, but the representation should accord with the number of freemen. That government is a collection or result of the wills of all. That if any government could speak the will of all it would be perfect; and that so far as it departs from this it becomes imperfect. It has been said that Congress is a representation of states; not of individuals. I say that the objects of it's care are all the individuals of the states. It is strange that annexing the name of 'State' to ten thousand men, should give them an equal right with forty thousand. This must be the effect of magic, not of reason. As to those matters which are referred to Congress, we are not so many states; we are one large state. We lay aside our individuality whenever we come here. The Germanic body is a burlesque on government: and their practice on any point is a sufficient authority & proof that it is wrong. The greatest imperfection in the constitution of the Belgic confederacy is their voting by provinces. The interest of the whole is states. The history of the constantly sacrificed to that of the small war in the reign of Q. Anne sufficiently proves this. It is asked Shall nine colonies put it into the power of four to govern them as they please? I invert the question and ask Shall two millions of people put it in the power of one million to govern them as they please? It is pretended too that the smaller colonies will be in danger from the greater. Speak in honest language & say the minority will be in danger from the majority. And is there an assembly on earth where this danger may not be equally pretended? The truth is that our proceedings will then be consentaneous with the interests of the majority, and so they ought to be. The probability is much greater that the larger states will disagree than that they will combine. I defy the wit of man to invent a possible case or to suggest any one thing on earth which shall be for the interests of Virginia, Pennsylvania & Massachusets, and which will not also be for the interest of the other states.

Source: Paul H. Smith, Gerard W. Gawalt, Rosemary Fry Plakas, and Eugene R. Sheridan, eds., *Letters of Delegates to Congress, 1774–1789,* 26 vols. (Washington, D.C.: Library of Congress, 1976–2000), 4:438–445.

Notes

1. Worthington Chauncey Ford and Roscoe R. Hill, eds., *Journals of the Continental Congress, 1774–1789* (Washington, D.C.: GPO, 1904–1937), 2:195–199, and 5:425, 433, 546–555. See also Edmund Cody Burnett, *The Continental Congress* (New York: W. W. Norton, 1964), 90–93, 213–229, 248–258; Merrill Jensen, *The Articles of Confederation* (Madison: University of Wisconsin Press, 1948), 84, 103, 114, 126–139; Paul H. Smith, Gerard W. Gawalt, Rosemary Fry Plakas, and Eugene R. Sheridan, eds., *Letters of Delegates to Congress, 1774–1789,* 26 vols. (Washington, D.C.: Library of Congress, 1976–2000), 4:251–252.

2. For background on the ratification of the Articles of Confederation see Burnett, *The Continental Congress,* 341–345, 499–500; Jensen, *The Articles of Confederation,* 185–238; Forrest McDonald, *E Pluribus Unum: The Formation of the American Republic, 1776–1790* (Indianapolis: Liberty Press, 1979), 38–42, 48; Smith et al., *Letters of Delegates to Congress, 1774–1789,* 8:xxvi.

3. Ford, *Journals of the Continental Congress, 1774–1789,* 9:907–925.

4. Jensen, *The Articles of Confederation,* 139–140.

5. Jensen, *The Articles of Confederation,* 243–244.

6. Merrill Jensen, *The New Nation: A History of the United States During the Confederation, 1781–1789* (New York: Alfred A. Knopf, 1967), 18–19.

7. Leonard W. Levy, "Articles of Confederation," in Leonard W. Levy, Kenneth L. Karst, and Adam Winkler, eds., *Encyclopedia of the American Constitution,* 2nd ed., 6 vols. (New York: Macmillan Reference USA, 2000), 1:76–77.

Northwest Ordinance
✳ 1787 ✳

The creation of the Northwest Ordinance of 1787 is regarded as one of the two greatest achievements of Congress under the Articles of Confederation, second in importance only to signing the 1783 Treaty of Peace with Great Britain. The Northwest Ordinance is also considered one of the three most influential documents in relation to the founding of our Nation — the other two being the Declaration of Independence and the Constitution. The Ordinance provided for the creation of new states and the orderly expansion of the 275,000 square miles of territory between the Appalachian Mountains, the Mississippi River, and the Great Lakes, an area that today encompasses Ohio, Indiana, Illinois, Michigan, Wisconsin, and part of Minnesota. The commitment to continental development embodied in the Ordinance was as crucial to the new nation's future as the nearly simultaneous decision to institute a more "energetic" national government. The principles the Ordinance espoused were drawn from a 1784 plan offered by Virginia politician Thomas Jefferson, a committee report, and extensive discussions among congressional delegates.

Members of Congress as well as presidents have acclaimed the Ordinance. Longtime U.S. representative and senator Daniel Webster of Massachusetts once said: "I doubt whether one single law of any lawgiver, ancient or modern, has produced effects of most distinct, marked, and lasting character than the Ordinance of 1787." President Theodore Roosevelt believed that because it was "so wide-reaching in its effects," the Ordinance should "rank among the foremost of American State papers." President Franklin D. Roosevelt called it the "third great charter ... the highway, broad and safe over which poured the westward march of our civilization," the plan on which the "United States was built." [1]

Congress wrestled with the issues addressed in the Ordinance for much of its history. The Ordinance itself, which Congress sporadically considered for more than a year, was completed at the same time the Framers of the new federal Constitution who were deliberating in Philadelphia fashioned their western policy. It was the last major piece of legislation passed by Congress under the Articles of Confederation. Despite predictions that a new Constitution-based government would suffer an early demise, historian Peter S. Onuf points out that the "drafters of the Ordinance proceeded in the faith that the convention would succeed in its task." Like the Framers, the drafters of the Ordinance probably exceeded their authority in promising to admit new states. "The Northwest Ordinance and the federal Constitution depended on each other. Without the Constitution, the Ordinance probably would have been a dead letter. Strikingly, the reverse is also probably true: the success of the new constitutional order depended on the Ordinance's commitment to a dynamic, expanding union of equal states." As Onuf, author of the most comprehensive study of the Ordinance stresses, "The Constitution did not *require* expansion; it only *enabled* the new federal government to fulfill promises made by the Confederation Congress in the Northwest Ordinance." [2] The reaffirmation and reenactment of the Ordinance in 1789 by the First Congress "made its provisions compatible with the new constitutional regime," Onuf points out, and the "constitutional future of the West seemed secure." [3]

During the 1780s, there was rapid and unregulated settlement of the West. This provoked the American Indians to fight to retain their lands, deprived Congress of a desperately needed source of revenue from land sales that could be used to relieve its huge burden of debt, and jeopardized the new nation's chance to avail itself of "rich natural endowments promising boundless prosperity and power." The Ordinance affirmed the new nation's commitment to continental development by establishing a framework for Western economic and political development and "was an integral part of America's new constitutional order." [4]

The Ordinance called for the territory to be initially administered by a governor, secretary, and three judges appointed by Congress until the population of the territory reached five thousand free male adults. At that time, a territory could elect a bicameral legislature and a nonvoting member of the House of Representatives. The Ordinance provided for the creation of at least three, but not more than five, states. When a designated area of territory attained a population of sixty thousand free inhabitants, it could apply to become a state by complying with specified requirements. The new states were to be admitted into the Union "on an equal footing with the original states in all respects whatso-

This map depicts the Northwest Territory following the Northwest Ordinance of 1787, which provided for the establishment of new states and the expansion of U.S. territory. The relationship of the new territory to the U.S. government was one under great debate by the Continental Congress.
Source: The Granger Collection, New York.

ever." The Ordinance was the first federal document to contain a bill of rights. It included the following:

- a guarantee of freedom of worship if it was conducted in "a peaceful and orderly manner";
- protection of an individuals' right to trial by jury and the writ of habeas corpus, proportionate representation in the legislature, judicial proceedings in keeping with common law practices, right of bail except for capital offenses, and moderate fines;
- a ban on cruel or unusual punishment, deprivation of liberty or property except by peer judgment or legal action, and laws that would interfere with or affect existing private contracts made in good faith without fraud;
- support for schools and education because "Religion, morality, and knowledge [were] necessary to good government and the happiness of mankind";
- a promise of "utmost good faith" and "justice and humanity" toward the Indians, guaranteeing them their "property rights and liberty" which could not be abridged except in "just and lawful wars authorized by Congress";
- a ban on "slavery and involuntary servitude in the territory," and a stipulation that fugitive slaves and servants from the original states must be returned to their lawful owners; and

- a declaration that navigable waters leading into the Mississippi and St. Lawrence rivers in the territory and their connecting carrying places were open to all American citizens without any tax or duty.[5]

Throughout the protracted struggle that eventually produced the Ordinance, it is evident that its proponents were convinced the union must survive. Congress also was committed to deriving its powers from the consent of the governed and securing the rights of the governed. The provisions of the Ordinance were designed to attract to the territory the type of people that would be the most reliable guardians of the union and to afford them an opportunity to see firsthand the relationship between popular government and individual rights. Following the Revolution, American leaders both dreamed of a continental empire and feared the collapse of their republican system. They worried that distant settlers might break away from the union, align themselves with a foreign power, and weaken, rather than strengthen, the nation.

While Congress succeeded in shaping a policy for expansion across the continent, its promises to racial minorities were less easily achieved. Slavery continued in a number of areas in the Northwest Territory for years after the Ordinance was passed, and the American Indians ultimately lost both their lands and way of life. Despite these realities, the Ordinance created a mechanism that made it possible not only to create the states of the Old Northwest but also a nation of fifty states stretching across the entire continent.

Historian Bruce Catton, in his final work, *The Bold and Magnificent Dream,* published posthumously in 1978 by his son William, captured both the spirit and essence of the Ordinance when he wrote:

> Once and for all, it determined what sort of country this was going to be; the concept of complete equality, so nobly voiced in the Declaration [of Independence], was written into the basic document that determined how the nation grew. It compelled men to look past their own dooryards to something unlimited beyond the horizon, and decreed that a man's place in the American Republic would be forever greater than his place as a resident of a single state.[6]

"One of the true marks of genius present in the Northwest Ordinance," historian Robert M. Sutton observed, "was its ability to recognize and soften deep-seated sectional rivalries." While state rivalries existed, particularly over issues involving trade, the real threat to the success of the new republic, Sutton reasoned, was sectional differences. "Commercial states versus agricultural states; merchants versus planters, slave states versus free states; large states versus small states; old states versus potential new states — the possibilities were limitless." The Ordinance "bridged the gap between wilderness and statehood" by providing "encouragement, incentives, and safeguards" and "the promise of statehood on a basis of equality with the original thirteen." It became "one of the great success stories of American history. Few documents in our national life have done more to encourage and perpetuate the American dream than did the Ordinance."[7]

CORRESPONDENCE BETWEEN JAMES MONROE AND THOMAS JEFFERSON ON THE DEBATE OVER THE NORTHWEST ORDINANCE

The official version of the Ordinance of 1787 and an abbreviated summary of the action that preceded its adoption are found in the *Journals of the Continental Congress*. During the past half-century, scholars, through painstaking research, have concluded that the Continental Congress repeatedly debated the issues dealt with in the Ordinance. Unfortunately, only scant remnants of that debate are found in the *Journals*. As is often the case in looking at actions by the Continental Congress, it is necessary to look beyond the official record. The give-and-take involved in establishing the Ordinance can be seen in records at the National Archives, state documents, and personal papers of Jefferson, Monroe, and other members of the Continental Congress.[8] The following excerpts from correspondence between Thomas Jefferson and James Monroe highlight their differing views, as well as those of many in the Continental Congress, on how to provide for the settlement and governance of the land the states had ceded to the national government. The Northwest Ordinance, as one author has aptly observed, "set the pattern for territorial governance and state-making that was ultimately applied to thirty-one of the fifty states."[9]

Two years prior to the Monroe-Jefferson exchange, the Continental Congress approved the Ordinance of 1784, which Jefferson had drafted. It reflected the future president's belief that the western territories should be self-governing and, when they reached a certain stage of growth, should be admitted to the Union as full partners with the original thirteen states. The Ordinance of 1784 called for the land north of the Ohio River, west of the Appalachian Mountains, and east of the Mississippi River to be divided into ten separate self-governing districts. The districts would remain as dependent territories until they had attained the same population as the least populous existing state, at which time they could petition Congress for statehood.

During its consideration of the Ordinance of 1784, Congress modified Jefferson's original draft to include a provision stating that a government could only be formed after the lands in the Northwest had actually been "offered for sale." Congress failed, however, to establish how the government would distribute the land or how the territory would be settled. The Land Ordinance of 1785 dealt with these issues by providing for the use of a rectangular survey system for the Northwest Territory. This plan divided the land into townships, set a price for the land, established land offices at convenient points for selling the land, and set aside land reserves for Revolutionary War veterans.

Several factors prevented the two ordinances from succeeding. A lack of adequate funding to maintain the system Congress had created blocked its implementation. Also, significant delays, first by Congress in establishing a land office, and then by surveyors in platting the land, prompted further disenchantment with the system. Amidst these concerns, modifications were sought regarding the size and number of new states, the population threshold for statehood, and the type of government to be imposed on the settlers. For all of these reasons, Congress chose the Northwest Ordinance over the Ordinance of 1784 to create new provisions for the governance of western settlers.[10]

By May 11, 1786, when Monroe wrote Jefferson, who at the time was minister to Paris, the Continental Congress had begun debating a plan authored by Monroe that was designed to reshape the Ordinance of 1784. Monroe unabashedly described the plan to Jefferson "in effect to be a colonial government similar to that which prevail'd in these States previous to the revolution, with this remarkable and important difference that when such districts shall contain the number of the least of the '13. original States for the time being' they shall be admitted into the confederacy."[11]

Monroe's "apparent repudiation of the constitutionalism that underlay the Ordinance of 1784," historian Arthur Bestor concludes, "turned out to be neither final nor complete." Bestor further states:

> Though the Northwest Ordinance did not grant self-government to western settlers at the outset as Jefferson had proposed to do, it reiterated in language as impressive as his the promise that new states would receive, at a predetermined point in their cycle of growth, not only every privilege of republican self-government but also unqualified admission to the Union "on an equal footing with the original States, in all respects whatever." Jefferson's idea of incorporating such guarantees in a solemn compact — an idea that Congress seemed ready to abandon in 1786 — was revived, and not only revived but expanded. Thanks to the skillful draftsmanship of Nathan Dane, the Articles of Compact of the Northwest Ordinance became a full articulated bill of rights, comparable to those that prefaced most state constitutions and unlike anything that had as yet been drawn up as part of the fundamental law of the Confederation.[12]

JAMES MONROE TO THOMAS JEFFERSON

MAY 11, 1786

In my last I mention'd to you that the propriety of the acts of Congress founded on the condition of cession from the States, fixing the limits of the States westward, was question'd. A proposition or rather a report is before Congress recommending it to Virga. and Mass. to revise their acts as to that condition so as to leave it to the U.S. to make what division of the same future circumstances may make necessary, subject to this proviso, "that the said territory be divided into not less than two nor more than five states." The plan of a temporary government to be instituted by Congress and preserv'd over such district untill they shall be admitted into Congress is also reported. The outlines are as follows. Congress are to appoint, as soon as any the lands shall be sold, a governor, Council, Judges, secretary to the Council, and some other officers; the Governor and Council to have certain powers untill they have a certain number inhabitants, at which they are to elect representatives to form a general assembly, to consist of the governor and council and said house of representatives. It is in effect to be a colonial government similar to that which prevail'd in these States previous to the revolution, with this remarkable and important difference that when such districts shall contain the number of the least numerous of the "13. original States for the time being" "they shall be admitted into the confederacy." The most important principles of the act at Annapolis are you observe preservd in this report. It is generally approv'd of but has not yet been taken up.

Sources: Julian P. Boyd et. al., eds., The Papers of Thomas Jefferson, 34 vols. (Princeton, N.J.: Princeton University Press, 1950–2006), 9: 510–511; Edmund C. Burnett, ed., *Letters of Members of the Continental Congress*, 8 vols. (Washington, D.C.: Carnegie Institute of Washington, 1921–1936), 8:385–286; and Paul H. Smith, Gerard W. Gawalt, Rosemary Fry Plakas, and Eugene R. Sheridan, eds., *Letters of Delegates to Congress*, 1774–1789, 26 vols. (Washington, D.C.: Library of Congress, 1976–2000), 23:278–279.

THOMAS JEFFERSON TO JAMES MONROE

JULY 9, 1786

Note: Jefferson, in his response of July 9, 1786, reminded Monroe that Congress had already approved a plan that called for the government of the western settlers to "treat them as fellow citizens." By giving them "a just share in their own government," Jefferson continued, "they will love us, and pride themselves in an union with us." If "we treat them as subjects," Jefferson warned, "they will abhor us as masters, and break from us in defiance."

★ ★ ★ ★

With respect to the new states were the question to stand simply in this form, How may the ultramontane territory be disposed of so as to produce the greatest and most immediate benefit to the inhabitants of the maritime states of the union? the plan would be more plausible of laying it off into two or three states only. Even on this view however there would still be something to be said against it which might render it at least doubtful. But it is question which good faith forbids us to receive into discussion. This requires us to state the question in it's just form. How may the territories of the Union be disposed of so as to produce the greatest degree of happiness to their inhabitants? With respect to the Maritime states nothing, or little remains to be done. With respect then to the Ultramontane states, will their inhabitants be happiest divided into states of 30,000 square miles, not quite as large as Pennsylvania, or into states of 160,000 square miles each, that is to say three times as large as Virginia within the Alleghaney? They will not only be happier in states of a moderate size, but it is the only way in which they can exist as a regular society. Considering the American character in general, that of those

---

Upon this plan we treat them as fellow citizens. They will have a just share in their own government, they will ... pride themselves in an union with us. Upon the other we treat them as subjects ... they will abhor us as masters, and break off from us in defiance.

— Thomas Jefferson to James Monroe

---

people particularly, and the inergetic nature of our governments, a state of such extent as 160,000 square miles would soon crumble into little ones. These are the circumstances which reduce the Indians to such small societies. They would produce an effect on our people similar to this. They would not be broken into such small peices because they are more habituated to subordination, and value more a government of regular law. But you would surely reverse the nature of things in making small states on the ocean and large ones beyond the mountains. If we could in our consciences say that great states beyond the mountains will make the people happiest, we must still ask whether they will be contented to be laid off into large states? They certainly will not; and if they decide to divide themselves we are not able to restrain them. They will end by separating from our confederacy and becoming it's enemies. We had better then look forward and see what will be the probable course of things. This will surely be a division of that country into states of a small, or at most of a moderate size. If we lay them off into such, they will acquiesce, and we shall have the advantage of arranging them so as to produce the best combinations of interest. What Congress has already done in this matter is an argument the more in favour of the revolt of those states against a different arrangement, and of their acquiescence under a continuance of that. Upon this plan we treat them as fellow citizens. They will have a just share in their own government, they will love us, and pride themselves in an union with us. Upon the other we treat them as subjects we govern them, and not they themselves; they will abhor us as masters, and break off from us in defiance. I confess to you that I can see no other turn that these two plans would take, but I respect your opinion, and your knowlege of the country too much, to be over confident in my own.

Source: Julian P. Boyd, et. al., eds., *The Papers of Thomas Jefferson*, 34 vols. (Princeton, N.J.: Princeton University Press, 1950–2006), 10:112–113.

Notes

1. Daniel Webster, "First Speech on Foot's Resolution," in *The Writings and Speeches of Daniel Webster*, 18 vols. (Boston: Little, Brown, 1903), 5:263; Theodore Roosevelt, *The Works of Theodore Roosevelt*, 20 vols. (New York: Charles Scribner's Sons, 1926), 9: 218; and "Franklin D. Roosevelt, "The President Hails the One Hundred and Fiftieth Anniversary of the Ordinance of 1787, April 30, 1935," in Samuel I. Rosenman, comp., *The Public Papers and Addresses of Franklin D. Roosevelt*, 13 vols. (New York: Random House, 1938–1950), 4:125. See also Phillip R. Shriver, "Freedom's Proving Ground: The Heritage of the Northwest Ordinance," *Wisconsin Magazine of History*, 72 (Winter 1988–1989), 126–131.

2. Peter S. Onuf, "For the Common Benefit: The Northwest Ordinance," *Timeline*, 5 (April–May 1988), 4.

3. Peter S. Onuf, *Statehood and Union: A History of the Northwest Ordinance* (Bloomington: Indiana University Press, 1987), xviii.

4. Ibid., 4, 9.

5. Worthington Chauncey Ford and Roscoe R. Hill, eds., *Journals of the Continental Congress, 1774–1789*, 34 vols. (Washington, D.C.: GPO, 1904–1937), 32: 334–343.

6. Bruce Catton and William B. Catton, *The Bold and Magnificent Dream: America's Founding Years, 1492–1815* (Garden City, N.Y.: Doubleday, 1978), 316–317.

7. Robert M. Sutton, "The Northwest Ordinance: A Bicentennial Souvenir," *Illinois Historical Journal*, 81 (Spring 1988), 20, 24.

8. Jack Ericson Eblen, *The First and Second United States Empires: Governors and Territorial Government, 1784–1912* (Pittsburgh: University of Pittsburgh Press, 1968), 17; Leonard Rapport, "Discussion of Sources," in John Porter Bloom, ed., *The American Territorial System* (Athens: Ohio University Press, 1973), 56–57.

9. Denis P. Duffey, "The Northwest Ordinance as a Constitutional Document," *Columbia Law Review*, 95 (May 1995), 930.

10. Robert F. Berkhofer Jr., "Jefferson, the Ordinance of 1874, and the Origin of the American Territorial System," *William and Mary Quarterly*, Third series, 29 (April 1972), 231–262; Duffey, "The Northwest Ordinance as a Constitutional Document," 935–936; Eblen, *The First and Second United States Empires: Governors and Territorial Government, 1784–1912*, 21–29; Onuf, *Statehood and Union: A History of the Northwest Ordinance*, 50–52; Richard P. McCormick, "The 'Ordinance' of 1784?" *William and Mary Quarterly*, Third series, 50 (January 1993), 112–122.

11. For background on the Northwest Ordinance debate see Michael Allen, *The Confederation Congress and the Creation of the American Trans-Appalachian Settlement Policy 1783–1787* (Lewiston, N.Y.: Edwin Mellen Press, 2006), 119–126; Eblen, *The First and Second United States Empires: Governors and Territorial Government, 1784–1912*, 29–51; Jack E. Eblen, "Origins of the United States Colonial System: The Ordinance of 1787," *Wisconsin Magazine of History*, 51 (Summer 1968), 305–307; H. James Henderson, *Party Politics in the Continental Congress* (New York: McGraw-Hill, 1974), 409–413.

12. Arthur Bestor, "Constitutionalism and the Settlement of the West: The Attainment of Consensus, 1754–1784," in John Porter Bloom, ed., *The American Territorial System* (Athens: Ohio University Press, 1973), 32–33.

Bill of Rights
✳ 1789 ✳

After the American colonies separated from England in 1776, each of the thirteen states of the newly independent United States wrote constitutions to replace their defunct colonial governments. Seven of the new constitutions included a declaration of fundamental and inalienable rights. The remaining six new states included elements of the English Bill of Rights of 1689 (in which Parliament limited Royal authority and guaranteed British citizens certain rights) in the bodies of their constitutions. Congress itself provided the first federal precedent for a bill of rights with the passage of the Northwest Ordinance of 1787, which included articles guaranteeing "fundamental principles of civil and religious liberty" in the new territories and future. Nearly all of these rights were to ultimately be expressed in the Constitution of 1787 or in the Constitution's first ten amendments of 1789, known as the Bill of Rights.

During the Constitutional Convention, the Framers continuously expressed concern about protecting individual liberties against an abusive government, but most concluded that a separate bill of rights was unnecessary. When Charles Pinckney of South Carolina formally raised the issue on August 20, 1787, the notion of a bill of rights was in part rejected because the Constitution contained strictly enumerated powers; as a consequence, the federal government was restricted from passing legislation ignoring individual rights. Such reasoning did not, however, alleviate the concerns of those delegates already opposed to the work of the Convention. On September 12 and again on September 14, only a few days before the Convention adjourned, George Mason of Virginia and Elbridge Gerry of Massachusetts were also unsuccessful in their efforts to include a declaration of basic individual liberties protected under the proposed Constitution then being drafted.

As Americans waited over the next ten months to see if the proposed Constitution would be approved by the state ratifying conventions, the absence of a bill of rights proved to be the chief impediment to its acceptance. Almost immediately, Antifederalists put Federalist supporters of the Constitution on the defensive. Although the ratifying conventions did not have the power to amend the Constitution, eventually the Federalists realized that political expediency dictated a switch in their position and they were forced to concede that a bill of rights might be necessary to calm apprehension about the proposed new government. To gain ratification, some even adopted a tactic of suggesting that states offer "recommendatory alterations" that could be adopted as soon as the new government was operational. Prominent among the Federalists who changed their position on the need for a bill of rights was James Madison, who made his views known at the Virginia ratifying convention. By the time the Constitution was declared ratified, eight states had suggested amendments designed specifically to safeguard individual rights as a condition for their ratification, and two states, North Carolina and Rhode Island, refused to even ratify the Constitution until a bill of rights was adopted.[1]

Subsequently, during his campaign to become a member of the first House of Representatives, Madison promised voters in his district that he would work for "such amendments as will, in the most satisfactory manner, guard essential rights, and render certain vexatious abuses of power impossible." To ease all doubt, Madison said that he would seek amendments protecting "all those rights, which have been thought in danger, such as the rights of conscience, the freedom of the press, trials by jury, exemption from general warrants &c."[2] Madison defeated his opponent, James Monroe, by a comfortable margin and went to the First Congress prepared to fulfill his campaign promise. Also, his close friend, Thomas Jefferson, who strongly favored a bill of rights, influenced Madison.

In George Washington's inaugural address on April 30, 1789, the new president acknowledged widespread demand for amendments to the Constitution but declined to make "particular recommendations on this subject,"[3] leaving that role up to Congress. In response, in an address to the president that Madison drafted, the House promised that the question of amendments "will receive all the attention demanded by its importance."[4]

Realizing that a national consensus favored a bill of rights, Madison drafted them himself. His initial attempt to gain support for the adoption of a bill of rights, however, received mixed reactions in large part because such matters as making the new government operational, organizing the judicial branch, fixing taxes and tariffs, and establishing an armed

James Madison won election to the House of Representatives in 1789 after promising voters that he would work for the protection of "essential rights." Along with Thomas Jefferson, Madison was one of the strongest proponents of the Bill of Rights.
Source: Library of Congress.

forces were considered more important. Further complicating his effort was opposition from the Antifederalist critics of the Constitution now worried that adoption of a bill of rights would further strengthen the strong central government they opposed. They sought instead a second constitutional convention or amendments that would limit the substantive powers of the government. Madison knew, however, that if he could get the amendments adopted, it would be very difficult for the Antifederalists to obtain passage of their proposals in the future. Ultimately, he was successful and his "accomplishment in the face of opposition and apathy entitles him to be remembered as 'father of the bill of rights' even more than as 'father of the Constitution.'"[5] By the time Madison announced on May 4, 1789, that he would soon be offering the promised amendments, the New York legislature had sent Congress an application calling for a second constitutional convention. The following day, Virginia submitted a similar application to the House. The timing of Madison's announcement was intended "to counter an incipient movement for a second constitutional convention to decide on amendments." With this action, "Madison deftly secur[ed]

the filing of both applications, instead of having them referred to the Committee of the Whole. When he officially introduced his proposed amendments, on June 8, he effectively ended any chance the applications might have otherwise have had for a second convention."[6]

In his masterful address that day, Madison declared that there was a great desire for a bill of rights. To "satisfy the public mind that their liberties will be perpetual," Congress needs to declare the "great rights" guaranteed under the Constitution, he stated. Madison went on to explain the proposed amendments and why they were needed. In response to critics who argued that a bill of rights was not necessary, Madison argued that such constitutional provisions would have "a salutary effect against the abuse of power," and secure "the great rights of mankind."[7] Madison's draft, which included all of the personal liberties brought forward during the ratification process, covered every provision that was eventually included in the Bill of Rights.

Six weeks later, on July 21, the House formed a select committee composed of a representative from each state to consider Madison's proposals. The committee, which included Madison, completed its work in a week. While the version it reported did not make any substantial modifications, it did make certain stylistic changes. The subsequent House debate on the amendments extended from August 13 through August 24 before the proposals were arranged into seventeen amendments and sent to the Senate for its consideration. While the House retained most of Madison's proposal during its extensive debate, his idea to incorporate the amendments in the text of the Constitution was not. Instead, the House accepted the recommendation of Roger Sherman of Connecticut that the amendments stand as independent provisions at the end of the Constitution. "This change," legal historian Bernard Schwartz has observed, "was of the greatest significance; it may be doubted that the Bill of Rights could have attained its position as the vital center of constitutional law, had its provisions been dispersed throughout the Constitution."[8]

The Senate work on the amendments, which began on September 2, was conducted behind closed doors, as were all Senate sessions prior to February 1794. Besides focusing on strengthening the language of amendments through changes in prose and combining related amendments, the Senate made several important substantive changes. By the time the Senate finished its work on September 9, it had reduced the seventeen House amendments to twelve. During the process, it eliminated several provisions that prohibited states from infringing on freedom of conscience, speech, press, and jury trial; an amendment limiting appeals to the Supreme Court; an amendment requiring strict separation of powers in the national government; and language exempting conscientious objectors from having to serve in the military.

A conference committee, which included Madison, then met to resolve the differences between the House and Senate versions of proposed amendments. The committee's report to the House on September 23 recommended that all of the Senate amendments be accepted and called for three changes. These included a minor alteration in an amendment on representation, strengthening the religious freedom guaranty clause, and reinserting the right of a jury trial by the locality (which the Senate had omitted). On September 24, the House voted 37–14 to agree to the committee report. The Senate concurred the following day. On October 2, President George Washington officially transmitted the proposed amendments to the states for ratification. More than two years passed, however, before Virginia, on December 15, 1791, became the eleventh state to ratify the first ten amendments, thereby fulfilling the constitutional requirements that three-fourths of the states approve amendments to the Constitution. Those ten amendments are known collectively as the Bill of Rights.[9]

Article I provides for the freedom of religion, speech, and the press; and for "the right of people peaceably to assemble, and to petition the government for redress of grievances." Article II guarantees the right of the people to bear arms. Article III forbids the government from quartering troops in private homes in times of peace without the consent of the owner, and in times of war only as prescribed by law. Article IV protects the people against unreasonable searches and seizures. Article V outlaws double jeopardy and the deprivation of life, limb, and property without due process of law. Articles VI and VII guarantee the right to a speedy and impartial jury trial and the right to defense counsel. Article VIII prohibits excessive bail or fines, or cruel and unusual punishment. Article IX declares that the enumeration of these rights can "not be construed to deny or disparage others retained by the people." Article X declares that "powers not delegated to the United States by the Constitution, nor prohibited by it to the States, are reserved to the States, or to the people." The two proposed amendments that did not become part of the Constitution prescribed the ratio of members in the House of Representatives and specified that no law varying the compensation of members should be effective until after an intervening election of representatives. More than two centuries later, on May 7, 1992, ratification of the congressional pay proposal was completed and it became the Twenty-seventh Amendment to the Constitution.

HOUSE DEBATE ON THE BILL OF RIGHTS

JUNE 8, 1789

MR. MADISON. This day, Mr. Speaker, is the day assigned for taking into consideration the subject of amendments to the Constitution. As I considered myself bound in honor and in duty to do what I have done on this subject, I shall proceed to bring the amendments before you as soon as possible, and advocate them until they shall be finally adopted or rejected by a Constitutional majority of this House. With a view of drawing your attention to this important object, I shall move that this House do now resolve itself into a Committee of the Whole on the state of the Union; by which an opportunity will be given, to bring forward some propositions, which I have strong hopes will meet with the unanimous approbation of this House, after the fullest discussion and most serious regard. I therefore move you, that the House now go into a committee on this business.

Mr. SMITH was not inclined to interrupt the measures which the public were so anxiously expecting, by going into a Committee of the Whole at this time. He observed there were two modes of introducing this business to the House. One by appointing a select committee to take into consideration the several amendments proposed by the State Conventions; this he thought the most likely way to shorten the business. The other was, that the gentleman should lay his propositions on the table, for the consideration of the members; that they should be printed, and taken up for discussion at a future day. Either of these modes would enable the House to enter upon business better prepared than could be the case by a sudden transition from other important concerns to which their minds were strongly bent. He therefore hoped that the honorable gentleman would consent to bring the subject forward in one of those ways, in preference to going into a Committee of the Whole. For, said he, it must appear extremely impolitic to go into the consideration of amending the Government, before it is organized, before it has begun to operate.

★ ★ ★ ★

Mr. JACKSON. I am of opinion we ought not to be in a hurry with respect to altering the Constitution. For my part, I have no idea of speculating in this serious manner on theory. If I agree to alterations in the mode of administering this Government, I shall like to stand on the sure ground of experience, and not be treading air. What experience have we had of the good or bad qualities of this Constitution? Can any gentleman affirm to me one proposition that is a certain and absolute amendment? I deny that he can. Our Constitution, sir, is like a vessel just launched, and lying at the wharf; she is untried, you can hardly discover any one of her properties. It is not known how she will answer her helm, or lay her course; whether she will bear with safety the precious freight to be deposited in her hold. But, in this state, will the prudent merchant attempt alterations? Will he employ workmen to tear off the planking and take asunder the frame? He certainly will not. Let us, gentlemen, fit out our vessel, set up her masts, and expand her sails, and be guided by the experiment in our alterations. If she sails upon an uneven keel, let us right her by adding weight where it is wanting. In this way, we may remedy her defects to the satisfaction of all concerned; but if we proceed now to make alterations, we may deface a beauty, or deform a well proportioned piece of workmanship. In short, Mr. Speaker, I am not for amendments at this time; but if gentlemen should think it a subject deserving of attention, they will surely not neglect the more important business which is now unfinished before them.

★ ★ ★ ★

MR. BURKE thought amendments to the Constitution necessary, but this was not the proper time to bring them forward. He wished the Government completely organized before they entered upon this ground. The law for collecting the revenue is immediately necessary; the Treasury Department must be established; till this, and other important subjects are determined, he was against taking this up. He said it might interrupt the harmony of the House, which was necessary to be preserved in order to despatch the great objects of legislation. He hoped it would be postponed for the present, and pledged himself to bring it forward hereafter, if nobody else would.

MR. MADISON. The gentleman from Georgia (Mr. JACKSON) is certainly right in his opposition to my motion for going into a Committee of the Whole, because he is unfriendly to the object I have in contemplation; but I cannot see that the gentlemen who wish for amendments to be proposed at the present session, stand on good ground when they object to the House going into committee on this business. When I first hinted to the House my intention of calling their deliberations to this object, I mentioned the pressure of other important subjects, and submitted the propriety of postponing this till the more urgent business was despatched; but finding that business not despatched, when the order of the day for considering amendments took place arrived, I thought it a good reason for a farther delay; I moved the postponement accordingly. I am sorry the same reason still exists in some degree, but it operates with less force, when it is considered that it is not now proposed to enter into a full and minute discussion of every part of the subject, but merely to bring it before the House, that our constituents may see we

pay a proper attention to a subject they have much at heart; and if it does not give that full gratification which is to be wished, they will discover that it proceeds from the urgency of business of a very important nature.... The applications for amendments come from a very respectable number of our constituents, and it is certainly proper for Congress to consider the subject, in order to quiet that anxiety which prevails in the public mind.... I wish then to commence the consideration at the present moment; I hold it to be my duty to unfold my ideas, and explain myself to the House in some form or other without delay. I only wish to introduce the great work, and, as I said before, I do not expect it will be decided immediately; but if some step is taken in the business, it will give reason to believe that we may come to a final result. This will inspire a reasonable hope in the advocates for amendments, that full justice will be done to the important subject; and I have reason to believe their expectation will not be defeated. I hope the House will not decline my motion for going into a committee.

MR. SHERMAN. I am willing that this matter should be brought before the House at a proper time. I suppose a number of gentlemen think it their duty to bring it forward; so that there is no apprehension it will be passed over in silence. Other gentlemen may be disposed to let the subject rest until the more important objects of Government are attended to; and I should conclude, from the nature of the case, that the people expect the latter from us in preference to altering the Constitution; because they have ratified that instrument, in order that the Government may begin to operate. If this was not their wish, they might as well have rejected the Constitution, as North Carolina has done until the amendments took place. The State I have the honor to come from adopted this system by a very great majority, because they wished for the Government; but they desired no amendments. I suppose this was the case in other States; it will therefore be imprudent to neglect much more important concerns for this. The executive part of the Government wants organization; the business of the revenue is incomplete, to say nothing of the judiciary business. Now, will gentlemen give up these points to go into a discussion of amendments, when no advantage can arise from them? For my part, I question if any alteration which can be now proposed would be an amendment, in the true sense of the word; but, nevertheless, I am willing to let the subject be introduced. If the gentleman only desires to go into committee for the purpose of receiving his propositions, I shall consent....

MR. WHITE. I hope the House will not spend much time on this subject, till the more pressing business is despatched; but, at the same time, I hope we shall not dismiss it altogether, because I think a majority of the people who have ratified the Constitution did it under the expectation that Congress would, at some convenient time, examine its texture and point out where it was defective, in order that it might be judiciously amended. Whether, while we are without experience, amendments can be digested in such a manner as to give satisfaction to a Constitutional majority of this House, I will not pretend to say; but I hope the subject may be considered with all convenient speed. I think it would tend to tranquilize the public mind; therefore I shall vote in favor of going into a Committee of the Whole, and, after receiving the subject, shall be content to refer it to a special committee to arrange and report. I fear, if we refuse to take up the subject, it will irritate many of our constituents, which I do not wish to do.

★ ★ ★ ★

Mr. PAGE. My colleague tells you he is ready to submit to the Committee of the Whole his ideas on this subject. If no objection had been made to his motion, the whole business might have been finished before this. He has done me the honor of showing me certain propositions which he has drawn up; they are very important, and I sincerely wish the House may receive them. … I venture to affirm, that unless you take early notice of this subject, you will not have power to deliberate. The people will clamor for a new convention; they will not trust the House any longer. Those, therefore who dread the assembling of a convention, will do well to acquiesce in the present motion and lay the foundation of a most important work. I do not think we need consume more than half an hour in the Committee of the Whole; this is not so much time but we may conveniently spare it, considering the nature of the business.

★ ★ ★ ★

MR. MADISON. I am sorry to be accessary to the loss of a single moment of time by the House. If I had been indulged in my motion, and we had gone into a Committee of the Whole, I think we might have rose and resumed the consideration of other business before this time; that is, so far as it depended upon what I proposed to bring forward. As that mode seems not to give satisfaction, I will withdraw the motion, and move you, sir, that a select committee be appointed to consider and report such amendments as are proper for Congress to propose to the Legislatures of the several States, conformably to the fifth article of the Constitution.

I will state my reasons why I think it proper to propose amendments, and state the amendments themselves, so far as I think they ought to be proposed. If I thought I could fulfil the duty which I owe to myself and my constituents, to let the subject pass over in silence, I most certainly should not trespass upon the indulgence of this House. But I cannot do this, and am therefore compelled to beg a patient hearing to what I have to lay before you.

★ ★ ★ ★

It cannot be a secret to the gentlemen in this House, that, notwithstanding the ratification of this system of Government by eleven of the thirteen United States, in some cases unanimously, in others by large majorities; yet still there is a great number of our constituents who are dissatisfied with it; among whom are many respectable for their talents and patriotism, and respectable for the jealousy they have for their liberty, which, though mistaken in its object, is laudable in its motive. There is a great body of the people falling under this description, who at present feel much inclined to join their support to the cause of Federalism, if they were satisfied on this one point. We ought not to disregard their inclination but, on principles of amity and moderation, conform to their wishes, and expressly declare the great rights of mankind secured under this Constitution. The acquiescence which our fellow citizens show under the Government calls upon us for a like return of moderation. But perhaps there is a stronger motive than this for our going into a consideration of the subject. It is to provide those securities for liberty which are required by a part of the community; I allude in a particular manner to those two States that have not thought fit to throw themselves into the bosom of the Confederacy. It is a desirable thing, on our part as well as theirs, that a reunion should take place as soon as possible.…

But I will candidly acknowledge, that, over and above all these considerations, I do conceive that the Constitution may be amended; that is to say, if all power is subject to abuse, that then it is possible the abuse of the powers of the General Government may be guarded against in a more secure manner than is now done, while no one advantage arising from the exercise of that power shall be damaged or endangered by it. We have in this way something to gain, and, if we proceed with caution, nothing to lose. And in this case it is necessary to proceed with caution; for while we feel all these inducements to go into a revisal of the Constitution, we must feel for the Constitution itself and make that revisal a moderate one. I should be unwilling to see a door opened for a reconsideration of the whole structure of the Government for a reconsideration of the principles and the substance of the powers given; because I doubt if such a door were opened, we should be very likely to stop at that point which would be safe to the Government itself.… I will not propose a single alteration which I do not wish to see take place, as intrinsically proper in itself, or proper because it is wished for by a respectable number of my fellow-citizens; and therefore I shall not propose a single alteration but is likely to meet the concurrence required by the Constitution. There have been objections of various kinds made against the Constitution.… [B]ut I believe that the great mass of the people who opposed it, disliked it because it did not contain effectual provisions against the encroachments on particular rights, and those safeguards which they have been long accustomed to have interposed between them and the magistrate who exercises the sovereign power; nor ought we to consider them safe, while a great number of our fellow-citizens think these securities necessary.

It is a fortunate thing that the objection to the Government has been made on the ground I stated; because it will be practicable on that ground, to obviate the objection so far as to satisfy the public mind that their liberties will be perpetual, and this without endangering any part of the Constitution, which is considered as essential to the existence of the Government by those who promoted its adoption. The amendments which have occurred to me, proper to be recommended by Congress to the State Legislatures, are these:

★ ★ ★ ★

The first of these amendments relates to what may be called a bill of rights. I will own that I never considered this provision so essential to the Federal Constitution as to make it improper to ratify it, until such an amendment was added; at the same time I always conceived, that in a certain form, and to a certain extent, such a provision was neither improper nor altogether useless. I am aware that a great number of the most respectable friends to the Government, and champions for republican liberty, have thought such a provision not only unnecessary, but even improper; nay, I believe some have gone so far as to think it even dangerous. Some policy has been made use of, perhaps, by gentlemen on both sides of the question: I acknowledge the ingenuity of those arguments which were drawn against the Constitution, by a comparison with the policy of Great Britain, in establishing a declaration of rights; but there is too great a difference in the case to warrant the comparison: therefore, the arguments drawn from that source were in a great measure inapplicable. In the declaration of rights which that country has established, the truth is, they have gone no farther than to raise a barrier against the power of the Crown; the power of the Legislature is left altogether indefinite. Although I know whenever the great rights, the trial by jury, freedom of the press or liberty of conscience, come in question in that body, the invasion of them is resisted by able advocates, yet their Magna Charta does not contain any one provision for the security of those rights, respecting which the people of America are most alarmed. The freedom of the press and rights of conscience, those choicest privileges of the people, are unguarded in the British Constitution....

The people of many States have thought it necessary to raise barriers against power in all forms and departments of Government, and I am inclined to believe if once bills of rights are established in all the States as well as the Federal Constitution, we shall find, that, although some of them are rather unimportant, yet, upon the whole, they will have a salutary tendency....In some instances they assert those rights which are exercised by the people in forming and establishing a plan of Government. In other instances, they specify those rights which are retained when particular powers are given up to be exercised by the Legislature. In other instances, they specify positive rights, which may seem to result from the nature of the compact. Trial by jury cannot be considered as a natural right but a right resulting from a social compact, which regulates the action of the community, but is, as essential to secure the liberty of the people as any one of the pre-existent rights of nature. In other instances, they lay down dogmatic maxims with respect to the construction of the Government; declaring that the Legislative, Executive, and Judicial branches shall be kept separate and distinct. Perhaps the best way of securing this in practice is, to provide such checks as will prevent the encroachment of the one upon the other.... [T]he great object in view is to limit and qualify the powers of Government, by excepting out of the grant of power those cases in which the Government ought not to act, or to act only in a particular mode. They point these exceptions sometimes against the abuse of the Executive power, sometimes against the Legislative, and, in some cases, against the community itself; or, in other words, against the majority in favor of the minority.

In our Government it is, perhaps, less necessary to guard against the abuse in the Executive Department than any other; because it is not the stronger branch of the system, but the weaker. It therefore must be levelled against the Legislative, for it is the most powerful, and most likely, to be abused, because it is under the least control.... The prescriptions in favor of liberty ought to be levelled against that quarter where the greatest danger lies, namely, that which possesses the highest prerogative of power. But this is not found in either the Executive or Legislative departments of Government, but in the body of the people, operating by the majority against the minority.

★ ★ ★ ★

It has been said, by way of objection to a bill of rights, by many respectable gentlemen out of doors, and I find opposition on the same principles likely to be made by gentlemen on this floor, that they are unnecessary articles of a Republican Government, upon the presumption that the people have those rights in their own hands, and that is the proper place for them to rest. It would be a sufficient answer to say, that this objection lies against such provisions under the State Governments, as well as under the General Government; and there are, I believe, but few gentlemen who are inclined to push their theory so far as to say that a declaration of rights in those cases is either ineffectual or improper. It has been said, that in the Federal Government they are unnecessary, because the powers are enumerated, and it follows, that all that are not granted by the Constitution are retained, that the Constitution is a bill of powers, the great residuum being the rights of the people; and, therefore, a bill of rights cannot be so necessary as if the residuum was thrown into the hands of the Government. I admit that these arguments are not entirely without foundation; but they are not conclusive to the extent which has been supposed. It is true, the powers of the General Government are circumscribed, they are directed to particular objects; but even if Government keeps within those limits, it has certain discretionary powers with respect to the means, which may admit of abuse to a certain extent, in the same manner as the powers of the State Governments under their constitutions may to an indefinite extent.

★ ★ ★ ★

It may be said, indeed it has been said, that a bill of rights is not necessary, because the establishment of this Government has not repealed those declarations of rights which are added to the several State constitutions that those rights of the people which had been established by the most solemn act, could not be annihilated by a subsequent act of that people, who meant and declared at the head of the instrument, that they ordained and established a new system, for the express purpose of securing to themselves and posterity the liberties they had gained by an arduous conflict.

★ ★ ★ ★

It has been objected also against a bill of rights that, by enumerating particular exceptions to the grant of power, it would disparage those rights which were not placed in that enumeration; and it might follow by implication, that those rights which were not singled out, were intended to be assigned into the hands of the General Government, and were consequently insecure. This is one of the most plausible arguments I have ever heard urged against the admission of a bill of rights into this system; but, I conceive, that it may be guarded against. I have attempted it, as gentlemen may see by turning to the last clause of the fourth resolution.

It has been said that it is unnecessary to load the Constitution with this provision, because it was not found effectual in the constitution of the particular States. It is true, there are a few particular States in which some of the most valuable articles have not, at one time or other, been violated; but it does not follow but they may have, to a certain degree, a salutary effect against the abuse of power. If they are incorporated into the Constitution, independent tribunals of justice will consider themselves in a peculiar manner the guardians of those rights; they will be a impenetrable bulwark against every assumption of power in the Legislative or Executive; they will be naturally led to resist every encroachment upon rights expressly stipulated for in the Constitution by the declaration of rights. Besides this security, there is a great probability that such a declaration in the federal system would be enforced; because the State Legislatures will jealously and closely watch the operations of this Government, and be able to resist with more effect every assumption of power, than any other power on earth can do; and the greatest opponents

to a Federal Government admit the State Legislatures to be sure guardians of the people's liberty. I conclude, from this view of the subject, that it will be proper in itself, and highly politic, for the tranquillity of the public mind, and the stability of the Government, that we should offer something in the form I have proposed, to be incorporated in the system of Government, as a declaration of the rights of the people.

★ ★ ★ ★

I wish, also, in revising the Constitution, we may throw into that section, which interdicts the abuse of certain powers in the State Legislatures some other provisions of equal, if

I have stated ... that no State shall violate the equal right of conscience, freedom of the press, or trial by jury in criminal cases; because it is proper that every Government should be disarmed of powers which trench upon those particular rights. — James Madison

not greater importance than those already made. The words, "No State shall pass any bill of attainder, *ex post facto law,*" &c., were wise and proper restrictions in the Constitution. I think there is more danger of those powers being abused by the State Governments than by the Government of the United States. The same may be said of other powers which they possess, if not controlled by the general principle, that laws are unconstitutional which infringe the rights of the community. I should, therefore, wish to extend this interdiction, and add, as I have stated in the 5th resolution, that no State shall violate the equal right of conscience, freedom of the press, or trial by jury in criminal cases; because it is proper that every Government should be disarmed of powers which trench upon those particular rights.... [I]t must be admitted, on all hands, that the State Governments are as liable to attack these invaluable privileges as the General Government is, and therefore ought to be as cautiously guarded against.

★ ★ ★ ★

These are the points on which I wish to see a revision of the Constitution take place. How far they will accord with the sense of this body, I cannot take upon me absolutely to determine; but I believe every gentleman will readily admit that nothing is in contemplation, so far as I have mentioned, that can endanger the beauty of the Government in any one important feature, even in the eyes of its most sanguine admirers. I have proposed nothing that does not appear to me as proper in itself, or eligible as patronized by a respectable number of our fellow-citizens; and if we can make the Constitution better in the opinion of those who are opposed to it, without weakening its frame, or abridging its usefulness in the judgment of those who are attached to it, we act the part of wise and liberal men to make such alterations as shall produce that effect.

Having done what I conceived was my duty, in bringing before this House the subject of amendments, and also stated such as I wish for and approve, and offered the reasons which occurred to me in their support, I shall content myself, for the present, with moving "that a committee be appointed to consider of and report such amendments as ought to be proposed by Congress to the Legislatures of the States, to become, if ratified by three-fourths thereof, part of the Constitution of the United States." By agreeing to this motion, the subject may be going on in the committee, while other important business is proceeding to a conclusion in the House. I should advocate greater despatch in the business of amendments, if I were not convinced of the absolute necessity there is of pursuing the organization of the Government; because I think we should obtain the confidence of our fellow-citizens, in proportion as we fortify the rights of the people against the encroachments of the Government.

★ ★ ★ ★

MR. SHERMAN. I do not suppose the Constitution to be perfect, nor do I imagine if Congress and all the Legislatures on the continent were to revise it, that their united labors

---

I do not suppose the Constitution to be perfect, nor do I imagine if Congress and all the Legislatures on the continent were to revise it, that their united labors would make it perfect. — Roger Sherman

---

would make it perfect. I do not expect any perfection on this side the grave in the works of man; but my opinion is that we are not at present in circumstances to make it better. It is a wonder that there has been such unanimity in adopting it, considering the ordeal it had to undergo; and the unanimity which prevailed at its formation is equally astonishing; amidst all the members from the twelve States present at the Federal Convention, there were only three who did not sign the instrument to attest their opinion of its goodness. Of the eleven States who have received it, the majority have ratified it without proposing a single amendment. This circumstance leads me to suppose that we shall not be able to propose any

alterations that are likely to be adopted by nine States; and gentlemen know, before the alterations take effect, they must be agreed to by the Legislatures of three-fourths of the States in the Union. Those States which have not recommended alterations, will hardly adopt them, unless it is clear that they tend to make the Constitution better. Now, how this can be made out to their satisfaction I am yet to learn; they know of no defect from experience. It seems to be the opinion of gentlemen generally that this is not the time for entering upon the discussion of amendments: our only question therefore is, how to get rid of the subject. Now, for my own part, I would prefer to have it referred to a Committee of the Whole, rather than a special committee, and therefore shall not agree to the motion now before the House....

MR. SUMTER. I consider the subject of amendments of such great importance to the Union, that I shall be glad to see it undertaken in any manner. I am not, Mr. Speaker, disposed to sacrifice substance to form; therefore, whether the business shall originate in a Committee of the Whole or in the House, is a matter of indifference to me, so that it be put in train. Although I am seriously inclined to give this subject a full discussion, yet I do not wish it to be fully entered into at present, but am willing it should be postponed to a future day, when we shall have more leisure. ... I hope ... this House, when they do go into the business, will receive those propositions generally. This, I apprehend, will tend to tranquilize the public mind, and promote that harmony which ought to be kept up between those in the exercise of the powers of Government, and those who have clothed them with the authority, or, in other words, between Congress and the people. Without a harmony and confidence subsist between them, the measures of Government will prove abortive, and we shall have still to lament that imbecility and weakness which have long marked our public councils.

Mr. VINING found himself in a delicate situation respecting the subject of amendments. He came from a small State, and therefore his sentiments would not be considered of so much weight as the sentiments of those gentlemen who spoke the sense of much larger States. Besides, his constituents had prejudged the question, by a unanimous adoption of the Constitution, without suggesting any amendments thereto. His sense accorded with the declared sense of the State of Delaware, and he was doubly bound to object to amendments which were either improper or unnecessary. But he had good reasons for opposing the consideration of even proper alterations at this time. He would ask the gentleman who pressed them, whether he would be responsible for the risk the Government would run of being injured by an interregnum? Proposing amendments at this time, is suspending the operations of Government, and may be productive of its ruin.

He would not follow the gentleman in his arguments, though he supposed them all answerable, because he would not take up the time of the House; he contented himself with saying, that a bill of rights was unnecessary in a Government deriving all its powers from the people; and the Constitution enforced the principle in the strongest manner by the practical declaration prefixed to that instrument; he alluded to the words, "We the people do ordain and establish."

★ ★ ★ ★

He found he was not speaking to the question; he would therefore return to it, and declare he was against committing the subject to a select committee; if it was to be committed at all, he preferred a Committee of the Whole, but hoped the subject would be postponed.

Mr. MADISON found himself unfortunate in not satisfying gentlemen with respect to the mode of introducing the business; he thought, from the dignity and peculiarity of the subject, that it ought to be referred to a Committee of the Whole. He accordingly made that motion first, but finding himself not likely to succeed in that way, he had changed his ground. Fearing again to be discomfited, he would change his mode, and move the propositions he had stated before, and the House might do what they thought proper with them. He accordingly moved the propositions by way of resolutions to be adopted by the House.

Mr. LIVERMORE objected to these propositions, because they did not take up the amendments of the several States.

Mr. PAGE was much obliged to his colleague for bringing the subject forward in the manner he had done. He conceived it to be just and fair. What was to be done when the House would not refer it to a committee of any sort, but bring the question at once before them? He hoped it would be the means of bringing about a decision.

Mr. LAWRENCE moved to refer Mr. MADISON'S motion to the Committee of the Whole on the state of the Union.

★ ★ ★ ★

At length Mr. LAWRENCE'S motion was agree to, and Mr. MADISON'S propositions were ordered to be referred to a Committee of the Whole.

Source: Excerpts from debates in the House of Representatives, *Annals of Congress,* June 8, 1789 (Washington: Gales and Seaton, 1834), 1:424–450.

Notes

1. To understand Madison's shift in thinking on a bill of rights see Stuart Leibiger, "James Madison and the Amendments to the Constitution, 1787–1789: 'Parchment Barriers,'" *Journal of Southern History,* 59 (August 1993), 441–468. A summary of the proposed amendments is found in Bernard Schwartz, *The Great Rights of Mankind: A History of the American Bill of Rights* (New York: Oxford University Press, 1977), 156–159.

2. The quotes are taken from a letter Madison wrote to Thomas Mann Randolph, January 13, 1789, and a Resident of Spotsylvania County, Virginia, January 27, 1789. The letters were subsequently published in the *Virginia Independent Chronicle* on January 28, 1789, and the (Fredericksburg, Virginia) *Herald* on January 29, 1789, respectively. Robert A. Rutland et al., eds., *The Papers of James Madison,* 17 vols. (Charlottesville: University Press of Virginia, 1962–1991), 11:416, 428. Also see James Madison to George Eve, January 2, 1789, ibid., 405.

3. *Annals of Congress,* 1st Cong., 1st sess., April 30, 1789, 1:28; John C. Fitzpatrick, ed., *The Writings of George Washington from the Original Manuscript Sources, 1745–1799,* 39 vols. (Washington, D.C.: GPO, 1931–1944), 30:295.

4. *Annals of Congress,* 1st Cong., 1st sess., May 5, 1789, 1:248.

5. Leonard W. Levy, "Bill of Rights (United States)," in Leonard W. Levy and Kenneth L. Karst, eds., *Encyclopedia of the American Constitution,* 6 vols., 2nd ed. (New York: Macmillan, 2000), 1:115.

6. Bernard Schwartz, *The Great Rights of Mankind: A History of the American Bill of Rights* (New York: Oxford University Press, 1977), 163.

7. *Annals of Congress,* 1st Cong., 1st sess., June 8, 1789, 1: 432–433, 439.

8. Schwartz, *The Great Rights of Mankind: A History of the American Bill of Rights,* 179.

9. U.S. Congress, Senate, *The Constitution of the United States of America: Analysis and Interpretation,* 108th Cong., 2nd sess., S. Doc. 108–117 (Washington, D.C.: GPO, 2004), 25, n. 2.

Judiciary Act of 1789

✳ 1789 ✳

The Framers of the Constitution agreed that there should be three branches of government — legislative, executive, and judicial. They created a Supreme Court, but they left to Congress the responsibility of creating lower, or inferior, federal courts from time to time as it deemed necessary. On April 7, 1789, a day after it initially achieved a quorum, the U.S. Senate's first order of business was the formidable task of establishing the judicial branch of government. Since a national judiciary had not existed under the Articles of Confederation, and the Constitution left many of the important details of the judicial branch to the discretion of Congress, the Senate created a committee to "bring in a bill for organizing the Judiciary of the United States." [1]

It was the responsibility of the newly created committee, which consisted of one senator from each of the states then represented in Congress, to deal with such questions as the number of justices that should sit on the Supreme Court and whether to establish inferior national courts, and if so, how many. Although little evidence of the committee's work has survived, "letters to constituents and friends, suggests that the committee followed the practice of the Continental Congress and the Constitutional Convention, that is, they proceeded by debating, and either adopting or rejecting, a series of general resolutions; the committee did not begin drafting an actual text until after certain basic resolutions were adopted." [2] By the end of April, the committee reached tentative agreement upon the broad outline of what should be included in the first judiciary act; on May 11, it appointed a three-member subcommittee to draft it. A month later, the full committee approved the subcommittee's draft language and reported it to the Senate.

Between June 22 and July 17, the Senate debated and modified the bill to establish a judicial system for the United States prior to its approval in a 14–6 vote. The Senate delivered the engrossed judicial bill to the House of Representatives on July 23. Debate took place in late August and early September. On September 17, the House passed the bill by a voice vote following more than fifty amendments. It has been asserted "that the House amendments were 'merely verbal in nature and made no essential alterations to the bill.'" The record of the House proceedings, however, does not substantiate this claim. [3] During the ensuing week, the Senate disagreed with four of the House amendments and amended a fifth. Without debate, the House then receded from the four amendments to which the Senate had disagreed and agreed to the Senate amendment. On September 24, 1789, President George Washington signed the Judiciary Act of 1789. [4]

"Conscious of the delicacy of their task, members of the First Congress naturally sought assistance from legal experts in their respective communities. The result was analogous to a modern-day congressional hearing, with the difference that most of the testimony was received by letter than in person." These solicitations for comments "were more than mere formalities." Congress members wanted to craft a bill that would "avoid a hostile reception" and as a consequence "paid close attention to the concerns of those who offered advice." In fashioning a federal judiciary, the drafters of the Judiciary Act of 1789 "overwhelmingly concerned themselves with creating a judicial system that safeguarded federal interests without antagonizing those who favored a strong role for the states." Their work "reflected not so much the powers granted by the Framers in 1787 as the powers that were acceptable to the nation in 1789." [5]

During the state ratification debates on the Constitution, the nature of the federal judiciary had been hotly debated between those who opposed a strong system of federal courts and those who welcomed a centralized federal judicial system. These differences carried over to the debates on the draft judiciary bill even though the Senate committee had carefully avoided giving the federal courts too much authority. Those opposed to the bill contended that a federal judiciary was not necessary and the states were capable of deciding federal issues. They also contended that the Constitution did not require Congress to create lower courts, but merely suggested that it could. Proponents, however, insisted that the Framers intended for Congress to establish lower courts to ensure the supremacy of federal law, which was less susceptible to state and local bias. Eventually, the proponents carried the day.

The compromise agreed upon "was as astute politically as it was legally. It was an ingenious collection of compromises,

President George Washington signed the Judiciary Act of 1789 on September 24 of that year, establishing a federal judiciary after heated debate in Congress over the necessity of a centralized judicial system.
Source: The Granger Collection, New York.

using both tight, detailed wording and broad, open-ended wording in different places; it established foundations upon which successors could be built." The act represented a practical compromise between those who sought to "establish an army of judges that would carry national authority into every county" and their counterparts who "desired a minimal national judiciary."[6]

In implementing the judiciary clause of the Constitution, Congress created a federal judiciary that specified that the Supreme Court would consist of a chief justice and five associate justices; thirteen district courts, corresponding roughly to state boundaries, with a judge for each; and three circuit courts, consisting of two Supreme Court judges and a district

judge. The Judiciary Act of 1789 also specified the precise jurisdictions of each of the three courts and established the office of attorney general. It was the responsibility of the Supreme Court to hear appeals from federal district and circuit courts; hear appeals from state courts in cases involving federal statutes and treaties; review state statutes that were argued to be incompatible with the Constitution, federal law, or treaties; and interpret any clause of the Constitution or of federal laws or statutes. In addition, the Supreme Court was given jurisdiction over disputes between states, between a state and citizens of another state, and against ambassadors, public ministers, and consuls or their domestics.

The district courts were given jurisdiction over minor criminal cases, admiralty and maritime cases, and civil actions on federal matters. The circuit courts were responsible for reviewing final decisions of district courts in civil and admiralty cases involving more than $50 or $300, respectively, and hearing serious criminal cases, civil cases involving more than $500 between parties from different states (or diversity cases) or in which an alien was a party, and civil cases involving more than $500 where the United States was a plaintiff or petitioner. A federal trial in diversity cases was not necessary, however, if a plaintiff chose to sue in a state court or if a defendant from another state was being sued in a state court for more than $500.

Although the "matters that can be heard by the federal courts have expanded far beyond the contemplation of the 1789 law," the three-tiered structure it established remains in effect today, and its procedural provisions still govern the basic operations of the federal courts."[7] Among the statutes enacted during the first session of the first Congress, "none was of greater prospective force than this act; none more astutely contrived." While the members of the Senate committee "charged with drafting this measure were federally minded and so politically disposed to take a bold view of the legislative authority conveyed by Article III," they were "wholly sensitive to the variety of criticisms that had been directed at the judicial, and, for the future success of their handiwork, were prepared to meet these." The Judiciary Act of 1789, one author has suggested, "must be viewed in a political context as an instrument of reconciliation deliberately framed to quiet still smoldering resentments."[8]

By adopting the Bill of Rights and enacting the Judiciary Act of 1789, which established the federal judiciary, Congress completed the work of the Constitutional Convention and helped to secure the legacy of the Revolution.

HOUSE DEBATE ON THE JUDICIARY ACT OF 1789

AUGUST 24, 1789

Mr. LIVERMORE. I fear this principle of establishing Judges of a Supreme Court will lead to an entire new system of jurisprudence, and fill every State in the Union with two kinds of courts for the trial of many causes. A thing so heterogeneous must give great disgust. Sir, it will be establishing a Government within a Government, and one must prevail upon the ruin of the other. Nothing, in my opinion, can irritate the inhabitants so generally, as to see their neighbors dragged before two tribunals for the same offence. Mankind in general are unfriendly to courts of justice; they are vexed with law-suits for debts or trespasses; and though I do not doubt but the most impartial administration of justice will take place, yet they will feel the imposition burdensome and disagreeable. People in general do not view the necessity of courts of justice with the eye of a civilian; they look upon laws rather as intended for punishment than protection; they will think we are endeavoring to irritate them, rather than to establish a Government to sit easy upon them.

It will be establishing a Government within a Government, and one must prevail upon the ruin of the other. — Samuel Livermore

---

Will any gentleman say that the Constitution cannot be administered without this establishment? I am clearly of a different opinion; I think it can be administered better without than with it. There is already in each State a system of jurisprudence congenial to the wishes of its citizens. I never heard it complained that justice was not distributed with an equal hand in all of them; I believe it is so, and the people think it so. We had better then continue them than introduce a system replete with expense, and altogether unnecessary.

Nor will this expense be inconsiderable; we must have a double suit of salary judges, attorneys general, marshals, clerks, and constables, together with jails and court-houses; and all this for what? To try a man over again who has been acquitted by the State courts, in cases of concurrent jurisdiction, or from an apprehension that the State courts may err. The State courts have hitherto decided all cases of a national or local import; and it was never heard that they determined with any degree of partiality. Perhaps a maritime case, that was carried by appeal before the court for final determination in cases of capture, where the judgment was reversed, may be thought an exception; but whether this case was decided rightly or wrongly at last, I shall not pretend to say at present. Now, if the State courts have hitherto had cognizance of similar cases, and proceeded on them with impartiality, what occasion is therefor a new institution? I cannot possibly conceive, unless it be to plague mankind.

But, besides the expense of judges, marshals, &c., there will be another difficulty; there must be procured jurors for such courts, for I presume it is not intended that they shall try causes [sic] without a jury. Now, how is this jury to be constituted? Are they to come to the Supreme Court from the county in which the offence has been committed, or is the court to go to that place? We have heard cases spoken of, to arise under the mountains of Carolina, and be dragged down to the sea-shore; but the inconvenience of three or four hundred miles is nothing compared with what may take place under this system. Certainly this consideration must offer difficulties to every gentleman's mind; difficulties which can easily be avoided by pursuing another route.

But after the trial follow judgment and execution. Now what mode will you pursue to complete your process? There are various ways of levying an execution in the different States; in some States the land is attached; in others, the personal estate; sometimes the debtor is confined in jail, or, in case he breaks jail, the county has to pay the debt. I hope the Government will not adopt this last mode, or escapes may be made in great number. I apprehend we shall find the execution offer no inconsiderable obstacle to our system.

Now, why engage in a plan so obnoxious and difficult without necessity? Gentlemen will not pretend to be afraid of erroneous decision, because they may be subject to appeal and revision, which furnishes as great security as it is possible to have in any system of jurisprudence whatever. For my part, I contemplate with horror the effects of the plan; I think I see a foundation laid for discord, civil wars, and all its concomitants. To avert these evils, I hope the House will reject the proposed system.

★ ★ ★ ★

AUGUST 29, 1789

Mr. Smith of South Carolina.... I readily agree ... that there are in every community some individuals who will see, with pain, every new institution in the shape of a constable, jail, or gibbet, and who think that law and courts are an abridgment of their liberty: but I should be very sorry to concur with him that this is a prevailing opinion. I think better of our constituents, and am persuaded they are sensible that those institutions are necessary for the protection of their lives and property; and grow out of the very nature of a federal Government. Care, indeed, should be taken to prevent their being grievous and oppressive; but as long as knaves and roues exist in the world, and monsters under the form of men, preying upon the innocent, so long will courts and all their concomitants be wanted to redress the wrongs of the latter, and repress the depredations of the former. But let me ask the gentleman whether a Court of Admiralty and a court for the trial of offences on the high seas, which he agrees ought to be established, will not require all these institutions, viz: court-houses, clerks, sheriffs, &c.? There can be no doubt of it. The extension of the jurisdiction of the district court, as far as I think it necessary, will not occasion any one article of expense, or any one institution that will not be necessary on the gentleman's plan. To suppose that there will be a clashing of jurisdiction between the State and district courts on all occasions, by having a double set of officers, is to suppose the States will take a pleasure in thwarting the Federal Government; it is a supposition not warranted by our fellow-citizens, who finding that these establishments were created for their benefit and protection, will rather promote than obstruct them; it is a supposition equally opposed to the power of direct taxation, and to the establishment of State and county courts which exist in the several States, and are productive of no such inconvenience. These several courts will have their limits defined, and will move within their respective orbits without any danger of deviation. Besides, I am not persuaded that there will be a necessity for having separate court-houses and jails; those already provided in the several States will be made use of by the district courts. I remember when the court for the trial of piracy, under the authority of Congress, was held at Charleston, the judges sat in the court-house; the prisoners were confined in the jail, were under the custody of the constable, and were executed by the orders of the sheriff of the district of Charleston. All these were State institutions, and yet the court was a federal court.

There is another important consideration; that is, how far the Constitution stands in the way of this motion. It is declared by that instrument that the judicial power of the United States shall be vested in one supreme, and in such inferior courts as Congress shall from time to time establish. Here is no discretion, then, in Congress to vest the judicial power of the United States in any other than the Supreme Court and the inferior courts of the United States. It is further declared that the judicial power of the United States shall extend to all cases of a particular description. How is that power to be administered? Undoubtedly by the tribunals of the United States; if the judicial power of the United States extends to those specified cases

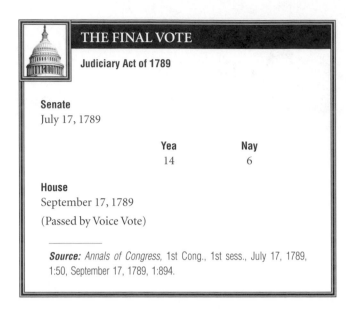

THE FINAL VOTE

Judiciary Act of 1789

Senate
July 17, 1789

	Yea	Nay
	14	6

House
September 17, 1789

(Passed by Voice Vote)

Source: Annals of Congress, 1st Cong., 1st sess., July 17, 1789, 1:50, September 17, 1789, 1:894.

it follows indisputably that the tribunals of the United States must likewise extend to them. What is the object of the motion? To assign the jurisdiction of some of these very cases to the State courts, to judges who, in many instances, hold their places for a limited period; whereas, the Constitution, for the greater security of the citizen, and to insure the independence of the federal judges, has expressly declared that they shall hold their commissions during good behaviour; to judges who are exposed every year to a diminution of salary by the State Legislatures; whereas, the Constitution, to remove from the federal judges all dependence on the Legislative or Executive, has protected them from any diminution of their compensation. Whether the expediency or the unconstitutionality of the motion be considered, there are more than sufficient reasons to oppose it. The district court is necessary, if we intend to adhere to the Constitution, and to carry the Government into effect. At the same time, I shall cheerfully assist in organizing this court in that mode, which will prevent its being grievous or oppressive, and will render it conducive to the protection and happiness of our constituents.

★ ★ ★ ★

MR. SEDWICK.… Is it not essential that a Government possess within itself the power necessary to carry its laws into execution? But the honorable gentleman proposes to leave this business to a foreign authority, totally independent of this Legislature, whether our ordinances shall have efficacy or not. Would this be prudent, even if it were in our power? Suppose a State Government was inimical to the Federal Government, and its judges were attached to the same local policy, they might refuse or neglect to attend to the national business; they might be corrupt, and in either case the public might sustain an essential injury. And where would be your redress? Shall we apply to the state Legislatures that patronize them? Can we impeach or have them tried? If we can, how is the trial to be had; before a tribunal established by the State? Can we expect in this way to bring them to justice? Surely no gentleman supposes we can. These are not chimerical suppositions; they are founded in nature, and such as may be expected.

★ ★ ★ ★

The administration of justice is the very performance of the social bargain on the part of Government. — Fisher Ames

---

When we are certain that the Government cannot be organized, without establishing its judicial tribunals; when we fear for its existence, (at least its existing with reputation and dignity) unless we provide for the due execution of national laws and national treaties; shall we forego them because gentlemen apprehend some small difficulties from interfering process? Sir, it has been already demonstrated that the interference will be trifling, if any; it will be too small to authorize us to blast the expected benefits arising from a complete and efficient system of government.

MR. AMES said, the remarks made by gentlemen on the importance of this question would be of some utility in deciding it. The judicial power is, in fact, highly important to the Government and to the people; to the Government, because by this means its laws are peaceably carried into execution. We know, by experience, what a wretched system that is which is divested of this power. We see the difference between a treaty which independent nations make and which cannot be enforced without war, and a law which is the will of the society. A refractory individual is made to feel the weight of the whole community. A Government that may make but cannot enforce laws, cannot last long, nor do much good. By the power, too, the people are gainers. The administration of justice is the very performance of the social bargain on the part of Government. It is the reward of their toils; the equivalent for what they grant. They have to plant, to water, to manure the tree, and this is the fruit of it. The argument, therefore, *a priori*, is strong against the motion; for while it weakens the Government, it defrauds the people. We live in a time of innovation; but until miracles shall become more common than ordinary events, and surprise us less than the usual course of nature, he should think it a wonderful felicity of invention to propose the expedient of hiring out our judicial power, and employing courts not amenable to our laws, instead of instituting them ourselves as the Constitution requires. We might with as great propriety negotiate and

assign over our legislative as our judicial power; and it would not be more strange to get the laws made for this body, than after their passage to get them interpreted, and executed by those whom we do not appoint and cannot control.

★ ★ ★ ★

MR. STONE.... [W]hat I am not satisfied of is, whether it is now essential that we proceed to make such establishments. I cannot conceive it to be now essential; because the business may be done without, and it is not commanded by the Constitution; if it is commanded by the Constitution, we have no power to restrain or modify it. If it is the right of an alien or foreigner to sue or be sued only in the courts of the United States, then they have a right to that jurisdiction complete, and then Congress must institute courts for taking exclusive cognizance of all cases pointed out in the Constitution; but this would be contrary to the principle of the bill, which proposes to establish inferior courts with concurrent jurisdiction with the State courts.

By the Constitution, Congress has a right to establish such inferior courts as they from time to time shall think necessary. If I understand the force of the words "from time to time," it is that Congress may establish such courts when they think proper. I take it they have used an other precaution; and this construction is guarded by another clause in the Constitution, where it is provided that the Constitution itself, and all laws made in pursuance thereof, as well as treaties, shall be the supreme law of the land, and the judges in every State are to be bound thereby; any thing in the State laws or constitutions to the contrary notwithstanding.

★ ★ ★ ★

If, then, the State courts have the power, your system is not necessary, unless they will not execute that power; it must therefore depend on your suspicion of their want of judgment or integrity. I declare I can contemplate a time, with great pain, when one of those cases may happen; but I believe the time is not yet arrived, and we ought not to adopt a system which presupposes it.

I know it is of great importance to have the decisions of the courts conformable; and I believe also it is of no inconsiderable importance to the Government, to have it operate as well on individuals as on States. It would be, if liked by the people, one of the strongest chains by which the Union is bound; one of the strongest cements for making this Constitution firm and compact. But I would not have the measure adopted at a time, and on a principle, which must have a direct contrary tendency. If we establish Federal courts, on the principle that the State courts are not able or willing to do their duty, we establish rivals. But if we honestly conduct upon the principle of the Constitution — *necessity,* we may expect some good to result from the exercise of our powers, and prevent any clashing of jurisdiction; but to act on other principles must introduce confusion.

★ ★ ★ ★

The clew of separate jurisdiction will twine into such a state of perplexity, as to render it impossible for human wisdom to disentangle it without injury.

★ ★ ★ ★

MR. MADISON said, it would not be doubted that some Judiciary system was necessary to accomplish the objects of the Government and that it ought to be commensurate with the other branches of the Government. Under the late confederation, it could scarcely be said that there was any real Legislative power — there was no Executive branch, and the Judicial was so confined as to be of little consequence; in the new Constitution a regular system is provided; the Legislative power is made effective for its objects; the Executive is co-extensive with the Legislative, and it is equally proper that this should be the case with the Judiciary. If the latter be concurrent with the State jurisdictions, it does not follow that it will for that reason be impracticable. It is admitted that a concurrence exists in some cases between the Legislative authorities of the Federal and State Governments; and it may be safely affirmed that there is more, both of novelty and difficulty in that arrangement, than there will be in the other.

★ ★ ★ ★

[A] review of the constitution of the courts in many States will satisfy us that they cannot be trusted with the execution of the Federal laws. In some of the States, it is true, they might, and would be safe and proper organs of such a jurisdiction; but in others they are so dependent on State Legislatures, that to make the Federal laws dependent on them, would throw us back into all the embarrassments which characterized our former situation.

★ ★ ★ ★

MR. BURKE said he had turned himself about to find some way to extricate himself from this measure; but which ever way he turned, the Constitution still stared him in the face, and he confessed he saw no way to avoid the evil. He made this candid confession to let them know why he should be a silent spectator of the progress of the bill; and he had not the most distant hope that the opposition would succeed. If any substitute could be devised that was not contrary to the Constitution, it should have his support, but he absolutely despaired of finding any. He was, however, satisfied that the people would feel its inconvenience, and express their dislike

to a Judicial system which rendered them insecure in their liberties and property; a system that must be regarded with jealousy and distrust.

★ ★ ★ ★

AUGUST 31, 1789

MR. LIVERMORE thought this law would entirely change the form of Government of the United States.... This new fangled system would eventually swallow up the State courts, as those who were in favor of this rapid mode of receiving debts, would have recourse to them. He then adverted to the clashing circumstances that must arise in the administration of justice, by these independent courts having similar powers. Gentlemen, said he, may be very facetious respecting dividing the body; but these are serious difficulties; the instances mentioned by the gentleman from South Carolina do not apply, the officer here is the same; the same sheriff has the precepts committed to him; and the execution does not clash; the same jail answers for both.

★ ★ ★ ★

Mr. VINING said he conceived that the institution of general and independent tribunals were essential to the fair and impartial administration of the laws of the United States. That the power of making laws, of executing them, and a judicial administration of such laws, is in its nature inseparable and indivisible, if not, "justice might be said to be lame as well as blind among us."

★ ★ ★ ★

He wished, he said, to see justice so equally distributed, as that every citizen of the United States should be fairly dealt by, and so impartially administered, that every subject or citizen of the world, whether foreigner or alien, friend or foe, should be alike satisfied; by this means, the doors of justice would be thrown wide open, emigration would be encouraged from all countries into your own, and, in short, the United States of America would be made not only an asylum of liberty, but a sanctuary of justice. The faith of treaties would be preserved inviolate; our extensive funded system would have its intended operation; our navigation, impost, and revenue laws would be executed so as to insure their many advantages, whilst the combined effect would establish the public and private credit of the Union.

MR. STONE. — I am mistaken if the whole subject has yet come before us in its full extent, and I think it ought to be thoroughly investigated before it is decided upon.

I declare myself, Mr. Chairman, much pleased with the discussion, and am gratified with the different points of view in which it has been placed; but I conceive there is a variety of considerations arising out of the subject which have not yet been touched upon. I have seriously reflected, sir, on the subject, and have endeavored to give the arguments all the weight they deserve. I think, before we enter into a view of the convenience of the system, it will be right to consider the Constitutional ground on which we stand.

Gentlemen, in their arguments, have expressly or impliedly declared that the Constitution, in this respect, is imperative — that it commands the organization of inferior courts. If this doctrine is true, let us see where it will carry us. It is conceded on all hands that the establishment of these courts is immutable. If the command of the Constitution is imperative, we must carry it through all its branches; but if it is not true we may model it so as to suit the convenience of the present time. It appears from the words of the Constitution, that Congress may, from time to time, ordain and establish inferior courts, such as they think proper. Now, if this is a command for us to establish inferior courts, if we cannot model or restrain their jurisdictions, the words which give us the power from time to time so to do, are vain and nugatory. Do the words "from time to time" leave any thing to our discretion? Or must we establish in our own minds a given length of time to gratify its meaning? Are we to compare it with the case of a census, and confine it to a subsequent term of ten years? If you establish inferior courts upon this principle, you have expended your whole power upon the subject for that length of time, and cannot interfere until the term arrives which you have fixed in your own mind for the power to return. But the words "ordain and establish" will not only go to the appointment of Judges of inferior courts, but they comprehend every thing which relates to them; we have good authority for this opinion, because one branch of the Legislature has expressly laid it down in the bill before us; they have modified the tribunal; they have restrained its jurisdiction; they have directed appeals only to be had in certain cases; they have connected the State courts with the district courts in some cases; this shows that, in their opinion, the articles of the Constitution gave them a latitude. It is not said in that instrument that you shall exercise the judicial power over all those cases, but that the judicial power shall extend to those cases. If it had been the idea of the convention that its Judiciary should extend so as positively to have taken in all these cases, they would have so declared it, and been explicit; but they have given you a power to extend your jurisdiction to them, but have not compelled you to that extension. Several gentlemen have mistaken this idea, and that on very different ground. The gentleman from Virginia has compared the exercise of the Judiciary to that of the Executive and Legislative powers, and seems from his arguments to infer that if you do not extend the Judiciary power, so as to take in all those cases which are specified in the Constitution, that you will leave the Judiciary defective.

The gentleman from New York seems to think it will be an abandonment of our Judicial power altogether. To what does

the Legislative power of this Government extend? To a variety of cases which are not yet put in action; for instance, the Legislative power extends to excises and direct taxes. If you conceive the Judiciary incomplete, because you have not strained it to its utmost extension, cannot you see, from the same principle, that the Legislative power is not complete unless you extend it as far as you have the power? Do you divest yourself of the power by not exercising it? Certainly not. Suppose you were to lay as heavy a land tax as the people could bear, (and this is in our power by the terms of the Constitution,) and suppose the people were to ask you why you had done so, when there was no absolute necessity for it, would you answer that the Constitution has given us the power, therefore we must exercise it? Certainly not. The Constitution has given us power to admit that a suit in certain cases shall be brought for six-pence; this we may authorize to be done in an inferior court — from the District Court it is carried to the Circuit Court, and may be brought up into the Supreme Court. This power, I say, we have by the Constitution....

★ ★ ★ ★

Mr. GERRY. — We are to administer this Constitution, and therefore we are bound to establish these courts, let what will be the consequence. Gentlemen say they are willing to establish Courts of Admiralty; but what is to become of the other cases to which the Continental jurisdiction is extended by the Constitution? When we have established the courts as they propose, have fixed the salaries, and the Supreme Executive has appointed the Judges, they will be independent, and no power can remove them; they will be beyond the reach of the Executive or Legislative powers of this Government; they will be unassailable by the State Legislatures; nothing can affect them but the united voice of America, and that only by a change of Government. They will, in this elevated and independent situation, attend to their duty — their honor and every sacred tie oblige them. Will they not attend to the Constitution as well as your laws? The Constitution will undoubtedly be their first rule; and so far as your laws conform to that, they will attend to them, but no further. Would they then be confined by your laws within a less jurisdiction than they were authorized to take by the Constitution? You must admit them to be inferior courts; and the Constitution positively says, that the Judicial powers of the United States shall be so vested. They would then inquire what were the Judicial powers of the Union, and undertake the exercise thereof, notwithstanding any Legislative declaration to the contrary; consequently their system would be a nullity, at least, which attempted to restrict the jurisdiction of inferior courts.

It has been said, that much inconvenience will result from the clashing of jurisdiction. Perhaps this is but ideal; if, however, it should be found to be the case, the General Government must remove the obstacles. They are authorized to suppress any system injurious to the administration of this Constitution, by the clause granting to Congress the power of making all laws necessary and proper for carrying into execution the powers of the Constitution, or any department thereof. It is without a desire to increase the difficulties of the proposed arrangements, that I make these observations, for I am desirous of promoting the unity of the two Governments, and this, I apprehend, can be done only by drawing a line between the two Judicial powers.

Source: Excerpts from debates in the House of Representatives, *Annals of Congress,* August 24, 1789, August 29, 1789, and August 31, 1789 (Washington: Gales and Seaton, 1834), 1:784–830.

Notes

1. *Journal of the First Session of the Senate of the United States* (Washington: Gales and Seaton, 1820), 10. For background on the members of the committee see Julius Goebel Jr., *Antecedents and Beginnings to 180: History of the Supreme Court of the United States,* Vol. 1, (New York: Macmillan, 1971), 458–460.

2. Wilfred J. Ritz, edited by Wythe Holt and L. H. LaRue, *Rewriting the Judiciary Act of 1789: Exposing Myths, Challenging Premises, and Using New Experiences* (Norman: University of Oklahoma Press, 1990), 16. See also Goebel, *Antecedents and Beginnings to 1801,* 460–462.

3. Quote is found in Goebel, *Antecedents and Beginnings to 1801,* 504. For a discussion of the House amendments, see ibid., 504–507. At least two authors have suggested that the House amendments made only small alterations in the bill. See Ritz, *Rewriting the Judiciary Act of 1789,* 17; and Charles Warren, "New Light on the History of the Judiciary Act of 1789," *Harvard Law Review,* 37 (November 1923), 130, n. 178.

4. Goebel, *Antecedents and Beginnings to 1801,* 494–508.

5. Maeva Marcus and Natalie Wexler, "The Judiciary Act of 1789: Political Compromise or Constitutional Interpretation?" in Maeva Marcus, *Origins of the Federal Judiciary: Essays on the Judiciary Act of 1789* (New York: Oxford University Press, 1992), 14–15, 29–30.

6. Ritz, *Rewriting the Judiciary Act of 1789,* 22.

7. Stephen B. Presser, "Judiciary Act of 1789," in Stanley I. Kutler, ed., *Dictionary of American History,* 10 vols., 3rd ed. (New York: Charles Scribner's Sons, 2003), 5:499.

8. Goebel, *History of the Supreme Court of the United States,* 457–458.

Jay Treaty
✳ June 1795; March–April 1796 ✳

Midway through his second term as president, George Washington faced his first major foreign policy and political crisis when the United States became entangled in a war between Great Britain and France. Initially, the conflict, which began in February 1793, enabled Americans to build a flourishing trade with France's Caribbean colonies, but in June and again in November 1793, the British issued orders to disrupt such commerce. Enforcement of these orders led to the seizure of American ships, confiscation of their cargoes, and impressments or imprisonment of American seamen.

At the time, relations between Great Britain and France were further strained by American and British violations of the Paris Peace Treaty of 1783. In the Old Northwest, there was a longstanding frontier dispute over British refusal to abide by provisions of the treaty that called for them to evacuate their military posts there. The British held on to the posts both to impede Western settlement by Americans and to retain control of the lucrative fur trade in the area. Also, settlers in the Ohio country believed the British had instigated Indian massacres of pioneers to drive out settlers. American violations of the terms of the treaty reflected the weakness of the new national government — state governments had enacted laws blocking the repayment of pre-Revolutionary War debts owed to British creditors and Americans continued to discriminate against those who had been loyal to England during the war.

Disagreement over how to handle the delicate situation led to a split within Washington's administration between members of the Federalist and Democratic-Republican parties. Federalists such as Secretary of the Treasury Alexander Hamilton sought a peaceful solution because British exports to the United States were the chief source of tariff income, which was needed to finance the delicate fiscal system he had created. Secretary of State Thomas Jefferson and the other Republicans, however, were committed to France; they reasoned that the United States must firmly insist that Britain honor its treaty obligations.

War with Great Britain was averted when a U.S. delegation headed by U.S. Supreme Court chief justice John Jay successfully completed negotiations with England. The Anglo-American Treaty of Amity, Commerce, and Naviga-

tion (better known as the Jay Treaty), which was signed on November 19, 1794, provided for evacuation of British military forces from the Northwest, settlement of boundary disputes between the two nations, payment by Americans for pre-Revolutionary debts to British merchants, and compensation by Britain for its seizure of American merchant ships and cargo. The treaty placed British trade with the United States on a most-favored-nation basis and gave Americans the right to trade in the British East Indian ports. Joint commissions were provided for in the treaty to adjudicate pre-Revolutionary debts, boundary questions, and compensation for illegal maritime seizures.[1]

The Jay Treaty allowed the United States to postpone war with Great Britain for eighteen years and settled several longstanding problems involving the two nations. When Republicans learned the terms of the treaty in March 1795, however, they immediately sought to arouse public opposition against its ratification and protests arose from all parts of the country. They contended that the treaty was in violation of French-American treaties and it failed to deal with several of the issues that had brought the United States and Great Britain to the brink of war. The treaty did not guarantee neutral maritime rights, address the impressment of American seamen, or include compensation for the British removal of slaves from the South during the Revolutionary War. Also, Southern planters were disgruntled over the treaty because it guaranteed payment of private pre–Revolutionary War debts (much of which were owed by Virginians). Even the president and some Federalist members of Congress were dissatisfied with the treaty, but after considerable deliberation Washington decided to sign it.[2]

Following a highly partisan debate, the Senate ratified the treaty on June 24, 1795, exactly by the constitutionally required two-thirds vote 20–10. Passage was only assured, however, after the Senate struck from the treaty Article XII, which imposed a 70-ton limit on American ships trading with the West Indies. Nine months later, House Republicans attempted to block implementation of the treaty through the appropriation process. While the treaty had been negotiated by ministers approved by the president and the Senate, ratified by the Senate, and signed by the president, it established

Thomas Jefferson's supporters burn John Jay in effigy following the Jay Treaty of 1794. Those opposed to the treaty argued that it violated French-American treaties and did not address all of the issues that drove Britain and America to the brink of war.
Source: The Granger Collection, New York.

arbitration commissions that could not operate without a congressional appropriation. The Republicans, who felt Jay had sold out to Britain and betrayed the nation's alliance with France, asserted that the House, through its power over appropriations, had the right to consider the expediency of executing the treaty. The president and the Federalists argued that the House had no right to do this, since once the treaty is ratified the government is honor bound to execute its terms.

On March 2, 1796, Rep. Edward Livingston of New York offered a resolution requesting the president to provide the chamber with copies of all papers relevant to the treaty. A lengthy debate ensued over the constitutionality of the request before the House on March 24 finally approved 62–37 a revised resolution that excepted such "papers as any existing negotiation may render improper to be disclosed."

Pivotal to its approval was the contention that the treaty involved appropriations and the regulation of commerce, both of which were properly within the purview of the House. As a consequence, the mission's papers contained information essential to determining appropriate action.[3] The president, however, denied the demand for the papers, stressing that concurrence of the two houses was not required to give validity to a treaty. He maintained that turning over the papers would "establish a dangerous precedent," and "that the boundaries fixed by the [C]onstitution" between the branches of government needed to be preserved.[4]

The House countered by insisting it had a right to the papers. Rep. James Madison, DR-Va., attempted to refute the president in a floor speech that lasted several hours,[5] but Washington never released the papers. By asserting his executive prerogative, Washington set an important precedent. Now the question became whether to appropriate the funds needed to implement the treaty despite the president's stance. The most strenuous Republican objections at this point focused on two issues: the lack of compensation for confiscated slaves and payment of private debts to British merchants.

At the outset of the effort to block implementation of the treaty, Madison and other House Republican leaders believed they had a twenty-one-vote majority and defeat of the treaty was certain. Several forces, however, worked together to weaken the Republican strength. Four factors prompted a large number of representatives from New York, New Jersey, and Pennsylvania to ultimately vote for the appropriation: (1) pressure from business interests and the clergy; (2) a large pro-Washington sentiment; (3) threat of the Federalist-controlled Senate rejecting the widely acclaimed Pinckney Treaty if the Jay Treaty was blocked; and (4) fear of a foreign war and possible disruption of the Union. Also, the Federalists were able to mobilize 10,200 pro-treaty petitioners that further eroded Republican strength.[6]

The climax of a month-long House debate came on April 28, 1796, when Rep. Fisher Ames, F-Mass., overcame a debilitating illness to present a brilliant defense of the Jay Treaty in one of the most famous speeches in the history of the House. Ames condemned the Republicans for exaggerating the powers of the House and reminded his colleagues that the treaty, more than anything else, was the only means for avoiding war.[7] The following day, Rep. Frederick A. C. Muhlenberg, DR-Penn., as chairman of the committee of the whole, broke a tie vote to accept a resolution stating "[t]hat it is expedient to make the necessary appropriations for" implementing the treaty. When the House voted on April 30, 1796, ten Republicans had changed their position on implementation funding and two others chose not to vote. By the narrow margin of 51–48, the Republican effort to thwart implementation was overcome and soon thereafter an $80,808 appropriation to carry the treaty into effect was approved by Congress and signed into law by the president.[8]

The treaty resulted in Britain being able to retain the United States as its best foreign customer and keep the United States neutral during the conflict with France. France, however, regarded the treaty as a violation of its commercial treaty with the United States and, as Alexander DeConde has written, engaged in a kind of undeclared naval war with America between 1797 and 1800.[9]

At home, the House struggle between the Federalists and Republicans over the Jay Treaty prompted first the Federalists, followed by the Republicans in Congress, to begin holding party caucuses. These events were of great importance in the institutional development of the nation's legislature as well as political parties in the United States.

SPEECH OF REPRESENTATIVE JAMES MADISON IN OPPOSITION TO THE JAY TREATY

MARCH 10, 1796

Mr. Madison said that the direct proposition before the House, had been so absorbed by the incidental question which had grown out of it, concerning the Constitutional authority of Congress in the case of Treaties, that he should confine his present observations to the latter.

On some points there could be no difference of opinion; and there need not, consequently, be any discussion. All are agreed that the sovereignty resides in the people. That the Constitution, as the expression of their will, is the guide and the rule to the Government; that the distribution of powers made by the Constitution, ought to be sacredly observed by the respective departments. That the House of Representatives ought to be equally careful to avoid encroachments on the authority given to other departments, and to guard their own authority against encroachments from the other departments. These principles are as evident as they are vital and essential to our political system.

The true question, therefore, before the Committee, was not whether the will of the people expressed in the Constitution was to be obeyed, but how that will was to be understood; in what manner it had actually divided the powers delegated to the Government; and what construction would best reconcile the several parts of the instrument with each other, and be most consistent with its general spirit and object.

★ ★ ★ ★

It was to be regretted, he observed, that on a question of such magnitude as the present, there should be any apparent inconsistency or inexplicitness in the Constitution, that could leave room for different constructions. As the case, however, had happened, all that could be done was to examine the different constructions with accuracy and fairness, according to the rules established therefor, and to adhere to that which should be found most rational, consistent, and satisfactory.

★ ★ ★ ★

[T]he question immediately under consideration, and which the context and spirit of the Constitution must decide, turned on the extent of the Treaty power in relation to the objects specifically and expressly submitted to the Legislative power of Congress.

It was an important, and appeared to him to be a decisive, view of the subject, that if the Treaty power alone could perform any one act for which the authority of Congress is required by the Constitution, it may perform every act for which the authority of that part of the Government is required. Congress have power to regulate trade, to declare war, to raise armies, to levy, borrow, and appropriate money, &c. If by Treaty, therefore, as paramount to the Legislative power, the PRESIDENT and Senate can regulate trade, they can also declare war, they can raise armies to carry on war, and they can procure money to support armies. These powers, however different in their nature or importance, are on the same footing in the Constitution, and must share the same fate. A member from Connecticut [Mr. Griswold] had admitted that the power of war was exclusively vested in Congress; but he had not attempted, nor did it seem possible, to draw any line between that and the other enumerated powers. If any line could be drawn, it ought to be presented to the Committee; and he should, for one, be ready to give it the most impartial consideration. He had not, however, any expectation that such an attempt could succeed; and therefore should submit

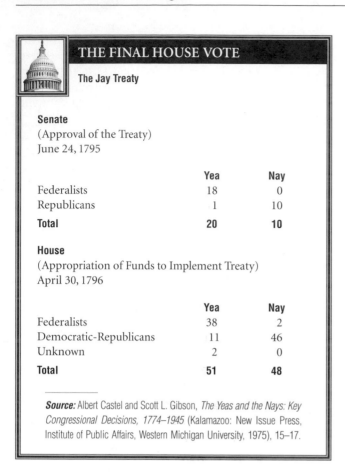

THE FINAL HOUSE VOTE

The Jay Treaty

Senate
(Approval of the Treaty)
June 24, 1795

	Yea	Nay
Federalists	18	0
Republicans	1	10
Total	**20**	**10**

House
(Appropriation of Funds to Implement Treaty)
April 30, 1796

	Yea	Nay
Federalists	38	2
Democratic-Republicans	11	46
Unknown	2	0
Total	**51**	**48**

Source: Albert Castel and Scott L. Gibson, *The Yeas and the Nays: Key Congressional Decisions, 1774–1945* (Kalamazoo: New Issue Press, Institute of Public Affairs, Western Michigan University, 1975), 15–17.

if Congress have no will but to obey, and if to disobey be Treason and rebellion against the constitutional authorities? Under a Constitutional obligation with such sanctions to it, Congress, in case the PRESIDENT and Senate should enter into an alliance for war, would be nothing more than the mere heralds for proclaiming it. In fact, it had been said, that they must obey the injunctions of a Treaty as implicitly as a subordinate officer, in the Executive line, was bound to obey the Chief Magistrate; or as the Judges are bound to decide according to the laws.

★ ★ ★ ★

It was to be presumed, that in all such cases, the Legislature would excise its authority with discretion, allowing due weight to the reasons which led to the Treaty, and to the circumstance of the existence of the Treaty. Still, however, this

---

If [the House] must carry all Treaties into effect, it would no longer exercise a Legislative power; it would be the mere instrument of the will of another department, and would have no will of its own. — James Madison

---

to the serious consideration of the Committee, that, although the Constitution had carefully and jealously lodged the power of war, of armies, of the purse, &c., in Congress, of which the immediate Representatives of the people, formed an integral part, yet, according to the construction maintained on the other side, the PRESIDENT and Senate by means of a Treaty of Alliance with a nation at war, might make the United States parties in the war. They might stipulate subsidies, and even borrow money to pay them, they might furnish Troops to be carried to Europe, Asia, or Africa; they might even undertake to keep up a Standing Army in time of peace, for the purpose of co-operating, on given contingencies, with an ally, for mutual safel[t]y or other common objects. Under this aspect, the Treaty power would be tremendous indeed.

The force of this reasoning is not obviated by saying that the PRESIDENT and Senate would only pledge the public faith, and that the agency of Congress would be necessary to carry it into operation. For, what difference does this make, if the obligation imposed, be as is alleged, a Constitutional one;

House, in its Legislative capacity, must exercise its reason; it must deliberate; for deliberation is implied in legislation. If it must carry all Treaties into effect, it would no longer exercise a Legislative power; it would be the mere instrument of the will of another department, and would have no will of its own. Where the Constitution contains a specific and peremptory injunction on Congress to do a particular act, Congress must, of course, do the act, because the Constitution, which is paramount over all the departments, has expressly taken away the Legislative discretion of Congress. The case is essentially different where the act of one department of Government interferes with a power expressly vested in another, and no where expressly taken away: here the latter power must be exercised according to its nature; and if it be a Legislative power, it must be exercised with that deliberation and discretion which is essential to the nature of Legislative power.

Source: Excerpts from debates in the House of Representatives, *Annals of Congress,* March 10, 1796 (Washington: Gales and Seaton, 1849), 5: 487–495.

SPEECH OF REPRESENTATIVE FISHER AMES IN SUPPORT OF APPROPRIATING FUNDS TO IMPLEMENT THE JAY TREATY

APRIL 28, 1796

It would be strange that a subject which has roused in turn all the passions of the country, should be discussed without the interference of any of our own. We are men, and, therefore, not exempt from those passions; as citizens and Representatives, we feel the interest that must excite them. The hazard of great interests cannot fail to agitate strong passions: we are not disinterested, it is impossible we should be dispassionate. The warmth of such feelings may becloud the judgment, and, for a time, pervert the understanding; but the public sensibility and our own, has sharpened the spirit of inquiry, and given an animation to the debate. The public attention has been quickened to mark the progress of the discussion, and its judgment, often hasty and erroneous on first impressions, has become solid and enlightened at last. Our result will, I hope, on that account be the safer and more mature, as well as more accordant with that of the nation. The only constant agents in political affairs are the passions of men — shall we complain of our nature? Shall we say that man ought to have been made otherwise? It is right already, because He, from whom we derive our nature, ordained it so; and because thus made and thus acting, the cause of truth and the public good is the more surely promoted.

But an attempt has been made to produce an influence of a nature more stubborn and more unfriendly to truth. It very unfairly pretended that the Constitutional right of this House is at stake, and to be asserted and preserved only by a vote in the negative. We hear it said that this is a struggle for liberty, a manly resistance against the design to nullify this assembly, and to make it a cypher in the Government. That the PRESIDENT and Senate, the numerous meetings in the cities, and the influence of the general alarm of the country, are the agents and instruments of a scheme of coercion and terror, to force the Treaty down our throats, though we loathe it, and in spite of the clearest convictions of duty and conscience.

It is necessary to pause here and inquire, whether suggestions of this kind be not unfair in their very texture and fabric, and pernicious in all their influences? They oppose an obstacle in the path of inquiry, not simply discouraging, but absolutely insurmountable. They will not yield to argument; for, as they were not reasoned up, they cannot be reasoned down. They are higher than a Chinese wall in truth's way, and built of materials that are indestructible. While this remains, it is in vain to argue; it is in vain to say to this mountain, be thou cast into the sea. For, I ask of the men of knowledge of the world, whether they would not hold him for a blockhead that should hope to prevail in an argument whose scope and object it is to mortify the self-love of the expected proselyte? I ask, further, when such attempts have been made, have they not failed of success? The indignant heart repels a conviction that is believed to debase it.

The self-love of an individual is not warmer in its sense, or more constant in its action, than what is called in French *l'esprit de corps,* or the self-love of an assembly; that jealous affection which a body of men is always found to bear towards its own prerogatives and power. I will not condemn this passion.... It cherishes the principle of self-preservation; and, without its existence, and its existence with all the strength we see it possess, the privileges of the Representatives of the people, and immediately the liberties of the people, would not be guarded, as they are, with a vigilance that never sleeps, and an unrelaxing constancy and courage.

If the consequences, most unfairly attributed to the vote in the affirmative, were not chimerical, and worse, for they are deceptive, I should think it a reproach to be found even moderate in my zeal to assert the Constitutional powers of this assembly; and, whenever they shall be in real danger, the present occasion affords proof that there will be no want of advocates and champions.

Indeed, so prompt are those feelings, and were once roused, so, difficult to pacify, that, if we could prove the alarm was groundless, the prejudice against the appropriations may remain on the mind, and it may even pass for an act of prudence and duty to negative a measure which was lately believed by ourselves, and may hereafter be misconceived by others, to encroach upon the powers of the House. Principles that bear a remote affinity with usurpation on those powers will be rejected, not merely as errors, but as wrongs. Our sensibilities will shrink from a post where it is possible they may be wounded, and be inflamed by the slightest suspicion of an assault.

While these prepossessions remain, all argument is useless; it may be heard with the ceremony of attention, and lavish its own resources, and the patience it wearies, to no manner of purpose. The ears may be open, but the mind will remain locked up, and every pass to the understanding guarded.

Unless, therefore, this jealous and repulsive fear for the rights of the House can be allayed, I will not ask a hearing.

I cannot press this topic too far — I cannot address myself with too much emphasis to the magnanimity and candor of those who sit here, to suspect their own feelings, and while they do, to examine the grounds of their alarm. I repeat it, we must conquer our persuasion, that this body has an interest in one side of the question more than the other, before we attempt to surmount our objections. On most subjects, and solemn ones too, perhaps in the most solemn of all, we form our creed from inclination than evidence.

Let me expostulate with gentlemen to admit, if it be only by way of supposition and for a moment, that it is barely possible they have yielded too suddenly to their alarms for the powers of this House; that the addresses which have been made with such variety of forms, and with so great dexterity in some of them, to all that is prejudice and passion in the heart, are either the effects or the instruments of artifice and deception, and then let them see the subject once more in its singleness and simplicity.

It will be impossible on taking a fair review of the subject, to justify the passionate appeals that have been made to us to struggle for our liberties and rights, and the solemn exhortation to reject the proposition, said to be concealed in that on your table, to surrender them forever. In spite of this mock solemnity, I demand, if the House will not concur in the measure to execute the Treaty, what other course shall we take? How many ways of proceeding lie open before us?

In the nature of things there are, but three — we are either to make the Treaty — to observe it — or break it. It would be absurd to say we will do neither. If I may repeat a phrase, already so much abused, we are under coercion to do one of them, and we have no power, by the exercise of our discretion, to prevent the consequences of a choice.

★ ★ ★ ★

On this subject you need not suspect any deception on your feelings. It is a spectacle of horror which cannot be overdrawn. It you have nature in your hearts, it will speak a language compared with which all I have said or can say will be poor and frigid.

Will it be whispered that the Treaty has made me a new champion for the protection of the frontiers? It is known that my voice, as well as my vote, have been uniformly given in conformity with the ideas I have expressed. Protection is the right of the frontier; it is our duty to give it.

★ ★ ★ ★

By rejecting the posts, we light the savage fires — we bind the victims. This day we undertake to render account to the widows and orphans whom our decision will make; to the wretches that will be roasted at the stake; to our country; and I do not deem it too serious to say, to conscience, and to God — we are answerable; and if duty be anything more than a word of imposture, if conscience be not a bug-bear, we are preparing to make ourselves as wretched as our country.

This day we undertake to render account to the widows and orphans whom our decision will make; to the wretches that will be roasted at the stake; to our country; and I do not deem it too serious to say, to conscience, and to God. — Fisher Ames

---

There is no mistake in this case; there can be none. Experience has already been the prophet of events, and the cries of our future victims have already reached us. The Western inhabitants are not a silent and uncomplaining sacrifice. The voice of humanity issues from the shade of their wilderness. It exclaims that while one hand is held up to reject this Treaty, the other grasps a tomahawk. It summons our imagination to the scenes that will open. It is no great effort of the imagination to conceive, that events so near are already begun. I can fancy that I listen to the yells of savage vengeance, and the shrieks of torture. Already they seem to sigh in the West wind; already they mingle with every echo from the mountains.

★ ★ ★ ★

Let me cheer the mind, weary no doubt and ready to despond on this prospect, by presenting another, which it is yet in our power to realize. Is it possible for a real American to look at the prosperity of this country without some desire for its continuance, without some respect for the measures which, many will say, produced, and all will confess, have preserved it? Will he not feel some dread that a change of system will reverse the scene? The well-grounded fears of our citizens in 1794 were removed by the Treaty, but are not forgotten. Then they deemed war nearly inevitable, and would not this adjustment have been considered at that day as a happy escape from the calamity? The great interest, and the general desire of our people, was to enjoy the advantages of neutrality. This instrument, however misrepresented, affords America that inestimable security. The causes of our disputes are either cut up by the roots, or referred to a new negotiation, after the end of the European war. This was gaining everything, because it confirmed our neutrality, by which our citizens are gaining every thing. This alone would justify the engagements of the Government. For, when the fiery vapors of the war lowered in the skirts of our horizon, all our wishes were concentered in this one, that we might escape the desolation of the storm. This Treaty, like a rainbow on the edge of the cloud, marked to our eyes the space where it was raging, and afforded at the same time the sure prognostic of fair weather. If we reject it, the vivid colors grow pale; it will be a baleful meteor, portending tempest and war.

Source: Excerpts from debates in the House of Representatives, *Annals of Congress,* April 28, 1796 (Washington: Gales and Seaton, 1849), 5: 239–1263.

Notes

1. For a comprehensive examination of the Jay Treaty, see Samuel Flagg Bemis, *Jay's Treaty: A Study in Commerce and Diplomacy* (Westport, Conn.: Greenwood Press, 1975); Jerald A. Combs, *The Jay Treaty: Political Battleground of the Founding Fathers* (Berkeley: University of California Press, 1970).

2. Albert Castel and Scott L. Gibson, *The Yeas and the Nays: Key Congressional Decisions* 1774–1945 (Kalamazoo: New Issues Press, Institute of Public Affairs, Western Michigan University, 1975), 16; Combs, *The Jay Treaty,* 160–161, 185–186; James Roger Sharp, *American Politics in the Early Republic: The New Nation in Crisis* (New Haven, Conn.: Yale University Press, 1993), 117–118, 121–123.

3. For the March 24, 1796, vote, see *Annals of Congress,* 4th Cong., 1st sess., March 24, 1796, 5:800–801. Language of this resolution is found in ibid, 759. For the entire debate, see ibid., March 7–April 6, 1796, 426–783.

4. George Washington to the House of Representatives, March 30, 1796, in John C. Fitzpatrick, ed. *The Writings of George Washington,* 39 vols. (Washington, D.C.: GPO, 1931–1944), 35:3, 5.

5. *Annals of Congress,* 4th Cong., 1st sess., April 6, 1796, 5:772–781.

6. Alexander DeConde, *Entangled Alliance: Politics & Diplomacy Under George Washington* (Durham, N.C.: Duke University Press, 1958), 137–138; Castel and Gibson, *The Yeas and the Nays,* 17; and Combs, *The Jay Treaty,* 181–185.

7. *Annals of Congress,* 4th Cong., 1st sess., April 28, 1796, 5: 1239–1263.

8. *Annals of Congress,* 4th Cong., 1st sess., April 30, 1796, 5: 1281–1296; and 1 Stat. 459.

9. DeConde, *Entangled Alliance: Politics & Diplomacy Under George Washington,* 510–511.

War of 1812
✳ November 1811–June 1812 ✳

Following nearly two decades of congressionally authorized military actions against Indians, France, and the Barbary pirates, Congress declared its first war in June 1812. Seven months earlier, President James Madison had alerted Congress to a number of hostile and discriminatory actions by Great Britain that required Congress to prepare for war. He stressed that the British had "trampl[ed] on rights which no independent nation can relinquish," and suggested that Congress "will feel the duty of putting the United States into an armor and an attitude demanded by the crisis, and corresponding with the national spirit and expectations."[1]

Between November 1811 and June 1812, Congress, in response to the president's plea, approved ten different bills designed to enhance the nation's military preparedness. These measures provided for expansion of the army, recruitment of short-term volunteers, use of the militia, appropriations for the purchase of ordinance and construction of coastal fortifications, a war loan, expansion of the navy, and establishment of a quartermaster's department within the army. Also, Congress sanctioned a ninety-day embargo that prohibited American ships from sailing to foreign ports and a ninety-day prohibition against the export of goods and money.[2]

Passage of these measures in large part may be attributed to Madison's Democratic-Republican Party, which had sizeable majorities in both houses of Congress (93–128 House seats and 24–32 Senate seats), and for the first time was led by capable and firm leaders who supported the administration. Henry Clay, the "most able and articulate of the War Hawks, who supported the movement toward war, led the Republican Party's effort as Speaker in his first term in the House." Clay "insured that the War Hawks dominated the Twelfth Congress." While "most of war preparations were adopted by large majorities, the voting masked deep-seated differences among the various factions" within the Republican Party reflected in accompanying floor debate. Still, the War Hawks hoped that their actions "would promote patriotism and prepare the American people psychologically and militarily for war," and President Madison "hoped for the same result."[3]

To a large extent, the congressional debate over whether to go to war with Great Britain took place in the House of Representatives, whose proceedings at the time were published more completely than were those of the Senate. Among the most articulate opponents of the war was Rep. Daniel Sheffey, F, Va. Rep. Robert Wright, DR, Md., a Revolutionary veteran and an ardent supporter of the war party, provided vehement arguments on behalf of the War Hawks.

Despite the preparations for war, most Americans remained skeptical about its prospects. During the first six months of 1812, the British made overtures designed to stave off a war, but each was rejected or arrived too late. Then on June 1, after the latest news received from Great Britain continued to be disappointing, President Madison sent a message to Congress charging the British with inflicting a long list of "injuries and indignities" on the United States. The British were assailed for impressing American seamen, violating U.S. rights to neutral seas, blockading U.S. ports, refusing to revoke the Orders of Council (discriminatory economic measures against America), and provoking Indian raids against settlers in the Northwest Territory. War, Madison reasoned, was the only alternative. The president emphasized that these actions amounted to "a state of war against the United States," and a declaration of war "is a solemn question, which the Constitution wisely confides to the Legislative Department of the Government."[4]

Madison's message was referred to the House Committee on Foreign Affairs, which acted quickly in strongly advocating a declaration of war. "The mad ambition, the lust for power, and commercial avarice of Great Britain," the committee concluded, "have left to neutral nations an alternative only between the basic surrender of their rights and a manly vindication of them." Two days later, the House voted 79–49 to support a declaration of war. Senate debate on the war declaration was more protracted. After a select committee reported a bill to declare war, a motion was made to return the bill to the committee with instructions to merely authorize warships and privateers to make reprisals against Great Britain. That motion carried 17–13. When the modified bill was reported for final action, however, a motion to accept the committee's changes failed by a tie vote of 16–16. Other attempts to limit the war to the high seas also failed. Ultimately, the Senate would deliberate for two weeks before

The British bombed Fort McHenry, near Baltimore, during the War of 1812. On June 1, 1812, President James Madison requested that Congress make a declaration of war, which occurred on June 17 after two weeks of debate.

Source: Library of Congress.

finally voting in favor of a declaration of war on June 17, 19–13. The following day, President Madison signed the declaration of war, which authorized him to use "the whole land and naval force of the United States."[5]

Congress's decision for war was not a sudden one. A number of historians have concluded that it was made because the peaceful policies of diplomacy and commercial restriction operative since 1806 no longer offered hope of redress. The debate in the Twelfth Congress reflected the fact that the War Hawks had attempted to "supply the means for waging war before it was actually declared." Although both houses of Congress ultimately approved the war bill, the vote "was the closest vote on any declaration of war in American history. Only 61 percent of the voting members supported the bill." Approximately "81 percent of the Republicans in both houses of Congress voted for the measure 98–23, while all the Federalists voted against it 93–0."[6]

The United States was, however, hardly prepared for war. Its preparations were woefully inadequate and resulted in insufficient and ill-trained troops. The war proved to be "the most unpopular war that this country has ever waged," historian Samuel Eliot Morison has observed, and "while it lasted," domestic opposition to the war was as widespread as any in American history, including the Vietnam War. Donald R.

Hickey characterized it as "one of the worst-managed wars in American history. Although much of the responsibility rests with President James Madison, Congress must share the blame. Throughout the war both Houses suffered from deep divisions, and endless debate and hostility to the administration combined to prevent or delay much-needed legislation." Northeastern financiers refused to subscribe to national war loans, sectarian pacifists clung to their demands for peace, and mainstream American churches waged "a veritable civil war" over the righteousness of the struggle against the British. As a consequence, Hickey emphasizes, "instead of winning much-needed concessions from the British on the maritime issues in dispute, the United States was lucky to escape from the conflict without making major concessions itself."[7]

The War of 1812 lasted thirty-two months, producing heavy losses along the Canadian front, a costly British embargo of the eastern seaboard, and the burning of Washington, D.C. (including the Capitol, the White House, and most of the executive branch buildings). During the war, Congress "was slow to adopt the measures needed to support the war effort," and economic conditions became so severe in the Northeast that several states assembled at the Hartford Convention to discuss the merits of seceding from the Union. Although the United States did not achieve any of the goals it had gone to war for, the news of its end was received joyfully throughout the country. When it was over, Morison quipped, it became "our most popular war," perhaps in large part because the United States had not been defeated by Great Britain. After the war, Hickey found, people quickly forgot how uncooperative Congress had been during the war. But they never forgave the Federalists for opposing the contest, and the rapid disintegration of the party in the postwar era served as a lesson for congressional opponents of future wars."[8] The Treaty of Ghent, which was signed on December 24, 1814, and unanimously ratified by the Senate on February 16, 1815, ended any secession ideas harbored in New England.

The "Second War of Independence," as the War of 1812 is often called, enhanced "the reputation that the United States enjoyed in Europe. Although the nation's performance in this war was mixed, it nevertheless earned the respect of Europe." The War of 1812 "also left an enduring political legacy. A number of statesmen — James Monroe, John Quincy Adams, Andrew Jackson, and William Henry Harrison — were able to parlay their public service during the war into the presidency."[9]

REPRESENTATIVE ROBERT WRIGHT ARGUES THE NECESSITY OF WAR

DECEMBER 11, 1811

Mr. SPEAKER, I must beg the indulgence of the House while I deliver my opinion on the subject now under consideration, the most important submitted to the Congress of the United States. I, sir, shall take the liberty of varying the question from the honorable member from Virginia (Mr. Randolph,) who yesterday considered it a question of peace or war. I shall consider it as a question of war or submission, dire alternatives, of which, however, I trust no honest American can hesitate in choosing, when the question is correctly stated and distinctly understood. The gentleman from Virginia contends that it is a dispute about the carrying trade, brought on us by the cupidity of the American merchants, in which the farmer and planter have little interest; that he will not consent to tax his constituents to carry on a war for it; that the enemy is invulnerable on the "mountain wave," the element of our wrongs, but should they violate the "*natale solum*," he would point all the energies of the nation and avenge the wrong. Was that gentleman stricken on the nose by a man so tall that he could not reach his nose, I strongly incline to think his manly pride would not permit him to decline the conflict. Sir, the honorable member is incorrect in his premises, and, of course, in his conclusions. I will endeavor to convince him of this, and shall be gratified if I can enlist his talents on the side of a bleeding country. Sir, the violations of the commercial rights of which we complain do not only embrace the carrying trade, properly so called, but also the carrying of the products of our own soil, the fruits of our own industry; these, although injurious only to our property, are just causes of war. But, sir, the impressment of our native seamen is a stroke at the vitals of liberty itself, and although it does not touch the "*natale solum*" yet it enslaves the "*nativos filios*" — the native sons of America; and, in the ratio that liberty is preferable to property, ought to enlist the patriotic feelings of that honorable member, and make his bosom burn with that holy fire that inspired the patriots of the Revolution.

Sir, the carrying trade — by which I mean the carrying articles the growth produce, or manufacture of a foreign clime — except articles contraband of war — is as much the right of the American people as the carrying the products of their own soil, and is not only secured by the law of nations, but by the positive provisions of the British Treaty. To us sir, it is an all-important right.

★ ★ ★ ★

Mr. Speaker, I hope if the gentleman from Virginia will not defend the carrying of foreign articles, he will defend the carrying the products of our own soil, a right most disgracefully violated. When our own citizens have been carrying provisions — the produce of their own soil, in their own ships — to feed the armies of England, and her allies on the continent of Europe, they have been captured on their homeward-bound passage, on their own coast, and condemned in a British Court of Admiralty. If this does not inspire him, yet I am not without hopes that when he reflects on the impressment of our native American seamen, while carrying the products of our own industry to market, thousands of whom, at this moment, are languishing under the ignominious scourge, on board the infernal floating castles of Great Britain, he will feel like an American, devoted to avenge their wrongs.

★ ★ ★ ★

Mr. Speaker, I regret that the gentleman from Virginia should ascribe to gentlemen of the West, a disposition for war, with a view to raise the price of their hemp; or to the gentlemen of the North, with a view to raise the price of their beef and flour. These, sir, are selfish motives, and such I cannot, for a moment, believe, will be taken into consideration; they will, with every other section of the Union, unite in deciding it on its merits; they will count the wrongs we have sustained; they will reflect that the honor, the interest, and the very independence, of the United States, is directly attacked; they will as guardians of the nation's rights, agreeably to the advice of the Administration, "put the United States into an armor and an attitude demanded by the crisis, and the correspondent with the national spirit and expectations;" … and I hope they will decide with me, that submission is a crime; and sir, if they will examine a document on the table, I mean the returns of the twelfth Congress, and compare them with the eleventh, they will find nearly one half of the eleventh Congress removed. This, sir, may correctly be considered as the sentence of the nation against the doctrine of submission; it is certainly an expression of the nation's will, in a language not to be misunderstood, and too serious in application not to be respected.… Mr. Speaker, I cannot forebear the remark that, while the gentleman from Virginia ascribes to the West and to

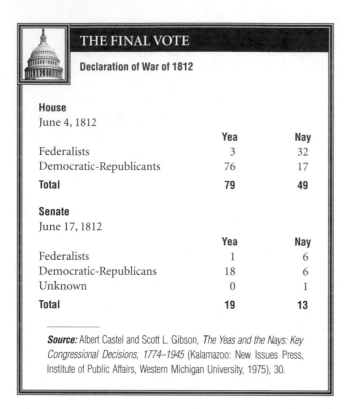

THE FINAL VOTE

Declaration of War of 1812

House
June 4, 1812

	Yea	Nay
Federalists	3	32
Democratic-Republicans	76	17
Total	**79**	**49**

Senate
June 17, 1812

	Yea	Nay
Federalists	1	6
Democratic-Republicans	18	6
Unknown	0	1
Total	**19**	**13**

Source: Albert Castel and Scott L. Gibson, *The Yeas and the Nays: Key Congressional Decisions, 1774–1945* (Kalamazoo: New Issues Press, Institute of Public Affairs, Western Michigan University, 1975), 30.

the North interested motives, he confesses that the situation of the blacks in the State he represents, impressed as they are with the new French principles of liberty, and their desire for the fraternal hug, are seriously to be feared; that these new principles have been taught them by the pedlers from the East, who, while they sell trinkets, inculcate these doctrines. He suffers his fears for the State he represents, in the event of war, on account of the blacks, to interest him; and had he not told us that, if the "natale solum" was touched, or that, if there was a British agency in the late attack on Governor Harrison, he would go to war, I should have been ready to conclude that, as the state of the blacks would be a permanent objection, no cause could occur that would induce him to go to war.

★ ★ ★ ★

Sir, I sincerely regret that the gentleman from Virginia should treat, with so much freedom, that class of society, which, in case of a war, must make the standing army. It was illy calculated to aid the recruiting service, to call them "the scourings of the seaports, to be collected by the scavengers of the army," "the engines of despotism," ever dangerous to liberty. This could have no good effect. That there is a mixed society in the seaports I admit — adventurers from all nations — but the great mass of our people are truly respectable; and I trust the honesty of their principles is not to be measured by any standard of' wealth.... I wish gentle-

men, when they speak of the soldiery, would recollect how they came into this House, and by whose blood the independence of the United States was purchased. Sir, if they will examine their own history: they will find that the tax in blood was paid by the poor in the ratio of sixty-four to four, the number of privates when compared with the officers; and, indeed, they will find that many of the best officers were poor. Sir, we know many of the privates of that army who are now among the most respectable of our citizens.

★ ★ ★ ★

But Mr. Speaker, the gentleman from Virginia could he be reconciled to a war and a regular army, would have, as he tells, insuperable difficulties on account of a commander-in-chief. He says we have no WASHINGTON, and that our present chieftain is an acquitted felon. Sir, our WASHINGTON was little known at the commencement of the Revolution, nor after he was known could his distinguished character secure him against intrigues to remove him from the command of the Army, however, they fortunately failed. I am truly sorry, sir, that the delicacy of the situation of the gentleman from Virginia, and the more delicate situation of General Wilkinson (now under a trial by a court martial,) had not restrained his invectives. In such a case the press is muzzled nor ought such freedom of speech to be indulged in this House.

★ ★ ★ ★

But, sir, from a militia of nearly eight hundred thousand, we can never be at a loss to create a regular army of the thirty or forty thousand; nor, sir, can our liberties ever be endangered by that army, while we have an armed militia of seven hundred thousand, composed at least of as good materials; nor, sir, can we, even should General Wilkinson be slandered

> *[T]he impressment of our native seamen is a stroke at the vitals of liberty itself, and ... ought to enlist the patriotic feelings of that honorable member, and make his bosom burn with that holy fire that inspired the patriots of the Revolution.* — Robert Wright

out of the confidence of the nation. We certainly have patriots and soldiers of talent and enterprise, who would have the confidence of the nation, and who would lead her Army to honor and glory and crown their arms with success.

Source: Excerpts from debates in the House of Representatives, *Annals of Congress*, 12th Cong., 1st sess., December 11, 1811 (Washington: Gales and Seaton, 1853), 23:467–475.

REPRESENTATIVE DANIEL SHEFFEY OPPOSES THE WAR OF 1812

JANUARY 3, 1812

Mr. Speaker, it was not my intention to have disturbed the tranquillity with which this measure has hitherto progressed through the House; but considering the deep interest which this country has at stake, and which is so intimately connected with the present question, I have thought it my duty to state the reasons which influence my vote. I feel the greater solicitude to do so, because, as will have been perceived in several stages of the bill under consideration. I differ essentially with a great majority of the representatives of the people of the United States. They suppose that this course is indispensable to maintain the rights and honor of the country, and that the means which they are about to provide by this bill are calculated to attain the ends in view; while I conceive their projects pregnant with every mischief — with the ruin of our liberties. In the expression of this opinion, let me not be understood as disposed in any degree to impeach the purity of their motives. I have no doubt that every member acts under the high sense of duty which he owes to his country, and which the occasion is particularly calculated to inspire. While I make this sincere and unsophisticated declaration, I hope a correspondent indulgence and liberality will be extended to me.

I had hoped, if it was seriously intended to change the state of this nation, and to barter the blessings of peace, which we have enjoyed for so many years, for the evils and calamities of war, that the question would have been propounded to us in a direct and unequivocal shape; that we should have been called upon to determine whether the injuries of which we justly complain, are to be redressed by the employment of the physical force of the country. If such had been the explicit determination of the majority, much as I deprecate the evils which must inevitably attend a state of war, I should have cordially united with them in calling forth our energies and providing the means, calculated to terminate it speedily and successfully.... It has, however, pleased those who direct the affairs of this nation in this House to pursue a different course. Instead of designating the object for the attainment of which the force provided by the bill under consideration is to be employed, so far as it respects any declaration of this House, that is still unascertained; so that we are reduced to the necessity of opposing the grant of the means, because we are opposed to the subject to which they are probably to be applied. Through this bill, we must perceive the ulterior intention of the majority; which, as avowed, is nothing more or less than an offensive war against Great Britain.

★ ★ ★ ★

I am not one of those ... who suppose that "Great Britain has done us no essential injury." Far from it. I am fully sensible of the indignities offered to us, and the repeated violations of our rights as a neutral nation on her part; but this is not enough for me, I must be persuaded that there is a rational hope that war will remedy the evil which we experience, and that it will not bring with it others much more to be dreaded than that under which we labor. Were these things as little questionable as the course of the British Government has been unjust, I should have no hesitation in uniting my efforts to obtain justice by force.

★ ★ ★ ★

On the subject of the impressment of our seamen, much has been said in the course of this debate.... I feel for our unfortunate countrymen in that situation, and readily admit that there is cause of complaint against Great Britain, arising from that source. But, on this subject, it is important to view the question on both sides, to enable us to ascertain whether we are not claiming more than we can ever rationally expect to obtain. Our native citizens, or those who were members of this community at the close of the Revolutionary war, are unquestionably entitled to exemption from impressment. But we claim it for every person who shall sail under our flag — at least, for those that have been naturalized since the period mentioned. I confess I am not disposed to enter into a war for the security on the high seas of the latter class. I think we do enough (more than any other Government on earth does) when we place those persons upon a perfect equality, as it respects the enjoyment of every right within our territorial jurisdiction.... Allegiance is due from every person in a social state to some Government ... since the dawn of civil liberty, it has been considered as a duty growing out of an implied compact between the governors and governed, and indissoluble like other compacts, without the mutual assent of the contracting parties. On this principle is founded the doctrine of perpetual allegiance recognised throughout Europe, and the British pretensions, by which they reclaim their subjects found on board of our merchant vessels, where they allege they are not entitled to protection, no more than enemy's property and contraband goods, for which they have an unquestionable right to search. Thus, while they claim the right of impressing their own subjects only, the similarity of manners and language, and the abuses of power by British officers, causes the impressment of many of our native citizens.

In considering this part of the subject, I deem it unnecessary to investigate the *justice* of the doctrine for which Great Britain contends, or how far it corresponds with the abstract

---

We must be conscious that we cannot impose our principles *on other nations, with whom it is our interest to cultivate a good understanding.* — Daniel Sheffey

---

"right of man;" I speak of the fact. It is enough for us to know that these pretensions exist, have long existed, and will not be abandoned. We must be conscious that we cannot *impose our principles* on other nations, with whom it is our interest to cultivate a good understanding; but that on every subject where our rights or pretensions may conflict, both parties must cherish a spirit of conciliation and concession, as the only mode by which we can be brought together to prevent collision, from which neither can derive any substantial benefit.

★ ★ ★ ★

From what I have said it will be apparent that I do not oppose this measure on the ground that there is not ample cause of war against Great Britain. The reverse is explicitly admitted. But shall the blood and treasure of this nation be lavished against the Orders in Council, as so much paper, or are we to contend for some substantial good, which we should otherwise enjoy, and of which their operation deprives us? I presume there is scarcely a man in this country, however infected he may be with the war mania, who could act so madly, as to propose a warfare to procure the mere nominal repeal of Orders in Council, when it was evident it would be unattended with a single practical benefit. No! the nominal repeal of the Orders in Council is not your object. It is the substantial commercial benefit which you conceive will follow that act, that forms the essence of the controversy. The unmolested commerce to France and her dependencies is the boon for which you are going to war. This is the real object, disguise it as you will. And it is not the commerce which we formerly enjoyed (as gentlemen would seem to suppose) which is in controversy.... The municipal regulations, which have been substituted for the Berlin decree, so far as it respects the practical effect, have destroyed by far the most profitable and important branch of our trade to the French Empire, which consisted in the products and manufactures of other

countries.... Of so much more importance was this export trade to us than that of our own commerce, that in 1807, before the British Orders in Council existed, the domestic exports to France (including Belgium) amounted to about two millions seven hundred thousand dollars only; while the amount of exports to the same country of foreign manufactures and products (chiefly colonial) was nearly ten millions. In the same year the whole of our domestic exports to every part of the world amounted to about forty-eight millions and a half; of which the amount I have stated was exported to France, and about twenty-eight millions to Great Britain and her possessions and dependencies, in the four quarters of the globe....[E]stimating our exports to Great Britain and her present possessions and dependencies as they stood in 1807, the amount would be about thirty-two millions — about two-thirds of the whole amount of our domestic exports to every part of the world. Thus, while we are about engaging in a war for commerce, we abandon the greater, absolutely, and contend for the lesser. We relinquish our commerce with Great Britain and her possessions at the threshold, (for during hostilities I presume we shall have none.) and go to war for what we can get of the commerce of France, Italy, Holland, Hamburg, and the Hanse Towns. I leave Spain and Portugal and their American provinces out of the question, as the fate of those countries hangs in suspense.

But this is not all. We may expect to see, and the day is not distant, when the dominions of France shall not afford us a market for a single article, but all commerce with her shall either be interdicted by her own Government, or abandoned by our merchants as unworthy their pursuit.

★ ★ ★ ★

But we have been told that all calculations, as to objects, means, or consequences, are to be laid out of the question, as sordid and low-minded. That feeling our country's rights violated and her honor assailed, we ought to march heedlessly on to seek redress at every hazard. I confess I was astonished to hear such a course recommended. In the most unimportant concerns of life, a prudent man calls to his aid his best reason and deliberate judgment. But it seems in the great concerns of the nation where its peace is at stake and its future destiny hazarded, we must close our eyes, set all prudence at defiance, and move boldly on to our object, and not disgrace ourselves by consulting lessons of wisdom and experience which lie in our way.... I cannot consent to purchase national misery, even should it be accompanied with what gentlemen call national honor.... In the whole history of our Government, prudence has been considered as essential to regulating our measures, particularly those which affect foreign nations. We have not suffered ourselves to be led away by our feelings, but were governed by the very calculations which gentlemen now affect so much to despise.... Can the waste of our blood and treasure heal the wounds which the nation's fancied honor may have received? Are we to draw upon us all the miseries that attend war, and all the dangers with which it is surrounded without any practical good in prospect, when perhaps at the end of seven years we shall be compelled to sit down and acquiesce under the system against which the war is waged, merely to have it to say — that we acted like men of spirit?

★ ★ ★ ★

The present state of the European world, is the primary cause from which those principles that have so seriously affected our commerce have received their origin. And to me it appears vain to expect that our neutral rights will be respected, until the causes which have subverted every venerable principle, once a rule of conduct between nations, shall no longer exist. We may make arrangements with France for the revocation of her decrees, and with England, for the revocation of her Orders in Council. But there will be no permanent security; we must participate in the evils (in some shape) which have fallen on the community of civilized man.

★ ★ ★ ★

There is one consideration distinct from all others, which ought to inspire us with caution in entering into the contest between the two great belligerents: England is contending not only for her own existence, but in doing so, she secures us from the attempt to subjugate us to the power of France, to which we should be otherwise exposed. I feel my self under no obligation for any good intention towards us on her part; it is a sense of her own danger, and her struggle for security that produces the effect; but the fact is unquestionably so. Viewing the character of him who has enslaved Europe, I cannot believe otherwise than that if England shall fall, we shall not remain unassailed.

★ ★ ★ ★

We have been emphatically asked, (by Mr. SPEAKER,) "what are we to gain by peace?" I was astonished at the question. What are we to gain by peace? What are we not to lose by war? Liberty! security! and happiness! are the great blessings which we hazard! Leave me these, and take your trade to the Continent, or your Orders in Council. With all the difficulties which we encounter, and the ills which befall us, we are still the freest and happiest nation on which the sun shines. I fear, sir, we shall draw upon us the just displeasure of Heaven, if we estimate her bounties, lavished upon us with such profuse hand, so lightly.

Source: Excerpts from debates in the House of Representatives, *Annals of Congress,* 12th Cong., 1st sess., January 3, 1812 (Washington: Gales and Seaton, 1853), 23:619–635.

Notes

1. *Annals of Congress,* 12th Cong., 1st sess., 23: 13 (Nov. 5, 1811).

2. 2 Stat. 671–674, 676–677, 682–683, 684–685, 685–686, 695, 696–699, 699–700, 700–701, 704, 705–707, 707–708 (1811–1812).

3. Donald R. Hickey, *The War of 1812: A Forgotten Conflict* (Urbana: University of Illinois Press, 1989), 30, 37; Donald R. Hickey, *The War of 1812: A Short History* (Urbana: University of Illinois Press, 1995), 11–12.

4. *Annals of Congress,* 12th Cong., 1st sess., 23:1629 (June 1, 1812).

5. *Annals of Congress,* 12th Cong., 1st sess., 23:1547 (June 25, 1812). For a copy of the entire report of the House Committee on Foreign Relations, see *Annals of Congress,* 12th Cong., 1st sess., 23: 1546–1554. The House and Senate debate on the war resolution is found in *Annals of Congress,* 12th Cong., 1st sess., 23:1630–1638 (June 3–June 4, 1812), 265–298 (June 5–June 17, 1812). For a copy of the war resolution, see 2 Stat. 755 (1812). See also Hickey, *The War of 1812: A Forgotten Conflict,* 44–45.

6. Reginald Horsman, *The Causes of the War of 1812* (Philadelphia: University of Pennsylvania Press, 1962), 261; Hickey, *The War of 1812: A Forgotten Conflict,* 46.

7. Quotes are found in Samuel Eliot Morison, "Dissent in the War of 1812," in Samuel Eliot Morison, Frederick Merk, and Frank Freidel, *Dissent in Three American Wars* (Cambridge, Mass.: Harvard University Press, 1970), 3–4; William Gribbin, *The Churches Militant: The War of 1812 and American Religion* (New Haven, Conn.: Yale University Press, 1973), 103.

8. Morison, "Dissent in the War of 1812," 4. See also William Ray Barlow, "Congress During the War of 1812," Ph.D. dissertation, Ohio State University, 1961.

9. Hickey, *War of 1812: A Forgotten Conflict,* 307.

Missouri Compromise
✳ 1819–1821 ✳

During Congress's first twenty years, the issue of slavery never once aroused more than passing interest. Then almost unexpectedly, early in 1819, slavery erupted into a sectional controversy that would dominate the American political landscape for nearly a half century before finally exploding into a civil war between the Northern and Southern states. The application of the citizens of Missouri to become a state prompted the first major clash over slavery since the Constitutional Convention of 1787. Previously, nine additional states had been admitted to the Union, largely without controversy. Missouri proved to be different because slavery, in the absence of any legal prohibition, had spread into the Missouri Territory following the 1803 purchase of Louisiana from France. The conflict over Missouri brought to the forefront of American consciousness the degree of irreconcilable differences between North and South on the issue of slavery.

Rep. James Tallmadge Jr., DR-N.Y., offered an amendment that prompted the opening debate over Missouri, enabling the people of the Missouri Territory to take the preparatory steps of statehood. Tallmadge's amendment barred any new slaves from entering the future state and freed any slaves born in Missouri — after the territory's admission into the Union — at age twenty-five. At the time there were eleven free states and ten slave states. Following a lengthy debate, the House voted separately on the two clauses of the Tallmadge amendment. The clause forbidding future slaves from entering Missouri passed 87–76. (Northerners voted 86–10 in favor and Southerners 66-1 against). The second clause, which called for slaves born in Missouri after statehood to be free at age twenty-five, passed by a narrower margin of 82–78. (Northerners voted 80–15 for the clause and Southerners voted 63–2 against it.) In the Senate, however, the first clause of the Tallmadge amendment (forbidding future slaves from entering the State) was rejected 22–16. The second clause (freeing slave offspring) was even more soundly defeated, 31–7. Five senators from free states voted with the South in rejecting the first clause. Nine additional Northern senators joined the majority in rejecting the second clause. No senator from a slave state favored either clause. The Missouri bill as modified was returned to the House, which on March 2, 1819, voted 78–76 not to concur with the Senate's action in striking the antislavery amendment from the Missouri bill. When informed of the Senate's unwillingness to change its position, the House again spurned the Senate position, 78–66. The following day, the Fifteenth Congress adjourned.[1]

Surprisingly, "when the Fifteenth Congress adjourned, the Missouri Controversy adjourned with it (except in Missouri and Illinois) and created scarcely a ripple of interest for the next eight months. Until the fall of 1819, it was rarely mentioned either in newspaper editorials or private correspondence." In fact, as historian Glover Moore has observed, the public's lack of concern over the Missouri dispute "would have remained so if it had not been subjected to a carefully organized barrage of propaganda and a series of mass meetings by means of which those who favored slavery restriction managed to invest their cause with the aura of a moral crusade."[2]

By the time the Sixteenth Congress reconvened on December 6, 1819, antislavery mass meetings were being held throughout the Northern states, and state legislatures and pamphleteers soon joined the fray. Further complicating the Missouri question was Maine's application for statehood on December 8, 1819, whose admission would add another Northern state, and Alabama's admission into the Union on December 14, which left the Senate evenly divided between North and South. With the addition of Alabama, the position of those opposed to the restriction of slavery in Missouri, who could count on the two slaveholding Illinois senators and at least two or three other Northern senators, became even stronger.

On December 30, backed by a clear-cut majority in the Senate, House Speaker Henry Clay, DR-Ky., informed his Northern colleagues that Southerners would block Maine's admission until the House consented to allow slavery in Missouri. The impasse between the North-controlled House, which insisted on the Tallmadge amendments, and the South-controlled Senate, which demanded admission of the enslaved Missouri without Tallmadge's dual restrictions, could not be broken in 1819. On January 3, 1820, the House passed a bill providing for the admission of Maine. Ten days later, the Senate took up the Maine bill together with an amendment suggested by the Senate Judiciary Committee, which incorporated in the House bill a provision enabling

Missouri to become a slave state.[3] As Clay predicted, the admission of Maine now became inseparably linked to Missouri's admission without a slavery restriction.

During the next several days, the Senate first debated whether to have the bill recommitted to the Judiciary Committee with instructions to strike out the provision relating to Missouri, and then whether to attach an antislavery provision to the amendment admitting Missouri. Ultimately, both motions were defeated. Then on February 3, Rep. Jesse B. Thomas, DR-Ill., a slaveholder, suggested that Congress link the admission of Missouri and Maine. Two weeks later, Thomas's proposal, which became the basis for the Missouri Compromise of 1820, was incorporated as an amendment to a Maine-Missouri bill. In essence, the compromise meant three things: Maine would be admitted as a free state and Missouri as a slave state, Arkansas and Oklahoma would be open to settlement by slaveholders, and slavery would be prohibited in the remainder of the Louisiana Territory north of 36° 30′, which comprised most of the area of nine future states. The Senate first approved Thomas's amendment and then the Maine-Missouri bill.[4]

The battle over Missouri, however, was far from over. When the House resumed consideration of the Missouri question, both the Thomas amendment and the amended Maine-Missouri bill were rejected. While most Americans were far more interested in the economic depression that gripped the nation at the time, on Capitol Hill "crowded galleries … heard orator after orator discuss the subject of slave restriction from every conceivable angle. Never before had the deliberations of Congress aroused a deeper interest, said the Washington *Intelligence*," and the "[t]hreats of disunion became commonplace in the winter of 1819–1820." With surprising accuracy, as the debate continued, several in Congress even predicted the Civil War of 1861–1865.[5]

On March 1, the House once again passed a Missouri bill restricting slavery, and the next day, the Senate once more struck out the slavery restriction clause and added the Thomas amendment. Then almost without warning on March 2, the hopeless deadlock was broken when a joint conference committee that was established to seek a workable compromise recommended that: (1) the Senate withdraw its

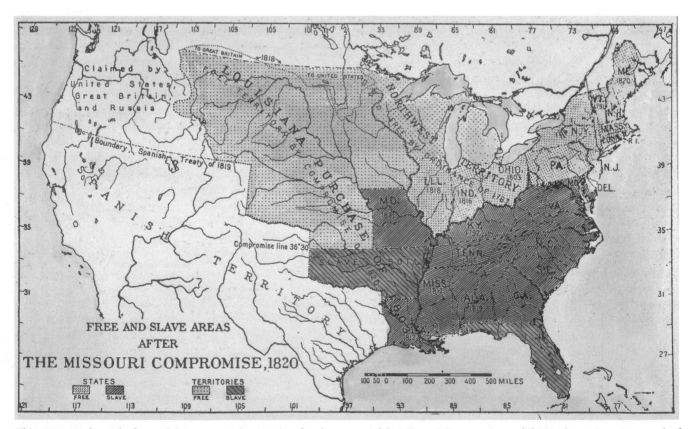

This 1820 map shows the free and slave states and territories after the passage of the Missouri Compromise, prohibiting slavery in regions north of 36° 30′. Debate on this decision marked the first congressional clash over slavery.
Source: The Granger Collection, New York.

amendments to the Maine bill, (2) both houses strike the slavery restriction clause from the House Missouri bill, and (3) a provision be added to the House Missouri bill excluding slavery from any part of the Louisiana Territory north of 36° 30′ not included within the boundaries of the proposed state of Missouri. After debating the merits of the compromise, the House agreed, 90–87, to remove the restriction against slavery in Missouri, and voted 134–42 to exclude slavery from the remainder of the Louisiana Territory north of 36° 30′. The Missouri Compromise proved successful because the House never voted on the compromise as a whole, but instead split it into sections and voted separately on each one to avoid attracting the diehards who were opposed to the Thomas amendment. Afterwards, Speaker Clay, who had worked hard to achieve the compromise, thwarted a last-ditch effort by Rep. John Randolph of Virginia to strike the antislavery clause from the Missouri bill.[6]

On March 3, the Senate withdrew its amendments to the Maine bill, and later the same day President James Monroe signed the legislation admitting Maine into the Union. Three days later, Monroe also signed legislation that authorized the people of Missouri to create a constitution and form a state government without a slavery restriction, and he prohibited slavery in the unorganized territory north and west of the new state. The Missouri Compromise of March 1820 did not, however, end the dispute. When the Missouri constitution was completed in July, it contained a clause barring free Negroes and mulattoes from entering the State. This clause revived the Missouri controversy and prompted a bitter debate with Northerners, who argued that it violated Article 4, Section 2, of the Constitution, which declared that "the citizens of each State shall be entitled to the privileges and immunities of the citizens of the several States." Finally, in February 1821, Henry Clay offered a joint resolution requiring the Missouri legislature to make a "solemn" promise that it would not enact any law that excluded any citizen "from the enjoyment of any of the privileges and immunities" to which they were entitled under the Constitution. The House voted in favor of Clay's resolution, 87–81, and the Senate concurred 28–14; it was incorporated in the Resolution for the Admission of Missouri, which became law on March 2. On August 10, 1821, President Monroe issued a proclamation announcing that the State of Missouri had "assented to the condition prescribed by Congress" and had been admitted to the Union. Clay's

role as a peacemaker in 1821 helped him to win the title of "Great Pacificator."[7]

The Missouri Compromise, which helped to preserve section peace and hold the Union together for the next three decades, introduced virtually every argument used to describe the slavery issue during that period. These diverse views are represented in excerpts from addresses of Sen. Rufus King, F, N.Y., who used "calm and dignified" oratory to present the antislavery cause, and Sen. William Pinkney, DR, Md., who, in "emotional and flowery, though none the less cogent"[8] language, espoused the South's case.

THE FINAL VOTE

Second Missouri Compromise
Henry Clay's Resolution

House
February 26, 1821

	Yea	Nay
Northeast	4	35
Middle States	22	37
Southeast	42	1
Northwest	0	8
Southwest	19	0
Total	**87**	**81**

Senate
February 28, 1821

	Yea	Nay
Northeast	5	6
Middle States	6	3
Southeast	5	2
Northwest	3	3
Southwest	9	0
Total	**28**	**14**

Source. Albert Castel and Scott L. Gibson, *The Yeas and the Nays: Key Congressional Decisions, 1774–1945* (Kalamazoo: New Issues Press, Institute of Public Affairs, Western Michigan University, 1975), 36.

SUBSTANCE OF TWO SPEECHES IN OPPOSITION TO THE MISSOURI COMPROMISE OF 1820 BY SENATOR RUFUS KING

FEBRUARY 9 AND FEBRUARY 11, 1820

The Constitution declares "that Congress shall have power to dispose of, and make all needful rules and regulations respecting the territory and other property of the United States." Under this power Congress have passed laws for the survey and sale of public lands, for the division of the same into separate territories; and have ordained for each of them a constitution, a plan of temporary government, whereby the civil and political rights of the inhabitants are regulated, and the rights of conscience and other natural rights are protected.

The power to make all needful regulations, includes the power to determine what regulations are needful; and if a regulation prohibiting slavery within any territory of the United States be, as it has been, deemed needful, Congress possesses the power to make the same, and moreover to pass all laws necessary to carry this power into execution.

The territory of Missouri is a portion of Louisiana, which was purchased of France, and belongs to the United States in full dominion; in the language of the constitution Missouri is their territory or property, and is subject, like other territories of the United States, to the regulations and temporary government which has been, or shall be prescribed by Congress. The clause of the constitution, which grants this power to Congress, is so comprehensive, and unambiguous, and its purpose so manifest, that the commentary will not render the power, or the object of its establishment, more explicit or plain.

The Constitution further provides that "new states may be admitted by congress in the Union" — as this power is conferred without limitation, the time, terms and circumstances of the admission of new states are referred to the discretion of congress; which may admit new states, but are not obliged to do so — of right no new state can demand admission into the Union, unless such demand be founded upon some previous engagement of the United States.

When admitted by congress into the Union, whether by compact or otherwise, the new state becomes entitled to the enjoyment of the same rights, and bound to perform the like duties as the other states; and its citizens will be entitled to all privileges and immunities of citizens in the several states.

The citizens of each state possess rights, and owe duties that are peculiar to and arise out of the constitution and laws of the several states. These rights and duties differ from each other in the different states, and among these differences none is so remarkable or important as that which proceeds from the constitution and laws of the several states respecting slavery; the same being permitted in some states, and forbidden in others.

The question respecting slavery in the old thirteen states had been decided and settled before the adoption of the constitution, which grants no power to congress to interfere with, or to change what had been so previously settled — the slave states therefore are free to continue or to abolish slavery. Since the year 1808 congress have possessed power to prohibit and have prohibited the further emigration or importation of slaves into any of the old thirteen states, and at all times under the constitution have had power to prohibit such migration or importation into any of the new states, or territories of the United States. — The Constitution contains no express provision respecting slavery in a new state that maybe admitted into the Union; every regulation upon this subject belongs to the power whose consent is necessary to the formation and admission of new states into the Union. Congress may therefore make it a condition of the admission of a new state, that slavery shall be forever prohibited within the same. We may, with the more confidence, pronounce this to be the true construction of the constitution, as it has been so amply confirmed by the past session of congress.

★ ★ ★ ★

Although congress possesses the power of making the exclusion of slavery a part or condition of the act admitting a new state into the Union, they may, in special cases, and for sufficient reasons, forbear to exercise this power.

★ ★ ★ ★

Admitting this construction of the constitution, it is alleged that the power by which congress excluded slavery from the states north-west of the river Ohio is suspended in respect to the state that may be formed in the province of Louisiana. The article of the treaty referred to declares: "That the inhabitants of the territory shall be incorporated in the

Union of the United States, and admitted as soon as possible, according to the principles of the federal constitution, to the enjoyment of all rights, advantages, and immunities of citizens of the United States; and in the mean time, they shall be maintained and protected in the free enjoyment of their liberty, property, and the religion which they profess."

Although there is a want of precision in the article, its scope and meaning cannot be misunderstood. It constitutes a stipulation, by which the United States engage that the inhabitants of Louisiana should be formed into a state or states, and as soon as the provisions of the constitution permit, that they should be admitted as new states into the Union on the footing of the other states; and before such admission, and during their territorial government, that they should be maintained and protected by congress in the enjoyment of their liberty, property, and religion. The first clause of this stipulation will be executed by the admission of Missouri as a new state into the Union as such admission will impart to the inhabitants of Missouri "all the rights advantages and immunities" which citizens of the United States derive from the constitution thereof; these rights may be denominated federal right, are uniform throughout the Union, and are common to all its citizens. But the rights derived from the constitution and laws of the states, which may be denominated state rights, in many particulars differ from each other. Thus while the federal rights of citizens of Massachusetts and Virginia are the same, their state rights are dissimilar, and different, slavery being forbidden in one, and permitted in the other state. This difference arises out of the constitutions and laws of the two states, in the same manner as the difference in the rights of the citizens of these states to vote for representatives in congress arises out of the state laws and constitution. In Massachusetts every person of lawful age, and possessing property of any sort of the value of two hundred dollars, may vote for representatives to congress. In Virginia no person can vote for representatives to congress unless he be a freeholder. As the admission of a new state into the Union confers upon its citizens only the rights denominated federal, and as these are common to the citizens of all the states, as well as those in which slavery is prohibited, as of those in which it is allowed, it follows that the prohibition of slavery in Missouri will not impair the federal rights of its citizens, and that such prohibition is not restrained by the clause of the treaty which has been cited.

The remaining clause of the article is expressly confined to the period of the territorial government of Missouri, to the time between the first occupation of the country by the United States and its admission as a new state into the Union. Whatever may be its import, it has no reference nor application to the terms of the admission, or to the condition of Missouri after it shall have been admitted into the Union. The clause is but the common formula of treaties by which inhabited territories are passed from one sovereign to another; its object is to secure such inhabitants the permanent or temporary enjoyment of their former liberties, property and religion; leaving to the new sovereign full power to make such regulations respecting the same as may be thought expedient, provided these regulations be not incompatible with the stipulated security.

★ ★ ★ ★

As all nations do not permit slavery, the term property, in its common and universal meaning, does not include or describe slaves. In treaties therefore between nations, and especially in those of the United States, whenever stipulations respecting slaves were to be made, the words "negroes" or "slaves" have been employed, and the omission of these words in this clause, increases the uncertainty whether, by the term property, *slaves* were intended to be included. But admitting that such was the intention of the parties, the stipulation is not only temporary, but extends no farther than to the property actually possessed by the inhabitants of Missouri when it was first occupied by the United States. Property since acquired by them, and property acquired or possessed by the new inhabitants of Missouri, has in each case been acquired under the laws of the United States, and not during and under the laws of the province of Louisiana. Should therefore the future introduction of slaves into Missouri be forbidden, the feelings of the citizens would soon become reconciled to their exclusion, and the inconsiderable number of slaves owned by the inhabitants at the date of the cession of Louisiana would be emancipated or sent for sale into states where slavery exists.

It is further objected, that the article of the act of admission into the Union by which slavery should be excluded from Missouri, would be nugatory, as the new state, in virtue of the sovereignty, would be at liberty to revoke its consent, and annul the article by which slavery is excluded.

Such revocation would be contrary to the obligations of good faith, which enjoins the observance of our engagements; it would be repugnant to the principles on which government itself is founded; sovereignty in every lawful government is a limited power, and can do only what is lawful to do — sovereigns, like individuals, are bound by their engagements, and have no moral power to break them. Treaties between nations repose on this principle. If the new state can revoke and annul an article concluded between itself and the United States, by which slavery is excluded from it, it may revoke and annul any other article of the compact; it may for example annul the article respecting public lands, and in virtue of its sovereignty, assume the right to tax and to sell the lands of the United States.

There is yet a more satisfactory answer to this objection. The judicial power of the United States is co-extensive with their legislative power, and every question arising under the constitution or laws of the United States is cognizable by the judiciary thereof. Should the new state rescind any of the articles of compact contained in the act of admission into the Union, that for example by which slavery is excluded, and should pass a law authorizing slavery, the judiciary of the United States, on proper application, would immediately deliver from bondage, any person detained as a slave in said state. And in like manner in all instances affecting individuals, the judiciary might be employed to defeat every attempt to violate the constitution and laws of the United States.

If Congress possesses the power to exclude slavery from Missouri, it still remains to be shown that they ought to do so. The examination of this branch of the subject, for obvious reasons, is attended with peculiar difficulty, and cannot be made without passing over arguments which to some of us might appear to be decisive, but the use of which, in this place, would call up feelings, the influence of which would disturb, if not defeat, the impartial consideration of the subject.

Slavery unhappily exists within the United States. Enlightened men in the states where it is permitted, and every where, out of them, regret its existence among us, and seek for the means of limiting and of mitigating it. The first introduction of slaves is not imputable to the present generation, nor even to their ancestors.... The laws and customs of the states in which slavery has existed for so long a period, must have had their influence on the opinions and habits of the citizens, which ought not to be disregarded on the present occasion.

Omitting therefore the arguments which might be urged, and which by all of us might be deemed conclusive, were this an original question, the reasons which shall be offered in favor of the interposition of the power of congress to exclude slavery from Missouri, shall be only such as respect the common defence, the general welfare, and that wise administration of the government, which, as far as possible, may produce the impartial distribution of benefits and burdens throughout the Union.

★ ★ ★ ★

The equality of rights, which includes an equality of burdens, is a vital principle in our theory of government, and its jealous preservation is the best security of public and individual freedom; the departure from this principle in the disproportionate power and influence allowed to the slaveholding states, was a necessary sacrifice to the establishment of the constitution. The effect of this concession has been obvious in the preponderance which it has given to the slaveholding states, over the other states. Nevertheless, it is an ancient settlement, and faith and honor stand pledged not to disturb it. But the extension of this disproportionate power to the new states would be unjust and odious. The states whose power would be abridged, and whose burdens would be increased by the measure, cannot be expected to consent to it; and we may hope that the other states are too magnanimous to insist on it.

The existence of slavery impairs the industry and the power of a nation; and it does so in proportion to the multiplication of its slaves. Where the manual labour of a country is performed by slaves, labour dishonours the hands of freemen.

If her labourers are slaves, Missouri may be able to pay money taxes, but will be unable to raise soldiers, or to recruit seamen, and experience seems to have proved that manufacturers do not prosper where the artificers are slaves. In case of foreign war, or domestic insurrection, misfortunes from which no states are exempt, and against which all should be reasonably prepared, slaves not only do not add to, but diminish the faculty of self-defence; instead of increasing the public strength, they lessen it, by the whole number of free persons, whose place they occupy, increased by the number of freemen that may be employed as guards over them.

The motives for the admission of new states into the Union are the extension of the principles of our free government, the equalizing of the public burdens and the consolidation of the power of the confederated nation. Unless these objects be promoted by the admission of new states, no such admission can be expedient or justified.

The states in which slavery already exists are contiguous to each other; they are also the portion of the United States nearest to the European colonies in the West Indies; colonies whose future condition can hardly be regarded as problematical. If Missouri and the other states that may be formed to the west of the river Mississippi, are permitted to introduce and establish slavery, the repose, if not the security of the Union may be endangered; all the states south of the river Ohio and west of Pennsylvania and Delaware, will be peopled with slaves, and the establishment of new states west of the river Mississippi will serve to extend slavery instead of freedom over that boundless region.

Such increase of the states, whatever other interest it may promote, will be sure to add nothing to the security of the public liberties, and can hardly fail hereafter to require and produce a change in our government.

On the other hand, if slavery be excluded from Missouri, and the other new states which may be formed in this quarter, not only will the slave markets be broken up, and the principles of freedom be extended and strengthened, but an exposed and important frontier will present a barrier, which will check and keep back foreign assailants, who may be as brave, and, as we hope, will be as free as ourselves. Surrounded in this manner by connected bodies of freemen, the states where slavery is allowed will be made more secure against domestic insurrection, and less liable to be affected by what may take place in the neighboring colonies.

It ought not to be forgotten, that the first and main object of the negotiation which led to the acquisition of Louisiana, was the free navigation of the Mississippi, a river that forms the sole passage from the western states to the ocean. This navigation, although of general benefit, has been always valued and desired, as of peculiar advantage to the western states; whose demands to obtain it, were neither equivocal nor unreasonable. But with the river Mississippi, by a sort of coercion, we acquired by good or ill fortune, as our future measures shall determine, the whole province of Louisiana. As this acquisition was made at the common expense, it is very fairly urged that the advantages to be derived from it should also be common. This it is said will not happen, if slavery be excluded from Missouri, as the citizens of states where slavery is permitted, will be shut out, and none but citizens of states where slavery is prohibited, can become inhabitant of Missouri.

★ ★ ★ ★

We may renew our efforts, and enact new laws with heavier penalties, against the importation of slaves: the revenue cutters may more diligently watch our shores and the naval force may be employed on the coast of Africa, and on the ocean, to break up the slave trade — but these means will not put an end to it; so long as markets are open for the purchase of slaves so long they will be supplied; and so long as we permit the existence of slavery in our new and frontier states, so long slave markets will exist. The plea of humanity is equally inadmissible; since no one who has ever witnessed the experiment, will believe the condition of slaves is made better by breaking up, and separation of their families, nor by their removal from old states to the new ones; and the objection to the provision of the bill, excluding slavery from Missouri, is equally applicable to the like prohibitions of the old states: these should be revoked in order that the slaves now confined to certain states may for their health, and comfort, and multiplication, be spread over the whole Union.

That the condition of slaves within the United States has been improved; and the rigours of slavery mitigated, by the establishment and progress of our free governments, is a fact that imparts consolation to all who have taken pains to inquire concerning it. The disproportionate increase of free persons of colour, can be explained only by the supposition that the practice emancipation is gaining ground; a practice which there is reason to believe would become more general, if a plan could be devised by which the comfort and morals of the emancipated slaves could be satisfactorily provided for; for it is not to be doubted that the public opinion everywhere, and especially in the oldest state of the Union, is less favorable than formerly to the existence of slavery. Generous and enlightened men in the states where slavery exists have discovered much solicitude on the subject: a desire has been manifested that emancipation might be encouraged by the establishment of a place, or colony, without the United States,

to which free persons of colour might be removed: and great efforts for that purpose are making, with a corresponding anxiety for their success. These persons, enlightened and humane as they are known to be, surely will be unwilling to promote the removal of the slaves from the old states, to the new ones; where their comforts will not be multiplied, and where their fetters may be riveted forever.

Slavery cannot exist in Missouri without the consent of Congress; the question may therefore be considered, in certain lights, as a new one, it being the first instance in which an inquiry respecting slavery, in a case so free from the influence of the ancient laws, and usages, and manners of the country, has come before the Senate.

★ ★ ★ ★

If slavery by permitted in Missouri, with the climate, and soil, and in the circumstance of this territory, what hope can be entertained that it will ever be prohibited in any of the new states that will be formed of the immense region west of the Mississippi? Will the co-extensive establishment of slavery and of new states throughout this region, lessen the danger of domestic insurrection, or of foreign aggression? Will this manner of executing the great trust of admitting new states into the Union, contribute to assimilate our strength and Union? Will the militia of the nation, which must furnish our soldiers and seamen, increase as slaves increase? Will the actual disproportion in the military service of the nation, be thereby diminished? A disproportion that will be, as it has been, readily borne, as between the original states, because it arises out of their compact of union, but which may become

> [W]e are now about to pass our original boundary; if this can be done without affecting the principles of our free governments, it can be accomplished only by the most vigilant attention to plant, cherish and sustain the principles of liberty in the new states that may be formed beyond our ancient limits.
>
> — Rufus King

a badge of inferiority, if required for the protection of those who being free to choose persist in the establishment of maxims, the inevitable effect of which, will deprive them of the power to contribute to the common defence, and even of the ability to protect themselves. There are limits within which our federal system must stop; no one has supposed that it could be indefinitely extended — we are now about to pass our original boundary; if this can be done without affecting the principles of our free governments, it can be accomplished only by the most vigilant attention to plant, cherish and sustain the principles of liberty in the new states that may be formed beyond our ancient limits: with our utmost caution in this respect, it may be justly apprehended that the general government must be made stronger as we become more extended.

But, if instead of freedom, slavery is to prevail and spread, as we extend our dominion, can any reflecting man fail to see the necessity of giving to the general government, greater powers to enable it to afford the protection that will be demanded of it; powers that will be difficult to control, and which may prove fatal to the public liberties?

Sources: Charles R. King, ed., *The Life and Correspondence of Rufus King* (New York: G.P. Putnam's Sons, 1900), 690–703. Sen. King's remarks were not published in the *Annals of Congress*, but reference to them is found in "Missouri Question," *Annals of Congress*, February 11, 1820 (Washington: Gales and Seaton, 1855), 35:372–373.

SPEECH BY SENATOR WILLIAM PINKNEY IN SUPPORT OF THE MISSOURI COMPROMISE OF 1820

FEBRUARY 15, 1820

I believe, Mr. President, that I am about as likely to retract an opinion which I have formed, as any member of this body, who, being a lover of truth, inquires after it with diligence before he imagines that he has found it; but I suspect that we are all of us so constituted as that neither argument nor declamation, levelled against recorded and published decision, can easily discover a practicable avenue through which it may hope to reach either our heads or our hearts. I mention this, lest it may excite surprise, when I take the liberty to add, that the speech of the honorable gentleman from New York, upon the great subject with which it was principally occupied, has left me as great an infidel as it found me. It is possible, indeed, that if I had had the good fortune to hear that speech at an earlier stage of this debate, when all was fresh and new, although I feel confident that the analysis which it contained of the Constitution, illustrated as it was by historical anecdote rather than by reasoning, would have been just as unsatisfactory to me then as it is now, I might not have been altogether unmoved by those warnings of approaching evil which it seemed to intimate, especially when taken in connection with the observations of the same honorable gentleman on a preceding day, "that delays in disposing of this subject, in the manner he desires, are dangerous, and that we stand on slippery ground." I must be permitted, however (speaking only for myself), to say, that the hour of dismay is passed. I have heard the tones of the larum bell on all sides, until they have become familiar to my ear, and have lost their power to appall, if indeed, they ever possessed it. Notwithstanding occasional appearances of rather an unfavorable description, I have long since per-

suaded myself that the Missouri Question as it is called, might be laid to rest, with innocence and safety, by some conciliatory compromise at least, by which, as is our duty, we might reconcile the extremes of conflicting views and feelings, without any sacrifice of Constitutional principle; and in any event; that the Union would easily and triumphantly emerge from those portentous clouds with which this controversy is supposed to have environed it.

I confess to you, nevertheless, that some of the principles announced by the honorable gentleman from New York, (Mr. King), with an explicitness that reflected the highest credit on his candor, did, when they were first presented, startle me not a little. They were not perhaps entirely new. Perhaps I had seen them before in some shadowy and doubtful shape,

> If shape it might be called, that shape had none Distinguishable in member, joint, or limb.

But in the honorable gentleman's speech they were shadowy and doubtful no longer. He exhibited them in forms so boldly and accurately defined, with contours so distinctly traced, with features so pronounced and striking, that I was unconscious for a moment that they might be old acquaintances. I received them as *novi hospites* within these walls, and gazed upon them with astonishment and alarm. I have recovered, however, thank God, from this paroxysm of terror although not from that of astonishment.... I have what I may be allowed to call a proud and patriotic trust, that they will give countenance to no principles, which, if followed out to their obvious consequences, will not only shake the goodly fabric of the Union to its foundations, but reduce it to a melancholy ruin. The people of this country, if I do not wholly mistake their character, are wise as well as virtuous. They know the value of that federal association which is to them the single pledge and guarantee of power and peace. Their warm and pious affections will cling to it as to their only hope of prosperity and happiness, in defiance of pernicious abstractions, by whomsoever inculcated, or howsoever seductive and alluring in their aspect.

★ ★ ★ ★

Sir, it was but the other day that we were forbidden (properly forbidden, I am sure, for the prohibition came from you) to assume that there existed any intention to impose a prospective restraint on the domestic legislation of Missouri — a restraint to act upon it contemporaneously with its origin as a State, and to continue adhesive to it through all the stages of its political existence. We are now, however, permitted to know that it is determined by a sort of political surgery to amputate one of the limbs of its local sovereignty, and thus mangled and disparaged, and thus only, to receive it into the bosom of the Constitution. It is now avowed that, while Maine is to be ushered into the Union with every possible demonstration of studious reverence on our part, and on hers with colors flying, and all the other graceful accompaniments of honorable triumph, this ill-conditioned upstart of the West, this obscure foundling of a wilderness that was but yesterday the hunting-ground of the savage, is to find her way into the American family as she can with an humiliating badge of remediless inferiority patched upon her garments, with the mark of recent, qualified manumission upon her, or rather with a brand upon her forehead to tell the story of her territorial vassalage, and to perpetuate the memory of her evil propensities.

★ ★ ★ ★

The clause of the Constitution which relates to the admission of new States is in these words: "The Congress may admit new States into this Union," &c., and the advocates for restriction maintain that the use of the word "may" imports discretion to admit or to reject; and that in this discretion is wrapped up another — that of prescribing the terms and conditions of admission in case you are willing to admit: *Cujus est dare ejus est disponere.* I will not for the present inquire whether this involved discretion to dictate the terms of admission belongs to you or not. It is fit that I should first look to the nature and extent of it.

I think I may assume that if such a power be any thing but nominal, it is much more than adequate to the present object; that it is a power of vast expansion, to which human sagacity can assign no reasonable limits; that it is a capacious reservoir of authority, from which you may take, in all time to come, as occasion may serve, the means of oppression as well as of bene-

faction.... There are those in this house who appear to think, and I doubt not sincerely, that the particular restraint now under consideration is wise, and benevolent, and good: wise as respects the Union, good as respects Missouri, benevolent as respects the unhappy victims whom, with a novel kindness, it would incarcerate in the South, and bless by decay and extirpation. Let all such beware, lest in their desire for the effect which they believe the restriction will produce they are too easily satisfied that they have the right to impose it. The moral beauty of the present purpose, or even its political recommendations (whatever they may be) can do nothing for a power like this, which claims to prescribe conditions *ad libitum,* and to be competent to this purpose because it is competent to all.

★ ★ ★ ★

Slavery, we are told in many a pamphlet, memorial, and speech, with which the press has lately groaned, is a foul blot upon our otherwise immaculate reputation. Let this be conceded — yet you are no nearer than before to the conclusion that you possess power which may deal with other subjects as effectually as with this. Slavery, we are further told with some pomp of metaphor, is a canker at the root of all that is excellent in this republican empire, a pestilent disease that is snatching the youthful bloom from its cheek prostrating its honor and withering its strength. Be it so — yet if you have power to medicine to it in the way proposed and in virtue of the diploma which you claim you have also power in the distribution of your political alexipharmics to present the deadliest drugs to every territory that would become a State, and bid it drink or remain a colony for ever. Slavery we are also told, is now "rolling onward with a rapid tide towards the boundless regions of the West," threatening to doom them to sterility and sorrow, unless some potent voice can say to it, thus far shalt thou go and no farther. Slavery engenders pride and indolence in him who commands and inflicts intellectual and moral degradation on him who serves. Slavery, in fine, is unchristian and abominable. Sir, I shall not stop to deny that slavery is all this and more; but I shall not think myself the less authorized to deny that it is for you to stay the course of this dark torrent, by opposing to it a mound raised up by the labors of this portentous discretion on the domain of others; a mound which you cannot erect but through the instrumentality of a trespass of no ordinary kind — not the comparatively innocent trespass that beats down a few blades of grass which the first kind sun or the next refreshing shower may cause to spring again — but that which levels with the ground the lordliest trees of the forest, and claims immortality for the destruction which it inflicts.

★ ★ ★ ★

We are told that, admitting a State into the Union is a compact. Yes; but what sort of a compact? A compact that it shall be a member of the Union, as the Constitution has made it. You cannot new fashion it. You may make a compact to admit, but when admitted, the original compact prevails. The Union is a compact, with a provision of political power and agents for the accomplishment of its objects. Vary that compact as to a new State; give new energy to that political power so as to make it act with more force upon a new State than upon the old; make the will of those agents more effectually the arbiter of the fate of a new State than of the old, and it may be confidently said that the new State has not entered into this Union, but into another Union. How far the Union has been varied is another question. But that it has been varied is clear.

If I am told, that by the bill relative to Missouri, you do not legislate upon a new State, I answer that you do; and I answer further, that it is immaterial whether you do or not. But it is upon Missouri, as a State, that your terms and conditions are to act. Until Missouri is a state, the terms and conditions are nothing. You legislate in the shape of terms and conditions, prospectively; and you so legislate upon it, that when it comes into the Union it is to be bound by a contract degrading and diminishing its sovereignty, and is to be stripped of rights which the original parties to the Union did not consent to abandon, and which that Union (so far as depends upon it) takes under its protection and guarantee.

Is the right to hold slaves a right which Massachusetts enjoys? If it is, Massachusetts is under this Union in a different character from Missouri. The compact of Union for it, is different from the same compact of Union for Missouri. The

---

It is immaterial whether you legislate for Missouri as a State or not. The effect of your legislation is to bring it into the Union with a portion of its sovereignty taken away.
— William Pinkney

---

power of Congress is different — every thing which depends upon the Union is, in that respect, different.

But it is immaterial whether you legislate for Missouri as a State or not. The effect of your legislation is to bring it into the Union with a portion of its sovereignty taken away.

★ ★ ★ ★

It is said that the word *may* necessarily implies the right of prescribing the terms of admission. Those who maintain this are aware that there are no express words (such as upon such terms and conditions as Congress *shall* think fit), words which it was natural to expect to find in the Constitution, if the effect contended for were meant. They put it, therefore, on the word *may,* and on that alone.

★ ★ ★ ★

In a word, the whole amount of the argument on the other side is, that you may refuse to admit a new State and that therefore, if you admit, you may prescribe the terms.

The answer to that argument is, that even if you can refuse, you can prescribe no terms which are inconsistent with the act you are to do. You can prescribe no condition which, if carried into effect, would make the new State less a sovereign State than, under the Union as it stands, it would be. You can prescribe no terms which will make the compact of Union between it and the original States essentially different from that compact among the original States. You may admit, or refuse to admit: but if you admit, you must admit a State in the sense of the Constitution — a State with all such sovereignty as belongs to the original parties: and it must be into *this Union* that you are to admit it not into a Union of your own dictating, formed out of the existing Union by qualifications and new compacts, altering its character and effect, and making it fall short of its protecting energy in reference to the new State, whilst it acquires an energy of another sort — the energy of restraint and destruction.

★ ★ ★ ★

No State, or Territory, in order to become a State, can alienate or surrender any portion of its sovereignty to the Union, or to a sister State, or to a foreign nation. It is under an incapacity to disqualify itself for all the purposes of government left to it in the Constitution, by stripping itself of attributes which arise from the natural equality of States and which the Constitution recognizes, not only because it does not deny them, but presumes them to remain as they exist by the law of nature and nations. Inequality in the sovereignty of states is unnatural, and repugnant to all the principles of that law. Hence we find it laid down by the text-writers on public law, that "Nature has established a perfect equality of rights between independent nations;" and that, "whatever the quality of a free sovereign nation gives to one, it gives to another." The Constitution of the United States proceeds upon the truth of this doctrine. It takes the States as it finds them, *free and sovereign alike by nature.* It receives from them portions of their power for the general good, and provides for the exercise of it organized political bodies. It diminishes the individual sovereignty of each, and transfers, what it subtracts, to the Government which it creates: it takes from all alike, and leaves them relatively to each other equal in sovereign power.

★ ★ ★ ★

One of the most signal errors with which the argument on the other side has abounded, is this of considering the proposed restriction as if levelled at the introduction or establishment of slavery. And hence the vehement declamation which, among other things, has informed us that slavery originated in fraud or violence.

The truth is, that the restriction has no relation, real or pretended, to the right of making slaves of those who are free, or of introducing slavery where it does not already exist. It applies to those who are admitted to be already slaves, and who, with their posterity, would continue to be slaves if they should remain where they are at present; and to a place where slavery already exists by the local law. Their civil condition will not be altered by their removal from Virginia, or Carolina, to Missouri. They will not be more slaves than they now are. Their abode, indeed, will be different, but their bondage the same. Their numbers may possibly be augmented by the diffusion, and I think they will. But this can only happen because their hardships will be mitigated and their comforts increased. The checks to population which exist in the older States will be diminished. The restriction, therefore, does not prevent the establishment of slavery, either with reference to persons or place; but simply inhibits the removal from place to place (the law in each being the same) of a slave, or make his emancipation the consequence of that removal. It acts professedly merely on slavery as it exists, and thus acting restrains its present lawful effects. That slavery, like many other human institutions, originated in fraud or violence, may be conceded: but, however it originated it is established among us, and no man seeks a further establishment of it by new importations of freemen to be converted into slaves. On the contrary, all are anxious to mitigate its evils by all the means within the reach of the appropriate authority, the domestic Legislatures of the different States.

★ ★ ★ ★

Of the Declaration of our Independence, which has also been quoted in support of the perilous doctrines now urged upon us, I need not now speak at large. I have shown on a former occasion how idle it is to rely upon that instrument for such a purpose, and I will not fatigue you by mere repetition. The self-evident truths announced in the Declaration of Independence are not truths at all, if taken literally; and the practical conclusions contained in the same passage of that Declaration prove that they were never designed to be so received.

The Articles of Confederation contain nothing on the subject; whilst the actual Constitution recognizes the legal existence of slavery by various provisions. The power of prohibiting the slave trade is involved in that of regulating commerce, but this is coupled with an express inhibition to the exercise of it for twenty years. How, then, can that Constitution which expressly permits the importation of slaves authorize the National Government to set on foot a crusade against slavery?

The clause respecting fugitive slaves is affirmative and active in its effects. It is a direct sanction and positive protection of the right of the master to the services of his slave as derived under the local laws of the States.

★ ★ ★ ★

The power is "to admit new States into this Union;" and it may be safely conceded that here is discretion to admit or refuse. The question is, what must we do if we do any thing? What must we admit, and into what? The answer is a State — and into this Union.

★ ★ ★ ★

[Mr. Pinkney concluded by expressing a hope that (what he deemed) the perilous principles urged by those in favor of the restriction upon the new State would be disavowed or explained, or that at all events, the application of them to the subject under discussion would not be pressed, but that it might be disposed of in a manner satisfactory to all by a prospective prohibition of slavery in the territory to the north and west of Missouri.]

Source: Excerpts from the House of Representatives, *Annals of Congress*, February 15, 1820 (Washington: Galoc and Conton, 1055), 35, 389–417).

Notes

1. *Annals of Congress*, 15th Cong., 2nd sess., 33:1166 (February 13, 1819), 1170 (February 15, 1819), 1214–1215 (February 16, 1819), 34:1272–1273 (February 19, 1819), 1433–1438 (March 2, 1819). See also Glover Moore, *The Missouri Controversy, 1819–1821* (Lexington: University of Kentucky Press, 1953), 33–59.

2. Moore, *The Missouri Controversy, 1819–1821*, 65–66.

3. *Annals of Congress*, 16th Cong., 1st sess., 35:841 (December 30, 1819), 849 (January 3, 1820), 85 (January 13, 1820).

4. *Annals of Congress*, 16th Cong., 1st sess., 35:101–118 (January 14, 1820), 314–359, (February 1, 1820), 363 (February 3, 1820), 424 (February 16, 1820), 426–428 (February 17, 1820), 428–430 (February 18, 1820). For an analysis of the Senate vote on the Maine-Missouri bill containing the Thomas amendment. See also Albert Castel and Scott L. Gibson, *The Yeas and the Nays: Key Congressional Decisions, 1774–1945* (Kalamazoo: New Issues Press, Institute of Public Affairs, Western Michigan University, 1975), 35–36.

5. Moore, *The Missouri Controversy, 1819–1821*, 91–93.

6. *Annals of Congress*, 16th Cong., 1st sess., 35:467–469 (March 2, 1820); 36:1572–1573 (March 1, 1820), 1576–1588 (March 2, 1820). See also Moore, *The Missouri Controversy, 1819–1821*, 100–103. For an analysis of the House vote on the Maine-Missouri bill containing the Thomas amendment. See also Castel and Gibson, *The Yeas and the Nays*, 35–36.

7. 3 Stat. 544, 545–548; 3 Stat. Appendix II; *Annals of Congress*, 16th Cong., 2nd sess., 37:1228, 1236–1240 (February 26, 1821), 389–390 (February 28, 1821); Moore, *The Missouri Controversy, 1819–1821*, 134–159; Castel and Gibson, *The Yeas and the Nays*, 36–37.

8. Moore, *The Missouri Controversy, 1819–1821*, 99.

Webster-Hayne Debate
✳ January 1830 ✳

During the nation's first four decades under the Constitution, the federal government routinely sold public lands as a means of raising money to build roads and canals, which enabled thousands of Americans an opportunity to begin anew in the rapidly developing west. This policy was rarely challenged until late December 1829, when Sen. Samuel A. Foot of Connecticut called attention to the recent report of the commissioner of the Land Office. The report revealed that more than 72 million acres of surveyed public land remained unsold. Before any additional surveys were conducted, Foot called for the sale of public lands to be limited for a time to those already offered for sale. He also proposed an inquiry into the practicality of abolishing the office of surveyor general — the most important office in the General Land Office.[1] Foot's routine motion of inquiry was not expected to provoke debate. Within a month, however, his proposal to limit the sale of public lands in the rapidly developing West prompted one of the most famous constitutional debates ever conducted in the Senate.

The ensuing exchange over the Foot Resolution thrust to the forefront of public consciousness "two opposing philosophies of American government — nationalism and states' rights." What started out as a debate "over public lands" quickly broadened to a discussion about the recently enacted protective "tariff, slavery, local patriotism, and sectionalism," before finally centering on "a discussion of the Constitution and the nature of the American Union."[2] While the dramatic encounter on the nature of the Union between Sen. Daniel Webster of Massachusetts and Sen. Robert Y. Hayne of South Carolina received the most focus, nearly half of the members of the Senate (twenty-one of forty-eight) delivered speeches on the Foot Resolution. The sixty-five speeches that make up the debate "analyzed, evaluated, and offered predictions concerning the changing political, constitutional, and economic conditions of the country."[3]

Sen. Thomas Hart Benton of Missouri, in an emotional speech on January 18, 1830, denounced the resolution as an effort by Easterners to "check" Western immigration and prosperity by keeping oppressed workers in the East from moving West. Eastern "manufacturers," Benton declared, "want poor people to do the work for small wages; these poor people wish to go to the West and get land; to have flocks and herds — to have their own fields, orchards, gardens, and meadows — their own cribs, barns, and dairies, and to start their children on a theater where they can contend with equal chances for the honors and dignities of the country." The high price of western lands, Benton emphasized, threatened to create "a fund for corruption — fatal to the sovereignty and independence of the states." Realizing that Southern help was needed to defeat the resolution, Benton encouraged the South to forge an alliance with the West against the Northeast.[4]

On January 19, Hayne realized that the West and South both opposed the economic policies favored by the Northeast and went even farther in opposing the Foot Resolution. He pledged Southern support for the West on land policy in the hope of gaining that section's support for a lower tariff, which was favored by the South. The South wanted a lower tariff, which was opposed by Northeastern manufactures, because it would increase foreign competition and reduce their profits. The opposing views on public lands, Hayne observed, were clear. "On one side, it is contended that the public land ought to be reserved as a permanent fund for revenue and future distribution among the states; while on the other it is insisted that the whole of these lands of right belong to, and ought to belong to, the states in which they lie." Invoking strict constructionist and states' rights views against federal interference, Hayne asserted that "the very life of our system is the independence of the States, and that there is no evil more to be depreciated than the consolidation of this Government."[5] With his initial remarks, Hayne turned the dispute into a confrontation between those favoring state sovereignty and those supportive of national sovereignty.

In response, Webster, the recognized champion of New England, expressed displeasure over the tendency of some Southerners to "habitually speak of the Union in terms of indifference, or even of disparagement,"[6] and delivered a lengthy attack on the doctrine of nullification, which he knew Westerners deplored. Webster argued "that the logic, tendency, and practical effect of nullification, if permitted to be developed and employed, would be to destroy the Union and foment lawlessness and revolutionary violence. As a peaceful alternative," he "offered the theory of the Union as a sovereign

Senator Daniel Webster replies to Robert Hayne during their debate concerning a proposal to place limitations on public lands in the rapidly expanding West. At issue was federal versus state rights, a debate that continues in some fashion into the modern day.
Source: The Granger Collection, New York.

national government, created by the people of the United States as a whole, with authority to decide on the lawfulness and constitutionality of its origins."[7] Webster also took time to recount the underlying devotion of the East and New England to the West. With his first reply to Hayne, Webster cleverly shifted the focus of the debate to an exchange over the purpose of the Union, and thrust the issue of nullification to the forefront of what had quickly become a public debate.

When Hayne delivered his reply to Webster on January 25, the crowded Senate galleries heard a sarcastic and provocative defense of the doctrine of state sovereignty and nullification, and an attack of New England's "disloyalty" during the War of 1812. According to Hayne, states had the right to both judge whether the actions of the federal government violated the Constitution and "to protect her citizens from the operation of unconstitutional laws." He argued that Webster's contention that "the Federal Government is the exclusive judge of

the extent as well as limitations of its powers" was "utterly subversive of the sovereignty and independence of the states."[8]

Hayne's rebuttal set the stage for one of the most eloquent speeches ever delivered on the Senate floor. Webster, in his famous "Second Reply to Hayne," delivered over two days January 26 and 27, defended his section's patriotism and then upheld the concept of nationalism as opposed to nullification, which, if adopted, would turn the union into a "rope of sand." Webster continued by arguing that the Constitution confers on the federal government the "power of deciding ultimately and conclusively … the just extent of its authority." Largely ignoring Hayne's economic grievance, Webster instead sought to rally the nation's disparate groups behind his image of the nation held together by the joint ideals of liberty and union, the premises upon which the Constitution was framed. He showed the fallacy of twenty-four separate states interpreting the Constitution, maintained that the historic document was the work of the people, and contended that "Liberty and Union" were "now and forever, one and inseparable."[9] Webster, as one writer has aptly observed, "could see no middle ground, no way to have a combination of autonomous states and a national intent, no way to reconcile sectional interests except in uniting on common aspirations."[10]

Future president Woodrow Wilson, writing three-quarters of a century after the historic confrontation, characterized the Webster-Hayne debate as "the formal opening of the great controversy between the North and the South concerning the nature of the Constitution which bound them together."[11] Unveiled was the tension that existed between those who wanted the states to be the ultimate governmental authority and those who instead preferred federal authority to be predominate. While Hayne and Webster's speeches between January 19 and January 27, 1830, packed the Senate galleries and captured the preponderance of the nation's attention, intermittent debate on the Foot Resolution continued for another four months before it ultimately died on May 21, 1830.

Aside from foreshadowing the developing sectional crisis between North and South, Webster and Hayne provided the nation a "comprehensive review of politics and constitutionalism in the United States since the American Revolution." Webster's orations on the new, growing spirit of nationalism helped forestall the threatened alliance between the South and West against the protective tariff. Equally important, Webster, by shifting the emphasis of the debate, "provoked the responses of other senators that give the debate its landmark significance in constitutional history. ... Considered together, these speeches demonstrate the responsibility for constitutional construction and commitment to constitutional values that were the basic features of legislative practice in the nineteenth century."[12]

SENATOR ROBERT Y. HAYNE'S REPLY TO SENATOR DANIEL WEBSTER

JANUARY 25, 1830

In 1825, the gentleman [Daniel Webster] told the world, that the public lands "ought not to be treated as a treasure." He now tells us, that "they must be treated as so much treasure." What the deliberate opinion of the gentleman on this subject may be, belongs not to me to determine; but, I do not think he can, with the shadow of justice or propriety, impugn my sentiments, with the shadow of justice or propriety, while his own recorded opinions are identical with my own.... If, in the deeds of cession, it has been declared that the grants were intended for "the common benefit of all the States," it is clear, from other provisions, that they were not intended merely as so much property: for, it is expressly declared that the object of the grants is the erection of new States; and the United States, in accepting the trust, bind themselves to facilitate the foundation of the States, to be admitted into the Union with all the rights and privileges of the original states. This, sir, was the great end to which all parties looked, and it is by the fulfilment of this high trust, that "the common benefit of all the States" is to be best promoted.

★ ★ ★ ★

It has been reserved to the gentleman from Massachusetts, while he vaunts his own personal devotion to Western interests, to claim for the entire section of country to which he belongs, an ardent friendship for the West, as manifested by their support of the system of Internal Improvement, while he casts in our teeth the reproach that the South has manifested hostility to Western interests in opposing appropriations for such objects.... He has fallen into this error from not having duly weighed the force and effect of the reproach which he was endeavoring to cast upon the South. In relation to the other point, the friendship manifested by New England towards the West in their support of the system of internal improvement. ... It must be well known to everyone whose experience dates back as far as 1825, that, up to a certain period, New England was generally opposed to appropriations for internal improvements in the West.

★ ★ ★ ★

Sir, let me tell that gentleman that the South repudiates the idea that a pecuniary dependence on the federal government is one of the legitimate means of holding the states together. A moneyed interest in the Government is essentially a base interest; and just so far as it operates to bind the feelings of those who are subjected to it to the government; just so far as it operates in creating sympathies and interests that would not otherwise exist; is it opposed to all the principles of free government and at war with virtue and patriotism. ... Sir,

I would lay the foundation of this Government in the affections of the people; I would teach them to cling to it by dispensing equal justice, and, above all, by securing the "blessings of liberty to themselves and to their posterity."

The honorable gentleman from Massachusetts has gone out of his way to pass a high eulogium on the state of Ohio. In the most impassioned tones of eloquence, he described her majestic march to greatness. … When … the gentleman proceeded to contrast the State of Ohio with Kentucky, … for the purpose of pointing out the superiority of the former, and of attributing that superiority to the existence of slavery, in the one state, and its absence in the other, I thought I could discern the very spirit the Missouri question intruded into this debate, for objects best known to the gentleman himself.

★ ★ ★ ★

The impression which has gone abroad, of the weakness of the South, as connected with the slave question, exposes us to such constant attacks, has done us so much injury, and is calculated to produce such infinite mischiefs, that I embrace the occasion presented by the remarks of the gentleman from Massachusetts, to declare that we are ready to meet the question promptly and fearlessly. It is one from which we are not disposed to shrink, in whatever form or under whatever circumstances it may be pressed upon us. We are ready to make up the issue with the gentleman, as to the influence of slavery on individual and national character — on the prosperity and greatness, either of the United States, or of particular States…. Sir, we will not consent to look at slavery in the abstract…. If slavery, as it now exists in this country, be an evil, we of the present day found it ready made to our hands. Finding our lot cast among a people, whom God had manifestly committed to our care. … We met it as a practical question of obligation and duty. We resolved to make the best of the situation in which Providence had placed us, and to fulfil the high trust which had devolved upon us as the owners of slaves, in the only way in which such a trust could be fulfilled, without spreading misery and ruin throughout the land. We found that we had to deal with a people whose physical, moral, and intellectual habits and character, totally disqualified them from the enjoyment of the blessings of freedom. We could not send them back to the shores from whence their fathers had been taken; their numbers forbade the thought, even if we did not know that their condition here is infinitely preferable to what it possibly could be among the barren sands and savage tribes of Africa; and it was wholly irreconcilable with all our notions of humanity to tear asunder the tender ties which they had formed among us, to gratify the feelings of a false philanthropy. What a commentary on the wisdom, justice, and humanity, of the Southern slave owner is presented by the example of certain benevolent associations and charitable individuals elsewhere…. By means of missionaries and polit-

ical tracts … Thousands of these deluded victims of fanaticism were seduced into the enjoyment of freedom in our Northern cities. And what has been the consequence? Go to these cities now, and ask the question. Visit the dark and narrow lanes, and obscure recesses, which have been assigned by common consent as the abodes of those outcasts of the world — the free people of color. Sir, there does not exist, on the face of the whole earth, a population so poor, so wretched, so vile, so loathsome, so utterly destitute of all the comforts, conveniences, and decencies of life, as the unfortunate blacks of Philadelphia, and New York, and Boston. Liberty has been to them the greatest of calamities, the heaviest of curses.

★ ★ ★ ★

When the gentleman from Massachusetts adopts and reiterates the old charge of weakness as resulting from slavery, I must be permitted to call for the proof of those blighting effects which he ascribes to its influence…. [I]t may be well doubted whether slaveholding states, by reason of the superior value of their productions, are not able to maintain a number of troops in the field, fully equal to what could be supported by states with a larger white population, but not possessed of equal resources.

It is a popular error to suppose, that, in any possible state of things, the people of a country could ever be called out *en masse*, or that a half, or a third, or even a fifth part of the physical force of any country could ever be brought into the field. The difficulty is not to procure men, but to provide the means of maintaining them; and in this view of the subject, it may be asked whether the southern states are not a source of strength and power, and not of weakness, to the country? Whether they have not contributed, and are not now contributing, largely, to the wealth and prosperity of every state in this Union?…. It is not true, as has been supposed, that the

> *[A]s to the doctrine that the Federal Government is the exclusive judge of the extent as well as the limitations of its powers, it seems to me to be utterly subversive of the sovereignty and independence of the States.*
> — Robert Y. Hayne

advantages of this labor is confined almost exclusively to the southern states. Sir, I am thoroughly convinced that, at this time, the States North of the Potomac actually derive greater profits from the labor of our slaves, than we do ourselves. It appears, from our public documents, that, in seven years, (from 1821–1827 inclusive) the six Southern States exported to the amount of one hundred and ninety millions three hundred and thirty-seven thousand two hundred and eighty-one dollars; and imported to the value of fifty-five millions six hundred and forty-six thousand three hundred and one dollars. Now, the difference between these two sums, near one hundred forty millions of dollars, passed through the hands of the Northern merchants, and enabled them to carry on their commercial operations with all the world.... It will be seen, therefore, at a glance, how much slave labor has contributed to the wealth and prosperity of the United States; and how largely our Northern brethren have participated in the profits of that labor.

★ ★ ★ ★

There is a spirit, which, like the father of evil, is constantly "walking to and fro about the earth, seeking whom it may devour." It is the spirit of false philanthropy. The persons whom it possesses do not indeed throw themselves into the flames, but they are employed in lighting up the torches of discord throughout the community. Their first principle of action is to leave their own affairs, and neglect their own duties, to regulate the affairs and the duties of others.... It is a spirit which has long been busy with the slaves of the South, and is even now displaying itself in vain efforts to drive the Government from its wise policy in relation to the Indians....

But, sir, whatever difference of opinion may exist as to the effect of slavery on national wealth and prosperity, if we may trust to experience, there can be no doubt that it has never yet produced any injurious effect on individual or national character.

★ ★ ★ ★

Sir, as to the doctrine that the Federal Government is the exclusive judge of the extent as well as the limitations of its

powers, it seems to me to be utterly subversive of the sovereignty and independence of the States. It makes but little difference, in my estimation, whether Congress or the Supreme Court, are invested with this power. If the Federal Government, in all or any of its departments, are to prescribe the limits of its own authority; and the States are bound to submit to the decision, and are not to be allowed to exercise and decide for themselves when the barriers of the constitution shall be overleaped, this is practically "a government without limitation of powers." The States are at once reduced to mere petty corporations, and the People are entirely at your mercy. I have but one more word to add. In all the efforts that have been made by South Carolina to resist the unconstitutional laws which Congress has extended over them, she has kept steadily in view the preservation of the Union, by the only means by which she believes it can be long preserved — a firm, manly, and steady resistance against usurpation. The measures of the Federal Government have, it is true, prostrated her interests, and will soon involve the whole South in irretrievable ruin. But this evil, great as it is, is not the chief ground of our complaints. It is the principle involved in the contest — a principle which, substituting the discretion of Congress for the limitation of the constitution, brings the States and the people to the feet of the Federal Government, and leaves them nothing they can call their own.... Sir, if, in acting on these high motives, if animated by that ardent love of liberty which has always been the most prominent trait in the Southern character, we should be hurried beyond the bounds of a cold and calculating prudence, who is there, with one noble and generous sentiment in his bosom, that would not be disposed in the language of Burke to exclaim — "You must pardon something to the spirit of liberty."

Source: *Register of Debates in Congress,* January 25, 1830 (Washington: Gales and Seaton, 1830), 6:44–58.

SENATOR DANIEL WEBSTER'S REPLY TO SENATOR ROBERT Y. HAYNE

JANUARY 26 AND 27, 1830

Mr. President — I ask for the reading of the resolution before the Senate.

The Secretary read the resolution, as follows:

"Resolved. That the Committee on Public Lands be instructed to inquire and report the quantity of public lands remaining

unsold within each State and Territory, and whether it be expedient to limit for a certain period the sales of the public lands to such lands only as have heretofore been offered for sale, and are now subject to entry at the minimum price. And, also, whether the office of Surveyor-General, and some of the land offices, may not be abolished without detriment to the public interest; or whether it be expedient to adopt measures to hasten the sales and extend more rapidly the surveys of the public lands."

We have thus heard, Sir, what the resolution is which is actually before us for consideration; and it will readily occur to every one, that it is almost the only subject about which something has not been said in the speech, running through two days, by which the Senate has been entertained by the gentleman from South Carolina.... He has spoken of every thing but the public lands; they have escaped his notice. To that subject, in all his excursions, he has not paid even the cold respect of a passing glance.

★ ★ ★ ★

I spoke, sir, of the Ordinance of 1787, which prohibits slavery, in all future times, northwest of the Ohio, as a measure of great wisdom and foresight, and one which had been attended with highly beneficial and permanent consequences. I suppose that, on this point, no two gentlemen in the Senate could entertain different opinions. But the simple expression of this sentiment has led the gentleman, not only into a labored defense of slavery, in the abstract, and on principle, but also into a warm accusation against me, as having attacked the system of domestic slavery now existing in the Southern States. For all this, there was not the slightest foundation, in any thing said or intimated by me.... I said, only, that it was highly wise and useful, in legislating for the Northwestern country while it was yet a wilderness, to prohibit the introduction of slaves; and I added, that I presumed there was no reflecting and intelligent person, in the neighboring State of Kentucky, who would doubt that, if the same prohibition had been extended, at the same early period, over that commonwealth, her strength and population would, at this day, have been far greater than they are. If these opinions be thought doubtful, they are nevertheless, I trust, neither extraordinary nor disrespectful.

★ ★ ★ ★

There is not, and never has been, a disposition in the North to interfere with these interests of the South. Such interference has never been supposed to be within the power of government; nor has it been in any way attempted. The slavery of the South has always been regarded as a matter of domestic policy, left with the States themselves, and with which the federal government had nothing to do.... The gentleman, indeed, argues that slavery, in the abstract, is no evil. Most assuredly I need not say I differ with him, altogether and most widely, on that point. I regard domestic slavery as one of the greatest evils, both moral and political. But whether it be a malady, and whether it be curable, and if so, by what means; or, on the other hand, whether it be the *vulnus immedicabile* of the social system, I leave it to those whose

right and duty it is to inquire and to decide. And this I believe, Sir, is, and uniformly has been, the sentiment of the North.

★ ★ ★ ★

The domestic slavery of the South I leave where I find it — in the hands of their own Governments.... I go for the Constitution as it is, and for the Union as it is. But I am resolved not to submit in silence to accusations, either against myself individually or against the North, wholly unfounded and unjust.

★ ★ ★ ★

We approach, at length, sir, to a more important part of the honorable gentleman's observations. Since it does not accord with my views of justice and policy to give away the public lands altogether, as a mere matter of gratuity, I am asked by the honorable gentleman on what ground it is that I consent to vote them away in particular instances? How, he inquires, do I reconcile with these professed sentiments, my support of measures appropriating portions of the lands to particular roads, particular canals, particular rivers, and particular institutions of education in the West? This leads, sir, to the real and wide difference in political opinion between the honorable gentleman and myself. On my part, I look upon all these objects as connected with the common good, fairly embraced in its object and its terms; he, on the contrary, deems them all, if good at all, only local good. This is our difference. ... We look upon the States, not as separated, but as united. We love to dwell on that Union, and on the mutual happiness which it has so much promoted, and the common renown which it has so greatly contributed to acquire. In our contemplation, Carolina and Ohio are parts of the same country. ... We do not impose geographical limits to our patriotic feeling or regard. ... We who come here, as agents and representatives of these narrow-minded and selfish men of New England, consider ourselves as bound to regard with an equal eye the good of the whole, in whatever is within our powers of legislation.

★ ★ ★ ★

I understand the honorable gentleman from South Carolina to maintain, that it is a right of the State Legislatures to interfere, whenever, in their judgment, this Government transcends its constitutional limits, and to arrest the operation of its laws.

I understand him to maintain this right, as a right existing under the constitution, not as a right to overthrow it on the ground of extreme necessity, such as would justify violent revolution.

I understand him to maintain an authority, on the part of the States, thus to interfere, for the purpose of correcting the exercise of power by the General Government, of checking it, and of compelling it to conform to their opinion of the extent of its powers.

I understand him to maintain, that the ultimate power of judging of the constitutional extent of its own authority is not lodged exclusively in the General Government, or any branch of it; but that, on the contrary, the States may lawfully decide for themselves, and each State for itself, whether, in a given case, the act of the General Government transcends its power.

I understand him to insist, that, if the exigency of the case, in the opinion of any State Government, require it, such State Government may, by its own sovereign authority, annul an act of the General Government which it deems plainly and palpably unconstitutional.

This is the sum of what I understand from him to be the South Carolina doctrine, and the doctrine which he maintains. I propose to consider it, and compare it with the constitution. Allow me to say, as a preliminary remark, that I call this the South Carolina doctrine, only because the gentleman himself has so denominated it. I do not feel at liberty to say that South Carolina, as a State, has ever advanced these sentiments.

★ ★ ★ ★

We, sir, who oppose the Carolina doctrine, do not deny that the people may, if they choose, throw off any government when it becomes oppressive and intolerable, and erect a better in its stead. We all know that civil institutions are established for the public benefit, and that, when they cease to answer the ends of their existence, they may be changed. But I do not understand the doctrine now contended for to be that, which, for the sake of distinction, we may call the right of revolution. I understand the gentleman to maintain, that, without revolution, without civil commotion, without rebellion, a remedy for supposed abuse and transgression of the powers of the General Government lies in a direct appeal to the interference of the State Governments. [Mr. Hayne here rose: He did not contend, he said, for the mere right of revolution, but for the right of constitutional resistance. What he maintained was, that in case of a plain, palpable violation of the constitution by the General Government, a State may interpose; and that this interposition is constitutional.] Mr. Webster resumed: So, sir, I understood the gentleman, and am happy to find that I did not misunderstand him. What he contends for is, that it is constitutional to interrupt the administration of the constitution itself, in the hands of those who are chosen and sworn to administer it, by the direct interference, in form of law, of the States, in virtue of their sovereign capacity. The inherent right in the people to reform their government I do not deny; and they have another right, and that is, to resist unconstitutional laws, without overturning the Government. It is no doctrine of

mine that unconstitutional laws bind the people. The great question is, whose prerogative is it to decide on the constitutionality or unconstitutionality of the laws? On that, the main debate hinges.... I do not admit, that, under the constitution and in conformity with it, there is any mode in which a State Government, as a member of the Union, can interfere and stop the progress of the general government, by force of her own laws, under any circumstances whatever. This leads us to inquire into the origin of this Government and the source of its power. Whose agent is it? Is it the creature of the State legislatures, or the creature of the people? If the government of the United States be the agent of the State Governments, then they may control it, provided they can agree in the manner of controlling it; if it be the agent of the people, then the people alone can control it, restrain it, modify, or reform it. It is observable enough, that the doctrine for which the honorable gentleman contends leads him to the necessity of maintaining, not only that this General Government is the creature of the States, but that it is the creature of each of the States severally, so that each may assert the power for itself of determining whether it acts within the limits of its authority. It is the servant of four and twenty masters, of different wills and different purposes, and yet bound to obey all. This absurdity (for it seems no less) arises from a misconception as to the origin of this Government and its true character. It is, sir, the people's constitution, the people's Government, made for the people, made by the people, and answerable to the people. The people of the United States have declared that this constitution shall be the supreme law. We must either admit the proposition, or dispute their authority. ... The National Government possesses those powers which it can be shown the people have conferred on it, and no more. All the rest belongs to the State Governments, or to the people themselves. So far as the people have restrained State sovereignty, by the expression of their will, in the Constitution of the United States, so far, it must be admitted, State sovereignty is effectually controlled. I do not contend that it is, or ought to be, controlled farther. The sentiment to which I have referred propounds that State sovereignty is only to be controlled by its own "feeling of justice;" that is to say, it is not to be controlled at all, for one who is to follow his own feelings is under no legal control. Now, however men may think this ought to be, the fact is, that the people of the United States have chosen to impose control on State sovereignties. There are those, doubtless, who wish they had been left without restraint; but the constitution has ordered the matter differently. ... Such an opinion, therefore, is in defiance of the plainest provisions of the constitution.

★ ★ ★ ★

I must now beg to ask, sir, whence is this supposed right of the States derived? Where do they find the power to interfere with the laws of the Union? Sir, the opinion which the honorable gentleman maintains is a notion founded in a total misapprehension, in my judgment, of the origin of this Government, and of the foundation on which it stands. I hold it to be a popular Government, erected by the people; those who administer it, responsible to the people; and itself capable of being amended and modified, just as the people may choose it should be. ... We are here to administer a constitution emanating immediately from the people, and trusted by them to our administration. It is not the creature of the State Governments. It is of no moment to the argument, that certain acts of the State Legislatures are necessary to fill our seats in this body. That is not one of their original State powers.... It is a duty which the people, by the constitution itself, have imposed on the State Legislatures; and which they might have left to be performed elsewhere, if they had seen fit.

★ ★ ★ ★

The people, then, sir, erected this government. They gave it a constitution, and in that constitution they have enumerated the powers which they bestow on it. They have made it a limited Government. They have defined its authority. They have restrained it to the exercise of such powers as are granted; and all others, they declare, are reserved to the States or the people. But, sir, they have not stopped here. If they had, they would have accomplished but half their work. No definition can be so clear, as to avoid possibility of doubt; no limitation so precise, as to exclude all uncertainty. Who, then, shall construe this grant of the people? Who shall interpret their will, where it may be supposed they have left it doubtful? With whom do they repose this ultimate right of deciding on the powers of the Government? Sir, they have settled all this in the fullest manner. They have left it with the Government itself, in its appropriate branches. Sir, the very chief end, the main design, for which the whole constitution was framed and adopted, was to establish a Government that should not be obliged to act through State agency, or depend on State opinion and State discretion. The people had had quite enough of that kind of government under the Confederation.... But, sir, the people have wisely provided, in the Constitution itself, a proper, suitable mode and tribunal for settling questions of constitutional law.... How has it accomplished this great and essential end? By declaring, sir, that "the Constitution, and the laws of the United States made in pursuance thereof, shall be the supreme law of the land, any thing in the constitution or laws of any State to the contrary notwithstanding."

This, sir, was the first great step. By this the supremacy of the Constitution and laws of the United States is declared. The people so will it. No State law is to be valid which comes in conflict with the constitution, or any law of the United States passed in pursuance of it. But who shall decide this question of interference? To whom lies the last appeal? This, sir, the constitution itself decides also, by declaring "that the judicial power shall extend to all cases arising under the Constitution and laws of the United States." These two provisions cover the whole ground. They are, in truth, the key-stone of the arch. With these, it is a constitution; without them, it is a confederacy.

★ ★ ★ ★

Sir, I deny this power of State Legislatures altogether. It cannot stand the test of examination. Gentlemen may say, that, in an extreme case, a State Government might protect the people from intolerable oppression. Sir, in such a case, the people might protect themselves, without the aid of the State Governments. Such a case warrants revolution. It must make, when it comes, a law for itself.... They have chosen to repose this power in the general government, and I think it my duty to support it, like other constitutional powers.

★ ★ ★ ★

I profess, sir, in my career hitherto, to have kept steadily in view the prosperity and honor of the whole country, and the preservation of our Federal Union. It is to that Union we owe our safety at home, and our consideration and dignity abroad. It is to that Union that we are chiefly indebted for whatever makes us most proud of our country. That Union we reached only by the discipline of our virtues in the severe school of adversity.... I have not allowed myself, sir, to look beyond the Union, to see what might lie hidden in the dark recess behind. ... [N]or could I regard him as a safe counsellor, in the affairs of this Government, whose thoughts should be mainly bent on considering, not how the Union may be best preserved, but how tolerable might be the condition of the people when it should be broken up and destroyed.... When my eyes shall be turned to behold for the last time, the sun in heaven, may I not see him shining on the broken and dishonored fragments of a once glorious Union; on States dissevered, discordant, belligerent; on a land rent with civil feuds, or drenched, it may be,

> [W]hence is this supposed right of the States derived? Where do they find the power to interfere with the laws of the Union? ... We are here to administer a constitution emanating immediately from the people, and trusted by them to our administration. It is not the creature of the State Governments.
>
> — Daniel Webster

in fraternal blood! Let their last feeble and lingering glance rather behold the gorgeous ensign of the republic, now known and honored throughout the earth, still full high advanced, its arms and trophies streaming in their original lustre, not a stripe erased or polluted, nor a single star obscured, bearing for its motto, no such miserable interrogatory as, What is all this worth? Nor those other words of delusion and folly, Liberty first and Union afterwards; but every where, spread all over in characters of living light, blazing on all its ample folds, as they float over the sea and over the land, and in every wind under the whole heavens, that other sentiment, dear to every true American heart — Liberty *and* Union, now and for ever, one and inseparable!

Source: *Register of Debates in Congress,* January 26–27, 1830 (Washington: Gales and Seaton, 1830), 6:58–80.

Notes

1. *Register of Debates in Congress,* 21st Cong., 1st sess., 6:3–4 (Dec. 6, 1830).

2. Fletcher M. Green, "Webster-Hayne Debate," in *Dictionary of American History,* 8 vols., rev. ed. (New York: Charles Scribner's Sons, 1976), 7:265.

3. Herman Belz, ed., *The Webster-Hayne Debate on the Nature of the Union* (Indianapolis: Liberty Fund, 2000), ix.

4. Quote is found in *Register of Debates in Congress,* 21st Cong., 1st sess., 6:24 (Jan. 18, 1830). See also Ibid., 22–27.

5. *Register of Debates in Congress,* 21st Cong., 1st sess., 6:33–34 (Jan. 19, 1830).

6. *Register of Debates in Congress,* 21st Cong., 1st sess., 6:38 (Jan. 20, 1830).

7. Belz, *The Webster-Hayne Debate on the Nature of the Union,* xi.

8. *Register of Debates in Congress,* 21st Cong., 1st sess., 6:52, 58 (Jan. 25, 1830).

9. *Register of Debates in Congress,* 21st Cong., 1st sess., 6:74, 76, 80 (Jan. 27, 1830).

10. Richard L. Grossman, ed., *Bold Voices* (Garden City, N.Y.: Doubleday, 1960), 98.

11. Woodrow Wilson, *Division and Union, 1829–1909* (New York: Longman's, Green, 1912), 44.

12. Belz, *The Webster-Hayne Debate on the Nature of the Union,* xii–xiii.

Veto of the Second Bank of the United States

✳ July 1832 ✳

Early in the 1830s, the Bank of the United States, with stately headquarters in Philadelphia and branches in twenty-nine other cities, was America's most influential financial institution. By law, the government owned one-fifth of its stock, and the bank served as the only place federal funds could be deposited. It provided credit to growing businesses, issued bank notes that served as a dependable medium of exchange throughout the country, and exercised a restraining effect on the ill-managed state banks. Much of the credit for the bank's success was due to the efforts of Nicholas Biddle, its president since 1823.

The bank was not without its enemies. It was unpopular among debtor groups, particularly in the South and West, and Southern states' rights groups questioned its constitutionality. The bank's most powerful political opponent, President Andrew Jackson, used his first annual message to Congress (1829) to question the bank's constitutionality, and express doubts about its expediency and perceived failure to establish "a uniform and sound currency." Jackson instead favored a government-owned institution with severely limited operations. Subsequently, when Jackson's intent to eliminate the bank became clear, Biddle and his advisors started to have concerns about the bank's future and decided not to wait until 1836 when the bank's charter expired: they instead opted to apply to Congress much earlier for a renewal.

With the assistance of Sen. Daniel Webster of Massachusetts and Sen. Henry Clay of Kentucky, Biddle prepared a rechartering memorial that was presented to Congress on January 9, 1832. Clay, the National Republicans' unanimous choice for president that year, reasoned that forcing a vote on the bank before the November election would give him a major national issue to use against Jackson in the upcoming campaign.[1]

After a lengthy debate over the petition, which continued into mid-March 1832, the House of Representatives appointed a seven-member committee to investigate possible misconduct and violations of the bank's charter. Following a month of hearings, a majority of the committee "condemned the bank, declaring that it was unconstitutional and antagonistic to the free enterprise system," and recommended that no action be immediately taken on rechartering. In a separate report, the three members of the minority criticized the treatment of Biddle during the hearings and contended that the majority report "showed an ignorance of banking matters." The adverse "report is of importance in [American] financial history," Margaret G. Myers emphasized, "because it laid the basis not only for the destruction of the Bank but also for a series of governmental actions which within a decade completely changed the relations of the government to the money market."[2]

On June 11, 1832, despite the committee's negative report and critical coverage by several prominent newspapers, the Senate passed a rechartering bill, 28–20; on July 3, the House concurred, 106–84.[3] As Clay had hoped, Jackson vetoed the bill on July 10.

The veto message declared the Bank to be unconstitutional. President Jackson reasoned that it was a monopoly that received special government privileges, catered to the privileged, and was controlled by foreigners. Particularly significant was his contention that the president, as well as Congress, possessed the coordinate power to determine questions of constitutionality, despite the Supreme Court's decision in *McCulloch v. Maryland,* 17 U.S. 316 (1819), which declared that Congress had the right to charter a bank. Jackson's rejection cited economic, political, social, nationalist, and constitutional arguments.[4]

Jacksonian historian Robert Remini has characterized the message as "one of the strongest and most controversial presidential statements ever written" and "the most important … ever issued by a president." During the previous four decades under the Constitution, presidents had used the veto only nine times and only three had dealt with important issues — and only to set aside legislation considered unconstitutional. "In effect," Remini contends, "it claimed for the President the right to participate in the legislative process." With it, Jackson invaded what had previously been the "exclusive province of

The 1833 cartoon satirizes the opposition of Nicholas Biddle, Daniel Webster, and Henry Clay to President Andrew Jackson's order for the removal of federal deposits from the Bank of the United States. Jackson believed the bank failed to provide a stable currency and was unconstitutional.
Source: Library of Congress.

Congress." His view meant that Congress "must now consider the President's wishes on all bills *before* enacting them, or risk a veto." It established an important precedent that significantly strengthened the presidency, "essentially altered the relationship between the legislative and judicial branches of the government," and gave the President a "distinct edge" in "becoming the head of the government, not simply an equal partner."[5]

The initial test of Jackson's expanded influence over legislation occurred shortly after the veto, when Congress faced the decision of whether to accept the president's position or reject it by overriding the veto. On July 11, 1832, those in the overcrowded Senate gallery heard Senator Webster seek to refute what he perceived to be the president's contemptuous constitutional arguments, his disregard for the Supreme Court, and his attempt to deprive Congress of its full legislative authority. "According to the doctrines put forth by the President," Webster declared, "although Congress may have passed a law, and although the Supreme Court may have pronounced it constitutional, yet it is, nevertheless, no law at all, if he, in his good pleasure, sees fit to deny its effect; in other words, to repeal or annul it." Webster reminded his col-

leagues, that "no President, and no public man, ever before advanced such doctrines in the face of the nation. There never was before a moment in which any President would have been tolerated in asserting such a claim to deposit power." Webster further protested, "What Jackson claims for the President" is "not the power of approval, but the primary power of originating laws."[6]

Senator Clay agreed with Webster on virtually every point, calling the president's action a "perversion of the veto power" never intended by the Framers of the Constitution. The veto, Clay declared, "is an extraordinary power, which, though tolerated by the constitution, was not expected, by the convention, to be used in ordinary cases. It was designed for instances of precipitate legislation, in unguarded moments." Presidents understood that it was to be used sparingly. Now, however, we "hear quite frequently, in the progress of [guiding] measures through Congress, the statement that the President will veto them, urged as an objection to their passage." Such reasoning, if allowed to continue, Clay emphasized, would result in the president effectively intruding into the legislative process and forcing his will upon Congress, an action that "is hardly reconcilable with the genius of representative government." The president's action under the Constitution are confined to the "consummated proceedings" of the two houses of Congress and "does not extend to measures in their incipient stages, during their progress through the Houses, nor to the motives by which they are actuated."[7]

Sen. Thomas Hart Benton of Missouri responded to the criticisms of Webster and Clay by defending Jackson's veto as the only means of referring "a measure to the people, for their consideration, and to stay its execution until the people could pass upon it, and to adopt or reject it at an ensuing Congress." Benton saw the disrespectful attack on the president by some in the Senate as part of a vicious campaign, financed by Biddle, to abuse and discredit the president before the American public and ensure his defeat at the polls in November. Benton called Webster and Clay "duplicate Senators" who sought to fault the president when it was clear that the Bank of the United States was a "dangerous" institution controlled by the "moneyed power of the republic" who were determined to control the next presidential election, and then all elections.[8]

Despite the great oratorical skills of Webster and Clay, the Senate debate ended with the override attempt falling far short of the two-thirds majority needed. The 22–19 vote[9] proved a precursor of the fall election as the issue of the Bank remained at the forefront of public consciousness throughout the 1832 presidential election. Clay, however, was unsuccessful in using the veto to deny Jackson a second term as Jackson soundly defeated Clay that November.

Neither the president nor Congress, however, was finished with the debate over the Bank. The ramifications of veto extended well beyond the 1832 presidential election. Jackson believed his resounding electoral victory provided him a popular mandate to sever the relationship between the state government and the bank. While he could not legally abolish the institution before the expiration of its charter, he decided to weaken it by removing the government's deposits from the Bank. When two successive secretaries of the Treasury — Louis McLane and William J. Duane — refused to support the president's decision to transfer government deposits to selected state banks, popularly called "pet banks," he fired them and appointed Attorney General Roger B. Taney secretary of the Treasury. In the fall of 1833, Taney issued an order setting the president's plan in motion. The following March, in an unprecedented decision, the Senate censured President Jackson for exceeding the power conferred upon him by the Constitution in removal of the deposits.

SENATOR HENRY CLAY ATTACKS PRESIDENT JACKSON'S VETO OF THE SECOND BANK OF THE UNITED STATES

JULY 12, 1832

A bill to recharter the bank had recently passed Congress, after much deliberation. … [T]he President has rejected the bill, and transmitted to the Senate an elaborate message, communicating at large his objections. The constitution requires that we should reconsider the bill, and that the question of its passage, the President's objections notwithstanding, shall be taken by yeas and nays. Respect to him, as well as the injunctions of the constitution, require that we should deliberately examine his reasons, and reconsider the question.

The veto is hardly reconcilable with the genius of representative Government. It is totally irreconcilable with it, if it is to be frequently employed in respect to the expediency of measures, as well as their constitutionality. It is a feature of our Government borrowed from a prerogative of the British King. And it is remarkable that in England it has grown obsolete, not having been used for upwards of a century.

★ ★ ★ ★

It cannot be imagined that the convention contemplated the application of the veto to a question which has been so long, so often, and so thoroughly scrutinized, as that of the Bank of the United States, by every department of the Government, in almost every stage of its existence, and by the people, and by the State Legislatures. Of all the controverted questions which have sprung up under our Government, not one has been so fully investigated as that of its power to establish a Bank of the United States.... Mr. Madison, himself opposed to the first Bank of the United States, yielded his own convictions to those of the nation, and all the departments of the Government thus often expressed. Sub-

---

The veto is hardly reconcilable with the genius of representative Government. — Henry Clay

---

sequent to this true, but strong statement of the case, the present Bank of the United States was established.

★ ★ ★ ★

After the President had directed public attention to this question, it became not only a topic of popular conversation, but was discussed in the press, and employed, as a theme in popular elections. I was myself interrogated on more occasions than one, to make a public expression of my sentiments.

★ ★ ★ ★

The President thinks that the precedents, drawn from the proceedings of Congress, as to the constitutional power to establish a bank, are neutralized.

★ ★ ★ ★

Congress, by various other acts, in relation to the Bank of the United States, has again and again sanctioned the power. And I believe it may be truly affirmed that, from the commencement of the Government to this day, there has not been a Congress opposed to the Bank of the United States upon the distinct ground of a want of power to establish it.

★ ★ ★ ★

The interest which foreigners hold in the existing Bank of the United States is dwelt upon in the message as a serious objection to the recharter. But this interest is the result of the assignable nature of the stock; and if the objection be well founded, it applies to Government stock, to stock in local banks, in canal and other companies, created for internal improvements, and every species of money or moveables in which foreigners may acquire an interest. The assignable character of the stock is a quality conferred, not for the benefit of foreigners, but for that of our own citizens. And the fact of its being transferred to them is the effect of the balance of trade being against us — an evil, if it be one, which the American system will correct. All Governments wanting capital resort to foreign nations possessing it in superabundance, to obtain it.... The confidence of foreigners in our stocks is a proof of the solidity of our credit. Foreigners have no voice in the administration of this bank; and if they buy its stock,

they are obliged to submit to citizens of the United States to manage it.

★ ★ ★ ★

The President assigns in his message a conspicuous place to the alleged injurious operation of the bank on the interests of the Western people.... The people of all the West owe to this bank about thirty millions, which have been borrowed from it; and the President thinks that the payments for the interest, and other facilities which they derive from the operation of this bank, are so onerous as to produce "a drain of their currency, which no country can bear without inconvenience and occasional distress." His remedy is to compel them to pay the whole of the debt which they have contracted in a period of four years. Now Mr. President, if they cannot pay the interest without distress, how are they to pay the principal? If they cannot pay a part, how are they to pay the whole?

★ ★ ★ ★

The President tells us that, if the Executive had been called upon to furnish the project of a bank, the duty would have been cheerfully performed; and he states that a bank, competent to all the duties which may be required by the Government, might be so organized as not to infringe on our own delegated powers, or the reserved rights of the States. The President is a co-ordinate branch of the legislative department. As such, bills which have passed both Houses of Congress, are presented to him for his approval or rejection. The idea of going to the President for the project of a law, is totally new in the practice, and utterly contrary to the theory of the Government. What should we think of the Senate calling upon the House, or the House upon the Senate, for the project of a law?

★ ★ ★ ★

The message states that "an investigation unwillingly conceded, and so restricted in time as necessarily to make it incomplete and unsatisfactory, discloses enough to excite suspicion and alarm." As there is no prospect of the passage of this bill, the President's objection not withstanding, by a constitutional majority of two-thirds, it can never reach the House of Representatives. The members of that House, and especially its distinguished chairman of the Committee of Ways and Means, who reported the bill, are therefore cut off from all opportunity to defend themselves. Under these circumstances, allow me to ask how the President has ascertained that the investigation was unwillingly conceded? I have understood directly the contrary; and that the chairman already referred to, as well as other members in favor of the renewal of the charter, promptly consented to and voted for the investigation. And we all know that those in support of the renewal could have prevented the investigation, and that

THE FINAL VOTE

Veto to Recharter the Bank of the United States

	Senate Vote June 11, 1832		House Vote July 3, 1832	
	Yea	Nay	Yea	Nay
Northeast	11	1	24	12
Middle States	7	3	47	21
Northwest	5	1	10	5
Southeast	0	8	13	31
Southwest	5	7	12	15
Total	**28**	**20**	**106**	**84**

The House tallies reflect voting after the third reading of the bill rechartering the Bank of the United States.

A Senate override attempt on July 13, 1832, of President Andrew Jackson's veto of the bill fell short of the needed two-thirds majority, 22–19.

Source: Albert Castel and Scott L. Gibson, *The Yeas and the Nays: Key Congressional Decisions, 1774–1945* (Kalamazoo: New Issues Press, Institute of Public Affairs, Western Michigan University, 1975), 44.

they did not. But suspicion and alarm have been excited. Suspicion and alarm! Against whom is this suspicion? The House, or the bank, or both?

Mr. President, I protest against the right of any Chief Magistrate to come into either House of Congress, and scrutinize the motives of its members; to examine whether a measure has been passed with promptitude or repugnance; and to pronounce upon the willingness or unwillingness with which it has been adopted or rejected.

★ ★ ★ ★

There are some parts of this message that ought to excite deep alarm; and that especially in which the President announces that each public officer may interpret the constitution as he pleases. His language is: "Each public officer, who takes an oath to support the constitution, swears that he will support it as he understands it, and not as it is understood by others."

★ ★ ★ ★

"The opinion of the judges has no more authority over than the opinion of Congress has over the judges; and, on that point, the President is independent of both." Now, Mr. President, I conceive, with great deference, that the President

has mistaken the purport of the oath to support the constitution of the United States. No one swears to support it as he understands it, but to support it simply as it is in truth. All men are bound to obey the laws, of which the constitution is supreme; but must they obey them as they are, or as they understand them? If the obligation of obedience is limited and controlled by the measure of information.... We should have nothing settled, nothing stable, nothing fixed. There would be general disorder and confusion throughout every branch of administration, from the highest to the lowest officers — universal nullification. For what is the doctrine of the President, but that of South Carolina applied throughout the Union? The President independent both of Congress and the Supreme Court! Only bound to execute the laws of the one and the decisions of the other as far as they conform to the constitution of the United States, as he understands it! Then it should be the duty of every President, on his installation into office, to carefully examine all the acts in the statute book, approved by his predecessors, and mark out those which he was resolved not to execute, and to which he meant to apply this new species of veto, because they were repugnant to the constitution, as he understands it. And, after the expiration of every term of the Supreme Court, he should send for the record of its decisions, and discriminate between those which he would, and those which he would not execute, because they were or were not agreeable to the constitution, as he understands it.

There is another constitutional doctrine contained in the message, which is entirely new to me. It asserts that "the Government of the United States have no constitutional power to purchase lands within the States," except "for the erection of forts, magazines, arsenals, dock yards, and other needful buildings;" and even for these objects only "by the consent of the Legislature of the State in which the same shall be." Now, sir, I had supposed that the right of Congress to purchase lands in any State was incontestable: and, in point of fact, it probably, at this moment, owns lands in every State of the Union, purchased for taxes, or as a judgment or mortgage creditor. And there are various acts of Congress which regulate the purchase and transfer of such lands. The advisers of the President have confounded the faculty of purchasing lands with the exercise of exclusive jurisdiction, which is restricted by the constitution to the forts and the other buildings described.

★ ★ ★ ★

Mr. President, we are about to close one of the longest and most arduous sessions of Congress under the present constitution; and, when we return among our constituents, what account of the operations of their Government shall we be bound to communicate? We shall be compelled to say that the Supreme Court is paralyzed, and the missionaries retained in prison in contempt of its authority, and in defiance of numerous treaties and laws of the United States; that the Executive, through the Secretary of the Treasury, sent to Congress a tariff bill which would have destroyed numerous branches of our domestic industry, and led to the final destruction of all; that the veto has been applied to the Bank of the United States, our only reliance for a sound and uniform currency; that the Senate has been violently attacked for the exercise of a clear constitutional power; that the House of Representatives has been unnecessarily assailed; and that the President has promulgated a rule of action for those who have taken the oath to support the constitution of the United States, that must, if there be practical conformity to it; introduce general nullification, and end in the absolute subversion of the Government.

Source: *Register of Debates in Congress,* July 12, 1832 (Washington: Gales and Seaton, 1833), 8:1265–1274.

SENATOR THOMAS HART BENTON DEFENDS PRESIDENT JACKSON'S VETO OF THE SECOND BANK OF THE UNITED STATES

JULY 18, 1832

[Mr. Benton] first vindicated the use and origin of the veto, as derived from the institution of the tribunes of the people among the Romans, and its exercise always intended for the benefit of the people; and under our constitution, its only effect to refer a measure to the people, for their consideration, and to stay its execution until the people could pass upon it, and to adopt or reject it at an ensuing Congress. It was a power eminently just and proper in a representative government, and intended for the benefit of the whole people; and, therefore, placed in the hands of the magistrate elected by the whole.

★ ★ ★ ★

Why debate the bank question now, he exclaimed, and not debate it before? Then was the time to make converts; now, none can be expected. Why are lips unsealed now, which were silent as the grave when this act was on its passage through the Senate.... With what object do they speak? Sir! exclaimed Mr. B., this *post facto* debate is not for the Senate, nor the President, nor to alter the fate of the bank bill. It is to rouse the officers of the bank — to direct the efforts of its mercenaries in their designs upon the people — to bring out its stream of corrupting influence, by inspiring hope, and to embody all its recruits at the polls to vote against President Jackson.

★ ★ ★ ★

The bank is in the field (said Mr. B.), a combatant, and a fearful and tremendous one in the presidential election. If she succeeds, there is an end of American liberty — an end of the republic. The forms of election may be permitted for a while, as the forms of the consular elections were permitted in Rome during the last of the republic; but it will be for a while, only.

★ ★ ★ ★

The Bank is in the field, and the West — the Great West is the selected theater of her operations. There her terrors, her seductions, her energies, her rewards and her punishments are to be directed. The senator from Massachusetts opened yesterday with a picture of the ruin in the West, if the bank were not rechartered; and the senator from Kentucky, Mr. Clay, wound up with a retouch of the same picture to day, with a closeness of coincidence which showed that this part of the battle ground had been reviewed in company by the associate generals and duplicate senators. Both agree that the West is to be ruined if the bank be not rechartered; and rechartered it cannot be, unless the *veto* President is himself *vetoed.*

★ ★ ★ ★

Thirty millions is the bank debt in the West; and these thirty millions they threaten to collect by writs of execution if Jackson is re-elected; but if he is not elected, and, somebody else be elected, then they promise no forced payments shall be exacted, — hardly any payment at all! The thirty millions it is pretended will almost be forgiven; and thus a bribe of thirty millions is deceitfully offered for the Western vote, with a threat of punishment, if it be not taken! ... Mr. B. had read in Roman history of the empire being put up to sale; he had read of victorious generals, returning from Asiatic conquests loaded with oriental spoil, bidding in the market for the consulship and purchasing their elections with the wealth of conquered kingdoms, but he had never expected to witness a bid for the presidency in this young and free republic.

★ ★ ★ ★

Mr. B.... affirmed, that the debt had been created for the very purpose to which it was now applied; an electioneering,

---

The bank is in the field . . . , a combatant, and a fearful and tremendous one in the presidential election. If she succeeds, there is an end of American liberty. — Thomas Hart Benton

---

political purpose; and this he proved by a reference to authentic documents.

First. He took the total bank debt, as it existed when President Jackson first brought the bank charter before the view of Congress in December, 1829, and showed it to be $40,216,000; then he took the total debt as it stood at present, being $70,428,000; and thus showed an increase of thirty millions in the short space of two years and four months. This great increase had occurred since the President had delivered opinions against the bank, and when as a prudent, and law abiding institution, it ought to have been reducing and curtailing its business, or at all events, keeping it stationary.... After having shown this enormous increase in the sum total of the debt, Mr. B. went on to show where it had taken place; and this he proved to be chiefly in the West, and not merely in the West, but principally in those parts of the West in which the presidential election was held to be most doubtful and critical.

★ ★ ★ ★

Mr. B. went on to show, from the time and circumstances and subsequent events, that they were created for a political purpose, and had already been used by the bank with that view. He then recurred to the two-and-twenty circulars, or writs of execution, as he called them; issued against the South and West, in January and February last, ordering curtailments of all debts, and the supply of reinforcements to the Northeast. He showed that the reasons assigned by the bank for issuing the orders of curtailments were false. ... The true reasons were political: a foretaste and prelude to what is now threatened. It was a manoeuvre to press the debtors — a turn of the screw upon the borrowers — to make them all cry out and join in the clamors and petitions for a renewed charter!

★ ★ ★ ★

Messrs. C. and W. had attacked the President for objecting to foreign stockholders in the Bank of the United States. Mr. B. maintained the solidity of the objection, and exposed the futility of the argument urged by the duplicate senators. They had asked if foreigners did not hold stock in road and canal companies? Mr. B. said, yes! but these road and canal companies did not happen to be the bankers of the United States! The foreign stockholders in this bank were the bankers of the United States. They held its moneys; they collected its revenues; they almost controlled its finances; they were to give or withhold aid in war as well as peace, and, it might be against their own government. Was the United States to depend upon foreigners in a point so material to our existence? The bank was a national institution. Ought a national institution to be the private property of aliens? It was called the Bank of the United States; and ought it to be the ban of the nobility and gentry of Great Britain? ... All the lessons of history, said Mr. B., admonish us to keep clear of foreign influence. The most dangerous influence from foreigners is through money. The corruption of orators and statesmen, is the ready way to poison the councils, and to betray the interest of a country.... What a temptation to them to engage in our elections. By carrying a President, and a majority of Congress, to suit themselves, they not only become masters of the moneyed power, but also of the political power of this republic.

★ ★ ★ ★

The duplicate senators, said Mr. B., have occupied themselves with criticising the President's idea of the obligation of his oath in constructing the constitution for himself. They also think that the President ought to be bound, the Congress ought to bound, to take the constitution which the Supreme Court may deal out to them! If so, why take an oath? The oath is to bind the conscience, not to enlighten the head. Every officer takes the oath for himself; the President took the oath for himself; administered by the Chief Justice, but not *to* the Chief Justice. He bound himself to observe the constitution, not the Chief Justice's interpretation of the constitution; and, his message is in conformity to his oath. This is the oath of duty and of right. It is the path of Jefferson, also, who has laid it down in his writings, that each department judges the constitution for itself; and that the President is as independent of the Supreme Court as the Supreme Court is of the President.

★ ★ ★ ★

The President is assailed for showing the drain upon the resources of the West, which is made by this bank. How assailed. With any documents to show that he is in error? No! not at all! No such document exist.

★ ★ ★ ★

Mr. B. rapidly summed up with a view of the dangerous power of the bank, and the present audacity of her conduct. She wielded a debt of seventy millions of dollars, with an organization which extended to every part of the Union, and she was sole mistress of the moneyed power of the republic.... What individual could stand in the States against the power of the bank, and that bank flushed with a victory over the conqueror of the conquerors of Bonaparte? The whole government would fall into the hands of this moneyed power. An oligarchy would immediately be established; and that oligarchy, in a few generations, would ripen into a monarchy.

Source: Thomas Hart Benton, *Thirty Years' View: Or, a History of the Working of the American Government for Thirty Years, From 1820–1850,* 2 vols. (New York: D. Appleton and Co., 1863), 1:255–262. (Note: The *Register of Debates* makes only brief mention of Benton's response to Webster and Clay.)

Notes

1. *Register of Debates in Congress,* 22nd Cong., 1st sess. (Jan. 9, 1832), 8: 53–54, 1502.

2. Quotes are found in Edward S. Kaplan, *The Bank of the United States and the American Economy* (Westport, Conn.: Greenwood Press, 1999), 133; Margaret G. Myers, *A Financial History of the United States* (New York: Columbia University Press, 1970), 91. See also *Register of Debates in Congress,* 22nd Cong., 1st sess. (March 14, 1832), 8: 2163–2164; Appendix (Report of Majority, May 14, 1832), 33–46; Appendix (Reports of the Minority, May 14, 1832), 46–73.

3. *Register of Debates in Congress,* 22nd Cong., 1st sess. (June 11, 1832), 8:1073–1074; (July 3, 1832), 3851–3852.

4. James D. Richardson, comp., *Compilation of the Messages and Papers of the Presidents,* 20 vols. (New York: Bureau of National Literature, 1897–1927), 3:1139–1154.

5. Robert V. Remini, *Andrew Jackson and the Course of American Freedom, 1822–1832* (New York: Harper and Row, 1981), 369–370; Robert V. Remini, *The Life of Andrew Jackson* (New York: Harper & Row, 1988), 229–230.

6. *Register of Debates in Congress,* 22nd Cong., 1st sess. (July 11, 1832), 8:1232, 1240.

7. *Register of Debates in Congress,* 22nd Cong., 1st sess. (July 12, 1832), 8: 1265, 1272–1273 . See also Robert V. Remini, *Henry Clay: Statesman for the Union* (New York: W. W. Norton, 1991), 399–400.

8. Quotes are found in Thomas Hart Benton, *Thirty Years' View: Or, a History of the Working of the American Government for Thirty Years, from 1820–1850,* 2 vols. (New York: D. Appleton and Co., 1863), 1:256–257, 260–261, 263. See also William Nisbet Chamber, *Old Bullion Benton, Senator from the New West: Thomas Hart Benton, 1782–1858* (Boston: Little Brown, 1956), 184–186; Benjamin Perley Poore, *Perley's Reminiscences of Sixty Years in the National Metropolis,* 2 vols. (Philadelphia: Hubbard Brothers, 1886), 1:144.

9. *Register of Debates in Congress,* 22nd Cong., 1st sess., (July 13, 1832), 8:1294–1296.

Force Bill

✶ December 1832–March 1833 ✶

Early in 1833, Congress began reconsideration of one of the nation's most volatile political issues — a revision of the Tariff of Abominations (1828). Passage of the Tariff Act of 1832 the previous July had reduced extremely high tariffs enacted four years earlier, but it did not satisfy those who were dependent upon trade rather than manufacturing, particularly Southerners. Because of its lack of industry, the South was dependent upon an export market for its three staple crops — cotton, tobacco, and rice — which accounted for nearly two-thirds of all American exports.

The protective tariff, Southerners argued, allowed American manufacturers to increase the price of goods sold in the United States and obligated Americans to pay more for imports. It "diminished the amount Americans could purchase, and consequently diminished the amount of cotton and other crops foreign nations could buy in exchange." The tariff aided Northern manufacturers, "but only at the cost of considerable damage to Southern agricultural trade." While the "economic validity of these arguments was suspect, their emotional impact was substantial." They embodied the fear that other "injurious policies" would be imposed on the South. For Southerners, the "tariff demonstrated that the North and West would ignore Southern claims of grave injury if the policy in question benefited them sufficiently. What was to stop them from abolishing slavery if they chose to?" [1]

Following the adjournment of Congress for the summer, President Andrew Jackson watched from his Tennessee home as Southern outrage over the Tariff of 1832 gained momentum. Then in November 1832, a convention of South Carolina nullifiers meeting in Columbia passed an Ordinance of Nullification, which declared the tariff laws of 1828 and 1832 unconstitutional, null and void, and not binding on the state after February 1, 1833. The ordinance further asserted that if the federal government attempted to force the state to enforce payment of the duties, South Carolina would consider secession from the Union; required all state office holders, except members of the legislature, to take an oath to obey, execute, and enforce the ordinance; and forbade appeal to the U.S. Supreme Court of any case in law or equity arising under the ordinance. A week later, the South Carolina state legislature, which had called the convention, passed three laws to enforce the ordinance. Among these were provisions authorizing the raising of a military force and appropriations for arms. [2]

President Jackson was both conciliatory and firm. In his annual message to Congress on December 4, 1832, he declared that nullification would "endanger the integrity of the Union." He expressed hope "that the laws themselves are fully adequate to the suppression of such attempts as may be immediately made," and he promised to give Congress "prompt notice" of any "exigency … rendering the execution of the existing laws impracticable." At this time, Jackson believed he needed no further power to repress nullification. His message also called for a substantial reduction in tariff rates, and he "stressed that the policy of protection must be ultimately limited to those articles of domestic manufacture which are indispensable to our safety in time of war." [3]

A week later, Jackson again rejected nullification as well as secession in a December 10 "Proclamation to the People of South Carolina." The president's statement asserted the supremacy of a sovereign and indivisible government. "Disunion by armed force is *treason*," Jackson stressed. The strongly worded proclamation declared that federal law was supreme, and any nullification of it by a state was an act of rebellion. In response, the South Carolina legislature adopted a series of resolutions on December 17 and Governor Robert Y. Hayne issued a counter proclamation. Just before the end of the year, John C. Calhoun resigned from the vice presidency, having been elected a U.S. senator to replace Hayne, who resigned to become governor. [4]

On January 16, 1833, President Jackson asked Congress to authorize him to take some specific actions that he felt would result in "fewer difficulties and less opportunity of actual collision between" the federal government and South Carolina as well as make the collection of tariffs more effective. Jackson's modest proposals, one historian observed, were "designed to keep the peace rather than make war. Jackson did not accuse the nullifiers of treason, and he asked for the right to use force only if the nullifiers struck first." However, his "reputation and the gravity of the crisis led Congress, the public, and students of nullification to call the document the 'Force Bill Message' and to treat it as though Jackson had asked for the power to crush South Carolina."[5]

The great debate over the Force Bill was destined to take place in the Senate. Following the reading of President Jackson's message in the Senate, Calhoun took the floor to accuse the administration of "despotism." Five days later, the Force Bill, reported by the Senate Judiciary Committee, included almost all of the president's proposals. Within hours, Calhoun introduced three resolutions that would test the principles on which the bill rested. The resolutions stated that the states constituting the United States were united by a "constitutional compact," each state had an "equal right to judge for itself" any alleged violation of the Constitution, and any assertion that the people of the United States "are now formed into one nation or people" was false.[6]

During the next several days, the tiny gallery and lobbies of the Senate were jammed, and Americans throughout the country eagerly followed reports of the debates on Calhoun's resolutions and the Force Bill. While William Campbell Preston of South Carolina and George Poindexter of Mississippi aptly argued the pros and cons of the Force Bill, the principal contest was between Calhoun, who led the opposition, and Daniel Webster of Massachusetts, who counteracted with a notable speech on nationalism and states' rights. In Calhoun's initial speech, given over two days (February 15–16), he denounced the Force Bill, asking, "how is it proposed to preserve the Union? By Force! Does any man in his senses believe that this beautiful structure, this harmonious aggregate of States, produced by joint consent of all, can be preserved by force?" The answer is "no; you cannot keep the States united in their constitutional and federal bonds by force." On February 16, Webster directed his rebuttal at South Carolina's interpretative resolutions and arguments on constitutional theory. Webster attacked Calhoun's premises by explaining that logical consequences of such reasoning could be seen in the feeble and impotent Confederacy that preceded the Constitution and the American Revolution. He concluded with a stirring declaration: "I shall exert every faculty I posses in aiding to prevent the Constitution from being nullified, destroyed, or impaired."[7]

While the debate over the Force Bill raged in Senate, Henry Clay of Kentucky came to the realization that some tariff revision was inevitable. On February 12, he introduced a compromise proposal that offered an opportunity to resolve the potentially dangerous dilemma that faced the nation. It provided for the gradual reduction of all tariffs over 20 percent every two years until 1842; at that time, the uniform rate would be 20 percent and the principle of protection would be abandoned. Clay reasoned that South Caro-

John C. Calhoun opposed the Force Bill, which was designed to prevent South Carolina from nullification of the Tariff of 1832.
Source: Library of Congress.

lina's nullification order did not block tariff revision. When consideration shifted to the Senate, Calhoun supported Clay's reasoning, stressing that "[h]e who loves the Union must desire to see this agitating question brought to a termination." Calhoun "believed that if the present difficulties were to be adjusted, they must be adjusted on the principles embraced in the bill" offered by his colleague from Kentucky. Since there were only "minor points of difference," he reasoned, there would be no difficulty in reaching agreement "when gentlemen met together in the spirit of mutual compromise which, he doubted not, would be brought unto their deliberations, without at all yielding the constitutional question as to the right of protection."[8]

Before the Senate could act on Clay's proposal, however, the Force Bill came to a vote on February 20. Despite Calhoun's fervent argument that Congress was creating a government by the "sword," the Senate passed the bill, 32–1. Only John Tyler of Virginia voted nay. Calhoun, Clay, and ten other nullifiers stalked out of the chamber without casting a vote. The House concurred on March 1 (149–47). Meanwhile, the compromise tariff, with strong support from the South and West, passed in the House (119–85) on February

26 and in the Senate on March 1 (29–16). Afterwards, Clay told a friend that March 1 might "perhaps be the most important Congressional day that ever occurred" and was the "most proud and triumphant day of my life." President Jackson signed both bills into law on March 2.[9] Passage of the Force Act and the Compromise Tariff ended any thoughts of nullification.

Upon learning that a compromise tariff was in the making, South Carolina suspended the Ordinance of Nullification on January 21 1833. Following passage of the Compromise Tariff, the South Carolina convention reassembled and formally rescinded the ordinance. To preserve its prerogative, the convention on March 18 adopted an ordinance declaring the Force Act null and void, and it adjourned the same day. Although the Force Bill debate "has never received the attention given to the Webster-Hayne debate, it was in many ways superior. The issue of states' rights and the Union had several years in which to mature, more was now at stake, the debate went over a longer period of time, and Calhoun was a far stronger opponent." The debate also had more "intellectual cogency, and the greater national crisis invested them with a heightened sense of drama."[10]

SENATOR JOHN C. CALHOUN'S COMPACT THEORY OF THE CONSTITUTION

FEBRUARY 15, 1833

Mr. CALHOUN rose. He knew not, he said, which was most objectionable, the provision of the bill, or the temper in which adoption had been urged. If extraordinary powers with which the bill proposed to clothe the Executive, to the utter prostration of the constitution and the rights of the States, be calculated to impress our minds with alarm at the rapid progress of despotism in our country, the zeal with which every circumstance calculated to misrepresent or exaggerate the conduct of Carolina in the controversy was seized on, with a view to excite hostility against her, but too plainly indicated the deep decay of that brotherly feeling which once existed between these States, and to which we are indebted for our beautiful federal system.

★ ★ ★ ★

The real question at issue is, has the Government a right to impose burdens on the capital and industry of one portion of the country, not with a view to revenue, but to benefit another? And he must be permitted to say that, after the long and deep agitation of this controversy, it was with surprise that he perceived so strong a disposition to misrepresent its real character. To correct the impressions which those misrepresentations were calculated to make, he would dwell on the point under consideration for a few moments longer.

The Federal Government has, by an express provision of the constitution, the right to lay duties on imports. The State has never denied or resisted this right, nor even thought of so doing. The Government has, however, not been content with exercising this power as she has the right to do, but had gone a step beyond it, by laying imports, not for revenue, but for protection. This the State considered as an unconstitutional exercise of power, highly injurious and oppressive to her and the other staple states, and had accordingly met it with the most determined resistance.... Congress had assumed, without any warrant from the constitution, the right of exercising this most important power, and had so exercised it as to impose a ruinous burden on the labor and capital of the State, by which her resources were exhausted, the enjoyments of her citizens curtailed, the means of education contracted, and all her interests essentially and injuriously affected.

★ ★ ★ ★

It has been said that South Carolina claims the right to annul the constitution and laws of the United States; ... Nothing can be more erroneous: her object is not to resist laws made in pursuance of the constitution, but those made without its authority, and which encroach on her reserved powers. She claims not even the right of judging of the delegated powers, but of those that are reserved; and to resist the former when they encroach upon the latter.

★ ★ ★ ★

[T]he great question is now presented — has Congress the right to pass this bill? — which he would next proceed to consider. The decision of this question involves the inquiry into the provisions of the bill. What are they? It puts at the disposal of the President the army and navy, and the entire militia of the country. It enables him, at his pleasure, to subject every man in the United States, not exempt from military duty, to martial law; to call him from his ordinary occupation to the field, and under penalty of fine and imprisonment inflicted by a court-martial to imbrue his hand in his brothers' blood. There is no limitation on the power of the sword, and that over the purse is equally without restraint; for among the extraordinary features of the bill, it contains no appropriation; which, under existing circumstances, is tantamount to an unlimited appropriation. The President may, under its authority, incur any expenditure, and pledge the national faith to meet it. He may create a new national debt, at the very moment of the termination of the former — a debt of millions, to be paid out of the proceeds of the labor of that section of the country whose dearest constitutional rights this bill prostrates! Thus exhibiting the extraordinary spectacle, that the very section of the country which is urging this measure, and carrying the sword of devastation against us, are at the same time incurring a new debt, to be paid by those whose rights are violated; while those who violate them are to receive the benefits, in the shape of bounties and expenditures.

And for what purpose is the unlimited control of the purse and of the sword thus placed at the disposition of the Executive? To make war against one of the free and sovereign members of this confederation, which the bill proposes to deal with, not as a state, but as a collection bandits or outlaws. Thus exhibiting the impious spectacle of the Government, the creature of the States, making war against the power to which it owes its existence.

The bill violates the constitution, plainly and palpably, in many of its provisions, by authorizing the President, at his pleasure, to place the different ports of the Union on an equal footing, contrary to that provision of the constitution which declares that no preference should be given to one part over another. It also violates the constitution by authorizing him, at his discretion, to impose cash duties in one port, while

---

It has been said that the bill declares war against South Carolina. No; it decrees a massacre of her citizens! — John C. Calhoun

---

credit is allowed in others; by enabling the President to regulate commerce, a power vested in Congress alone; and by drawing within the jurisdiction of the United States courts powers never intended to be conferred on them. As great as these objections were, they became insignificant in the provisions of a bill which, by a single blow, by treating the States as a mere lawless mass of individuals, prostrates all the barriers of the constitution.... It has been said that the bill declares war against South Carolina. No; it decrees a massacre of her citizens!

★ ★ ★ ★

It is said that the bill ought to pass, because the law must be enforced. The law must be enforced! The imperial edict must be executed. It is under such sophistry, couched in general terms, without looking to the limitations which must ever exist in the practical exercise of power, that the most cruel and despotic acts ever have been covered.... Yes, to this result you must come by this miserable sophistry, this vague abstraction, of enforcing the law without a regard to the fact whether the law be just or unjust, constitutional or unconstitutional.

In the same spirit we are told that the Union must be preserved, without regard to the means. And how is it proposed to preserve the Union? By force! Does any man in his senses believe that this beautiful structure, this harmonious aggregate of States, produced by the joint consent of all, can be preserved by force? Its very introduction will be certain destruction of this Federal Union. No, no; you cannot keep the States united in their constitutional and federal bonds by force. Force may, indeed, hold the parts together; but such union would be the bond between master and slave; a union of exaction on one side, and of unqualified obedience on the other.

★ ★ ★ ★

Disguise it as you may, the controversy is one between power and liberty; and he would tell the gentlemen who are opposed to him, that, strong as might be the love of power on their side, the love of liberty is still stronger on ours.

★ ★ ★ ★

Whatever opinion may exist upon other points, there is one in which he would suppose, there could be none: that this bill rests on principles which, if carried out, will ride over State sovereignties, and that it will be idle for any of its advocates hereafter to talk State rights.

★ ★ ★ ★

Mr. C. said that, in reviewing the ground over which he had passed, it would be apparent that the question in controversy involved that most deeply important of all political questions, whether ours was a federal or a consolidated Government — a question on the decision of which depends, as he solemnly believed, the liberty of the people, their happiness, and the place which we are destined to hold in the moral and intellectual scale of nations.

★ ★ ★ ★

That our government, for many years has been gradually verging to consolidation, that the constitution has gradually become a dead letter, and that all restrictions upon the power of Government have been virtually removed, so as practically to convert the General Government into a Government of an absolute majority, without check or limitation, cannot be denied by anyone who has impartially observed its operation.

It is not necessary to trace the commencement and gradual progress of the causes which have produced this change in our system; it is sufficient to state that the change has taken place within the last few years. What has been the result? Precisely that which might have been anticipated — the growth of faction, corruption, anarchy, and, if not despotism itself, it's near approach, as witnessed in the provisions of this bill.

★ ★ ★ ★

Let it never be forgotten, that power can only be opposed by power, organization by organization; and on this theory stands our beautiful federal system of Government. No free system was ever further removed from the principle that the absolute majority, without check or limitation, ought to govern. To understand what our Government is, we must look to the constitution, which is the basis of the system.

★ ★ ★ ★

To maintain the ascendancy of the constitution over the law-making majority is the great and essential point, on which the success of the system must depend. Unless that ascendancy can be preserved, the necessary consequence must be, that the laws will supersede the constitution; and, finally, the will of the Executive, by the influence of his patronage, will supersede the laws; indications of which are already perceptible. This ascendancy can only be preserved through the action of the States as organized bodies, having their own separate governments, and possessed of the right, under the structure of our system, of judging of the extent of their separate powers, and of interposing their authority to arrest the unauthorized enactments of the General Government within their respective limits.

★ ★ ★ ★

Against the view of our system which he had presented, and the right of the State to interpose, it was objected, that it would lead to anarchy and dissolution. He considered the objection as without the slightest foundation; and that, so far from tending to weakness or disunion, it was the source of the highest power and the strongest cement.

★ ★ ★ ★

In this great struggle between the delegated and reserved powers, so far from repining that his lot and that of those whom he represented is cast on the side of the latter, he rejoiced that such was the fact; for though we participate in but few of the advantages of the Government, we are compensated, and more than compensated, in not being so much exposed to its corruptions. Nor did he repine that the duty, so difficult to be discharged, of defending the reserved powers against apparently such fearful odds, has been assigned to them. To discharge it successfully requires the highest qualities, moral and intellectual; and should we perform it with a zeal and ability proportioned to its magnitude, instead of mere planters, our section will become distinguished for its patriots and statesmen. But, on the other hand, if we prove unworthy of this high destiny, if we yield to the steady encroachments of power, the severest calamity and most debasing corruption will overspread the land. Every Southern man, true to the interests of his section, and faithful to the duties which Providence has allotted him, will be forever excluded from the honors and emoluments of this Government, which will be reserved for those only who have qualified themselves, by political prostitution, for admission into the Magdalen Asylum.

Source: *Register of Debates in Congress,* February 15, 1833 (Washington: Gales and Seaton, 1833), 9:519–553.

SENATOR DANIEL WEBSTER DECLARES THAT THE CONSTITUTION IS NOT A COMPACT BETWEEN SOVEREIGN STATES

FEBRUARY 16, 1833

Mr. WEBSTER rose. The gentleman from South Carolina, said Mr. W., has admonished us to be mindful of the opinions of those who shall come after us. We must take our chance, sir, as to the light in which posterity will regard us. I do not decline its judgment, nor withhold myself from its scrutiny. Feeling that I am performing my public duty with singleness of heart and to the best of my ability, I fearlessly trust myself to the country, now and hereafter, and leave both my motives and my character to its decision.

★ ★ ★ ★

The honorable gentleman has declared, that on the decision of the question now in debate may depend the cause of liberty itself. I am of the same opinion; but then, sir, the liberty which I think is staked on the contest is not political liberty, in any general and undefined character, but our own well understood and long enjoyed American liberty.

★ ★ ★ ★

The gentleman's speech made some days ago, upon introducing his resolution, those resolutions themselves, and parts of the speech now just concluded, may probably be justly regarded as containing the whole South Carolina doctrine. That doctrine it is my purpose now to examine, and to compare it with the Constitution of the United States.... I shall take the instrument as they have established it and shall endeavor to maintain it in its plain sense and meaning, against opinions and notions which, in my judgment, threaten its subversion.

★ ★ ★ ★

Sir, since any State, before she can prove her right to dissolve the Union, must show her authority to undo what has been done, no State is at liberty to secede on the ground that she and other States have done nothing but accede. She must show that she has a right to reverse what has been ordained, to unsettle and overthrow what has been established, to reject what the people have adopted, and to break up what they have ratified; because these are the terms which express the transactions which have actually taken place. In other words, she must show her right to make a revolution.

★ ★ ★ ★

Where sovereign communities are parties, there is no essential difference between a compact, a confederation, and a league. They all equally rest on the plighted faith of the sovereign party. A league, or confederacy, is but a subsisting or continuing treaty.

The gentleman's resolutions, then, affirm, in effect, that these twenty-four United States are held together only by a subsisting treaty, resting for its fulfilment and continuance on no inherent power of its own, but on the plighted faith of each State; or, in other words, that our Union is but a league; and, as a consequence from this proposition, they further affirm that as sovereigns are subject to no superior power, the States must decide, each for itself, of any alleged violation of the league; and if such violation be supposed to have occurred, each may adopt any mode or measure of redress which it shall think proper.

★ ★ ★ ★

The result of the whole is, that any State may secede at pleasure; that any State may resist a law which she herself may choose to say exceeds the power of Congress; and that, as a sovereign power, she may redress her own grievances, by her own arm, at her own discretion, she may make reprisals; she may cruise against the property of other members of the league; she may authorize captures, and make open war.

If, sir, this be our political condition, it is time the people of the United States understood it.

★ ★ ★ ★

The Constitution does not provide for events which must be preceded by its own destruction. Secession, therefore, since it must bring these consequences with it, is revolutionary. And nullification is equally revolutionary.... [Nullification] attempts to supersede the supreme legislative authority. It arrests the arm of the executive magistrate. It interrupts the exercise of the accustomed judicial power. Under the name of an ordinance, it declares null and void, within the State, all the revenue laws of the United States.

While practical nullification in South Carolina would be, as to herself, actual and distinct revolution, its necessary tendency must also be to spread revolution, and to break up the constitution, as to all the other States. It strikes a deadly blow at the vital principle of the whole Union. To allow State resistance to the laws of Congress to be rightful and proper, to admit nullification in some States, and yet not expect to see a

---

To allow State resistance to the laws of Congress to be rightful and proper, to admit nullification in some States, and yet not expect to see a dismemberment of the entire government, appears to me the wildest illusion, and the most extravagant folly. — Daniel Webster

---

dismemberment of the entire government, appears to me the wildest illusion, and the most extravagant folly. The gentleman seems not conscious of the direction or the rapidity of his own course. The current of his opinions sweeps him along, he knows not whither.

★ ★ ★ ★

On entering into the Union, the people of each State gave up a part of their own power to make laws for themselves, in consideration that, as to common objects, they should have a part in making laws for other States. In other words, the people of all the States agreed to create a common government, to be conducted by common counsels.... If South Carolina now refuses to submit to this power, she breaks the condition on which other States entered into the Union. She partakes of the common counsels, and therein assists to bind others, while she refuses to be bound herself. It makes no difference in the case, whether she does all this without reason or pretext, or whether she sets up as a reason that, in her judgment, the acts complained of are unconstitutional.

★ ★ ★ ★

Mr. President, all popular governments rest on two principles, or two assumptions:

First. That there is, so far, a common interest among those over whom the Government extends, as that it may provide for the defence, protection, and good government of the whole, without injustice or oppression to parts.

Second. That the representatives of the people, and especially the people themselves, are secure against general corruption, and may be trusted, therefore, with the exercise of power. Whoever argues against these principles, argues against the practicability of all free governments. And whoever admits these, must admit, or cannot deny, that power is as safe in the hands of Congress as in those of other representative bodies. Congress is not irresponsible. Its members are agents of the people, elected by them, answerable to them, and liable to be displaced or superseded, at their pleasure; and they possess as fair a claim to the confidence of the people, while they continue to deserve it, as any other public political agents.

If, then, sir, the manifest intention of the convention, and the contemporary admission of both friends and foes, prove any thing; if the plain text of the instrument itself, as well as the necessary implication from other provisions, prove any thing; if the early legislation of Congress, the course of judicial decisions, acquiesced in by all the States for forty years, prove any thing, then it is proved that there is a supreme law, and a final interpreter.

★ ★ ★ ★

Mr. President, if the friends of nullification should be able to propagate their opinions, and give them practical effect, they would, in my judgment prove themselves the most skillful "architects of ruin," the most effectual extinguishers of high-raised expectation, the greatest blasters of human hopes that any age has produced.

★ ★ ★ ★

But, sir, if the government do its duty; if it act with firmness and with moderation, these opinions cannot prevail. Be assured, sir, be assured, that among the political sentiments of this people, the love of union is still uppermost. They will stand fast by the constitution, and by those who defend it. I rely on no temporary expedients — on no political combination — but I rely on the true American feeling, the genuine patriotism of the people; and the imperative decision of the public voice. Disorder and confusion, indeed, may arise; scenes of commotion and contest are threatened, and perhaps may come. With my whole heart, I pray for the continuance of the domestic peace and quiet of the country.... We cannot, we must not, we dare not, omit to do that which, in our judgment, the safety of the Union requires.... I am ready to perform my own appropriate part, whenever and wherever the occasion may call on me, and to take my chance among those upon whom blows may fall first and fall thickest. I shall exert every faculty I possess in aiding to prevent the constitution from being nullified, destroyed, or impaired; and even should I see it fall, I will still, with a voice feeble, perhaps, but earnest as ever issued from human lips, and with fidelity and zeal which nothing shall extinguish, call on the PEOPLE to come to its rescue.

Source: *Register of Debates in Congress,* February 16, 1833 (Washington: Gales and Seaton, 1833), 9:554–587.

Notes

1. Dall W. Forsythe, *Taxation and Political Change in the Young Nation, 1781–1833* (New York: Columbia University Press, 1977), 83–84.

2. Massachusetts General Court, Committee on the Library, *State Papers on Nullification* (Boston: Dutton and Wentworth, Printers to the State, 1834), 28–33; and *Register of Debates in Congress,* 22nd Cong., 2nd sess., 9, appendix, 162–163, 177–181.

3. James D. Richardson, comp., *A Compilation of the Messages and Papers of the Presidents,* 20 vols. (New York: Bureau of National Literature, 1897–1927), 3:1161–1162.

4. Ibid., 3:1205, 1217.

5. Ibid., 3:1192; and Donald B. Cole, *The Presidency of Andrew Jackson* (Lawrence: University Press of Kansas, 1993), 167. See also William W. Freehling, *Prelude to Civil War: The Nullification Controversy in South Carolina, 1816–1836* (New York: Oxford University Press, 1992), 284.

6. *Register of Debates in Congress,* 22nd Cong., 2nd sess., (January 22, 1833), 9:191–192.

7. *Register of Debates in Congress,* 22nd Cong., 2nd sess., (February 15, 1833), 9:539; February 16, 1833, 9:587.

8. *Register of Debates in Congress,* 22nd Cong., 2nd sess., (February 12, 1833), 9:472, 477–478.

9. *Register of Debates in Congress,* 22nd Cong., 2nd sess., (February 18, 1833), 9:591; (February 20, 1833), 688; (March 1, 1833), 9:1903; (February 26, 1833), 9:1810–1811; (March 1, 1833), 9:808–809; Henry Clay to James Barbour, March 2, 1833, in James F. Hopkins and others, eds., *The Papers of Henry Clay,* 11 vols. (Lexington: University of Kentucky Press, 1959–1992), 8:629.

10. Quotes are found in Cole, *The Presidency of Andrew Jackson,* 171; and Freehling, *Prelude to Civil War,* 286.

Censure of
President Andrew Jackson
✳ 1833–1834 ✳

During the fall of 1833, financial panic quickly spread throughout the nation as the Second Bank of the United States drastically curtailed its loans in retaliation for President Andrew Jackson's decision to remove the government's deposits from the bank and place them in state banks. Preceding the removal, Jackson took the unprecedented action of firing Secretary of the Treasury William J. Duane for refusing his request to issue the order to remove the deposits, even though that authority actually belonged to the Treasury secretary, not the president. With Duane's dismissal, Jackson broadened presidential power to the removal of Cabinet officers without notifying Congress, a step taken by no previous chief executive. Ultimately, the responsibility of issuing the removal order fell to the new secretary of the Treasure, former attorney general Roger B. Tancy. His order of September 25, 1833, called for the government to begin placing all future deposits in "pet banks," as the opposition called them, on October 1. It also stipulated that the government was to draw its operating funds from the bank until they were exhausted, which occurred in December.

The order predictably unleashed a storm of criticism both from the business community and politicians. Jackson made no pretense that the federal deposits were not safe in the bank. Instead he argued that the action was necessary "to preserve the morals of the people, freedom of the press, and the purity of the elective franchise." In essence, he felt that the "corrupting influences" of the bank had made it "an engine of opposition to the people instead of the agent of their will." Many, however, contended that the removals endangered the "very financial structure of the nation, and with it the American experiment in freedom and democracy." Jackson was not, however, without advantages in his battle to destroy the bank. According to Jacksonian historian Robert V. Remini, removal of the deposits by the president "strengthened his hand as party leader and head of the government." The American "people gravitated closer and closer to Jackson's position on the bank issue because it had become infused with moral overtones, namely, the struggle of honest working people against evil aristocrats who were scheming to rob and exploit them." [1]

After the Jackson administration began to deposit government funds in the pet banks, Nicholas Biddle, president of the Bank of the United States, called in loans and raised interest rates explaining that without federal deposits the bank's resources were stretched too thin. While Biddle realized his actions were likely to cause financial distress, he hoped a short recession would persuade Congress to renew the bank's charter and that Jackson would be forced to go along.

By the time the Twenty-third Congress convened early that December, the stage was set for a monumental political scrimmage. For the next four months, little other than the removal of the deposits occupied the attention of either the nation's legislators or its newspapers. The battle between Congress and the president began in earnest on December 11, when the Senate voted 23–18 to call upon President Jackson to submit a copy of a document drafted by Treasury Secretary Taney. It stated the reasons why federal funds needed to be withdrawn from the bank. Jackson responded by saying that the Senate had no right to demand such an executive communication. [2]

The president's refusal prompted Sen. Henry Clay of Kentucky on December 26 to introduce a resolution calling for the censure of both Jackson, for assuming an unconstitutional and "dangerous" power in removing the government deposits, and Secretary of the Treasury Taney, for providing reasons "unsatisfactory and insufficient" for the removal. Clay, in his accompanying two-day speech, denounced "the concentration of all power in the hands of one man," which, if left unchecked, will transform our government "into an elective monarchy — the worst of all forms of government." He also condemned President Jackson for dismissing Secretary of the Treasury Duane solely because he was unwilling to remove deposits from the bank. Sen. John C. Calhoun of South Carolina, Jackson's vice president for most of his first term, was equally zealous in his condemnation of the president in mid-January 1834. [3]

Sen. Thomas Hart Benton, D-Mo., responded to the attacks on the president over three days in early January 1834 by accusing his colleague of asking the Senate to usurp the House's power to impeach. If the Senate tried President Jackson, Benton warned, it would be "subject to trial itself — to be tried by the people, and have its sentence reversed."[4]

Early in 1834, as the debate over the bank grew more intense, interest rates, unemployment, and bankruptcies continued to increase as the nation's financial situation worsened. Bank supporters organized meetings around the country and sent petitions to Washington pleading for relief from the deepening recession that, they argued, had been caused by President Jackson's action. A "phalanx of orators and speakers" in Congress daily attacked the president and his administration. One of the most provocative moments in the continuing debate came on March 7, 1834, when Clay delivered a flamboyant address blaming Jackson for the economic panic that now gripped the nation.[5]

The controversy enabled a new political coalition — the Whig Party — to emerge and be embraced by the Clay-led, anti-Jackson forces in Congress. The Whigs, like Clay, favored a national bank, strong credit, and currency facilities, and they opposed strong executive leadership. As the Whig movement gained momentum, the alleged misdeeds of the Jackson administration increasingly attracted the nation's attention. Finally, on March 28, 1834, in an unprecedented action, the Senate approved a resolution censuring the president for assuming "upon himself authority and powers not conferred by the Constitution and laws" in removing the deposits. It also voted to censure Secretary Taney for offering "unsatisfactory and insufficient" reasons for removal of the deposits.

Within a week of Jackson's censure, the Democrat-controlled House reached a much different verdict. On April 4, the House Democrats were able to pass four resolutions favorable to the president by solid margins. These stated that the bank should not be rechartered, federal deposits should not be returned to the bank, deposits should continued to be placed in state banks, and the bank's activities should be investigated. When the Senate subsequently passed joint resolutions condemning Taney's reasons for the removals and proposing restoration of the deposits, the House tabled them.[6]

The president's reaction to the Senate's action was predictable: he was outraged. His protest message of April 15 emphasized that without any action by the House, he had been found guilty of an impeachable offense without a formal impeachment proceeding taking place. There was no doubt in Jackson's mind that he had acted within his constitutional rights. The "President is the direct representative of the American people," Jackson declared, and is "responsible to them." In essence, he claimed that only the office of the president embodied the entire electorate, and as spokesman of the people, Congress could not restrict his actions. Predictably, the Whigs insisted that the president was respon-

This 1834 cartoon illustrates Henry Clay's successful call for censure of President Andrew Jackson in response to his removal of federal funds from the National Bank. Clay stands over the seated Jackson, sewing his mouth shut, representative of the president's three-year censure from the Senate Journal.
Source: Library of Congress.

sible to Congress. Sen. Daniel Webster of Massachusetts denounced Jackson's comments as "outrageous contentions," as did Senators Clay and Calhoun, but the president's novel view that he represented the people found an immediate acceptance with the electorate. Quickly, an unprecedented bond developed between Jackson and the American people, and as a result, the "President, not Congress, had become the instrument of popular will."[7]

It took more than three years of repeated efforts by Senate Democrats to marshal enough votes to expunge Jackson's censure from the Senate *Journal.* Even when the Whigs knew they no longer had the votes to stop the expungement, Clay, Calhoun, Webster, and other prominent Whigs continued to expound at length reasons why the censure should stand. When the vote took place near midnight on January 16, 1837, about seven weeks before Jackson left the White House, the final tally was 24–19 in favor of expungement. The next day,

Benton, who had introduced the successful resolution, sent the president the pen used by the secretary of the Senate to expunge the censure from the *Journal*.[8]

Nicholas Biddle and the Bank of the United States did not fare nearly as well. Biddle contracted credit too far even for his own allies in the business community, who feared that in his effort to save the bank he was threatening their interests. To appease the business community, Biddle eventually reversed himself and began granting credit in abundance and on reasonable terms. His vacillating and unpopular tactics, however, ended any chance for the bank to continue as an influential political and economic force. When its federal charter expired in March 1836, the bank was rechartered with the title of the Bank of the United States of Pennsylvania. Meanwhile, state banks had flourished and helped generate a period of prosperity that lasted until after Jackson retired from office in March 1837.

"There is no question that the Second Bank of the United States needed curbing," Robert V. Remini contends, because it "concentrated too much power in private hands, power that was repeatedly misused." Jackson, however, "can be faulted for not substituting another," more efficient central banking system. While the death of the bank resulted in "a considerable political victory" for Jackson, "the country lost a valuable, albeit flawed, financial institution, and was left with a fragmented and chronically unstable banking system that would plague the economy for more than a century." Even "more important than the economic effects of the Bank was its significance in party development, and particularly in the growth of presidential power." The battle over the bank "became the instrument by which the powers of the President were vastly expanded," and in terms of party politics it "was the single most important event during the middle period of American history." Not only did the Bank War "give rise to the Whig party, but the clash between opposing Bank forces established rigid lines between the contending parties that lasted practically to the Civil War."[9]

SENATOR HENRY CLAY CALLS FOR THE CENSURE OF PRESIDENT ANDREW JACKSON

DECEMBER 26 AND DECEMBER 30, 1833

Mr. CLAY rose and offered the following resolutions:

1. Resolved. That by dismissing the late Secretary of the Treasury because he would not, contrary to his sense of his own duty, remove money of the United States in deposit with the Bank of the United States and its branches, in conformity with the President's opinion; and by appointing his successor to effect such removal, which has been done, the President has assumed the exercise of a power over the Treasury of the United States, not granted to him by the constitution and laws, and dangerous to the liberties of the people.

2. Resolved. That the reasons assigned by the Secretary of the Treasury for the removal of the money of the United States deposited in the Bank of the United States and its branches, communicated to Congress on the 3d day of December, 1833, are unsatisfactory and insufficient.

The resolutions having been read,

Mr. CLAY addressed the Senate as follows: We are, said he, in the midst of a revolution, hitherto bloodless, but rapidly tending towards a total change of pure republican character of the Government, and to the concentration of all power in the hands of one man. The powers of Congress are paralyzed, except when exerted in conformity with his will, by the frequent and an extraordinary exercise of the executive veto, not anticipated by the founders of the constitution, and not practised by any of the predecessors of the present Chief Magistrate. And, to cramp them still more, a new expedient is springing into use, of withholding altogether bills which have received the sanction of both Houses of Congress, thereby cutting off all opportunity of passing them, even if, after their return, the members should be unanimous in their favor. The constitutional participation of the Senate in the appointing power is virtually abolished, by the constant use of the power of removal from office without any known cause.

★ ★ ★ ★

The most extensive and most valuable public domain that ever fell to the lot of one nation is threatened with a total sacrifice. The general currency of the country, the life-blood of all its business, is in the most imminent danger of universal disorder and confusion. The power of internal improvement lies crushed beneath the veto. The system of protection of American industry was snatched from impending destruction at the last session; but we are now coolly told by the Secretary of the Treasury, without a blush, "that it is understood to be

---

We are, said he, in the midst of a revolution, hitherto bloodless, but rapidly tending towards a total change of pure republican character of the Government, and to the concentration of all power in the hands of one man. — Henry Clay

---

conceded on all hands that a tariff for protection merely is to be finally abandoned." By the 3d of March, 1837, if the progress of innovation continue, there will be scarcely a vestige remaining of the Government and its policy, as they existed prior to the 3d of March, 1829. In a term of years, a little more than equal to that which was required to establish our liberties, the Government will have been transformed into an elective monarchy — the worst of all forms of government.

★ ★ ★ ★

Mr. President, when Congress adjourned at the termination of the last session, there was one remnant of its powers — that over the purse — left untouched. The two most important powers of civil government are those of the sword and the purse; the first, with some restrictions, is confined by the constitution to the executive, and the last to the legislative department. If they are separate, and exercised by different responsible departments, civil liberty is safe; but if they are united in the hands of the same individual, it is gone. That clear-sighted and revolutionary orator and patriot Patrick Henry justly said, in the Virginia convention, in reply to one of his opponents, "Let him candidly tell me where and when did freedom exist, when the sword and purse were given up from the people? Unless a miracle in human affairs interposed, no nation ever retained liberty after the loss of the sword and purse. Can you prove, by any argumentative deduction, that it is possible to be safe without one of them? If you give them up, you are gone."

Up to the period of the termination of the last session of Congress, the exclusive constitutional power of Congress over the treasury of the United States had never been contested. Among its earliest acts was one establishing the Treasury Department, which provided for the appointment of a Treasurer, who was required to give bond and security, in a very large amount, "to receive and keep the moneys of the United States, and disburse the same upon warrants drawn by the Secretary of the Treasury, countersigned by the Comp-

troller, recorded by the Register, and not otherwise." Prior to establishment of the present Bank of the United States, no treasury or place had been provided or designated by law for the safe keeping of the public moneys, but the Treasurer was left to his own discretion and responsibility. When the existing bank was established, it was provided that public moneys should be deposited with it, and consequently that bank became the treasury of the United States; for, whatever place is designated by law for the keeping of the public money of the United States, under the care of the Treasurer of the United States, is, for the time being, the treasury.... [A]mong the last acts of the House of Representatives, prior to the close of the last session, was the adoption of a resolution, manifesting its entire confidence in the ability and solidity of the bank.

After all these testimonies to the perfect safety of the public moneys in the place appointed by Congress, who could have supposed that the place would have been changed? Who could have imagined that within sixty days of the meeting of Congress, and, as it were, in utter contempt of its authority, the change should have been ordered? Who would have dreamed that the Treasurer should have thrown away the single key to the treasury, over which Congress held ample control, and accepted in lieu of it, some dozens of keys, over which neither Congress nor he has any adequate control? Yet, sir, all this has been done; and it is now our solemn duty to inquire, 1st, by whose authority it has been ordered; and 2d, whether the order has been given in conformity with the constitution and laws of the United States.

★ ★ ★ ★

The first question, which I have intimated it to be my purpose to consider is, by whose authority, power, or direction, was the change of the deposites made? Now, is there any Senator who hears me that requires proof on this point? ... Does any one, and who, doubt that it was the act of the President? — that it was done by his express command? The President, on this subject, has himself furnished perfectly conclusively evidence, in the paper read by him to his cabinet.... Although the President has denied to the Senate an official copy of that singular paper, as a part of the people of the United States, for whose special benefit it was published, we have a right to use it.

The question is, by virtue of whose will, power, dictation, was the removal of the deposites effected? By whose authority and determination were they transferred from the Bank of the United States, where they were required by the law to be placed, and put in banks which the law had never designated? ... I want to know that power in the Government, that original and controlling authority, which required and commanded the removal of the deposites. And, I repeat the question, is there a Senator, or intelligent man in the whole country, who entertains a solitary doubt?

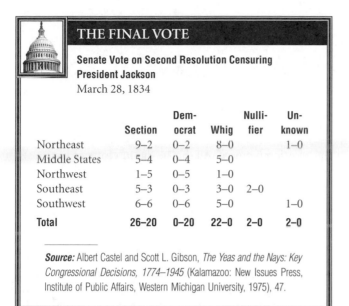

THE FINAL VOTE

Senate Vote on Second Resolution Censuring President Jackson
March 28, 1834

Section		Democrat	Whig	Nulli-fier	Un-known
Northeast	9–2	0–2	8–0		1–0
Middle States	5–4	0–4	5–0		
Northwest	1–5	0–5	1–0		
Southeast	5–3	0–3	3–0	2–0	
Southwest	6–6	0–6	5–0		1–0
Total	**26–20**	**0–20**	**22–0**	**2–0**	**2–0**

Source: Albert Castel and Scott L. Gibson, *The Yeas and the Nays: Key Congressional Decisions, 1774–1945* (Kalamazoo: New Issues Press, Institute of Public Affairs, Western Michigan University, 1975), 47.

I hear what the President himself says in his manifesto read to his cabinet: "The President deems it *his* duty to communicate in this manner to his cabinet the final conclusions of *his own mind,* and the reasons on which they are founded." And, at the conclusion of this paper, what does he say? "The President again repeats that he begs his cabinet to consider the proposed measure as *his own,* in the support of which he shall require no one of them to make a sacrifice of opinion or principle. *Its responsibility has been assumed,* after the most mature deliberation and reflection, as necessary to preserve the morals of the people, the freedom of the press, and the purity of the elective franchise, without which all will unite in saying that the blood and treasure expended by our forefathers, in the establishment of our happy system of government, will have been vain and fruitless. Under these convictions, he feels that a measure so important to the American people cannot be commenced too soon; and *he* therefore names the 1st day of October next as a period proper for the change of the deposites, or sooner, provided the necessary arrangements with the State banks can be made." Sir, is there a Senator who will now tell me that the removal was not the measure and the act of the President?

★ ★ ★ ★

[I]f the President had no power over the subject; if the constitution and laws, instead of conveying to him an authority to act as he has done, required him to keep his hands off the public treasury, and confided its care and custody to other hands, no reasons can justify the usurpation. What power has the President over the public treasury? That gives him but two clearly defined powers: one to appoint, with the concurrence of the Senate, and to remove the Government directors;

and the other, to order a *scire facias* when the charter shall be violated by the bank. There is no other power conferred on him by it…. The Secretary of the Treasury alone is designated. The President is not, by the remotest allusion, referred to. And, to put the matter beyond all controversy, whenever the Secretary gives an order or direction for the removal, he is to report his reasons — to whom? To the President? No! directly to Congress. Nor is the bank itself required to report its periodical condition to the President, but to the Secretary of the Treasury, or to Congress, through the organ of a committee…. The constitution had ordained that no money should be drawn from the treasury but in consequence of appropriations made by law. It remained for Congress to provide *how* it should be drawn. And that duty is performed by the act constituting the Treasury Department. According to that act, the Secretary of the Treasury is to prepare and sign, the Comptroller to countersign, the Register to record, and, finally, the Treasurer to pay a warrant issued, *and only issued,* in virtue of a prior act of appropriation.

★ ★ ★ ★

Is there a Senator who can hesitate to affirm, in the language of the resolutions, that the President has assumed a dangerous power over the treasury of the United States, not granted him by the constitution and the laws; and that the reasons assigned for the act, by the Secretary of the Treasury are insufficient and unsatisfactory?

The eyes and the hopes of the American people are anxiously turned to Congress. They feel that they have been deceived and insulted; their confidence abused; their interests betrayed; and their liberties in danger. They see a rapid and alarming concentration of all power in one man's hands. They see that, by the exercise of the positive authority of the Executive, and his negative power exerted over Congress, the will of one man alone prevails, and governs the republic. The question is no longer what laws will Congress pass, but what will the Executive not veto? The President, and not Congress, is addressed for legislative action…. We behold the usual incidents of approaching tyranny. The land is filled with spies and informers; and detraction and denunciation are the orders of the day. People, especially official incumbents in this place, no longer dare speak in the fearless tones of manly freemen, but in the cautious whispers of trembling slaves. The premonitory symptoms of despotism are upon us; and if Congress do not apply an instantaneous and effective remedy, the fatal collapse will soon come on, and we shall die — ignobly die — base, mean, and abject slaves; the scorn and contempt of mankind; unpitied, unwept, unmourned!

Source: *Register of Debates in Congress,* December 26 and December 30, 1833 (Washington: Gales and Seaton, 1834), 10:58–94.

SENATOR THOMAS HART BENTON DEFENDS PRESIDENT ANDREW JACKSON

JANUARY 2–3 AND JANUARY 7, 1834

Mr. B. then proceeded to the order of the day, the resolutions submitted by a Senator from Kentucky, [Mr. Clay,] on the removal of the public deposites from the Bank of the United States.

★ ★ ★ ★

Mr. B. said that the first of these resolutions contained impeachable matter, and was in fact, though not in form, a direct impeachment of the President of the United States. He recited the constitution provision, that the President might be impeached — 1st, for treason; 2d, for bribery; 3d, for high crimes; 4th, for misdemeanors; and, said that the first resolution charged both a high crime and a misdemeanor upon the President; a high crime, violating the laws and constitution, to obtain a power over the public treasure, to the danger of the liberties of the people; and a misdemeanor, in dismissing the late Secretary of the Treasury from office.

★ ★ ★ ★

We are, then, said Mr. B., trying an impeachment! … It is a proceeding in which the First Magistrate of the republic is to be tried without being heard, and in which his accusers are to act as his judges!

Mr. B. called upon the Senate to consider well what they did before they proceeded further in the consideration of this resolution.… It accused the President of violating the constitution, and itself committed twenty violations of the same constitution in making the accusation! It accused him of violating a single law, and itself violated all the laws of criminal justice in prosecuting him for it. It charged him with designs dangerous to the liberties of the citizens, and immediately trampled upon the rights of all citizens, in the person of their Chief Magistrate.

★ ★ ★ ★

The President, he repeated, was on trial for high crime, in seizing the public treasure in violation of the constitution. Was the charge true? Does the act which he has done deserve the definition which has been put upon it? He had made up his own mind that the public deposites ought to be removed from the Bank of the United States. He communicated that opinion to the Secretary of the Treasury; the Secretary refused to move them; the President removed him, and appointed a Secretary who gave the order which he thought

the occasion required. All this he did in virtue of his constitutional obligation to see the laws faithfully executed; and in obedience to the same sense of duty which would lead him to dismiss a Secretary of War, or of the Navy, who would refuse to give an order for troops to march, or a fleet to sail.

★ ★ ★ ★

The President is on trial for a misdemeanor — for dismissing his Secretary without sufficient cause. To this accusation there are ready answers: first, that the President may dismiss his Secretaries without cause; secondly that the Senate has no cognizance of the case; thirdly, that the Senate cannot assume to know for what cause the Secretary in question was dismissed.

★ ★ ★ ★

A great issue, said Mr. B., is made up, and between great parties, and generally affecting the property and liberty of the American people. It is an issue of fact. It is, whether the Bank of the United States has unnecessarily curtailed its debts, and oppressed the community, and used its immense power over the money market to promote its own objects at the present time.… The Senate has assumed to try this great issue; and how will they try it? By entering the arena, for and against the bank. By pleading like lawyers, and testifying as witnesses, and deciding as judges? Will they become compurgators for the bank? Will they enter the lists as champions, and that in a case in which the laws of chivalry do not admit of a champion; for the bank is neither a woman nor a priest? Will they convert the Senate into a bear garden, give and take contradictions, have a dog fight for the entertainment of the galleries, and acquit the bank by dint of numbers, without examination, and without trial?

Mr. B. held it to be impossible that the Senate of the United States could go on in this way, but that they were bound to proceed in the most solemn manner known to the history of parliamentary proceedings, namely, an examination of the president of the bank, and all other material witnesses, at the bar of the Senate. This, he said, was the course followed in England in similar conjunctures. It was done in the famous case of the South Sea directors; it was the proper course in all great national emergencies. It was the only way to obtain a PUBLIC TRIAL, such as the genius of our constitution delights in.… This case, above all others, demanded such a public trial. The gravity and enormity of the accusation, the dignity of the parties making it, the high trust of the parties denying it, the elevation of the tribunal before which it was made, and the deep interest to their property and liberty, which involved the whole body of the American people in the most anxious suspense for a just and impartial decision.... At the proper time, therefore, he (Mr. B.) should move to strike out the whole of the second resolution submitted by the Senator from Kentucky, [Mr. CLAY,] which undertook to pronounce judgement without trial, and to insert in place of it a resolution to summon Nicholas Biddle, president of the Bank of the United States, and such other persons as the Senate should direct, to appear at the bar of the Senate at some short and convenient day, to be examined upon oath as to the causes which led to the late large curtailment of the debts of the bank, and the manner of conducting the curtailment.

★ ★ ★ ★

The bank was created for the convenience of Government, as a thing necessary to the Government, and not for the benefit of itself. The benefits which might result to the stockholders were incidental and subordinate, and could be no part of the object of the Government in creating the bank. It was for its own convenience alone that the charter was granted; and upon that argument alone, worked up to the idea of necessity, could the charter be renewed.

The Government, then, was the judge of the convenience and of the necessity which should induce a recharter; and the institution itself had no right to demand it, much less to spend the Government's money to obtain. As individuals, the directors and stockholders may spend their own money, like other citizens; but the funds, of which they were the trustees, could only be used according to the terms of the trust; that is, in making profits for the stockholders, and defraying the necessary expenses of prudent and economical administration of its affairs.... To refuse to be discontinued, to demand a recharter, and to use its money to obtain it, is just as outrageous and unjustifiable as if the regiment of dragoons, raised last winter, and to be enlisted for three years, should refuse to be disbanded at the end of the time, and use their swords and pistols upon Congress to force a re-enlistment.... The bank, according to the decision of the Government, has become as unnecessary as an army in time of peace; but, like an army that refuses to be disbanded in time of peace, she revolts against the Government, sets up her will above that of the Government, and uses her appropriate weapon, money, to prolong and to perpetuate her existence.

★ ★ ★ ★

A civil Government must be first detested and despised by the people, before an armed force can overturn it. Not so with a moneyed power. It works by corruption. It saps the foundations of Governments. It destroys Government by rendering them odious, and not because they are odious. It prepares them for the arm of the military usurper; and if this Government shall ever be overthrown by a military chieftain, it will be after the indulgence of a course of conduct that shall deprive it of the confidence and esteem of the people. The moneyed power — the ass loaded with gold — is then so much more dangerous than an army, as it can use a more formidable weapon, and can attack the Government before it is corrupt; and, by corrupting it, fit it for overthrow by the military arm. Here, then, is a great moneyed power, wielding its tens of millions, holding half the specie of the country in its vaults, in open insurrection against the Government of the country, contending against it for power and pre-eminence, and boldly declaring, in a paper furnished by itself to the members of Congress, that it will be the exclusive judge of the amount of money, and the time and manner of using it, which it will choose to expend in this contest. Such is the declaration of directors, who themselves have no real interest in the bank, except the profitable business of managing it; who, holding their one, two, five, and ten shares, arrogantly wield the seventy thousand shares of the Government against itself. Mr. B. said, this was a crisis which the prophetic spirit Jefferson foresaw, and which thirty years ago, he foretold. It was an attempt to upset the Government — the popular elective Government — secured to the people by the constitution, and to substitute for it a bank government, representing, not the people, but the bloated oligarchy of a moneyed power.

> Here, then, is a great moneyed power, wielding its tens of millions, holding half the specie of the country in its vaults, in open insurrection against the Government of the country, contending against it for power and pre-eminence.... — Thomas Hart Benton

★ ★ ★ ★

He trusted that the facts and reasons which he had brought to bear upon the question, in addition to the intrinsic weight and palpable force of the Secretary's reasoning, were sufficient to show that the reasons assigned by him were sufficient to justify the act that he had done; at all events, that they ought not to be condemned as insufficient, without a rigorous investigation into their truth. This investigation was what he demanded; he did not want a verdict, either for or against the bank, without a trial. He believed that all those opposed to the bank were in favor of an investigation. He considered the House of Representatives, as being the grand inquest of the nation, the appropriate branch of the Legislature for originating accusations, and particularly charged with the moneyed concerns of the people, to be the proper place for investigating the truth of the charges against the institution. He would prefer that the whole matter should be left in that House, which was now fully occupied with the subject; but the control of this subject was in the hands of the friends of the bank, and, if they would prosecute it here, he must demand investigation into the truth of the Secretary's reasons before they were condemned.

Source: *Register of Debates in Congress,* January 2–3 and January 7, 1834 (Washington: Gales and Seaton, 1834), 10:97–139.

Notes

1. Quotes are found in Calvin Colton, *Life and Times of Henry Clay,* 2 vols. (New York: A. S. Barnes and Co., 1846), 2:97; Robert V. Remini, *The Life of Andrew Jackson* (New York: Harper and Row, 1988), 262. See also Remini, *The Life of Andrew Jackson,* 265–266.

2. *Register of Debates in Congress,* 23rd Cong., 1st sess., (December 11, 1833), 10:30–37.

3. *Register of Debates in Congress,* 23rd Cong., 1st sess., (December 26, 1833), 10:58–59; January 13–14, 1834, 10:206–223.

4. Thomas Hart Benton, *Thirty Years' View,* 2 vols. (New York: D. Appleton, 1863), 1:409.

5. Ibid., 1:424; *Register of Debates in Congress,* 23rd Cong., 1st sess., (March 7, 1834), 10:834–836.

6. *Register of Debates in Congress,* 23rd Cong., 1st sess., (March 28, 1834), 10:1185–1187; April 4, 1834, 10:3474–3478.

7. Remini, *The Life of Andrew Jackson,* 269–270.

8. *Register of Debates in Congress,* 23rd Cong., 1st sess., (January 16, 1837), 13:428–505; Benjamin Perley Poore, *Perley's Reminiscences of Sixty Years in the National Metropolis,* 2 vols. (Philadelphia: Hubbard Brothers, 1886), 1:142; Henry A. Wise, *Seven Decades of the Union* (Philadelphia: J. B. Lippincott, 1881), 143.

9. Quotes are found in Robert V. Remini, *Andrew Jackson and the Bank War: A Study in the Growth of Presidential Power* (New York: Norton, 1967), 176–177; Alan Brinkley, *American History: A Survey,* 11th ed. (Boston: McGraw Hill, 2003), 250.

House Gag Rule

✳ 1836–1844 ✳

During the 1830s, as antislavery sentiment spread throughout the Northern states, a network of abolition societies emerged in response. The New England Anti-Slavery Society was formed in 1831 and two years later, at a meeting in Philadelphia, delegates from Massachusetts, New York, and Pennsylvania established a national organization, the American Anti-Slavery Society (AAS). By 1835, there were 225 auxiliaries of the AAS, and by 1840, 1,650. Prominent among AAS activities was its "postal campaign," which launched in 1835. Under the leadership of Lewis Tappan, the AAS sought to inundate the South with anti-slavery publications in the hope of ultimately convincing the region to do away with the institution. Amidst Southern efforts to stop the circulation of abolitionist materials, Congress passed a law making it a federal misdemeanor for postmasters to detain or delay delivery of the mail, but it was never enforced. Eventually, the postal campaign was abandoned and replaced by a drive to present Congress with petitions on a variety of subjects related to slavery.[1]

Previously, Congress had largely ignored or given cursory treatment to slavery, with the exception of the debates over the congressional prohibition of the slave trade in 1808 and the Missouri Compromise in 1819–1820. By December 1835, however, it was clear that Congress could no longer ignore the slavery question. Early the following February, as debate over slavery continued to increase in intensity, Rep. Henry L. Pinckney of South Carolina introduced a resolution — soon to be known as the "gag rule" — designed to relieve the House from having to deal with a dramatic increase in antislavery petitions being submitted to Congress. Pinckney's resolution called for all antislavery petitions, as well as all pending resolutions and future propositions relating to the subject, to be referred to a select committee with instructions to report that Congress had no power to interfere with slavery in the states or the District of Columbia. This approach, he declared, was designed "to enlighten the public mind, to repress agitation, to allay excitement, to sustain and preserve the just rights of the slaveholding States and of the people of [the District of Columbia], and to establish harmony and tranquillity

amongst the various sections of the Union." Following extensive discussion, Pinckney's resolution was adopted on February 8, 1836.[2]

By 1836, slavery "seemed to be woven into the fabric of the nation's life." It had become a deeply rooted institution that many, such as Rep. James Henry Hammond of South Carolina, believed could not be abolished. During the next three months, as the select committee worked on its report, the House was frequently caught up in disputes over the propriety of antislavery petitions. The controversy reached an apex when the committee presented its report and the House spent more than a week discussing its contents. Finally on May 26, Congress adopted three resolutions, which stated that: (1) Congress had no authority to abolish slavery in the States, (2) Congress "ought not to interfere in any way with slavery in the District of Columbia," and (3) "all petitions, memorials, resolutions, propositions, or papers" dealing in any way with the subject of slavery would be laid on the table without being printed or referred, and no further action be taken on them.[3]

The Senate's response to the deluge of abolitionist petitions was not nearly as strong. Earlier, that same March, the Senate rejected the motion of Sen. John C. Calhoun of South Carolina to bar antislavery petitions; instead, it adopted a compromise motion offered by Sen. James Buchanan, D-Penn., that ostensibly affirmed the right of petition by allowing the Senate to receive the petitions and then reject them without referral or consideration.[4]

The House gag rule was drafted in response to Southern concerns over the significant increase in petitions sent to the House "praying" for the emancipation of slaves in the District of Columbia. The rule represented a significant shift in procedure. Between the first Congress and approval of the initial gag rule resolution, similar petitions had been sporadically received and referred to the appropriate committee and in the process received at least pro forma consideration.

Because the gag rule was first adopted in the form of a resolution, it automatically expired at the end of each session of

Congress and had to be readopted at the beginning of each new session, which it was in 1837, 1838, and 1839. Finally in 1840, over the vocal objections of abolitionists, proslavery elements in the House were successfully able to incorporate the gag rule in a standing chamber rule. Prior to its acceptance as a standing rule, the House debated the rule for several days before adopting it on January 28. The new rule provided "[t]hat no petition, memorial, resolution, or other paper praying the abolition of slavery in the District of Columbia, or any State or Territory, or the slave trade between the States and Territories of the United States in which it now exists, shall be received by this House, or entertained in anyway whatever." The rule, which was far more restrictive than earlier resolutions, prohibited even the reception of abolition petitions.[5]

Opponents of the gag rule were led by Rep. John Quincy Adams, W-Mass., the only former president to ever serve in the House. While not an abolitionist, Adams believed very strongly in the right of petition and that Congress should receive antislavery petitions even if no action was intended. He also maintained that in the event the slave states ever became a "theater of war, civil, servile, or foreign … the war powers of Congress [would] extend to interference with the institution of slavery in every way." During the 1836 roll call vote on the gag rule, Adams abstained, declaring the "resolution to be a direct violation of the Constitution of the United States, of the rules of [the] House, and the rights of [his] constituents." Initially, he was reluctant to be associated with the abolitionists and centered his advocacy on the belief that agreement with a petition's content should not be a prerequisite for its presentation. As the struggle continued, Adams "increasingly used the 'gag rule' battle as a pulpit to rail against slavery as a moral issue."[6]

During his relentless campaign to repeal the gag rule, or at least evade it, Adams at one point "threw the House into an uproar lasting for days, and nearly subjected himself to censure by the House, by asking whether he might present a petition purporting to come from slaves." On other occasions, he offered petitions calling for the repeal of the gag rule, and against the annexation of Texas, neither of which came under the rule. At the same time, antislavery colleagues continued their agitation by circumventing the rule by offering resolutions, petitions, and constitutional amendments that espoused antislavery views, but did not mention slavery specifically. Although a definitive list of all the antislavery petitions submitted while the gag rule controversy raged in the House has not been compiled, one scholar calculated that from December 1838 through March 1839 nearly 1,500 were presented, 693 of which Adams offered.[7]

Not until December 3, 1844, however, was Adams's relentless eight-year struggle to secure repeal of the gag rule finally realized. Ironically, the ending was somewhat anticlimactic. When Adams offered his resolution to repeal the gag rule at

While not an abolitionist himself, John Quincy Adams opposed the House Gag Rule, which prohibited debate over slavery in the House of Representatives. Calling the Gag Rule "a direct violation of the Constitution," Adams led a relentless campaign to have it repealed.
Source: Library of Congress.

the beginning of the Twenty-eighth Congress, the rule, which for eight "years had caused so much excitement, so many recriminations, such long debate, such heated argument, and such dire threat," was adopted "quietly, without debate or turbulence." Thus ended "one of the longest, most spectacular, and most important struggles ever waged in the American Congress." That evening, Adams wrote a simple account of the day's proceedings in his *Diary* and concluded the entry with the following thought, "Blessed, forever blessed, be the name of God." Adams's strong feelings about the gag rule and his persistent support of the right of petition earned him the sobriquet "Old Man Eloquent."[8]

One scholar has aptly noted that the real importance of the gag rule was that it "provided the first appeal broad enough to rouse every antislavery man to action" and "attached to the movement a veritable host of sympathizers who might not have joined it but for the additional spur of a seeming denial of petition." The rule also strengthened the antislavery movement by adding the issue of deprivation of the rights of petition to the list of indictments against the South and was a "constant source of publicity for the antislavery crusade." Many of the arguments voiced during the debate were later used even more extensively as the controversy over slavery gained strength.[9]

As a consequence of procedural barriers that the House, and to a lesser degree the Senate, developed in the 1830s, the effectiveness of petitions was greatly diminished. With the "decline of petitioning as a means for individual citizens to communicate grievances on issues of public policy to Congress," Americans largely relinquished a right specifically granted in the First Amendment to the Constitution — one that actually preceded the "free speech rights that grew out of the English parliamentary experience." Prior to the gag rule, the right of petition was a vehicle for mass agitation on a broad range of topics. In its aftermath, no group has ever again "exercised the right of petition on so grand a scale in a dialogue with congress on an important social issue."[10]

REPRESENTATIVE HENRY L. PINCKNEY'S INTRODUCTION OF THE HOUSE GAG RULE

FEBRUARY 8, 1836

Mr. PINCKNEY then submitted the following resolution:

Resolved. That all the memorials which have been offered, or may hereafter be presented, to this House, praying for the abolition of slavery in the District of Columbia, and also the resolutions offered by an honorable member from Maine, [Mr. JARVIS,] with the amendment thereto proposed by an honorable member from Virginia [Mr. WISE,] and every other paper or proposition that may be submitted in relation to that subject, be referred to a select committee, with instructions to report that Congress possesses no constitutional authority to interfere in any way with the institution of slavery in any of the States of this confederacy; and that, in the opinion of this House, Congress ought not to interfere in any way with slavery in the District of Columbia, because it would be a violation of the public faith, unwise, impolitic, and dangerous to the Union; assigning such reasons for these conclusions as, in the judgment of the committee, may be best calculated to enlighten the public mind, to repress agitation, to allay excitement, to sustain and preserve the just rights of the slaveholding States and of the people of this District, and to reestablish harmony and tranquillity amongst the various sections of the Union.

Mr. PINCKNEY said he would not detain the House long. He had offered the resolution before the House upon the most deliberate reflection, and after consultation with several highly respected and judicious friends, and because he honestly believed it to be the very best course that could be adopted in relation to the dangerous and exciting subject to which it refers. Mr. P. said he was aware of the responsibility he assumed, but knowing that he was acting for the highest good of the whole country, he was perfectly ready and willing to encounter it. He was acting for the true interests of his constituents, for the true welfare of his native State and of all the South, and, he was neither afraid nor ashamed to add, with a view to the peace and preservation of the Union. But, because he had dared to adopt this course, he had been bitterly assailed by a certain print, [the Telegraph,] and that, too, before he had even had an opportunity to assign his reasons. Sir, said Mr. P. let me say once for all that I am not to be driven by newspaper assaults, or calumnious imputations upon my motives, from my settled convictions of public duty, nor from my determined purpose to take high and patriotic ground upon this subject, and to prevent it, as far as I am able to do so, from being made a perpetual source of agitation to the ruin of the South, and the destruction of the Union. I have no fear that the assaults to which I have alluded will injure me in the estimation of the citizens of Charleston. My constituents have known me long, and they know me well. They know that I am utterly incapable of being tempted to desert my duty to them, in any matter in which their rights or interests are involved; and they will spurn the base imputation upon me, as all insult to themselves. But I do plead guilty to the heinous accusation of desiring harmony — of desiring to produce a safe, and advantageous, and honorable adjustment of this question. But how, Mr. Speaker! By evading the resolutions offered by the honorable members from Maine and Virginia, as I am charged with doing! No sir: all who know me, either here or in South Carolina, know that I never have evaded or avoided any vote on any question, upon which it has ever been my duty to act as a public representative. It is not my nature: it is not my character. I would disdain to shrink from an open avowal of my sentiments, or record of my vote, upon any question which any gentleman could make before this House. How then, sir! By retracing ground already gained,

THE FINAL VOTE

Adoption of House Gag Rule
May 26, 1836

	Section	Democrat	Whig	Unionist	Nullifier	Unknown
Northeast	12–21	12–4	0–17			
Middle States	41–26	40–7	1–19			
Northwest	12–14	11–5	1–9			
Southeast	27–7	17–5	5–1	3–0	0–1	2–0
Southwest	25–0	12–0	12–0			1–0
Total	**117–68**	**92–21**	**19–46**	**3–0**	**0–1**	**3–0**

Source: Albert Castel and Scott L. Gibson, *The Yeas and the Nays: Key Congressional Decisions, 1774–1945* (Kalamazoo: New Issues Press, Institute of Public Affairs, Western Michigan University, 1975), 47.

and yielding an advantage obtained from the enemy! No sir: for I know of no ground gained — no advantage obtained — but I am decidedly of opinion, on the contrary, that we have lost ground daily by the course that has been pursued, and that we shall lose more and more, the longer it is persisted in. This accusation, then, is absurd. I have evaded nothing: I have yielded nothing. I deny the imputation and every vile insinuation connected with it. But, sir, I do desire harmony — by producing harmonious, united, and efficient action — by taking higher ground than has yet been taken — by covering the whole field — by bringing up the main question and acting upon that; and by doing what no one else has yet attempted to do — by procuring a direct vote, and a practical result, upon the whole subject of the abolition of slavery! This is my object, sir. And am I to be denounced for this! Are my constituents to be incited to suspect me, because I am honestly endeavoring to bring this distracting controversy to the very best issue of which it is susceptible? Is it treason to the South, sir, that this House should declare, by a solemn and deliberate vote, that Congress possesses no constitutional authority to interfere with slavery in any of the States? Is it treason to the South, that this House should declare, by a solemn and deliberate vote, that Congress ought not, and will not, interfere in any way with slavery in the District of Columbia, because it would be a violation of the public faith, and dangerous to the Union? Has such a point as this ever been gained before? Has ever such a vote been taken, or such a declaration made, as this? Is it treason to the South to wish to allay excitement, and to repress agitation? Is it treason to the South, that a committee should be ordered to draught a report, as ably as they can to secure and maintain the just rights of the slaveholding States and of the people of this District, on the one side, and at the same time to restore concord and tranquility amongst the various sections of this confederacy, on the other? If this be treason to the South, sir, let my constituents judge me. I am responsible to them — but to no individual, be he who he may. If this be treason to the Union, let the people of America decide: for I cheerfully acknowledge that, as a citizen of the Union, I am also responsible to them. But, at all events, however I may be denounced for my audacity in having acted thus, I have the consolation to know that the propositions I have offered meet the cordial approbation of many members from the South, than whom there are no purer patriots, or more devoted southerners, upon this floor. Several of them have said that they would have rejoiced if this very course had been adopted at the beginning of the session; and I have every reason to believe that it will now be sustained by the almost undivided vote of the whole southern delegation. What, then, Mr. Speaker! am I and all the southern delegates who act with me, are all of us, traitors; and is the individual who has assailed me the only man who understands the interests, or cares for the rights and honor, of the South? But, sir, I feel that I ought to ask pardon of the House for speaking in this manner. It is exceedingly painful to me to speak of myself, at any time, or in any place, but especially before so respectable and enlightened an assembly as this; but, in justice to myself, I could not have avoided it upon the present occasion. Sir, I will only trouble the House, with one or two observations more. I wish my constituents to understand my motives. It is my duty, as the representative of the people of Charleston, to render an account to them, of every thing that I may say or do in my public capacity, and I wish them to understand me distinctly, that they may judge me correctly, and especially before any false impressions may have been created in their minds. I say, then, Mr. Speaker, that I have three great objects in offering this resolution. The first is, as far as possible, to arrest the discussion of the subject of slavery within these walls, which I believe to be useless —

worse than useless — pernicious to the South, and dangerous to the whole country. The second is, to bring the whole subject of the abolition of slavery to practical result, in a manner safe and advantageous to the South, satisfactory to the North, and calculated also to tranquillize the country and, to confirm the Union. My last object is — and this, indeed, substantially includes the whole — my last object is to put down the spirit of fanaticism, to repress the spirit of incendiary agitation, by disseminating throughout the country a calm and temperate report, emanating from this body, having the high sanction of the national Legislature, and calculated, both by its own arguments and the high source from which it issues, to produce that sound and rational state of public opinion, in the non-slaveholding States, which is equally due to the South and to the preservation of the Union. And, for this great purpose, sir, I would cover the whole ground, I would embrace the States, as well as the District of Columbia. I know no reasonable objection to doing so, and it is justified by precedent. It is the very course that was adopted by Congress in the memorable resolution of 1790 — a course that was sustained (I believe proposed) by the venerable Madison, and that received the unanimous sanction of the whole southern delegation of that day. I can see no reason why the same course should not receive the unanimous sanction of the whole southern delegation now. In my humble judgment, it is the only course by which we can bring this matter to an advantageous issue. Hitherto, we have been fighting about abstractions. Hitherto we have been contending about the right of petition, and other minor and unimportant points. We have been wasting our energies, and losing ground upon a false issue — an issue upon which the whole North is united, and the South divided, and very debate upon which, so far from doing the least good, only increases the spirit of abolition of the North, inflames excitement in the South, and is daily widening the breach between the different members of the Union. Now, sir, I am for overstepping these minor abstract points and taking high ground. I am for taking the question upon the whole subject. I would let the right of petition alone, as no way material to the true issue. I would have a broad and comprehensive declaration that Congress possess no authority over slavery, here or elsewhere, and will not interfere with it in any way whatever. Is not this the true position of the South, sir? I think it is, and my constituents, too, all of whom own slaves, will think upon it too. Sir, the abolitionists aim at general emancipation. No candid man can doubt it, or deny it. All their writings and publications prove it. You cannot read the proceedings of a single antislavery society, or a single production of incendiary press, without being thoroughly convinced that they contemplate abolition in the States as their grand ultimate object, and that they never will be satisfied with any thing short of it, as long as they have the slightest shadow of a hope. Now, sir, I would meet them, and defeat them, at once and forever, upon that. I consider that we do

but little, if we do not crush their hopes in relation to the States. There can be no doubt that all their attempts to procure abolition in the District, are, that it may constitute a foundation for their general scheme. They regard it as an entering wedge by which they may carry on their operations afterwards to an indefinite extent. Give them this District as a lever, and they will never cease until they bring this Government to act upon the States. I would therefore cut off all their hopes at once, as regards the States by saying to them, plainly and distinctly, that this Government possesses no power whatever by which they could be aided in their views. Satisfy them that they have no hope in relation to the States, and they will soon cease to trouble us in relation to the District. But, "to make assurance doubly sure," I would also extinguish their hopes as regards the District. I would meet them at every point, and put them down on all. I would say to them, that, so far from obtaining the aid of this Government in their designs upon the States, they shall never be permitted even to obtain a foothold here. They shall never be permitted to use this District for the purpose of convulsion and disunion. And surely, Mr. Speaker, if any thing on earth can repress the spirit

---

[S]o far from obtaining the aid of this Government in their designs upon the States, they shall never be permitted even to obtain a foothold here. They shall never be permitted to use this District for the purpose of convulsion and disunion. — Henry L. Pinckney

---

of incendiary agitation, such proceedings on the part of this House must produce that effect. And not only that, sir; it will not only tend, as I firmly believe, to check and repress the fanatics, but, what is still more important, it will tend, powerfully and irresistibly, to produce a high-toned, generous patriotism, an enlarged, magnanimous, American spirit, in the great body of the non-slaveholding States, eminently favorable to the cause of peace and to the constitutional rights and interest of the southern States. Only let this House adopt the course indicated in the resolutions I have offered, and my life upon it they will be sustained by every honest heart, by every true American patriot, in every non-slaveholding State in this great republic. Now, sir, this is the very result I desire to produce. The battle of abolition is to be fought, not at the South, but in the non-slaveholding States. The people of the non-slaveholding States are divided into two classes — the incendiary fanatics, who are plotting our destruction and the destruction of this Union; and the great body of the people, who respect the rights and feelings of their southern brethren, and are doing all that they can to put the fanatics down. What, then, is our policy? To make a new issue upon abstract points; to change the whole aspect of the question, by contending against the right of petition, and thus increase abolition, and drive our supporters from the field. No, sir, I would strengthen our friends, not weaken them. I would let them fight the abolitionists in their own way, and not hamper or trammel them, by making new contests, or creating new difficulties of any kind whatever. I do firmly and conscientiously believe that, if this course is adopted, they will succeed in putting the fanatics down, and putting an end to this most unnatural war. These, then, are my motives. These are my objects. I go for the suppression of abolition, I go to maintain the just rights of the South without invading the rights of others. I go to obtain a direct vote upon the whole subject of the abolition of slavery, without being involved in consti-

tutional contests upon any other points. In one word, I go for a decisive settlement of this question in the manner that I honestly think will best maintain the rights of the South and the peace and perpetuity of this Union. And as I do sincerely believe that the adoption of my resolutions, accompanied by a firm but temperate report, will produce these blessed results, so I shall esteem myself truly happy if I shall be the humble instrument of giving effectual and permanent repose to the South, (to which I am attached by every tie that can bind the heart of man to his natural soil,) and also accomplish the great object of placing this Union once more upon a firm, and solid, and immoveable foundation.

Source: *Register of Debates in Congress,* 24th Cong., 1st sess., February 8, 1836 (Washington: Gales and Seaton, 1836), 12:2491–2495.

REPRESENTATIVE JOHN QUINCY ADAMS OPPOSES THE HOUSE GAG RULE

JANUARY 22, 1840

Mr. ADAMS offered the following:

Resolved. That the following be added to the standing rules of the House to be numbered the 21st:

"Every petition presented by the Speaker, or by any other member, with a brief verbal statement of its contents, shall be received, unless objection be made of its reception for special reason; and whenever objections shall be made to the reception of a petition, the name of the member objecting and the reason of the objection shall be entered upon the *Journal*. The question in every such case shall be, Shall the petition be rejected? And no petition shall be rejected but by the majority of the members present."

Mr. ADAMS said it was his intention to detain the House but for a short period; indeed, he had been much inclined to suffer the question on the resolution, which after many attempts he had at length succeeded in presenting to the House, to be taken without debate. The proposition (said Mr. A.) is a very simple one, and relates to the reception of petitions presented to this House on any and all subjects. It is not confined to petitions praying for the abolition of slavery and the slave trade in the District of Columbia, not to any other class of petitions commonly known by the name of abolition petitions, a term exceedingly indefinite in itself, and in regard to which the House has had a ten days' debate without coming to any understanding as to what is meant by it. I shall not

now enter upon that subject at all, nor shall I discuss the subject of abolition, nor of slavery, nor of the slave trade in any form. If I were to do so I would think it necessary to enlarge the field very much. As it is, a vast amount of time has been expired without coming to an issue of any consequence whatever to this House or to the country. I say this because, on the propositions relating to memorials on abolition, the classes of these memorials are so very imperfectly defined that no man in this House knows what memorials have been received and what would be rejected under any of the resolutions which have been offered. To exemplify, the first call of these memorials pray for abolition of slavery and of the slave trade in the District of Columbia.

Well, gentlemen have wasted their eloquence in making constitutional objections against the reception of such memorials by this House, contending that Congress has no power to legislate on that subject. Admit that (which I do not,) but supposing it is a valid reason for the rejection of all petitions on this subject, there is another class which pray for the abolition of slavery and of the slave trade in the Territory of Florida. What becomes of all these constitutional objections when the question relates to the Territories? That case presents a different question, and must be met by a different argument. Supposing, however, both these classes of memorials to be included in your resolution, there is still another class, which pray that no new State shall be admitted into the Union whose constitution tolerates the existence of slavery. Not one of the arguments which we have supposed valid against the other classes of petitions applies to this class; and supposing you to exclude all which relate to slavery in this District or in the Territory, that does not exclude these, and as soon as one of them shall be prevented, the whole subject of slavery and of the slave trade will be as completely open to discussion as it would have been on the other classes of memorials. A fourth class relates to the admission of the Territory of Florida as a slave State. Congress has the constitutional power to admit or not to admit; the question then arises, shall Florida be received or not received? And here again is the whole subject open to discussion. I shall not enter on the discussion, but I say that these memorials throw the whole subject open as much as any of those which have been specified in the resolution under discussion.

But, besides all these, there is another, and a distinct class of petitions, which pray for the establishment of diplomatic relations with the republic of Hayti. I do not believe that it is in the mind of the gentleman of this House to raise a constitutional question on this subject. It is indisputably in the power of Congress to act on such a prayer; and when such a memorial shall be brought up here, the whole subject of slavery and of the slave trade is as fully open for discussion as it could have been a petition praying for the abolition of slavery in the District. I will not go further; but I put it to the gentlemen who complain of the waste of time, and of the agitation in the country, occasioned by the reception of abolition memorials, to inquire of themselves, and answer to themselves, how long they think that the discussion of slavery and of the slave trade can be excluded from this House? I ask whether they expect to suppress that discussion here by refusing to receive petitions for the abolition of slavery in the District of Columbia? Supposing a resolution passes that petitions on this specific subject shall be excluded, you do not get rid of the general subject; it goes further. I ask again, is there here any individual who has the slightest fear of any member rising in his place and offering a resolution to abolish slavery and the slave trade in the District of Columbia? I wish they would allow it to be done, that they may see what number of votes can be obtained in support of such a proposition. I say this in kindness to the South; if their object is to put down petitions of that character, I do in my conscience believe that the first thing they should do is admit them to be presented. If, out of the whole two hundred and forty votes, such a measure receives ten I shall be surprised. As to myself, I have long professed my belief on the subject. From the time I first entered this House, (which is now, I think, between eight and nine years,) I have always declared that I am not prepared for the immediate abolition of slavery in the District; and since the adjournment of the last Congress I have explicitly and publicly avowed my sentiments on that matter to the very petitioners who pray for it, and who sent me their memorials to be presented here. With the exception of my friend from Vermont, over the way, [Mr. SLADE,] who, I am obliged to believe, is prepared for such a measure, I do not know another gentleman in this House who I think would go for it. There may be many others; I do not say there are not; but I do not myself know of one, nor do I believe that ten votes could be got for such a proposition in the House. And even my friend from Vermont himself, whose able argument against slavery, delivered last week, was not as much attended to in this House as it will be by this nation — even he, who, I believe, once offered to introduce a bill for the subject, declared to us that the argument of the Abolitionists generally attributed far more importance to the measure than he himself did. I take it for granted that he would vote for such a measure; but I think it at the same time extremely likely that, when the House came to be divided, he would find himself in the "glorious majority of one."

I say again to gentlemen of the South, if you want peace, if your object is to allay agitation, if you want to see what is the real opinion of the Representatives of the North, be they Whigs or Administration men, offer yourselves, or get some one else to offer, a resolution for the immediate abolition of slavery in this District, and call the yeas and nays upon it; then you will understand what is our feeling on that subject, and what is the feeling of our constituents. As matters now stand, we often hear one of the gentlemen of the South speak our own opinions more nearly than anyone from the North. I believe that this is true in most cases. But what I now say is that you cannot suppress a discussion on slavery by suppressing petitions for its abolition in this District; and what I say of one class of petitions, I say of them all. I have now in my drawer not less than a hundred and fifty of them, waiting till we shall be allowed an opportunity to present them to the

---

I put it to the gentlemen who complain of the waste of time, and of the agitation in the country, occasioned by the reception of abolition memorials, to inquire of themselves, and answer to themselves, how long they think that the discussion of slavery and of the slave trade can be excluded from this House?
— John Quincy Adams

House; and I will here say that I think these petitioners have ground to inquire of this House how it happened that, while the reception of these petitions is preeminently and most emphatically the business of this House, we have been fifty days in session, and yet the Representatives from only two States have been permitted to present the petitions of their constituents. I have petitions of great importance on other subjects entirely distinct from abolition, which I am waiting to present here; but I cannot because this question is now brought up, and the House is openly called upon to suppress the right of petition; and we are here debating, from day to day, about excluding one petty class of petitions relating to an object from which none would vote if they were received. I hope to be discharged from the responsibility of consuming the time of the House on such a matter as this. I have been charged with it. The House has been heretofore debating for weeks, and I have been mostly unjustly charged with it all; but I cannot be charged with it now. I say to this House and to this nation that I have no part in the blame.

★ ★ ★ ★

I shall not now enter on the great and wide question of slavery or the slave trade in any State, District, Territory, dominion, or nation on the face of the globe. The subject is too large. I hope the day will come when I shall have an opportunity of delivering my opinions on that whole subject; but I assure gentlemen that I shall not attempt it on a little petty resolution about the reception of petitions. There are ways enough to get at the subject. I could bring it into this House to-morrow. I can tell gentlemen that it will come upon this House in forms very different from this; and to give the House a piece of my mind, I think it ought to have been before this House already. It should have formed one of the topics of the President's message. Here are at this moment four States of this Union on the verge of civil war, avowedly on this very subject; and we see no more mention of it in the message than if those States were in the moon. Do gentlemen from Virginia, from New York, from Georgia, from Maine, from New Hampshire, expect that this question is not to come before Congress; that it will not be discussed here in all its breadth and length and depth? Very well, gentlemen, go on, to sleep and to slumber; but remember you will be waked from your sleep by voices more than from the dead. I say again, to gentlemen of the North, and gentlemen of the South, you cannot keep that discussion out of this House; and you will soon give up trying to do so by passing small resolutions about abolition petitions.

★ ★ ★ ★

As a justification for my extreme anxiety on the subject of the right of petition, I will ask attention of the House to the order of business which these rules establish. What is it? The very first business in order is to receive petitions; and this regulation dates from the beginning of the Government. There is a reason for it. What is a Government instituted for, but to redress the grievances of the people? What is the object of all government? What are we here for? What is the Constitution

for? Why does Congress meet every year, if not for redress of grievances? All else is of subordinate importance. The appropriation bills are very important for the conducting of the Government, and for performing its duties of justice to the people. But what else have we to do but redress grievances? It is therefore just and reasonable that the first thing the House does should be to inquire what grievances are to be redressed. But how can we know this unless the people tell us? The right of petition, therefore, is essential to the very existence of government; it is the right of the people over the Government; it is their right, and they may not be deprived of it.

★ ★ ★ ★

If this House, on the force of these precedents, is justified in the principle that it may reject abolition petitions, I ask if the same precedent is not much more powerful, and still more in point, if applied to petitions which relate to the tariff? The parallel would then run on all fours. Then the precedent of the House Commons would be of authority. If it has any force in the one class of petitions; it has still more in relation to the other. I ask gentlemen from the North, and gentlemen from the South, are you ready to reject petitions against duties imposed for the revenue? The rule includes the resolutions of State Legislatures. I repeat, that if you can reject abolition memorials because the House of Commons rejects memorials against taxes, you can reject petitions against all taxation; and the president is of stronger authority. If you can do it in relation to one class, you can do it in relation to any other class; and if you can do it in relation to the petitions of whole classes of individuals, you can do it to the petition of any one individual. Nay, I think I heard it expressly argued here that the right to petition is not infringed on when you reject a single petition, because the Constitution says that the people have a right to "assemble" to petition Congress for a redress of grievances. So there must be an assembly of the people, or else the reject of their petitions is not unconstitutional! I say that argument will apply precisely. If once you admit the principle that the House has a discretionary power to reject petitions, the question will at last be made here, whether the petitioner is of the politics of the majority or of the minority. That will be the next step; and when that step is taken, what will have become of the right to petition?

★ ★ ★ ★

When you assume the right of petition, does not that right, in all sound logic and in all moral principle carry with it the duty to receive, hear, and, consider petitions? If not, then is the guarantee of that right the greatest of mockery? This House says to an American citizen, "O, yes, you have certainly the right to petition; but I will neither read, hear, nor consider your petition when you send it." Sir, what difference is there between saying this and telling the man at once, "You have not the right to petition us?" You only cheat the man by a false pretense, while you give him a right which you take care shall be of no avail. This is the objection I have to all resolutions which refuse the hearing of petitions. This House should speak the language of a great and generous nation; it should deal with the people in a fair, open, and candid way; and it is not so dealing to say to them, "We will receive your petitions, but we will not consider them." If you refuse to hear and consider, as well as receive, you do in substance deny the right to petition. Sir, decent language will not express what you do; it is conduct that would be unworthy of a single individual, and is vastly more so of the Representatives of this great and mighty nation.

I have already stated the substance of another objection to the resolution, namely, that it will not answer its purpose. If you succeed in rejecting all these memorials you have not thereby got rid of the question. You will have the question of slavery and of abolition forced upon you every day; you cannot keep it out of the House; and if you persevere you will before you are aware of it have a civil war raging, while you are excluding the only means that can put an end to it.

★ ★ ★ ★

It will be observed that [my] resolution, if adopted does not specify in what manner the petitions shall be treated after they are received. I say this by way of answering a large portion of the gentlemen on the other side who wasted a vast deal of argument by putting supposed cases of the presentation of absurd and unconstitutional petitions. I do not deny the right of the House to refuse to receive a petition when it is first presented, but I wish all petitions to be received unless their reception is specifically objected to. What shall be done with them afterwards is for the House to determine. What I want to settle is the principle that the right of petition includes within it the right of having a petition received, unless special objection exists against it; and to show whether this is the case I require the name of the person objecting and the reasons of the objection to be entered on the Journals of the House. Now it is possible for the House to adopt this resolution, and yet pass another that the petitions, when received, shall neither be read nor considered. But if the House shall adopt this resolution I confess that it is my impression that there is not a man in the House who will be willing to record as the ground of his objection to its being received that it is an abolition petition. There may be some, there may be many; but I believe that, if the question of reception is put to the House, they cannot get a majority to vote against it.

I do not believe that there is a man here who is willing to have such a thing go upon the record in a single case; and if there is — there may be many, for aught I know — but if there is, put the question to the decision of the House, and see how the majority will do. I do not believe that you can get a majority for it, if there is a man who would move it; and for

this reason: by receiving a petition you decide nothing, and I was willing to put upon the record my acknowledgment of the right of the House to reject petitions. I fully and freely admit it; but I say it must be done for a special reason, which must be assigned on the *Journal* to go before the world, before posterity; and if there is a gentleman here who would not scruple at putting his name to such an objection on the *Journal*, I will answer for it that in twenty years hence he and his children would blush to see his name with such an addition to it, come he from the North or the South, or where he may. If you adopt my resolution, you only settle the principle that all petitions shall be received, unless a special objection, which is to be entered on the *Journal*, shall be made, and then that there shall be a special vote upon it by the House. Rely upon it that, if this resolution passes, you will hear no more objections, not only to the reception of the petition, but to the reference; to the hearing of it; to considering it, which is as much the duty of the House as to receive it. I am willing to rest it upon this. I am willing to admit the right of the House to refuse to receive, in any case in which a majority of the House is willing that the reason for rejecting the petition shall go upon the Journal.

Source: *Congressional Globe*, 26th Cong., 1st sess., January 22, 1840 (Washington: Blair and Rives, 1847), appendix, 8:761–764.

Notes

1. 5 Stat. 87, sec. 32 (July 2, 1836); David C. Frederick, "John Quincy Adams, Slavery, and the Disappearance of the Right of Petition," *Law and History Review* (Spring 1991), 9:121; and Susan Wyly-Jones, "The Antiabolitionist Panic: Slavery, Abolition, and Politics in the South, 1835–1844," PhD diss., Harvard University, April 2000, 209–263, 271–288.

2. *Register of Debates in Congress*, 24th Cong., 1st sess., (February 4, 1836), 12:2482–2483; (February 8, 1836), 12:2491–2502.

3. Quotes are found in William Lee Miller, *Arguing About Slavery: The Great Battle in the United States Congress* (New York: Knopf, 1996), 9; *Register of Debates in Congress*, 24th Cong., 1st sess., (February 1, 1836), 12:2457; (May 26, 1836), 12:4050–4054.

4. George C. Rable, "Slavery Politics, and the South: The Gag Rule as a Case Study," *Capitol Studies*, (Fall 1975), 3:77–80; Wyly-Jones, "The Antiabolitionist Panic," 263–271.

5. *Congressional Globe*, 26th Cong., 1st sess., (January 28, 1840), 8:150–151. See also Miller, *Arguing About Slavery*, 214–215; Wyly-Jones, "The Antiabolitionist Panic," 291–359, 379.

6. *Register of Debates in Congress*, 24th Cong., 1st sess., (May 25, 1836), 12:4047; (May 26, 1836), 12:4050–4054; Richard P. Kollen, "The House Gag Rule Debate: The Wedge Dividing North and South," *Magazine of History* (Summer 1998), 12:56. See also Leonard L. Richards, *The Life and Times of Congressman John Quincy Adams* (New York: Oxford University Press, 1986), 115–125.

7. Quote is found in Robert P. Ludlum, "The Antislavery 'Gag Rule': History and Argument," *Journal of Negro History,* (April 1941), 26:208. See also, ibid., 209–213; and Dwight Lowell Dumond, *Antislavery: The Crusade for Freedom in America* (Ann Arbor: University of Michigan Press, 1961), 245–246.

8. Ludlum, "The Antislavery 'Gag Rule': History and Argument," 221; Bennett Champ Clark, *John Quincy Adams: "Old Man Eloquent"* (Boston: Little, Brown, 1932), 407; Charles Francis Adams, ed., *Memoirs of John Quincy Adams,* 12 vols. (Philadelphia: J. B. Lippincott, 1874–1877), 12:115–116. For summaries of the eight-year debate over the gag rule, see Ludlum, "The Antislavery 'Gag Rule': History and Argument," 203–243; Rable, "Slavery Politics, and the South," 69–86.

9. Ludlum, "The Antislavery 'Gag Rule': History and Argument," 243.

10. Frederick, "John Quincy Adams, Slavery, and the Disappearance of the Right of Petition," 113–114, 119.

Wilmot Proviso
✳ 1846–1847 ✳

On April 12, 1844, following considerable negotiation, Secretary of State John C. Calhoun concluded a treaty of annexation with the Republic of Texas. Under its terms, the public lands of Texas were ceded to the United States; the United States assumed up to a maximum of $10 million in Texas debt; and the citizens of Texas were extended "all the rights, privileges, and immunities, of citizens of the United States." While the treaty was under consideration, President John Tyler promised to use U.S. naval and military forces to protect Texas against a possible attack by Mexico.

The treaty, Tyler stressed in submitting it to the Senate for ratification, was in the interest of the entire nation, and would add a vast area of fertile lands, stimulate commerce, and afford protection to the Southern states. Former president Andrew Jackson, as well as a number of proslavery politicians, spoke out in favor of annexation while former president Martin Van Buren, former senator Henry Clay, W-Ky., and others denounced it. Many Northerners saw the acquisition as a Southern plot to spread slavery, a view strengthened by an indiscrete note Secretary Calhoun sent to the British minister in Washington strongly defending slavery. On June 8, the Senate soundly rejected annexation, 35–16.[1]

After Congress adjourned that summer, the debate over Texas shifted to the 1844 presidential campaign. James K. Polk, the Democratic candidate, ran on an expansionist platform that called for the acquisition of Texas. The Whig platform, upon which standard bearer Henry Clay campaigned, made no reference to Texas. Incumbent John Tyler, the first president to not run for reelection, withdrew as the nominee of the Tyler Democrats when it became clear he could not win. In a narrow victory, Polk captured the popular vote 1,339,494 to 1,300,004. James B. Birney, the Liberty Party antislavery candidate, received 62,130 votes. Polk garnered 170 electoral votes to Clay's 105.

In his final annual message that December, President Tyler urged Congress to use a joint resolution, requiring a simple majority of both houses, to acquire Texas, thereby obviating

the necessity of the two-thirds Senate vote required for ratification. An annexation resolution was approved in late February 1845, and on March 1, three days before the presidential mantle passed to Polk, Tyler signed it. The resolution, unlike the annexation treaty, called for Texas to enter the Union as a state rather than a territory. Within weeks, Mexico severed diplomatic relations with the United States and began increasing its military forces.[2]

That December, President Polk sent Congress a special message announcing that Texas had accepted the proposed terms for statehood, and on December 29 the Lone Star State was officially admitted to the Union. During the next several months, relations between Mexico and the United States continued to deteriorate. By the evening of May 9, 1846, news reached Washington that Mexican troops had crossed the Rio Grande River, killing eleven, wounding five, and capturing forty-seven American soldiers; Polk and his Cabinet were already discussing the propriety of asking for a war declaration. Two days later, Congress concurred and approved a $10 million appropriation to support the effort. Several factors contributed to the outbreak of hostilities — disagreement over the southwestern boundary of Texas; outstanding American claims against Mexico; Mexican outrage over the loss of Texas; difficulties in negotiating with Mexico; and Polk's determination to purchase the Mexican province of California or, if necessary, use force to obtain it.[3] The conflict continued until the fall of 1847. Under the Treaty of Guadalupe Hidalgo, which formally ended the war, Mexico relinquished all claims to Texas above the Rio Grande River and ceded New Mexico and California to the United States. The acquired territory included the present states of Arizona, California, and Nevada, and parts of Colorado, New Mexico, and Wyoming.

While peace was being secured both on the battlefield and among diplomats, Congress engaged in a historic debate over what America should look like politically once the fighting ceased. Soon after the outbreak of hostilities, President Polk asked Congress for $2 million to expedite peace negotiations with Mexico and, perhaps unwittingly, added the acquisition

President Zachary Taylor is depicted atop a scale on which he attempts to balance Northern and Southern interests on slavery in 1850. The left of the scale, labeled "Wilmot Proviso," depicts Northern interests, while the right depicts "Southern Rights." The proviso contributed to disputes culminating in the Civil War.

Source: Library of Congress.

of new territory to the bitter sectional debate over the expansion of slavery. For the preceding decade, Congress had fought endlessly over abolitionist petitions, slavery in the District of Columbia, and the annexation of Texas, and Northern Democrats had become increasingly more resentful of Southern dominance of their party and certain policies resulting from that domination. Against this backdrop, on August 8, 1846, Rep. David Wilmot, D-Penn., offered a rider to the funding resolution that called for slavery to be prohibited in any territory acquired from Mexico.

During the ensuing debate, Pro-Polk and Southern Democrats attempted to limit the resolution's applicability to the region north of the 36° 30′ parallel north (the Missouri Compromise line), but were unsuccessful, 89–54. Northern Democrats and Northern Whigs who were critical of what they considered to be Polk's pro-Southern policies joined together to pass the Wilmot amendment 83–64, and they approved the funding bill, as amended, 85–80. Those opposed to the amendment saw it as "an attempt to rob them of the anticipated fruits of the Mexican War and an indirect yet dan-

gerous attack on slavery itself. The dissolution of party lines on this issue presaged the eventual breakup of the Union."[4] A subsequent filibuster by Southern, antislavery senators prevented the Senate from voting on the amendment before the Twenty-ninth Congress adjourned.

When the peace negotiations bill (now $3 million) was reconsidered early in 1847, the House again attached the Wilmot Proviso. This time the Senate refused to even consider the appropriation until it was stricken. The opposition leader, Sen. John C. Calhoun, D-S.C., argued that Congress had no right to bar slavery from any territory. Territories, he reasoned, were the common property of all the states, and Congress lacked the authority to prevent individuals from taking their property into a territory. Therefore, slavery was legal in all the territories. If this principle was not upheld, the balance between free and slave states would be destroyed. Later in 1847, Sen. Lewis Cass, D-Mich., unsuccessfully sought to settle the issue by "popular sovereignty" — proposing that the settlers decide whether their territory would be free or slave.[5]

When both Democrats and Whigs in the 1848 presidential election essentially sidestepped the question of slavery in the territories, opponents of extension organized the Free-Soil Party. This party enjoyed some success before it ultimately disbanded. Its remnants were absorbed by the new formed Republican Party in 1854. Six years later, Republican Abraham Lincoln of Illinois was elected president on a platform that promised to fulfill the goal of the proviso and abolish slavery in the territories. The Wilmot Proviso, as it came to be called, reflected the political realities of the day. Northern Democrats such as Wilmot were fearful of allowing the expansion of slavery into the territories. What President Polk apparently failed to fully grasp, some scholars have contended, was that real debate was over whether slave owners, or antislave forces, would control the vast amount of new territory the United States would gain and would, in time, control the government there. Instead, Polk saw the proviso as purely an effort to embarrass him, since he and many others felt slavery would not prove practicable in the unproductive areas of northern Mexico.[6]

"If any event in American history can be singled out as the beginning of a path which led almost inevitably to sectional controversy and civil war," historian Eric Foner has written, "it was the introduction of the Wilmot Proviso." It "threw the issue of slavery into the center of the political arena — a place it would retain for twenty years." The proviso, Foner contends, "was a defensive, not an aggressive move by" Northern congressmen "to protect themselves in the face of growing antislavery sentiment in their constituents.… In attempting to assure their constituents that the Mexican War was not being waged to spread slavery, they stumbled upon a principle — the non-extension of slavery — which would shape the politics of two decades, make a sectional hero of previously undistinguished Wilmot," win him election to the Senate, and lead all but one of eight antislavery Democratic congressmen who worked on the proviso into the Republican Party.[7]

Southerners saw slaves as property and felt the Constitution protected their rights to property, thereby allowing owners to take slaves wherever they wished. This led them to oppose any attempt to bar slavery while the country was expanding and provoked Southern ideologues like Calhoun into formulating a Southern position that became more dogmatic and entrenched over time. While the Southern-dominated Senate was able to block the proviso, it was unable to halt the growing sectional rift between the North and South. The Compromise of 1850 expressly repudiated the proviso, and the Supreme Court declared its content unconstitutional in the *Dred Scott* decision (19 Howard 393 (1857)). "Judging by the furor it created," however, "the issue of slavery in the territories was one of the most significant in American history." Chaplain W. Morrison has noted that "not only did it give birth to the only major political party to emerge in the United States since the time of Andrew Jackson, the struggles it engendered culminated in southern secession and civil war."[8]

REPRESENTATIVE DAVID WILMOT DEFENDS HIS PROVISO

FEBRUARY 8, 1847

Sir, it will be recollected by all present, that, at the last session of Congress, an amendment was moved by me to a bill of the same character as this, in the form of a proviso, by which slavery should be excluded from any territory that might subsequently be acquired by the United States from the republic of Mexico.

Sir, on that occasion, that proviso was sustained by a very decided majority of this House. Nay, sir, more it was sustained, if I mistake not, by a majority of the Republican party on this floor. I am prepared, I think, to show that the entire South were then willing to acquiesce in what appeared to be, and, in so far as the action of this House was concerned, what was the legislative will and declaration of the Union on this subject. It passed this House. Sir, there were no threats of disunion sounded in our ears. It passed here and went to the Senate, and it was the judgment of the public, and of men well informed, that, had it not been defeated there for want of time, it would have passed that body and become the established law of the land. Sir, the charge was not then made upon me, nor upon those who acted with me, of having, by the introduction of that proviso at an untimely period, defeated a measure deemed necessary by the President for the establishment of peace between this country and Mexico.... Upon these facts, I assert that the President was willing to take the money and the proviso together, and the South were prepared to abide by the judgement and will of the nation.

★ ★ ★ ★

I was aware that the proviso met with no favor from the South. I did not mean to declare that it did; and if the gentleman so understood me, I was misunderstood. I did not intend to say that the South was favorable in any way to the proviso which I offered. Her Representatives resisted it; manfully, boldly resisted it. But sir, it *was passed*. There was then no cry that the Union was to be severed in consequence. The South, like brave men defeated, bowed to the voice and judgement of the nation. No, sir, no cry of disunion then. Why now? The hesitation and the wavering of northern men on the question has encouraged the South to assume a bolder attitude. This cry of disunion proceeds from no resolve of the South. It comes, sir, from the cowardice of the North. Why, in God's name, should the Union be dissolved for this cause? … If this were a question of compromise, I would yield much. Were it a question of this character, I would go as far as any man. But it is no question for compromise or concession. It is a question of naked and abstract right; and, in the language of my colleague from the Erie district, [Mr. THOMPSON,] sooner shall this right shoulder be drawn from its socket, than I will yield one jot or tittle of ground upon which I stand. No concessions, sir, no compromise. What, I repeat, do we ask? That free territory shall remain free. We demand the neutrality of this Government on the question of slavery.

But, sir, the issue now presented is not whether slavery shall exist unmolested where it now is, but whether it shall be carried to new and distant regions, now free, where the footprint of a slave cannot be found. This, sir, is the issue. Upon it I take my stand, and from it I cannot be frightened or driven by idle charges of abolitionism. I ask not that slavery be abolished. I demand that this Government preserve the integrity of *free territory* against the aggressions of slavery — against its wrongful usurpations. Sir, I was in favor of the annexation of Texas. I supported it with my whole influence

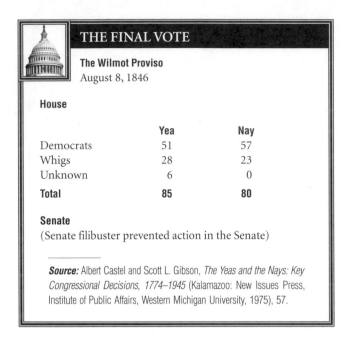

and strength. I was willing to take Texas as she was. I sought not to change the character of her institutions, Slavery existed in Texas — planted there, it is true, in defiance of law; still it existed.

★ ★ ★ ★

But, sir, we are told, that the joint blood and treasure of the whole country being expended in this acquisition, therefore it should be divided, and slavery allowed to take its share. Sir, the South has her share already; the instalment for slavery was paid in advance. We are fighting this war for Texas and for the South. I affirm it — every intelligent man knows it — Texas is the primary cause of this war. For this, sir, northern treasure is being exhausted, and northern blood poured out upon the plains of Mexico. We are fighting this war cheerfully, not reluctantly — cheerfully fighting this war for Texas; and yet we seek not to change the character of her institutions. Sir, the whole history of the question is a history of concessions on the part of the North. The money of the North was expended for the purchase of Louisiana, two-thirds of which was given to slavery. Again, in the purchase of Florida, did slavery gain new acquisitions. Slavery acquired an empire in the acquisition of Texas. Three slave States have been admitted out of the Louisiana purchase. The slave State of Florida has been received into the Union; and Texas annexed, with the privilege of making five States out of her territory. What has the North obtained from these vast acquisitions, purchased by the joint treasure and defended by the common blood of the Union? One State, sir, — one: young Iowa, just admitted into the Union, and not yet represented on the floor of the Senate. This, sir, is a history of our acquisitions since we became a nation. A history of northern concession — of southern triumphs.

Now, sir, we are told that California is ours; that New Mexico is ours — won by the valor of our arms. They are free. Shall they remain free? Shall these fair provinces be the inheritance and homes of the white labor of freemen or the black labor of slaves? This, sir, is the issue — this the question. The North has the right, and her representatives here have the power. Shall the right prevail? I fear not, sir. There is power more potent than the right. These fair provisions are ours — so held, and so regarded by the Administration. But of this I shall speak more fully hereafter. All we ask is, that their character be preserved. They are now free. It is a general principle of the law of nations, that in conquered or acquired territories, all laws therein existing, not inconsistent with its new allegiance, shall remain in force until altered or repealed.

★ ★ ★ ★

Sir, it has been objected to this measure that it was brought forward at an untimely period. An attempt has been made to cast both ridicule and reproach upon it. It is said that we are already quarrelling about territory which does not belong to us; that it will be in time to agitate this question when the country shall be acquired. Sir, I affirm that now is the time, the only time. To hesitate at such a crisis is to surrender the whole ground; to falter is to betray.

Sir, what is the policy of the Administration? It is fully disclosed; it is not disguised.... It is to require indemnity in territory. Peace is desired, eminently desired by the Administration and its friends; but with peace must come indemnity and territory.

★ ★ ★ ★

My amendment can interfere with the war only in two respects: either by frustrating its objectives, or weakening its support. The first it does not do, unless slavery is its objective; nor the second, unless for this cause the South are driven from its support. If the South are so driven, then it will be apparent to all that, on the part of the South, the war was prosecuted for the extension of slavery, and not the vindication of the rights and honor of the country. This is my

> *The treasure and blood of the North will not be poured out in waging a war for the propagation of slavery over the North American continent.* — David Wilmot

ground. If the war is not for slavery, then I am deceived as to it objects. The treasure and blood of the North will not be poured out in waging a war for the propagation of slavery over the North American continent. I trust that such is not its object; yet the attitude of the South on this question is susceptible of no other construction.

★ ★ ★ ★

The North has yielded until there is no more to give up. We have gone on, making one acquisition after another, until we have acquired and brought into the Union every inch of slave territory that was to be found upon this continent. Now, sir, we have passed beyond the boundaries of slavery and reached free soil.

★ ★ ★ ★

I have said before, that I have no morbid sympathies upon the subject of slavery; still I regard it as a great social and

political evil — a blight and deadly mildew upon any country or State in which it exists. I regard it as the most difficult and dangerous problem which we will have to work out in this free Government.

★ ★ ★ ★

As a friend of the Union, as a lover of my country, and in no spirit of hostility to the South, I offer my amendment. Viewing slavery as I do, I must resist its further extension and propagation on the North American continent. It is an evil, the magnitude and end of which, no man can see.

Source: *Congressional Globe,* 29th Cong., 2nd sess., February 8, 1847, (Washington: Blair and Rives, 1847), appendix, 16:314–318.

SENATOR JOHN C. CALHOUN OPPOSES WILMOT PROVISO

FEBRUARY 19, 1847

Mr. President, I rise to offer a set of resolutions in reference to the various resolutions from the State Legislatures upon the subject of what they call the extension of slavery, and the proviso attached to the House bill, called the three million bill. What I propose before I send my resolutions to the table, is to make a few explanatory remarks.

Mr. President, it was solemnly asserted on this floor, some time ago, that all parties in the non-slave States had come to a fixed and solemn determination upon two propositions. One was, that there should be no further admission of any States into this Union which permitted by their constitution the existence of slavery; and the other was, that slavery shall not hereafter exist in any of the Territories of the United States; the effect of which would be to give to the non-slaveholding States the monopoly of the public domain, to the entire exclusion of the slaveholding States. Since that declaration was made, Mr. President, we have abundant proof that there was a satisfactory foundation for it.... But we need not go beyond the walls of Congress. The subject has been agitated in the other House, and they have sent you up a bill "prohibiting the extension of slavery" (using their own language) "to any territory which may be acquired by the United States hereafter." At the same time, two resolutions which have been moved to extend the compromise line from the Rocky Mountains to the Pacific, during the present session, have been rejected by a decided majority.

Sir, there is no mistaking the signs of the times; and it is high time that the southern States, the slaveholding States, should inquire what is now their relative strength in this Union, and what it will be if this determination should be carried into effect hereafter. Sir, already we are in a minority — I use the word "we," for brevity sake — already we are in a minority in the other House, in the electoral college, and, I may say, in every department of this Government, except at present in the Senate of the United States: there, for the present, we have an equality. Of the twenty-eight States, fourteen are non-slaveholding and fourteen are slaveholding, counting Delaware, which is doubtful, as one of the non-slaveholding States. But this equality of strength exists only in the Senate.... There are two hundred and twenty-eight representatives, including Iowa, which is already represented there. Of these, one hundred and thirty-eight are from the non-slaveholding States and ninety from what are called the slave States, giving a majority in the aggregate to the former forty-eight. In the electoral college there are one hundred and sixty-eight votes belonging to the non-slaveholding States, and one hundred and eighteen to the slaveholding, giving a majority of fifty to the non-slaveholding.

We, Mr. President, have at present time only one position in the Government, by which we may make any resistance to this aggressive policy which has been declared against the South, or any, other than the non-slaveholding States may choose to take. And this equality in this body is of the most transient character.... sir, if this aggressive policy be followed — if the determination of the non-slaveholding States is to be adhered to hereafter, and we are to be entirely excluded from the territories which we already possess, or may possess — if this is to be the fixed policy of the Government, I ask, what will be our situation hereafter?

★ ★ ★ ★

Sir, if this state of things is to go on; if this determination, so solemnly made, is to be persisted in — where shall we stand, as far as this Federal Government of ours is concerned? We shall be at the entire mercy of the non-slaveholding States.

★ ★ ★ ★

Sir, can we find any hope by looking to the past? If we are to look to that — I will not go into the details — we will see from the beginning of this Government to the present day, as far as pecuniary resources are concerned — as far as the disbursement of revenue is involved, it will be found that we have been a portion of the community which has substantially supported this Government without receiving anything like a remuneration from it. But why look to the past — why should I go beyond this very measure itself? Why go beyond this determination on the part of the non-slaveholding States, that there shall be no further addition to the slaveholding States, to prove what our condition will be?

Sir, what is the entire amount of this policy? I will not say that it is so designed. I will not say from what cause it originated. I will not say whether blind fanaticism on one side, whether a hostile feeling to slavery entertained by many not fanatical on the other, has produced it; or whether it has been the work of men, who, looking to political power, have considered the agitation of this question as the most effectual mode of obtaining the spoils of Government. I look to the fact itself. It is a policy now openly avowed as one to be persisted in. It is a scheme, Mr. President, which aims to monopolize the powers of Government and to obtain sole possession of its territories.

Now, I ask, is there any remedy? Does the Constitution afford any remedy? And if not, is there any hope? These, Mr. President, are solemn questions — not only to us, but, let me say to gentlemen from non-slaveholding States: to them. Sir, the day that the balance between two sections of the country — the slaveholding States and the non-slaveholding States — is destroyed, is a day that will not be far removed from political revolution, anarchy, and wide-spread disaster. The balance of this system is in the slaveholding States. They are the conservative portion — always have been the conservative portion — always will be the conservative portion; and with a due balance on their part may, for generations to come, uphold this glorious Union of ours. But if this scheme should be carried out — if we are to be reduced to a handful

---

Sir, the day that the balance between two sections of the country — the slaveholding States and the non-slaveholding States — is destroyed, is a day that will not be far removed from political revolution, anarchy, and widespread disaster. — John C. Calhoun

---

— if we are to become a mere ball to play the presidential game with — to count something in the Baltimore caucus — if this is to be the result — wo, wo, I say, to this Union!

Now, sir, I put again the solemn question — does the Constitution afford any remedy? Is there any provision in it by which this aggressive policy — boldly avowed, as if perfectly consistent with our institutions and the safety and prosperity of the United States! — may be confronted? Is this a policy consistent with the Constitution? No, Mr. President, no! It is, in all its features, daringly opposed to the Constitution.

★ ★ ★ ★

How, then, do we stand in reference to this territorial question — this public domain of ours? Why, sir, what is it? It is the common property of the States of this Union. They are called "the territories of the United States." And what are the "United States" but the States united? Sir, these territories are the property of the States united; held jointly for their common use. And is it consistent with justice, is it consistent with equality, that any portion of the partners, outnumbering another portion, shall oust them of this common property of theirs — shall pass any law which shall proscribe the citizens of other portions of the Union from emigrating with their property to the Territories of the United States?

★ ★ ★ ★

Mr. President, not only is that proposition grossly inconsistent with the Constitution, but the other, which undertakes to say that no State shall be admitted into this Union which shall not prohibit by its constitution the existence of slaves, is equally a great outrage against the Constitution of the United States. Sir, I hold it to be a fundamental principle of our political system that the people have a right to establish what government they may think proper for themselves; that every State about to become a member of this Union has a right to form its own Government as it pleases; and that, in order to be admitted, there is but one qualification, and that is, that the government shall be republican.

★ ★ ★ ★

Mr. President the resolutions that I intend to offer present, in general terms, these great truths. I propose to have a vote upon them; and I trust there is no gentlemen here who will refuse it.

★ ★ ★ ★

Sir, here let me say a word as to the compromise line. I have always considered it as a great error — highly injurious to the South, because it surrendered, for mere temporary purposes, those high principles of the Constitution upon which I think we ought to stand.

★ ★ ★ ★

I see my way in the Constitution. I cannot in a compromise. A compromise is but an act of Congress. It may be overruled at any time. It gives us no security. But the Constitution is stable. It is a rock. On it we can stand. It is a firm and stable ground, on which we can better stand in opposition to fanaticism, than on the shifting sands of compromise.

Let us be done with compromises. Let us go back and stand upon the Constitution!

Well, sir, what if the decision of this body shall deny to us this high constitutional right, not the less clear because deduced from the whole body of the instrument and the nature of the subject to which it relates? What, then, is the question? I will not undertake to decide. It is a question for our constituents — the slaveholding States. A solemn and a great question. If the decision should be adverse, I trust and do believe that they will take under solemn consideration what they ought to do…. I am a southern man and a slaveholder; a kind and a merciful one, I trust — and none the worse for being a slaveholder. I say, for one, I would rather meet any extremity upon the earth than give up one inch of equality — one inch of what belongs to me as member of this great republic. What, acknowledge inferiority! The surrender of life is nothing to sinking down into acknowledged inferiority.

I have examined this subject largely — widely. I think I see the future if we do not stand up as we ought.

Source: *Congressional Globe,* 29th Cong., 2nd sess., February 19, 1847, (Washington: Blair and Rives, 1847), 16:453–455.

Notes

1. Randolph B. Campbell, *Gone to Texas: A History of the Lone Star State* (New York: Oxford University Press, 2003), 182–186; Justin H. Smith, *The Annexation of Texas* (New York: Baker and Taylor, 1911), 147–179, 188–189, 201–204; James D. Richardson, comp., *Compilation of Messages and Papers of the Presidents,* 20 vols. (New York: Bureau of National Literature, 1897–1927), 5:2160–2166, 2176–2180; *Congressional Globe,* 28th Cong., 1st sess., (June 8, 1844), 13:651–652.

2. Richardson, *Messages and Papers of the Presidents,* 5: 2193–2198; John L. Moore, Jon P. Preimesberger, and David R. Tarr, eds., *Congressional Quarterly's Guide to U.S. Elections,* 4th ed., 2 vols. (Washington, D.C.: CQ Press, 2001), 1:237–236, 446–447, 649, 732; *Congressional Globe,* 28th Cong., 2nd sess., (February 27, 1845), 14:358–363; (February 28, 1845), 14:371–372; and 5 Stat. 797–798.

3. Richardson, *Messages and Papers of the Presidents,* 5:2266; *Congressional Globe,* 29th Cong., 1st sess., (May 11, 1846), 15:791–795; (May 12, 1846), 15:795–804; 9 Stat. 9–10, 108; Campbell, *Gone to Texas: A History of the Lone Star State,* 188–189.

4. Quotes are found in Albert Castel and Scott L. Gibson, *The Yeas and the Nays: Key Congressional Decisions, 1774–1945* (Kalamazoo: New Issues Press, Institute of Public Affairs, Western Michigan University, 1975), 58. See also *Congressional Globe,* 29th Cong., 1st sess., (August 8, 1845), 15:1217–1218; (August 10, 1845), 15: 1220–1221.

5. Chaplain W. Morrison, *Democratic Politics and Sectionalism: The Wilmot Proviso Controversy* (Chapel Hill: University of North Carolina Press, 1967), 34–35, 90–91; Don E. Fehrenbacher, *Sectional Crisis and Southern Constitutionalism* (Baton Rouge: Louisiana State University Press, 1995), 25–44.

6. David M. Pletcher, *The Diplomacy of Annexation: Texas, Oregon, and the Mexican War* (Columbia: University of Missouri Press, 1973), 606–607; Sam W. Haynes, *James K. Polk and the Expansionist Impulse* (New York: Longman, 1997), 148–149.

7. Eric Foner, "The Wilmot Proviso Revisited," *Journal of American History* (September 1969), 56:262, 278–279.

8. Morrison, *Democratic Politics and Sectionalism: The Wilmot Proviso Controversy,* vii.

Compromise of 1850
✴ 1850 ✴

The Mexican Cession further intensified sectional conflict in the United States. With the acquisition of this new region, the South saw an opportunity to expand slavery beyond the limits established by the Missouri Compromise of 1820. Since that time, the balance between slave states and free states had been maintained. Texas, which already permitted slavery, was allowed to enter the Union in 1845 as a slave state. California, New Mexico, and Utah did not, however, have slavery, and when the United States prepared to take over these areas in 1846, there were conflicting suggestions on what should be done. When the discovery of gold in California precipitated the rush of one hundred thousand new settlers there in 1849, Congress faced an immediate need to resolve the crucial question of the status of the new territory before a government could be established there.

The North demanded that slavery be barred in America's new western holdings, while the South insisted on the right to expand the institution. A number of Northerners justified their opposition to adding new slave states by quoting statements by George Washington and Thomas Jefferson, as well as the Ordinance of 1787, which forbade the extension of slavery into the Northwest. Others suggested that the Missouri Compromise line of 36° 30′ be extended to the Pacific Ocean with free states north of it and slave states to the south. Still others proposed that the question be left to "popular sovereignty," with settlers entering the new territory being allowed to determine for themselves how to resolve the question. The dominant position among Southerners was that all of the lands acquired from Mexico be thrown open to slaveholders.

Once again Sen. Henry Clay, W-Ky, took the initiative to resolve the impasse, just as he had thirty years earlier during the debate over the spread of slavery that led to his Missouri Compromise. Early in 1850, shortly after returning to the Senate following a seven-year absence, Clay introduced a series of eight compromise resolutions he hoped would permanently end sectional strife and settle the major issues in dispute between the North and South. The resolutions com-

bined several previous proposals into one measure. For the next eight months, members of Congress, led by Clay, Sen. Daniel Webster, W-Mass., and Sen. John C. Calhoun, D-S.C., debated the complicated compromise. Clay's plan called for the admission of California as a free state; establishment of New Mexico and Utah as territories with no restrictions on slavery; resolution of the Texas–New Mexico boundary dispute by having the U.S. government assume Texas's pre-annexation debts; abolition of slave trade in the District of Columbia; adoption of a policy of noninterference with slavery in the District; enactment of a more stringent fugitive slave law; and a formal declaration by Congress that it had no authority over the interstate slave trade. With his proposed compromise, Clay, who was alarmed by Southern threats of disunion, seized for the Senate the initiative from President Zachary Taylor, who in his inaugural address revealed his plan for dividing the land acquired in the Mexican War into two free states — California and New Mexico.[1]

What emerged in response to Clay's resolutions was one of the most famous and eloquent debates in American history, which also proved to be the final performance of the great triumvirate of Clay, Calhoun, and Webster. Clay opened the debate on February 5, 1850, with a two-day defense of his measures. He appealed for mutual concessions and warned that secession was not a rightful remedy for Southern grievances. A sound compromise, he reasoned, should "settle all of the questions arising out of the subject of slavery," and "that neither of the two classes of States into which our country is unhappily divided should make a sacrifice of any great principle." He believed the series of resolutions he offered accomplished that objective. On March 4, Calhoun, who was dying of consumption, listened silently as Sen. James M. Mason, D-Va., read Calhoun's remarks in opposition. Calhoun maintained that the Union could only be saved by giving the South equal rights in the acquired territory, by halting the agitation of the slavery question, and by instituting a constitutional amendment that restored "to the South, in substance, the power she possessed of protecting herself before the

Henry Clay presents his compromise to the Senate on February 5, 1850, in his attempt to quell sectional differences by settling all major disputes between the North and South.
Source: The Granger Collection, New York.

equilibrium between the sections was destroyed by the action of this government."[2]

Three days later, Webster sought to refute Calhoun's charges against the North by framing Clay's proposal so as to make it more palatable to both the North and South. Webster began by saying: "I wish to speak today, not as a Massachusetts man, nor as a Northern man, but as an American.... I speak today for the preservation of the Union." There was, he contended, no necessity for congressional action on slavery in the acquired territory. Webster held that slavery had been excluded there by virtue of soil, climate, and geography. He balanced the grievances of the North and South by condemning abolitionism fanaticism and the constant Southern threats of secession. While Webster's speech drew a favorable response, it earned him the enmity of fellow New Englanders and charges of exploitation by Southern radicals.[3]

On April 18, Clay's proposal was referred to a special Committee of Thirteen chaired by the Kentuckian. Early in May, the committee reported three pieces of legislation: an omnibus bill that dealt with admitting California as a state, establishing territorial governments for New Mexico and Utah, and making proposals to Texas for the establishment of its western and northern boundaries; a stringent fugitive-slave bill; and a bill prohibiting slave trade in the District of Columbia. None of the three, however, were found acceptable. Also, the threat of a presidential veto of any compromise loomed. On July 9, 1850, however, President Taylor died. Already silenced were denunciations from Calhoun, who had passed away on March 31.

Although Taylor's successor, Millard Fillmore, did not support Clay's approach any more than Taylor did, Fillmore was helpful in developing an acceptable alternative. Also, Webster left the Senate on July 22 and used his new position as Fillmore's secretary of state to garner support for the legislation.[4]

During the final weeks of the battle, Sen. Stephen A. Douglas, D-Ill., replaced an exhausted Clay as leader of the compromise movement. By dividing the omnibus bill into separate measures and other parliamentary maneuvers, Douglas was able to fashion a different sectional majority in support of each bill that made passage possible. The bills, collectively known as the Compromise of 1850, provided for the admission of California as a free state; resolution of the Texas–New Mexico boundary dispute, together with the assumption of Texas's debt; establishment of territorial governments for New Mexico and Utah with a popular sovereignty clause; a stricter Fugitive Slave Act; and prohibition of the slave trade in the District of Columbia.[5] Senator Douglas, in reflecting on his role in the compromise, told his Senate colleagues on September 16:

> My object was to settle the controversy, and to restore peace and quiet to the country, and I was willing to adopt any mode of preceding and to follow any gentleman's lead which would bring us the desired results. When the rule omnibus was defeated, I fell back upon my own separate bills, which, fortunately for the country, received the sanction of the two Houses of Congress, and became the law of the land. ... No man and no party has acquired a triumph, except the party friendly to the Union triumphing over abolitionism and disunion.... The North has not surrendered to the South, nor has the South made humiliating any concession to the North. Each section has maintained its honor and its rights, and both have met on the common ground of justice.[6]

The compromise included elements that were questioned by partisans of both North and South. In the final analysis, however, it was recognized as the best possible solution to nearly intractable issues, and as such, was greeted with great relief and hope. In his annual message of December 2, President Fillmore told Congress that he regarded the compromise measures as "a final settlement of the dangerous and exciting subjects which they embraced."[7]

After Congress passed the compromise bills, "'wild jubilation' rocked Washington. There were bonfires and belching cannon salutes for the next 24 hours. All-night processions of celebrants roamed the streets looking to serenade the lawmakers responsible for the miracle. The main buildings in Washington were lit and illuminated, and exultant crowds shouted, 'The Union is saved.'" Webster believed that the country had "had a providential escape from very considerable dangers." Others, however, were hopeful, but doubted that the crisis was past. "In the long run," author Merrill D. Petersen quipped, it "bore more the character of truce than a final settlement."[8]

The "Compromise of 1850 was a temporary success in securing tranquility for the country." While it "delayed the Civil War ten years and therefore served an invaluable purpose," the sectional differences that threatened to disrupt the country at the midpoint of the nineteenth century unfortunately would reappear. "Hindsight," David M. Potter observed, "has long shown that the Compromise of 1850 did not bring either the security for the Union which many hoped for or the security for slavery which others feared. But at the time this was not evident." What it did do was avert a crisis in 1850, and "a settlement of issues which four preceding sessions of Congress had been unable to handle."[9]

SENATOR HENRY CLAY ARGUES FOR THE COMPROMISE OF 1850

JULY 22, 1850

Mr. President, in the progress of this debate it has been again and again argued that perfect tranquillity reigns throughout the country, and that there is no disturbance threatening its peace, endangering its safety, but that which was produced by busy, restless politicians. It has been maintained that the surface of the public mind is perfectly smooth and undisturbed by a single billow. I most heartily wish I could concur in this picture of general tranquillity that has

been drawn upon both sides of the Senate. I am no alarmist; nor, I thank God, at the advanced age at which His providence has been pleased to allow me to reach, am I very easily alarmed by any human event; but I totally misread the signs of the times, if there be that state of profound peace and quiet, that absence of all just cause of apprehension of future danger to this confederacy, which appears to be entertained by some other senators. Mr. President, all the tendencies of the times, I lament to say, are toward disquietude, if not more fatal consequences. When, before, in the midst of profound peace with all the nations of the earth, have we seen a convention, representing a considerable portion of one great part of the Republic, meet to deliberate about measures of future safety in connection with great interests of that quarter of the country? When before have we seen, not one, but more — some half a dozen — legislative bodies solemnly resolving that if any one of these measures — the admission of California, the adoption of the Wilmot proviso, the abolition of slavery in the District of Columbia — should be adopted by Congress measures of an extreme character, for the safety of the great interests to which I refer, in a particular section of the country, would be resorted to? For years, this subject of the abolition of slavery, even within this District of Columbia small as is the number of slaves here, has been a source of constant irritation and disquiet. So of the subject of the recovery of fugitive slaves who have escaped from their lawful owners: not a mere border contest, as has been supposed — although there, undoubtedly, it has given rise to more irritation than in other portions of the Union — but everywhere throughout the slave-holding country it has been felt as a great evil, a great wrong which required the intervention of congressional power. But these two subjects, unpleasant as has been the agitation to which they have given rise, are nothing in comparison to those which have sprung out of the acquisitions recently made from the Republic of Mexico. These are not only great and leading causes of just apprehension as respects the future, but all the minor circumstances of the day intimate danger ahead, whatever may be its final issue and consequence.

★ ★ ★ ★

Mr. President, I will not dwell upon other concomitant causes, all having the same tendency, and all well calculated to awaken, to arouse us — if, as I hope the fact is, we are all of us sincerely desirous of preserving this Union — to rouse us to dangers which really exist, without underrating them upon the one hand, or magnifying them upon the other.

★ ★ ★ ★

It has been objected against this measure that it is a compromise. It has been said that it is a compromise of principle, or of a principle. Mr. President, what is a compromise? It is a work of mutual concession — an agreement in which there are reciprocal stipulations — a work in which, for the sake of peace and concord one party abates his extreme demands in consideration of an abatement of extreme demands by the other party: it is a measure of mutual concession — a measure of mutual sacrifice. Undoubtedly, Mr. President, in all such measures of compromise, one party would be very glad to get what he wants, and reject what he does not desire, but which the other party wants. But when he comes to reflect

that, from the nature of the Government and its operations, and from those with whom he is dealing, it is necessary upon his part, in order to secure what he wants, to grant something to the other side, he should be reconciled to the concession which he has made, in consequence of the concession which he is to receive, if there is no great principle involved, such as a violation of the Constitution of the United States. I admit that such a compromise as that ought never to be sanctioned or adopted. But I now call upon any senator in his place to point out from the beginning to the end, from California to New Mexico, a solitary provision in this bill which is violative of the Constitution of the United States.

Sir, adjustments in the shape of compromise may be made without producing any such consequences as have been apprehended. There may be a mutual forbearance. You forbear on your side to insist upon the application of the restriction denominated the Wilmot proviso. Is there any violation of principle there? The most that can be said, even assuming the power to pass the Wilmot proviso, which is denied, is that there is a forbearance to exercise, not a violation of, the power to pass the proviso. So upon the other hand, if there was a power in the Constitution of the United States authorizing the establishment of slavery in any of the Territories — a power, however, which is controverted by a large portion of this Senate — if there was a power under the Constitution to establish slavery, the forbearance to exercise that power is no violation of the Constitution any more than the Constitution is violated by a forbearance to exercise numerous powers, that might be specified, that are granted in the Constitution, and that remain dormant until they come to be exercised by the proper legislative authorities. It is said that the bill presents the state of coercion — that members are coerced, in order to get what they want, to vote for that which they disapprove. Why, sir, what coercion is there? ... Can it be said upon the part of our Northern friends, because they have not got the Wilmot proviso incorporated in the territorial part of the bill, that they are coerced — wanting California, as they do, so much — to vote for the bill, if they do vote for it? Sir, they might have imitated the noble example of my friend [Mr. COOPER] from that State upon whose devotion to this Union I place one of my greatest reliances for its preservation. What was the course of my friend upon this subject of the Wilmot proviso? He voted for it; and could go back to his constituents and say, as all of you could go back and say to your constituents, if you chose to do so, "We wanted the Wilmot proviso in the bill; we tried to get it in; but the majority of the Senate was against it." The question then came up whether we should lose California, which has got an interdiction in her constitution, which in point of value and duration, is worth a thousand Wilmot provisos; we were induced, as my honorable friend would say, to take the bill and the whole of it together, although we were disappointed in our votes with respect to the Wilmot proviso — to take it, whatever omissions may have been made, on account of the superior amount of good it contains.

★ ★ ★ ★

Not the reception of the treaty of peace negotiated at Ghent, nor any other event which has occurred during my progress in public life, ever gave such unbounded and universal satisfaction as the settlement of the Missouri compromise. We may argue from like causes like effects. Then, indeed, there was great excitement. Then, indeed, all the legislatures of the North called out for the exclusion of Missouri and all the legislatures of the South called out for her admission as a State. Then, as now, the country was agitated like the ocean in the midst of a turbulent storm. But now, more than then, has this agitation been increased. Now, more than then, are the dangers which exist, if the controversy remains unsettled, more aggravated and more to be dreaded. The idea of disunion was then scarcely a low whisper. Now, it has become a familiar language in certain portions of the country. The public mind and the public heart are becoming familiarized with that most dangerous and fatal of all events, the disunion of the States. People begin to contend that this is not so bad a thing as they had supposed. Like the progress in all human affairs, as we approach danger it disappears, it diminishes in our conception and we no longer regard it with that awful apprehension of consequences that we did before we came into contact with it. Everywhere now there is a state of things, a degree of alarm and apprehension, and determination to fight, as they regard it, against the aggressions of the North. That did not so demonstrate itself at the period of the Missouri compromise. It was followed, in consequence of the adoption of the measure which settled the difficulty of Missouri, by peace, harmony, and tranquillity. So now, I infer, from the greater amount of agitation from the greater amount of danger, that, if you adopt the measures under consideration they, too, will be followed by the same amount of contentment, satisfaction, peace, and tranquillity, which ensued after the Missouri compromise.

★ ★ ★ ★

The responsibility of this great measure passes from the hands of the committee, and from my hands. They know, and I know, that it is an awful and tremendous responsibility. I hope that you will meet it with a just conception and a true appreciation of its magnitude, and the magnitude of the consequences that may ensue from your decision one way or the other. The alternatives I fear, which the measure presents, are concord and increased discord; a servile civil war, originating in its causes on the lower Rio Grande, and terminating possibly in its consequences on the upper Rio Grande in the Santa Fe country, or the restoration of harmony and fraternal kindness.

I believe from the bottom of my soul, that the measure is the reunion of this Union. I believe it is the dove of peace, which, taking its aerial flight from the dome of the Capitol, carries the glad tidings of assured peace and restored harmony to all the remotest extremities of this distracted land. I believe that it will be attended with all these beneficent effects. And now let us discard all resentment, all passions, all petty jealousies, all personal desires, all love of place, all hoaning after the gilded crumbs which fall from the table of power. Let us forget popular fears, from whatever quarter they may spring. Let us go to the limpid fountain of unadulterated patriotism, and, performing a solemn lustration, return divested of all selfish, sinister and sordid impurities, and think alone of our God, our country, our consciences, and our glorious Union; that Union without which we shall be torn into hostile fragments, and sooner or later become the victims of military despotism, or foreign domination.

Mr. President, what is an individual man? An atom, almost invisible without a magnifying glass — a mere speck upon the surface of the immense universe; not a second in time, compared to immeasurable, never-beginning, and never-ending eternity; a drop of water in the great deep, which evaporates and is borne off by the winds; a grain of sand, which is soon gathered to the dust from which it sprung. Shall a being so small, so petty, so fleeting, so evanescent, oppose itself to the onward march of a great nation, which is to subsist for ages and ages to come — oppose itself to that long line of posterity which, issuing from our loins, will endure during the existence of the world? Forbid it God! Let us look to our country and our cause, elevate ourselves to the dignity of pure and disinterested patriots, and save our country from all impending dangers. What if, in the march of this nation to greatness and power, we should be buried beneath the wheels that propel it onward. What are we — what is any man worth who is not ready and willing to sacrifice himself for the benefit of his country when it is necessary?

★ ★ ★ ★

If this Union shall become separated, new unions, new confederacies will arise. And with respect to this — if there be any — I hope there is no one in the Senate — before whose imagination is flitting the idea of a great Southern Confederacy to take possession of the Balize and the mouth of the Mississippi, I say in my place never! *never!* NEVER will we who occupy the broad waters of the Mississippi and its upper tributaries consent that any foreign flag shall float at the Balize or upon the turrets of the Crescent City — never — never! I call upon all the South. Sir, we have had hard words — bitter words, bitter thoughts, unpleasant feelings toward each other in the progress of this great measure. Let us forget them. Let us sacrifice these feelings. Let us go to the altar of our country and swear, as the oath was taken of old, that we will stand by her; that we will support her; that we will uphold her Constitution; that we will preserve her Union; and that we will pass this great, comprehensive and healing system of measures, which will hush all the jarring elements, and bring peace and tranquillity to our homes.

Let me, Mr. President, in conclusion, say that the most disastrous consequences would occur, in my opinion, were we to go home, doing nothing to satisfy and tranquillize the country upon these great questions. What will be the judgment of mankind, what the judgment of that portion of mankind who are looking upon the progress of this scheme of self-government as being that which holds the highest hopes and expectations of ameliorating the condition of mankind — what will their judgment be? Will not all the monarchs of the Old World pronounce our glorious Republic a disgraceful failure? What will be the judgment of our constituents, when we return to them and they ask us, How have you left your country? Is all quiet — all happy? Are all the seeds of distraction or division crushed and dissipated? And, sir, when you come into the bosom of your family, when you come to converse with the partner of your fortunes of your happiness, and of your sorrows, and when in the midst of the common offspring of both of you, she asks you, "Is there any danger of civil war? Is there any danger of the torch being applied to any portion of the country? Have you settled the questions which you have been so long discussing and deliberating upon at Washington? Is all peace and all quiet?" What response, Mr. President, can you make to that wife of your choice and those children with whom you have been blessed by God? Will you go home and leave all in disorder and confusion, all unsettled, all open? The contentions and agitations of the past will be increased and augmented by the agitations resulting from our neglect to decide them. Sir, we shall stand condemned by all human judgment below, and of that above it is not for me to speak. We shall stand condemned in our own consciences, by our own constituents, and by our own country. The measure may be defeated. I have been aware that its passage for many days was not absolutely certain. From the first to the last, I hoped and

believed it would pass, because from the first to the last I believed it was founded on the principles of just and righteous concession of mutual conciliation. I believe that it deals unjustly by no part of the Republic; that it saves their honor, and, as far as it is dependent upon Congress, saves the interests of all quarters of the country. But, sir, I have known that the decision of its fate depended upon four or five votes in the

---

[I]f defeated, it will be a triumph ... of a most extraordinary conjunction of extremes; a victory won by abolitionism; a victory achieved by free-soilism; the victory of discord and agitation over peace and tranquility.

— Henry Clay

Senate of the United States, whose ultimate judgment we could not count upon the one side or the other with absolute certainty. Its fate is now committed to the Senate, and to those five or six votes to which I have referred. It may be defeated. It is possible that, for the chastisement of our sins and transgressions, the rod of Providence may be still applied to us, may be still suspended over us. But, if defeated, it will be a triumph of ultraism and impracticability — a triumph of a most extraordinary conjunction of extremes; a victory won by abolitionism; a victory achieved by free-soilism; the victory of discord and agitation over peace and tranquillity; and I pray to Almighty God that it may not, in consequence of the inauspicious result, lead to the most unhappy and disastrous consequences to our beloved country.

Source: *Congressional Globe,* 31st Cong., 1st sess., July 22, 1850 (Washington: John C. Rives, 1850), appendix, 22:1405, 1407, 1413–1414.

SENATOR THOMAS HART BENTON OPPOSES THE COMPROMISE OF 1850

JUNE 10, 1850

I make the motion which supersedes all other motions, and which, itself, can only be superseded by a motion still more stringent — the motion to lie on the table. I move the indefinite postponement of this bill, and in the form required by our rules, which is to a day certain beyond the session; and, to make sure of that, I propose a day beyond

the life of the present Congress. It is the proper motion to test the sense of the Senate on the fate of a measure, and to save time which might be lost in useless amendments. I have waited a month for the larger amendments to be voted upon, and now deem it my duty to proceed with my motion, with a view to proceed with the bills singly, if this bill, of many in one, shall be put out of the way; but will withdraw it at any time to admit of votes on vital points. It is a bill of thirty-nine sections — forty, save one — an ominous number; and which, with the two little bills which attend it, is called a compromise, and is pressed upon us as a remedy for the national calamities. Now, all this labor of the committee, and all this remedy, proceed upon the assumption that the people of the United States are in a miserable, distracted condition; that it is their mission to relieve this national distress, and that these bills are the sovereign remedy for that purpose. Now, in my opinion, all this is a mistake, both as to the condition of the country, the mission of the committee, and the efficacy of their remedy. I do not believe in this misery, and distraction, and distress, and strife, of the people. On the contrary, I believe them to be very quiet at home, attending to their crops, such of them as do not mean to feed out of the public crib; and that they would be perfectly happy if the politicians would only permit them to think so. I know of no distress in the country, no misery, no strife, no distraction.… The Senator from Kentucky [Mr. Clay], chairman of the committee, and reporter of the bill, and its pathetic advocate, formerly delivered us many such recitals, about the times that the tariff was to be increased, the national bank charter to be renewed, the deposits to be restored, or a bankrupt act to be passed. He has been absent for some years; and, on returning among us, seems to begin where he left off. He treats us to the old dish of distress! Sir, it is a mistake. There is none of it; and if there was, the remedy would be in the hands of the people — in the hearts of the people — who love their country, and mean to take care of it — and not in the contrivances of politicians, who mistake their own for their country's distresses. It is all a mistake. It looks to me like a joke. But when I recollect the imposing number of the committee, and how "distinguished" they all were, and how they voted themselves free from instructions, and allowed the Senate to talk, but not to vote, while they were out, and how long they were deliberating: when I recollect all these things, I am constrained to believe the committee are in earnest. And as for the Senator himself, the chairman of the committee, the perfect gravity with which he brought forward his remedy — these bills and the report — the pathos with which he enforced them, and the hearty congratulations which he addressed to the Senate, to the United States, and all mankind on the appointment of his committee, preclude the idea of an intentional joke on his part. In view of all this, I find myself compelled to consider this proceeding as serious, and bound to treat it parliamentarily; which I now proceed to do.

★ ★ ★ ★

I proceed to the destruction of this monster. The California bill is made the scapegoat of all the sins of slavery in

the United States — that California which is innocent of all these sins.

★ ★ ★ ★

She is innocent of all the evils of slavery in the United States, yet they are all to be packed upon her back, and herself sacrificed under the heavy load. First, Utah and New Mexico are piled upon her, each pregnant with all the transgressions of the Wilmot proviso — a double load in itself — and enough, without further weight, to bear down California. Utah and New Mexico are first piled on; and the reason given for it by the committee is thus stated in their authentic report:

> The committee recommend to the Senate the establishment of those territorial governments; and, in order more effectually to secure that desirable object, they also recommend that the bill for their establishment be incorporated in the bill for the admission of California, and that, united together, they both be passed.

This is the reason given in the report; and the first thing that strikes me, on reading it, is its entire incompatibility with the reasons previously given for the same act. In his speech in favor of raising the committee, the Senator from Kentucky [Mr. CLAY] was in favor of putting the territories upon California for her own good — for the good of California herself — as the speedy way to get her into the Union, and the safe way to do it, by preventing an opposition to her admission which might otherwise defeat it altogether. This was his reason then, and he thus delivered it to the Senate.

> He would say now to those who desired the speedy admission of California, the shortest and most expeditious way of attaining the desired object was to include her admission in a bill giving governments to the territories. He made this statement because he was impelled to do so from what had come to his knowledge. If her admission as a separate measure be urged, an opposition is created which may result in the defeat of any bill for her admission.

These are the reasons which the Senator then gave for urging the conjunction of the State and the Territories — quickest and safest for California: her admission the supreme object, and the conjunction of the Territories only a means of helping her along and saving her. And unfounded as I deemed these reasons at the time, and now know them to be, they still had the merit of giving preference where it was due — to the superior object — California herself, a state, without being a state of the Union, and suffering all the ills of that anomalous condition. California was then the superior object; the Territories were incidental figures and subordinate considerations, to be made subservient to her salvation. Now all this is reversed. The territories take the superior place.

They become the object: the state the incident. They take the first — she the second place! And to make sure of their welfare — make more certain of giving governments to them — *inuendo,* such governments as the committee prescribe — the conjunction is now proposed and enforced. This is a change of position, with a corresponding change of reasons. Doubtless the Senator from Kentucky has a right to change his own position, and to change his reasons at the same time; but he has no right to ask other Senators to change with him, or to require them to believe in two sets of reasons, each contradictory to the other. It is my fortune to believe in neither.

★ ★ ★ ★

Mr. President, all the evils of incongruous conjunctions are exemplified in this conjunction of the territorial government bills with the California state admission bill. They are subjects not only foreign to each other, but involving different questions, and resting upon principles of different natures. One involves the slavery and antislavery questions: the other is free from them. One involves constitutional questions: the other does not. One is a question of right, resting upon the Constitution of the United States and the treaty with Mexico: the other is a question of expediency, resting in the discretion of Congress. One is the case of a State, asking for an equality of rights with the other States: the other is a question of territories, asking protection from States. One is a sovereignty — the other a property. So that, at all points, and under every aspect, the subjects differ; and it is well known that there are Senators here who can unite in a vote for the admission of California, who cannot unite in any vote for the territorial governments; and that, because these governments involve the slavery questions, from all which the California bill is free. That is the rock on which men and parties split here. Some deny the power of Congress *in toto* over the subject of slavery in territories: such as they can support no bill which touches that question, one way or the other. Others admit the power, but deny the expediency of its exercise. Others again claim both the power and the exercise. Others again are under legislative instructions — some to vote one way, some the other. Finally, there are some opposed

---

Vote for all — and call it a compromise! … No! rejection of the whole is the only course; and to begin anew, each bill by itself, the only remedy. — Thomas Hart Benton

---

to giving any governments at all to these Territories, and in favor of leaving them to grow up of themselves into future States. Now, what are the Senators, so circumstanced, to do with these bills conjoined? Vote for all — and call it a com-

promise! as if oaths, duty, constitutional obligation, and legislative instructions, were subjects of compromise. No! rejection of the whole is the only course; and to begin anew, each bill by itself, the only remedy.

★ ★ ★ ★

Mr. President, the moralist informs us, that there are some subjects too light for reason — too grave for ridicule; and in such cases, the mere moralist may laugh or cry, as he deems best. But not so with the legislator — his business is not laughing or crying. Whimpering, or simpering, is not his mission. Work is his vocation, and gravity his vein; and in that vein I proceed to consider this interjection of Texas, with all her multifarious questions, into the bowels of the California bill.

In the first place, this Texas bill is a compact, depending for its validity on the consent of Texas, and is put into the California bill as part of a compromise and general settlement of all the slavery questions; and, of course, the whole must stand together, or fall together. This gives Texas a veto upon the admission of California. This is unconstitutional, as well as unjust; for, by the Constitution, new states are to be admitted by Congress, and not by another state; and, therefore, Texas should not have a veto upon the admission of California.

★ ★ ★ ★

And here I find the largest objection to the extension of slavery — to planting it in new regions where it does not now exist — bestowing it on those who have it not. The incurability of the evil is the greatest objection to the extension of slavery. It is wrong for the legislator to inflict an evil which can be cured: how much more to inflict one that is incurable, and against the will of the people who are to endure it forever! I quarrel with no one for supposing slavery a blessing: I deem it an evil and would neither adopt it nor impose it on others. Yet I am a slaveholder, and among the few members of Congress who hold slaves in this District. The French proverb tells us that nothing is new but what has been forgotten. So of this objection to a large emancipation. Every one sees now that it is a question of races, involving consequences which go to the destruction of one or the other: it was seen fifty years ago, and the wisdom of Virginia balked at it then. It seems to be above human wisdom. But there is a wisdom above human! and to that we must look. In the meantime, not extend the evil.

★ ★ ★ ★

In refusing to extend slavery into these seventy thousand square miles, I act in conformity not only to my own long-established principles, but also in conformity to the long-established practice of Congress.

★ ★ ★ ★

This is the end of the committee's labor — five old bills gathered up from our table, tacked together, and christened a compromise! Now compromise is a pretty phrase at all times, and is a good thing in itself, when there happens to be any parties to make it, any authority to enforce it, any penalties for breaking it, or anything to be compromised. The compromises of the Constitution are of that kind; and they stand. Compromises made in court, and entered of record, are of that kind; and they stand. Compromises made by individuals on claims to property are likewise of that character; and they stand. I respect all such compromises. But where there happens to be nothing to be compromised, no parties to make a compromise, no power to enforce it, no penalty for its breach, no obligation on anyone — not even its makers — to observe it, and when no two human beings can agree about its meaning, then a compromise becomes ridiculous and pestiferous. I have no respect for it, and eschew it. It cannot stand, and will fall; and in its fall will raise up more ills than it was intended to cure. And of this character I deem this farrago of incongruous matter to be, which has been gathered up and stuck together, and offered to us "all or none," like "fifty-four forty." It has none of the requisites of a compromise, and the name cannot make it so.

★ ★ ★ ★

A compromise is a concession, a mutual concession of contested claims between two parties. I know of nothing to be conceded on the part of the slaveholding states in regard to their slave property. Their rights are independent of the federal government, and admitted in the Constitution — a right to hold their slaves *as property,* a right to pursue and recover them *as property,* a right to it as a *political element* in the weight of these states, by making five count three in the national representation. These are our rights by an instrument which we are bound to respect, and I will concede none of them, nor purchase any of them. I never purchase as a concession what I hold as a right, nor accept an inferior tide when I already hold the highest. Even if this congeries of bills was a compromise, in fact, I should be opposed to it, for the reasons stated. But the fact itself is to me apocryphal. What is it but the case of five old bills introduced by different members as common legislative measures — caught up by the Senator from Kentucky, and his committee, bundled together, and then called a compromise! Now, this mystifies me. The same bills were ordinary legislation in the hands of their authors; they become a sacred compromise in the hands of their new possessors. They seemed to be of no account as laws; they become a national panacea as a compromise. The difference seems to be in the change of name.

★ ★ ★ ★

Mr. President, it is time to be done with this comedy of errors. California is suffering for want of admission. New Mexico is suffering for want of protection. The public business is suffering for want of attention. The character of Congress is suffering for want of progress in business. It is time to put an end to so many evils; and I have made the motion intended to terminate them, by moving the indefinite postponement of this unmanageable mass of incongruous bills, each an impediment to the other, that they may be taken up one by one, in their proper order, to receive the decision which their respective merits require.

────

Source: Congressional Globe, 31st Cong., 1st sess., June 10, 1850 (Washington: John C. Rives, 1850), appendix, 22:676–684.

Notes

1. *Congressional Globe,* 31st Cong., 1st sess., (January 29, 1850), 22:244–252; Merrill D. Petersen, *The Great Triumvirate: Webster, Clay, and Calhoun* (New York: Oxford University Press, 1987), 454–460.

2. *Congressional Globe,* 31st Cong., 1st sess., (February 5, 1850), appendix, 22:115–127; March 4, 1850, 22:451–455.

3. *Congressional Globe,* 31st Cong., 1st sess., (March 7, 1850), appendix, 22:269–276; Petersen, *The Great Triumvirate: Webster, Clay, and Calhoun,* 462–466.

4. *Congressional Globe,* 31st Cong., 1st sess., 2 vols., (April 18, 1850), 22:770–774; (May 8, 1850), 22:944–956; Holman Hamilton, *Prologue to Conflict: The Crisis and Compromise of 1850* (Lexington: University of Kentucky Press, 1964), 107–108; Michael F. Holt, *The Political Crisis of the 1850s* (New York: John Wiley and Sons, 1978), 76–87; Elbert B. Smith, *The Presidencies of Zachary Taylor and Millard Fillmore* (Lawrence: University Press of Kansas, 1988), 191; John C. Waugh, *On the Brink of War: The Compromise of 1850 and How It Changed the Course of American History* (Wilmington, Del.: Scholarly Resources, 2003), 177–180.

5. Texas and New Mexico Act (9 Stat. 446–452); California admitted as a free state 9 Stat. 452–453; Utah Act (9 Stat. 453–458); Fugitive Slave Act 9 Stat. 462–465; District of Columbia Slave Trade Act (9 Stat. 467–468); Hamilton, *Prologue to Conflict: The Crisis and Compromise of 1850,* 132–151; David M. Potter, *The Impending Crisis, 1848–1861* (New York: Harper and Row, 1976), 109–120; Robert W. Johannsen, *Stephen A. Douglas* (New York: Oxford University Press, 1973), 294–298.

6. *Congressional Globe,* 31st Cong., 1st sess., (September 16, 1850), 22:1830.

7. James D. Richardson, *Messages and Papers of the Presidents,* 20 vols. (New York: Bureau of National Literature, 1897–1925), 6:2629.

8. Quotes are found in Waugh, *On the Brink of War: The Compromise of 1850 and How It Changed the Course of American History,* 187, 190; Charles M. Wiltse and Michael J. Birkner, eds., *The Papers of Daniel Webster,* 7 vols. (Hanover, N.H.: University Press of New England, 1986), 7:143, 144, 155; Petersen, *The Great Triumvirate: Webster, Clay, and Calhoun,* 475.

9. Quotes are found in Hamilton, *Prologue to Conflict: The Crisis and Compromise of 1850,* 184–185; Potter, *The Impending Crisis, 1848–1861,* 120.

Kansas-Nebraska Act
✳ 1854 ✳

Enactment of the Compromise of 1850 resulted in a momentary lull in debate over the slavery question. Both North and South hoped it would not erupt again, but it was far from forgotten. At the outset of the Thirty-second Congress, Sen. Stephen A. Douglas, D-Ill., told his colleagues that the compromise should be considered a "final settlement" of the slavery issue. It was time, he reasoned, to "cease agitating, stop the debate, and drop the subject." Forty-four members of Congress even signed a pledge that they would only support political candidates totally committed to the settlement. When Sen. Charles Sumner of Massachusetts sought the repeal of the Fugitive Slave Act in August 1852, only three other senators were willing to support him. That November, Democrat Franklin Pierce captured the presidency by endorsing the compromise and pledging not to let slavery become a political issue again. He carried with him substantial majorities in the Senate and House.[1]

Despite the congressional compromise on slavery, the issue continued to intrude on the national consciousness. Harriet Beecher Stowe's celebrated novel, *Uncle Tom's Cabin*, published in March 1852, helped convert thousands to the merits of the antislavery movement. Stowe's portrayal of the tragic aspects of slavery sold more than three hundred thousand copies in its first year alone. David M. Potter said that "[h]istory cannot evaluate with precision the influence of the novel upon public opinion, but the northern attitude toward slavery was never the same after *Uncle Tom's Cabin*. Men who had remained unmoved by real fugitives wept for Tom under the lash and cheered for Eliza with the bloodhounds on her track." Despite "a supreme effort to avert the dangers of the [Wilmot] Proviso and restore sectional harmony," the compromisers of 1850 had enacted in the Fugitive Slave Law "a firebrand vastly more inflammatory than the Wilmot Proviso."[2]

Still, little sense existed of the impending crisis that would consume the nation in less than a decade. For now the question of the best route for a transcontinental rail route had become a more prominent topic of debate. Because the set-

tlement of Western territories depended upon the construction of the rail line, where it was finally located was of tremendous importance. In early March 1853, the effort ended in a sectional deadlock. The best Congress could do was approve funding for the secretary of war to make explorations and surveys for determining the most practical and economic rail route between the Mississippi River and the Pacific Ocean.[3]

The next Congress shifted its attention once again to the question of how the vast remaining portion of the Louisiana Purchase west of Iowa and Missouri should be formed into territories and started on the road to statehood. It was a question irrevocably bound to the bitter sectional controversies over the extension of slavery into both the territories and path of the projected transcontinental railroad. Four previous attempts to organize a single territory out of this area had been defeated in Congress. The most recent of these efforts had been approved by the House, but it failed to secure passage in the Senate.[4]

On December 14, 1853, Sen. Augustus C. Dodge, D-Iowa, introduced a bill to organize a territory of Nebraska that made no mention of slavery. It was assumed that any bill dealing with Nebraska would leave in place the three-decade-old Missouri Compromise prohibition against slavery in the portion of the Louisiana Purchase north of 36° 30′. The measure was referred to the Senate Committee on Territories, chaired by Senator Douglas, who realized that the South would oppose the bill as drafted because it would prepare the way for a new free state in the area north of 36° 30′. His solution was a new bill that made concessions designed to ensure its passage.

The recast measure made no mention of the Missouri Compromise or the status of slavery in the new territory. It simply stated that when the new territory or any portion of the territory was "admitted as a State or States," it would "be received into the Union, with or without slavery, as their constitution may prescribe at the time of admission." Southerners, however, were quick to point out that the 1820 Missouri

Compromise still applied. At their insistence, Douglas agreed to an amendment by Sen. Archibald Dixon, W-Ky., explicitly repealing the 1820 ban on slavery north of 36° 30′. It declared that the Missouri Compromise line had been "superseded" by popular sovereignty wording of the Compromise of 1850. Douglas also agreed to divide the proposed new territory into two territories — the southern to be called Kansas and the northern to be called Nebraska. Douglas and several other Democrats then persuaded President Pierce, who wanted to evade the issue of repealing the Missouri Compromise, that the bill would not pass without a direct repeal that he supported. On January 23, Douglas's Committee on Territories reported the measure. [5]

When introducing the Kansas-Nebraska Act, Douglas declared that it was in harmony with the "great principle of self government" already enacted in the Compromise of 1850. Those measures, he emphasized, "established … that people should be allowed to decide the questions of their domestic institutions, subject only to such limitations and restrictions as are imposed by the Constitution of the United States, instead of having them determined by an arbitrary or geographical line." [6]

During the next four months, Capitol Hill was embroiled in discussion of the measure as Douglas; his strongest ally, Senate president pro tempore David Atchison, D-Mo.; and other supporters continued to argue that the Compromise of 1850 has already superseded the Missouri Compromise and that the proposed Kansas-Nebraska Act merely extended that action. The majority of Northern congressmen, however, denounced the Kansas-Nebraska Act as a betrayal of both the Missouri Compromise and Compromise of 1850. Sen. Salmon P. Chase of Ohio insisted that no one who had voted for the 1850 act felt it superseded the Missouri Compromise. Chase, together with five other Democrats, published an "Appeal of the Independent Democrats in Congress to the People of the United States," in the National Era, an antislavery Washington weekly that portrayed Douglas's bill "as a gross violation of a sacred pledge." They predicted that the Kansas-Nebraska Act would have a dire effect on western immigration, warned the country that freedom and union were in peril, and implored all Christians to rise in protest against this "enormous crime." Chase repeated these themes in a Senate address on February 3, 1854. Despite the best effort of Chase and others, the Senate debate, which continued until March 3, ended with the passage of the Douglas bill, 37–14. [7]

While the debate in the Senate had been heated, it was complex in the House where every member faced reelection, and "the rising tide of indignation in the North was frightening to many Democrats who would have to face angry voters, indignant at contrivers or supporters of this measure." House Democrats had a huge 159–75 majority, but 92 of the 159 came from Northern constituencies outraged over the Sen-

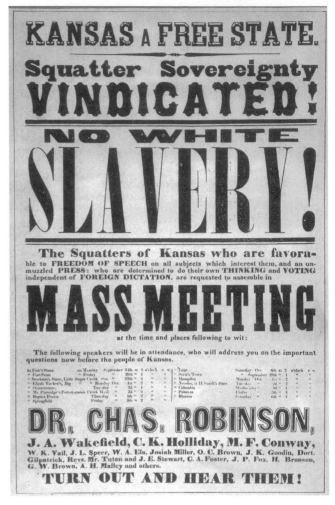

This 1854 poster is calling for a meeting of the Kansas settlers opposed to slavery following the Kansas-Nebraska Act. The act led to civil war in "Bleeding Kansas," where pro- and anti-slavery forces rose in violent opposition to one another, battling for control over the territory.
Source: The Granger Collection, New York.

ate's decision to void the Missouri Compromise and include an amendment offered by John M. Clayton, W-Del., prohibiting unnaturalized foreign immigrants from participation in the organization of the territories. Initially, a group consisting of nearly two-thirds of the northern Democrats revolted in hopes of obtaining a more palatable bill, but eventually several were persuaded to support an almost identical House bill sponsored by Rep. William A. Richardson, D-Ill. "Had it not been for the support of the thirteen southern Whigs," however, "the now impotent Democratic majority could not have carried the bill." [8]

Initially, the House referred the measure to the Committee of the Whole, where it was placed at the bottom of a lengthy calendar of bills under consideration. Not until May

8 did bill supporters succeed in laying all of the other bills aside so the Richardson bill could be considered. Debate continued until May 22, when it was finally taken up without the Clayton amendment, and was passed 113–100. The House ultimately approved the bill because the South voted almost unanimously for it, whereas the North divided its opposition. The Senate concurred in omitting the Clayton amendment, realizing that the House would never approve its retention. President Pierce signed the Act on May 30.[9]

"No piece of legislation in American history produced so many immediate, sweeping, and ominous consequences."[10] It dashed President Pierce's hopes of reelection; divided and destroyed the Whig Party; left the Democratic Party with little influence in the North and as a proslavery party in the South; and ushered in a new political organization, the Republican Party, as an immediate political force that included anti-Nebraska Democrats, northern Whigs, Know-Nothings, and nativist groups. The Act also deepened suspicions between the North and South, which ultimately led to veritable civil war in "Bleeding Kansas," where proslavery and antislavery forces battled over control of the territory with such passion that reconciliation was not possible. Even more important, the Kansas-Nebraska Act set the stage for Southern secession and the Civil War in 1861.

SENATOR STEPHEN A. DOUGLAS ARGUES FOR THE KANSAS-NEBRASKA BILL

MARCH 3, 1854

It has ... been urged in debate that there is no necessity for these territorial organizations; and I have been called upon to point out any public and national considerations which require action at this time. Senators seem to forget that our immense and valuable possessions on the Pacific are separated from the States and organized Territories on this side of the Rocky Mountains by a vast wilderness, filled by hostile savages — that nearly a hundred thousand emigrants pass through this barbarous wilderness every year, on their way to California and Oregon — that these emigrants are American citizens, our own constituents, who are entitled to the protection of law and government, and that they are left to make their way, as best they may, without the protection or aid of law or government. The United States mails for New Mexico and Utah, and official communications between this Government and the authorities of those Territories, are required to be carried over these wild plains, and through the gorges of the mountains, where you have made no provisions for roads, bridges, or ferries to facilitate travel, or forts or other means of safety to protect life. As often as I have brought forward and urged the adoption of measures to remedy these evils, and afford security against the damages to which our people are constantly exposed, they have been promptly voted down as not being of sufficient importance to command the favorable consideration of Congress. Now, when I propose to organize the Territories, and allow the people to do for themselves what you have so often refused do for them, I am told that there are not white inhabitants enough permanently settled in the country to require and sustain a government. True there is not a very large population there, for the very good reason that your Indian code and intercourse laws exclude the settlers, and forbid their remaining there to cultivate the soil. You refuse to throw the country open to settlers, and then object to the organization of the Territories, upon the ground that there is not a sufficient number of inhabitants.

★ ★ ★ ★

We have been told by nearly every Senator who has spoken in opposition to this bill, that at the time of its introduction the people were in a state of profound quiet and repose — that the antislavery agitation had entirely ceased — and that the whole country was acquiescing cheerfully and cordially in the compromise measures of 1850 as a final adjustment of this vexed question. Sir, it is truly refreshing to hear Senators, who contested every inch of ground in opposition to those measures, when they were under discussion, who predicted all manner of evils and calamities from their adoption, and who raised the cry of appeal, and even resistance, to their execution, after they had become the laws of the land — I say it is really refreshing to hear these same Senators now bear their united testimony to the wisdom of those measures, and to the patriotic motives which induced us to pass them in defiance of their threats and resistance — and to their beneficial effects in restoring peace, harmony, and fraternity to a distracted country. These are precious confessions from the lips of those who stand pledged never to assent to the propriety of those measures, and to make war upon them so long

THE FINAL VOTE

Kansas-Nebraska Act

Senate
March 3, 1854

	Yea	Nay
Democrats	32	4
Whigs	5	7
Freesoilers	0	3
Total	**37**	**14**

House
May 22, 1854

	Yea	Nay
Democrats	99	45
Whigs	13	50
Freesoilers	0	3
American	1	2
Total	**113**	**100**

Source: Albert Castel and Scott L. Gibson, *The Yeas and the Nays: Key Congressional Decisions, 1774–1945* (Kalamazoo: New Issues Press, Institute of Public Affairs, Western Michigan University, 1975), 69.

the country, whenever any new Territory was to be acquired or organized. We were also aware that in 1850, the right of the people to decide this question for themselves, subject only to the Constitution, was submitted for the doctrine of congressional intervention. This first question, therefore, which the committee were called upon to decide, and indeed the only question of any material importance in framing this bill was this: shall we adhere to and carry out the principle recognized by the compromise measures of 1850, or shall we go back to the old exploded doctrine of congressional interference, as established in 1820, in a large portion of the country, and which it was the object of the Wilmot proviso to give a universal application, not only to all the territory which we then possessed, but all which we might hereafter acquire? There are no alternatives. We were compelled to frame the bill upon the one or the other of these two principles. The doctrine of 1820, or the doctrine of 1850, must prevail. In the discharge of the duty imposed upon us by the Senate, the committee could not hesitate upon this point, whether we consulted our own individual opinions and principles, or those which were known to be entertained and boldly avowed by a large majority of the Senate. The two great political parties of the country stood solemnly pledged before the world to adhere to the compromise measures of 1850 "in principle and substance." A large majority of the Senate — indeed, every member of the body, I believe, except the two avowed Abolitionists, [Mr. CHASE and Mr. SUMNER,] profess to belong to one or the other of these parties, and hence were supposed to be under a high moral obligation to carry out "the principle and substance" of those measures in all new territorial organizations.

★ ★ ★ ★

Mr. President, the opponents of this measure have had much to say about the mutations and modifications which this bill has undergone since it was first introduced by myself, and about the alleged departure of the bill, in its present form, from the principle laid down in the original report of the committee as a rule of action in all future territorial organizations. Fortunately there is no necessity, even if your patience would tolerate such a course of argument at this late hour of the night, for me to examine these speeches in detail, and reply to each charge separately. Each speaker seems to have followed faithfully in the footsteps of his leader in the path marked out by the Abolition confederates in their manifesto, which I took occasion to expose on a former occasion. You have seen them on their winding way, meandering the narrow and crooked path in Indian file, each treading close upon the heels of the other, and neither venturing to take a step to the right or left, or to occupy one inch of ground which did not bear the footprint of the Abolition champion. To answer one, therefore, is to answer the whole. The statement to which they seem to attach the most importance, and which they have repeated oftener, perhaps, than any other, is,

as they shall remain upon the statute-book. I well understand that these confessions are now made, not with the view of yielding their assent to the propriety of carrying those enactments into faithful execution, but for the purpose of having a pretext for charging upon me, as the author of this bill, the responsibility of an agitation which they are striving to produce. They say that I, and not they, have revived the agitation. What have I done to render me obnoxious to this charge? They say that I wrote and introduced this Nebraska bill. That is true; but I was not a volunteer in the transaction. The Senate, by a unanimous vote, appointed me chairman of the Territorial Committee, and associated five intelligent and patriotic Senators with me, and thus made it our duty to take charge of all Territorial business. In like manner, and with the concurrence of these complaining Senators, the Senate referred to us a distinct proposition to organize this Nebraska Territory, and required us to report specifically upon the question. I repeat, then, we were not volunteers in this business. The duty was imposed upon us by the Senate. We were not unmindful of the delicacy and responsibility of the position. We were aware that from 1820–1850, the abolition doctrine of congressional interference with slavery in the Territories and new States had so far prevailed as to keep up an incessant slavery agitation in Congress, and throughout that, pending the compromise measures of 1850, no man in or out of Congress ever dreamed of abrogating the Missouri compromise; that from that period down to the present session nobody supposed that its validity had been impaired or any thing done which rendered it obligatory upon us to make it inoperative hereafter; that at the time of submitting the report and bill to the Senate, on the 4th of January last, neither I nor any member of the committee ever thought of such a thing; and that we could never be brought to the point of abrogating the eighth section of the Missouri act until after the Senator from Kentucky introduced his amendment to my bill.

★ ★ ★ ★

They wish to have the people believe that the abrogation of what they call the Missouri compromise was the main object and aim of the bill, and that the only question involved is whether the prohibition of slavery north of 36° 30' shall be repealed or not? That which is a mere incident they choose to consider the principal. They make war on the means by which we propose to accomplish an object instead of openly resisting the object itself. The principle which we propose to carry into effect by the bill is this: That *Congress shall neither legislate slavery into any Territories or state, nor out of the same; but the people shall be left free to regulate their domestic concerns in their own way, subject only to the Constitution of the United States.*

In order to carry this principle into practical operation, it becomes necessary to remove whatever legal obstacles might be found in the way of its free exercise. It is only for the purpose of carrying out this great fundamental principle of self-government that the bill renders the eighth section of the Missouri act inoperative and void.

★ ★ ★ ★

[M]y accusers attempt to raise up false issue, and thereby divert public attention from the real one by the cry that the Missouri compromise is to be repealed or violated by the passage of this bill. Well, if the eighth section of the Missouri act, which attempted to fix the destinies of future generations in those Territories for all time to come, in utter disregard of the rights and wishes of the people when they should be received into the Union as States, be inconsistent with the great principles of self-government and the Constitution of the United States, it ought to be abrogated. The legislation of 1850 abrogated the Missouri compromise, so far as the country embraced within the limits of Utah and New Mexico was covered by the slavery restriction. It is true, that those acts did not in terms and by name repeal the act of 1820, as originally adopted, or as extended by the resolutions annexing Texas in 1845, any more than the report of the Committee on Territories proposed to repeal the same acts this session. But the acts of 1850 did authorize the people of those Territories to

exercise "all rightful powers of legislation consistent with the Constitution" not excepting the question of slavery; and did provide that, when those Territories should be admitted into the Union, they should be received with or without slavery as the people thereof might determine at the date of their admission.

★ ★ ★ ★

Our object was to leave the people entirely free to form and regulate their domestic institutions and internal concerns in their own way, under the Constitution; and we deemed it wise to accomplish that object in the exact terms in which the same thing had been done in Utah and New Mexico by the acts of 1850. This was the principle upon which the committee voted; and our bill was supposed, and is now believed, to have been in accordance with it. When doubts were raised whether the bill did fully carry out the principle laid down in the report, amendments were made from time to time, in order to avoid all misconstruction, and make the true intent of the act more explicit.

★ ★ ★ ★

There is nothing [in the Missouri Compromise] in the terms of law that purports to be a compact, or indicates that it was anything more than an ordinary act of legislation. To prove that it was more than it purports to be on its face, gentlemen must produce other evidence, and prove that there was such an understanding as to create a moral obligation in the nature of a compact.

★ ★ ★ ★

If the act of 1820, called the Missouri compromise, was a compact, it was violated and repudiated by a solemn vote of the House of Representatives in 1821, within eleven months, after it was adopted. It was repudiated by the North by a majority vote, and that repudiation was so complete and successful as to compel Missouri to make a new compromise, and she was brought into the Union under the new compromise of 1821, and not under the act of 1820.

★ ★ ★ ★

Mr. President, I have also occupied a good deal of time in exposing the cant of these gentlemen about the sanctity of the Missouri compromise, and the dishonor attached to the violation of plighted faith. I have exposed these matters in order to show that the object of these men is to withdraw from public attention the real principle involved in the bill. They well know that the abrogation of the Missouri compromise is the incident and not the principal of the bill. They well understand that the report of the committee and the bill propose to establish the principle in all territorial organizations, that the question of slavery shall be referred to the people to regulate for themselves, and that such legislation should be had as was necessary to remove all legal obstructions to the free exercise of this right by the people.

★ ★ ★ ★

Now, sir, if these gentlemen have entire confidence in the correctness of their own position, why do they not meet the issue boldly and fairly, and controvert the soundness of this great principle of popular sovereignty in obedience to the Constitution? They know full well that this was the principle upon which the colonies separated from the crown of Great Britain, the principle upon which the battles of the Revolution were fought, and the principle upon which our republican system was founded. They cannot be ignorant of the fact that the Revolution grew out of the assertion of the right on the part of the imperial Government to interfere with the internal affairs and domestic concerns of the colonies.

★ ★ ★ ★

The Declaration of Independence had its origin in the violation of that great, fundamental principle which secured to the colonies the right to regulate their own domestic affairs in their own way; and the Revolution resulted in the triumph of that principle, and the recognition of the right asserted by it. Abolitionism proposes to destroy the right and extinguish the principle for which our forefathers waged a seven years' bloody war, and upon which our whole system of free government is founded. They not only deny the application of this principle to the Territories, but insist upon fastening the prohibition upon all the States to be formed out of those Territories. Therefore, the doctrine of the Abolitionists — the doctrine of the opponents of the Nebraska and Kansas bill,

---

[T]he doctrine of the Abolitionists — the doctrine of the opponents of the Nebraska and Kansas bill, and the advocates of the Missouri restriction — demands congressional interference with slavery, not only in the Territories, but in all the new States to be formed therefrom. — Stephen A. Douglas

---

and the advocates of the Missouri restriction — demands congressional interference with slavery, not only in the Territories, but in all the new States to be formed therefrom. It is the same doctrine, when applied to the Territories and new States of this Union, which the British Government attempted to enforce by the sword upon the American colonies. It is this fundamental principle of self-government which constitutes the distinguishing feature of the Nebraska

bill. The opponents of the principle are consistent in opposing the bill. I do not blame them for their opposition. I only ask them to meet the issue fairly and openly, by acknowledging that they are opposed to the principle which it is the object of the bill to carry into operation. It seems that there is no power on earth, no intellectual power, no mechanical power, that can bring them to a fair discussion of the true issue. If they hope to delude the people and escape detection for any considerable length of time under the catchwords "Missouri compromise" and "faith of compacts," they will find that the people of this country have more penetration and intelligence than they have given them credit for.

★ ★ ★ ★

You cannot fix bounds to the onward march of this great and growing country. You cannot fetter the limbs of the young giant. He will burst all your chains. He will expand, and grow, and increase, and extend civilization, christianity, and liberal principles. Then, sir, if you cannot check the growth of the country in that direction, is it not the part of wisdom to look the danger in the face, and provide for an event which you cannot avoid? I tell you, sir, you must provide for lines of continuous settlement from the Mississippi valley to the Pacific ocean. And in making this provision, you must decide upon what principles the Territories shall be organized; in other words, whether the people shall be allowed to regulate their domestic institutions in their own way, according to the provisions of this bill, or whether the opposite doctrine of congressional interference is to prevail. Postpone it, if you will; but whenever you do act, this question must be met and decided.

The Missouri compromise was interference; the compromise of 1850 was non-interference, leaving the people to exercise their rights under the Constitution. The Committee on Territories were compelled to act on this subject. I, as their chairman, was bound to meet the question. I chose to take the responsibility, regardless of consequences personal to myself.

★ ★ ★ ★

On every other political question these have always supporters and opponents in every portion of the Union — in each State, county, village, and neighborhood — residing together in harmony and good fellowship, and combating each other's opinions and correcting each other's errors in a spirit of kindness and friendship. These differences of opinion between neighbors and friends, and the discussions that grow out of them, and the sympathy which each feels with the advocates of his own opinions in every portion of this widespread Republic, adds an overwhelming and irresistible moral weight to the strength of the Confederacy. Affection for the Union can never be alienated or diminished by any other party issues than those which are joined upon sectional or geographical lines. When the people of the North shall all be rallied under one banner, and the whole South marshaled under another banner, and each section excited to frenzy and madness by hostility to the institutions of the other, then the patriot may well tremble for the perpetuity of the Union. Withdraw the slavery question from the political arena, and remove it to the States and Territories, each to decide for itself, such a catastrophe can never happen. Then you will never be able to tell, by any Senator's vote for or against any measure, from what State or section of the Union he comes.

Why, then, can we not withdraw this vexed question from politics? Why can we not adopt the principle of this bill as a rule of action in all new territorial organizations? Why can we not deprive these agitators of their vocation, and render it impossible for Senators to come here upon bargains on the slavery question? I believe that the peace, the harmony, and perpetuity of the Union require us to go back to the doctrines of the Revolution, to the principles of the Constitution, to the principles of the Compromise of 1850, and leave the people, under the Constitution, to do as they may see proper in respect to their own internal affairs.

Source: Congressional Globe, 33rd Cong., 1st sess., March 3, 1854, (Washington: John C. Rives, 1854), appendix, 31:325–338.

SENATOR SALMON P. CHASE OPPOSES THE KANSAS-NEBRASKA ACT

FEBRUARY 3, 1854

I enter into this debate, Mr. President, in no spirit of personal unkindness. The issue is too grave and too momentous for the indulgence of such feelings. I see the great question before me, and that question only.

Sir, these crowded galleries, these thronged lobbies, this full attendance of the Senate, prove the deep, transcendent interest of the theme.

A few days only have elapsed since the Congress of the United States assembled in this Capitol. Then no agitation seemed to disturb the political elements. Two of the great political parties of the country, in their national conventions, had announced that slavery agitation was at an end, and that henceforth that subject was not to be discussed in Congress or out of Congress. The President, in his annual message, had referred to this state of opinion, and had declared his fixed purpose to maintain, as far as any responsibility attached to him, the quiet of the country.

★ ★ ★ ★

A few of us, indeed, doubted the accuracy of these statements, and the permanency of this repose. We never believed that the acts of 1850 would prove to be a permanent adjustment of the slavery question. We believed no permanent adjustment of that question possible except by a return to that original policy of the fathers of the Republic, by which slavery was restricted within State limits, and freedom without exception or limitation, was intended to be secured to every person outside of State limits and under the exclusive jurisdiction of the General Government.

But, sir, we only represented a small, though vigorous and growing, party in the country. Our number was small in Congress. By some we were regarded as visionaries — by some as factionists; while almost all agreed in pronouncing us mistaken.

And so, sir, the country was at peace. As the eye swept the entire circumference of the horizon and upward to midheaven not a cloud appeared; to common observation there was no mist or stain upon the clearness of the sky.

But suddenly all is changed. Rattling thunder breaks from the cloudless firmament. The storm bursts forth in fury. Warring winds rush into conflict.

★ ★ ★ ★

Now, sir, who is responsible for this renewal of strife and controversy? Not we, for we have introduced no question of territorial slavery into Congress — not we who are denounced as agitators and factionists. No, sir: the quietists and the finalists have become agitators; they who told us that all agitation was quieted, and that the resolutions of the political conventions put a final period to the discussion of slavery.

This will not escape the observation of the country. It is *Slavery* that renews the strife. It is Slavery that again wants room. It is Slavery, with its insatiate demands for more slave territory and more slave States.

And what does Slavery ask for now? Why, sir, it demands that a time-honored and sacred compact shall be rescinded — a compact which has endured through a whole generation — a compact which has been universally regarded as inviolable,

North and South — a compact, the constitutionality of which few have doubted, and by which all have consented to abide.

It will not answer to violate such a compact without a pretext. Some plausible ground must be discovered or invented for such an act; and such a ground is supposed to be found in the doctrine which was advanced the other day by the Senator from Illinois, that the compromise acts of 1850 "superseded" the prohibition of slavery north of 36° 30′, in the act preparatory for the admission of Missouri. Ay, sir, "superseded" is the phrase — "superseded by the principles of the legislation of 1850, commonly called the compromise measures."

★ ★ ★ ★

Sir, this is a novel idea. At the time when these measures were before Congress in 1850, when the questions involved in them were discussed from day to day, from week to week, and from month to month, in this Senate Chamber, who ever heard that the Missouri prohibition was to be superseded? What man, at what time, in what speech, ever suggested the idea that the acts of that year were to affect the Missouri compromise?

★ ★ ★ ★

Now, sir, let us come to the last session of Congress. A Nebraska bill passed the House and came to the Senate, and was reported from the Committee on Territories by the Senator from Illinois, as its chairman. Was there any provision in it which even squinted toward this notion of repeal by supersedure? Why, sir, Southern gentlemen opposed it on the very ground that it left the Territory under the operation of the Missouri prohibition. The Senator from Illinois made a speech in defence of it. Did he invoke Southern support upon the ground that it superseded the Missouri prohibition? Not at all. Was it opposed or vindicated by anybody on any such ground? Every Senator knows the contrary.

★ ★ ★ ★

On the 4th day of January, the Committee on Territories, through their chairman, the Senator from Illinois, made a report on the territorial organization of Nebraska; and that report was accompanied by a bill. Now, sir, on that 4th day of January, just thirty days ago, did the Committee on Territories entertain the opinion that the compromise acts of 1850 superseded the Missouri prohibition? If they did, they were very careful to keep it to themselves. We will judge the committee by their own report. What do they say in that? In the first place, they describe the character of the controversy, in respect to the Territories acquired from Mexico. They say that some believed that a Mexican law prohibiting slavery was in force there, while others claimed that the Mexican law became inoperative at the moment of acquisition, and that

slave-holders could take their slaves into the Territory and hold them there under the provisions of the Constitution. The territorial compromise acts, as the committee tell us, steered clear of these questions. They simply provided that the States organized out of these Territories might come in with or without slavery, as they should elect, but did not affect the question whether slaves could or could not be introduced before the organization of State governments. That question was left entirely to judicial decision.

★ ★ ★ ★

The Committee on Territories declared that it was not wise, that it was not prudent, that it was not right, to renew the old controversy, and to arouse agitation. They declared that they would abstain from any recommendation of a repeal of the prohibition, or of any provision declaratory of the construction of the Constitution in respect to the legal points in dispute.

Mr. President, I am not one of those who suppose that the question between Mexican law and the slave-holding claims was avoided in the Utah and New Mexico Act; nor do I think that the introduction into the Nebraska bill of the provisions of those acts in respect to slavery would leave the question between the Missouri prohibition and the same slaveholding claims entirely unaffected. I am of a very different opinion. But I am dealing now with the report of the Senator from Illinois, as chairman of the committee, and I show, beyond all controversy, that that report gave no countenance whatever to the doctrine of repeal by supersedure.

Well, sir, the bill reported by the committee was printed in the *Washington Sentinel* on Saturday, January 7th. It contained twenty sections; no more, no less. It contained no provisions in respect to slavery, except those in the Utah and New Mexico bills. It left those provisions to speak for themselves. This was in harmony with the report of the committee. On the 10th of January — on Tuesday — the act appeared again in the *Sentinel*; but it had grown longer during the interval. It appeared now with twenty-one sections. There was a statement in the paper that the twenty-first section had been omitted by a clerical error.

But, sir, it is a singular fact that this twenty-first section is entirely out of harmony with the committee's report. It undertakes to determine the effect of the provision in the Utah and New Mexico bills. It declares, among other things that all questions pertaining to slavery in the Territories, and in the new States to be formed therefrom, are to be left to the decision of the people residing therein, through their appropriate representatives. This provision, in effect, repealed the Missouri prohibition, which the committee, in their report, declared ought not to be done. Is it possible, sir, that this was a mere clerical error? May it not be that this twenty-first section was the fruit of some *Sunday work;* between Saturday the 7th, and Tuesday the 10th?

But, sir, the addition of this section, it seems, did not help the bill. It did not, I suppose, meet the approbation of Southern gentlemen, who contended that they have a right to take their slaves into the Territories, notwithstanding any prohibition, either by Congress or by Territorial Legislature. I dare say it was found that the votes of these gentlemen could not be had for the bill with that clause in it. It was not enough that the committee had abandoned their report, and added this twenty-first section, in direct contravention of its reasonings and principles. The twenty-first section itself must be abandoned, and the repeal of the Missouri prohibition placed in a shape which would not deny the slave-holding claim.

The Senator from Kentucky [Mr. Dixon], on the 16th of January, submitted an amendment which came square up to repeal, and to the claim. That amendment, probably, produced some fluttering and some consultation. It met the views of Southern Senators, and probably determined the shape which the bill has finally assumed. Of the various mutations which it has undergone, I can hardly be mistaken in attributing the last to the amendment of the Senator from Kentucky. That there is no effect without a cause, is among our earliest lessons in physical philosophy, and I know of no causes which will account for the remarkable changes which the bill underwent after the 16th of January, other than that amendment, and the determination of southern Senators to support it, and to vote against any provision recognizing the right of any Territorial Legislature to prohibit the introduction of slavery.

It was just seven days, Mr. President, after the Senator from Kentucky had offered his amendment, that a fresh amendment was reported from the Committee on Territories in the shape of a new bill, enlarged to forty sections. This new bill cuts off from the proposed Territory half a degree of latitude on the south, and divides the residue into two Territories — the southern Territory of Kansas, and the northern Territory of Nebraska. It applies to each all the provisions of the Utah and New Mexico bills; it rejects entirely the twenty-first clerical-error section, and abrogates the Missouri prohibition.

★ ★ ★ ★

The truth is, that the Compromise acts of 1850 were not intended to introduce any principles of territorial organization applicable to any other Territory except that covered by them. The professed object of the friends of the compromise acts was to compose the whole slavery agitation. There were various matters of complaint. The non-surrender of fugitives from service was one. The existence of slavery and the slave-trade here in this District and elsewhere, under the exclusive jurisdiction of Congress, was another. The apprehended introduction of slavery into the Territories furnished other grounds of controversy. The slave States complained of the free States, and the free States complained of the slave States. It was supposed by some that this whole agitation might be

stayed, and finally put at rest by skillfully adjusted legislation. So, sir, we had the omnibus bill, and its appendages the fugitive slave bill, and the District slave trade suppression bill. To please the North — to please the free States — California was to be admitted, and the slave depots here in the District were to be broken up. To please the slave States, a stringent fugitive slave act was to be passed and slavery was to have a chance to get into the new Territories. The support of the Senators and Representatives from Texas was to be gained by a liberal adjustment of boundary, and by the assumption of a large portion of their State debt. The general result contemplated was a complete and final adjustment of all questions relating to slavery. The acts passed. A number of the friends of the acts signed a compact pledging themselves to support no man for any office who would in any way renew the agitation. The country was required to acquiesce in the settlement as an absolute finality. No man concerned in carrying those measures through Congress, and least of all the distinguished man whose efforts mainly contributed to their success, ever imagined that in the Territorial acts, which formed a part of the series, they were planting the germs of a new agitation.

★ ★ ★ ★

Mr. President, three great Eras have marked the history of this country in respect to slavery. The first may be characterized as the Era of ENFRANCHISEMENT. It commenced with the earliest struggles for national independence. The spirit which inspired it animated the hearts and prompted the efforts of Washington, of Jefferson, of Patrick Henry, of Wythe, of Adams, of Jay, of Hamilton, of Morris, in short, of all the great men of our early history. All these hoped — all these labored for — all these believed in, the final deliverance of the country from the curse of slavery. That spirit burned in the Declaration of Independence, and inspired the provisions of the Constitution, and the Ordinance of 1787. Under its influence when in full vigor, State after State provided for the emancipation of the slaves within their limits, prior to the adoption of the Constitution. Under its feebler influence at a later period, and during the administration of Mr. Jefferson, the importation of slaves was prohibited into Mississippi and Louisiana, in the faint hope that those territories might finally become free States. Gradually that spirit ceased to influence our public councils, and lost its control over the American heart and the American policy.

★ ★ ★ ★

[The] second era was the Era of CONSERVATISM. Its great maxim was to preserve the existing condition. Men said: Let things remain as they are; let slavery stand where it is; exclude it where it is not; refrain from disturbing the public quiet by agitation; adjust all difficulties that arise, not by the application of principles, but by compromises.

★ ★ ★ ★

The Era of CONSERVATISM passed, also by imperceptible gradations, into the Era of SLAVERY PROPAGANDISM. Under the influences of this new spirit we opened the whole territory acquired from Mexico, except California, to the ingress of slavery. Every foot of it was covered by a Mexican prohibition; and yet, by the legislation of 1850, we consented to expose it to the introduction of slaves. Some, I believe, have actually been carried into Utah and New Mexico. They may be few, perhaps, but a few are enough to affect materially the probable character of their future governments. Under the evil influences of the same spirit, we are now called upon to reverse the original policy of the Republic; to support even a

> *No great question so thoroughly possesses the public mind as this of slavery.... It will light up a fire in the country which may, perhaps, consume those who kindle it.* — Salmon P. Chase

solemn compact of the conservative period, and open Nebraska to slavery.

Sir, I believe that we are upon the verge of another era. That era will be the Era of REACTION. The introduction of this question here, and its discussion, will greatly hasten its advent. We, who insist upon the denationalization of slavery, and upon the absolute divorce of the General Government from all connection with it, will stand with the men who favored the compromise acts, and who yet wish to adhere to them in their letter and in their spirit, against the repeal of the Missouri prohibition. But you may pass it here. You may send it to the other House. It may become a law. But its effect will be to satisfy all thinking men that no compromises with slavery will endure, except so long as they serve the interests of slavery; and that there is no safe and honorable ground for non-slaveholders to stand upon, except that of restricting slavery within State limits, and excluding it absolutely from the whole sphere of Federal jurisdiction. The old questions between political parties are at rest. No great question so thoroughly possesses the public mind as this of slavery. This discussion will hasten the inevitable reorganization of parties upon the new issues which our circumstances suggest. It will light up a fire in the country which may, perhaps, consume those who kindle it.

Source: Congressional Globe, 33rd Cong., 1st sess., February 3, 1854 (Washington: John C. Rives, 1854), appendix, 31:133–140.

Notes

1. *Congressional Globe,* 32nd Cong., 1st sess., (December 23, 1851), appendix, 25:68; (August 26, 1852), appendix, 25:1102–1125; David M. Potter, *The Impending Crisis, 1848–1861* (New York: Harper and Row, 1976), 121–122, 139, 143.

2. Potter, *The Impending Crisis, 1848–1861,* 130, 140.

3. 10 Stat. 291, sec. 10; Potter, *The Impending Crisis, 1848–1861,* 146–151.

4. P. Orman Ray, *The Repeal of the Missouri Compromise, Its Origin and Authorship* (Cleveland: Arthur H. Clark, 1909), 95–99.

5. Robert W. Johannsen, *Stephen A. Douglas* (New York: Oxford University Press, 1973), 410–417; Potter, *The Impending Crisis, 1848–1861,* 158–163.

6. *Congressional Globe,* 33rd Cong., 1st sess., (January 30, 1854), 28:275. Historians disagreed over Douglas's motives in introducing the Kansas-Nebraska Act, which reopened the sectional conflict he had helped temporarily resolve four years earlier. They have emphasized his desire for the presidency, his wish to cement the bonds of the Democratic Party, his interest in expansion and railroad building, or his desire to activate the unimpressive Pierce administration. Potter, *The Impending Crisis, 1848–1861,* 153 (n. 18), 169–171; Roy F. Nichols, "The Kansas-Nebraska Act: A Century of Historiography," *Mississippi Valley Historical Review,* September 1956, 43: 187–197. Douglas, in a contemporary letter, declared that his purpose was to remove the "barbarian wall" created by the occupancy of Indian tribes in the West which prevented "further progress of emigration, settlement and civilization in that direction," and "to authorize and encourage a continuous line of settlements to the Pacific Ocean." In that correspondence, he emphasized that the central idea of continental expansion included railroad development. Stephen A. Douglas to J. H. Crane, D. M. Johnson, and L. J. Eastin, December 17, 1853, in Robert W. Johannsen, ed., *The Letters of Stephen A. Douglas* (Urbana: University of Illinois Press, 1961), 269–270.

7. *Congressional Globe,* 33rd Cong., 1st sess., (January 30, 1854), 31:280–282; (February 3, 1854), appendix 28:133–140; (March 3, 1854), 28:532; (May 22, 1854), 28:1254, appendix, 31:133–140; Johannsen, *Stephen A. Douglas,* 418–419; Potter, *The Impending Crisis, 1848–1861,* 155–165; Frederick J. Blue, *Salmon P. Chase: A Life in Politics* (Kent, Ohio: Kent State University Press, 1987), 93–96; John Niven, *Salmon P. Chase: A Biography* (New York: Oxford University Press, 1995), 149–152.

8. Potter, *The Impending Crisis, 1848–1861,* 165–167; Nichols, "The Kansas-Nebraska Act: A Century of Historiography," 208–211.

9. Robert R. Russell, "The Issues in the Congressional Struggle Over the Kansas-Nebraska Bill, 1854," *Journal of Southern History,* May 1963, 29:208–209; Nicole Etcheson, *Bleeding Kansas: Contested Liberty in the Civil War Era* (Lawrence: University of Kansas Press, 2004), 19–20.

10. Alan Brinkley, *American History: A Survey,* 11th ed. (Boston: McGraw-Hill, 2003), 360.

Pacific Railroad Act
✸ 1862 ✸

"Next to winning the Civil War and abolishing slavery," historian Stephen E. Ambrose writes, "building the first transcontinental railroad, from Omaha, Nebraska to Sacramento, California, was the greatest achievement of the American people in the nineteenth century." The idea of a rail route to the Pacific was first advocated in the 1830s, and by the late 1840s it came to be viewed by many as a necessity. By then, the United States had become a nation where slavery divided the North and the South and a scarcity of transportation divided the East from the newly acquired Western territories. As a result of the settlement of the Oregon question with Great Britain (1846) and the Treaty of Guadalupe Hidalgo with Mexico (1848), which ended the Mexican American War, — the United States had gained control of parts of present-day Colorado, Arizona, New Mexico, and Wyoming, as well as the whole of California, Oregon, Nevada, and Utah. Congress began its consideration of a rail route to the Pacific in 1845. The debate continued for the next seventeen years before Congress reached a resolution.[1]

Proponents argued that the railway was needed to (1) defend the nation's Pacific territories from foreign intrusion, (2) suppress the Indians, (3) cement ties with California and Oregon, (4) speed settlement of the West, (5) relieve problems in American cities by offering new opportunities in the West, (6) create new markets for merchants and manufacturers, (7) provide a trade route to India and China, (8) lower transportation costs by eliminating the need for freight and passengers to be carried across the continent or transported around Cape Horn, and (9) stimulate industry. The project's economic and political implications sparked a spirited rivalry between cities seeking to become the route's eastern terminus and further intensified growing tension between the North and South as each section envisioned the benefits of a rail line running through its region.[2]

Congress allocated funds for a Pacific Railway survey in 1849, but the money was never used. Four years later, Secretary of War Jefferson Davis was authorized "to make such explorations and surveys as he may deem advisable, to ascer-

tain the most practical and economical route for a railroad from the Mississippi River to the Pacific Ocean." Davis's report proved to be "almost as valuable as those of Lewis and Clark." It "contained descriptions of every possible feature of the physical and natural history of the country," "studies of weather," and descriptions of five possible rail routes. Unfortunately, while the report was important to Western settlement, it was not what it claimed to be — a railroad survey. "Not a single qualified railroad engineer had gone into the field with the various parties," and "many questions fundamental to railroad construction had not been addressed." Still, the report did show practical routes to the west, "and members of Congress had now no excuse for further delay in satisfying the general demand of the public for a Pacific railway." There was general agreement on the need for the railway, but debate continued over the "choice of route" and "whether the road should be a private, government, or mixed enterprise."[3]

That spring, the predominant view — to have the federal government build or at least initiate and control the railway — began to be replaced by the idea "that anyone that wished to build a Pacific railway should have an opportunity to do it." The government would support the effort through right-of-way grants, land grants, and bonds. Soon, however, Congress's most enduring and compelling concern — slavery — once again became an issue. The previous May, Congress had repealed the Compromise of 1850, which supposedly settled the question of slavery in the territories. In its place, Congress approved the Kansas-Nebraska Act, which left the decision of whether those two territories would enter the Union as slave or free states up to their inhabitants. The Senate passed Pacific railway bills in 1855 and 1859, but the House took no action. A bill calling for both Northern and Southern routes passed in the House in late 1860, and an amended Senate version was later approved, but by then Congress was preoccupied with the Civil War. The war "removed Congress from the advocates of a southern route and many who opposed giving federal aid to the project. It also strengthened the argument of military

The May 10, 1869, completion of the Transcontinental Railroad at Promontory Point, Utah, where the Central Pacific and Union Pacific Railroads were joined. The specific route and amount of funding for the railroad were determined through the Pacific Railroad Act in 1862.
Source: The Granger Collection, New York.

necessity." One route now seemed likely, but still unresolved were its location and the scope of government aid.[4]

Ultimately, the most persuasive lobbyist proved to be Theodore D. Judah, a celebrated engineer, who in 1857 published his *Practical Plan for Building the Pacific Railroad*. Subsequently, Judah completed an engineering survey that identified a practical route over the Sierra Nevada Mountains and presented facts designed to attract investors; secured the financial backing of several California businessmen, including Governor Leland Stanford; and worked tirelessly on Capitol Hill. In January 1862, Judah's efforts moved Rep. Aaron A. Sargent, R-Calif., to boldly take the House floor, amidst a debate on slavery, to speak on the history of efforts to secure the railway; the military necessity of the route; the economic and military importance of the West Coast; and

Judah's survey. Sargent's remarks prompted the creation of a special subcommittee to draft a proposed bill. Judah was appointed clerk of the new subcommittee and the House and Senate Select Committees on the Pacific Railroad.[5]

While there was little Senate debate in 1862 on the Pacific Railroad Act, a "ferocious" House debate focused on (1) limiting the railway to a single route, (2) determining the amount of money and land the builders of the railway received, and (3) ensuring that the project would be completed. The debate showed that most members were willing to come to grips "with the intricate problem of adjusting differences over routes and terminuses, and the character and extent of aid to be offered." A majority of the House was supportive, with Representative Sargent delivering the most thorough speeches. Several Easterners favored the idea but felt the enormous costs of the war had already severely strained the federal treasury. Rep. William P. Sheffield of Rhode Island believed that Congress already faced "duties more difficult, more arduous, and of greater magnitude than were ever devolved upon any preceding Congress — the duty of preserving this Government from destruction." That goal could not be achieved, he reasoned, "unless we maintain the credit of the country."[6]

When the debate ended, on May 6 the House passed the bill by a comfortable margin, 79–49. An amended Senate version was passed on June 20, 35–5, and five days later the House concurred. President Abraham Lincoln signed the bill on July 1. The act created the Union Pacific Railroad Company to build westward from Omaha, Nebraska (it fixed the latitude and gave President Lincoln the authority to name the eastern terminus). The act's objective was to connect with the Central Pacific Railroad (later the Southern Pacific), which was commissioned to begin construction at the same time in Sacramento, California. The act granted each railroad a 400-foot-wide right-of-way and five alternate sections of land on each side line for every mile laid. It also provided for the issuance of 30-year, 6-percent U.S. government bonds to be issued at a rate of $10,000 a mile for track laid on flat land, $32,000 a mile in foothills, and $48,000 in mountainous terrain.[7]

In 1864, after the Central Pacific had laid only 18 miles of track and the Union Pacific had yet to lay a rail, Congress passed a second Pacific Railroad Act to provide further means for the two companies to build capital. The second Pacific Railroad Act doubled the land grants and reduced the right-of-way grants from 400 feet to 200 feet. It was Congress's intent to have the land grants give the railroads an asset that could be used to help finance construction. Initially, the bonds were of little help because money was needed to begin construction. The second act also extended the Central Pacific's authorization to lay rail another 150 miles east into Nevada. Subsequently, in 1866, the Central Pacific received permission to build until it met up with the Union Pacific. Before the transcontinental railroad was completed at Promontory Point, Utah, on May 10, 1869, both companies faced unprecedented construction problems, severe weather, and the hostility of Native Americans.[8]

REPRESENTATIVE AARON A. SARGENT ON THE NECESSITY OF A PACIFIC RAIL ROUTE

JANUARY 31, 1862

Mr. Chairman, I did not rise for the purpose of discussing the slavery question in any of its aspects. Sufficient time has been abstracted from the deliberations of the House on both sides of this Chamber to lead to results upon that matter. Although I have settled convictions upon the duty of Congress and the Executive in the disposal of that question which has disturbed our international relations for half a century, and finally involved us in a disastrous war, I prefer to express these convictions by my votes upon the pending measures, and to use the hour accorded to me by the courtesy of the committee in the presentation of my views of a matter which has heretofore at this session been neglected in both houses, and in which the interests and safety of my constituents, the continuance of our Pacific Empire, and the good name of the nation are involved. I shall treat the question as not one of local importance, for the whole country is interested in our action upon it, and the whole country must suffer by our supineness.

Sir, one year ago this House, after full consideration, passed a bill for the construction of a railroad and telegraph line from the valley of the Mississippi to the Pacific, for the reasons, as indicated in the title of the bill, that military and other purposes of public interest were subserved thereby. The vote by which that bill was passed was the consummation of a long struggle in this House, upon one side of which was arrayed the progressive, far-seeing men of the country, representing constituencies controlling large capital, and anxious for the inauguration of this great national measure. Energy, wisdom, and patriotism distinguished the efforts of the men who fought for this great object through many stormy debates in Congress. Upon the other side were ranged in stolid opposition the men who ever hang upon the wheels of progress; those who delay enterprises of great pith and moment by scruples concerning powers and minor expediencies; the men who could discern constitutional power to indefinitely expand the territory of the Union, but none for its improvement; the men

THE FINAL VOTE

The First Pacific Railroad Act

House
May 6, 1862

	Yea	Nay
Republicans	59	20
Democrats	14	19
Unionists	6	10
Total	**79**	**49**

Senate
June 20, 1862

	Yea	Nay
Republicans	25	3
Democrats	6	2
Unionists	4	0
Total	**35**	**5**

Source: Albert Castel and Scott L. Gibson, *The Yeas and the Nays: Key Congressional Decisions, 1774-1945* (Kalamazoo: New Issues Press, Institute of Public Affairs, Western Michigan University, 1975), 75.

who were governed by local prejudices, more than by considerations of general good. Sectional prejudice, rival routes, and schemes, timidity, indifference, all weighed in the scale, and delayed the consummation for many a weary year achieved by that vote passing a Pacific railroad bill.

★ ★ ★ ★

To-day this great work is not further advanced, so far as Congress is concerned, than it was at the date of the passage of that bill. Although both Houses are now filled with the avowed friends of the measure, it almost seems as if its fate would be to be betrayed with a kiss. I now conceive it my duty — representing, as I do, a people whose safety, perhaps their power to remain a part of this Union depends upon it — to speak plainly upon it, to arouse this House from its inaction, and convince it, if I am able, that this railroad is a necessity of the times — a great war measure — to be inaugurated now, if regard is to be paid to the most vital interests of the country.

★ ★ ★ ★

The Pacific railroad has been a subject of so great interest, and such acknowledged importance, that it has been incorporated into the platform of each party at every Presidential election since 1852, and has often been the subject of special recommendations from the Presidents to Congress. Does this mean nothing? Is it a settled policy to acknowledge its necessity before and ignore its usefulness after a Presidential election? ... A pledge made under these circumstances becomes a responsibility when that party succeeds to power.

★ ★ ★ ★

The admission of new States or Territories into the Union necessarily involves new duties and responsibilities upon the parent Government. All are mutually interested in the welfare, protection and perpetuity of the Union.... It is clearly the imperative duty of the Congress of the United States, therefore, to assume the responsibilities imposed by the Constitution, and grant to the several States the protection they need, and which they justly claim as a constitutional right. Under the authority to declare war and repel invasion, Congress has the undisputed power to assume the construction of any work of public utility or necessity which the exigencies of war may demand.

★ ★ ★ ★

Then, sir, if there be no question as to the powers of Congress, let us inquire as to its duties in relation to this matter.

Between the Atlantic coast and the western verge of the valley of the Mississippi was but lately contained the wealth, power, and influence of this great Republic. Until after the Mexican war the entire country lying still further west to the Pacific was a vast territory, nearly uninterrupted wilderness, sparsely settled, and of which little was known. Our only possession on the Pacific coast was Oregon Territory, the home of a few thousand of our citizens, and the trade of which was comparatively unimportant. British America and the Russian possessions occupied the territory north to Behring Straits, while Mexico and a few minor States were in the possession of

> *[T]his railroad is a necessity of the times — a great war measure — to be inaugurated now, if regard is to be paid to the most vital interests of the country.* — Aaron A. Sargent

the coast to the Isthmus of Panama. As a result of that war the new territory of California and New Mexico was added to our possessions, comprehending a line of seacoast extending from the thirty-fifth to the forty-second parallel of north latitude, equal in extent to the entire Atlantic sea-board from Maine to Florida. Almost simultaneously with the acquisition of this territory were discovered the extensive gold regions of Sierra Nevada, the result of which has been the influx of population into this new country unparalleled in the annals of history. Within the past twelve years a steady stream of immigration has poured into those new possessions by every available route.… [A]t the present time, a population of over half a million souls are pursuing their daily avocations upon the shores of the Pacific.… The steady tide of gold of over $500,000,000 which has during the past twelve years flowed from thence to benefit the older States of the Atlantic slope, fully attests the energy and industry of the citizens of the Pacific.

Sir, it is these people who earnestly demand through us, their congressional Representatives, to be heard upon the great questions which affect their welfare. The States of California and Oregon are realities.… And they claim to be heard at this Congress upon the subject of their necessities by the mouth of their chosen and honored Representatives. Their great want is action; *action* on the subject of a railroad communication with the Atlantic States.

The position of the people of California, and of the whole Pacific coast, in the event of a war with any maritime Power, is an unenviable one. We are not situated as are our sister States of the Atlantic slope. The eastern States possess within themselves elements of power and self-reliance which will enable them to sustain themselves in time of either peace or war.

★ ★ ★ ★

But how is it with us? Members of the same Confederation, we are more distant from our mother land than is India from the British isles. In case of a foreign war, we possess neither the power nor means to successfully defend ourselves from the assaults of our foes. The Isthmus route, now available and open, will then be closed. Our only water communication will be via Cape Horn — a journey of over fifteen thousand miles, requiring from four to five months to make the passage in clipper ships.… No, sir, the first result of a foreign war will be the entire destruction of our commerce. We are confined like the fox in his hole, unable to advance or retreat.

★ ★ ★ ★

But a little over a year ago all was sunshine with us. If any member of this House had risen in his seat only two short years ago and predicted the events of the now past year as they have occurred, he would have been deemed a visionary or a madman. Had he told us that a rebellion would be inaugurated so powerful as to require the organization of an army of half a million of men to quell it, would he have been believed? Had he told us … that two of our then honorable Senators would become traitors and rebels to this Government, and as such would be taken by a war vessel belonging to this Government … to invoke the aid of foreign governments to assist in our overthrow; that their detention by us would result in a war with England, would he not have been suspected of idle dreaming or willful folly? Yet all this, and more, has occurred; and to-day we are trying to provide means to pay or secure to be paid a debt of $1,000,000,000 on

account of this war, of which we have but just commenced the first campaign.

★ ★ ★ ★

This is why, I repeat, it is the duty of wise statesmanship to provide for the future. We know that we are passing through a fiery ordeal. We have just escaped the brink of a precipice — the horrors of a war with the most powerful nation on the earth; a war which, while it would affect the Atlantic States disastrously, would have brought total ruin and desolation to the inhabitants of the Pacific coast, unless they threw themselves without resistance into the arms of the foreign foe. It is the right of those people to ask, it is the duty of Congress to provide, means of protection; and we believe that protection is best afforded, can, in fact, be only afforded by the immediate construction of a railroad connecting the Atlantic States with those of the Pacific.

★ ★ ★ ★

Many obstacles which have heretofore delayed action on this measure are now removed.… The danger of a foreign war has aroused the public mind to the absolute necessity of a railroad to the Pacific. The late interference of the New Granadian authorities with the transit of our prisoners across the Isthmus of Panama warns us of the insecurity of that route. The only objection which I hear urged is the inability of Government to assume new obligations, or to add to the present large debt incurred in quelling the rebellion.

Sir, the argument that this Government is ever too poor to do *equal* justice to all the members of its family is not a fair argument. But it can be shown clearly that this assumed additional debt will not become a burden upon the Treasury of the country. There are two methods by which Government can consistently lend its aid, and by which that aid will prove effectual, both of which contemplate a future reimbursement of the aid advanced; while from the enhanced value of the lands along the line, the development of mineral wealth, and from the rapid settlement of the country, now a wilderness, through which the road will pass, the Government will prove a gainer in a business point of view.

★ ★ ★ ★

It is well known that the surveys made by the Government engineers were not close railroad surveys, but barometrical reconnaissances, which, while affording data sufficiently accurate from which to deduce general results, do not furnish information of the character necessary to determine with accuracy the cost of a line over a difficult country.

★ ★ ★ ★

Since that time reconnaissances have been made of several routes through central California, resulting in the discovery of an entirely new route across the Sierra Nevada mountains, upon which an accurate, scientific railroad survey has recently been made by T. D. Judah, Esq., an accomplished civil engineer, who has done more to advance the great Pacific railroad work by years of labor and devotion than any other man in the country. His surveys develop the fact that, with less maximum grades than those employed on the Baltimore and Ohio railroad, this route effects a saving in distance of nearly two hundred miles, and a saving in cost of nearly fifteen millions of dollars — no mean items in reckoning the length and cost of a Pacific railroad.

★ ★ ★ ★

Sir, if fortunately I may be able by my efforts of this day to excite an active interest in this great and necessary military work, I shall have justified my consumption of the time of the committee. Commercial considerations I have not dwelt upon, although important. If the House wills to aid this grand national measure, I may by and by crave its indulgence in further discussion of details.

I have spoken from a full heart, and from long and anxious study; and I beg that this session may not pass away without the inauguration of a Pacific railroad upon one of the plans which I have presented, or some other that shall commend itself to the wisdom of the House.

Source: *Congressional Globe*, 37th Cong., 2nd sess., January 31, 1862 (Washington: John C. Rives, 1862), 32:599–603.

REPRESENTATIVE WILLIAM F. SHEFFIELD VOICES OPPOSITION TO THE PACIFIC RAILROAD ACT

APRIL 18, 1862

Mr. Chairman, I never read this bill until last evening, when I cursorily glanced over it. I did not intend to vote for it from the beginning, and therefore had no occasion to read it. I believe that there are times and seasons for all things; that every day brings its trials and its duties, and in the providence of God, upon this Congress have been cast duties and responsibilities delicate and arduous; duties more difficult, more arduous, and of greater magnitude than were ever devolved upon any preceding Congress — the duty of preserving this Government from destruction. It is our duty to first perform this higher office before we undertake to embark in an inferior and subordinate enterprise.

The first great object which is devolved upon us to accomplish, is to preserve the Government in its integrity and purity as we inherited it from our ancestors. We cannot do that unless we maintain the credit of the country. What is this project which we are now called upon to adopt? It is to involve the Government still further in a vast expenditure of money.... It is the construction of a railroad from some part of the State of Kansas to the Pacific ocean. It is a magnificent enterprise, and I would be glad to see it carried out, if it could be done without risking the credit of the Government — the integrity of that Government which has protected us so long and so well.

★ ★ ★ ★

Gentlemen may say that money is not required for immediate expenditure. What of that? Our bonds when we issue them bear upon them the pledge of the faith of the nation, and that faith must be redeemed. Our constituents will demand that it shall be redeemed. And those bonds will go into the market, and compete with the bonds we are issuing to raise money to carry on this Government, and to suppress the cruel rebellion which is waged against it. The idea of borrowing money for such an enterprise as this at such a time, and under such circumstances, is wild and chimerical in the extreme, and ought to receive the condemnation of every intelligent gentleman in the country.

This bill provides for the construction of a chain of railroads, to be composed of several links, one of which is to be in Missouri, one in Kansas, one in California, one in Nevada, and the other connecting links to be constructed under the provisions of this act.

I believe involved in that scheme is the means of making this railroad, if it is ever constructed under this bill, one of the most stupendous swindling enterprises ever forced upon a people. Let us look for a moment at some of the provisions of the bill. For instance, the road is to pass through the Territory of Nevada. The corporation to construct the road through that Territory is to be organized under an act of the Legislative Assembly of that Territory. Is it not quite possible that the people who embark in this enterprise may get possession of that corporation and may construct that part of the road? The Government may have a mortgage upon all of the road without that Territory, which it would be induced

> I believe involved in that scheme is the means of making this railroad, if it is ever constructed under this bill, one of the most stupendous swindling enterprises ever forced upon a people. — William F. Sheffield

to foreclose. The Nevada corporation would, nevertheless, control the entire line of road, run it, and receive the profit from it.

★ ★ ★ ★

Mr. Chairman, the gentleman from Missouri, [Mr. BLAIR,] when he was upon the floor yesterday, suggested that members representing districts in the eastern States were opposed to this bill because it was a western scheme. I wish the gentleman had postponed his attempt to get up this sectional party and another sectional strife, until we had overcome the one which we are now trying to put down. I deny, most emphatically, this allegation, and I should have been glad if he had omitted to make this charge.

★ ★ ★ ★

The gentleman from Missouri referred to the battle recently fought in the West, and he told us that the West had done all the fighting in the present war. They have done well and nobly, and I rejoice in it. These men who have won victories at Springfield, Fort Henry, Fort Donelson, Island No. 10, and Pittsburg Landing, are the descendants of the Pilgrim fathers. They are our countrymen, our own kindred, and we glory in their achievements as we do in those of our own sons. But the gentleman forgot some matters when he spoke of the army of the West and its achievements. He forgot the part taken in obtaining these victories by eastern men. General Halleck is from Oneida county, New York. Commodore Foote, who has done as much for the glory of our arms as any other man in the public service, is from the State of Connecticut. Lyon, one of the early victims and martyrs in this great cause, was also from Connecticut. From Massachusetts came Mitchell, who is now performing deeds which are adding to the glory of the American flag. These are our fellow-citizens. They are our countrymen. Their achievements

are the property of the nation, and their glory belongs to our common country — to us at the East as well as to the men of the West

★ ★ ★ ★

The gentleman from Maine [Mr. FESSENDEN,] has stated that we must vote for this Pacific railroad because it is a plank in the Chicago platform, which we introduced here as a kind of political bible. At the time that plank was adopted by the Chicago convention, I indorsed it in its length and breadth, and under the same circumstances I would reindorse it to-day. But the times and circumstances then were, however, very different from what they are now. The times have changed, and to be wise we must change with them. The gentleman tells us that we are now to be governed by a party creed. Mr. Chairman, I have but one party, and that party is the country; I have but one platform, and that platform is the Federal Constitution; one political object to attain, and that is the preservation of this Government. On the 12th of April a year ago, when the shot went against the walls of Sumter, which aroused the nation and shocked the world, I gave up all my party predilections in favor of the country and its cause.... We must look at this great question before us as it is to affect the integrity of the Union.... Gentlemen who urge this measure cannot have considered its financial bearings. If they had done so, they would pause before they undertook to embark the Government in a scheme of this character. I would gladly have voted for a bill for this purpose under other circumstances.... The exigencies of the times demand of us, as the Representatives of the people, that we should devote our attention to that one object, the accomplishment of which is nearer to the hearts of the loyal people than any other — the object of suppressing the insurrection and restoring the union of the States as it came to us from the hands of our fathers.

Source: *Congressional Globe,* 37th Cong., 2nd sess., April 18, 1862 (Washington: John C. Rives, 1862), 32:1727–1728.

Notes

1. Stephen E. Ambrose, *Nothing Like It in the World: The Men Who Built the Transcontinental Railroad, 1863–1869* (New York: Simon and Schuster, 2000), 17. See also John P. Davis, *The Union Pacific Railway: A Study in Railway Politics, History, and Economics* (Chicago: S.C. Griggs, 1894), 35–95; Thamar Emelia Dufwa, *Transcontinental Railroad Legislation, 1835–1862* (New York: Arno Press, 1981), 17–106; Robert William Fogel, *The Pacific Railroad: A Case in Premature Enterprise* (Baltimore: Johns Hopkins Press, 1960), 19–50; Lewis H. Haney, *A Congressional History of Railways in the United States,* 2 vols. (Madison, Wis.: Democrat Printing Co., 1910), 2:49–64.

2. Fogel, *The Pacific Railroad,* 20–21; William F. Huneke, *The Heavy Hand: The Government and the Union Pacific, 1862–1898* (New York: Garland, 1985), 10–11.

3. 10 Stat. 219 (March 3, 1853); Ambrose, *Nothing Like It in the World,* 59; John Hoyt Williams, *A Great and Shining Road: The Epic Story of the Transcontinental Railroad* (New York: Time Books, 1988), 25; Davis, *The Union Pacific Railway,* 60; and Maury Klein, *Union Pacific: Birth of a Railroad, 1862–1893* (New York: Doubleday, 1987), 10.

4. Davis, *The Union Pacific Railway,* 67; Klein, *Union Pacific,* 13; and Williams, *A Great and Shining Road,* 36.

5. Carl I. Wheat, "A Sketch of the Life of Theodore D. Judah," *California Historical Society Quarterly,* (September 1925), 4:253. See also Stuart Daggett, *Chapters on the History of the Southern Pacific* (New York: A. M. Kelley, 1966), 46–47; Helen Hinckley Jones, *Rails from the West: A Biography of Theodore D. Judah* (San Marino, Calif.: Golden West Books, 1969), 41–133; Williams, *A Great and Shining Road,* 29–44; "State of the Union," *Congressional Globe,* (January 31, 1862), 32:599–603.

6. Robert R. Russel, *Improvement of Communication with the Pacific Coast as an Issue in American Politics, 1783–1864* (Cedar Rapids: Iowa: Torch-Press, 1948), 296–297; "Pacific Railroad," *Congressional Globe,* (April 18, 1862), 32:1727. See also "Pacific Railroad," *Congressional Globe,* (April 17, 1862), 32:1699–1700, 1707; April 18, 1862, 32:1727–1728.

7. 12 Stat. 489–498 (July 1, 1862).

8. 13 Stat. 356–365 (July 2, 1864).

Homestead Act
✳ 1862 ✳

"One of the truly epochal laws of American history," proffered historian Paul Gates, is the Homestead Act, signed by President Abraham Lincoln on May 20, 1862. It allowed citizens to settle up to 160 acres of surveyed but unclaimed public land, and to receive title to it after making improvements and residing there continuously for five years. The homesteader had to be the head of a household and at least twenty-one years old. The act was "an aggressive move by a Northern Congress against the South as the nation fell into civil war" as well as "an anachronistic throwback to an earlier period in American history, a memorial of sorts to Thomas Jefferson and his naive vision of a nation sustained by virtuous and independent yeomen tilling small farms." Following Jefferson's death in 1826, laborers on the Eastern seaboard and others began appealing for public land grants to American workers. Subsequently, George Henry Evans, editor of the *Workingman's Advocate,* Horace Greeley, editor of the influential *New York Tribune,* and several other reformers joined the effort to generate "popular interest for free homesteads." Supporters petitioned Congress and kept the issue at the forefront from 1845 to 1862. The land question at times generated dissension on a level with slavery as well as debate over the territories. Congress introduced the first homestead bill in 1844, and subsequent bills passed in the House in 1852, 1854, and 1859, but each subsequently died in the Senate. Both the House and Senate finally agreed on an emasculated homestead bill in 1860, only to see President James Buchanan veto the measure.[1]

When the first homestead bill passed in 1852, most House Southerners favored the bill. Passage of the Kansas-Nebraska Act in 1854 left it to the people of those territories to decide whether they desired slavery, prompting a dramatic change in Southerners. Suddenly, the slavery issue became a more important argument against homesteading than either agrarianism or the protective tariff. Southerners contended free land was unconstitutional, would destroy land values in the South, significantly reduce the income of Eastern farmers, and spark the migration of Europe's unskilled and illiterate to the United States. More importantly, Southerners feared their "peculiar institution" would be injured if free blacks were covered by a homestead bill. To succeed, a free land bill now had to overcome the resistance of Southern planters as well as Eastern speculators who profited from western land sales. When the panic of 1857 largely ended speculative sales, those who supported slavery then stood alone in opposition.[2]

Late in the 1850s, the ascendant Republican Party tacitly agreed that a free land policy could accommodate both homestead supporters and those seeking to block further expansion of slavery. With their party platform of 1860, the Republicans formally abandoned their general condemnation of slavery, and merely opposed its extension into the territories. This allowed Western Democrats indifferent to slavery, as well as the Eastern laboring classes for whom slavery was a secondary concern, to join the party. It also made the homestead idea acceptable to antislavery Easterners fearful that free land might trigger Western migration from their states. The homestead idea was portrayed as a way for the poor to achieve economic independence and become part of the middle class.[3]

When the House again took up the homestead bill early in 1859, it passed with little discussion because, as Rep. Galusha A. Grow, R-Penn., noted, similar bills had already passed in the House and debate on the issue had been going on for years. The bill was subsequently tabled in the Senate when Vice President John C. Breckinridge cast the deciding vote. A year later, when Grow reintroduced his bill, Southerners attempted to table it, but it was eventually approved. Meanwhile, the Senate began consideration of a less objectionable bill offered by Andrew Johnson, D-Tenn., which excluded future aliens and foreigners. When Benjamin F. Wade, R-Ohio, attempted to substitute the House bill for the Senate bill, Southerners harshly attacked the maneuver, charging that the bill's supporters favored it as an abolitionist measure and that it was a ploy to attract votes in the upcoming presidential campaign. Ultimately Johnson withdrew his original bill and, by the authority of the Senate Committee on Public

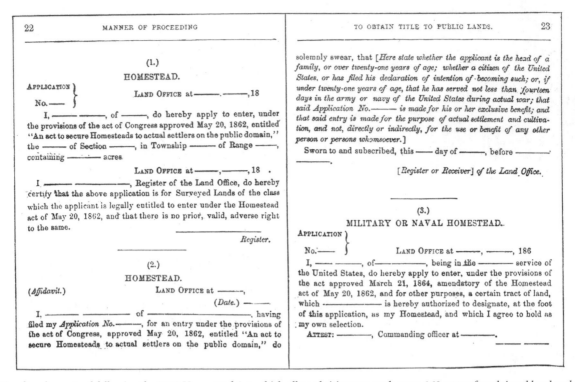

An application for a homestead following the 1862 Homestead Act, which allowed citizens to settle up to 160 acres of unclaimed land and to receive ownership of it after living on it and improving upon it for five consecutive years. Repealed in 1976, 287.5 million acres of land were sold or granted under the act's provisions.
Source: The Granger Collection, New York.

Lands, introduced a new compromise bill that elicited bitter Southern opposition. Slavery and racial sentiments permeated the rhetoric.[4]

Giving public land to the people, Rep. Stephen C. Foster, R-Maine, predicted, would halt calls to prohibit slavery in the territories, resolve the Indian problem, permit the territories to become "organized and compactly-settled states," eliminate the need for a large standing army, and extinguish Mormon polygamy. "[I]nstead of injuring the eastern states by drawing off their population," Foster declared, the law "will give them new life and enterprise. The unemployed will find employment; the homeless will find homes; manufactures and commerce will be invigorated by the new markets which will open in the immense and fertile regions which remain to be settled." Conversely, Sen. James M. Mason, D-Va., saw the bill as an effort by Republicans to gain control of the government so they could "act directly on the condition of African bondage in the southern states." The homestead bill "has no longer the narrow and contracted purpose of giving land to the landless, and providing homes for men who will never occupy them; it has no longer that diminishing character of philanthropic exercise of power on the part of this government, instituted for a very different purpose; it is a political engine, and a potent one." The Senate finally approved a modified bill on May 10, 44–8. Resolving the differences

between the House and Senate versions required the efforts of three different conference committees. On June 19, both houses overwhelmingly accepted a compromise bill; the Senate vote was 36–2, and the House vote was 115–51.[5]

President James Buchanan, however, vetoed the bill. He found the bill objectionable because: (1) it did not require foreign applicants to be the head of the household if they declared their intention to become a citizen, (2) Congress constitutionality did not have the right to donate lands to individuals or to states, and (3) the price of 25 cents per acre was too low given that earlier settlers had paid $1.25 per acre for their land. The same day, the Senate's attempt to override the veto failed by one vote, 27–18 to attain the two-thirds majority required by the Constitution.[6]

In 1861, the elections of 1860 led to Republicans gaining control of both the House and Senate. Abraham Lincoln won the presidency by running on a platform with a plank that demanded homestead legislation. Passage of a homestead bill seemed assured. Approval, however, did not occur until May 1862, more than a year after the secession of the Southern states had seen the most vociferous opponents of the act leave Congress. The House vote of February 28, 1862, was 107–16; the Senate vote of May 6 was 33–7. Congress passed the Pacific Railroad Act, six weeks after the Homestead Act was signed into law, and in May 1869 the transcontinental railroad across the American frontier was completed. The railroad provided easier transportation for homesteaders, and new immigrants were lured westward by railroad companies eager to sell off excess land at inflated prices. It also provided ready access to manufactured goods and catalog houses like Montgomery Ward that offered farm tools, barbed wire, linens, weapons, and even houses delivered via the rails. By the time the Homestead Act was repealed in 1976, 287.5 million acres of the public domain had been sold or granted under its provisions.[7]

REPRESENTATIVE STEPHEN C. FOSTER'S "REPUBLICAN LAND POLICY—HOMES FOR THE MILLION"

APRIL 24, 1860

The proper disposition to be made of the public lands has been, from the origin of the Government, a subject of grave interest, upon which the great parties of the day have been divided. The treaty of 1783, by which Great Britain acknowledged the independence of her revolted colonies, fixed the western limits of the Confederacy at the Mississippi river. At that day, the whole valley of the great river was an unbroken wilderness; and, indeed, the settlements were almost confined to the belt of land near the sea-shore. The western portions of the now old States were at that period as wild and as unknown to civilized man as the Rocky Mountain regions are to us to-day. If we look at the modern maps of the United States, the area included within the original limits of the Union will appear small; but the proportion of land to the number of the inhabitants was, at the commencement of our national existence, far greater than it is at the present time. We have made vast acquisitions of territory; but the increase of population has outstripped territorial expansion in a fourfold degree.

This single comparison illustrates the immense progress which the country has made in subduing the wilderness and subjecting it to the uses of civilized life. It also gives promise of still greater and more rapid victories of peace and industry in the near future. Within the space of a lifetime our population has advanced from the Atlantic slope of the Alleghanies, in compact array of States, to the western frontiers of Missouri and Iowa. We have planted States on the Pacific, and, interspersed between these disjointed parts of the Confederacy, we have planted colonies, numbering tens of thousands of intelligent freemen, which, under the fostering care of the Federal Government, are destined to become States, and to complete the chain of civilization from ocean to ocean.

In my judgment, the Government of the Union is called upon by every consideration of humanity and expediency to encourage the settlement of the Territories as rapidly as possible. We now have two frontiers exposed to the predatory attacks of savage Indians. The States on this side of the continent have a western frontier; the States on the Pacific have an eastern frontier. From whatever cause it may happen, whether from the warlike habits of the Indians or from the unjust encroachments of white men upon these children of the forest, we know that a state of almost perpetual hostility exists between the people of the frontiers and the savage tribes. This state of things will become worse and worse, so long as the Territories remain wild and unsettled, and the Indians continue their savage customs.

In view of what has been accomplished during the last eighty years from small beginnings, and with small means, we hazard little in the prediction that the whole of our Territories may, within twenty years more, become organized and compactly-settled States. Eighty years ago, our population was three million. It is now more than thirty million. Within that period, those three million, and their descendants, together with immigrants from Europe, have settled and subdued a wilderness larger than that which now remains in its wild state. Can not thirty-odd million, backed by an increasing tide of European immigration, accomplish as much within the next two decades as three million accomplished in eighty years? Is it too much to anticipate the obliteration of our frontiers within that period?

If we consult merely economical considerations, it seems to me that the Federal Government is bound to pursue a policy which will facilitate the speedy settlement of the Territories. Why do we keep a standing Army of twenty thousand men, at a cost of $20,000,000 per annum? It is not to protect the people of the United States from aggression upon each other. It is not to defend them against the assaults of the great Powers of the earth. It is well understood that our immense and rapidly-growing commerce is our best protection against

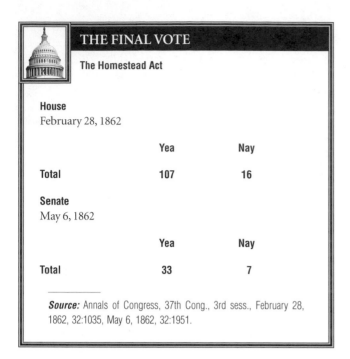

THE FINAL VOTE

The Homestead Act

House
February 28, 1862

	Yea	Nay
Total	107	16

Senate
May 6, 1862

	Yea	Nay
Total	33	7

Source: Annals of Congress, 37th Cong., 3rd sess., February 28, 1862, 32:1035, May 6, 1862, 32:1951.

the really formidable nations of the earth. They cannot afford to go to war with us; our trade is too important, too necessary to their prosperity, to permit the idea of war. We fear nothing from abroad; nothing from domestic insurrection or revolution. Why then, I repeat, do we keep a standing Army at a cost of $20,000,000 per annum? The reason is obvious. It is to prevent the roving bands of Indians in the Territories from preying upon the frontier settlers. These Indian savages are few in numbers; but their trade is war, and their means of subsistence altogether precarious. They are not engaged in cultivating the earth, nor even in pastoral pursuits. Their habits are those of mere savages, and their pursuits, hunting, fishing, and war. When the first two fail them, they resort to the third. They rob caravans, they murder and despoil emigrants, and they attack settlements.

Now, sir, there is but one remedy for these Indian depredations, and that is, the purchase and settlement of their lands. This can be accomplished in a very few years, if the policy of the Federal Government is made to conform to the natural tendency of American population. Let us aid and encourage the settlement of the Territories by granting the public lands to actual settlers. The actual settlers are the men who make the new States; it is their labor which confers value upon the lands; they make marts for the commerce and manufactures of the older States, and they are entitled to the lands. Pass this bill, and every foot of our Territories will, within twenty years, be as secure against Indian depredations as Ohio or Kentucky is to-day.

But what is to become of the Indians? I would not ignore their rights. Far from it. I would be more just and kind to

them than this Government or people have ever been. But I deny the right of a handful of savages to monopolize a continent, when millions of men, more intelligent and better every way, need homes. I would pay the Indians liberally for their lands, and secure to them and their posterity perpetual homesteads; and I would extend to them every facility for learning the arts of civilized life. Above all, their present vagabond and destructive habits of hunting and war should be broken up. They should be assigned a permanent home, and confined to it. They can never become civilized until they become fixed to the soil, and learn to live by its cultivation. They are now scattered over a million of square miles of territory, and are nevertheless dying for want of the comforts of life. A hundredth part of that space, if cultivated, would support ten times their number.

★ ★ ★ ★

There is another evil which the remoteness and wildness of our immense Territories has fostered into fearful importance. I allude to polygamy, that foulest product of the nineteenth century, which seems to denote a decline in civilization. Mormonism, we are aware, sprung up in the older States; but polygamy was unheard of until the Saints removed beyond the reach of civilization. In Missouri and Illinois that fanatical and persecuted sect was suspected of some practices inconsistent with morality, but it was not until they felt themselves secure in the mountain fastnesses of Utah, a thousand miles beyond the frontiers of civilization, that they threw off all disguise, and shocked the moral sense of the country and the world by the open practice of polygamy. They feel secure from molestation in that remote and not easily accessible region. We know what their history has been. They have trampled on the laws of the Congress, and notwithstanding that millions of money have been spent in sending an army to subdue them, they still revel in licentiousness, insult your judges, mock your army, and murder your citizens.

★ ★ ★ ★

The only way to render the abolition of polygamy effectual is to encourage the settlement of the Territories as rapidly as possible. To effect this result, no plan could be better devised than the homestead bill which lately passed this body, but which, I fear, is doomed to hang up for a long time in the other wing of the Capitol, if it ever passes that body. If such a law were passed, a very few years would suffice to fill the Territories with population, and to overwhelm the polygamists of Utah beneath the advancing tread of Christian civilization.

★ ★ ★ ★

Sir, there are three measures of Republican policy which admirably harmonize with each other and cooperate for the common defense and the general welfare of the Union. These are, the homestead for actual settlers on the public lands, the construction of a Pacific railroad, and the suppression of polygamy. The most effectual way to bring about this last result is to adopt the other two. It is to be hoped that a bill for the construction of a Pacific railroad will be adopted during the present session of Congress. This Congress has it in its power to make itself memorable, through all coming time, by the inauguration of the homestead and the Pacific railroad. They should go together, because they will mutually assist each other. The railroad will make the lands more desirable to settlers, and the settlers will make the construction of the road easier, and add to its utility when completed.

These two great measures, if adopted, would develop the resources of the country; they would people the wilderness, and convert it into smiling fields and peaceful homes for millions of Christian families. This influx of population, as I have pointed out, is the only sure remedy for polygamy; and thus three seemingly independent measures are so intimately blended in their beneficent consequences, as to appear parts of one common policy.

But there are other consequences which must result from these great measures. I have already alluded to one of first-rate importance. By the settlement of the public lands, the frontiers will be obliterated, Indian wars will be abolished, and a large standing Army rendered unnecessary. There is still another incidental benefit which must flow from the passage of these important measures. It addresses itself peculiarly to southern men. They are bitterly hostile to the old Jeffersonian policy of excluding slavery from the Territories; and for a generation past, the very pivot on which their politics has turned has been this question of the power of Congress over slavery in the Territories. The most effectual remedy for the evil of which they complain is to be found in the transformation of the Territories into States.

★ ★ ★ ★

Now, would not this be better than to keep up the agitation in Congress, and run the risk of bringing the Wilmot proviso upon you? Will you not join us in superseding the Wilmot proviso, by the passage of the homestead and the Pacific railroad bills?

We learn from the reports of the Secretary of the Interior, that the Government had, up to September 30, 1859, disposed of 380,000,000 acres of land. Of this vast aggregate, only 147,000,000 acres, or a little more than one third had been sold for cash; while 241,000,000 acres were donated to individuals, corporations, and States. The old parties have had their separate and conflicting policies in regard to the proper disposition of the public lands, but neither policy has prevailed. The Whig policy was to divide the proceeds of sales among the States. This was never done but in one instance, when some twenty million dollars were donated to the States, if I am not mistaken, under the form of a loan or deposit. That measure was never regarded with general favor, and

some of the States for a long period refused to receive their distributive shares. The Democratic policy was to put the proceeds of the land sales into the Treasury, and disburse them as ordinary revenue, thus saving the necessity of taxation to that amount. This scheme may appear very plausible to the lovers of economy, who happen not to be acquainted with Democratic practice; but the above statement, from official sources, must open the eyes of all such persons to the true state of the case. Only about one third of the lands disposed of have been sold for cash; the remaining two thirds have been given away. But it must not be supposed that the one third sold has brought $1.25 per acre into the Treasury. Far from it. Out of the proceeds of sale must be taken the whole expense of surveys and sales, and of the Land Office bureau. When these expenses are deducted, the actual clear receipts into the Treasury will scarcely reach $100,000,000.

I will not undertake to say that the two thirds of the public land which have been given away, have been improperly disposed of. I admit that the bounties to soldiers, and the grants for purposes of education, have been generally well bestowed. It may be admitted, also, that the grants for railroad purposes have generally tended to promote the welfare of the new States, although they have, at the same time, more immediately benefitted the wealthy few engaged in the construction of the roads. The mass of the people have come in for incidental benefits; but the donations of the Government have been made to the wealthy classes. Thus while the country is amused and cheated with the idea which the Democratic party has ever held up to view — that the public lands are to be sold, and their proceeds put into the Treasury, in order to save the necessity of taxation — they are in fact voted away by millions of acres to States and corporations. This practice of giving away the public lands is becoming the general rule, and selling them the exception.

★ ★ ★ ★

Now, sir, the country is growing tired of this mockery. Whatever honest and unsophisticated Democrats may have thought of the avowed policy of the party twelve or twenty years ago, it is now clear that that policy has never been put in practice; or that, if it ever was the practice, it has for many years ceased to be, and that it will never be again.

★ ★ ★ ★

I find in the annual report of the Commissioner for December, 1857, that up to that period 24,247,335 acres of land had been granted under various acts of Congress passed since 1850, to the States for the construction of certain railroads.

★ ★ ★ ★

The lands donated to railroad companies answer a useful end; but they also are held out of market in order, at a future day, to be rendered valuable by the progress of settlements around them. It is thus the fate of the honest laboring masses to be imposed upon and speculated upon, whether the public lands are sold to capitalists or donated to the States for the construction of railroads.

★ ★ ★ ★

Sir, I think it is about time to change this policy. The Democratic policy has now been ostensibly in operation since the foundation of the Government, and its effect has been, to make the rich, richer, and the poor, poorer. Now, let us try the Republican policy, which is to give the public lands to actual settlers, in tracts of one hundred and sixty acres each. Whoever chooses to reside five years on a quarter section of the public domain will amply repay the Government for it, since he will be a pioneer of civilization and Christianity; he will, to that extent, curtail the area of the savage wilderness, and limit the territory to be defended by the Army. He will become a sentinel on the outposts of civilization, and his compensation will be not more than adequate to the service he will render his country. Sir, the idea of giving away the public domain to the people is no new one. Indeed, I incline to the opinion that the idea of selling them is new. The first settlers on this continent, we are informed by history, received the most magnificent donations of land from those who had no right to give them, namely, the monarchs of Europe. The court favorites were munificently endowed with provinces and principalities, and these favorites, I believe, sub-granted them to actual settlers, at nominal prices, or at no price whatever.

★ ★ ★ ★

If we go to the great cities and see thousands of men and women crowded together, like pigs in a sty; if we reflect that their great numbers furnish a supply of labor out of all proportion to the demand; and that this undue competition for employment has reduced them to poverty and to vice, do we not wonder why such things are to be witnessed in a country which has a territory half as large as Europe without inhabitants? Is it wise, is it humane, is it just, to withhold from these people lands which have remained untilled, perhaps, since the dawn of creation? By giving them away, we change the wilderness into fruitful fields; we increase the productive capacity of the land; we set thousands of idle hands to work; we enhance the wages of labor in the eastern cities, by diverting the excess of laborers into new channels of employment, and we create new markets in the West for the manufactures of the East.

It is a great mistake to suppose that the development and settlement of the West will be injurious to the eastern States.

A little reflection will satisfy us that emigration westward, so far from injuring the East, by draining off its population, is the very thing to make the East great and prosperous. What would New York, and Boston, and Philadelphia, and Baltimore be to-day, but for the constant tide of emigration that has for more than half a century flown westward? Where would be their markets for their manufactures and their importations from abroad, if the great West had not been settled? The emigrants from New England, New York, and Pennsylvania, from Maryland, Virginia, and the Carolinas, to the Mississippi valley and to the Pacific shores, have made the

---

The unemployed will find employment; the homeless will find homes; manufactures and commerce will be invigorated by the new markets which will be opened in the immense and fertile regions which remain to be settled. — Stephen C. Foster

---

Erie canal, the Central and Erie railroads, the Pennsylvania, Maryland, and Virginia railroad connections with the Ohio necessary. Without emigration to the West those great highways of our internal commerce would never have existed; the manufactures of New England, Philadelphia, and Baltimore, would never have been heard of; and the commerce of New York would have remained what it was sixty years ago.

The homestead law, instead of injuring the eastern States by drawing off their population, will give to them new life and enterprise. The unemployed will find employment; the homeless will find homes; manufactures and commerce will be invigorated by the new markets which will be opened in the immense and fertile regions which remain to be settled.

★ ★ ★ ★

Sir, is it not a shame and a reproach to a Government like ours, which professes to be a Government of the people, that it should contain, at one and the same time, millions of families without house and home, and a thousand million acres of land which have not known the plow, or seed-time and harvest, since they came forth fresh from the Creator's hand?

Source: *Congressional Globe*, 36th Cong., 1st sess., April 24, 1860 (Washington: John C. Rives, 1860), appendix, 29:244–246.

SENATOR JAMES M. MASON SPEAKS OUT AGAINST THE HOMESTEAD ACT

APRIL 10, 1860

Mr. President, the discussion of to-day, I think, has shed a flood of light upon this great political movement called the homestead bill. The bill came from the House of Representatives. A majority of the Senate, according to my recollection, having the entire control of the subject, have determined that the bill, in some shape, shall pass this body. What form it is to assume, remains yet to be seen. The bill came from the House of Representatives; and I understand the honorable Senator who has just taken his seat, who is a leading, and a deservedly leading, member of the dominant party in that House, to announce here to-day that this bill is a measure intended for empire, command, control, over the destinies of this continent; and he is right. Sir, it lets a flood of light in upon the subject. The honorable Senator has chosen — and it is a part of the policy of this measure of empire — to connect, as indissolubly belonging to it, the whole slave question with the homestead policy. The honorable Senator has told us that the great feature of this policy is, by the gratuitous distribution of the public lands, to plant throughout the whole country now open for settlement a free white population to preoccupy it. The Senator is right; with the objects in view by the bill that has been sent to us by the other House, the question of slavery is connected with it, and cannot be separated. Sir, the purpose is avowed; and if it were not avowed, it would manifest itself; the purpose is avowed, by means of the gratuitous distribution of the public lands, to preoccupy the Territories by population from the free States, and thus incidentally, but of necessity, to exclude slavery. The Senator has been candid in that avowal. The Senator has proclaimed that it was a measure for empire, for political control, and for political ascendency.

★ ★ ★ ★

There is no doubting the quarter from which this bill comes; there is no doubting the policy that it is intended to ingraft upon the country, and there is no doubt that the solid and compact phalanx which we here see on the right of the Chamber is embarked in that policy. Sir, I appeal to the honorable Senator from Tennessee, who comes from a different constituency, to see this thing now in its true light.

★ ★ ★ ★

I know very well that in the organization of the Territories of Oregon and Washington, according to my recollection, there was a policy to invite emigration there by giving men lands on the terms mentioned in the law. I do not remember whether I voted for it; I dare say I did. The policy there was to invite a population into a country without people. Whether it was an ill or a wise policy I will not now undertake to say; but I demand the attention of the Senator from Tennessee — representing a constituency totally different from the constituency of gentlemen on the opposite side of the Chamber, and having a policy totally different in the political power, or the mode in which it is to be controlled in this Government — I demand his attention to the fact, no matter what the policy of those laws was; look at the purpose of this, a purpose avowed, openly avowed on this floor — and I know of no better means by which that policy could be attained than this very scheme of a gratuitous distribution of the public lands, wherever they may be located — for the purpose of planting a population there from the free States, and excluding the slave population.

If the bill passes, how will it be followed up? We have had some experience of the agencies that are introduced by the opposite party in the United States. If the bill passes granting a quarter section of land to those who will go and take possession of it, you will have emigrant aid societies chartered for the purpose of sending people there to take possession, and you will have the honorable Senator from Tennessee and his constituency ministering to that policy, aiding in it, and confirming it. Sir, I give the honorable Senator full credit, if it be a credit — he is the best judge of that — for having been the early friend of what I think he miscalls "the homestead policy." He introduced it at an early day in this Chamber, soon after he came here. According to my recollection, when he represented his constituents in the other branch of the Legislature, he introduced the same policy there; and, if he thinks it a good policy, let him think so. I call his attention to the uses to which it is to be put now.

Why, sir, since I have been a Senator on this floor, an honorable gentleman who came, I think, from the State of Wisconsin — represented by the Senator who has so ably and so frankly discussed this question this morning — a gentleman who has not been a member of this body for many years, a Senator from Wisconsin, (Mr. Walker,) brought in annually what he called his homestead bill. There was a congress at one time in the city of New York, and they memorialized the two Houses to give land to the landless, in the terms used in the resolutions of that congress; and what countenance did it receive here? The bill was introduced from year to year; it has been introduced by the honorable Senator from

Tennessee since he came upon this floor. What countenance did it get? Generally a very meager vote. Where does it stand now? It is brought up as a political engine from the other wing of the Capitol, introduced and sustained here by the compact vote of the Opposition. What is the Opposition? A party calling themselves the Republican party. What is their purpose? To get the control of this Government, that they may act directly on the condition of African bondage in the southern States.

Honorable gentlemen on the other side of the Chamber have, more than once, many of them, disclaimed any connection with the Abolition party. They claim that there is a party somewhere among them of Abolitionists, *pure et simple* fanatics; men who have no political purpose except that of destroying the condition of slavery. I have heard honorable Senators on that side of the Chamber say they had no political affiliation with such a party. Sir, I put it to the country and to the world, what cohesion, what principle of cohesion, is there in this so-called Republican party but its opposition to the condition of slavery? Take that from them, and their life-blood is gone, and they would not exist a day.

Sir, are we to go back to our ABC's in politics, or in the affairs of nations? Have we not seen, within a few years, one of the most distinguished Senators here putting his standard far in advance even of that very Abolition party, for the purpose of compelling them to unite with this so-called Republican party? I allude to the speech made by a Senator from New York, [Mr. SEWARD,] somewhere in his own State — at Rochester, or Syracuse, or some one of those places. In that celebrated speech he spoke of an irrepressible conflict, in which he declared, as the destiny of this country, that it must all be subjected to the dominion of the white race, without any intermixture of African slavery, or that African slavery must extend over the whole continent. That was his theory; and he illustrated it by saying that one of two things must happen — either that the slaveholders of the South would be cultivating with slaves the rye and the wheat fields of the North, or that the white people of the North would he cultivating exclusively the rice and cotton fields of the South. "We must be homogeneous," was his doctrine; and the illustration was, that there was a conflict irrepressible to bring it about. That is the policy of this Republican party. That is the policy which is to be attained by this great engine of the distribution of the public lands. That is the intent and design of the bill which has been brought in from the other House, and received the compact vote of the Opposition on the other side of the Chamber; and that is the bill which the honorable Senator from Tennessee, representing a very different constituency, as I understand it, is prepared to give his countenance and his vote to.

Now, Mr. President, we are indebted to the honorable Senator from Wisconsin for lifting the vail from this measure. It has no longer the narrow and contracted purpose of giving land to the landless, and providing homes for men who will never occupy them; it has no longer that diminished character of philanthropic exercise of power on the part of this Government, instituted for a very different purpose; it is a political engine, and a potent one. It has already received the sanction of the other branch of the Legislature, where there is a majority — I do not know whether a numerical — but a controlling majority of the Opposition; and it is before us now, to be passed in the Senate, for the purpose of effecting that great object. It is the Emigrant Aid Society's policy upon a wider scale. It is not to be sustained by voluntary contributions, but it is to be purchased at the price of the public domain gratuitously given. That is the policy of the present homestead bill. I desire that my people should know it, if it is to pass into a law, I desire that my people should have another evidence of the practical working of this Federal Government, if it gets into the hands of those who not only have no sympathy with, but who have a determination to destroy that condition of society which is mixed up with the very existence of the South. I desire my people to see it, and to note it as another evidence of the practical working of this Government when it falls into those hands.

Sir, I have spoken of this measure altogether as a measure of policy, as a mode of attaining empire and of using it when it is attained. It is an agrarian policy. It is an utter departure from the spirit, intent, and meaning of the Constitution which holds these States together. But, besides, it is bad policy as a measure of philanthropy; it is an encouragement to pauperism. The honorable Senator from Texas has been kind enough to show me — I am indebted to his kindness for it — that on the law quoted by the honorable Senator from Tennessee, the yeas and nays were not called for, so as to vindicate my personal vote, if it is worth vindicating; but, as I said before, I am perfectly indifferent. I may have voted for such a bill as that; very possibly I did; but not this policy, with a disposition to invite population into a territory without population.

★ ★ ★ ★

If the honorable Senator from Tennessee can find any vindication of a vote for this bill, in any policy that may have been adopted to bring population into territories where there was none, he is welcome to it. Let him settle that with his constituents. I do not intend to hold him to an account; I have no right to do so; but I intended most respectfully and civilly to call his attention to the political uses which are to be made of the measure for which he is responsible on this floor. I confess that when I first saw that this measure had been taken up as a party measure in the other House by those who are in opposition to the party now in possession of the Government, upon the eve of a presidential election, the impression I entertained, though I did not express it, was that it was only a magnificent bid for the Presidency, to conciliate or to buy up the popular vote. It seems I was mistaken. It has a larger, a wider, a grander end in view; one much more worthy of the great political struggle that must exist between parties in this country. Its end is to attain political power — I will not say fairly and honestly — but to attain political power by parceling out the public property gratuitously amongst those who would come and take it, and the end of the political power was to operate against the condition of slavery.

★ ★ ★ ★

It is a vastly different thing between sending a population into a territory not populated, for political ends to be attained there, and a measure of this kind, by which the public lands are to be gratuitously given in every State and Territory where we have public lands, for the purpose of infusing a population, to attain a great political end of a political party. I say again, if the honorable Senator from Tennessee can vindicate his support of this measure by any policy of that sort, let him do it. The things are very different; widely different. We are to have, as I have said, an emigrant aid society, not aided by the private contributions of individual members of a political party, but an emigrant aid society aided by the legislation of the Federal Government to bring about political ends hostile to the South, and intended to destroy the social condition of the South. That is the purpose. It is in that light I present it to the honorable Senator and to the country.

★ ★ ★ ★

I cannot imagine a greater curse that can be inflicted on the white race anywhere, than to send them a parcel of negroes in any other condition than that of slavery. I cannot imagine a greater curse that could be inflicted on the black race — the negroes — than to set them free to work out in freedom their own salvation. It would end — as the honorable Senator must know, or will know if he looks at the condition of negroes in freedom — in their relapsing into utter and brutal barbarism. Why, sir, what is the experience of our country? If honorable

---

I cannot imagine a greater curse that can be inflicted on the white race anywhere, than to send them a parcel of negroes in any other condition than that of slavery. I cannot imagine a greater curse that could be inflicted on the black race ... than to set them free to work out in freedom their own salvation.

— James M. Mason

Senators will open their eyes to the existing facts, wherever the black race has been elevated on this continent, it has been elevated in the condition of slavery. Where they have been

humanized, civilized, or christianized, it has been while they were in the condition of slaves; and when they have been emancipated, and gone to live by themselves, they have fallen from the degeneration of their race, of necessity, from causes over which we have no control, and can exercise none — fallen into absolute, brutal barbarism.

★ ★ ★ ★

We all know that it is part of the history of man that we are very prone to make facts conform to our theories; and we all know that there is no part of the habitable civilized world where this idea of abolitionism has taken more hold than upon some of the British statesmen — the sentimentalists of Great Britain; and I have seen, from time to time, as that Senator has, in their views and in their speeches in Parliament, directly opposite statements as to the condition of things in the British West Indies. I have understood, on the best information I can get, that since the emancipation of the negro race in the British West Indies, the value of property there, dependent altogether upon labor to make it productive, has diminished not less than seventy-five per cent; and the reason of it is, that they have no labor. I know, because it has passed within my personal knowledge, that Great Britain was at one time ready and anxious to get an importation of free negroes, if they would go voluntarily from this country to her possessions in the West Indies, to see if she could use that labor, when there was abundance of the same sort of machines capable of labor that would not do it. The honorable Senator from Wisconsin comes from one of the new States, where, I presume, there are very few negroes; but there are other Senators, who come from old States, where there are vast numbers of them, and I put it to them whether, in any of the old States, or in any States where there are a large number of free negroes, they ever find them, left to themselves, be it in a city or in a village or in the country, where they are not in a state a very few degrees removed from actual barbarism?

★ ★ ★ ★

I made the inquiry, and it was fair that it should be answered, whether, in the experience of Senators who came from those States where there remained a comparatively large colored population in freedom, they had not retrograded, and whether, wherever they were found in masses, wherever they were congregated and left to communities by themselves, they did not show a strong proclivity to the barbarism from which they emerged when they were brought to this continent. That has been my experience, so far as I have had a personal knowledge, or so far as I have derived it from the observations of others. It may be that in the New England States for aught I know to the contrary, and more especially in the State of Massachusetts, it is impossible for a negro, any more than it is for a white man, to be idle and to be dependent. Everything works there. If a man or a woman gets poor, they pick him or her up and put him or her in the work-house and make them work; and I dare say if the statistics of the State were looked to, it would be found that a large portion of the negro population of that State were now subjected to coercive labor somewhere and in some form.

★ ★ ★ ★

What is to be done with blacks who are now emancipated, I am not prepared to say. It is a great problem that is to be worked out. We had thought at one time, when they were emancipated in the slave States, that they would find a refuge in the free States. The free States are expelling them. Why? If they formed a desirable population they would not do so. If they were not *fruges consumere nati* they would not be for expelling them; they would tolerate them. I agree that something is to be done with them or for them. What it will be, I am not now prepared to say; but from regard for them, that regard which we ought to feel for everything that pertains to animal life, to ascend no higher, I would be the last to advise that they should be sent into the tropics to shift for themselves. Something better may be done for them at home. As to the slave population, I agree with the Senator from South Carolina: if a problem, it has worked itself out; the thing is settled here, so far as the South is concerned or the opinions and purposes of the South, or their ability to make their opinions and their purposes good. It will become, as it has already begun to be, the established policy of the South to have no more emancipation. Let them continue in bondage as they now exist, as the best condition for both races.

Source: *Congressional Globe,* 36th Cong., 1st sess., April 10, 1860 (Washington: John C. Rives, 1860), 29:1634–1637.

Notes

1. Paul W. Gates, *Free Homesteads for All Americans: The Homestead Act of 1862* (Washington, D.C.: Civil War Centennial Commission, 1962), 1, 5–6; William Deverell, "The American West," in Julian E. Zelizer, ed., *The American Congress: The Building of Democracy* (Boston: Houghton Mifflin, 2004), 269. See also Roy M. Robbins, *Our Landed Heritage: The Public Domain, 1776–1936* (Princeton: Princeton University Press, 1942), 105; George M. Stephenson, *The Political History of the Public Lands, from 1840 to 1862: From Pre-Emption to Homestead* (New York: Russell and Russell, 1917), 116.

2. Robbins, *Our Landed Heritage: The Public Domain, 1776–1936,* 116, 175–178. See also Stephenson, *The Political History of the Public Lands, from 1840 to 1862: From Pre-Emption to Homestead,* 168–169.

3. Deverell, "The American West," 270; and Eric Foner, *Free Soil, Free Labor, Free Men: The Ideology of the Republican Party Before the Civil War* (Oxford: Oxford University Press, 1995), 28–29.

4. "Homestead Bill," *Congressional Globe,* (January 26, 1859), 28:612–613. See also ibid., (February 1, 1859), 28:726; (February 17, 1859), 28:1076; and *Congressional Globe,* (March 12, 1860), 29:1115; (March 22, 1860), 29:1297–1298; (April 11, 1860), 29:1650–1652; Benjamin Horace Hibbard, *A History of the Public Land Policies* (New York: P. Smith, 1939), 373–379; Robbins, *Our Landed Heritage: The Public Domain, 1776–1936,* 179–181; Stephenson, *The Political History of the Public Lands, from 1840 to 1862: From Pre-Emption to Homestead,* 195–212.

5. "The Republican Land Policy—Homes for the Millions," *Congressional Globe,* (April 24, 1860), appendix, 29:244–246; "Homestead Bill," *Congressional Globe,* (April 10, 1860), 29:1635. See also "Homestead Bill," *Congressional Globe,* (May 10, 1860), 29:2043; (June 19, 1860), 29:3159, 3179; Hibbard, *A History of the Public Land Policies,* 377–379; Robbins, *Our Landed Heritage: The Public Domain, 1776–1936,* 181.

6. Hibbard, *A History of the Public Land Policies,* 379–380; Robbins, *Our Landed Heritage: The Public Domain, 1776–1936,* 181; Stephenson, *The Political History of the Public Lands, from 1840 to 1862: From Pre-Emption to Homestead,* 215.

7. "Homestead Bill," *Congressional Globe,* (February 28, 1862), 32:1030–1035; (May 6, 1862), 32:1951; 12 Stat. 392–394 (May 20, 1862); U.S. Department of Interior, Bureau of Land Management, *Public Land Statistics, 2006* (Washington, D.C.: Bureau of Land Management, April 2007), 6.

Fourteenth Amendment
✷ 1866–1868 ✷

President Abraham Lincoln, in his second inaugural address of March 4, 1865, appealed to the nation to forget vengeance as it looked toward the future. "With malice toward none; with charity for all," he pleaded, "let us strive on to finish the work we are in, to bind up the nation's wounds … to do all which may achieve and cherish a just and lasting peace."[1] While Lincoln lived long enough to see the surrender of the Confederacy at Appomattox, Virginia, on April 9, he was deprived of the opportunity to continue his pursuit of a "just and lasting peace."

Just six days after Confederate general Robert E. Lee's surrender, the North was plunged into mourning when President Lincoln was assassinated at Ford's Theater in Washington, D.C., by actor and Confederate sympathizer John Wilkes Booth. Secretary of State William H. Seward was also assaulted in his home at the same time but survived his wounds. Lincoln's assassination, along with the subsequent discovery that Booth was part of a wider conspiracy intending also to murder Vice President Andrew Johnson and Union general Ulysses S. Grant, reinforced the determination of radical elements in the Republican Party to impose a harsh Reconstruction program on the defeated Southern states. With Lincoln's assassination, Vice President Johnson assumed the presidency. The principal questions facing both the new chief executive and Congress were: (1) how to restore the Union and reintegrate the defeated South, and (2) what status to accord former slaves. Conflict between the White House and Congress over Reconstruction began with President Lincoln's December 1863 Proclamation of Amnesty. It called for the creation of loyal state governments in which a minority of voters (at least 10 percent of those who had cast votes in the 1860 election) took an oath of allegiance to the Union and accepted emancipation.

Radical Republicans in Congress faulted Lincoln's plan as being excessively lenient and pushed to require at least half the eligible voters to take an oath of allegiance. Although the Thirty-eighth Congress in 1864 reached agreement on a Reconstruction plan to bring the South back into the Union, President Lincoln refused to sign the Wade-Davis Bill and used a pocket veto to kill the proposal. He considered restoration of the Union to be presidential prerogative. Sen. Ben-

jamin F. Wade, R-Ohio, and Rep. Henry W. Davis of Maryland, cosponsors of the plan, together with the other Radical Republicans, favored congressional control of Reconstruction. A critical clause in the Wade-Davis Bill required that 50 percent (rather than 10 percent, as Lincoln favored) of those who cast votes in the 1860 elections take an oath of allegiance to the U.S. Constitution as well as the slavery-related laws and proclamations issued during the War.[2]

Lincoln's veto angered Radical Republicans and foreshadowed his successor's disastrous confrontation with Congress. After Congress refused to seat delegates from Arkansas and Louisiana, as they prepared for readmission under Lincoln's plan, there were hints of a more rigorous administration policy. Lincoln's assassination, however, left unanswered exactly what he intended. Republicans mistakenly assumed they had an ally in Andrew Johnson. They were shocked when Johnson announced his Reconstruction plan on May 29, 1865, while Congress was in a long recess. The plan called for Southerners who took an oath of allegiance to receive a pardon, amnesty, and restoration of their property, except for slaves. Next, delegates were to be elected to state conventions that would be required to proclaim that secession was illegal, repudiate state debts incurred during the rebellion, and ratify the Thirteenth Amendment, which abolished slavery. Former Confederate military and civil officers were barred from participating in this process, as were ex-Confederates with a taxable income of $20,000 or more. Johnson's action in carrying out his plan quickly aroused criticism, however, as he began to hand out pardons to individuals who initially had been disqualified on the basis of wealth or position. At the same time, several Southern states adopted "black codes" that placed legal and economic restrictions on former slaves and refused to ratify the Thirteenth Amendment or repudiate their Confederate debt.[3]

When the Thirty-ninth Congress convened on December 4, it too refused to seat representatives from the seceded states. Instead, it appointed a Joint Committee of Fifteen consisting of nine representatives and six senators to which all matters pertaining to the restoration of the South were to be referred. The committee was charged with investigating conditions in the former Confederate states and formulating Reconstruction

John A. Bingham argued for the passage of the Fourteenth Amendment, which established due process and equal protection under the law. Those opposed to it declared that it violated states' rights and was therefore unconstitutional.
Source: Library of Congress.

strengthened and extended the Freedmen's Bureau, which Congress had created a year earlier to assist destitute former slaves in making the transition to freedom and to administer abandoned farm lands in the war-devastated South. The second proposal made blacks U.S. citizens with the same civil rights as other citizens and conferred enforcement powers on the president and the federal judiciary. The bills were sent to President Johnson for his signature in February and March, respectively, and were immediately vetoed. The Senate, on February 19, attempted to override the Freedmen's Bureau veto but failed, 30–18. A second attempt to extend the bureau was greeted with another veto, but this time Congress prevailed when it overrode the president's action in July. Johnson's veto of the 1866 Civil Rights Act was more easily overridden. The Senate vote of April 6 was 33–15 while the House vote three days later stood at 122–41.[5]

It was against this backdrop on April 30, 1866 that the Joint Committee on Reconstruction proposed a constitutional amendment declaring that all persons born or naturalized in the United States were U.S. citizens, as well as citizens of their respective states, and that a citizen's rights could not be abridged or denied without due process of law. Any state that enacted or enforced a law denying suffrage to any male citizen was subject to proportional reductions in its representation in the House of Representatives. It also excluded all former Confederate officials from holding federal or state office, repudiated the Confederate debt, and maintained the "validity of the United States public debt." Six weeks of extensive debate followed, typified by the remarks of Rep. Andrew J. Rogers, D-N.J., who contended that the proposed Fourteenth Amendment violated states' rights, and Rep. John A. Bingham, R-Ohio, who argued it did not. On June 8, the Senate approved a revised amendment, 33–11. On June 13, the House concurred, 120–32, and sent it to the states for ratification. Abolitionists criticized the amendment for not going far enough. Southerners denounced its restrictions on ex-Confederates. President Johnson questioned the right of Congress to adopt an amendment without the participation of Southern senators and representatives. The Republicans were able, however, to turn the 1866 congressional elections into a highly successful referendum on the amendment, as they retained sizeable majorities in both houses of Congress.[6]

Ratification of the Fourteenth Amendment was not a prerequisite for readmission of former Confederate states to the Union. Prior to 1868, however, Tennessee was the only Southern state to ratify the amendment and the only one to be readmitted. Not until Congress required ratification of the amendment as a necessary precondition for readmission to the Union did enough Southern states join with Northern and Western states to attain the twenty-four of thirty-seven states required for the Fourteenth Amendment to become part of the Constitution in July 1868.[7]

policy. To thwart Johnson's Reconstruction plan, the Radical Republicans knew it had to be answered in a way that would appeal to moderates. That task fell to Rep. Thaddeus Stevens, D-Penn., who was destined to dominate the Joint Committee's work. His speech of December 18 succinctly laid out the Reconstruction policy of Radical Republicans. Stevens's remarks were countered by those of Henry Jarvis Raymond of New York, chairman of the Republican National Committee, and an influential force in Johnson's effort to obtain the vice presidential nomination in 1864. Raymond urged the adoption of a lenient post-war policy toward the South and opposed the Radical Republicans who wanted harsher measures. Together, the remarks of Stevens and Raymond mirrored the divergent views the Joint Committee ultimately tried to address when it proposed the Fourteenth Amendment. Rep. Frederick Enoch Woodbridge, R-Vt., aptly observed at the time that Congress was "not writing history which is difficult," but "making history, which is more difficult."[4]

Meanwhile in the Senate, moderate and Radical Republicans joined together early in 1866 to approve two proposals drafted by Judiciary Committee chairman Lyman Trumbull, D-Ill., to invalidate the "black codes." The first proposal

During the interim, one of the fiercest political struggles in U.S. history played itself out in Washington. In the process, Congress overrode presidential vetoes of the First, Second, and Third Reconstruction Acts, which were designed to provide for the more effective government of the rebel States, and the Tenure of Office Act, which made it an impeachable offense for a president to remove appointed officeholders without first consulting the Senate. Radical Republicans saw the latter measure as a means of assuring that implementation of their Reconstruction plan was not undermined by unsympathetic Johnson appointees. When in February 1868 Johnson tested the constitutionality of the Tenure of Office Act by firing Secretary of War Edwin M. Stanton, the House adopted a resolution to impeach the president for "high crimes and misdemeanors in office." In early March, the House adopted eleven articles of impeachment — the majority of which charged Johnson with violating the Tenure of Office Act. The second longest impeachment trial in the nation's history followed in the Senate before Johnson escaped conviction by a single vote, a two-thirds majority being necessary (thirty-five senators voted "guilty" and nineteen "not guilty") on three separate articles. Following Johnson's acquittal by the Senate, seven states — Arkansas, North Carolina, South Carolina, Louisiana, Georgia, Alabama, and Florida — satisfied the requirements of the Reconstruction Acts, including ratification of the Fourteenth Amendment, and were readmitted into the Union. Both admission bills overcame presidential vetoes.[8]

REPRESENTATIVE ANDREW J. ROGERS DECLARES THAT THE FOURTEENTH AMENDMENT VIOLATES STATES' RIGHTS

FEBRUARY 26, 1866

No resolution proposing an amendment to the Constitution of the United States had been offered to this Congress more dangerous to the liberties of the people and the foundations of this Government than the pending resolution. When shifted from top to bottom it will be found to be the embodiment of centralization and the disfranchisement of the States of those sacred and immutable State rights which were reserved to them by the consent of our fathers in our organic law.

When the gentleman says the proposed amendment is intended to authorize no rights except those already embodied in the Constitution, I give him the plain and emphatic answer — if the Constitution provides the requirements contained in this amendment, why, in this time of excitement and public clamor, should we attempt to again ingraft upon it what is already in it?

★ ★ ★ ★

The gentleman takes the position that there is nothing in this proposed amendment with regard to privileges and immunities of citizens of the several States attempted to be ingrafted in the instrument, except those which already exist in it. If those rights already exist in the organic law of the land, I ask him, what is the necessity of so amending the Constitution as to authorize Congress to carry into effect a plain provision which now, according to his views, inheres in the very organic law itself? I know what the gentleman will attempt to say in answer to that position: that because the Constitution authorizes Congress to carry the powers conferred by it into effect, privileges and immunities are not considered within the meaning of powers, and therefore Congress has no right to carry into effect what the Constitution itself intended when it provided that citizens of each State should have all privileges and immunities of citizens in the several States.

★ ★ ★ ★

This proposed amendment goes much further than the Constitution goes in the language which it uses with regard to the privileges and immunities of citizens in the several States. It proposes so to amend it that all persons in the several States shall by act of Congress have equal protection in regard to life, liberty, and property. If the bill to protect all persons in the United States in their civil rights and furnish the means of their vindication, which has just passed the Senate by almost the entire vote of the Republican party be constitutional, what, I ask, is the use of this proposed amendment? What is the use of authorizing Congress to do more than Congress has already done, so far as one branch is concerned, in passing a bill to guaranty civil rights and immunities to the people of the United States without distinction of race or color? If it is necessary now to amend the Constitution of the United States in the manner in which the learned gentleman who reported this amendment proclaims, then the vote of the Senate of the

THE FINAL VOTE

Fourteenth Amendment

Senate
June 8, 1866

	Yea	Nay
Republicans	32	2
Democrats	0	6
Unionists	0	3
Total	**33**	**11**

House
June 13, 1866

	Yea	Nay
Republicans	120	0
Democrats	0	32
Total	**120**	**32**

Source: Albert Castel and Scott L. Gibson, *The Yeas and the Nays: Key Congressional Decisions, 1774–1945* (Kalamazoo: New Issues Press, Institute of Public Affairs, Western Michigan University, 1975), 86.

United States in passing that bill guarantying civil rights to all without regard to race or color was an attempt to project legislation that was manifestly unconstitutional, and which this proposed amendment is to make legal.

★ ★ ★ ★

No sentiment of disloyalty to the great doctrines of self-government embodied in the Constitution has or shall ever beat or throb in my heart. To the maintenance of those doctrines I have devoted the whole of my time in this body, and to them and the safeguards of constitutional liberty I shall devote the balance of my life. In devotion to and love of my country, I will yield to no man on earth. My only hope for liberty is in the full restoration of all the States, with the rights of representation in the Congress of the United States upon no condition but to take the oath laid down in the Constitution. In the legislation by the States they should look to the protection, security, advancement, and improvement, physically and intellectually, of all classes, as well the blacks as the whites. Negroes should have the channels of education opened to them by the States, and by the States they should be protected in life, liberty, and property, and by the States should be allowed all the rights of being witnesses, of suing and being sued, of contracting, and doing every act or thing that a white man is authorized by law to do. But to give to them the right of suffrage, and hold office, and marry whites, in my judgment is dangerous and never ought to be extended to them by any State. However, that is a matter belonging solely to the sovereign will of the States. I have faith in the people, and dark and gloomy as the hour is, I do not despair of free government. I plant myself upon the will of God to work out a bright destiny for the American people.

★ ★ ★ ★

I know human nature is frail. We are not so constituted that we can all think alike. I have no feelings against those who disagree with me, and my only regret is that they cannot look at the situation of our country from a stand above and beyond party. I have been treated with great respect by those who disagree with me, and feel bound to believe that they are moved by honest convictions of duty, and in all charitableness I am willing to accord to them the same rights I claim for myself. Let us treat our southern brethren with kindness. They deserve our sympathy and support, for sorely have they been chastened. God gave His only begotten Son to save the world. Can we not give up our passions and prejudices to save the Union? When you refuse representation you dissolve the Union, prostrate the Constitution, and erect an imperial despotism over nearly one third of the Union. The despotisms of Europe will shout over our fall, while the people of Ireland and all the downtrodden masses will shed tears, mingled with blood. Holding eleven States as conquered provinces, and the enforcement of taxes upon them, must alienate all the affections of the South, and finally end in revolution and blood. Congress has no power to dissolve the Union. I cannot join with northern disunionists in such an abominable act.

I call upon the people of the South to fill up the ranks and make a more determined effort to get into the Union than they did to get out. Let the angel of love blot out the memories of the past insurrection, and hover her wings over a united Union.

Who gave the Senate the constitutional power to pass that bill guarantying equal rights to all, if it is necessary to amend the organic law in the manner proposed by this joint resolution? This is but another attempt to consolidate the power of the States in the Federal Government. It is another step to an imperial despotism. It is but another attempt to blot out from that flag the eleven stars that represent the States of the South and to consolidate in the Federal Government, by the action of Congress, all the powers claimed by the Czar of Russia or the Emperor of the French. It provides that all persons in the several States shall have equal protection in the right of life, liberty, and property. Now, it is claimed by gentlemen upon the other side of the House that negroes are citizens of the United States.

★ ★ ★ ★

This amendment would make all citizens eligible, negroes as well as whites. For if negroes are citizens, they are natural born, because they are the descendants of ancestors for several generations back who were born here as well as themselves. The negroes cannot be citizens in a new State in which they may take up their residence unless they are entitled to the privileges and immunities of the citizens resident in that State. Most of the States make a distinction in the rights of married women. This would authorize Congress to repeal all such distinctions.

★ ★ ★ ★

Now, sir, the words "privileges and immunities" in the Constitution of the United States have been construed by the courts of the several States to mean privileges and immunities in a limited extent. I was so expressly decided in Massachusetts by Chief Justice Parker, one of the ablest judges who ever sat upon the bench in the United States. Those words, as now contained in the Constitution of the United States, were used in a qualified sense, and subject to the local control, dominion, and the sovereignty of the States. But this act of Congress proposes to amend the Constitution so as to take away the rights of the States with regard to the life, liberty, and property of the people, so as to enable and empower Congress to pass laws compelling the abrogation of all the statutes of the States which makes a distinction, for instance, between a crime committed by a white man and a crime committed by a black man, or allow white people privileges, immunities, or property not allowed to a black man.

★ ★ ★ ★

The effect of this proposed amendment is to take away the power of the States; to interfere with the internal police and regulations of the States; to centralize a consolidated power in this Federal Government which our fathers never intended should be exercised by it. All men who are honest, and love their country, and who believe in the doctrines upon which the constitutional liberty of this country is founded, must admit that the rights of the States were the most jealous rights which our fathers had in view; and when they wrested from England the independence of the several States, they wrested them as thirteen independent States and nations, free from each other, with all rights and privileges given to the people to exercise, carry into effect, and control a Government according to their own exclusive will and judgment.

★ ★ ★ ★

Does this amendment propose to leave the several States foreign to each other as regards the regulation of property and of estates, the laws of marriage and divorce, and the protection of the powers of those who live under their jurisdiction? No, sir; it proposes to take away all those rights of a State, and under this broad principle of equality which during the last five years has been proclaimed throughout the land to empower the Federal Government to exercise an absolute, despotic, uncontrollable power of entering the domain of the States and saying to them, "Your State laws must be repealed wherever they do not give to the colored population of the country the same rights and privileges to which your white citizens are entitled." I will not vote for any amendment to the organic law that is to affect the eleven southern States as long as those States are denied representation. The courts have decided that guarantees, privileges, and immunities are not powers, and when the Constitution authorized Congress to make all laws necessary and proper to carry into execution the powers vested in the Government, it meant powers strictly. Upon this point the honorable gentleman who reported this resolution [Mr. BINGHAM] and I agree. That powers do not mean guarantees and privileges we all agree; and because of that this amendment in part is deemed necessary.

Now, sir, another reason why our fathers never intended that Congress should have the right to interfere in the case of the clause of the organic law which says that "the citizens of each State shall be entitled to all privileges and immunities of citizens in the several States," is this: that the eighth section of the first article designates and names the particular powers which Congress may exercise. It is therefore clear that the framers of the Constitution intended to exclude the exercise of all powers except those expressly named. You nowhere find in the Constitution the grant of any power such as is now proposed to be exercised. You nowhere find Congress endowed with the right to interfere with the eminent domain and the sovereign power of a State. But each State has sovereign jurisdiction and power over the property, the liberty, the privileges, and immunities, and the lives of its citizens.

★ ★ ★ ★

It was State rights that our fathers in framing the Constitution sought to preserve in all their just majesty. Through seventy-five years we have enjoyed these rights; and I desire that they shall be handed down unimpaired to our children and our children's children forever. I affirm that when you attempt to take away those rights by constitutional amendment, you make one more stride toward a consolidation of power in one central Government; one more stride toward despotism; one more stride toward the destruction of those great principles which Washington and Jefferson and Madison regarded as the vitalizing ideas of our republican system; one more stride toward the enslavement of your posterity, whose liberties can only be guarantied by the maintenance of the great principles which our revolutionary fathers vindicated and sought to transmit for the benefit of their posterity.

Sir, one great object which is now sought is to prevent eleven sovereign States of this Union from being represented in the Halls of Congress while they are compelled to bear their full burden of taxation. The tendency of this effort must be to widen and deepen that gulf between the North and

South which has been created by northern fanaticism and southern rebellion. The purpose is to make that gulf so broad and vast that the southern States shall never be permitted to take their place in this Union except as mere dependencies of a consolidated central power, by virtue of which Congress shall exercise an unlimited control over the municipal concerns of these States, embracing in its jurisdiction all the most valued rights of life, liberty, and property, which our Constitution designed to be under the guardianship of the individual States, which alone can give the citizen the adequate measure of protection.

Sir, I defy any man upon the other side of the House to name to me any right of the citizen which is not included in the words "life, liberty, property, privileges, and immunities," unless it should be the right of suffrage; and that has been decided by the circuit court of the United States in *Cornfield vs. Cornell*, 4 Washington's Circuit Court Reports, pages 380 and 381, to be included in the words "privileges and immunities;" that "privileges and immunities" are so broad as even to include the right of suffrage. I will not affirm that that position is correct, nor will I deny it; but if it be correct, as that high court has solemnly decided, it is easy to perceive why our fathers refused to authorize Congress to legislate on this subject by granting no power to it to legislate upon the guarantees of the organic law, and confining its legislation to the powers granted. That clause in the organic law which says that no person shall be deprived of life, liberty, or property without due process of law, as well as the other guarantees of the Constitution, have been repeatedly decided by the Supreme Court of the United States to apply only to cases affecting the Federal Government, and not to apply to such cases as are exercised by the States. For instance, if a State should condemn a man to death without due process of law, or take his property for public use without any compensation, the clauses of the Constitution of the United States would have no application to such cases; but if the Federal Government should do the same thing, then these clauses in the organic law would apply. This position no lawyer in this House will deny.

★ ★ ★ ★

This Congress, not satisfied with the powers already given by the Constitution of the United States, not believing that they have authority to pass this civil rights bill which passed through the Senate of the United States, not believing according to the letter and spirit of the Constitution, within the meaning of the word "powers," there is any authority in Congress to carry into effect the immunities and privileges which are contained in this section, they now attempt to ingraft and implant upon the Federal system of this country for all time to come, a despotic and supreme power which would sap the very life-blood of the States and deprive them of the most precious and heretofore indestructible rights which they have

enjoyed from the formation of the Government down to this time. It cannot be expected that the southern States or any one of the border States in this Union will indorse through their Legislatures an amendment of this character. If this amendment were submitted to the people it would not receive the sanction of one State except Massachusetts. The name of this committee ought to be changed from the committee on reconstruction to the committee on destruction. It is a source of despotism and partakes of the character of the English Inquisition and the Jacobin committees of France. It usurps the power to regulate the affairs of the Union, sits in secret inquisition over the liberties of the people, issues edicts and mandates to Congress, and with imperial dignity orders Congress to pass laws which would sap the life-blood of the nation, prostrate the Constitution, break down the Union, and destroy the rights and liberties of the people of America. Its conduct has been recorded for posterity to judge of, and that judgment will consign its acts to oblivion and eternal shame. It was established to prevent the southern States from having representation in the Union, to reduce them to conquered provinces, and to blot from the flag of our country eleven of its stars, and to allow none to even come in by act of Congress, until it would ratify these abominable, despotic, and accursed amendments to the Constitution. This is wicked, pestilent, and odious despotism. I say that the liberties of France were no more invaded, when Napoleon sought to regulate the destinies of France. The bloody acts of Nero and Caligula were not conceived in a more determined hatred of law, liberty, and order, than are the results of the action of this committee. I do not believe they intend to do wrong, but they are mad and know not what they do. They

---

The bloody acts of Nero and Caligula were not conceived in a more determined hatred of law, liberty, and order, than are the results of the action of this committee. — Andrew J. Rogers

---

are like John Brown, who believed he was doing God's will in the murders at Harper's Ferry. I know they would not do an intentional wrong, but fanaticism has made them delirious in their vengeance upon the South. Do not inaugurate this spirit of despotism within the portals of this Capitol dedicated to the immortal Washington.

But of all the amendments that have been proposed there are none so dangerous and outrageous as this.

Source: *Congressional Globe,* 39th Cong., 1st sess., February 26, 1866 (Washington: F. & J. Rives, 1866), appendix, 36:133–136.

REPRESENTATIVE JOHN A. BINGHAM ARGUES THAT THE FOURTEENTH AMENDMENT DOES NOT VIOLATE STATES' RIGHTS

FEBRUARY 28, 1866

[T]he people of the United States have intrusted to the present Congress in some sense the care of the Republic, not only for the present, but for all the hereafter. [The Joint Committee on Reconstruction] would not have sent to this House for its consideration this proposition [Fourteenth Amendment] but for the conviction that its adoption by Congress and its ratification by the people of the United States is essential to the safety of all the people of every State. I repel the suggestion made here in the heat of debate, that the committee or any of its members who favor this proposition seek in any form to mar the Constitution of the country, or take away from any State any right that belongs to it, or from any citizen of any State any right that belongs to him under that Constitution. The proposition pending before the House is simply a proposition to arm the Congress of the United States, by the consent of the people of the United States, with the power to enforce the bill of rights as it stands in the Constitution today.

★ ★ ★ ★

Gentlemen admit the force of the provisions in the bill of rights, that the citizens of the United States shall be entitled to all the privileges and immunities of citizens of the United States in the several States, and that no person shall be deprived of life, liberty, or property without due process of law; but they say, "We are opposed to its enforcement by act of Congress under an amended Constitution, as proposed." That is the sum and substance of all the argument that we have heard on this subject. Why are gentlemen opposed to the enforcement of the bill of rights, as proposed? Because they aver it would interfere with the reserved rights of the States! Who ever before heard that any State had reserved to itself the right, under the Constitution of the United States, to withhold from any citizen of the United States within its limits, under any pretext whatever, any of the privileges of a citizen of the United States, or to impose upon him, no matter from what State he may have come, any burden contrary to that provision of the Constitution which declares that the citizen shall be entitled in the several States to all the immunities of a citizen of the United States?

What does the word immunity in your Constitution mean? Exemption from unequal burdens. Ah! say gentlemen who oppose this amendment, we are not opposed to equal rights; we are not opposed to the bill of rights that all shall be protected alike in life, liberty, and property; we are only opposed to enforcing it by national authority, even by the consent of the loyal people of all the States.

★ ★ ★ ★

Why, I ask, should not the "injunctions and prohibitions," addressed by the people in the Constitution to the States and the Legislatures of States, be enforced by the people through the proposed amendment? By the decisions read the people are without remedy. It is admitted ... that the State Legislatures may by direct violations of their duty and oaths avoid the requirements of the Constitution, and thereby do an act which would break up any government.

★ ★ ★ ★

The question is, simply, whether you will give by this amendment to the people of the United States the power, by legislative enactment, to punish officials of States for violation of the oaths enjoined upon them by their Constitution? That is the question, and the whole question. The adoption of the proposed amendment will take from the States no rights that belong to the States. They elect their Legislatures; they enact their laws for the punishment of crimes against life, liberty, or property; but in the event of the adoption of this amendment, if they conspire together to enact laws refusing equal protection to life, liberty, or property, the Congress is thereby vested with power to hold them to answer before the bar of the national courts for the violation of their oaths and of the rights of their fellow-men. Why should it not be so? That is the question. Why should it not be so? Is the bill of rights to stand in our Constitution hereafter, as in the past five years within eleven States, a mere dead letter? It is absolutely essential to the safety of the people that it should be enforced.

★ ★ ★ ★

Is it not essential to the unity of the people that the citizens of each State shall be entitled to all the privileges and immunities of citizens in the several States? Is it not essential to the unity of the Government and the unity of the people that all persons, whether citizens or strangers, within this land, shall have equal protection in every State in this Union in the rights of life and liberty and property? Why, sir, what an anomaly is presented to-day to the world! We have the power to vindicate the personal liberty and all the personal rights of the citizen on the remotest sea, under the frowning batteries of the remotest tyranny on this earth, while we have not the power in time of peace to enforce the citizens' rights to life, liberty, and property within the limits of South Carolina after her State government shall be recognized and her constitutional relations restored.

★ ★ ★ ★

As the whole Constitution was to be the supreme law in every State, it therefore results that the citizens of each State, being citizens of the United States, should be entitled to all the privileges and immunities of citizens of the United States in every State, and all persons, now that slavery has forever perished, should be entitled to equal protection in the rights of life, liberty, and property.

As a further security for the enforcement of the Constitution, and especially of this sacred bill of rights, to all the citizens and all the people of the United States, it is further provided that the members of the several State Legislatures and all executive and judicial officers both of the United States and of the several States, shall be bound by oath or affirmation to support this Constitution. The oath, the most solemn compact which man can make with his Maker, was to bind the State Legislatures, executive officers, and judges to sacredly respect the Constitution and all the rights secured by it. And yet there is still another provision lest a State Legislature, with the approval of a State Executive, should in disregard of their oath, invade the rights of any citizen or person by unjust legislation, violative alike of the Constitution and the rights secured by it, which is very significant and not to be overlooked, which is,

"And the judges of every State shall be bound by the Constitution of the United States, anything in the constitution and laws of any State to the contrary notwithstanding."

With these provisions in the Constitution for the enforcement in every State of its requirements, is it surprising that the framers of the Constitution omitted to insert an express grant of power in Congress to enforce by penal enactment these great canons of the supreme law, securing to all the citizens in every State all the privileges and immunities of citizens, and to all the people all the sacred rights of person — those rights dear to freemen and formidable only to tyrants — and of which the fathers of the Republic spoke, after God had given them the victory, in that memorable address in which they declared, "Let it be remembered that the rights for

which America has contended were the rights of human nature?" Is it surprising that essential as they held the full security to all citizens of all the privileges and immunities of citizens, and to all the people the sacred rights of person, that having proclaimed them they left their lawful enforcement to each of the States, under the solemn obligation resting upon every State officer to regard, respect, and obey the constitutional injunction?

What more could have been added to that instrument to secure the enforcement of these provisions of the bill of rights in every State, other than the additional grant of power which we ask this day? Nothing at all. And I am perfectly confident that that grant of power would have been there but for the fact that its insertion in the Constitution would have been utterly incompatible with the existence of slavery in any State; for although slaves might not have been admitted to be citizens they must have been admitted to be persons. That is the only reason why it was not there. There was a fetter upon the conscience of the nation; the people could not put it there and permit slavery in any State thereafter. Thank God, that fetter has been broken; it has turned to dust before the breath of the people speaking as the voice of God and solemnly ordaining that slavery is forever prohibited everywhere within the Republic except as punishment for crime on due conviction. Even now for crimes men may be enslaved in States, notwithstanding the new amendment.

As slaves were not protected by the Constitution, there might be some color of excuse for the slave States in their disregard for the requirement of the bill of rights as to slaves and refusing them protection in life or property; though, in my judgment, there could be no possible apology for reducing men made like themselves, in the image of God, to a level with the brutes of the field, and condemning them to toil without reward, to live without knowledge, and die with-out hope.

But, sir, there never was even colorable excuse, much less apology, for any man North or South claiming that any State Legislature or State court, or State Executive, has any right to deny protection to any free citizen of the United States within their limits in the rights of life, liberty, and property. Gentlemen who oppose this amendment oppose the grant of power to enforce the bill of rights. Gentlemen who oppose this amendment simply declare to these rebel States, go on with your confiscation statutes, your statutes of banishment, your statutes of unjust imprisonment, your statutes of murder and death against men because of their loyalty to the Constitution and Government of the United States.

That is the issue that is before the American people; and God helping me, without respect for persons in high places who show a disposition to betray this great cause, I will not betray it, so long as it is given me to know the right.

Pending this great issue, what utterances do we hear? You have, in the first place, the utterances of him whom we elected Vice President of the United States, and who is now, by the work of an assassin, President of the United States, and of whom I have been accustomed to speak with great respect. The House and the country will remember that at the opening of this session I declared in my place here that if an issue was to be made between the President and the Representatives of the people it must be made by him and not by us. It has been made by him.

★ ★ ★ ★

What, in brief, are those utterances? Why, says the President in his speech — not in his message to Congress, but in his speech, which is received with so many laudations in certain quarters, and over which, it seems, the gentleman from New Jersey [Mr. ROGERS] and his party held a sort of general jubilation — "Let all those lately in insurrection against the Government and laws of the United States, who will now declare their allegiance and take the oath, be admitted into this Union, and by their representatives into the councils of this nation."

Take the oath! What oath? Not the oath of the Constitution which they have broken, but the oath prescribed by the President himself, and which, except in the tribunals of military justice, has no more force or effect than the paper upon which it is printed. Ay, take the oath! "Swear him, and let him go." It would be about as reasonable, under existing circumstances, to swear that venomous reptile which was the symbol of South Carolina's treason — the rattlesnake — and let it go.

★ ★ ★ ★

It has been announced by persons in high places unofficially that no amendment should be made to the Constitution; that there is no danger to be apprehended from the million men lately in arms against the Republic; that all the lately rebellious States should be admitted at once to representation without any condition; that the loyal people of the United States who have saved their Government from overthrow by the wager of battle have no right to require any security for the future; that nothing remains for them to do but to kill the fatted calf and to welcome back the returning prodigal traitors by the million.

★ ★ ★ ★

I desire to proceed with the argument to make good the declaration that there is danger to the Republic unless the loyal people who have saved this country by arms shall save it also by laws, which they can only do within the limits of organized States, restored to their constitutional relations to the Government, by and through an amendment to your Constitution.

★ ★ ★ ★

How will you prevent that overpowering majority from taking possession of those reconstructed governments? Do you call it a "republican government" within the meaning of the Constitution to maintain a minority in power indefinitely in a State by Federal bayonets? I do not, nor does any other intelligent man. What then? Why, according to the programme before us, those rebels are all to be sworn in — sworn in upon an oath that makes no conditions, as announced in the President's speech the other day at the White House, save that they will hereafter support the Constitution. They are all to be sworn in and to be allowed to assume the control of their respective States. Where is the power in Congress, unless this or some similar amendment be adopted, to prevent the reenactment of those infernal statutes of banishment and confiscation and imprisonment and murder under which people have suffered in those States during the last four years? Let some man answer. Why, sir, the gentleman from New York [Mr. HALE] himself yesterday gave up the argument on this point. He said that the citizens must rely upon the State for their protection. I admit that such is the rule under the Constitution as it now stands.

I beg leave to read, in confirmation of the truth of what I say, an utterance made in the hearing of the whole people of this country in 1788, when the Constitution was on trial for its deliverance. I read from No. 45 of the *Federalist*, a paper written by James Madison:

> "The powers reserved to the Federal States will extend to all the objects which, in the ordinary course of affairs, concern the lives, liberties, and properties of the people, and the internal order, improvement, and prosperity of the State."

★ ★ ★ ★

Sir, the great question is presented for the consideration of the House and the country, shall these States, all of them, be restored in their present condition, and with no new securities taken by the people for the future? Shall South Carolina be thus restored, for example, nine tenths of her people who vote having been rebels in arms or directly engaged in rebellion against the country, and her Governor having been an active member of the rebel senate at Richmond during the four years' trial, now acting Governor over the loyal men of the State? Is that State to be restored without the power in Congress to protect the few loyal white men there against State statutes of confiscation and statutes of banishment? And for the emancipated slaves of South Carolina are you to have no power save to prohibit their reduction again to slavery except as punishment for crimes against the laws of South Carolina? Let some gentleman who opposes this amendment stand up in his place and answer to the country how, after these States are restored to political power, the Government of the United States can by law intervene, except as to slavery, under the Constitution of the United States, as it now stands, to protect the loyal white minority or the loyal but disfranchised colored majority in that State against banishment?

★ ★ ★ ★

I speak in behalf of this amendment in no party spirit, in no spirit of resentment toward any State or the people of any State, in no spirit of innovation, but for the sake of a violated Constitution and a wronged and wounded country whose heart is now smitten with a strange, great sorrow. I urge the amendment for the enforcement of these essential provisions of your Constitution, divine in their justice, sublime in their humanity, which declare that all men are equal in the rights of life and liberty before the majesty of American law.

I urge the amendment for the enforcement of these essential provisions of your Constitution, divine in their justice, sublime in their humanity, which declare that all men are equal in the rights of life and liberty before the majesty of American law. — John A. Bingham

---

Representatives, to you I appeal, that hereafter by your act and the approval of the loyal people of this country, every man in every State of the Union in accordance with the written words of your Constitution, may, by the national law, be secure in the equal protection of his personal rights. Your Constitution provides that no man, no matter what his color, no matter beneath what sky he may have been born, no matter in what disastrous conflict or by what tyrannical hand his liberty may have been cloven down, no matter how poor, no matter how friendless, no matter how ignorant, shall be deprived of life or liberty or property without due process of law — law in its highest sense, that law which is the perfection of human reason, and which is impartial, equal, exact justice; that justice which requires that every man shall have his right; that justice which is the highest duty of nations as it is the imperishable attribute of the God of nations.

Source: *Congressional Globe,* 39th Cong., 1st sess., February 28, 1866 (Washington: F. & J. Rives, 1866), 36:1088–1094.

Notes

1. James D. Richardson, comp., *Compilation of Messages and Papers of the Presidents,* 20 vols. (New York: Bureau of National Literature, 1897–1927), 8:3478.

2. Herman Belz, *Reconstructing the Union: Theory and Policy During the Civil War* (Ithaca, N.Y.: Cornell University Press, 1969), 126–167, 168–243; David Herbert Donald, Jean H. Baker, Michael F. Holt, *The Civil War and Reconstruction* (New York: W. W. Norton, 2001), 419–420, 508–518.

3. Belz, *Reconstructing the Union: Theory and Policy During the Civil War,* 304–311; Donald, *The Civil War and Reconstruction,* 518–527; J. G. Randall and David Donald et al., *The Civil War and Reconstruction* (Boston: D.C. Heath, 1961), 558–561; Joseph T. Sneed, *Footprints on the Rocks of the Mountain: An Account of the Enactment of the Fourteenth Amendment* (San Francisco: TYSAM Press, 1997), 7–12.

4. *Congressional Globe,* 39th Cong., 1st sess., (December 18, 1865), 36: 72–75; (December 21, 1865), 36:120–126; (February 28, 1866), 36: 1088.

5. Horace Edgar Flack, *The Adoption of the Fourteenth Amendment* (Baltimore: Johns Hopkins Press, 1908), 11–53; Donald et al., *The Civil War and Reconstruction,* 524–535; Randall and Donald, *The Civil War and Reconstruction,* 576–580; Sneed, *Footprints on the Rocks of the Mountain,* 171–-298.

6. Flack, *The Adoption of the Fourteenth Amendment,* 55–139; Donald et al., *The Civil War and Reconstruction,* 543–555; Randall and Donald, *The Civil War and Reconstruction,* 580–586; Sneed, *Footprints on the Rocks of the Mountain,* 298–460.

7. 14 Stat. 428–429; Alan P. Grimes, *Democracy and the Amendments to the Constitution* (Lexington, Mass.: Lexington Books, 1978), 50. See also 15 Stat. 706–707, 710–711; Joseph B. James, *The Framing of the Fourteenth Amendment* (Urbana: University of Illinois Press, 1956), 169.

8. Donald et al., *The Civil War and Reconstruction,* 556–573.

Impeachment of
Andrew Johnson

✵ 1868 ✵

On March 2, 1867, Congress overrode President Andrew Johnson's veto of the Tenure of Office Act — perhaps the most volatile of a series of acts designed by Radical Republicans in Congress to curtail presidential power. The Tenure of Office Act required the president to seek the advice and consent of the Senate before removing any federal official it had confirmed. If the Senate was not in session, the president could suspend an appointee, but if when the Senate reconvened it refused to concur in the removal, the official had to be reinstated. Whether the act applied to individuals appointed by a previous president was unclear. Violation of the act could result in impeachment by the House and removal from office by the Senate.

The first test of the act came during the summer of 1867, while Congress was in recess, after President Johnson asked Secretary of War Edwin M. Stanton for his resignation. When Stanton refused, Johnson suspended him and named former Union general Ulysses S. Grant as his *interim* replacement. Stanton, who had been appointed by Johnson's predecessor, Abraham Lincoln, had become increasingly at odds with the president and most of his cabinet, and was perceived as conspiring with Radical Republicans in Congress to thwart the administration's Reconstruction policies. Johnson subsequently submitted his reasons for suspending Stanton to the Senate when Congress reconvened on December 12.[1]

When the Senate refused to concur with the president's action on January 13, 1868, by a 35–6 vote, Johnson reinstated Stanton. Five weeks later, however, on February 21, he fired Stanton, arguing that the Tenure of Office Act was an unconstitutional infringement on executive power. Later the same day, Lorenzo Thomas, adjutant general of the Army, was appointed secretary of war. Congress quickly became involved in the dispute when Sen. Charles Sumner, R-Mass., one of the upper chamber's leading Radical Republicans, sent Stanton a one-word telegram: "Stick," and Rep. John Covode, R-Penn., introduced a resolution to impeach the president for "high crimes and misdemeanors in office." Impeachment opponents unsuccessfully echoed the sentiments of Rep. James Brooks, D-Maine, who implored the House to beware of the "terrible, fatal precedent" it would set. Instead, Congress followed the lead of men such as Rep. Thaddeus

Stevens, R-Penn., who characterized the president as "a great malefactor."[2]

On February 22, the Committee on Reconstruction favorably reported the Covode Resolution, and two days later, the House voted 126–47 to impeach Johnson and approved two special impeachment committees — one to prepare and report articles of impeachment and the other to "communicate to the Senate the action of the House in ordering an impeachment of the President." On March 2 and 3, the House adopted eleven articles of impeachment — nine involving the president's violation of the Tenure of Office Act, a tenth relating to his "ridiculous harangues" in speeches against Congress, and an eleventh omnibus article. Also, it selected seven of its members as managers to present and argue the charges before the Senate.[3]

The Senate trial began with procedural motions on March 5, 1868, with the chief justice of the U.S. Supreme Court, Salmon P. Chase, presiding. On March 30, Rep. Benjamin F. Butler, R-Mass., delivered the opening argument for the House managers. Historian David Dewitt characterized Butler's three-hour denunciation of Johnson as "a lawyer's tainted plea with a dash of the demagogue." Butler contemptuously dismissed arguments that Stanton was not covered by the Tenure of Office Act, read portions of Johnson's 1866 speeches that were the basis of the tenth article of impeachment, and referred to the president as "his accidental Chief" and "the elect of an assassin." Following Butler's remarks, other House managers spent seven days introducing documentary evidence and calling witnesses who supported the impeachment articles that the House prepared. On April 9, the managers concluded their case.[4]

Later the same day, former Supreme Court justice Benjamin Curtis delivered the opening argument in the president's defense. Curtis claimed that Stanton was not covered by the Tenure of Office Act since Johnson's predecessor had appointed him, and that the president had not violated the act because he had not succeeded in removing Stanton. Also, the act unconstitutionally infringed on the presidency. As for the impeachment article based on Johnson's 1866 speeches, "The House of Representatives ha[d] erected itself into a school of manners … and they desire the judgment of this body whether the President has not been guilty of

Pennsylvania Representative Thaddeus Stevens closing the debate on the impeachment of President Andrew Johnson on March 2, 1868 for his "high crimes and misdemeanors in office."
Source: Library of Congress.

indecorum." Conviction on the tenth article of impeachment, Curtis reasoned, would violate the free speech clause of the First Amendment.[5]

Among the witness called by the president's counsel were Lorenzo Thomas, Johnson's choice to be secretary of war, and Secretary of the Navy Gideon Welles. The latter testified that Cabinet members had told Johnson they felt the Tenure of Office Act was unconstitutional, and Secretary of State William Seward and Secretary of War Stanton agreed to prepare a draft of a veto message. Welles's testimony, Curtis reasoned, showed that the president honestly believed the law to be unconstitutional. Over the House managers' objection, Chief Justice Chase ruled the evidence admissible but was overruled by the Senate 29–20, and the testimony was not allowed.[6]

Final arguments extended from April 22 to May 6, with the House managers speaking for six days and counsel for the

president using five. The managers' case ranged from constitutional concerns to personal attacks on Johnson. Representative Stevens labeled Johnson a "wretched man" who had committed perjury in taking the presidential oath because he only intended to obey the laws he had personally approved. The "track of infamy which must mark his name, and that of his posterity," Stevens declared, "will indeed be long and dark." Rep. John A. Bingham, R-Ohio, brought the crowded galleries to their feet with his thunderous closing: "May God forbid that the future historian shall record of this day's proceedings, that by reason of the failure of the legislative power of the people to triumph over the usurpations of an apostate President, through the defection of the Senate of the United States, the just fabric of American empire fell and perished from the earth!"[7]

William M. Evarts, a prominent Republican lawyer representing the president, contended in his closing argument that violation of the Tenure of Office Act did not rise to the level of an impeachable offense. In his closing argument for Johnson, former attorney general Henry Stanberry compared conviction to a despicable crime.[8]

For most of May 11, the Senate debated the merits of the case behind closed doors. At noon on May 16, it reassembled to vote on impeachment Article XI, which charged Johnson with bringing disrespect to Congress and its Reconstruction policies. When the votes were tallied, thirty-five senators voted "guilty" and nineteen voted "not guilty" — one vote short of the two-thirds majority needed for conviction. By an identical vote on May 26, Johnson again escaped conviction on Article II (of violating the Tenure of Office Act) and Article III (appointing Thomas to be secretary of war *ad interim* without the advice and consent of the Senate).[9] At this point, the Senate voted to adjourn the trial *sine die* without considering the remaining articles.

Although the rules of the Senate required that its members "proceed to vote without debate," on May 11 and May 16, each senator was "permitted to file [an opinion] within two days after the vote." In arguing for conviction, Sen. Charles Sumner, R-Mass., characterized the trial as "one of the last great battles with slavery. Driven from these legislative Chambers; driven from the field of war, this monstrous power has found a refuge in the Executive Mansion, where, in utter disregard of the Constitution and laws, it seeks to exercise its ancient far-reaching sway." Instead of "cooperating with Congress, by execution of laws passed by it," Sen. John Sherman, R-Ohio, declared, Johnson had "thwarted and delayed their execution, and sought to bring the laws and the legislative power into contempt. Armed by the Constitution and the laws, with vast powers, he has neglected to protect loyal people in the rebel States, so that assassination is

organized all over those States, as a political power to murder, banish and maltreat loyal people, and to destroy their property."[10]

Sen. James W. Grimes, R-Iowa, however, could not "agree to destroy the harmonious working of the Constitution for the sake of getting rid of an unacceptable President. Whatever may be my opinion of the incumbent, I cannot consent to trifle with the high office he holds." As a consequence, while he differed "with the President respecting his political views and measures," and deeply regretted the difference between the president and Congress, Grimes explained, "I am not able to record my vote that he is guilty of high crimes and misdemeanors by reason of those differences." For the Senate "to convict and dispose of the Chief Magistrate of a great nation," Sen. Lyman Trumbull, D-Ill., reasoned, "when his guilt was not made palpable by the record, and for insufficient cause, would be fraught with far greater danger to the future of the country than can arise from leaving Mr. Johnson in office for the remaining months of his term, with powers curtailed and limited as they have been by recent legislation."[11]

Nearly two decades after these remarks were penned, Congress repealed the Tenure of Office Act in 1887, after President Grover Cleveland challenged its constitutionality. With the repeal, Congress formally abrogated its claim "to control presidential discretion in suspending or removing officials in the executive branch." Finally, in 1926, Chief Justice (and former president) William Howard Taft found the act to be unconstitutional in his majority opinion in *Myers v. United States*, 272 U.S. 52. Taft reasoned that it was absolutely essential that presidents be able to remove subordinates freely, saying "to hold otherwise would make it impossible for the President, in case of political differences with the Senate or Congress, to take care that the laws be faithfully executed."[12]

REPRESENTATIVE JAMES BROOKS IMPLORES THE HOUSE AGAINST IMPEACHING PRESIDENT ANDREW JOHNSON

FEBRUARY 22, 1868

I am utterly inadequate to discharge the duty which has devolved upon me on this august day, the anniversary of the birthday of the Father of his Country. I am utterly unable upon this occasion either to do my duty to the people or to express myself with that deep solemnity which I feel in rising to resist this untoward, this unholy, this unconstitutional

proceeding. Indeed, I know not why the ghost of impeachment has appeared here in a new form. We have attempted to lay it hitherto, and we have successfully laid it, upon the floor of this House. But a minority of the party on the other side, forcing its influence and its power upon a majority of a committee of this House, has at last succeeded in compelling its

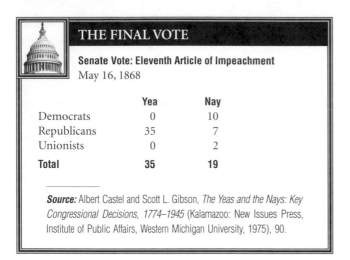

THE FINAL VOTE

Senate Vote: Eleventh Article of Impeachment
May 16, 1868

	Yea	Nay
Democrats	0	10
Republicans	35	7
Unionists	0	2
Total	**35**	**19**

Source: Albert Castel and Scott L. Gibson, *The Yeas and the Nays: Key Congressional Decisions, 1774–1945* (Kalamazoo: New Issues Press, Institute of Public Affairs, Western Michigan University, 1975), 90.

party to approach the House itself in a united, and therefore in a more solemn form, and to demand the impeachment of the President of the United States.

Sir, we have long been in the midst of a revolution. Long, long has our country been agitated by the throes of that revolution. But we are now approaching the last and the final stage of that revolution in which, like many revolutions that have preceded it, a legislative power not representing the people attempts to depose the executive power, and thus to overthrow that constitutional branch of the Government.

There is nothing new in all this. There is nothing new in what we are doing, for men of the present but repeat the history of the past. We are traversing over and over again the days of Cromwell and Charles I and Charles II, and we are traversing over and over again the scenes of the French revolution, baptized in blood in our introductory part, but I trust in God never again to be baptized by any revolutionary proceeding on the part of this House.

The President of the United States, we have been told on other occasions, has deserved impeachment if for nothing else than that he was an obstruction in the way of restoring certain States to this Union; or rather, in better phrase, an obstruction to the party which would be, but is not yet, in full power. Sir, we are all obstructions to that party. My associates, I myself — we all have been and intend to be through all time obstructions in the way of their high-handed proceedings; and if the President of the United States is to be removed as an obstruction and as in the way of the party in power it is equally within that power, by the exercise of a tyrannical majority on the floor of this House, to remove every obstruction here and to have the sole control of the Government themselves. But I bid them beware, and in no spirit of defiance, but from love to my country and the institutions of my country — I solemnly bid them beware before they proceed further in their revolutionary steps.

Suppose you should succeed in passing your resolution of impeachment; suppose you achieve a majority in this House and obtain all you want in the Senate — what then? You can impeach the President of the United States for the hat he wears or for the color of his coat, if you choose, and can arraign him before the Senate, before the judicial tribunal of the Senate, under the merest forms and pretense whatever. You have the power if not the right. But I speak in behalf of those who have sworn to support the Constitution, in behalf of my associates here upon this floor of this House, in behalf of those thundering majorities whose voices are roaring outside of this Capitol and waiting but for a constitutional opportunity to enter herein. And I bid you beware that in so doing you follow every form of the Constitution

---

[S]uppose you achieve a majority in this House and obtain all you want in the Senate — what then? You can impeach the President of the United States for the hat he wears or for the color of his coat, if you choose.... — James Brooks

---

and every form of the common law, or your impeachment will avail you nothing. The President is to be tried before the Senate of the United States through all the forms of law whatsoever, and before you can thus reach your final result he will be removed from your authority by ceasing any longer to be the constitutional President of the United States. If you proceed further; if, as threatened, you suspend him; if you throw him out of office by any other process than impeachment, I tell you in behalf of thousands and tens of thousands and hundreds of thousands and millions of the people of this country we will never, never, so help me God! never, never submit. [Derisive laughter on the Republican side of the House.]

★ ★ ★ ★

I will call the attention of the House to the issue presented here. What is that simple issue? It is an issue for office — only an issue for office. Who has the right to-day to act as Secretary of War, Mr. Stanton or Adjutant General Thomas? Which of them now holds that office? Which of them rightfully occupies that place? It is a mere question of law. The right of trial of a title to office is like the right of trial to property — that and nothing more. In that respect this case presents nothing extraordinary, for over and over again the question who shall be the legal possessor of an office has hitherto been tried by the courts of law. But now for the first time it is proposed to take from the courts of law the control of this question and remove it from judicial investigation and direction. The Reconstruction Committee steps in here and proposes to adjudicate the question for itself and to impeach the President of the United States.

Why, sir, has the gentleman from Pennsylvania [Mr. STEVENS] or have his associates forgotten the case of *Marbury vs. Madison*, almost at the very origin of this Government, in the year 1800, when John Adams went out of office and Thomas Jefferson came in? Here in the District of Columbia Marbury was appointed a justice by Mr. Adams, the outgoing President, and a commission executed, but its delivery was refused by Mr. Madison, the Secretary of State who succeeded under Mr. Jefferson. What was done then? Was the House of Representatives called upon to interfere? Was an impeachment demanded then, as now? Was Mr. Madison or Mr. Jefferson arraigned before the bar of the Senate on the grand inquest of this House for not enforcing an act upon his Secretary of State? No. All parties then cheerfully resorted to the supreme tribunal of the land, and by the simple process of a *mandamus* all asked for an adjudication of the question there. And here is a like legal question — who is and who is not now the legal acting Secretary of War? in order to settle which question this House proposes to snatch the case from the courts and to adjudicate it here by the removal of the President of the United States.

Sir, the President of the United States has as much right to judge of the constitutionality of a law as has the Congress of the United States. The Executive is as much a branch of the Government, aye, is as much the Government, and in some respects more the Government, as the Congress of the United States. And yet, because he has exercised what in good faith he has believed to be his constitutional authority as President of the United States, under an act of Congress, to put in the Department of War a gentleman to act *ad interim*, the honorable gentleman from Pennsylvania [Mr. STEVENS] and those associated with him, upon the instant, impromptu, in a single day, in utter violation of the rules and ordinances of this House, summon us here to settle at once, not whether this or that person legally and constitutionally holds the office of Secretary of War, but to convict the President of crimes and misdemeanors because he honestly holds to one construction of the law while you hold to another.

★ ★ ★ ★

The President of the United States has given his opinion upon the official tenure-of-office act and upon the Constitution of the United States by the appointment of Adjutant General Thomas as Secretary of War *ad interim,* and because of the exercise of that constitutional right we are called upon here at once to pronounce him guilty of high crimes and misdemeanors and to demand his deposition and degradation therefor.

★ ★ ★ ★

Before any adjudication whatsoever, when he is in the exercise of his legal right of construing the Constitution of the United States and the official tenure act, you step in, pronounce him guilty of high crimes and misdemeanors, you impeach him, and attempt his deposition. You make a rule violating the Constitution, and you then impeach the President because he wishes to test the constitutionally of your rule. In other words, you claim the right to throw the President out of office, to abrogate or change the executive department of the Government, to strip it of its prerogatives and power, whenever, by a mere act of Congress, you can overrule a veto; and when you have thus done, unless the Executive obeys your act implicitly, without any investigation or legal adjudication, you claim the right to snatch the case in contest from the Supreme Court of the United States and adjudicate it here in this House and in the Senate through the impeachment power, which destroys that Executive, even if he could afterward rule that all that has been done is right. You have a right, you contend, to pass any illegal and unconstitutional laws; you have a right to disfranchise all of the people of the United States, if you so choose, that are not of your party, you have a right to eject every Democratic member upon the floor of this House by some disqualifying law that you have passed; and if the President of the United States maintains and executes the laws as they have been adjudged by the courts hitherto you have a right then to impeach and depose him because in the exercise of this trust he has been executing what he deems to be the laws and the Constitution of the United States.

Sir, in my judgment, these doctrines and these principles are not maintainable, or if they are then we have ceased to have a written Constitution, and the whole Government which we have is an arbitrary majority on this floor or some arbitrary majority in the Senate. What is the Government? What is the Constitution? What is the law? What is the beauty of our free institutions? The arbitrary rule of a temporary House of Representatives or a temporary Senate? The mere will, the caprice, the tyranny of a majority of members of Congress elected two or four or six years ago?

★ ★ ★ ★

Sir, the history of all such acts as this has been written by many historians and illuminates many pages of the past; but here, for the first time in the history of our country; here, on the natal day of Washington, whose farewell address invokes peace; quiet, forgetfulness of party, and devotion to the public good, whose very presence should inspire us on a great occasion like this, you, by a mere party majority, in order to obtain possession of the Executive of the United States and to have the distribution of a few offices — you propose to depose the President of the United States and to substitute a

President of your own, the present President of the Senate, in his stead.

Sir, the people will understand this. They expect party struggles and struggles for power; they comprehend what are the legitimate authority and prerogatives of a party; but now, for the first time in the history of our country, does a party, in order to maintain itself in power, without which it could not be in power, attempt to overthrow a judicial tribunal of the country, to overthrow the executive department, and thereby to abolish two coordinate and component departments of the Government, for a few miserable offices, for the control of a few wretched places.

★ ★ ★ ★

Go on; go on, if you choose. If I were your trusted adviser and wished to accomplish your overthrow I would hurry you on. Andrew Johnson has no power now as President of the United States. He is without authority or influence or patronage, you have so manacled whatever influence or patronage that he has. By your violent acts, by your unconstitutional proceedings, by your revolutionary overthrow of executive rights, you may succeed, if not in reelecting him to that office, at least in immortalizing him on the pages of history as the most glorious defender of liberty that ever lived under any constitutional Government. You may strip him of his office, but you will canonize him among those heroic defenders of constitutional law and liberty in whose ranks it is the highest glory of human ambition to shine. You may sacrifice him as a President, but long, long after the very name of President — a free President — shall have been forgotten in the clouds of the past his will be blazoned forth in the foreground of the present as the Pole star of liberty and law to be reverenced among men.

But why is this attempted? Because it is believed that the northern people of this country are now with the Democratic party; because it is believed now, previous to a presidential election, it is necessary so to manipulate and control the executive and judicial departments of the Government, by the annexation of some African states of the South, that the so-called Republicans of the North, in spite of the majority of the northern people, shall obtain control and possession of this Government. The sacrifice of two of the three branches of Government is deemed indispensably necessary to keep the Republican party in power.

★ ★ ★ ★

I beg the House to consider the higher duties which it owes to this country and to itself than this impeachment of a President of their own choosing, because he has not construed the laws as they understand them. We have higher, nobler, and better duties to discharge than those due to party. We who may be here now will not be here hereafter, but what we are doing will be remembered through all time. Our children will come after us. History will make the record of our startling proceedings. Above all, we establish a precedent which will be used in republican forms of Government throughout all time to the injury and overthrow of free institutions. It is a beautiful fact in the history of our country in times past that whatever party might be in power, Republican or Democratic, Federal or Whig, which ever had the control of the Government, hitherto the institutions of the country have been respected by the party in power. No party has ever attempted to obtain power in the overthrow and destruction of our form of Government. No Administration was more odious than that of Adams prior to the year 1800, but the Democrats of that day, though denounced, traduced, and imprisoned even, awaited the verdict of the ballot-box. They never attempted to destroy the institutions of the country.

★ ★ ★ ★

I beg the party upon the other side to consider the fatal danger of establishing such a precedent as this. Suppose you succeed, suppose you make the President of the Senate President of the United States, you settle that hereafter a party having a sufficient majority in the House and the Senate can depose the President of the United States. You establish a precedent which all future parties in all time to come will look to.... In the name of all history as well as all right, in the name of the present, in the name of the future, in the name of your children and of mine and of our children's children, I implore you to respect the institutions of your country and to fly from and beware of this terrible, fatal precedent of the deposition of the executive branch of the Government.

Source: *Congressional Globe,* 40th Cong., 2nd sess., February 22, 1868 (Washington: F. & J. Rives and George A. Bailey, 1868), Supplement 39:1336–1339.

REPRESENTATIVE THADDEUS STEVENS ON THE IMPEACHMENT OF PRESIDENT ANDREW JOHNSON

MARCH 2, 1868

Mr. STEVENS, of Pennsylvania. Never was a great malefactor so gently treated as Andrew Johnson. The people have been unwilling to blot the records of their country by mingling his crimes with their shame — shame for endurance for so long a time of his great crimes and misdemeanors. The committee have omitted entirely his wicked abuse of the patronage of the Government, his corruption of the voters of the nation by seducing them with the offers of office, and intimidating them by threats of expulsion, all for the purpose of making them abandon their honest principles and adopt the bastard policy which he had just conceived, a crime more heinous than that which brought many ancient agitators to the block. To this he was prompted by the same motive which made the angels fall. Soon after the death of Mr. Lincoln and the surrender of the so-called confederate army and possessions, the whole government of the territory, persons and property of the territory claimed and conquered from the so-called confederate States of America devolved upon the Congress of the United States, according to the most familiar and well-adjudicated principles of national and municipal law, leaving nothing for the President to do but execute the laws of Congress and govern them by military authority until Congress should otherwise direct. Yet Andrew Johnson, assuming to establish an empire for his own control and depriving Congress of its just prerogative did erect North Carolina and the other conquered territories into States and nations, giving them governments of his own creation and appointing over them rulers unknown to the laws of the United States, and who could not by any such laws hold any office therein. He fixed the qualifications of electors, directed who should hold office, and especially directed them to send representatives to both branches of Congress, ordering Congress to admit them when they should arrive. When Congress refused and asserted its sovereign prerogative to govern those territories, except during their military occupation, by their own inherent power, he treated their pretensions as idle and refused to obey them. When Congress subsequently passed acts dated, March 2, 1867, and their supplements, to reconstruct those governments under republican forms by the votes of the people, he pronounced them unconstitutional, and after they had become laws he advised the people not to obey them, thus seeking to defeat instead of to execute the laws of Congress. All this was done after Congress had

declared these outlying States as possessing no governments which Congress could recognize, and that Congress alone had the power and control over them. This monstrous usurpation, worse than sedition and little short of treason, he adhered to, by declaring in his last annual message and at other times that there was no Congress, and that all their acts were unconstitutional. These, being much more fundamental offenses, and, in my judgment, much more worthy of punishment, because more fatal to the nation, the committee have omitted in their articles of impeachment, because they were determined to deal gently with the President. Encouraged by this impunity, the President proceeded to new acts of lawless violence and disregard of the express enactments of Congress. It is those acts, trivial by comparison, but grave in their positive character, for which the committee has chosen to call him to answer, knowing that there is enough among them, if half were omitted, to answer the great object and purpose of impeachment. That proceeding can reach only to the removal from office, and anything beyond what will effect that purpose, being unnecessary, may be looked upon as wanton cruelty. Hence the tender mercies of this committee have rested only on the most trifling crimes and misdemeanors which they could select from the official life of Andrew Johnson.

I will begin with the articles in their inverse order and devote a few minutes to each. The tenth article charges the President with attempting to induce the commander of this military district, Major General Emory, to disregard the law, by which he considered that he was bound to act, requiring orders to be issued through the General of the Army. The President declared it to be unconstitutional and contrary to the General's commission. About the fact there can be no doubt. There could be but one purpose, and that was to use the Army, if possible, for his operations against Congress. By the ninth article it is charged that the President violated the act regulating the tenure of certain civil officers by appointing Lorenzo Thomas Secretary of War *ad interim* on the 21st day of February, 1868, and declaring that he had that day removed Edwin M. Stanton from the office of Secretary for the Department of War, the Senate being then in session, and not having consented to said removal. He ordered the said Lorenzo Thomas to seize the property of the War Department and act in place of Edwin M. Stanton, and delivered to said Thomas a letter of authority in writing authorizing him to do said acts. About the fact there can be no doubt, as the certified records aver it. What defense the President will make for this violation, direct and palpable, of the civil-tenure bill, we must wait and see.

The eighth article charges that the President conspired with Lorenzo Thomas to seize, take, and possess the property of the United States in the War Department, in violation of the act of March 2, 1867, before referred to. This fact is also proved by the records.

The seventh article charges that the President entered into a conspiracy with Lorenzo Thomas to prevent Edwin M. Stanton, Secretary for the Department of War, from holding the office of Secretary of War, to which he had been appointed under the laws of the United States. All this is proved by a letter of authority produced by General Thomas when he repeatedly demanded possession of the office from the incumbent, and needs no further proof till there be a satisfactory answer.

Article six charges that the President conspired with Thomas to seize the property of the United States in the War Department, contrary to both the act of July, 1861, and the act of March 2, before referred to. This is all proved by the same letter of authority issued by the President to said Thomas, and repeatedly produced by the latter to the Secretary of War in his attempt to gain possession of said property. As I am now only showing the evidence that will be given, it would be wrong to anticipate the defense by argument, until we see the authority upon which it rests.

Article five charges that the President conspired with Lorenzo Thomas to hinder the execution of the tenure-of-office bill, passed March 2, 1867, and to prevent Edwin M. Stanton, Secretary of War, from holding said office. The same evidence is conclusive upon this point.

The fourth article charges that the President, in conspiracy with Lorenzo Thomas and with other persons unknown, did attempt, by intimidation and threats, to prevent Edwin M. Stanton, then and there Secretary of the Department of War, from holding said office, contrary to the provisions of the act of July 31, 1866. The third article charges that the President, on the 21st day of February, 1868, while the Senate was in session, did appoint Lorenzo Thomas Secretary of War *ad interim* without the advice and consent of the Senate, no vacancy having happened during the recess of the Senate nor then existing. The commission produced by Major General Thomas and the copy given in evidence place that fact beyond dispute.

By the second section of the second article of the Constitution the President is empowered to make appointments to office by and with the advice and consent of the Senate, but not while the Senate is in session without such consent. The appointment, therefore, of General Thomas was a palpable violation of the Constitution.

The first article charges that the President, in violation of the Constitution and laws of the United States, issued an order removing Edwin M. Stanton from the office of Secretary of War, commissioned by and with the advice and consent of the Senate, having suspended Mr. Stanton from his office during the recess of the Senate and within twenty days after the meeting of the next session of the Senate, on the 12th day of December, having reported to the Senate such suspension, with the evidence and reasons for his action, and the Senate on the 13th of January, having considered the evidence, refused to concur in the suspension, whereby the said Edwin M. Stanton, by virtue of the tenure-of-office bill, did forthwith resume the functions of his office, of which the said President had due notice, as appears from the records whereupon the President assumed to remove the Secretary from office and to appoint Brevet Major General Lorenzo Thomas Secretary *ad interim,* and ordered the delivery of possession, which order was unlawfully issued, in violation of the act to regulate the tenure of certain civil offices, and contrary to the provisions of said act, and contrary to the provisions of the Constitution of the United States, without the advice and consent of the Senate then being in session.

I had thought that the article which I hold in my hand was one of the articles reported; I had understood it was to be put in as one of the articles, but when I came to read them, after they were printed, I found that there were two articles that are nearly alike, tautological, I think; but this was not in, and I suspect it was omitted by mistake. I will therefore read it and call it one and a half, as, in my judgment, it is the gist and vital portion of this whole prosecution:

> On the 12th day of August 1867, during the recess of Congress, Andrew Johnson, President of the United States, did suspend from office Edwin M. Stanton, Secretary of the Department of War, he having been duly appointed and then in possession and in discharge of the duties of said office, and did, as he was bound to do by the act entitled "An act regulating the tenure of certain civil offices," report to the Senate at its next meeting such suspension, with his reasons for his action in the case. By the second section of said act it is provided, that "if the Senate shall refuse to concur in such suspension, such officer so suspended shall forthwith resume the functions of his office, and the powers of the person so performing its duties in his stead shall cease." While the Senate was considering the sufficiency of the reason, reported, and at other times, Andrew Johnson, President, as aforesaid, formed a deliberate design and determination to prevent the execution of that portion of the law and to prevent the said Edwin M. Stanton from forthwith resuming the functions of his office, notwithstanding the Senate should decide in his favor, thereby committing a high misdemeanor in office. And, when he was defeated in accomplishing his design by the integrity and fidelity of the Secretary *ad interim,* he sought to arrive at the same end by giving a letter of authority to one Lorenzo Thomas, Adjutant General of the Army, to

act as Secretary of War *ad interim,* and to take all the records, books, papers, and other public property of said Department into his custody, the Senate being then in session; and he severely censured the former Secretary *ad interim* for not yielding to his efforts to make him betray his trust.

I wish this to be particularly noticed, for I intend to offer it as an amendment. I wish gentlemen to examine and see that this charge is nowhere contained in any of the articles reported, and unless it be inserted there can be no trial upon it; and if there be shrewd lawyers, as I know there will be, and cavilling judges, and, without this article, they do not acquit him, they are greener than I was in any case I ever undertook before the court of quarter sessions. If it be inserted his own letters show both the removal and the attempt to defeat the reinstatement of the Secretary of War, although the Senate should decide in his favor. How, then, can he or his counsel hope to escape, even if there were no other charge — it is worth all of them put together — from conviction, unless it be upon what I know they will rely on, the unconstitutionality of the tenure-of-civil-office act. Let us for a moment look and see what chance he has to escape there. I may say that the Senate have four times voted upon the constitutionality of that very bill. On the 19th day of February, 1867, the Senate passed that bill by a vote of yeas 29, nays 9. I am sorry to say that it was a party vote, but every Republican voted in its favor. Let me see the recreant who will now dare to tread back upon his steps and vote upon the other side.

Gentlemen remember that we had a committee of conference upon the bill, and the votes were — yeas 22, nays 10; every Republican present voting, after a long discussion, in

---

Unfortunate man! thus surrounded, hampered, tangled in the meshes of his own wickedness — unfortunate, unhappy man, behold your doom. — Thaddeus Stevens

---

favor of the constitutionality of the measure. Then came the veto of the President and his reasons therefor, when the bill was again submitted to the Senate and passed by yeas 35, nays 11; every Republican present voting in favor of the bill. I will not go further, although I could trace one or two other incidental votes of precisely the same character.

Now, if my article is adopted, let him hope who dares to hope that so high a body as the Senate will betray its trust, will forget its own acts, will tread back upon its own action, will

disgrace itself in the face of the nation. Point me to one who dare do it, and I will show you one who will dare the infamy of posterity.

What chance, then, would Andrew Johnson have had we not left out the article I desire to move as an amendment, in order to give him a loophole of escape. Gentlemen can see how fair we are. If my article be inserted what chance has Andrew Johnson to escape, even if all the rest of the articles should fail? Unfortunate man! thus surrounded, hampered, tangled in the meshes of his own wickedness — unfortunate, unhappy man, behold your doom.

Source: *Congressional Globe,* 40th Cong., 2nd sess., March 2, 1868 (Washington: F. & J. Rives and George A. Bailey, 1868), supplement, 39:1612–1613.

Notes

1. James D. Richardson, comp., *Compilation of Messages and Papers of the Presidents,* 20 vols. (New York: Bureau of National Literature, 1897–1927), 8:3781–3792.

2. David Miller Dewitt, *The Impeachment and Trial of Andrew Johnson* (Madison: State Historical Society of Wisconsin, 1967), 408; *Journal of the Executive Proceedings of the Senate,* 40th Cong., 2nd sess., January 13, 1868, 16:129–130; *Congressional Globe,* 40th Cong., 2nd sess., (February 21, 1868), 39:1329–1330; (February 22, 1868), 39:1339; (March 2, 1868), 39:1612.

3. *Congressional Globe,* 40th Cong., 2nd sess., (February 22, 1868), 39:1336–1355, 1358–1369; (February 24, 1868), 39:1382–1402; (March 2, 1868), 39:1613–1619; (March 3, 1868), 39:1638–1642.

4. Supplement of *Congressional Globe Containing the Proceedings in the Senate Sitting for the Trial of Andrew Johnson, President of the United States,* 40th Cong., 2nd sess., (March 30, 1868), 39:34, 40; (March 31, April 1–4, April 9, 1868), 39:53–123.

5. Supplement of *Congressional Globe Containing the Proceedings in the Senate Sitting for the Trial of Andrew Johnson, President of the United States,* 40th Cong., 2nd sess., March 30, 1868, 39:123–136. Quote is found at ibid., 39:135.

6. April 10, 1868, ibid., 39:136–150; April 17–18, 1868, ibid., 8:221–235.

7. Quotes are found in ibid., April 27, 1868, 39:323; May 6, 1868, 39:405.

8. Ibid., April 28, 1868, 39:337–341; April 29, 1868, 39:343–350; April 30, 1868, 39:351–361; May 1, 1868, 39:361–368; May 2, 1868, 39:378–379.

9. Ibid., May 16, 1868, 410–412; May 26, 1868, 412–415.

10. Ibid., 463, 450.

11. Ibid., 424, 420.

12. 24 Stat. 500; Leonard D. White, *The Republican Era, 1869–1901: A Study in Administrative History* (New York: Macmillan, 1958): 31; *Myers v. United States,* 272 U.S. 164 (1926).

Fifteenth Amendment
✳ 1869 ✳

Early in 1867, Congress enfranchised adult male blacks in the District of Columbia, the territories, Nebraska, and eleven former Confederate states. During the next two years, however, supporters of black suffrage realized no further gains. Adult black males still could vote in only twenty of thirty-seven states, and seventeen of the loyal Union States still denied black suffrage. Between 1865 and 1868, Northern voters had "rejected Negro suffrage by a generally substantial vote." Outside the South, only five New England states where black populations were small (Maine, Massachusetts, New Hampshire, Rhode Island, and Vermont), and four Midwestern states (Iowa, Minnesota, Nebraska, and Wisconsin) allowed them to vote.[1]

By the end of 1868, it had become clear to those politicians who favored Negro suffrage "that only federal action could circumvent state action...." State opposition to black suffrage in the North "remained strong enough to intimidate most congressmen." When the Republican national convention met in Chicago on May 20 and 21, a vigorous struggle erupted among the framers of the party's platform over how to handle the potentially "dangerous and debilitating" issue of black suffrage. In the end, they "devised a double standard by endorsing black voting in the South while trying not to antagonize white voters in the North." It allowed Northern states to "decide black suffrage without federal interference" but forced Southern states to "accept black voting as a matter of national policy."[2]

When the black Southern vote proved decisive in Ulysses S. Grant's victory over Horatio Seymour for the presidency in 1868, the Republicans recognized they needed to enfranchise "more blacks, who would be expected to vote Republican in masse" and create "a possible counterbalance against a resurgent Democratic party." While they had captured the White House and maintained substantial majorities in the House 149–63 and Senate 56–11, Grant's electoral college margin, 214–80 was much larger than his popular margin 53 percent to 47 percent. Without the Southern black vote, Grant would have still won the electoral vote but would have lost his popular margin. The election results "engendered within the Republican ranks a sense that the Fortieth Congress," which ended on March 4, 1869, "might be the last

opportunity to pass" a constitutional amendment that would finally settle the suffrage issue. Also, some Republicans "wished to advance the cause of equal rights and impartial justice. The idealistic motive reinforced the pragmatic one."[3]

Two years earlier, congressional Republicans had worked to enfranchise Southern blacks because they needed black votes to counter white votes in the South. Now, it was apparent they also "needed the support of northern and border blacks, especially in closely balanced states, and were willing to run limited risks and promote political reforms in order to maintain power." At the same time, the Republicans wanted to "protect black voting in the South by federal election enforcement." To achieve these two objectives, they decided to work for a constitutional amendment that would guarantee black suffrage in all the states, instead of a federal statute, which could be more easily repealed. While most Republican members of Congress agreed on these goals, they "differed on how to achieve their common goals."[4]

Radical Republicans wanted to bar the federal and state governments from disfranchising voters because of race, property, literacy, and other classifications. Moderate Republicans believed in limited suffrage for black men, with states retaining authority over other voting qualifications. Republicans from New England and the Far West favored state literacy and nativity qualifications for voters (aimed at Irish and Chinese immigrants). These differences produced three strikingly dissimilar proposals. The first prohibited states from denying citizens the vote because of their race, color, or the previous experience of being a slave. The second prevented states from denying the vote to anyone based on literacy, property, or the circumstances of their birth. The third stated plainly and directly that all male citizens who were 21 or older had the right to vote.

The congressional debates on which language should be adopted often "extended into all-night sessions, taxed the patience of congressmen, consumed three hundred pages in the *Congressional Globe,* and produced incredible parliamentary triangles." While the debate was protracted, "there was little question that the enfranchisement of the Negro was the object" being sought, and the "primary goal was the enfranchisement of Negroes outside the deep South." The Democrats,

President Ulysses S. Grant, center, signs the Fifteenth Amendment. Several versions of the amendment were proposed and met with vigorous debate in the House and Senate. Congress finally agreed to a moderate version that prevented restricting the right to vote "on account of race, color, or previous condition of servitude."
Source: Library of Congress.

historian William Gillette observed, "were under no illusion about what a constitutional amendment was designed to achieve, [and] fought hard against it in any form, for they knew that Republican supremacy in the North was at stake." The debate frequently focused on "protecting the Southern Negro vote by outlawing literacy tests and poll taxes," but in the end "both the bans and guarantees were scrapped." Only the primary and secondary objectives, respectively — "to make Negro voters in the North," and "to keep Negro votes in the South" — were realized.[5] The two most divisive issues among Republicans were universal suffrage and the right to hold office.

The first Senate proposal was reported by Judiciary Committee chairman William M. Stewart, R-Nev., who told the Senate the amendment was "a declaration to make all men, without regard to race or color, equal before the law." Despite Stewart's plea for a quick vote, Sen. James Dixon, R-Conn.,

responded by identifying the three major ideological issues — the capabilities of various races, female suffrage, and the role of the federal government — that would dominate the lengthy and often chaotic Senate debate.[6]

Initially, the House passed a moderate version and the Senate a radical one. Then the House rejected the Senate resolution and approved its own radical amendment, while the Senate passed a moderate one. The Senate later agreed to a modified version of a bill offered by Sen. Henry Wilson, R-Mass., guaranteeing Negroes both the right to vote as well as to hold office. The modified amendment guaranteed the right to hold office, but did not, as Wilson's original version did, bar states from setting qualifications for holding office. The House rejected the Senate amendment on February 15.[7]

Two days later, following twelve hours of debate, the Senate adopted a new proposal, introduced by Senator Stewart, that stipulated that the "right of citizens of the United States to vote, and hold office shall not be denied or abridged by the United States or any State on account of race, color, or previous condition of servitude." The new Senate version retained the office-holding guarantee, which the House version did not, but eliminated the clause pertaining to the ability of the states to set voting qualifications. The House did not like the Senate's revised amendment much more than its earlier proposal and instead adopted yet another proposal. The Lower Chamber's fresh submission, tendered by Rep. John A. Bingham, R-Ohio, proposed to ban nativity, property, and creed (but significantly not education) as tests of suffrage, a ban the House had, in effect, rejected previously in the first proposal (the Wilson proposal) adopted by the Senate.[8]

Although many viewed the stalemate as intractable, a House/Senate conference committee was able to report a moderate solution that would win acceptance. The committee's solution was to drop the office-holding guarantee and ban most suffrage tests. The proposed Fifteenth Amendment stipulated that: "The rights of citizens of the United States to vote shall not be denied or abridged by the United States or by any State on account of race, color, or previous servitude." It closely paralleled the initial House version. The favorable House vote was 144–44. A 39–13 Senate vote sent it forward to the states for ratification.[9]

Section two of the Amendment authorized Congress to enforce the Amendment "by appropriate legislation." A subsequent act approved on April 10, 1869, required that the three Southern States still outside the Union (Texas, Mississippi, and Virginia) ratify the amendment as a condition for readmission into the Union.[10]

Although the final form of the Fifteenth Amendment was moderate compared to some of the other versions adopted by both the House and the Senate, it nevertheless represented a significant change in the U.S. Constitution. The compromise declared that neither the states nor the federal government could limit citizens' voting rights "on account of race, color,

THE FINAL VOTE

The Fifteenth Amendment

House
February 25, 1869

	Yea	Nay
	144	44

Senate
February 26, 1869

	Yea	Nay
	39	13

Source: Congressional Globe, 40th Cong., 3rd sess., February 25, 1869, 40:1563–1564, February 26, 1869, 40:1638–1641.

or previous condition of servitude." It did not, however, "protect access to public office, nor did it prohibit literacy, property, or nativity tests for suffrage. Members feared such far-reaching reform might be politically dangerous and imperil chances of ratification. The amendment represented more the pragmatic instincts of moderate Republicans and practical Radicals than the idealistic views for doctrinaire Radical Republicans."[11]

Some scholars have argued that the primary objective of the Amendment was to enfranchise the Northern and border state blacks. Others contend that supporters were primarily motivated by a conscious belief that it was the right thing to do. Despite these differing perspectives, there is general agreement that if the Republicans had not acted when they did, the opportunity to enact both the Fourteenth and Fifteenth Amendments might have been lost forever.

SENATOR WILLIAM M. STEWART INTRODUCING THE FIFTEENTH AMENDMENT

JANUARY 28, 1869

Mr. President, I do not propose to occupy the time of the Senate in discussing this great question at any length. It is the culmination of a contest which has lasted for thirty years. It is the logical result of the rebellion, of the abolition of slavery, and of the conflicts in this country during and before the war. Every person in the country has discussed it; it has been discussed in every local paper, by every local speaker; it has been discussed at the firesides; and now we are to place the grand result, I hope, in the Constitution of the United States. And let me remind my fellow Senators that it is well that this work be now done, for we have realized the force of the very pointed sentence which was read here from the Swiss address,

---

This amendment is a declaration to make all men, without regard to race or color, equal before the law.... It must be done.
— William M. Stewart

---

that "undetermined questions have no pity for the repose of mankind." This question can never rest until it is finally disposed of. This amendment is a declaration to make all men, without regard to race or color, equal before the law.

★ ★ ★ ★

It must be done. It is the only measure that will really abolish slavery. It is the only guarantee against peon laws and against oppression. It is that guarantee which was put in the Constitution of the United States originally, the guarantee that each man shall have a right to protect his own liberty. It repudiates that arrogant, self-righteous assumption, that one man can be charged with the liberties and destinies of another. You may put this in the form of legislative enactment; you may empower Congress to legislate; you may empower the States to legislate, and they will agitate the question. Let it be made the immutable law of the land; let it be fixed; and then we shall have peace. Until then there is no peace. I cannot add to the many eloquent speeches that have been made on this great question in this House. I will not attempt it. I want a vote. I will not occupy time. The proposition itself is more eloquent than man can be. It is a declaration too high, too grand, too noble, too just, to be ornamented by oratory. I hope we shall soon have a vote upon the question.

★ ★ ★ ★

Mr. President, there have been fourteen amendments to the Constitution of the United States heretofore ratified. They have all been submitted to the State Legislatures for ratification, and have been ratified by the various Legislatures. That has been the course pursued from the beginning of this Government until now. Never before was it pretended that such a ratification was not a ratification by the people. In the beginning of the Constitution it is declared that "we, the people, do ordain this Constitution," &c.; and in this Constitu-

tion ordained by the people a mode of amending it was pointed out by the people; and that was to submit the amendment to the individual States. In the Chicago platform we did take the position that this matter to a certain extent belonged to the States; and that is what influenced several members of the Senate against legislation who had formerly thought there was power to legislate directly upon this subject; they thought they were committed to submit it to the several States. The platform says that so far as the rebel States are concerned it is the duty of Congress to maintain equal suffrage. It says further that the other question should be submitted to the several States; and it not to be pretended that that platform meant that it should be submitted for ratification in any unusual manner. We have adopted this manner adopted from the foundation of the Government of taking the sense of the people.

A literal construction of the amendment would prevent any action whatever, because the Constitution does not point out any mode of taking the popular vote. In neither of the modes prescribed by the Constitution do the people act directly. There is no way of amending the Constitution so as to let the people act directly on the amendment. As the Constitution is now, you can submit the question to the Legislature or to a convention in the State — to no other body. It has been thought that the Legislature reflected more directly the will of the people than a convention irregularly called; and hence from the foundation of the Government all constitutional amendments proposed by Congress have been submitted to the State Legislatures for action.

Sir, it is very strange that whenever the Constitution of the United States can be construed to deny rights it is sacred with some; but whenever it can be used to secure right and liberty we are complained of for following the Constitution. Does the Senator from Indiana suppose that the Republican party intended in the Chicago convention to change the Constitution or to limit the power of Congress to submit propositions to the several States under the Constitution? No such construction is fair; no such construction can be maintained. The people understood perfectly well that Congress had power to submit amendments to the Constitution and ask for the action of the several States. They did regard that as a pledge against legislation; and that is the embarrassment in the way of legislation; but they did not regard it as a pledge against submitting propositions to amend the Constitution in the ordinary way.

Source: Congressional Globe, 40th Cong., 3rd sess., January 28, 1869 (Washington: F. & J. Rives and George A. Bailey, 1869), 40:668–674.

SENATOR THOMAS A. HENDRICKS OPPOSES THE FIFTEENTH AMENDMENT

FEBRUARY 8, 1869

Where, Mr. President, does the power of amendment stop? I say the power of amendment is limited to the correction of defects that might appear in the practical operations of the Government; but the power of amendment does not carry with it the power to destroy one form of government and establish another. I will ask the distinguished Senator who has just propounded the question to me, whether under the form and pretext of an amendment you can change the office of the chief Executive of this nation and make him cease to be a President and make him a king?

★ ★ ★ ★

I understand that answer given by the Senator to be that under the constitutional provision for amendment, under the proceeding for amendments, the Congress of the United States by a two-thirds vote of each body, three-fourths of the States ratifying it, may change this Government from a Republic and make it a monarchy.

We have now a distinct proposition before us. I am not going to talk in this general way about what the people of the United States may do. They may revolutionize, perhaps; there may be a revolution, and the present Government may go down under that revolution, and a monarchy may be its result. Perhaps we are in the midst of such a revolution as that now. Perhaps, we have gone very rapidly and far in that direction of revolution; but I am speaking of the power of Congress and three fourths of the States to amend the Constitution of the United States; and now I understand it to be averred as a doctrine of the party that the President may be displaced and a king established in his stead.

★ ★ ★ ★

Mr. President, I believe that there is a limit to the power of two thirds of Congress and of three fourths of the States to amend the Constitution of the United States. I believe that they have a right to amend the Constitution in those respects wherever defects appear in the practical operations of the Government to make it more complete and satisfactory; but they have no power, in my judgment, so to amend the Constitution as to change the character and the nature of the Government. This is, as was well expressed by the Senator from Tennessee this evening, not purely a confederacy, nor is it altogether a popular Government. It is a Government of the people and at the same time a confederacy. The States, before

the formation of the Federal Government, were independent States. They had the right to go into the confederacy or not to go into it as they pleased. It was not obligatory upon Pennsylvania to become a party to the confederacy, and if the other States had agreed to the Constitution and Pennsylvania had not agreed to it, Pennsylvania would not have been part of the Government; and that was provided in the Constitution itself, for the very last provision of the Constitution is that —

"The ratification of the conventions of nine States shall be sufficient for the establishment of this Constitution between the States so ratifying the same."

★ ★ ★ ★

Mr. President, my objection, which I now choose to state to the amendment proposed and pending before the Senate, is that it does change the nature of the Government, it does take away from the States a power which they retained and which is necessary to that independence and sovereignty of the States which the original compact contemplated they should enjoy.

Now, Mr. President, in using the term "sovereignty of the States" I do not mean that the States have control of every subject. In that sense the States are not sovereign; in that sense the Federal Government is not sovereign; but in the language of the courts the States are sovereign within the sphere of their jurisdiction or reserved powers, while the General Government is sovereign within the sphere of its jurisdiction. I think that the right to control the suffrage for the election of State officers is essential to the independence of the States, is essential to the very nature of the Government itself.

In further illustration of the question asked by the Senator from Wisconsin, I may say that the Constitution might be so amended as to regulate the suffrage in the election of Federal officers. I think that for the purpose of electing members of Congress, by an amendment of the Constitution the qualifications of the voters might be defined, and that would not change the nature of the Government; it would change, to some extent, the mode of selecting Federal Officers. But when the Constitution of the United States comes to regulate the mode of selecting State officers, and takes away from the States the control of that question, you materially change the framework of the Government itself. I can conceive of no power so important to a State as to

189

decide who shall be her officers and in what mode these officers shall be selected, whether by all the people or by a portion of the people. It is for her to select her own officers, to define who shall be her officers and how they shall be chosen, and if you take that power away from a government and confer it upon another government you have materially and very essentially changed the nature of the relations between the two.

★ ★ ★ ★

Now, sir, it is of the very essence of the relations between the States and the General Government that the States shall retain the control of a large class of subjects. All questions of a domestic sort, the regulation of property, the descent of estates, the courts that regulate such questions — these are exclusively within the control of the States; their regulation requires that the State shall have a Legislature, that it shall make laws; and if it make laws as an independent and sovereign State over these subjects it must have the control and selection of the law-makers. And if you take away from the State the power to select the law-makers you take away from the State the control of the subjects that the laws may operate upon. So when the Constitution of the United States takes away from the State the control over the subject of suffrage it takes away from the State the control of her own laws upon a

---

[W]hen the Constitution of the United States takes away from the State the control over the subject of suffrage it takes away from the State the control of her own laws upon a subject that the Constitution of the United States intended she should be sovereign upon. — Thomas A. Hendricks

---

subject that the Constitution of the United States intended she should be sovereign upon. But I have said more upon this question than I intended to do.

Now, Mr. President, if it were the pleasure of Congress to change the Constitution upon a subject so important as this ought it not to be clear and beyond all doubt that it would result in public good? I know there are very many distinguished men in the Republican party who have recently expressed the opinion that universal suffrage would be an evil; that these colored people, just come out of a condition of slavery, were not qualified to exercise the suffrage for the good of the public. I know that opinion was expressed by very many within a short time past.

★ ★ ★ ★

We have had but a very short experience on this question. A year ago, or a little more, suffrage was conferred upon the colored people in some of the States by Congress. Governments have been going on in those States in some way or other for this short period. I submit to Senators that the propriety of it has not been sufficiently tested to justify Congress in making a permanent change for all the States. A test of a year in those States of the South is not a satisfactory test. If so short a period could furnish a test, the success of government in those States has not been such as to justify very high hopes in that direction. I am sure no Senators will claim that society is in a more secure condition by the introduction of this element into the political power of the States. But I do not intend to discuss that question at any length. I now reach the question that is suggested by the Senator from Vermont.

I have not been satisfied, as many gentlemen of the Republican party recently were not satisfied, that it is wise to extend the suffrage to the colored people. If any State chooses to do it under the existing Constitution it is her own right to do so. I make no war upon that. That is right, because it is in the sense of the Constitution right, the State having the power to do so. But I am not satisfied, I never have been satisfied, that it is wise to make suffrage universal so as to include that race; and I think upon this subject there are some Senators in this Hall who are going to vote for this amendment who will agree with me. I will come to that directly.

I do not believe that the negro race and the white race can mingle in the exercise of political power and bring good results to society. We are of different races. Men may argue about it as much as they please; we know that in many respects there is a great difference between the races. There is a difference not only in their physical appearance and conformation, but there is a difference morally and intellectually; and I do not believe that the two races can mingle successfully in the management of government. I believe that it will bring strife and trouble to the country.

★ ★ ★ ★

Some Senator this evening said that intelligence and virtue were essential to the safe exercise of the suffrage. I think that race does not now bring to the mass of the intelligence of this country an addition. I do not think it ever will. That race in its whole history has furnished no evidence of its capacity to lift itself up. It has never laid the foundation for its own civilization. Any elevation that we find in that race is when we find it coming in contact with the white race. The influence of the white race upon the colored man has carried him up somewhat in the scale of civilization, but when dependent upon himself he has never gone upward. I am willing that that shall be tested by the history and experience of two thousand years back. While the tendency of the white race is upward, the tendency of the colored rate is downward; and I have always supposed it is because in that race the physical predominates over the moral and intellectual qualities.

★ ★ ★ ★

While the white man for two thousand years past has been going upward and onward, the negro race wherever found dependent upon himself has been going downward or standing still. Look at Africa and Europe, and I need make no argument on the subject — Europe with the advancement that she has made, with her advancement in the arts and sciences, in learning, in the development of wealth, in the comforts of the people, as compared with the condition of affairs in Africa. What has this race ever produced? What invention has it ever produced of advantage to the world? You need not say it is because of slavery, for we all know it is not. This race has not been carried down into barbarism by slavery. The influence of slavery upon this race — I will not say it is the influence of slavery — but the influence of the contact of this race with the white race has been to give it all the elevation it possesses, and independent and outside of that influence it has not become elevated anywhere in its whole history.

★ ★ ★ ★

There are some Senators here who do not want the Chinese to vote. The Senators from Oregon and California, I think, are all opposed to the Chinese voting; and I think the Senator from Nevada [Mr. STEWART] is; and why? I believe they said they were pagans, but they are not such pagans as we find in Africa. China is the original home of a civilization that the world honors to this day. Why, sir, in China they had many of the rare and useful inventions long before they were known in Europe. It is said that gunpowder was known in China before it was in Europe.

★ ★ ★ ★

Of course I am in favor of naturalizing no [individual who does not acknowledge an allegiance to the Government of the United States]; and anybody who is naturalized under our law must abjure all allegiance to any other Government, and in the most formal manner possible recognize the authority of our Government. The Senator is not in favor, I believe, of allowing the Chinese to vote, while he is in favor of allowing the negro to vote; and I am speaking of the position occupied by the Senators from the Pacific coast upon this particular question. It does not suit them to have the Chinese vote, for some reason or other. I guess it is not popular out there to have the Chinese vote, and they are opposed to it. I would not wish to force the Chinese vote upon the people of the Pacific coast unless they wanted it themselves; and if I desired to amend the Constitution so as to force the Chinaman to vote in California, I would say, "Let the people of California have a chance to express their

wish on that subject;" and if they voted it down I would not attempt to force it upon them. They are the best judges of the interests of their society and that which will contribute to the strength and purity of their State government. And the same is true in Indiana. But Nevada, with her twenty-five thousand people, has just as large a vote upon the adoption of this constitutional amendment as Indiana with her fifteen hundred thousand. But Nevada does not want the Chinaman, and she does want the colored man to vote. She has no colored people, but she has Chinamen. That is the style of this controversy. It suits certain purposes that the suffrage should be extended to the negro; it does not suit for other purposes that it should be extended to other races.

Source: Congressional Globe, 40th Cong., 3rd sess., February 8, 1869 (Washington: F. & J. Rives and George A. Bailey, 1869), 40:988–990.

Notes

1. 14 Stat. 375–376, 379–380, 428–430; Xi Wang, *The Trial of Democracy: Black Suffrage and Northern Republicans, 1860–1910* (Athens: University of Georgia Press, 1997), 40–42, Forrest G. Wood, *Black Scare: The Racist Response to Emancipation and Reconstruction* (Berkeley: University of California Press, 1968), 82–85.

2. William Gillette, *The Right to Vote: Politics and the Passage of the Fifteenth Amendment* (Baltimore: Johns Hopkins Press, 1969), 25–32; William Gillette, "Fifteenth Amendment (Framing and Ratification)," in Leonard W. Levy, Kenneth L. Karst, and Adam Winkler, eds., *Encyclopedia of the American Constitution*, 6 vols. (New York: Macmillian, 2000), 3:1039.

3. Quotes are found in Earl M. Maltz, *Civil Rights, The Constitution, and Congress, 1863–1869* (Lawrence: University Press of Kansas, 1990), 142; Gillette, "Fifteenth Amendment (Framing and Ratification)," 1039.

4. Gillette, "Fifteen Amendment (Framing and Ratification)," 1039–1040; William Gillette, "Fifteenth Amendment," in Donald C. Bacon, Roger H. Davidson, and Morton Keller, *The Encyclopedia of the United States Congress*, 4 vols. (New York: Simon and Schuster, 1995), 2:831–832.

5. Gillette, *The Right to Vote: Politics and the Passage of the Fifteenth Amendment*, 46, 48–50.

6. *Congressional Globe*, 40th Cong., 3rd sess., (January 28, 1869), 40:668, 705–708.

7. *Congressional Globe*, 40th Cong., 3rd sess., (January 20, 1869), 40:742–745; (February 9, 1869), 40:1035, 1040; (February 15, 1869), 40:1226; Gillette, *The Right to Vote: Politics and the Passage of the Fifteenth Amendment*, 50–60.

8. *Congressional Globe*, 40th Cong., 3rd sess., (February 17, 1869), 40:1318; (February 20, 1869), 40:1428; Gillette, *The Right to Vote: Politics and the Passage of the Fifteenth Amendment*, 67.

9. *Congressional Globe*, 40th Cong., 3rd sess., (February 25, 1869), 40:1563–1564, (February 26, 1869), 40:1638–1641.

10. See 15 Stat. 346; 16 Stat. 40–41.

11. Gillette, "Fifteenth Amendment (Framing and Ratification)," 832.

Civil Rights Act of 1875
✳ 1875 ✳

During the years immediately after the Civil War, Congress approved the Thirteenth, Fourteenth, and Fifteenth Amendments, and several statutes designed to eliminate the discrimination that would limit the freedom of recently emancipated slaves. None of these legislative initiatives, however, mentioned public education or public accommodations. Sen. Charles Sumner, R-Mass., first sought to partially rectify this omission in March 1867 with a proposed amendment to the Second Reconstruction Act that would have desegregated public schools. Three years later, he offered a broader proposal to abolish racial segregation generally "Negroes," he held, "should not merely have the right to vote, and certain legal rights in the courtroom and in the handling of their property and labor, but also equality in education and public facilities." His bill called for equal access for all citizens — regardless of race — to schools, churches, hotels, theaters, restaurants, cemeteries, public transportation, and national and state jury duty.[1]

Variations of the bill were debated over the next five years as Republicans repeatedly accused the Southern states of failing to enforce the constitutional and statutory rights of African Americans. The most frequent objection of the Democrats was that the bill had no relevancy on constitutional rights. Instead, it sought "to regulate the association, companionship, tastes and feelings of the people." Some predicted "it would result in the abolition of the fledgling Southern school systems," "unrestrained growth of miscegenation," or "federal tyranny over the states." Others thought the jury clause unconstitutional, thought the church clause an infringement on religious rights, or feared the decline of local autonomy. Twice, the Senate Judiciary Committee reported the bill adversely before Sumner was able to attach it as a rider to a measure granting universal amnesty to former Confederate leaders, but it failed to pass. In May 1872, in Sumner's absence, the Senate did pass a civil rights bill that omitted the provisions regarding schools and juries, but the House took no action.[2]

The constitutional basis for the bill, at least in part, was believed to rest on that section of the Fourteenth Amendment that prohibited states from abridging the "privileges and immunities" of U.S. citizens. This argument became more tenuous after the Supreme Court in the *Slaughterhouse Cases*, 83 U.S. 36 (1873), ruled that a Louisiana law that allowed a company the exclusive right to butcher all livestock in New Orleans did not abridge the privilege and immunities clause. The Courts drew a distinction between federal and state citizenship, declaring that the Amendment only applied to federal rights and left the protection of state rights up to the states themselves.[3]

Senator Sumner did not reintroduce his bill until early December 1873. Two weeks later, House Judiciary Committee chairman Benjamin Butler reported his own civil rights bill. The Butler bill was debated on the House floor the following day, and again for three days in January 1874, before being withdrawn and returned to the committee. Highlighting that debate was a spirited exchange between Rep. Alexander H. Stephens, D-Ga., the former vice president of the Confederacy, and Robert B. Elliott, R-S.C., one of four blacks representing that state. The Stephens-Elliott debate overshadows all other speeches delivered on the civil rights bills of the 1870s.

Denying any prejudice against blacks, Stephens said he believed all people under federal jurisdiction should be afforded equal protection and redress under the law. He did not, however, think Congress had the authority to pass and enforce a measure that infringed upon the power of state governments to determine their citizens' rights. "If there is one truth which stands out prominently above all others in the history of these States," he emphasized, "it is that the germinal and seminal principle of American constitutional liberty is the absolute unrestricted right of State self-government in all purely internal municipal affairs." The bill was "inexpedient," neither helpful to the black populace nor to the nation. Although congressional reaction to the speech was mixed, in ensuing speeches most Democrats based their own arguments off of that of Stephens.[4]

Elliott regretted it was "necessary to advocate a bill which simply asserts equal rights and equal public privileges for all classes of American citizens"; and "that the dark hue of my skin may lend a color to the imputation that I am controlled by motives personal to myself in my advocacy of this great measure of national justice." The bill before the House, he

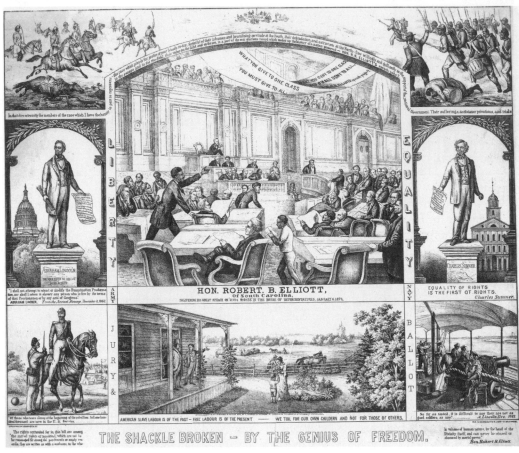

African American congressman Robert B. Elliot delivers his civil rights speech to the House of Representatives on January 6, 1874. Elliot's eloquence, knowledge, and use of reason convinced many Republican congressman that African Americans were equal to European Americans.
Source: The Granger Collection, New York.

said, sought neither "to confer new rights, nor to place rights conferred by state citizenship under the protection of the United States, but simply to prevent and forbid inequality and discrimination on account of race, color, or previous condition." Its passage "will determine the civil status, not only of the [N]egro, but of any other class of citizens who feel themselves discriminated against." Prominent newspapers praised Elliott; many spoke of "the nobility of his appeal to reason, the eloquence of his style, the dignity of his bearing, and the brilliance of his grasp of the constitutional issues"; and "white Republicans who spoke after him used his speech as definitive proof that African Americans were the equal of European Americans."[5]

Still, it was only after Senator Sumner's death on March 11, 1874, that momentum began to grow for passage of a civil rights bill. Senate debate began on May 20. Opponents proposed that the provisions dealing with schools and cemeteries be dropped, and they reiterated their belief that the bill was unconstitutional. Supporters stressed that the success of the civil rights movement depended on desegregated schools,

denied politics was a motivating factor, and emphasized the "equal protection" clause of the Fourteenth Amendment to counter the *Slaughterhouse* decision. Following a twenty-hour Democratic filibuster, the Senate passed a bill, 29–16, containing language similar to Sumner's except for the clause relating to churches.[6]

When Congress reconvened in December 1874, more than half of the House Republicans were lame ducks, having lost their seats in the November elections. Now they had only four months to approve a civil rights bill before the Democrats assumed control of the chamber. In mid-December, Chairman Butler reported a revised bill that called for "separate but equal" schools in the hope of satisfying desegregation opponents. The Democrats responded by making dilatory motions and staging a forty-eight-hour filibuster before Speaker James G. Blaine, R-Maine, brokered a compromise that allowed the bill to be called up for debate. The "acrimonious and highly personal" exchanges that followed climaxed with Rep. John Y. Brown, D-Ky., accusing the Republicans of conspiring to overthrow the Constitution and being censured for attacking Butler's motives, personal life, and social standing. The extreme remarks of House Democrats backfired and actually united Republicans in a way "that policy could not." Prior to the final House vote of February 4, the references to cemeteries and churches were stricken, and a preamble calling for equal treatment of the Negro was added before it passed 162–99. Unsuccessful Senate attempts to weaken the bill's penalties and to reinsert the provision barring discrimination in churches preceded approval by a 38–26 vote on February 27.[7]

During the next eight years, several state courts rejected petitioners' claims under the act before the Supreme Court took up five of the cases in one day. In the *Civil Rights Cases,* 109 U.S. 3 (1883), the Court ruled that the federal government could not bar discrimination by private individuals or businesses. While the Fourteenth Amendment allowed Congress to forbid state action interfering with the rights of blacks, it did not permit legislation aimed at private racial discrimination. "Despite its failure in practice," historian James M. McPherson observed, "the Civil Rights Act of 1875 was a symbolic victory for the equalitarian ideals of the Reconstruction and an historical bridge between the Fourteenth Amendment and the Civil Rights Act of 1964." Kirt H. Wilson, in his book-length study of the 1875 act, writes that the "debate over its passage was nothing less than a crucible in which the thoughts and judgments that would determine the future of race relations were formed."[8]

REPRESENTATIVE ALEXANDER H. STEPHENS OPPOSES THE CIVIL RIGHTS ACT OF 1875

JANUARY 5, 1874

Mr. Speaker, before entering upon the discussion of the question now before the House, I have done what I never did but once before in addressing a legislative body; and that is, I have reduced to writing, in advance, what I propose to say. This I have done on the present occasion, as I did on the former one alluded to, because of the very great gravity, importance, and magnitude of the subject; involving, as it does, several of the most essential principles of all good government, and especially those upon which rests, the whole fabric of our complex system of free institutions.

I feel on entering upon it as the highest judicial tribunal of our land felt, as proclaimed from the bench when the same questions, in part, for the first time, came before that body for adjudication. They said, in what is known as the Slaughterhouse cases, (16 Wallace, 36–83,) referred to the other day by Mr. BECK, of Kentucky:

We do not conceal from ourselves the great responsibility which this duty devolves upon us. No questions so far-reaching and pervading, so profoundly interesting to the people of this country, and so important in their bearing upon the relations of the United States and of the several States to each other and to the citizens of the States and of the United States, have been before this court during the official life of any of its present members.

When learned judges pause in hesitation where safely to tread, in view of their responsibility in expounding laws, well may legislators pause in view of their responsibility in making them. It is in view of this responsibility on me at this time I feel the necessity of the greatest possible care in duly considering and properly weighing every word that may be uttered by me in the discharge of the high duty now resting upon me, that there may be no misunderstanding of what I may say, and no grounds for any erroneous report or misrepresentation of my own utterances as they go forth in my own words. Steady as well as skilled should be the hand of him who puts the probe about the "heart-strings of life" of any one single human being, however humble; much more should it be so with him who deals with questions affecting the vital functions of commonwealths, whether State or Federal. No graver or more serious question will perhaps come before this Congress — not even the currency or Cuba questions — than the matter now under consideration. In giving my opinions on it I shall be governed solely by my own convictions of right and duty, looking to the best interest of the people of the several States of our Union, in view of the powers with which I am clothed. What I propose to submit is intended mainly for the consideration of members of this House, and without any regard to their party distinctions. I shall assume, having no right to question it, that we all feel alike a heavy responsibility for our acts, not only to our immediate constituents, but to the judgment of mankind; and that, too, not only of those of this generation, either of one section of the Union or another, but for all time to come;

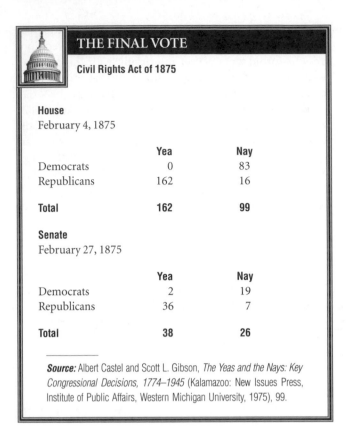

THE FINAL VOTE

Civil Rights Act of 1875

House
February 4, 1875

	Yea	Nay
Democrats	0	83
Republicans	162	16
Total	**162**	**99**

Senate
February 27, 1875

	Yea	Nay
Democrats	2	19
Republicans	36	7
Total	**38**	**26**

Source: Albert Castel and Scott L. Gibson, *The Yeas and the Nays: Key Congressional Decisions, 1774–1945* (Kalamazoo: New Issues Press, Institute of Public Affairs, Western Michigan University, 1975), 99.

entertain no feelings of that kind, and am not governed in my action here, nor elsewhere, by any influence of that sort.

In the third place, according to the method in which I propose to treat the subject, I wish now to say that my opinion of justice and its proper administration is not founded upon the doctrine of that dogma so generally announced and so pernicious in principle — "the greatest good to the greatest number." The true rule with me, even in our old organized system of State polity at the South, was, "the greatest good to all without detriment to any."

While I do not hold the doctrine of the equality of races of men, yet I do maintain the great truth, however paradoxical it may appear to some, that all men are created equal. This great truth was first enunciated by a council of States on the 4th of July, 1776. It was then adopted and proclaimed as it came from the pen of Jefferson, the chief apostle of liberty on this continent. This truth was never meant, however, in my opinion, to convey the idea that men were created equal in all respects, either in physical, mental, or moral development; but it was meant to assert the great law of nature, that all men have an equal right to justice, and to stand, so far as governmental powers are concerned or exercised over them, perfectly equal before the law. This is the right of all classes of men, whether white, red, brown, or black. This American principle is as broad as our jurisdiction, and as catholic as the doctrines of Him who first announced to the world the true principle of justice; that is, "As ye would that men should do to you, do ye also to them likewise."

★ ★ ★ ★

I am opposed to the passage of this measure, or any one kindred to it, even if any of the rights proposed to be secured

---

I am opposed to the passage of this measure ... because of the want of the necessary power, under the Constitution on the part of Congress to apply the appropriate remedy by the enactment of any such law as this bill proposes. — Alexander H. Stephens

---

by it were properly just in themselves, because of the want of the necessary power, under the Constitution, on the part of Congress to apply the appropriate remedy by the enactment of any such law as this bill proposes. I presume that it will not be assuming too much to take it for granted that it will be admitted by every member of the House that the powers of Congress are specific as well as limited, and that all the powers which Congress can, legislatively or otherwise, rightfully exercise are held by delegation from the people of the several

for our deeds, whatever they may be, whether of evil or good, will live after us.

★ ★ ★ ★

In assigning my reasons for opposing this measure, I shall state them, first, negatively; and, secondly, affirmatively. First, I shall state several grounds upon which I do not oppose it; next, some of the grounds upon which I do oppose it.

In this order, I announce, in the first place, that I am not opposed to it because of any opposition I have to doing full and ample justice to every human being within the legitimate jurisdiction of our Federal legislative powers. The chief end of all governments, whether State or Federal, should be the protection of rights. The great struggle of humanity from the first organization of society has been a strife between power and right. This has been the case in every form in which government has developed itself in all ages, climes, and countries, whether in monarchies, absolute or limited, in oligarchies or aristocracies, or democracies or republics, whether single or Federal.

★ ★ ★ ★

In the second place, my opposition to this bill springs from no prejudice, in the slightest degree, against any man, woman, or child within the limits of the United States, on account of race or color or previous condition of servitude. I

States of the Union. Where, then, in the Constitution is to be found the power which authorizes the passage of this measure? The power under which it is claimed, as I understand it, is derived chiefly from the first and fifth sections of the fourteenth article of amendment. It is true, in this connection, I have frequently seen reference made, also, to the fifteenth article of amendment. To see how far the power is sustained by the claim, we must therefore look into the purport and meaning of both these articles of amendment as they stand, without any consideration at this time as to their history, or how they became incorporated into the organic law of the Union.

★ ★ ★ ★

The reading of the Fifteenth Amendment shows it has no application whatever to the subject. Its main object was to deny to both Congress and the States the exercise of a certain power.

And as to the first section of the fourteenth, all I have to say here is that it very clearly appears from its words that it has but two objects. These were, first, to declare the colored race to be citizens of the United States, and of the States, respectively, in which they reside; and, secondly, to prohibit the States, severally, from denying to the class of citizens, so declared, the same privileges, immunities, and civil rights which were secured to the citizens of the several States, respectively, and of the United States, by the Constitution as it stood before citizenship to the colored race was declared by this amendment.

As to the fifth section of the Fourteenth Amendment and the second section of the fifteenth, so far as they relate to the subject-matter of the body of each amendment, respectively, their clear meaning and import are to provide security to the colored race in the enjoyment of the privileges, immunities, and rights so declared, in the same way and in like manner as was provided for the security of like privileges, immunities, and rights of the citizens of the several States, respectively, by the Constitution before this amendment, and that no other remedy for a violation of the prohibitions on State action in either of these amendments was contemplated than such as existed for like violations of like prohibitions anterior to the amendments. The exercise of no new power was conferred by either of these new amendments. The denial of the exercise of any number of powers by the United States, severally, does not, most certainly, confer its exercise upon the Congress of the States. Neither of these amendments confer, bestow, or even declare, any rights at all to citizens of the United States, or to any class whatever. Upon the colored race they neither confer, bestow, or declare civil rights of any character — not even the right of franchise. They only forbid the States from discriminating, in their laws against the colored race in the bestowment of such rights as they may severally deem best to bestow upon their own citizens. Whatever rights they grant

to other citizens shall not be denied to the colored race as a class. This is the whole of the matter. The question, then, is, how can Congress enforce a prohibition of the exercise of these powers by a State? Most assuredly in the same way they enforced or provided for violations of like prohibitions anterior to these amendments.

The proper remedies before were, and now are, nothing but the judgments of courts, to be rendered in such way as Congress might provide, declaring any State act in violation of the prohibitions to be null and of no effect, because of their being in violation of this covenant between the States as set forth in the Constitution of the United States. No new power over this matter of a different nature or character from that previously delegated over like subjects was intended to be conferred by the concluding sections of either the fourteenth or fifteenth article of amendment.

★ ★ ★ ★

If it is within the reserved powers of the States to deny the right of admission to the bar to any who may be held to be her citizens or citizens of the United States, is it not much more one of her reserved rights to say who may, or who may not, be admitted into her public schools or other institutions?

★ ★ ★ ★

Among the affirmative reasons for my opposition to this bill, I oppose it because of its inexpediency. Even if the power were, without question or doubt, vested in Congress to pass municipal regulations of this sort to operate over the people of the several States of the Union, I think it would be exceedingly injudicious and unwise to exercise it. Better leave all such matters to the States. In point of fact, I do not believe the colored people of Georgia have any desire for mixed schools, and very little, indeed, for mixed churches, as contemplated by this measure.

★ ★ ★ ★

Interference by the Federal Government, even if the power were clear and indisputable, would be against the very genius and entire spirit of our whole system. If there is one truth which stands out prominently above all others in the history of these States, it is that the germinal and seminal principle of American constitutional liberty is the absolute unrestricted right of State self-government in all purely internal municipal affairs. The first union of the Colonies, from which sprang the Union of the States, was by joint action to secure this right of local self-government for each. It was when the chartered rights of Massachusetts were violated by a British Parliament the cry first went up from Virginia, "The cause of Boston is the cause of us all!" This led to the declaration and establishment of the independence not of the whole people of the united Colonies as one mass, but of the independence of each of the original thirteen Colonies, then declared by themselves to be, and afterward acknowledged by all foreign powers to be, thirteen separate and distinct States.

★ ★ ★ ★

Let us not do by the passage of this bill what our highest judicial tribunal has said we have no rightful power to do. If you who call yourselves republicans shall, in obedience to what you consider a party behest, pass it in the vain expectation that the republican principles of the old and true Jeffersonian school are dead, be assured you are indulging a fatal delusion. The old Jeffersonian democratic republican principles are not dead, and will never die so long as a true devotee of liberty lives. They may be buried for a period, as Magna Charta was trodden under foot in England for more than half a century; but these principles will come up with renewed energy as did those of Magna Charta, and that, too, at no distant day: Old Jeffersonian democratic republican principles dead, indeed! When the tides of ocean cease to ebb and flow, when the winds of heaven are hushed into perpetual silence, when the clouds no longer thunder, when earth's electric bolts are no longer felt or heard, when her internal fires go out, then, and not before, will these principles cease to live; then, and not before, will these principles cease to animate and move the liberty-loving masses of this country. Dead, indeed!

Source: *Congressional Record,* 43rd Cong., 1st sess., January 5, 1874 (Washington, D.C.: GPO, 1874), 2:378–382.

REPRESENTATIVE ROBERT B. ELLIOTT ARGUES FOR THE CIVIL RIGHTS ACT OF 1875

JANUARY 6, 1874

While I am sincerely grateful for this high mark of courtesy that has been accorded to me by this House, it is a matter of regret to me that it is necessary at this day that I should rise in the presence of an American Congress to advocate a bill which simply asserts equal rights and equal public privileges for all American citizens. I regret, sir, that the dark hue of my skin may lend a color to the imputation that I am controlled by motives personal to myself in my advocacy of this great measure of national justice. Sir, the motive that impels me is restricted by no such narrow boundary, but is as broad as your Constitution. I advocate it, sir, because it is right. The bill, however, not only appeals to your justice, but demands a response from your gratitude.

In the events that led to the achievement of American Independence the negro was not an inactive or unconcerned spectator. He bore his part bravely upon many battle-fields, although uncheered by that certain hope of political elevation which victory would secure to the white man. The tall granite shaft, which a grateful State has reared above its sons who fell in defending Fort Griswold against the attack of Benedict Arnold, bears the name of Jordan, Freeman, and other brave men of the African race who there cemented with their blood the corner-stone of the Republic. In the State which I have the honor in part to represent the rifle of the black man rang out against the troops of the British crown in the darkest days of the American Revolution. Said General Greene, who has been justly termed the Washington of the North, in a letter written by him to Alexander Hamilton on the 10th day of January, 1781, from the vicinity of Camden, South Carolina:

> There is no such thing as national character or national sentiment. The inhabitants are numerous, but they would be rather formidable abroad than at home. There is a great spirit of enterprise among the black people and those that come out as volunteers are not a little formidable to the enemy.

At the battle of New Orleans, under the immortal Jackson, a colored regiment held the extreme right of the American line unflinchingly, and drove back the British column that pressed upon them, at the point of the bayonet. So marked was their valor on that occasion that it evoked from their great commander the warmest encomiums, as will be seen from his dispatch announcing the brilliant victory.

As the gentleman from Kentucky, [Mr. BECK,] who seems to be the leading exponent on this floor of the party that is arrayed against the principle of this bill, has been pleased, in season and out of season, to cast odium upon the negro and to vaunt the chivalry of his State, I may be pardoned for calling attention to another portion of the same dispatch. Referring to the various regiments under his command, and their conduct on that field which terminated the second war of American Independence, General Jackson says:

At the very moment when the entire discomfiture of the enemy was looked for with a confidence amounting to certainty, the Kentucky re-enforcements, in whom so much reliance had been placed, ingloriously fled.

In quoting this indisputable piece of history, I do so only by way of admonition and not to question the well-attested gallantry of the true Kentuckian, and to suggest to the gentleman that it would be well that he should not flaunt his heraldry so proudly while he bears this bar-sinister on the military escutcheon of his State — a State which answered the call of the Republic in 1861, when treason thundered at the very gates of the capital, by coldly declaring her neutrality in the impending struggle. The negro, true to that patriotism and love of country that have ever characterized and marked his love of continent, came to the aid of the Government in its efforts to maintain the Constitution. To that Government he now appeals; that Constitution he now invokes for protection against outrage and unjust prejudices founded upon caste.

But, sir, we are told by the distinguished gentleman from Georgia [Mr. STEPHENS] that Congress has no power under the Constitution to pass such a law, and that the passage of such an act is in direct contravention of the rights of the States. I cannot assent to any such proposition. The constitution of a free government ought always to be construed in favor of human rights. Indeed, the Thirteenth, Fourteenth, and Fifteenth Amendments, in positive words, invest Congress with the power to protect the citizen in his civil and political rights. Now, sir, what are civil rights? Rights natural, modified by civil society. Mr. Lieber says:

> By civil liberty is meant, not only the absence of individual restraint, but liberty within the social system and political organism — a combination of principles and laws which acknowledge, protect, and favor the dignity of man. ... Civil liberty is the result of man's two-fold character as an individual and social being, so soon as both are equally respected. — Lieber on *Civil Liberty,* page 25.

Alexander Hamilton, the right-hand man of Washington in the perilous days of the then infant Republic, the great interpreter and expounder of the Constitution, says:

> Natural liberty is a gift of the beneficent Creator to the whole human race; civil liberty is founded on it; civil liberty is only natural liberty modified and secured by civil society. Hamilton's *History of the American Republic,* vol. 1, page 70.

Are we then, sir, with the amendments to our Constitution staring us in the face; with those grand truths of history before our eyes; with innumerable wrongs daily inflicted upon five million citizens demanding redress, to commit this question to the diversity of State legislation? In the words of Hamilton —

Is it the interest of the Government to sacrifice individual rights to the preservation of the rights of an artificial being, called States? There can be no truer principle than this, that every individual of the community at large has an equal right to the protection of Government. Can this be a free Government if partial distinctions are tolerated or maintained?

The rights contended for in this bill are among "the sacred rights of mankind, which are not to be rummaged for among old parchment or musty records; they are written as with a sun beam, in the whole volume of human nature, by the hand of the Divinity itself, and can never be erased or obscured by mortal power."

But the Slaughter-house cases! — the Slaughter-house cases!

The honorable gentleman from Kentucky, always swift to sustain the failing and dishonored cause of proscription, rushes forward and flaunts in our faces the decision of the Supreme Court of the United States in the Slaughter-house cases, and in that act he has been willingly aided by the gentleman from Georgia. Hitherto, in the contests which have marked the progress of the cause of equal civil rights, our opponents have appealed sometimes to custom, sometimes to prejudice, more often to pride of race, but they have never sought to shield themselves behind the Supreme Court. But now, for the first time, we are told that we are barred by a decision of that court from which there is no appeal. If this be true we must stay our hands. The cause of equal civil rights must pause at the command of a power whose edicts must be obeyed till the fundamental law of our country is changed.

★ ★ ★ ★

Mr. Speaker, I venture to say here in the presence of the gentleman from Kentucky, and the gentleman from Georgia, and in the presence of the whole country, that there is not a line or word, not a thought or dictum even, in the decision of the Supreme Court in the great Slaughter-house cases which casts a shadow of doubt on the right of Congress to pass the pending bill, or to adopt such other legislation as it may judge proper and necessary to secure perfect equality before the law to every citizen of the Republic. Sir, I protest against the dishonor now cast upon our Supreme Court by both the gentleman from Kentucky and the gentleman from Georgia. In other days, when the whole country was bowing beneath the yoke of slavery, when press, pulpit, platform, Congress, and courts felt the fatal power of the slave oligarchy, I remember a decision of that court which no American now reads without shame and humiliation. But those days are past. The Supreme Court of to-day is a tribunal as true to freedom as any department of this Government, and I am honored with the opportunity of repelling a deep disgrace which the gentleman from Kentucky, backed and sustained as he is by the gentleman from Georgia, seeks to put upon it.

★ ★ ★ ★

The question which was before the court was not whether a State law which denied to a particular portion of her citizens the rights conferred on her citizens generally, on account of race, color, or previous condition of servitude, was unconstitutional because in conflict with the recent amendments, but whether an act which conferred on certain citizens exclusive privileges for police purposes was in conflict therewith, because imposing an involuntary servitude forbidden by the thirteenth amendment, or abridging the rights and immunities of citizens of the United States, or denying the equal protection of the laws, prohibited by the Fourteenth Amendment.

★ ★ ★ ★

The decision of the Supreme Court is to be found in the 16th volume of Wallace's Reports, and was delivered by Associate Justice Miller. The court hold, first, that the act in question is a legitimate and warrantable exercise of the police power of the State in regulating the business of stock-landing and slaughtering in the city of New Orleans and the territory immediately contiguous. Having held this, the court proceeds to discuss the question whether the conferring of exclusive privileges, such as those conferred by the act in question, is the imposing of an involuntary servitude, the abridging of the rights and immunities of citizens of the United States, or the denial to any person within the jurisdiction of the State of the equal protection of the laws.

That the act is not the imposition of an involuntary servitude the court hold to be clear, and they next proceed to examine the remaining questions arising under the Fourteenth Amendment. Upon this question the court hold that the leading and comprehensive purpose of the Thirteenth, Fourteenth, and Fifteenth Amendments was to secure the complete freedom of the race, which, by the events of the war, had been wrested from the unwilling grasp of their owners. I know no finer or more just picture, albeit painted in the neutral tints of true judicial impartiality, of the motives and events which led to these amendments.

★ ★ ★ ★

These amendments, one and all, are thus declared to have as their all-pervading design and end the security to the recently enslaved race, not only their nominal freedom, but their complete protection from those who had formerly exercised unlimited dominion over them. It is in this broad light that all these amendments must be read, the purpose to secure the perfect equality before the law of all citizens of the United States. What you give to one class you must give to all; what you deny to one class you shall deny to all, unless in the exercise of the common and universal police power of the State you find it needful to confer exclusive privileges on certain citizens, to be held and exercised still for the common good of all.

Such are the doctrines of the Slaughter-house cases — doctrines worthy of the Republic, worthy of the age, worthy of the great tribunal which thus loftily and impressively enunciates them.

★ ★ ★ ★

The only ground upon which the grant of exclusive privileges to a portion of the community is ever defended is that the substantial good of all is promoted; that in truth it is for the welfare of the whole community that certain persons should alone pursue certain occupations. It is not the special benefit conferred on the few that moves the legislature, but the ultimate and real benefit of all, even of those who are denied the right to pursue those specified occupations. Does the gentleman from Kentucky say that my good is promoted when I am excluded from the public inns? Is the health or safety of the community promoted? Doubtless his prejudice is gratified. Doubtless his democratic instincts are pleased; but will he or his able coadjutor say that such exclusion is a lawful exercise of the police power of the State, or that it is not a denial to me of the equal protection of the laws? They will not so say.

But each of these gentlemen quote at some length from the decision of the court to show that the court recognizes a difference between citizenship of the United States and citizenship of the States. That is true, and no man here who supports this bill questions or overlooks the difference. There are privileges and immunities which belong to me as a citizen of the United States, and there are other privileges and immunities which belong to me as a citizen of my State. The former are under the protection of the Constitution and laws of the United States, and the latter are under the protection of the constitution and laws of my State.

★ ★ ★ ★

The distinction between the two kinds of citizenship is clear, and the Supreme Court have clearly pointed out this distinction, but they have nowhere written a word or line which denies to Congress the power to prevent a denial of equality of rights, whether those rights exist by virtue of citizenship of the United States or of a State. Let honorable members mark well this distinction. There are rights which are conferred on us by the United States. There are other rights conferred on us by the States of which we are individually the citizens.

★ ★ ★ ★

Now, sir, recurring to the venerable and distinguished gentleman from Georgia, [Mr. STEPHENS,] who has added his remonstrance against the passage of this bill, permit me to say that I share in the feeling of high personal regard for that gentleman which pervades this House. His years, his ability, and his long experience in public affairs entitle him to the measure of consideration which has been accorded to him on this floor. But in this discussion I cannot and I will not forget that the welfare and rights of my whole race in this country are involved. When, therefore, the honorable gentleman from Georgia lends his voice and influence to defeat this measure, I do not shrink from saying that it is not from him that the American House of Representatives should take lessons in matters touching human rights or the joint relations of the State and national governments. While the honorable gentleman contented himself with harmless speculations in his study, or in the columns of a newspaper, we might well smile at the impotence of his efforts to turn back the advancing tide of opinion and progress; but, when he comes again upon this national arena, and throws himself with all his power and influence across the path which leads to the full enfranchisement of my race, I meet him only as an adversary; nor shall age or any other consideration restrain me from saying that he now offers this Government, which he has done his utmost to destroy, a very poor return for its magnanimous treatment, to come here and seek to continue, by the assertion of doctrines obnoxious to the true principles of our Government, the burdens and oppressions which rest upon five millions of his countrymen who never failed to lift their earnest prayers for the success of this Government when the gentleman was seeking to break up the Union of these States and to blot the American Republic from the galaxy of nations. [Loud applause.]

Sir, it is scarcely twelve years since that gentleman shocked the civilized world by announcing the birth of a government which rested on human slavery as its corner-stone. The progress of events has swept away that *pseudo*-government which rested on greed, pride, and tyranny; and the race whom he then ruthlessly spurned and trampled on are here to meet him in debate, and to demand that the rights which are enjoyed by their former oppressors — who vainly sought to overthrow a Government which they could not prostitute to the base uses of slavery — shall be accorded to those who even in the darkness of slavery kept their allegiance true to freedom and the Union.

★ ★ ★ ★

No language could convey a more complete assertion of the power of Congress over the subject embraced in the present bill than is here expressed. If the States do not conform to the requirements of this clause, if they continue to deny to any person within their jurisdiction the equal protection of the laws, or as the Supreme Court had said, "deny equal justice in its courts," then Congress is here said to have power to enforce the constitutional guarantee by appropriate legislation. That is the power which this bill now seeks to put in exercise. It proposes to enforce the constitutional guarantee against inequality and discrimination by appropriate legisla-

tion. It does not seek to confer new rights, nor to place rights conferred by State citizenship under the protection of the United States, but simply to prevent and forbid inequality and discrimination on account of race, color, or previous

---

The Constitution warrants it; the Supreme Court sanctions it; justice demands it.
— Robert B. Elliott

---

condition of servitude. Never was there a bill more completely within the constitutional power of Congress. Never was there a bill which appealed for support more strongly to that sense of justice and fair-play which has been said, and in the main with justice, to be a characteristic of the Anglo-Saxon race. The Constitution warrants it; the Supreme Court sanctions it; justice demands it.

★ ★ ★ ★

The results of the war, as seen in reconstruction, have settled forever the political status of my race. The passage of this bill will determine the civil status, not only of the negro, but of any other class of citizens who may feel themselves discriminated against. It will form the cap-stone of that temple of liberty, begun on this continent under discouraging circumstances, carried on in spite of the sneers of monarchists and the cavils of pretended friends of freedom, until at last it stands in all its beautiful symmetry and proportions, a building the grandest which the world has ever seen, realizing the most sanguine expectations and the highest hopes of those who, in the name of equal, impartial, and universal liberty, laid the foundation stones.

Source: *Congressional Record,* 43rd Cong., 1st sess., January 6, 1874 (Washington, D.C.; GPO, 1874), 2:407–410.

Notes

1. Bertram Wyatt-Brown, "The Civil Rights Act of 1875," *Western Political Quarterly* 18 (December 1965): 18:763. See also John S. Ezell, "The Civil Rights Act of 1875," *Mid-America: An Historical Review,* 50 (October 1968): 252–253.

2. Wyatt-Brown, "The Civil Rights Act of 1875," 765. See also ibid., 765–766; Ezell, "The Civil Rights Act of 1875," 254–257; Alfred H. Kelly, "The Congressional Controversy Over School Segregation, 1867–1875," *American Historical Review* 64 (April 1959): 547–552; Kirt H. Wilson, *The Reconstruction Desegregation Debate: The Politics of Equality and the Rhetoric of Place, 1870–1875* (East Lansing: Michigan State University Press, 2002), 20–23.

3. *Slaughter-House Cases,* 83 U.S. 36 (1873).

4. "Civil Rights," *Congressional Record,* January 5, 1874, 2:381; Wilson, *The Reconstruction Desegregation Debate,* 30. See also "Civil

Rights," *Congressional Record,* January 5, 1874, 2:378–382; Richard Malcolm Johnston and William Hand Browne, *Life of Alexander H. Stephens* (Philadelphia: J.B. Lippincott, 1878), 521–527.

5. "Civil Rights," *Congressional Record,* January 6, 1874, 2:407, 410; Peggy Lamson, *The Glorious Failure: Black Congressman Robert Brown Elliott and the Reconstruction in South Carolina* (New York: Norton, 1973), 181; Wilson, *The Reconstruction Desegregation Debate,* 31–32.

6. Ezell, "The Civil Rights Act of 1875," 257–258; Wilson, *The Reconstruction Desegregation Debate,* 33–35.

7. Ezell, "The Civil Rights Act of 1875," 260; Wilson, *The Reconstruction Desegregation Debate,* 38. See also Ezell, "The Civil Rights Act of 1875," 258–264; Kelly, "The Congressional Controversy Over School Segregation, 1867–1875," 555–562; Wilson, *The Reconstruction Desegregation Debate,* 36–42; Wyatt-Brown, "The Civil Rights Act of 1875," 771–774; 18 Stat. 335–337 (March 1, 1875).

8. James M. McPherson, "Abolitionists and the Civil Rights Act of 1875," *Journal of American History,* 52 (December 1965): 493; Wilson, *The Reconstruction Desegregation Debate,* 15. See also *Civil Rights Cases,* 109 U.S. 3 (1883); John Hope Franklin, "The Enforcement of the Civil Rights Act of 1875," *Prologue: The Journal of National Archives* 6 (Winter 1974): 225–235.

Compromise of 1877

✳ 1877 ✳

Immediately following the 1876 presidential election, a majority of the nation's newspapers reported the election of Democrat Samuel J. Tilden of New York as the nation's nineteenth chief executive. That verdict, of course, proved premature. Tilden won two hundred fifty thousand more popular votes and eighteen more undisputed electoral votes 184–165 than Republican Rutherford B. Hayes of Ohio. Neither candidate, however, received a majority of undisputed electoral votes, as the electoral votes of four states — Louisiana (8), South Carolina (7), Florida (4), and Oregon (1) — were called into question. Tilden needed only one of those votes to reach the one hundred eighty-five required to become president, while Hayes needed all twenty. Election irregularities in the first three states that made it difficult to determine which candidate had won, together with the disqualification of an elector in Oregon, prompted each party to send election certificates to Washington, which they claimed contained the legitimate election results.

The Constitution stipulated that both the Senate and the House be present when the electoral certificates from each state were opened and counted, but it provided no guidance regarding disputed certificates. Congressional Democrats, who controlled the House, believed the electoral count should be carried out in accordance with Article II of the Constitution. Under this procedure, the House was charged with electing the president, with each state delegation having one vote. The Republicans claimed that the Twelfth Amendment was applicable. It directed the president of the Senate, "in the presence of the Senate and House of Representatives [to] open all the certificates and the votes shall then be counted." This left the decision, they argued, with Sen. Thomas W. Ferry, R-Mich., who became the Senate's president in 1875 following the death of Vice President Henry Wilson. Despite their conflicts, both parties insisted on their rightness, and the resultant stalemate created nationwide anxiety.[1]

Soon after the Forty-fourth Congress convened on December 4, 1876, both the House and the Senate created bipartisan committees to study ways of resolving the impasse. A month-and-a-half later, the two committees jointly reported a bill calling for a fifteen-member independent Electoral Commission composed of five senators (three Republicans and two Democrats), five representatives (three Democrats and two Republicans), and five Supreme Court justices (two Democratic justices, two Republican justices, and a fifth chosen by the other four). The presumption was that the fifth justice would be independent David Davis of Illinois. The commission was to have final authority over disputed electoral votes, unless both houses of Congress overruled it.

At the height of the House debate, Rep. George F. Hoar, R-Mass., who, as a member of the joint committee was instrumental in fashioning the proposed Electoral Commission Act, proclaimed that the bill was "one of the greatest in history." Other countries had equaled the United States "with great achievements in war and peace, in art, in literature, in commerce," but this act "shall stand without a rival" for a thousand years. To support his contention, Hoar offered an effective speech in support of the bill, in which he noted the constitutional impropriety of the Senate's presiding officer determining congressional electoral contests. Hoar warned of deadlock and encouraged a bipartisan solution that all parties could accept as fair.[2]

Ironically, members of Hoar's own party came out as the harshest critics of the Electoral Commission plan. The most emotional retort was offered by Rep. James A. Garfield, R-Ohio, who, like Hoar, would be subsequently selected to serve on the commission. Garfield predicted that the bill would "destroy forever the constitutional plan of electing a President. Pass this bill and the old constitutional safeguards are gone.... If we adopt it, we shirk a present difficulty, but in doing so we create far greater ones for those who come after us. What to us is a difficulty will be to them a peril." Despite Garfield's concerns, the Senate (47–17) and House (191–86) overwhelmingly approved the bill. Democrats strongly supported it, while a majority of Republicans stood in opposition. The Democrats were momentarily optimistic, believing Justice Davis would support Tilden's election. Even before the House vote, their confidence began to dissipate as they learned that the Illinois legislature had selected Davis to be a U.S. senator. Davis subsequently declined to serve on the commission, and Joseph P. Bradley, a New Jersey Republican, who the Democrats considered the most independent of the remaining justices, took his place.[3]

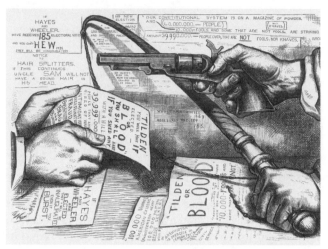

Thomas Nast's 1877 cartoon depicts controversy over the contested 1876 presidential election between Samuel Tilden and Rutherford B. Hayes. Hayes was declared president at 4:10 a.m. on March 2, 1877, after an 18-hour session in the House of Representatives with the compromise argued for by George F. Hoar and many hours of fillibusters to prevent it.

Source: The Granger Collection, New York.

On February 1, 1877, Congress met in a joint session to count the electoral votes; Senate president Ferry opened the state electoral certificates alphabetically until the certificates from Florida were presented. After objections were raised concerning the Florida certificates, the matter was referred to the Electoral Commission, which, after considerable discussion, decided not to examine evidence beyond that submitted with the certificates. The commission awarded Florida to Hayes, 8–7. Identical decisions were rendered in each of the three other disputed cases as well. Justice Bradley, in each instance, joined with the Republicans in favoring the Hayes electors. As stipulated by the Electoral Commission Act, the commission reported each determination to the House and Senate. The two chambers then met separately to decide whether to accept or reject the commission's findings. Only if both houses of Congress rejected a finding could it be overturned.

Predictably, the Senate agreed with the commission's decisions, while the House, after considerable debate, rejected them. As the electoral count progressed, House Democrats became increasingly agitated and threatened to launch a filibuster, but it never materialized because an agreement was reached between Hayes's forces and Southern conservative Democrats. While exactly what was agreed to remains in dispute, the agreement apparently called for the withdrawal of federal troops from the three contested Southern states and permitted the elected Democratic governors there to take office, signaling the end of Reconstruction. The Southerners, in turn, pledged to support the equal rights of blacks. Some have argued at length that the compromise also included promises of patronage favors and federal support for Southern railroads and internal improvements.[4]

At 10:00 a.m. on March 1, the House began an eighteen-hour session that, according to one account, was "probably the stormiest ever witnessed in any House of Representatives." The filibusters ruled until near the end when Rep. William M. Levy, D-La., took the floor to assure his fellow Democrats that he had solemn assurances from both Hayes's friends and President Ulysses. S. Grant of a "policy of conciliation toward the Southern States," and that neither "Federal authority or the army" would be used "to force upon those states governments not of there choice, but in the case of these states will leave their own people to settle the matter peaceably, of themselves." Levy's remarks served to silence the filibusters and a few hours later the House voted. At 4:10 a.m. on March 2, 1877, Senator Ferry announced that Rutherford B. Hayes had been elected president with 185 electoral votes. The following evening, Hayes took the oath of office privately at the White House because March 4 fell on a Sunday. The formal inauguration followed on Monday. Within two months, Hayes withdrew federal troops from the South and appointed former senator David M. Key, D-Tenn., postmaster general. It was to be another decade before Congress passed permanent legislation that addressed disputed electoral votes.[5]

REPRESENTATIVE GEORGE FRISBIE HOAR PRAISES THE COMPROMISE OF 1877

JANUARY 25, 1877

Mr. Speaker, the danger which our wisest writers on the Constitution years ago predicted and dreaded now confronts the American people. The Constitution contains no express provision for that determination of disputed questions of law or fact which it terms counting the electoral vote. The wisest students of its complicated mechanism have expressed their fear that it would give way, not in resisting foreign force or civil dissension, not even by decay or corruption, but because of its vague and imperfect provisions for determining that most vital of all questions, the title to executive power. With that peril, under circumstances of special difficulty, we have now to deal.

In estimating this danger I am not affected by any fear of civil war or any menace of violence. Such threats, if made in the spirit of empty bluster, deserve nothing but contempt; if serious, the swift and indignant scorn and condemnation of the whole people. I do not dwell upon any apprehension of violent resistance to the lawful authority of the Government. The evil of civil war — so great that even to threaten it is a grievous crime — is only surpassed by the greater evil of yielding one jot of lawful authority to menace. But I do hold that nothing could be more injurious to the whole Republic, nothing more destructive to the principles that I myself hold dear, than that a man holding them shall be placed in the presidential office whom at least one-half of the American people will regard as an usurper by an act of power which at least one-half of the people will regard as an usurpation. If any gentleman thinks otherwise, his judgment differs from mine as to the influences which commend the truth to the approbation of mankind.

I shall not attempt to add another to the arguments of the constitutional question: With whom is the power to determine those grave questions of law and fact which may arise in determining what votes have been lawfully cast for President and Vice-President by the electoral colleges? I admit that those persons who believe that the Constitution requires the President of the Senate in all cases to perform that office must deem this bill unconstitutional. I do not expect the votes of such persons for the bill, unless they think that the recent almost unanimous acquiescence of Senate and House in a different construction, supported by a current of great authorities, including John Marshall, Daniel Webster, and Abraham Lincoln, may induce them to treat the question as concluded, or at least so far to yield their individual judgment as to deal with it as one of doubt. This consideration may perhaps especially commend itself to those gentlemen who have honestly changed their opinions on a grave question of constitutional law in the presence of a great temptation. Fortunate is that statesman to whom long-settled and matured convictions are sufficient for the solution of the ever now and various problems of his public life,

> *Who in the height of conflict keeps the law*
> *In calmness mode, and sees what he foresaw.*

For myself three considerations make me deem it incredible that the framers of the Constitution or the people who accepted it ever meant or could mean to intrust the power of deciding these vast questions to the President of the Senate,

subject to no control of the two Houses of Congress or of the law-making power.

First. They were a generation of men that dreaded above all other things the usurpation of executive power.

Second. They expected that the President of the Senate would ordinarily be one of the candidates whose claim to the office was to be decided. They provided that two persons should be voted for President, of whom that one having the second highest number of votes was to become Vice-President, and President of the Senate. The President of the Senate, therefore, must within four years have been a leading candidate for the Presidency. The habit of continuing the same persons in public station doubtless led them to anticipate that he would be a leading candidate for the succession, as has first happened when Adams succeeded Washington, when Jefferson succeeded Adams, when Van Buren succeeded [Jackson] and in many cases of unsuccessful completion. The same suggestions apply to all cases where the Vice-President is a candidate for re-election.

Third. As in Great Britain, from which our institutions were derived, Parliament for centuries has regulated the inheritance of the crown and determined all questions of right to the succession, so, in every American State in existence when the Constitution of the United States was adopted, the Legislature at that time, either itself, elected the governor or counted the votes of the people and decided all disputes as to the popular choice.

As the Vice-President —

Says Alexander Hamilton —

may occasionally be a substitute for the President, all the reasons which recommend the mode of election prescribed for the one apply with great if not equal force to the manner of appointing the other.

There are three other theories, with none of which is this bill in conflict:

First. That the President of the Senate must count the vote in the absence of concurrent action by the two Houses, or of other provision by the law-making power.

Second. That under the power expressly conferred by the Constitution upon Congress to make "all laws which shall be necessary and proper for carrying into execution the foregoing powers, and all other powers vested by this Constitution in the Government of the United States, or in any department or officer thereof," the law-making power may provide a method for counting the vote.

Third. That the power of counting the vote is vested by the Constitution in the two Houses voting separately. The two Houses of Congress are the tribunal which according to this bill is to execute this grave authority. If they have it by the

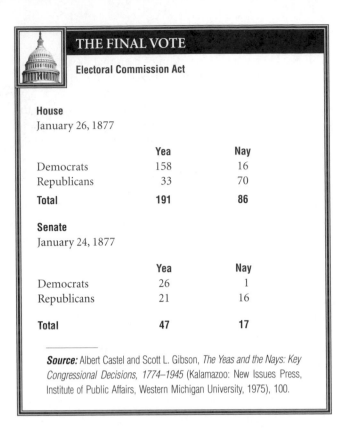

THE FINAL VOTE

Electoral Commission Act

House
January 26, 1877

	Yea	Nay
Democrats	158	16
Republicans	33	70
Total	**191**	**86**

Senate
January 24, 1877

	Yea	Nay
Democrats	26	1
Republicans	21	16
Total	**47**	**17**

Source: Albert Castel and Scott L. Gibson, *The Yeas and the Nays: Key Congressional Decisions, 1774–1945* (Kalamazoo: New Issues Press, Institute of Public Affairs, Western Michigan University, 1975), 100.

Constitution, it is left undisturbed. If it needs the forces of the law-making power to confer it, this bill confers it. The only case when any other aid comes in is when the two members of which the final tribunal is composed differ in their judgment. Certainly it is within the law-making power to provide what shall happen when the members of a constitutional tribunal composed of even numbers are equally divided in judgment. We may surely provide by law that, if the Supreme Court composed of six or ten members be equally divided in opinion, the judgment of the court below shall stand or a report of a reference shall be accepted. The commission is not an umpire. It is not an arbitration. It is an agency inferior to the two Houses, reporting to them, its action wholly subject to theirs, but only to stand when the two Houses are divided. The warmest advocate of the constitutional powers of the Houses must concede that this bill comes within the very letter of the definition of the law-making powers of Congress; a "law necessary and proper for carrying into execution the powers vested in the Government and in every department thereof." Unless this power exist in Congress of providing by law for the case where the two members of this tribunal composed of an even number, House and Senate, stand divided on any question one to one, the advocates of the power of the two Houses to count the vote must believe that the framers of the Government meant it should perish when the not improbable case should arise of a division it sentiment

between two political bodies on any question of law or fact which should arise in counting the vote.

Some gentlemen have spoken of this as a *compromise* bill. There is not a drop of compromise in it. I do not mean that, after it was found that the principle of securing an able and impartial tribunal conformed to the opinions and desires of all the committee, there was not some yielding of individual views as to detail. But how can that man be said to compromise who, having a just and righteous claim, asserts it, maintains it, enforces it by argument and proof, yields no jot or tittle of it before a tribunal so constituted as to insure its decision in accordance with justice and righteousness so far as the lot of humanity will admit? I think justice and right are compromised when they are submitted for their decision to force. They are compromised when they can only be maintained by doubtful disputed exercises of power. They never can be compromised when they are permitted to stand before a tribunal clothed with judicial powers, surrounded by judicial safeguards, invested with legal authority by the law-making power of the country.

Let it not be said that this reasoning implies that truth and error stand on an equality; that it makes no difference whether matters be settled right or wrong provided only they be settled. It is precisely because truth and error differ; it is because of the *vast* difference between the righteous result and its antagonist, that we propose to submit the differences between them not to force, not to heat and passion, but to that tribunal which, among all mechanisms possible to be executed by law, is least liable to be diverted from the truth.

But it is charged that this commission is in the end to be made up of seven men who of course will decide for one party, and seven men who of course will decide for the other,

---

Some gentlemen have spoken of this as a compromise bill…. [H]ow can that man be said to compromise who … yields no jot or tittle of it before a tribunal so constituted as to insure its decision in accordance with justice and righteousness so far as the lot of humanity will admit?

"[J]ustice and right are compromised when they are submitted for their decision to force." — George Frisbie Hoar

---

and who must call in an umpire by lot, and that therefore you are in substance and effect putting the decision of this whole matter upon chance. If this be true, never was a fact so humiliating to the Republic confessed since it was inaugurated. Of the members of our National Assembly, wisest and best selected for the gravest judicial duty ever imposed upon man, under the constraint of this solemn oath can there be found in all this Sodom not ten, not one to obey any other mandate but that of party? Far otherwise was the thought of Madison when with exultant aspiration he commended the Constitution to his countrymen:

> In cases where it may be doubtful on which side Justice lies, what better umpires could be desired by two violent factions, flying to arms and tearing the state to pieces, than the representatives of confederate States not heated by the local flame? To the impartiality of judges they would unite the affection of friends. Happy would it be if such a remedy for its infirmities could be enjoyed by all free governments; if a project equally effectual could be established for the universal peace of mankind. — James Madison in *Federalist Papers No. 43.*

But I especially repudiate this imputation when it rests upon those members of the commission who are to come from the Supreme Court. It is true there is a possibility of bias arising from old political opinions even there, and this, however minute, the bill seeks to place in exact equilibrium. But this small inclination, if any, will in my judgment be overweighted a hundred-fold by the bias pressing them to pre-

serve the dignity, honor, and weight of their judicial office before their countrymen and before posterity. They will not consent by a party division to have themselves or their court go down in history as incapable of the judicial function in the presence of the disturbing element of partisan desire for power, in regard to the greatest cause ever brought into judgment. Mr. Speaker, the act we are about to do will, in my judgment, be one of the greatest in history. Our annals have been crowded with great achievements in war and peace, in art, in literature, in commerce. But other countries, other republics have equaled us in these things. But in this great act we shall stand without a rival or an example. For a thousand years our children, with tears of joy and pride, will read that while in the fierce strife for executive power the sun of other republics has gone down in darkness and in blood, in their own country, too, the same great peril has arisen. Their sky has been darkened by the same cloud; their ship with its costly freight of love and hope encountered the same storm and was driven near the same rock; but in the midst of storm and darkness and conflict the August and awful figure of law rose over the face of the waters, uttering its divine, controlling mandate, Peace, be still! [Applause.]

Source: *Congressional Record*, 44th Cong., 2nd sess., January 25 (Washington: GPO, 1877), 1877, 5:940–942.

REPRESENTATIVE JAMES A. GARFIELD CRITICIZES THE COMPROMISE OF 1877

JANUARY 25, 1877

Mr. Speaker, nothing but the gravity of this subject would induce me to make a speech in my present condition of voice. But I must attempt it and trust that the kindness of the House will enable me to be heard.

I desire in the outset to recognize whatever of good there is in this bill. It has some great merits which I cheerfully recognize. It is intended to avoid strife in a great and trying crisis of the nation. It is intended to aid in tiding over a great present difficulty, possibly a great public danger. It will doubtless bring out a result. And when it has brought out a result it will leave the person who is declared to be the elect of the nation with a clearer title, or rather with a more nearly undisputed title, than any method that has yet been suggested.

These are certainly great results. At a time like this, no man should treat lightly a bill which may and probably will produce them all. Furthermore, I feel bound to say, if I were to speak of this bill only as a partisan — a word much abused just now — I should say that I am not afraid of its operation.

The eminent gentlemen who are to compose the commission, eminent for their character and abilities, will, I have no doubt, seek to do and will do justice under its provisions. And therefore, believing as I do that Rutherford B. Hayes has been honestly and legally elected President of the United States, I confidently expect that this commission will find that to be the fact and will declare it. Should they find otherwise, all good men everywhere will submit to their decision.

But neither the wishes nor the fate of Mr. Hayes or Mr. Tilden should be consulted in considering this bill. I presume no one here is authorized to speak for either of these gentlemen on the question. I certainly am not. It is our business to speak for ourselves and for the people whom we represent.

★ ★ ★ ★

On this occasion, as on all others, let us seek only that which is worthy of ourselves and of our great country.

★ ★ ★ ★

Let us for a moment forget Hayes and Tilden, republicans and democrats; let us forget our own epoch and our own generation; and, entering a broader field, inquire how this thing which we are about to do will affect the great future of our Republic; and in what condition, if we pass this bill, we shall transmit our institutions to those who shall come after us. The present good which we shall achieve by it may be very great, yet if the evils that will flow from it in the future must be greater, it would be base in us to flinch from trouble by entailing remediless evils upon our children.

In my view, then, the foremost question is this: What will be the effect of this measure upon our institutions? I cannot make that inquiry intelligibly without a brief reference to the history of the Constitution and to some of the formidable questions which presented themselves to our fathers nearly a hundred years ago, when they set up this goodly frame of government.

Among the foremost difficulties, both in point of time and of magnitude, was how to create an executive head of the nation. Our fathers encountered that difficulty the first morning after they organized and elected the officers of their constitutional convention. The first resolution introduced by Randolph, of Virginia, on the 29th day of May, recognized that great question and invited the convention to its examination. The men who made the Constitution were deeply read in the profoundest political philosophy of their day. They had learned from Montesquieu, from Locke, from Fenelon, and other great teachers of the human race that liberty is impossible without a clear and distinct separation of the three great powers of government.

★ ★ ★ ★

In the course of their deliberations upon the subject, there were suggested seven different plans, which may be grouped under two principal heads or classes. One group comprised all the plans for creating the Chief Executive by means of some one of the pre-existing political organizations of the country. First and foremost it proposed to authorize one or both Houses of the National Legislature to elect the Chief Executive. Another was to confer that power upon the governors of the States or upon the Legislatures of the States. Another, that he should be chosen directly by the people themselves under the laws of the States. The second group comprised all the various plans for creating a new separate instrumentality for making the choice.

At first the proposition that the Executive should be elected by the National Legislature was received by the convention with almost unanimous approval; and for the reason that up to that time, Congress had done all that was done in the way of National Government. It had created the nation, had led its fortunes through a thousand perils, had declared

and achieved independence, and had preserved the liberty of the people in the midst of a great war. Though Congress had failed to secure a firm and stable Government after the war, yet its glory was not forgotten. As Congress had created the Union it was most natural that our fathers should say Congress shall also create the Chief Executive of the nation. And within two weeks after the convention assembled, they voted for that plan with absolute unanimity.

But with equal unanimity they agreed that this plan would be fatal to the stability of the Government they were about to establish, if they did not couple with it some provision that should make the presidential office independent of the power that created him. To effect this they provided that the President should be ineligible for re-election. They said it would never do to create a Chief Executive by the voice of the National Legislature, and then allow him to be re-elected by that same voice; for he would thus become their creature. And so, from the first day of their work in May to within five days of its close in September, they grappled with the mighty question.

★ ★ ★ ★

At the close of the great discussion, when the last vote on this subject was taken by our fathers, they were almost unanimous in excluding the National Legislature from any share whatever in the choice of the Chief Executive of the nation. They rejected all the plans of the first group, and created a new instrumentality. They adopted the system of electors. When that plan was under discussion, they used the utmost precaution to hedge it about by every conceivable protection against the interference or control of Congress.

In the first place, they said the States shall create the electoral colleges. They allowed Congress to have nothing whatever to do with the creation of the colleges, except merely to fix the time when the States should appoint them. And in order to exclude Congress by positive prohibition, in the last days of the convention they provided that no member of either House of Congress should be appointed an elector; so that not even by the personal influence of any one of its members could the Congress interfere with the election of a President.

The creation of a President under our Constitution, consists of three distinct steps: First, the creation of the electoral colleges; second, the vote of the colleges; and third, the opening and counting of their votes. This is the simple plan of the Constitution.

The creation of the colleges is left absolutely to the States, within the five limitations I had the honor to mention to the House a few days ago: first, that it must be a *State* that creates it; second, that the State is limited as to the number of electors they may appoint; third, that electors shall not be members of Congress, nor officers of the United States; fourth, that the time for appointing electors may be fixed by Congress; and fifth, the date when their appointment is announced, which must be before the time for giving their votes, may also be fixed by Congress.

These five simple limitations, and these alone, were laid upon the States. Every other act, fact, and thing possible to be done in creating the electoral colleges, was absolutely and uncontrollably in the power of the States themselves. Within these limitations Congress has no more power to touch them in this work than England or France. That is the first step.

The second is still plainer and simpler, namely, the work of the colleges. They were created as an independent and separate power, or set of powers, for the sole purpose of electing a President. They were created by the States. Congress has just one thing to do with them, and only one; it may fix the day when they shall meet. By the act of 1792, Congress fixed the day as it still stands in the law; and there the authority of the Congress over the colleges ended.

There was a later act, of 1845, which gave to the States the authority to provide by law for filling vacancies of electors in these colleges, and Congress has passed no other law on the subject.

The States having created them, the time of their assemblage having been fixed by Congress, and their power to fill vacancies having been regulated by State laws, the colleges are as independent in exercise of their functions as is any department of, the Government within its sphere. Being thus equipped, their powers are restrained by a few simple limitations laid upon them by the Constitution itself: first, they must vote for a native-born citizen; second, for a man who has been fourteen years a resident of the United States; third, at least one of the persons for whom they vote must not be a citizen of their own State; fourth, the mode of voting and certifying their returns is prescribed by the Constitution itself. Within these simple and plain limitations, the electoral colleges are absolutely independent of the States and of Congress.

★ ★ ★ ★

These colleges are none the less sovereign and independent because they exist only for a day. They meet on the same day in all the States; they do their work summarily, in one day, and dissolve forever. There is no power to interfere, no power to recall them, no power to revise their action. Their work is done; the record is made up, signed, sealed, and transmitted; and thus the second great act in the presidential election is completed. I ought to correct myself: the second act *is* the presidential election. The election is finished the hour when the electoral colleges have cast their votes and sealed up the record.

Still there is a third step in the process; and it is shorter, plainer, simpler than the other two. These sealed certificates of the electoral colleges are forwarded to the President of the Senate, where they rest under the silence of the seals for more than two months. The Constitution assumes that the result of the election is still unknown. But on a day fixed by law, and

the only day, of all the days of February, on which the law commands Congress to be in session, the last act in the plan of electing a President is to be performed. How plain and simple are the words that describe this third and last step! Here they are:

> The President of the Senate shall, in the presence of the Senate and House of Representatives, open all the certificates, and the votes shall then be counted.

Here is no ambiguity. Two words dominate and inspire the clause: They are the words *open* and *count*. These words are not shrouded in the black-letter mysteries of the law. They are plain words, understood by every man who speaks our mother-tongue, and need no lexicon or commentary.

★ ★ ★ ★

No further act is required. The Constitution itself declares the result.

> The person having the greatest number of votes for President shall be President, if such number be a majority of the whole number of electors appointed.

If no person has such majority, the House of Representatives shall immediately choose a President; not the House as organized for legislation, but a new electoral college is created out of the members of the House, by means of which each State has one vote for President, and only one.

★ ★ ★ ★

Such, Mr. Speaker, was the grand and simple plan by which the framers of the Constitution empowered all the people, acting under the laws of the several States, to create special and select colleges of independent electors to choose a President, who should be, not the creature of Congress, nor of the States, but the Chief Magistrate of the whole nation, the elect of all the people.

When the Constitution was completed and sent to the people of the States for ratification, it was subjected to the severest criticism of the ablest men of that generation. Those sections which related to the election of President not only escaped censure but received the highest commendation. The sixty-seventh number of the Federalist, written by Alexander Hamilton, was devoted to this feature of the instrument. That great writer congratulated the country that the convention had devised a method that made the President free from pre-existing bodies that protected the process of election from all interference by Congress and from the cabals and intrigues so likely to arise in legislative bodies.

★ ★ ★ ★

Though the Constitution has sought to keep Congress away from all the process of making a President, this bill creates and places in the control of Congress the enginery by which Presidents can be made and unmade at the caprice of the Senate and House. It grasps all the power, and holds States and electors as toys in its hands. It assumes the right of Congress to go down into the colleges and inquire into all the acts and facts connected with their work. It assumes the right of Congress to go down into the States, to review the act of every officer, to open every ballot-box, and to pass judgment upon every ballot cast by seven millions of Americans.

★ ★ ★ ★

The radical and incurable defect of this bill is that it puts a vast, cumbrous machine in the place of the simple, plain

---

The radical and incurable defect of this bill is that it puts a vast, cumbrous machine in the place of the simple, plain plan of the Constitution; it adopts a method which invites and augments the evils from which we now suffer. — James A. Garfield

---

plan of the Constitution; it adopts a method which invites and augments the evils from which we now suffer.

★ ★ ★ ★

Mr. Speaker, I have trespassed too long upon on the indulgence of the House; but I cannot withhold from the gentleman from Massachusetts [Mr. HOAR] the tribute of my admiration for the earnestness and eloquence with which he closed his defense of this measure. I even shared his enthusiasm when looking forward to the future of this nation he pictured to our imagination the gratitude of those who may occupy these Halls a hundred years hence, for the wisdom which planned and virtue which adopted this act, which my friend believes to be the great act of the century; an act that solves a great national difficulty, that calms party passion, that averts the dangers of civil war. Let us hope, Mr. Speaker, that they will not be compelled to add that, though this act enabled the men of 1877 to escape from temporary troubles, yet it entailed upon their children evils far more serious and perils far more formidable; that it transmitted to them shattered institutions, and set the good ship of the Union adrift upon an unknown and harborless sea. I hope they may not say that we built no safeguard against dangers except the slight ones that threatened us. It would be a far higher tribute if they could say of us: "The men of 1876, who closed the cycle of the first century of the Republic, were men who, when they encountered danger, met it with clear-eyed wisdom and calm courage. As the men of 1776 met the perils of their time without flinching, and

through years of sacrifice, suffering and blood conquered their independence and created a nation, so the men of 1876, after having defended the great inheritance from still greater perils, bravely faced and conquered all the difficulties of their own epoch, and did not entail them upon their children.

"No threats of civil war, however formidable, could compel them to throw away any safeguard of liberty. The preservation of their institutions was to them an object of greater concern than present ease or temporary prosperity; and instead of framing new devices which might endanger the old Constitution, they rejected all doubtful expedients; and, planting their feet upon the solid rock of the Constitution, they stood at their posts of duty until the tempest was overpassed, and peace walked hand in hand with liberty, ruled by law." [Applause.]

During the many calm years of the century, our political pilots have grown careless of the course. The master of a vessel sailing down Lake Ontario has the whole breadth of that beautiful inland sea for his pathway. But when his ship arrives at the chute of the La Chine there is but one path of safety. With a steady hand, a clear eye, and a brave heart, he points his prow to the well-fixed landmarks on the shore, and with death on either hand, makes the plunge and shoots tire rapids in safety.

We too are approaching the narrows; and we hear the roar of angry waters below, and the muttering of sullen thunder overhead. Unterrified by breakers or tempest, let us steer our course by the Constitution of our fathers, and we shall neither sink in the rapids, nor compel our children to "shoot Niagara" and perish in the whirlpool. [Great Applause.]

Source: *Congressional Record,* 44th Cong., 2nd sess., January 25 (Washington: GPO, 1877), 1877, 5:968–973.

Notes

1. John Copeland Nagle, "How Not to Count Votes," *Columbia Law Review,* 104 (October 2004): 1738. See also Roy Morris Jr., *Fraud of the Century: Rutherford B. Hayes, Samuel Tilden, and the Stolen Election of 1876* (New York: Simon and Schuster, 2003), 164–197; Keith Ian Polakoff, *The Politics of Inertia: The Election of 1876 and the End of Reconstruction* (Baton Rouge: Louisiana State University Press, 1973), 201–231.

2. "Counting the Electoral Vote," *Congressional Record,* January 25, 1877, 5:941; and Richard E. Welch Jr., *George Frisbie Hoar and the Half-Breed Republicans* (Cambridge, Mass.: Harvard University Press, 1971), 62–63. See also U.S. Congress, House, *Counting the Electoral Vote,* report to accompany H.R. 4454, 44th Cong., 2nd sess., H. Rept. 108 (Washington: GPO, 1877); Paul Leland Haworth, *The Hayes-Tilden Disputed Presidential Election of 1876* (New York: Russell and Russell, 1966), 190–207.

3. Welch, *George Frisbie Hoar and the Half-Breed Republicans,* 63; and "Counting the Electoral Vote," *Congressional Record,* January 25, 1877, 5:970, 973. See also 19 Stat. 228 (January 29, 1877); Haworth, *The Hayes-Tilden Disputed Presidential Election of 1876,* 207–219;

Morris, *Fraud of the Century: Rutherford B. Hayes, Samuel Tilden, and the Stolen Election of 1876,* 197–219; Nagle, "How Not to Count Votes," 1743–1746; Polakoff, *The Politics of Inertia: The Election of 1876 and the End of Reconstruction,* 269–284; William H. Rehnquist, *Centennial Crisis: The Disputed Election of 1876* (New York: Knopf, 2004), 113–119, 141–160.

4. U.S. Electoral Commission (1887), *Proceedings of the Electoral Commission and of the Two Houses of Congress in Joint Meeting Relative to the Count of the Electoral Votes Cast December 6, 1876, for the Presidential Term Commencing March 4, 1877* (Washington, D.C.: GPO, 1877); Haworth, *The Hayes-Tilden Disputed Presidential Election of 1876,* 222–271; Morris, *Fraud of the Century: Rutherford B. Hayes, Samuel Tilden, and the Stolen Election of 1876,* 220–237; Polakoff, *The Politics of Inertia: The Election of 1876 and the End of Reconstruction,* 286–312; Rehnquist, *Centennial Crisis: The Disputed Election of 1876,* 177–178; C. Vann Woodward, *Reunion and Reaction: The Compromise of 1877 and the End of Reconstruction* (Boston: Little, Brown, 1966), 3–14, 155–203. For differing perspectives on the compromise, see Alan Peskin, "Was There a Compromise of 1877?" *Journal of American History* 60 (June 1973): 63–75; Michael Les Benedict, "Southern Democrats in the Crisis of 1876–1877: A Reconsideration of Reunion and Reaction," *Journal of Southern History* 46 (November 1980): 489–524.

5. Haworth, *The Hayes-Tilden Disputed Presidential Election of 1876,* 276; "Counting of the Electoral Vote," *Congressional Record,* March 1, 1877, 5:2047. See also "Counting the Electoral Vote," *Congressional Record,* March 1, 1877, 5:2068; Polakoff, *The Politics of Inertia: The Election of 1876 and the End of Reconstruction,* 312–313.

Reed's Rules

✳ 1890 ✳

Among Speakers of the House of Representatives, none have understood the chamber's legislative procedure better, nor had as great an impact on reforming that procedure, than Thomas B. Reed, R-Maine. By the time he was elected Speaker in December 1889, Reed had already earned a reputation for parliamentary prowess during his decade as a representative. As Speaker, he was ready to initiate what would become the most dramatic procedural changes in the institution's history.

The previous March, Reed laid out his intentions in a *Century Magazine* article that captured his frustration with obstructions in the House that had reduced the chamber's business to a "minimum." "The blocking of the public business by a set of rules which can be wielded by two or three men," he emphasized, "has aroused and interested the country, for the rights of all are immediately concerned…. Ever since the slavery question came to trouble the peace of the country the rules of the House have been framed with the view of rendering legislation difficult." The only remedy, Reed believed, was "to return to the first principles of democracy and republicanism alike." It was his contention that: "Our government was founded on the doctrine that if 100 citizens think one way and 101 think the other, the 101 are right. It is the old doctrine that the majority must govern. Indeed, you have no choice. If the majority do not govern, the minority will; and if the tyranny of the majority is hard, the tyranny of the minority is simply unendurable." As a consequence, the [procedural] rules of the House should be arranged so that the majority has sway, but should also provide for debate and careful consideration. Afterwards "there ought to be no hindrance to action except those checks and balances which our Constitution wisely provides."[1] Six months later, in a *North American Review* article, Reed made clear his intention to "establish rules which will facilitate the public business — rules unlike those of the present House, which only delay and frustrate action."[2]

At the time, two delaying tactics were most common: the disappearing quorum and the use of dilatory motions. Under House rule, a member could bring the business of the chamber to a halt by refusing to vote, thereby depriving the House of the quorum needed to conduct official business. Also, members opposing legislative action frequently demanded votes on motions such as those to recess or adjourn, simply for the purposes of delay.

While the Republicans held only a tenuous seven-vote advantage 166–159, they were determined to control House proceedings and put an end to delaying tactics. Such maneuvers, they felt, had allowed obstructionists to thwart opportunities for a more active legislative agenda by using House procedures to protect their concerns and perceptions. Leading Democrats defended existing House procedures as necessary for the protection of minority views and interests. Soon after the congressional elections of 1888, the Republicans began to plot their strategy for reforming the rules of the House. Reed provided the formula for achieving that goal.

With his election as Speaker, Reed also became the *ex officio* chairman of the powerful Committee on Rules, as had his predecessors for nearly a quarter century. These two leadership positions afforded Reed the power to bring about the rules changes he and his party sought. Because the House is not a continuing body like the Senate, it must at the beginning of each new Congress adopt a new set of procedural rules that govern the chamber's proceedings for the next two years. To gain control over the obstructionists, Reed instructed the Rules Committee to withhold its proposals "pending the development of a revised code [of rules] and the settlement cases of contested elections." Then, with the House "operating under the general rules of parliamentary law," Reed, "as the presiding officer … consistently refused to accept dilatory motions."[3]

The Democrats, anticipating that the Republicans would settle all disputed elections in favor of their party's candidate, planned to obstruct the election cases until the Rules Committee brought forth a set of rules they found acceptable. Their tactic was to refuse to vote on such cases and thereby deny the Republicans the quorum they needed to conduct business. Heretofore, even if members were in the chamber when their name was called, they were not counted unless they responded. Reed challenged this practice on January 29, 1890, eight weeks after the Fifty-first Congress convened, ruling that if members were in the chamber during a roll call they could be counted for the purposes of establishing a quorum even if they did not respond to the roll call.

PUCK.

"THE MINORITY BE D——D!"

Thomas B. Reed, elected Speaker of the House in 1888, implemented policy against the disappearing quorum, preventing representatives present from refusing to vote and earning himself names such as "tyrant" and "despot." Some members ran to hide as Reed called out their names for the congressional record to record their non-vote.
Source: Library of Congress.

His ruling against the disappearing quorum was prompted by a Democratic effort to obstruct debate on a Committee on Elections report that awarded a contested election seat to a Republican. When the quorum count was taken, one hundred sixty-one members voted yea, two voted nay. The vote fell two short of a quorum even though there were more than one hundred sixty-three members on the House floor at the time. Reed, however, ignoring Democrats' calls of "no quorum," directed the "Clerk to record the names of the following members present and refusing to vote."[4]

As Reed began to read the names of members he could see in the chamber that had not voted, the House erupted with Democrats, led by former Speaker Charles F. Crisp, D-Ga., strenuously objecting to the Speaker's action. There were new protests each time the Speaker called another name to add to the list that would make up a quorum. Amidst the tempestuous proceedings, Reed ignored the opposition and continued to call names for the clerk to list. Not until Reed reached the name of Rep. James B. McCreary, D-Ky., did he pause, as the

Kentuckian declared: "I deny your right, Mr. Speaker, to count me as present, and I desire to read from parliamentary law on the subject." Relying on common sense, Reed replied: "The Chair is making a statement of fact that the gentleman from Kentucky is present. Does he deny it?" Despite numerous objections and near pandemonium, Reed stood fast. Following the laughter and applause from the Republicans, and groans and imprecations from the Democrats, Reed continued until he had called the names of forty-one nonvoting members present in the chamber. Then he announced that a quorum was in fact present and that the resolution to consider the election contest had passed. The actual vote for consideration of the contested election case was one hundred sixty-one voting aye, two voting no, and one hundred sixty-five not voting. Representative Crisp appealed the ruling, but it was finally laid on the table by a majority of the counted quorum.[5]

The fight over the disappearing quorum, however, was far from over. The following day, when Reed once again refused to entertain appeals on the grounds that the House had already decided the question of the disappearing quorum, some on the floor denounced him with epithets such as "czar," "despot," and "tyrant." In between, Rep. Benjamin Butterworth, R-Ohio, delivered a resounding defense of Reed and Henry G. Turner, D-Ga., a stinging critique of Reed's actions. The following excerpts from their comments well illuminate the emotions of the moment. During the final day of the debate, the Democrats sat silently when their names were reached on roll calls. "Near the end, realizing that they were getting nowhere with their protests, members of the recalcitrant minority began trying to escape the eye of the quorum-counting Speaker by lurking under desks, dodging behind screens, or bolting for the exits." Some even suffered physical injuries in their attempts to hide from Reed.[6]

Attention next shifted to adoption of a new rules package that was introduced on February 6, accompanied by a lengthy majority and minority report. The proposed new rules, which were largely the work of Reed, made no change in twenty-nine of the forty-seven rules used by the previous Congress. A number of the remaining eighteen contained changes to bring about conformity in the "vitally important changes made in a few essential particulars, or to remove potential obstructions." There were only four important changes, "but they were revolutionary in character." These were designed to eliminate dilatory motions, to count nonvoting members as present, to increase the efficiency of deliberations in the Committee of the Whole, and to develop a new system for dealing with the order of business. As proposed, the new rules afforded the majority party greater control over legislative procedures, primarily by enhancing the prerogatives of the Speaker. These changes, together with the Speaker's previously existing authority to appoint members of standing committees and direct legislative business as chairman of the Rules Committee, significantly enhanced his power.[7]

Debate on the rules opened on February 10 and continued for the next four days before being adopted by a vote of 161–144, with twenty-three members not voting. With their adoption, "a momentous change had been effected in congressional procedure." Although "both the rules and their author were savagely assailed, and part of the gains were lost in the next Congress, most of the changes proved so reasonable and so valuable that they were soon restored." Although the Republicans only had the slimmest of majorities in the Fifty-first House, under new rules and Speaker Reed's leadership they achieved the "most productive [Congress] since the Civil War."[8] Its landmark legislation included the Dependent and Disability Pension Act, Sherman Anti Trust Act, Sherman Silver Purchase Act, McKinley Tariff, Court of Appeals Act, Immigration Act of 1891, Meat Inspection Act of 1891, General Land Revision Act of 1891, and International Copyright Act.

When the Democrats regained control of the House in the Fifty-second Congress, Speaker Crisp, who had led the protest against the abolition of the disappearing quorum, suddenly found it advantageous to retain the rule. While the "Democrats were correct in their concern that the Reed reforms would lead to the unmitigated tyranny of the majority … their fear was misdirected." Ultimately, "it was not the quorum count or the rule against dilatory motions that facilitated the centralization of power in the House; instead it was the [S]peaker's control over floor recognition, the committee system, and the Rules Committee." During the next two decades, "Reed's Rules provided the institutional framework for a period of strong Speakers and centralized party leadership in the House that continued until the House revolted against Speaker Joseph G. Cannon in 1910."[9]

REPRESENTATIVE HENRY G. TURNER'S CRITIQUE OF REED'S RULES

JANUARY 30, 1890

What is our situation? I shall endeavor to state it without heat or passion and with a sincere desire on my part to be fair in the discussion of the most important question of procedure that ever arose in this House.

I believe that if the wild view — I speak respectfully — presented on this appeal by gentlemen on the other side is once ingrafted into the practice of the House of Representatives it will inaugurate a reign of anarchy and profligacy unprecedented in the annals of this country.

On this the 30th day of January, two months after this session began, the House of Representatives is without a single rule of procedure. At the same time, sir, there are seventeen election contests pending to be decided by the House. We are now asked to consider one of these cases with no rule but the will of the Speaker to guide us. Time and again we have asked for rules, and they have been denied us. We are to engage in a struggle for a seat in this House under these extraordinary circumstances. Let it be further borne in mind that a seat just now is very valuable, because the rolls of this House on the last vote show four votes less than a majority for the party that elected the Speaker.

During the last Congress, when we had rules, gentlemen on that side, with great unanimity, refrained from voting when an election contest was pending.

★ ★ ★ ★

Mr. Speaker, if I have done injustice to the honorable gentleman from Iowa, I hope he will take the earliest opportunity to correct it. It is possible that the gentleman may have voted on the occasion to which I have referred. I know distinctly the gentleman from Ohio, Mr. McKINLEY, the gentleman from Illinois, Mr. CANNON, and the gentleman from Maine [Mr. REED], and various other gentlemen who are authorities on the question now pending never seemed to feel any compunction at all when they refrained from voting on a question of the character of that which is now pending. When was it, Mr. Speaker, this change of heart occurred? It is certain that these conversions have occurred since the last election. It is perhaps due to the Speaker to say that on the 4th of July last at Woodstock, Conn., that honorable gentleman saw fit to present some views evidently intended to prepare the country for our present predicament. That gentleman began his address on that occasion by misquoting a celebrated saying of the Duke of Wellington, in which he says: "It was no less a person, I believe, than field marshal the Duke of Wellington, who said, 'There is only one thing more demoralizing than a defeat and that is a victory.'"

The gentleman inverted the saying of the duke, but he stated a truth inadvertently [laughter and applause on the Democratic side] with more pith than did the famous warrior. [Laughter and applause.]

I shall endeavor to show that in his decision, from which an appeal is now pending, he has been again unmindful of the truths of history, and that victory to his party to-day may be more demoralizing than defeat!

That speech was evidently intended to prepare the country for the coup which now menaces us from the Speaker's chair. He then said:

> The victories of peace, though less demoralizing, require, like the victories of war, that they should be attended to if any advantage is to be derived from them.
>
> But I desire to say to you that a majority of twelve or twenty gives a right to the people of the United States to expect what they demand, while the majority of three or five requires that the people of the United States shall be ready to take what they can with outstretched hands, or else be thankful for nothing. [Laughter.]
>
> The Constitution, like England at Trafalgar, expected every man to do his duty, and now we are in such a condition that any man who is shameless enough may stop the legislation of the country, and men who are in the minority, simply

because they are in the minority, stop the progress of the public business, and they have received, thus far, no efficient rebuke from the people.

I do not deny the propriety of tactics for debate, but I do declare that filibustering to prevent the transaction of the public business is dishonest, unpatriotic, and unconstitutional. [Applause.]

Why did gentlemen on this side, under the lead of the honorable gentleman from Maine, habitually, for years, do these very same dishonest, unpatriotic, and unconstitutional things? [Applause on the Democratic side.] Are there any new authorities on this subject that have transpired since the Fiftieth congress? What new luminary has appeared to emblazon the parliamentary sky?

The only change, Mr. Speaker, that has occurred since these practices of the Republican party in the last Congress, consists in the fact that an election has recently occurred which has given them a lean majority.

But there are three things involved in this appeal. In the first place, has the Speaker the power to single out gentlemen on this floor and name them as contumacious delinquents, and invoking upon them the rebuke which stigmatizes them as "dishonest and unpatriotic?" Why, sir, the day has never been when the Speaker could from his high place name any man for censure or for rebuke or for animadversion without the authority of the House of Representatives. [Applause on the Democratic side.]

Not long since, sir, I think during the pendency of the famous cloture proceedings in the English House of Commons, one of the propositions there made was to give to the speaker of the House power to name a member as disorderly. Here the Speaker, without rule, without authority even from his own party, names members of this House, at the desk, one by one, as men who have not done their duty. Why, sir, he could not while in the chair even offer a resolution to that effect. Can he do what he could not ask the House to do?

If the gentlemen on the other side desire that to be done, let me beg them that it be done in a decent and orderly way. Let the majority propose a resolution charging us with contumacy.

On such a resolution we would have the common American right to be heard before condemnation.

The pending appeal from the Speaker's decision also denies his right to direct entries to be made on the *Journal of the House* which would not otherwise have been made. The Speaker is the creature of the House. When was this new function conferred upon him? The Constitution says that "each House shall keep a *Journal* of its proceedings," the House, not the Speaker. And how is it that the House performs that duty? By the election of an officer especially charged with this responsibility, and that officer is the organ of the House in the keeping of its minutes. The Speaker has no more control over those minutes than I have. I am his peer on this floor, and I direct the Clerk to omit my name from his *Journal*. [Applause on the Democratic side.]

But there is another great question included in the appeal now pending. The Constitution provides that "a majority of each [House] shall constitute a quorum to do business."

One hundred and sixty-five members constitute a majority of the House. But on the call of the yeas and nays, which the Constitution requires to be entered on the *Journal*, it appeared that one hundred sixty-one gentlemen voted in the affirmative and two voted in the negative. Less than a quorum having voted on the proposition, the result was a nullity according to the Constitution, as could have been shown by simply citing the *Journal*. The Speaker nevertheless decided that a quorum was present, and, to support his decision, directed the Clerk to note on the *Journal* that certain gentlemen, naming them, were present and refused to vote. This unprecedented action of the Speaker is now under review or appeal. From the foundation of the Government it has been held by the presiding officer that a failure of a quorum to appear on the call of the yeas and nays alone nullified the result. And every House since the Revolution has followed that practice.

In the discussion of this matter I shall not go over the ground which has been so ably presented to the public in the North American Review, in an article reviewing the whole subject, by the honorable gentleman from Texas, Mr. MILLS; nor shall I cite again the precedents presented so ably by my colleague [Mr. CRISP] on yesterday; nor will I attempt to reinforce the very clear and conclusive argument of the gentleman from Kentucky, Mr. CARLISLE, based upon the language of the Constitution.

Mr. Speaker, fifty Congresses have come and gone. The great men of the country, from the North and from the South, from the East and from the West, including Clay, Calhoun, and Webster and every man who has been Speaker of the House or President of the Senate and every President of the United States who ever served in Congress, have established the unbroken practice for which I contend to-day.

Ten thousand men, chosen by the people of this country, have occupied seats in the two branches of Congress since the foundation of the Government. Three generations of statesmen have succeeded each other in these halls. In all that multitude of authority there can not be found more gentlemen supporting the view of the Speaker than I can count on the fingers of one hand.

I call up this long array of eminent and distinguished men, our predecessors, and cite their united voices against the present Speaker. If he were to take a division of that great host he could not have a dozen supporters.

It is true that Mr. Tucker, of Virginia, did, in the Forty-sixth Congress, propose a rule providing that in a certain case, well defined, the Clerk should record certain gentlemen as present to make a quorum when they had been arrested and distinctly refused to vote; but he had the courage to abandon his position under fire. There is no such rule. Shall the Speaker make it?

Now, how is it at the other end of the National Legislature? That is supposed to be a legislative body which consists of the most experienced and distinguished men in this country, elected for six years, called the ambassadors of the States, and sometimes, by way of distinction, called the upper branch of Congress. The long catalogue of great men who have sat there and who have succeeded the fathers have themselves established a practice under this provision of the Constitution. Every President of that body, from Adams and Jefferson to INGALLS and MORTON, and every individual Senator from the beginning of the Government has sanctioned the construction of the Constitution for which I contend.

Will the authority of all these distinguished men, who were sworn to support the Constitution, avail nothing against this temptation which a party exigency suggests? For a century Congress has been executing the Constitution according to its plain import and the construction for which I contend.

To find a precedent for his view the Speaker has to turn his back on Congress and the House over which he presides. — Henry G. Turner

---

To find a precedent for his view the Speaker has to turn his back on Congress and the House over which he presides. [Applause on the Democratic side.]

★ ★ ★ ★

Again I ask gentlemen to pause before they commit us to this fatal step. I have no doubt what the result will be when this issue goes to the country; but as an American citizen, taking pride in the character and stability of our institutions, I ask you to put this temptation behind. That flag which is so appropriately placed above the Speaker's chair is itself a defiance of arbitrary power. [Applause on the Democratic side.] And everywhere else on earth, on land, on sea — everywhere on the face of the earth it is the standard of popular freedom. Shall it be said that here alone, of all other places in this country, there is the despotic sway of a single man? [Applause on the Democratic side.]

Source: *Congressional Record*, 51st Cong., 1st sess., January 30, 1890 (Washington: GPO, 1890), 21:985–986.

REPRESENTATIVE BENJAMIN BUTTER-WORTH DEFENDS SPEAKER REED

JANUARY 30, 1890

Mr. Speaker, I do not think any gentleman upon this floor underestimates the importance of having a right determination of the question which is submitted for our consideration and action. The ruling of the Speaker in the matter complained of, the correctness of which is indirectly, if not directly, called in question, is, I admit, not in the line of precedent in this House. But, on the contrary, it is, as asserted by my honorable friends on the other side of the Chamber, a radical departure from an almost unbroken line of precedent, and condemns a practice which has been tolerated by this body for possibly half a century — a practice which is, I may say, in a measure sanctified by antiquity, if antiquity can sanctify that which is in itself wrong.

This question goes to the power of majorities to rule in this Government, as my honored colleague [Mr. McKINLEY] has pertinently suggested. In determining this question we are called upon to decide whether the Constitution contains within itself the elements of suicide. This is a government of the people. Expressed in another way, it is a Government of majorities. The majority may exercise that authority in legislation and in Government which is conferred by and is in furtherance of the provisions of the Constitution. The majority of this House may do what it will, so long as it confines its action to the letter and spirit and keeps within the purview of the provisions of the organic law. We derive from the Constitution our power to act, and there we search to ascertain what we may do.

This is a legislative body, charged with certain duties under the Constitution. What are they? To transact that public business which is committed to our care.

★ ★ ★ ★

A GOVERNMENT OF MAJORITIES

This is either a government of majorities under the Constitution or it is a government of minorities. That it is a government is certain, and it is either the one or the other, for certainly it can not be both at the same time. If it is not a government of majorities it is a government of minorities.... Abraham Lincoln used to say that, after all, the plain, common-sense view of an instrument was the better view of it, and I apply that principle in this case, because the Constitution of the United States was written for the plain people of this country, who are the source of power. [Applause.]

Each House shall be the judge of the elections, returns, and qualifications of its own members, and a majority of each shall constitute a quorum to do business.

The language plainly and unmistakably fixes the number of members necessary to do business; that is, a less number can not do business. What was the object in fixing the number essential to be present to do business? The discussion in the convention which framed the Constitution indicates clearly the object. It was that a few members should not get together and enact laws for the people, nor yet that there should be required a number so large and unwieldy as to be cumbrous and make it impossible or difficult to transact business.

★ ★ ★ ★

What The Fathers Had In View

The fathers did contemplate as possible the secession of members of this body, thereby rendering it impossible to legislate, and inaugurating revolution, if you please; but, by the same token, under the inspiration and leadership of Madison and Randolph, they provided against the dangers that might wait on that secession by authorizing the members present in the House to bring the seceders back to their places.

For what? To make them stand up and say "ay" or "no?" We have no power to do that; we can use neither the rack nor the thumbscrew; our instrumentalities can only be applied to the consciences of men; but we bring them here in order that there may be *present to do* business the number required by the Constitution for that purpose. [Applause.]

★ ★ ★ ★

Authority To Compel Attendance Not Given In Vain

This was discussed further until finally Mr. Randolph and Mr. Madison, for the purpose of defeating the efforts of seceding members, moved to add at the end of Article 6, Section 3, the words: And may be authorized to compel the attendance of absent members in such manner and under such penalties as each House may provide. Compel them to attend — for what? To leave the House in precisely the same condition as before they were brought in — a condition which rendered it necessary to bring them in to change and improve it? Yet just this absurdity is involved in the proposition of the honorable gentlemen on the other side. Was this authority conferred by the Constitution only to enable us to go through the farce of bringing in the absentees and learning after each member has been seated in his place that, while under the Constitution he is actually personally present to make a quorum to do business, yet when an attempt is made to do the thing which required his presence he at once, by merely closing his mouth, becomes constructively absent? Or he may, in fact, while present, arise in his place and assert that he is absent, and we must take his word for it. [Laughter and applause.] Could any proposition be more absurd? And is it in this spirit we are to execute the law?

We Are Here For Business

I ask again, what was the object of conferring this power to compel the attendance of a quorum? Obviously to do business. And why? Because that is "what we are here for," and the Government itself must perish unless we do the business for which we are here assembled. The Constitution, I repeat, provides that a majority of each House shall constitute a quorum to do business, and the same Constitution provides that if it shall please a number of the members to secede from the House, in order that no business may be done, such members may be compelled to come in. For what? Incontestably to secure the presence in this legislative hall of the number of members which the Constitution says must be present in order to constitute a quorum to do business, and in the absence of which number this body has no power to proceed.

Yet our honored Democratic friends say that, although we may be brought here, yet the object of our being brought in can not be effective, since our presence, if we remain silent, is as potent to stop legislation as our absence would be; and beyond that they assert that, though present, if silent they are not participating, and whether they participate or not is left to the discretion of each member, he being answerable alone to himself and his constituents. And thus the provision of the Constitution intended to prevent the disaster which might result from the secession of members becomes a screaming farce, notwithstanding their presence in the House under its provision, since it is utterly nugatory so far as the results intended are concerned. To state the case as it is is to argue it and expose its absurdity, not to use a stronger term.

The honorable gentleman from Kentucky said that the Speaker who now occupies the chair is the first in the history of the Republic to hold that a bill could pass this House without a constitutional majority. I challenge the correctness of the honorable gentleman's statement. The Speaker has never held or pretended to hold that a bill can pass without receiving the necessary constitutional majority — I say it with all deference. The Speaker of this House has neither said nor intimated, at least within my hearing — and I have attended all the sittings here — that it was competent for this House to pass a bill except by a constitutional majority. He did say that bills have often passed, though receiving but one or two votes, but under well known parliamentary usage that the assent of all was conclusively presumed, there being no question of a quorum made.

★ ★ ★ ★

How Is A Quorum Determined?

The point we are considering is not as to whether a constitutional majority is required to do business — nobody doubts that — or whether there shall be a majority of a quorum to pass a bill — that is conceded — but *how shall the presence of a quorum in this* House be determined? That is the question we are endeavoring to answer — a question of fact, as a friend near me suggests. It is a question of fact. What number is required to constitute a quorum *is a question of law. Whether that number of members are present is a question of fact. That a majority of a quorum is necessary to pass a bill is *matter of law.* Whether a majority so voted is a *question of fact,* which can only be determined by a count.

★ ★ ★ ★

It Might Lead To Ruin

Sir, suppose the minority of this House should decide that they would not participate in its proceedings, no matter why. Suppose that it occurred that a number of members on this side were, by sickness, kept at their homes, and, without counting members of the minority, it should be impossible to pass an appropriation bill. Suppose it was the last day of the session, and the minority, as they do to-day, should sit in their places and refuse to participate, refuse to vote for or against appropriations absolutely necessary to carry on the Government. Mr. Speaker, would not that minority be participating? And, let me ask, what would be the effect of that participation? Although the wheels of Government might stand still, yet in the presence of an unexampled and unequaled surplus in the Treasury, with one hundred and sixty-three of us here and with one hundred and fifty of you here also, making one hundred more than a quorum present to do business, still, according to your view of the Constitution, we would not be able, in case you sat silent, to appropriate one poor farthing out of the national Treasury to carry on the Government.

You sit here in the flesh, bodily present, charged by the Constitution and the laws of your country with certain duties which you have sworn to perform. The Speaker sees you; we see you; nay, the country sees you; yet the country starves to death by your inaction, and that on your theory that though actually present you are constructively absent. Is that revolution or not? [Applause.] Gentlemen, if that is not revolution, will you point me to a method, an instrumentality which would put its fingers more certainly with a death-grip upon the throat of the Republic? And yet you say to me that, though present, if silent you are not "participating." Why, the

---

The Speaker sees you; we see you; nay, the country sees you; yet the country starves to death by your inaction. — Benjamin Butterworth

---

distinguished Speaker might as well sit down upon my lean friend from Alabama, sit comfortably on him, and against his protest say, "I am not participating in this proceeding." [Loud laughter and applause.]

★ ★ ★ ★

Clearly it is the right, and I might say the duty, of the majority to propose measures to this House. It is the obvious duty of the majority to present to this body such measures for consideration as ought to be brought before it. That is just what the majority has done or attempted. What followed? You have in effect asserted that not the majority, but the minority shall determine what measures shall be introduced and when they shall be introduced, and that is, I insist, to proclaim in the teeth of the Constitution that a minority, and not a majority, shall rule in this country.

You assert that it is your right to say to us what measures we shall consider. It would follow that you may also say what measures we shall not consider. If you, as a minority, can say arbitrarily, as you now propose, what bill shall not pass, you may by the same token and the same authority decide, as arbitrarily, what bill shall pass; and thus the majority under the Constitution must abdicate in favor of the sovereign will (for in that case it would be sovereign) of the minority of the House of Representatives, and this is the spectacle you gentlemen this day present to the country.

★ ★ ★ ★

Silence Can Be Revolutionary

If the gentleman is not in his seat, that is a question of fact, not of parliamentary law, and the only practical question before us is whether in point of fact it is true or not that he is there. If his silence alone is to determine the negative, as he says it is, then of course we are at the end of our legislative tether, and your silence stops legislation, it stops the wheels of the Government, it stops the House of Representatives from performing its constitutional functions, and if that is not revolutionary then I have no conception of what the term implies. [Applause on the Republican side.]

★ ★ ★ ★

The Minority Must Not Rule

There could be no greater danger to constitutional government than to put it within the power of the minority absolutely and arbitrarily to stop the wheels of legislation. There lies the danger. The record discloses that that is the danger of which the fathers spoke and against which they tried, nay did provide by the clause of the Constitution to which I have referred. That is the danger of which Bancroft wrote in commenting upon the views of the fathers:

That there may be a secession of members and thereby render the House powerless to do business.

★ ★ ★ ★

The Fathers Anticipated Secession

The fathers recognized the probability of that situation. They recognized all the facts that form and constitute a part of the problem with which they were dealing. They realized that in the nature of things it must occur that in the House and in the Senate the margin of majority might be small. They provided not that there should be a quorum made up of the majority side of the House, but a quorum to consist of a majority of the Members or Senators, and a quorum so constituted can do business. And it was further provided that to pass a bill there shall be not a majority of the votes of all the members, but a majority of a quorum; and they conferred the power to compel the attendance of a quorum; and, when secured, what folly to suggest that it can be dissipated by the magic influence of profound silence!

★ ★ ★ ★

An Absurd Proposition

Now, Mr. Speaker, it is a strange proposition that under this Constitution of ours the House can make a quorum by bringing in two sick men if they belong to the majority side, but it may bring one hundred fifty able bodied Representatives of the minority and place them in their seats and still lack a quorum by two, or three, or four! [Laughter.] That is, two sick men of the majority are more potent to make a quorum than one hundred fifty members of the minority, if the one hundred fifty will only sit in their places and keep still. What an absurdity upon the face of it that is, no matter how sanctified by age! It is the weapon of the revolutionist; it is the weapon of anarchy; it is the weapon of all that wars against the objects and purposes of the Constitution in the matter of giving expression to the will of the majority in this country, and the majority represent the sovereign will of the people.

★ ★ ★ ★

Tyranny, And Tyranny

Sir, the majority of this House does not rule even for a day. Let the peculiar organization or constitution of our Government be not forgotten. We do not pass laws; the Senate, not elected at the same time with ourselves, must concur; a President must approve; the Supreme Court may also pass upon our measures; all these stays in the line of legislative procedure stand between us and any arbitrary or wanton outrage upon the rights of the people so far as the majority is concerned. But what shall stand between the people and outrage if the minority may arbitrarily stop the wheels of legislation for an indefinite time?

★ ★ ★ ★

The Rights Of The People Vindicated

It is of the highest importance to secure to and maintain the rights of the minority; but it can not be justly claimed that such security can only be found in laying the majority at their feet, shorn of all power as a representative body except to meet and adjourn until they consent to abdicate their functions as a majority, with no higher mission in proposing measures than to ascertain the will of an arbitrary and controlling minority. But the sovereign will of the people is represented in the majority. Its power is limited by the Constitution, but under no circumstances is it transferred to the minority. Until the Constitution of our country shall be overthrown by revolution or otherwise, the decision of the Speaker, in giving expression to the will of the majority, must be held to be a vindication of the rights and privileges of the people of this country. [Long-continued applause.]

★ ★ ★ ★

The Speaker's Ruling Is Sound

The ruling of the Speaker is in the line of Democratic and Republican precedent. It is supported by the ablest Democratic constitutional lawyers in the country. It is not partisan in its nature, but results from the demand of the minority side of the House, a demand they seek to enforce, that the majority shall abdicate its rights, its powers, and its functions, and thus not only ignore, but before the country betray the will of the people, which is or ought to be sovereign. And that sovereignty can only find expression when the majority rules in the State and in the nation. And the Speaker, in the discharge of his duty, has so held, and his decision will have the approval of the patriotic people of this nation, and to that tribunal of last resort we with confidence appeal.

Source: Congressional Record, 51st Cong., 1st sess., January 30, 1890 (Washington: GPO, 1890), 21:986–993.

Notes

1. Thomas B. Reed, "Rules of the House of Representatives," *Century Magazine* 37 (March 1889): 792–795.

2. Thomas B. Reed, "Obstruction in the National House," *North American Review* 149 (October 1889): 428.

3. Ronald M. Peters Jr., *The American Speakership: The Office in Historical Perspective* (Baltimore: Johns Hopkins University Press, 1990), 63.

4. *Congressional Record,* 51st Cong., 1st sess., January 29, 1890, 21:949.

5. Quote is found at ibid. See also ibid., 21:949–960.

6. Booth Mooney, *Mr. Speaker: Four Men Who Shaped the United States House of Representatives* (Chicago: Follett, 1964), 66.

7. William A. Robinson, *Thomas B. Reed: Parliamentarian* (New York: Dodd, Mead, 1930), 223–227.

8. Robinson, *Thomas B. Reed: Parliamentarian,* 231; Peters, *The American Speakership,* 69.

9. Peters, *The American Speakership,* 74–75; Randall Strahan, "Reed's Rules," in Roger C. Bacon, Roger H. Davidson, and Morton Keller, *The Encyclopedia of the United States Congress,* 4 vols. (New York: Simon and Schuster, 1995) 3:1691.

Revenue Act of 1894
✴ 1894 ✴

Early in 1894, the House of Representatives was the setting for particularly impressive oratory displays by Rep. Bourke Cockran, D-N.Y., and Rep. William Jennings Bryan, D-Neb. Perhaps not since the classic Webster-Haynes debate in the Senate had Congress witnessed such a contest, in which the very issues seemed to be so clearly embodied in the men who articulated them." The exchange between Cockran and Bryan was sparked by the insertion of income tax provisions into what would become the Wilson-Gorman Tariff Act, a measure designed "to shift the tax burden from the working poor to the wealthy"; "to redistribute the *tax burden*, not society's wealth", and "to tap corporate wealth and check corporate abuse." The idea was not a new one. During the preceding two decades, Congress introduced nearly seventy income tax bills.[1]

The 1894 income tax had limited coverage — calling for a 2 percent tax on "gains, profits and incomes" of more than $4,000 — which affected a group of approximately eighty-five thousand individuals out of a population of sixty-five million. The measure, the first federal income tax since the Civil War, was struck down by the Supreme Court in *Pollock v. Farmers' Loan & Trust Company*, 157 U.S. 429 (1895), as a breach of the constitutional provision requiring that direct taxes be apportioned among the states according to population. The ruling blocked Congress's attempts to institute an income tax law without first amending the Constitution to authorize it. The issue, however, did not die. Between 1895 and 1909, thirty-three different proposed constitutional amendments were offered to overturn the *Pollock* decision as the protax arguments of 1894 repeatedly put forward.[2]

Those same arguments laid the foundation for the Sixteenth Amendment (1913), which "paved the way for the institutionalization of a tax base that had been fundamentally structured in 1894." The amendment granted Congress the power to collect money from the American people based on their income rather than apportioning taxes among the several states on an equal basis as originally provided in the Constitution. The basic structure of the first income tax law enacted after the amendment's ratification (included in the Underwood-Simmons Tariff Act of 1913) was similar in structure to the 1894 tax. Both measures arose in the midst of U.S. industrialization, when corporations began to dominate the national economy and a new working class of industrialists and financiers evolved. The existing tax system was ill-equipped to handle these changes. The 1913 legislation borrowed provisions from the 1894 act and was readily adopted.[3]

Preceding the inclusion of the tax provisions in the Revenue Act of 1894, the *New York Tribune* conducted a two-year study to determine how many millionaires there actually were in the United States to "disprove the charges levied against the Republican party, that its high-tariff policy had created robber barons and innumerable millionaires." The results, which the *Tribune* published in five installments and later as a pamphlet, identified only 1,125 out of 4,047 millionaires who obtained their wealth through "protected" industries. The results did not, however, deter the Populist Party in 1892 from inserting a plank in its party platform calling for a graduated income tax. With the onset of a deep depression in 1893, revenue from the existing tariff was insufficient to meet federal expenses, and President Grover Cleveland called upon Congress, in his annual message of December 4, for "a small tax upon incomes deriving from certain corporate investments."[4]

Early in January 1894, Bryan and Rep. Benton McMillin, D-Tenn., chairman of the House Committee on Ways and Means, persuaded the committee to support a tax on all net incomes of corporation and individual incomes over $4,000. Next, they convinced the House Democratic caucus to extend the ongoing Wilson-Gorman Tariff debate an additional three days to permit a discussion of the internal revenue provisions reported by the Ways and Means Committee. McMillin opened with an eloquent defense and justification for the tax before blaming Republicans for encouraging the concentration of wealth in America through unjust taxation. Other supporters contended that the tax would secure a contribution from the wealthy proportionate to the governmental protection and benefits they received, encourage economy in government, and constrain the accumulation of huge fortunes, which the American people had come to regard as a threat to democracy.

Opponents of the income tax, most of whom resided in eastern urban areas, derided it as "class legislation," some

W. Bourke Cockran, who debated with William Jennings Bryan about the Revenue Act of 1894. Cockran opposed the act, which was eventually passed and led to the to the American income tax.
Source: The Granger Collection, New York.

going so far as to label it communistic or the tool of socialist labor. They maintained that the income tax could only be justified as a war measure; would be an unfair burden on the rich and the business community; would encourage fraud, perjury, and lying; and was sectional biased in favor of the South and against the North. "The friends and enemies of the income tax struggled," the *New York World* wrote, "like athletes on a football field. Up and down and back and forth they tugged and tussled" until the showdown between the two most eloquent partisans, Cockran and Bryan, squared off on the afternoon of January 30. British prime minister Winston Churchill would later name Cockran as his model in developing his own speaking style. Bryan, twenty years Cockran's junior, was just beginning his extraordinary public career. The contrast between their use of imagery was dramatic. Cockran's allusions stemmed from his vast knowledge of history, while Bryan drew on the Bible and poetry.[5]

This proposal, Cockran declared, would force "us to support the platform of the Populist Party." Imposing a "direct tax on 85,000 persons out of a population of 65,000,000" is "an assault on Democratic institutions," and "the most dan-

gerous feature of the proceedings and operations of the government since its establishment." If allowed to become law, it would serve as the forerunner of "oppressive class legislation" and would eventually wrest control of government away from the majority through its limitations on their shares of "the burdens of government." It is "not imposed to raise revenue, but to gratify vengeance. It is not designed for the welfare of the whole people, but for the oppression of a part of the people." It would tax "industry and thrift, and is therefore a manifestation of hostility to that desire for success which is the main spring of human activity."[6]

Bryan began what many consider his best House speech, by saluting Cockran's rhetorical gifts. "If this were a mere contest in oratory," he said, "no one would be presumptuous enough to dispute the prize with the distinguished gentlemen from New York." He preferred a graduated income tax, but the proposal at hand was better than nothing at all. It was not inequitable, and it did not penalize the rich since their holdings were more in need of protection by armies and navies than those of the poor. What it might do was prompt increased perjury or fraud by the rich, or cause them to leave the country. At the time, the Cockran-Bryan exchange was not front-page news. Only later did the historic significance of their remarks become apparent. On February 1, 1894, the House approved the tax amendment, 182–48, and then approved the Wilson-Gorman Tariff, 204–140.

When the Senate took up the matter, the arguments echoed those espoused in the House. Those opposed viewed it as unnecessary; discriminatory; a violation of states rights; inquisitorial; an inducement for sectional and class legislation; a deterrent to the poor feeling more of a responsibility for the government as well as a deterrent to growth in the business community. Defenders claimed it was not unconstitutional, unjust, or sectional; not likely to encourage perjury; or to be more inquisitive than state property taxes. On July 3, 1894, the Senate passed its verison of the Wilson-Gorman Tariff, that also contained income tax provisions, 39–34. Following a month's deliberation the House approved the Senate bill on August 13, 182–106, and it became law on August 28. Despite significant criticism by writers and advocacy groups, the public felt the tax would begin to correct existing wealth and income inequalities and lead to the creation of a more balanced tax system.[8]

Reaction to the Supreme Court's voiding of the income tax a few months later was immediate and extreme. It captured "the popular imagination, and fostered the impression that the rich were escaping the burden of taxes." More than a decade of legislative efforts to overturn the decision followed before protax supporters finally gained the opening they needed in 1909 when Sen. Joseph W. Bailey, D-Texas, and Sen. Albert B. Cummins, R-Iowa, offered income tax amendments during the Payne-Aldrich Tariff bill debate. Senate Finance Committee chairman Nelson W. Aldrich, R-R.I., tried to derail the proposals by urging that they be dropped in favor of a constitutional amendment granting Congress the power to levy and collect taxes. He hoped his plan would delay passage of an income tax, and he felt that three-fourths of the states would never ratify the amendment. The strategy backfired. In July 1909, both the House 318–14 and Senate 77–0 approved the proposed amendment by deceptive wide margins, and President William Howard Taft added his endorsement. The Sixteenth Amendment was declared as having been ratified by the requisite number of states on February 25, 1913.[9]

REPRESENTATIVE W. BOURKE COCKRAN OPPOSES THE REVENUE ACT OF 1894

JANUARY 30, 1894

I feel assured that every member of the House will yield me implicit belief when I say it is with feelings of the most profound regret that I find myself compelled to intervene in this debate for the second time. I had hoped that the great measure of industrial emancipation of which general debate closed two weeks ago would be allowed to go before the country unvexed and undisturbed by factional disputes, that this experiment of tariff reform would be submitted to the American people free from all embarrassing side issues; that the Democratic party would proceed to redeem its pledges to the country before it began to indulge the vagaries of its individual members.

We on this side of the Chamber who are opposed to the pending amendment find a new test placed upon our loyalty. We are willing to support a tariff for revenue in obedience to the instructions of the great parliament of our party, but we are now commanded by a caucus of the Democratic members of this body to incorporate in the tariff bill a provision imposing a direct tax on 85,000 persons out of a population of over 65,000,000. The Democratic party has never approved such a system of taxation, but has always opposed it. The Populist party, apparently animated by a spirit of hostility to all wealth which is not possessed by its members, declared in favor of a tax on the incomes of a small number of citizens, and it is now proposed by the authors of this internal-revenue amendment to make our loyalty to the principles of the Democratic party a means of forcing us to support the platform of the Populist party.

Mr. Chairman, a proposal to tax any legitimate source of revenue would furnish no reason to a Democrat for separating from his associates and opposing this measure or any part of it. But when the proposal goes further than a mere scheme for raising revenue — when by the common declaration of all those who support it the amendment offered by the gentleman from Tennessee [Mr. MCMILLIN] is deliberately designed to create a special class for purposes of taxation, then those of us who regard the equality of all before the law as a fundamental feature of republican institutions, are compelled by loyalty to our consciences to oppose the decrees of the caucus.

Sir, I oppose this amendment because I regard the proposal of the gentleman from Tennessee as an assault on Democratic institutions. Its adoption would be the most dangerous feature of the proceedings and operations of this Government since its establishment. Its enactment will be the entering wedge in a system of oppressive class legislation, which is certain to provoke retaliatory measures and which, by excluding the majority of our citizens from participation in the burdens of government, will ultimately result in limiting their participation in the control of the Government.

★ ★ ★ ★

Throughout this whole discussion our main contention has been that the McKinley tariff is an economic failure; that it has diminished our trade, because it has restricted the free interchange of our commodities with the commodities produced by the other countries of the world.

We have repudiated with emphasis the theory that an increase in our imports would mean an injury to our business. We have insisted that this reduction in the tariff will stimulate both exports and imports. And now, after we have made these professions, after we have induced the country to believe them and to shape its legislation upon them, we find the reform itself discredited in the house of its friends, assailed by its supporters, the charges made by the Republican party against our doctrines reechoed by gentlemen on this side, who assert that the enactment of this measure will result in a decrease of the revenue, which is, virtually, a declaration that it will not increase the business of the country nor broaden the prosperity of the people.

★ ★ ★ ★

Are we by our acts to discredit the issue on which our party has won its greatest victory, while we profess faith in it

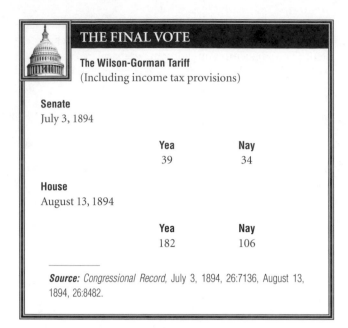

THE FINAL VOTE

The Wilson-Gorman Tariff
(Including income tax provisions)

Senate
July 3, 1894

	Yea	Nay
	39	34

House
August 13, 1894

	Yea	Nay
	182	106

Source: Congressional Record, July 3, 1894, 26:7136, August 13, 1894, 26:8482.

with our lips? When we show distrust of our own professions, can we expect the country to put faith in them? The pretense that an income tax has been made necessary by the reduction of tariff rates is too transparent to disguise the motives which govern the authors of this proposal. This tax is not imposed to raise revenue, but to gratify vengeance. It is not designed for the welfare of the whole people, but for the oppression of a part of the people.

This tax is not imposed to raise revenue, but to gratify vengeance. It is not designed for the welfare of the whole people, but for the oppression of a part of the people. — W. Bourke Cockran

---

We have heard but one argument in support of this proposal, and that was the argument voiced by the gentleman from Tennessee [Mr. MCMILLIN] that all other taxes were taxes upon consumption, while this would be a tax upon something else.

I do not think the gentleman succeeded in defining exactly the place where this special tax would fall, but it is perfectly clear that the distinction which he intended to make between existing systems of taxation and the plan now proposed was that all existing taxes fell on consumption, while this new tax was to fall somewhere else.

★ ★ ★ ★

The report which accompanied this amendment pursues the same enlightened course of argument and supports the

assertion that an income tax is no more inquisitorial in its character than a custom tax or an internal-revenue tax by stating that under existing laws whisky is taken from the hands of the owner and detained in the custody of the Government, and the baggage of travelers is examined at the steamship wharf. How does the detention of whisky in bond operate as an inquisition? Is it suspected that when the doors of the warehouse are closed the customs officer will constitute himself an inquisition and proceed with an inquiry into the quality of the liquid that is committed to his care? [Laughter.]

★ ★ ★ ★

By this legislation you place the Government in an attitude of hostility to the true patriots of this country, to the men by whose industry land is made valuable, by whose intelligence capital is made fruitful; and it is a woeful condition of society, it is a situation pregnant with evil and with ruin, when the productive masses, the creators of wealth, the architects of prosperity have reason to fear that the success of their industry will provoke the hostility of their government.

★ ★ ★ ★

Sir, I oppose this bill, not in the interests of the rich, but in the interests of the poor. I oppose this bill because I will not consent by any act of mine to place the humblest or the poorest of my fellow-citizens on a political plane one shade lower than that occupied by the richest and the proudest. I oppose this bill because its inevitable effect will be to impair the right of all the people to equality in control of the Government by establishing an inequality in the support of the Government.

★ ★ ★ ★

I oppose this measure because it involves a recognition of the principle that property, as distinguished from men, should bear the burdens of government.

★ ★ ★ ★

Gentlemen attempt to justify this legislation by the maxim that all men should bear a fair proportion of the burdens of the Government. Why, it is upon that principle alone that I base my opposition to this measure. You do not seek to make all men bear their proportionate share of the burdens of the Government; you are attempting to make a few men bear all the burdens of this taxation. If this be a Government of men, taxes must be levied on men and not on property. The amount which the Government exacts from the citizen should be proportionate to the amount of his wealth, but the tax should none the less be imposed on the owners of property, and not on the property itself. When all men are taxed according to fixed and equitable rules, whatever may be the amount of the burden imposed on each individual, the Government rests on men, not on things; on throbbing hearts and loyal shoulders, not on senseless property and soulless wealth.

★ ★ ★ ★

I do not believe that the poor of this country desire special privileges; I believe they are content with equality. During a long experience of politics in the great city of New York, I have never yet known the poor to assail the property of the rich; but I have known the rich to assail the political privileges of the poor.

★ ★ ★ ★

Mr. Chairman, I do not believe the humble people of this country, the people who are not possessed of $4,000 in annual rental or income, are in favor of this bill. I believe that this country is still capable of self-government. I believe that citizens whose intelligent industry, whose orderly daily lives, whose obedience to law, whose wonderful moral and commercial achievements are the marvel of the world, will stand immovably by those principles of equity and justice which have opened the pathway of prosperity to all the people.

★ ★ ★ ★

The imposition of such a tax is but a gentle, playful exercise of a dangerous power. It is merely showing demagogues the path of demagogy. The demand for a use of the taxing power which will result in substantial spoliation will soon be heard in every Populist meeting. The men who offer this amendment as a sop to the discontented will be swept away by the rising tide of socialism. They will discover, when too late, that in overturning the barriers which separate liberty from anarchy they have liberated ten thousand furies who will sweep over them and overwhelm them in a mad procession of anarchy and disorder.

★ ★ ★ ★

I am not in the least alarmed for the rich. I think this legislation will ultimately be injurious to them, because it will disturb the equality of all men before the law, which is after all their best protection, and which is the protection and stimulus of every man who hopes to be rich. But the men who seek to use the power of government to oppress the thrifty will be the first victims of inequality in the law. When the fruits of industry are threatened the industrious have always been able to strip the lawless of power for mischief. The growth of institutions has been the triumphant struggle of commerce to secure protection for property.

★ ★ ★ ★

We in this country who have for over a century enjoyed institutions which are based on the absolute political equality of all citizens, which were especially framed for the defense of liberty, we, who have seen our country grow as no country has ever grown, because within our limits property has been more secure than anywhere else on the globe, behold ourselves to-day threatened with a system of taxation which aims to create a class distinction between a small body of citizens and the great majority of the people who till the soil, who support this Government, upon whose patriotism, industry, and equality all the future glory and greatness of this nation must depend. [Applause.]

The Treasury Department informs us that but 85,000 persons enjoy incomes exceeding $4,000 a year. The men who are in possession of wealth thus seem to be a small part of the community, but the men who hope to possess wealth embrace a vast majority of the population. It is our proudest boast that every man in this country, no matter how humble his home, no matter how poor his family, no matter how dismal the circumstances which surround him, enjoys the opportunity and therefore the hope of achieving prosperity.

★ ★ ★ ★

So we see the Democratic party in the throes of a great struggle, apparently anxious to drive from their ranks the men who have been faithful in battle and in peace, in storm and in sunshine. I beseech you to pause before you enter upon a course which will prove disastrous to yourselves. You gentlemen who surround me have more at stake in the success of the Democratic party than we have who warn you of the danger which is involved in this legislation. You may pass this bill without our assistance, but you can not maintain the supremacy of our party if you array against it the sober, conservative judgment of the productive masses of this country. We have defended you in the past when your rights as citizens were imperiled, and we have aided you to baffle your enemies. We are anxious to win fresh victories for you and with you. We stand firmly and squarely for every question of policy upon which the party has ever pronounced. In the attitude which we have taken to this amendment we stand with the apostles of Democracy who have given the law to the party for over one hundred years.

★ ★ ★ ★

I oppose this income tax because it is not imposed for the protection of all the people but for the oppression of a part of the people. I oppose it because it is a violation of the principles upon which our institutions are founded by which this country has achieved a material prosperity which has astounded the world, and a moral influence which has edified and dignified the human race. I oppose it because it is a tax on industry and thrift and is therefore a manifestation of hostility to that desire for success which is the mainspring of human activity.

Source: *Congressional Record*, 53rd Cong., 2nd sess., January 30, 1894 (Washington: GPO, 1894), appendix, 26:462–469.

REPRESENTATIVE WILLIAM JENNINGS BRYAN REPLIES TO REPRESENTATIVE W. BOURKE COCKRAN

JANUARY 30, 1894

Mr. Chairman, if this were a mere contest in oratory, no one would be presumptuous enough to dispute the prize with the distinguished gentleman from New York [Mr. COCKRAN]; but clad in the armor of a righteous cause I dare oppose myself to the shafts of his genius, believing that "pebbles of truth" will be more effective than the "javelin of error," even when hurled by the giant of the Philistines. [Applause.]

What is this bill which has brought forth the vehement attack to which we have just listened? It is a bill reported by the Committee of Ways and Means as the complement of the tariff bill. It, together with the tariff measure already considered, provides the necessary revenue for the support of the Government. The point of attack is the income tax, individual and corporation (which is expected to raise about $30,000,000), and to that I will devote the few minutes which are allowed for closing the debate.

The gentleman from New York insists that sufficient revenue will be raised from the tariff schedules, together with the present internal-revenue taxes, and that it is therefore unnecessary to seek new objects for taxation. In this opinion he is not supported by the other members of the committee, and we have been constrained to follow our own judgment rather than his. The internal-revenue bill which is now pending as an amendment to the tariff bill imposes a tax of 2 percent upon the net incomes of corporations, and in the case of corporations no exemption is allowed.

I need not give all the reasons which led the committee to recommend this tax, but will suggest two of the most important. The stockholder in a corporation limits his liability. When the statute creating the corporation is fully complied with[,] the individual stockholder is secure, except to the extent fixed by the statute, whereas the entire property of the individual is ordinarily liable for his debts. Another reason is that corporations enjoy certain privileges and franchises. Some are given the right of eminent domain, while others, such as street-car companies, are given the right to use the streets of the city — a franchise which increases in value with each passing year. Corporations occupy the time and attention of our Federal courts and enjoy the protection of the Federal Government, and as they do not ordinarily pay taxes the committee felt justified in proposing a light tax upon them.

Some gentlemen have accused the committee of showing hostility to corporations. But, Mr. Chairman, we are not hostile to corporations; we simply believe that these creatures of the law, these fictitious persons, have no higher or dearer rights than the persons of flesh and blood whom God created and placed upon his footstool! [Applause.]

The bill also imposes a tax of 2 percent upon individual incomes in excess of $4,000. We have proposed the maximum of exemption and the minimum of rate. The principle is not new in this country. For nearly ten years, during and after the war, an income tax was levied, varying from 21 to 10 percent, while the exemption ranged from $600 to $2,000.

★ ★ ★ ★

The committee presents the bill after careful consideration, but will cheerfully accept any changes which the wisdom of the House may suggest. The bill not only exempts from taxation, but from annoyance as well, every person whose income is below $3,500. This is an important feature of the bill. In order to guard against fraud the bill provides that every person having an income of more than $3,500 shall make a return under oath, but no tax is collected unless the net income exceeds $4,000. The bill also provides severe penalties to restrain the tax-collector from disclosing any information gained from the returns made by citizens.

OBJECTIONS ANSWERED

Mr. Chairman, let us consider the objections which have been made. The gentleman from New York [Mr. BARTLETT] who addressed the House this forenoon, spent some time in trying to convince us that, while the Supreme Court had without dissent affirmed the constitutionality of an income tax, yet it might at some future time reverse the decision, and that, therefore, this bill ought to be rejected. This question has been settled beyond controversy. The principle has come before the court on several occasions, and the decisions have always sustained the constitutionality of the income tax.

★ ★ ★ ★

The gentleman from New York [Mr. COCKRAN] has denounced as unjust the principle underlying this tax. It is hardly necessary to read authorities to the House. There is no more just tax upon the statute books than the income tax, nor can any tax be proposed which is more equitable; and the principle is sustained by the most distinguished writers on political economy. Adam Smith says:

> The subjects of every State ought to contribute to the support of the Government, as nearly as possible in proportion to their respective abilities; that is, in proportion to the revenue which they respectively enjoy under the protection of the State. In the observation or neglect of this maxim consists what is called the equality or inequality of taxation.

The income tax is the only one which really fulfills this requirement. But it is said that we single out some person with a large income and make him pay more than his share. And let me call attention here to a fatal mistake made by the distinguished gentleman from New York [Mr. COCKRAN]. You who listened to his speech would have thought that the income tax was the only Federal tax proposed; you would have supposed that it was the object of this bill to collect the entire revenue from an income tax. The gentleman forgets that the pending tariff bill will collect upon imports more than one hundred and twenty millions of dollars — nearly ten times as much as we propose to collect from the individual income tax. Everybody knows that a tax upon consumption is an unequal tax, and that the poor man by means of it pays far out of proportion to the income which he enjoys.

★ ★ ★ ★

The gentleman from New York [Mr. COCKRAN] said that the poor are opposed to this tax because they do not want to be deprived of participation in it, and that taxation instead of being a sign of servitude is a badge of freedom. If taxation is

---

If taxation is a badge of freedom, let me assure my friend that the poor people of this country are covered all over with the insignia of freemen. — William Jennings Bryan

---

a badge of freedom, let me assure my friend that the poor people of this country are covered all over with the insignia of freemen. [Applause.]

Notwithstanding the exemption proposed by this bill, the people whose incomes are less than $4,000 will still contribute far more than their just share to the support of the Government. The gentleman says that he opposes this tax in the interest of the poor! Oh, sirs, is it not enough to betray the cause of the poor — must it be done with a kiss? [Applause.]

★ ★ ★ ★

Is It Inquisitorial?

The gentleman from New York says that this tax is inquisitorial, that it pries into a man's private business. I sent to New York and obtained from the city chamberlain copies of assessment blanks used. The chamberlain writes:

> The matter of assessing personal taxes is arrived at by interrogation of the persons assessed by either of the commissioners, which is a very rigorous cross-examination in reference to the amount of personal property they have, and reductions are only made by an affidavit asking for the same and sworn to before a tax commissioner of this county.

The citizen, after giving in detail his stock in various banks makes oath that —

> the full value of all personal property, exclusive of said bank shares owned by deponent (and not exempt by law from taxation) on the second Monday in January, 189-, did not exceed $— ; that the just debts owing by deponent on said date amounted to $—, and that no portion of such debts has been deducted from the assessment of any personal property of deponent, other than said bank shares, or has been used as an offset in the adjustment of any assessment for personal property whether in this or in any other county or State, for the year 189-, or incurred in the purchase of nontaxable property or securities, or for the purpose of evading taxation.

Is the proposed tax any more inquisitorial than that?

★ ★ ★ ★

Gentlemen say that some people will avoid the tax, and that therefore it is unfair to the people who pay. What law is fully obeyed? Why are criminal courts established, except to punish people who violate the laws which society has made? The man who pays his tax need not concern himself about the man who avoids it, unless, perhaps, he is willing to help prosecute the delinquent. The man who makes an honest return and complies with the law, pays no more than the rate prescribed, and if the possessors of large fortunes escape by fraud the payment of one-half their income tax, they will still contribute far more than they do now to support the Federal Government, and to that extent relieve from burdens those who now pay more than their share.

The gentleman from New York is especially indignant because incomes under $4,000 are exempt. Why, sir, this is not a new principle in legislation. The exemption of very small incomes might be justified on the ground that the cost of collection would exceed the amount collected, but it is not necessary to urge this defense. The propriety of making certain exemptions is everywhere recognized. So far as I have been able to investigate, every country which now imposes or has imposed an income tax has exempted small incomes from taxation. Nearly if not all of our States exempt certain kinds of property, or property to a certain amount. If an exemption tends toward socialism, as urged by the gentleman from New York [Mr. COCKRAN] and the Chamber of Commerce, is it possible that socialism has taken possession of the States of New York and Connecticut?

★ ★ ★ ★

The gentlemen who are so fearful of socialism when the poor are exempted from an income tax view with indifference those methods of taxation which give the rich a substantial exemption. They weep more because fifteen millions are to be collected from the incomes of the rich than they do at the collection of three hundred millions upon the goods which the poor consume. And when an attempt is made to equalize these burdens, not fully, but partially only, the people of the South and West are called anarchists.

I deny the accusation, sirs. It is among the people of the South and West, on the prairies and in the mountains, that you find the staunchest supporters of government and the best friends of law and order.

You may not find among these people the great fortunes which are accumulated in cities, nor will you find the dark shadows which these fortunes throw over the community, but you will find those willing to protect the rights of property, even while they demand that property shall bear its share of taxation. You may not find among them so much of wealth, but you will find men who are not only willing to pay their taxes to support the Government, but are willing whenever necessary to offer up their lives in its defense.

★ ★ ★ ★

Mr. George K. Holmes, of the Census Department, in an article recently published in the *Political Science Quarterly*, gives some tables showing the unequal distribution of property, and says:

> Otherwise stated, 91 percent of the 12,690,152 families of the country own no more than about 29 percent of the wealth, and 9 percent of the families own about 71 percent of the wealth.

Is it unfair or unjust that the burden of taxation shall be equalized between these two classes? Who is it most needs a navy? Is it the farmer who plods along behind the plow upon his farm, or is it the man whose property is situated in some great seaport where it could be reached by an enemy's guns? Who demands a standing army? Is it the poor man as he goes about his work, or is it the capitalist who wants that army to supplement the local government in protecting his property when he enters into a contest with his employés? For whom

are the great expenses of the Federal Government incurred? Why, sir, when we ask that this small pittance shall be contributed to the expenses of the Federal Government, we are asking less than is just rather than more. But the gentleman from New York fears that this amendment will embarrass the bill, and denounces the action of the caucus as treason.

★ ★ ★ ★

There is not a man whom I would charge with being willing to expatriate himself rather than contribute from his abundance to the support of the Government that protects him. If "some of our best people" prefer to leave the country rather than pay a tax of 2 percent, God pity the worst. [Laughter.]

If we have people who value free government so little that they prefer to live under monarchical institutions, even without an income tax, rather than live under the stars and stripes and pay a 2 per cent tax, we can better afford to lose them and their fortunes than risk the contaminating influence of their presence. [Applause.]

Source: *Congressional Record*, 53rd Cong., 2nd sess., January 30, 1894 (Washington: GPO, 1894), 26:1655–1658.

Notes

1. Alan P. Grimes, *Democracy and the Amendments to the Constitution* (Lexington, Mass.: Lexington Books, 1978), 70; Richard J. Joseph, *The Origins of the American Income Tax: the Revenue Act of 1894 and Its Aftermath* (Syracuse, N.Y.: Syracuse University Press, 2004), 75.

2. Grimes, *Democracy and the Amendments to the Constitution*, 69, 73. See also Joshua D. Brinen, "Sixteenth Amendment," in Kris E. Palmer, ed., *Constitutional Amendments: 1789 to the Present* (Detroit: Gale, 2000), 393.

3. Joseph, *The Origins of the American Income Tax*, xiv, 3–4; Brinen, "Sixteenth Amendment," 281.

4. Grimes, *Democracy and the Amendments to the Constitution*, 69. The complete *Tribune* study is found in Sidney Ratner, *New Light on the History of Great Fortunes: American Millionaires of 1892 and 1902* (New York: A.M. Kelley, 1953), 1–93. See also ibid., xi–xx; George K. Holmes, "The Concentration of Wealth," *Political Science Quarterly*, 8(December 1893): 589–600; Joseph, *The Origins of the American Income Tax*, 47–51; Robert Stanley, *Dimensions of Law in the Service of Order: Origins of the Federal Income Tax, 1861–1913* (New York: Oxford University Press, 1993), 111–113, 115.

5. Steven R. Weisman, *The Great Tax Wars: Lincoln to Wilson, the Fierce Battles Over Money and Power That Transformed the Nation* (New York: Simon and Schuster, 2002), 133; *New York World*, January 31, 1894, 7. See also Grimes, *Democracy and the Amendments to the Constitution*, 71; Sidney Ratner, *American Taxation: Its History as a Social Force in Democracy* (New York: Norton, 1942), 174–178; Ralph G. Martin, *Jennie: The Life of Lady Randolph Churchill*, 2 vols. (New York: New American Library, 1971), 2:40–43; Weisman, *The*

Great Tax Wars, Lincoln to Wilson, the Fierce Battles Over Money and Power That Transformed the Nation, 136–138.

6. *Congressional Record,* 53rd Cong., 2nd sess., January 30, 1894, appendix, 26:462–463, 468.

7. *Congressional Record,* 53rd Cong., 2nd sess., January 30, 1894, 26:1655–1658; February 1, 1894, 26:1795–1797. See also Joseph, *The Origins of the American Income Tax,* 64–66.

8. *Congressional Record,* July 3, 1894, 26:7136; August 13, 1894, 26:8482; Joseph, *The Origins of the American Income Tax,* 66–86. For the income tax provisions in the Wilson-Gorman Tariff are found in 28 Stat. 553–560, Sections 27–37 (August 28, 1894).

9. David E. Kyvig, "Can the Constitution Be Amended? The Battle Over the Income Tax, 1895–1913," *Prologue: Journal of the National Archives,* 20 (Fall 1988): 189–195; Joseph R. Long, "Tinkering with the Constitution," *Yale Law Journal,* 24 (May 1915): 576. See also Brinen, "Sixteenth Amendment," 393–394; Ratner, *American Taxation: Its History as a Social Force in Democracy,* 212–214.

Treaty of Paris and American Policy Regarding the Philippines

⊹ 1898; 1899–1901 ⊹

From April 25 to August 12, 1898, the United States waged a one hundred nine day war against Spain in its colonial possessions of Cuba and the Philippines. For at least three years preceding the war, Congress debated what role, if any, the United States should play in an ongoing war between Cuban citizens seeking independence and the Spanish government, which had controlled the island for three centuries. Although both Republicans and Democrats took up the Cuban cause in the 1896 presidential campaign, the U.S. government avoided any direct involvement. Neutrality appeared far less likely after February 15, 1898, when an explosion sank the American battleship USS *Maine*, which had been sent to Havana harbor to protect American property and citizens. Two hundred sixty American sailors were killed in the blast. Afterwards, "Remember the Maine!" quickly became a popular rallying cry as sentiment rapidly grew for a war against Spain.

Initially, President William McKinley assumed an antiwar stance, but he gave way to the demand for war on April 11, 1898, when he asked Congress for "forcible intervention" of the United States to secure peace in Cuba. Recognition of Cuban independence quickly followed. On April 20, Congress approved a joint resolution that demanded the withdrawal of Spanish armed forces, empowered the president to use American forces to carry out the demand, and declared that the United States could not annex Cuba and must "leave the government and control of the island to its people." The last clause, offered by Sen. Henry M. Teller, R-Col., which stipulated that the United States could not annex Cuba, came to be known as the Teller Amendment. Five days later, Congress approved a declaration of war against Spain.[1]

American military victories at Manila Bay that May and in Cuba in July left the Spanish land forces isolated from their homeland and, after brief resistance, brought about their surrender to U.S. military forces. In both theaters the decisive military event was the complete destruction of a Spanish naval squadron. Armistice negotiations in Washington, D.C., terminated the Spanish-American War on August 12. During the subsequent peace conference in Paris, the main sticking point was the future of the Philippines Islands. President McKinley demanded that Spain cede the islands to the United States. Spain initially resisted strongly but eventually agreed to a payment of $20 million. Spain also surrendered all claims to Cuba and agreed to assume the liability for the Cuban debt, estimated at $400 million. As indemnity, Spain ceded the island of Puerto Rico and other islands then under their sovereignty in the West Indies, as well as the island of Guam, to the United States.[2]

A turning point in American history occurred the following spring when the Senate approved the annexation of the Philippines, a significant change in American expansion policy that had, up until then, favored contiguous continental territorial gains. In acquiring the Philippines, the United States began a strategic policy that committed it to a presence in Asia, supplementing what until this time had been a "relatively homogenous population" with millions of "ethnic aliens." Past U.S. territorial acquisitions soon became states, operating under their own governments, but the Philippines had no chance at statehood and required control by force.[3]

Congressional debate over the Philippines covered two distinct phases. The first lasted from December 1898 to mid-February 1899, as the Senate debated the question of whether the Treaty of Paris should be ratified. The second phase, which lasted the next two years, was devoted to a discussion of the appropriate American policy toward the Philippines.

A majority of Americans strongly endorsed the treaty, as did Senate Republicans, who held a 47–34 advantage over the chamber's Democrats. Most of the Senate's five Populists also were supporters. A majority of Democrats opposed it. Most of the Senate debate was held behind closed doors in executive sessions. Several treaty-related resolutions, however, were considered in open sessions. The first, offered by Sen. George G. Vest, D-Mo., declared that constitutionally, the federal government could not permanently hold territories without the prospect of statehood. Sen. George Frisbie Hoar, R-Mass., one of only two Senate Republicans to ultimately oppose ratification, vigorously supported Vest's contention. Annexing foreign territory and governing it without the consent of its inhabitants, he declared, was totally contrary to both the Declaration of Independence and the Constitution. Others contended that the treaty would destroy America's

233

AT THE PARTING OF THE WAYS HE HESITATES.

In Doubt Himself, President McKinley Finds Enough Advisers Who Think They Know the True Path of National Progress.

This 1899 cartoon depicts President McKinley's choice after the 1898 Treaty of Paris on whether to follow the path of expansionism. The debate over the treaty and its implications for American policy in the Philippines is representative of the way that debates regarding the role of the United States in Pacific nations continued for many years.

Source: The Granger Collection, New York.

republican institutions, inevitably draw the country into international disputes over the Far East, deprive Americans of any moral right to uphold the Monroe Doctrine, and do little for foreign trade.[4]

Among treaty supporters, Sen. Orville H. Platt, R-Conn., offered the most effective constitutional argument. The right to acquire territory, Platt contended, was a sovereign right belonging to the United States by virtue of its national sovereignty. "I deny," he declared "that there is any constitutional right or moral obligation to fit the territory for statehood or to ever admit it as a state. To claim that there is is to deny the inherent sovereign right of this people, this nation, to do what any nation may do anywhere." An indignant Sen. Henry Cabot Lodge, R-Mass., questioned why anyone should fear for the welfare of the Filipinos under the U.S. government. The consequences of rejecting the treaty, Lodge declared,

would be disastrous. "Suppose we reject the treaty," "continue the state of war," and "repudiate the President." The United States will be branded "as a people incapable of great affairs or of taking rank where we belong, as one of the greatest of the great world powers." Sen. Knute Nelson, R-Minn., declared: "The American people are possessed of a genuine spirit of liberty.... We come as ministering angels, not as despots."[5]

The heated exchanges concluded on February 6, 1899, when the chamber approved the controversial Treaty of Paris by one vote 57–27 more than the necessary two-thirds majority required by the Constitution. Two days earlier, word came that fighting had broken out between Filipino insurgents and American troops, thereby opening the Philippine War, which lasted for more than three years. Even if the treaty had been rejected that February, McKinley still would have won ratification in March when the next Congress convened and the Republicans gained an additional six seats. Democratic Party leader Rep. William Jennings Bryan, D-Neb., personally persuaded a number of treaty opponents to vote for it on the grounds that it would end the war and Philippine independence might be more readily secured. Much of the credit, however, must go to President McKinley. Senator Lodge said of him: "[P]olitical expediency in expansion, and extensive patronage arrangements and promises of good committee assignments were made in his name.... Throughout the ratification fight he was 'extremely anxious' but showed 'great firmness of strength.'"[6]

Over the next two years, Congress devoted considerable attention to determining exactly what American policy would be toward the Philippines, before approving the Spooner Amendment in 1901. The amendment authorized the president to establish a civil government for the Philippines, formally ending the U.S. military regime in the islands. During 1900, the Senate chamber was the scene of two floor speeches that together reflect a debate that continues to this day over U.S. standing in the world and its relations with Pacific nations. The January 9 speech of Sen. Albert J. Beveridge, R-Ind., "was filled with the braggadocio of racial superiority and the belief that the United States was God's chosen instrument to bring order to the world." Senator Hoar's speech of April 17 "stands in marked contrast to the jingoism" of Senator Beveridge's speech and "remains a timeless argument against one nation imposing rule upon another nation without the consent of the governed."[7]

SENATOR ALBERT J. BEVERIDGE ON U.S. POLICY REGARDING THE PHILIPPINES

JANUARY 9, 1900

Mr. President, I address the Senate at this time because Senators and Members of the House on both sides have asked that I give to Congress and the country my observations in the Philippines and the far East, and the conclusions which those observations compel; and because of hurtful resolutions introduced and utterances made in the Senate, every word of which will cost and is costing the lives of American soldiers.

Mr. President, the times call for candor. The Philippines are ours forever, "territory belonging to the United States," as the Constitution calls them. And just beyond the Philippines are China's illimitable markets. We will not retreat from either. We will not repudiate our duty in the archipelago. We will not abandon our opportunity in the Orient. We will not renounce our part in the mission of our race, trustee, under God, of the civilization of the world. And we will move forward to our work, not howling out regrets like slaves whipped to their burdens, but with gratitude for a task worthy of our strength, and thanksgiving to Almighty God that He has marked us as His chosen people, henceforth to lead in the regeneration of the world.

PHILIPPINES COMMAND THE PACIFIC

This island empire is the last land left in all the oceans. If it should prove a mistake to abandon it, the blunder once made would be irretrievable. If it proves a mistake to hold it, the error can be corrected when we will. Every other progressive nation stands ready to relieve us.

But to hold it will be no mistake. Our largest trade henceforth must be with Asia. The Pacific is our ocean. More and more Europe will manufacture the most it needs, secure from its colonies the most it consumes. Where shall we turn for consumers of our surplus? Geography answers the question. China is our natural customer. She is nearer to us than to England, Germany, or Russia, the commercial powers of the present and the future. They have moved nearer to China by securing permanent bases on her borders. The Philippines give us a base at the door of all the East.

Lines of navigation from our ports to the Orient and Australia; from the Isthmian Canal to Asia; from all Oriental ports to Australia, converge at and separate from the Philippines. They are a self-supporting, dividend-paying fleet, permanently anchored at a spot selected by the strategy of Providence, commanding the Pacific. And the Pacific is the ocean of the commerce of the future. Most future wars will be conflicts for commerce. The power that rules the Pacific, therefore, is the power that rules the world. And, with the Philippines, that power is and will forever be the American Republic.

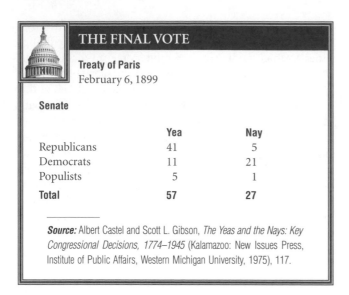

★ ★ ★ ★

Value of China's Trade

… That statesman commits a crime against American trade — against the American grower of cotton and wheat and tobacco, the American manufacturer of machinery and clothing — who fails to put America where she may command that trade…. The Philippines command the commercial situation of the entire East…. And yet American statesmen plan to surrender this commercial throne of the Orient where Providence and our soldiers' lives have placed us. When history comes to write the story of that suggested treason to American supremacy and therefore to the spread of American civilization, let her in mercy write that those who so proposed were merely blind and nothing more.

★ ★ ★ ★

Nothing is so natural as trade with one's neighbors. The Philippines make us the nearest neighbors of all the East. Nothing is more natural than to trade with those you know. This is the philosophy of all advertising. The Philippines bring us permanently face to face with the most sought-for customers of the world. National prestige, national propinquity, these and commercial activity are the elements of commercial success. The Philippines give the first; the character of the American people supply the last. It is a providential conjunction of all the elements of trade, of duty, and of power. If we are willing to go to war rather than let England have a few feet of frozen Alaska, which affords no market and commands none, what should we not do rather than let England, Germany, Russia, or Japan have all the Philippines? And no man on the spot can fail to see that this would be their fate if we retired.

★ ★ ★ ★

We Will Hold It Fast, And Hold It Forever

… Two years ago there was no land in all the world which we could occupy for any purpose. Our commerce was daily turning toward the Orient, and geography and trade developments made necessary your commercial empire over the Pacific. And in that ocean we had no commercial, naval, or military base. Today we have one of the three great ocean possessions of the globe, located at the most commanding commercial, naval, and military points in the eastern seas, within hail of India, shoulder to shoulder with China, richer in its own resources than any equal body of land on the entire globe, and peopled by a race which civilization demands shall be improved. Shall we abandon it?

★ ★ ★ ★

Military Situation — Otis Defended

The military situation, past, present, and prospective, is no reason for abandonment. Our campaign has been as perfect as possible with the force at hand. We have been delayed, first, by a failure to comprehend the immensity of our acquisition; and, second, by insufficient force; and, third, by our efforts for peace.

★ ★ ★ ★

Those who complain do so in ignorance of the real situation. We attempted a great task with insufficient means; we became impatient that it was not finished before it could fairly be commenced; and I pray we may not add that other element of disaster, pausing in the work before it is thoroughly and forever done. That is the gravest mistake we could possibly make, and that is the only danger before us.

★ ★ ★ ★

Our Efforts To Secure Peace

Our mistake has not been cruelty; it has been kindness…. Before the outbreak our general in command appointed a commission to make some arrangement with the natives mutually agreeable…. It was treated with contempt.

★ ★ ★ ★

"The Blood Of Our Soldiers"

Mr. President, reluctantly and only from a sense of duty am I forced to say that American opposition to the war has been the chief factor in prolonging it.

★ ★ ★ ★

[T]his has aided the enemy more than climate, arms, and battle.

★ ★ ★ ★

The Filipinos Are Children Utterly Incapable of Self-Government

But, Senators, it would be better to abandon this combined garden and Gibraltar of the Pacific, and count our blood and treasure already spent a profitable loss, than to apply any academic arrangement of self-government to these children. They are not capable of self-government. How could they be? They are not of a self-governing race. They are Orientals, Malays, instructed by Spaniards in the latter's worst estate.

★ ★ ★ ★

People Indolent — No Competition With Our Labor

… No one need fear their competition with our labor. No reward could beguile, no force compel, these children of indolence to leave their trifling lives for the fierce and fervid industry of high-wrought America. The very reverse is the fact. One great problem is the necessary labor to develop these islands — to build the roads, open the mines, clear the wilderness, drain the swamps, dredge the harbors. The natives will not supply it. A lingering prejudice against the Chinese may prevent us from letting them supply it. Ultimately, when the real truth of the climate and human conditions is known, it is barely possible that our labor will go there. Even now young men with the right moral fiber and a little capital can make fortunes there as planters.

★ ★ ★ ★

Kind of American Officials Necessary

… The men we send to administer civilized government in the Philippines must be themselves the highest examples of our civilization…. They must be men of the world and of affairs, students of their fellow-men, not theorists nor dreamers. They must be brave men, physically as well as morally. They must be as incorruptible as honor, as stainless as purity, men whom no force can frighten, no influence coerce, no money buy…. Better pure military occupation for years than government by any other quality of administration. Better abandon this priceless possession, admit ourselves incompetent to do our part in the world-redeeming work of our imperial race; better now haul down the flag of arduous deeds for civilization and run up the flag of reaction and decay than to apply academic notions of self-government to these children or attempt their government by any but the most perfect administrators our country can produce. I assert that such administrators can be found.

★ ★ ★ ★

Dominant Notes Of Our First And Second Centuries

Mr. President, self-government and internal development have been the dominant notes of our first century; administration and the development of other lands will be the dominant notes of our second century. And administration is as high and holy a function as self-government, just as the care of a trust estate is as sacred an obligation as the management of our own concerns.

★ ★ ★ ★

Administration of good government is not denial of liberty. For what is liberty? It is not savagery. It is not the exercise of individual will. It is not dictatorship. It involves government, but not necessarily self-government. It means law. First of all, it is a common rule of action, applying equally to all within its limits. Liberty means protection of property and life without price, free speech without intimidation, justice without purchase or delay, government without favor or favorites. What will best give all this to the people of the Philippines-American administration, developing them gradually toward self-government, or self-government by a people before they know what self-government means?

True Interpretation Of Declaration Of Independence

The Declaration of Independence does not forbid us to do our part in the regeneration of the world. If it did, the Declaration would be wrong, just as the Articles of Confederation, drafted by the very same men who signed the Declaration, was found to be wrong. The Declaration has no application to the present situation. It was written by self-governing men for self-governing men.

★ ★ ★ ★

Phrase "Consent Of The Governed" Misunderstood

The Declaration does not contemplate that all government must have the consent of the governed. It announces that man's "inalienable rights are life, liberty, and the pursuit of happiness; that to secure these rights governments are established among men deriving their just powers from the consent of the governed; that when any form of government becomes destructive of those rights, it is the right of the people to alter or abolish it." "Life, liberty, and the pursuit of happiness" are the important things; "consent of the governed" is one of the means to those ends.

If "any form of government becomes destructive of those ends, it is the right of the people to alter or abolish it," says the Declaration. "Any forms" includes all forms. Thus the Declaration itself recognizes other forms of government than those resting on the consent of the governed. The word "consent" itself recognizes other forms, for "consent" means the understanding of the thing to which the "consent" is given; and there are people in the world who do not understand any form of government.

★ ★ ★ ★

Words Of Empire Expressly In Constitution

No; the oceans are not limitations of the power which the Constitution expressly gives Congress to govern all territory the nation may acquire. The Constitution declares that "Congress shall have power to dispose of and make all needful rules and regulations respecting the territory belonging to the United States." Not the Northwest Territory only; not Louisiana or Florida only: not territory on this continent only, but any territory anywhere belonging to the nation. The founders of the nation were not provincial. Theirs was the geography of the world.

★ ★ ★ ★

Power Implied To Govern As We Please

The power to govern all territory the nation may acquire would have been in Congress if the language affirming that power had not been written in the Constitution. For not all powers of the National Government are expressed. Its principal powers are implied. The written Constitution is but the index of the living Constitution. Had this not been true, the Constitution would have failed. For the people in any event would have developed and progressed. And if the Constitution had not had the capacity for growth corresponding with the growth of the nation, the Constitution would and should have been abandoned as the Articles of Confederation were abandoned. For the Constitution is not immortal in itself, is not useful even in itself. The Constitution is immortal and even useful only as it serves the orderly development of the nation. The nation alone is immortal. The nation alone is sacred. The Army is its servant. The Navy is its servant. The President is its servant. This Senate is its servant. Our laws are its methods. Our Constitution is its instrument.

★ ★ ★ ★

The Whole Question Elemental

Mr. President, this question is deeper than any question of party politics; deeper than any question of the isolated policy of our country even; deeper even than any question of con-

stitutional power. It is elemental. It is racial. God has not been preparing the English-speaking and Teutonic peoples for a thousand years for nothing but vain and idle self-contemplation and self-admiration. No! He has made us the master organizers of the world to establish system where chaos reigns. He has given us the spirit of progress to overwhelm the forces of reaction throughout the earth. He has made us

---

God has not been preparing the English-speaking and Teutonic peoples for a thousand years for nothing but vain and idle self-contemplation and self-admiration. No! He has made us the master organizers of the world to establish system where chaos reigns. — Albert J. Beveridge

---

adepts in government that we may administer government among savage and senile peoples. Were it not for such a force as this the world would relapse into barbarism and night. And of all our race. He has marked the American people as His chosen nation to finally lead in the regeneration of the world. This is the divine mission of America, and it holds for us all the profit, all the glory, all the happiness possible to man. We are trustees of the world's progress, guardians of its righteous peace. The judgment of the Master is upon us: "Ye have been faithful over a few things; I will make you ruler over many things."

★ ★ ★ ★

God's Hand In All

… Mr. President and Senators, adopt the resolution offered, that peace may quickly come and that we may begin our saving, regenerating, and uplifting work. Adopt it, and this bloodshed will cease, when these deluded children of our islands learn that this is the final word of the representatives of the American people in Congress assembled. Reject it, and the world, history, and the American people will know where to forever fix the awful responsibility for the consequences that will surely follow such failure to do our manifest duty. How dare we delay when our soldiers' blood is flowing? [Applause in the galleries.]

Source: *Congressional Record*, 56th Cong., 1st sess., January 9, 1900 (Washington: GPO, 1900), 33:704–712.

SENATOR GEORGE FRISBIE HOAR ON SELF-GOVERNMENT FOR THE PHILIPPINES

APRIL 17, 1900

Wherever the Republic has gone thus far, wherever her name is known, it is an example of the equality of manhood and the freedom of man. This has made her the great benefactor in the Western Hemisphere. But if you have your way, she is to appear in the East to set an example of caste. Do you think with her great problem unsolved, with ten millions of her own people, now thirty-six years after the emancipation proclamation, still waiting for the promise of their perfect freedom to be fulfilled, you are asked to subject ten millions more, of an alien race, to a government in which they have no share, and an authority in which they have no voice. The people which were seventy millions are to be eighty millions — eighty millions, and every fourth man a serf — eighty millions, every fourth man, practically an inferior — at the end of the nineteenth century, twenty millions (near seven times the number with which the nation began) practically without the rights of citizenship.

I think the American people will conclude in the end that we shall get no trade advantage either in the Philippine Islands or in China by the forcible subjugation of this people. On the contrary, we injure our trade prospects when we alienate the affection of those people by an unjust attack upon their independence. But there is no space to argue this point now. Dr. Franklin said:

> To me it seems that neither the obtaining or retaining any trade, how valuable soever, is an object for which men may justly spill each other's blood. That the true and sure means of extending and securing commerce are the goodness and cheapness of commodities, and that the profits of no trade can ever be equal to the expense of compelling it and holding it by fleets and armies.

The Doctor, I suppose, was a traitor and a little American. But we are told if we oppose the policy of our imperialistic and expanding friends we are bound to suggest some policy of our own as a substitute for theirs. We are asked what we would do in this difficult emergency. It is a question not difficult to answer. I for one am ready to answer it.

1. I would declare now that we will not take these islands to govern them against their will.
2. I would reject a cession of sovereignty which implies that sovereignty may be bought and sold and delivered without the consent of the people. Spain had no rightful sovereignty over the Philippine Islands[.] She could not rightfully sell it to us. We could not rightfully buy it from her.
3. I would require all foreign governments to keep out of these islands.
4. I would offer to the people of the Philippines our help in maintaining order until they have a reasonable opportunity to establish a government of their own.
5. I would aid them by advice, if they desire it, to set up a free and independent government.
6. I would invite all the great powers of Europe to unite in an agreement that that [sic] independence shall not be interfered with by us, by themselves, or by any one of them with the consent of the others. As to this I am not so sure. I should like quite as well to tell them it is not to be done whether they consent or not.
7. I would declare that the United States will enforce the same doctrine as applicable to the Philippines that we declared as to Mexico and Haiti and the South American Republics. It is true that the Monroe Doctrine, a doctrine based largely on our regard for our own interests, is not applicable either in terms or in principle to a distant Asiatic territory. But undoubtedly, having driven out Spain, we are bound, and have the right, to secure to the people we have liberated an opportunity, undisturbed and in peace, to establish a new government for themselves.
8. I would then, in a not distant future, leave them to work out their own salvation, as every nation on earth, from the beginning of time, has wrought out its own salvation. Let them work out their own salvation, as our own ancestors slowly and in long centuries wrought out theirs; as Germany, as Switzerland, as France, in briefer periods, wrought out theirs; as Mexico and the South American Republics have accomplished theirs, all of them within a century, some of them within the life of a generation. To attempt to confer the gift of freedom from without, or to impose freedom from without

on any people, is to disregard all the lessons of history. It is to attempt

"A gift of that which is not to be given
By all the blended powers of earth and heaven."

9. I would strike out of your legislation the oath of allegiance to us and substitute an oath of allegiance to their own country.

Mr. President, if you once get involved and entangled in this policy of dominion and empire, you have not only to get the assent of three powers — House, Senate, and President — to escape from it, but to the particular plan and scheme and method of such escape. My friends say they are willing to trust the people and the future. And so am I. I am willing to trust the people as our fathers trusted them. I am willing to trust the people as they have, so far, trusted themselves; a people regulated, governed, constrained by the moral law, by the Constitution and by the Declaration. It is the constitutional, not the unconstitutional, will of the American people in which I trust.

★ ★ ★ ★

I love and trust the American people. I yield to no man in my confidence in the future of the Republic. To me the dearest blessings of life, dearer than property, dearer than home, dearer than kindred, are my pride in my country and my

---

I disavow and spurn the doctrine that has been more than once uttered by the advocates of this policy of imperialism on the floor of the Senate, that the sovereignty of the American people is inferior to any other because it is restrained and confined within constitutional boundaries. — George Frisbie Hoar

---

hope for the future of America. But the people that I trust is the people that established the Constitution and which abides by its restraints. The people that I trust is the people that made the great Declaration, and their children, who mean forever to abide by its principles. The country in whose future I have supreme and unbounded confidence is the Republic, not a despotism on the one hand, or an unchecked and unlicensed democracy on the other. It is no mere democracy. It is the indissoluble union of indestructible States. I disavow and spurn the doctrine that has been more than once uttered by the advocates of this policy of imperialism on the

floor of the Senate, that the sovereignty of the American people is inferior to any other because it is restrained and confined within constitutional boundaries.

★ ★ ★ ★

Mr. President, there lies at the bottom of what is called imperialism a doctrine which, if adopted, is to revolutionize the world in favor of despotism. It directly conflicts with and contradicts the doctrine on which our own revolution was founded, and with which, so far, our example has revolutionized the world. It is the doctrine that when, in the judgment of any one nation or any combination of nations, the institutions which a people set up and maintain for themselves are disapproved they have a right to overthrow that government and to enter upon and possess it themselves.

★ ★ ★ ★

Our imperialistic friends seem to have forgotten the use of the vocabulary of liberty. They talk about giving good government. "We shall give them such a government as we think they are fitted for." "We shall give them a better government than they had before." Why, Mr. President, that one phrase conveys to a free man and a free people the most stinging of insults. In that little phrase, as in a seed, is contained the germ of all despotism and of all tyranny. Government is not a gift. Free government is not to be given by all the blended powers of earth and heaven. It is a birthright. It belongs, as our fathers said and as their children said, as Jefferson said and as President McKinley said, to human nature itself. There can be no good government but self-government.

★ ★ ★ ★

I have failed to discover in the speech, public or private, of the advocates of this war, or in the press which supports it and them, a single expression anywhere of a desire to do justice to the people of the Philippine Islands, or of a desire to make known to the people of the United States the truth of the case. Some of them, like the Senator from Indiana and the President of the Senate, are outspoken in their purpose to retain the Philippine Islands forever, to govern them ourselves, or to do what they call giving them such share in government as we hereafter may see fit, having regard to our own interest, and, as they sometimes add, to theirs. The others say, "Hush! We will not disclose our purpose just now. Perhaps we may," as they phrase it, "give them liberty some time. But it is to be a long time first."

The catchwords, the cries, the pithy and pregnant phrases of which all their speech is full, all mean dominion. They mean perpetual dominion. When a man tells you that the American flag must not be hauled down where it has once floated, or demands of a shouting audience, "Who will haul it down?" if he mean anything, he means that that people shall be under our dominion forever.

★ ★ ★ ★

Why, the tariff schemes which are proposed are schemes in our interest and not in theirs.... The good government you are to give them is a government under which their great productive and industrial interests, when peace comes, are to be totally and absolutely disregarded by their government. You are not only proposing to do that, but you expect to put another strain on the Constitution to accomplish it.

Why, Mr. President, the atmosphere of both legislative chambers, even now, is filled with measures proposing to govern and tax these people for our interest, and not for theirs.

★ ★ ★ ★

Is there any man so bold as to utter in seriousness the assertion that where the American flag has once been raised it shall never be hauled down? I have heard it said that to haul down or to propose to haul down this national emblem where it has once floated is poltroonery. Will any man say it was poltroonery when Paul Jones landed on the northeast coast of England that he took his flag away with him when he departed? Was Scott a poltroon, or was Polk a poltroon? Was Taylor a poltroon? Was the United States a nation of poltroons when they retired from the City of Mexico or from Vera Cruz without leaving the flag behind them? Were we poltroons when we receded from Canada? If we had made the attack on the coast of Spain, at one time contemplated during this very war, were we pledged to hold and govern Spain forever or disgraced in the eyes of mankind if we failed to do it?

★ ★ ★ ★

Mr. President, this talk that the American flag is never to be removed where it has once floated is the silliest and wildest rhetorical flourish ever uttered in the ears of an excited populace. No baby ever said anything to another baby more foolish.

Now, what are the facts as to the Philippine Islands and the American flag? We have occupied a single city, part of one of four hundred islands, and with a population of 120,000 or thereabouts out of 10,000,000. The Spanish forces were invested and hemmed in by the people of those islands, who had risen to assert their own freedom when we got there. Now, what kind of Americanism, what kind of patriotism, what kind of love of liberty is it to say that we are to turn our guns on that patriot people and wrest from them the freedom that was almost within their grasp and hold these islands for our own purposes in subjection and by right of conquest because the American flag ought not to be hauled down where it has once floated, or, for the baser and viler motive still, that we can make a few dollars a year out of their trade?

Mr. President, this is the doctrine of purest ruffianism and tyranny. There is nothing of the Declaration of Independence in it. There is nothing of the Constitution of the United States in it. There is nothing of the fathers in it. There is nothing of George Washington in it, or of Thomas Jefferson. There is nothing in it of the old Virginia or of the old South Carolina or of the old Massachusetts. If every territory over which the flag of a country has once floated must be held and never shall be yielded again to the nation to which it belonged, every war between great and powerful nations must be a war of extermination or a war of dishonor alike to the victor and to the vanquished.

We expected, did we not, at the time of our declaration of war that we would not wrest Cuba from Spain for any purpose of our own aggrandizement, but only that there might be established there a free government for the people thereof, and that the people of Cuba were, and of right ought to be, a free, independent state; that our flag would float in Cuba while the operation of the war was going on as it has floated in glory and in honor.

★ ★ ★ ★

When the authority of the United States, in the days of Franklin Pierce and James Buchanan, undertook to subjugate the free men of Kansas and Nebraska, they stood for their freedom. They denied the right of James Buchanan or of Franklin Pierce to make this holy symbol the emblem of the government of man, or any race of men, against its will.

Now, Mr. President, it seems to me that these are grave questions. They are things worth thinking of by American Senators and American statesmen. They go down to the roots of our national life. They are not of yesterday, of to-day, or to-morrow alone. They were thought of when our country was settled. They were debated during the century's long strife that preceded the Revolution. The minds of the Fathers were full of them. Their answer to them was written in the imperishable lines of the Declaration of Independence, and in the constitutions of the States and of the nation. We have been brought up to think of them through the whole of our first century of greatness and of glory. We reaffirmed our doctrine about them again when we celebrated our centennial in 1876. They were daily and nightly on the thoughts of Abraham Lincoln and Charles Sumner. If Lincoln and Sumner should repeat what they thought of them now, they would be denounced as "little Americans," as "squaw men," and blacklisted as traitors.

Now, what is the answer we get when we repeat the old doctrine, not in our own language, but in the language of the Fathers, and of Lincoln, and of Sumner? Why, the answer — there are some creditable exceptions — but in general the answer we get is that there is a soldier in uniform somewhere shooting somebody; that the American flag is flying, and some poor devils, who ran when they come in sight of it, half armed, half disciplined, half clad, half fed, have got these ideas into their heads also, and are fighting for them and dying for them, and thinking we are invading them and are firing at our flag. Are you afraid of them? No. Are they formidable? No. Does the condition, according to your theory, of foreign war exist? No. But so long as the flag of the United States, standing for seventy million people — the richest, strongest, brightest, as we claim, on the face of the earth, anywhere the wide world over, is resisted there can be no question of liberty, honor, constitutional liberty, or national obligation considered throughout this broad continent.

★ ★ ★ ★

Certainly the flag should never be lowered from any moral field over which it has once waved. To follow the flag is to follow the principles of freedom and humanity for which it stands. To claim that we must follow it when it stands for injustice or oppression is like claiming that we must take the nostrums of the quack doctor who stamps it on his wares, or follow every scheme of wickedness or fraud, if only the flag be put at the head of the prospectus. The American flag is in more danger from the imperialists than there would be if the whole of Christendom were to combine its power against it. Foreign violence at worst could only rend it. But these men are trying to stain it.

It is claimed — what I do not believe — that these appeals have the sympathy of the American people. It is said that the statesman who will lay his ear to the ground will hear their voice. I do not believe it. The voice of the American people does not come from the ground. It comes from the sky. It comes from the free air. It comes from the mountains, where liberty dwells. Let the statesman who is fit to deal with the question of liberty or to utter the voice of a free people lift his ear to the sky — not lay it to the ground.

★ ★ ★ ★

Mr. President, I know how imperfectly I have stated this argument. I know how feeble is a single voice amid this din and tempest, this delirium of empire. It may be that the battle for this day is lost. But I have an assured faith in the future. I have an assured faith in justice and the love of liberty of the American people. The stars in their courses fight for freedom. The Ruler of the heavens is on that side. If the battle to-day go against it, I appeal to another day, not distant and sure to come. I appeal from the clapping of hands and the stamping of feet and the brawling and the shouting to the quiet chamber where the Fathers gathered in Philadelphia. I appeal from the spirit of trade to the spirit of liberty. I appeal from the Empire to the Republic. I appeal from the millionaire, and the

boss, and the wire-puller, and the manager to the statesman of the elder time, in whose eyes a guinea never glistened, who lived and died poor, and who left to his children and to his countrymen a good name far better than riches. I appeal from the Present, bloated with material prosperity, drunk with the lust of empire, to another and a better age. I appeal from the Present to the Future and to the Past. [Applause in the galleries.]

Source: *Congressional Record,* 56th Cong., 1st sess., April 17, 1900 (Washington: GPO, 1900), 33:4303–4306.

Notes

1. "Policy Concerning Cuba," *Congressional Record,* April 11, 1898, 31:3668–3672, 3704–3703; 30 Stat. 738–739 (April 20, 1898).

2. A copy of the treaty is found in 30 Stat. 1754–1762 (December 10, 1898). See also Ivan Musicant, *Empire by Default: The Spanish-American War and the Dawn of the American Century* (New York: Henry Holt, 1998), 586–627; William J. Pomeroy, *American Neo-Colonialism: Its Emergence in the Philippines and Asia* (New York: International Publishers, 1970), 35–58; David F. Trask, *The War With Spain in 1898* (New York: Macmillan, 1981), 423–468.

3. Richard Hofstadter, "Manifest Destiny and the Philippines," in Daniel Aaron, ed., *America in Crisis* (Hamden, Conn.: Archon Books, 1971), 187.

4. "Acquisition of Territory," *Congressional Record,* December 6, 1898, 32:20. See also "Acquisition of Territory," *Congressional Record,* January 9, 1899, 32:493–502; Julius W. Pratt, *Expansionists of 1898: The Acquisition of Hawaii and the Spanish Islands* (New York: P. Smith, 1951), 348–352; Pomeroy, *American Neo-Colonialism: Its Emergence in the Philippines and Asia,* 58–60.

5. "Acquisition of Territory," *Congressional Record,* December 19, 1989, 32:296; January 24, 1899, 32:959; January 20, 1899, 32: 838.

6. Paolo E. Coletta, "The Peace Negotiations and the Treaty of Paris," in Paolo E. Coletta, ed., *Threshold to American Internationalism: Essays on the Foreign Policies of William McKinley* (New York: Exposition Press, 1970), 163; Paolo E. Coletta, "Bryan, McKinley, and the Treaty of Paris," *Pacific Historical Review,* May 1957, 26:142–143. See also "Acquisition of Territory," *Congressional Record,* February 6, 1899, 32:1480–1495; U.S. Congress, Senate, *Journal of the Executive Proceedings of the Senate,* 55th Cong., 3rd sess., February 6 1899, 32:1282–1284.

7. Raymond W. Smock, ed., *Landmark Documents on the U.S. Congress* (Washington, D.C.: Congressional Quarterly, 1999), 274, 282. See also P.L. 803, 31 Stat. 910 (March 2, 1901); "Policy Regarding the Philippines," *Congressional Record,* January 9, 1900, 33:704–712; "The Philippine Islands," *Congressional Record,* April 17, 1900, 33:4303–4305.

House Revolt Against Speaker Cannon

✳ 1910 ✳

When Joseph Gurney Cannon, R-Ill., became Speaker of House of Representatives at age sixty-seven, he was at the time the oldest and the longest-serving representative ever to be elected to preside over the chamber. "No one in the House could equal his personal popularity or experience. The slight man with white, thinning hair, chin whiskers, and a cigar planted between his lips was considered by many to be practically an institution of the House." While Cannon was not considered a brilliant lawmaker and rarely authored or introduced legislation, he was a "fiercely loyal" member of the Republican party and was able to speak with "political savvy and pure blarney" to vanquish "whatever he may have lacked in brilliance or imagination."[1]

For seven years, from March 1903 until March 1910, Cannon, known by both friend and foe as Uncle Joe, possessed power unprecedented in his predecessors. He was "second to the president of the United States in influencing national affairs." His power stemmed in large part from House rules. As Speaker he appointed the chairman and all of the members of the House's standing committees, and he also served as chairman of the powerful five-man Committee on Rules, which set the floor agenda for the consideration of bills. As Rules Committee chair, Cannon could stifle legislation he opposed and attach nongermane amendments to bills, riders that might not have passed floor votes as separate measures. Once a proposal reached the House floor, his power as Speaker gave him incredible control over what legislation moved forward, or, more often than not, which bills were blocked.[2]

As Speaker, Cannon ruled the House with such an iron fist that his nickname soon changed from "Uncle Joe" to "Czar Cannon." Every representative holding a prominent place in the chamber owed his position directly to the Speaker, and he did not hesitate to remove those who were not loyal. Eventually, Cannon's conservative philosophy and abuse of his powers for personal considerations created an antagonism between the Speaker and rank-and-file Republicans who were just beginning to develop independent attitudes that eventually incited a revolt by progressive insurgents and Democrats. In the latter stages of his speakership, he was often depicted in the popular literature of the day as a

"tyrant," an unbending autocrat. This is a characterization still prominent in scholarly literature a century later. Both President Theodore Roosevelt and his successor, William Howard Taft, who occupied the White House during Cannon's reign, would have preferred another Speaker, but they knew Cannon was far too popular and powerful to replace. His support ranged from industrialists to farmers to colleagues within Congress, each finding in Cannon positions, roles, or favors to their benefit. Removing him as Speaker risked angering these groups and breaking party unity.[3]

By March 1909, however, it was apparent that there was growing opposition to Cannon on both sides of the aisle. At the beginning of the Sixty-first Congress, twelve Republicans refused to vote for him for Speaker, after which then-minority leader James Beauchamp "Champ" Clark, D-Mo., proposed a resolution to strip the Speaker of most of his authority to make committee assignments and deny him membership on the Rules Committee. What Cannon apparently did not fully grasp at the time was that the rise of Republican insurgents, coupled with the ongoing opposition of the Democratic leadership who were actively plotting against the Speaker, energized those indisposed to him who sought to change House rules and even remove him as presiding officer. Also, such publications as the *Baltimore Sun,* *Colliers,* and *Success* alerted the public to Cannon's less than benevolent character. In spite of the negative press coverage and the response it engendered, Cannon did not alter his leadership style.[4]

The first insurgent victory came in January 1910, when the Speaker and more than thirty of his loyal supporters were not even in the House chamber. Rep. George W. Norris, R-Neb., led a successful effort to have the whole House, instead of the Speaker alone, select members for a joint House-Senate select committee created to investigate charges against Secretary of the Interior Richard A. Ballinger. Although his success in this instance was clearly limited, Norris "had kept in his pocket for some time a well-worn copy of a resolution" to strip the Speaker of his committee appointment power and anxiously awaited the appropriate time to offer it.[5]

Norris's opportunity came on March 17, 1910, when Cannon "unwittingly recognized the man who would bring his

Congressman Joseph Cannon's nickname changed from "Uncle Joe" to "Czar Cannon" during his term as Speaker of the House, when his style of leadership alienated both Democrats and members of his Republican Party, who conspired to remove him from power.
Source: Library of Congress.

reign as 'czar' to an end," and Norris was allowed to present his long-held resolution. It called for the House rules to be amended to increase the membership of the Rules Committee from five to fifteen members, to permit the committee to select its own chairman, and to make the Speaker ineligible for membership on the committee. Rules Committee member John Dalzell, R-Penn., immediately raised a point of order against the resolution, claiming that it was not privileged. Norris countered by arguing that because the Constitution provides that "[e]ach House may determine the rules of its proceedings," the resolution was privileged. At this time, determining what was to be considered by the full House was largely at the Speaker's discretion. He could have immediately sustained Dalzell's point of order, but he did not have enough loyalist votes to sustain a motion against Morris because more than a hundred members, mostly Republicans, had left for their districts to attend St. Patrick's Day festivities and parades the following day. The Republicans started to filibuster in order to postpone Cannon's decision until the needed stalwarts could get back to Washington.[6]

The "hotly emotional debates" that ensued lasted for twenty-six hours. Cannon supporters argued that a majority within the Republican Party had selected the leaders who were authorized to act on their behalf. Those who rejected that leadership were rejecting the Republican Party and its popular mandate to manage the House. Rep. Jacob S. Fassett, R-N.Y., reminded the insurgents that they had not "received a commission" to betray their party and "were elected by majorities that expected [them] to act with the majority of [their] party associates on all party matters." While a "man ought to have opinions and convictions," he "ought not to be a political chocolate eclair. He always has a right to his individual liberty of opinion and action; always, however, within the limits of trust which has been bestowed upon him which he has accepted from his party to act with the majority." Insurgents such as Rep. John M. Nelson, R-Wis., contended that party leaders must be attentive to the need for change and that their power was not absolute. "We Republicans who protest against the Speaker's domination do not wish to put the gentlemen on the other side into control of the House," Nelson declared, but desired to overthrow the "arbitrary, artificial, and unrepublican system" Cannon imposed. "We do not need to be kept on leading strings. We are free representatives of the people, and we want freedom here for every Member of every party."[7]

Finally, at 2:00 p.m. on March 18, following a two-hour break, Cannon announced he was ready to rule on the Dalzell point of order. A postponement motion, however, delayed the procedural showdown until 12:05 the next day. During the interim, an ongoing effort to work out a compromise fell apart because of Cannon's unwillingness to give up membership on the Rules Committee and because of his objection to a change in Norris's resolution that required the committee's members be chosen by the entire House. When the House reconvened, Cannon ruled in favor of Dalzell's motion, an action immediately overturned by the House membership, 182–162. The Norris resolution was then adopted, 191–156, after being amended.[8] For the first time in fifty-two years, the occupant of the Speaker's chair was no longer a member or chair of the Rules Committee.

Cannon responded to his overthrow with a floor speech "that very nearly snatched victory from the jaws of defeat." He acknowledged there was no longer a coherent Republican majority in the House, and it was now the prerogative of the new majority, a "combination of Democrats and insurgents[,] to choose a new Speaker in harmony with its aims and purposes." He emphasized, however, that he would not step down unless a motion for him to do so was introduced. "Election of a new Speaker," Cannon declared, "might greatly endanger the final passage of all legislation necessary to redeem Republican pledges and fulfill Republican promises." "A resignation," he noted, "is in and of itself a confession of weakness or mistake or an apology for past actions." Rep. Albert S. Burleson, D-Texas, accepted Cannon's challenge by offering a resolution calling for the Speaker's removal, but a majority of the insurgents were reluctant to break completely with their Republican colleagues and rejected Burleson's resolution 192–155.[9]

Cannon did not, however, go away quietly. As the midterm congressional campaigns went into full swing during the summer and fall of 1910, Cannon lashed out at the insurgents, saying that he would "leave the Republican party and climb a tree or join the Democrats," if ever it was necessary to use an adjective to describe Republicans. Cannon also made it clear he would consider reelection as Speaker. These and similar comments served to make Cannonism the most important issue in an election that saw the Republicans lose fifty-four House seats and ten Senate seats. While the Republicans were able to retain control of the Senate, the Democrats became the majority party in the House for the first time in sixteen years. Cannon won reelection, but turned over the Speaker's gavel to former minority leader Clark on March 11, 1911. A month later, House Democrats, with Clark's blessing,

further reduced the Speaker's powers, adopting new rules that transferred to the House Ways and Means Committee the power to appoint standing committees, subject to the approval of the whole House.

Today, the Speakership of Joseph G. Cannon is most often remembered for the rules revolution of 1910. Even if he had chosen to be less autocratic, one historian suggests, it was Cannon's misfortune to preside over the House as it was beginning a transition from organizational rules that centralized the majority's power in the Speaker to a system emphasizing seniority and autonomous committees. The Cannon revolution demonstrated that he considered the reforms the insurgents and Democrats sought of little value and clearly unacceptable. A decade earlier, his autocratic approach might well have won him acclaim. In 1910, however, his failure to accommodate the growing sentiment among House members for a larger role in determining public policy cost him the Speakership.[10]

REPRESENTATIVE JACOB S. FASSETT DECLARES THAT THOSE WHO REJECT SPEAKER JOSEPH G. CANNON ARE REJECTING THE REPUBLICAN PARTY

MARCH 17, 1910

Mr. Speaker and gentlemen of this House, on both sides and in the middle of the aisle, I am going to beg your indulgence, because this debate has taken a little wider latitude than a close discussion of the resolution introduced, upon its merits or upon its parliamentary force and value, and has entered somewhat into the fundamental principles of party government and political administration, if I also depart from the subject immediately in hand.

As my good friend — and I hope he is my good friend — [Mr. CLARK of Missouri], the leader of the minority, said the other day: "We may fool all of the people some of the time and some of the people all of the time, but we can not fool all of the people all of the time," and that was originally said by that great Republican, our first President, Abraham Lincoln. We are playing politics and we are playing for great stakes. We are robust partisans, every one of us. The Democratic minority — and I applaud it for the fact — is playing for points. It is straining every nerve to outmaneuver the Republican majority in this House. This is a great arena, wherein political giants and a few political dwarfs are engaged in struggling

for the possession of the Government of the greatest people in the world. [Loud applause.]

We have developed inside of the Constitution, and outside of the Constitution, in accordance with the genius of our blood and our people, a government of a great people by great parties, parties that depend for their charters upon the votes of a free people from the various sections of the country, the highest source from which governmental charters have ever proceeded, ever can proceed, or ever will proceed. Men who hold elective office in this country hold such office in every case because the majority of the qualified electors in their districts have given them a mandate to proceed to carry out the promises which the party the candidates represent had made; and good faith and the rules of the game require that men who have received such a trust shall discharge it for the benefit of the estate in strict accord with the terms of the trust. Any man is reprobated properly who betrays any trust that is given to him, whether it be as an alderman, a supervisor, a member of the assembly, a state senator, or as a Member of Congress.

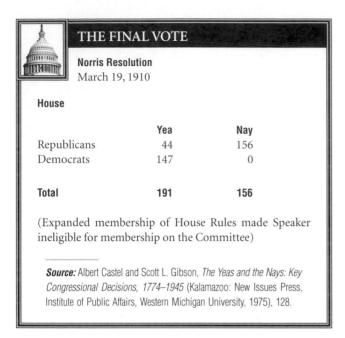

THE FINAL VOTE

Norris Resolution
March 19, 1910

House

	Yea	Nay
Republicans	44	156
Democrats	147	0
Total	**191**	**156**

(Expanded membership of House Rules made Speaker ineligible for membership on the Committee)

Source: Albert Castel and Scott L. Gibson, *The Yeas and the Nays: Key Congressional Decisions, 1774–1945* (Kalamazoo: New Issues Press, Institute of Public Affairs, Western Michigan University, 1975), 128.

In this House we are divided by one great line of separation, invisible, but recognizable as clearly as that center aisle is recognizable. On one side are men who have come from constituencies who believe, however misguidedly, in the promises and platforms, in the principles, and in the purposes of the Democratic party. On the other side are men who come here because a majority of the people in their districts, seeing them nominated upon Republican platforms, accepting the Republican trust, believed they were going to come here as Republicans and govern themselves according to the purposes of the entire Republican party officially expressed. So every man who is a man, and not a jellyfish, is a partisan. It is not wrong to be a partisan, especially when partisanship addresses itself to the highest purposes of patriotism. We were all elected by partisans because we were partisans, and as such represented party purposes as expressed by party platforms. None of us received any commission to betray his party at any time, but each of us was elected by majorities which expected us to act with the majority of our party associates on all party matters. I take it that no Democrat was elected to cooperate with our party, nor was any Republican elected to hand over the Republican control of this House to our political opponents.

A man ought to have opinions and convictions. He ought not to be a political chocolate eclair. He has a right to his individual liberty of opinion and action; always, however, within the limits of the trust which has been bestowed upon him and which he has accepted from his party to act with the majority.

Now, parties, like governments, provide machinery whereby men may adjust differences of opinion. If we have two hundred men on this side, I believe they are likely to have, if not two hundred different opinions, at least two hundred different kinds of opinion on almost any one of the great questions that concern the people of the United States, and we have planned to meet together and compare views. In my judgment, the place to adjust differences of opinion on unimportant questions, and on important questions of public policy and party policy is not in public, where one minority uniting with another minority may make a temporary majority; but in the family caucus, where we may adjust our opinions and govern ourselves, as responsible government must always be controlled, by an expression properly taken in a proper place, of the will of the majority of those qualified to speak. In this way only can party efficiency and unity be maintained and party responsibility as distinguished from personal whim be preserved.

Now, we have heard a great deal here about what the majority of this House can do. We have heard some of the humorous remarks of the Speaker quoted with approval, and to-day, with a grim approval by the leader of the minority, that a majority of this House could pass anything. It is true, and the majority of this House ought to be able to control the action of this House. Apart from courteous treatment, apart from reasonable consideration to the minority, the majority ought absolutely to control everything that the House does, everything that emanates from this House. We Republicans were put here by the American people for that purpose. They had tried you gentlemen on the other side of the aisle, and, as John Sharp Williams once said here on the floor, they are afraid of you. They have tried us, and he said they had grown tired of us, but still we are here. Now, we have the power. The people gave it to us as Republicans. We may surrender it. We may give you any part or all of our power, but if we strip ourselves of every particle of our power we can not strip ourselves of one iota of our responsibility, a responsibility we accepted as Republicans from Republicans. [Applause.]

And when your turn comes, my Democratic friends, which I trust heaven may long defer, and you sit in the seats of the mighty, and you are in control, and you are confronted with the problem of reconciling your many irreconcilable bundles of alleged principles, announced in all your platforms, you will have to be responsible to the country; and the majority that ought to control in the House of Representatives or the Senate is not a temporary affiliation of two minorities, but the majority commissioned by the American people, with responsibility for all legislation and the enactment of all laws. [Applause.]

Now, with reference to the so-called insurgents, I think our friends on the other side are congratulating themselves a little too soon. They are apt to refer to the insurgents as near Democrats or mercerized Republicans. [Laughter.]

They were almost on the point in their Democratic family caucus the other day of passing resolutions denouncing the Republican insurgents because they had gone back on the Democrats. [Laughter and cries of "No!" "No!" on the Democratic side.]

Well, I should say that my information came from the newspapers of this city, and I have never heard it denied. If it is not true, then my remark has no application.

★ ★ ★ ★

But I advise you under all the circumstances, and not depending on what I have seen in the papers, but from what I have heard here on this floor, that you should study the meaning and application of the word "parallax." Parallax, as I understand it, is the distance that divides the point where an object seems to be from one standpoint, and seems to be from another standpoint, from the point where the object really is. [Laughter.]

It is very necessary to understand their parallax in order to understand the movements of the heavenly bodies. It is necessary to understand the parallax of the insurgents to know exactly where they stand. I undertake to say that when you welcome them as assistant Democrats you do gross violence to their most sacred convictions. I undertake to say that were I as a regular to denounce them as irregular, they would fling back the taunt into my face and say, "Not so. Do you suppose from fair Washington or bleeding Kansas or fertile Nebraska I come as a Democrat to help Democracy, to be an assistant Democrat? Not so. I am progressive. I am a better Republican than you are. I am not joining the Democracy in an attempt to peddle political patent medicine. I am for the enactment of a political pure-food law. I want the label to correspond with the package and the package contents to correspond with the label." So they lay the flattering unction to their souls that they are progressive Republicans.

They are not for what your platform declares for. They do not believe in your follies of cheap money, of fiat money, or free trade. They believe in Republican principles; they are here after having been nominated on a Republican platform, and they see the light in accordance with the intelligence God has given them, to see the light. They are earnest men, striving to outdo us in making the American people believe the Republican party is the only party that has a consistent programme and a constructive statesmanship that will result in the benefit to the American people, as demonstrated in all points by the history of fifty years. [Applause on the Republican side.]

I do not agree with these gentlemen that they ought to take the power that the whole people have given to the entire Republican majority and hand it over to the Democratic minority in anything that goes to affect the vital energy, the unity, the efficiency of the Republican majority elected by the people to the House of Representatives. [Applause on the Republican side.]

Now, Mr. Speaker, for seven years the present occupant of the Chair has been known to us and to the country as our Speaker, "Uncle Joe." He is the same man now as then, with the same attitude toward men and toward the rules, the fairest presiding officer I have ever had the good luck to sit beneath. Twice by unanimous vote of Democrats and Republicans publicly thanked for his fairness. [Applause.]

Lauded in private, exalted and reverenced in secret, but under the pressure of untoward and abhorrent forces, which I will not stop to recount, he is held up by political opponents for selfish reasons as a political bugaboo by the very men who will extol him in private. I say that his record in the Speaker's chair challenges comparison with the record made by any presiding officer since the beginning of this country. [Applause on the Republican side.]

And the only critics of the Speaker, without exception, will be men who are sore, men who are angry, because, like my friend from New York [Mr. FISH], their particular legislative

---

And the only critics of the Speaker, without exception, will be men who are sore, men who are angry, because, like my friend from New York … , their particular legislative baby has not been taken out of the committee cradle first. — Jacob S. Fassett

---

baby has not been taken out of the committee cradle first. [Laughter and applause.]

There are thirty thousand legislative babies in our committee crib. Some must come out first; but without discussing that, Mr. Speaker, the organization of this House is the same, and the rules are the same, that we have lived under for the seven years under which we blessed the country in the Fifty-eighth, Fifty-ninth, and the Sixtieth Congresses. Then we had these same rules. Then we had this same crystallized wisdom of one hundred and thirty years of parliamentary experience to guide us. At any time the minority could, if it pleased, pass two weeks in roll calls to call the attention of the country to things both sides agreed to. The minority is protected by law the same as the weak man is protected by laws outside. And look at the record! Look at the splendid Republican laws Congress has rolled up under these rules and under this Speaker — a magnificent record, unsurpassed, nay, unparalleled for constructive statesmanship and for beneficent results to our people, in the history of the legislation in any country. I need not ask you to take my word alone. I have a witness whom I will summon presently.

This is not a question, gentlemen — be not deceived — this is not a question merely of a change of rules. It is a question of a change of party control. It is a question of losing grip. It is a question of whether or not the powers of this Republican majority are to be emasculated by an unnatural and abhorrent alliance with our natural born enemies. [Laughter and applause on the Republican side.]

If these rules are to be changed, they should be changed as the tariff was changed, not by their enemies, but by their friends. No; the first man to run to the cover of an efficient code of rules, mark my words, if the country should establish the Democracy in power, would be our friends on the other side, and the man over the hurdles first would be the distinguished orator from Missouri, who expects to be the Democratic Speaker. [Laughter and applause.]

Do you suppose he would consent to trust fifteen of the wild, untamed steeds of the Democracy to fix his rules or to name his committees which are to make him responsible to the great forty-six States of this Union? No; the gentleman is far too canny, too wise, too prudent, and too experienced. We have much at stake, far higher and greater than satisfaction of any man's resentment; it is the success of the Republican party's programme — the programme we were sent here by Republicans to carry out. It is the success of Taft's administration. [Applause on the Republican side.]

It is the success or defeat of our great party. The country is not ready yet to transfer from us to our friends on the other side, of fifty years of proven incompetency, the powers of this country to carry out the wishes of this people. But I summon a gentleman as a witness to the essential excellence of these rules, as a witness to the essential excellence of this Speaker, as a witness to the efficiency of the House of Representatives, in which many of you took part — I summon as a witness —

★ ★ ★ ★

[T]hose men who are eager here to assert their independence on this side, it seems to me, should again do, as we have all done in the past, subordinate their personal preferences to the opinions of an overwhelming majority of their Republican associates. In the light of the greater need of the greater people outside, in the need for remedial legislation, in view of the

voices summoning us from every valley, from every hill, from every industry, every enterprise, let us do our work as Republicans because the Republican people summoned us to it.

These summonses and these voices, the incarnate voice of the Republican people of the United States of America, should drown out and overwhelm and smooth down beneath their waves every unimportant difference, and we should unite, as representing the American people and as a majority that has been given the power to accomplish that which we set out to do, as Republicans. In spite of the promises, in spite of the cajoleries, in spite of the denunciations and maledictions, in spite of the prophecies of disaster that emanate from our eager opponents, let us remain true as a Republican majority. [Applause on the Republican side.]

Gentlemen, fellow-Republicans, many of us have grown old and gray in the service. We never have before been confronted with so critical a time as now. [Laughter and applause on the Democratic side.]

Aye, Mr. Speaker, I measure every word I say; the time is critical. The rejoicing of those men on the other side, because they think already they have the victory in their hands, who wish to destroy Republican prestige and Republican domination in the Nation, these all admonish us to fidelity to our oath of office, fidelity to our manhood, fidelity to fifty years of Republican history. Fair play with our constituents at home demands of us that we retain the control and exercise the control, as they elected us to do, as Republicans. For we shall be held responsible for the control of this branch of Congress as Republicans, and not as allies of the Democracy. We have no right to surrender our trust. [Loud and continued applause on the Republican side.]

Source: *Congressional Record,* 61st Cong., 2nd sess., March 17, 1910 (Washington: GPO, 1910), 45:3302–3304.

REPRESENTATIVE JOHN M. NELSON PROTESTS SPEAKER JOSEPH G. CANNON'S DOMINATION

MARCH 17, 1910

Mr. Speaker, with mingled feelings of diffidence and hope I rise to address the House. The opportunity for which we have labored long and earnestly is at hand. The overthrow, in part, of the Speaker's arbitrary power is now possible. Let us, therefore, force the issue and face the duty of the hour with the courage the cause demands. Our cause is righteous. Pub-

lic sentiment is with us. I see the beginning of the end of a long and arduous contest. For nearly three years it has been my chief purpose to study, to understand, and, so far as possible, to arouse sentiment here and elsewhere against these unjust, unfair, and arbitrary rules. In so doing I have sought to avoid personal notoriety or self-exploitation, preferring to remain a silent, but conscientious, student of general legislation, well knowing that it is not so much what one says here as how one votes here that counts for the general good.

Believing, however, that upon this matter I have special knowledge, I deem it my duty to reply to the gentleman from New York [Mr. FASSETT], who has charged some of us with the heinous crime of helping Democracy. I would ask the honorable gentleman if he thinks we act from unworthy motives? He must know how unpleasant is the duty before us; how difficult it has been made by the so-called regulars; how much we risk by provoking the displeasure of our party associates in pursuing our determined course. All that men prize here of patronage, of privilege, and of power we have had to forego for the sake of principle. Have we not been punished by every means at the disposal of the powerful House orga-

---

Members long chairmen of important committees, others holding high rank ... have been ruthlessly removed, deposed, and humiliated before their constituents and the country because ... they would not cringe or crawl before the arbitrary power of the Speaker and his House machine. — John M. Nelson

---

nization? Members long chairmen of important committees, others holding high rank — all with records of faithful and efficient party service to their credit — have been ruthlessly removed, deposed, and humiliated before their constituents and the country because, forsooth, they would not cringe or crawl before the arbitrary power of the Speaker and his House machine.

Plenty of proof is at hand. Let me cite an example or two. The distinguished gentleman from Wisconsin [Mr. COOPER] was made chairman of the Committee on Insular Affairs by Speaker Henderson at the urgent request of President McKinley, because the Chief Executive desired a man at the head of that great committee who would not permit the exploitation of the Philippine Islands. What was done to him by the present Speaker? What was done to Mr. FOWLER, Mr. NORRIS, Mr. HAUGEN, and many others? The Speaker did not hesitate to swing the headsman's ax nor the regulars to rejoice when an insurgent's head fell into the basket.

The gentleman from New York says we have grievances. Aye, we have, and many; but the gentleman does not state that these grievances arose after we had begun this fight on the Speaker's power and for the restoration of representative government in the House. The gentleman well knows that we are not seeking self-interest. We are fighting for the right of free,

fair, and full representation in this body for our respective constituencies. The so-called insurgent Republican represents as good citizenship as the regular does. The two hundred thousand or more citizens of the second district of Wisconsin have some rights of representation here under our Constitution. But what is that right under the despotic rules of this body? Merely the privilege to approve the will of a Representative from another State invested with despotic power under artificial, unfair, and self-made rules of procedure.

We know, indeed, by bitter experience what representation means under these rules. It means that we must stand by the Speaker, right or wrong, or suffer the fate that we have endured. Let no one accuse us, therefore, of an alliance with Democracy for unworthy purposes. We are fighting with our Democratic brethren for the common right of equal representation in this House, and for the right of way of progressive legislation in Congress; and we are going to fight on at any cost until these inestimable rights have been redeemed for the people. [Applause.]

The gentleman eloquently appealed to the spirit of party. I appeal to the spirit of country. Let me call the gentleman's attention to that part of George Washington's Farewell Address in which he speaks of the spirit of party and the despotism it may lead to if unchecked. Looking with prophetic eye into the future, scanning the reefs and rocks upon which the new ship of state might founder, he sounded this warning to us and to unborn generations of Americans. Hear his words:

> I have already intimated to you the danger of parties in the state, with particular reference to the founding of them on geographical discriminations. Let me now take a more comprehensive view, and warn you in the most solemn manner against the baneful effects of the spirit of party generally.
>
> The spirit, unfortunately, is inseparable from our nature, having its root in the strongest passions of the human mind. It exists under different shapes in all governments, more or less stifled, controlled, or repressed, but in those of the popular form it is seen in its greatest rankness and is truly their worst enemy.
>
> The alternate domination of one faction over another, sharpened by the spirit of revenge natural to party dissension, which in different ages and countries has perpetrated the most horrid enormities, is itself a frightful despotism.

This "spirit of revenge natural to party dissension," of which Washington warns us, has played its part in the creation of these rules and the parliamentary precedents that sustain the Speaker's despotic power. I have had the opportunity and the desire to investigate this subject, and I pause here to say that the rules in themselves are not so objectionable, but that a few changes might work wonders, if it were not for the mass of complicated, inconsistent, and arbitrary decisions that have grown up, some of them even contradicting the rules in express terms, and all tending to enlarge the importance of the presiding officer and to lessen the representative power of the House.

The history of the rules, as studied under the light of the precedents, proves that they have grown up under the united influences of party spirit and self-interest, and thus has gradually been formed in the Speaker's office the despotism from which we are now in open rebellion. How vividly Speaker Reed, when he was once in the minority, pictured the workings of this system, even in its infancy and youth; how "the few" — the Speaker and his lieutenants — "intrenched in the forms and usages," "the combination and concert of old Members knowing the rules," could "keep the many entirely out of control," "govern the House," "perpetuate their own rule," and thereby protect "vested interests and vested wrongs."

The eloquent gentleman from New York [Mr. FASSETT] says the majority must control, but what is the majority? Speaker Reed emphatically said:

> There is no greater fallacy than this idea that majority and minority are predicated of political parties only.

Why should the subject of the rules be a party matter? At what convention did the Republican party adopt the present rules of the House? The Speaker says he represents the majority. But how? He and his chief lieutenants — favorites or personal friends, a small minority within the majority — call themselves the party and then pass the word on to the rank and file of the Republican membership to line up or be punished. What is the controlling force? Party principles? No. The Speaker's power under the rules — his patronage, the appointment of all committees, the fifty-six desirable chairmanships, the control of recognition on the floor, the close corporation of the Committee on Rules consisting of the Speaker himself and his two assistants — all these forces unite to form an autocracy against which we are in rebellion to-day. We are no less Republicans because we would be free Members of Congress. We do not need to be kept in leading strings. We are free representatives of the people, and we want freedom here for every Member of every party. [Applause.]

★ ★ ★ ★

Love of party is good; love of country is better. The right should stand before reelection; and so believing, many of us have chosen to accept ostracism here from place and power and to risk defeat at home to change these rules. Has not the press been filled with the direst threats, inspired by the powers that be? Opponents are to be brought out against us, patronage to be taken away, and campaign funds to be used to effect our defeat; and all this because we would not bend our necks to the Speaker's yoke.

But the House machine is not the Republican party. We have no cause to fear. The people are with us. Now that the issue has been presented; now that the opportunity is at hand to amend these rules in one vital respect, let us do so, and perhaps help save the Republican party. If we go home to our constituents and tell them that these rules are still in force and that they are to stay in force, what will be their verdict? If we liberalize these rules now, if we change them by enlarging the Committee on Rules and disqualifying the Speaker from membership upon it, as is proposed by the pending resolution, to that extent we eliminate this issue from the campaign; and what is vastly more important, we make it easier to secure progressive legislation in the House, redeem our platform pledges, and prove our party faithful to its high trust.

The gentleman from New York [Mr. FASSETT] has read a letter by President Roosevelt, which he seeks to construe as an indorsement of the work of the House under these rules and the present Speaker. This letter was written four years ago for campaign purposes. It is true that the railway rate bill, the pure-food bill, and the meat-inspection bill had been favorably acted upon by Congress, but is there a man here who does not know that these great measures for the betterment of conditions among the people were forced through this House by the "big stick" in spite of the rules and the Speaker? I do not wish to violate any of the proprieties, but I know that President Roosevelt gave a subsequent indorsement under the promise that his policies would be enacted into law — a promise that was never performed. I know something of the feelings and thoughts of one President, although the impropriety of relating a conversation with him prevents me from giving them expression. I will say, however, as an offset to what the gentleman would have us believe, that there will be no commendation, in my judgment, for these rules, either from the former President or, for that matter, by the present one.

Mr. Speaker, I feel deeply on this subject. I have long been interested in it. I believe I can say without immodesty that I was the first Republican to raise this issue before the Congress and before the country. More than two years ago, after having studied the history of our rules, and what others have said on this subject, and after making comparison with the parliamentary practices of other nations, I first discussed these rules in a public address before my constituents, and then at the first session of the Sixtieth Congress I deliberately sought to make their revision a paramount national issue. Unceasingly, persistently, and self-sacrificingly I have labored to bring this issue to a head. And I rejoice that the crisis has come. I welcome it. Let there be no faint hearts nor drooping courage nor spirit of compromise among us. The conflict is irrepressible. Let us meet it now like men.

We seek to redress a grievous wrong. No such usurpation of power exists in any other parliamentary nation. Elsewhere the occupant of the chair is an impartial presiding officer. Elsewhere the rules have been worked out on a basis of equality. No man has more opportunity, more rights, or more freedom than his colleagues. But with us it is a matter of privilege; here legislation goes by favor, and the Speaker is the dispenser of opportunity and power. He is the hub of the parliamentary wheel, his lieutenants are the spokes, and the House revolves around him.

We wish to change this arbitrary, artificial, and unrepublican system. We do not desire to deprive any Member of rights. We wish merely some rights for ourselves. We Republicans who protest against the Speaker's domination do not wish to put the gentlemen on the other side into control of the House. Outside of this question we do not propose to act with them as a body. We have formed no permanent alliance. On matters of legislation each one of us will act as his conscience dictates. However, in the patriotic movement to restore legislative right to the American people, we welcome gladly any help that will relieve us from the intolerable tyranny of one-man power in the House of Representatives. [Loud applause.]

Source: Congressional Record, 61st Cong., 2nd sess., March 17, 1910 (Washington: GPO, 1910), 45:3304–3305.

Notes

1. Scott William Rager, "Uncle Joe Cannon: The Brakeman of the House of Representatives, 1903–1911," in Roger H. Davidson, Susan Webb Hammond, and Raymond W. Smock, *Masters of the House: Congressional Leadership Over Two Centuries* (Boulder, Col.: Westview Press, 1998), 65, 67.

2. Ibid., 64, 68.

3. Ibid., 72.

4. *Congressional Record,* 61st Cong., 1st sess., March 15, 1909, 45:18, 21–22; Rager, "Uncle Joe Cannon: The Brakeman of the House of Representatives, 1903–1911," 73–77. See also Ronald M.

Peters Jr., *The American Speakership: The Office in Historical Perspective* (Baltimore: Johns Hopkins University Press, 1997), 83.

5. Rager, "Uncle Joe Cannon: The Brakeman of the House of Representatives, 1903–1911," 77–78; *Congressional Record,* 61st Cong., 2nd sess., January 7, 1910, 45:383–406. See also Kenneth William Hechler, *Insurgency: Personalities and Politics of the Taft Era* (New York: Columbia University Press, 1940), 64, 67; Blair Bolles, *Tyrant from Illinois: Uncle Joe Cannon's Experiment with Personal Power* (New York: Norton, 1951), 211–214.

6. Rager, "Uncle Joe Cannon: The Brakeman of the House of Representatives, 1903–1911," 78; *Congressional Record,* 61st Cong., 2nd sess., March 17, 1910, 45:3292. See also *Congressional Record,* 61st Cong., 2nd sess., March 17, 1910, 45:3292–3335; March 18, 1910, 45:3388–3416; Bolles, *Tyrant from Illinois: Uncle Joe Cannon's Experiment with Personal Power,* 215–220; Hechler, *Insurgency: Personalities and Politics of the Taft Era,* 68–71; Richard Lowitt, *George W. Norris: The Making of a Progressive, 1861–1912* (Syracuse, N.Y.: Syracuse University Press, 1963), 170–176.

7. Rager, "Uncle Joe Cannon: The Brakeman of the House of Representatives, 1903–1911," 78; *Congressional Record,* 61st Cong., 2nd sess., March 19, 1910, 45:3302, 3304. See also Bolles, *Tyrant from Illinois: Uncle Joe Cannon's Experiment with Personal Power,* 220–222; and Lowitt, *George W. Norris: The Making of a Progressive, 1861–1912,* 170–176.

8. Rager, "Uncle Joe Cannon: The Brakeman of the House of Representatives, 1903–1911," 78–79; Hechler, *Insurgency: Personalities and Politics of the Taft Era,* 71–72; *Congressional Record,* 61st Cong., 2nd sess., March 18, 1910, 45:3416–3417; March 19, 1910, 45:3425–3436. See also Bolles, *Tyrant from Illinois: Uncle Joe Cannon's Experiment with Personal Power,* 222–224; Lowitt, *George W. Norris: The Making of a Progressive, 1861–1912,* 180–182.

9. *Congressional Record,* 61st Cong., 2nd sess., March 19, 1910, 45:3436–3439; Rager, "Uncle Joe Cannon: The Brakeman of the House of Representatives, 1903–1911," 79–80.

10. Rager, "Uncle Joe Cannon: The Brakeman of the House of Representatives, 1903–1911," 80–84.

Seventeenth Amendment:
The Popular Election of Senators
✳ 1911–1912 ✳

Since the Constitutional Convention of 1787 finished its work, more than eleven thousand proposals have been offered in Congress to amend the venerable parchment. Of the twenty-seven amendments subsequently adopted, few took longer to be approved by Congress than the Seventeenth, which provided for the popular election of U.S. senators. Prior to its ratification, state legislatures elected senators. While other constitutional amendments have affected the power of the federal government as well as citizen participation and protests, only the Seventeenth Amendment "has fundamentally altered the design of the original structure of the government."[1]

The precedent for senators to be elected by their state legislators originated with the election of delegates to the Constitutional Convention. The Framers of the Constitution believed that having state legislatures elect senators would cement their connection to the national government and increase the chances of the Constitution being ratified. The expectation was that senators would be able to do their work without regional pressure from the populace. The Senate, unlike the House of Representatives, was not intended to represent the people directly — it was to represent the state as a whole and protect against federal encroachment upon the constitutional rights of the states.

Prior to the 1850s, the process of having the state legislatures elect senators worked relatively smoothly. As political differences between the parties in various states became more common, however, contentious battles in state legislatures began to emerge as the struggle to elect senators reflected the increasing regional tensions over slavery and states' rights. Following the Civil War, as the number of problematic senatorial elections increased, Congress in 1866 approved legislation regulating the time and manner for electing senators. The law required the chambers of each state legislature to meet separately and, by an open vote, to name as Senator. If there was a disagreement between chambers, the two houses were to meet jointly until a prospective senator received a majority vote.[2]

The new law, however, proved ineffective in solving a number of problems that advocates of direct election identified. They argued that the system the Framers designed was not democratic and denoted a "lack of confidence" in the judgment of the American people; encouraged corruption in state legislatures that frequently resulted in the "selection of men whose only claim to office is their great wealth or subserviency to corporate interests"; and allowed for protracted legislative deadlocks over the elections that on a number of occasions deprived states of full Senate representation. "Over time," one scholar has observed, "election of senators by state legislatures came to be associated with stalemate, corruption, plutocracy, and reaction; by contrasts, direct election of senators was associated with reform, integrity, democracy, and progress."[3]

For advocates of direct election, "it was clear that the control of corporate power in America would never come about until the method of selecting senators was removed from the control of corporate interests. The way to remove the influence of the 'special interests,' it was argued, was to have the senators elected directly by the voters of each state."[4]

Between 1886 and 1912, groups of citizens, associations, and state legislatures sent Congress more than four hundred petitions calling for direct elections of senators. In addition, Congress received applications from twenty-eight states that prompted the most serious demand in American history for a second constitutional convention. By 1912, thirty-three states had taken matters into their own hands through the use of direct primaries, and twelve states had adopted some form of what came to be known as the Oregon System. This method asked candidates for the state legislature to pledge to vote for the senatorial candidate who won the popular vote. Also, various minor political parties had for some time incorporated the direct election of senators into their party platforms — Prohibition Party (1872, 1876, 1904, 1908, 1912), American Prohibition Party (1884), Anti-Monopoly Party (1884), Union Labor Party (1888), National Party (1896), People's Party (1896), People's (Fusion Faction) Party, and Independent Party (1908). At the turn of the century the Democratic Party (1900, 1904, 1908, 1912) followed suit.[5] The challenge was persuading Congress, and in particular the Senate, to approve the change.

In 1826, Rep. Henry R. Storrs of New York offered the first congressional proposal calling for the direct election of

Utah senator George Sutherland in 1911 introduced an amendment to allow for individual states to regulate senate elections. The Sutherland amendment ultimately failed, but in 1912 the Seventeenth Amendment was ratified, allowing for direct election of senators.
Source: Library of Congress.

senators. It would be another eighty-six years, however, before Congress finally sent the proposed change to the states for ratification in 1912. During the interim, nearly two hundred proposals were introduced in Congress. Most were offered between 1872 and 1912, a period during which popular election proponents routinely introduced proposals every Congress, and, beginning in 1893, annually. Five of the proposed amendments passed the House in 1893, 1894, 1898, 1900, and 1902 respectively, but in each instance the Senate fiercely resisted the change and refused to bring the question to a vote, despite frequent vacancies and disputed election results.[6]

Finally, in January 1911, Sen. William E. Borah, R-Idaho, chairman of the Senate Judiciary Committee, favorably reported the first direct election resolution to reach the Senate floor. As reported, the proposal, which had been introduced by Sen. Joseph L. Bristow, R-Kan., included a "race rider" that guaranteed to individual states regulatory control over senatorial elections. Attachment of the rider prompted Sen. George Sutherland, R-Utah, to introduce an amendment sanctioning federal supervision of congressional elections.

Debate over the Sutherland amendment continued until near the end of February, when it passed 50–37. On February 28, for the first time in history, the Senate voted on a constitutional amendment providing for the direct election of senators. When the votes were counted, fifty-four favored the amendment, and thirty-three opposed its passage. It failed by four votes to receive the requisite two-thirds majority.[7]

Supporters of direct election were not, however, to be denied. Early in April 1911, at the outset of a special session of the Sixty-second Congress, called by President William Howard Taft to review a reciprocal trade agreement with Canada, Rep. William W. Rucker, D-Mo., introduced H.J. Res. 39, which provided for direct election of senators and state control of elections. Within a week, the Rucker resolution was favorably reported. Then on April 13, Rep. Horace Olin Young, R-Mich., offered an amendment similar to the Sutherland amendment. Following a six-hour debate, the Young amendment failed and the House passed the Rucker resolution, as reported, 296–16. The House debate accentuated the broad diversity of opinion on the question.[8]

On May 1, H.J. Res. 39 was favorably reported by the Senate Judiciary Committee, but two weeks later Senator Bristow offered a substitute resolution that, while providing for the direct election of senators, struck the provision calling for exclusive state control over senatorial elections. In the aftermath, seven days of intense debate ensued, filled with personal attacks fueled by sectionalism and partisanship. When the June 12 vote on the Bristow amendment ended in a 44–44 tie, Vice President James S. Sherman cast the deciding vote in favor of the substitute. Later the same day, the Senate adopted the Bristow Amendment, 64–24. The House, however, refused to concur, and the Senate insisted on its amendment and requested a conference.[9]

During the next nine months, the conference committee met sixteen times without reaching an agreement. Finally on April 23, 1912, Sen. Clarence D. Clark, R-Wy., successfully persuaded his Senate colleagues to insist on the Bristow Amendment. When Clark's motion was read in the House on May 13, Representative Rucker, the author of H.J. Res. 39, moved that the House agree to the Bristow Amendment. While many Southern members of the House disagreed on the grounds that the Bristow Amendment would bring ruin to the South, and many others did not particularly agree with the amendment, most felt they must act. Failure to do so would probably end any opportunity to send a direct election amendment to the states for ratification in the foreseeable future. Against this backdrop, Rucker's motion to accept the Bristow Amendment was accepted, 238–39.[10] On May 17, 1912, the Seventeenth Amendment was sent to the states for their consideration and was quickly ratified by the states in a little more than a year. The following year marked the first time all senatorial elections were held by popular vote.

SENATOR WILLIAM E. BORAH SUPPORTS THE POPULAR ELECTION OF SENATORS

JUNE 12, 1911

Unsettled questions have no pity for the contentment of mankind. For nearly a hundred years this question has been seriously debated among the people. For more than fifty years there has been an earnest and persistent demand that the matter be submitted to a vote in the respective legislatures. Thirty-two States of the Union have in some form of resolution called for this change. Millions of people have in some form or other asked that we submit it. To deny this right to have it submitted is to repudiate the first principles of a free government. To refuse the people the right after this long-standing, earnest, patient plea to vote upon modifications of their Government is to plant the seeds of distrust and dissatisfaction in the minds of those without whose loyalty and confidence we have no government. It is unwise. It is the most disastrous course which men who would preserve the underlying principles of our Government could possibly take. It is a defiant challenge of the people to have a voice in their Government. Men who would not give the right even to vote upon such a subject would, undoubtedly, if they could, deny the people any say or voice in matters of government.

It has been declared many times that there is no public or general demand for this change in the Constitution; that the people do not want it. It is urged with much scorn and more voice that the movement has its support with a few men who are seeking cheap notoriety. Those men who so declare, by refusing to submit the question, convict by their own act their words of insincerity. Such insincere and fallacious assertions can never mislead any mind except the self-infatuated minds which give them birth. This amendment can never be adopted unless there is an overwhelming public sentiment for it. It requires three-fourths of the States to adopt; it only requires one-fourth to defeat. Are you not willing to submit the matter where the people must win by such great odds if they win at all? If there is no public sentiment, no earnest, widespread, public demand, then there is no danger of submission. On the other hand, if there are three-fourths of the States of the Union in favor of it, who will be so bold as to say that they are not to have a chance to vote upon it? The fact is that those who oppose this measure, while professing great reverence and love for the Constitution, nevertheless defy it. The right to amend the Constitution is just as much a part of the Constitution, just as obligatory upon men sworn to support it, as any other part of that instrument. When the people petition for the exercise of this power, and through long years and repeated exertions seek the right so given, to deny it is to deny them a right guaranteed by the Constitution.

But those who oppose this measure seem unwilling to submit to the crucial test of truth — that is, debate before the tribunal which is to finally decide it. If Senators who think this change unwise have faith in their arguments; if they believe that experience and reason and patriotism are against the change, will they not then consent to pass this contest from this forum to the forum of public opinion? If you are not afraid of your cause, and if you do not distrust your argument by which you seek to sustain your position, then it must be that you distrust the judgment and the patriotism of that tribunal to which you are asked to submit it. If one or the other were not true, you would at least be willing to give the people a chance to vote. A man who will not submit his cause to a tribunal created to determine such matters in an orderly way knows or feels either that his cause is not just or that the tribunal is unfit.

At the last session, while this question was before us, we listened to a most polished and effective eulogy by the Senator from Massachusetts upon the men who framed the Constitution. I agree with him fully in all he says in respect to the character and ability, the unselfish devotion, and unmatched patriotism of that remarkable group of men. I do not expect time to record the appearance of another Hamilton any sooner than it will record the appearance of another Shakespeare. I do not expect the future to see another Madison any sooner than it will see the return of a Robert Burns. Mr. President, if I could see this Government operate just as the fathers made it, I would never challenge their wisdom nor stray for one moment from the path they pointed out to their children. I do not want any different principles of government than the principles which they indorsed and approved, but I do want those. I want to see the old Government brought back to where they left it — in the absolute control of the people, operating alone in their behalf. Whatever changes in details are necessary to accomplish this we ought to make.

The first seventy years of the Republic are gone. They were years in which there were no influences sufficiently strong to prevent the powers of government from operating in the manner in which the fathers expected them to operate. They were years in which there were no influences sufficiently strong to turn the agencies of government into the agencies of particular interests or to wholly private and

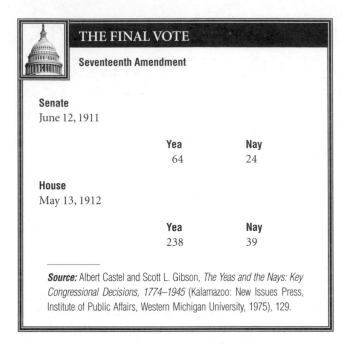

selfish purposes. But that is not true now. The last forty years have worked a marvelous change. We have other influences to deal with. We have influences of which they never dreamed, influences stronger in wealth and power than the Government itself at that time. These things do not require changes in the principles of the fathers, but they do require readjustment and a redistribution of powers. They require the adaptation of government to modern conditions. They require that we accept the wisdom of the fathers as a guide for brave, strong men confronted with a new condition of affairs, and not as a fetich before which slavish devotees bow in nerveless, lethargic adoration. Mr. Madison said in the constitutional convention:

> If an election by the people or through any other channel than the State legislature promised as incorrupt and Impartial a preference there could surely be no necessity for an appointment by those legislatures.

Had he been able to see what we see and know what we know, with that idea revolving in his mind, what do you think the father of the Constitution would have done? Had he looked upon vacant chairs here because of deadlocks in the legislature; had he seen as we saw last winter nearly one-half of a State legislature fleeing like fugitives across a State line and then negotiating with their colleagues like contending foes; had the men who surrounded Madison passed through the filth and corruption through which this Senate has been delving its way this last year; had they been thwarted and frustrated and defied in the effort to secure facts concerning the integrity of an election; had they believed that State legislatures would be turned by this duty from lawmaking bod-

ies dealing conscientiously with affairs of state into political combinations, torn and distracted by purely convention duties, venalized and corrupted by powerful interests who care nothing for the State, but everything for the membership of this body; if they had seen what we see, does any man doubt, in view of their declarations, that the fathers would have taken this duty from the legislature and given it directly to the people? The things which the fathers did are not right merely because they did them, but they, too, must stand the test of reason and the test of time and experience. I repeat, sir, that I join with those who give praise and honor to the fathers. But I do not believe in that kind of hero worship which makes the worshipers the nerveless, spineless, slavish devotees of a dead past. I believe in the hero worship which vitalizes and inspires, which realizes that all the great names which adorn the past are as sounding brass and tinkling cymbals, except as they inspire us for those achievements which in the language of Mr. Lincoln serves to keep the jewel of liberty in the family of men.

Those who are seeking to bring about this reform are not disturbed by the charge of being demagogues or sensation hunters or slaves to popular sentiment. The world has always had to deal with a very large and a very respectable class of people whose intellectual orbs are in the back of their head, and the rest of the world has learned patience and tolerance because of their affliction. There were able and brilliant and patriotic men who plead for the old Confederacy and against the adoption of the Constitution. A few weeks ago there was a great debate in the Senate of China over dispensing with the Chinaman's queue. The progressives favored the measure. The regulars, loyal to the institutions of the fathers, plead for the maintenance of those customs under which they had prospered and grown to power. To dispense with the queue

---

The things which the fathers did are not right merely because they did them, but they, too, must stand the test of reason and the test of time and experience. — William E. Borah

---

would be to strike at the very foundation of civil liberty and to turn the future over to an unthinking horde of sensation hunters trailing after new fads and worshiping in strange temples. It was a great debate, and men were moved to great feats of oratorical power.

I do not recall these things in disrespect of those who differ from us on this question. I only want to remind them that questions like this can not be met by charging its advocates with insincerity and demagogy. This question can only be met by argument, by reason, by a plea to the consciences and convictions of men. Those who favor this change are determined and uncompromising. They will never quit until the cause is decreed against them in the only forum which has jurisdiction to render final judgment. Realizing that they must have two-thirds of the votes of Congress, that they must have three-fourths of the States, that they must meet able and determined opposition, that they must win against a thousand conservative forces — even with this handicap they are anxious for the final test of battle. They are willing to submit this to the judgment and intelligence of the American people.

Notoriety could be secured by easier and cheaper methods; sensations could be more easily obtained; but, armed with a just cause, encouraged in the belief that a question is never settled until it is settled right, those who urge this measure will continue to do so until it is written by the hand of public opinion into the great charter.

Source: *Congressional Record*, 62nd Cong., 1st sess., June 12, 1911 (Washington: GPO, 1911), 47:1891–1892.

SENATOR AUGUSTUS O. BACON ARGUES AGAINST THE POPULAR ELECTION OF SENATORS

JUNE 12, 1911

I think I may safely say that there was but one single provision in the Constitution to which all of the States objected, but one single provision of the Constitution to which all of the States urged serious objections and criticisms; a provision to which they, every State — the records of which have been preserved — objected. The provision thus objected to is that which gives to Congress the ultimate power to regulate the times, places, and manner of electing Members of Congress. All of the States made formal protest to this particular provision and finally agreed to the Constitution, subject to the assurance that the powers conferred by this provision would only be used to the extent as expressed in the amendment which I have to-day offered, to wit, that the power to regulate the manner of elections would only be exercised when the State legislatures failed or refused to make the necessary regulations, or were for any reason incapable of making them.

I want to say, Mr. President, that the language of this amendment is copied almost verbatim, and in the essential part of it verbatim, from the resolution which was adopted by the convention of the State of New York when it adopted the Constitution. I am going to read, sir, although I did so upon a former occasion, the utterances of these various conventions on this subject at the time they acted upon the question whether or not they would adopt the Constitution of the United States and become a part of the Government formed thereby.

★ ★ ★ ★

No Senator who has ever read those debates, not only the debates of the Constitutional Convention but the debates in the several conventions of the States, can rise in his place to-day and say he has read them and believed for a moment that a single one of these States would have adopted the Constitution with any such proposition embodied in it.

★ ★ ★ ★

They objected to it most strenuously. They contended that that was a right which belonged to each State. There was then no cloud upon the horizon which indicated the coming of a sectional storm. It was not to guard against any special and particular evil which was apprehended, but those rugged men who had so recently been through a contest by means of which they had achieved their liberty stood more than a hundred years nearer to the times of autocratic rule than we stand. They stood more than a hundred years nearer the exhibition of great central power, situated beyond their borders and controlling their local affairs. They had devoted seven years in proclaiming their rights to free themselves of such outside domination and while there was then no particular menace from any particular quarter, they were grounded in the great fundamental proposition that they should control absolutely their own local affairs, and most particularly their elections, and that no general government should ever assume to control those local affairs for them.

★ ★ ★ ★

Mr. President, I think it is capable of easy demonstration that the adoption of an amendment giving to a direct vote of the people the choice of Senators, leaving at the same time the language of the fourth section of the first article of the Constitution to apply to that changed condition, does make a most radical change in the law, and that there will be a control

257

by the General Government of the election of Senators which the General Government has not now under the present law.

★ ★ ★ ★

Is there any Senator here who will say that under the present law under which Senators are elected by the legislatures Congress can pass or enforce any law which shall apply to the legislature of a State in managing and controlling the legislature in electing a Senator in the same way and by the same means that Congress can under that clause of the Constitution now exercise in managing and controlling the elections of Representatives? It is impossible under that clause of the Constitution for Congress to undertake to control the elections of Senators.... Although the language of the Constitution as to prescribing regulations for the control of elections is now the same for Representatives as for Senators, who is there who can rise in his place and say that Congress, without an absolute revolution in the Government, without overturning the autonomy and sovereignty of the States, without an utter destruction of our form of government, can undertake to prescribe registration laws for the legislatures, can undertake to supervise the election of a Senator by a legislature, to invade the halls of a legislature and set up the judges of the election, to put marshals appointed by Federal judges in the legislative halls, to see that the legislature elects Senators right, to send the armed forces of the United States with their guns and their sabers into the halls of the legislature to enforce the law with reference to the election of Senators?

★ ★ ★ ★

One of the arguments which has been pressed with great earnestness and with unremitting perseverance has been the one I have attempted to answer this afternoon — that the change in the law submitting the election of Senators to the direct vote of the people, with no supervision other than that which is now contained in the Constitution, would not change in effect the present Constitution as regards the control of those elections by the Government. If I have not demonstrated the fact that it would make a change of a most radical and far-reaching character, then, Mr. President, it is because I have not the command of language in order to express the thoughts which are in my mind and the arguments which have presented themselves to me.

★ ★ ★ ★

Conceding that the effect will be to change the control of the United States Government now in the election of Senators, and that in that change it only gives the Government of the United States the same power over the election of Senators that it now has over the election of Representatives, why, it is asked, should there be any reason why the Government of the United States should not have the same control over the election of Senators as it has over the election of Representatives? Well, sir, I want to give several reasons. Some of them have been given heretofore, and I shall do no more than touch them, at least those of them that I understand to have been already discussed. There are one or two of them, however, that I do not recollect having heard discussed, which I may speak of a little more at length.

In the first place, as I have endeavored to demonstrate, the power now claimed and which at times has been exercised in the control of the election of Representatives is altogether greater than that contemplated or intended by the framers of the Constitution, and if any change is to be made it should be a change which would take away the power to interfere with the elections of Representatives and not a change to give further power to interfere with the election of Senators.

In the next place, as has been repeatedly said here, and not very long ago said by my learned friend, the Senator from Mississippi [Mr. WILLIAMS], on my left, a Senator occupies a very different relation to the Government in his representation of a State here from what a Representative occupies in his representation of a given number of people. A Senator represents not only the people found within the State, but he represents the corporate entity of the State. He represents more than that, Mr. President; he represents that which the Supreme Court of the United States in more than one decision has recognized, to wit, the sovereignty of a State.

★ ★ ★ ★

The Supreme Court of the United States has more than once said that within its sphere the State is as much a sovereign as the United States in its sphere, and the Senator represents here not only the people and all the material interests within a State, but he represents the corporate entity and the sovereignty of the States.

Certainly, Mr. President, there is the strongest of reasons why the State should control the selection of the men who are thus to represent the State in this high Council of States. In one case the representation is a representation which includes a certain number of people, greater in the aggregate in one State than in another, equal in representation in the one district as in another, whether in the same State or not. It is a representation of that which is more particularly national. In the other it is the representation of that which is an entity in itself, and which has the same dignity each that another has, regardless of how much greater in area or population the one may be than the other.

★ ★ ★ ★

It is possible in the future, as it has been in the past, that it will be greatly to the interest of the interests to control the Senate. The control of one or two Representatives in the other House is a minor matter, because of the great number of men there, aside from the greater difference still of the functions which they perform: but the control of a few men in the Senate is a matter of most vital importance. The control of the election of one man in the Senate may change the practical control of the Government. It may be at some time that there is some Senator who is particularly disagreeable to certain influences. He may be a man who stands not in awe of the powers that be, political, financial, or otherwise. To control such a man as that in the other House would have very little influence upon the destinies of the country or upon the laws which are to be passed or the legislative functions to be performed, but to control the election or return of such a man in the Senate may be a matter of the vastest importance.

★ ★ ★ ★

It may sound like a startling statement, but the Constitution of the United States gives to the States through their representation in the Senate a greater power in the control of the Federal Government than it gives to all the people of the United States combined. It gives to the Senate in the carrying on of the Federal Government a greater power than it gives to any other agency, or any other part of the Government, or of the country, or that which makes up the Government. There are some things denied to the Executive; there are some things denied to the House of Representatives; there are some things which the Senate can do in connection with the Executive; there are some things which the Senate can do in connection with the House of Representatives; but there is nothing that can be done without the Senate. With the House of Representatives it can pass a law with the approval of the President of the United States, and it can pass a law with the disapproval of the President of the United States. It can repeal a law over the objection of the President of the United States. With the President of the United States the Senate can make a treaty, which is the supreme law of the land, against the wish of the House of Representatives. With the House of Representatives the Senate can subsequently, by the enactment of a statute, repeal that treaty against the wish of the President of the United States. The Senate in conjunction with the House can declare and make war against a foreign nation contrary to the wish and over the objection of the President; and then the Senate and the President, acting together in making a treaty, may stop that war and make peace with that country against the wish and over the objection of the House of Representatives. The Senate of the United States, in cooperation with the President, can make any officer of the United States from the Chief Justice down to a marshal of a district, and the Senate of the United States, acting with the House of Representatives, can turn that man out of office without the consent and against the wish of the President of the United States. So I might go on. There are some things which can be done without the House of Representatives and against the wish of the House; there are some things which can be done without the Executive and against the wish of the Executive; there are some things which can be done by the Senate in conjunction with the one over the objection of the other, and vice versa; but there is no single thing which either the House of Representatives can do or the Executive can do without the consent of the Senate. The Senate is the great conservative, central feature of the Government, and the reason of it is this: That the States, each possessing supreme power in itself, were, when the Federal Government was formed, not willing to make the Federal Government unless in the making of it the States should not only have reserved to them the right of controlling their individual and local matters, but also unless the States should have the most prominent and active and controlling part in every function of the Government through their equal and direct representation in the Senate.

★ ★ ★ ★

The creation and peculiar constitution of the Senate was the great covenant entered into between the States when they framed and adopted the Constitution, and when these great and varied powers were conferred upon those who should represent them in the Senate. What a mockery, what an absolute mockery, to talk about the retention of such power; what an absolute mockery to say that no great function of the Government can be performed unless the States shall consent to it through their Senators, and then pass a law which will say that the States must be overseen in the selection of their Senators; that the States must be controlled; that the States must be supervised and directed when they are to select the men who are to perform this high and mighty function.

★ ★ ★ ★

The House of Representatives sent us a joint resolution, which was a recognition of this right of the States. They sent us a joint resolution in which they say they recognize that the General Government or the people of the other States should not interfere in the local election of Senators; yet it is proposed that we, the special guardians of these mighty functions, we whose duty it is to uphold this aegis of power, we who should magnify our office that we shall be the ones, over the objection of the House of Representatives, to strike down this power of the States and put it in the power of the General Government, or of a dominant party in the Government — to practically dictate, when political or other influences shall demand it, who shall be declared to be the representative of a State in the Senate. Why, Mr. President, I say, of all men, why should we be the ones to sanction or permit such a thing? It would be bad enough for the House of Representatives to send us a joint resolution such as that now proposed by the substitute of the Senator from Kansas [Mr. BRISTOW], which is the same amendment as that offered previously by the Senator from Utah [Mr. SUTHERLAND]; it would be bad enough if they had sent such a resolution to us, and if they had done so we by right should have refused to concur in it; we should have replied, "In the name of our States, in the name of the great foundation principles of our Government, in the name of those sovereignties who surrendered in part their sovereignty upon the assurance that their right to control their elections should not be destroyed, we reject the proposition." Unless the Senate does consent, the practical exercise of the right to control the election of Senators can not be taken from the States.

★ ★ ★ ★

It is bad enough when we permit others to rob us of our rights; it is bad enough when we permit others to take from us that which belongs to us; it is bad enough when we let those who do it only by the strong hand tear from our brows the authority and the dignity which belong to us; but it is an unspeakable thing that we should do it ourselves. Why, Mr. President, I am reminded of the fabled eagle, who, when stricken and dying on the plain, found in that dying moment its chief agony when it saw that the shaft which had pierced its vitals had been guided by a feather which had fallen from its own wing. When this amendment has been adopted by the States in the form in which it is now proposed to impose it upon us, it will be an irrevocable act. In my opinion, the great dignity and security and stability of office in the Senate will be gone; in my opinion, the great function of the States that through their representatives in this body should exercise a controlling power that the people themselves do not exercise, and that they should exercise a power that all the other influ-

> *It is bad enough when we permit others to rob us of our rights; it is bad enough when we permit others to take from us that which belongs to us … but it is an unspeakable thing that we should do it ourselves.* — Augustus O. Bacon

ences put together in the Government do not equal — when, Mr. President, we strike that down, in my opinion we have done that which will unsettle the foundations and destroy the stability of this Government.

Source: *Congressional Record,* 62nd Cong., 1st sess., June 12, 1911 (Washington: GPO, 1911), 47:1892–1898.

Notes

1. Alan P. Grimes, *Democracy and the Amendments to the Constitution* (Lexington, Mass.: Lexington Books, 1978), 2.

2. 14 Stat. 243–244. For an overview of the election of senators by state legislatures, see George H. Haynes, *The Senate of the United States: Its History and Practice,* 2 vols. (Boston: Houghton Mifflin, 1938), 1:81–115.

3. Herman Ames, *The Proposed Amendments to the Constitution of the United States* (New York: B. Franklin, 1970), 62–63; Ralph A. Rossum, *Federalism, the Supreme Court, and the Seventeenth Amendment: The Irony of Constitutional Democracy* (Lanham, Md.: Lexington Books, 2001), 187–192. For an extensive contemporary discussion of the arguments for and against the direct election of senators, see George H. Haynes, *The Election of Senators* (New York: Henry Holt, 1906), 153–258.

4. Grimes, *Democracy and the Amendments to the Constitution,* 75.

5. Ibid., Haynes, *The Election of Senators,* 100–129; Donald Bruce Johnson, comp., *National Party Platforms,* rev. ed., 2 vols. (Urbana: University of Illinois Press, 1978), 1:46, 53, 64, 84, 101, 106, 115, 118, 133, 137, 149, 154, 156, 170, 182; Ralph A. Rossum, *Federalism, the Supreme Court, and the Seventeenth Amendment* (Lanham, Md.: Lexington Books, 2001), 192–194; Jean Elizabeth Mazzaferro, "Bicameralism, Federalism, and Passage of the Seventeenth Amendment)" (Ph.D. diss., Claremont Graduate University, 2004), 99–103.

6. Wallace Worthy Hall, "The History and Effect of the Seventeenth Amendment" (Ph.D. diss., University of California, Berkeley, 1936), Appendices A and C; Mazzaferro, "Bicameralism, Federalism, and Passage of the Seventeenth Amendment," 82–91; Ames, *The Proposed Amendments to the Constitution of the United States,* 60–62; Michael Angelo Musmanno, *Proposed Amendments to the Constitution: A Monograph on the Resolutions Introduced in Congress Proposing Amendments to the Constitution of the United States of America* (Westport, Conn.: Greenwood Press, 1976), 218–219; U.S. Congress, Senate, *Proposed Amendments to the Constitution of the United States Introduced in Congress From December 4, 1889, to July 2, 1926,* S. Doc. 93, 69th Cong., 1st sess. (Washington: GPO, 1926), 144.

7. *Congressional Record,* 61st Cong., 3rd sess., January 11, 1911, 46:766; January 13, 1911, 46: 847; February 24, 1911, 46:3307–3308; February 28, 1911, 46:3638–3639.

8. *Congressional Record,* 62nd Cong., 1st sess., April 5, 1911, 47: 85; April 12, 1911, 47:183; April 13, 1911, 47:203–243; Mazzaferro, "Bicameralism, Federalism, and Passage of the Seventeenth Amendment," 113–161.

9. *Congressional Record,* 62nd Cong., 1st sess., May 1, 1911, 47, 787–788; May 15, 1911, 47:1205; June 12, 1911, 47:1879–1924; June 27, 1911, 47:2548–2549; Mazzaferro, "Bicameralism, Federalism, and Passage of the Seventeenth Amendment," 162–286.

10. *Congressional Record,* 62nd Cong., 2nd sess., April 23, 1912, 47:5169–5172; May 13, 1812, 47:6346–6367; Mazzaferro, "Bicameralism, Federalism, and Passage of the Seventeenth Amendment," 287–309.

Federal Reserve Act
✴ 1912–1913 ✴

Throughout much of the nineteenth century, a succession of financial panics plagued the United States. It was a period during which bank failures, business bankruptcies, and economic downturns were frequently attributed to a poorly regulated banking system and an inflexible money supply. Not until the panic of 1907, however, did reform efforts begin to gain momentum. While relatively brief, the panic produced severe runs on banks and trust companies, a significant increase in bankruptcies and unemployment, and a sharp economic downturn. Despite "its vast gold reserves and a modern industrial economy," the United States "was the only major country to suffer such a complete break-down of its credit system." Two basic problems highlighted the nation's financial shortcomings — an inelastic currency and immobile reserves. Because the supply of national bank note currency was tied to government bonds, it changed in response to the bond market rather than the needs of business. Even when reserves were sufficient, it was difficult to move money to where it was needed most since fifty different cities served as reserve depositories.[1]

Initially, Congress passed the Aldrich-Vreeland Currency Act of 1908 to address some of the most glaring flaws in the nation's currency and credit structure. The act's more lasting significance, however, proved to be those provisions establishing a bipartisan congressional commission to analyze and provide recommendations on restructuring the U.S. banking and currency system. In creating the bipartisan National Monetary Commission, Congress circumvented its "committee system deadlocked by the conflict between rival banking factions" and "allowed New York and Chicago [banking] factions to hammer out their differences before engaging congressional committees." Previously, "bankers had focused on getting the committee in which they held special influence to produce a completely one-sided bill, which tended to polarize and stalemate reform." The commission allowed for a compromise to be negotiated without considerable outside scrutiny.[2]

The eighteen-member commission included an equal number of senators and representatives. Sen. Nelson W. Aldrich, R-R.I., coauthor of the Currency Act, acted as chair. By and large, the commission members lacked formal experience in banking and financial matters, so experts were used to organize investigations and prepare draft recommendations. Over four years, the commission published twenty-three volumes that presented "an unparalleled opportunity for those who [were] interested in American financial problems to make a comparative study of conditions and experiences" in the United States and abroad.[3]

In November 1910, as the commission continued its work, Senator Aldrich and a group of experienced bankers met secretly at financier J. P. Morgan's duck hunting club at Jekyll Island, a resort island off the coast of Georgia, to draft a banking reform bill. When Aldrich placed the plan before the Monetary Commission in mid-January 1911, only the drafters knew of its specific origin and they were intent on not having the public learn of their role. After the public learned of Jekyll Island with the publication of Aldrich's authorized biography in 1930, it became a favorite source of conspiracy theories.[4]

The plan called for the establishment of a "National Reserve Association" chartered by the federal government to act as the government's fiscal agent, both to hold government deposits and to conduct foreign exchange activities. Fifteen regional banks, owned and operated by private banks overseen by a Washington, D.C., office, were to subscribe to the association's $300 million capital stock. The plan allowed each regional bank to make emergency loans to member banks, create money when needed to meet a demand upon deposits, and establish foreign branches. Overall policymaking rested almost exclusively with bankers with the federal government having only a minimum role.

During the next two years, Aldrich's "Suggested Plan for Monetary Legislation" became the focal point of the debate over banking reform. The opportunity for immediate action, however, had been lost when the Democrats in the fall of 1910, for the first time since 1894, gained control of the House and deprived Aldrich's Republicans of a working majority in Congress. It was clear that modifications were needed to win over the banking community. To further this effort, to generate congressional support, and to educate the public on the need for reform, supporters organized the National Citizen's League. In March 1911, Aldrich retired from the Senate, but having more time to devote to the cause did not help. The modified plan he inserted in the Monetary Commission's report to Congress ten months later reflected several changes favored by bankers, but it failed to adequately address its primary political shortcoming — that still too much policy control was left with bankers.[5]

While the Aldrich Plan had no realistic chance of becoming law, it did stimulate debate and demonstrated the need for compromise. Rep. Charles A. Lindbergh, R-Minn., spearheaded the opposition, characterizing the plan as "the greatest monstrosity that was ever placed before the [American] people." The plan, Lindbergh reasoned, was a "wonderfully clever" scheme hatched by Wall Street to control the nation's banks. President William Howard Taft promised Aldrich his support, but adverse reaction to the plan tempered the administration's enthusiasm and then the White House became entangled in a controversy over formation of the National City Company, the country's largest bank holding affiliate. The size and scope of the new firm created by New York's National City Bank, the nation's largest bank, aroused concerns that the bank would control the Reserve Association.[6]

Meanwhile, in February 1912, the House authorized its Committee on Banking and Currency to create a special subcommittee to investigate banking and currency conditions in the United States. In response the committee created not one, but two, special subcommittees. The first, headed by committee chairman Arsène P. Pujo, D-La., was mandated to conduct a "fair" and "sane" investigation. The second, chaired by Rep. Carter Glass, D-Va., who was slated to become committee chairman upon Pujo's retirement at the end of the current Congress, was given responsibility for drafting a banking reform bill that addressed the issues raised by the investigation. Subsequently, the powers of the Pujo subcommittee were expanded "to compel testimony from bankers, to investigate a broad range of financial abuses, and to broaden the scope of the investigation to include a determination of the "'concentration of money and credit.'"[7]

For the next several months, the Pujo hearings dominated newspaper headlines with revelations indicating that the concentration of money and credit was increasing and New York banks were "the most active agents in forwarding and bringing about the concentration and control of money and credit in the United States." The "Money Trust" hearings, as they were called, first "eroded the delicate consensus among bankers by driving a wedge between New York and Chicago bankers," and then prompted a revolt among small bankers, farmers, and small businesses. During the 1912 presidential campaign that fall, the Republicans omitted any reference to the Aldrich plan in their party platform, while the Democrats and Theodore Roosevelt's Progressive Party both attacked the plan. As the Pujo hearings unfolded, Representative Carter, together with H. Parker Willis, a former professor of eco-

President Woodrow Wilson proposed a restructuring of the U.S. banking and currency system for greater regulation and flexibility. Despite opposition claiming the reforms would hand control over to Wall Street, the Federal Reserve Act became law.
Source: The Granger Collection, New York.

nomics who served as advisor to the Banking Committee, worked on a new proposal.[8]

After the Democrats gained control of both the House and Senate in November 1912, and their presidential candidate, Woodrow Wilson, captured the White House, the stage was set for enactment of a reform measure. Representative Glass and the Democrats faced the challenge of drafting a proposal that incorporated the basic features of the Aldrich plan while ensuring that New York banks could not control the new system. Initially, Glass and Willis presented President Wilson a plan for a decentralized privately controlled system. Wilson countered with a system based on a "central board with substantial powers to coordinate and control the individual banks."[9]

To gauge support for Wilson's central control board, Glass conducted a series of hearings on banking and currency reform between January 7 and February 17, 1913, that revealed that most major bankers were receptive to the idea. With this support in hand, Glass and Willis drafted a new bill for the president's consideration. Like the National Reserve Association, however, the Glass-Willis Federal Reserve Commission had only token government representation and little chance of being adopted by Congress in the wake of the "Money Trust" investigations.[10]

Finally, following a series of White House conferences between June 11 and June 18, 1913, Democratic leaders developed the Glass-Owen Bill. The new proposal, which was introduced in both the House and the Senate on June 26, shifted supervision, control, and coordination of the central bank in Washington from private bankers to government officials and presidential appointees approved by the Senate. It called for semi-autonomous regional banks operated by private bankers. To supply the elastic currency required by the economy, the central bank would re-discount bank notes and issue a new national currency, Federal Reserve notes. National banks were required to become members of the Federal Reserve System, while state-chartered banks were not. During the congressional debates that followed, Wall Street bankers worked hard to reduce the level of governmental control and increase banker representation on the Federal Reserve Board to no avail.[11]

What Congress crafted in the end was a regional, rather than fully centralized, approach to banking reform. While the bill bore the imprimatur of the Democrats, it closely followed the Aldrich plan in many of its provisions. The Federal Reserve Act (Glass-Owen Act) created twelve Federal Reserve Banks that were to act as central banks for all national banks and other member state financial institutions. The banks were not federal bodies, but private entities owned by the member banks. A Federal Reserve Board was formed to oversee the system and establish policy. Board members were to be appointed by the president, providing a considerable measure of federal direction over the system. Under the act, all federally chartered banks were required to join the Federal Reserve System. "While bankers lost the battle to gain full private control over the Federal Reserve System," the act signed by President Wilson on December 23, 1913, included compromises hammered out in both chambers and in conference that "increased the prospects of monetary policy independence" and were considered to be "acceptable alternatives."[12]

REPRESENTATIVE CHARLES A. LINDBERGH CRITICIZES THE FEDERAL RESERVE ACT

FEBRUARY 27, 1912

Mr. CHAIRMAN AND GENTLEMEN: We are responsible for the banking and currency system. We make the statute laws and the bankers follow the inevitable law of human nature in conducting their business to meet the demands of commerce and trade. They follow the statute laws as far as they are required to and no further, when to follow the law would be an obstruction to business. In all other fields of industry as well, every advantage of circumstances is made use of to strengthen the grasp of each special business. Those in business do that as a result of human nature, and I do not criticize the bankers for doing what others do. But we, as Representatives of all the people, should know human nature and enact laws that will relieve the special kinds of business of the opportunity and therefore of the temptation to take advantage of the public.

Considering the bad laws under which the banks are compelled to operate, they have done much better in facilitating exchange and accommodating the demands of commerce than we might expect. If it were not that special interests had possessed themselves of the great city banks to control the finances for their own purposes we should have had less complaint. But there are fundamental defects in the system and it is up to the people, through Congress, to provide a remedy.

We have gone far wrong and should not expect to correct the errors of the past in one swing of the pendulum. If we were to adopt a correct banking and currency system that would make things adjust to their natural order we would immediately have on our hands a violent panic. We would want to repeal it before we could get it into working order, because the most of us would think the law was the real cause of the panic, whereas, in truth, the cause would arise out of the confusion of adjusting, the same as there is confusion in moving from one house to another. On the other hand, we may modify our present defective system so as to be followed by a boom that will later fasten on us economic evils a thousand times worse than a panic. We are living under the influences of evils resulting from methods of patchwork of such systems now. We are going through what we may term dry-rot, brought on so gradually that few people realize why it is that things are wrong.

If Congress would adopt a system of laws with a view to correcting the present economic evils, to take effect at a practical time in the future, and laws to arrange for the adjustment in the intervening time, so that we should have no confusion in readjustment, there would be such prosperity as the world has not dreamed of so far, because we now have all the instruments of production that, with proper application of our energy, would produce plenty for all. But the trouble is that the changes demanded are so abrupt in their application that the confusion of adjustment — in some cases the anticipation — brings chaos and not enough know the cause to be willing to endure it till order can be restored and real prosperity brought about. We shall have to take notice of actual conditions and be governed in our action by what on all the circumstances seems likely of practical application, but in no way adopt any plan that will fasten on posterity greater evils.

There has been proposed what is commonly termed the Aldrich plan, which it is sought to have adopted by Congress as the future monetary and banking system of the country. There is more of veiled design in that plan than in any measure that I have ever studied.

★ ★ ★ ★

It is admitted on all sides that our banking and currency systems are not at all what they should be, and these people take advantage of that situation in presenting their plan. But mark this: The selfsame people who are presenting the new are mainly, if not wholly, responsible for the old. In other words, the money system is being revised by its friends. If we were dealing with men who had heretofore shown a desire to promote the general welfare, we might be justified in at least assuming that they would continue to do so, but the very parties we are now asked to trust are those who heretofore robbed. I believe, in any event, to make the public safe, whether we deal with alleged friends or rogues.

★ ★ ★ ★

If the country does not arouse to the importance of defeating this Aldrich scheme, it will later arise in wrath and at great expense and sacrifice to remove from themselves the added burdens of its iniquity. Never before were the money kings so bold as they are in this case, to openly ask the people to submit to binding themselves and their posterity to pay this additional toll.

★ ★ ★ ★

The proponents of the Aldrich plan have gone to great lengths and have taken extreme pains to assure the people that Wall Street could not control the National Reserve Association. It has even been tried to make it appear that the National Monetary Commission discriminated against the

banks of New York and other eastern cities. It is a sad admission for a national commission to make that it discriminates. It is because of discrimination in our national legislation and in the application of laws that most of us are now compelled to work two or more days for one day's pay, while the major portion of the results of our productive energies are diverted to the pockets of money kings. Through such discrimination most of us pay more in service or products for money than

---

It is because of discrimination in our national legislation and in the application of laws that most of us are now compelled to work two or more days for one day's pay, while the major portion of the results of our productive energies are diverted to the pockets of money kings. — Charles A. Lindbergh

---

we can buy with it, and the great majority of us, however industrious and frugal we may be, remain poor so long as we do that.

★ ★ ★ ★

It would be interesting to inquire why no powerful citizens' leagues are formed to advocate other important problems than this Aldrich plan. The transportation system is most unjust in its discrimination, but there are no national citizens' leagues to advocate its correction. If it were corrected, it would save the people hundreds of millions. The unjust tariff discrimination is another important problem, but there are no citizens' leagues attending to that. That, too, would, if properly adjusted, save the people vast sums. We have the great labor problems which if properly adjusted would save the wage earners and the people in general billions of dollars, and yet we have no national citizens' leagues formed to correct it. And so I might run through a long list of problems, vastly important to the people, and yet not one, except this Aldrich plan, has been dignified by the formation of national citizens' leagues. Is it because the people are by the Aldrich plan to give billions of dollars to a private monopoly that there are such numerous leagues springing up? Draw your own inference. Certain interests got busy inspiring citizens' leagues. I believe in citizens' leagues, but I would like to see them started voluntarily by the people themselves. I do not believe in a few men getting together and appointing themselves to the offices of a so-called citizens' league and then solicit citizens to join simply to say "amen." What we in Congress want are actual citizens' leagues, inspired from among the citizens themselves.

★ ★ ★ ★

This plan is monstrous. More so than any thing that was ever offered or proposed. It would practically put the people of this Government and the Government itself into a receivership. It would place within the control of a few the means of commercial exchange by the use of which they would control the material merchantable substances of the earth and compel the rest of us to eat out of their hands on such terms as they fixed. I must nevertheless speak of the plan in measured terms, for when I stop to consider how the people have permitted themselves to become slaves of false systems, I realize the possibility of their submitting even to this additional burden.

I appeal to all the people and to the business interests and to bankers who should seek independence to study with care the proposed plan. The subject is so important that it can not be fairly neglected.

★ ★ ★ ★

The trouble with Congress is that Members are looking after some special interest instead of serving the public. As long as that practice prevails we shall have the cost of living high and the pay of wage earners and other producers low.

If Congress would do its duty, the people would be very prosperous whenever and wherever the natural conditions were suitable for prosperity. I can not see that there is anything to boast of in having prosperity for the rich alone. It does seem that a little consideration for the fitness of things would make people object to the Government serving special interests to obtain advantages over the people. It does seem that it would be unfair and beyond the conscience of those whom the public has entrusted to look after the general welfare that such persons should recommend or vote for the Aldrich bill, to incorporate a private corporation and give to it the name of the National Reserve Association, as if it were to serve a national function, when it would be, in fact, a private monopoly, with practically unlimited powers to control the general finances. I can not understand the citizenship and civic mind of a party who would give such power to a private concern, but I do know that the selfish interests are using every subterfuge in an attempt to fool the people.

Source: *Congressional Record,* 62nd Cong., 2nd sess., February 27 (Washington, GPO, 1912), 1912, appendix, 48:55–64.

SENATOR ROBERT L. OWEN SPEAKS IN SUPPORT OF THE FEDERAL RESERVE ACT

NOVEMBER 24, 1913

This bill probably is the most important measure that has been presented to the country since the Civil War. The American banking system has had some very serious defects. The principal defect of our system has been that the country has had no adequate protection against panics, so that from time to time the country has been shaken to its foundations by the severest financial panics, throwing into chaos our commerce, our manufactures, and our industries, from which the recovery in some cases has taken as much as four or five years. This bill is intended to correct the chief defects in our system.

The last great panic which shocked this country was that of 1907, in which, beginning in January with some measure of unrest, interest rates began to go through violent fluctuations, running on the New York Stock Exchange from as low as 11 percent to as high as 45 percent in January, 1907; a like fluctuation in March from 2 to 25 percent; and in October going through such fluctuations so that on the New York Stock Exchange money commanded as high as 125 percent interest, with the most tremendous fluctuations in the price of stocks, and, indeed, in the price of other forms of property which apparently had no relation whatever to the stock exchange, because of the interruption of the credit system of the country.

These extreme disturbances in the interest rates were attended with the most tremendous changes in the selling price of the principal stocks.

★ ★ ★ ★

Because of the tremendous national catastrophe of 1907, which Senator Aldrich estimated to have cost us over two thousand millions of dollars, the entire country demanded some prompt relief. A measure was brought in in Congress by Mr. Aldrich which finally culminated in the legislation known as the Vreeland-Aldrich Act, which undertook to give some measure of temporary relief by the organization of credit associations by which currency to the possible extent of $500,000,000 could be obtained against the combined assets of the associations. While that measure was very defective in numerous particulars, and while it did not at all reach the fundamental defects of our banking system, it at least afforded some measure of protection in abating a panic and in moderating its injurious effects.

★ ★ ★ ★

The Vreeland-Aldrich bill of 1908 took the preliminary steps, however, looking to a thoroughgoing investigation of the banking system of the United States. The National Monetary Commission was authorized to make a searching investigation and inquiry and to make proper report to the Congress of the United States as to suitable remedies. This commission made a careful and searching investigation of the banking systems of the entire civilized world, giving a complete report of the banking systems of the German Empire, of France, of Belgium, of Holland, of England, of the European countries, and also of Japan, Canada, and Mexico, giving a full account of the banking systems of the various States and of the United States.

The report of the National Monetary Commission was published during several years in thirty-three volumes and a vast amount of literature assembled, making a library of between two thousand five hundred and three thousand volumes. This work involved a public expenditure of nearly $300,000. At its conclusion the National Monetary Commission recommended a central bank controlled by the banks of the country, a voluntary association, however, with numerous powers, which I will not here recount. See Senate bill 7, present session.

This measure was presented throughout the country in the various States before numerous gatherings of bankers and business men and credit men. It was urged very strongly by a vigorous propaganda, and finally was approved by the American Bankers' Association.

★ ★ ★ ★

At all events, Mr. President, the people of the United States profoundly objected to the Aldrich plan of a central bank because the plan proposed to put into the hands of private persons the control of the credit system of the United States, which already had been so far concentrated in private hands as to have become a national scandal and a national danger of vast importance.

The bill was condemned by public sentiment, so far that although it was presented to the Senate of the United States, with the party in power supposed to be very friendly to those who were advancing the bill, that measure never received any consideration in the last Congress and has not been seriously advanced in this Congress, although it was introduced into the Senate as Senate bill No. 7.

Mr. President, not only has this matter, therefore, been considered during the last five years, but during the summer before last, beginning in May, 1912, there was a very careful examination made by one branch of the Committee on Banking and Currency of the House of Representatives, under the management of Mr. Pujo, acting as chairman of that subcommittee of the Committee on Banking and Currency of the House of Representatives, into the so-called Money Trust.

★ ★ ★ ★

The Pujo examination verified what was generally well understood, that so far had the concentration of financial and commercial power proceeded in this country that a handful of men exercised practically commercial and financial supremacy over the people of the United States; that they could at their will shake the foundations of the country; that they could at their pleasure cause not only stringency, but, what is far more dangerous, could carry those stringencies of credit to a point of absolute and overwhelming panic that could close the doors of the banks of this country from the Atlantic to the Pacific in a single day.

I shall not pretend to believe for one moment that the panic of 1907 was an accident. It is a long story. I can not at this time go into that story, but I profoundly believe that the result in October, 1907, was a part of a concerted plan by which a few men did two things, first, enriched themselves on the one hand at the expense of the Nation, and administered what they conceived to be a terrifying political rebuke to the administration then in power.

I have always contended that a drastic congressional investigation of this panic should have been made and its promoters and beneficiaries exposed to full public view.

The Pujo investigation did not end this inquiry into our banking system. The chairman of another branch of the Committee on Banking and Currency of the House of Representatives, Mr. GLASS, of Virginia, who is justly entitled to very great credit in preparing and helping to perfect this bill, began the consideration of the question with a view to framing a bill to afford adequate remedy to this country against the exercise of individual unrestrained and irresponsible power over the business men of this country. That committee patiently heard the representatives of the great banking institutions of the country, of the great commercial houses of the country, of financial experts, and their investigations were printed in a volume of over seven hundred printed pages.

Nor was that the end of the investigation. I refer to these investigations because it has been given out to the country in various ways that the Congress of the United States was dealing with this matter with extreme haste, that Congress was rushing through a measure affecting the interests of the country without suitable inquiry or examination. I remind Senators that when the Aldrich bill was proposed to be submitted to the Senate the very men who recently have said "do not be in haste" were at that time urging haste on a proposal which would have concentrated in private hands the control of the credit system of the United States.

But this was not all. In addition to the investigation of the Monetary Commission, the investigation of the Pujo committee, of the Glass committee, numerous hearings were extended to representatives of the American Bankers' Association by those who were charged with the duty of making a preliminary draft for the consideration of their colleagues, and when these hearings had been much extended finally there was a preliminary draft made of this bill.

But before it was ever submitted it was considered by many thoughtful, careful men, various amendments suggested, various amendments made, and finally it was brought into the Committee on Banking and Currency of the House of Representatives and there discussed. It was afterwards discussed in the Democratic conference of Members of the House of Representatives, and then discussed on the floor of the House of Representatives, and finally came to this body on the 18th of September last. But before it came here the members of the Banking and Currency Committee of the Senate had been giving this matter attention, had been studying it, had been considering it, and they began their formal hearings on the 2d of September last. Sixteen days before the bill reached the Senate they began to take evidence upon this question, and finally concluded the taking of evidence on the 25th of October, and submitted it to the Senate in three volumes, including something over three thousand two hundred printed pages of matter. We heard at length the representatives of the banks, the representatives of business interests, of credit associations, of clearing houses, of financial experts, and of interested citizens not claiming to be experts. The committee with great patience and industry, gave a careful consideration to various groups of people, and finally submitted to the Senate as a Senate document these hearings.

So, Mr. President, it is impossible for anyone to contend that the Congress of the United States has not given this matter the most infinite pains and considerate care.

★ ★ ★ ★

PURPOSES OF THE MEASURE

The purposes of this measure are:

First. To insure the stability of our commerce, of our manufacturing enterprises, of our industries, and the safety of our merchants and manufacturers and business men generally.

Second. To make available effective commercial credit for individuals engaged in manufacture, in commerce, in finance, and in business to the extent of their just deserts.

Third. To put an end to the pyramiding of the bank reserves of the country and the use of such reserves for gambling purposes on the stock exchange.

Fourth. To keep constantly employed the productive energies of the Nation. And this consideration is of vital impor-

tance to the laboring men of the country who are dependent for their daily bread upon constant, regular employment. Our crimes, our vices, our chief social evils come from lack of regular remunerative employment.

★ ★ ★ ★

Concentration And Mobilization

Mr. President, we are proposing to concentrate these funds; and there will be concentrated in the hands of these eight regional banks, or reserve banks, approximately $400,000,000 of reserves. We propose a capital of $106,000,000, amounting to 6 percent of the capital and surplus of the national banks of the country, of which we propose that one-half shall be paid in during a period of six months after the system is established, making a total payment of $53,000,000 on capital stock. We propose that the Government funds shall be concentrated in these banks to a certain extent, amounting probably to one hundred and fifty or two hundred million dollars. Then we propose by this system to mobilize these reserves.

★ ★ ★ ★

These elastic Federal reserve notes are the best-secured notes that ever have been devised in any banking system in the world.
— Robert L. Owen

It is unnecessary for me to point out how in the United States this has so far failed that in times of stringency, much more in times of panic, men go trembling, with hat in hand, seeking credit to which they are entitled and which they ought to have merely for the asking upon the class of securities which they can offer.

But we have gone further in proposing this plan of mobilization in the present bill. We have provided for the issuance of elastic currency, by which the Government of the United States places its strong hand behind the banking system of the United States in the support of our commerce and industry. These elastic Federal reserve notes are the best-secured notes that ever have been devised in any banking system in the world.

★ ★ ★ ★

Interest Rate

Another very important feature of the bill is that it places in the hands of the Federal reserve board the power to fix the rate of interest. This power primarily is placed in the hands of the Federal reserve bank directors; but the final determination of the rate is put in the hands of the Federal reserve board, in order to obtain the power which is necessary to protect the country as to the gold reserve by raising the rate where necessary; to protect the country against undue inflation; against undue expansion; against a speculative fever, by raising the rate, and, by forecasting the future, to protect the country in advance against any dangerous improvidence that might be brought about, by whatever cause.

Another very important feature is that allowing the Federal reserve board to fix the interest rate enables a standard to be set by which the business men of the country can hope to ascertain and know reasonably in advance what money will cost them in their enterprises, and, by knowing that they will have a stable rate of interest, to forecast the future with some degree of certainty.

One of the great injuries to this country has been that business men have been deterred from going into enterprises of various kinds because they could not foresee the future. They could not foretell what violent fluctuations of interest rates might occur. They could not tell when some tremendous stringency of credit might take place.

Source: *Congressional Record,* 63rd Cong., 1st sess., November 24, 1913 (Washington: GPO, 1913), 50:5992–5996.

Notes

1. J. Lawrence Broz, *The International Origins of the Federal Reserve System* (Ithaca, N.Y.: Cornell University Press, 1997), 165. See also Milton Friedman and Anna Jacobson Schwartz, *A Monetary History of the United States, 1867–1960* (Princeton, N.J.: Princeton University Press, 1963), 156–168.

2. Quotes are found in Broz, *The International Origins of the Federal Reserve System*, 173. See also 35 Stat. 552.

3. Quote is found in A. Piatt Andrew, "Problem Before the National Monetary Commission," *Annals of the American Academy of Political and Social Science* 36(November 1910):5. See also Broz, *The International Origins of the Federal Reserve System*, 174; N. A. Weston, "Studies of the Monetary Commission," *Annals of the*

American Academy of Political and Social Science 49 (January 1922):17–27.

4. Nathaniel Wright Stephenson, *Nelson W. Aldrich: A Leader in American Politics* (New York: Charles Scribner's Sons, 1930), 373–379; Richard T. McCulley, *Banks and Politics During the Progressive Era: The Origins of the Federal Reserve System, 1897–1913* (New York: Garland, 1992), 222–224.

5. Broz, *The International Origins of the Federal Reserve System*, 176–190; McCulley, *Banks and Politics During the Progressive Era*, 224–247, 256; U.S. Congress, Senate, *Suggested Plan for Monetary Legislation Submitted to the National Monetary Commission by Hon. Nelson W. Aldrich*, 61st Cong., 3rd sess., S. Doc. 784 (Washington: GPO, 1911). For a copy of the commission's report, see U.S. Congress, House, *Report of the Committee Appointed Pursuant to House Resolutions 429 and 504 to Investigate the Concentration of Control of Money and Credit*, 62nd Cong., 3rd sess., H. Rept. 1593 (Washington: GPO, 1913).

6. Quotes are found in U.S. Congress, House Committee on Rules, *House Resolution No. 314*, hearings, 62nd Cong., 2nd sess., December 15, 1911 (Washington: GPO, 1911), 42; *Congressional Record*, 62nd Cong., 2nd sess., February 24, 1912, 48: 2408; and *Congressional Record*, 62nd Cong., 1st sess., June 13, 1911, 47: 1992. See also McCulley, *Banks and Politics During the Progressive Era*, 257–259.

7. *Congressional Record*, 62nd Cong., 2nd sess., February 24, 1912, 48:2382–2419; April 25, 1912, 48:5336–5346; McCulley, *Banks and Politics During the Progressive Era*, 263–264.

8. Quote is found in Broz, *The International Origins of the Federal Reserve System*, 192; McCulley, *Banks and Politics During the Progressive Era*, 279. See also McCulley, *Banks and Politics During the Progressive Era*, 266–280; U.S. Congress, House Subcommittee of the Committee on Banking and Currency, *Money Trust Investigations*, 3 vols., hearings, 62nd Cong., 2nd and 3rd sess. (Washington: GPO, 1913).

9. Broz, *The International Origins of the Federal Reserve System*, 196.

10. Ibid., 196–197; McCulley, *Banks and Politics During the Progressive Era*, 293–297.

11. Broz, *The International Origins of the Federal Reserve System*, 197–200; McCulley, *Banks and Politics During the Progressive Era*, 297–301.

12. Broz, *The International Origins of the Federal Reserve System*, 200.

Eighteenth Amendment

✳ 1917 ✳

For nearly fourteen years, from January 20, 1920, when the Eighteenth Amendment went into effect, until it was repealed by the Twenty-first Amendment on December 5, 1933, breweries, distillers, and saloons in the United States were forced to close their doors. It is the only successful attempt to place a limit on individual liberty in the Constitution, the sole instance where a constitutional provision was designed "to use the power of law to improve the national character by regulating individual conduct," and the only constitutional amendment to be repealed. Prohibition had a devastating effect on all commercial enterprises associated with the manufacture and sale of liquor, which represented the seventh largest industry in the United States constitutionally speaking, the Eighteenth Amendment was incredibly significant. "Like the Thirteenth Amendment, the Eighteenth altered private property rights, ended a vast and profitable business activity, and fundamentally transformed American society."[1]

Congress's willingness to embark on what President Herbert Hoover characterized as "a great social and economic experiment, noble in motive and far-reaching in purpose," climaxed a century-long effort by religious, moral, political, and medical activists to stamp out the evils they associated with alcoholic beverages. Scattered efforts of action against distilled spirits date to the American colonial period, and in the 1850s, Maine and twelve other states passed mostly short-lived prohibition laws. Subsequently, in 1869, three years after the Prohibition Party was founded, it used its party's platform to signal the birth of the movement for a constitutional amendment establishing prohibition as a national policy. The first congressional proposal followed in 1876. The 1870s and 1890s saw local or state dry politicians take over and enforce a statewide prohibition on alcohol, but they remained in a minority until the late nineteenth century.[2]

Far more influential were the Anti-Saloon League (ASL), and to a lesser extent, the Women's Christian Temperance Union (WCTU). Within thirty years of its 1873 inception, the WCTU had become the nation's largest women's organization in the country. The WCTU worked tirelessly to publicize the evils of alcohol and its connection with family violence, unemployment, poverty, and disease until the ASL joined the temperance movement. Together, the two organizations began to press for a specific legislative solution. By 1900, the ASL, which began eight years earlier as a loose federation of Ohio Protestant churches, had become a national association with "a powerful network of temperance activists connected to the influential voices and votes of American Protestants." The ASL's success stemmed from its use of three tactics: (1) attacking the "liquor industry rather than individual drinkers," (2) avoiding the support of individual officeholders or candidates rather than political parties, and (3) working "incrementally for realistic gains." Initially, it focused on local referenda banning alcohol sales, and then in 1907 aligned with the WCTU "to achieve statewide prohibition by statute or constitutional amendment."[3]

While initially both organizations focused a majority of their efforts at the local and state level, they also in the 1890s established legislative offices in Washington. A significant turning point in their lobbying efforts came in 1913, when Congress resoundingly overrode President William Howard Taft's veto of the Webb-Kenyon Act prohibiting the interstate shipment of alcohol into states barring its production or sale. Webb-Kenyon's passage opened the door for the ASL and others to pursue Prohibition by amendment to the U.S. Constitution. They began cautiously recognizing that "[m]illions of Americans, especially those tied to the European cultural traditions, enjoyed alcoholic beverages and deeply resented any attempts to criminalize their social customs."[4]

Looking ahead, however, the ASL reasoned it needed to act soon. During the previous two decades, the country had added twelve western states, nearly all of them dry and progressive. While the 1910 congressional reapportionment increased the strength of rural districts, most of which favored prohibition, it was estimated that the 1920 reapportionment would incorporate close to six million new immigrants and strengthen House wet representation by over three dozen seats. Wet representation in the Senate would also benefit. The drys strategized that a quick move to enact a prohibition amendment would, once ratified, safeguard it from any further congressional interference. The speed with which the drys moved on the amendment left the wets unprepared.[5]

With America's entry into World War I on April 6, 1917, supporting the troops overseas required sacrifices at home that

Supporters of Prohibition believed that alcohol played a significant role in the day's social problems, including violence, unemployment, and disease. At the outbreak of World War I, debate on the issue became limited and the Eighteenth Amendment passed, despite numerous objections.

Source: Library of Congress.

included restrictions on the use of grain and sugar so they could be used by the Army and U.S. allies. Prohibiting the manufacturing and consumption of liquor now became a patriotic as well as a moral issue. Also, prohibitionists probably benefited from beer being associated with war foe Germany. These realities and sentiments, coupled with a fear of the power of the Anti-Saloon League, prompted many in Congress to vote for the Eighteenth Amendment. At the time, one journalist even contended that numerous members of Congress were more fearful of the League than they were the president.[6]

That fear clearly contributed to the absence of extensive congressional consideration in 1916 and 1917 of the issue's merits. Prohibitionists "discovered that the war power was a handy tool to use against their enemies. The emergency surrounding the war mobilization precluded long debate on the prohibition amendment." No hearings were held on the question and little time was set aside for discussion. Those exchanges that did take place "pitted supporters of national morality against defenders of individual liberty." Opponents portrayed the amendment as "an improper interference with states' rights," an unjust destruction of legitimate businesses, an inappropriate national regulation of personal behavior, and undemocratic since it "could be ratified by thirty-six states with an aggregate population nine million fewer than that of the remaining twelve states." Supporters countered with the evils of alcohol and saloons, a study showing how much grain prohibition would save, and an argument that

"they were only using the constitutional procedures made available to them by the Founding Fathers."[7]

Initial Senate approval of the amendment on August 1, 1917, was by a 65–20 vote (76 percent). The House vote on December 17, 1917, while closer, 282–128 (69 percent), still exceeded the requisite two-thirds needed by nine votes (273 votes needed). The following day, with no debate, the Senate concurred 47–8 with House modifications granting Congress concurrent power to enforce the amendment, and extending the ratification period from six to seven years.[8] The Eighteenth Amendment was declared ratified on January 16, 1919, and became effective one year later.

Three months prior to the amendment's January 16, 1920, effective date, Congress overrode President Woodrow Wilson's veto of the Volstead Act, which placed responsibility for enforcement of the Eighteenth Amendment with the Internal Revenue Bureau; defined intoxicating beverages as those containing more than 0.5 percent alcohol; and specified penalties for the manufacturing, transportation, sale, and possession of liquor. Subsequently, efforts by beer makers and distributors, personal liberty leagues, and constitutional scholars to have the amendment and Volstead Act declared unconstitutional were unsuccessful. Over time, the more powerful opposition proved to be the American people. Ultimately, widespread bootlegging, graft, corruption, disregard for the law, and popular opposition prompted the amendment's repeal.[9]

A number of very different factors gave impetus to the prohibition movement as it moved across the American landscape. Prohibition was an important facet of the cultural wars that the United States experienced as record numbers of immigrants flocked to the country in the late nineteenth and early twentieth centuries. It intensified as the country grappled with the rapid growth of cities, expansion of industry, anxieties over national identity, and increased patriotism accompanying the country's entry into World War I. At the time, many Americans were fearful that their political and social institutions were not up to the challenge. They were also alarmed by the power wielded by big business and monopolies, appalled by political corruption, and concerned about environmental as well as health concerns being raised by doctors and social workers. Prohibitionists saw the production, transportation, sale, and consumption of liquor as the embodiment of all that was wrong with America, and they believed that their movement solved all of the nation's economic, political, and moral problems. The repeal of prohibition, as historian Thomas R. Pegram aptly reminds us, "became a reminder of the perils of moral regulation that has chastened Congress ever since."[10]

SENATOR WILLIAM S. KENYON SUPPORTS THE EIGHTEENTH AMENDMENT

AUGUST 1, 1917

Mr. KENYON. Mr. President, I want to take ten minutes to express a view or two on the pending subject; and in view of the fact that a bill at present in conference seeks to stop the manufacture of whisky as a food-conservation proposition, but not to stop the manufacture of beer. I desire to submit just an observation or two on that and other propositions in general relating to the subject. That part of my remarks will consist of questions which some proponents of the liquor traffic may perhaps answer in the further progress of this debate.

Why do we prohibit the boys in the Army and Navy from having booze and insist that those who remain at home shall have it?

If liquor is a bad thing for the boys in the trenches, why is it a good thing for those at home?

When they are willing to die for us, should we not be willing to go dry for them?

Will a sober nation not win the war quicker than a drunken nation?

When the food controller asks everyone in the country to conserve the food supply, why must the food supply going into beer be excepted?

Is it not as much waste of foodstuff to put it into beer as to put it into whisky? If more foodstuff goes into beer than into whisky, why do we prevent foodstuff going into whisky and permit it going into beer?

Will rebellions come in the cities, as we have been told, if the workers do not have their beer?

Sixty per cent of the Nation, territorially, is dry. Are the feelings of people living in that territory entitled to any consideration?

If the beer drinkers are going to rebel unless they get their beer, will the temperance people rebel unless they get temperance?

Does the rule only work one way?

Why do not the temperance people claim that they will rebel also? No one has heard any such thing from them, nor will anybody hear such thing.

The temperance people will be for the Nation no matter if beer and whisky be forced on them. Their patriotism does not depend on having their own way.

Is patriotism purchased by beer worth while anyway?

If some one were taking as much foodstuff as goes into booze and dumping it into the sea, what would the people of the Nation say?

If some one should advance the argument that this was necessary in order to appease certain people who believed in dumping foodstuffs into the sea, and that if they did not do it would arouse riots, would we accede to their request?

★ ★ ★ ★

Is it reasonable to ask the temperance people of the country to conserve and save every particle of food and at the same time permit some of it to go into booze?

Is beer more essential to the American people than bread?

What kind of people are they in this country who are not willing to give up their liquor to help their country?

Is the food conservation to be for the benefit of the many or is it to be limited in order that the few may have their drinks?

Have we reached a point in this country where the war can not be won unless people who drink are permitted to tickle their stomachs with wines and beer?

Will beer patriots win the war anyhow?

Are the interests of brewers in this country more important than the winning of the war?

Are we willing to sacrifice everything in the country to win the war, except beer?

If the temperance forces in the Senate were responsible for delaying the food bill as charged by certain liquor-interest papers, why is it that the food bill has been delayed for three weeks after the temperance sections of the bill were settled?

With the great demand for labor in this country and the high wages, could there ever be a better time, as far as the laboring men are concerned, for the transition from a wet to a dry Nation?

When there is a shortage of labor in the important and necessary work to carry on the war, why waste labor in making booze?

If booze is essential to win the war, why stop selling it to the soldiers?

Mr. President, I have listened to the argument as to State rights; but I have discovered that the doctrine of State rights absolutely vanishes in Congress whenever an appropriation is attached to a bill.

The advance in this country of the temperance cause has been due to the fight against the American saloon. That is what has been at the bottom of it. That has brought us to the issue of national prohibition.

THE FINAL VOTE

The Eighteenth Amendment (Prohibition)
December 18, 1917

Senate
August 1, 1917

	Yea	Nay
Republicans	27	8
Democrats	38	12
Total	**65**	**20**

House
December 17, 1917

	Yea	Nay
Republicans	139	59
Democrats	140	67
Socialists	0	1
Independents	2	0
Prohibitionists	1	1
Total	**282**	**128**

Source: Albert Castel and Scott L. Gibson, *The Yeas and the Nays: Key Congressional Decisions, 1774–1945* (Kalamazoo: New Issues Press, Institute of Public Affairs, Western Michigan University, 1975), 139–140.

more manhood, and sent more people to an early grave than any other influence in our land.

Its day has come. No subterfuge can long save it. It will be dragged into the open, the influences behind it stripped of their masks. A mighty public conscience is aroused, moving on rapidly, confidently, undismayed, and undeceived. Behind it are the churches of the Nation — Protestant and Catholic — schools, colleges, and homes. This public conscience is not discouraged by defeat or deceived by any cunning devices, by any shams or pretenses. Its cause is the cause of humanity, of righteousness, and God, Almighty fights with it.

It has no desire to injure the saloon keeper. It would help him, but it asks no quarter of the saloon and it proposes to give none. The forces fighting the saloon are not composed of mollycoddies. The most far-seeing business minds of the country are in the ranks.

Men will have to take their places in this fight. They can not sit on the fence. This fight is no place for the political coward to stand between the lines. He will be shot from both directions.

No denunciation, no slurs, no jests on the floor of the Senate, no hurling of epithet, no cheap ribaldry in the cloakrooms will stop this fight. It is going on in Congress, and it is

---

No denunciation, no slurs, no jests on the floor of the Senate ... will stop this fight. It is going on in Congress, and it is going on in the Nation until the tear-producing, orphan-making, home-wrecking, manhood-debauching, character-destroying, hell-filling saloon business is banished from this country. — William S. Kenyon

---

This amendment is to give to the States the right to speak their desire on this question. Why should they not have such right? The American people are tired of saloons.

No one rises on this floor or elsewhere to defend the American saloon directly.

The American saloon has no conscience. It never did a good act or failed to do a bad one.

It is a trap for youth; a destroyer for the old; a foul spawning place for crime; a corrupter of politics; knows no party; supports those men for office whom it thinks can be easiest influenced; has no respect for law or the courts; debauches city councils, juries, and everyone it can reach; is powerful in the unity of its vote, and creates cowards in office.

It flatters, tricks, cajoles, and deceives in order to accomplish its purpose; it is responsible for more ruin and death than all the wars the Nation has ever engaged in; has corrupted more politics, ruined more lives, widowed more women, orphaned more children, destroyed more homes, caused more tears to flow, broken more hearts, undermined

going on in the Nation until the tear-producing, orphan-making, home-wrecking, manhood-debauching, character-destroying, hell-filling saloon business is banished from this country. The American saloon is just as certainly doomed as slavery is doomed.

A saloonless Nation means an efficient Nation, better able to cope with any problem threatening it from without or within.

Source: *Congressional Record*, 65th Cong., 1st sess., August 1, 1917 (Washington: GPO, 1917), 55:5639–5640.

SENATOR JOHN W. WEEKS OPPOSES THE EIGHTEENTH AMENDMENT

AUGUST 1, 1917

Mr. President, it is my purpose to vote against the submission of this proposition to the States; and having but a limited time in which to discuss the proposition, I want to give the reasons, so far as I can within that time, for my action.

The pending question is one which should be considered by Congress solely on its merits and not on the assumption that it has reached a state of agitation and resulting favor which justifies its being submitted to the States without any reference to the individual opinions of Senators as to the advisability of such action. When a referendum is submitted in a State the people of that State have an opportunity to decide what action they wish to take; and, while I think that in many cases they decide public questions without the knowledge and information they should have before passing on proposed laws, yet it is their own fault if they do not decide the question wisely. This case is entirely different, and it should not be misunderstood by Senators, many of whom seem to have the impression that in passing along this important question to the States they are performing their full duty.

It is true that the advocates of national prohibition — very largely those connected with the Anti-Saloon League — are urging this matter and doing so with the argument that they are not asking any Member of Congress to declare that he is in favor of national prohibition, but simply that he shall not "become an avowed exponent and protector of the liquor traffic by refusing to vote to allow the people of the Nation, by States, through their Representatives, to determine this question."

★ ★ ★ ★

I am now, and always have been, a believer in local option, and firmly believe that this is a question which should be decided by the people of the several States in accordance with their own wishes. The police powers are inherent in the States, and the question of controlling the sale of spirits largely comes within that constitutional provision.

Formerly there was some logic in the position taken by many that if liquor were sold in any States it could be shipped into other States against the wishes of the people of the States that had adopted prohibition. That condition has been cured by the Webb-Kenyon bill, for which I voted, which prohibits the shipment of liquor into dry territory; and the act making this prohibitive has been declared constitutional by the Supreme Court, so there is no possibility of such complaint if the officers of the States are attending to their duties. Moreover, in order to prevent or discourage the purchase of liquor in dry territory, a bill passed Congress last winter prohibiting the carrying by mail of newspapers into dry territory if they contained liquor advertisements. I voted for that bill, and I shall vote for any other legislation to protect the desires of those living in territory which has become dry.

One of the serious weaknesses of this proposed measure is that it may be brought before the legislatures of the several States as many times as its proponents desire, or until the legislatures of three-fourths of the States are found favorable to the proposition. If it were submitted at one time, it might be found that the legislatures of twenty-five or thirty States would be favorable to it and the legislatures of the other States unfavorable; but it can be brought up again and again in the States which have not adopted the provision until a legislature may be found, years hence, favorable to it. By that time, there might be legislatures in some of the States which had adopted the amendment unfavorable to it, but they could not retrace their steps. That makes the whole question a constant irritant in connection with our elections, distracting attention from the issues which divide political parties, and very largely breaking down the party spirit and action which I believe essential to the best interests of the Republic.

No law can be enforced unless it accords with public sentiment; in fact, when a law does not conform to public sentiment, ordinarily, there is no attempt to enforce it.

★ ★ ★ ★

I do not wish to unnecessarily emphasize the financial phase of this question, for if all the people of the country could decide that they prefer to raise the revenue incident to this business in some other way I should not care to advance that argument in any form, but, as a matter of fact, it has been a large factor in our national revenues, and when we return to normal times we shall find some difficulty and a good deal of opposition to substituting other sources of revenue for it. Neither can the revenue question be entirely confined to national receipts; they are important in a local way. All large cities, which vote more or less frequently on this subject and vote for the maintenance of a license system, obtain from this source a very considerable revenue, which will be taken from them against their will if this proposition prevails. Then, again, there is no attempt made by the proponents of this legislation to make provision for any compensation on account of the destruction of a business which has continued to exist during the entire life of the Republic by national license. I am opposed to confiscation of property in any form at any time, whether or not I entirely approve of the individuals engaged in this business or the character of the business conducted. When we propose confiscation we are inaugurating a policy which is likely to be most far-reaching in its effect. Some one may conclude that some other form of business is not entirely for the public interest, and the fact that we have established a confiscation precedent may result in its being extended to other fields.

Finally, it seems to me that the individual has rights which should be protected. The vast majority of those who indulge in stimulants, in these days especially, do so to a very moderate degree. I am not satisfied that the multitudinous statistics which are given out about the harm coming from wines and light beers are well founded.

★ ★ ★ ★

There are innumerable things in which we indulge which are undoubtedly more or less harmful to individuals, and I think that statement would be equally true in its application to food consumed in unreasonable quantities and at unreasonable times.

There are innumerable things in which we indulge which are undoubtedly more or less harmful to individuals, and I think that statement would be equally true in its application to food consumed in unreasonable quantities and at unreasonable times.

— John W. Weeks

When the rights of individuals who are temperate are taken from them, not by those living within the same political division or even by the same number of people in some other political section, it seems to me that the action is illogical, unfair, and from every standpoint undesirable. I firmly believe that the world is advancing satisfactorily in its relation to this question; that the good old times are a myth, as far as it is concerned; that the modern business man or professional man will not tolerate in an associate or employee a failure to observe proper temperance rules; and anyone who observes the social practices of to-day and compares them with those of twenty-five years ago must readily admit that gradually we are coming to a real temperance in the use of all forms of stimulants, and a temperance which not only satisfies the individual but does no real injustice to the community. Pro-

gressing as we are in this respect, it seems to me particularly unfortunate that what many will consider an unreasonable course is likely to be taken by the National Government. They will resent it, and properly so, in my opinion. I honestly believe that this ill-advised attempt, if it succeeds, will be harmful rather than beneficial to real temperance. I hope not, as far as I am concerned, because I shall be glad to see moderation in the use of stimulants as in all other matters, but I am fearful that the result will be unsatisfactory even to those who are most urgent in pressing this proposition.

Source: *Congressional Record,* 65th Cong., 1st sess., August 1, 1917, 55:5643–5645.

Notes

1. Quotes are found in Richard B. Bernstein, "Eighteenth Amendment," in *Constitutional Amendments: 1789 to the Present,* ed. Kris E. Palmer (Detroit: Gale, 2000), 420; David E. Kyvig, *Explicit and Authentic Acts: Amending the U.S. Constitution, 1776–1995* (Lawrence: University Press of Kansas, 1996), 226.

2. U.S. President, Herbert Hoover, *Public Papers of the Presidents of the United States: Herbert Hoover, 1929* (Washington: GPO, 1974), 511. See also Thomas R. Pegram, "Prohibition," in *The American Congress: The Building of Democracy* ed. Julian E. Zelizer (Boston: Houghton Mifflin, 2004), 414; Bernstein, "Eighteenth Amendment," 423.

3. Pegram, "Prohibition," 414–415.

4. Ibid., 419–420.

5. Ibid., 421. See also Bernstein, "Eighteenth Amendment," 424.

6. Alan P. Grimes, *Democracy and the Amendments to the Constitution* (Lexington, Mass.: Lexington Books, 1978), 85; Albert Castel and Scott L. Gibson, *The Yeas and the Nays: Key Congressional Decisions, 1774–1945* (Kalamazoo: New Issues Press, Institute of Public Affairs, Western Michigan University, 1975), 140; Thomas R. Pegram, *Battling Demon Rum: The Struggle for a Dry America, 1800–1933* (Chicago: Ivan R. Dee, 1998), 147.

7. Richard F. Hamm, *Shaping the Eighteenth Amendment: Temperance Reform, Legal Culture, and the Polity, 1880–1920* (Chapel Hill: University of North Carolina Press, 1995), 240–241; Bernstein, "Eighteenth Amendment," 425; Grimes, *Democracy and the Amendments to the Constitution,* 85–86.

8. *Congressional Record,* 65th Cong., 1st sess., August 1, 1917, 55:5636–5666; and *Congressional Record,* 65th Cong., 2nd sess., December 17, 1917, 56:422–470; December 18, 1917, 56:477–478. Those fearful that the seven-year time limitation ultimately agreed upon would prove a handicap had no need to worry as ratification was completed on January 16, 1919, thirteen months after the amendment was submitted to the states.

9. Bernstein, "Eighteenth Amendment," 426–427. See also 41 Stat. 305–323.

10. Pegram, "Prohibition," 414.

Nineteenth Amendment (Women's Suffrage)

✳ 1919 ✳

For more than half of the United States' history, women were not allowed to vote. Only with the ratification of the Nineteenth Amendment in 1920 was that right guaranteed. While the Constitution as originally drafted did not preclude women from voting, it was implied by American society. Voting requirements were left to the states, and only a very small number offered women suffrage. Also, legal and social customs kept most women from having money or property, marital rights, or the right to speak at public gatherings. Not until July 1848, after Lucretia Mott and Elizabeth Cady Stanton organized the first women's rights convention in Seneca Falls, New York, was the movement begun that sought to address these inequities. The attendees approved a Declaration of Sentiments and resolutions that addressed inequality in suffrage, laws, human rights, marriage, divorce, legal matters, employment, involvement in religious gatherings and public meetings, personal freedom, punishment for transgressions, and promoting righteous causes. Only the suffrage resolution, which had difficulty obtaining a majority, failed to pass unanimously. [1]

During the next two decades, women's suffrage slowly won acceptance thanks to the tireless efforts of Mott, Stanton, Susan B. Anthony, and other early leaders of the movement, and the significant contributions of women in the Civil War. After the war, suffragists and former abolitionists joined to organize the American Equal Rights Association (AERA). Under Mott's leadership, the AERA worked for the suffrage of women as well as African Americans. Many women were disappointed when the Fourteenth and Fifteenth Amendments pointedly failed to address woman suffrage. Stanton and Anthony became so outraged over the omission that they were eventually expelled by the AERA for their harsh comments. Soon afterwards, the two women formed the National Woman Suffrage Association (NWSA) as they continued their quest to secure a woman suffrage amendment. Not long after the NWSA's creation, a third association, the American Woman Suffrage Association (AWSA), was formed under the leadership of Lucy Stone. This group also endorsed a federal constitutional amendment, but focused mainly on state suffrage amendments. [2]

In 1878, Sen. Aaron A. Sargent, R-Calif., a close friend of Susan B. Anthony, was persuaded to introduce the woman suffrage amendment that incorporated the same language as Congress would approve four decades later. The Senate Committee on Privileges and Elections held hearings on the measure before issuing an adverse report. The "Susan B. Anthony Amendment," as it came to be known, was reintroduced each session of Congress for the next eighteen years and was the subject of hearings several of those years. In 1882, both the House and Senate created Select Committee on Woman Suffrage that favorably reported the measure, but no further action was taken. The measure was also favorably reported by the Senate committee the next two Congresses and debated by the full Senate in December 1886 and January 1887, before being rejected, 34–16. [3]

After it had become increasingly apparent that both the NWSA and AWSA were steadily diminishing in importance, the two groups in 1890 put aside their differences and formed a new organization, the National American Woman Suffrage Association (NAWSA). The NAWSA's primary objective was state-by-state suffrage with a federal constitutional amendment as a secondary goal. At the turn of the century, however, its efforts had produced limited success with only four states granting full-woman suffrage and a few others permitting limited suffrage. In Washington, the Susan B. Anthony Amendment continued to be introduced each year but was never favorably reported by a congressional committee. [4]

Congressional opposition persisted for several reasons. Southern disenfranchisement of black males persisted through poll taxes and other restrictions despite the ratification of the Fourteenth and Fifteenth Amendment, and there was equal resistance to enfranchising black females. The Susan B. Anthony Amendment threatened those who wanted the issue of racial discrimination in politics reopened as well as Westerners who were concerned about enfranchising women of all races. Then there were those who were uneasy about thousands of immigrant women from Southern Europe, who knew little about America, having the right to vote. In the East, different social conditions aroused fear among politicians and the business community that giving women the right to vote would lead to all sorts of unwanted political and legal reforms. Among the most ardent opposition came from the conviction of the liquor industry that

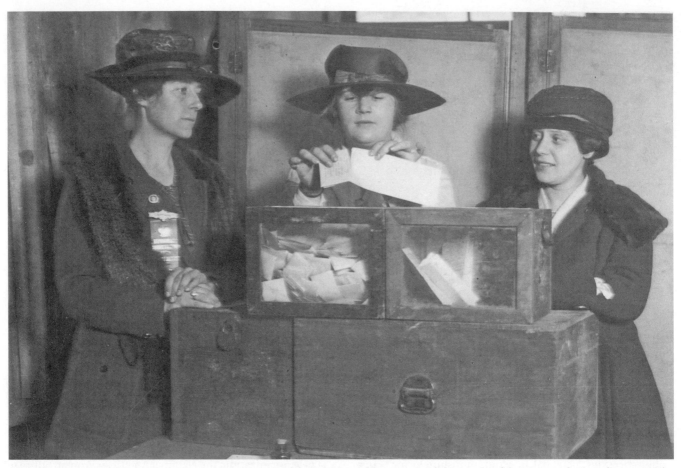

Suffragists casting votes in New York City in 1917 were part of the movement that encouraged the passage of the Nineteenth Amendment. Legislation giving women the right to vote was ignored or voted down for at least a decade in Congress before the Nineteenth Amendment was eventually ratified.

Source: Library of Congress.

women, if given suffrage rights, would side with the temperance movement and harm their business.[5]

Still, the NAWSA persevered, growing from thirteen thousand in 1893, to two million in 1917. Amidst this growth, the association in 1908 began a drive to obtain one million signatures on a petition calling on President Theodore Roosevelt to use his State of the Union Message to endorse women's suffrage. Although Roosevelt said that such a petition would not influence him, the NAWSA persisted and collected four hundred thousand signatures in two years. By default, Roosevelt became a supporter in 1912, when as the presidential candidate of the newly formed Progressive Party, he ran on a platform containing a plank favoring woman suffrage. The Progressives did not win the White House that fall, but the election proved to be a turning point in the movement as four new states approved woman suffrage. Women now enjoyed full suffrage in nine states and the right to vote on such issues as schools, taxes, and bond referendums in twenty-nine others. In 1913, Illinois became the first state to approve presi-

dential suffrage, and suffragists Alice Paul and Lucy Burns formed the Congressional Union, an auxiliary of the NAWSA, to persuade Congress to pass a suffrage amendment.[6]

Soon afterwards, the Congressional Union split with the NAWSA and began a strenuous campaign to hold the Democrats responsible for failing to pass a suffrage bill. In March 1914, largely because of the efforts of the NAWSA, the Anthony amendment was brought to a vote in the Senate but failed to earn the required two-thirds majority by a wide margin, 34–35. The following January, the House also rejected the measure, 204–174. Although suffragists could not yet claim a legislative victory, the Congressional Union in the fall of 1914 was able to use its organizational power to unseat twenty-three out of forty-three Western Democrats. Subsequently, in 1916, the NAWSA, using a two-million-dollar bequest and a winning plan devised by Carrie Chapman Catt for building support in the thirty-six states likely to approve a federal amendment, refocused on that goal. Catt also worked very hard to secure President Woodrow Wilson's support and he eventually agreed to speak at the NAWSA convention that September, but he stopped short of endorsing woman suffrage.[7]

Early in January 1917, the National Woman's Party (which had united with the Congressional Union Party) began picketing the White House to call attention to what it saw as Wilson's hypocritical message on democracy and women's suffrage. Police arrested more than two hundred of the picketers, ninety-seven of whom later were convicted and sent to jail when the protests grew larger and louder. The D.C. Court of Appeals subsequently invalidated the arrests and sentences, but the dramatic militancy of the Woman's Party served to make the NAWSA, which had distanced itself from the picketers, appear much more moderate and acceptable to mainstream politicians. Six states responded by altering their laws to permit women to vote in presidential elections, and a seventh approved a constitutional amendment enfranchising women in all elections. By this point, Rep. Jeannette Rankin, R-Mont., the first woman elected to Congress, had taken her seat, and the United States had entered World War I. As America mobilized, perceptions changed as women in unprecedented numbers joined the rapidly depleting industrial and public service workforce. Their important role in the war effort gained national attention. Although many suffragists were antiwar and the Woman's Party made no formal effort to support the war, the NAWSA lent significant assistance to the cause.[8]

On January 9, 1918, President Wilson finally issued a statement declaring his support for the Anthony Amendment. The following day, after two months of debate, the House reversed its stance of three years earlier and approved the amendment by one vote more than the required two-thirds majority 274–136. The dramatic shift in support for women's suffrage in the House can be attributed to two factors not present earlier — the significant role of women in the war effort, and the passage of the Eighteenth Amendment the previous December, which eliminated the fear that woman suffrage would bring on prohibition.[9]

Shifts in public opinion were less of a concern to senators. They faced reelection far less often and had little or no experience facing voters since the adoption of the Seventeenth Amendment only four years earlier provided for their popular election. Also in the Senate, where seats were allotted by state rather than population, Southern opposition was much stronger. Southern Senators felt passage of the suffrage amendment would make it more difficult for their region to continue barring African Americans from voting. The day before the Senate was to vote, President Wilson on September 30 made a surprise and unprecedented appearance in the Senate chamber to urge passage of the amendment. Wilson's eloquent speech had little effect on the opponents of the amendment as the Senate voted 53–31, three votes short of the required two-thirds. It would be another year-and-a-half

before the Senate, where antisuffrage Southern Democrats were proportionally stronger, approved the amendment. During the interim, the NAWSA responded by making good on its earlier promise to work to defeat certain incumbent senators who had voted against suffrage, including two long-term leaders. Following the election, a Senate vote by a "lame duck" session of the Sixty-fifth Congress came up one vote short[10]

By May 1919, when the Sixty-sixth Congress convened, thirty-nine states had granted women the right to vote in at least some elections, and President Wilson reiterated his recommendation that Congress act on the woman suffrage amendment. On May 21, the House quickly agreed, this time 304–90. Although the House vote was not close, the following excerpts from the debate show a clear flavor for the range of emotions that prevailed. After debating the measure on June 3 and 4, the Senate passed the amendment 56–25, with two votes to spare. Most speeches were offered by the opposition who, like those in the House, focused on states' rights themes, enfranchisement of African American women, and the fear that women voters would support social reform legislation. By mid-June 1920, thirty-five of the thirty-six states needed for ratification had voiced their approval, and attention shifted to Tennessee, where President Wilson had persuaded the governor to call a special legislative session. The Tennessee Senate added its support on August 13, and five days later the Tennessee House concurred. Before the results

THE FINAL VOTE

The Nineteenth Amendment (Women's Suffrage)

House
May 21, 1919

	Yea	Nay
Republicans	200	22
Democrats	102	68
Independents	1	0
Prohibitionists	1	0
Total	**304**	**90**

Senate
June 4, 1919

	Yea	Nay
Republicans	41	8
Democrats	15	17
Total	**56**	**25**

Source: Congressional Record, 66th Cong., 1st sess., May 21, 1919, June 4, 1919 (Washington: GPO, 1919), 58:93–94, 635.

could be forwarded to Washington, however, an injunction was granted on August 21 prohibiting the governor from certifying the state's ratification. Two days later, the Tennessee Supreme Court overturned the injunction and the governor certified the results. On the morning of August 26, 1920, Secretary of State Bainbridge Colby declared that the amendment had been ratified by the requisite number of states and was part of the Constitution. Subsequently, antisuffragist members of the state legislature succeeded in expunging the House vote, but Secretary of State Colby was unpersuaded by the arguments that Tennessee's ratification was unconstitutional. A month later, Connecticut became the thirty seventh state to ratify the amendment.[11]

While some politicians found women's suffrage appealing because it would correct a long-term injustice, social reformers saw it as a way to win the support of potential voters, even though that expectation aroused opposition to the movement. Adoption of the Nineteenth Amendment generated much activity in Congress between 1920 and 1925. Laws concerning women with disabilities, mother and infant health, and equal pay were among the issues subject to legislation. By 1925, however, Congress could feel relief that women were not, as had been feared, voting as a block or otherwise changing the ways of politics. The strength of an organized women's movement returned to again pressure Congress almost half a century later.[12]

REPRESENTATIVE ADOLPHUS P. NELSON ARGUES FOR THE NINETEENTH AMENDMENT

MAY 21, 1919

Mr. Speaker and gentlemen of the House, I am for this resolution and desire to speak in its behalf, because I believe that the time is now here when we ought to express ourselves in favor of one-half of the loyal, patriotic, and conscientious citizenship of our country — the faithful women who have stood by us in the hour of need and in the hour of the greatest crisis of our history. Equal suffrage for the women of the United States is certain to come. It is futile to stem the ever-growing tide in its favor any longer. Delay will only intensify its demand. Our people are impatient. They demand this simple act of justice to our great American womanhood. The Republican Party will to-day add additional honor to its glorious history of statesmanlike achievements by overwhelmingly passing this amendment to our Constitution. [Applause.]

Wyoming was the first Territory in the Union to adopt equal suffrage, in 1869, and the first State to incorporate equal suffrage into its State constitution, 1890, and Congress gave its first official approval of equal suffrage when it admitted Wyoming as a State, July 10, 1890. State after State has followed in adopting equal suffrage until now complete enfranchisement of women is given in fifteen States; right to vote for presidential electors in eleven States; full suffrage at primary election in two States; and partial suffrage in thirteen States. This means that forty-one out of the forty-eight States of the Union have already granted women the right of the ballot in some form and to some degree. I am proud this afternoon to say that in my own State of Wisconsin the legislature recently granted to

women suffrage as far as it relates to presidential electors, and if the United States Senate promptly acts upon this joint resolution and passes it, as we confidently believe it will, my own Legislature of Wisconsin, which is still in session, I think will, without question, promptly ratify this amendment, and the State of Wisconsin will thus become one of the first States in the Union to ratify the equal suffrage amendment.

I believe that the time is now ripe for this Congress to vote to submit to the several States of the Union for ratification the constitutional amendment making equal suffrage a part of the Constitution of the United States. The privilege of ratifying the amendment by three-fourths of the States should no longer be denied. In the interest of justice, right, and equality, the equal-suffrage amendment should be passed by this Congress and be speedily ratified by the several States. Woman has demonstrated in the awful war just ended, as well as in every crisis of the world's history, her undisputed right to equal suffrage. President Wilson has said: "This war could not have been fought had it not been for the services of the women." Gen. Pershing says: "This war is being fought by women; it is women who suffer and lend courage to us; women are the ones who will deserve honor for their aid in establishing democracy." Gen. Wood says: "The support and efforts of American women made our part in the war possible." Ex-President Roosevelt, the matchless leader of American thoughts and ideals, and one of the three greatest statesmen of our history, was very pronounced in his views in favor of woman suffrage.

In home, in religion, in education, in society, and in the very fundamentals of civilization itself, it has been woman who has been the molder of our highest ideals and purposes and the inspiring genius for the achievement of liberty, justice, and democracy. In all the great spiritual, moral, and social movements and reforms of the world for the uplift and blessing of the human race, women have taken a conspicuous part and have been willing to suffer and die that civilization might be advanced and the blessings of liberty vouchsafed. The family, the church, the school, and the State are dependent upon women for their highest development and largest achievement. [Applause.]

Taxation without representation should no longer apply to womankind. Only those who place the rights of property over the rights of humanity can possibly oppose women's suffrage. Disfranchisement of women is merely a relic of barbarism and is founded on the old spirit that might makes right. Real democracy is built on equality and justice and a

---

Real democracy is built on equality and justice and a government by the consent of the governed. Real democracy, therefore, demands the full enfranchisement of women.

— Adolphus P. Nelson

---

government by the consent of the governed. Real democracy, therefore, demands the full enfranchisement of women.

In the work of the Red Cross — the great mother of the world — in the hospitals and trenches on the battle fields of Flanders and France, and in all the tasks that lie at the very heart of civilization, women have displayed a patriotism and heroism born of devotion, sacrifice, and service that has meant and means to-day a larger interpretation of the "Fatherhood of God and the brotherhood of man" in which there shall be no supermen of autocracy to despoil and crucify by acts of tyranny, but supermen of democracy to sacrifice and die for the freedom of mankind and the liberation of the world. The heroic and supreme sacrifices of our women inspire us to-day to permit our women to contribute jointly with our men in the work of our reconstruction period that is before us, our utmost power of service to the end that not only our own Nation but the whole human family shall be enriched spiritually, physically, socially, and economically.

The world is now calling as never before for both men and women of great brains and noble hearts to meet our large and complex problems of national and international reconstruction. Problems that will tax to the very limit our best statesmanship must be solved patiently and wisely yet heroically and resolutely, ever looking to the interest not only of our

own Nation but to the lasting interest of all mankind. With the allied powers we have won a triumphant and glorious victory over militarism, materialism, and autocracy, but if this great victory is to bear fruit for the interest and benefit of future generations we must now unite in a peace program of reconstruction that will challenge our highest resolves and greatest determinations. In this great work we need the constant aid and counsel of our women in order that we may unitedly accomplish the best results. We need the aid of our American womanhood to build a democracy competent, constructive, and achieving.

Nothing less than absolute equality will begin to do justice to our glorious American womanhood. Right, justice, liberty, and democracy will then be our common aspiration, attained by a united citizenship of men and women who shall believe in a culture, a religion, a government, and a civilization subject not to the distinction of sex, but to the highest law of morals and justice, and which shall make right might and righteousness power and help usher in the glad day when the whole world shall be a glorious sisterhood of democracies dedicated to the welfare of all mankind. [Applause.]

The battle for the equal-suffrage amendment in the United States was begun by Susan B. Anthony, and the first amendment was drafted by her in 1875. The proposed amendment to the Federal Constitution to give the right of the ballot to women reads:

> The right of citizens of the United States to vote shall not be denied or abridged by the United States or by any State on account of sex.

This amendment is practically the same as the one proposed by Susan B. Anthony in 1875. The amendment was first introduced by Senator Sargent, of California, January, 1878. It was voted on in the Senate four times, as follows: In 1887, yeas seventeen, nays thirty-four; in 1914, failing by eleven votes; in 1918, failing by two votes; February, 1919, failing again by one vote. In the House it was voted on in 1915, failing by seventy-eight of the necessary two-thirds vote. On January 10, 1918, it passed by one vote over the necessary two-thirds majority.

WHERE WOMEN VOTE

The twenty-eight States in which women now have presidential suffrage control about 55 percent of the Electoral College, over one-half of the Senate, 45 percent of the House, and 55 percent of the votes in the party conventions. Full suffrage is granted to women in the following States:

Wyoming, granted 1869.
Colorado, granted 1893.
Utah, granted 1896.
Idaho, granted 1896.
Washington, granted 1910.
California, granted 1911.

Kansas, granted 1912.
Arizona, granted 1912.
Oregon, granted 1912.
Nevada, granted 1914.
Montana, granted 1914.
New York, granted 1917.
Michigan, granted 1918.

Oklahoma, granted 1918.
South Dakota, granted 1918.
Texas, granted 1919.
Tennessee, granted 1919.

Source: *Congressional Record*, 66th Cong., 1st sess., May 21, 1919 (Washington: GPO, 1919), 58:83–84.

REPRESENTATIVE FRANK CLARK OPPOSES THE NINETEENTH AMENDMENT

MAY 21, 1919

I am opposed to submitting this amendment to the States for several reasons, Mr. Speaker, and one is because the franchise is not a right which attaches or belongs to any person of any sex or race. It is a privilege to be granted or withheld at the pleasure of the States. The power to control and regulate the suffrage was not delegated in the Constitution to the Federal Government, but was expressly retained by the several States, and these States have exclusively exercised this power ever since the Union was established. No member of the convention which framed our Federal Constitution suggested that the power should be delegated to the Federal Government, but by unanimous consent it was left as a reserved right to the respective States. Why should the States now delegate to the General Government a power which in the unanimous judgment of the fathers of the Republic it was deemed wise to retain when the organic law was written? I respectfully submit, Mr. Speaker, that a radical change in the structure of a great government should not be made unless it should be indisputably established that the proposed change is not only for the betterment of mankind, but that it is necessary for the welfare of the people.

What is it that we are asked to do here? We are asked to pass this joint resolution and thereby submit to the legislatures of the several States for ratification or rejection an amendment to the Constitution of the United States, which amendment confers upon women the privilege of voting. What is the duty of a Representative? I ask my colleagues to listen to this: What is the duty of a Representative in Congress when he is confronted with a proposition to submit an amendment to the Constitution?

Just two or three days ago everyone of us took a solemn oath "to uphold and defend the Constitution of the United States against all enemies, foreign and domestic," and that Constitution itself, with unerring certainty, points out our duty in this emergency. The Constitution provides that "the Congress, whenever two-thirds of both Houses shall deem it necessary, shall propose amendments to this Constitution." It does not provide that whenever two-thirds of both Houses think it "advisable." It does not provide that whenever two-thirds of both Houses think it "politic." It does not provide that whenever two-thirds of both Houses think it "expedient." It does not provide that whenever two-thirds of both Houses "believe their seats are in jeopardy." It does not provide that whenever "a few women in the country desire it." But it provides that whenever two-thirds of both Houses, before the bar of their consciences, under their oaths to defend the Constitution, deem it to be necessary to propose the amendments.

Why is it necessary? Is the Republic in danger? Is there any great public purpose to be subserved? Does the welfare of the country demand it? Why is it necessary? Not only must the Representative in his solemn judgment be convinced that it is necessary, but he ought to be able to point out the necessity which impels him to vote that way. Oh, my friends, some gentlemen say they will vote for it "because their people want it." That does not meet the constitutional requirement. Some people are for it "because the good women of the country say they want it." That does not meet the constitutional requirement under your oath to uphold and defend the Constitution. You can not excuse yourself upon the proposition that somebody wants it or that you believe it is a good thing. If the fathers who framed the organic law had intended that, they would have put in that solemn instrument that whenever two-thirds believed that it is a good thing, or that so many people want it, they will vote for it.

Oh, my friends, can you put your hands upon your hearts to-day, before God and man, with due respect to your oaths to uphold the Constitution, and say that you believe that it is absolutely necessary that this amendment be submitted to the American people? You can not say it. No; you can not say it. I have heard gentlemen give their reasons for voting for it. Some of them say one thing and some say another, but I want to tell you what I believe. It strikes me that a great political storm cloud has appeared on the horizon and many are running to cover. There are a whole lot of people who, if Indian nomenclature were adopted at this time, might properly be dubbed "Young-men-afraid-of-their-jobs." That is what is the matter with a great lot of people. [Laughter.]

Oh, my friends, let us stand here to protect the Constitution which we swore we would protect. The fathers put that in the Constitution because they did not think that that great instrument ought to be lightly amended, because they did not think that we ought to tinker with it in obedience to the demand of every passing fancy. They knew that these "isms" would arise. They knew that these fantastic propositions would come up in the future to meet and plague the people of this country, and they decided to fix the Constitution so that it would be hard to amend, and then not amended until the welfare of the people absolutely demanded it. And yet here we tinker with a Constitution that for a century and a third and more has stood the test of all the changes of time.

My fellow countrymen, I am opposed to woman suffrage straight out from the shoulder, every day in the week and every week in the year. I am against it because I agree with the great leader from Illinois [Mr. MANN], that the place for the women is at home. That is where they belong. That is where he said they belonged. I agreed with him then and I agree with what he then said now. [Applause.]

★ ★ ★ ★

I was amused when some gentlemen were talking to-day about women being entitled to this privilege because they had made this great fight for world liberty and world democracy. I am willing to leave it to the mothers of the sons who went to France. If you will leave it to them and cut out the agitators and soapbox orators, you will see that the vote would be overwhelmingly against it. The real mothers — I do not mean all of them, but the great majority of them — do not want it. The men of America have protected them for a century and a third, and they will do it yet. But when this comes, women have got to take their stand on a level with the men. There will be no more legislation in the different States in her interests. There will be no more legislation in the National Government in her interest. Take the case to-day in every State in the Union and let a man and a woman have a law case before the court and the jury and the man has as much chance as the proverbial snowball down in some other country. But when this comes, she will have to "stand up to the rack, fodder or no fodder."

★ ★ ★ ★

This resolution takes the matter of the regulation of the suffrage entirely out of the power of the respective States of the Union and confers upon the Federal Government the unrestricted power to regulate elections and prescribe the qualifications of voters.

I am aware that some Representatives, and especially some from the South, who are supporting this resolution are endeavoring to justify their support of it by claiming that the States will still control in this regard, notwithstanding the incorporation of this amendment in the organic law. The last paragraph of the amendment provides "Congress shall have power to enforce this article by appropriate legislation." This provision either means what it says or it means nothing. It gives to Congress the full, absolute, unrestricted, and exclusive power to "enforce this article," and to enforce it "by appropriate legislation." The amendment gives to all women — white, black, and any other color — the right to vote, and invests Congress with complete power to carry it into effect by the enactment of any legislation which Congress may deem to be "appropriate." This opens up anew the negro question in all the Southern States, and I warn my colleagues from the South who are supporting this measure that they are "playing with fire," which is likely to produce another "reconstruction" conflagration in our Southland.

I am not an alarmist, Mr. Speaker, nor am I an extremist. The negro in the South to-day is as a class satisfied. He is treated fairly and justly under the law and is content to leave politics alone. He is now not a factor in politics and has no desire to become a factor. The two races understand each other perfectly, and are now dwelling in the same territory in amity, with nothing to disturb these relations. So far as I am concerned — and I am sure I speak for the real representative sentiment of the southern people — I would do the negro no harm, and would protect and defend him in the enjoyment of his every legal right. We do protect him under our laws in the full enjoyment of life, liberty, and the pursuit of happiness, and no States in any portion of this country will go further to conserve his rights in these respects than will the States in the section from which I hail. But we had as well be plain. This does not mean that we will tolerate conditions of social equality with the negro or that we will allow the vicious and ignorant to control in our political affairs.

★ ★ ★ ★

Make this amendment a part of the Federal Constitution and the negro women of the Southern States, under the tutelage of the fast-growing socialistic element of our common country, will become fanatical on the subject of voting and will reawaken in the negro men an intense and not easily quenched desire to again become a political factor. White Bolsheviki will readily be found to organize and train this mass of ignorance and vice to the end that they may be elevated to places of honor and power, and they will make promises of social position and anything else to their deluded followers in order to accomplish their own ignoble purposes. But, say my southern colleagues who are enamored of this new and to Democrats strange doctrine, this will not happen. Let us see.

★ ★ ★ ★

Mr. Speaker, another objection which I have to woman suffrage is the fact that it will unquestionably materially aid the growth of socialism in this country. It will not only add

---

I may be old-fashioned and out of date, but I believe in the home woman. I believe in the American mother who presides in queenly dignity over an American home. She needs no ballot for her protection. — Frank Clark

---

to the growth of socialism, but will likewise contribute to the upbuilding of feminism and Bolshevism in America. Every Socialist and every Bolshevist throughout the land wherever you find him is an ardent advocate of woman suffrage, and he wants it by Federal amendment.

★ ★ ★ ★

Mr. Speaker, again I desire to call the attention of my colleagues in this House to the seriousness of amending the organic law of the Republic. It should not be amended except the necessity to amend for the public welfare is made plainly to appear, and I respectfully submit that no such necessity is apparent. I may be old-fashioned and out of date, but I believe in the home woman. I believe in the American mother who presides in queenly dignity over an American home. She needs no ballot for her protection. God bless her; she is and always will be protected by the deep and undying love of the American man. I want her to forever occupy the commanding place which she fills in our economic affairs, respected, honored, and revered. I would not drag her from the lofty pedestal on which she has been placed by the undying love of the American man — the pedestal of sisterhood, wifehood, and motherhood — to the low level of ward politics. God forbid.

Source: *Congressional Record*, 66th Cong., 1st sess., May 21, 1919 (Washington: GPO, 1919), 58:88–92.

Notes

1. Eleanor Flexner and Ellen Fitzpatrick, *Century of Struggle: The Woman's Rights Movement in the United States* (Cambridge, Mass.: Belknap Press of Harvard University Press, 1996), 66–72; Alexander Keyssar, *The Right to Vote: The Contested History of Democracy in the United States* (New York: Basic Books, 2000), 173–176; Mary Hertz Scarbrough, "Nineteenth Amendment," in *Constitutional Amendments: 1789 to the Present*, ed. Kris E. Palmer (Detroit: Gale, 2000), 429–433.

2. Scarbrough, "Nineteenth Amendment," 430–440. For a time in the 1870s, the AWSA also tried to gain women's suffrage through court challenges. Between 1870 and 1910, the AWSA was involved in 480 "campaigns in thirty-three states resulting in only seventeen state referendum votes in eleven states ... and only two victories." ibid., 441.

3. Flexner and Fitzpatrick, *Century of Struggle: The Woman's Rights Movement in the United States*, 165–167; *Congressional Record*, 49th Cong., 2nd sess., January 25, 1887, 18:987–1003.

4. Flexner and Fitzpatrick, *Century of Struggle: The Woman's Rights Movement in the United States*, 208–217; Scarbrough, "Nineteenth Amendment," 441; David E. Kyvig, *Explicit and Authentic Acts: Amending the U.S. Constitution, 1776–1995* (Lawrence: University Press of Kansas 1996), 227.

5. Alan P. Grimes, *Democracy and the Amendments to the Constitution* (Lexington, Mass.: Lexington Books, 1978), 91–92, 94; Kyvig, *Explicit and Authentic Acts: Amending the U.S. Constitution, 1776–1995*, 232; Scarbrough, "Nineteenth Amendment," 441.

6. Scarbrough, "Nineteenth Amendment," 442–444.

7. Flexner and Fitzpatrick, *Century of Struggle: The Woman's Rights Movement in the United States*, 258–272.

8. Keyssar, *The Right to Vote: The Contested History of Democracy in America*, 214. See also Flexner and Fitzpatrick, *Century of Struggle: The Women's Rights Movement in the United States*, 292–299; Keyssar, *The Right to Vote: The Contested History of Democracy in America*, 214–215.

9. *Congressional Record*, 65th Cong., 2nd sess., January 10, 1918, 56:762–811; October 1, 1918, 56:10976–10988; Grimes, *Democracy and the Amendments to the Constitution*, 92.

10. *Congressional Record*, 65th Cong., 2nd sess., October 1, 1918, 56:10976–10988; *Congressional Record*, 65th Cong., 3rd sess., February 10, 1919, 57:3053–3062; Arthur S. Link, ed., *The Papers of Woodrow Wilson* (Princeton, N.J.: Princeton University Press, 1884), 51:158–161; Flexner and Fitzpatrick, *Century of Struggle: The Woman's Rights Movement in the United States*, 302–304; Keyssar, *The Right to Vote: The Contested History of Democracy in the United States*, 216; Kyvig, *Explicit and Authentic Acts: Amending the U.S. Constitution, 1776–1995*, 234–235; Scarbrough, "Nineteenth Amendment," 446.

11. *Congressional Record*, 66th Cong., 1st sess., May 21, 1919, 58:78–94; June 4, 1919, 58:615–635; Flexner and Fitzpatrick, *Century of Struggle: The Woman's Rights Movement in the United States*, 307–317; Scarbrough, "Nineteenth Amendment," 446–447; Anastatia Sims, "Armageddon in Tennessee: The Final Battle Over the Nineteenth Amendment," in *One Woman, One Vote: Rediscovering the Woman Suffrage Movement*, ed. Marjorie Spruill Wheeler (Troutdale, Ore: New Sage Press, 1995), 332–352.

12. Grimes, *Democracy and the Amendments to the Constitution*, 96. See also Keyssar, *The Right to Vote: The Contested History of Democracy in America*, 218–221.

League of Nations
✳ 1919 ✳

Despite a three-year effort by President Woodrow Wilson to remain neutral as war raged in Europe, events in early 1917 made American entrance into World War I virtually inevitable. That January, Germany began unrestricted submarine warfare against neutral as well as enemy ships. A month later, a message intercepted and decoded by British intelligence was transmitted to the State Department outlining a proposed Mexican-German alliance if war broke out between Germany and the United States. In return, Mexico would regain its "lost territory in New Mexico, Texas, and Arizona." Disclosure of the Zimmerman Telegram, as it came to be known, further inflamed growing anti-German sentiment within the United States. Soon thereafter, a revolution in Russia toppled the Czarist government and replaced it with a republican government, sparing the United States of allying with a despotic monarchy. Then on April 2, 1917, two weeks after German submarines torpedoed three American ships, Wilson asked Congress for a declaration of war. The Senate approved the declaration on April 4, 82–6, and the House on April 6, 373–50. At the time, an Allied victory was less than certain. During the next eighteen months, nearly 4.8 million Americans would serve in the U.S. armed forces. Before the Germans were defeated and the official Armistice declared on November 11, 1918, the war claimed nine million lives, including 112,432 Americans.

Peace negotiations ensued in Paris the following January at a conference attended by leaders from Great Britain, France, Italy, Japan, and the United States. Wilson personally headed the U.S. delegation, and in so doing became the first president to visit Europe while in office. Both his announcement that he would go to Paris as well as his failure to include any senators or Republican leaders in the five-member delegation accompanying him aroused considerable criticism. The latter omission was particularly hard to understand given that the November 1918 congressional elections had seen the Republicans regain control of both the House 240–190 and Senate 49–47.[1]

The challenge of "defending Wilson's actions even before the first meeting in France took place" fell to Sen. Gilbert M. Hitchcock, D-Neb., first as chairman of the Committee on Foreign Affairs and then as Democratic minority leader.

Hitchcock "had grave reservations about the failure of the president to take some senators with him" and "saw the president's decision as giving opponents of the Treaty an edge they might otherwise not have had." Still, as a party leader, he felt obligated to defend the president and the League of Nations, the centerpiece of Wilson's efforts in Paris. Hitchcock's effort is exemplified in his remarks of February 27, 1919. The war, he told his Senate colleagues, has shaken the "confidence of men in government," and "it will not be restored until governments devise some way to end war."[2] Hitchcock saw the League of Nations as that way. It was a theme he would repeat often over the next several months.

At Paris, initially, the peace aims of the British and French "followed traditional lines of territorial and colonial ambitions, combined with guarantees of military security and reparations from the defeated," while "American peace aims were expressed in President Woodrow Wilson's ideal of self-determination and his Fourteen Points" proposal for ending the war first delivered in an address before a joint session of Congress on January 8, 1918. The most significant point, number fourteen, called for the establishment of a "general association of nations . . . for the purpose of affording mutual guarantees of political independence and territorial integrity to great and small states alike." Preventing war was of utmost concern to Wilson in his rationale for a League of Nations.[3]

President Wilson played a leading role in getting the Allies to agree on the Treaty of Versailles, the peace treaty with Germany signed on June 28, 1919. Except for a brief visit to the United States between February 24 and March 5, Wilson remained in Europe. As negotiations continued, Americans began to express increased concern about the wisdom and fairness of the president's approach. Opposition developed among various ethnic groups, who felt their particular concerns were being neglected, as well as among others lacking strong ties to the Old World, who were exhausted by the war, tired of the wrangling over peace, and anxious to get back to their domestic pursuits. The biggest hurdle, however, was the Senate, where beginning in March 1919, the Republicans held a two-vote advantage. Wilson could count on most fellow Democrats, but also needed Republican votes to secure the constitutionally mandated two-thirds majority required for

TRIUMPHAL ENTRY INTO NORMALCY

Senator Henry Cabot Lodge, left, with Philander Chase Knox, led the opposition against the United States entering the League of Nations. This 1921 cartoon satirizes the opposition as an outdated "Triumphant Entry into Normalcy." The opposition, however, successfully defeated U.S. participation in the League.
Source: The Granger Collection, New York.

ratification. When he submitted the treaty to the Senate on July 10, he wanted it ratified without either amendments or reservations. Subsequently, "he agreed in principle to interpretive restrictions separate from the instrument of ratification." That concession proved insufficient, as did meetings with individual senators. Leading the opposition was Sen. Henry Cabot Lodge, R-Mass., chairman of the Senate Committee on Foreign Relations, who held a deep distaste for the president personally, and Sen. William E. Borah, R-Idaho.[4]

A particular source of criticism, the Covenant of the League of Nations (Article X), prescribed the use of collective security actions to guarantee the status quo in the postwar world. Lodge and several other senators opposed having American soldiers protect the territorial integrity of other nations and serving under the command of foreigners. Other critics pointed to the League's voting procedures that assigned a single vote to the United States, but allowed the British to control its own vote as well as those of its dominions and colonies — Australia, Canada, India, New Zealand, and South Africa. A number of senators felt Wilson had misused his office at the expense of Congress and that the League Covenant failed to adequately recognize Congress's constitutional powers.[5]

Senator Lodge realized he needed time to develop increased opposition to the president. He spent the first two weeks of Foreign Relation Committee hearings on the treaty reading the entire two hundred sixty-four-page document into the record. Next the committee devoted six weeks to public hearings before reporting the treaty to the full Senate on September 10, with forty-five amendments and four reservations. During the hearings, Wilson invited committee members to the White House where he patiently answered questions for several hours in an unsuccessful effort to gain support. When this effort proved futile, on September 3, Wilson departed on a twenty-three-state, eight-thousand-mile railroad trip to persuade the American people to push the Senate for an unqualified ratification of the treaty. The president's "speaking tour failed. Far from winning the support of senators, Wilson antagonized many. When compromise was overdue, he showed himself unyielding."[6]

Meanwhile, on the Senate floor, a coalition of Senate Democrats and moderate Republicans repeatedly rejected the Foreign Relations Committee amendments as well as those offered by individual senators. Finally, Lodge, anxious to prevent a split between Republican moderates and the "irreconcilables" (sixteen Republican senators adamantly opposed) proposed fourteen reservations to U.S. participation in the League and adherence to the treaty. From his sickbed, Wilson denounced the Lodge reservations. On November 19, Senate Democrats loyal to Wilson joined with Republican irreconcilables to defeat the treaty with the reservations attached 55–39. Later the same day, loyal Democrats supported the measure, but reservationists joined irreconcilables to reject the treaty without the reservations 53–38.[7] The "conventional wisdom about Congress is that floor debate in the House or the Senate seldom changes votes." Yet when Senator Borah took to the floor that day and railed against the proposed League, "few who heard the speech failed to realize that it was a masterpiece of oratory and superb timing, perhaps unmatched since the days of Daniel Webster, Henry Clay, and John C. Calhoun." Without question "Henry Cabot Lodge deserved the lion's share of the credit for defeating the bill to create the League," but it was Borah "who carried the day with his passionate opposition to the league."[8]

Early in 1920, the Senate again took up the treaty and after a lengthy debate, the Senate voted on the treaty with modified Lodge reservations on March 19. Although Wilson had communicated his displeasure to Democratic senators, his control over his party was waning. A number of Democrats deserted the president and voted in favor of the proposal, but the final tally of forty-nine in favor and thirty-five opposed fell seven votes short of the required two-thirds total for ratification. In this instance, the loyalist Democrats teamed with the irreconcilables to stop the measure.[9]

Some believe that if a Republican had occupied the White House — or perhaps a Democrat other than Wilson — the treaty would have gained approval. While the president faced considerable hostility from Republicans, as could be expected, members of his own party showed signs of resentment as well. Close Wilson advisor Colonel Edward House echoed this feeling in his diary. The United States's failure to join the League of Nations, he felt, was not based on "partisanship as much as bitter hatred of the President and this hatred [was] largely shared by Democratic Senators." Others contend that "[n]either Wilson nor his Republican foes evidenced any willingness to compromise their fundamental differences."[10]

In mid-May 1920, Congress enacted a measure declaring a formal end to the war, but Wilson promptly vetoed it. The president remained resolute. He chose to take the matter to the electorate, and used the election of 1920 as a "solemn referendum" on the treaty. Wilson's recent history of taking issues to the public had not been successful and this effort failed as well. Pledging to return the country to "normalcy," Sen. Warren G. Harding, R-Ohio, was elected president and his fellow Republicans won a smashing victory. Wilson slipped into a bitter and short retirement before his death on February 3, 1924. A congressional joint resolution ended the war with Germany and Austria-Hungary in July 1921. President Harding chose not to resubmit the Treaty of Versailles to the Senate for ratification.

SENATOR GILBERT M. HITCHCOCK ON THE TROUBLE WITH SENATORS WHO OPPOSE THE LEAGUE OF NATIONS

FEBRUARY 27, 1919

Which shall it be, Mr. President — war, and continued preparations for war, or a league of nations? Those are the alternatives.

Heretofore the world, through all the centuries down to the present time, has been afflicted and inflicted with the curse of war. The larger part of governmental appropriations, here and elsewhere, has been for the burdens of war. Through all the centuries this has continued. Every generation has sent its men to the slaughter. One eloquent critic of this proposed league of nations has read into the *Record* recently a list of fifty wars that have devastated the Old World during the last century. America has not been free from the curse. Besides our own Revolutionary War, our Civil War, and our Indian wars, we have had the War with Mexico, the War with Spain, the War with Germany and Austria-Hungary, and we have felt, even though using every effort to keep out of war, its awful effects. Our experiences in the war from which we are just now emerging have convinced us that we are a part of the world; that whenever the world is convulsed with war we are going to suffer from it, and probably participate in it. We, too, therefore, find ourselves face to face with the question, Shall it be war, and preparations for war, or shall it be a league of nations?

Senators who criticize the league of nations seem to ignore the alternative. Let us face it. What if we have no league of nations?

★ ★ ★ ★

What if the peace to be signed becomes like other peaces that have been signed — merely a truce while nations make ready for another war? That inevitably means a resumption of war preparations on an increased scale.

★ ★ ★ ★

I am speaking now only of preparations for war, Mr. President; but what of actual war?

First, we have the cost in money, the least important and the least terrible penalty we pay for war. The war just concluded is estimated to have cost the seven nations which bore its burden something like one hundred and forty thousand million dollars. The taxpayers of those nations will stagger under that burden for generations yet unborn if no relief is afforded in the cost of war preparations. The late war cost 6,000,000 lives and millions more of cripples. It has destroyed hundreds of towns. It has widowed millions of wives. It has brought in its train the inevitable consequences of war — pestilence and famine. One of the war diseases alone has cost this country over 306,000 lives of the civilian population. It has let loose and inflamed the passions and lusts of men and crushed and humiliated millions of women. Massacre, torture, and assassinations have accompanied it. Law and order have been overthrown. Bolshevism and anarchy have been propagated. The confidence of men in government has been shaken. It will never be restored until governments devise some way to end war.

★ ★ ★ ★

Humanity will not long tolerate a condition of recurring war over questions between governments that can be settled

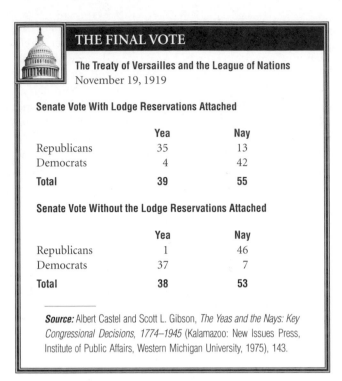

THE FINAL VOTE

The Treaty of Versailles and the League of Nations
November 19, 1919

Senate Vote With Lodge Reservations Attached

	Yea	Nay
Republicans	35	13
Democrats	4	42
Total	**39**	**55**

Senate Vote Without the Lodge Reservations Attached

	Yea	Nay
Republicans	1	46
Democrats	37	7
Total	**38**	**53**

Source: Albert Castel and Scott L. Gibson, *The Yeas and the Nays: Key Congressional Decisions, 1774–1945* (Kalamazoo: New Issues Press, Institute of Public Affairs, Western Michigan University, 1975), 143.

by peaceful methods along the lines of justice and reason. The mass of men will not allow themselves to be forever led to the slaughter uselessly and unnecessarily. The taxpayers will not submit indefinitely to spoliation by enormous taxes to make unending preparation for unceasing wars.

Senators who oppose the league of nations have apparently ignored the enormous evil from which the world suffers. They have apparently ignored the rising tide of protest not only among the people of the United States but among the people of the whole civilized world against war. If we fail to adopt an internationalism of governments that will unite to end the wars we shall be face to face with the internationalism of the individual socialist. We can not ignore the fact that the Russian millions are now thoroughly committed to the communistic government. We can not deny the fact that France and Italy, the one a republic and the other a limited monarchy, are largely under the control of socialistic ideas and socialistic leaders. No other leader could get control in the state of public opinion. We can not ignore the fact that Germany is being rapidly and radically reorganized into a socialistic nation of 75,000,000 souls. We are impressed by the growth of socialism in Great Britain and the acceptation of socialistic ideas by British leaders.

★ ★ ★ ★

I therefore repeat, we must choose between the internationalism of the league of nations bound together in a society for mutual protection, with honor and justice and liberty

and self-government as the standard, and the internationalism of the Socialist.

★ ★ ★ ★

The purpose of the league of nations set forth in the articles is to maintain international peace. To this end its members agree that they will in no case resort to war with each other until they have submitted to arbitration the dispute between them, or submitted to an inquiry by the executive council, and not even then will any member resort to war until the arbitration has concluded or the inquiry of the executive council has been finished, and not even then until three months thereafter. There is thus provided by this ingenious machinery, whenever a dispute arises between any of the nations in the league, a cooling-off time of from nine months to one year, a time sufficient in all human probability to end the danger of war between the contestants.

The nations further agree, moreover, that they will not even then, after the lapse of three months, resort to war against a member of the league which complies with the award of the arbitrators or the recommendation of the executive council if it is unanimous. There we have another block to war. There is an almost insuperable obstacle in the way of war, a solemn covenant between the nations which have entered into the league.

These agreements render war between members of the league as nearly impossible as human ingenuity can devise. To my mind it is unthinkable that any nation admitted to the league will violate this solemn covenant. I think we have passed the age when a national covenant will be considered as a scrap of paper.

★ ★ ★ ★

When I hear Senators describe the danger which they see in entering the league, when I hear one Senator condemn one article and another a different article, and another propose a change here and another a change there, I begin to wonder whether all this great labor of the leading nations of the world, represented by their ablest men, having all possible counsel, has really created a thing which is so weak and miserable, so dangerous and so fatal to the welfare of the members that are going into it. One would think that this league, with the loftiest purposes, designed by the ablest men, inspired by the most noble spirit, was nothing but a fabric of faults, a creation of mistakes.

★ ★ ★ ★

When I hear these gentlemen ready to prescribe for the league of nations, one on one thing and one on another, one tearing this out and another tearing that out, it seems to me that in considering this noble creation of these great men, representing the leading countries of the world, the political critics view the league to be in position of a man who has been listening to quack doctors and reading patent-medicine advertisements of ills that are only imaginary.

★ ★ ★ ★

Mr. President, we have been told in a single speech on the floor of the Senate that the control of the league would be in the hands of European monarchs and Asiatic despots; that it might be controlled by the British Empire, or, if the British Empire should lose control, the Germanic nations might get control, or that, if they did not get control, the Bolsheviki might get control. In fact, in that single speech every possible method of control was suggested except the very obvious one that the league and the executive council of the league are going to be in control of the great democracies of the world, five of them being named as permanent members of the executive council and controlling it.

★ ★ ★ ★

We have been told also that when a nation enters this league it yields to the arbitrament of the league its national life. What nonsense when, under one of the covenants of the league, all the nations that join in it solemnly pledge themselves to preserve and protect the political independence of each member, including its territorial integrity.

Then, we have been told that we would be compelled to contribute to a force that might be used by the league against us, whereas the only provision for contributing a force is in case one of the nations becomes an outlaw, and then the other nations contribute to bring it within control of civilization again. There is no standing army; there is no league navy; each nation maintains its nationality.

★ ★ ★ ★

We have been told that if we joined the league we would place ourselves at the mercy of Mexico, which might despoil our citizens, commit outrages on our borders, and enjoy the benefits of the guaranty of the league as to its political independence and territorial integrity. Yet the fact is that under the terms of the league Mexico is ineligible to admission to membership in the league. Mexico can not perform, and does not perform, her international obligations, and no such nation can gain admission.

We have been told that if we enter this league we will abandon the Monroe doctrine; that is, we will abandon our right to attack any nation which may seek to gain a foothold on the Western Hemisphere. The Monroe doctrine was enunciated when each nation had to look out for itself, and we took that step to look out for ourselves; but the purpose of the league of nations includes the very purpose of the Monroe doctrine; that is, to prevent aggression of nations upon each other, whether upon the continent where they exist or upon any other continent. Anything that has the character of an attack

upon any American Republic or even an unfriendly act against the United States would call for action by the league. Instead of being compelled to defend the Western Hemisphere alone, we would, if necessary, have the sympathy and help of every member of the league.

We have been told that this is one of those entangling alliances against which Washington warned us. I deny it. There is just as much difference between an entangling alliance and the league of nations as there is between a horse-chestnut and a chestnut horse. When Washington gave his warning the world was full of entangling alliances; nations were endeavoring to secure power by alliances with other nations. Why? To fight wars. They were not doing it to main-

---

We have been told that this is one of those entangling alliances against which Washington warned us. I deny it. There is just as much difference between an entangling alliance and the league of nations as there is between a horse-chestnut and a chestnut horse. — Gilbert M. Hitchcock

---

tain peace; they were doing it to fight wars. That age has passed away; the league of nations is to wipe out all entangling alliances and bring about an honorable union among the nations of the world to end war and preserve peace.

★ ★ ★ ★

We have been told here in the Senate that if we entered this league of nations Japan would compel the United States to arbitrate the immigration question, and, if she succeeded, compel this country to admit her nationals. What nonsense! There are two answers to this proposition. The first is that if Japan could compel arbitration by the executive council, she nevertheless could not hope to win a verdict favorable to her contention. She is the only nation of her race represented among the eight Caucasian members of the executive council. She could not hope to get the vote of Great Britain, who sits on the executive council with her, when Great Britain is so tremendously interested in the immigration question as affecting Canada and her other dominions, Australia being even a stronger illustration.

★ ★ ★ ★

We have been told that if we should agree to the league proposal for the limitation of armaments we would interfere with the power of Congress and impair the sovereignty of the country. Nothing is more ridiculous. A hundred years ago the

United States and Great Britain entered into a contract, which was ratified by the Senate of the United States, limiting naval armaments on the Great Lakes between Canada and the United States. Did that limit the sovereignty of the United States?

★ ★ ★ ★

We have been told that we would destroy our Americanism and our nationalism if we entered this league; and the eloquent Senator from Idaho [Mr. BORAH], in a brilliant peroration here the other day, brought before our eyes the personality of Theodore Roosevelt as the very embodiment of Americanism, which we should cherish and which we should live up to. Has the Senator forgotten that Theodore Roosevelt himself ardently advocated a reduction of armaments by agreement between the nations? Has he forgotten that Theodore Roosevelt advocated a league of nations? Has he forgotten that Theodore Roosevelt even went so far as to declare that force should be placed behind a league of nations to maintain the peace of the world? Who can doubt that if Theodore Roosevelt were President of the United States to-day he would be bending every energy, as Woodrow Wilson is bending every energy, to establish a league of nations to preserve the peace of the world?

★ ★ ★ ★

Mr. President, that is the trouble with Senators who oppose the league of nations. They are thinking of the days that are gone, and gone forever. The conquering empires of the world have been wiped out. The fall of Russia and Germany and Austria-Hungary removed from the world the last representatives of the conquering spirit and of autocratic power. The world is now democratic. Senators should cease to turn their eyes to the past and turn them to the present and see what we have before us. The world of democracy has come into its own. Yes; that is the mistake; too many are turning their eyes to the past and forgetting that we have come into a new world.

Source: *Congressional Record*, 65th Cong., 3rd sess., February 27, 1919 (Washington: GPO, 1919), 57:4414–4418.

SENATOR WILLIAM E. BORAH OPPOSES THE LEAGUE OF NATIONS

NOVEMBER 19, 1919

Mr. President, I am not misled by the debate across the aisle into the view that this treaty will not be ratified. I entertain little doubt that sooner or later — and entirely too soon — the treaty will be ratified with the league of nations in it, and I am of the opinion with the reservations in it as they are now written. There may possibly be some change in verbiage in order that there may be a common sharing of parentage, but our friends across the aisle will likely accept the league of nations with the reservations in substance as now written. I think, therefore, this moment is just as appropriate as any other for me to express my final views with reference to the treaty and the league of nations. It is perhaps the last opportunity I shall have to state, as briefly as I may, my reasons for opposing the treaty and the league.

Mr. President, after Mr. Lincoln had been elected President before he assumed the duties of the office and at a time when all indications were to the effect that we would soon be in the midst of civil strife, a friend from the city of Washington wrote him for instructions. Mr. Lincoln wrote back in a single line, "Entertain no compromise; have none of it." That states the position I occupy at this time and which I have, in an humble way, occupied from the first contention in regard to this proposal.

My objections to the league have not been met by the reservations. I desire to state wherein my objections have not been met. Let us see what our attitude will be toward Europe and what our position will be with reference to the other nations of the world after we shall have entered the league with the present reservations written therein. With all due respect to those who think that they have accomplished a different thing and challenging no man's intellectual integrity or patriotism, I do not believe the reservations have met the fundamental propositions which are involved in this contest.

When the league shall have been formed, we shall be a member of what is known as the council of the league. Our accredited representative will sit in judgment with the accredited representatives of the other members of the league to pass upon the concerns not only of our country but of all Europe and all Asia and the entire world. Our accredited representatives will be members of the assembly. They will sit there to represent the judgment of these 110,000,000 people — more then — just as we are accredited here to represent our constituencies. We can not send our representatives to sit in council with the representatives of the other great nations of the world with mental reservations as to what we shall do in case their judgment shall not be satisfactory to us. If we go to the council or to the assembly with any other purpose than that of complying in good faith and in absolute integrity with all upon which the council or the assembly may pass, we shall soon return to our country with our self-respect forfeited and the public opinion of the world condemnatory.

Why need you gentlemen across the aisle worry about a reservation here or there when we are sitting in the council and in the assembly and bound by every obligation in morals, which the President said was supreme above that of law, to comply with the judgment which our representative and the other representatives finally form? Shall we go there, Mr. President, to sit in judgment, and in case that judgment works for peace join with our allies, but in case it works for war withdraw our cooperation? How long would we stand as we now stand, a great Republic commanding the respect and holding the leadership of the world, if we should adopt any such course?

★ ★ ★ ★

We have said, Mr. President, that we would not send our troops abroad without the consent of Congress. Pass by now for a moment the legal proposition. If we create executive functions, the Executive will perform those functions without the authority of Congress. Pass that question by and go to the other question. Our members of the council are there. Our members of the assembly are there. Article 11 is complete, and it authorizes the league, a member of which is our representative, to deal with matters of peace and war, and the league through its council and its assembly deals with the matter, and our accredited representative joins with the others in deciding upon a certain course, which involves a question of sending troops. What will the Congress of the United States do? What right will it have left, except the bare technical right to refuse, which as a moral proposition it will not dare to exercise? Have we not been told day by day for the last nine months that the Senate of the United States, a coordinate part of the treaty-making power, should accept this league as it was written because the wise men sitting at Versailles had so written it, and has not every possible influence and every source of power in public opinion been organized and directed against the Senate to compel it to do that thing? How much stronger will be the moral compulsion upon the Congress of the United States when we ourselves have indorsed the proposition of sending our accredited representatives there to vote for us?

★ ★ ★ ★

Do our Democratic friends ever expect any man to sit as a member of the council or as a member of the assembly equal in intellectual power and in standing before the world with that of our representative at Versailles? Do you expect a man to sit in the council who will have made more pledges, and I shall assume made them in sincerity, for self-determination and for the rights of small peoples, than had been made by our accredited representative? And yet, what became of it? The unanimous consent was obtained nevertheless.

But take another view of it. We are sending to the council one man. That one man represents 110,000,000 people.

Here, sitting in the Senate, we have two from every State in the Union, and over in the other House we have Representatives in accordance with population, and the responsibility is spread out in accordance with our obligations to our constituency. But now we are transferring to one man the stupendous power of representing the sentiment and convictions of 110,000,000 people in tremendous questions which may involve the peace or may involve the war of the world.

★ ★ ★ ★

You have put in here a reservation upon the Monroe doctrine. I think that, in so far as language could protect the Monroe doctrine, it has been protected. But as a practical proposition, as a working proposition, tell me candidly, as men familiar with the history of your country and of other countries, do you think that you can intermeddle in European affairs; and, secondly, never to permit Europe to [interfere in our affairs].

★ ★ ★ ★

If the league includes the affairs of the world, does it not include the affairs of all the world? Is there any limitation of the jurisdiction of the council or of the assembly upon the question of peace or war? Does it not have now, under the reservations, the same as it had before, the power to deal with all matters of peace or war throughout the entire world? How shall you keep from meddling in the affairs of Europe or keep Europe from meddling in the affairs of America?

★ ★ ★ ★

In opposing the treaty I do nothing more than decline to renounce and tear out of my life the sacred traditions which throughout fifty years have been translated into my whole intellectual and moral being. I will not, I can not, give up my belief that America must, not alone for the happiness of her own people, but for the moral guidance and greater contentment of the world, be permitted to live her own life. Next to the tie which binds a man to his God is the tie which binds a man to his country, and all schemes, all plans, however ambitious and fascinating they seem in their proposal, but which would embarrass or entangle and impede or shackle her sovereign will, which would compromise her freedom of action, I unhesitatingly put behind me.

Sir, since the debate opened months ago those of us who have stood against this proposition have been taunted many times with being little Americans. Leave us the word American, keep that in your presumptuous impeachment, and no taunt can disturb us, no gibe discompose our purposes. Call us little Americans if you will, but leave us the consolation and the pride which the term American, however modified, still imparts. Take away that term and though you should coin in telling phrase your highest eulogy we would hurl it back as common slander.... If we have erred it is because we have placed too high an estimate upon the wisdom of Washington and Jefferson, too exalted an opinion upon the patriotism of the sainted Lincoln. And blame us not therefore if we have, in our limited vision, seemed sometimes bitter and at all times uncompromising, for the things for which we have spoken, feebly spoken, the things which we have endeavored to defend, have been the things for which your fathers and our fathers were willing to die.

Senators, even in an hour so big with expectancy we should not close our eyes to the fact that democracy is something more, vastly more, than a mere form of government by which society is restrained into free and orderly life. It is a moral entity, a spiritual force, as well. And these are things which live only and alone in the atmosphere of liberty. The foundation upon which democracy rests is faith in the moral instincts of the people. Its ballot boxes, the franchise, its laws, and constitutions are but the outward manifestations of the deeper and more essential thing — a continuing trust in the moral purposes of the average man and woman. When this is lost or forfeited your outward forms, however democratic in terms, are a mockery.

★ ★ ★ ★

Sir, we are told that this treaty means peace. Even so, I would not pay the price. Would you purchase peace at the cost of any part of our independence? We could have had peace in 1776 — the price was high, but we could have had it. James Otis, Sam Adams, Hancock, and Warren were surrounded by those who urged peace and British rule. All through that long and trying struggle, particularly when the clouds of adversity lowered upon the cause, there was a cry of peace — let us have peace. We could have had peace in 1860; Lincoln was counseled by men of great influence and accredited wisdom to let our brothers — and, thank Heaven, they are brothers — depart in peace. But the tender, loving Lincoln, bending under the fearful weight of impending civil war, an apostle of peace, refused to pay the price, and a reunited country will praise his name forever more — bless it because he refused peace at the price of national honor and national integrity. Peace upon any other basis than national independence, peace purchased at the cost of any part of our national integrity, is fit only for slaves, and even when purchased at such a price it is a delusion, for it can not last.

But your treaty does not mean peace — far, very far, from it. If we are to judge the future by the past it means war. Is there any guaranty of peace other than the guaranty which comes of the control of the war-making power by the people? Yet what great rule of democracy does the treaty leave unassailed? The people in whose keeping alone you can safely lodge the power of peace or war nowhere, at no time and in no place, have any voice in this scheme for world peace. Autocracy which has bathed the world in blood for centuries reigns supreme. Democracy is everywhere excluded. This, you say, means peace.

★ ★ ★ ★

With a ruthlessness unparalleled your treaty in a dozen instances runs counter to the divine law of nationality. Peoples who speak the same language, kneel at the same ancestral tombs, moved by the same traditions, animated by a common hope, are torn asunder, broken in pieces, divided, and parceled out to antagonistic nations. And this you call justice. This, you cry, means peace. Peoples who have dreamed of independence, struggled and been patient, sacrificed and been hopeful, peoples who were told that through this peace conference they should realize the aspirations of

---

No; your treaty means injustice. It means slavery. It means war. And to all this you ask this Republic to become a party. You ask it to abandon the creed under which it has grown to power and accept the creed of autocracy, the creed of repression and force.
— William E. Borah

---

centuries, have again had their hopes dashed to earth. One of the most striking and commanding figures in this war, soldier and statesman, turned away from the peace table at Versailles declaring to the world, "The promise of the new life, the victory of the great humane ideals for which the peoples have shed their blood and their treasure without stint, the fulfillment of their aspirations toward a new international order and a fairer and better world, are not written into the treaty." No; your treaty means injustice. It means slavery. It means war. And to all this you ask this Republic to become a party. You ask it to abandon the creed under which it has grown to power and accept the creed of autocracy, the creed of repression and force.

Mr. President, I turn from this scheme based upon force to another scheme, planned one hundred fory-three years ago in old Independence Hall, in the city of Philadelphia, based upon liberty. I like it better. I have become so accustomed to believe in it that it is difficult for me to reject it out of hand. I have difficulty in subscribing to the new creed of oppression, the creed of dominant and subject peoples. I feel a reluctance to give up the belief that all men are created equal — the eternal principle in government that all governments derive their just powers from the consent of the governed. I can not get my consent to exchange the doctrine of George Washington for the doctrine of Frederick the Great translated into mendacious phrases of peace. I go back to that serene and masterful soul who pointed the way to power and glory for the new and then weak Republic, and whose teachings and admonitions even in our majesty and dominance we dare not disregard.

I know well the answer to my contention. It has been piped about of late from a thousand sources — venal sources, disloyal sources, sinister sources — that Washington's wisdom was of his day only and that his teachings are out of fashion — things long since sent to the scrap heap of history — that while he was great in character and noble in soul he was untrained in the arts of statecraft and unlearned in the science of government. The puny demagogue, the barren editor, the sterile professor now vie with each other in apologizing for the temporary and commonplace expedients which the Father of his Country felt constrained to adopt in building a republic!

What is the test of statesmanship? Is it the formation of theories, the utterance of abstract and incontrovertible truths, or is it the capacity and the power to give to a people that concrete thing called liberty, that vital and indispensable thing in human happiness called free institutions, and to establish over all and above all the blessed and eternal reign of order and law? If this be the test, where shall we find another whose name is entitled to be written beside the name of Washington? His judgment and poise in the hour of turmoil and peril, his courage and vision in times of adversity, his firm grasp of fundamental principles, his almost inspired power to penetrate the future and read there the result, the effect of policies, have never been excelled, if equaled, by any of the world's commonwealth builders. Peter the Great, William the Silent, and Cromwell the Protector, these and these alone perhaps are to be associated with his name as the builders of States and the founders of governments. But in exaltation of moral purpose, in the unselfish character of his work, in the durability of his policies, in the permanency of the institutions which he more than anyone else called into effect, his service to mankind stands out separate and apart in a class by itself. The works of these other great builders, where are they now? But the work of Washington is still the most potent influence for the advancement of civilization and the freedom of the race.

Reflect for a moment over his achievements. He led the Revolutionary Army to victory. He was the very first to suggest a union instead of a confederacy. He presided over and counseled with great wisdom the convention which framed the Constitution. He guided the Government through its first perilous years. He gave dignity and stability and honor to that which was looked upon by the world as a passing experiment, and finally, my friends, as his own peculiar and particular contribution to the happiness of his countrymen and to the cause of the Republic, he gave us his great foreign policy under which we have lived and prospered and strengthened for nearly a century and a half. This policy is the most sublime confirmation of his genius as a statesman. It was then, and it is now, an indispensable part of our whole scheme of government. It is to-day a vital, indispensable element in our entire plan, purpose, and mission as a nation. To abandon it is nothing less than a betrayal of the American people. I say betrayal deliberately, in view of the suffering and the sacrifice which will follow in the wake of such a course.

Source: *Congressional Record*, 66th Cong., 1st sess., November 19, 1919 (Washington: GPO, 1919), 58:8781–8784.

Notes

1. Herbert F. Margulies, *The Mild Reservationists and the League of Nations Controversy in the Senate* (Columbia: University of Missouri Press, 1989), 8–9; Ralph Stone, *The Irreconcilables: The Fight Against the League of Nations* (Lexington: University of Kentucky Press, 1970), 33–36.

2. Thomas W. Ripley, *Gilbert Hitchcock of Nebraska — Wilson's Floor Leader in the Fight for the Versailles Treaty* (Lewiston, N.Y.: Edwin Mellen Press, 1998), 161–165; *Congressional Record*, 65th Cong., 3rd sess., February 27, 1919, 57:4414. See also Kurt Wimer, "Senator Hitchcock and the League of Nations," *Nebraska History* 44 (September 1963): 189–204.

3. Quotes are found in Antoine Capet, "Versailles, Treaty of," in *Dictionary of American History*, 3rd ed., 10 vols., ed. Stanley I. Kutler (New York: Charles Scribner's Sons, 2003), 8:315; Thomas A. Bailey, "Woodrow Wilson Wouldn't Yield," *American Heritage* 8 (June 1957): 21–22.

4. Margulies, *The Mild Reservationists*, 40–41, 99–100; Stone, *The Irreconcilables*, 107, 119; Herbert F. Margulies, "The Moderates in the League of Nations Battle: An Overlooked Faction," *The Historian* 60 (Winter 1998): 275.

5. Margulies, *The Mild Reservationists*, 16, 21–34, 65, 74–75.

6. Quote is found in Margulies, *The Mild Reservationists*, 94. See also ibid., 72–77, 94–110; U.S. Congress, Senate Committee on Foreign Relations, *Treaty of Peace with Germany,* hearings, 66th Cong., 1st sess., S. Doc. 106 (Washington: GPO, 1919); U.S. Congress, Senate, *Treaty of Peace with Germany: Report of the Conference Between Members of the Senate Committee on Foreign Relations and the President of the United States at the White House, Tuesday, August 19, 1919*, 66th Cong., 1st sess., S. Doc. 76 (Washington: GPO, 1919); Stone, *The Irreconcilables*, 124–127; Arthur Walworth, *Woodrow Wilson*, 3rd ed. (New York: Norton, 1978), 348–352.

7. Lloyd E. Ambrosius, *Woodrow Wilson and the American Diplomatic Tradition: The Treaty Fight in Perspective* (Cambridge: Cambridge University Press, 1987), 176–224; Margulies, *The Mild*

Reservationists, 94, 119–184; Stone, *The Irreconcilables,* 128–146; *Congressional Record,* 66th Cong., 1st sess., November 19, 1919, 58:8786, 8803.

8. Raymond W. Smock, ed., *Landmark Documents on the U.S. Congress* (Washington, D.C.: Congressional Quarterly, 1999), 315. See also *Congressional Record,* 66th Cong., 1st sess., November 19, 1919, 58:8781–8784.

9. Ambrosius, *Woodrow Wilson and the American Diplomatic Tradition,* 241–250; Stone, *The Irreconcilables,* 165–170.

10. Quotes are in Kurt Wimer, "The League of Nations: A Victim of Executive-Legislative Rivalry," *The Lock Haven Review,* series 1, no. 2, 1960, 11; Ambrosius, *Woodrow Wilson,* 172.

Smoot-Hawley Tariff

✷ 1929–1930 ✷

During the presidential campaign of 1928, Republican standard bearer Herbert Hoover pledged to help the belcaguered American farmer who had fallen victim to declining prices as foreign agricultural imports increased significantly following World War I. The solution was simple: provide increased protection by raising tariffs on imported agricultural products. That fall, the Republicans not only retained the White House, but significantly increased their majorities in both the House from 237 to 267 seats and Senate from 49 to 56 seats. Hoover told the nation in his March 1929 inaugural address that: "Action upon some of the proposals upon which the Republican Party was returned to power, particularly further agricultural relief and limited changes in the tariff, cannot in justice to our farmers, our labor, and our manufacturers be postponed." Congress, he continued, would soon be called into special session to address these issues.[1]

Hoover's subsequent message to Congress called for a limited upward revision of tariff rates with general increases on farm products and adjustment of a few industrial rates. Within eighteen months, however, his call for "limited changes in the tariff" was transformed into the quintessential protectionist legislation of the twentieth century as requests for increased protection flooded in every spectrum of American society. Through effective lobbying, a bill meant to provide relief for farmers became a means for substantial increases on many classes of manufactured goods, on the theory that restricting imports would stimulate the faltering U.S. economy. Over time, the results made the Smoot-Hawley Tariff among the most notorious pieces of legislation in American history.

In the "twentieth century, only a few other traumatic events — Munich, the German invasion of France in 1940, Pearl Harbor, Yalta, and Vietnam — have seared the public consciousness similarly and become enduring metaphors for public policy failures." "Interestingly, these "latter crises emerged from military defeats or perceived diplomatic failures, not from political combat over domestic legislation."[2]

Although the consensus view among economic historians is that while the collapse of international trade in the 1930s can at least partially be attributed to Smoot-Hawley, its effect on the Great Depression was far less dramatic than many have claimed. Scholarly studies have attributed its adoption to a variety of forces including party politics, an ideological attachment to protectionism, and an unprecedented lobbying campaign by agricultural and industrial special interest groups. Critiques of its economic consequences have been offered by scholars, the media, and presidents of both major political parties. Several factors caused it to become infamous:

- congressional debate on the bill kept it continuously in public view for eighteen months;
- the bill was not only far more complicated than previous tariff measures but more controversial as well;
- Congress transformed President Hoover's promise for limited changes into an overhaul of the entire tariff schedule;
- public opposition was extremely vocal in response to the unprecedented special interest lobbying that attended consideration of the bill;
- it provoked a storm of foreign retaliatory measures and contributed to a drastic decline in international trade;?
- other nations perceived it as a symbol of American willingness to improve its own lot at the expense of other countries; and
- a series of economic catastrophes occurred soon after its passage.[3]

Congressional consideration of the bill sponsored by Sen. Reed Smoot, R-Utah, chairman of the Senate Committee on Finance, and Rep. Willis C. Hawley, R-Ore., chairman of the House Committee on Ways and Means, extended from January 1929 through June 1930. During those eighteen months, Smoot-Hawley was subjected to lengthy hearings and heated debate and prompted continuing controversy.

House hearings on the tariff began on January 7, 1929. They lasted forty-three days and five nights, and included 1,131 witnesses. On May 9, the House Committee on Ways and Means reported a bill that was essentially presented to the committee's minority members as an accomplished fact. When House floor debate began later the same day, opportunities for either debate or amendment were markedly restricted. By virtue of a rule passed by the House, general

Representative W. C. Hawley, chair of the House Tariff Committee, and Senator Reed Smoot, of the Senate Finance Committee, combined efforts on legislation that became the Smoot-Hawley Tariff. The legislation served as one of the major pieces of protectionist legislation in the twentieth century.
Source: Library of Congress.

floor debate on the bill was closed and the Ways and Means Committee was given priority in offering amendments. This ensured that the committee would have control over whatever changes were made in the bill. The Democrats unsuccessfully decried the rule as the most restrictive ever employed by the House to pass legislation, as the Chamber House passed a bill calling for eight hundred forty-five tariff increases and eighty-two reductions.[4]

Next, the Senate Committee on Finance held more than five weeks of hearings on the bill. Published transcripts of those proceedings contained the testimony of 1,004 witnesses and two hundred forty-nine pages of protests from foreign countries. The committee's report of September 4 included four hundred fifty-three amendments that adjusted the House increases but did little to aid farmers.

Senate floor consideration offered a stark contrast to that of the House. Initially, the Senate, while sitting as Committee of the Whole for six months from early September to early March, entered into an open-ended debate that permitted senators to offer amendments and request votes on specific tariff rates that resulted in six hundred twenty tariff increases

and two hundred two reductions. During the subsequent floor debate, further amendments resulted in seventy-five tariff increases and thirty-one reductions before the bill passed on March 24, 53–31 vote. Preceding that vote, the Senate abolished its Committee of the Whole procedure for bills and resolutions after claims of senator vote-trading (one senator supporting another senator's amendment to gain support for one the first senator had offered) surfaced in the press.[5]

A House-Senate conference was then created to resolve the differences between the tariff bills passed by the two chambers. Arriving at a resolution of these differences required an unusually complex process that involved two conference committees, the first of which dealt with matters reported in disagreement by the other, over the course of two months. Each report was initially subjected to points of order in the Senate because it included new matter. When the points of order were sustained, the reports were returned to conference and reported without the objectionable matter. Each chamber then considered both of the revised conference reports together.[6]

Final Senate debate prompted observations similar to those espoused by others in ensuing decades. Sen. George W. Norris, R-Neb., declared that Smoot-Hawley "was conceived and written in the interest of victorious business organizations who are using their power ... to put through Congress one of the most selfish and indefensible tariff measures that has ever been considered by the American people." Sen. Robert M. LaFollette Jr., R-Wis., felt the "shameful logrolling methods by which the bill has been forced through both Houses of Congress [would] do more to discredit and destroy an embargo tariff system, erected by twisting and warping the doctrine of protection, than all the tariff revisions of the past." Conversely, Sen. James E. Watson, R-Ind., acknowledged that the nation was "in the midst of financial depression" but confidently predicted that if the bill passed, the "Nation will be on the upgrade financially, economically, and commercially within thirty days, and that within a year from this time we shall have regained the peak of prosperity and the position we lost" with the stock market crash of October 1929.[7]

On June 13, the Senate agreed to the conference report, which contained higher tariff rates than the chamber originally passed, by just two votes, 44–42. The next day, the House concurred, 222–153. During the previous eighteen months, some twenty thousand pages of hearing testimony and twenty-eight hundred pages of the *Congressional Record* were needed to capture the totality of the debate. Despite widespread protests and strenuous objections by prominent individuals, including one thousand twenty-eight of the nation's leading economists who signed a petition condemning the tariff, President Hoover signed Smoot-Hawley on June 17, 1930.[8]

SENATOR ROBERT M. LAFOLLETTE OPPOSES THE SMOOT-HAWLEY TARIFF

JUNE 11, 1930

Mr. President, the pending conference report on the Hawley-Smoot tariff bill represents the twenty-first general revision of tariff duties in the history of this country.

This report levies import taxes on a greater number of articles at higher rates of duty than any tariff bill brought into this chamber for approval since Alexander Hamilton drafted the first tariff bill of 1789. In one hundred forty-one years since the establishment of the protective system the rates provided in the pending report have not been equaled nor, except in time of war or under abnormal conditions of panic, have they been even nearly approximated. Considering the number of articles included on the dutiable list this report erects the highest and longest tariff wall in American history.

★ ★ ★ ★

That is the point at which we have arrived after more than fourteen months since consideration of this bill commenced in the lower House. That is the nature of the legislation we are asked to approve at the end of a session of Congress called by President Hoover to fulfill the Republican pledge of a "limited revision" of the tariff, primarily in the interests of agriculture.

I appreciate the fact that this bill has been subjected to analysis and scrutiny such as no previous tariff measure has received. It is apparent that the supporters of the bill are impatient to secure its final enactment and to divert the attention of the public to other questions. Nevertheless, I believe that the struggle that has been waged here in the Senate during the last eight months has involved principles that should not be brushed lightly aside now, and that will survive the passage of this bill. I shall not be deterred, therefore, from discussing the conference report in the light of those principles and asserting what seem to me to be compelling objections against its adoption by the Senate and its approval by the President.

I contend that the pending bill is a complete betrayal of President Hoover's pledge, solemnly given to the American people throughout the 1928 campaign, that he would favor a "limited revision" of the tariff as a means toward giving agriculture equality with industry.

In the face of the pledge to give agriculture equality with industry made by the Republican Party in 1924, and by both parties in 1928, the pending bill places new burdens upon the farmer which increase the disparity against him, deny him relief, and leave him without hope of sharing in any substantial benefits of the protective system, considering agriculture as a whole.

PENDING BILL TURNS THE CLOCK BACK 20 YEARS

This bill turns the clock back twenty years in the tariff history of this country. It undoes the work of a whole generation of progressive Republicans who commenced their struggle under Dolliver and La Follette in the Senate and NORRIS in the House against the domination of the party and the Government by Aldrich and Cannon. That struggle was waged on behalf of the common man, asserting his right to control his own Government and his right to an equal share in the benefits it should afford. This bill brings the Republican Party to the crossroads at which it stood in 1909, under the control of the Old Guard leaders who wrote the Payne-Aldrich Act at the dictation of special interests and led the party to disaster in 1912. The rates in this bill have been dictated by the same interests that wrote the schedules of the Payne-Aldrich Act.

★ ★ ★ ★

Republican Party Betrayed Its Pledge In 1909

After the Payne-Aldrich Act had been passed in 1909 and the Republican Party had been driven from power by the outraged citizens of the country, the Democrats in 1913 revised the tariff downward by passing the Underwood Act. The Underwood Act was subject to the same criticism that can be made against all tariff legislation enacted without adequate data from reliable sources on costs of production, but I maintain it was an honest attempt to carry out the pledge to revise the Payne-Aldrich rates downward, and in the 1916 election the people sustained it. After the World War the rates were revised upward by the passage of the Fordney-McCumber Act of 1922. It was enacted on the plea that cheap foreign-made goods would flood the markets of this country upon the return of Europe from a war to a peace basis. It was enacted at a time when the attention of the American people was absorbed by other issues that had arisen out of the World War.

★ ★ ★ ★

Fordney-McCumber Act Violated Republican Platform

No one has ever successfully defended the economic soundness of the existing Fordney-McCumber Act. Its

THE FINAL VOTE

The Smoot-Hawley Tariff

Senate
June 13, 1930

	Yea	Nay
Republicans	38	13
Democrats	6	28
Farm Laborers	0	1
Total	**44**	**42**

House
June 14, 1930

	Yea	Nay
Republicans	203	20
Democrats	19	132
Farm Laborers	0	1
Total	**222**	**153**

Source: Congressional Record, 71st Cong., 2nd sess., June 13, 1930, 72:10635, June 14, 1930, 72:10789–10790.

schedules were written on the same unscientific basis as previous bills. The recommendations of the Tariff Commission were ignored and the principle that had been written into Republican platforms that tariff rates should equal the difference in the costs of production at home and abroad plus a reasonable profit was defied. The excessive rates in the Fordney-McCumber Act have only been justified by the defenders of that act on the specious argument that under its operation the country has been "prosperous." The truth is that from 1923 to the present hour, while the Fordney-McCumber Act has been in effect, agriculture, our great basic industry, has been struggling for its very existence, and to-day under the operation of that act we are in the midst of grave industrial and business depression.

★ ★ ★ ★

Demand For Tariff Equality

It was inevitable, Mr. President, that these conditions should breed general dissatisfaction with the excessive rates and inequalities of the Fordney-McCumber Act. Beginning a few years ago the farmers and business men of the West and the South adopted formal resolutions giving notice to the country that unless they were to be accorded some measure of equal protection with other industries in other sections they would no longer sustain the Republican conception of a protective tariff system.

The American Farm Bureau Federation in 1923 published an analysis showing that when increases in agricultural rates were set off against the increases on industrial rates voted in 1922 the net loss to the farmers of the country amounted to not less than $300,000,000 a year. The United States Senate itself is on record as condemning the inequalities of the Fordney-McCumber Act. On January 16, 1928, the Senate adopted, by a vote of 54–34, a resolution offered by the junior Senator from South Dakota, as follows:

Resolved. That many of the rates in existing tariff schedules — Referring, of course, to the Fordney-McCumber Tariff Act — are excessive, and that the Senate favors an immediate revision downward of such excessive rates, establishing a closer parity between agriculture and industry, believing it will result to the general benefit of all.

Is there any man in this Chamber who contends that these two conference reports conform to the declaration of policy contained in the McMaster resolution?

Six months after that resolution was adopted the Republican National Convention met at Kansas City. The senior Senator from Utah [Mr. SMOOT], coauthor of the pending bill, presided over the resolutions committee during the convention. Before this committee appeared accredited representatives of agriculture asking legislation to enable the farmer to control and market his surplus products. That plan of farm relief had already twice been approved by a Republican Congress but had been vetoed in 1927 and 1928 by President Coolidge. This plan of farm relief received the approval of fifteen of the members of the committee on resolutions at the Republican National Convention. As the Wisconsin member of the committee on resolutions I submitted a minority platform. It enumerated the inequalities of which I have spoken here to-day. It rejected in its entirety the plan of aiding agriculture through upward revision of the Fordney-McCumber Act. A minority plank on agriculture was submitted to the convention with the support of fifteen of the leading farm States which likewise rejected and repudiated the theory that equality for agriculture could be attained through upward revision of the tariff.

But, Mr. President, the coauthor of the pending bill submitted to the convention as the chairman of the resolutions committee a platform holding out to the farmer the false hope that the Republican Party would solve his problems through tariff revision and that platform was adopted over the protest of two hundred seventy-seven delegates from the farm States. The Republican national convention thus refused to the farmer the remedy he sought. It offered him the remedy of tariff revision and imposed it upon him against his will.

President Hoover Declared Tariff Revision Foundation Of Farm Relief

In his address of acceptance on August 11, 1928, President Hoover undertook to interpret the Kansas City platform. In that address he said:

> The most urgent economic problem in our Nation to-day is in agriculture. It must be solved if we are to bring prosperity and contentment to one-third of our people directly and to all of our people indirectly. We have pledged ourselves to find a solution.

Mr. Hoover then listed the remedies which he proposed as a solution for this problem. As the first and most important item upon that list, emphasized above all others, Mr. Hoover placed revision of the tariff. He said:

> An adequate tariff is the foundation of farm relief. Our consumers increase faster than our producers. The domestic market must be protected. Foreign products raised under lower standards of living are to-day competing in our home markets. I would use my office and influence to give the farmer the full benefit of our historic tariff policy.

Mr. President, no Senator can successfully defend the proposition that the pending bill carries out that pledge.

★ ★ ★ ★

Senator Smoot's Figures Give Misleading Impression—Revision Limited

On May 27 the author of this bill, the senior Senator from Utah, presented certain figures which he declared represented an analysis of the bill "by the best informed body of tariff specialists ever assembled." The Senator undertook to demonstrate that the pending bill represents the "limited" revision of the Fordney-McCumber rates "written primarily for agriculture" which was pledged by President Hoover in the 1928 campaign.

For the purposes of this discussion, Mr. President, I do not question the accuracy of the figures estimating the duties under the present law and under the proposed bill and the ad valorem equivalents based on 1928 imports which the Senator has presented. I am willing to assume that these figures have been furnished the Senator by the United States Tariff Commission and for the purpose of a comparison between the rates of the proposed bill and the existing law I accept them as accurate.

When the Senator undertakes, however, to compute the percentage of increase of the proposed rates over the existing rates I reject his method as totally inaccurate and assert that it conveys an entirely erroneous understanding of the increases which are carried in this conference report. The method employed by the Senator leads him to the conclusion

that taking the ad valorem equivalents of the duties for the bill as a whole the proposed bill represents an increase of 6.86 percent over the existing Fordney-McCumber rates.

Pending Bill Boosts Rates 20 Percent

The fact is, Mr. President, that the proposed Hawley-Smoot bill represents an increase of 20 percent above the rate structure of the existing Fordney-McCumber Act. This increase is clearly shown in the ad valorem equivalents for each of the fifteen schedules of the bill and by a comparison of the computed ad valorem duties under the act of 1922 and the pending bill, estimated on the basis of imports for 1928.

★ ★ ★ ★

It is absurd to speak of this bill as a tariff for the benefit of agriculture when we realize that $10,000,000,000 worth of agricultural commodities, which are on an export basis, will not derive one nickel of benefit from the rates carried in this bill; that only a partial and probably temporary benefit from these paper rates will accrue to the producers of another $3,000,000,000 worth of commodities; and that the full benefit of the new duties will reach only the producers of some $368,000,000 worth of our annual agricultural production.

★ ★ ★ ★

Bill Should Be Defeated In The Senate

Throughout the consideration of this bill in the Senate the President has not once, by word or deed, lent the slightest aid or encouragement to those who have been making the fight against the excessive industrial rates of duty carried in this bill.... There has not been one day during the last fourteen months that the President might not have terminated the debate and forced the withdrawal of this bill by repudiating the general upward revision of industrial rates, in violation to the pledge he made to the American people as the leader of his party and the Chief Executive of the Nation.

★ ★ ★ ★

The enactment of this measure is a gross betrayal of the pledge given to a third of our population, engaged in agriculture, who have formed the backbone of the Republican Party for more than seventy years. To put this bill on the statute books is to ignore the protest of the most enlightened and progressive of our industrial and financial leaders. The passage of this bill permits the interests which have fattened on tariff favors through monopoly practices to take advantage of the farmer's necessity to satisfy their own avarice and to increase the disparity which already exists between agriculture and industry under the present law.

★ ★ ★ ★

Mr. President, Senators may have decided to pass this bill and to put it on the statute books. They may ignore the protests which business and industrial leaders have made

---

The enactment of this measure is a gross betrayal of the pledge given to a third of our population, engaged in agriculture, who have formed the backbone of the Republican Party for more than seventy years.

—Robert M. LaFollette

---

against the bill. They may spurn the judgment of one thousand twenty-eight economists who have analyzed the effects of this bill upon our industrial and economic life. They may brazenly repudiate the pledge which President Hoover and

the Republican Party made to agriculture in 1928 — namely, that they would revise the tariff in the interest of agriculture and that it was the foundation of farm relief.

Mr. President, a majority of Senators in this Chamber may assume the attitude which Nelson W. Aldrich took on the floor of the Senate and say that prophecies as to dire results growing out of its passage are purely partisan political statements. I say to you here and now, if you pass this bill, every Senator who is up for reelection who votes for it will have to meet that as the primary issue of his campaign in 1930; and, Mr. President, when they meet that issue, those who voted for this bill will regret that they have violated the pledge for a limited revision in the interest of agriculture and that they have ignored the protests of those who are most vitally interested in the economic effects of this measure. I venture the prediction that the American people will reject this iniquitous bill at the polls.

Source: *Congressional Record*, 71st Cong., 2nd sess., June 11, 1930 (Washington: GPO, 1930), 72:10448–10455.

SENATOR JAMES E. WATSON SPEAKS IN SUPPORT OF THE SMOOT-HAWLEY TARIFF

JUNE 13, 1930

There has been no alteration in the last hundred years in the method of attacking tariff legislation. The methods are always the same and, in some respects, those who attack and those who assail have every advantage, because of modern publicity methods.

Two courses always are open to those who are the proponents of a tariff measure. The first is to permit the opponents of the proposition to do all the talking, and in that way promote the speedy passage of the measure. The other is to answer every thing that is said and every argument that is made, and in that way greatly prolong the discussion and delay the passage of the tariff bill. Always the proponents of tariff, measures have chosen the former course, because while a tariff bill is under discussion, business lags and industry falters. The manufacturer knows not how much to buy. He has no idea what the market of to-morrow will have to furnish, or what the price is to be, and is more or less in a fog of uncer-

tainty. Therefore an undue prolongation of any tariff discussion leads more or less to business depression and to commercial uncertainty in the land.

It has been so in the case of every bill that has ever passed, it is so with this one, and it is my prediction to-day, deliberately made on the floor of the United States Senate, that after the passage of this bill this afternoon the skies will clear, and within a comparatively brief time the sun again will shine, and bring back prosperous conditions and happy days to the people of the United States. If I did not believe that to be true — and it has proved true in the passage of every tariff act in the history of the Nation — I would oppose this bill instead of favoring it.

★ ★ ★ ★

My friend the senior Senator from, Utah [Mr. SMOOT] was the one man who stood up to defend the rates in this tariff bill. In the first place, he knew more about it than anybody else. He wanted no help; he needed no help; he got no help.

★ ★ ★ ★

Mr. President, a singular thing happened in the history of this tariff bill. The day after it was reported from the Ways and Means Committee the very able publicity bureau that was set up by the Democratic Party began to issue its blasts against the bill, when it was not possible for that bureau to have had much information concerning it, for its consideration had been carried on in such secrecy, by the committee that even other Members of the House could not ascertain what its provisions were. But the Democratic publicity bureau said, "This is an iniquitous tariff, it is illogical, and inequitable, and un-American, and unholy." They kept up those blasts against it day after day and week after week and month after month. The proponents of the measure offered no suggestions, because if a man says a tariff bill is infamous and illogical it takes a speech to combat it and show that these charges are not true.

★ ★ ★ ★

It is easy for men to say a tariff bill is infamous and outrageous. That requires no argument. It is based on no facts. It requires no logic. It simply acclaims, and yet because it is antagonistic and strikes at something, it gets the headlines of the newspapers and simmers down in the imagination of the people, and after a while a lot of folks begin to think, "Maybe there is something wrong with the tariff bill," although they do not have any reason for it or any basis for it, and never have, because when the bill has been passed, when it is put in operation it will open the mills and restore prosperity. The answer to all these charges is the actual demonstration of the workings of the tariff bill. That is what has happened before and that is what will happen again.

★ ★ ★ ★

I could go back to quote from speeches of John C. Calhoun and Thomas H. Benton on the tariff. I am perfectly familiar with those speeches. Calhoun and Benton were the first men ever to use the expression "A tariff of abominations." That expression has been made use of millions of times by those who have opposed tariff bills, all over the Republic and on the floor of the Senate and the floor of the House from that day to this — "A tariff of abominations." How often we heard that expression used in this Chamber. I could take the speeches of John C. Calhoun and Thomas H. Benton, containing what they said about the tariff bill of 1828, and the expressions and the characterizations employed by those who fought the Dingley bill, the Payne-Aldrich bill, and the Fordney-McCumber bill as they came from the mouths of Senators and Members of the House of 1898, of 1908, of 1922, and put them in the mouths of the men who have opposed the bill now before us, and I would

not have to change a word. I could put those speeches in the *Record* of to-day as the expressions of the men who have opposed this bill and it would not have been necessary for them to utter a single word, for they have only repeated in regard to this measure what has been said time and time again in regard to every other tariff measure of like character since 1824. It would have been unnecessary to dot an "i" or cross a "t," because they are exactly the same characterizations in the same language, used by the descendants of those illustrious men, and always with the same inevitable result.

That is where the expressions originated. John C. Calhoun was the first fiery and spectacular orator ever thus to attack a tariff measure, and it has come down the line from that day to this. His descendants have used it with more or less telling effect to stir up feeble souls and to terrify the timid. They have

---

John C. Calhoun was the first fiery and spectacular orator ever thus to attack a tariff measure.... [His descendents] have filled the air with goblins and spooks and gnomes and specters that are about to descend upon us and "get" us if we pass this tariff bill.

— James E. Watson

---

filled the air with goblins and spooks and gnomes and specters that are about to descend upon us and "get" us if we pass this tariff bill. Well, we have gone on and passed tariff bills just the same, and prosperity has come back to the people.

★ ★ ★ ★

We have been told in the past that the laboring people of America would be reduced to a condition of peonage if we passed protective tariff bills. Under the dominating effect of the successive protective-tariff measures, Mr. President, we brought our people to that high place where in 1917 they were enabled to help the world. It has been said that we have never done anything for the world and that we are not now doing anything for Europe; and our friends on the other side stand upon the floor and say that the way to cure unemployment in the United States is to pull down the tariff, to permit from abroad unlimited importations, made by people who receive one-fourth as much as our laboring people receive. That is the remedy proposed to cure unemployment in America. Was there ever such a farcical suggestion made in the face of an intelligent people in an effort to convince them?

★ ★ ★ ★

My friends over on the other side are far more interested in shrinkage than they are in expansion. [Laughter.]

They are glad to see things diminished and dwarfed in the United States and not brought up to a high plane. Here is the difference between our philosophy and yours, my dear friends. We believe in production. We believe that production in the United States should be full and abundant and full rounded and ripe every day and everywhere. We believe that our natural resources should be utilized to the limit. We believe that our inventive genius should be called upon every day to bring into being new forms of machinery. We believe that our railroads should operate every day and employ all of these 1,750,000 men and pay them American wages. We believe that American labor should be employed to the full in order that in turn they may buy the products of the American farmer right at home, for the farther the farmer goes from his home to find his market the greater the freight rates. Therefore it is our policy to put the factory and the farm alongside each other in order that each may find a ready market right at his door for what he produces.

That has been our policy from the beginning. On the other hand, you said we were robbing the many to feed the few, and you wanted to pull down the tariff and bring in unlimited products from abroad, made by people who get from one-fourth to one-half what our people get; and you said that that would make things cheap in America.

There never was a more fallacious doctrine preached to the people, from an economic standpoint, than this doctrine of cheapness. Ben Harrison, President of the United States from my State, compressed it all into an argument when, he said, "A cheap coat means a cheap man under the coat." What did he mean by that? Why, the man that made the cheap coat got cheap wages for making it; and cheap wages always make a cheap man. We want wages high. That is one thing in which I agree with Henry Ford. I want high wages, paid in American money.

★ ★ ★ ★

Foreign Protests

Let it be remembered that 66 percent of all the imports coming into this country under the present law come in free of duty. Only 34 percent of all we buy will pay a tariff. This policy of isolation gentlemen talk about, this policy of shutting ourselves off from Europe they discuss, is all the height of absurdity, in view of the statement that 66 percent, or two-thirds of all we bring in, comes in absolutely free of any tariff exaction, and that but one-third pays any tariff rate at all.

★ ★ ★ ★

Conclusion

The pending bill meets the prescription of the President for a tariff on competitive articles where there is injurious competition equal to the difference in labor costs at home

and abroad; in fact, it falls short of that prescription in many instances at a time when Europe, adopting our mass production and management methods, is preparing an invasion of our markets, which, unless halted, will greatly intensify our unemployment situation.

Only recently Henry Ford and Alfred P. Sloan, president of the General Motors, have issued statements denouncing the pending bill. Henry Ford is a genius and a wizard in invention and production, but helpless in political problems. However, he certainly knows which side his bread is buttered on, and does not intend if the bread falls that the buttered side shall be next to the ground. He has recently moved all of his tractor production to Ireland, where labor costs are just half what they are in Detroit. General Motors have made a tie-up with the German motor industry, where wages are only about 40 percent of what they are here. The motives of these international financiers and industrialists are obvious, and portend only unemployment or cheapened labor in this country.

In other words, these great masters of production, after having enriched themselves and their corporations in this country, are using the wealth they thus obtained to set up competitive institutions in foreign countries and produce their products by men who receive from one-fourth to one-half the wages paid in their factories in the United States. They want free trade in those articles in order that they may compete in our market with the products of their own mills in this country, where they pay 50 percent more wages than in producing the competing products in foreign countries. They thus want to use the wealth they obtained in the United States to destroy the very conditions which made possible the accumulation of that wealth by transferring to foreign nations that production.

The whole of internationalism is of one piece. The third article of the League of Nations covenant calls for the removal of trade barriers and for equality of economic opportunities for nations, involving a leveling of wages and living standards throughout the world, with manifest great sacrifice of our standards of living and wages in America. This is the big objective of all this foreign program. The assault on our tariff is a part of the movement which, if successful, would put such a strain on our economic and social order that it would necessarily blow up, and would kill the goose that laid the golden eggs for these international bankers and industrialists themselves.

Let us stick to the protective-tariff system. It has been the policy of the Government four-fifths of the time from Washington's day down to this. Under it we have prospered as no other nation in the recorded history of the earth has prospered, until to-day our people are the wonder and the envy of the earth.

It is quite true that we are in the midst of a financial depression produced by manifest causes that I shall not here discuss and which do not pertain to this subject, but I here and now predict, and I ask my fellow Senators to recall this prediction in the days to come, that if this bill is passed this Nation will be on the upgrade financially, economically, and commercially within thirty days, and that within a year from this time we shall have regained the peak of prosperity and the position we lost last October, and shall again resume our position as the first and foremost of all the peoples of history in all the essential elements of individual and national greatness.

Source: *Congressional Record,* 71st Cong., 2nd sess., June 13, 1930 (Washington: GPO, 1930), 72:10625–10634.

Notes

1. U.S. President, *Public Papers of the President of the United States: Herbert Hoover, 1929* (Washington: GPO, 1974), 10.

2. Alfred E. Eckes Jr., *Opening America's Market: U.S. Foreign Policy Since 1776,* (Chapel Hill: University of North Carolina Press, 1995), 100. See also ibid., 100–103.

3. Douglas A. Irwin, "The Smoot-Hawley Tariff: A Quantitative Analysis," *The Review of Economics and Statistics,* May 1998, 80:326; Douglas A. Irwin, "From Smoot-Hawley to Reciprocal Trade Agreements: Changing the Course of U.S. Trade Policy in the 1930s," in *The Defining Moment: The Great Depression and the American Economy in the Twentieth Century,* ed. Michael D. Bordo, Claudia Goldin, and Eugene N. White (Chicago: University of Chicago Press, 1998), 334–335; Joseph M. Jones Jr., *Tariff Retaliation: Repercussions of the Smoot-Hawley Bill* (Philadelphia: University of Pennsylvania Press, 1934). See also Colleen M. Callahan, Judith A. McDonald, and Anthony Patrick O'Brien, "Who Voted for Smoot-Hawley?" *Journal of Economic History* 54 (September 1994): 683–690; Eckes, *Opening America's Market: U.S. Foreign Policy Since 1776,* 100–139; Barry Eichengreen, "The Political Economy of the Smoot-Hawley Tariff," *Research in Economic History* 12(1989): 1–43; Robert Pastor, *Congress and the Politics of U.S. Foreign Economic Policy, 1929–1976* (Berkeley: University of California Press, 1980); E. E. Schattschneider, *Politics, Pressures and the Tariff* (New York: Prentice-Hall, 1935); F. W. Taussig, *The Tariff History of the United States* (New York: G. P. Putnam's Sons, 1931), 489–526.

4. Douglas A. Irwin and Randall S. Kroszner, "Log-Rolling and Economic Interests in the Passage of the Smoot-Hawley Tariff," *Carnegie–Rochester Conference Series on Public Policy* 45 (December 1996): 175, 178. See also *Congressional Record,* 71st Cong., 1st sess., (May 14–May 28, 1929) 71:1867–1878, 2089–2106; *Congressional Record,* 71st Cong., 2nd sess., June 14, 1930, 72:10761.

5. Irwin and Kroszner, "Log-Rolling and Economic Interests in the Passage of the Smoot-Hawley Tariff," 180, 193. See also *Congressional Record,* 71st Cong., 2nd sess., June 13–14, 1930, 72:10615–10636, 10694–10790; *Congressional Record,* 71st Cong., 2nd sess., May 16, 72: 9055–9056, June 14, 1930, 10761.

6. Gilbert Y. Steiner, *The Congressional Conference Committee: Seventieth to Eightieth Congress* (Urbana: University of Illinois Press, 1951), 43–47.

7. *Congressional Record,* 71st Cong., 2nd sess., June 11–13, 1930, 72:10155, 10540, 10654.

8. *Congressional Record,* 71st Cong., 2nd sess., June 13, 1930, 72:10635, June 14, 1930, 72:10789–10790. Arthur W. Macmahon, "Second Session of the Seventy-First Congress, December 2, 1929, to July 3, 1930; Special Session of the Senate, July 7–21," *American Political Science Review* 24 (November 1930: 924–925; and William O. Scroggs, "Revolt Against the Tariff," *North American Review* 230(July 1930):18–24.

Supreme Court Nomination of John J. Parker

✵ 1930 ✵

At 1:30 on the afternoon of May 7, 1930, the U.S. Senate rejected the nomination of John J. Parker of North Carolina to be an associate justice of the Supreme Court of the United States, 41–39. It marked the first time since 1894 that the Senate failed to confirm a nominee to the highest court in the land, and it would remain the lone Supreme Court rejection in the twentieth century until 1968. It is also historically significant because:

It symbolized labor's resurgence in the 1930s; it was one of the first important victories of the National Association for the Advancement of Colored People (NAACP); it reflected a growing opposition to the predominant philosophy of the Supreme Court, an opposition which would reach a climax in 1937; it raised fundamental questions as to the role of pressure groups in a democracy; and it demonstrated how an apparently routine appointment can become a personal and a partisan campaign for office.[1]

Sixteen years after the Parker nomination was rejected, the *American Bar Association Journal* concluded that it "was one of the most regrettable combinations of error and injustice that has ever developed as to a nomination of the great court." When Parker was nominated there were few signs of the trouble ahead. He had served as a judge on the U.S. Fourth Circuit Court of Appeals since 1925, and he was a well-regarded jurist. Preceding his nomination, the Justice Department conducted a thorough examination of Parker's opinions, and Attorney General James DeWitt concluded that he was highly qualified for consideration as an associate justice. The Hoover administration anticipated little opposition to Parker, who they considered a moderately conservative Republican.[2]

Initially, Sen. Lee S. Overman, D-N.C., chairman of the Senate Judiciary Committee subcommittee appointed to consider the nomination, wrote Parker that all three members of the panel supported his nomination and that they probably would not hold a hearing since there had been only one minor objection. The lone dissenter, the American Federation of Labor (AFL), opposed Parker on the grounds that in a 1927 case involving the United Mine Workers and the Red Jacket Consolidated Coal and Coke Company of West Virginia, he had upheld an earlier injunction issued by a federal district

court that prevented the union from interfering in the operations of certain West Virginia coal mines. The case stemmed from several instances of violence attending attempts by the union to organize workers at mines operating under closed non-union shop agreements known as "yellow dog" contracts. Parker's ruling, which the U.S. Supreme Court declined to hear on appeal, prohibited unions from trying to sell such employees on the idea of joining a union.[3]

Within a week, however, Parker received a second letter from Overman indicating that a hearing would be held, and he anticipated possible opposition when the full Judiciary Committee considered the nomination. By the time the hearings convened on April 5, the protests against Parker had gained significant momentum. Overman's effort to defend him in a lengthy review of the judge's credentials, together with a detailed memorandum refuting the AFL charges, failed to achieve their intended affect. AFL president William Green, whose appearance marked the first ever by an organized group at a hearing on a Supreme Court nomination, argued that the nominee did not possess the qualifications required of a Supreme Court justice. Of particular concern was the nominee's judicial attitude, perspective on human relations in industry, position on yellow dog contracts, and attitude toward labor. Also, he felt Parker had lived in a narrow environment, had limited experience, and was not acquainted with modern-day economics.[4]

By far the most injurious testimony, however, was that of Walter White, secretary of the NAACP. White submitted for the record a statement made by Parker during an unsuccessful 1920 campaign for the governorship of North Carolina in which he was quoted as saying that the "Negro" had "not yet reached the stage of development where he can share the burden and responsibility of government." White explained that a telegram sent to Parker inquiring of his present views on the subject had gone unanswered, and the NAACP assumed Parker had not changed his attitude. Although White had never heard of Parker prior to his nomination, and knew of nothing else that indicated either an unfriendly or unjust attitude toward African Americans except for the 1920 statement, he felt "that no man who entertains such ideas of utter disregard for integral parts of the Federal Constitution is fit

Senator Robert Ferdinand Wagner was instrumental in blocking the nomination of John J. Parker to the Supreme Court. Parker's antiunion position in some cases served as one of Wagner's strongest objections.
Source: The Granger Collection, New York.

to occupy a place on the bench of the United States Supreme Court." At the same time, the NAACP used the collective forces of the National Association of Colored Women and some two hundred African American newspapers to pressure individual senators.[5]

On April 14, as expected, the subcommittee favorably reported the nomination to the full Judiciary Committee, 2–1, Sen. William E. Borah, R-Idaho, being the lone dissenter. The Senate Republican leadership, however, was worried about the effect a united African American vote might have on midterm congressional elections in southern and border states, and that Republican senators facing a reelection in those states might vote against Parker to avoid defeat at the polls. Hoover was urged to reconsider the nomination or at least have Parker defend himself; the president stood firm and the nominee remained silent. By April 21, the efforts to discredit Parker had eroded support to such an extent that ten of the sixteen members of the Senate Judiciary Committee voted to adversely report his nomination. Not until April 24, just four days before the full Senate began its debate on the nomination, did Parker finally issue carefully worded statements denying impropriety with respect either to his decision in the Red Jacket case or his remarks during the 1920 gubernatorial campaign.[6]

During the lengthy, and often sharp and boisterous debate that occupied the attention of the Senate from April 28 until May 7, the arguments offered at the subcommittee hearing were often restated and amplified. "Judged by the available record," Sen. Robert F. Wagner, D-NY., declared, Judge Parker "is obviously incapable of viewing with sympathy the aspirations of those who are aiming for a higher and better place in the world." "His sympathies," Wagner continued, "naturally flow out to those who are already on top, and he used the authority of his office and the influence of his opinions to keep them on top and to restrain the strivings of others, whether they be an exploited economic group or a minority racial group. Among the new concerns raised was an allegation appearing in a newspaper account quote by Sen. Hugo Black, D-Ala., that accused Parker with impropriety while arguing a lumber fraud case as government prosecutor with the U.S. Department of Justice, and an observation by Sen. Thaddeus H. Caraway, D-Ark., who found it "strange that this lawyer who posses all the virtue and all the character attributed to him was so unknown." How he was able to "conceal all these virtues," Caraway was "never able to find out."[7]

Senator Borah offered one of the longest and most bitter attacks on Parker as he denounced yellow dog contracts and the nominee's decision in the Red Jacket case. Sen. Simeon D. Fess, D-Ohio, contended Parker was a victim of a crusade by labor groups, the NAACP, and certain senators devised to "break down the present American judiciary." Sen. Daniel O. Hastings, R-Del., charged that Borah and other senators were only interested in having men on the Supreme Court who shared their social and economic views. Opponents saw Parker as lacking the "intellect, learning, character, judicial temperament, courage, capabilities, and experience" required of a Supreme Court justice; a proven racist; a nominee selected purely for political reasons; an individual lacking independence; and a man who favored "big business" and believed "in the virtue of large aggregations of wealth." One senator even claimed certain colleagues were being offered bribes in the form of federal judgeships if they would support Parker.[8]

When the final vote, 41–39, was tallied, seventeen Republicans abandoned Hoover's nominee. Defeat resulted from several factors. Particularly critical were the Progressive Republicans on the Judiciary Committee who refused to allow Parker to defend himself before the committee, controlled the writing of the committee's adverse report, and strenuously opposed him during the floor debate, as did most Progressives. Joining the Progressives in opposition were the AFL, the NAACP, Democrats retaliating against a perceived partisan appointment, and several groups seeking either an increased influence on the governmental process or with their constituents. Had one additional senator voted for Parker, Vice President Charles Curtis would have cast the tie-breaking vote that turned the tide.[9]

SENATOR WILLIAM W. HASTINGS SUPPORTS THE NOMINATION OF JOHN J. PARKER TO THE SUPREME COURT

APRIL 30, 1930

I am wondering whether the Senate is going either to agree or even to argue that a judge who has rendered a decision in the circuit court is to be condemned for rendering that sort of a decision when the identical question has been submitted to the Supreme Court, the same sort of argument made that it is contended ought to have been made in that case, and the Supreme Court denied the writ of certiorari. I am wondering whether the Senate of the United States is willing to take that as evidence that this man is unfit to sit on the bench of the Supreme Court.

It seems to me that it is impossible for any person to take these cases and criticize them and urge that Judge Parker ought not to be confirmed because of them — these five cases that I have referred to, one of them being the one in which he himself participated. If Parker is not to be confirmed, what shall we do with great old Harlan, and Fuller, and Brewer, and White, and Peckham, and Day, and the other men who have been upon the Supreme Court Bench and have sustained this sort of a contract? If it be successfully argued here against the man who comes before us for confirmation for that great office that he ought not to be confirmed because he holds to these views, when the only expression he has made is when he was in a court below the Supreme Court, and in which he properly held that he was bound by the decisions of the Supreme Court, we shall go far afield and it seems to me that we shall have to get away from that proposition to find a sufficient excuse to reject this man.

It is not these propositions that are bothering a lot of people here. There are other things that are distressing them more than these. I submit that no lawyer can reasonably reject the opinion of Judge Parker and say that that unfits him for a position on the Supreme Bench unless he has in his mind something else; and this is what it seems to me may be in the minds of Senators as was suggested by the Senator from Ohio [Mr. FESS] yesterday.

I am wondering whether we are about to adopt a new attitude with respect to the Supreme Court. Can it be said that the Senate of the United States ought to adopt as a policy a plan to put on the Supreme Court only persons who have certain fixed ideas as to the interpretation of the law? Shall that be the policy of the United States Senate? Shall that be the policy of the President of the United States?

I have heard it suggested in campaigns no longer ago than the last campaign, that a certain candidate for President, if he should become President, would fill the Supreme Court with men who had ideas agreeing with his upon the wet and dry question. I considered it an insult to suggest that a candidate for the Presidency of the United States should adopt any such policy as that. Are we to make the Supreme Court of the United States a part of our political scheme of things?

We adopt platforms, both the Democratic and the Republican platforms, and probably other parties here and there occasionally adopt platforms, in which we set forth certain policies which we favor. Shall we include in those platforms a policy which will undertake to control the Supreme Court of the United States and say to the people of this country, "We want you to vote for this man for President because he holds to certain ideas with respect to the character of men who ought to be appointed to the Supreme Court — not the character of man that we have all been taught for years and years is required, namely, that he should have ability, that he should have learning, that he should have character — not that. That is not all that is demanded now, but much more. What is demanded is that he shall be first against the "yellow dog" contract in particular; that he shall be liberal, and no longer conservative." Is that to be our attitude? Is that the policy that we are about to adopt?

I say that it is not only a dangerous policy but it is not a practical policy. Men can not be appointed to the Supreme Court that we know beforehand will constantly and forever follow a particular line of thought. They must of necessity be left to their own judgment, having before them the Constitution of the land and the laws which have been passed by Congress and the various States of the Union. When we leave that we leave a practical thing, and we embark upon a dangerous thing.

But, my friends, it is not the Red Jacket case that is about to defeat Parker. It is not that. I think it may be true that what are called the "liberals" of this country, as shown by the letter that was read and placed in the *Record* yesterday from the president of the American Federation of Labor, are undertaking to stir this country, to stir the Senate, to reject this man in order that they might have an opening wedge to this plan which they think is wise for the country. That may be true. It may be true that that is what has stirred up the labor unions of this country. It may be true that that is what has caused resolutions to be passed in every city, town, and hamlet all over this country. It may be true that that is what has brought forth the telegrams to every Senator sitting in this body with

---

Are we to make the Supreme Court of the United States a part of our political scheme of things? — William W. Hastings

---

respect to this matter. But I submit that when you get down and talk to the laboring man and tell him what it all means, when you get down and explain to him what all this fuss is about, when you get down and explain to him that Parker is just as safe for labor as any other man that the President could select, you will have no trouble in getting him to understand this. I know the laboring man. I have lived with him. I have slept with him. I have eaten with him. I know his thoughts. I have worked for him. I have great sympathy for his ideals and what he is attempting to accomplish; but I say that I resent his efforts to come here and undertake to control the only independent body that there is in this land. I resent any effort to make out of that body a party scheme — a scheme which will unquestionably in the end bring chaos to this country and to all the people living in it.

That is what I object to. I am in favor of giving the laboring man what help we can by such legislation as is necessary, but I am opposed to giving him legislation that is not in conformity with the Constitution.

That is not the only trouble some of us here have. We have another problem on our hands. There is another great body of citizens in this country of ours who are greatly interested in this, and interested why? In my judgement, they are interested because they have been stirred to an interest which they did not know they had.

It has been less than five years since this nominee received the unanimous approval of the Senate of ours. Where, then, were the people who are now so active? Why did they not discover before some of these great objections to Parker? It had been ten years before that when he had made his political speech in North Carolina. Why did not the colored people then become aroused and object to him as a member of the part of the judiciary which is next to the Supreme Court, namely, the circuit court? No; the colored people of North Carolina were not alarmed, and, therefore, there was no danger of the colored people in other parts of the country being alarmed. But as the Senator from Ohio, clearly pointed out, there is a determined effort to stir up every organization and every citizen of the country for one purpose; and that is what has brought the colored man into this.

Somebody complains that Parker, from what he said in North Carolina about the colored people, can not be in favor of the Fourteenth and Fifteenth Amendments of the Constitution of the United States, and that his statement practically said so. What he did say when he was a candidate for Governor of the State of North Carolina, was that he would support the constitution of North Carolina so long as it was not in conflict with the Constitution or any provision of the Constitution of the he United States. It cannot be argued here that he is not for the Fourteenth and Fifteenth Amendments, because this very year he upheld the Fourteenth Amendment in a segregation case growing out of an ordinance passed in the city of Richmond.

That is the situation here, and that is giving us on this side of the Chamber much concern, because we are afraid that these colored people will be stirred to the point where they will believe that we voted to confirm a nominee to the Supreme Court who would not give them a fair chance.

There is no man living anywhere who knows Judge Parker's record who fears that he will not support every particle of the Constitution. There is not a colored man in North Carolina who believes that he is biased against the colored race. That charge is not true and the colored people of North Carolina know it is not true. But the colored people of the North are stirred, and it is the colored people of the North who throw out threats as to what they will do if Parker is confirmed.

It may be that it is a serious thing. I do not know how serious it is for me. I have been in the public service for more than twenty-five years, but I have never been a candidate for any elective office. It is true that I had hope to be a candidate to succeed myself in this body, with the idea that I might be of some service to my State, and might add some little service to the Nation. I still hope to be in that position, and I have to go out and defend myself against what I am going to do in this case. I am going to have to defend myself against the labor organizations, which have been friendly to me ever since I was able to vote. I am going to have to defend myself against the colored man, whose champion I have been for more than twenty years. I know I will have to do that, and, with that realization before me, what should I do in this case? I am just as certain that Parker ought to be confirmed as I am certain that Hughes should have been confirmed. I am just as certain that if he is confirmed to the bench of the Supreme Court of the United States in after years those of us who were instrumental in helping him to get there will be proud of what we did. I am just as certain of that as I can be.

What shall I do in this embarrassing position? Shall I withdraw what I have said here and keep my mouth closed or shall I get up and say in the Senate what I believe to be true, and give my reasons for it?

Oh, it may be that the workingman and the labor organizations are important; I am reasonably certain that they are important, not only to the country, but to the laboring people everywhere. I am certain of that, but I say that in this kind of crisis, I can not permit the labor organizations to mold my conscience and turn it out, where, if I look at it, I can not recognize it myself, and where, if my children should see it, they would not believe it was the conscience of their father.

I do not propose that the colored people of this country shall take my judgment and fashion it in such a way that when they get through with it will look like a weak, miserable candidate for the United States Senate. Instead of a man who is sitting there now and endeavoring to do his duty as he sees it.

Am I to sacrifice principle for political expediency? Oh, no. Before that is done, I hope nature may close my lips so that I can not cast another vote in this body. I hope that before that is done the people of my State will take from me whatever responsibility and whatever power they have given me in this great office.

No, no. I can not stand for that. But when it is all over, I hope to have some good, able friend to say, "He sacrificed his political career, but he did it upon the altar of what he believed to be right," and if, that can be said, I care not what else may be said.

Source: *Congressional Record*, 71st Cong., 2nd sess., April 30, 1930 (Washington: GPO, 1930), 72:8032–8033.

SENATOR ROBERT F. WAGNER OPPOSES THE NOMINATION OF JOHN J. PARKER TO THE SUPREME COURT

APRIL 30, 1930

Mr. President, it is my intention to vote to sustain the committee which has reported adversely on Judge Parker's nomination as Justice of the Supreme Court. My present purpose is, in justice to myself, to set forth the reasons which prompted me to come to this conclusion and to persuade, if I can, my colleagues whose minds are still open on this question, likewise to vote to reject the nomination.

I do not often enter upon the terrain of debate in which the Senate is now engaged, because frankly, I dislike to discuss men. I prefer to consider problems. It is only under compulsion of the constitutional duty of advice and consent in the nomination of Supreme Court judges — duty too important to be shirked — that I permit myself to express my thoughts on the pending question.

Let me say at the outset that I do not question Mr. Parker's integrity, nor do I doubt that he possesses a knowledge of the law. That is but the lawyer's stock in trade. It determines admission to the bar; it is alone insufficient for elevation to the highest court. To pass upon a nomination of that office it is first necessary to survey the requirements of the post, to plumb its profound responsibilities, to calculate its importance in terms of its influence upon the welfare of our country. Only then is it possible to make an appropriate comparison between the magnitude of the place to be filled and the size of the man who has been called to fill it.

The judicial process has been studied for thousands of years. Few students of the subject in our day have been rewarded with as rich an insight into that process as Benjamin Cardozo, Chief Judge of the New York Court of Appeals. In his well-known volume, the Nature of the Judicial Process, he emphasizes that an important phase of the work of judges is lawmaking, and that the decisions they render are law in the making. The present Chief Justice of the United States Supreme Court many years ago expressed a similar thought in an epigrammatic phrase when he said:

The Constitution is what the judges say it is.

We are to-day all fully aware that the Constitution we live under and the laws we are judged by are not a lifeless set of wooden precepts moved about according to the rules of a mechanical logic. At least I should say that the law is never that in the hands of great judges. The Constitution of the United States to-day is what the judges of the past have made it and the Constitution of the future will be what the judges appointed in our day will make it; and it is, therefore, by the standard of makers of the Constitution that nominees for the Supreme Bench must be judged.

★ ★ ★ ★

Appointments to the Supreme Court must be by long-time standards. They certainly should not be made by reference to immediate political opportunities. Presidential administrations come and go; laws are made and repealed; alongside of these judicial pronouncements are relatively immortal.

No man of ordinary capacity who merely happens to fit into the political and geographical necessities of the moment can pass muster if tested by these standards. The peculiar quality required of a Supreme Court judge can best be described by the term "statecraft." Its possession is indispensable.

The Constitution ... to-day is what the judges of the past have made it and the Constitution of the future will be what the judges appointed in our day will make it; and it is, therefore, by the standard of the makers of the Constitution that nominees for the Supreme Bench must be judged. — Robert F. Wagner

---

One of our closest observers of the work of the Supreme Court, Felix Frankfurter, in his recent lecture at Yale University, expressed this idea effectively:

> With the great men of the Supreme Court, constitutional adjudication has always been "statecraft." As a mere lawyer Marshall had his superiors among his colleagues. His supremacy lay in recognition of the practical needs of the Government. Those of his successors whose labors history has validated were men who brought to their task insight into the problems of their generation. The great judges are those to whom the Constitution is not primarily a text for interpretation, but the means of ordering the lives at a progressive people.

At the present time three problems of major importance divide the Supreme Court. The first deals with the question: What are the limits within which a State may exercise its police powers and taxing powers to accomplish ends loosely referred to as social welfare? New problems, generally arising out of present-day urban and industrial conditions, have been met by the several States in a variety of ways. Many of the methods attempted by the States have been declared invalid by a divided court. The problem is not yet settled. In the nature of things it can never be settled. Every new decision is but the driving of a new stake in the boundary line between permissible action and prohibited action. The nature of the personnel of the Supreme Court will determine whether the area of permitted action shall be wide and free or narrowly restricted.

The second of these problems is identified with the relatively new and expanding field of public-utility regulation.

The third is concerned with industrial relations: What is the scope of permissible action by employees in attempting to further their economic interest?

Little, if anything, is known of the nominee's attitude or experience in dealing with the first two problems. On the third his record discloses an opinion sanctioning the anti-union or so-called "yellow-dog" promise. It is an opinion which obviously merits special consideration.

★ ★ ★ ★

It is extraordinarily simple and easy to insert "yellow-dog" contracts into terms of employment. If employers should be foolish enough to use them, and the courts should enforce them by injunction, then the well-organized, responsible trade unionism we have known is doomed. Only underground, rebellious, revolutionary, secret association will flourish in its place. The injunction will silence the voice of every responsible union organizer. But the underground revolutionist who pays little attention to law and less to injunctions will flourish like a green bay tree.

These are considerations which appeal to the lay mind as well as to the professional. One need not have read Blackstone to understand that there is something inherently unfair in such an arrangement. No acquaintance with Supreme Court decisions is necessary to understand the probable effects of such a régime upon the future of industrial relationship. Nor is it necessary for us to consider at this time whether an employer may insist that only unorganized labor shall be employed in his plant.

For purposes of present discussion it is sufficient to inquire whether, if he so insists, he must educate his employees to be satisfied with his terms or whether the courts will tender him immune from the flow of ideas and the current of world discussion and the persuasion of workmen that in the union lies their salvation.

★ ★ ★ ★

To the worker organization means bargaining power, security, self-respect. So long as he continues unorganized he must accept terms of employment just as they are as tendered. It is only through organization that he achieves the power to withhold that which he sells. The arrangement known as the antiunion or "yellow-dog" contract is ordinarily an undertaking on the part of the employee that he will continue to remain in the same helpless condition which compelled him to make the "yellow-dog" promise in the first instance. Is it good social policy to give full play to a device to accomplish that which medievalism accomplished through class stratification? Is it sound American practice to permit that system to be reproduced on this continent?

★ ★ ★ ★

It was this sort of agreement that was presented to Judge Parker in the Red Jacket case.

The Red Jacket Mining Co. employed each man with the understanding that he would not join the union as long as he worked for the Red Jacket Co. The United Mine Workers, nevertheless, sent agents to persuade the employees of the Red Jacket Co. to join the union. The Red Jacket did not attempt to meet argument with argument.

It did not even go through the form of attempting to persuade its men that its method of employment was superior and that they ought not to join the union. It did not exercise the power which it possessed to fire the men who joined. Instead it appealed to the equity court to restrain the organizers from persuading its employees to join the union. How did Judge Parker react to this application? Did he inquire into or consider the inequality of bargaining power between the Red Jacket Co. and each of its employees? Did he consider the consequences to unionism if such applications were generally granted? Did he inquire into the consonance of such a limitation upon public speech with American institutions? Did it occur to him that if such an injunction issued it would mean that under the protecting wing of the Federal courts every form of bondage could be imposed upon workers and that all resistance on their part would be rendered futile?

Mr. President, the most devastating criticism of Mr. Parker, the one fact which alone, in my judgment, is sufficient to disqualify him to hold the position to which he has been nominated is the fact that he failed totally to react. The application aroused in him no response. It called forth in him no evaluation of this device in the government of our people or its effect upon industrial relations. He was not what Cardoza called "the skeptic on the bench." The instrument was labeled a contract, and he accepted it as labeled, without question, without doubt, without thought, totally oblivious of its possibly catastrophic effects upon the future. That failure to be aware of the fact that he was in the presence of an important problem shows a lack of statecraft which is the sine qua non of the high judicial office to which he has been nominated.

★ ★ ★ ★

Out of a host of principles of law pertinent to the Red Jacket case the first that comes to mind is the general rule that no contract is entitled to enforcement if it is in conflict with public policy.

The great value of this rule lies in its flexibility, in its power to comprehend new standards and new conditions. It is one of the great moving forces in the law which enables it to be stable and yet not to stand still. Whether a particular contract violates public policy in 1930 can not be determined by reading the precedents in Coke on Littleton. It is the public welfare of this generation that the law seeks to conserve.

What is the evidence on the question of public policy?

There is the story of every commission that has gone into the coal fields that the "yellow-dog" contract and the injunc-

tion which it gives rise are supplanting civil law and government. There is the deliberate conclusion of mature students of the subject that they are rendering impossible the solution of the labor problem. There is the testimony of one commission that many coal operators regard this so-called contract as immoral. There is the historical fact that State legislatures believe that it ought to be a criminal offense to make such a contract.

All this is cumulative evidence that the antiunion promise is in conflict with public policy. Certainly, no court of equity ought to give it validity.

Another well established principle has decisive bearing upon the issue raised in the Red Jacket case — the principle that courts will not enforce a harsh and unfair bargain. Compare the give and take in this employment arrangement. What do the employees and employers exchange? Primarily work for wages. But what does the employee secure in return for his additional promise not to join a union? Does the company promise not to fire him when and as it pleases? It does not. Does the company promise not to join a combination of employers to force wages down? It does not. The employer continues unhampered. His liberty of action is in no wise curtailed, but the worker has surrendered his power of self-defense against possible economic oppression. Such a bargain is harsh and unfair. It is not entitled to the extraordinary protection of an injunction.

These are general principles of universal application. They should have governed the disposition of the Red Jacket case.

But in addition, Mr. President, there is one clear-cut, conclusive reason why on Judge Parker's own statement of facts this injunction should never have issued. I have reference to the very simple fact that the employees were urged to do only that which they were at perfect liberty to do under the very terms of their contract. Such was the fact as found by the district court and approved by Judge Parker. On any theory of law whatsoever, there was, therefore, no interference with anyone's rights and no violation of law to be enjoined.

★ ★ ★ ★

The one and only inference that can be and drawn from the Parker decision is that he holds it unlawful for a union to organize workers in a trade and persuade them to go on — contract or no contract. There is precedent for this idea; but, Mr. President, Judge Parker will have to go much farther back than the Hitchman case to it. He might discover it in that benevolent age of a hundred years ago, in which also flourished the fellow-servant rule and similar barbarisms of our law. Only there can Judge Parker find the precedent or inspiration for the conclusion that must be drawn from his opinion. He said the union was not unlawful of itself. It was lawful as long as it was willing peacefully to curl up and die. But it became unlawful the minute it tried to extend its membership, its scale of wages, and its conditions of employment into the coal fields of West Virginia.

The implications of the case are far wider than the sanctioning of the "yellow-dog" contract. It threatens the right of self-organization by workers in any manner whatever.

★ ★ ★ ★

Mr. President, I see a deep and fundamental consistency between Judge Parker's views of labor relation and his reported attitude toward the colored people of the United States. They both spring from a single trait of character. Judged by the available record, he is obviously incapable of viewing with sympathy the aspirations of those who are aiming for a higher and better place in the world. His sympathies naturally flow out to those who are already on top, and he has used the authority of his office and the influence of his opinion to keep them on top and to restrain the strivings of the others, whether they be an exploited economic group or a minority racial group. Otherwise, would it not be strange that the man whose Red Jacket opinion is defended as resulting from the constraint of a Supreme Court precedent should feel so lightly the restraints of the Constitution itself in his expressed views of the colored people?

In my State, I am happy to say, men and women participate fully and freely in every phase of democratic government and in every branch of the arts and sciences, without regard to race or creed or color.

From the contributions to its development by the negro as well as the white man the State of New York has grown to the position it holds to-day. We have never had cause to regret that in New York color does not determine the rights of citizenship or access to private opportunities. I am sure we never shall.

Judge Parker's reference to the colored race is to my mind, an insufferable and unjustified affront to millions of American citizens.

Mr. President, Judge Parker's sympathies as reflected in the record are not mine. His attitudes I do not share. But more important than either of these, in my judgment, is that measured by the standards erected, Judge Parker is found wanting. He lacks the statecraft essential to the office which he seeks. Guided by my conscience in the exercise of the duty imposed by the Constitution, I must withhold from the President my consent to this nomination, and in imparting the advice required under the constitutional mandate I satisfy myself to quote once again from Chief Judge Cardozo that it would be well for the President to —

… Know that the process of judging is a phase of a never-ending movement, and that something more is exacted of those who are to play their part in it than imitative reproduction, the lifeless repetition of a mechanical routine.

<hr>

Source: *Congressional Record,* 71st Cong., 2nd sess., April 30, 1930 (Washington: GPO, 1930), 72:8033–8037.

Notes

1. Richard L. Watson, Jr., "The Defeat of Judge Parker: A Study in Pressure Groups and Politics," *Mississippi Valley Historical Review* 50 (September 1953): 218.

2. "John J. Parker: Senior Circuit Judge: Fourth Circuit," *American Bar Association Journal,* December 1946 32 (857–858); William C. Burris, *Duty and the Law: Judge John J. Parker and the Constitution* (Bessemer, Ala.: Colonial Press, 1987), 72–73.

3. Burris, *Duty and the Law: Judge John J. Parker and the Constitution,* 73–75. See also Peter Graham Fish, "*Red Jacket* Revisited: The Case That Unraveled John J. Parker's Supreme Court Appointment," *Law and History Review* 5 (Spring 1987): 51–104; Watson, "The Defeat of Judge Parker: A Study in Pressure Groups and Politics," 216–217; *"Yellow Dog" Contract: Menace to American Liberties* (Washington, D.C.: American Federation of Labor, 1930).

4. U.S. Congress, Senate Subcommittee of the Committee on Judiciary, *Confirmation of Hon. John J. Parker to be an Associate Justice of the Supreme Court of the United States,* hearings, 71st Cong., 2nd sess., April 5, 1930 (Washington: GPO, 1930), 1–60.

5. *Confirmation of Hon. John J. Parker to be an Associate Justice of the Supreme Court of the United States,* hearings, 74–75; Watson, "The Defeat of Judge Parker: A Study in Pressure Groups and Politics," 218. See also Kenneth W. Goings, *"The NAACP Comes of Age": The Defeat of Judge John J. Parker* (Bloomington: Indiana University Press, 1990).

6. "Committee, 10 to 6, Rejects Parker," *New York Times,* April 22, 1930, 1; Watson, "The Defeat of Judge Parker: A Study in Pressure Groups and Politics," 221–222.

7. *Congressional Record,* 71st Cong., 2nd sess., April 28, 1930, 72:7811, 7822; ibid., April 30, 1930, 72:8037; William C. Burris, *The Senate Rejects a Judge: A Study of the John J. Parker Case* (Chapel Hill, N.C.: University of North Carolina, Department of Political Science, 1962), 15. *Congressional Record.*

8. *Congressional Record,* 71st Cong., 2nd sess., April 29, 1930, 72:7930–7939, 7949, 7950, 7953; April 30, 1930, 72:8032–8033, 8037, 8038–8039, 8182; May 6, 1930, 72:8343, 8358–8360; May 6, 1930, 72:8426, 8426–8427.

9. Burris, *Duty and the Law: Judge John J. Parker and the Constitution,* 94–100; Burris, *The Senate Rejects a Judge: A Study of the John J. Parker Case,* 22–31.

Roosevelt's Court-Packing Plan
✳ 1937 ✳

"No event of twentieth-century American constitutional history is better remembered," wrote William E. Leuchtenburg, "than Franklin D. Roosevelt's ill fated 'Court-packing scheme of 1937.'"[1] The previous November, Roosevelt had been reelected president by crushing Republican candidate Alf Landon in one of the most lopsided presidential elections in American history. He won nearly 61 percent of the popular vote, and by a 523–8 margin in the electoral college, captured forty-six of the country's forty-eight states. In the process he led the Democrat Party to overwhelming majorities in both the House, 331–89 and Senate, 76–16. Despite an unprecedented popular mandate, Roosevelt faced the prospect in his second term of seeing the closely divided Supreme Court continue, as it had in the previous two years, to strike down significant portions of New Deal legislation designed to help the nation recover from the agricultural, industrial, and social problems of the Great Depression.

When he had begun his first term in 1933, the makeup of the Court was relatively balanced with the conservative coalition of Justices James Clark McReynolds, Willis Van Devanter, George Sutherland, and Pierce Butler often clashing with the liberal Justices, Louis Dembitz Brandeis, Harlan Fiske Stone, and Benjamin Nathan Cardozo. Justice Owen Josephus Roberts and Chief Justice Charles Evans Hughes remained more or less moderate. Initially, the Court accepted most of Roosevelt's programs, but beginning in 1935, the Court, under Chief Justice Hughes, had ruled in several cases that the executive branch had unconstitutionally assumed powers reserved for the legislature. In the process, the Court invalidated portions of several New Deal measures.

Roosevelt interpreted his overwhelming 1936 electoral victory as an approval of New Deal policies that had put millions of Americans back to work and given people hope. With an enormous popular mandate in hand, FDR turned full attention to the challenge posed by the Court instead of waiting for vacancies to occur, or hoping that the election results had changed the views of some of the justices.[2] Having a strong sense of his historic role, Roosevelt refused to be remembered as allowing the Court to frustrate his efforts to end the country's economic crisis. He was instead determined to liberalize the Court.

Several possible approaches were discussed by the president and Attorney General Homer S. Cummings including various constitutional amendment proposals designed to enlarge federal power at the expense of the Supreme Court. An amendment, however, was ultimately rejected as being too slow a process and too easy to defeat. Instead, Roosevelt settled on a judicial reform proposal that allowed the president to appoint: (1) up to six new justices to the Supreme Court for every member who had served for ten years and did not resign or retire within six months after his seventieth birthday; and (2) forty-four new judges to lower courts using the same criteria. A number of provisions designed to streamline judicial action were also in the measure.[3]

When Roosevelt announced what his critics immediately dubbed as the "Court-Packing" plan in a special message to Congress on February 5, 1937, he caught the nation, Congress, the Cabinet, and his closest friends by surprise. Although his ostensible purpose was to increase the efficiency of the judiciary, he was clearly motivated by the consistent opposition that New Deal legislation had encountered in the federal courts, most notably the Supreme Court's recent invalidation of such laws as the National Industrial Recovery Act, Railroad Retirement Act, Agricultural Adjustment Act, Bituminous Coal Act, and Municipal Bankruptcy Act. He hoped to use the plan to appoint six new justices and gain control over the hostile Supreme Court.

Aged and infirm judges and insufficient personnel, the President told Congress, had overburdened the federal courts. While in "exceptional cases, of course judges like other men, retain to an advance age full mental and physical vigor. Those not so fortunate are often unable to perceive their own infirmities." The Framers in granting life tenure for judges, Roosevelt declared, did not intend "to create a static judiciary. A constant and systematic addition of younger blood will revitalize the courts and better equip them to recognize and apply the essential concepts of justice in the light of the needs and the facts of an ever-changing world."[4]

Roosevelt's plan, which was revealed at a White House press conference prior to being sent to Capitol Hill, stunned congressional leaders who were being excluded from its drafting, provoked vigorous public opposition, and prompted

In order to preserve large portions of his New Deal plan, President Franklin D. Roosevelt aimed to reform the now-divided Supreme Court to make it more receptive to his legislation. Despite his large public popularity, Roosevelt's 1937 "court-packing plan" had difficulty passing the Senate.

Source: The Granger Collection, New York.

the American people that has occurred since the days preceding the Civil War."[6]

Despite significant opposition, chiefly because of the huge Democratic majorities in Congress, most observers agreed that Roosevelt had the votes needed to enact the Judicial Reorganization Bill. On March 4, the president launched a personal campaign on behalf of the proposal at a Democratic Victory dinner in Washington, arguing that national progress was being blocked by the prejudices of the Court majority and that his plan would restore, rather than threaten, the balance of power among the three branches of government. Roosevelt continued his drive for approval on March 9 in a national radio address, "the only time he used one of his famous fireside chats to ask the nation to pressure Congress in behalf of his policies."[7]

Shortly thereafter, the Court launched a significant counterattack. Early in March, Chief Justice Hughes, in a letter to the Senate Judiciary Committee approved by Justices Brandeis and Van Devanter, refuted Roosevelt's claim that the Court was not keeping up with its caseload and provided records demonstrating the Court's efficiency. Hughes' letter countered each of the arguments put forth by the White House. More importantly, from late March through May, the Court reversed its course and unexpectedly upheld the Frazier-Lemke Farm Mortgage Moratorium Act of 1935, the Social Security Act, the Wagner National Labor Relations Act, and a Washington state minimum wage law for women that closely resembled one it had struck down only a few months earlier. Also in May, conservative Justice Van Devanter announced his retirement, assuring Roosevelt a liberal majority with his first appointment to the Court.[8]

Roosevelt was not, however, ready to concede. In early June, he agreed to allow Senate Majority Leader Joseph Robinson, D-Ark., to develop a compromise bill that authorized the president each year to appoint an additional justice for each member of the Court who was seventy-five. In mid-June, the Senate Judiciary Committee by a 10–8 vote recommended against passage of the bill. Its scathing report to the full Senate characterized the bill as "a needless, futile and utterly dangerous abandonment of constitutional principle" that if enacted would "make this government one of men rather than of law." The committee concluded that it "should be so emphatically rejected that its parallel will never again be presented to the free representatives of the free people of America."[9]

Now the burden of gaining approval of the plan was left to the persuasive powers of Senator Robinson, the expectant nominee for the vacancy created by Justice Van Devanter's retirement. By the time the bill reached the Senate floor on July 6, the chamber was so evenly divided on the plan it was unclear how the final vote would unfold. Then suddenly, a week into an acrimonious floor debate, the president lost his final advantage when Robinson was stricken with a fatal heart attack. Just prior to Robinson's death, Sen. Joseph C. O'Ma-

bitter debate in Congress. Many saw it as an attempt to overturn the American constitutional system of checks and balances and destroy the independence of the judiciary. Judges, state bar associations, and conservatives who opposed the New Deal denounced Roosevelt as a would-be dictator, and Democrats and sympathetic New Deal liberals unexpectedly criticized the president as well. He further antagonized potential supporters within his own party by refusing to consider changes in the bill. Angered that they had not been consulted and aggravated by what they saw as territorial encroachment, Senate Democrats provided some of the strongest resistance.[5]

The plan was expostulated at town meetings, country stores, rallies, club meetings, and churches. Constituents overwhelmed members of Congress with mail, and critical articles, editorials, and letters to the editor dominated the media. In proposing the plan, *The Congressional Digest* reasoned, Roosevelt "precipitated the biggest fight the Senate has engaged in since the memorable battle over President Woodrow Wilson's proposal that the United States join the League of Nations. So far as its importance is concerned, some observers are of the opinion that the basic issues involved make the present controversy the most important to

honey, D-Wy., captured the tenor of growing sentiment among Senators when he characterized the court-packing bill as vesting "in any occupant of the White House," whether the President be good or bad, the power, if he so wished, "to wreck every vestige of human liberty under the Stars and Stripes. On July 22, 168 days after the reorganization plan was first introduced, the bill was recommitted back to the Judi-

ciary Committee, 70–20, where it died. Instead, in August, Congress passed a diminished reform measure, incorporating some of the resident's recommendations, but leaving the number of Supreme Court justices unchanged.[10] Over the next four years, however, a combination of deaths and retirements enabled Roosevelt to make seven appointments to the Court.

SENATOR JOSEPH T. ROBINSON SUPPORTS PRESIDENT ROOSEVELT'S COURT-PACKING PLAN

JULY 6, 1937

As everyone who hears me realizes there has been great diversity of opinion not only among those who are opposed to any legislation providing for the reorganization of the Federal courts, but also among those who feel that conditions justify, if they do not require, a change in our statutes relating to the questions at issue.

THE SUBSTITUTE

The substitute amendment provides for the appointment of one Justice in each calendar year in relation to Justices of the Supreme Court as may be serving after they have reached the age of seventy-five years. There seems to be wide-spread if not general or universal sentiment in favor of the retirement of Justices who have attained that age. It is not that all men who reach seventy-five lose their powers of reasoning or of judgment, but it is that by common acceptance those who have passed beyond seventy-five usually are in a state of mental and physical decline. Our statutes have recognized the wisdom and the necessity for judges who have the physical vigor to perform the tasks that are assigned to them. Heretofore provision has been made for voluntary retirement at the age of seventy years, and that policy has not only been approved in general public opinion but it has been advocated by some Justices of the Supreme Court who now have passed far beyond seventy years, and who quite naturally are unable to apply to themselves the theory and the doctrine they have sought to apply to other judges.

The statute, as proposed in the pending amendment in the nature of a substitute, permits the appointment by the President of one additional Justice of the Supreme Court in each calendar year where a Justice or Justices are serving beyond the age of seventy-five. I know it has been said by some, and I expect that it will be repeated in the memorable debate that is to follow my statement, that the principle incorporated in

this legislation in the particular to which I am now referring is erroneous, that it is disregardful of the spirit of the Federal Constitution, that it tends to give to the President dictatorial powers. Later, during the course of the debate, it may be my privilege to elaborate the arguments which appear to me consistently to refute the contention. It suffices for my purpose on this occasion to say that during the course of this prolonged controversy Senators who lead the opposition to any legislation have introduced constitutional amendments substantially conforming to the provisions of this bill.

No moral or legal reason can be assigned in justification to resorting to the complicated and difficult process of constitutional amendment in preference to the legislative process if it appears that the legislative proposal is itself within the Constitution. I make the declaration now, in order that it may be considered by those who oppose the position I take, that no serious question has been raised by any lawyer, either in this body or in the country at large, that it is within the power of the Congress to enact the legislation contemplated in the proposed substitute; and, if that be true, then the only question left in that particular is one of policy. Manifestly it is neither necessary nor desirable to resort to the slow and difficult process of amending the Constitution if substantially the same ends may be brought about by the enactment of legislation.

★ ★ ★ ★

No lawyer would say that Congress has the power to limit the tenure of a Justice of the Supreme Court to less than life and good behavior, and therefore, no proposal of that nature is presented. But there is, and there has been for more than fifty years, a feeling in the country among those who constitute its citizenship that men are not always conscious of the time when they have passed the climax of their usefulness. It is well illustrated in politics. One who has served long and well is seldom, if ever, conscious of his failing powers, and he keeps on running for office, running and running and run-

---

It is not that all men who reach seventy-five lose their powers of reasoning or of judgment, but it is that by common acceptance those who have passed beyond seventy-five usually are in a state of mental and physical decline. — Joseph T. Robinson

---

ning, until everyone gets tired of him and until some man whom he considers his inferior defeats him for office. [Laughter.]

★ ★ ★ ★

I have often thought that politics is not an occupation; it is a disease [Laughter]; and, by the Eternal when it gets in the blood and brain, there is no cure for it. [Laughter.]

★ ★ ★ ★

I have seen dozens of men, discredited and rejected by their constituents, sit on the fence and in the exercise of their "imaginatory" powers — I quote now the Senator from Vermont — see strange hands beckoning them out of the darkness and hear mysterious voices calling them back to run for office again.

★ ★ ★ ★

In October 1914, when the Associate Justice, Mr. McReynolds, was Attorney General, he submitted a report which no doubt is in the mind and memory of my good friend the Senator from Indiana [Mr. Minton]. In the performance of his duties he sent an urgent recommendation to Congress, and I shall now read it:

> Judges of the United States courts, at the age of seventy, after having served ten years, may retire upon full pay. In the past many judges have availed themselves of this privilege. Some, however, have remained upon the bench long beyond the time they are adequately able to discharge their duties, and in consequence the administration of justice has suffered. I suggest an act —

Not a constitutional amendment remind the Senator from Nebraska [Mr. Burke]; just an act —

> I suggest an act providing that when any judge of a Federal court below the Supreme Court fails to avail himself of the privilege of retiring now granted by law, that the President be required, with the advice and consent of the Senate, to

appoint another judge who would preside over the affairs of the court and have precedence over the older one. This will insure at all times the presence of a judge sufficiently active to discharge promptly and adequately the duties of the court.

It is true that Mr. Justice McReynolds then Attorney General, limited his recommendation to the inferior courts the circuit and district courts of the United States, but there is no difference in principle if the doctrine be applied to the Supreme Court as well as to the inferior courts.

★ ★ ★ ★

I think there is no limitation in the Constitution on the power of the Congress to prescribe the number of Justices that shall compose the Supreme Court. I would not say it is sound policy to exercise that power for a bad motive, but the power exists, and that is sufficient for this argument.

★ ★ ★ ★

Independence of the judiciary does not involve or imply usurpation by the judiciary.... My theory is that the demand for this legislation arises principally — not entirely, but principally — out of the fact that the judiciary, not only in the Supreme Court but even in the lower courts have from time to time confused the question of power with the issue of policy. Do you get it? They have decided that the exercise of a power by the Congress is unconstitutional in some instances when they disapproved the public policy involved in the legislation. That is wrong; and the efforts to prevent it have no sensible relation to the independence of the judiciary. The judiciary must be independent in the sphere ascribed to it by the Constitution. It must not be an outlaw in any other sphere. The mere fact that there is no appeal from the Supreme Court of the United States gives that Court no right to violate constitutional limitations imposed by law and by reason on its own authority.

★ ★ ★ ★

There is not any way by which the Congress can prevent a judge from doing the wrong thing; but the theory of the bill is that it will gradually place on the bench those who will respect, as a primary consideration, the limitations on their own authority. I do not ask you to take my word. I will ask you to take the word of the Senator from Idaho himself.

In 1930, I think, the Senator from Idaho arose on the floor and made an eloquent appeal against the confirmation of a great Chief Justice, solely on the theory that that Chief Justice was disposed to decide questions of public policy rather than questions of limitation on the power of the lawmaking body. The Senator from Idaho may take from now until the end of the threatened filibuster to explain his attitude on that occasion; and he was not alone in that attitude. At the same time a dozen other Senators, among them the brightest and the bravest who are opposing this bill, sought to prevent the confirmation of Mr. Chief Justice Hughes on the theory that Mr. Hughes would lead the Court out of the proper sphere of judicial determination into the realm of legislation. They could not say anything against his character other than that. They could not question his personal integrity, but they fought him to the bitter death; and I cabled back from London, where I had gone on a mission for the Government, my vote in support of Mr. Hughes, because I believed him to be an honest and an able man. The issue was acute, it was tense; it was hard fought, and there was a large vote in the Senate. At one time it was thought doubtful whether he would be confirmed. The opposition rested their argument solely on the ground that he would legislate as a judge.

★ ★ ★ ★

After a judge is confirmed he is on the bench for life, and there is no opportunity of knowing what he is going to decide except to use the method employed by the Senator from Idaho and the Senator from Virginia and say, "From what he has done heretofore, from the clients he has represented, from the methods used in other matters, I think he will be unfair to the public, unconsciously unfair to the public."

Of course, if one knows about those things at the time confirmation occurs and has not confidence in the judge, he would do just what these senators did in opposing Mr. Justice Hughes. I cannot say that their judgement of Mr. Hughes is confirmed by the history of his actions as the Chief Justice. I have great respect for the able lawyer. I regard him as a learned and conscientious man, and do not wish to be construed as giving endorsement to the arguments which were employed against his confirmation. I voted for his confirmation.

Source: *Congressional Record*, 75th Cong., 1st sess., July 6, 1937 (Washington: GPO, 1937), 81:6789–6794.

SENATOR JOSEPH C. O'MAHONEY OPPOSES ROOSEVELT'S COURT-PACKING PLAN

JULY 12, 1937

CENTRALIZED JUSTICE THE ISSUE

… [I]t ought to be clear to the Senate and to the country that we are not discussing a personal issue; we are discussing a system for the reorganization of the judiciary of the United States. The issue before this body is not the election of 1940, as some Senators seem to imagine; the issue before this body is not the New Deal, as some Senators would like to have the country believe; the issue before this body is not the record of Franklin D. Roosevelt, as some Senators would like us to believe. The issue before this body is whether or not we are going to adopt a system for the judiciary of the United States vastly different from anything which has ever existed in the history of our Government.

We are rapidly approaching the one hundred and fiftieth anniversary of the adoption of the Constitution of the United States under which our judicial system was established; and we are now asked to consider a bill which, if enacted would revolutionize that system. The measure before us today and which will be before us tomorrow and many a day hence, I gather from the attitude of Senators, should not be entitled "A bill to reform the judiciary," as it is sometimes called in the public press; it should be called a bill to centralize the administration of justice and to give the central establishment at Washington greater control over the local administration of justice than it has ever had in this democracy.

Do we desire to centralize the administration of justice? Presidents come and Presidents go. The present occupant of the White House will not always occupy that distinguished position with the great ability and charm with which he now occupies it. Some other President will succeed him, and when he does, if this bill should become a law, it would apply to him as well as to the present occupant of the White House.

So I say, Mr. President, this is not a personal issue; this is not a question of whether or not we are going to give a certain amount of power to Franklin D. Roosevelt. The issue before us in whether we are going to give this power to any President who may occupy the White House, no matter who he may be. I shall not engage in any invidious comparisons; I shall not mention names; but there must come to the mind of every Member of this body, as there must come to the minds of all the citizens of the United States, the names of Presidents in whom they would not for three minutes entrust the power which is proposed to be vested in the President by the pending measure.

A New System is Proposed

Remember we are acting upon a system. Let no one forget it. If this measure should be enacted into law, this generation may pass and the next generation will be operating under the system proposed, which would mark a revolutionary change from the system which has been handed down to us by the constitutional fathers.

Let us consider the bill. What proponent has yet stood upon this floor and explained the first section of the proposed substitute? Was it explained by the sponsors of the bill? Did the eminent chairman of the Judiciary Committee of the Senate of the United States, the Senator from Arizona [Mr. Ashurst], whose name is attached to this measure, explain the bill? Did the eminent Senator from Kentucky [Mr. Logan], whose name is attached to this measure, rise in his place to explain its purport and effect? He spoke not a single word of that character. Did the Senator from New Mexico [Mr. Hatch], who lends his name to it, give any explanation of the measure? Not a word or a syllable. And when those of us who are opposed to the measure undertake to discuss it we are told that we are filibusterers and are preventing the transaction of the public business.

What business can be more important, Senators of the United States, than the establishment of the judicial system under which you, your children, and your children's children will be governed so long as this measure remains upon the statute books, if it is passed? Good Presidents come and good Presidents go and bad Presidents come and bad Presidents go, and the power that is proposed to be vested by this bill in any occupant of the White House could be used by a man if he were so minded, to wreck every vestige of human liberty under the Stars and Stripes. Let us consider it.

When the original bill was proposed it provided that in the instance of each member of the judiciary who had attained the age of seventy years and had served for ten years and within six months had not retired or resigned, the President should appoint another Justice.

It was mandatory. He had no discretion about it at all. The solemn duty was laid upon him by the terms of the bill to send the nomination to the Senate of the United States for every man on the bench of the given age and service. As it was written it would probably have resulted in the immediate appointment of six Justices.

Discretionary Appointments

The resentment of the country to the plan was so sweeping and so strong that it was abandoned, or at least we are told it was abandoned, and here as a substitute we have a bill which, instead of saying that the President "shall" appoint says he "may" appoint. The President now has the discretion

to appoint an additional Justice when a sitting Justice reaches the age of seventy-five years. Why the discretion? Is the President to be permitted to say, "In my judgment new blood is not necessary now. It is true these men are seventy-five years of age. It is true that there ought to be new blood; but I am satisfied, I shall make no appointments."

Understand, Mr. President, I am speaking in an impersonal manner. I am not speaking of the present occupant of the White House. I am speaking of any occupant of the White House. If the power is discretionary then it follows as the night follows the day that the occupant of the White House

---

Good Presidents come and good Presidents go and bad Presidents come and bad Presidents go, and the power that is proposed to be vested by this bill in any occupant of the White House could be used by a man if he were so minded, to wreck every vestige of human liberty.... — Joseph C. O'Mahoney

---

at some future time, if not at this time, may say, "I am satisfied with the decisions of Justice A, who is seventy-five years of age, and I shall not send a new nomination."

Why the difference between "shall" and "may"? When it was pointed out on the first day of the debate, the Senator from New Mexico [Mr. Hatch] immediately announced his belief that the appointment should be mandatory, and I understand now from the newspapers that the Senator from Kentucky [Mr. Logan] says the same thing. How does it happen that, after the lapse of all these months, the proponents of the substitute come upon the floor not knowing exactly what the bill proposes? Who is the legislative draftsman who substituted "may" for "shall"? It was not the chairman of the Judiciary Committee [Mr. Ashurst]. It was not the Senator from New Mexico [Mr. Hatch]. It was not the Senator from Kentucky [Mr. Logan]. It was not the Senator from Arkansas [Mr. Robinson] who proposed the substitute. Who substituted "may" for "shall"?

The Accumulation of Appointments

That is not all. The new bill provides that:

Not more than one appointment of an additional Justice as herein authorized shall be made in any calendar year.

What is the explanation for that limitation? Obviously if new blood is necessary, if age be a crime, if, when Justices reach the age of seventy-five they are no longer fit to sit upon the bench, why should they not be removed and why should there be only one substitute Justice when perhaps there may be four or five who have reached the alleged age of senility? If the rule is good for one it is good for all.

Oh, but this limitation was put in for the purpose of preventing judgments of the Court from being influenced by the appointments. How simple-minded we are all supposed to be!

★ ★ ★ ★

Mr. President, we have here a substitute which provides, first, for concentration of power by giving the appointing authority wholly new powers in the selection of Justices of the Supreme Court in the manner I have described; for concentration of power in the transfer of judges both circuit and district, through all parts of the country; for additional concentration of power through the operation of the newly established office of proctor; and, finally — the fourth phase of concentration — permission to the United States Government to intervene in every case in which the constitutionality of a law drawn in question, and to appeal these cases, regardless of the desires or will of the litigants.

Does this consolidation have any significance for the people of the United States? I think it cannot be denied that it does. It has a tremendous significance, a significance which I venture to say is not realized by many persons in the United States. Perhaps not many in Congress or in the administration realize the great danger that confronts them.

★ ★ ★ ★

Big Business and Big Government

There is no Member of this body who does not know that the great glory of the American judicial system is the independence of the courts. The independent judiciary was the greatest advance in the history of government, and it has been one of our great prides that it has been protected in the United States, and that it is the ideal of our people.

★ ★ ★ ★

Independent Judiciary Essential

Mr. President, I suppose there is no great statesman of our country who has not at one time or another declared his belief in the independence of the courts. In the same month in which the Declaration of Independence was signed, Thomas Jefferson wrote a letter to the distinguished George Wythe, of Virginia, from which I wish to read an extract. It was dated July 1776 and reads:

The dignity and stability of government in all its branches, the morals of the people, and every blessing of society, depends so much upon an upright and skillful administration of justice that the judicial power ought to be distinct from both the legislature and executive, and independent upon both, that so it may be a check upon both, as both should be checks upon

that. The judges, therefore, should always be men of learning and experience in the laws, of exemplary morals, great patience, calmness, and attention; their minds should not be distracted with jarring interests, they should not be dependent upon any man or body of men. To these ends they should hold estates for life in their offices, or in other words, their commissions should be during good behavior, and their salaries ascertained and established by law.

For misbehavior, the grand inquest of the colony, the house of representatives, should impeach them before the Governor and council, when they should have time and opportunity to make their defense; but if convicted, should be removed from their offices and subjected to such other punishment as shall be thought proper.

Every law student who remembers his Blackstone remembers the lectures of that distinguished British jurist and his pronouncement upon this subject. I quote from Blackstone's *Commentaries*, volume 1, chapter 7, page 268:

In this distinct and separate existence of the judicial power in a peculiar body of men nominated indeed, but not removable at pleasure, by the crown, consists one main preservative of the public liberty; which cannot subsist long in any state unless the administration of common justice be in some degree separated from the legislative and also from the executive power. Where it joined with the legislative, the life, liberty, and property of the subject would be in the hands of arbitrary judges, whose decisions would be then regulated only by their own opinions, and not by any fundamental principles of law; which, though legislators may depart from, yet judges are bound to observe. Were it joined with the executive, this union might soon be an overbalance for the legislative. For which reason, by the statute of 16 Car. I., c. 10, which abolished the court of star chamber, effectual care is taken to remove all judicial power out of the hands of the King's privy council, who, as then was evident from recent instances, might soon be inclined to pronounce that for law which was most agreeable to the prince or his officers. Nothing, therefore, is more to be avoided, in a free constitution, than uniting the provinces of a judge and a minister of state.

★ ★ ★ ★

The object of the creation of the independent judiciary — and I could quote at length from the distinguished statesmen of the past — was to preserve the individual citizen from the power of the Government. That is the purpose of the independent judiciary, to make the judges free of the executive arm so that there may be no danger of a miscarriage, so that there may be no danger that the executive arm of the Government may impose its will in decision of cases. But now we have a bill before us which tears this principle down and tends to make the judiciary the agent of the Government. Do you wonder I call it revolutionary?

Source: *Congressional Record*, 75th Cong., 1st sess., July 12, 1937 (Washington: GPO, 1937), 81:7038–7039, 7045–7047.

Notes

1. William E. Leuchtenburg, "The Origins of Franklin D. Roosevelt's 'Court-Packing' Plan," *The Supreme Court Review* 347 (1966). See also William E. Leuchtenburg, "Franklin D. Roosevelt's Supreme Court 'Packing' Plan," in *Essays on the New Deal by Wilmon H. Droze, George Wolfskill, and William E. Leuchtenburg*, ed. Harold M. Hollingsworth and William F. Holmes (Austin: University of Texas at Arlington by the University of Texas Press, 1969), 69–71.

2. Leuchtenburg, "The Origins of Franklin D. Roosevelt's 'Court-Packing' Plan," 382.

3. Joseph Alsop and Turner Catledge, *The 168 Days* (Garden City, NY: Doubleday, Doran, 1938), 23–38, 43–49, 54–55; Leuchtenburg, "The Origins of Franklin D. Roosevelt's 'Court-Packing' Plan," 383–400.

4. Samuel I. Rosenman, comp., *The Public Papers and Addresses of Franklin D. Roosevelt*, 13 vols. (New York: Russell and Russell, 1938–1950), 6:54–55. See also Alsop and Catledge, *The 168 Days*, 55–60, 66.

5. Patrick Maney, "The Forgotten New Deal Congress," in *The American Congress: The Building of Democracy*, ed. Julian E. Zelizer (Boston: Houghton Mifflin, 2004), 461. See also Alsop and Catledge, *The 168 Days*, 68–106.

6. "The Supreme Court Controversy," *The Congressional Digest*, March 1937, 66; Alfred Haines Cope and Fred Krinsky, eds., *Franklin D. Roosevelt and the Supreme Court*, rev. ed. (Lexington, Mass.: D.C. Heath, 1969), 28; Leuchtenburg, "Franklin D. Roosevelt's Supreme Court-'Packing' Plan," 77.

7. Samuel Kernell, *Going Public: New Strategies of Presidential Leadership*, 3rd ed. (Washington, D.C.: Congressional Quarterly, 1997), 128.

8. U.S. Congress, Senate Committee on the Judiciary, *Reorganization of the Federal Judiciary,* hearings on S. 1392, 75th Cong., 1st sess. (Washington: GPO, 1937), 491; Alsop and Catledge, *The 168 Days*, 135–147; Leonard Baker, *Back to Back: The Duel Between FDR and the Supreme Court* (New York: Macmillan, 1967), 153–164; Leuchtenburg, "Franklin D. Roosevelt's Supreme Court-'Packing' Plan," 93–97.

9. U.S. Congress, Senate Committee on the Judiciary, *Reorganization of the Federal Judiciary,* S. Rept. 711, 75th Cong., 1st sess. (Washington: GPO, 1937), 23. See also Baker, *Back to Back: The Duel Between FDR and the Supreme Court,* 145–173, 177–183, 206.

10. For Sen. O'Mahoney's observation see *Congressional Record*, July 12, 1937, 81:7038. See also *Congressional Record*, 75th Cong., 1st sess., July 22, 1937, 81:7375–7381; 50 Stat. 751–754.

Fair Labor Standards Act
✳ 1937–1938 ✳

On six occasions between May 1937 and April 1938, President Franklin D. Roosevelt asked Congress for a law establishing a national minimum hourly wage, a maximum full-time standard workweek, and child labor standards. Ultimately, his appeals resulted in the Fair Labor Standards Act (FLSA). The debate preceding its passage was one of the bitterest in the annals of Congress.

During the previous century, a number of states had passed laws limiting the working hours of women and children, but the drive for federal regulation did not begin until 1932, when the American Federation of Labor (AFL) called on Congress to reduce the work week to thirty hours to increase employment opportunities. Although Roosevelt did not commit to a thirty-hour work week in his 1932 presidential campaign, he did recognize the despair confronting those who earned the least and promised to help them.[1]

Following his election, Roosevelt selected Francis Perkins, an acknowledged expert on labor legislation and social reform as secretary of labor and in the first hundred days pressed for passage of the National Industrial Recovery Act (NIRA). The act included provisions authorizing the formation of industrial codes governing labor practices that had the force of law when approved by the president. To administer the act, he created the National Industrial Recovery Administration, which tried to enforce minimum wage and maximum hour standards. After the Supreme Court ruled the NIRA unconstitutional in *A.L.A. Schechter Poultry Corp. v. United States* (1935), Roosevelt and his closest advisors began contemplating ways of restoring the minimum-age and maximum-hours standards.

During his 1936 reelection campaign, the importance of higher labor standards permeated Roosevelt's speeches and news conferences. That spring, after shocking everyone with his proposal to "pack" the Supreme Court with up to six new judges favorable to New Deal legislation, the Court reversed itself in upholding a Washington state minimum wage law for women, the Farm Mortgage Moratorium Act of 1935, the Social Security Act, and the Wagner Labor Relations Act. Now the stage was set for a minimum wage and hour bill. America, Roosevelt told Congress, should be able to "devise ways and means of insuring to all our able-bodied working men

and women a fair day's pay for a fair day's work" and "extend the frontiers of social progress." No "self-supporting and self-respecting democracy can" justify the child labor or offer an "economic reason for chiseling workers' wages or stretching workers' hours.... Goods produced under conditions which do not meet rudimentary standards of decency should be regarded as contraband and ought not to be allowed to pollute the channels of interstate trade."[2]

The administration's bill, which was prepared by Secretary of Labor Francis Perkins, and presidential advisors Benjamin V. Cohen and Thomas J. Corcoran, was introduced by Hugo Black, D-Ala., and William Connery, D-Mass., chairmen of the Senate Committee on Education and Labor and the House Committee on Labor, respectively. Black-Connery called for an unstated minimum wage (widely assumed to be 40 cents an hour), a maximum work week (assumed to be forty hours) for workers involved in interstate commerce, and a prohibition on child labor. Workers involved in agricultural or supervisory positions, and firms with fewer than six employees, were exempt from its coverage. A five-member Labor Standards Board would have discretionary power to set higher wage and lower hour requirements for those industries that demonstrated an "inadequacy or ineffectiveness of facilities for collective bargaining."[3]

Black-Connery incited intense debate on Capitol Hill as well as among the media and public. Joint House and Senate committee hearings in June 1937 revealed significant opposition from the business community (including the National Association of Manufacturers and United States Chamber of Commerce), the AFL, and conservative Republican and Democrats in the South and rural West. By the time the Senate passed the bill on July 31, several industries had lobbied successfully for exemptions and enhanced regional wage differentials, and the regulation of child labor was virtually eliminated.[4]

That fall, the House debated at length a significantly different version of the bill reported by the Labor Committee and two other drafts before sending the measure back to committee for further consideration. This action concluded a special session called by the president to deal with the wages-and-hours bill among other issues, and it marked the

President Franklin D. Roosevelt asked Congress to establish fair labor standards, including child labor laws to protect workers like those then common in factories. Though industries successfully limited the legislation, the core of Roosevelt's intentions remained in the Fair Labor Standards Act.
Source: The Granger Collection, New York.

first time Roosevelt was beaten on a major piece of legislation on the House floor. For much of the session, a coalition of nine southern Democrats and Republicans on the fourteen-member Rules Committee refused to provide for the bill's consideration on the floor. Eventually, Rep. Mary T. Norton, D-N.J., chair of the Labor Committee since Representative Connery's death the proceeding summer, persuaded a majority of the House, 218, to sign a discharge petition circumventing the Rules Committee's scheduling authority. The bill failed, however, to garner significant floor votes as did a substitute AFL proposal offered by Norton to place the labor standards administrator in the Department of Justice.[5]

Many felt the bill was dead, but Roosevelt refused to concede. Instead, he asked Secretary Perkins to shorten the bill and used his January 1938 annual message to offer conciliatory overtures to the South, to business, and to the AFL in asking once again for "legislation to end starvation wages and intolerable hours."[6] These gestures and decisive Senate primary victories in Alabama and Florida by staunch administration supporters dramatically altered the debate. Amid these events, Norton's Labor Committee reported a much more simplified bill that set the minimum wage at 25 cents with nickel increases each year until it reached 40 cents, and a forty-four-hour workweek that decreased two hours annually until it reached forty. After Sen. Claude Pepper, D-Fla., an

ardent supporter of the bill, won the second Southern primary, the mood of the House changed and Norton was able to secure the two hundred eighteen member signatures needed to discharge her bill from the Rules Committee.

On May 24, the Norton bill passed the House, 314–97. While a conference committee worked to resolve the difference between the House and Senate versions, Southern senators threatened to filibuster any bill reported by the conference unless a regional differential was included. Instead, they got limited wage flexibility through industry wage boards. The House passed the conference report, 291–89 vote, on June 14, and the Senate concurred the same day without a recorded vote. Roosevelt signed the act on June 25. Four months later it became effective. With the passage of the act, the federal government for the first time assumed social responsibility for helping the American worker.[7]

Although the act's coverage, administrative authority, investigative power, and standards were all weakened by the tortuous congressional amendment process, that it passed at all is a tribute to Roosevelt's commitment to secure a minimum wage and hour bill. "The demand for the passage of this legislation," Rep. George Schneider, R-Wis., reasoned, "is not based soley on humanitarian grounds. From a purely business and financial standpoint, as well as for humanitarian reasons, a law providing for minimum wages, maximum hours, and the abolition of child labor is absolutely necessary." Throughout the thirteen month FLSA debate, there were members who fulminated against "sweatshop and starvation wages," "intolerable labor conditions, and unfair employers," and oppressive child labor. They called for "fair" standards assuring a "decent" wage or a wage sufficient to maintain "reasonable comfort." The act, proponents stressed, would correct conditions under which "one-third of the population" were "ill-nourished, ill-clad, and ill- housed," and "preserve for the future our entire system of private enterprise." Shorter hours, it was argued, would "create new jobs … for millions of our unskilled unemployed," and minimum wages would "underpin the whole wage structure … at a point from which collective bargaining could take over."[8]

Opponents called the bill "a bad bill badly drawn" a "political and not economic" solution. It would "increase unemployment not decrease it," create a "tyrannical industrial dictatorship," and lead to a loss of protection, freedom, independence, incentive, and "nearly all those spiritual values which have contributed to the superb achievements of the American people in business, in culture, in art, and in those social virtues which we have dubbed during the New Deal as 'social justice.'" Prosperity, they argued, relies on the "genius" of American business. How is business going to "find any time left to provide jobs if we are to persist in loading upon it these everlastingly multiplying governmental mandates and delivering it to the mercies of multiplying and hampering Federal bureaucracy?" Others saw it as an attack on "States' rights," an attempt under the "sorry pretense of regulating commerce … to deserve the reserved powers of the states over their local concerns." The sentiments of Rep. Edward E. Cox, D-Ga., which follow, capture much of the essence of those opposed to Fair Labor Standard Act.[9]

While subsequent debates on Federal wage and labor standards have devoted considerable attention to economic analysis, Congress relied on the work of economists far less during the 1937–1938 debates.[10]

REPRESENTATIVE EDWARD E. COX OPPOSES THE FAIR LABOR STANDARDS ACT

MAY 24, 1938

The statement of our esteemed colleague, the gentleman from Mississippi [Mr. RANKIN], in which he denounced the pending bill as a raid upon the South and the West, prompts me to remark that the phrase, "Our country, one and indivisible forever," is but the expression of a hope and is not a statement of fact.

This country, Mr. Chairman, is divided into three distinct economic and social sections, the North, South, and West, with three distinct cultures and three distinct ways of life. The South had its cultural beginning in Jamestown in 1607, the North its beginning in Massachusetts thirteen years later, the one cavalier and the other puritan. There was cooperation between the two to the extent that a general government was established upon a basis of compromise. Following the setting up of that general government, the two sections entered upon their effort toward expansion and were, of course, attracted to the West. The rivalry between the two sections the North and the South, each in its effort to spread its influence into the West, led to the War between the states.

After the war was over the South turned to the task of rebuilding herself with naked hands and worn-out tools. The Federal Government came down upon that stricken area of our country and wrested local government from the control of the people. It set up a carpetbag rule which it supported by the bayonet. It took the franchise from the people who had developed southern civilization and gave it to their former slaves. It denied the people of that section, who had fought in defense of their homes and their civilization, the right to a seat in this body. It established a pension system which the South, stricken and impoverished though it was, was compelled in part to support, and which resulted in the accumulation of wealth in the North that was used for the industrialization of that area to the further disadvantage of the South. [Applause]

★ ★ ★ ★

The tariff has poured billions of dollars into the lap of the North — the greatest gift that any modern government ever bestowed on one group of people at the expense of other groups. The Government has showered thousands of other blessings on the North at the expense of the South and West. It is in complete command of the mighty forces of the industrial, political, and social revolution in America.

With one-fifth of the area and with less than three-fifths of the population of the country, the North owns above ninety percent of the wealth of the Nation. The South, with little more than one-fourth of the area and a little more than one-fourth of the population, owns less than five percent of the total wealth. The North owns the greater number of the banks, the insurance companies, the railroads, telegraph, and telephone companies, aviation and radio, the utilities, all branches of manufacturing, stocks and bonds, mining and oil. Through the corporate device it has swallowed America.

Now, Mr. Chairman, let us discuss the bill.

Invoking its constitutional power to regulate commerce among the several states, Congress in this wage-hour bill proposal is endeavoring to set up Federal control over all the activities of the people.

Calling the measure a "great humanitarian act" and saying that it will relieve the conditions of substandard workers is the mere spreading of honey to catch flies, for it is neither the one nor will it accomplish the other.

Disguised as a labor act, providing a "floor for wages and a ceiling for hours," which is a rhetorical phrase that means nothing, it is actually a social-security measure, under which industry and labor are to be made the instruments of social-security experiments. Industrial questions are to be lifted out of the economic field and treated as social problems.

The bill puts into the hands of the Secretary of Labor the power of control over the production activities of operators who either buy or sell in interstate commerce or who compete in a purely local market with interstate operators. No regard is to be taken of the right of a free person to sell his labor at his own price or of another to buy it, and none is to be taken of the inability of an employer to pay the required wages.

No greater powers were ever given any one person than those put into the hands of the Secretary of Labor under this bill. To exercise wisely and without damage or injustice, these despotic powers would call for superhuman judgment and understanding, which it is doubted the Secretary possesses.

The administration of the act would call for an army of snoopers, inspectors, counselors, and other agents, particularly susceptible to partisan abuses and political manipulations, and would throw all business and industry into the political field.

Both employers and employees would do well to remember that Federal control is a two-edged sword that cuts both ways. The powers so vested in Federal authority could as easily be used by a government hostile to free industry to crush it, as it could be used by a government hostile to labor to enslave it. Remembering also the Secretary's attitude toward the sit-down strike, for months unable to determine that the seizing, the holding, and the confiscation of other peoples' property constituted a violation of law, and remembering the Secretary's close tie-up with the radical labor element of the country, and the support given the National Labor Relations Board, the partners of the C. I. O. in its partisan and prejudicial administration of the one-sided National Labor Relations Act, it is not unreasonable to wonder how this law would be administered.

This wage-hour bill is political and not economic; it will increase unemployment and not decrease it; it is bad and not good; it will destroy and not save.

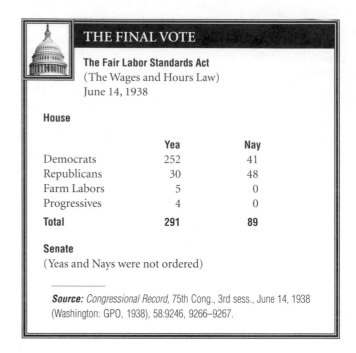

THE FINAL VOTE

The Fair Labor Standards Act
(The Wages and Hours Law)
June 14, 1938

House

	Yea	Nay
Democrats	252	41
Republicans	30	48
Farm Labors	5	0
Progressives	4	0
Total	**291**	**89**

Senate
(Yeas and Nays were not ordered)

Source: *Congressional Record*, 75th Cong., 3rd sess., June 14, 1938 (Washington: GPO, 1938), 58:9246, 9266–9267.

The enactment of this measure, supplementing the National Labor Relations Act, would result in a wave of organization by the C. I. O. throughout the country and particularly, in the South. The well-known and undenied communistic leadership of the C. I. O. in its field operations would be given an open field to spread communistic doctrines throughout the South and other parts of the country, and the labor and social unrest that would necessarily and inevitably result would change for the worse the whole industrial and social atmosphere of these regions.

The measure is monopolistic and so intended. It will destroy small industry, a purpose for which it is designed. It will freeze industrial development to those areas where now existing and foreclose the possibility of spread into outlying areas.

Under the sorry pretense of regulating commerce, the real purpose of the bill is to set up Federal dominion over the activities of the people. It is an attempt to regulate all industry and to destroy the reserved powers of the States over their local concerns. It is a proposal to push an alleged Federal power to the point of wiping out the distinction between commerce among the several States and the internal commerce of a State. It is not an honest effort to regulate commerce, but to use the commerce powers of the Constitution to regulate employer-employee relations, which, standing alone, are of purely State concern.

The courts have uniformly held that production is a local activity concerning which it is not within the competency of the Congress to legislate. The decisions of the Supreme Court, in the Labor Board cases, decided in April 1937, do not support the claims of advocates of control.

The adoption of the measure would constitute the greatest single step toward centralized bureaucracy yet taken in the history of the Nation. It would lead to Federal control of wages generally, governmental regulation of hours and working conditions, and price fixing by government decree. And when this door is opened to the invasion of Federal interference with free competition, free labor, competitive price adjustment, and collective bargaining, we will have abandoned the capitalistic system as it has always operated and we will have undergone regimentation of industry and labor, just as surely as it exists anywhere in the world today.

The act is unconstitutional, in that it attempts to establish Federal control over all production under the pretense of regulating interstate commerce. If this principle is ever established, then those meager powers kept by the States will be gone, and liberty, as understood and practiced by the people, will be a thing of the past.

The attempt to create the impression throughout the country that all those who love their fellow man favor this act, while those who oppose it are motivated by greed and a desire to see that the poor stay poor, is simply a demagogic appeal to prejudice.

That this whole idea is alien to our American ideals and customs, that it is incompatible with our democratic system of government, that it seeks to away from the people the right to live their lives in their own way and to interpret their own needs in their own native voice; that is, in part, the product of those whose thinking is rooted in an alien philosophy and who are bent upon the destruction of our whole constitutional system and the setting up of a red-labor communistic despotism upon the ruins of Christian civilization is apparent to all who read understandingly.

Source: *Congressional Record,* 75th Cong., 3rd sess., May 24, 1938 (Washington: GPO, 1938), 83:7418, 7420–7421.

REPRESENTATIVE GEORGE SCHNEIDER SUPPORTS THE FAIR LABOR STANDARDS ACT

JUNE 14, 1938

Mr. Speaker, the conference report on the bill calling for minimum wages, maximum hours, and the abolition of child labor is now before us. I believe that this report should and will be adopted by this House. And when it will be passed by both House and Senate and signed by the President, history will record that it took three sessions of the present Congress to force this achievement.

On August 17, 1937, in connection with the bill then pending, providing for minimum wages, maximum hours, and the abolition of child labor, I declared:

Regardless of what happens to the present bill at this session, I am convinced that a minimum-wage and maximum-hour law will be enacted by Congress in the very near future. The abominable conditions which the hearings on this bill reveal must bring action soon. I am certain that the American people expect Congress to act and to act without delay.

PRESENT BILL A BEGINNING IN RIGHT DIRECTION

At that time — about a year ago, during the first session of this Congress — I pointed out that I was not completely sat-

isfied with all of the provisions contained in the then pending bill. Nevertheless, I declared that as a Progressive, I was glad that the Congress was moving along the right road. To be frank, I must state that some of the provisions embodied in this conference report are not altogether to my liking or to the liking of friends of labor. However, I accept the present report as a beginning, with the firm expectation that the law will be amended and improved by succeeding Congresses.

In that spirit I hail the report and congratulate the President of the United States and the forward-looking legislators who sponsored and fought for this labor bill. As a member of the Labor Committee of the House of Representatives, I may be pardoned in claiming a modest part in the formulation and advocacy of legislation calling for minimum wages, maximum hours, and the abolition of child labor.

The measure as reported out by the conference report applies to interstate business exclusively. This is, of course, very well known. It must be repeated, however, to avoid any misunderstanding of the bill, that it does not in any way, shape, or form affect intrastate or purely local or State business. It covers only interstate commerce; that is, business which is interstate in character.

Main Provisions of Bill

Mr. Speaker, the present bill provides for an absolute bedrock minimum wage for the first year of 25 cents an hour, and for the second year of its operation of 30 cents per hour. The law does not go into effect until one hundred twenty days

---

The attempt to create the impression through-out the country that all those who love their fellow man favor this act, while those who oppose it are motivated by greed and a desire to see that the poor stay poor, is simply a dem-agogic appeal to prejudice. — Edward E. Cox

---

after it is signed by the President. This period of time is to enable those employees affected to adjust themselves to the new provisions.

By starting with such a low minimum wage of 25 cents an hour for the first year, the law will not affect any industry disastrously. However, it is well to realize that Congress, by the passage of this act, is going on record to the effect that an industry or business of an interstate character which cannot pay at least 25 cents an hour to its employees has no justification or reason for existence.

In the matter of maximum hours, the proposed act provides for forty-four hours per week for the first year, forty-two hours the second year, and forty hours thereafter, with certain exceptions. Now, on the basis of forty-four hours per week and 25 cents per hour the first year, a minimum wage of $11 a week is thus provided for. Will anyone say that a worker should receive less than the paltry sum of $11 a week to keep body and soul together? Then, after a whole year goes by with a maximum workweek of forty-two hours and a wage of 30 cents an hour, a minimum wage of $12.60 per week is thus called for. The measure also permits a higher wage, up to 40 cents per hour, barring certain exceptions.

★ ★ ★ ★

An administrator of the law is to be set up, appointed by the President, who will issue the official orders. He and his division are to be located in the Department of Labor. He is to appoint representative advisory boards for an industry, to investigate and recommend what exceptions, if any, are to be made for certain industries from the cents minimum wage per hour, or the forty hours maximum work week. The goal set for the act is 40 cents per hour and forty hours per week.

Mr. Speaker, this bill provides for the abolition of child labor in the production of goods for interstate commerce. The labor of children is defined to include all those under the age of sixteen, and also those between sixteen and eighteen in hazardous occupations. The Chief of the Children's Bureau of the United States Department of Labor will provide by special order for the employment of children from the age of fourteen to sixteen in any occupation in which employment is confined to periods which will not interfere with their schooling, and under conditions which will not interfere with their health or well-being.

Does Not Cover Agriculture

As already pointed out, the bill does not apply to local or exclusively intrastate business. Likewise, it does not cover those engaged in agricultural pursuits. Nor do the provisions embrace those employed in the first processing of dairy products. Similar exceptions are made for perishable fruit and vegetable first processing during busy seasons for limited periods. The bill also exempts those who are employed in a bona fide executive, administrative, professional, or local retailing capacity.

HUMANITARIAN REASONS

This bill calling for minimum wages, maximum hours, and the abolition of child labor is the result of years of education. The evils which it seeks to remedy have been brought vividly to the attention of the American people and Congress. First and foremost there is an overwhelming sentiment, as indicated by national polls, in favor of this act, based on humanitarian grounds. The American people are now aware of a situation where the helpless, unorganized, and submerged one-third of the population are being exploited mercilessly and ruthlessly. They are determined to put a stop, once and for all, to the human degradation caused by the payment of sweatshop and starvation wages, by the working of men and women for very long hours, and the employment of children in their tender years. The Congress now has a chance to speak out and adopt this proposed measure, which, despite any of its shortcomings, will go a long way to end the exploitation of the poorest paid, the hardest worked, and the most defenseless toilers. In this rich country of ours there is absolutely no justification whatever for starvation wages, overlong hours of toil, and child labor.

The demand for the passage of this legislation is not based solely on humanitarian grounds. From a purely business and financial standpoint, as well as for humanitarian reasons, a law providing for minimum wages, maximum hours, and the abolition of child labor is absolutely necessary.

★ ★ ★ ★

Business, and Financial Reasons

Mr. Speaker, from a business and financial standpoint, it must be remembered that the decent employer and decent community are in competition with the unfair employer and low-standard community. In fact, the situation now faces us in the United States where the fair employer and the decent community can no longer survive against cutthroat competition of the ruthless, chiseling, and exploiting employer and his industrial serflike community. The issue then becomes clear: Who shall be favored? Shall it be the fair employer and the decent community of free workers or shall it be the unfair and exploiting employer and the community of serfs? Congress can give its answer by the passage of the pending bill and the conference report.

Migration of Industry to Low-Wage Areas

Am I exaggerating the situation? Here are some facts concerning the migration of industry. The American Federation of Full-Fashioned Hosiery Workers recently listed fifty-eight mills which sold their equipment and moved from the city of Philadelphia and immediate vicinity since 1929. Between 1929 and 1937 there was an increase of full-fashioned hosiery machines in the South from 730 to 2,807, or increase of 385 percent. The low-wage areas are drawing the industry to themselves like magnets.

★ ★ ★ ★

Migration of industry is not only taking place from the North to the South; it is also occurring from high-wage to low-wage areas inside the North and within Northern States. The needle trades — making men's and women's clothing and accessories — are in a state of flux, as well as textiles, where industry is constantly going "out of town;" that is, leaving the cities for the small towns and rural areas. Some of the lowest wages are found in these out-of-the-way places in the North. It is hardly necessary to pile up evidence; the facts are so numerous and well-known. The evils attendant to migration of industry come home to the older worker especially.

★ ★ ★ ★

No Democracy Can Survive Submerged Workers

Mr. Speaker, a new sense of stability and security will enter communities which have been threatened with unfair competition and the great fear of migration. The hearings and the debates on this legislation have proved beyond any question of doubt that it is not only the representatives of labor and liberal thought who favor it. Industry after industry and state after State, which are suffering from the disastrous effects of unfair competition, have demanded a floor to wages. The fair employer and the decent community are united with all progressive and humanitarian folks on behalf of this bill…. No democracy can thrive or survive with a debased and poverty-stricken mass. No; the people cannot and will not tolerate exploitation, sweatshop wages, killing hours, and child labor,

regardless of the callousness, selfishness, and indifference of a few.

[I]t is well to realize that Congress, by the passage of this act, is going on record to the effect that an industry or business of an interstate character which cannot pay at least 25 cents an hour to its employees has no justification or reason for existence. — George Schneider

---

★ ★ ★ ★

Prevents Reductions in Wages

Mr. Speaker, this legislation providing for minimum wage, maximum hours, and the abolition of child labor is most necessary at this time to restore wages to the barest minimum and to prevent any further cuts below it. The mistaken belief that some employers have, that we can promote recovery by means of wage reductions, is checked by strong labor organizations which have the power of resistance. But the employer intent on wage cuts meets with little or no resistance from the poorest paid and poorest organized workers. Hence, he reduces purchasing power still more, and depresses the industry still further, and tears down old standards. By the passage of this legislation the wage-cutting employer will be prevented from trying to smash his way to recovery over the living standards of the defenseless and helpless submerged one-third of the population; whose standards are already too low, and which, instead of being further reduced, should and will be raised by the pending measure.

★ ★ ★ ★

The present bill, calling for minimum wages, maximum hours, and the abolition of child labor, will benefit the farmer, because it will increase the purchasing power of his best customers, the workers in the cities, and especially those who need more food and will be enabled to buy it.

Both the monopoly and highly competitive industry can still pay a minimum wage as fixed under this act, and will not need to charge the farmer a single penny more for their goods. The monopolist of course, fixes his price according to what the traffic will bear and not according to the cost of labor. The competitive industry can introduce more efficient methods and thereby offset any slight wage increase without raising its prices. No; the solution to the agricultural problem is to give the farmer his cost of production. The farmer has nothing to lose by the city worker's obtaining at least a bare minimum wage.

Conclusion

Mr. Speaker, this legislation constitutes a historic beginning in the United States. It is a declaration by Congress, after a lapse of twenty-two years since the passage of the Child Labor Law of 1916, which was declared unconstitutional, that it can and will abolish child labor in interstate commerce. In the field of wages and hours it is truly a tremendous stride forward as a piece of Federal legislation. This law, by applying to the entire country, so far as interstate commerce is concerned, treats all industries, all areas, all employers alike. It is fair and just to all, while at the same time it reaches out and protects the weakest and most exploited of workers. It brings at least some necessities and comforts into the lives of millions of Americans. From the humanitarian and materialistic standpoint, I am certain this legislation will be accepted almost everywhere by the overwhelming majority of the people. Mr. Speaker, I shall close as I began with the thought that this bill, when enacted into law will receive constant study in practice, and from our experience we will improve it in succeeding Congresses. Meanwhile and today, the conference report should be supported so that legislation providing for minimum wages, maximum hours, and the abolition of child labor may be placed on the statute books of the United States.

Source: *Congressional Record,* 75th Cong., 3rd sess., June 14, 1938 (Washington: GPO, 1938), 83:9259–9262.

Notes

1. George E. Paulsen, *A Living Wage for the Forgotten Man: The Quest for Fair Labor Standards 1933–1941* (Selinsgrove, Penn.: Susquehanna University Press, 1996), 8; John S. Forsythe "Legislative History of the Fair Labor Standards Act," *Law and Contemporary Problems,* Summer 1939 6 (474; Howard D. Samuel, "Troubled Passage: The Labor Movement and the Fair Labor Standards Act," *Monthly Labor Review,* 123 (December 2000): 32–33.

2. Samuel I. Rosenman, comp., *The Public Papers and Addresses of Franklin D. Roosevelt,* 13 vols. (New York: Russell and Russell, 1938–1950), 1937, 6:209–212.

3. Paul H. Douglas and Joseph Hackman, "The Fair Labor Standards Act of 1938 I," *Political Science Quarterly,* 53 (December 1938): 493–499; Forsythe, "Legislative History of the Fair Labor Standards Act," 465–466; Jonathan Grossman, "Fair Labor Standards Act of 1938: Maximum Struggle for Minimum Wage," *Monthly Labor Review* 101 (June 1978): 24–25.

4. Douglas and Hackman, "The Fair Labor Standards Act of 1938 I," 500–506; Forsythe, "Legislative History of the Fair Labor Standards Act," 467–470; Paulsen, *A Living Wage for the Forgotten Man,* 85–97.

5. James G. Patterson, *Congressional Conservatism and the New Deal: The Growth of the Conservative Coalition in Congress, 1933–1939* (Lexington: University of Kentucky Press, 1967), 193–197; Douglas and Hackman, "The Fair Labor Standards Act of 1938 I," 508–511; Grossman, "Fair Labor Standards Act of 1938: Maximum Struggle for Minimum Wage," 26; Forsythe, "Legislative History of the Fair Labor Standards Act," 470–472; Paulsen, *A Living Wage for the Forgotten Man,* 98–113.

6. Rosenman, *The Public Papers and Addresses of Franklin D. Roosevelt,* 1938, 7:6.

7. Irving Bernstein, *A Caring Society: The New Deal, the Worker, and the Great Depression* (Boston: Houghton Mifflin, 1985), 141–143; Grossman, "Fair Labor Standards Act of 1938: Maximum Struggle for Minimum Wage," 26–29; Douglas and Hackman, "The Fair Labor Standards Act of 1938," 511–515; Forsythe, "Legislative History of the Fair Labor Standards Act," 472–273; Paulsen, *A Living Wage for the Forgotten Man,* 115–130; Patterson, *Congressional Conservatism and the New Deal,* 243–246.

8. For Rep. Schneider's remarks see *Congressional Record,* June 14, 1938, 83:9360. Other member quotations from the *Congressional Record* are found in Grossman, "Fair Labor Standards Act of 1938: Maximum Struggle for Minimum Wage," 25; William G. Whittaker, *The Fair Labor Standards Act: Analysis of Economic Issues in the Debates of 1937–1938* (Washington, D.C.: Congressional Research Service, October 10, 1989), 18, 21.

9. Member quotations from the *Congressional Record* are found in Grossman, "Fair Labor Standards Act of 1938: Maximum Struggle for Minimum Wage," 25; Whittaker, *The Fair Labor Standards Act,* 5, 14–15. For Rep. Cox's remarks see, *Congressional Record,* May 24, 1938, 83:7418–7421.

10. Whittaker, *The Fair Labor Standards Act,* 39.

Burke-Wadsworth Bill (Selective Training and Service Act of 1940)
✴ 1940 ✴

Amidst growing American concern about the ability of the United States to avoid involvement in the escalating war in Europe, President Franklin D. Roosevelt in mid-May 1940 asked Congress for more than a billion dollars in additional funding for military weapons and equipment. Omitted from his message was any mention of the estimated 750,000 trained men needed to support the military buildup. By June 1940, nearly two-thirds of Americans believed Germany would attack the United States if France and Britain surrendered, but only one in fourteen advocated declaring war against the Nazis. While 64 percent favored conscription (the draft), White House mail ran two-to-one against a draft. Clearly, for most Americans the perplexing question was how to defend the United States without becoming involved in the war.[1]

While legislation calling for the first peacetime draft in American history was predictable, what is surprising is that a determined group of private citizens originated and saw through to fruition the Selective Service Training Act of 1940. It was born in early May, when nine World War I veterans met at New York's Harvard Club to plan for the twenty-fifth anniversary of the Plattsburg Movement, a privately initiated program responsible for recruiting and training nearly one hundred thousand businessmen and community leaders to be officers during World War I. The idea they accepted was offered by Grenville Clark, a prominent New York attorney, who suggested they stage a campaign for compulsory military training and service. Within two weeks, the group of one hundred men formed the National Emergency Committee (NEC) of the Military Training Camps Association. As the movement gained momentum, the army was forced to significantly alter its plans, Congress and the White House embraced new strategies, and virtually every American household was affected.[2]

In May and June of 1940, War Department planning under the direction of its chief of state, Gen. George C. Marshall, was focused solely on defending the Western Hemisphere. While Marshall recognized that conscription was unavoidable, he careful avoided prematurely committing either himself or the army on the issue. President Roosevelt's first priority was to overcome the isolationist sentiment in Congress so he could transfer the military equipment, planes, and naval craft that the British needed to defend themselves as quickly as politically feasible. Taking a stand on selective service, Roosevelt felt, could jeopardize that goal and have broad political ramifications as well. Instead, he initially favored comprehensive vocational training for industrial workers. Grenville Clark saw the situation as more urgent and advocated selective service as prudent preparation for likely intervention in the war.[3]

Unable to gain the support of the administration, the NEC turned to Rep. James W. Wadsworth Jr., R-N.Y., who chaired the House Committee on Military Affairs, and Sen. Edward R. Burke, D-Neb., a lame duck anti–New Deal Democrat, to guide the bill through Congress. S. 4164 was introduced in the Senate on June 20, 1940, and H.R. 10132, the House companion bill, the following day. Overnight, thanks to an organized NEC propaganda effort, the Burke-Wadsworth bill, as it came to be known, was catapulted into a major issue. Coinciding with the bill's introduction was an announcement by Roosevelt that he intended to nominate Henry L. Simpson and Frank Knox to head the War and Navy departments respectively. These appointments marked a decisive turning point. Clark had quietly lobbied for both nominees, who coincidently favored a peacetime draft.[4]

At the hearings on the Burke-Wadsworth bill, influential and articulate witnesses, including Clark, pled the case for compulsory military training. They argued that the very essence of American democracy was at grave risk, and the nation needed an adequate force of trained soldiers to protect its security. Voluntary enlistments historically had proven inadequate. General Marshall added his support after meeting with Secretary Stimson. Civil rights, antiwar, and women's groups, and most organized labor leaders, however, questioned the seriousness of the threat. The bill, they contended, would destroy American civil liberties and lead to a dictatorship. While their arguments were often not as skillfully presented as those of the bill's advocates, their intensity and sincerity gained widespread support because many Americans wanted to believe that a draft was unnecessary. Religious opinion on conscription was equally divided as was that of the educational world. Sensing that both conscription

President Franklin Roosevelt, left, reads the first draft serial number for the first peacetime compulsory military service in 1940. Secretary of War Henry L. Stimson, center, selected the number. Many witnesses at hearings on the Burke-Wadsworth Bill argued for compulsory military training.
Source: The Granger Collection, New York.

and war were likely, they concentrated on the issues of conscientious objectors. Their effort was rewarded when the House and Senate reported conscription bills that contained conscientious objectors provisions.[5]

As both the Senate and House floor moved closer to a floor vote in August, NEC leaders were worried both about a dramatic increase of opposition mail and telegrams being sent to Capitol Hill and Roosevelt's lack of endorsement of the bill despite a demand by Sen. Styles Bridges, R-N.H., that the president formally clarify his position. Then, unexpectedly, at an August 2 press conference just three days before the Senate reported the bill, Roosevelt gave his unequivocal approval of the draft, saying he "considered it essential to adequate national defense."[6]

Morris Sheppard, D-Tex., chairman of the Armed Services Committee, formally opened the Senate floor debate by emphasizing that the "doctrines and aggressions of certain dictator-controlled nations" had made it necessary for the United States to create "a nucleus of armed forces in air, on sea, and on land … to overcome attack on the United States or the Western Hemisphere." Given the immediate emergency, a draft was the only way "the burdens will be borne equally by all classes, regardless of economic means." Anti-

conscriptionists stressed that volunteering had not failed; Japan, Germany, and Italy did not pose an immediate threat; and peacetime conscription was undemocratic and gave the president too much power. Sen. George W. Norris, I-Neb., asserted it would "turn the clock back a thousand years." D. Worth Clark, D-Idaho, portrayed proponents as seeking to "take advantage of the hysteria" sweeping the country to create a permanent system by which every boy in the country would "grow up to be a soldier, to be regimented and subjected to the militarism which is repugnant to every American instinct and institution." Sen. Robert A. Taft, R-Ohio, whose remarks were more thoughtful and less emotional, warned against overstating the emergency.[7]

When it became apparent that opponents did not have the Senate votes to prevent the passage of Burke-Wadsworth, their attention shifted to delaying tactics intended to weaken the bill through amendments. The most important, authored by Sen. Francis T. Maloney, D-Conn., authorized the president prior to December 1 to call for no more than four hundred thousand volunteers. If that figure was not reached by January 1, he could then institute the draft. During ensuing days, Maloney's proposal gained significant support, before President Roosevelt told a White House press conference on

August 23, that he was "absolutely opposed to postponement" of the draft. Opponents received another setback when Wendell Willkie, the recently nominated Republican standard bearer in the November presidential election, "announced that he favored the immediate enactment of the draft." The long Senate debate ended on August 28, with the Senate rejecting an eleventh-hour substitute offered by Sen. Carl Hayden, D-Ariz., as well as the Maloney amendment. Hayden's option, which called for a sixty-day trial, lost on close vote, 43 against, 41 for, 12 not voting. Maloney's amendment fell, 50–35. The final, anticlimatic vote, 58–31, to approve the bill followed.[8]

Debate in the House was much briefer because Andrew J. May, D-Ky., chairman of the House Committee on Military Affairs, obtained a special rule from the House Rules Committee limiting general debate to only two days. The House proceedings, though brief, prompted spirited remarks by both proponents and opponents and at one point prompted one House member to call another "a traitor" and the other retaliating "with a staggering right to the jaw, the best punch landed in the past fifty years according the House doorkeeper." The biggest surprise was a move by Rep. Hamilton Fish, R-N.Y., to resurrect the Hayden amendment, the plan that had failed by only two votes in the Senate. As in the Sen-

ate, the House vote for compromise was very close, but in this case the opposition won 207–200. The Senate, however, rejected a motion to instruct its conferrees to accept the Fish amendment, and Willkie and President Roosevelt both condemned it. Confronted with this strong opposition, the conference committee deleted the Fish amendment. After the Senate sent the bill back to the conference committee a second time for an additional adjustment, both chambers finally approved Burke-Wadsworth by substantial margins.[9]

The debate over the nation's first peacetime conscription illuminates the evolution of American policy and attitudes toward the Second World War, and it marked the effective end of the isolationist tradition. While the nation remained officially at peace, civilians began to be drafted into the armed forces to face the possible threat of aggression from abroad. "Because the draft touched nearly every family," it has been written, "no measure during the months before Pearl Harbor" generated more public controversy.[10] A year later, the House, by one vote, agreed to keep draftees in the army beyond their one-year training period, and after the United States entered World War II in December 1941, the draft served as the means for raising nearly two-thirds of the sixteen million Americans who engaged in the conflict.

SENATOR MORRIS SHEPPARD ARGUES FOR THE BURKE-WADSWORTH BILL

AUGUST 9, 1940

Mr. President, the matter of our national defense is so vital, the time elements involved in the establishment of a sound defense so insistent that failure to take the necessary steps in time might result in perilous consequences.

The doctrines and aggressions of certain dictator-controlled nations become every day more menacing toward free and independent democratic countries and the bloody conflicts they have imposed on many of such countries outside the United States, and are still imposing on those they have not already conquered, in a crusade which evidently they do not propose to end until all democracy and freedom shall have been blasted from the earth, call for the immediate establishment by us of a nucleus of armed forces in air, on sea, on land, properly equipped and capable of expansion within adequate time into proportions sufficient to overcome attack on the United States or the Western Hemisphere.

This is the best assurance of the preservation of our liberties and the liberties of the Western Hemisphere.

This is the strongest and most permanent guaranty against our involvement in any war.

Aside from the existence of present dictatorships and the existing world situation, we need a permanent defense policy to protect us against aggression from all war until that day shall come for which we most fervently pray when "the blast of war's great organ shall no longer shake the skies."

Here let us examine our present defense requirements. We cannot draw a line around the sea and land frontiers of continental United States, as it was attempted to do during our consideration of the bill which preceded this, and say that this alone is what we will defend.

The Panama Canal, Hawaii, Puerto Rico, and Alaska are vital links in our defense chain. These areas are often referred to as outposts. This is in error. Outposts are usually considered as warning or delaying forces to be withdrawn when they have accomplished their mission, or when they are overwhelmed, or when their position shall have become untenable.

There can be no withdrawal from Panama, Hawaii, Puerto Rico, or Alaska without vital disaster to the Nation. To permit

---

Aside from the existence of present dictatorships and the existing world situation, we need a permanent defense policy to protect us against aggression from all war until that day shall come for which we most fervently pray when "the blast of war's great organ shall no longer shake the skies." — Morris Sheppard

---

these strategical areas to fall into the hands of any enemy would jeopardize the security of continental United States itself.

★ ★ ★ ★

Moreover, if there is one policy involving a foreign angle to which the American people subscribe, it is embodied in the doctrine that the western world belongs to the western nations.

A violation of this policy by invasion from Europe, which is prohibited by our Monroe Doctrine, would probably not occur as a sudden overt act. It could easily take the form of a step-by-step movement, or of the continuance of a peaceful penetration by foreign nationals of some of our western nations, until definite and powerful minorities would be established, with the result that hostile nations might already have secured a foothold in areas that would threaten the most important link in our national defense — the Panama Canal.

With the Panama Canal out of commission, permanently, or for a prolonged period of time, our Navy as at present constituted would be helpless as the guardian of the oceans, and our present defense system would collapse. It is to be hoped that it will never be necessary to fight to preserve the Monroe Doctrine and the freedom of the Western-Hemisphere from aggression and conquest; but if we must fight, prompt action will be imperative. Inability to act promptly would in the end necessitate a long and costly war. But what is more important, the knowledge on the part of invaders that we have the ability to act promptly would be the best form of security against the necessity for action.

It is gratifying to note that along all the necessary channels of action we are taking intensive steps to bring about a proper state of national defense. One of such steps was the passage yesterday by the Senate of the bill for the training and use of the National Guard and other Reserve components of the Army of the United States.

Another such step is the bill now before us, a bill for the training of a vast citizenship reserve in military science and practice.

This bill does not substitute the compulsory for the volunteer system of enlistment for military purposes.

It combines the compulsory with the volunteer system, because the needed number of men within the necessary time cannot be secured by the volunteer system alone.

To be specific, four hundred thousand men, the number needed to carry out the plan of our War Department in connection with the first increment by the 1st of October, cannot be secured by the volunteer system alone. The situation is such that every day is vital to a proper national defense at the earliest practicable time.

The volunteer system continues to be the system of our Regular Army, because the Regular Army does not need men in the vast numbers required by the proposed training system in so short a time.

The volunteer system continues to be the system of the Navy, the Marine Corps, the Officers Reserve Corps, the Regular Army Reserve, for the same reason.

The compulsory system is added in the present bill to the volunteer system to meet an immediate emergency in which the time element is a tragic necessity and because the volunteer system cannot obtain the necessary numbers within the time needed in the Nation's defense.

We want to start four hundred thousand men in training in October, four hundred thousand in April, and additional increments from time to time of a size demanded by what may be an increasing emergency, each year or a lessening emergency until the bill ceases to operate in 1945, unless Congress should extend it.

Why should not a combination of systems be used to insure the result desired?

When the bill ceases to operate, the compulsory phase of enlistment ceases also to operate.

The volunteer system continues as the permanent peacetime policy.

★ ★ ★ ★

Although large numbers of men are subject to registration and are liable for military training and service, only comparatively few of those registered will actually be selected and inducted for military training and service. The numbers to be so selected and inducted will depend upon the requirements of the War and Navy Departments. In other words, many are registered and are liable for service, but comparatively few will actually be inducted.

Under this bill about 12 million men will be registered. Of this number, the number actually inducted for training during the five years of the bill's operation will finally be determined by Congress through its power of appropriation. It is planned to submit to Congress estimates for the induction of four hundred thousand trainees this fall and four hundred thousand next spring. Further plans have not been perfected.

★ ★ ★ ★

Those who are liable for service will be classified, depending upon their degree of availability for military service; but all, regardless of their classification, will continue to be liable for military service. The classification will be made by local boards composed of civilians, who will be neighbors of the men to be classified.

It is deemed advisable to have all male aliens, though not liable for training and service, registered and classified so as to obtain information essential for the most efficient operation of the system — such as, for example, information as to the particular type of jobs they are engaged in and fitted for. In this connection, it is important to ascertain the available source of the various types of skilled workers, so as to determine in what proportion the skilled workers are available for the various armed forces and necessary industries. It is important to note that the bill does not provide for the selection and induction of men for industry or agriculture, as some opponents might have people believe. It is solely a bill for the procurement of men for military functions in the armed forces. Certain men are not primarily taken for the armed forces for the reason that they should be left at home to follow their jobs, which at the time are thought to include necessary functions for fostering defense preparedness.

★ ★ ★ ★

It is believed that voluntary enlistment permitted simultaneously with compulsory selection will not, if properly controlled, interfere with or change the ultimate democratic, impartial, and speedy results which compulsory selection would attain by itself. It is believed that a system of voluntary enlistment operating alone, and without a system of compulsory selection operating simultaneously with it, would fail to produce now, and hereafter as needed sufficient numbers of qualified men in an impartial, efficient, speedy, and democratic manner. The experiences of past wars show that systems providing for volunteering solely, and without compulsory selection, failed to obtain sufficient numbers of qualified men in sufficient time and in a sufficiently steady, uniform stream. Volunteering did not produce a sufficient volume of men; and even the insufficient volume decreased and ended abruptly.

★ ★ ★ ★

The bill is based on the traditional principle that every citizen owes a duty to defend the Nation. Under the terms of the bill, the burdens of military service will be borne not only by the willing and by those compelled to volunteer because of lack of funds — as is true under a volunteer system operating alone — but such burdens will be borne equally by all classes, regardless of economic means.

We must not fail to realize that in order to have benefits we must assume some burdens and discomforts. It is high time for us to check up and take stock of our moral fiber and character. We cannot ignore the facts. They must be faced.

★ ★ ★ ★

It is intended that there shall exist and be maintained a reasonably small Regular Army of approximately three hundred seventy-five thousand men to be maintained as a permanent nucleus, capable of expansion by utilizing the National Guard and the trainees reserve in such numbers as may be required by any emergency. The trainees will be trained in groups for periods of one year, after which they will be transferred to the trainees' reserve, and will be free to go home to private life and employment, subject to recall as previously stated. Within as reasonable a period of time as possible, there will be available sufficient numbers of men who have served their training period and who have been transferred to the reserves, so that there will be available for purposes of defense and protection of the Nation, should the occasion arise, a vast number of trained reserves not being maintained in the regular armed forces who can spring to arms at a moment's notice. The result will be great elasticity, which will enable rapid expansion, but which will also permit contraction, which is a very important factor overlooked by many.

★ ★ ★ ★

Quotas will be based upon the number of men who are liable for military training and service, but who have not been placed in a deferred class after being classified. World War experience demonstrated the unfairness of basing quotas according to the total male population or even according to all of the men liable for military training and service, including those classified into deferred classes. The unfairness resulted from the fact that some States and localities were discovered to have either great numbers of nondeclarant aliens or others in deferred classes, whereas other states and localities had very few. In other words, it was ascertained that there was an unequal distribution of those classified in deferred classes. When such unfairness was recognized it was decided to base quotas on the number of men in the first class, or, in other words, upon the number of men liable for military service but not deferred.

★ ★ ★ ★

Under this bill no large Regular Army is contemplated. The induction is merely for a one-year period, unless extended by Congress. This bill provides the means for commencing the training of men in military capacities for one-year training periods and is part of our military policy which contemplates a Regular Army of approximately three hundred seventy-five thousand trained men, a National Guard of approximately two hundred fifty thousand trained men, and such number of trained Reserves as may be necessary to supplement the Regular Army and National Guard. In the absence of further action by Congress, trainees will go home to private lives after a one-year training period, unless at that time they enlist in the Regular Army or the National Guard.

Source: *Congressional Record*, 76th Cong., 3rd sess., August 9, 1940 (Washington: GPO, 1940), 86:10092–10096.

SENATOR ROBERT A. TAFT OPPOSES THE BURKE-WADSWORTH BILL

AUGUST 14, 1940

Mr. President, I wish to state to the Senate my reasons for opposing the adoption at this time of a compulsory draft of men into the United States Army. No measure considered since I have been in the Senate has sought to change so much the basic theory of American life, or, in my opinion, will have a more profound effect on our political and governmental ideas. There is a general agreement that the bill, in the words of the distinguished chairman of the Military Affairs Committee can be justified only by a tragic necessity. The question we must consider, therefore, is whether or not a necessity exists. I am opposed to the bill because in my opinion, no necessity exists requiring such tragic action.

Of course I realize that some persons look on the bill as a good thing in itself even in peacetime and when no emergency exists. The sponsor of the bill, the Military Training Camps Association, has advocated the bill, or something like it, ever since 1920. Secretary Stimson, Assistant Secretary Patterson, Col. Julius Adler, who testified that he wanted to train a reserve of 20 million men, Mr. Grenville Clark and others who testified for the bill have been members of this group for many years. But their appeal was overwhelmingly rejected before the European war. They have availed themselves of the present emergency to propose this bill, at first without administration support. They have established a national emergency committee, which is now soliciting contributions to a fund of $100,000 "to help enact the Burke-Wadsworth bill into legislation." This money is apparently to be used to spread all over the country the belief that anyone who opposes the bill is un-American and unpatriotic.

★ ★ ★ ★

In the atmosphere of excitement and prejudice created by this kind of propaganda, it is difficult to consider calmly the issues which are really involved. But I do desire to discuss the actual situation which exists today, and the necessity for the revolutionary measure before us. I take it that the majority of the Senate does not agree on compulsory military training as a peacetime measure. They do agree with the distinguished chairman of the Military Affairs Committee, who said the other day in the Senate:

> The compulsory system is added in the present bill to the volunteer system to meet an immediate emergency in which the time element is a tragic necessity and because the volunteer system cannot obtain the necessary numbers within the time needed the Nation's defense.
>
> So the question is not the general advantages of military training, but it is whether there is now an absolute necessity for this kind of tragic action.

★ ★ ★ ★

[A]s a practical matter, the President is nearly always made a dictator in wartimes. But if we begin to do that every time Congress thinks there is an emergency, which is the theory we have pursued for some years, it takes very little, after a while, to make an emergency. In other words, it is urged now that in time of peace we shall confer the power of conscripting men by force of dragging them from their homes and putting them into the Army. That is a very different thing to my mind, from doing the same thing in wartimes. In wartimes a democracy temporarily creates a dictatorship. But it is recognized that when the war is over the dictatorship will end, although there always may be danger that at the end of the war it may not end. It has ended with us after every war.

★ ★ ★ ★

I say that if Congress can declare an emergency like this in time of peace, now, it can declare it in time of peace after the war. There is no way to draw the line. No one can see the distinction. War is war, and when war is over there is peace, and everyone knows that is the time when the emergency power should end.

★ ★ ★ ★

A PEACETIME DRAFT IS CONTRARY TO LIBERTY AND AMERICAN PRECEDENT

We should avoid a draft if it can possibly be done. The distinguished chairman of the Military Affairs Committee spoke of its tragic necessity. In war it may be necessary, but I agree with him that it is tragic to permit the Government to take a man already well established in his life work, and compel him to give up that work in time of peace and enter the Army. That is certainly not liberty or freedom, whether it is democracy or not. The basis of our Government has been the right of individuals to choose their own way of life, to find the niche they fit, to rise to positions of interest and power no matter how humble their beginnings may be. Probably no quality is so essential to success as persistence and thoroughness. To take a man when he has gotten well started, and compel him to be absent for a year, undoes the progress he has made in his chosen occupation, and is more than likely to affect his whole life unfavorably.

It is said that a compulsory draft is a democratic system. I deny that it has anything to do with democracy. It is neither democratic nor undemocratic. It is far more typical of totalitarian nations than of democratic nations. The theory behind it leads directly to totalitarianism. It is absolutely opposed to the principles of individual liberty which have always been considered a part of American democracy. To choose one man in ten by lot, and require him to leave his home against his will, is more like roulette than it is like democracy. Many people came to this country for the single purpose of avoiding the requirements of military service in Europe. This country has always been opposed to a large standing army, and it has been opposed to the use of the draft except in time of war when it may be absolutely necessary. I shrink from the very setting up of thousands of draft boards, with clerks and employees, and endless paper work and red tape; from the registration of 12 million men and the prying into every feature of their physical condition, their religious convictions, their financial status, and even their hobbies.

★ ★ ★ ★

The draft is said to be democratic because it hits the rich as well as the poor. Since the rich are about 2 percent of the total, it is still true that 98 percent of those drafted are going to be the boys without means. In fact, it is probable that under the volunteer system you would get a greater percentage of wealthy boys than under the draft. These boys all go to college and the percentage of enlistment from the colleges has always been higher, because the need for the defense of this country against countries thousands of miles distant is brought home to those in the colleges more forcibly than it is to the boy who is employed locally, and to whom international affairs are a great many thousand miles away.

The principle of a compulsory draft is basically wrong. If we must use compulsion to get an army, why not use compulsion to get men for other essential tasks? We must have men to manufacture munitions, implements of war, war vessels, and other equipment. Why not draft labor for these occupations at wages lower than the standard? There are many other industries absolutely essential to defense, like the utility industries, the railroads, the coal-mining industry. Why not draft men for those industries also at $21 a month? Protection is absolutely essential against domestic violence. If we draft soldiers, why not draft policemen and firemen for city and state service? The maintenance of an army on inadequate pay is merely a matter of precedent with no justification under our form of government. To a certain extent the draft act recognizes that the Government may compel men to remain in war industries, for they are exempted for that purpose, but told that if they leave that industry they must at once become subject to draft. The logical conclusion of this peacetime conscription bill is that we should draft all labor and assign all men to the jobs we think they ought to have.

★ ★ ★ ★

[T]he logical conclusion of peacetime conscription is that we should draft all labor and assign all men to the jobs we think they ought to have. Apparently that is the logical conclusion reached by the Senator from Florida. Certainly it is the conclusion reached by one of the strong advocates of conscription, Mr. Walter Lippmann. He says this of the Burke-Wadsworth bill:

> The foundation of the system is the registration of all adult males and their classification according to their training. All registered males are then legally liable to national service, they may be selected to work or to fight, depending upon their abilities and the national need. Under such a system it is not only possible to recruit in an orderly way the relatively small number who can usefully be trained and equipped, it is possible to call all the others as they are needed to jobs when they are needed or to be trained for technical tasks which will be multiplied greatly if we really mean to build the new Navy, the new air force, and the new Army. If, therefore, the conscription bill is to serve its real purpose, it must not be regarded as a mere device for putting one man out of twenty-five into uniform. It must be regarded as a method of mobilizing the men of the country for the much larger and more complicated task of industrial preparedness.

That is Mr. Lippmann's analysis of the original Burke-Wadsworth bill. The substance and purposes of the two bills are not different, for the naval or military service of the

United States in time of war may easily be extended to any important industry.

In short, the logic behind the bill requires a complete regimentation of most labor, and the assignment of jobs to every man able to work. This is actually done today in the Communist and Fascist states, which we are now apparently seeking to emulate.

Many organizations ordinarily conservative have gone on record in favor of the conscription of property in time of war if men are conscripted. They were joined last week by Mrs. Franklin D. Roosevelt. I do not agree that the arguments for one are the same as the arguments for the other, but if men are to be conscripted in peacetime, there certainly seems no reason why the Government should not arbitrarily direct the method in which all property shall be used in formulating a general-defense program. If men are selected by lot to serve at $21 a month, it may be argued that manufacturers should be selected by lot, and those selected, be required to produce munitions at a loss, at least to the extent that such loss only impairs their surplus and does not result in bankruptcy. Certainly taxes should be immediately raised so that property will at least contribute the entire cost of the present program instead of having the Government borrow the money from the banks and pay it off later out of taxes on property and consumers alike.

The argument in favor of conscription proves too much. If the emergency is as great as alleged, then we should adopt a completely socialized state and place ourselves and our property at the disposal of the Government. This is fascism. It could only be justified if it were the only possible alternative to the subjugation of the United States by fascism from without.

★ ★ ★ ★

How Large An Army Do We Need to Meet New World Conditions?

In my opinion, we must have an armed force sufficiently large to repel any attack which might be made. If the possible attackers in the future build up instruments of war which might be used against us, we must build faster.

★ ★ ★ ★

Can The Men Be Obtained Without Conscription?

Can we permanently maintain our naval forces at their increased strength, and an army of seven hundred fifty thousand men, with 1,250,000 reserves by voluntary enlistment, without compelling men to serve against their will? Surely, as a permanent policy, the question answers itself. It is only a question of making the service sufficiently attractive. We seem to be assuming that it is a sacrifice to go into the Army; that it is the most unpleasant occupation in the United States,

and one which every boy instinctively avoids. That should be far from the case. In time of war the Army is dangerous; but if we prepare adequately we should not be at war, and the Army for the most part is a peacetime, highly specialized occupation, with only a chance of danger. Experience shows that men do not avoid an occupation because there is a chance of danger. There are dangerous civilian occupations — work with high-tension wires, work in tunnel construction, work in coal mines — and there is never any difficulty in finding men interested in those occupations. The Army has many advantages — a clean and regular life without responsibility, an attraction in the very discipline and order which appeals to some men and offends others very greatly.

There are few occupations in which men could be induced to volunteer for $21 a month, and yet today we are enlisting, over twenty-five thousand men a month. In July we enlisted over thirty thousand.

★ ★ ★ ★

The voluntary-enlistment plan has not broken down. In spite of inadequate pay and three-year enlistments, it has accomplished everything which has been asked of it. Up to this time Congress has not even declared that a larger army is necessary. We can hardly blame the enlistment system for not providing an army which we have not actually authorized. No appeal has been made by the President for enlistment. Surely a general campaign led by the President, and organized on a voluntary basis throughout the United States, can secure even half a million men if that many should be necessary. There are many million men unemployed.

★ ★ ★ ★

I am absolutely convinced that an attempt to raise whatever army is necessary by a volunteer appeal, if that attempt has the wholehearted cooperation of the administration and the army will unquestionably meet with success; that it will furnish four hundred thousand men before the complicated draft is working.

Conclusion

Finally Mr. President, I refer again to the fact that the Chairman of the Military Affairs Committee has referred to the draft as a tragic necessity. The draft would be tragic but I do not agree that it is a necessity. There are other means that can be taken, means more consistent with Americanism, means more likely to preserve the liberty and freedom for which America was established, means likely to secure a better army. Surely if we draft one boy in ten by lot, there are many who will be continually disgruntled at their bad luck and only anxious to get through the twelve months as best they may. Surely, if we treat the Army as an occupation which any man might prefer, and take those who do prefer it, we will have a more earnest, interested, permanent, and enthusiastic force than if we treat it as an occupation to be avoided, for which men can be obtained only by force. In this moment of

---

[I]f we treat the Army as an occupation which any man might prefer, and take those who do prefer it, we will have a more earnest, interested, permanent, and enthusiastic force than if we treat it as an occupation to be avoided, for which men can be obtained only by force. — Robert A. Taft

---

excitement and hysteria, do not break down the fundamental principles of the American Republic. Do not overestimate the emergency and sink all the principles we love in the slough of totalitarian defense.

Source: *Congressional Record,* 76th Cong., 3rd sess., August 14, 1940 (Washington: GPO, 1940), 86:10296–10311.

Notes

1. J. Garry Clifford and Samuel R. Spencer Jr., *The First Peacetime Draft* (Lawrence: University Press of Kansas, 1986), 13, 48. See also George H. Gallup, *The Gallup Poll: Public Opinion, 1935–1971,* 3 vols. (New York: Random House, 1972), 1:226, 229.

2. Clifford and Spencer, *The First Peacetime Draft,* 5, 28. For how Clark came up with the idea, see ibid., 23–24; John O'Sullivan, *From Voluntarism to Conscription* (New York: Garland, 1982), 14–16.

3. Clifford and Spencer, *The First Peacetime Draft,* 51–54.

4. Ibid., 93. See also ibid., 63–69, 88.

5. Ibid., 104, 126, 155. See also ibid., 140–155; O'Sullivan, *From Voluntarism to Conscription,* 30–43; U.S. Congress, Senate Committee on Military Affairs, *Compulsory Military Training and Service,* hearings on S. 4164, 76th Cong., 3rd sess., July 3, 5, 10–12, 1940 (Washington: GPO, 1940); U.S. Congress, House Committee on Military Affairs, *Selective Compulsory Military Training and Service,* hearings on H.R. 10132, 76th Cong., 3rd sess., July 10, 11, 24–26, 30–31, Aug. 2, 12–14, 1940 (Washington: GPO, 1940).

6. Samuel I. Rosenman, comp., *The Public Papers and Addresses of Franklin D. Roosevelt,* 13 vols. (New York: Russell and Russell, 1938–1950), 9 (1940):321. See also Clifford and Spencer, *The First Peacetime Draft,* 170–171.

7. Quotes are found in *Congressional Record,* 76th Cong., 3rd sess., August 9, 1940, 86:10092–10093; August 12, 1940, 86:10117, 10119; August 12, 1940, 86:10117–10118. See also *Congressional Record,* 76th Cong., 1st sess., August 14, 1940, 86:10296–10311; O'Sullivan, *From Voluntarism to Conscription,* 44–70.

8. Rosenman, *The Public Papers and Addresses of Franklin D. Roosevelt,* 9 (1940):337; Clifford and Spencer, *The First Peacetime Draft,* 204; *Congressional Record,* 76th Cong., 3rd sess., August 28, 1940, 86:11112–11142.

9. Clifford and Spencer, *The First Peacetime Draft,* 210, 220; O'Sullivan, *From Voluntarism to Conscription,* 76–79; *Congressional Record,* 76th Cong., 3rd sess., September 5, 1940, 86:11572–11574; September 7, 1940, 86:11748.

10. Clifford and Spencer, *The First Peacetime Draft,* 4.

Lend-Lease Act
✵ 1941 ✵

Shortly after Germany's invasion of Poland on September 3, 1939, President Franklin D. Roosevelt used one of his fireside chats to warn Americans that when "peace has been broken anywhere, the peace of all countries everywhere is in danger." He declared that the United States would "remain a neutral nation" but emphasized, "I cannot ask that every American remain neutral in thought." At the time, an overwhelming majority of Americans wanted to stay out of the emerging conflict in Europe, which in coming months would see Germany assault Denmark, Norway, Belgium, Holland, Luxembourg, and France. With the collapse of France in June 1940, reality set in that a woefully unprepared United States might have to soon defend itself. Congress approved the Selective Training and Service Act of 1940, the first national peacetime draft in U.S. history, and two tax measures designed to produce the funds needed to sustain an expanded defense program. American anxiety over German conquests in Western Europe further increased beginning in August 1940 as Germany attempted to bomb Great Britain into submission.[1]

A month after the bombing began, Roosevelt signed an executive agreement transferring fifty mothballed American destroyers to Britain in exchange for ninety-nine-year leases of air and naval bases in the Caribbean and Newfoundland. For the British, the destroyers-for-bases deal was seen as a means of combating Germany's submarine attacks and repelling an invasion by German dictator Adolf Hitler's armies. In the United States, it ignited a bitter debate over whether we should offer such aid or maintain strict neutrality. Ultimately, British Royal Air Force (RAF) fighter pilots repelled the assault by the German Air Force (Luftwaffe), forcing Hitler to cancel his planned invasion of Britain and shift the Luftwaffe to indiscriminate night bombings of British cities. By then the Nazis dominated virtually all of Western and Central Europe and it seemed likely Britain would be unable to hold out against Hitler's economic and industrial resources. At the same time the war in Europe continued to expand, tension between the United States and Japan increased dramatically during the final months of 1940 as the Japanese entered into a military and economic alliance with Germany and Italy.[2]

Early in December, British prime minister Winston Churchill wrote Roosevelt a letter describing in stark terms Britain's substantial losses as a result of the Blitz (German air assault on Britain) and German U-boat attacks. "Unless we can establish our ability to feed this island, to import the munitions of all kinds which we need, unless we can move our armies" Churchill warned, "we may fall by the way, and the time needed by the United States to complete her defensive preparations may not be forthcoming." Britain was essentially bankrupt and did not have the resources to pay for armaments ordered from the United States, let alone future orders. Unless President Roosevelt found a way to aid Britain, it simply could not afford to continue the War.[3]

Although the Johnson Debt-Default Act of 1934 prohibited the United States from lending Britain the money it needed to buy supplies, President Roosevelt was deeply moved by Churchill's letter. Following a few days of contemplation, he announced at a December 17 news conference the lend-lease concept he had developed to aid the British without referring to loans, credits, or subsidies. Using a now famous analogy, he compared lend-lease to a neighbor whose home catches on fire and you lend him your garden hose to put out his fire without worrying about how much it costs. Afterwards if the hose was damaged while he used it, the borrower would be expected to replace it. Building on the concept's favorable reception, Roosevelt made lend-lease the central theme of a December 29 fireside chat. He told the American people that the Nazis, if not stopped, would "enslave the whole of Europe" and "dominate the rest of the world." If Britain falls, "all of us, in all the Americas, would be living at the point of a gun — a gun loaded with explosive bullets, economic as well as military." The United States "must be the great arsenal of democracy. For us this is an emergency as serious as war itself." That night, the Luftwaffe staged the largest bombing raid of the war on London, so as to dispel any hope that Roosevelt might offer. The bombers wreaked severe damage on the city, but Londoners tuned into the president's broadcast just as Americans did.[4]

Roosevelt used his January 6, 1941, State of the Union Message to formally ask Congress for the power to sell, exchange, lend, or lease war equipment to any nation whose

Demonstrators gather in 1940 to protest the Lend-Lease Act, also known as H.R. 1776. Public debate over the act was widespread, and congressional exchanges were bitter and partisan, though enough support existed for the bill to pass.
Source: The Granger Collection, New York.

defense was considered vital to the defense of the United States. He also emphasized the need of a rapid reorientation of America's industrial base toward armaments production and argued that British survival was critical to American security. The ultimate defeat of the Axis nations, he stressed, would constitute a victory for the Four Freedoms characterized as underlying the American political system — freedom of speech and expression, freedom of religion, freedom from want, and freedom from fear. The actual drafting of the "Lend-Lease Bill," which began shortly thereafter, was done in Henry Morgenthau's Treasury Department, particularly by Edward H. Foley and Oscar S. Cox. It was formally introduced in the House as H.R. 1776, with obvious symbolism, on January 10, by House majority leader John W. McCormack, D-Mass. Senate majority leader Alben W. Barkley, D-Ky., offered the Senate companion measure, S. 275, the same day. Under the proposed act, the U.S. government could make defense articles available to "any country whose defense the President deems vital to the defense of the United States." Administration of Lend-Lease was entrusted to the president,

with Congress exercising its constitutional control over appropriations.[5]

Roosevelt's proposal prompted one of America's most emotional and significant foreign relations debates. The Committee to Defend America by Aiding the Allies rallied supporters while the America First Committee and peace groups mobilized the opposition. The pros and cons were argued at social gatherings and formal meetings and in radio broadcasts, newsreels, pamphlets, and articles. People representing virtually every possible perspective made their views known to members of Congress and the White House. All eighteen of the public opinion polls conducted at the time indicated that at least 50 percent favored Lend-Lease, but the exchanges between members of Congress remained fierce, bitter, and partisan.[6]

Although it was clear from the outset that the administration had the votes it needed, there was general agreement that a full debate was needed to achieve widespread public support and Roosevelt had to be willing to accept amendments. The crucial House battle was fought in the Foreign Affairs Com-

THE FINAL VOTE

Lend-Lease Act

Senate
March 8, 1941

	Yea	Nay
Democrats	50	13
Republicans	10	17
Progressives	0	1
Total	**60**	**31**

House
March 11, 1941

	Yea	Nay
Democrats	218	15
Republicans	96	54
Progressives	3	0
Farm Labors	0	1
American Labor	0	1
Total	**317**	**71**

Sources: "Promotion of National Defense," *Congressional Record*, March 8, 1941, 87:2097; "Promotion of National Defense," *Congressional Record*, March 11, 1941, 87:2170.

mittee where the committee's hearings captured the nation's attention and rated front-page newspaper coverage. Two major opposition themes emerged: the powers granted by the bill would make the president a virtual dictator and were probably designed to get America into the war. Following the hearings, the committee approved four amendments that had the blessing of the administration. On February 8, 1941, nine days after H.R. 1774 was favorably reported by the Foreign Affairs Committee, the House voiced its approval, 260–165, after adding two additional amendments. The most important stipulated that a congressional resolution could terminate the president's powers prior to the act's expiration date.[7]

For the Senate hearings, the opposition called witnesses with a broad range of ideological beliefs. While a significant number saw limited aid to Great Britain as beneficial, they reasoned that Lend-Lease would thrust the United States into the war. A stirring endorsement by Wendell Wilkie, the Republican standard-bearer in the 1940 presidential campaign, however, provided the greatest benefit to the administration. Early on, Wilkie had "warned his party that if they blindly opposed the bill and presented itself to the American people as the isolationist party, it would 'never again control American government.'" Sen. Barkley opened the floor debate by telling his Senate colleagues that supporters of Lend-Lease believed it offered the "surest method by which we can avoid participation actively in this war and at the same time help those nations which are heroically grappling with a universal enemy to preserve the doctrines of our fathers and the aspirations of our own hearts." Speaking in opposition later that same day, Senator Arthur H. Vandenberg, R-MI., said his "greatest fundamental objection" to Lend-Lease was "that it invites and authorizes the President of the United States to enter the continental arena of 'power politics,' which has been the curse of the Old World and the cradle of its incessant wars for a thousand years, invites and authorizes him to become the power politician No. 1 of this whole mad world." During the ensuing floor debate the Republicans repeatedly sought to limit the expansion of presidential power under the act, but were unable to generate public support for such action. Their lengthy speeches extended the debate for more than two weeks, but the effort did not move the American people to rise up in condemnation, as they had when Roosevelt attempted to pack the Supreme Court in 1937.[9]

Senate opponents of Lend-Lease were, however, able to secure amendments that required the administration to use Lend-Lease funds for transactions after the bill was enacted, and they emphasized it did not change existing law regarding the use of American forces. On March 8, an exhausted Senate approved Lend-Lease, 60–31. Three days later, the House approved the final text, 317–71. Afterwards, Prime Minister Churchill rose in Parliament to describe Lend-Lease as "the most unsordid act in the history of any nation." In Washington, President Roosevelt told the annual White House Correspondents' Association dinner that "great debate" on Lend-Lease had gone far beyond the "halls of Congress. It was argued in every newspaper, on every wave length, over every cracker barrel in all the land; and it was finally settled by the American people themselves." With its passage, the United States became the "arsenal of democracy" for a vast coalition of allied nations forming around Britain and the United States, and the country began to help those nations whose defense was considered vital to our defense. Altogether, the program provided more than $50 billion worth of aid to the war against Nazi Germany, Fascist Italy, and Imperial Japan.[9]

SENATOR ALBEN W. BARKLEY SUPPORTS THE LEND-LEASE ACT

FEBRUARY 17, 1941

Mr. President, I approach the discussion of this historic measure with a profound appreciation of the events which have preceded its introduction and the policy which is set out and may be inferred from the terms of the bill itself.

The importance of the subject, the consequences which may flow from its enactment and administration, the anxiety and suspense with which the American people are today tip-toeing to catch the latest word concerning events over which they now have no control, but which may for generations and centuries determine the fate of America and the world, require of us the utmost sincerity, calmness, frankness, and courage in our approach to and our discussion of this tremendous subject.

I trust, therefore, that we may preserve the dignity and the freedom from personalities for which the Senate of the United States should be distinguished. I trust that none of us may be provoked into a departure from this high standard.

There are two things which, in my judgment, the American people desire to preserve. One is the peace of this Nation and of this hemisphere. The other is the freedom and independence of this Nation and of this hemisphere. They want to preserve them both at the same time, if this is possible. If they cannot both be preserved at once and simultaneously, then our history has belied our character if they are not willing to make whatever effort is essential and undergo whatever sacrifice is required to preserve the freedom and independence of this Nation and this hemisphere, and the method of life and the form of culture which they have established.

In the language of Grover Cleveland, speaking on another subject, it is a condition and not a theory which confronts us as a nation today. But even in the discussion and the consideration of the condition which confronts us we cannot completely escape the theories which are promulgated in various quarters touching the origin of the condition and responsibility for it.

I have said that the American people desire peace. They desire it here in the United States. They desire it in all the Americas. They desire it in all the world. They have made greater sacrifices to secure it and to perpetuate it than have been made by almost any other nation in history, unless it be those nations now engaged in defending their right to the liberty and self-government which we ourselves have always cherished.

If we had the time or the inclination to seek the causes of the present conflict in the realms of ancient, medieval, or modern history, we should find the exploration interesting,

and fascinating, but probably futile — futile because the pattern of the present war in Europe and Asia is something that has no counterpart in all history.

Some of those who discuss present world conditions like to trace them back to the Treaty of Versailles and the first World War. I do not wish to deny that there were injustices in that treaty. If men and nations could recall past deeds, they would no doubt find many occasions and causes to change their actions and their attitudes.

But if it be said that the Treaty of Versailles was a dictated peace, it is equally true that the treaty which terminated the Franco-Prussian War, out of which it was said the World War grew, was also a dictated peace. We have all observed the striking scene as depicted in the painting which shows the imposing forms of Bismarck and Von Moltke compelling France to sign on the dotted line of a dictated peace.

History records few instances in which a victorious war has not resulted in a dictated peace. During the World War, before the entry of the United States, President Wilson advanced the idea of a peace without victory. While it was a noble ideal, the suggestion was not followed and would not have been followed if Germany had won that war.

While it may be true that the dictated treaties which have followed the World War, the Franco-Prussian War, and all the wars that have been fought between nations and races and tribes from the beginning of history, might be marshaled in a long line of contributing causes to the present world conflict, it is futile to assume that any one of them is entitled to major responsibility for what is now being attempted by those who have instigated this war.

This is not a war merely of boundaries. It is not a war to eliminate corridors entirely. It is not a war merely to relieve minorities of some injustice inflicted upon them by a boundary line. This may have been the pretext upon which it was begun. But its genesis lies deeper than mere physical delineations upon a map.

It is a war of ideas, a war of philosophies, a war to impose upon the world a system of moral, economic, and political controls to which it has never been subjected in all its history. These controls are diametrically opposed to the theory of freedom and democracy. They are opposed to the doctrine of self-government. They are avowedly antagonistic to Christianity or any other form of religion except the worship of the state; that state to be under the autocratic domination of authoritarian theories and actions which deny the people any voice in their government or their society. The result is economic bondage, it is religious bondage, it is political bondage, and it is intellectual bondage. It is impossible to have intellectual freedom where the soul of man is enslaved. It is impossible to have economic freedom where the political rights of man are trampled under foot.

Can there be any doubt of the intention of Hitler to impose this revolting system upon the whole world, the United States? Although Hitler calls it a revolution of young nations and young people against old and decadent nations, we have already recognized it for what it is, an inhuman and bestial revolution against every freedom for which men have striven through centuries of hardship.

★ ★ ★ ★

[C]an we doubt that one of the motives for this war is the economic domination of the world? And can we doubt that economic domination will be followed by political intrigue and infiltration; and that economic and political domination will produce a prodigious effort at military domination in all countries upon which this system shall be imposed?

If Hitler should win, we will face, therefore, not only a hostile Germany but a hostile world. If he wins, he will control all of Europe. And if Mussolini should survive, through him, or over him, he will control all of Africa. If he wins in Europe and in Africa, we must presuppose that Japan as one of the Axis powers will control if she does not occupy all of China and the entire Pacific west of Hawaii, including Malaya and the Dutch East Indies. Should the Axis Powers win, they will have a naval strength two and a half times that of the United States, leaving out of consideration the British Navy, and this strength would be still further augmented by the capture of all or any considerable part of that navy.

In the event of a victory for Hitler and his allies, they would have control of foreign exchange and of trade and of raw materials in Europe and Asia, including materials vital to our national defense and national life. They would control investments in stocks in the Western Hemisphere outside the United States which were heretofore held by Dutch, Belgian, Scandinavian, Polish, Czech, French, and British countries. Through the control of the products we need; through their ability to sell cheaper, unless we abandon our standards of living; through all the trade and industrial and economic advantages which would accrue to Hitler by such a victory, the Nazis would have the superb weapons they now seek to forge in order to destroy us.

★ ★ ★ ★

We sometimes look upon ourselves as a self-sufficient nation, and some of our people now and then boast that we can continue to live and maintain our standards of life no matter who controls the world.

Is it true? Let us see. Only about one-half of the strategic materials vital to our life and our defense are available in the Western Hemisphere. There are fourteen of such strategic materials listed by the Munitions Board, and only three of them are to be had in any quantity from Latin America, and only half of them are available in small quantities.

★ ★ ★ ★

In the light of these conditions, which could be given in greater detail if time permitted, are we justified in assuming that the American people are not interested in the kind of world which we are to live in after this present conflict is over? Are we to assume that the American people are unwilling to throw the weight of their material assistance into the scales in order to avert the kind of world from the economic viewpoint alone of which I have been speaking? I am unwilling to indulge in any such assumption.

But I stated at the beginning of these remarks that this war is not only an economic war, but that it is an attack against all the moral and religious standards which have lifted our civilization out of the depths of barbarism and paganism.

★ ★ ★ ★

There is but one way to stop a conqueror. That way is to defeat him. The only way to stop Hitler is to defeat him; and if we do not help Great Britain and other nations now fighting him to defeat him over there we shall some day have to surrender to him or defeat him over here.

★ ★ ★ ★

I do not pretend that there are not risks, no matter what we do or fail to do. It may be a choice of risks. If we do nothing, we run the risk of being hemmed in and fenced off as a sort of unilateral concentration camp. We run the risk of see-

---

The only way to stop Hitler is to defeat him; and if we do not help Great Britain and other nations now fighting him to defeat him over there we shall some day have to surrender to him or defeat him over here. — Alben W. Barkley

---

ing the rest of the world overrun, and then being compelled to fight a hostile world or be overrun ourselves.

On the other hand, if we take the action which is contemplated in the legislation now before us, while that course is not free from risks, the chances are that the foul aggressor, who now boasts that he has his eyes upon us, may be stopped in his tracks, and all that we love and cherish for ourselves and for other peoples may experience a revival that will cheer the hearts and bolster the spirits of hundreds of millions who are bowed today beneath the yoke of grief and oppression.

The American people must make this choice, and we, Mr. President, as their representatives, must make it, too. I believe the American people have made it. What is our verdict to be, as their spokesmen here in this forum called the Senate of the United States?

That we have determined to arm ourselves against the danger which all now recognize is demonstrated by the willingness with which our people have accepted the appropriation of billions of dollars and will accept increased debt and taxation.

It is demonstrated by their willingness to have their young men undergo training for national defense. It is demonstrated by the concentration of all our efforts as a nation to the task of preparation.

★ ★ ★ ★

The overwhelming majority of the American people, regardless of race, religion, color, politics, or origin, are determined that we shall not suffer the fate of the victim nations of Europe; and they, in equal numbers, have determined that one of the best methods by which to stave off that fate is to give material aid to England and the other nations which are battling for their right to exist.

Under the Neutrality Act, no matter how desperately these nations may need the weapons they must have for their survival, and no matter how essential their defense may be to our own national welfare, they cannot obtain such weapons now in this country unless they have the cash in American dollars with which to pay for them.

No financial institution in America can lend such a nation the money with which to pay for these weapons. No American factory can give them credit for one airplane, one rifle, or one bullet. The nation involved must pay for these things in cash, no matter how hard pressed and no matter how willing the American factory might be to extend them credit.

This law, while called a neutrality law, has worked to the disadvantage of nations which had not previously armed to the teeth or whose industrial facilities are not sufficient to provide them with weapons of defense.

Therefore, in order that the nations whose defense is essential to ours may continue to fight, in order that we may keep war and all its horrible effects from our shores, we must consider the method by which we may afford them the maximum quantities of defense implements and at the same time not become actively engaged as a participant in the war which is threatening to overcome them.

This is the object sought by the passage of the measure now under consideration in the Senate.

★ ★ ★ ★

This measure does not surrender the right of Congress to declare war. It not only preserves that constitutional right, which cannot be abrogated, but it requires the President to come to Congress for the appropriations necessary to administer it, and also the authority to make contracts for future execution.

- This measure does not confer upon the President the right to convoy ships across the ocean.
- It does not confer upon him the right to send American troops to Europe.
- It does not confer upon him the authority to send American ships into war zones.
- It does not confer upon him the power to seize foreign ships in the ports of the United States.

It does not confer upon him the power to impose a censorship, or to restrict the freedom of speech or of the press or of worship or assembly. These rights have been abolished in the dictator nations, but they have not been restricted in any respect in the United States, and will not be under the terms of this measure.

This measure confers upon the President no power to seize property or to conscript labor, or to nullify the laws enacted for the protection of labor in the United States.

It gives him power to do the things set out in the measure. He may possess other powers given him in the Constitution or in other laws not in conflict with this; but this measure does no more nor less than what it says.

★ ★ ★ ★

We do not want war. We hate war. Most of us here have seen the ravages of war, and we have seen the devastation and the suffering which it has always entailed. We do not want these ravages and this suffering to come to our shores. We believe that this measure offers the surest method by which we can avoid participation actively in this war and at the same time help those nations which are heroically grappling with a universal enemy to preserve the doctrines of our fathers and the aspirations of our own hearts.

Source: *Congressional Record*, 77th Cong., 1st sess., February 17, 1941 (Washington: GPO, 1941), 87:1033–1039.

SENATOR ARTHUR H. VANDENBERG OPPOSES THE LEND-LEASE ACT

FEBRUARY 18, 1941

Mr. President, this is a momentous debate, because it leads to momentous conclusions which inevitably affect the peace, the security, and the free institutions of the United States for generations to come. Indeed its acknowledged aim is finally to influence the security and the lives of men, according to Presidential definition, "everywhere in the world." The Congress heretofore has never faced such infinite horizons. It has never been invited to such limitless adventure. It has never confronted a prospectus fraught with heavier consequence to the American way of life.

Unfortunately, in the midst of ruthless world-wide wars from which our Western Hemisphere is thus far alone immune, there is no clear road ahead, regardless of what our decisions may be. In our anomalous role of an unneutral nonbelligerent, none among us is entitled dogmatically to say, "This is the safe sure way." There are risks at every turn. There is destiny in every choice. There ought to be humility as well as courage in each one of us.

Out of this controversy, when the final answer is written for America, must come the nearest possible approach to that national unity which is our source of greatest strength when we face the world. I, for one, shall seek it. In pursuit of it, if we ever respected each other's motives and sought to avoid the acrimony and the intolerance which kill reason with the poisons of prejudice, hysteria, and hate, here is the essential occasion. And I commend that thought to some of our external critics. If we ever strove to reject the substitution of anathema for argument, now is the essential time. If we ever needed the gift of divine-guidance, the hour has struck. Yet if we ever needed the brave truth, as God gives it to each one of us to see the truth, the Republic needs it now. Under such critical circumstances, Mr. President, and in the presence of such sinister portent, it must be with a sense of profound — aye, oppressive — responsibility that any Senator addresses himself to the pending text.

In what I hope may be fidelity to this spirit — and with complete respect for the opinions of those who disagree with me — I state my reasons for opposing H. R. 1776 which, by title, is intended "to promote the defense of the United States and for other purposes." If it is for "the defense of the United States" then the "other purposes" should be abandoned. If and when they are, I can heartfully go along. But as it stands, and as it seems destined to stand when all effective amendments have been rejected here as elsewhere, I must oppose it because I deeply believe that, in its pending form, it is a potential and needless threat to the peace and security of the United States; that it impairs democracy at home in the promise of supporting it abroad; that it may lead us ever closer to dire involvement in the fires of war itself; that it could strip us of the essential means, in the last analysis, to implement our own pledge to maintain hemispherical defense in this New World, most emphatically and particularly including Canada; that it still nullifies the constitutional checks and balances, in respect to this issue, which have been the bulwark of one hundred fifty years of American freedom — still nullifies them despite certain partially corrective amendments which the bill now carries; that it is unnecessary as a means to achieve, short of war, that "aid to England" which has come to be our dominating aspiration which I share, and that it should either be sharply amended or rejected in favor of other, direct and simple means to reach this goal.

I hasten to say that no Senator who supports this bill accepts this indictment for a single instant. Neither does that major body of public opinion in the country which is urging its adoption. In some instances, proponents frankly state that if war is the consequence of this new policy they are prepared to take it. But the vast majority assert it is the road to peace; and that the temporary impairment of our democracy is a useful price to pay for its ultimate salvation. That is where our fundamental difference of opinion stems.

★ ★ ★ ★

In my view, this so-called lending-leasing bill not only invites us closer to the grim event of war itself — for reasons upon which I shall presently enlarge — but it lends essential congressional prerogatives to the President and leases a new portion of the Constitution to the White House — and all unnecessary in order to aid England short of war. It is not embraced within my mandate. It will not proceed with my support until the democratic process ordains otherwise.

Let me repeat that this implies no lack of willingness — yea, of anxiety — to aid the Allies within the self-saving limitations heretofore defined; and only those critics in whom an obsession has overcome the power to think will read it otherwise. God knows it implies no hospitality to Hitlerism. Indeed, if the Axis Powers should so tragically misconstrue the attitude of those of us who take this position as being sympathetic with their bloody aims, they have but to defile the hem of Columbia's garment to find all of us irresistibly upon the forward march — including war itself — to defend democracy in this New World.

★ ★ ★ ★

My greatest fundamental objection to it is that it invites and authorizes the President of the United States to enter the continental arena of "power politics," which has been the curse of the Old World and the cradle of its incessant wars for a thousand years, invites and authorizes him to become power politician No. 1 of this whole mad world.

★ ★ ★ ★

Oh, I am fully conscious of the fact that our constitutional theory of government commits exclusive control over foreign contacts and negotiations to the President, although foreign commitments belong equally with Congress. But this proposed new power is vastly more. Nothing remotely like it exists anywhere on earth today unless it be in Rome, Moscow, or Berlin.

★ ★ ★ ★

This bill says to the President: "Solely in your own discretion and solely on your own authority you pick our allies and our enemies anywhere you please all around the globe; you reward them as you personally may wish out of this vast reservoir of our own hard-pressed resources; you bid as you please for whatever alliances you see fit; you underwrite the wars of others as your wisdom indicates to be essential to our own defense; you make whatever undeclared wars you please, so long as you think it comports with our defense necessity. You may make the decision. You do it all. And all that Congress humbly and most respectfully requests is that you tell us once every ninety days what is going on — and you need not do even that if you deem it incompatible with the public welfare."

★ ★ ★ ★

Mr. President, this is a new role for America, a complete departure from history and traditions. But, most important of all, America accepts a responsibility not only for what happens here but for what happens wherever this war is raging anywhere around the world. It accepts an American responsibility from which we can never depart when once we have embraced it. The world's power politician No. 1 is created by this bill. Not even Jove, with his monopoly of lightning bolts, was more powerful on Mount Olympus.

★ ★ ★ ★

Mr. President, I do not believe that we keep the American way of democracy or the spirit of constitutional government when we thus transfer vast resources to the sole bounty of the President to roam a war-torn world and to reward whatever alien nation he may please, in whatever way he pleases, for whatever war action he deems ultimately helpful to the defense of the United States. Furthermore, I reject and deny the novel doctrine implicit in this new philosophy — a doctrine denied by a century and a half of our forward-marching history — that our American defense is thus at the mercy of any such far-flung manipulation of power politics in the Old World. I simply cannot accept the novel theory that our safety and our peace and happiness require of us that we shall make our White House the war capital of half the earth or more, and our President the No. 1 power politician of the world. I do not believe it contributes to our peace. I do not believe it defines our appropriate role in World War No. 2.

I simply cannot accept the novel theory that our safety and our peace and happiness require of us that we shall make our White House the war capital of half the earth or more, and our President the No. 1 power politician of the world. — Arthur H. Vandenberg

---

★ ★ ★ ★

I know it is said we might better have Roosevelt for a temporary dictator than to have Hitler for a permanent one. Mr. President, I do not believe that either is necessary. As for the former, I concede the need for substantial elasticity in executive authority to meet the ever-shifting, new techniques of modern war; and I will grant it. But I do not for an instant concede that this elasticity needs extend to fundamental decisions affecting the very life of the Republic itself; that it needs to contemplate today, while we are still at peace, for the present President of the United States greater powers than Wilson, at war, had in 1917–18 or that Churchill, at war, has in 1941.

★ ★ ★ ★

This leads me to my second fundamental objection to this bill. Everyone admits that it is a matter of all-controlling judgment how much of our defense equipment — our ships, our guns, our planes — shall go abroad and how much shall stay at home. I believe the President once said, for example, that the division of planes should be on a 50–50 basis. I believe, however, that our recent division has been running more nearly 90–10 — the 10 for us. Spokesmen for the Navy Department said last June they could not spare destroyers. A month later fifty destroyers were traded for naval-base leases. Last week one of our very able clipper ambassadors — and I speak of him with great respect — suggested that our immediate contribution to Britain should be from five–ten destroyers a month. He intimated that he had highest authority for the feasibility of his suggestion. But he was followed within twenty-four hours by a sharp statement from our Secretary of the Navy that no destroyers whatever can be spared. Then his statement was swiftly followed by a White House luncheon concerning the outcome of which we are not advised. I am simply illustrating the wide range of opinions which may be involved in this vital matter of judgment as to where we shall draw the line in depleting our own defense resources to build up the resources of an ally.

★ ★ ★ ★

The whole impetus and implication of this new policy is to defend America abroad. I accept the thesis that there is, today, powerfully much that we can do to defend America abroad. Let us do it as effectively and as fully as our own situation will permit. But, I resist the thesis that this is paramount to defending America at home. The two objectives must be parallel. The discriminating decision — since it may prove to be a life-and-death decision for us — should be the decision of our whole Government, and not the sole decision of him who under the terms of this bill becomes head armorer to all the world.

★ ★ ★ ★

Mr. President, I have never faced an issue which has disturbed me, in mind and soul, more than this one. I say, at the end as I said in the beginning, that no one of us may be sure that he is right in decisions that must be taken in the midst of such cataclysm. I envy those who know that they know — though assurance fails to validate to me the pontifical conclusions they announce. In such a situation it seems unescapably plain to me that there is greatest safety for our own America in leaning upon the consensus of many minds rather than upon just one. This, indeed, is the American constitutional theory and system. Dictators may be more expeditious. But the democratic process is the safer one.

★ ★ ★ ★

I freely concede that isolation — that much-bandied and abused word — is impossible in this foreshortened world. We cannot escape world repercussions, though we can be more nearly self-contained than any other nation on earth.

★ ★ ★ ★

I would not proceed on theory that if England falls, we fall too. Despite our fervent hopes for her, I would not encourage

England, magnificent exemplar of Anglo-Saxon fortitude, to believe that such is our commitment. I would proceed on the theory that America, after sending material aid to those who sustain our point of view, survives no matter what happens across any seas, and I would prepare accordingly. It is my firm faith that this can be done. I would not give up democracy at home in an effort to save it abroad.

Source: Congressional Record, 77th Cong., 1st sess., February 18, 1941 (Washington: GPO, 1941), 87:1101–1108.

Notes

1. Samuel I. Rosenman, comp., *The Public Papers and Addresses of Franklin D. Roosevelt,* 13 vols. (New York: Russell and Russell, 1938–1950), 8 (1939):461–463; 54 Stat. 516–527, 885–897, 974–1018.

2. Philip Goodhart, *Fifty Ships That Saved the World: The Foundation of the Anglo-American Alliance* (London: Heinemann, 1965); William L. Langer and S. Everett Gleason, *The Challenge to Isolation, 1937–1940* (New York: Harper and Brothers, 1952), 742–776; Winston S. Churchill, *The Second World War,* vol. 2, *Their Finest Hour* (Boston: Houghton Mifflin, 1949), 398–416.

3. Churchill, *Their Finest Hour,* 558–567. See also William L. Langer and S. Everett Gleason, *The Undeclared War, 1940–1941* (New York: Haper & Brothers Publishers, 1953), 231–237.

4. Rosenman, *The Public Papers and Addresses of Franklin D. Roosevelt,* 9 (1940):607, 634, 635, 643. See also Langer *The Undeclared War, 1940–1941,* 231–251.

5. Warren F. Kimball, *The Most Unsordid Act: Lend-Lease, 1939–1941* (Baltimore: Johns Hopkins Press, 1969), 151–153; Langer, *The Undeclared War, 1940–1941,* 252–258; Rosenman, *The Public Papers and Addresses of Franklin D. Roosevelt,* 9 (1940): 663–672.

6. Wayne S. Cole, *Roosevelt & the Isolationists, 1932–45* (Lincoln: University of Nebraska Press, 1983), 414, 421. See also Kimball, *The Most Unsordid Act: Lend-Lease, 1939–1941,* 191–192.

7. Quotes are found in Kimball, *The Most Unsordid Act: Lend-Lease, 1939–1941,* 162, 165. See also ibid., 156–176, 203–207; Langer, *The Undeclared War, 1940-1941,* 262–276.

8. Langer, *The Undeclared War, 1940–1941,* 259.

9. "Promotion of National Defense," *Congressional Record,* March 8, 1941, 87:2097; "Promotion of National Defense," *Congressional Record,* March 11, 1941, 87:2178; Kimball, *The Most Unsordid Act: Lend-Lease, 1939–1941,* 216–220; Churchill, *Their Finest Hour,* 569; Rosenman, *The Public Papers and Addresses of Franklin D. Roosevelt,* 9 (1941):63.

10. Kimball, *The Most Unsordid Act: Lend-Lease, 1939–1941,* 216–220; Churchill, *Their Finest Hour,* 569; and Rosenman, *The Public Papers and Addresses of Franklin D. Roosevelt,* 9 (1940):63.

Atomic Energy Act of 1946
✳ 1946 ✳

Prior to August 5, 1945, when the United States dropped the first atomic bomb on Hiroshima, Japan, neither Congress nor the American people were aware that scientists were working on such a destructive weapon. Only a few in the Roosevelt administration, and the scientists and military leaders involved in the Manhattan Project, the top secret project started prior to World War II, had knowledge of the government's effort to develop the first nuclear weapons.[1]

Vannevar Bush, who, at President Franklin D. Roosevelt's behest, led the effort to build the first atomic bomb, and his deputy, James B. Conant, took the initial lead in the debate over management of America's domestic nuclear program. In September 1944, they suggested to Secretary of War Henry L. Stimson the creation of a postwar twelve-member commission, which included four members of the military, to control large-scale production as well as research involving minute amounts of material. The following May, two months before a New Mexico test showed the bomb would work, Stimson, with the approval of President Harry S. Truman, who succeeded Roosevelt following his April 12, 1945, death, appointed an advisory committee to develop a legislative proposal for regulating and controlling the development of atomic energy in the United States. Given that Congress likely would want to appoint a permanent commission to deal with the issue, Stimson considered his appointees an "Interim Committee."[2]

At its first meeting in July 1945, the Interim Committee considered, but did not adopt, a draft atomic energy bill prepared by two War Department lawyers, Brig. Gen. Kenneth C. Royall and William L. Marbury. The bill called for a part-time, nine-member commission consisting of five civilians and two representatives each from the Army and the Navy. In contrast to the Bush-Conant plan, it provided for a stronger military presence on a smaller-sized commission.[3]

Following the bombing of Hiroshima, Truman asked Congress to promptly consider the establishment of an appropriate commission to control the production and use of atomic energy in the United States. Two months later, on October 3, he sent Congress a special message on atomic energy that included the Royall-Marbury draft. The same day, Rep. Andrew J. May, D-Ky., chairman of the House Com-

mittee on Military Affairs, and Sen. Edwin Johnson, D-Col., a senior member of the Senate Military Affairs Committee, introduced identical bills incorporating the language found in Truman's message.[4]

Although the May-Johnson bills specifically placed peacetime control of atomic energy with civilians, critics denounced the bill as giving control to the military. Such a conclusion was understandable given that several provisions allowed for military domination. Six days after the bill was introduced, Gen. Leslie R. Groves (head of the Manhattan Engineer Project), Bush, and Conant told the House Military Affairs Committee that the sweeping powers granted the proposed commission were necessary and only government control could prevent misuse of atomic power. A second day of hearings, held after several prominent scientists complained that the bill was designed to maintain military control and imposed far too harsh penalties for security violations, did little to breach the gap between the military and the scientists. The committee reported a slightly amended bill on November 5, 1945.[5]

The president began having misgivings about aspects of the bill after learning of the scientists' objections. House Speaker Sam Rayburn, D-Tex., upon conferring with Truman, postponed floor debate on the bill until a newly created Special Senate Committee on Atomic Energy could prepare alternative legislation. While Senator Brien McMahon, D-Conn., the committee's chairman, did not care for May-Johnson, he felt none of the committee's members knew enough about atomic energy to draft a substitute bill. That challenge McMahon left to James R. Newman, head of the Office of War Mobilization and Reconversion, who he persuaded to become the committee's special counsel, and Dr. Edward U. Condon, director of the National Bureau of Standards, who was selected as the committee's scientific advisor.[6]

During the fall of 1945, the committee, at Newman's suggestion, devoted considerable time to learning about the atomic bomb and its military significance. The committee's bill, prepared "under the joint guidance of Senator McMahon and the Administration, and in consultation with the scientists and other agencies of the government," was introduced on December 20. It called for five civilian commissioners and

Secretary of War Henry L. Stimson created an "Interim Committee" to develop legislation regulating and controlling the development of atomic energy in the United States. The legislation produced eventually led to the hotly debated Atomic Energy Act.
Source: Library of Congress.

four directors of operating divisions, all presidential appointees. The military was excluded from its membership.[7]

Senate hearings on the bill began in late January 1946. Early in the four-week-long hearings, President Truman sent a letter to McMahon (drafted by Newman) congratulating him on the hearings and emphasizing that: (1) any atomic energy commission Congress established "should be exclusively composed of civilians," (2) an "absolute Governmental monopoly of ownership, production, and possession of all fissionable materials" was imperative, (3) there should be access to atomic energy devices through private licensing, and (4) any legislation "must assure genuine freedom to conduct independent research and guarantee that controls over dissemination of the information will not stifle scientific progress." General Groves, new Secretary of War Robert P. Patterson Sr., and Secretary of the Navy James V. Forrestal, however, all expressed deep concern about the bill's weak security provisions and lack of military representation.[8] Their arguments were not without effect.

Afterwards, the committee met in executive session daily for six weeks before reporting an extensively modified bill. A key figure during those sessions was Senator Arthur H. Vandenberg, R-Mich., who felt the decisions made by the commission should be reviewed by the military when the

circumstances warranted. The revised bill called for a presidentially appointed five-member commission and general manager; four operating divisions — research, production, engineering, and atomic applications — whose directors would be selected by the commission; and a scientific advisory committee, military liaison committee appointed by the military, and joint congressional committee on atomic energy. The Senate passed the bill on June 1, by a voice vote, following brief debate.[9]

Attention now focused on the House Committee on Military Affairs, which the administration had deserted once public opinion turned against the May-Johnson Bill. Now it was "expected to give preferred treatment to a bill written by the Senate committee which had untiringly attacked the May-Johnson proposal." On June 3, Speaker Rayburn told the press that Truman preferred the Senate bill. The committee, however, was not persuaded, and following its hearings, amended the bill to restore military control over the commission before reporting the measure.

During the heated House floor debate, opponents of the Senate bill focused on three primary themes: the complete and absolute authority given the proposed commission over the licensing of patents, a belief the bill would remove all existing statutory provisions against the disclosure of secrets that are in the national interest, and a need for significantly more military representation on the commission. Three days into the debate, a vote was taken on whether to return the bill to committee. By nine votes, 93 yeas, 102 nays, it survived and immediately telegrams were dispatched to supporters who had already gone home to pursue reelection. In the meantime, several important amendments were made that significantly strengthened the military influence on the commission.[10]

Just when the bill seemed destined to be killed or recommitted, Rep. Jerry Voorhis, D-Calif., made a stirring appeal. Although he opposed most of the amendments, he implored the House not to recommit the bill. "We must be able to deal with this our greatest problem if we are to prove that democratic parliamentary legislative Government can justify its continuance in the new and admittedly dramatic and in some respect fearsome age in which we live." As those in the House galleries applauded, the mood in the chamber seemed to change as Voorhis reminded those listening that the issue before them was "a matter for the ages." Following his remarks, the House adopted the amendments, voted not to recommit the bill, 195–146, and then adopted the bill, 265–79.[11]

Next, House and Senate conferees met to strike a compromise between the differing versions of the bills approved by the two chambers. Ultimately, conferees from both chambers acquiesced on several amendments. Senate conferees prevailed on the key issue of civilian control, but the final measure included a strong advisory role for the military.

Although few in Congress advocated military control, most did not want the military totally excluded. The final version of the bill passed both houses on July 26, 1946. A week later, President Truman's signature officially transferred control of the world's most powerful weapon from the military to a five-member civilian panel.[12]

REPRESENTATIVE CLARE BOOTHE LUCE SUPPORTS THE ATOMIC ENERGY ACT OF 1946

JULY 17, 1946

Mr. Chairman, if a man, in order to get home safely, must walk along the brink of an abyss, he does well to take that trip with his eyes open and in clear weather. We want, if we can, to avoid the abyss of atomic warfare. It seems that the only road home does skirt that abyss; and unhappily, it is the totalitarian road of the legislation before us. Let us take it if we must. But, in the name of all our liberties, let us take it with our eyes wide open.

I arise in support of S. 1717, an act for the control and development of atomic energy, with a very heavy heart, indeed. We all remember — I believe somewhat unpleasantly — the President's recent emergency strike-control bill. Well, that bill was a tender affirmation of pre-New Deal rugged individualism compared with the socialistic character of this bill. Some sections of S. 1717 might have been written by the most ardent Soviet Commissar. Indeed, the patent provisions section — section II — are paralleled nowhere except in Soviet patent law. I urge upon my colleagues, whose legal training equips them to do so, to give their sharpest attention to the amendments offered on this section of the bill.

I am not alone in my opinion of the bill's politically revolutionary character. Through the entire course of the Senate debate on June 15 the author himself, the brilliant and able Senator from Connecticut [Mr. McMAHON] candidly stated that it was unique in American history.

★ ★ ★ ★

A study of the McMahon committee's lengthy hearings will reveal how profoundly disturbed all the Members were by the socialistic implications of this unprecedented piece of legislation.

The deceptive language of the declaration of policy to the contrary, there is not one single provision in this bill which will be of substantial aid in promoting world peace, except as it allows for the integration of domestic with international control of atomic energy. Nor is there in it — to quote the New Deal jargon of the preamble again — anything that will increase the standard of living. And as for strengthening free competition in private enterprise — another favorite preamble phrase of the New Dealers — there is many a section which does precisely the opposite. Provision after provision muzzles free competition and depresses incentive and production in all mining, industrial, patent, and invention fields which impinge at any point on the manufacture of nuclear energy.

Why then did the Senate support it so unanimously, and why must the House support it after amendment?

We must support it because nuclear energy, still in its infancy, contains horrible powers for mass destruction. And we dare not, in these oppressive and troubled times, leave the raw materials and processes of nuclear fissions, which even if developed in all good faith for peaceful purposes, are rapidly convertible to bomb manufacture, in the hands of private citizens.

S. 1717 is a tragically necessary defense measure in a world which may again, in five or ten years, flame into total war.

Let me quote a paragraph from the so-called Acheson or State Department report on the international control of atomic energy:

> Today, the United States has a monopoly in atomic weapons. We have strategic stock piles; we have extensive facilities for making the ingredients of atomic bombs and for making the bombs themselves; we have a large group of people skilled in the many arts which have gone into this project; we have experience and knowledge obtainable only in the actual practice of making atomic weapons; we have considerable theoretical knowledge of the field which may appear inadequate in future years, but which enables us to evaluate not only the performance of the past, but also what the future is likely to hold.

The chief merit, if not the only merit of this bill, is that it allows our Government to maintain and protect our monopoly of atomic weapons by seizing, operating, and using all

THE FINAL VOTE

Atomic Energy Act
July 26, 1946

Conference Report accepted by voice vote of both the Senate and House.

Source: "Development and Control of Atomic Energy — Conference Report," *Congressional Record,* July 26, 1946, 92:10167–10168, 10189–10199.

available source materials, stock piles, facilities, installations, information and know-how for making bombs.

Atomic energy today is preponderantly a weapon — a weapon of catastrophic character. This bill controls and safeguards for the United States of America all atomic weapons of the present, and permits the development of bigger and better — or one should say — worse ones, if this Nation should, in spite of all its sincere efforts in the direction of international control, be forced into a world wide race in atomic armament.

It seems to me that there is nothing to be gained by this House trying to deceive itself, or the American people about the true intent of this legislation, which is to secure and promote, for so long as we can, or until international atomic control is achieved, our national monopoly of this fearful weapon. Moreover, even if we deceived ourselves today into believing that this is preponderantly a bill for the peaceful development of atomic energy, we should not in the least deceive our world neighbors who will see at once right through the sweet and peaceful language of the preamble to the explosive heart of the matter: the bill's intent is to enable our Nation to amass an adequate stock pile of bombs for the purpose of defense and attack in war — should war again be suddenly thrust upon us, and to keep pace, in the research, and experimental fields with new processes in nuclear fission. It is the latter urgency which above all requires civilian control and civilian participation. That is why we must not leave the matter in the hands of the military who, while they can preserve the atomic status quo, can never make advances in this field. Under a civilian commission alone can such advances in this twilight peacetime be made.

★ ★ ★ ★

When — or rather, if — a reliable and effective mechanism for the international control of atomic energy can be formed in the UN, the domestic controls provided by this bill can be quickly and smoothly geared into the controls of that authority.

To be sure, the best opinion, as reflected in the State Department and Baruch reports, holds that it may be several, or even many years before such a world authority can be set up, and made effective. Every provision of this domestic bill will have to be duplicated on an international scale. Any world authority to be effective must begin with world ownership of all atomic raw materials, and provide rigid international inspection and licensing systems. The acceptance of these prime conditions may call for a greater abandonment of national sovereignty than some nations will endure. Still, the creation of effective world authority, along the lines laid down by Mr. Baruch, is not impossible, though I confess it seems to me unlikely. Nevertheless, to this noble task we must dedicate all our efforts. We must pray, in the name of survival itself, that the UN can be employed for atomic control.

But, until that day comes, it is plain that this Nation must embrace, however, reluctantly, the legislation before us, which is a complete device for domestic control of a highly expensive, highly complicated, highly industrialized, and highly dangerous process, which is rapidly convertible to the purposes of war.

And now, while I support this bill as a defense measure in a world which is no nearer peace than it was ten years ago, I feel that there should be laid before you the very real dangers to our American way of life involved in keeping this bill on the books as permanent legislation.

If all peace treaties had been signed and agreeably accepted; if the desperate political chaos of Central Europe and Asia had begun to resolve itself into democratic order; if Soviet Russia showed a sincere inclination to retire to her prewar borders, and to disband her Trojan horse political parties in our own and other countries; if the United Nations were really one big happy family; and if there were not, according to the State Department report, "the already launched international armament race"; in short if we entertained the heart-warming hope of world peace, instead the soul-sickening fear of a third world war, I should fight this bill to the last ounce of my strength. For in such circumstances, this bill could, and perhaps would, then be used as a perfect instrument for the socialization of America.

★ ★ ★ ★

Neither Senator McMAHON, nor we, nor the scientists, nor anybody with a logical mind can have the proposition two ways: either atomic energy molds us, as he first claimed, or we mold atomic energy, as he afterwards stated. The latter is, of course, the truth. The plain fact is that this man-made law will mold the use of God-given atomic energy. Nor was this bill written, as the able Senator claimed "out of the sheer necessity inherent in that" — inhuman — "tremendous force." This bill was written out of the human horror and fear that gripped the Senators when they thought of the tremendous human forces in other lands that might one day be able to hurl atomic bombs in a surprise attack on us. Human fears alone — chiefly of foreign powers — devised this law, which is — or should be — a law for keeping us supreme in the field of nuclear fission, and at the same time keeping the knowledge of how to make bombs away from our enemies. The able Senator said that this bill was forged in the fires of democratic action. It was not. It was forged in the fires of totalitarian action which are sweeping toward the West, and have already begun to burn holes in the fabric of our democratic civilization. Our fears concerning the future intentions of aggressive totalitarian nations dictated this bill; and its provisions were born of a psychological necessity, and not a scientific one: the dread of sudden attack, and the belief that one way perhaps to forestall it, was to be in a position to retaliate overwhelmingly.

We have devised this law, not to encourage the free enterprise system, or industrial research, or even the means of curing cancer and leukemia, but to protect ourselves so long as we can from greedy and lawless enemies.

★ ★ ★ ★

There is nothing in the "logic of atomic energy" which requires that atomic energy must be used to sovietize America. Only a human mind is capable of logic, or for that matter, of illogic, as when a man speaks of the logic of atomic energy. If America is eventually sovietized, as a result of the wartime discovery of atomic energy, it will be because the Congress, in fear and funk, allowed itself to be duped by the belief so dear to the heart of the mystical Marxian that logical matter disposes of mindless man, rather than that logical man disposes of mindless matter. Energy and matter, which we now know to be one, are both amoral. Man only is moral or immoral. We have only to reflect that if all the large nations of the world were led today by moral men instead of immoral ones, atomic energy, like all the other power sources, coal gas, oil, electricity, which we have developed in the ways of peace before, would not require such totalitarian legislation as this for their peaceful development.

The really immoral feature of this bill is that it implies, if indeed it does not state, that in time, atomic energy itself can and will automatically provide "the answers to the atomic age" without any mental effort on our part; that it will one day solve all our social, political, and economic problems, like some powerful, alert, conscious, genii out of a bottle. Well, it will not. Not any more than coal, or gas, or oil, or electricity, or radar, or radio, or television have solved in the past the recurrent problems of war and peace.

The plain fact is, that whether we pass this bill or not, we are still going to have to face, in the years ahead, the problem of industrial unrest, the problem of famine and revolution in Europe, and, above all, the problems created by Soviet ambitions and Soviet ideologies. The discovery of nuclear fission has not changed, and will not solve, one underlying problem in the world today. At worst, in the form of bombs it can aggravate them greatly. At best, in the form of heat or electri-

cal energy, or cancer and leukemia cures, it can ameliorate them only slightly.

Moreover, today and tomorrow we will do well to remember that every scientist who testified before our committee, or the Senate committee, said that in from five to fifteen years Soviet Russia, and any industrial nation with access to sources of uranium and thorium can make atomic bombs — and they insisted of a destructive capacity so much greater that the present bombs will look by comparison like fire crackers. So this bill, which can never solve our domestic economic problem, except as some in this House may imagine that communism is a cure-all, gives us only a temporary respite from the fear of atomic warfare, even as a defense measure. Only a wholly effective system of world nuclear control can guarantee us for the next two decades against atomization.

★ ★ ★ ★

Mr. Chairman, the real problem of the age is how shall we find economic and physical security, while at the same time safeguarding our political liberties. This legislation, S. 1717, epitomizes this crucial problem of our age. It does without any shadow of doubt, promise us at least five years of security from atomic attack. But its essential principle, which is state monopoly and control in the hands of a few administrative appointees, strikes fear to the heart of political liberty.

Patrick Henry said "Give me liberty or give me death."

Perhaps before this debate is over many of you may feel inclined to echo Patrick Henry's noble words.

But let me point this out: If your choice were truly a personal one, that is to say, if you, as one individual preferred death to losing your political liberties — you would be justified and even honored for making it.

If you vote against this bill you may be choosing death for millions of your fellow citizens by atomization. — Clare Boothe Luce

---

But your choice is not personal, unhappily. If you vote against this bill you may be choosing death for millions of your fellow citizens by atomization.

I, for one, dare not make such a ghastly choice. I support S. 1717, because I believe it offers the best possible solution to the problem of defending countless American lives in a world which is neither at war, nor at peace.

Source: *Congressional Record*, 79th Cong., 2nd sess., July 17, 1946 (Washington: GPO, 1946), 92:9261–9264.

351

REPRESENTATIVE CHARLES H. ELSTON OPPOSES THE ATOMIC ENERGY ACT OF 1946

[T]his bill is both dangerous and unnecessary. It is dangerous because it sets up a Government bureau with more power and authority than has ever been granted before. This bureau, under the provisions of the bill as now written, would have life and death control over the industry of the Nation whenever we reach the place where atomic energy may become useful for industrial purposes, in fact, even before that time. Moreover, the armed forces would become subservient to this power even in matters of national defense so far as the use of atomic energy is concerned. Furthermore, it removes incentives provided by our patent laws to inventors, and adopts a patent system found only in Soviet Russia. The fact that the Constitution of the United States gives to every inventor the exclusive right to his discoveries has meant nothing to the proponents of this legislation for under the provisions of this bill patents relating to the use of atomic power are either revoked or become the property of the Government.

Although the measure relates to the use of atomic power for military as well as civilian purposes, every conceivable effort has been made to eliminate representatives of the armed forces from representation on that all powerful bureau know as the Atomic Energy Commission. In its introductory section this bill is presented to us through a series of misrepresentations. For example, section 1 provides that it is "declared to be the policy of the people of the United States that, subject at all times to the paramount objective of assuring the common defense and security, the development and utilization of atomic energy shall, so far as practicable, be directed toward improving the public welfare, increasing the standard of living, strengthening free competition in private enterprise, and promoting world peace."

If enacted into law this bill would do exactly the reverse of these things. If the paramount objective is to assure the common defense and security, why has so desperate an effort been made to completely eliminate the armed forces from representation on the Commission or in any department under the supervision the Commission? Even though the bill purports to deal with atomic weapons and national defense, every attempt to give the Army and the Navy some representation has been resisted to the utmost. The House Committee on Military Affairs was bitterly assailed by the supporters of the bill generally because it dared to amend the act as it

came from the Senate so as to provide that at least one member of the Commission and the head of the Division of Military Application should be from the armed forces. The only argument I have heard against it is the rather specious claim that it is not in keeping with our traditions for a military man to serve on a policy-making commission — that military men are only interested in war, and that other nations might frown upon their presence on the Commission. In this connection I wonder why the civil functions of the War Department are so conveniently forgotten. If there has been any Government agency that has been free from criticism and that has been elevated above the run-of-mine Washington bureau, it has been the Corps of Army Engineers which has for so many years been responsible for our rivers and harbors and flood-control projects. In this work they have handled billions of dollars and have performed work in no way related to war. Yet I have never heard that it was not in keeping with American tradition for them to exercise these functions.

★ ★ ★ ★

I for one am not willing to turn this Nation into a totalitarian state merely because there may be some confusion about proposed legislation. Since some speakers today have indicated that they are for the legislation solely for security reasons, I would say that is all the more reason why things should remain as they are. I am not willing to substitute a politically minded bureau, such as this bill would set up, for trained military personnel so long as we are in any danger.

★ ★ ★ ★

They say that if the Army is represented on the Commission this country might go ahead and manufacture atomic bombs and atomic weapons. The answer to that I believe is that any time the President of the United States wants the manufacture of atomic bombs to cease all he has to do is to give a simple order to stop.

You will no doubt hear it loudly proclaimed that the armed services have been taken care of in the Senate bill by providing for a military liaison committee. Read the section creating this committee and you will see that it has been given no authority whatsoever. Aside from the fact that the Atomic

Energy Commission shall consult with the liaison committee, and that they shall keep each other informed as to atomic energy matters in the War and Navy Departments, the liaison committee has nothing to do. Actually nothing is provided for in this section that could not and should not be done between any government departments as a matter of simple courtesy and expediency. Since the Commission must deal with matters' of national defense, I do not know how it could function without consultation with the War and Navy Departments. The appeals which the services are permitted to make to the Secretaries of War and Navy, and through them to the President, would be permitted without this legislation. In a word, this section is nothing more or less than a sop handed out to convey the erroneous impression that our armed forces are given some recognition. Even this was denied in the beginning despite the fact that the atomic bomb was developed under the supervision of the Army and all secrets in connection therewith are in its custody.

Before we look into the powers of the Commission and the extent to which it encroaches upon private industry and interferes with our American way of life, you will note that section 9 requires the Army to transfer to the Commission forthwith upon the passage of the bill, all facilities, equipment, and material devoted to atomic energy, research, and development. This would include even the Oakridge plant, together with any bombs now in existence, as well as formulas and secrets in connection with the atomic bomb and other atomic weapons. So at the start, even before the war is officially over, the branches of the services charged under the Constitution with the defense of the Nation are required to turn over to a civilian Government bureau of political appointees weapons which the services may require for the defense of the country. If this does not jeopardize the security of the Nation then the Bikini tests and the results at Hiroshima and Nagasaki were incorrectly reported.

So much for security. As to other powers of the Commission, let us examine a few of them. In the field of research the Commission may make grants-in-aid and loans to public or private institutions or persons even in connection with research for industrial purposes. Thus the Commission has the power to favor one school or university as against another, and to favor industries, companies, or individuals to the detriment of others. As no person or company would have the right to engage in research on their own part, you perhaps begin to appreciate what is meant by the term "life-and-death control of industry."

★ ★ ★ ★

Bear in mind, Mr. Chairman, that the Commission will become the owner of all fissionable material regardless of who may now possess it. It can be parceled out for industrial purposes only with the consent of the Commission. As the time may come when atomic energy power may supplant many other forms of power, and become vital to every industry in the Nation, it is not difficult to understand the extent to which the Atomic Commission would control the industries of the country.

If any person, industry or company should be dissatisfied with the distribution or refusal of the Commission to distribute any fissionable or by-product materials, such person or company may obtain a review of the determination of the Commission by an appeal. But let us examine into the types of appeal afforded. On a matter as important as this, one would feel the appeal should be to the courts, or at least to an unbiased or disinterested tribunal of some sort. Such is not the case, however. Section 5 (d)(2) makes the Commission the judge, jury, and executioner so far as appeals under this section are concerned. The Board of Appeals created by this section shall consist of three members who shall be appointed by the Commission. Should any person feel himself aggrieved by a decision of the Board of Appeals his only further appeal is to the Commission itself. Even this right is not guaranteed as it is provided that "the Commission may in its discretion review and revise any decision of such board of appeal." Here, I submit we see bureaucracy at its worst.

★ ★ ★ ★

One of the most objectionable features of this bill is section 7, which contains the licensing provisions. Under this section it shall be unlawful for any person to manufacture, produce, or export any equipment or device utilizing fissionable material or to utilize atomic energy except under and in accordance with a license issued by the Commission. Do not be misled by subsection (b) which requires a report to Congress before such licenses may be issued. If you will examine that section you will find that there is but one report to be made to Congress. That report will be made when, in the opinion of the Commission, any industrial, commercial, or other nonmilitary use of atomic energy has been sufficiently developed to be of practical value. In that report the Commission will set forth all the facts with respect to such use, and the report will contain the Commission's estimate of the social, political, economic, and international effects of such use. After ninety days subsequent to the making of such report, the Commission will have unlimited authority to issue licenses for the utilization of atomic energy to such persons and on such terms as it sees fit.

★ ★ ★ ★

When we reach section 10 of the bill we see unfolded a strange philosophy for America. Let me read the pertinent part of this section:

It shall be the policy of the Commission to control the dissemination of restricted data in such a manner as to assure the common defense and security. Consistent with such policy the Commission shall be guided by the following principles:

(1) That information with respect to the use of atomic energy for industrial purposes should be shared with other nations on a reciprocal basis as soon as the Congress declares by joint resolution that effective and enforceable international safeguards against the use of such energy for destructive purposes have been established.

In other words, hereafter it shall be the policy of this country, as soon as international safeguards have been established, to share the use of atomic energy secrets and power with the other Nations of the world. When in all the history of this Nation has it been required that anything developed for the benefit of American industry shall be shared with other Nations? American industry leads the world today because of American inventive genius and our free enterprise system, but now we have a new philosophy. Do not lose sight of the fact that this sharing plan pertains to the use of atomic energy for industrial purposes only. It has no relation to the outlawing of atomic energy for military purposes which, I am sure, every thinking person favors when it can be done without endangering our own security. Judge for yourselves what this international plan will mean to American industry.

Not only must we share such information with other nations, but we must make sure they get the information. Section 10 (b) authorizes the Commission to establish such information services, publications and even libraries, as it sees fit. These may be established anywhere in the world. I know, of course, that someone will say that this sharing of information must be on a reciprocal basis, but who determines what shall be reciprocated? The Commission, of course. Since we apparently have all the information regarding atomic energy, what are we to get in return? Perhaps good will. So far as this section is concerned, the Commission would have authority to exchange atomic secrets for industrial purposes for good will as the Commission is the sole judge.

The patent section of the bill is definitely unconstitutional in its present form. Article I, section 8, clause 8, of the Constitution provides —

The Congress shall have . . . power to promote the program of science and useful arts by securing for limited times for authors and inventors the exclusive right to their respective writings and discoveries.

This section has been interpreted on many occasions by the courts, and the leading decisions on the subject are set forth in the minority views which accompanied this bill. For example, it is said in *Solomons v. United States* (137 U. S. 342, 346), that —

The Government has no more power to appropriate a man's property invested in a patent than it has to take his property in vested in real estate.

The only testimony presented to our committee on the subject of patents came from Mr. Conder C. Henry, formerly Assistant Commissioner of Patents. He said, and I quote:

By removing the incentives provided by our patent laws, the bill is a radical departure from anything known in our history. The only parallel I can find to it is the Soviet patent law.

He further stated that hundreds of inventions used at Oak Ridge and elsewhere in the development of the atomic bomb had previously been made by private inventors. Moreover, he pointed out that under our present patent system the interests of the Government were fully safeguarded without encroaching upon the constitutional rights of any person. This same system should and can continue, and it is my purpose to offer as I did in committee, an amendment to strike section 11 from the bill.

Section 15 of the act creates a new congressional committee with full legislative authority, and this comes at a time when Congress is recommending fewer committees — even a consolidation of the Military and Naval Committees.

In the enforcement provisions of the act the Commission is given the broad power to make regulations and orders and enforce them by punishing offenders with a fine as high as $20,000 and imprisonment for not more than twenty years; or both. This section, I believe, violates the rule laid down by the Supreme Court of the United States in the case of *Schechter v. United States* (295 U. S. 495), wherein it was held that Congress cannot delegate to any Government agency the power to make regulations having the force of law without laying down the policies and establishing the appropriate standards.

★ ★ ★ ★

Why do they say this legislation is needed? The principal claim is that it will impress the rest of the world that we have taken the matter out of the hands of the military and invested it with civilians. If that be the purpose, this legislation very definitely is not needed as the President can order the military authorities to cease any of their military activities at any time, including the manufacture of atomic bombs or the use of atomic energy in any way.

Another claim is that peace of the world requires international control of atomic energy. If that be so point out a single thing in this bill dealing with international control or in any manner related to it. International control can come about only by international agreement. If any legislation is needed to augment such an agreement it necessarily would come after the international agreement was entered into.

Do we need this legislation to begin negotiations for such an agreement? The best answer is — such negotiations have begun before the duly constituted United Nations Atomic Energy Commission. Mr. Baruch submitted a proposal to this

Commission a month ago. But it takes two or more to enter into an agreement, and Russia has flatly rejected Mr. Baruch's plan. Not only has she rejected it, but she has submitted a counterproposal which never could be agreed to if we have any regard at all for the security of this country.

So if we do not need this bill to remove an impression that we are militaristically inclined and we do not need it for the purpose of helping to bring about international control of atomic energy, what do we need it for? If it seeks to do anything further than to place shackles on American industry

---

If it seeks to do anything further than to place shackles on American industry and barriers against inventive genius and ingenuity such purpose does not appear from the language of the bill. — Charles H. Elston

---

and barriers against inventive genius and ingenuity such purpose does not appear from the language of the bill.

If this Nation is concerned lest the other nations of the world think we are assuming too much of a military attitude we perhaps should explain why we are spending hundreds of millions of dollars in proceeding with the Bikini tests. Is it consistent to carry on these demonstrations and at the same time try to fool the American people into believing we can pacify the world by creating another bureau and many expensive bureaucrats to further regiment the lives of our people and further encroach upon their liberties?

If this measure were to stop with encroachment upon American freedom it would be bad enough, but not necessarily fatal, as such an invasion might be corrected by subsequent legislation, although I have found that liberty and freedom, once surrendered, are not easy to regain. There is always another emergency offered as an excuse for retaining them. On the other hand, if the security of the country is involved, legislation might be helpless to correct the error.

As I see it, the bill before us today, if enacted into law, will definitely jeopardize the Nation's security. At the moment the secrets of the atomic bomb and the bomb itself are safely in the hands of the military authorities in the keeping of that branch of the Government charged by the Constitution with the responsibility of defending the Nation. That is where I submit it should remain until our safety is assured under

international agreements actually entered into and until machinery has been set up in the world adequate to enforce such agreements.

Source: *Congressional Record*, 79th Cong., 2nd sess., July 17, 1946 (Washington: GPO, 1946), 92:9272–9275.

Notes

1. Byron S. Miller, "A Law is Passed — The Atomic Energy Act of 1946," *The University of Chicago Law Review* 15 (Summer 1948): 801.

2. U.S. Congress, House Committee on Military Affairs, *Atomic Energy*, hearings on H.R. 4280, 79th Cong., 1st sess., October 9, 1945 (Washington: GPO, 1945), 4; Richard G. Hewlett and Oscar E. Anderson, *A History of the United States Atomic Energy Commission*, 2 vols. (University Park: Pennsylvania State University Press, 1962), 1:345.

3. Hewlett and Anderson, *A History of the United States Atomic Energy Commission*, 1:412.

4. Nelson W. Polsby, *Political Innovation in America: The Politics of Policy Initiation* (New Haven, Conn.: Yale University Press, 1984), 22–23.

5. Quote is found in Miller, "A Law is Passed — The Atomic Energy Act of 1946," 803. See also Hewlett and Anderson, *A History of the United States Atomic Energy Commission*, 1:429–439.

6. Polsby, *Political Innovation in America: The Politics of Policy Initiation*, 27.

7. Miller, "A Law is Passed — The Atomic Energy Act of 1946," 807. See also Hewlett and Anderson, *A History of the United States Atomic Energy Commission*, 1:436–455.

8. Harry S. Truman, *Memoirs*, 2 vols. (Garden City, N.Y.: Doubleday, 1955–1956), 2: 3–5. See also Hewlett and Anderson, *A History of the United States Atomic Energy Commission*, 1:488–504.

9. Hewlett and Anderson, *A History of the United States Atomic Energy Commission*, 1:504. See also ibid., 504–516; Miller, "A Law is Passed — The Atomic Energy Act of 1946," 807–813; Polsby, *Political Innovation in America: The Politics of Policy Initiation*, 30–31.

10. Quotes are found in Hewlett and Anderson, *A History of the United States Atomic Energy Commission*, 517; *Congressional Record*, July 17, 1946, 92:9261, 9272. See also Hewlett and Anderson, *A History of the United States Atomic Energy Commission*, 517–528.

11. Rep. Jerry Voorhis, "Atomic Energy Act of 1946," *Congressional Record*, remarks in the House, July 20, 1946, 92:9555. See also Hewlett, *A History of the United States Atomic Energy Commission*, 528.

12. "Development and Control of Atomic Energy — Conference Report," *Congressional Record*, July 26, 1946, 92:10167–10168, 10189–10199; PL. 585, 60 Stat. 755–775, August 1, 1946.

McCarthyism
✳ 1950–1954 ✳

In Wheeling, West Virginia, on February 9, 1950, Sen. Joseph R. McCarthy, R-Wis., told a Lincoln Day dinner audience of Republican women that he had in his "hand a list of two hundred five [individuals] who were known to the Secretary of State as being members of the Communist party and who nevertheless, are still working and shaping policy in the State Department." Although Congress had been conducting investigations of Communist subversion and espionage for more than two decades, his sensational accusation still shocked the nation. It thrust the obscure first-term senator into national prominence and launched a period of intensified postwar communist investigations, during which both the Senate and the nation were gripped by fear and distrust. Eventually, McCarthyism became synonymous with political actions that blatantly disregarded the civil liberties of Americans.[1]

Soon after the Wheeling event, the McCarthy crusade reached the Senate floor where the ineffectiveness of the Democratic majority in upstaging him prompted four months of hearings by a special subcommittee of the Senate Foreign Relations Committee, chaired by Sen. Millard F. Tydings, D-Md. Rather than discredit McCarthy, the Tydings hearings thrust him forward as the nation's principal pursuer of communists. The committee's three hundred forty-seven-page report, which was extremely critical of McCarthy, coupled with Tydings's equally blunt remarks on the Senate floor when the full Senate took up the report, branded the panel's effort as partisan. McCarthy labeled the report "a signal to the traitors, Communists and fellow travelers in our government that they need have no fear of exposure from [the Truman] administration," and his influence continued to soar. Then in April 1951, President Harry S. Truman fired Gen. Douglas MacArthur, commander of United Nations forces in Korea, after the two disagreed on strategic plans for the conflict. Truman's decision angered many Americans who perceived a lost opportunity to deliver a deadly blow to communism. McCarthy saved his harshest criticism for Secretary of State Dean Acheson and Secretary of Defense George C. Marshall. Particularly brutal was his stinging sixty-thousand-word *Congressional Record* attack on Marshall, who was accused of "a conspiracy so immense and an infamy so black as to dwarf any previous such venture in the history of man." Marshall was assailed for Truman's removal as well as for suggestions and decisions while a general in World War II and as secretary of state following the war.[2]

Prior to 1953, McCarthy identified communists employed by the federal government and then expected Senate investigative committees to find proof of their wrongdoing. After the Republicans recaptured the Senate in the 1952 elections, McCarthy became chairman of the Committee on Government Operations and the panel's Permanent Subcommittee on Investigations. He used the latter position to hire staff pledged to helping him expose traitors within the government. Together, McCarthy and Roy M. Cohn, the subcommittee's chief counsel, held four-hundred forty-five preliminary inquiries and one hundred fifty-seven investigations in 1953 alone, a workload negatively impacted on the quality of the subcommittee's research and preparation. The inconclusiveness of the investigations was overshadowed by McCarthy's performances before the television cameras.[3]

McCarthy's hearings first focused on the Voice of America and the International Information Agency, and then they shifted to the Central Intelligence Agency and Government Printing Office. Witnesses first appeared before congressional investigative committees at a closed executive session, which permitted him to manipulate the media by furnishing opportunistic summaries of the proceedings just before their deadlines. Statutes and court rulings, he believed, granted him the right to question anyone suspected of being a communist or communist sympathizer. Nothing was too private or personal. His tactics included verbal abuse, intimidation, and firings without due process. Only a few followed the lead of CBS's Edward R. Murrow, who used his popular TV show, *See It Now*, to expose McCarthy's total disregard for those he attacked.[4]

During his most controversial hearings, McCarthy tried to expose communist infiltration into the Army Signal Corps Center at Fort Monmouth, New Jersey. He both harassed and browbeat the Army officers who appeared as witnesses which, as usual, generated headlines. His harshest attack was saved for Brig. Gen. Ralph W. Zwicker, the commanding officer who had alerted him to Irving Peress, an Army dentist who was promoted and then honorably discharged while

Congress in 1954 voted to censure Senator Joseph McCarthy for his committee hearings seeking to reveal communists within the government. McCarthy's blatant disregard for civil liberties and increasingly aggressive tactics led to the Senate censure.
Source: The Granger Collection, New York.

under investigation by Army intelligence and the FBI. Rather than praising Zwicker, McCarthy blamed him for allowing the promotion and berated and insulted him. When the *New York Times* published a transcript of the closed-door session, even McCarthy's allies were outraged.[5]

Amidst the Zwicker controversy, McCarthy accused President Dwight D. Eisenhower of only belatedly joining the anticommunist cause. Secretary of Defense Charles E. Wilson answered by giving each member of McCarthy's subcommittee a report prepared by Army counsel John G. Adams that accused McCarthy and Cohn of attempting to intimidate the Army on behalf of Private G. David Shine, a former subcommittee staffer. McCarthy responded with what proved to be a bogus memorandum that assailed his Army accusers as prevaricators who lacked integrity. Finally, the subcommittee felt compelled to replace Cohn, investigate the various allega-

tions and counter allegations, and temporally remove McCarthy as chairman. The televised Army-McCarthy hearings, chaired by Rep. Karl E. Mundt, R-S.D., preempted regular daytime programming for more than a month. As an estimated twenty million viewers watched, McCarthy was outmatched by Joseph N. Welch, special Army counsel. McCarthy's mean-spirited performance further eroded his quickly evaporating support, while Welch quickly established himself as a skillful and often flamboyant opponent and relied on humor, logic, and moral outrage to outmaneuver the senator.[6]

The McCarthy-Welch face-off reached a climax when the senator attacked Frederick Fisher, a young partner in Welch's law firm who sought a job with the subcommittee even though he had belonged to the National Lawyers Guild, a subversive group, in the 1940s. Welch responded by explaining that while Fisher was in law school, and for a few months afterwards, he had belonged to the Guild, and now was a secretary of the Young Republicans in Newton, Massachusetts. Upon learning of Fisher's past affiliation, Welch explained, he told him to abandon his plan of working for the subcommittee. Then turning to McCarthy, Welch added: "Little did I dream you could be so reckless and so cruel as to do an injury to that lad…. Let us not assassinate this lad further, Senator. You have done enough. Have you no sense of decency, sir, at long last? Have you left no sense of decency?"[7]

Welch's retort was devastating. For weeks afterwards, the sequence was replayed on television and newsreels, in editorials and commentary. On July 30, following the conclusion of the hearings, Sen. Ralph E. Flanders, R-Vt., who in preceding months had delivered some of the most pointed attacks on McCarthy, introduced a resolution to censure McCarthy. A week later, Sen. Arthur V. Watkins, R-Utah, was selected to chair a select committee created to hear the charges against McCarthy. Late in September, the committee concluded censure was warranted, and in December McCarthy was formally condemned, 67–22, for bringing the Senate "into dishonor and disrepute and thus impairing its dignity." When the Eighty-fourth Congress convened in January 1955, McCarthy lost his chairmanship as a consequence of the Democrats regaining control of the Senate and quickly faded into obscurity before dying prematurely at age forty-eight.[8]

While a number of senators would eventually speak out against McCarthy, particularly during the debate over the censure resolution, Sen. Margaret Chase Smith, R-Maine, was among the first to openly question his charges in her June 1, 1950, "Declaration of Conscience." McCarthy was not mentioned by name, but everyone knew to whom she was referring in declaring that the Senate had been "debased to the level of a forum of hate and character assassination sheltered by the shield of congressional immunity." Afterwards, McCarthy "ridiculed Smith and her seven cosigners as 'Snow White and the Seven Dwarfs,'" and "removed her as a member of the Permanent Subcommittee on Investigations." His "allies took every occasion to smear Smith. But in 1954, she had the satisfaction of casting a vote for McCarthy's censure and effectively ending" the tactics "she had so effectively denounced "as a political attempt to ride 'the Four Horsemen of Calumny — fear, ignorance, bigotry and smear.'"[9]

SENATOR JOSEPH R. McCARTHY ON COMMUNISTS IN GOVERNMENT SERVICE

FEBRUARY 20, 1950

Mr. McCARTHY. Mr. President, I wish to discuss a subject tonight which concerns me more than does any other subject I have ever discussed before this body, and perhaps more than any other subject I shall ever have the good fortune to discuss in the future. It not only concerns me, but it disturbs and frightens me.

About ten days ago, at Wheeling, W. Va., in making a Lincoln Day speech, I made the statement that there are presently in the state Department a very sizable group of active Communists. I made the further statement, Mr. President, that of one small group which had been screened by the President's own security agency, the State Department refused to discharge approximately two hundred of those individuals.

The Secretary of State promptly denied my statement and said there was not a single Communist in the State Department. I thereafter sent a telegram to the President, which I should like to read at this time:

President HARRY S. TRUMAN
White House, Washington, D. C.

In the Lincoln Day speech at Wheeling Thursday night I stated that the State Department harbors a nest of Communists and Communist sympathizers who are helping to shape our foreign policy. I further stated that I have in my possession the names of fifty-seven Communists who are in the State Department at present. A State Department spokesman promptly denied this, claiming that there is not a single Communist in the Department. You can convince yourself of the falsity of the State Department claim very easily. You will recall that you personally appointed a board to screen State Department employees for the purpose of weeding out fellow travelers — men whom the board considered dangerous to the security of this Nation. Your board did a painstaking job, and named hundreds which had been listed as dangerous to the security of the Nation, because of communistic connections.

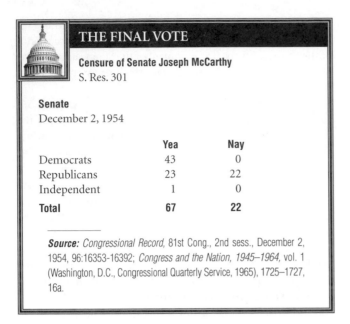

THE FINAL VOTE

Censure of Senate Joseph McCarthy
S. Res. 301

Senate
December 2, 1954

	Yea	Nay
Democrats	43	0
Republicans	23	22
Independent	1	0
Total	**67**	**22**

Source: Congressional Record, 81st Cong., 2nd sess., December 2, 1954, 96:16353-16392; *Congress and the Nation, 1945–1964,* vol. 1 (Washington, D.C., Congressional Quarterly Service, 1965), 1725–1727, 16a.

While the records are not available to me, I know absolutely of one group of approximately three hundred certified to the Secretary for discharge because of communism. He actually only discharged approximately eighty. I understand that this was done after lengthy consultation with the now-convicted traitor Alger Hiss. I would suggest, therefore, Mr. President, that you simply pick up your phone and ask Mr. Acheson how many of those whom your board had labeled as dangerous Communists he failed to discharge. The day the House Un-American Activities Committee exposed Alger Hiss as an important link in an international Communist spy ring you signed an order forbidding the State Department's giving any information in regard to the disloyalty or the communistic connections of anyone in that Department to the Congress.

Despite this State Department black-out, we have been able to compile a list of fifty-seven Communists in the State Department. This list is available to you but you can get a much longer list by ordering Secretary Acheson to give you a list of those whom your own board listed as being disloyal and who are still working in the State Department. I believe the following is the minimum which can be expected of you in this case.

1. That you demand that Acheson give you and the proper congressional committee the names and a complete report on all of those who were placed in the Department by Alger Hiss, and all of those still working in the State Department who were listed by your board as bad security risks because of their communistic connections.

2. That you promptly revoke the order in which you provided under no circumstances could a congressional committee obtain any information or help in exposing Communists.

Failure on your part will label the Democratic Party of being the bedfellow of international communism. Certainly this label is not deserved by the hundreds of thousands of loyal American Democrats throughout the Nation, and by the sizable number of able loyal Democrats in both the Senate and the House.

Mr. President, the only answer I have received to this telegram was the statement by the President at his press conference to the effect that there was not a word of truth in the telegram.

Subsequently, the Democratic leader of the Senate [Sen. Scott Wike Lucas of Illinois] — at least, the alleged leader — made a speech in Chicago in which he repeated substantially what the President said, except that he went one step further and stated:

> If I had said the nasty things that McCarthy has about the State Department, I would be ashamed all my life.

He also said there was not a word of truth in my charge. I think it is unfortunate, not because I am concerned with what the senior Senator from Illinois happens to think, but because he occupies such an important position. I believe, if we are going to root out the fifth column in the State Department, we should have the wholehearted cooperation of both Democrats and Republicans —

Mr. LUCAS. Mr. President, will the Senator yield?

Mr. McCARTHY. Wait until I finish. If the Senator will stay with me for the next few hours he will learn a great many facts. I have never refused to yield to any Senator, and I do not intend to refuse. The Senator from Illinois will have full time in which to answer any question he wishes to ask, but let me first finish my sentence. I started to say that I think it is especially bad because it indicates a preconceived decision not to work with us in attempting to ferret out Communists. I do not feel that the Democratic Party has control of the executive branch of the Government any more. If it had with the very able Members on the other side of the aisle, we would not find the picture which I intend to disclose. I think a group of twisted-thinking intellectuals have taken over both the Democratic and Republican Parties to try to wrest control from them.

I shall be glad now to yield to the Senator from Illinois.

Mr. LUCAS. Mr. President, I should like to say to the Senator that there is no one in the Senate or in the country who is any more opposed to Communist domination of any nation or Communist infiltration into any country than is the Senator from Illinois. What I am asking the Senator to do — and I hope he will do it, and the country wants him to do it — is to follow through with the speech which he made in Wheeling, W. Va., in which he stated more than two hundred persons working in the State Department were known to the Secretary of State to be members of the Communist Party. If the Senator made that statement — and that is what has been reported — I want him to name those Communists. If there are card-carrying Communists in the State Department the Senator from Illinois will go along with the Senator from

---

Failure on your part will label the Democratic Party of being the bedfellow of international communism. Certainly this label is not deserved by the hundreds of thousands of loyal American Democrats throughout the Nation, and by the sizable number of able loyal Democrats in both the Senate and the House. — Joseph R. McCarthy

---

Wisconsin in any way possible to remove those Communists from the rolls.

The Senator does not have to do as he did in Salt Lake City and say, "I am not charging these four people with being Communists." The Senator is privileged to name them all in the Senate, and if those people are not Communists he will be protected. That is all I want the Senator to do. If the Senator names those two hundred five card-carrying Communists and he proves to be right, the Senator from Illinois will apologize for anything he has said about the Senator from Wisconsin.

Mr. McCARTHY. I wish to thank the distinguished Senator from Illinois for his views, but I should like to assure him that I will not say anything on the Senate floor which I will not say off the floor. On the day when I take advantage of the security we have on the Senate floor, on that day I will resign from the Senate. Anything I say on the floor of the Senate at any time will be repeated off the floor.

Mr. LUCAS. Mr. President, will the Senator yield?

Mr. McCARTHY. Not until I have finished answering the question of the Senator from Illinois. The Senator called my attention to something, and I am glad he did; otherwise I might have overlooked it. Incidentally, the speech in Reno, Nev., and that in Wheeling, W. Va., were recorded, so there is no question about what I said. I do not believe I mentioned the figure two hundred five. I believe I said "over two hundred." The President said, "It is just a lie. There is nothing to it."

I have before me a letter which was reproduced in the *Congressional Record* on August 1, 1946, at page A4892. It is a letter from James F. Byrnes, former Secretary of State. It deals with the screening of the first group, of about 3,000. There were a great number of subsequent screenings. This was the beginning.

Mr. LUCAS. Mr. President, will the Senator yield?

Mr. McCARTHY. Please let me finish. The Senator will have all the time in the world to ask questions, and I shall be very glad to yield to the Senator for that purpose, and he can even make short speeches and take all the time he wants.

Mr. LUCAS. Mr. President, the Senator from Illinois —

Mr. McCARTHY. I do not yield at this time.

The PRESIDING OFFICER. The Senator from Wisconsin declines to yield.

Mr. McCARTHY. The letter deals with the first group of 3,000 which was screened. The President — and I think wisely so — set up a board to screen the employees who were coming to the State Department from the various war agencies of the War Department. There were thousands of unusual characters in some of those war agencies. Former Secretary Byrnes in his letter, which is reproduced in the *Congressional Record*, says this:

Pursuant to Executive order, approximately four thousand employees have been transferred to the Department of State from various war agencies such as the OSS, FEA, OWI, OIAA, and so forth. Of these four thousand employees, the case histories of approximately three thousand have been subjected to a preliminary examination, as a result of which a recommendation against permanent employment has been made in 285 cases by the screening committee to which you refer in your letter.

In other words, former Secretary Byrnes said that two hundred eighty-five of those men are unsafe risks. He goes on to say that of this number only seventy-nine have been removed. Of the fifty-seven I mentioned some are from this group of two hundred five, and some are from subsequent groups which have been screened but not discharged.

I might say in that connection that the investigative agency of the State Department has done an excellent job. The files show that they went into great detail in labeling Communists as such. The only trouble is that after the investigative agency had properly labeled these men as Communists the State Department refused to discharge them.

★ ★ ★ ★

Mr. LUCAS. Mr. President, did the Senator say at Wheeling, W. Va., last Thursday night that two hundred five persons working for the State Department were known by the Secretary of State to be members of the Communist Party, or words to that effect? Did he call the attention of the country to the fact that two hundred five men in the State Department were card-carrying Communists? Did the Senator say that? That is what I should like to know.

Mr. McCARTHY. Mr. President, I ask unanimous consent at this time to insert in the *Record* a copy of the speech which I made at Wheeling, W. Va.

Mr. LUCAS. Cannot the Senator answer "Yes" or "No?"

Mr. McCARTHY. I will ask the Senator please not to interrupt me. I will give him all the chance in the world.

Mr. LUCAS. I asked the Senator a very simple question.

Mr. McCARTHY. I ask at this time unanimous consent to be allowed to insert in the *Record* a copy of the speech which I made at Wheeling, W. Va., and at Reno, Nev. It was the same speech.

Mr. LUCAS. Mr. President, I object.

Mr. McCARTHY. In that case I shall read the speech into the RECORD.

Mr. LUCAS. We want to hear it.

[Senator McCarthy then read a transcript of the Wheeling speech, periodically yielding to answer questions from vari-ous senators. *Congressional Record*, 81st Cong., 2nd sess., February 20, 1950, 96:1954–1957. For a copy of the tape recorded version of the speech, which contains portions omitted from the *Congressional Record* version, see Robert C. Byrd, *The Senate 1789–1989: Classic Speeches, 1830–1993,* ed. Wendy Wolff (Washington: GPO, 1994), 611–616.]

Source: *Congressional Record*, 81st Cong., 2nd sess., February 20, 1950 (Washington: GPO, 1950), 96:1952–1954.

SENATOR MARGARET CHASE SMITH'S DECLARATION OF CONSCIENCE

JUNE 1, 1950

Mr. President, I would like to speak briefly and simply about a serious national condition. It is a national feeling of fear and frustration that could result in national suicide and the end of everything that we Americans hold dear. It is a condition that comes from the lack of effective leadership either in the legislative branch or the executive branch of our government. That leadership is so lacking that serious and responsible proposals are being made that national advisory commissions be appointed to provide such critically needed leadership.

I speak as briefly as possible because too much harm has already been done with irresponsible words of bitterness and selfish political opportunism. I speak as simply as possible because the issue is too great to be obscured by eloquence. I speak simply and briefly in the hope that my words will be taken to heart.

Mr. President, I speak as a Republican. I speak as a woman. I speak as a United States Senator. I speak as an American.

The United States Senate has long enjoyed worldwide respect as the greatest deliberative body in the world. But recently that deliberative character has too often been debased to the level of a forum of hate and character assassination sheltered by the shield of congressional immunity.

It is ironical that we Senators can in debate in the Senate, directly or indirectly, by any form of words, impute to any American who is not a Senator any conduct or motive unworthy or unbecoming an American — and without that non-Senator American having any legal redress against us — yet if we say the same thing in the Senate about our colleagues we can be stopped on the grounds of being out of order.

It is strange that we can verbally attack anyone else without restraint and with full protection, and yet we hold ourselves above the same type of criticism here on the Senate floor. Surely the United States Senate is big enough to take self-criticism and self-appraisal. Surely we should be able to take the same kind of character attacks that we "dish out" to outsiders.

I think that it is high time for the United States Senate and its members to do some real soul searching and to weigh our consciences as to the manner in which we are performing our duty to the people of America and the manner in which we are using or abusing our individual powers and privileges.

I think that it is high time that we remembered that we have sworn to uphold and defend the Constitution. I think that it is high time that we remembered that the Constitution as amended, speaks not only of the freedom of speech but also of trial by jury instead of trial by accusation.

Whether it be a criminal prosecution in court or a character prosecution in the Senate, there is little practical distinction when the life of a person has been ruined.

Those of us who shout the loudest about Americanism in making character assassinations are all too frequently those who, by our own words and acts, ignore some of the basic principles of Americanism —

- The right to criticize.
- The right to hold unpopular beliefs.
- The right to protest.
- The right of independent thought.

The exercise of these rights should not cost one single American citizen his reputation or his right to a livelihood nor should he be in danger of losing his reputation or livelihood merely because he happens to know someone who holds unpopular beliefs. Who of us does not? Otherwise none of us could call our souls our own. Otherwise thought control would have set in.

Those of us who shout the loudest about Americanism in making character assassinations are all too frequently those who, by our own words and acts, ignore some of the basic principles of Americanism.
— Margaret Chase Smith

The American people are sick and tired of being afraid to speak their minds lest they be politically smeared as "Communists" or "Fascists" by their opponents. Freedom of speech is not what it used to be in America. It has been so abused by some that it is not exercised by others.

The American people are sick and tired of seeing innocent people smeared and guilty people whitewashed. But there have been enough proved cases, such as the Amerasia case, the Hiss case, the Coplon case, the Gold case, to cause nation wide distrust and strong suspicion that there may be something to the unproved, sensational accusations.

As a Republican, I say to my colleagues on this side of the aisle that the Republican party faces a challenge today that is not unlike the challenge which it faced back in Lincoln's day. The Republican party so successfully met that challenge that it emerged from the Civil War as the champion of a united nation — in addition to being a party which unrelentingly fought loose spending and loose programs.

Today our country is being psychologically divided by the confusion and the suspicions that are bred in the United States Senate to spread like cancerous tentacles of "know nothing, suspect everything" attitudes. Today we have a Democratic administration which has developed a mania for loose spending and loose programs. History is repeating itself — and the Republican party again has the opportunity to emerge as the champion of unity and prudence.

The record of the present Democratic administration has provided us with sufficient campaign issues without the necessity of resorting to political smears. America is rapidly losing its position as leader of the world simply because the Democratic administration has pitifully failed to provide effective leadership.

The Democratic administration has completely confused the American people by its daily contradictory grave warnings and optimistic assurances, which show the people that our Democratic administration has no idea of where it is going.

The Democratic administration has greatly lost the confidence of the American people by its complacency to the threat of communism here at home and the leak of vital secrets to Russia through key officials of the Democratic administration. There are enough proved cases to make this point without diluting our criticism with unproved charges.

Surely these are sufficient reasons to make it clear to the American people that it is time for a change and that a Republican victory is necessary to the security of the country. Surely it is clear that this nation will continue to suffer so long as it is governed by the present ineffective Democratic administration.

Yet to displace it with a Republican regime embracing a philosophy that lacks political integrity or intellectual honesty would prove equally disastrous to the nation. The nation sorely needs a Republican victory. But I do not want to see the Republican party ride to political victory on the Four Horsemen of Calumny — fear, ignorance, bigotry, and smear.

I doubt if the Republican party could do so, simply because I do not believe the American people will uphold any political party that puts political exploitation above national interest. Surely we Republicans are not that desperate for victory.

I do not want to see the Republican party win that way. While it might be a fleeting victory for the Republican party, it would be a more lasting defeat for the American people. Surely it would ultimately be suicide for the Republican party and the two-party system that has protected our American liberties from the dictatorship of a one-party system.

As members of the minority party, we do not have the primary authority to formulate the policy of our government. But we do have the responsibility of rendering constructive criticism, of clarifying issues, of allaying fears acting as responsible citizens.

As a woman, I wonder how the mothers, wives, sisters, and daughters feel about the way in which members of their families have been politically mangled in Senate debate — and I use the word "debate" advisedly.

As a United States senator, I am not proud of the way in which the Senate has been made a publicity platform for irresponsible sensationalism. I am not proud of the reckless abandon in which unproved charges have been hurled from this side of the aisle. I am not proud of the obviously staged, undignified countercharges which have been attempted in retaliation from the other side of the aisle.

I do not like the way the Senate has been made a rendezvous for vilification, for selfish political gain at the sacrifice of individual reputations and national unity. I am not proud of the way we smear outsiders from the floor of the Senate and hide behind the cloak of congressional immunity and still place ourselves beyond criticism on the floor of the Senate.

As an American, I am shocked at the way Republicans and Democrats alike are playing directly into the Communist design of "confuse, divide, and conquer." As an American, I do not want a Democratic administration white wash or cover up any more than I want a Republican smear or witch hunt.

As an American, I condemn a Republican Fascist just as much as I condemn a Democrat Communist. I condemn a Democrat Fascist just as much as I condemn a Republican Communist. They are equally dangerous to you and me and to our country. As an American, I want to see our nation recapture the strength and unity it once had when we fought the enemy instead of ourselves.

It is with these thoughts that I have drafted what I call a Declaration of Conscience. I am gratified that the Senator from New Hampshire [Mr. TOBEY], the Senator from Vermont [Mr. AIKEN], the Senator from Oregon [Mr. MORSE], the Senator from New York [Mr. IVES], the Senator from Minnesota [Mr. THYE], and the Senator from New Jersey [Mr. HENDRICKSON] have concurred in that declaration and have authorized me to announce their concurrence.

The declaration reads as follows:

STATEMENT OF SEVEN REPUBLICAN SENATORS

1. We are Republicans. But we are Americans first. It is as Americans that we express our concern with the growing confusion that threatens the security and stability of our country. Democrats and Republicans alike have contributed to that confusion.

2. The Democratic administration has initially created the confusion by its lack of effective leadership, by its contradictory grave warnings and optimistic assurances, by its complacency to the threat of communism here at home, by its oversensitiveness to rightful criticism, by its petty bitterness against its critics.

3. Certain elements of the Republican party have materially added to this confusion in the hopes of riding the Republican party to victory through the selfish political exploitation of fear, bigotry, ignorance, and intolerance. There are enough mistakes of the Democrats for Republicans to criticize constructively without resorting to political smears.

4. To this extent, Democrats and Republicans alike have unwittingly, but undeniably, played directly into the Communist design of "confuse, divide, and conquer."

5. It is high time that we stopped thinking politically as Republicans and Democrats about elections and started thinking patriotically as Americans about national security based on individual freedom. It is high time that we all stopped being tools and victims of totalitarian techniques — techniques that, if continued here unchecked, will surely end what we have come to cherish as the American way of life.

Margaret Chase Smith,
Maine.

Charles W. Tobey,
New Hampshire.

George D. Aiken,
Vermont.

Wayne L. Morse,
Oregon.

Irving M. Ives,
New York.

Edward J. Thye,
Minnesota.

Robert C. Hendrickson,
New Jersey.

Source: *Congressional Record,* 81st Cong., 2nd sess., June 1, 1950 (Washington: GPO, 1950), 96:7894–7895.

Notes

1. Ronald D. Elving, "McCarthy and the Climate of Fear," in *Congress and the Great Issues: 1945–1995,* ed. Ronald D. Elving (Washington, D.C.: Congressional Quarterly, 1996), 27; Donald A. Ritchie, "McCarthyism in Congress: Investigating Communism," in *The American Congress: The Building of Democracy,* ed. Julian E. Zelizer (Boston: Houghton Mifflin, 2004), 515. In actuality, McCarthy had no list. Robert Griffith, *The Politics of Fear: Joseph McCarthy and the Senate,* 2nd ed. (Amherst: University of Massachusetts Press, 1987), 49–51; David M. Oshinsky, *A Conspiracy So Immense: The World of Joe McCarthy* (New York: The Free Press, 1983), 108–112.

2. For quotes see "Text of McCarthy Reply," *New York Times,* July 18, 1950, 16; Senator Joseph R. McCarthy, "The History of George Catlett Marshall," *Congressional Record,* 82nd Cong., 1st sess., June 14, 1951, 97:6556. See also *Congressional Record,* 81st Cong., 2nd sess., February 20, 1950, 96:1952–1981; July 20, 1950, 96:10697–10717; *Congressional Record,* 82nd Cong., 1st sess., April 24, 1951, 97:4264–4267; June 14, 1951, 97:6556–6603; U.S. Congress, Senate Committee on Foreign Relations, *State Department Employee Loyalty Investigation,* S. Rept. 2108, 81st Cong., 2nd sess. (Washington: GPO, 1950); William S. White, "Red Charges by M'Carthy Ruled False," *New York Times,* July 18, 1950, 1, 17; Griffith, *The Politics of Fear: Joseph McCarthy and the Senate,* 100–101, 132–133, 142–146; Oshinsky, *A Conspiracy So Immense: The World of Joe McCarthy,* 194–202; Thomas C. Reeves, *The Life and Times of Joe McCarthy* (Lanham, Md.: Madison Books, 1997), 222–314, 370–372; Elving, "McCarthy and the Climate of Fear," 31–32; Ritchie, "McCarthyism in Congress: Investigating Communism," 519.

3. Ritchie, "McCarthyism in Congress: Investigating Communism," 521; Griffith, *The Politics of Fear: Joseph McCarthy and the Senate,* 207–220.

4. Ritchie, "McCarthyism in Congress: Investigating Communism," 524.

5. Robert W. Merry, "McCarthy's Self-Destruction," in *Congress and the Great Issues: 1945–1995* ed. Ronald D. Elving (Washington,

D.C.: Congressional Quarterly, 1996), 39, 41–42. See also Oshinsky, *A Conspiracy So Immense: The World of Joe McCarthy,* 457–463; Reeves, *The Life and Times of Joe McCarthy,* 561–637, 639, 641–642. See also Reeves, *The Life and Times of Joe McCarthy,* 459–559.

6. Merry, "McCarthy's Self-Destruction," 41–43; Ritchie, "McCarthyism in Congress: Investigating Communism," 526. See also Oshinsky, *A Conspiracy So Immense: The World of Joe McCarthy,* 390–456.

7. U.S. Senate, Committee on Government Operations, Special Subcommittee on Investigations, *Special Senate Investigation on Charges and Counter-Charges Involving: Secretary of the Army Robert T. Stevens, John G. Adams, H. Struve Hensel, and Senator Joe McCarthy, Roy M. Cohn, and Francis P. Carr,* hearings, 83rd Cong., 2nd sess., June 9, 1954 (Washington: GPO, 1954), 2428–2429. See also Merry, "McCarthy's Self-Destruction," 43; see also Oshinsky, *A Conspiracy So Immense: The World of Joe McCarthy,* 457–463; Reeves, *The Life and Times of Joe McCarthy,* 561–637.

8. *Congressional Record,* 81st Cong., 2nd sess., December 2, 1954, 96:16353–16392; Merry, "McCarthy's Self-Destruction," 43; Ritchie, "McCarthyism in Congress: Investigating Communism," 526. See also Oshinsky, *A Conspiracy So Immense: The World of Joe McCarthy,* 457–494; Griffith, *The Politics of Fear: Joseph McCarthy and the Senate,* 295–317.

9. Robert C. Byrd, *The Senate 1789–1989: Classic Speeches, 1830–1993* (Washington, D.C.: GPO, 1994), 620. See also *Congressional Record,* 81st Cong., 2nd ses., June 1, 1950, 96:7894–7895; Margaret Chase Smith, *Declaraion of Conscience,* ed. William C. Lewis Jr. (Garden City, N.Y.: Doubleday, 1972), 3–61.

"Great Debate" of 1951

✳ 1951 ✳

Following World War II, Korea was divided at the Thirty-eighth parallel with the United States occupying the southern portion of the country and the Soviet Union (U.S.S.R.) the northern. In 1948, South Korean elections led to the formation of the Republic of Korea, and in North Korea the Democratic People's Republic of Korea was formed. On June 25, 1950, a year after the withdrawal of U.S. forces there, North Korean communists invaded South Korea. President Harry S. Truman responded by ordering U.S. Air and Naval forces to provide support for South Korean forces and by sending the Seventh Fleet to the area to prevent an attack on or from Formosa (present day Taiwan). Subsequently, the United Nations Security Council approved an American-sponsored resolution that denounced the surprise attack and called for a cessation of hostilities. When the United Nations requested its members to provide military assistance to repel the invasion, the president committed American ground forces, and General Douglas MacArthur was named commander of the U.N. forces. Truman did not, however, ask Congress for a declaration of war.[1]

As the war gained momentum, U.N. forces drove the aggressors north back across the Thirty-eighth parallel with the intention of unifying the entire peninsula, an action provoking a Chinese communist counterattack that penetrated to twenty-five miles south of Seoul. Meanwhile, European officials grew increasingly worried about a possible hostile Soviet Union move in Europe. When President Truman announced his intent to substantially increase U.S. forces in Western Europe as part of a projected NATO buildup, France refused to countenance German rearmament. Only after the Chinese became involved in Korea did the North Atlantic Council agree to an integrated defense force; this also prompted Truman to choose Gen. Dwight D. Eisenhower as Supreme Allied Commander.

NATO's unprecedented display of unity prompted former president Herbert Hoover to deliver a national radio address denouncing the "rash involvement of our forces in hopeless campaigns." He felt the United States should cut off aid until the Europeans, whose "will to defend themselves is feeble," could develop enough forces to "erect a sure dam against the Red flood." To preserve the "Gibraltar of Western Civiliza-tion" on this side of the Atlantic, the United States needed to expand its air and naval forces, rearm Japan, and stiffen its Pacific frontier in Formosa and the Philippines. Joseph P. Kennedy, former U.S. ambassador to Great Britain, raised similar issues, urging that the United States get out of both Korea and Europe. Truman partisans, as well as the president, criticized both men for supporting a return to pre–World War II isolationist policies.[2]

Later, others credited Hoover and Kennedy with launching the "Great Debate" of 1951 in the Senate that centered on the future direction of American foreign policy as well as the question of whether the president or Congress would determine that direction. Anger and frustration over the situation in Korea, a perceived excessive use of executive power, and impatience with European allies provoked the three-month debate. The confrontation between advocates of presidential power and proponents of congressional power elicited bitter, vindictive, and often excessive claims. Congressional critics of Truman's foreign policy focused their condemnation on the president's plan to send additional U.S. forces to Western Europe.[3]

The leading Truman critics were Sen. Robert A. Taft, R-Ohio, and Sen. Kenneth S. Wherry, R-Neb. Since 1945, Taft contended in a two-hour, ten-thousand-word floor speech on January 5, 1951, the administration had formulated policy without consulting either Congress or the American people. Taft sharply disputed the president's right "to agree to send American troops to fight in Europe…. Without authority [Truman] involved us in the Korean War. Without authority he apparently is now adopting a similar policy in Europe." Taft favored enhancing U.S. military prowess while limiting its relationship with NATO. Three days later, Senator Wherry introduced a resolution expressing the sense of the Senate that American ground forces not be sent to Europe "pending the adoption of a policy with respect thereto by the Congress." Wherry argued that there was neither constitutional authority nor precedent to support the president's decision to send armed forces to NATO countries.[4]

Sen. Paul H. Douglas, D-Ill.; Sen. Thomas T. Connally, D-Tex., chairman of the Foreign Relations Committee; and Sen. Wayne L. Morse, R-Ore., all offered salient rebuttals of

After debating the issue of U.S. troop commitment overseas, the Senate issued two resolutions. The first approved Dwight D. Eisenhower's appointment as supreme commander of NATO. The second requested the president consult with other parties in government before committing U.S. troops to Europe.
Source: Associated Press.

Taft's arguments on strategic issues. Western Europe, they emphasized, was strategically important because of its industrial potential and airbases within striking distance of the Soviet Union. A high defense budget was, to their thinking, almost inevitable. They also took issue with Taft's deep concerns about the United States making a disproportionate contribution to European security. Senator Connally made a point of emphasizing that "[t]he scope of the authority of the President as Commander in Chief to send the armed forces to any place required by the security interests of the United States has often been questioned, but never denied by authoritative opinion." A more conciliatory group of senators from both parties generally supported Truman's decision to send troops to Europe, but agreed that there need to be more congressional participation prior to the implementation of such a decision. Only then would it be possible to "move forward as a team."[5]

Hoping to defuse the controversy, the administration arranged Capitol Hill appearances in January for General Eisenhower, who had recently returned from a European fact-finding mission. Eisenhower told an informal joint session of Congress that the United States must give Western Europe assistance "because there is no acceptable alternative,"

a theme repeated in subsequent meetings with congressional committees. Democrats lauded Eisenhower's report. Republicans were divided. In February, the Senate Foreign Relations and Armed Services Committees held twelve days of joint hearings on the troop question. Despite the administration's belief to the contrary, the committee concluded that a resolution was needed that would mollify congressional anxieties while expressing approval of the president's decision.[6]

What resulted were two resolutions: S. Res. 99 required only Senate action; S. Con. Res. 18 required House approval as well. Both approved the appointment of Eisenhower to be NATO commander and expressed the sense of the Senate (or Congress) that while the United States should contribute its "fair share" of NATO's forces, the Europeans should make the major contribution. The resolutions also requested that the president, before committing troops to Europe, consult with the secretary of defense, the Joint Chiefs of Staff, the NATO commander, and the Foreign Affairs Committees; and required the Joint Chiefs of Staff to certify that NATO countries were providing their share of the troops. After two weeks of contentious debate, the Senate approved an amended version of S. Res. 99, 69–21, and an identical S. Con. Res. 18, 45–41. The House never acted on S. Con. Res. 18. Since congressional resolutions only expressed nonbinding sentiments, however, neither resolution had the force of a public law.[7]

President Truman hailed the adoption of S. Res. 99 as a "clear endorsement" of his troop assignment plans, saying it showed "there has never been any real question" that the United States "would do its part in helping create an integrated European defense force."[8] His April 5, 1951, statement made no mention of the Senate's claim to a voice in future troop commitments. What resulted from the "Great Debate" was a consensus that Europe's defense was important to American security as well as a decision by the Senate to reject the Wherry Resolution and other resolutions that would have barred the president from sending additional troops to Europe without congressional approval.

SENATOR ROBERT A. TAFT OPPOSES ASSIGNMENT OF ADDITIONAL U.S. FORCES TO EUROPE

JANUARY 5, 1951

During recent years a theory has developed that there shall be no criticism of the foreign policy of the administration, that any such criticism is an attack on the unity of the Nation, that it gives aid and comfort to the enemy, and that it sabotages any idea of a bipartisan foreign policy for the national benefit. I venture to state that this proposition is a fallacy and a very dangerous fallacy threatening the very existence of the Nation.

In very recent days we have heard appeals for unity from the administration and from its supporters. I suggest that these appeals are an attempt to cover up the past faults and failures of the administration and enable it to maintain the secrecy which has largely enveloped our foreign policy since the days of Franklin D. Roosevelt. It was a distinguished Democrat, President Woodrow Wilson, who denounced secret diplomacy and demanded open covenant openly arrived at. The administrations of President Roosevelt and President Truman have repudiated that wise democratic doctrine and assumed complete authority to make in secret the most vital decisions and commit this country to the most important and dangerous obligations. As I see it, Members of Congress, and particularly Members of the Senate, have a constitutional obligation to reexamine constantly and discuss the foreign policy of the United States. If we permit appeals to unity to bring an end to that criticism, we endanger not only the constitutional liberties of the country, but even its future existence.

★ ★ ★ ★

Certainly when policies have been determined, unity in execution is highly desirable, and in the preparation for and the conduct of war it is essential. During recent months, the Republican minority has joined in granting to the President those powers which may be necessary to deal with the situation. We have not hesitated to pass a draft law, a law granting extensive powers of economic control, and almost unlimited appropriations for the Armed Forces. No action of the minority can be pointed to as in any way blocking or delaying the mobilization of our resources and our Armed Forces. If there has been any delay in the rearming, it has been in the administrative branch of the Government.

But it is part of our American system that basic elements of foreign policy shall be openly debated. It is said that such debate and the differences that may occur give aid and comfort to our possible enemies. I think that the value of such aid and comfort is grossly exaggerated. The only thing that can give real aid and comfort to the enemy is the adoption of a policy which plays into their hands as has our policy in the Far East. Such aid and comfort can only be prevented by frank criticism before such a policy is adopted.

Whatever the value of unity, it is also true that unity carried to unreasonable extremes can destroy a country. The Kaiser achieved unity in Germany. Hitler again achieved the same unity at the cost of freedom many years later. Mussolini achieved unity in Italy. The leaders of Japan through a method of so-called thought control achieved unity in Japan. In every case, policies adopted by these enforcers of unity led to the destruction of their own country. We have regarded ourselves as safe and a probable victor in every war. Today it is just as easy for us to adopt a false foreign policy leading to the destruction of our people as for any other nation to do so. The best safeguard against fatal error lies in continuous criticism and discussion to bring out the truth and develop the best program.

I have referred to the general tendency toward secrecy on the part of recent administrations. At Tehran and Yalta we secretly agreed to a zone of influence for Soviet Russia in Europe extending through the Baltic states and the Balkans and into the eastern zones of Austria and Germany. The result was to establish Russia in a position of power in central Europe which today threatens the liberty of Western Europe and of the United States itself. Our leaders secretly agreed to turn over control of Manchuria to Russia, and later hampered the operations of the Nationalist Government in combat against the Communists without consultation of any kind with Congress. In Germany our leaders adopted the Morgenthau plan while constantly denying that they were doing anything of the kind, and without submitting the questions in any way to Congress for discussion. The President without authority, as I pointed out in my speech on June 28, 1950, committed American troops to Korea without any consultation whatever with Congress and, in my opinion, without authority of law. He did not even tell Congress there was a war for two weeks after we were engaged. The President claims the right without consultation with Congress to decide whether or not we should use the atomic bomb.

We see now the beginning of an agreement to send a specified number of American troops to Europe without that question ever having been discussed in the Congress of the United States. The Atlantic Pact may have committed us to send arms to the other members of the pact, but no one ever maintained that it committed us to send many American troops to Europe. A new policy is being formulated without consulting the Congress or the people.

In other cases policies have been developed to a point where the honor of this country is committed before any serious debate by the public is permitted. Thus in the case of the Marshall plan and the Atlantic Pact, the programs were broached in the most general terms, then substantially advanced by the State Department through secret briefing conferences with many friendly groups and thorough indoctrination of friendly editors, columnists and commentators before they were submitted to the public or to Congress. After that if anyone dared to suggest criticisms or even a thorough debate, he was at once branded as an isolationist and a saboteur of unity and the bipartisan foreign policy.

More and more it has become customary to make agreements instead of treaties thus bypassing the power intended to be conferred on the Senate to pass on the wisdom of important principles of foreign policy. It is still fashionable to meet any criticism by cries of isolationism just as Mr. Hoover's recent speech has been treated. Criticisms are met by the calling of names rather than by intelligent debate.

I do not intend to say that a bipartisan foreign policy could not be adopted, but there has been no real bipartisan policy, at any rate since the 1948 election. It is a proper ideal and the minority will always be ready to answer any appeal for advice and cooperation. Only there cannot be a bipartisan foreign policy unless it is a policy on which both parties agree, and it is unlikely that there can be such agreement unless the administration is more inclined to give consideration to the views of the minority and to modify its own views than it has done in recent months. We certainly would be prepared to make concessions, but certainly the policy of concessions should not be a one-way street. I quite realize the difficulty of any President in consulting the minority in advance on every question of foreign policy, and I do not blame him for his failure to urge or adopt a bipartisan policy. But certainly the Republican minority cannot be attacked for failure to agree on policies on which they have not even been consulted or on policies which they may regard as detrimental to the welfare of the Nation.

The result of a general practice of secrecy in all the initial steps of foreign policy has been to deprive the Senate and Congress of the substance of the powers conferred on them by the Constitution.

We would be lacking in the fulfillment of our obligations and false to our oaths if we did not criticize policies which may lead to unnecessary war, policies which may wreck the internal economy of this country and vastly weaken our economic abilities through unsound taxation or inflation, policies which may commit us to obligations we are utterly unable to perform, and thus discredit us in the eyes of the world. Criticism and debate are essential if we are to maintain the constitutional liberties of this country and its democratic heritage. Under the present administration, at any rate, criticism and debate I think are essential to avoid danger and possible destruction of our Nation.

LIBERTY AND PEACE OF THE AMERICAN PEOPLE SHOULD BE THE BASIC AIMS OF OUR FOREIGN POLICY

The principal purpose of the foreign policy of the United States is to maintain the liberty of our people. Its purpose is not to reform the entire world or spread sweetness and light

---

The principal purpose of the foreign policy of the United States is to maintain the liberty of our people. Its purpose is not to reform the entire world or spread sweetness and light and economic prosperity to peoples who have lived and worked out their own salvation for centuries.... — Robert A. Taft

---

and economic prosperity to peoples who have lived and worked out their own salvation for centuries, according to their customs, and to the best of their ability. We do have an interest, of course, in the economic welfare of other nations and in the military strength of other nations, but only to the extent to which our assistance may reduce the probability of an attack on the freedom of our own people.

After liberty, peace must be the goal of our policy and of our leaders — more than has been in recent years. In order to assure progress and happiness for our people, we must avoid war like poison, except when it is absolutely essential to protect our liberty. War not only produces pitiful human suffering and utter destruction of things worth while but it actually may end our own liberty, certainly for the time being. From our experience in the last two world wars, it actually promotes dictatorship and totalitarian government throughout the world. It is almost as disastrous for the victor as for the vanquished. War is to be preferred only to the destruction of our liberty.

It seems to me most unwise ever to admit that war is inevitable until it has occurred, and it seems to me that today our policy and the thinking of too many Americans are based too much on the premise that war is inevitable. It is a possibility which we must face, and for which we must prepare, but the theory of a preventive war, so closely related to the acceptance of that thesis, is contrary to every American principle and every moral principle.

The Menace Of Communism

The present situation arises out of the menace of communism and the military strength of Soviet Russia. Soviet Russia has broken every treaty. It has suppressed liberty everywhere within its zone of influence. It engineered a forcible seizure of the Government in Czechoslovakia. It promoted the military aggression of the North Koreans. It promoted the military aggression of the Chinese Communists. Those diplomats and soldiers who have had to deal with the Russians find them always unreasonable, uncompromising, and truculent. There is sufficient evidence of a determined plan to communize the entire world, which can be clearly envisioned from the writings of Lenin and Stalin, just as Hitler's intention could be found in Mein Kampf. Such a plan is evidenced by the formation of Communist organizations throughout the entire world, acting as agents for the Russian Government, and promoting the communizing of every country by propaganda and infiltration into labor unions, organizations of all kinds, and the government itself. We have seen how successful effort has been in this country.

Does this Russian plan include a military conquest of the world, where infiltration is unsuccessful? It is now clear that it does include the use of satellite troops to attack neighboring countries in cases where such military aggression may not necessarily lead to a third world war. Up to this time, apparently, the Russians have not been willing to use their own armies in deliberate military aggression, for fear of precipi-

tating such a war, but it is pointed out that that may be because they are not yet ready.

I myself do not see any conclusive evidence that they expect to start a war with the United States. Certainly I see no reason for a general panic on the assumption that they will do so. We have clearly notified them that any attack in Europe upon the members of the Atlantic Pact means a third world war, and we are obligated to enter such a war under the terms of the Atlantic Pact. Look at it from any point of view — and, I think, particularly from the Russian point of view — and it is difficult to see how the Russians today could reasonably entertain the hope that they can conquer the world by military action. It must seem to their thinkers an extremely difficult undertaking.

★ ★ ★ ★

It seems to me that our battle against communism is in fact a world-wide battle and must be fought on the world stage. What I object to is undertaking to fight that battle primarily on the vast land areas of the continent of Europe or the continent of Asia where we are at the greatest possible disadvantage in a war with Russia.

★ ★ ★ ★

There are some places where it may even be wise to commit some land troops if we can see a reasonable chance of success. Korea does not seem to be such an area, but the entire continent of Africa is connected with Asia, and certainly we should assist in defending the Suez Canal as a means of maintaining our connections by sea, and northern Africa where we hold valuable air bases. It may be possible to assist Spain. I should suppose that Singapore and the Malay peninsula could be defended by land troops if sea and air power is available on both sides of the peninsula. The extension of such aid by land troops, however, is a dangerous experiment as we found in Korea. I doubt if we should enter into any commitments in advance, or undertake the job at all unless we are sure it is well within our capacity, and almost certain of success.

★ ★ ★ ★

Conclusion

The threat of communism is real. Those who are directing its affairs are brilliant and unprincipled. America must be the leader in the battle to prevent the spread of communism and preserve the liberty of the world. In the field of military operations our strongest position is in the air and on the sea, and we should not attempt to be also a controlling power on the land. We should not be a military aggressor or give the impression of military aggression or incite a war which might otherwise never occur. Operations on the continents of

Europe and Asia, if any, should be undertaken only with the greatest care, and under careful limitation. We must not so extend ourselves as to threaten economic collapse or inflation, for a productive and free America is the last bastion of liberty. And finally the policy we adopt must be approved by Congress and the people after full and free discussion. The commitment of a land army to Europe is a program never

approved by Congress, into which we should not drift. The policy of secret executive agreements has brought us to danger and disaster. It threatens the liberties of our people.

Source: *Congressional Record*, 82nd Cong., 1st sess., January 5, 1951 (Washington: GPO, 1951), 97:55–61.

SENATOR THOMAS T. CONNALLY FAVORS ASSIGNMENT OF ADDITIONAL U.S. FORCES TO EUROPE

JANUARY 11, 1951

Mr. President, this is a solemn and serious hour when we are to consult each other regarding the paramount interests and security of the people of the United States.

Nearly one hundred seventy-five years ago our forefathers dissolved the political bands that bound the Colonies to England. They did so because their inalienable rights of life, liberty, and the pursuit of happiness were in danger.

As the Eighty-second Congress debates the President's state of the Union message, every American expects to preserve for our Nation, with his life if necessary, those same inalienable rights. Indeed, I am sure we are all agreed that the policy is to maintain the liberty and the security of our people.

We are today engaged in a notable debate. The debate is not on the ends of our foreign policy, but on the means to the end. We bring to this debate a great tradition. That is the tradition of the free exchange of ideas that has taken place on the floor of the Senate since our Government was founded. Our debates here reflect and distill the thinking of our rulers — the American people. Out of this debate will come new ideas, new conclusions, and, I hope, a new unity.

The distinguished Senator from Ohio [Mr. TAFT] suggested last week that appeals for unity from administration sources may be attempts to cover past faults and failures. That is not the case. The unity I ask for is the unity that comes in a democracy as the result of our confidence in the ability of the American people to hear all sides of issues, to determine the merits of the proposals, and then pull toward a common goal.

I hope sincerely that we will not spend our time here fighting the battles of the past. There have been times when consultation between the administration and the Congress has

been forgotten. There have been times when the American people have not had sufficient information to enable them to pass judgment on the issues before our Government. I think there have also been times when opponents of administration policy have not been willing to discuss issues on their merits, or have cultivated issues for their own purposes. But let us look ahead to the tremendous problems we face.

Thomas Jefferson once remarked that "error of opinion may be tolerated where reason is left free to combat it." In these halls we will hear error of opinion, but reason is free. What I ask now is that we meet fairly and squarely the issues that face the United States. Our discussions here can help the people of this great Nation to know and understand the tremendous responsibilities our size and strength and freedom impose upon us.

PRINCIPLES UNDERLYING UNITED STATES POLICY SINCE WORLD WAR II

During the past five years, certain basic themes and principles of American foreign policy have emerged on which the programs that express our policy have been built. I review them now because they need frequent restatement so that in the pressure of this crisis we will not lose sight of them.

I want to emphasize in the first place, as strongly as I can, that the primary objective of this Government has always been the security of the United States. Closely linked to this fundamental is our continuing effort to contribute to the world framework for a just and lasting peace. As one means to these ends, we have given, and will continue to give, unflagging support to the United Nations. That is, and must remain, a cornerstone of our international policy.

While the United Nations must remain the cornerstone of our policy, I do believe that its members must take careful and solemn note of the growing concern of the American people that the United Nations is not fulfilling its great promise. I say in all sincerity to each and every Member of the United Nations that if the international community is not willing now as a matter of principle to recognize aggression for what it is, whenever and wherever it occurs, then the United Nations will die as surely as the tree without a tap root.

Mr. President, I say these things because the primary purpose of the organization of the United Nations was to resist aggression and to settle international disputes by peaceful means.

It was aggression in June when the North Korean Communists attacked the Republic of Korea. It is aggression today when Chinese Communists attack our UN forces. If the United Nations wants to retain the confidence and support of our people, it must not run to cover when the going becomes a little rough.

It has been said that "peoples and governments never have learned anything from history, or acted on principles deduced from it." The League of Nations failed because the great powers, despite the constant urging and pleadings of the small states, would not back up the League. The United States learned that lesson. But now, strange as it seems, we are confronted by the uncertainty and unwillingness of the smaller powers to accept the fundamental principle of the Charter that the United Nations will take effective collective measures to suppress aggression. That means aggression by great powers as well as by small powers.

Our determined adherence to the United Nations demonstrates our flat rejection of the thesis that war is inevitable. We believe that war can be avoided and that the differences between the free world and the Soviet Union which are at the root of every current major problem can be resolved by negotiation and agreement.

But we know now that war can be avoided only if the free nations have the economic and military strength to guarantee such rough handling of acts of aggression that the Communist imperialists will abandon aggression as a tactic. This economic and military power will also enable the free world to make certain that the Soviet Union will live up to its agreements both in letter and in spirit.

This principle has been described as the building of situations of strength. It has been put to the test at various points during the past five years, and in each instance where we have led from strength we have always been able to resolve the issue in our favor — whether in Berlin, in connection with the airlift, or Italy, or Greece, or Western Europe. The political, economic, and military programs which have been developed since the end of World War II have all been keyed to the creation of the necessary strength in areas that are threatened by Soviet imperialism.

I believe that the reception given these measures in the Senate — evidenced by votes of approval which, without exception, were overwhelming — is proof of wide support for them on the Senate floor, and that in each instance the measures were a clear expression of the popular will.

★ ★ ★ ★

The Issues We Must Debate

I have already commented on our great tradition of debate in this body. I stand for the freedom of debate. That freedom is greater even than the freedom of the press and many of the other freedoms we enjoy. It is free so that the people of the United States may know the issues and may know the attitude of their representatives on the floor of the Senate.

Last Friday the senior Senator from Ohio set forth his views on the foreign policy of the United States. He discussed a number of issues that go to the heart of our foreign policy. His statement has attracted considerable attention in the United States and in foreign countries, some friendly, some unfriendly. As a consequence of this debate I expect there will be reactions that many of us do not expect.

My information regarding the impact of the speech upon the people of Western Europe is that many of them have been stunned in view of the North Atlantic Pact, our signature to the pact, and the suggested repudiation of the pact. I recall vividly, and I know many other Senators will also recall, the ceremony which was held on the occasion of the signing of the North Atlantic Pact. The high representatives of the nations who were parties to the agreement appeared and with appropriate ceremony affixed their signatures to the great document in behalf of the peace and security of the North Atlantic area. No wonder they are stunned, and no wonder many of them feel despair, unless they know that we will remain true to our obligations and to our pledged faith.

★ ★ ★ ★

I desire to take this occasion to say to our friends in Europe that they must seek to understand the United States. We believe that the destiny of our country is best guided by the people of our country. In the debate that is now underway all points of view will be expressed. Our friends abroad will hear many things they do not like. They will hear many things they do like. I am sure that they will find that the American people will be ready in the future, as they have in the past, to stand with their full strength on the side of the freedom, the tradition, and the culture that is European in origin and ours by adoption.

Let me first speak for a moment about the subject of attaining security for the United States and some of the questionable conclusions which have been advanced from several quarters in recent days.

The charge has been made that the President has violated the Constitution of the United States by sending troops to

Korea. The President's power to send additional troops to Europe has also been challenged. The scope of the authority of the President as Commander in Chief to send the Armed Forces to any place required by the security interests of the United States has often been questioned, but never denied by authoritative opinion.

Mr. President, the Constitution provides that the President of the United States shall be Commander in Chief of the Armed Forces. When was the Constitution adopted? It was adopted, of course, after the Revolutionary War and after the experience of the states under the Confederation. Why was it provided that the President should be the Commander in Chief of the Army and Navy? The founding fathers still had vividly in their recollection the mistakes and troubles of the Continental Congress in trying to conduct the military affairs of the United States. They remembered that General Washington had to overcome many difficulties by reason of the activities of certain Members of the Continental Congress. Under the Confederation the same troubles existed. So the Constitution provided that the President should be Commander in Chief of the Armed Forces. If our forefathers had wanted Congress to be the Commander in Chief, they would have said so. But they did not. They said that the President of the United States should be Commander in Chief of the Armed Forces. That principle has never been seriously questioned as a legal proposition. It follows, furthermore, that with such power the President of the United States has the authority to send the Armed Forces to any part of the world if the security and safety of the United States are involved.

★ ★ ★ ★

A Positive Policy

Mr. President, the underlying fallacy of the suggestions I have been considering derives from the failure to assign appropriate weight to the actual components that make up American security.

There are three major factors, which have been dominant in keeping the uneasy peace which has prevailed since the Japanese surrendered. They are the three main elements which have deterred the Soviet Union from all-out aggression. The existence of the first has given us an interval of time that is all too brief to develop the second and the third.

The first great deterrent, of course, is American supremacy in atomic weapons. Beyond doubt, our possession of a quantity of atomic bombs combined with the operation of bombers capable of delivering them has held the Soviet in check. This deterrent will be effective until such time as the Soviet is able to build up a stockpile of bombs sufficient to challenge American superiority.

The second great deterrent is the tremendous productive capacity represented by the combination of our own industrial might plus that of Western Europe and the Ruhr.

The third is the fact that in this struggle for survival the vast majority of the nations of the world stand with us against the forces of evil and tyranny.

★ ★ ★ ★

The United States today bears a tremendous responsibility. I believe that never before has one nation had the destiny of mankind so within its control. True, we say that the Soviet Union can decide whether there will be war or peace in our time. But it is the United States that can decide whether life, liberty, and the pursuit of happiness, or death, tyranny, and misery are to be the fate of mankind.

True, we say that the Soviet Union can decide whether there will be war or peace in our time. But it is the United States that can decide whether life, liberty, and the pursuit of happiness, or death, tyranny, and misery are to be the fate of mankind. — Thomas T. Connally

---

This responsibility is upon the people of the United States and upon us, their elected representatives.

We have a great people, a people peculiarly adapted to leadership of the free world. We draw our heritage from more races and creeds than any other nation on earth. We have banded ourselves together in a union based on the dignity of the individual. Our people have created a productive system that is stronger and more efficient and better for the common man than is any other on earth. We have created a government able to express the will of the people and incorporate that will in our national policy.

★ ★ ★ ★

We bear a heavy responsibility today in the United States Senate. What we say here, what we do here, can give the people of the world hope, or turn them away in despair from the citadel of freedom.

While this is a terrible responsibility which our country bears, it is also a rare opportunity.

The President of the United States asked that we stand together as Americans and that we stand together with all men everywhere who believe in human liberty. We will do no less. We can do no more. Let the unfair critics sheathe their swords. Let us not employ our weapons against each other. Let us face the enemy together in defense of our security and liberty.

With the unity of purpose that comes from the justice of our cause, and with firm belief in the divine guidance that has made our country great, we face the future with courage and determination.

Source: Congressional Record, 82nd Cong., 1st sess., January 11, 1951 (Washington: GPO, 1951), 97:140–146.

Notes

1. Burton I. Kaufman, *The Korean War: Challenges in Crisis, Credibility, and Command*, 2nd ed. (New York: McGraw-Hill, 1997), 19. See also Louis Fisher, "The Korean War: On What Legal Basis Did Truman Act," *American Journal of International Law* 89 (January 1995): 21–22, 32–39; Robert F. Turner, "Truman, Korea, and the Constitution: Debunking the 'Imperial President' Myth," *Harvard Journal of Law and Public Policy* 19 (Winter 1996): 563–583.

2. Herbert Hoover, "Our National Policies in This Crisis" (December 20, 1950), *Vital Speeches of the Day*, January 1, 1951, 17:165–167. See also Joseph P. Kennedy, "Present Policy Is Politically and Morally Bankrupt" (December 12, 1950), Ibid., 170–173; Ted Galen Carpenter, "United States' NATO Policy at the Crossroads: The 'Great Debate' of 1950–51," *International History Review*, 8 (August 1986): 389–399, 405.

3. Carpenter, "United States' NATO Policy at the Crossroads," 405; Phil Williams, *The Senate and U.S. Troops in Europe* (New York: St. Martin's Press, 1985), 58.

4. "Constructive Criticism of Foreign Policy Is Essential to the Safety of the Nation," *Congressional Record*, January 5, 1951, 97:59. See also "S. Res. 8," *Congressional Record*, January 8, 1951, 97:93; "Assignment of Ground Troops for Service in Europe," Ibid., January 16, 1951, 97:325–329.

5. Quotes are found in "Presidential Power to Deploy Troops Abroad," *Congressional Record*, January 17, 1951, 97:384; "Necessity to Meet Fairly and Squarely the Issues Facing the United States," *Congressional Record*, January 11, 1951, 97:142. See also David R. Kepley, *The Collapse of the Middle Way: Senate Republicans and the Bipartisan Foreign Policy, 1948–1952* (New York: Greenwood Press, 1988), 107–109; Williams, *The Senate and U.S. Troops in Europe*, 58–67

6. Quote is found in U.S. Congress, Senate Committee on Foreign Relations and Senate Committee on Armed Services, *Assignment of Ground Forces to Duty in the European Area, Hearings on S. Con. Res. 8, Febuary 1, 1951* (Washington: GPO, 1951), 4. See also Williams, *The Senate and U.S. Troops in Europe*, 69–83; *Congressional Quarterly Almanac*, 1951 (Washington, D.C.: Congressional Quarterly, 1952), 223–224, 229–230.

7. "Assignment of Ground Forces to Duty in the European Area," *Congressional Record*, April 4, 1951, 97:3282, 3293–3294. See also *Congressional Quarterly Almanac*, 1951, 230–232; Williams, *The Senate and U.S. Troops in Europe*, 92–107; Kepley, *The Collapse of the Middle Way*, 109–115.

8. *U.S. President (Truman), Public Papers of the Presidents of the United States*, 1951 (Washington: GPO, 1965), 217.

Civil Rights Act of 1964

✳ 1964 ✳

During the 1960 presidential campaign, Sen. John F. Kennedy, D-Mass., promised to support civil rights initiatives and made a concerted effort to attract the African American vote. He was rewarded with better than 68 percent of the black vote at a time when the Republicans were still competitive with the African American electorate. To fulfill his civil rights commitment, however, Kennedy would undoubtedly antagonize southern Democrats whose support proved essential in defeating Vice President Richard Nixon in one of the closest elections in American history. Not until June 11, 1963, during a nationally televised address, did President Kennedy finally announce his intention to send Congress a bill guaranteeing equal treatment of every American regardless of race. Hours earlier the nation had watched the federalized Alabama National Guard order Governor George Wallace to stand aside after he attempted to bar two black students from enrolling at the all-white University of Alabama.

Also, still fresh on the minds of many were the vivid television images of recent violence and racial strife in Birmingham that exposed viewers to police dogs attacking protesters; crowds of black school children being dispersed by clubs, high-pressure fire hoses, and electric cattle prods; and the arrests of thousands of demonstrators. The Southern Christian Leadership Conference (SCLC), led by Dr. Martin Luther King Jr., organized the Birmingham marches of April and May 1963. Their supporters sought to end the city's discriminatory hiring as well as its segregated lunch counters, fitting rooms, and department store restrooms. The ill-advised intimidation effort resulted in civil leaders signing an agreement acceding to some of the SCLC's key demands. Just as calm began to settle on the city, bombs rocked the home of King's younger brother and the SCLC headquarters in the Gaston Motel. These assaults triggered a four-hour riot injuring more than fifty people.[1]

"Short of a declaration of war," writes historian Robert D. Loevy, "few bills presented to Congress have had as violent and confrontational an origin" as Kennedy's civil rights bill. The bill was first referred to the Judiciary Committee, chaired by Rep. Emanuel Celler, D-N.Y. While the Judiciary Committee's Subcommittee No. 5 still considered the bill, two other important events occurred that focused additional attention on the need for civil rights legislation. On August 28, more than two hundred thousand civil rights supporters participated in the March on Washington and heard King's "I Have a Dream" speech. Two weeks later, on September 16, white supremacists bombed the Sixteenth Street Baptist Church in Birmingham, Alabama, a staging area for many of the demonstrations that spring. People across the country were appalled upon learning the Church blast had killed four young girls attending Sunday School. President Kennedy spoke for millions of shocked and outraged Americans when he expressed "a deep sense of outrage and grief" over the killings.[2]

Celler's committee significantly strengthened the bill before reporting it on November 20. Because debate is limited in the House, the bill did not immediately go to the floor for consideration, but went first to the Rules Committee, where the length of time as well as the manner in which it would be debated was decided. In 1963, the committee's chairman, Rep. Howard W. Smith, D-Va., a conservative southern Democrat, was ardently opposed to the civil rights bill and made clear his intention to delay its consideration indefinitely. The assassin's bullet that killed President Kennedy in Dallas that November had a profound impact on the political situation concerning civil rights. His successor, former vice president Lyndon Johnson, was seen by some as a southerner who had less than a year to convince skeptical Northern and Western liberals he could win his own full term as president. Earlier, as Senate majority leader, Johnson helped engineer the Civil Rights Act of 1957, but no one knew if the Texan would continue that fight or placate his fellow southerners. Five days after the assassination, Johnson responded by telling a joint session of Congress: "No memorial oration or eulogy could more eloquently honor President Kennedy's memory than the earliest passage of the civil rights bill for which he fought so long.... We have talked long enough in this country about equal rights.... It is time now to write the next chapter, and to write it in the books of law."[3]

Supporters first had to get the bill out of the Rules Committee. Celler filed a discharge petition, which, if signed by a majority of the House, would allow the bill to be debated by the full House. Initially, supporters struggled to obtain the sig-

Rev. Martin Luther King Jr. and President Lyndon B. Johnson shake hands at the signing of the Civil Rights Act of 1964. Public support for the legislation grew after President John F. Kennedy's assassination, and the only major amendment during House debate added provisions against discrimination of sex.

Source: The Granger Collection, New York.

natures necessary, but by late December the president's constant advocacy had shifted public opinion in many wavering member's home districts. To prevent the embarrassment of a successful petition, Chairman Smith finally allowed the bill to pass through the committee two months and ten days after the Judiciary Committee reported it. During the ensuing nine-day House floor debate, the only major amendment to the bill actually furthered the cause of civil rights by outlawing discrimination on the basis of sex as well as race. On February 10, 1964, the House overwhelmingly passed the bill, 290–130.[4]

The real battle proved to be in the Senate, where chamber rules allow unlimited debate. Southern Senators had long made use of the lack of limitation as part of a strategy for blocking civil rights bills by filibuster, the practice of preventing legislation from coming to a vote. Only if two-thirds of the Senate votes to end debate — that is, invoked cloture — does a filibuster end. Although cloture votes had been attempted many times on civil rights bills, none had ever succeeded. Also, strong presidential primary showings in Wisconsin and Indiana by George Wallace led southern Senators to hope their colleagues would come to believe that civil rights was no more popular in the north than in the south. Wallace's failure to win the Maryland primary, however, dampened the momentum of the movement and prevented any kind of national movement against civil rights.[5]

When the bill reached the Senate, majority leader Mike Mansfield, D-Mont., moved to place it directly on the Senate calendar, thereby bypassing the Judiciary Committee, chaired by Sen. James O. Eastland, D-Miss. Although this procedural maneuver provoked a small filibuster by southern Democrats, Mansfield prevailed. What followed, however, was the longest continuous floor debate in Senate history, eighty-three consecutive legislative days — from March 9 to June 17, 1964. As a small group of southern Senators attempted to kill the bill, President Johnson kept the pressure on with regular weekly statements reiterating his desire for a strong bill. Still, passage ultimately depended on getting the Senate to vote for cloture. Senators from small states, mainly in midwestern and western states, viewed the filibuster as the only instrument they had to protect themselves from the large states, and these were the senators southern Democrats hoped would refuse to support cloture.[6]

Only minority leader Everett McKinley Dirksen, R-Ill., could persuade small-state Republicans. Winning him over fell to Democratic whip Hubert Humphrey, D-Minn., floor manager for the bill, and to the co-floor manager, minority whip Thomas H. Kuchel, R-Calif. Early in May, Dirksen invited Humphrey to his office to negotiate amendments acceptable to fellow party members. Justice Department officials and other senators also attended. In mid-May, the revised bill was completed, and Dirksen began the job of winning support for the compromise. The capstone of his effort occurred on June 10, 1964. "There are many reasons why cloture should be invoked and a good civil rights measure enacted," Dirksen told Senate colleagues, and then quoted Victor Hugo, who, on the night he died, entered these words in his diary: "Stronger than all the armies is an idea whose time has come." "The time," Dirksen reasoned, "has come for equality of opportunity in sharing of government, in education, and in employment. It will not be stayed or denied. It is here." Many feel, however, that Dirksen's heroic leading role would not have happened without Humphrey's skillful floor leadership. The motion for cloture passed, 71–29, the first time cloture was invoked in a civil rights debate.[7]

On June 18, hours before the final Senate vote, Sen. Richard B. Russell, D-Ga., voiced the sentiments of opponents, who, he declared, had "given their last particle of ability and the last iota of physical strength in the effort to hold back the overwhelming combination of forces supporting this bill until its manifold evils could be laid bare before the people of the country." The following day, it passed in the Senate, 73–27. On July 2, the House adopted the bill, 289–126, and President Johnson then signed the act. While the Civil Rights Act of 1964 did not solve all of the nation's racial problems, its significance cannot be overstated. The weakness of its voting rights section sparked black demonstrations that proved to be a large factor in the Voting Rights Act of 1965, which generated far less debate.[8]

SENATOR EVERETT McKINLEY DIRKSEN SUPPORTS THE CIVIL RIGHTS ACT OF 1964

JUNE 10, 1964

Mr. President, it is a year ago this month that the late President Kennedy sent his civil rights bill and message to the Congress. For two years, we had been chiding him about failure to act in this field. At long last, and after many conferences, it became a reality.

After nine days of hearings before the Senate Judiciary Committee, it was referred to a subcommittee. There it languished and the administration leadership finally decided to await the House bill.

In the House it traveled an equally tortuous road. But at long last, it reached the House floor for action. It was debated for sixty-four hours; one hundred fifty-five amendments were offered; thirty-four were approved. On February 10, 1964, it passed the House by a vote of, 290–130. That was a 65 percent vote.

It was messaged to the Senate on February 17 and reached the Senate Calendar on February 26. The motion to take up and consider was made on March 9. That motion was debated for sixteen days and on March 26 by a vote of, 67–17, it was adopted.

It is now four months since it passed the House. It is three-and-one-half months since it came to the Senate Calendar. Three months have gone by since the motion to consider was made. We have acted on one intervening motion to send the bill back to the Judiciary Committee and a vote on the jury trial amendment. That has been the extent of our action.

Sharp opinions have developed. Incredible allegations have been made. Extreme views have been asserted. The mail volume has been heavy. The bill has provoked many long-distance telephone calls, many of them late at night or in the small hours of the morning. There has been unrestrained criticism about motives. Thousands of people have come to the Capitol to urge immediate action on an unchanged House bill.

For myself, I have had but one purpose and that was the enactment of a good, workable, equitable, practical bill having due regard for the progress made in the civil rights field at the State and local level.

I am no Johnnie-come-lately in this field. Thirty years ago, in the House of Representatives, I voted on antipoll tax and antilynching measures. Since then, I have sponsored or cosponsored scores of bills dealing with civil rights.

At the outset, I contended that the House bill was imperfect and deficient. That fact is now quite generally conceded.

But the debate continued. The number of amendments submitted increased. They now number nearly four hundred. The stalemate continued. A backlog of work piled up. Committees could not function normally. It was an unhappy situation and it was becoming a bit intolerable.

It became increasingly evident that to secure passage of a bill in the Senate would require cloture and a limitation on debate. Senate aversion to cloture is traditional. Only once in thirty-five years has cloture been voted. But the procedure for cloture is a standing rule of the Senate. It grew out of a filibuster against the armed ship bill in 1917 and has been part of the Standing Rules of the Senate for forty-seven years. To argue that cloture is unwarranted or unjustified is to assert that in 1917, the Senate adopted a rule which it did not intend to use when circumstances required or that it was placed in the rulebook only as to be repudiated. It was adopted as an instrument for action when all other efforts failed.

Today the Senate is stalemated in its efforts to enact a civil rights bill, one version of which has already been approved by the House by a vote of more than 2 to 1. That the Senate wishes to act on a civil rights bill can be divined from the fact that the motion to take up was adopted by a vote of, 67–17.

There are many reasons why cloture should be invoked and a good civil rights measure enacted.

First. It is said that on the night he died, Victor Hugo wrote in his diary, substantially this sentiment:

> Stronger than all the armies is an idea whose time has come.

The time has come for equality of opportunity in sharing in government, in education, and in employment. It will not be stayed or denied. It is here.

The time has come for equality of opportunity in sharing in government, in education, and in employment. It will not be stayed or denied. It is here. — Everett McKinley Dirksen

---

The problem began when the Constitution makers permitted the importation of persons to continue for another twenty years. That problem was to generate the fury of civil strife seventy-five years later. Out of it was to come the Thirteenth Amendment ending servitude, the Fourteenth Amendment to provide equal protection of the laws and dual citizenship, the Fifteenth Amendment to prohibit government from abridging the right to vote.

Other factors had an impact. Two and three-quarter million young Negroes served in World Wars I, II, and Korea. Some won the Congressional Medal of Honor and the Distinguished Service Cross. Today they are fathers and grandfathers. They brought back impressions from other countries where no discrimination existed. These impressions have been transmitted to children and grandchildren. Meanwhile, hundreds of thousands of colored have become teachers and professors, doctors and dentists, engineers and architects, artists and actors, musicians and technicians. They have become status minded. They have sensed inequality. They are prepared to make the issue. They feel that the time has come for the idea of equal opportunity. To enact the pending measure by invoking cloture is imperative.

Second. Years ago, a professor who thought he had developed an incontrovertible scientific premise submitted it to his faculty associates. Quickly they picked it apart. In agony he cried out, "Is nothing eternal?" To this one of his associates replied, "Nothing is eternal except change."

Since the act of 1875 on public accommodations and the Supreme Court decision of 1883 which struck it down, America has changed. The population then was 45 million. Today it is 190 million. In the Pledge of Allegiance to the Flag we intone, "One Nation, under God." And so it is. It is an integrated Nation. Air, rail, and highway transportation make it so. A common language makes it so. A tax pattern which applies equally white and nonwhite makes it so. Literacy makes it so. The mobility provided by 80 million autos makes it so. The accommodations laws in thirty-four States and the District of Columbia makes it so. The fair employment practice laws in thirty States make it so. Yes, our land has changed since the Supreme Court decision of 1883.

As Lincoln once observed:

> The occasion is piled high with difficulty and we must rise with the occasion. As our case is new, so we must think anew and act anew. We must first disenthrall ourselves and then we shall save the Union.

To my friends from the South, I would refresh you on the words of a great Georgian named Henry W. Grady. On December 22, 1886, he was asked to respond to a toast to the new South at the New England society dinner. His words were dramatic and explosive. He began his toast by saying:

> There was a South of slavery and secession — that South is dead. There is a South of union and freedom — that South thank God is living, breathing, growing every hour.

America grows, America changes. And on the civil rights issue we must rise with the occasion. That calls for cloture and for the enactment of a civil rights bill.

Third. There is another reason — our covenant with the people. For many years, each political party has given major consideration to a civil rights plank in its platform. Go back and reexamine our pledges to the country as we sought the suffrage of the people and for a grant of authority to manage and direct their affairs. Were these pledges so much campaign stuff or did we mean it? Were these promises on civil rights but idle words for vote-getting purposes or were they a covenant meant to be kept? If all this was mere pretense, let us confess the sin of hypocrisy now and vow not to delude the people again.

To you, my Republican colleagues, let me refresh you on the words of a great American. His name is Herbert Hoover. In his day he was reviled and maligned. He was castigated and calumniated. But today his views and his judgment stand vindicated at the bar of history. In 1952 he received a volcanic welcome as he appeared before our national convention in Chicago. On that occasion he commented on the Whig Party, predecessor of the Republican Party, and said:

> The Whig Party temporized, compromised upon the issue of freedom for the Negro. That party disappeared. It deserved to disappear. Shall the Republican Party receive or deserve any better fate if it compromises upon the issue of freedom for all men?
>
> To those who have charged me with doing a disservice to my party because of my interest in the enactment of a good civil rights bill — and there have been a good many who have made that charge — I can only say that our party found its faith in the Declaration of Independence in which a great Democrat, Jefferson by name, wrote the flaming words:
>
> We hold these truths to be self-evident that all men are created equal.

That has been the living faith of our party. Do we forsake this article faith, now that equality's time has come or do we stand up for it and ensure the survival of our party and its ultimate victory. There is no substitute for a basic and righteous idea. We have a duty — a firm duty — to use the instruments at hand — namely, the cloture rule — to bring about the enactment of a good civil rights bill.

Fourth. There is another reason why we dare not temporize with the issue which is before us. It is essentially moral in character. It must be resolved. It will not go away. Its time has come. Nor is it the first time in our history that an issue with moral connotations and implications has swept away the resistance, the fulminations, the legalistic speeches, the ardent but dubious arguments, the lamentations and the thought patterns of an earlier generation and pushed forward to fruition.

More than sixty years ago came the first efforts to secure Federal pure food and drug legislation. The speeches made on this floor against this intrusion of Federal power sound fantastically incredible today. But it would not be stayed. Its time had come and since its enactment, it has been expanded and strengthened in nearly every Congress.

When the first efforts were made to ban the shipment of goods in interstate commerce made with child labor, it was regarded as quite absurd. But all the trenchant editorials, the bitter speeches, the noisy onslaughts were swept aside as this limitation on the shipment of goods made with sweated child labor moved on to fulfillment. Its time had come.

More than eighty years ago came the first efforts to establish a civil service and merit system to cover Federal employees. The proposal was ridiculed and drenched with sarcasm. Some of the sharpest attacks on the proposal were made on this very Senate floor. But the bullet fired by a disappointed office seeker in 1880 which took President Garfield's life was the instrument of destiny which placed the Pendleton Act on the Federal statute books in 1883. It was an idea whose time had come.

When the New York Legislature placed a limit of ten hours per day and six days per week upon the bakery workers in that state, this act was struck down by the U.S. Supreme Court. But in due time came the eight-hour day and the forty-hour week and how broadly accepted this concept is today. Its time had come.

More than sixty years ago, the elder La Follette thundered against the election of U.S. Senators by the state legislatures. The cry was to get back to the people and to first principles. On this Senate floor, Senators sneered at his efforts and even left the Chamber to show their contempt. But fifty years ago, the Constitution was amended to provide for the direct election of Senators. Its time had come.

Ninety-five years ago came the first endeavor to remove the limitation on sex in the exercise of the franchise. The comments made in those early days sound unbelievably ludicrous. But on and on went the effort and became the Nineteenth Amendment to the Constitution. Its time had come.

When the eminent Joseph Choate appeared before the Supreme Court to assert that a Federal income tax statute was unconstitutional and communistic, the Court struck down the work of Congress. Just twenty years later in 1913 the power of Congress to lay and collect taxes on incomes became the Sixteenth Amendment to the Constitution itself.

These are but some of the things touching closely the affairs of the people which were met with stout resistance, with shrill and strident cries of radicalism, with strained legalisms, with anguished entreaties that the foundations of the Republic were being rocked. But an inexorable moral force which operates in the domain of human affairs swept these efforts aside and today they are accepted as parts of the social, economic and political fabric of America.

Pending before us is another moral issue. Basically it deals with equality of opportunity in exercising the franchise, in securing an education, in making a livelihood, in enjoying the mantle of protection of the law. It has been a long, hard furrow and each generation must plow its share. Progress was made in 1957 and 1960. But the furrow does not end there. It requires the implementation provided by the substitute measure which is before us. And to secure that implementation requires cloture.

Let me add one thought to these observations. Today is an anniversary. It is in fact the one hundreth anniversary of the nomination of Abraham Lincoln for a second term for the Presidency on the Republican ticket. Two documents became the blueprints of his life and his conduct. The first was the Declaration of Independence which proclaimed the doctrine that all men are created equal. The second was the Constitution, the preamble to which began with the words:

> We, the people…do ordain and establish this Constitution for the United States of America.

These were the articles of his superb and unquenchable faith. Nowhere and at no time did he more nobly reaffirm that faith than at Gettysburg one hundred one years ago when he spoke of "a new nation, conceived in liberty and dedicated to the proposition that all men are created equal."

It is to take us further down that road that a bill is pending before us. We have a duty to get that job done. To do it will require cloture and a limitation on debate as provided by a standing rule of the Senate which has been in being for nearly fifty years. I trust we shall not fail in that duty.

That, from a great Republican, thinking in the frame of equality of opportunity — and that is all that is involved in this bill.

To those who have charged me with doing a disservice to my party — and there are many — I can only say that our party found its faith in the Declaration of Independence, which was penned by a great Democrat, Thomas Jefferson by name. There he wrote the great words:

> We hold these truths to be self-evident, that all men are created equal.

That has been the living faith of our party. Do we forsake this article of faith, now that the time for our decision has come?

There is no substitute for a basic ideal. We have a firm duty to use the instrument at hand, namely, the cloture rule, to bring about the enactment of a good civil rights bill.

I appeal to all Senators. We are confronted with a moral issue. Today let us not be found wanting in whatever it takes by way of moral and spiritual substance to face up to the issue and to vote cloture.

Source: *Congressional Record,* 88th Cong., 2nd sess., June 10, 1964 (Washington: GPO, 1964), 110:13319–13320.

SENATOR RICHARD B. RUSSELL JR. OPPOSES THE CIVIL RIGHTS ACT OF 1964

JUNE 18, 1964

SENATE'S LONGEST DEBATE

Mr. President, the moving finger is writing the final act of the longest debate and the greatest tragedy ever played out in the Senate of the United States.

Within a short time, the battle that began on this floor on March 9 will be concluded with the passage of H.R. 7152 — a bill bearing the attractive but false title of the "Civil Rights Act of 1964."

The Senate will have no further opportunity to express itself on this proposed legislation. It has already been arranged for the other body to accept the bill in the form it leaves the Senate. It will then go to the President to be signed into law with the great fanfare, ceremony, pomp, and circumstance.

In view of the political nature of the proposed legislation, I doubt that the Executive Office — large as it is — can accommodate the rejoicing and admiring throng.

Today marks the 82d day this matter has been considered by the Senate. Some six thousand three hundred-pages in the *Congressional Record* and an estimated ten million words have been devoted to the debate thus far.

In point of historical fact the longest previous debate in the history of the Senate was over the ship subsidy and took place in the early 1920s. However, that was an off-and-on discussion spread over seventy-five days with frequent interruptions including a Christmas recess. The only other two debates that have lasted as long as two months were the Oregon bill in 1846 and the communications satellite bill in 1962.

Mr. President, the historian of the future will find little significance in the duration of the debate, but he will find much to consider and study in the fundamental issues involved and the impact of this legislation upon our form of government. It will take little effort or intelligence to recognize that the year 1964 marked a turning point in our history. This legislation and other actions will profoundly affect the American way of life and the rights and individual liberties of every American of whatever race, religion, or place of residence.

Indeed, Mr. President, history may well record this as the last sustained fight to keep inviolate the federal system with its division of powers between the States and the Central Government, and the delicate system of checks and balances between the three branches of our National Government that have been dependent upon respect shown by each branch for the doctrine of the separation of powers between the three equal but coordinate branches.

All of the eloquence that has been poured out here in this Chamber this afternoon in behalf of the bill will apply to any piece of proposed legislation that may be brought forward to use the Federal power to enforce absolute conformity of thought and action by every one of our citizens.

Central Issue

I cannot escape the conclusion that the central issue at stake in this debate has been the preservation of the dual system of divided powers that has been the hallmark of the genius of the Founding Fathers.

I am proud to have been a member of that small group of determined Senators that since the 9th of March has given the last particle of ability and the last iota of physical strength in the effort to hold back the overwhelming combination of forces supporting this bill until its manifold evils could be laid bare before the people of the country.

The depth of our conviction is evidenced by the intensity of our opposition. There is little room for honorable men to compromise where the inalienable rights of future generations are at stake.

No group of men could have worked harder in a nobler cause. Undismayed and unintimidated by forces marshaling incomparably greater strength than available to us, we have fought the good fight until we were overwhelmed and gagged. With apologies to no one, the opponents of this legislation have since the 9th day of March presented, as forcefully and persuasively as our ability would permit, the reasons we believe that this bill is not only in conflict with the Constitution but also is not in the best interests of the people of the Nation, of any race, or any creed.

No little group has ever faced greater odds. *The Wall Street Journal*, in an article critical of the strategy of the opponents, described the forces arrayed against us as:

> The full force of an administration whose southern chief needed to establish his civil credentials; and the combined pressure of powerful unions, numerous women's groups, scores of civil rights organizations, and for the first time, intensive lobbying by organized religion.

That last line does not apply to all of the men of cloth in this country, nor to those of any one creed or faith. Thousands of them did not permit themselves to have their vestments dragged in the mire of political turmoil. All religious faiths have some expression of peace and good will in their creeds and support the rights of property. But there were many ministers who, having failed completely in their effort

The depth of our conviction is evidenced by the intensity of our opposition. There is little room for honorable men to compromise where the inalienable rights of future generations are at stake. — Richard B. Russell Jr.

to establish good will and brotherhood from the pulpit, turned from the pulpit to the powers of the federal Government to coerce the people into accepting their views under threat of dire punishment.

While there is a great deal of difference in the methods applied, the philosophy of coercion by the men of cloth in this case is the same doctrine that dictated the acts of Torquemada in the infamous days of the Spanish Inquisition.

This is not all, Mr. President. The fact that the great metropolitan press, the radio and television, and other media of communicating news and formulating public opinion strongly support the bill made it all but impossible for us to get our case before the country. They magnified all that was said or done in the emotional appeals for support of the legislation and minimized or omitted the arguments as to its dangers. The same thing may be said about the efforts of many editorial writers, and the production of numerous columnists and commentators.

People Should Decide

Despite all of these odds, Mr. President, our presentation of the evils contained in the bill were finally penetrating to the American people. The people were beginning to stir. Indeed, the people were sufficiently informed to cause the chief proponents and the principal architects of the bill to deny them an opportunity to express their will in a national referendum for the unabashed reason that the people would defeat the bill if they were permitted to speak in a fair election.

It is impossible, Mr. President, to foresee all of the evils that are bound to flow from the enactment of this bill. It grants powers to appointive officials not only to pick the objects of their enforcement power, but to define the offense with which the alleged culprit will be charged.

★ ★ ★ ★

This bill is not only the greatest delegation of power and authority by the legislative branch to the executive ever seen;

it represents an admission of inadequacy and an abdication of responsibility by the national legislature which to all intents and purposes amounts to surrender of any claim to equality with the other two branches of the Government. It is an abandonment by the legislative branch of any defense whatever of the principal doctrine of separation of powers.

This bill would empower the executive branch to reach the long arm of regulation and intimidation into labor unions, business, commerce and industry in many areas into which the Federal power has not heretofore been permitted to intrude.

It places onerous requirements upon all people undertaking to earn a living in the way of reports and record keeping, and requires almost weekly obeisance to some bureaucrat in Washington. All of this falls upon the once free enterprise system that is the genesis of our greatness.

It bestows greater powers upon the Attorney General to invade and control the private lives of the American people than has ever been exercised by any other individual in our free system.

It so greatly enlarges the powers of the Federal Government over affairs that, under our constitutional concept, have been the sole concern of States and local governments as to make those governments mere puppets of the gigantic bureaucracy which this legislation strengthens and enlarges.

The bill is a drastic infringement by the Federal Government upon the basic human rights of every American citizen of every race to own and control property honestly gained as well as to be selective in choosing those with whom he wishes to associate.

Special-Privilege Legislation

In short, Mr. President, this is not a civil rights bill. It is a bill granting plenary powers to bureaucrats to enable them to create a horde of special benefits for a selected group of citizens in defiance of our exalted Jeffersonian doctrine of equal rights to all and special privileges to none.

It is impossible to exaggerate the latent opportunities for evil and oppression in the bill that are available to a power-seeking administrator.

This measure can be indicted on many other counts; and all counts could be sustained in the mind of anyone who examined it objectively. It should be defeated. It had its genesis in politics. It is punitive in its nature, and it is certain to be sectional in its application.

The South will be tossed from pillar to post in the tug of war between the two political parties. They will play as a record on a machine, again and again, the false picture of the South which has been established by constant years of propaganda in bidding for the favor of those who live in the more populous States.

The fact that this bill is more fraught with political implications and considerations than any that has been before

Congress in generations is apparent from much of the strange maneuvering that took place in the Senate over the past several days.

No secret has been made of the fact that both political parties consider that there is a direct relationship between forcing and liquidating this issue and the approaching National Conventions of the Republican and Democratic Parties. Very few are so naive as to be unaware of the fact that those in high positions of both parties will immediately seek to derive some political gain from the passage of the bill.

I resent — and resent bitterly — the attempt to make the people and the section from whence I come, and whom I have the honor to represent, the eternal whipping boy for the political aggrandizement of any politician or official of any political party.

It is now accepted, after halfhearted attempts at denial, that the main thrust of this bill is aimed at the Southern States. This is especially true with regard to its harshest and most coercive sections.

Hypocrisy reaches a new high in this measure undertaking to bring about a maximum degree of racial mixing in the schools and in the businesses of the South, while other States utilize as a defense against Federal invasion of their so-called equal accommodations and fair employment statutes, which in many cases are more fiction than fact and have long been dormant.

The veriest tyro at the law — indeed anyone who is able to understand the English language — can grasp that the bill is so drafted as to exempt or delay the application of its worst provisions in every section of the country save the Southern States. Many Senators, in responding to the expressed fears of their constituents as to this extension of Federal power, have assured them again and again that the bill would not be applicable in their State, but is applicable only to the South. I have in my files the newsletters of several Senators from States, where minority groups are so small as to be inconsequential, solemnly assuring their constituents that the bill is aimed only at the white people of the South.

South a Mistreated Minority

In all of the sanctimony about protecting the rights of minorities, let us understand fully that the bill is aimed at what has become the most despised and mistreated minority in the country — namely, the white people of the Southern States. The approach is more subtle and hypocritical in this bill, but its purposes are identical with those that prompted Charles Sumner, Thaddeus Stevens, and Ben Wade in the reconstruction legislation of the 1860's.

Mr. President, the people of the South are citizens of this Republic. They are entitled to some consideration. It seems to me that fair men should recognize that the people of the South, too, have some rights which should be respected. And though, Mr. President, we have failed in this fight to protect them from a burgeoning bureaucracy that is already planning and organizing invasion after invasion of the South, preceded by thousands of young people who have been recruited in the greatest crusade since the Children's Crusade of the Middle Ages, our failure cannot be ascribed to lack of effort. Our ranks were too thin, our resources too scanty, but we did our best. I say to my comrades in arms in this long fight that there will never come a time when it will be necessary for any one of us to apologize for his conduct or his courage.

Mr. President, those of us who have been upon this floor day after day for more than three months have used every weapon available. We have sought to appeal to the sense of fairness and justice of the Members of this body. Finding that the ears of our colleagues were closed and that a majority had already signed in blood to "follow the leaders," we undertook to go over their heads and appeal to the American people.

There is reason to believe that the long and arduous fight that we have waged has caused hundreds of thousands of people to look beyond the attractive and misleading title of this bill and consider — objectively and dispassionately — the far-reaching implications of this measure and its effect upon the future of every American, no matter what the color of his skin or his place of residence.

Until we were gagged, we made no secret of the fact that we were undertaking to speak in detail and at length in an effort to get the message across to the American people. We did not deceive anyone as to our purposes.

Source: *Congressional Record*, 88th Cong., 2nd sess., June 18, 1964 (Washington: GPO, 1964), 110:14299–14301.

Notes

1. Carl M. Brauer, *John F. Kennedy and the Second Reconstruction* (New York: Columbia University Press, 1977), 30–60, 230–330; Robert D. Loevy, *To End All Segregation: The Politics of the Passage of the Civil Rights Act of 1964* (Lanham, Md.: University Press of America, 1990), 12–17, 33.

2. Quotes are found in Loevy, *To End All Segregation: The Politics of the Passage of the Civil Rights Act of 1963*, 33; U.S. President (Kennedy), *Public Papers of the Presidents of the United States, 1963* (Washington, D.C.: GPO, 1964), 681. See also Loevy, *To End All Segregation: The Politics of the Passage of the Civil Rights Act of 1963*, 62–63.

3. Loevy, *To End All Segregation: The Politics of the Passage of the Civil Rights Act of 1964*, 7, 29–70, 90–92; Charles W. Whalen and Barbara Whalen, *The Longest Debate: A Legislative History of the 1964 Civil Rights Act* (Cabin John, Md.: Seven Locks Press, 1985), 75–79.

4. Hugh Davis Graham, *The Civil Rights Era: Origins and Development of National Policy, 1960–1972* (New York: Oxford University Press, 1990), 134–139; Loevy, *To End All Segregation: The Politics of the Passage of the Civil Rights Act of 1964*, 99–101, 113–124; Whalen and Whalen, *The Longest Debate: A Legislative History of the 1964 Civil Rights Act*, 84–123.

5. Loevy, *To End All Segregation: The Politics of the Passage of the Civil Rights Act of 1964,* 216–223, 261–266.

6. Loevy, *To End All Segregation: The Politics of the Passage of the Civil Rights Act of 1964,* 1, 167–185; Whalen and Whalen, *The Longest Debate: A Legislative History of the 1964 Civil Rights Act,* 131–135, 200.

7. Quote is found in "Civil Rights Act of 1964," *Congressional Record,* June 10, 1964, 110:13319. See also Graham, *The Civil Rights Era: Origins and Development of National Policy, 1960–1972,*

141–152; Loevy, *To End All Segregation: The Politics of the Passage of the Civil Rights Act of 1964,* 225–230, 242, 255–260, 266–268, 316–321; Robert Mann, *The Walls of Jericho: Lyndon Johnson, Hubert Humphrey, Richard Russell, and the Struggle for Civil Rights* (New York: Harcourt Brace, 1996), 428; Whalen and Whalen, *The Longest Debate: A Legislative History of the 1964 Civil Rights Act,* 148–197.

8. "Civil Rights Act of 1964," *Congressional Record,* June 18, 1964, 110:14300. See also "Civil Rights Act of 1964," *Congressional Record,* June 19, 1964, 110:14511, July 2, 1964, 110:15897.

Medicare and Medicaid
✳ 1965 ✳

On July 20, 1965, with former president Harry S. Truman at his side, President Lyndon B. Johnson signed legislation that provided, for the first time, government health insurance for the elderly as well as the poor. Enactment of Medicare and Medicaid culminated more than two decades of fierce debate in Congress. In a touching tribute to Truman, the first president to endorse the idea of federal health care insurance, Johnson praised him for planting "the seeds of compassion and duty ... which flowered into care for the sick, and serenity for the fearful."[1]

The Truman Library ceremony was a historic moment in a long and bitter political struggle to create a government-financed health care system in the United States. It originated in nineteenth-century Europe and intensified after World War II with the convergence of several highly significant economic and medical developments. The most important resulted from the increased production of penicillin during the war and subsequent development of other antibiotics. With physicians better able to fight infection, new surgical techniques resulted that greatly enhanced the capability to affect diseases and dramatically increased the demand for medical care. Also, a spectacular growth in the economy and a federal policy that excluded health insurance coverage from taxable income helped drive up health care costs and made far more noticeable the plight of the elderly, half of whom had no insurance and virtually no access to employers' tax-subsided insurance.

President Franklin D. Roosevelt considered endorsing a government health insurance plan in 1935, but advisers convinced him it would jeopardize passage of the Social Security Act. Instead, he authorized staff to continue studying the question, and congressional proposals incorporating those findings were later introduced. When Truman became president, he sent Congress the first official White House proposal. It fell victim to a very conservative Congress, a war-delayed reaction to the New Deal, high taxes, the regimentation and control imposed during the war, and big government. Then the cold war eclipsed domestic issues; organized labor began looking to employers for health insurance coverage; and the American Medical Association (AMA) commenced contending, as it would for the next two

decades, that the U.S. national health insurance would lead to socialized medicine and be exorbitantly costly and that a better option was private insurance companies.[2]

At the beginning of 1952, the strength of the AMA's opposition was sufficient enough to prompt Truman not to mention his proposal in the State of the Union Address. Instead, he announced the creation of a Commission on the Health Needs of the Nation to study the problem. Some of the most important work on what would become Medicare, however, was done during Truman's presidency. Following the 1950 midterm elections, his administration reintroduced the idea of limiting health insurance to Social Security beneficiaries. For some time, Social Security officials had felt they could not fully protect the elderly from economic dependency unless the safety net included some form of medical insurance.[3]

President Dwight D. Eisenhower opposed government health insurance, but did sign four bills in 1956 that suggested the idea of making health insurance available to Social Security beneficiaries might be revisited. These acts established a health protection program for military dependents, expanded payments to medical vendors for welfare recipients, provided benefits for the permanently disabled age fifty and older, and appropriated funds to study the problems of aging and the aged. A year later, Rep. Aime J. Forand, D-R.I., introduced a revised version of the beneficiaries-only health insurance. By mid-1960, members of both parties conceded that assisting the elderly poor with their medical expenses was a federal obligation. In response, House Ways and Means Committee Chairman Wilbur Mills, D-Ark., developed a new approach that financed elderly medical care through federal grants rather than Social Security. It quickly passed the House.[4]

In the Senate, Robert S. Kerr, D-Okla., offered a bill incorporating much of the Mills plan which became known as the Kerr-Mills Bill. The ensuing debate offered a preview of the upcoming presidential campaign that saw the Republican contender, Vice President Richard M. Nixon, lobbying on the Senate floor to defeat a rival proposal offered by his Democratic opponent, John F. Kennedy, D-Mass., and Senate colleague Clinton P. Anderson, D-N.M. If Kennedy-Anderson passed, and President Eisenhower carried out his threat to veto the bill, Nixon knew it would become the most prominent issue of the campaign. Nixon's strategy worked. The Senate rejected Kennedy-Anderson overwhelmingly and passed Kerr-Mills, which subsequently became law. Opponents of placing health insurance under Social Security hoped that Kerr-Mills would serve as an alternative, but a number of experts considered it a logical prerequisite to a bona fide health insurance program.[5]

During the 1960 campaign, Kennedy made Medicare a major issue by attacking Kerr-Mills as inadequate. After he won the presidency, Kennedy's proposal received increased emphasis as prominent members of both parties began to publicly endorse it, and a presidential Task Force on Health and Social Security for the American People was created. Social Security expert William Cohen, who headed the task force, subsequently became assistant secretary of health, education, and welfare and took charge of the fight for health insurance for the elderly. A vote on Medicare, however, was postponed until after the 1962 midterm elections because the Democrats did not have the House votes needed for passage. Amidst this void, opponents and proponents escalated their activities. The administration's push climaxed on May 20

when the president addressed a rally of nearly twenty thousand seniors in Madison Square Garden, and some three dozen other rallies were held around the country to generate support for Medicare. In a carefully planned counter-event, the AMA aired its response two days later in a televised broadcast from a dramatically empty Garden to symbolize the AMA's "underdog" status.[6]

Despite the administration's effort, a majority of the House Ways and Means Committee still opposed Medicare, and a compromise Senate floor amendment to a House-passed welfare benefits measure also failed. Afterwards, President Kennedy angrily vowed to make Medicare an issue in the 1962 midterm elections, but foreign affairs dominated the fall campaigns in the aftermath of the Cuban missile crisis. Following the election, there was a lull in agitation for Medicare as the administration became preoccupied with drafting a civil rights bill, a trade expansion bill, a nuclear test ban treaty, and tax reform. Kennedy's tragic assassination on November 22, 1963, prompted a surge of sympathy for his legislative program, and his successor, former vice president Lyndon B. Johnson, immediately acted upon these sentiments by asking Congress to pass Medicare. The Senate

Medicare and Medicaid were debated for almost two decades before being signed into law by President Lyndon Johnson in 1965.
Source: Associated Press.

moved quickly to include a health insurance plan as part of a Social Security amendments bill. House conferees, led by Rep. Mills, however, refused to accept the proposal, prompting the *New York Times* to predict that Medicare was probably destined for "the limbo of perennial issues."[7]

The *Times's* pessimism was misplaced, and the 1964 election dispelled any lingering doubts about passage of Medicare. Johnson was returned to office by the largest plurality in history, and the Democrats gained their biggest congressional majorities since the New Deal. Mills realized that there was now pressure to come up with an acceptable bill, but he remained concerned with the financing of the bill. In early January 1965, Mills announced he would soon present a new redesigned Medicare bill, and in so doing sought to balance the various interests that would be responsible for administering the program or had some stake in its operation — physicians, nurses, hospital administrators, nursing home representatives, state health and welfare officials, labor leaders, insurance industry representatives, federal officials, and many others. Ultimately, he settled on a bill that contained three distinct parts: Medicare Part A, a payroll tax program that automatically covered hospital care for all Social Security recipients; Medicare Part B, a voluntary supplement program that covered physician care, and an expanded Kerr-Mills program that addressed the care of the needy. In the process, Mills

transformed a bill providing medical insurance for the elderly into an antipoverty program called Medicare.[8]

Following a spirited debate, the Ways and Means Committee reported the bill. In the House, the two hundred ninety-six-page measure was considered under a closed rule, meaning that the chamber had to act on the measure without considering any floor amendments. During the House debate, Rep. John W. Byrnes, R-Wis., and others argued that the hospital fund would endanger the Social Security retirement fund. Mills, however, was thoroughly convinced it would be actuarially sound. Following House approval, the Senate Finance Committee had two weeks of hearings and extended executive sessions. During the ensuing three-day floor debate, senators offered five hundred thirteen amendments and added $1.5 billion in expenditures. A conference committee took more than a week to reconcile the differences between the two chambers before the bill was approved by the House on July 27, 307–116, and the Senate the following day, 70–24. In the preceding eight years since the introduction of the Forand Bill in 1957, Congress had considered some eighty different government-financed health care alternatives, held eight different sets of hearings on the issue, and devoted countless hours of floor debate to the subject. Interestingly, the bill that Congress finally approved was by far the most comprehensive of any of the bills considered.[9]

REPRESENTATIVE WILBUR MILLS PRESENTS HIS PLAN FOR FINANCING HOSPITAL CARE FOR THE AGED OVER 65

APRIL 7, 1965

Mr. Chairman, we are beginning the consideration, in the Committee of the Whole, of H.R. 6675, a bill reported by the Committee on Ways and Means after consideration this year of many, many days in executive session involving a subject matter that has been before the Committee for a number of years, subject matter on which the Committee on Ways and Means has conducted over the course of that time more days of public hearings than on any other matter within the jurisdiction of the Committee on Ways and Means in the same period of time. This is pointed out by the gentleman from New York [Mr. KEOGH] during the debate a few minutes ago.

Mr. Chairman, the bill, H.R. 6675, involves some matters that have not been in bills submitted in prior years to the Committee on Ways and Means as a single package or previously reported by the Committee on Ways and Means.

It is significant, however, Mr. Chairman, that the bill, H.R. 6675, contains all except one of the provisions that were in the bill last year that was reported from the committee providing for social security amendments and which the House passed by an overwhelming vote, as I recall, with only eight Members voting against that bill. At that time the committee thought it advisable to include a provision to permit firemen and policemen under existing State and local government pension plans so they could elect among themselves to come under social security. That provision was stricken by Senate action in the Finance Committee as it considered the bill last year and is not in this year's bill.

★ ★ ★ ★

In bringing to you the contents of this bill permit me to divide the bill into four parts, for each of these four parts

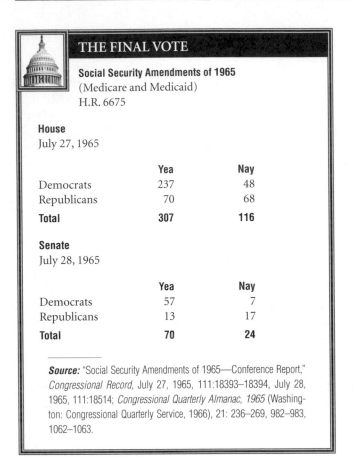

THE FINAL VOTE

Social Security Amendments of 1965
(Medicare and Medicaid)
H.R. 6675

House
July 27, 1965

	Yea	Nay
Democrats	237	48
Republicans	70	68
Total	**307**	**116**

Senate
July 28, 1965

	Yea	Nay
Democrats	57	7
Republicans	13	17
Total	**70**	**24**

Source: "Social Security Amendments of 1965—Conference Report," *Congressional Record*, July 27, 1965, 111:18393–18394, July 28, 1965, 111:18514; *Congressional Quarterly Almanac, 1965* (Washington: Congressional Quarterly Service, 1966), 21: 236–269, 982–983, 1062–1063.

constitutes a separate subject matter for a monumental bill within itself.

These four parts are, first, the part dealing with the medical care of our elderly citizens; the second, the part dealing with maternal and child health, crippled children, and mentally retarded programs; the third part revising and improving the benefit and coverage provisions of the old-age, survivors, and disability insurance program; and fourth, the part improving and expanding the public assistance programs themselves.

Now, let us return to the first of these. What, in a brief way, is the committee bill proposing to do with respect to health insurance and medical care of those over sixty-five? The bill divides in that respect into three parts. There is within the bill what we have called a basic plan providing protection against the cost of hospital and nursing home care, financed through a separate payroll tax and using a separate trust fund.

The proposed basic hospital insurance would be provided — on the basis of a new section in title II of the act — for people aged sixty-five and over who are entitled to monthly social security benefits or to annuities under the Railroad Retirement Act. In addition, people who are now aged sixty-five or will reach age sixty-five within the next few years and who are not insured under the social security or railroad programs would nevertheless be covered under the basic plan. In July 1966, when the program would become effective, about 17 million people aged sixty-five and over who are eligible for social security or railroad retirement benefits, and about 2 million aged who would be covered under a special transitional provision, would have the proposed basic hospital insurance.

★ ★ ★ ★

Currently, 93 percent of the people reaching age sixty-five are eligible for benefits under social security or railroad retirement and this percentage will rise to close to 100 percent as the program matures. Thus, over the long run all older people will earn entitlement for the proposed hospital insurance.

Persons entitled to benefits under the hospital insurance plan would be eligible to have payments made for inpatient hospital care and for important additional benefits covering posthospital home extended care, posthospital home health services, and certain outpatient hospital diagnostic studies.

★ ★ ★ ★

The second part of the medical package provides for a voluntary supplementary program providing and making available money for the payment of physicians' fees and other medical and health services which would be financed through a small monthly premium paid by the individual, equally matched by an amount from the general funds of the Treasury of the United States.

The voluntary supplementary plan would provide protection that builds upon the protection provided by the hospital insurance plan. It would cover physicians' services, additional home health visits, care in psychiatric hospitals, and a variety of medical and other services not covered under the hospital insurance plan. The beneficiary would pay the first $50 of expenses he incurs each year for services of the type covered under the plan. Above this deductible amount, the plan would pay 80 percent of the reasonable costs in the case of services provided by an institution or home health agency and 80 percent of reasonable charges for other covered services, with 20 percent being paid by the beneficiary.

★ ★ ★ ★

In developing this comprehensive health insurance program for the aged the Committee on Ways and Means was mindful that a program is no better than its administration. The committee proposals reflect a conviction that the administrative challenges brought by this new program can be met by the combined efforts of voluntary organizations and the Government. The governmental part of this challenge will nevertheless remain large. It will fall mainly to the Social Security Administration. We believe that this agency's outstanding record for service and efficiency will be carried forward into the new program.

The Social Security Administration, however, will face a major job of advance planning and preparation to bring the health insurance programs into operation by next year. Extensive negotiations will be required to complete agreements and financial arrangements with fiscal intermediaries, insurance carriers, State agencies, and others. Broad-scale consultation will also be required with professional organizations representing the Nation's hospitals and others who furnish reimbursable health services. Operational policies and record keeping procedures will have to be worked out on a scope never before undertaken in the health field. This will entail, among other things, putting into the hands of 19 million aged people information about the two health insurance programs, answering inquiries on the benefits of the voluntary insurance plan, setting up records for those who elect the plan, and preparing and delivering identification cards for all eligible aged.

In addition to this vast enrollment task, the Social Security Administration will have a tremendous job of taking and developing new claims in order to establish the basic eligibility of the aged who have been uninsured for cash benefits and from all others over sixty-five who have not yet applied for social security benefits.

★ ★ ★ ★

I must admit that the benefits in the committee bill cost money — yes, they cost money. Let us see what they cost. Let us see what we are doing in this bill to provide for those costs.

The health care program costs include those for the supplementary program, for the basic program, and for the medical assistance for the aged improvements. The basic program, which I have said is financed by the payroll tax device, will in the first full year of its operation, 1967, produce a cost of $2,300 million on the basis of using high cost estimates, which we think is the conservative way to determine what something will cost when you have to provide a tax for it.

The voluntary supplementary health benefits program will have a cost out of the Federal Treasury beginning on July 1, 1966, of approximately $600 million per year, while for the same period there will also be a cost of $275 million for uninsured persons covered by the hospital insurance program.

★ ★ ★ ★

Now as to the health part of the bill. We have worked out a separate tax and separate trust fund. Let no one mislead you with statements, general in nature as they appear to be, and be not misled by minority views expressed in the report that this separation is illusory.

Some statements have recently been made that I have, in effect, gone back on my previously expressed position that there must be a separation between the cash benefits system and the proposed hospital benefits program. I emphatically state, here and now, that this is not the case. My conviction is that there must be separation and the bill I bring to you reflects this belief. For years I have maintained that the basis difference between the two types of benefits makes it essential that we have two separate systems. During many hours of questioning the Government witnesses before our committee, particularly the Chief Actuary, I brought out the different nature of the cost assumptions which underlie the hospital program as distinguished from the cash program. I pointed out that some assumptions which were conservative under one program had exactly the reverse effect when applied to the other program. Thus, as the committee drew up the bill, at every opportunity I urged that provisions be inserted which would provide meaningful separation between the two systems.

★ ★ ★ ★

[T]he bill before you today … provides for a redistribution of the revenues from the combined old-age and survivors benefit insurance tax. This new allocation, which will put the disability insurance fund on a sound actuarial basis to make up for some unfavorable cost experience in recent years, would not be possible as to hospital benefits under your committee's bill. Under H.R. 6675 any adjustment of revenue because of either unfavorable or favorable experience will have to be done by a change in the tax rate or earnings base — or both — of a separate hospital insurance tax.

The hospital benefit program will thus be financed from its own tax and there will be no shifting of funds — either way — from the old-age, survivors, or disability program.

★ ★ ★ ★

On the basis of legislation that has been presented to the Ways and Means Committee, it does not appear that there is much doubt any more in the minds of many that we do have a problem of meeting the medical costs in the United States with respect to certain people in our population. These are our grandfathers who are living longer today than did their loved ones before them. We owe that to the great miracles which have been performed by medical science. But in the process of having performed those miracles, problems have resulted. Today's problems, as a result, are certainly greater in magnitude than those the generations before had, because of the greater length of time beyond retirement and before death, and because of the vicissitudes of illness of more and more of these people as a result of the length of their lives.

★ ★ ★ ★

I have said consistently that I did not think that all of the medical costs that are incurred by those over sixty-five could be financed only through a payroll tax, because conceivably the payroll tax would be so high finally as to interfere with our capacity to compete in the world, with the payroll being charged as a cost of doing business. I have said repeatedly that we cannot run the risk of bankrupting the Federal Treasury once and for all by putting this entire cost upon the general fund of the Treasury. I think that the program has to be dealt with in a combination approach of two things: use of payroll tax and use of general fund revenues. That is what the committee has done. That is the only difference, apparently, that exists today between my distinguished friend who has offered his bill and the committee's proposition.

Just how do we finance the proposal? Because his proposition would be voluntary, with no compulsion under a payroll tax, it would be financed by the payment of the individual and from the general funds of the Treasury. In total, his plan would be financed just as our supplementary plan would be.

Now, how did we divide the health insurance provisions of H.R. 6675? Which did we put in which pocket and out of what account does it come and why? There are very, very important reasons why we propose to finance the benefits the way we do. It is the way that has been debated completely but which has been disregarded by the very people with whom we were trying to work. What did we do? We picked this single biggest element, namely, the cost of being in a hospital, and we financed that by the payroll tax to let the person during his working years, through small amounts of money paid per week, per month, or per year, make advance payments to that trust fund entirely on his own and from his employer and by the self-employed on their own account.

★ ★ ★ ★

I would want you to know that finally it has been possible for us, after all these years, to develop a proposition that I could wholeheartedly and conscientiously, with every bit of the energy at my command, support. That has not been the case with reference to propositions in the past. Here, Mr. Chairman, I believe we have finally worked out a satisfactory and reasonable solution of an entire problem, not just a partial solution of a major problem. I feel that we have done it in a way, Mr. Chairman, that will commend it to the people for whom we do it and that they will realize that in spite of all that has been said in the past, in spite of all the ways that have

---

Here, Mr. Chairman, I believe we have finally worked out a satisfactory and reasonable solution of an entire problem, not just a partial solution of a major problem. — Wilbur Mills

---

been suggested in the past, finally the Committee on Ways and Means has produced the proper way to do it and that is the way that good legislation is developed.

★ ★ ★ ★

I would suggest, therefore, that when tomorrow comes, we not toy with the bill by considering a motion to recommit, but that we take the bill as reported to the House from the Committee on Ways and Means and pass this bill as we have passed every other bill dealing with amendments to the Social Security Act in the past — by an overwhelming majority.

Source: *Congressional Record,* 89th Cong., 1st sess., April 7, 1965 (Washington: GPO, 1965), 111:7208–7215.

REPRESENTATIVE JOHN W. BYRNES OPPOSES REPRESENTATIVE MILLS'S PLAN FOR FINANCING HOSPITAL CARE FOR THE AGED OVER 65

APRIL 7, 1965

Let me point out this at the very beginning, that we on the committee, Democrats and Republicans alike, are in general agreement with respect to those provisions in the bill as reported by the committee relating to the old-age and survivors system, the disability system, and even as far as the Kerr-Mills system is concerned. That is not to say we have agreed on everything that is in the bill today, but generally we could have accepted them and they could have passed this House without a dissenting vote if we had limited it to that.

Yes, and we are in agreement in the committee, Democrats and Republicans alike, that our aged people face a problem with respect to providing for their medical care. We acknowledged that as far back as 1950, when we authorized the Federal Government to participate in subsidizing the benefit payments made by States to certain of its aged people who were in need.

We recognized it again when we enacted in the first instance the Kerr-Mills bill, and we still recognize that this is a problem of our older people.

We all feel, Democrats and Republicans alike, that something should be done, that action is called for. Our difference, and it is an important difference, is as to how. How do we do it? How do we meet the problems of people in a way that is best for them and is best for the Nation and in the best interest of all our people?

Let me, in my discussion of the bill before us and the issue before us, say a few words about the changes that have been made in the basic Social Security Act. I am most pleased at some of the changes that have been made because they are changes that I have been advocating for some time. We are finally moving in this bill to correct what I consider to be some very serious inequities and some injustices.

I would mention first the benefit level. It was last year when this matter of increasing the level of benefits under the old-age and survivors and disability insurance was under consideration that I proposed, and in fact, moved in the committee that the benefit level be increased by 7 percent. We were told at that time by the administration, and this position was supported by the majority on the committee, that it had to be held to a 5 percent increase and that it had to be held there in order to accommodate a medical care program under the social security system.

Do not forget that history because it is important to remember when the proponents of the committee bill say the medical program can have no effect on the cash benefits, that we do not have to worry about superimposing a medical care program on the old-age and survivors insurance system.

It was as recent as last year that we were told — yes; the cost of living has increased 7 or 8 percent since we last increased the cash benefit level, but you cannot increase benefits by 7 percent and still have enough of the payroll tax left to finance a medical care program under social security.

That, my friends, is what is also to happen again in the future if we tie a hospitalization program to the old-age and survivors insurance system, as is done in this bill as reported by the committee.

There is going to come a day when you will recognize the need for increased cash benefits in that program and you will be foreclosed from doing so because you will have preempted the payroll tax and the source of revenue from that source for the purposes of medical care, and you will not have sufficient left to do what should be done with respect to cash benefits.

★ ★ ★ ★

I would propose to replace the provisions of the bill as reported by the committee relating to medical care for the aged over sixty-five.

The bill I propose, which I have introduced, includes all of the social security amendments, all of the public welfare amendments, all of the amendments to the Kerr-Mills Act, to which I have, however, added specifically the option for the States to adopt the elder care program. The only difference between the bill I have proposed and will offer as a substitute and the bill as reported by the committee is in the approach to the problem of health insurance for the aged.

The substitute bill provides a program of health insurance which is admittedly the most comprehensive available today. The substitute adopts the approach used by the private insurance industry and it is patterned after the system of insurance that we have provided for our own Federal employees. The benefits are patterned on the high option of the Government-wide indemnity contract negotiated between the Civil Service Commission and private carriers for the benefit of Federal employees. It makes no distinction between medical services in the hospital or out of the hospital and it thus avoids placing unnecessary reliance on hospitalization, as I feel the committee bill does, which is the area admittedly where the costs are the greatest and the most likely to rise in the future.

The program is also patterned after the program we make available to our Federal employees in that we provide for a sharing of premium costs. The individual participates on a voluntary basis. He has the choice as to whether he wants to take the insurance policy or not. He pays a part of the premium costs. The Federal Government pays the balance of the premium costs.

For parts 1 and 2 of title I of the committee bill — these are the sections which provide for the hospitalization and related medical services — I substitute a single comprehensive program of Federal insurance. The program incorporates the medical program of the committee bill into a single package of benefit, with more extensive coverage — yes, and a savings in costs.

Now, there is nothing complicated about the proposal. We rely upon and adopt the procedures which are followed by private carriers in their contracts with the Civil Service Commission for our Federal employees.

★ ★ ★ ★

All persons aged sixty-five or over would be eligible — eligible on a uniform basis — for insurance and protection equivalent to the Government-wide indemnity benefit plan of the Federal Government. Their participation would be voluntary. There would be no means test. Enrollment would be during an initial enrollment period followed by periodic enrollment periods. This is the same system we use for our own Federal employees. For those under social security or the railroad retirement, enrollment would be exercised by the assignment of a premium contribution or a checkoff against the individual's current social security benefits. Those not under social security, would execute an application accompanying it with their initial premium contribution. State agencies would be granted an option to purchase the insurance for their old-age assistance and medical assistance for the aged recipients at a group rate. Premium contributions by the individual would be based on the cash benefits which they received under OASDI.

★ ★ ★ ★

The estimates of the cost of this program have been made by the chief actuary of the Department of Health, Education, and Welfare, who has also made the estimates of the cost of the committee bill. On February 9, shortly after I introduced the bill embodying the provisions of this alternative plan, the actuary, in whom I have a great deal of confidence, estimated that this program would cost on an average of $20 a month for each participant. That is the premium you would have to charge if the program were fully financed by premiums.

On February 16, a week later, however, the same actuary gave us an estimate of $16. Now I am told that if the same assumptions were used that have been used in estimating the cost of the committee bill the estimate might be back up to $20 per month. There has been a new estimate of the cost of our program on the same actuarial basis, using the same conservative assumptions; and the estimate now comes to a benefit level cost of approximately $20 per month per individual. That is the benefit side.

But where do we have the savings? Where is the difference in the cost between the two plans? In the first place, the program I advocate is voluntary, whereas the hospitalization program under the committee plan is compulsory.

The voluntary aspect of the program automatically reduces the cost; it reduces the cost of the voluntary program of supplemental benefits in the committee. I believe the estimate of utilization under that program is something like 85 or 90 percent.

★ ★ ★ ★

The cost of the hospital and the voluntary supplemental services under the committee bill in the first full year of operation is $2.8 billion of taxpayers' funds, either payroll taxpayers or general taxpayers. Under our substitute, the total cost as far as the general taxpayer is concerned in the first full year of operation is $2 billion. There is where the difference in cost is, Mr. Chairman, and it is there in black and white. We do not have to do any searching for it. A large part of the savings results from the fact that the substitute program is on a voluntary basis. Hospitalization under the committee bill is compulsory. In addition the substitute bill is contributory. I believe experts in the field will agree that the contributory factor is a substantial element in reducing abuses; namely, excessive utilization of benefits.

Then, finally, Mr. Chairman, I would also point out that the bill I propose provides for a special recoupment of the subsidy from those who are well able to pay the full cost of their subsidy. We do it by way of a special tax applied to those people with an individual income of over $5,000 a year and we recoup $100 for each $100 of income i[n] excess of $5,000 up to a recoupment of $100 which represents the amount of subsidy contained in the policy that they purchase from the Government. Therefore, no one can contend that we are providing a benefit for the rich and a benefit to those who can well afford to take care of themselves.

But may I point this out, Mr. Chairman? My objection to the committee bill is not on the basis of the cost. My objection is to the means used to finance the benefits; namely the payroll tax.

The committee bill would finance the major cost of medical care for the aged — the hospitalization program — through the social security system. One hundred percent of that cost will be paid for by today's workers — and tomorrow's workers — for 19 million persons over age sixty-five. These 19 million persons will pay nothing. This amounts to approximately two-thirds of the total cost of the combined package of benefits.

The administration bill would finance the balance of its package — the medical services — one-half out of general revenues and one-half by premium contributions.

In summary, the committee bill finances two-thirds of the cost through the social security system, one-sixth of the cost through general revenues, and one-sixth of the cost by premium contributions.

The substitute bill would finance two-thirds of the cost through the general revenues and one-third of the cost by premium contributions.

The committee bill would finance the major cost of medical care for the aged and the hospitalization program through the social security system, and you cannot get away from it.

★ ★ ★ ★

My primary concern — and I am certain the chairman of our committee shares the concern — is to protect cash ben-

My primary concern ... is to protect cash benefits under social security. That is the foremost and basic need of the elderly. Cash benefits will be secure only so long as we do not overburden the payroll tax system which is used to finance those benefits. — John W. Byrnes

efits under social security. That is the foremost and basic need of the elderly. Cash benefits will be secure only so long as we do not overburden the payroll tax system which is used to finance those benefits.

★ ★ ★ ★

If we pass the committee bill, we will be taking an unprecedented step in the field of social security. We will be tying into the social security system a service benefit. Not the payment of a specified amount of dollars at some future date, but payment for a specified service — hospitalization — regardless of what that service might cost.

That is why I am unalterably opposed to financing hospitalization through the social security system. You have been told that this is a separate tax with a separate fund, and everyone will know what the hospitalization program costs in terms of the payroll tax.

Once we embark on the program, will that make any difference?

★ ★ ★ ★

Once we tie the hospitalization program to the payroll tax we are only kidding ourselves when we say that it can be separated from the cash benefits.

The same worker, the same employer, the same wage, all must finance both programs. Every percentage point that we levy as a tax for hospital benefits means that much less available as a tax to finance cash benefits. That is the crux of the matter.

No one can honestly say that in levying this tax to finance hospital benefits we are not jeopardizing our ability at some future date to provide for an increase in cash benefits. And I happen to believe — and I believe our chairman shares my belief — that the most important consideration should be our ability to maintain cash benefits at a level which will preserve the purchasing power of those benefits to our aged citizens.

★ ★ ★ ★

I would summarize by saying that the differences of opinion — the point of conflict in our whole discussion is with reference to the medical provisions as contained in the committee bill. I propose a voluntary system instead of a compulsory system. I propose that it be financed not on the regressive payroll tax but that it be financed on the basis of our progressive tax system. I propose a system that is more comprehensive as far as the benefits are concerned.

Under the alternative proposal, the matter of need is recognized by a recoupment provision. We make sure that you are not just giving a gratuity to those who are well able to take care of their own medical needs.

Source: *Congressional Record,* 89th Cong., 1st sess., April 7, 1965 (Washington: GPO, 1965), 111:7219–7223.

Notes

1. U.S. President (Lyndon Johnson), *Public Papers of the Presidents: Lyndon B. Johnson, 1965,* 2 vols. (Washington, D.C.: GPO, 1966), II:812.

2. Peter A. Corning, *The Evolution of Medicare ... From Idea to Law* (Washington, D.C.: U.S. Social Security Administration, Office of Research and Statistics, 1969), 30–56; Frank D. Campion, *The AMA and U.S. Health Policy Since 1940* (Chicago: Chicago Review Press, 1984), 21–29.

3. Corning, *The Evolution of Medicare ... From Idea to Law,* 69; Philip J. Funigiello, *Chronic Politics: Health Care Security from FDR to George W. Bush* (Lawrence: University Press of Kansas, 2005), 88.

4. Corning, *The Evolution of Medicare ... From Idea to Law,* 74; Funigiello, *Chronic Politics: Health Care Security from FDR to George W. Bush,* 103.

5. Corning, *The Evolution of Medicare ... From Idea to Law,* 87; Funigiello, *Chronic Politics: Health Care Security from FDR to George W. Bush,* 108–109.

6. Corning, *The Evolution of Medicare ... From Idea to Law,* 87–89, 96. Critical analyses of President Kennedy's speech are found in Funigiello, *Chronic Politics: Health Care Security from FDR to George W. Bush,* 119; Sheri I. David, *With Dignity: The Search for Medicare and Medicaid* (Westport, Conn.: Greenwood Press, 1985), 71–72.

7. Editorial, "Double Defeat," *New York Times,* October 3, 1964, 28. See also Corning, *The Evolution of Medicare ... From Idea to Law,* 96–109; David, *With Dignity: The Search for Medicare and Medicaid,* 75–121; Funigiello, *Chronic Politics: Health Care Security from FDR to George W. Bush,* 122–137.

8. Corning, *The Evolution of Medicare ... From Idea to Law,* 112; David, *With Dignity: The Search for Medicare and Medicaid,* 121–130; Funigiello, *Chronic Politics: Health Care Security from FDR to George W. Bush,* 137–148; Theodore R. Marmor, *The Politics of Medicare,* 2nd ed. (New York: A. de Gruyter, 2000), 45–53.

9. "Social Security Amendments of 1965," *Congressional Record,* 89th Cong., 1st sess., April 7, 1965, 111:7208–7215, 7219–7226; "Social Security Amendments of 1965 — Conference Report," *Congressional Record,* July 27, 1965, 111:18393–18394, July 28, 1965, 111:18514; 79 Stat. 286–423, P.L. 89–97 (July 30, 1965); Corning, *The Evolution of Medicare ... From Idea to Law,* 117; David, *With Dignity: The Search for Medicare and Medicaid,* 130–141; Funigiello, *Chronic Politics: Health Care Security from FDR to George W. Bush,* 152–153.

Voting Rights Act of 1965

✳ 1965 ✳

At the beginning of 1965, despite provisions in the Civil Rights Acts of 1957, 1960, and 1964 designed to protect the right to vote, millions of southern African Americans were still being denied that right. Deciding the time had come to lead in the struggle for voting rights, Dr. Martin Luther King Jr. and his associates joined a Selma, Alabama, voter registration campaign with the intention of provoking a confrontation that would make disenfranchisement the country's predominant legislative issue. Only three hundred thirty-five out of the nine thousand eight hundred seventy-seven registered voters in Selma at the time were black. By mid-February 1965, more than two thousand four hundred blacks who had marched from Selma's Brown Chapel to the Dallas County Courthouse to register to vote had been arrested and jailed by Sheriff Jim Clark, as was King. Following his release, several members of Congress visited King to pledge their support and met with President Lyndon B. Johnson who pledged to send Congress a voting rights bill. Shortly after King returned to Selma, Clark and his deputies arrested one hundred sixty-five black students and used cattle prods and night sticks on a two-mile forced march through the countryside.[1]

King retained the attention of the media as well as Washington by heightening the intensity of the Selma demonstrations and organizing protests in surrounding areas. A February 18 demonstration in nearby Marion turned violent when the local sheriff and Alabama state police attacked protesters, and demonstrator Jimmie Lee Jackson was shot and later died. At Jackson's funeral, King announced plans for a fifty-four-mile march from Selma to the state capitol in Montgomery. On "Bloody Sunday," as it is now known, Alabama state troopers and Sheriff Clark's deputies used clubs, tear gas, and bullwhips to attack six hundred marchers who were crossing Selma's Edmund Pettus Bridge on the road to Montgomery. The March 7 assaults received extensive television and newspaper coverage. Two days later, after accepting a Johnson administration compromise that called for an abbreviated march by the demonstrators and restraint by Alabama troopers, the protesters won a partial victory. That afternoon, King led a second group of marchers that included black and white clergymen across Pettus Bridge to within fifty feet of state troopers. There the demonstrators sang, knelt in prayer, and

then returned to Selma without incident. The peace, however, was short lived. That evening, three white clergymen who had participated in the march were attacked, and one of them, Rev. James Reeb, a Unitarian clergyman from Boston, was killed.[2]

As tension in Selma continued to grow, President Johnson met with Alabama governor George C. Wallace to emphasize that he held him personally responsible for protecting protesters when they marched to Montgomery. It was a responsibility the president would assume if Wallace did not accept it. Two days later, Johnson urged a joint session of Congress to pass a voting rights bill that would "strike down restrictions to voting in all elections—Federal, State, and local—which have been used to deny Negroes the right to vote," and "establish a simple, uniform standard" of voter registration. Most in Congress hailed Johnson's "We Shall Overcome" speech, and a poll showed that a majority of Americans favored his proposal. Under the protection of the federalized National Guard of Alabama, regular army units, and local police, the five-day march to the state capitol concluded on March 25 with King telling a huge crowd that the "confrontation of good and evil compressed in the tiny community of Selma [had] generated the massive power to turn the whole nation to a new course."[3]

Prior to the march, Johnson's voting rights bill was introduced in the House H.R. 6400 and the Senate S. 1564. Hearings on the bills took eight days in the House and nine in the Senate. Afterwards, the administration, in consultation with majority leader Mike Mansfield, D-Mont., and minority leader Everett McKinley Dirksen, R-Ill., agreed to include several amendments suggested at the Senate Judiciary Committee hearings in a substitute bill reported by the committee. The House Judiciary Committee reported an amended bill as well. On the Senate floor, civil rights advocates faced the prospect of a southern filibuster, as they had in pushing the 1964 Civil Rights Act. Once again, Senator Dirksen was the key to defeating the filibuster since conservative Republicans were reluctant to take action that limited Senate debate and thought the voting rights bill granted too much power to the federal government at the expense of the states. Although the expected filibuster never materialized, opponents did attempt to alter the bill's main provisions through numerous unsuccessful amendments.[4]

Activists march from Selma to Montgomery, Alabama, to register to vote. While voting provisions were included in the previous civil rights acts, discrimination and the denial of this right continued throughout the South, ultimately leading to the Voting Rights Act of 1965.
Source: Library of Congress.

Senator Dirksen began the twenty-eight-day debate by asking: "How … shall there be government by the people if some of the people cannot speak? How obtain the consent of the governed when a segment of those governed cannot express themselves? How strange that nearly two centuries after Thomas Jefferson wrote those words into the Declaration of Independence, assuring to the governed a reasonable chance to consent or descent, the problem still vexes the national Government." It is "quite clear that additional legislation is needed if the unequivocal mandate in the Fifteenth Amendment to the Constitution of the United States is to be enforced and made effective and if the Declaration of Independence is to be made truly meaningful." Speaking in opposition, Sen. Sam Ervin, D-S.C., who offered most of the constitutional arguments against the bill, predicted that if the voting rights act was "to be a prototype of the legislation which the American people can expect from Congress in the future, we will not be able to keep the Republic which the Founding Fathers gave us."[5]

During the course of the debate, Mansfield and Dirksen introduced a substitute measure that deleted a controversial provision banning state poll taxes, but Dirksen still had difficulty in gaining support for cloture, the only procedure by which the Senate can, by a three-fifths vote, place a time limit on consideration of a bill. Significant contention still existed between those who wanted an outright ban on poll taxes, and there were those not certain that Congress had the constitutional right to legislate such a ban. Finally, another Mansfield-Dirksen amendment was agreed to that added a congressional declaration that poll taxes infringed on the constitutional right to vote and extended the time for paying them if federal courts upheld their constitutionality. With the poll tax issue resolved, a cloture motion was adopted, 70–30, on May 25, and the bill passed, 77–19, the next day.[6]

House floor debate, which was more perfunctory, momentarily intensified when minority leader Gerald R. Ford, R-Mich., and Rep. William M. McCulloch, R-Ohio, the Judiciary Committee's ranking Republican, accused the president of being a "Lyndon-Come-Lately" to civil rights issues, after he criticized the House for offering a weaker, substitute bill H.R. 7896. While southern segregationists supported the Ford-McCulloch alternative, liberals and moderates rejected it, and H.R. 6400 won, 333–85, later that day. When the conference committee met to resolve the differences between the House and Senate bills, a stalemate ensued after House conferees insisted that legislation, rather than court challenges, be used to abolish poll taxes. The impasse continued for two weeks before King, who strongly favored including a repeal of the poll tax in the voting rights bill, reluctantly agreed with President Johnson to yield on that issue. A modified bill was then reported. It was approved by the House on August 3, 328–74, and the Senate on August 4, 79–18.[7]

At the August 6, 1965, signing ceremony broadcast nationwide from the rotunda of the U.S. Capitol, President Johnson described the Voting Rights Act of 1965 as "one of the most monumental laws in the entire history of American freedom … a victory for the freedom of the American Nation." The act, he declared, would "strike away the last major shackle of those fierce and ancient bonds." The Supreme Court upheld the constitutionality of the Voting Rights Act in *South Carolina v. Katzenbach* (1966) as "rational means to effectuate the constitutional prohibition of racial discrimination in voting."[8] The act was unique in that it departed from the pattern of earlier bills by providing for direct federal action to enable African Americans to register and vote. Today, the Voting Rights Act of 1965 is generally recognized as one of the seminal pieces of legislation enacted by Congress.

SENATOR EVERETT McKINLEY DIRKSEN SUPPORTS THE VOTING RIGHTS ACT OF 1965

APRIL 22, 1965

Mr. President, I can see the Continental Congress in session one hundred eighty-nine years ago. It was June. It was considering a resolution by Richard Henry Lee of Virginia. The purport of the resolution was that the Colonies are and of right should be free and independent states. That resolution was referred to a committee consisting of Jefferson, Adams, Franklin, Roger Sherman, and Robert Livingston. Jefferson undertook the task of formulating a declaration to carry out the sense of that resolution. What he wrote and what was approved was the Declaration of Independence.

How significant it is as a world document and how highly it is esteemed in the American tradition can be noted from the care that has been lavished upon its preservation. First, it was kept in the archives of the State Department. When the British invaded our Capital in 1812, it was removed to Virginia. When it was returned to Washington, it was kept in the Patent Office. Later it was placed in the Library of Congress. Today, it reposes in the National Archives in a glass case, bound in bronze and sealed in helium that light, dampness, or insects will not mar it.

One especial sentiment in that document is appropriate to this occasion. After asserting that man is endowed with certain inalienable, God-given rights, Jefferson then wrote:

Governments are instituted among men, deriving their just powers from the consent of the governed.

What a strange, amazing concept in a world of kings, czars, and emperors who had fastened upon mankind the belief that they rule by divine mandate. Was this a whimsy from the pen of the great Virginian? Was it a mockery or did it have purpose. How well we know that it did have purpose for it became the very foundation of the system of government which the Constitution makers promulgated in Philadelphia eleven years later. In his own way, Abraham Lincoln reaffirmed it at Gettysburg fourscore and seven years later when he expressed the prayerful hope that government of the people, for the people, and by the people would not perish from the earth.

How then shall there be government by the people if some of the people cannot speak? How obtain the consent of the governed when a segment of those governed cannot express themselves?

How strange that nearly two centuries after Thomas Jefferson wrote those words into the Declaration of Independence, assuring to the governed a reasonable chance to consent or dissent, the problem still vexes the National Government.

Can there be any doubt that this is the problem before us? Men are taxed, but not permitted to pass upon those who impose such taxes. Can this be the consent of the governed?

Men are compelled to render military service but not permitted to pass upon those who decree such service. Is that the consent of the governed?

Men are fined and imprisoned under laws dealing with crime and social infractions but not permitted to pass upon the authors of such laws. Is this the consent of the governed?

Men are compelled to send their children to schools which are supported with their taxes but not permitted to pass upon those who make the laws and issue the regulations under which their children are educated. Is this the consent of the governed?

Men pay for a variety of services such as gas, electricity, telephone service, railroad fares, airplane fares, the rates for which are predicated upon laws enacted by men whom they are not permitted to select. Is this the consent of the governed?

Bloody strife and a century of history have brought no solution to the problem. The final fulfillment of the basic concept set forth in the Declaration of Independence has not been achieved. And now, one hundred years to the month after civil strife came to an end, we seek a solution which overrides emotion and sentimentality, prejudice, and politics and which will provide a fair and equitable solution.

This is the fourth civil rights measure to come before Congress in the last eight years. The act of 1957 provided the right to go to court and to secure the aid of the Attorney General in providing injunctive relief where voting rights were denied. It also created the Civil Rights Commission with subpoena power to make investigations in this field and report to the Congress. The act of 1960 enlarged the powers of the Attorney General to investigate and find a pattern or practice under which voting rights were denied and then file suit so that a court could issue an order showing that the plaintiff in the suit was qualified to vote. Then came the Civil Rights Act of 1964 under which three-judge courts could deal with vot-

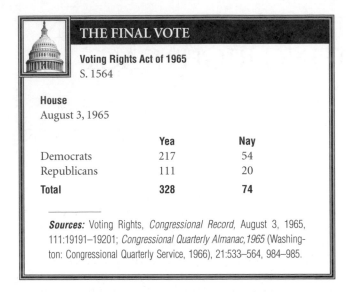

THE FINAL VOTE

Voting Rights Act of 1965
S. 1564

House
August 3, 1965

	Yea	Nay
Democrats	217	54
Republicans	111	20
Total	**328**	**74**

Sources: Voting Rights, *Congressional Record,* August 3, 1965, 111:19191–19201; *Congressional Quarterly Almanac, 1965* (Washington: Congressional Quarterly Service, 1966), 21:533–564, 984–985.

ing rights actions. But discrimination in the matter of voting rights has continued and the data and information collected by the Civil Rights Commission and the Department of Justice makes it quite clear that additional legislation is needed if the unequivocal mandate in the Fifteenth Amendment to the Constitution of the United States is to be enforced and made effective and if the Declaration of Independence is to be made truly meaningful.

Mr. President, that is a preliminary statement. It does not undertake to deal with any analysis of the bill that is before the Senate. That will come later. But I believe that it is necessary to lay down a philosophical predicate that is the inspiration for the endeavor that is before us at the present time. The story could be multiplied ad infinitum. One could deliver a long dissertation, going back to an unsolved problem in the Constitution. The Framers of the Constitution picked the year 1808 in which to continue the importation of persons. Parenthetically, the Constitution does not use the word "slaves" or the word "slavery," but it speaks about the continued importation of persons until 1808, and provides that such importation shall not be denied until that time. The only limitation on that trade was that there could be imposed a $10 capitation tax. So importation continued.

At long last, after fifty years and a bloody strife, that institution came to an end, and those people were here. The question was how to deal with them realistically and recognize the fact that they were human beings. They were people with souls, and they were entitled to equality if the Declaration of Independence and the Constitution meant anything whatsoever.

After that strife came the Thirteenth Amendment abolishing the hideous institution that had grown up in our country.

Then in 1868 came the Fourteenth Amendment, with a further expansion of rights, privileges, and immunities.

Then came the Fifteenth Amendment in 1870. That amendment dealt very specially with citizens of the United States. That is what we are concerned with at the present time. The amendment stated that the right of citizens of the United States to vote shall not be abridged or denied by the United States or any State on account of race or color. That is as short, as explicit, and as clear as the English language could make it.

The authors of the amendment went further. They said that the Congress shall have power by appropriate legislation to enforce the amendment.

It is on the basis of that authority that we proceed with the measure that is now before the Senate.

Mr. President, this has been no easy chore. It has been one of the most difficult, intricate, and abstruse subjects with which I have contact in all of my legislative career. I am not insensible of those requirements by way of the qualification for electors that appears in article I of the Constitution. But I am not insensible either to the mandate in the Fifteenth Amendment and how it shall be consummated and made effective.

It has taken a long time, under the peculiar procedure that has inhibited our action, even to file a document, which I presume I cannot call a "report." It is entitled "Joint Statement of Individual views of Mr. DODD, Mr. HART, Mr. LONG of Missouri, Mr. KENNEDY of Massachusetts, Mr. BAYH, Mr. BURDICK, Mr. TYDINGS, Mr. DIRKSEN, Mr. HRUSKA, Mr. FONG, Mr. SCOTT, and Mr. JAVITS of the Committee

> *But discrimination in the matter of voting rights has continued and … [it is] quite clear that additional legislation is needed if the unequivocal mandate in the Fifteenth Amendment … is to be enforced and made effective and if the Declaration of Independence is to be made truly meaningful.*
>
> — Everett McKinley Dirksen

on the Judiciary, supporting the adoption of Senate 1564, the Voting Rights Act of 1965."

I wish to pay testimony not only to the members of my staff, who are gracing the Senate Chamber today, but also the staff of the majority leader and the staff of the Attorney General, because they worked until the hour of 11:58 last night, two minutes before the deadline that was set for the filing of this report. It is an excellent piece of work. Perhaps in the interest of accuracy I had better strike that word "report" and say "the filing of this document." It is an excellent piece of work. Some time later I intend to read a good deal of the document into the *Congressional Record,* because many hours and weeks of endeavor have gone into the document; and it deserves wider currency than a report or a document usually receives.

Source: *Congressional Record,* 89th Cong., 1st sess., April 22, 1965 (Washington: GPO, 1965), 111:8292–8293.

SENATOR SAM ERVIN OPPOSES THE VOTING RIGHTS ACT OF 1965

MAY 26, 1965

Mr. President, Benjamin Franklin stated at the completion of the work of the Constitutional Convention of 1787:

We have given this country a republic if it can keep it.

I say in all solemnity, and in all sincerity that if the pending bill is to be a prototype of the legislation which the American people can expect from the Congress in the future, we will not be able to keep the Republic which the Founding Fathers gave us. The Founding Fathers were perhaps the best qualified men who ever lived to write a Constitution. They had studied the long and bitter struggle of man for the right of self-government and for freedom from governmental tyranny. They had found these tragic words inscribed upon each page of that history:

No man or set of men can be safely trusted with unlimited governmental power.

This discovery inspired them to write a Constitution which specified the powers that the Federal Government was to take, the powers which the States were to retain, and the rights which the citizens were to have even against Government.

The bill before the Senate does offense not only to constitutional safeguards but also to the essential elements of fair play. The Founding Fathers did not merely define the powers the Federal Government was to take. They wrote into the Constitution specific limitations upon the powers of the Federal Government. One of those limitations appears in section 9 of article I of the Constitution. It states in plain words that Congress shall not have the power to pass a bill of attainder or an ex post facto law.

A bill of attainder is a legislative act which imposes punishment upon named individuals or ascertainable groups of individuals without judicial trial. The bill condemns five States as a whole and parts of two other States without notice,

without an opportunity to be heard, without evidence, and without a trial. By an artificial and deceptive triggering process, it declares that five States and substantial portions of two other States are guilty of violating the Fifteenth Amendment. Thirty-four counties of the State which I have the honor, in part, to represent are condemned by this artificial and deceptive formula of violating the Fifteenth Amendment upon the pretext that the election officials in them use literacy tests to deny citizens the right to vote on the basis of their race or color. That is the condemnation made by the triggering process of the bill. The condemnation is made despite the fact that records assembled by U.S. Civil Rights Commission show that during recent years nine hundred ninety-seven of every one thousand persons of both races who took the literacy in North Carolina were judged literate and were registered to vote.

The administration, through its representative, the Attorney General, demands the passage of the bill. The Attorney General came before the Senate Judiciary Committee and admitted that the Department of Justice had no evidence that any of the thirity-four counties of North Carolina are engaged in violating the Fifteenth Amendment. A tragic day has been reached in the history of the Nation when its chief law officer comes before a committee of Congress and demands that thirty-four counties of my State, which he admits to be innocent, be adjudged guilty of a violation of the Constitution.

When the Attorney General asked why he advocates a bill of this type, he says that the judicial processes are too slow and cumbersome. In other words, he advances as the only argument for the passage of the bill the excuse which a mob gives when it denies a man a fair trial in a court of justice and lynches him.

That excuse goes along very well with the provisions of the bill, because the bill would lynch provisions of the Constitution, which every officer of the Federal Government is bound by a solemn oath or affirmation to support.

I believe that every qualified citizen of every race ought to enjoy the right to vote, and that any election official who wil[l]fully denies him such right ought to be punished. For this reason I offered amendments which would have made it possible to secure the registration of qualified citizens in all areas of the country without substantial delay in a manner consistent with constitutional principles and the essentials of fair play. Unfortunately for good government these amendments were defeated.

When the Constitution divided the powers of government between the Federal Government on the one hand, and the States, on the other, it declared, by section 2 of article I and section 2 of article II of the original Constitution, and by the Tenth Amendment, and by the Seventeenth Amendment, that the power to prescribe qualifications for voting belongs to the States, not to Congress. According to every decision handed down by the Supreme Court of the United States from the beginning of the Republic to this hour, the power which those provisions of the Constitution give to the State to pre-

---

I say in all solemnity, and in all sincerity that if the pending bill is to be a prototype of the legislation which the American people can expect from the Congress in the future, we will not be able to keep the Republic which the Founding Fathers gave us. — Sam Ervin

---

scribe qualifications for voting include the power to establish and to use a literacy test as one of the qualifications for voting.

★ ★ ★ ★

The bill would rob seven States of their power to establish and use literacy tests without notice, without an opportunity to be heard without evidence, and without a trial. It would do so not withstanding the fact that every decision handed down by the Supreme Court on this subject, from the day George Washington took his first oath of office as President of the United States to this very second, has declared that the power to prescribe qualifications for voting, including the power to prescribe a literacy test, belongs to the States under the provisions of the Constitution of the United States.

This being so, the proponents of the bill lay themselves open to the charge that they have no confidence whatever in the judicial stability of the Supreme Court. I say this because the bill can not be adjudged valid by the Court unless it repudiates every decision it has made on the subject.

The proponents of the bill also lay themselves open to the charge that they manifest little confidence in the intellectual integrity of the Supreme Court. This is true because the second section of article I of the Constitution and the Seventeenth Amendment state in simplest words that in order to be eligible to vote for Senators and Representatives in Congress persons must possess the qualifications of electors of members of the most numerous branch of the State legislature. It would have been impossible for the Founding Fathers and those who drafted and ratified the Seventeenth Amendment to have selected clearer words in which to express that all the States of the Union, including Alabama, Georgia, Louisiana, Mississippi, North Carolina, South Carolina, and Virginia, have the power to prescribe who shall vote for Senators and Representatives in Congress within their borders by prescribing the qualifications of those eligible to vote for members of their respective legislatures.

The pending measure would ignore those plain words of the 2d section of article I and the Seventeenth Amendment and deprive seven states of the power which these plain words vest in them to determine the persons eligible to vote for Senators and Representatives in Congress.

Another principle which was written into the Constitution by implication, and, which has been declared by the Supreme Court again and again in matters involving the powers of newly admitted States is that the Constitution of the United States creates a union of States of equal dignity and power.

The pending measure would ignore that constitutional principle and declare that seven States are not States of equal dignity and power with the other forty-three States. Consequently, this is a bill to make the constitutional angels weep. The legislative physicians who have concocted the strange nostrum contained in the bill are unwilling for their States to take their own medicine.

Hence, the bill is cleverly designed to exempt their States from its provisions. It is to be used as an instrument of chastisement for selected areas of the country which it is now politically profitable to chastise and which are without protection against the injustices embodied in the bill unless the Constitution of the United States is still a living document affording them the protection which the pending measure would deny to them.

No action taken in connection with the consideration of the pending bill illustrates in a more glaring manner the attitude which this bill expresses toward constitutional government than the action of the Senate in respect to the amendment designed to rob the State of New York of its constitutional power to prescribe literacy in English as a test for voting in that State.

★ ★ ★ ★

Notwithstanding the Constitution of the United States, which gives the State of New York the power to prescribe lit-

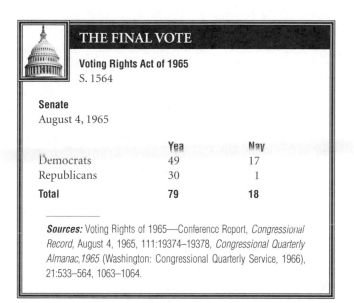

THE FINAL VOTE

Voting Rights Act of 1965
S. 1564

Senate
August 4, 1965

	Yea	Nay
Democrats	49	17
Republicans	30	1
Total	**79**	**18**

Sources: Voting Rights of 1965—Conference Report, *Congressional Record,* August 4, 1965, 111:19374–19378, *Congressional Quarterly Almanac,1965* (Washington: Congressional Quarterly Service, 1966), 21:533–564, 1063–1064.

eracy in English as a prerequisite to the right to vote, and not withstanding all of the decisions of the Supreme Court of the United States placing that interpretation upon the Constitution of the United States, and not withstanding the decisions of the highest court in the state of New York, the court of appeals, and the three-judge Federal court sitting in New York, that New York State had the power under the Constitution to prescribe literacy in English as a prerequisite to the right to vote, the Senate, by an overwhelming vote, incorporated that amendment in the bill.

When the Constitution of the United States was drawn, it divided the legislative powers of government between the Congress on the one hand, and the legislatures of the states on the other. Under the decisions of the Supreme Court of the United States construing that separation of governmental powers, it has been held what ought to be self-evident — that the states of the Union have the same legislative power in the fields assigned to them by the Constitution as the Congress has in the fields assigned to it by the Constitution.

Notwithstanding the plain words of the Constitution and the clear decisions of the courts construing those plain words, that the States have the right to prescribe the qualifications for voting, including a literacy test, and that they have the constitutional power under section 4 of article I of the Constitution to designate the procedures for voting in Federal elections in the absence of express congressional legislation on the subject, the bill before the Senate provides that in seven states legislative acts adopted by those States in the plain exercise of their constitutional power cannot be made effective until they are approved by an executive officer of the Federal government, the Attorney General of thee United States, or by a Federal court sitting in the District of Columbia.

This offends the Constitution because it robs those States of their undoubted power to pass laws and make them immediately effective.

It is also an offense to the constitutional principle that the powers of the Federal Government itself are divided among the Congress, the President, and the Federal courts.

I say this because the bill would vest in the Attorney General what is in essence judicial power.

If Congress can vest power in the Attorney General to pass on the validity of an act of a State legislature before it can become effective in one case, it can vest that power in the Attorney General in all cases. If Congress can vest that power in the Attorney General in respect to seven states, it can vest that power in the Attorney General with respect to all fifty states.

There are more strange things about the bill than time permits me to discuss, but the strangest thing is that the proponents of the bill admit that those of us who oppose it are on sound constitutional ground when we say that the Constitution of the United States gives the States power to prescribe literacy tests.

They also admit that we are on sound constitutional ground when we say that Congress cannot abolish by congressional act any of the powers conferred upon the States by the Constitution.

They say, "We are not doing that. All we are doing is to suspend the power of seven States to use literacy tests as qualifications for voting. We admit that the power to do so is vested in these seven States by the Constitution."

If Congress can suspend any power vested in Alabama by the Constitution, it can suspend any power vested in Kentucky by the Constitution. If Congress can suspend any power vested in Mississippi by the Constitution, it can suspend any power vested in the State of Michigan by the Constitution. If Congress can suspend power vested in North Carolina by the Constitution, it can suspend power vested in all fifty States by the Constitution. I deny the theory which underlies the bill; namely, that Congress can suspend any provision of the Constitution. This theory is utterly inconsistent with the Constitution and utterly repugnant to the reasons which gave it birth.

★ ★ ★ ★

The pending bill is absolutely incompatible with devotion to the rule of law or respect for the judicial process.

Although Congress has created ninety-one Federal district courts in the United States and given them virtually identical jurisdiction in all other instances, this bill provides that only one of the ninety-one Federal district courts, to wit, the District Court of the District of Columbia, can exercise jurisdiction in cases arising under the provisions of the pending bill.

Mr. President, the judicial process was invented by man in his most exalted and most enlightened hour. Its purpose was to repeal the law of the jungle, and establish in its place the law of civilization. The judicial process was invented by man for one purpose and one purpose only — to enable government to perform in a just manner its most sacred task, the administration of justice. The judicial process contemplates that no person, natural or artificial, shall be condemned and punished for alleged wrongdoing without notice, without evidence, without an opportunity to be heard, and without a judicial trial.

The pending bill scarcely pays lip service to the judicial process. It says to each State and to each political subdivision condemned by the triggering device: "You are condemned without notice. You are condemned without evidence. You are condemned without an opportunity to be heard. You are condemned without a judicial trial."

After condemning the State or political subdivision without notice, without evidence, without an opportunity to be heard, and without a judicial trial, the bill then makes false obeisance to the judicial process by saying, in substance, to the condemned State or political subdivision: "While all the other ninety Federal district courts in the United States are closed to you and denied power to harken to your plea, you may journey anywhere from your location, be it 250 or 1,000 miles distant, to the District Court of the District of Columbia, and exonerate yourself from your congressional condemnation if you satisfy such court of two things:

"First. That you have not violated the Fifteenth Amendment in the past, or if you have, you have fully corrected your past violations.

"Second. That you will not violate the Fifteenth Amendment at any time during the foreseeable future."

The bill withholds the substance of the judicial process from those it condemns without notice, evidence, opportunity to be heard, and a judicial trial. I do not know of a worse offense which can be committed by a legislative body than to do what the pending bill would do with respect to the judicial process, to take a process which was created to do justice and pervert it, distort it, and prostitute it, so that justice cannot be done.

Source: *Congressional Record,* 89th Cong., 1st sess., May 26, 1965 (Washington: GPO, 1965), 111:11732–11734.

Notes

1. David J. Garrow, *Protest at Selma: Martin Luther King, Jr., and the Voting Rights Act of 1965* (New Haven, Conn.: Yale University Press, 1978), 39–61; *Congressional Quarterly Almanac, 1965,* (Washington, D.C.: Congressional Quarterly Service, 1966), 21:538–540; Nick Kotz, *Judgment Days: Lyndon Baines Johnson, Martin Luther King, Jr., and the Laws That Changed America* (Boston: Houghton Mifflin, 2005), 250–281; Stephen Tuck, "Making the Voting Rights Act," in *The Voting Rights Act: Securing the Ballot* ed. Richard M. Valelly (Washington, D.C.: CQ Press, 2006), 78–83.

2. Garrow, *Protest at Selma: Martin Luther King, Jr., and the Voting Rights Act of 1965,* 61–91; Kotz, *Judgment Days: Lyndon Baines Johnson, Martin Luther King, Jr., and the Laws That Changed America,* 275–296; Tuck, "Making the Voting Rights Act," 83–85.

3. Quotes are found in U.S. President (Lyndon Johnson), *Public Papers of the Presidents of the United States: Lyndon Johnson, 1965,* 2 vols. (Washington, D.C.: GPO, 1966), 1:283; James Melvin Washington, ed., *A Testament of Hope: The Essential Writings of Martin Luther King, Jr.* (San Francisco: Harper and Row, 1986), 228. See also Garrow, *Protest at Selma: Martin Luther King, Jr., and the Voting Rights Act of 1965,* 99–118; Kotz, *Judgment Days: Lyndon Baines Johnson, Martin Luther King, Jr., and the Laws That Changed America,* 303–325.

4. *Congressional Quarterly Almanac, 1965,* 541–545, 556–559; Garrow, *Protest at Selma: Martin Luther King, Jr., and the Voting Rights Act of 1965,* 145; Kotz, *Judgment Days: Lyndon Baines Johnson, Martin Luther King, Jr., and the Laws That Changed America,* 328–329.

5. "Voting Rights Act of 1965," *Congressional Record,* April 22, 1965, 111:8293; May 26, 1965, 11732.

6. *Congressional Quarterly Almanac, 1965,* 544; Garrow, *Protest at Selma: Martin Luther King, Jr., and the Voting Rights Act of 1965,* 123–127; Stephen F. Lawson, *Black Ballots: Voting Rights in the South, 1944–1969* (New York: Columbia University Press, 1976), 316–318.

7. David S. Broder, "Johnson's Charge Stirs G.O.P. Wrath," *New York Times,* July 13, 1965, 22; Julius Duscha, "LBJ Called Laggard on Rights Issue," *Washington Post,* July 13, 1965, A1; *Congressional Quarterly Almanac, 1965,* 564; Kotz, *Judgment Days: Lyndon Baines Johnson, Martin Luther King, Jr., and the Laws That Changed America,* 330–331; Lawson, *Black Ballots: Voting Rights in the South, 1944–1969,* 319–321.

8. U.S. President (Lyndon Johnson), *Public Papers of the Presidents of the United States, 1965,* 2 vols. (Washington, D.C.: GPO, 1966), 2:840–841, 843; *South Carolina v. Katzenbach, Attorney General,* 383 U.S. 324 (1966). See also 79 Stat. 437–446, P.L. 89–110 (August 6, 1965).

War Powers Resolution of 1973

✷ 1973 ✷

Early in November 1973, nine months before the fallout over the Watergate scandal prompted his resignation, Congress dealt President Richard M. Nixon a stunning political rebuke by overriding his veto of the War Powers Resolution. The intention of the resolution was to limit the president's power to commit U.S. forces abroad without congressional approval. Nixon contended the restrictions it imposed "upon the authority of the President were both unconstitutional and dangerous to the best interests of our Nation," would seriously damage "our ability to respond to international crisis," "undercut the ability of the U.S. to act as effective influence for peace," and would give "every future Congress the ability to handcuff every future President."[1]

Under the Constitution, Congress has the power to declare war and raise and support the armed forces (Article I, Section 8), while the president is commander in chief Article II, Section 2. It is generally agreed that as commander in chief the president has the power to repel attacks against the United States and the responsibility for leading the armed forces. During the Korean and Vietnam Wars, the United States was involved for many years in intense conflict without a declaration of war. While decisions about goals and strategy in both wars were dominated by the president, Congress regularly approved military appropriations and renewed the draft, without which neither war would have continued. By the time the United States pulled out of Vietnam, however, many on Capitol Hill were deeply concerned about the erosion of congressional authority to decide when the nation should become involved in a war or commit armed forces in conflicts that might lead to war. Passage of the War Powers Resolution of 1973 culminated a three-year congressional debate on the issue.

Preceding the floor debate on the Resolution, there were eight days of congressional hearings — six in the Senate and two in the House — to more precisely clarify the competing constitutional claims of Congress and the president. While both the House and Senate conceded that, constitutionally, the president could in an emergency commit U.S. forces abroad without their approval, they differed on how to guarantee Congress participated in the process. The House wanted to require the president: (1) to consult with Congress before sending troops into hostile or possibly hostile situations, or if unable to, to report to Congress within seventy-two hours the rationale and circumstances for his decision; and (2) to remove the troops if Congress did not declare war within one hundred twenty days or specifically authorize the use of force. Anytime during the one hundred twenty days, Congress could direct disengagement by passing a concurrent resolution. The Senate sought to limit unilateral action by the president to three situations: (1) to repel, retaliate, or forestall an armed attack on the United States, its territories, or possessions; (2) to repel, retaliate, or forestall an armed attack on U.S. forces in other locations; and (3) to rescue endangered American citizens in foreign countries or at sea.[2]

The original House-passed bill H.J. Res. 542 required the president to report to the Speaker of the House and president pro tempore of the Senate in writing any commitment or substantial enlargement of U.S. forces abroad within seventy-two hours, placed a one hundred twenty-day limit on the power of the president to send troops into combat without congressional consent, and granted Congress power to stop U.S. troop participation earlier if both houses adopted a concurrent resolution, which would not require presidential approval. President Nixon's declaration of opposition to the "dangerous and unconstitutional" termination timetable in the bill had little effect on the outcome.[3]

The original Senate bill S. 440, approved two days later, spelled out the emergency situations under which the president could commit U.S. forces; set a deadline of thirty days on any U.S. commitment that had not received congressional sanction; and granted Congress the power to stop U.S. troop participation earlier through a congressional act or joint resolution, which required presidential approval or a veto override. After completing action on S. 440, the Senate took up the House bill and voted to substitute the text of S. 244 for the House text.[4]

A conference committee appointed to resolve the differences between the House and Senate versions prepared the compromise measure presented to President Nixon. It included several important concessions by Senate conferees. Instead of using the Senate's delineation of circumstances under which the president could commit U.S. troops abroad,

President Richard Nixon shakes hands with armed forces in Vietnam in July 1969. After the undeclared wars of Korea and Vietnam, Congress wanted more checks on war powers. Three years of debate produced the 1973 War Powers Resolution.
Source: National Archives.

the conferees allowed the president to take such action without specific congressional authorization for up to sixty days, or ninety days if necessary for safe withdrawal of troops. The resolution required the president to notify Congress within forty-eight hours of introducing troops into hostilities. The limit on troop commitments could only be extended if Congress: (1) declared war, (2) specifically authorized its continuation, or (3) was unable to meet as a result of an attack on the United States. The most controversial provision, which many consider unconstitutional, permitted Congress at any time to terminate troop commitments through passage of a concurrent resolution — an action that would not require presidential approval.[5]

On October 10, the House approved the conference committee report, 238–123. Two days later, the Senate vote was 75–20.[6] President Nixon's veto was predictable. Many felt there was little chance of a successful override in the House. Vigorous lobbying by advocates and opponents, an ongoing Middle East crisis, and recent administration calamities, however, left the outcome uncertain. Still fresh were the

memories of Vice President Spiro Agnew's resignation prior to pleading *nolo contendere* (no contest) to criminal charges of tax evasion and money laundering while governor of Maryland, as well as the "Saturday Night Massacre" that led to the resignation of Attorney General Elliot Richardson and Deputy Attorney General William Ruckelshaus because they were unwilling to carry out the president's order to fire Watergate special prosecutor Archibald Cox.

Although the Senate override effort of November 7, 1973 succeeded by a comfortable thirteen-vote margin, 75–18, the House vote a few hours earlier was far more suspenseful. The final House tally was 284–135, just four votes more than the two-thirds majority required by the Constitution. The final exchanges on the House floor were spirited. Rep. Clement J. Zablocki, D-Wis., leader of the chamber's war powers movement, felt Congress had a "historic opportunity to reassert its constitutionally mandated obligation in the area of war powers." He saw the "war powers resolution [as] purely and simply a legitimate effort by Congress to restore its rightful and responsible role under the Constitution." Countering Zablocki's reasoning was Rep. Gerald R. Ford, R-Mich., who would soon be confirmed as former vice president Agnew's replacement. "We cannot deny," Ford declared, "that this bill does not really fashion a partnership. It makes us, the Congress, a partner by inaction. If congress wants to assume the role that is essential for that partnership, we have to redesign the legislation."[7]

In the Senate, Sen. Thomas F. Eagleton, D-Mo., an author of the original Senate bill, portrayed the conference version as giving the president "more authority … than perhaps he ever dreamed he had. Not only President Nixon, but every president of the United States will have at least the color of legal authority, the advance blessing of congress, given on an open, blank check basis, to take us to war. It is a horrible mistake."[8] Speaking for the majority of the Senate that supported the override effort were Sen. John C. Stennis, D-Miss., Sen. Jacob Javits, R-N.Y., Sen. Edmund Muskie, D-Maine, Sen. Mark O. Hatfield, R-Ore., and Sen. Robert J. Dole, R-Kan.

Usually the War Powers Resolution is "described as a concerted effort to 'reassert' congressional prerogatives," presidential scholar Louis Fisher writes, "but it has not halted executive domination over military operations." Supporters hoped it would increase executive accountability and congressional oversight, but both its legitimacy and utility have long been questioned by those both inside and outside Congress. Presidents have consistently maintained that the resolution's consultation, reporting, and congressional authorization requirements amount to an unconstitutional impediment to executive authority. Much of its ineffectiveness arose from the incompatibility of House- and Senate-passed bills. The conferees, under pressure to produce a bill, agreed on compromise language that broadened the power of the president rather than weakened it. Despite objections, two-thirds of each chamber voted to oppose Nixon. To do otherwise, some feared, would be interpreted as an endorsement of the views on executive power advanced in the president's veto message. Others thought it would accelerate demands for Nixon's impeachment. Still others wished to finally prevail after eight unsuccessful override attempts during the Ninety-third Congress.[9]

SENATOR THOMAS F. EAGLETON OPPOSES OVERRIDE OF PRESIDENT'S VETO OF WAR POWERS ACT

NOVEMBER 7, 1973

Mr. President, I rise to speak in support of the President's veto of the so-called war powers bill, and therefore in opposition to the attempt to override it.

The term "war powers" is a generic term dealing with the authority of the President and Congress to commit American Armed Forces into hostilities or into a theater of the world where there is the imminent threat of hostilities. The proposed legislation has had a long and tortuous and, at times, intriguing road. It was three years ago or more when the first war powers bills were introduced, initially by Senator JAVITS, then one by me, and then one by the distinguished Senator from Mississippi (Mr. STENNIS).

The Senate Committee on Foreign Relations held extensive hearings, and a bill was fashioned that defined the parameters of responsibility of the President and Congress.

In essence, the Senate bill said the following: The decision to go to war, under our Constitution, is a decision for Congress to make. That is what Hamilton and Madison, who worked on that section of the Constitution, intended. Fresh from the control of King George, they no longer wanted one man, however decent, however benign, to make the troublesome and difficult decision to commit the United States to war.

They wanted this to be a collective judgment, made by the Congress of the United States, and therefore they reposed in Congress the authority to declare war.

The Senate bill is premised on that sound constitutional precept. And no valid bill can be premised on any other precept and be constitutional. The Senate bill then went on, as it properly had to because of court decisions, and historical precedent to delineate three emergency situations that would permit the President to act on his own without prior authority.

The general premise is that Congress is to declare war. Congress is to decide. But there are three exceptions to that premise recognized in law, and those exceptions were ratified in the Senate bill.

First. An attack on the continental limits of the United States. If we are attacked, the President can respond — obviously so.

Second. An attack on U.S. forces legally deployed abroad — for example NATO. In the case of an attack on our forces in Germany, the President could respond to maintain their self-defense.

Third. The most obscure one, but one that is blessed by previous court decisions — the right to rescue American citizens. The President would have the authority to rescue American nationals abroad in time of danger, but only under carefully circumscribed conditions.

Those were the three limited exceptions in which the President could act under the Senate bill; and even with those limited exceptions, he could act for only a brief period of time — thirty days. If Congress did not ratify the action beyond that time, it would terminate within thirty days. This parameter recognized that the act of repelling attacks is finite and that the defensive action is transformed to an offensive action requiring congressional sanction.

That was the basic thrust of the Senate bill. That was the form it was in when it went to that mysterious conclave called the conference committee. The Senate bill disappeared in conference. What came out is a total, complete distortion of the war powers concept, because what came out has nothing to do with emergency authority of the President. It has nothing to do with the central point of contention over war powers.

There are some precatory words about emergency authority in the conference version, but it is just that, meaningless. It is pious, nonoperative, nonbinding, nonenforceable language. What the conference bill now says is this, and the country had better know it. The country does not know it yet, because the media coverage of the bill still says that this limits the President's war powers. It does not. The bill gives the President of the United States unilateral authority to commit American troops anywhere in the world, under any

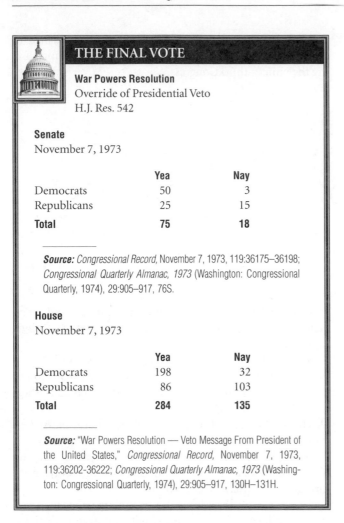

THE FINAL VOTE

War Powers Resolution
Override of Presidential Veto
H.J. Res. 542

Senate
November 7, 1973

	Yea	Nay
Democrats	50	3
Republicans	25	15
Total	**75**	**18**

Source: Congressional Record, November 7, 1973, 119:36175–36198; *Congressional Quarterly Almanac, 1973* (Washington: Congressional Quarterly, 1974), 29:905–917, 76S.

House
November 7, 1973

	Yea	Nay
Democrats	198	32
Republicans	86	103
Total	**284**	**135**

Source: "War Powers Resolution — Veto Message From President of the United States," *Congressional Record*, November 7, 1973, 119:36202-36222; *Congressional Quarterly Almanac, 1973* (Washington: Congressional Quarterly, 1974), 29:905–917, 130H–131H.

conditions he decides, for sixty–ninety days. He gets a free sixty days and a self-executing option for an additional thirty days, making ninety.

Mr. President, the express train already has left to make this bill law. We had to beg another hour to debate the most important question a free society can face — war. And we are going to debate it for two hours. If we are going to debate a pay raise for Senators we debate it for a week, but just two hours on war.

What this bill says is that the President can send us to war wherever and whenever he wants to. Troops could be deployed tomorrow to the Mideast under this bill without prior authority. All the President has to do is to make a telephone call to Senator MANSFIELD and Senator SCOTT and say, "The boys are on the way. I think you should know." Consultation. There they are; sixty to ninety days. Once those troops are committed the history of this country is replete with examples; that once committed they remain.

How sharp can memories be? My God, we just got out of a nightmare that lasted nine years in Southeast Asia in what at the outset was going to be a sort of mop-up action. At the time of the Gulf of Tonkin incident most thought that in sixty

to ninety days we would have that one resolved. Once those troops were committed in August 1964, at the time of the Gulf of Tonkin incident, they remained for nine years. They left nine years later, fifty thousand dead later, over three hundred fifty thousand wounded later, and with the expenditure of so many billions of dollars I cannot add it up; lots of blood, lots of sweat, and lots of tears. Yet we attempt to engrain in this bill the unilateral presidential decisionmaking authority to commit more troops anywhere in the world. The Mideast is the most obvious example in current affairs.

Under this bill the President can commit troops without any ratification by Congress; he can send American troops into Egypt, Syria, Israel, or anywhere else. All he has to do is make the telephone call to Senator MANSFIELD and to Senator SCOTT.

He could commit troops to Chile. Suppose a few weeks ago, at the time of the assassination of President Allende, he had decided that there were vital American interests involved in Chile, and he thinks it is in our interest to have a military presence in Chile. Under this bill the troops could be sent there with no declaration of war by Congress.

This bill attempts by legislation to leave out of the Constitution that provision that says Congress shall declare war. One does not have to be a Harvard lawyer, one does not have to be a Philadelphia lawyer, or a law school graduate; all one needs is to have basic common sense to know that by legislation the Constitution of the United States cannot be amended, but that is what this bill attempts to do.

There is no doubt about what I am saying. It will be refuted by the Senator from New York or some other Senators. The Senator from New York and the Senator from Maine (Mr. MUSKIE) sent around a "Dear Colleague" letter. On page 3 they state:

Nothing in the war powers resolution could have hampered the President in his handling of the recent Middle East crisis. The bill would have allowed the President to put our armed forces on alert, to order movements of our fleets and to resupply the Israelis with military equipment. The bill would have required the President only to report to the Congress within forty-eight hours with respect to the deployment of U.S. Armed Forces in foreign territory, airspace and waters.

Hear that again:

The bill would have required the President only to report to the Congress within forty-eight hour in writing with respect to the deployment of U.S. Armed Forces in foreign territory, airspace and waters.

That is what this bill is all about. It is not mysterious; it is very clear. Despite what has been written and said about it, it does not limit the power of the President of the United States to wage war by himself.

Quite to the contrary. It attempts to emblazon into law, that unilateral decisionmaking process.

I am dumbfounded, because for five years I sat here during the whole evolution of McGovern-Hatfield resolutions, Goodell resolutions, Cooper-Church resolutions; through hundreds of hours of debate, in which Senator after Senator decried the fact that a President had got us involved in a nightmare, and that we should not get involved in such a nightmare again; and that no one man could ever get us involved in a nightmare again; and was not it awful? We debated that question during the five years that I have been here — and the war lasted a total of nine.

With that memory so fresh, how can it be that we would now turn around and sanction the very thing that we castigated for all those years of debate since the original Gulf of Tonkin resolution in August 1964? Were this debate to take place ten years from now, perhaps I might understand. Memories do grow dim with time. We all get a bit forgetful as the rush of events fades from our memory. But how can we forget so quickly? We just cannot forget in the same calendar year in which American troops were withdrawn from Southeast Asia; now, in the same year, within a matter of weeks, how can we give unbridled, unlimited total authority to the President to commit us to war?

We just cannot forget in the same calendar year in which American troops were withdrawn from Southeast Asia; now, in the same year, within a matter of weeks, how can we give unbridled, unlimited total authority to the President to commit us to war?

— Thomas F. Eagleton

In one of the early days after I had come to the Senate, I was seated, having lunch, in the little dining room where Senators sometimes dine. I was so new that I sat at the head of the table by mistake. I sat in the chair that, by custom, was traditionally reserved for the late Senator Richard Russell of Georgia. No one told me to the contrary. Senator Russell came in to eat. He took another chair, he being the very fine gentleman that he was. Finally, somebody winked at me and told me I was in the wrong place. So I traded chairs, but I sat next to Senator Russell.

Somewhere in the conversation, the discussion turned to war, how we get into it, and how hard it is to get out of it. It perhaps is not very well known, but Senator Russell had personal misgivings in the sense of why we were there and what national security interests were being served by our massive presence there.

But he said:

Whatever misgivings I had about that war — and I counseled with President Eisenhower about it in the early days; I counseled with President Kennedy about it; and I counseled with President Johnson about it — whatever misgivings I had, whatever doubts I had, so long as our flag is committed and our troops have been sent, I have got to support those troops and I have to support the flag when the decision is made.

That was what Senator Russell told me. He was a very wise man, one of the wisest ever to serve in this body. Those words of his are better than any I could summon. Once the commitment has been sent, the die is cast.

And the die may be cast for sixty days, ninety days, sixty months, ninety months, or nine years. And if the troops are sent by the President to Egypt, they are there, and more troops will follow, Mr. President, and more planes, and more bombs. If the troops are sent to Chile, more troops will follow. Or if they are sent wherever the President wants them to be sent, because that is what this bill permits him to do, to send them wherever he wants, for whatever reason.

I think this is the most dangerous piece of legislation that I have seen in my brief five years in the Senate. The bill has the name "war powers." It has a nice title. It was nobly conceived, I think, in its inception, but it has been horribly bastardized to the point of being a menace. But we will go ahead, in about an hour and forty-five minutes, and we will override the President's veto.

Some of my colleagues will celebrate. The President has beaten us 8 to 0 so far in the veto league, so some of us are eager for our first victory. And so there will be some handshakes and some jubilation. But what a mistake we are about to make.

If we want to defeat Richard Nixon by overriding this veto, we are going to give him more authority, and legalize it, than perhaps he ever dreamed he had. Not only President Nixon, but every President of the United States, will have at least the color of legal authority, the advance blessing of Congress, given on an open, blank check basis, to take us to war. It is a horrible mistake, Mr. President.

Mistakes are made by mortal men. We all in this body are that, and we have no divine attributes; but most of the mistakes that we make; first, we can live with or; second, can be rectified at a later date. But this kind of mistake will haunt us the rest of our lives.

It will haunt us every time in the future that an American boy dies somewhere in the world in a Presidentially initiated war. The blood of those young men will be ours because we are giving away the authority that sends them to die, and we are giving up the greatest responsibility that the Constitution gives to the Congress — the power to declare war.

Former Under Secretary of State Katzenbach, at the time of his testimony before the Foreign Relations Committee indicated that that provision of the Constitution was outmoded in this atomic, nuclear space age; that these subtle niceties about Congress declaring war were a little antiquated. That may well be. I do not think so, but Mr. Katzenbach did; and if they are, there is a way to change that. Amend the Constitution if we want to say that — if we want to say that in this day and age, only the President has the omniscience to know when and why we go to war. So be it. I would oppose such a method, but that is the way to accomplish it. But this bill is not the method, Mr. President.

Nevertheless, we shall go ahead. But I hope every Member of the Senate who votes on this measure realizes what he is doing. I hope that he is not voting to override simply because this is a way of making the score eight to one.

I hope Senators are not voting to override because they really think they have captured some of the decisionmaking process insofar as war-making is concerned.

If they think they are doing that, Mr. President, they are very, very wrong. I am sure those who vote to override will do it sincerely and with a full and decent heart. Mistakes, as I say, can be made by decent men. Mistakes can be made by men of good will, but still the same, it is a mistake; and that is what this bill in its present form is — a mistake, a serious mistake, a nightmarish mistake.

Source: *Congressional Record,* 93rd Cong., 1st sess., November 7, 1973, 119:36176–36178.

SENATOR JACOB JAVITS FAVORS OVERRIDING THE PRESIDENT'S VETO OF WAR POWERS ACT

NOVEMBER 7, 1973

Mr. President, I have heard with the deepest feeling the views of my colleague from Missouri, and of my colleague from Texas. I assure them, as allegedly the basic author of this measure, that there will be no shallow sense of jubilation tonight. There will be no handshaking, there will be no congratulations, there will be no champagne as in a partisan or common occurrence political victory. This is not that kind of an occasion. This is the most somber and historic business before the American people, and with the war powers resolution's passage, after two hundred years, at least something will have been done about codifying the implementation of the most awesome power in the possession of any sovereignty and giving the broad representation of the people in the Congress a voice in it. This is critically important for we have just learned the hard lesson that wars cannot be successfully fought except with the consent of the people and with their support. That is the essence of our society.

The Vietnam war literally brought this country to its knees because, without going into the technicalities of what Congress might or might not have done to assert its authority, the fact is that on the record it was essentially a Presidential war — as was so viewed around the world. The United States was saved miraculously from disgrace and defeat because the people and the Congress, even though they thoroughly dis-

approved, still exercised the patience to see it liquidated without terribly undue damage. We still do not know what that damage was or may prove to be in history.

All of us who advocated this measure before the Senate, and it has had three years of consideration, with a most tremendous volume of expert testimony given by constitutional authorities and experts of all sorts, extended debate on two occasions in the Senate and then again on the conference report, on all of the very arguments which we hear now made, and which were made then and yet the Senate voted to affirm the conference report 75–20. The Senate acted then 75–20 in the teeth of the President's threat to veto.

That is what he then told the minority leader of the House of Representatives. Notwithstanding this, the House of Representatives passed it by a vote of almost 2–1 and the Senate passed it by a margin of over 3–1.

Now why, Mr. President? Why?

Congress passed it because Members considered it, as I believe we must consider it today, in the light of its terms.

We have had a lot of conversation today, which is interesting and highly rhetorical, but does not go to the terms of the bill. At long last, Congress is determined to recapture for ourselves, the representatives of the people at the state level in the

Senate and as the House did on the local level, the awesome power to make war.

At long last, Congress is determined to recapture for ourselves, the representatives of the people at the state level in the Senate and as the House did on the local level, the awesome power to make war. — Jacob Javits

---

The first point I should like to make is, let us not confuse this with foreign policy.

Foreign policy does not mean war and war does not mean foreign policy unless there is a breakdown or failure of foreign policy.

No one is impairing the President's authority to carry on the foreign policy of the country. But we are affecting materially his authority, in the name of foreign policy, to take the Nation into war. When we judge, by this measure that an incident would become a war, then we, and we alone, have the right to decide that it shall go on into war or that it shall stop. For, the Constitution lays upon the Congress, unmistakably, the responsibility of deciding whether or not the state of our Nation should be changed from peace to war.

We accomplish that in this bill by depriving the President of authority to make that decision himself at the given time when, according to the dictates of experience and history, an incident becomes a war.

The President cannot under the Constitution control us as to war by his power of veto. In that case, Congress would not have any real say, because he would only need one-third plus one of either House to exercise his will against the majority of Congress and the people it represents.

In this bill, we have embodied a methodology — the very word I have used, and the very word that Senator EAGLETON, Senator STENNIS, Senator TAFT, and many other Senators have used — a methodology by which Congress could, if it wished, insert upon its concurrence in the awesome decision of war.

If we analyze the arguments against this measure, they are, that to assure the President the flexibility to carry on the foreign policy of the country, according to the arguments of those who are in Senator TOWER'S school, we must also give him the power to make war on his own.

We say "No."

That is what this is all about.

We say "No."

We say there is a world of difference, a chasm, between carrying on the foreign policy and plunging the Nation into war. If Mr. Brezhnev has the authority do that, we disapprove of it. We disapprove of the system under which Mr. Brezhnev operates. Indeed, if that system can have anything said about it, that is exactly what is threatening the world and what is threatening the detente.

We reject that. The House has rejected it and we should reject it.

That is what is at stake here.

Senator EAGLETON'S arguments confound me and sadden me. They sadden me because he had a big hand in this bill and was really one of its most eloquent advocates.

Specifically, those significant provisions remaining in this bill are essentially his contribution.

The imperfection which is seen in the bill by him and, as I say it saddens me and confounds me, is that we give the President powers he does not have.

On the contrary, we have made crystal clear in section 8(d) that we do not alter the constitutional authority of the Congress or the President. We say it in just so many words.

Beyond that, Mr. President, I must say that the President, after all, is the fellow whose ox is being gored. He is the one who is seeking to protect what he considers to be his prerogatives in respect of the war power.

With respect to this bill, the President of the United States says in his veto message:

> … it would seriously undermine this Nation's ability to act decisively and convincingly in times of international crisis.

By this he means his power is very reduced, and drastically so.

So, the man whose ox is gored and whose power is being affected sees the situation exactly 180 degrees opposite from the way my colleague from Missouri does. It seems to me that that is the best evidence as to whether we are granted additional authority to him.

The President is left with his true, preexisting constitutional authority as Commander in Chief to deploy the forces of the United States, assuming he can get the Congress to raise the forces and to finance them. We do impose a reporting requirement in the case of significant peacetime deployments. It is not just a little piece of paper that we require. It requires that the President shall submit to the Speaker of the House and the President pro tempore of the Senate a report in writing, within forty-eight hours of any unusual, significant peacetime deployment, spelling out the circumstances.

★ ★ ★ ★

Mr. President, he is required to state "the constitutional and legislative authority under which such introduction took place."

That leaves him all the necessary flexibility.

Mr. President, this brings me the part of our letter — Senator MUSKIE'S and mine — to which Senator EAGLETON referred. He did not read far enough.

We said that nothing in the war powers resolution could have hampered the President in his handling of the recent Middle East crisis. He placed our forces on alert as he thought desirable and advisable. But Mr. President, if we read on in that paragraph it says as follows:

> It is important to note that during the recent crisis at no point were United States Armed Forces engaged in hostilities or in situations where imminent involvement in hostilities was clearly indicated by the circumstances. The actions taken by the President related solely to the state of readiness of U.S. Armed Forces and did not involve the provisions of the bill.

Of course, Mr. President, if he had introduced our forces further than he did, in terms of the imminent danger of hostilities or in terms of the actual involvement in hostilities, the bill would have and should have become operative. That is exactly the purpose and intention of the bill and exactly the way it reads.

★ ★ ★ ★

Whatever may be the President's constitutional authority, he has it, whatever it may be. We give him no new grant of constitutional authority. Hence, in terms of the constitutional authority to put our forces into war, I adhere to the construction of the Constitution which says he may only do that where our territory or our forces are in danger.

As a matter of fact, the writers of the Constitution said in the event of "sudden attack." That is quite a separate question, in my judgment, and it has nothing to do with this bill, which neither makes nor unmakes that situation. That is the important point about reading the bill. In my judgment, before the President put forces into those areas, he should come to Congress for its authority, by resolution.

★ ★ ★ ★

We have taken the precaution of reciting in section 2(c), which was hotly debated in conference, what we consider to be a declaration. We could not go the distance that the Senate bill went. If we had tried to do that, we would not be here today; we probably would have no bill. It is far more important in terms of the future of our Nation than to be sticklers on that point.

In section 2(c) we have declared what we understand to be the constitutional authority of the Commander in Chief, and it means in this respect putting our forces in imminent danger of hostilities or in the hostilities, only exercised pursuant, to a declaration of war, specific statutory authorization, or a national emergency created by attack upon the United States, its territories, its possessions, or its Armed Forces.

One of the closely considered questions before the conference was over the omission of the rescue of individual American citizens. Our decision was that we felt that the recital of it was undesirable and unnecessary, in that it was so much a question of degree as to when an incident such as that could be converted into a conflagration that we would rather not state it. If a President felt, under given circumstances, that that was his constitutional authority under the terms of this bill, we could contest it or not in the particular circumstance. Other than that, we did declare, our finding. It is not as strong in this respect as the Senate bill, which actually specified those as the President's emergency powers and no more.

★ ★ ★ ★

I differ deeply, decidedly, and as profoundly as any human being can with the Senator from Missouri that this historic recapture by Congress of its powers is worth running down the drain simply because we have been unable to get that particular statutory definition which the Senator, in my judgment, has permitted to completely obscure what should be our judgment.

★ ★ ★ ★

If the Senate fails to override this veto, we will leave him [the President] the very illimitably claimed power we are trying to curb. So, by the idealism the Senator [from Missouri] thinks he is obeying, he is running the one chance down the drain by which we do something to negate that claim to imperial power.

Source: *Congressional Record,* 93rd Cong., 1st sess., November 7, 1973, 119:36187–36189.

Notes

1. U.S. President, *Public Papers of the Presidents of the United States, Richard Nixon, 1973* (Washington, D.C.: GPO, 1975), 893–895.

2. Louis Fisher, *Constitutional Conflicts Between Congress and the President* (Lawrence: University Press of Kansas, 1997), 279–280. See also U.S. Congress, House Committee on Foreign Affairs, Subcommittee on National Security Policy and Scientific Developments, *War Powers,* hearings, 93rd Cong., 1st sess., March 7, 8, 13, 14, 15, 20, 1973 (Washington, D.C.: GPO, 1973); U.S. Congress, Senate Committee on Foreign Relations, *War Powers Legislation, 1973,* hearings, 93rd Cong., 1st sess., April 11–12, 1973 (Washington, D.C.: GPO, 1973).

3. U.S. President, *Public Papers of the Presidents of the United States, Richard Nixon, 1973,* 893. See also "War Powers of Congress and the President," *Congressional Record,* July 18, 1973, 119:24653–24708; U.S. Congress, House Committee on Foreign Affairs, *War Powers Resolution of 1973,* report to accompany H.J. Res. 542, 93rd Cong., 1st sess., H. Rept. 93-287 (Washington, D.C.: GPO, 1973).

4. "War Powers Act," *Congressional Record,* July 20, 1973, 119: 25093–25120; U.S. Congress, Senate committee on Foreign Relations, *War Powers,* report to accompany S. 440, 93rd Cong., 1st sess. (Washington, D.C.: GPO, 1973).

5. U.S. Congress, Conference Committees, *War Powers,* conference report to accompany H.J. Res. 542, 93rd Cong., 1st sess., H. Rept. 93-547 (Washington, D.C.: GPO, 1973).

6. "War Powers Resolution of 1973 — Conference Report," *Congressional Record,* October 10, 1973, 119:33548–33569; "Conference Report on House Joint Resolution 542, "War Powers Resolution of 1973," *Congressional Record,* October 12, 1973, 119:33858–33874.

7. For quotes see "War Powers Resolution — Veto Message from the President of the United States," *Congressional Record,* November 7, 1973, 119:36202–36204. See also "War Powers Resolution — Veto Message from the President of the United States," *Congressional Record,* November 7, 1973, 119:36202–36222; "War Powers Resolution — Veto Message from the President of the United States," *Congressional Record,* November 7, 1973, 119:36202–36222; "War Powers of Congress and the President," *Congressional Record,* November 7, 1973, 119:36175–36198.

8. "War Powers of Congress and the President," *Congressional Record,* November 7, 1973, 119:36178. See also "War Powers of Congress and the President," *Congressional Record,* November 7, 1973, 119:36175–36198.

9. Louis Fisher, *Presidential War Power,* 2nd ed., rev. (Lawrence: University Press of Kansas, 2004), 145. See also ibid., 145–147; Louis Fisher, "War Power," in *The American Congress: The Building of Democracy* ed. Julian E. Zelizer (Boston: Houghton Mifflin, 2004), 690–692.

Impeachment of President Richard M. Nixon

✳ 1974 ✳

Early in the morning of June 17, 1972, five men were arrested for breaking into the Democratic National Committee headquarters at the Watergate hotel-apartment-office complex in Washington, D.C. The burglars, it turned out, were employees of the Committee for the Reelection of the President (CRP), there to fix bugging equipment placed on phones during an earlier break-in. White House involvement became apparent when police found the White House phone number of E. Howard Hunt on two of the burglars. Officially, the White House had hired Hunt, a former CIA operative, as a part-time security consultant. In actuality, Hunt, together with G. Gordon Liddy, counsel to CRP's Finance Committee, headed a group cryptically called the "plumbers" unit, which was responsible for discouraging and plugging White House information leaks.

Although the media treated the break-in as a minor burglary, the prolonged and bungled cover-up that followed precipitated a political scandal of unprecedented historic proportions. During the ensuing twenty-five months, *Washington Post* reporters Bob Woodward and Carl Bernstein, a federal grand jury, two different special prosecutors, the Senate Select Committee on Presidential Campaign Activities (popularly known as the Senate Watergate Committee), and the House Judiciary Committee unraveled a web of political spying and sabotage. In the process, the American people learned that White House advisors of President Richard M. Nixon, and employees of his reelection committee, had engaged in criminal acts, suppressed civil liberties, levied domestic warfare against political opponents through espionage, created an enemies list, and sought to intimidate the media.[1]

Under the chairmanship of Sen. Sam Ervin, D-N.C., the Watergate Committee played a pivotal role in gathering evidence that led to the indictment of forty members of the Nixon administration. Between May 17 and August 7, 1973, television cameras captured the dramatic testimony of former White House counsel John Dean and other administration officials. Dean, the first presidential aide to accuse Nixon of direct involvement in Watergate, implicated others as well, including former attorney general John Mitchell, who headed CRP. Former White House aide Alexander P. Butter-

field, however, offered the most important revelation — that tape recordings of presidential conversations had been made since early 1971. When Nixon asserted executive privilege in refusing to turn over relevant tapes to the committee or Special Prosecutor Archibald Cox, U.S. District Court judge John J. Sirica, who presided over the Watergate break-in and cover-up trials, ordered the release of tapes containing nine presidential conversations for a private judicial review. The U.S. Court of Appeals subsequently upheld Sirica's August 29, 1973, order two weeks later.[2]

Amidst the continuing battle over the tapes, Vice President Spiro Agnew was accused of having accepted bribes and kickbacks while governor of Maryland. In exchange for an agreement on the part of the Justice Department not to further prosecute the case, Agnew plea-bargained, admitting "*nolo contendere*" (no contest) to a lesser charge of tax evasion, and resigned on October 10, 1973. Two days later, Nixon nominated House minority leader Gerald R. Ford, R-Mich., to be vice president. In accordance with the Twenty-fifth Amendment, Ford was subsequently confirmed by two-thirds of the House and Senate before taking the oath of office on December 6.[3]

While awaiting Ford's confirmation, Nixon announced a "compromise" plan to provide the summaries of Watergate-related tapes. When Special Prosecutor Cox rejected the "compromise," the president directed Attorney General Richardson and his then deputy, William Ruckelshaus, to fire Cox. When both refused and resigned, Solicitor General Robert H. Bork, acting head of the Justice Department, dismissed Cox. The so-called "Saturday Night Massacre" of October 20 precipitated a firestorm of public outrage and the possibility of impeachment began to take shape in Congress. Finally, Nixon agreed to obey Sirica's order, but first a White House lawyer told the court that two of the tapes did not exist, and then a crucial, eighteen and a half-minute portion of one tape, which had never been out of White House custody, was found to have been erased.[4]

Two months later, the House by a 410–4 vote, authorized its Judiciary Committee to investigate whether grounds existed for impeachment of the president. From late February to mid-July 1974, the panel examined the documents and testimony gathered by the Watergate Committee. Meanwhile, Special Prosecutor Jaworski, who had replaced Cox, filed criminal charges against a number of Nixon administration officials. In March, former attorney general Mitchell and several former White House aides, including top presidential aides H. R. Haldeman and John Ehrlichman, were indicted for conspiracy to cover up the Watergate break-in, and the president was named as an unindicted coconspirator.

As the Judiciary Committee's probe continued, Nixon became the first president in American history to be subpoenaed to furnish information to an impeachment inquiry. Also in May 1974, Special Prosecutor Jaworski asked the Supreme Court for a prompt ruling on the president's use of executive privilege to avoid fully complying with subpoenas, and the committee began closed hearings to consider possible grounds for impeachment. On July 24, 1974, in *United States v. Nixon,* 418 U.S. 683, the Court ruled unanimously that the "demands of due process of law in the fair administration of criminal justice" superseded the president's claim of executive privilege, and it ordered him to provide the tapes of sixty-four conversations subpoenaed by Jaworski. That evening, the president announced he would comply with the Court's "decision in all respects."[5]

Less than an hour later, the Judiciary Committee began its final deliberations on the possible impeachment of the president. "Make no mistake about it. This is a turning point, whatever we decide," Chairman Peter W. Rodino Jr., D-N.J., told the committee. "Our judgment is not concerned with an individual but with a system of constitutional government," he said. Rep. Trent Lott, R-Miss., in defense of Nixon, argued there was "not one iota of evidence that the President had any prior knowledge whatsoever of the Watergate break-in" or participated "in the Watergate coverup." Conversely, Rep. Lawrence J. Hogan, R-Md., found it "impossible … to condone or ignore the long train of abuses to which [Nixon] has subjected the Presidency and the people of this country.… I cannot, in good conscience, turn away from the evidence of evil that is to me so clear and compelling." Another speech, by Rep. Barbara Jordan, D-Tex., catapulted her to

Make no mistake about it. This is a turning point, whatever we decide. Our judgment is not concerned with an individual but with a system of constitutional government.
— Peter W. Rodino Jr.

instant nationwide fame. Jordan declared, "I am not going to sit here and be an idle spectator to the diminution, the subversion, the destruction of the Constitution" by the president

and his administration. She then in methodical and determined tones unfolded the constitutional standards the president appeared to have violated.[6]

Altogether, the committee spent nearly thirty-six hours over a six-day period debating proposed impeachment articles. On July 27, the panel voted 27–11 to recommend the first article of impeachment against the president (obstruction of justice). Second (abuse of power) and third (contempt of Congress) articles were passed on July 29 and July 30, by votes of 28–10 and 21–17, respectively. House floor debate on the articles was scheduled to begin two weeks later, but the August 5 release of three transcripts of conversations between Nixon and Haldeman less than a week after the Watergate break-in left even his most ardent supporters stunned. The so-called "smoking gun tape" of June 23, 1973, showed direct involvement of the president in the cover-up of the Watergate burglary and provided incontrovertible evidence of his leading role in the obstruction of justice. On the evening of August 8, he told a national television audience of his decision to relinquish the presidency. At noon on the following day, Vice President Ford, who was sworn in as the nation's thirty-eighth president, became the only person to serve as the chief executive without having been elected either

President Richard M. Nixon announces his resignation in a television address on August 8, 1974. Nixon resigned before Congress could impeach him over the Watergate scandal.
Source: The Granger Collection, New York.

president or vice president. Although Nixon's resignation obviated the need for an impeachment, criminal prosecution was still a possibility until President Ford pardoned him on September 8.[7]

That November, the fallout from Watergate helped the Democrats gain five seats in the Senate and forty-nine in the House. Later, Congress approved legislation that made exten-sive changes in campaign financing, and in 1986, passed the Freedom of Information Act, which required new financial disclosures by key government officials. The scandal also inspired the mass media to became far more aggressive in reporting on the activities of politicians and prompted the frequent use of the suffix "gate" to subsequent episodes of political corruption.

HOUSE JUDICIARY COMMITTEE DEBATES THE IMPEACHMENT OF PRESIDENT RICHARD M. NIXON, AND REPRESENTATIVE PETER W. RODINO JR., CHAIRMAN OF THE HOUSE JUDICIARY COMMITTEE, SPEAKS ON IMPEACHMENT

JULY 24, 1974

Before I begin, I hope you will allow me a personal refer-ence. Throughout all of the painstaking proceedings of this committee, I as the chairman have been guided by a simple principle, the principle that the law must deal fairly with every man. For me, this is the oldest principle of democracy. It is this simple, but great principle which enables man to live justly and in decency in a free society.

It is now almost fifteen centuries since the Emperor Jus-tinian, from whose name the word "justice" is derived, estab-lished this principle for the free citizens of Rome. Seven centuries have now passed since the English barons pro-claimed the same principle by compelling King John, at the point of the sword, to accept a great doctrine of Magna Carta, the doctrine that the king, like each of his subjects, was under God and the law.

Almost two centuries ago the Founding Fathers of the United States reaffirmed and refined this principle so that here all men are under the law, and it is only the people who are sovereign. So speaks our Constitution, and it is under our Constitution, the supreme law of our land, that we proceed through the sole power of impeachment.

We have reached the moment when we are ready to debate resolutions whether or not the Committee on the Judiciary should recommend that the House of Representatives adopt articles calling for the impeachment of Richard M. Nixon.

Make no mistake about it. This is a turning point, what-ever we decide. Our judgment is not concerned with an indi-vidual but with a system of constitutional government.

It has been the history and the good fortune of the United States, ever since the Founding Fathers, that each generation of citizens, and their officials have been, within tolerable limits, faithful custodians of the Constitution and of the rule of law.

For almost two hundred years every generation of Amer-icans has taken care to preserve our system, and the integrity of our institutions, against the particular pressures and emer-gencies to which every time is subject.

This committee must now decide a question of the highest constitutional importance. For more than two years, there have been serious allegations, by people of good faith and sound intelligence, that the President, Richard M. Nixon, has com-mitted grave and systematic violations of the Constitution.

Last October, in the belief that such violations had in fact occurred, a number of impeachment resolutions were introduced by Members of the House and referred to our committee by the Speaker. On February 6, the House of Rep-resentatives, by a vote of 410–4, authorized and directed the Committee on the Judiciary to investigate whether sufficient grounds exist to impeach Richard M. Nixon, President of the United States.

THE FINAL VOTE

House Judiciary Committee Recommends
Three Articles of Impeachment

Article 1. Obstruction of Justice
July 27, 1974

	Yea	Nay
Democrats	21	0
Republicans	6	11
Total	**27**	**11**

Article 2. Abuse of Power
July 29, 1974

	Yea	Nay
Democrats	21	0
Republicans	7	10
Total	**28**	**10**

Article 3. Contempt of Congress
July 30, 1974

	Yea	Nay
Democrats	19	2
Republicans	2	15
Total	**21**	**17**

Source: U.S. Congress, House Committee on the Judiciary, *Debate on Articles of Impeachment*, 93rd Cong., 2nd sess., hearings, July 27, 29, and 30, 1974, 329–331, 445–447, 488–489; "Impeachment: 3 Articles Sent to House Floor," *Congressional Quarterly Weekly Report*, August 3, 1974, 32:2018–2021.

The Constitution specifies that the grounds for impeachment shall be, not partisan consideration, but evidence of "treason, bribery, or other high crimes and misdemeanors."

Since the Constitution vests the sole power of impeachment in the House of Representatives, it falls to the Judiciary Committee to understand even more precisely what "high crimes and misdemeanors" might mean in the terms of the Constitution and the facts before us in our time.

The Founding Fathers clearly did not mean that a President might be impeached for mistakes, even serious mistakes, which he might commit in the faithful execution of his office. By "high crimes and misdemeanors" they meant offenses more definitely incompatible with our Constitution.

The Founding Fathers, with their recent experience of monarchy and their determination that government be accountable and lawful, wrote into the Constitution a special oath that the President, and only the President, must take at his inauguration. In that oath, the President swears that he will take care that the laws be faithfully executed.

The Judiciary Committee has for seven months investigated whether or not the President has seriously abused his power, in violation of that oath and the public trust embodied in it.

We have investigated fully and completely what within our constitution and traditions would be grounds for impeachment. For the past ten weeks, we have listened to the presentation of evidence in documentary form, to tape recordings of nineteen Presidential conversations, and to the testimony of nine witnesses called before the entire committee.

We have provided a fair opportunity for the President's counsel to present the President's views to the committee. We have taken care to preserve the integrity of the process in which we are engaged.

We have deliberated. We have been patient. We have been fair. Now, the American people, the House of Representatives, the Constitution, and the whole history of our Republic demand that we make up our minds.

As the English statesman, Edmund Burke said during an impeachment trial in 1788: "It is by this tribunal that statesmen who abuse their power are accused by statesmen and tried by statesmen, not upon the niceties of a narrow jurisprudence, but upon the enlarged and solid principles of state morality."

Under the Constitution and under our authorization from the House, this inquiry is neither a court of law nor a partisan proceeding. It is an inquiry which must result in a decision — a judgment based on the facts.

In his statement of April 30, 1973, President Nixon told the American people that he had been deceived by subordinates into believing that none of the members of his administration or his personal campaign committee were implicated in the Watergate break-in, and that none had participated in efforts to cover up that illegal activity.

A critical question this committee must decide is whether the President was deceived by his closest political associates or whether they were in fact carrying out his policies and decisions. This question must be decided one way or the other.

It must be decided whether the President was deceived by his subordinates into believing that his personal agents and key political associates had not been engaged in a systematic coverup of the illegal political intelligence operation, of the identities of those responsible, and of the existence and scope of other related activities; or whether, in fact, Richard M. Nixon, in violation of the sacred obligation of his constitutional oath, has used the power of his high office for over two years to cover up and conceal responsibility for the Watergate burglary and other activities of a similar nature.

In short, the committee has to decide whether in his statement of April 30 and other public statements the President was telling the truth to the American people, or whether that statement and other statements were part of a pattern of conduct designed not to take care that the laws were faithfully executed, but to impede their faithful execution for his political interest and on his behalf.

There are other critical questions that must be decided. We must decide whether the President abused his power in the execution of his office.

The great wisdom of our founders entrusted this process to the collective wisdom of many men. Each of those chosen to toil for the people at the great forge of democracy — the House of Representatives — has a responsibility to exercise independent judgment. I pray that we will each act with the wisdom that compels us in the end to be but decent men who seek only the truth.

Let us be clear about this. No official, no concerned citizen, no Representative, no member of this committee, welcomes an impeachment proceeding. No one welcomes the day when there has been such a crisis of concern that he must decide whether "high crimes and misdemeanors," serious abuses of official power or violations of public trust, have in fact occurred.

Let us also be clear. Our own public trust, our own commitment to the Constitution, is being put to the test. Such tests, historically, have come to the awareness of most peoples too late — when their rights and freedoms under the law were already so far in jeopardy and eroded that it was no longer in the people's power to restore constitutional government by democratic means.

Let us go forward. Let us go forward into debate in good will, with honor and decency, and with respect for the views of one another. Whatever we now decide, we must have the integrity and the decency, the will, and the courage to decide rightly.

Let us leave the Constitution as unimpaired for our children as our predecessors left it to us.

Source: U.S. Congress, House Committee on the Judiciary, *Debate on Articles of Impeachment,* 93rd Cong., 2nd sess., hearings, July 24, 1974 (Washington, D.C.: GPO, 1974), 1–4.

REPRESENTATIVE LAWRENCE J. HOGAN SUPPORTS IMPEACHMENT

JULY 25, 1974

More than a century ago, in a time of great national trial, Abraham Lincoln told a troubled and bitterly divided Nation: "We cannot escape history. We of this Congress and this administration will be remembered in spite of ourselves. No personal significance or insignificance can spare one or another of us. The fiery trial through which we pass will light us down in honor or dishonor to the last generation."

Today, we are again faced with a national trial. The American people are troubled and divided again, and my colleagues on this committee know full well that we cannot escape history, that the decision we must jointly make will itself be tested and tried by our fellow citizens and by history itself.

The magnitude of our mission is awesome. There is no way to understate its importance, nor to mistake its meaning. We have unsheathed the strongest weapon in the arsenal of congressional power; we personally, members of this committee, have felt its weight, and have perceived its dangers.

The Framers of the Constitution, fearing an Executive too strong to be constrained from injustice or subject to reproof, arrayed the Congress with the power to bring the Executive into account, and into peril of removal, for acts of, "treason, bribery, or other high crimes and misdemeanors." Now, the

first responsibility facing members of this committee was to try to define what is an impeachable offense is. The Constitution does not define it. The precedents which are sparse do not give us any real guidance as to what constitutes an impeachable offense. So each of us in own conscience, in our own mind, in our own heart, after much study, had to decide for ourselves what constitutes an impeachable offense. Obviously, it must be something so grievous that it warrants the removal of the President of the United States from office. I do not agree with those that say an impeachable offense is anything that Congress wants it to be and I do not agree with those who say that it must be an indictable offense. But somewhere in between is the standard against which we must measure the President's conduct.

There are some who say that he should be impeached for the wrongdoing of his aides and associates. I do not concur in that. I think we must find personal wrongdoing on his part if we are going to justify his impeachment.

The President was elected by an overwhelming mandate from the American people to serve as their President for four years and we obviously must be very, very cautious as we attempt to overturn this mandate and the historic proportions that this deliberation has. After a member decides what to his mind constitutes an impeachable offense he then has to decide what standard of proof he would use in trying to determine whether or not the President of the United States had committed an impeachable offense. Now, some have said that we are analogous to a grand jury and a grand juror only need find probable cause that a criminal defendant had committed an offense in order to send the matter to trial. But because of the vast ramifications of this impeachment, I think we need to insist on a much higher standard. Our counsel recommended clear and convincing proof. That is really the standard for civil liability, that or a preponderance of evidence, and I think we need a higher standard than that when the question is removing the President of the United States from office.

So I came down myself to the position that we can have no less a standard of proof than we insist on when a criminal trial is involved, where to deny an individual of his liberty we insist that the case against him be proved beyond a reasonable doubt. And I say that we can insist on no less when the matter is of such overriding import as this impeachment proceeding.

I started out with a presumption of innocence for the President because every citizen of this country is entitled to a presumption of innocence, and my fight for fairness on this committee is obvious to my thirty-seven friends and colleagues who I think will corroborate that I was as outspoken as every member — any member of this committee in calling our very fine staff to task when I thought they were demonstrating bias against the President, when I thought they were leaving from the record parts of the evidence which were exonerating of the President. I thought with the chairman and the majority, with some of colleagues on this side, insisting that every element of fairness be given to the President, that his counsel should sit in on deliberation and offer arguments and evidence and call witnesses and my friend from Alabama mentioned that earlier, Mr. Flowers. But he will also have to confess that most of these concessions to fairness were made only after partisan dispute and debate which is what our whole legislative process is about in the Congress.

So I do not concede to anyone on this committee any position of fighting harder and stronger that the President get a fair hearing of the evidence and while I do have some individual specific objections to isolated incidents of unfairness, I think on the whole, the proceeding has been fair.

Now, I am a Republican. Party loyalty and personal affection and precedents of the past must fall, I think, before the arbiter of men's actions, the law itself. No man, not even the President of the United States, is above the law. For our system of justice and our system of government to survive, we must pledge our highest allegiance to the strength of the law and not to the common frailties of men.

Now, a few days ago, after having heard and read all the evidence and all the witnesses and the arguments by our own

staff and the President's lawyer, I came to a conclusion, and I felt that the debates which we began last night were more or less pro forma and I think they have so far indicated that. I feel that most of my colleagues before this debate began had made up their mind on the evidence, and I did, so I saw no reason to wait before announcing the way I felt and how I was going to vote.

No man, not even the President of the United States, is above the law. For our system of justice and our system of government to survive, we must pledge our highest allegiance to the strength of the law and not to the common frailties of men. — Lawrence J. Hogan

---

I read and reread and sifted and tested the mass of information and then I came to my conclusion, that Richard Nixon has beyond a reasonable doubt committed impeachable offenses which in my judgement, are of sufficient magnitude that he should be removed from office.

Now, that announcement was met with a great deal of criticism from friends, from Government officials, from colleagues in Congress. I was accused of making a political decision. If I had decided to vote against impeachment, I venture to say that I would also have been criticized for making a political decision. One of the unfortunate things about being in politics is that everything you do is given evil or political motives. My friend from Alabama, Mr. Flowers, said that the decision that we make is one that we are going to have to live with the rest of our lives. And for anyone to think that this decision could be made on a political basis with so much at stake is something that I personally resent.

It is not easy to [align] myself against the President, to whom I gave my enthusiastic support in three presidential campaigns, on whose side I have stood in many a legislative battle, whose accomplishments in foreign and domestic affairs I have consistently applauded.

But it is impossible for me to condone or ignore the long train of abuses to which he has subjected the Presidency and the people of this country. The Constitution and my own oath of office demand that I "bear true faith and allegiance" to the principles of law and justice upon which this Nation was founded, and I cannot, in good conscience, turn away from the evidence of evil that is to me so clear and compelling.

Source: U.S. Congress, House Committee on the Judiciary, *Debate on Articles of Impeachment*, 93rd Cong., 2nd sess., hearings, July 25, 1974 (Washington, D.C.: GPO, 1974), 61–63.

REPRESENTATIVE TRENT LOTT FINDS GROUNDS FOR IMPEACHMENT LACKING

JULY 25, 1974

This has truly been an awesome, time-consuming and exhausting task, and I really wonder if any of us here really can appreciate what this moment in history could mean to the future of our country. And while at various points along the way I have really been somewhat disgusted with this committee's proceedings, such as when we spent an hour earlier this week trying to decide not whether or not to have television cameras, but whether or not to have lights for the television cameras. I must admit in all candidness that it has been very fair and I must take this opportunity to thank the chairman for his consideration of this particular member.

And also, Mr. Chairman, I was particularly impressed with several of the comments that you made in your opening statement last night. And I would like to refer to those.

> Make no mistake about it, this is a turning point whatever we decide. Our judgment is not concerned with an individual, but with a system of constitutional government.

I believe that.
Further quoting:

> For almost two hundred years, every generation of Americans has taken care to preserve our system and the integrity of our institutions against the particular pressures and emergencies to which every time is to that subject.

And I subscribe to that.
Quoting further:

> The Founding Fathers clearly did not mean that a President might be impeached for mistakes, even serious mistakes.

These quotes I would like to direct some of my attention to. But first, let me go back and put our present situation into the proper perspective. We are now in the final stages of review of some fifteen months of the most intensive investigation of any President of the United States, perhaps of any man. The Senate select committee or the Watergate Committee spent some months and over $2 million in its investigation. The grand jury in Washington, D.C., has spent over $225,000 in their proceedings since June 1972. The Special Prosecutors have been at their task since May 1973 and at a cost of over $2.8 million. And the House Judiciary Committee staff of some 100 have been working since January at a cost of over $1.17 million.

There are reams of paper, thousands of pages, volumes of material, grand jury evidence, other congressional committee investigation papers and transcripts, tapes, logs, handwritten memos, and on, and on, and on. The sheer weight in pounds is overwhelming.

Could any man withstand such scrutiny, could any man go through all of this without some evidence of a questionable statement under pressure, or while frustrated, or even without revealing some mistakes? I submit no. And where was the similar counterbalancing presentation of the other side of the story? Was the whole picture revealed properly? Was it in the Senate Watergate Committee? No.

Was it in the grand jury or even in this committee? In this committee the staff was nonpartisan, and I must give credit where credit is due, for a fair presentation, until, of course, very recently and that is understandable. But, except for a last-minute shift in the minority counsel, the arguments against impeachment, the cons, the other side of the story, would not have been presented.

Yes, the President's counsel, James St. Clair, was properly allowed to sit in this presentation of evidence and eventually to participate on a limited basis. His was the only argument on behalf of the President until the last presentation by Mr. Garrison. However, he was the President's counsel, not the committee counsel, not my counsel.

There was not a staff structure for a balanced presentation, in my opinion, and perhaps I share the blame for that.

An interesting aside is the fact that, as I get into procedure, is that last night at 7:30 we received the proposed articles of impeachment, the night the debate began. Quite often we have been faced with being hit at the last minute with what we are fixing to vote on, but regardless of that, we are now preparing to vote on articles of impeachment.

I have tried to maintain a restrained position because I think it has been incumbent upon every member to listen and keep his mouth shut until he had enough to make his decision. But, I must also be frank in saying that I have approached this task from the standpoint that the President was innocent, like any man, under such proceedings, and should be presumed innocent until there was clear and convincing evidence to the contrary. You cannot impeach a

President because you don't like his philosophy, or on the basis of innuendo or contradicted evidence.

In my opinion, you cannot impeach a President for a half a case, or on the basis of parts of several cases put together.

And we are not faced with impeaching John Dean or John Mitchell, or Magruder or any of these others. We are faced with impeaching the President. The line must be drawn directly to the President, clearly to the President.

This has not been done.

The President had several aides that served him and this country poorly. The legal processes are now dealing with them. But, for every bit of evidence implicating the President, there is evidence to the contrary. What is at stake here is the Presidency, and this is what has worried me all along.

In my part of the country we do worry about these institutions, we do still hold institutions that made this grand country great, dear, and important. We have to consider the best interests of this country now and in the long run. We cannot allow political considerations or circumstantial evidence to be the basis for impeaching the first President of the United States in over one hundred years. And I might add, in so many ways, the best President in that period of time.

I think this is a classic example here of how perhaps all of us in this committee have gotten so deep in the forest that we

---

We cannot allow political considerations or circumstantial evidence to be the basis for impeaching the first President of the United States in over one hundred years. And I might add, in so many ways, the best President in that period of time. — Trent Lott

---

have lost sight of the forest. We are now analyzing every diseased tree and I think we have got to look beyond that.

Let us take a look at a couple of specifics. There is not one iota of evidence that the President had any prior knowledge whatsoever of the Watergate break-in. And I don't want to get into quoting half a passage. But I guess we could do that on each one, one would be quoting something and the other to the contrary and that's my point. So much contradicting evidence.

The President himself, in the transcript of March 13, referred to the Watergate break-in like this. "What a stupid thing, pointless. That was the stupid thing."

The President did not participate in the Watergate coverup. True, he did not immediately throw all possibly involved immediately to the wolves. Would you, without knowing all of the facts [dismiss] your principle aide?

But, upon learning from Dean on March 21 the real seriousness of what was happening, he started taking a series of actions to find really what the truth, the whole story, was. The President on March 22 said that Hunt could not demand blackmail money, they just wouldn't go along with that, and he instructed Dean to prepare a report for him of what had really gone on. He never got that report.

The Attorney General was advised to report directly to the President. Members of the White House were instructed to go to the grand jury and to tell the truth. I think it is important that you have got to look at what eventually happened. I think that you must consider the fact that the President waived executive privilege for his closest aides, including his counsel.

That is what really happened.

And we could go on, and on and on.

With regard to Ellsberg's psychiatrist break-in, Charles Colson testified before this committee that he was convinced that the President did not know in advance of the break-in.

I will make no comment on the part of the article that deals with the contempt of Congress charge because I think it is so ludicrous that it deserves no comment.

Now, what is really the genesis of all of this? What was the beginning of the whole thing? Now, I am not saying that or other things weren't important and I had my difficult moments, particularly with the conversation of March 21, which I have satisfied myself that the President did not order that payment.

But, the beginning really was with the bombing of Cambodia and the impoundment of funds. And look at that. The bombing of Cambodia led to the eventual end of the longest war in this country's history. It was one of the important ingredients.

And then impoundment. Presidents have been impounding funds since Thomas Jefferson, and Kennedy and Johnson both percentage-wise impounded more than President Nixon. I think it is interesting in a recent article in the *Washington Post* of August 2, 1971, where it came out that under the Kennedy administration, through Assistant Attorney General Burke Marshall there was a plan called Stick it to Mississippi, my home State.

"Stick it to Mississippi." Remember that. And what was involved was the impoundment of funds on some three dozen projects to force Mississippi to comply with certain Justice Department decrees and court decrees. It is impoundment. It is impoundment any way you look at it. But, when it is impoundment of some other area, then it is a different horse.

Now, many of those here have talked about the youth of America, and although I have grown older in the last few months, I guess I am still the youngest member of this committee. And I have been concerned at what impact Watergate would have on the young people of America. But, I think maybe in the final analysis they see all of this more clearly than we do. And I really think the young people that I have talked to, and I have talked to a lot of them, have dedicated themselves to making this system better by working within the system. And no matter what we finally do in Congress, the Presidency will be treated more carefully by future Presidents. So I think we must take care to see that we don't do irreparable damage to the longest single existing form of government in the history of man.

My question, in the final analysis, will be this: As strongly as I, as I disapproved of the policies of President Kennedy and Johnson, would I have voted to impeach them based on the evidence before this committee.

Source: U.S. Congress, House Committee on the Judiciary, *Debate on Articles of Impeachment*, 93rd Cong., 2nd sess., hearings, July 25, 1974 (Washington, D.C.: GPO, 1974), 86–90.

REPRESENTATIVE BARBARA JORDAN ARGUES IN FAVOR OF IMPEACHMENT

JULY 25, 1974

Earlier today we heard the beginning of the Preamble to the Constitution of the United States, "We, the people." It is a very eloquent beginning. But when that document was completed on the 17th of September in 1787 I was not included in that "We, the people." I felt somehow for many years that George Washington and Alexander Hamilton just left me out by mistake. But through the process of amendment, interpretation and court decision I have finally been included in "We, the people."

Today, I am an inquisitor, I believe hyperbole would not be fictional and would not overstate the solemness that I feel right now. My faith in the Constitution is whole, it is complete, it is total. I am not going to sit here and be an idle spectator to the diminution, the subversion, the destruction of the Constitution.

"Who can so properly be the inquisitors for the nation as the representatives of the nation themselves?" (*Federalist Papers* No. 65). The subject of its jurisdiction are those offenses which proceed from the misconduct of public men. That is what we are talking about. In other words, the jurisdiction comes from the abuse of violation of some public trust. It is wrong, I suggest, it is a misreading of the Constitution for any member here to assert that for a member to vote for an Article of Impeachment means that that member must be convinced that the President should be removed from office. The Constitution doesn't say that. The powers relating to impeachment are an essential check in the hands of this body, the legislature, against and upon the encroachment of the Executive. In establishing the division between the two branches of the legislature, the House and the Senate, assigning to the one the right to accuse and to the other the right to judge, the Framers of this Constitution were very astute. They did not make the accusers and the judges the same person.

We know the nature of impeachment. We have been talking about it a while now. "It is chiefly designed for the President and his high ministers" to somehow be called into account. It is designed to "bridle" the Executive if he engages in excesses. "It is designed as a method of national inquest into the conduct of public men" (Hamilton, *Federalist Papers* No. 65). The Framers confined in the Congress the power if need be, to remove the President in order to strike a delicate balance between a President swollen with power and grown tyrannical; and preservation of the independence of the Executive. The nature of impeachment is a narrowly channeled exception to the separation of powers maxim, the Federal Convention of 1787 said that. It limited impeachment to high crimes and misdemeanors and discounted and opposed the term, "maladministration." "It is to be used only for great misdemeanors," so it was said in the North Carolina ratification convention. And in the Virginia ratification convention: "We do not trust our liberty to a particular branch. We need one branch to check the others."

The North Carolina Ratification Convention: "No one need be afraid that officers who commit oppression will pass with immunity."

"Prosecutions of impeachments will seldom fail to agitate the passions of the whole community," said Hamilton in the *Federalist Papers* No. 65. "And to divide it into parties more or less friendly or inimical to the accused." I do not mean political parties in that sense.

The drawing of political lines goes to the motivation behind impeachment; but impeachment must proceed within the confines of the constitutional term, "high crimes and misdemeanors."

Of the impeachment process, it was Woodrow Wilson who said that "nothing short of the grossest offenses against the plain law of the land will suffice to give them speed and effectiveness. Indignation so great as to overgrow party interest may secure conviction; but nothing else can."

Commonsense would be revolted if we engaged upon this process for petty reasons. Congress has a lot to do. Appropriations, tax reform, health insurance, campaign finance reform, housing, environmental protection, energy sufficiency, mass transportation. Pettiness cannot be allowed to stand in the face of such overwhelming problems. So today we are not being petty. We are trying to be big because the task we have before us is a big one.

This morning in a discussion of the evidence we were told that the evidence which purports to support the allegations of misuse of the CIA by the President is thin. We are told that that evidence is insufficient. What that recital of the evidence this morning did not include is what the President did know on June 23, 1972. The President did know that it was Republican money, that it was money from the Committee for the Re-Election of the President, which was found in the possession of one of the burglars arrested on June 17.

What the President did know on June 23 was the prior activities of E. Howard Hunt, which included his participation in the break-in of Daniel Ellsberg's psychiatrist, which included Howard Hunt's participation in the Dita Beard ITT affair, which included Howard Hunt's fabrication of cables designed to discredit the Kennedy administration.

We were further cautioned today that perhaps these proceedings ought to be delayed because certainly there would be new evidence forthcoming from the President of the United States. There has not even been an obfuscated indication that this committee would receive any additional materials from the President. The committee subpoena is outstanding and if the President wants to supply that material, the committee sits here.

That fact is that on yesterday, the American people waited with great anxiety for eight hours, not knowing whether their President would obey an order of the Supreme Court of the United States.

At this point I would like to juxtapose a few of the impeachment criteria with some of the President's actions.

Impeachment criteria: James Madison, from the Virginia Ratification Convention. "If the President be connected in any suspicious manner with any person and there be grounds to believe that he will shelter him, he may be impeached."

We have heard time and time again that the evidence reflects payment to the defendants of money. The President had knowledge that these funds were being paid and that these were funds collected for the 1972 Presidential campaign.

We know that the President met with Mr. Henry Petersen twenty-seven times to discuss matters related to Watergate and immediately thereafter met with the very persons who were implicated in the information Mr. Petersen was receiving and transmitting to the President. The words are, "if the President be connected in any suspicious manner with any

person and there be grounds to believe that he will shelter that person, he may be impeached."

Justice Story: "Impeachment is intended for occasional and extraordinary cases where a superior power acting for the whole people is put into operation to protect their rights and rescue their liberties from violations."

We know about the Huston plan. We know about the break-in of the psychiatrist's office. We know that there was absolute complete direction in August 1971 when the President instructed Ehrlichman to "do whatever is necessary." This instruction led to a surreptitious entry into Dr. Fielding's office.

"Protect their rights." "Rescue their liberties from violation."

The South Carolina Ratification Convention impeachment criteria: Those are impeachable "who behave amiss or betray their public trust."

Beginning shortly after the Watergate break-in and continuing to the present time the President has engaged in a series of public statements and actions designed to thwart the lawful investigation by Government prosecutors. Moreover, the President has made public announcements and assertions bearing on the Watergate case which the evidence will show he knew to be false.

These assertions, false assertions, impeachable, those who misbehave. Those who "behave amiss or betray their public trust."

James Madison again at the Constitutional Convention: "A President is impeachable if he attempts to subvert the Constitution."

The Constitution charges the President with the task of taking care that the laws be faithfully executed, and yet the President has counseled his aides to commit perjury, willfully disregarded the secrecy of grand jury proceedings, concealed surreptitious entry, attempted to compromise a Federal judge while publicly displaying his cooperation with the processes of criminal justice.

"A President is impeachable if he attempts to subvert the Constitution."

If the impeachment provision in the Constitution of the United States will not reach the offenses charged here, then perhaps that eighteenth century Constitution should be abandoned to a twentieth century paper shredder.

— Barbara Jordan

If the impeachment provision in the Constitution of the United States will not reach the offenses charged here, then perhaps that eighteenth century Constitution should be abandoned to a twentieth century paper shredder. Has the President committed offenses and planned and directed and acquiesced in a course of conduct which the Constitution will not tolerate? That is the question. We know that. We know the question. We should now forthwith proceed to answer the question. It is reason, and not passion, which must guide our deliberations, guide our debate, and guide our decision.

Source: U.S. Congress, House Committee on the Judiciary, *Debate on Articles of Impeachment,* 93rd Cong., 2nd sess., hearings, July 25, 1974 (Washington, D.C.: GPO, 1974), 111–113.

Notes

1. For detailed studies of Watergate, see Carl Bernstein and Bob Woodward, *All the President's Men* (New York: Simon and Schuster, 1974); Fred Emery, *Watergate: The Corruption of American Politics and the Fall of Richard Nixon* (New York: Times Books, 1994); Stanley I. Kutler, *The Wars of Watergate: The Last Crisis of Richard Nixon* (New York: Knopf, 1990); Michael Schudson, *Watergate in American Memory: How We Remember, Forget, and Reconstruct the Past* (New York: Basic Books, 1992); *Watergate: Chronology of a Crisis* (Washington, D.C.: Congressional Quarterly, 1975).

2. U.S. Congress, Senate Select Committee on Presidential Campaign Activities, *Presidential Campaign Activities of 1972, Senate Resolution 60: Watergate and Related Activities,* hearings, 93rd Cong., 2nd sess. (Washington, D.C.: GPO, 1973–74), 26 vols.; *Nixon v. Sirica,* 487 F. 2d 700 (D.C. Cir. 1973).

3. Emery, *Watergate: The Corruption of American Politics and the Fall of Richard Nixon,* 377–384; Kutler, *The Wars of Watergate: The Last Crisis of Richard Nixon,* 391–399, 417–421.

4. *Watergate: Chronology of a Crisis,* 293–464.

5. *United States v. Nixon,* 418 U.S. 683, 713 (1974); U.S. President (Nixon), *Public Papers of the Presidents of the United States, 1974* (Washington, D.C.: GPO, 1975), 606.

6. U.S. Congress, House Committee on the Judiciary, *Debate on Articles of Impeachment,* 93rd Cong., 2nd sess., hearings, July 24, 25, 26, 27, 29, and 30, 1974 (Washington, D.C.: GPO, 1974), 2, 63, 88, 111.

7. U.S. Congress, House Committee on the Judiciary, *Debate on Articles of Impeachment,* 93rd Cong., 2nd sess., hearings, July 27, 29, and 30, 1974, 329-331, 445-447, 488-489; U.S. Congress, House Committee on the Judiciary, *Impeachment of Richard M. Nixon, President of the United States,* 93rd Cong., 2nd sess., H. Rept. 93-1305 (Washington: GPO, Aug. 20, 1974), 1-11; "Impeachment: 3 Articles Sent to House Floor," *Congressional Quarterly Weekly Report,* August 3, 1974, 32:2018-2021; *Watergate: Chronology of a Crisis,* 734-791.

Panama Canal Treaties

✳ 1978 ✳

On September 7, 1977, after thirteen years of negotiations, the United States and Panama signed two treaties providing for the termination of U.S. jurisdiction over the Panama Canal Zone and restoration of Panamanian control in 2000. In return, Panama agreed to keep the canal open and accessible, and guaranteed the United States priority usage in emergency situations. Latin American leaders publicly supported the accords, but they were never popular in the United States and became a serious political liability for many pro-treaty senators as well as the administration of President Jimmy Carter. Few foreign policy debates have aroused as much controversy and occupied as much of the Senate's time. Despite numerous public opinion polls showing sizeable constituent opposition to the pacts, and exceedingly passionate opponents, pro-treaty senators ultimately secured the votes needed to surrender control of the canal to the Panamanians. Influential backers of the treaties included former president Gerald R. Ford and former secretaries of state Henry A. Kissinger and Dean Rusk.[1]

One leading opponent was former California governor Ronald Reagan, who had made the canal a central issue in his attempt to wrestle the 1976 Republican presidential nomination away from incumbent president Ford. Once the treaties were signed, Reagan sought rejection of the accords, stressing the possibility of increased Russian and Cuban influence in Panama. Others felt retaining the canal was necessary to protect the nation's security and commercial interests, and the stature of the United States abroad would suffer if it ceded control of the waterway.

Usually treaties are approved by two-thirds of the Senate without any House action, but because these agreements contained provisions that dealt with the disposal of U.S. property, some contended approval by both houses of Congress was needed. The administration maintained that Senate consent to the treaties was sufficient.[2]

The Senate hearings on the treaties featured members of Congress; administration officials; and prominent military, religious, business, professional, and academic leaders. By the time the Senate began floor consideration of the treaties, the historical and economic arguments had already been widely discussed. Still, the ensuing deliberations prompted the second longest treaty debate in U.S. history, except for the Treaty of Versailles, and was the first to be broadcast live on radio (by National Public Radio) from the Senate chamber. The thirty-eight days of continuous debate in February, March, and April 1978 were historically significant, but the Senate's deliberative reputation was not enhanced by the performance. *Washington Post* correspondent Marquis Child called it "an intolerable charade … since all the arguments pro and con have been rehearsed a dozen times." Sen. Patrick Leahy, D-Vt., likened it to a "long-running" television soap opera. "You could listen to the debate for several days, leave for a week or two, and come back to it having missed very little. All the arguments are being forwarded again and again."[3]

The debate, however, was far from superfluous. Because the opposition was sufficient to threaten passage of one or both of the treaties, the debate was a much more important influence for the undecided than usual. Sen. Robert P. Griffin, R-Mich., the only member of the Foreign Affairs Committee who voted against approval of the pacts, called them "a dangerous step, a gamble for the United States and the security of the United States." Others, such as Sen. James Allen, D-Ala.; Sen. Robert J. Dole, R-Kan.; Sen. Jesse Helms, R-N.C.; Sen. Paul D. Laxalt, R-Nev.; and Sen. Orrin G. Hatch, R-Utah, saw ratification as undermining American prestige and defense posture. Pro-treaty senators contended that public support for the treaties was growing as the American public became more educated about the issues and their concerns were increasingly alleviated. Anti-treaty senators denied such claims, insisted that an overwhelming majority of Americans continued to oppose the treaties, and cited polls to show persistent opposition to the treaties despite the inordinate efforts of the White House and major news sources to convince the public otherwise.[4]

Ironically, perhaps the most noteworthy speech did not have the Panama Canal treaties as its central theme. Instead, Sen. Thomas J. McIntyre, D-N.H., used his courageous remarks to expose "the techniques used to exploit the issue of the canal," which he felt, were "the most compelling to date that an ominous change is taking place in the very character and direction of American politics." McIntyre, who decided to vote for the treaties after "six months of hard study," spoke

President Jimmy Carter shakes hands with Panama's leader Omar Torrijos in 1977 after they signed the Panama Canal Treaty. Senate deliberations about the treaties became the second longest in history and were the first to be broadcast on the radio.
Source: Associated Press.

of his deep concern of tactics used by a handful "that threaten amity, unity, and the purposely course of government in order to advance a radical ideology that is alien to mainstream political thought." Afterwards, a fellow senator arose to declare that McIntyre's speech "could have been made in the Roman Senate in the days of its honor," but it did not prevent him from narrowly losing a bid for a fourth term that fall.[5]

The critical turning point actually came shortly before the debate began when Senate minority leader Howard Baker, R-Tenn., endorsed the treaties and agreed to co-sponsor, with Senate majority leader Robert C. Byrd, D-W.Va., two leadership amendments that clarified America's right to defend the canal and to have priority passage in military emergencies. Next, Byrd chose to have the Senate first consider the neutrality treaty, which required Panama to keep the canal open and accessible. He hoped security-conscious colleagues would be content with making amendments to the neutrality treaty and not modify the basic treaty, which transferred control of the canal to the Panamanians. His instincts were

correct. The two amendments to the neutrality treaty, observers conclude, account for several senators who had opposed the treaties to become supporters.[6]

Gaining approval, however, was not easy. How, opponents asked, would the United States exercise its right to defend the canal, since the treaties provided for the removal of all U.S. troops and since one of the amendments prohibited interference in the "internal affairs" of Panama? While the second amendment theoretically guaranteed the right of priority passage during emergencies, neither a description nor definition of emergency was specified. What would happen if the United States felt there was an emergency and Panama did not concur? Ultimately, the Senate approved both amendments by overwhelming majorities on March 9, but only after adopting a reservation proposed by Sen. Dennis W. DeConcini, D-Ariz., who clarified the first amendment. The nonbinding language added to the neutrality treaty affirmed America's right to take unilateral action in Panama to restore operations of the canal if it were closed for any reason. A week later, on March 16, 1978, the neutrality pact was ratified, 68–32.[7]

An outpouring of Panamanian anger over the DeConcini reservation delayed ratification of the basic treaty for a month while Senator Byrd and treaty floor managers, Sen. Frank Church, D-Idaho, and Sen. Paul Sarbanes, D-Md., worked out compromise language stating that the United States would not intervene in the "internal affairs of Panama" or interfere with "its political independence or sovereign integrity" in keeping the canal open, neutral, or secure. Finally, on April 18, the Senate, by an identical 68–32 vote, ratified the basic treaty. While the leadership amendments left the question of military rights ambiguous, pro-treaty supporters were able to persuade hesitant colleagues that the amendments had placated the American people. Along the way, seventy-five amendments designed to either dramatically modify or kill the treaties were rejected.[8]

Jimmy Carter's success in gaining ratification of the Panama Canal Treaties, he later concluded, may well have been the single most important factor in him losing his 1980 reelection bid. In his memoirs he wrote that the treaty fight was "the most difficult political battle [he] had ever faced."[9]

SENATOR ROBERT P. GRIFFIN OPPOSES PANAMA CANAL TREATIES

FEBRUARY 8, 1978

Mr. President, as the only and lonely member of the Committee on Foreign Relations who voted against approval of the treaties, I wish at the outset to thank the distinguished chairman of the committee (Mr. SPARKMAN) and the ranking minority member (Mr. CASE) for their courtesy and their consideration during the course of the committee's deliberations. I wish to say now, as I have said before, that I respect our two Senate leaders and those of our colleagues who have reached a conclusion contrary to mine — those who are convinced in their own minds that these treaties do represent and serve the best interests of our Nation. I salute them for having the courage of their convictions, because I believe, with Edmund Burke, that a Senator does owe his constituents his judgment and should not sacrifice it to public opinion alone.

However, Mr. President, I also believe that when the call on the merits of an issue is a[s] close as this is, or as close as I perceive it to be, the judgment of the people ought not to be taken lightly. Very honestly and frankly, I have come to the conclusion that, in this situation, as so often is the case, the people are right.

Mr. President, as nearly as I can boil down the basic arguments of many people around the country who believe these treaties should be approved, there are three:

First. They believe, and are told that the Panama Canal is obsolete or becoming obsolete — that we really do not need it anymore or will not need it very long.

That is not the case. Far from it. The canal is vital to U.S. security, important to our economy — and will be more, not less, important in the years ahead — as I will detail at a later point in my statement.

Second. A second argument is that unless these treaties are ratified, unknown terrorists and radicals will blow up the canal.

Like many other Americans, I am shocked and repulsed by such an argument, or suggestion, particularly when it is put forth by officials in high places in our Government. Surely, if we want self-respect as well as the respect of others, we cannot make our foreign policy on such a basis. Furthermore, as I will explain, I am deeply concerned that approval of these treaties will render the canal more vulnerable, not less, to the dangers of terrorism and sabotage in the years ahead.

Finally, the argument is made that we should ratify these treaties to divest ourselves of the guilt and stigma we are supposed to feel concerning the U.S. role in connection with the 1903 treaty and our operation of the Panama Canal.

Frankly, along with most Americans, I am proud of the United States' role in building, operating, and maintaining the engineering masterpiece that is the Panama Canal. I do not think there is reason to be ashamed or to apologize. The canal has been good for the United States — and good for Panama — and good for the world.

On the other hand, for other positive reasons — and because times and circumstances do change — I am willing to recognize, as one Senator, that a major revision in our treaty relationship with the Republic of Panama is in order — that it could serve the interests of both countries.

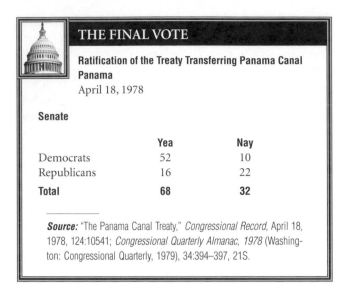

THE FINAL VOTE

Ratification of the Treaty Transferring Panama Canal
Panama
April 18, 1978

Senate

	Yea	Nay
Democrats	52	10
Republicans	16	22
Total	**68**	**32**

Source: "The Panama Canal Treaty," *Congressional Record*, April 18, 1978, 124:10541; *Congressional Quarterly Almanac, 1978* (Washington: Congressional Quarterly, 1979), 34:394–397, 21S.

My problem, as a lawyer and as a Senator, is that after carefully studying the text of these treaties, and the accompanying documents, I could come to no conclusion other than that they are fatally flawed — that they are riddled with ambiguities — that the security interests of the United States are not adequately protected — and that the defects are so serious and basic that they cannot be remedied by trying to rewrite the treaties here on the Senate floor.

Being the lone dissenter on the Foreign Relations Committee — and for that reason alone — I find myself thrust into the role of floor manager for the opposition. I wish to make it clear, however, that my views — and what I say — will not necessarily reflect the views of other Senators who oppose these treaties. Each of them will, of course, speak for himself as this debate proceeds.

★ ★ ★ ★

Under the Constitution, the Senate's role is one of "advice and consent." Instead of consenting to these treaties, I believe it would be a wiser course for the Senate to exercise only its "advice" authority. In other words, without rejecting the treaties outright, the Senate, after examining these treaties in detail, ought to advise the President to send the negotiators back to the drawing boards with instructions to persist until more acceptable treaties can be fashioned.

Despite all of his knowledge about the history of the canal, or perhaps because of it, David McCullough, the distinguished author of "The Path Between the Seas[,]" acknowledged before the Senate Foreign Relations Committee that he had experienced great difficulty in reaching a personal decision about the merit of these treaties. Although he finally decided, on balance, to support the treaties, when he

appeared before the committee he made this profound and perceptive point:

> … If we say "yes" to these [treaties] in a grudging way … [because we think] we have painted ourselves into a corner and we have to get out … [that would be] unfortunate … [and] just as wrong, and in some ways a greater mistake than to say "no" in the spirit of saying "no" because [it should be] done right — because we don't want to have to come back in fifteen or twenty years and have to do it all over again.

So, it would be my hope, Mr. President, that the Senate will consider and act in that spirit with respect to the treaties now before us.

In other words, I concur with those of my colleagues who believe and who will argue in the weeks to come that rejection of these treaties would be unfortunate and would adversely affect our relations with our allies in the hemisphere. But I also believe that it would be wrong to reject these treaties in effect by adopting substantive amendments on the Senate floor — that could do even more to poison the air of friendship than outright rejection.

★ ★ ★ ★

Mr. President, I wish to review with the Senate some of the basic concerns I have with respect to these treaties. I will discuss the broad issue of the canal and U.S. security; the question of a new or second canal, as well as some other concern.

Military experts may disagree as to the advisability of ratifying these treaties, but it is clear there is general agreement that the Panama Canal is very important — if not vital — to the security of the United States.

Indeed, as the Soviet Navy continues to grow larger and larger, while our own Navy shrinks in size — the canal becomes more — not less — important.

★ ★ ★ ★

The sobering fact is that the rapidly expanding Soviet Navy raises real concerns about future control of the maritime "choke points" of the world — one of which is the Panama Canal.

★ ★ ★ ★

If access to the canal were denied to ships of the American navy, the trip from ocean to ocean would involve an eight thousand mile journey around Cape Horn — an extra seventeen days for a warship traveling at twenty knots.

★ ★ ★ ★

Even if we accept the decision to turn the canal over to Panama in the year 2000, our security interests still require, in my view, that the treaties be negotiated to include certain fundamental safeguards:

First. We need more control and jurisdiction between now and the year 2000 to insure that we will be able effectively to operate and defend the canal.

Second. We must have the right, in unambiguous terms, beyond the year 2000 to use military force, if necessary, to protect the neutrality of the canal against any threat — even a domestic Panamanian threat, or particularly an internal threat from within Panama, because that poses the greatest danger.

Third. We need to maintain our option to negotiate for construction of a second (perhaps sea-level) canal outside of Panama, should that prove necessary because of Panamanian intransigence, or desirable because of economic or security considerations.

As drawn, the Canal Treaty and the Neutrality Treaty do not provide these important safeguards.

Even if it is conceded that the United States is not now sovereign in the Panama Canal Zone, there is no question that under the treaty of 1903, The United States has all the rights, power, and authority as if it were sovereign. I strongly suggest that control on that order is important if the United States is to be able effectively to operate and maintain the Panama Canal between now and the year 2000. In other words, if we are going to keep the canal for twenty-three years, it is essential during that period at least for the United States to retain adequate control and jurisdiction.

Under the proposed Panama Canal Treaty, the United States would have the responsibility to operate the canal during the next twenty-three years with employees — both United States and Panamanian — who would be subject, even while performing their duties with respect to the canal, to the laws of Panama, the police of Panama, and the courts of Panama.

In other words, shortly after the ratification, we would be in the position of trying to operate and maintain the canal in a foreign country — rather than in a canal zone under our jurisdiction.

I am deeply concerned that instead of solving problems, this arrangement is pregnant with the seeds of acrimony and conflict.

★ ★ ★ ★

In a country where anti-Americanism has a proven political value, and where courts may be heavily influenced by the ruler in power, one is left to wonder whether such a treaty arrangement could even be used as the basis for harassing U.S. military and civilian personnel to force them out of the country.

★ ★ ★ ★

In view of the great importance of keeping the canal open, it would be ironic indeed, it would be tragic if the Senate, by approving these treaties, should trigger an exodus that closes down the canal.

I am concerned not only with the mishmash of jurisdiction and responsibility that would exist between now and the year 2000 under the proposed treaties, but also about the situation that would prevail under the so-called Neutrality Treaty after the year 2000 — particularly in light of differences in interpretation which have existed, and in some vital respects continue to exist, between the officials of our two countries.

★ ★ ★ ★

On the record, it is painfully obvious that the United States and Panama have been in disagreement — and still disagree, despite the October 14 Carter-Torrijos joint statement — on at least two major points:

Our administration tells the American people that the United States will have the right to defend the canal after the year 2000 against any threat to its neutrality, including an internal threat from within Panama. But spokeswomen for Panama assert that the United States will have such a right only if the canal is threatened by a foreign power.

Our administration tells the American people that the United States can determine unilaterally when such a right to defend the canal can be exercised. But Panamanian spokesmen insist that U.S. forces can come in only when requested or when the action is agreed to by Panama.

We would be living in a fool's paradise to assume that these contradictory interpretations will simply go away if this treaty arrangement is ratified.

It is essential, Mr. President, that we avoid being placed in the dilemma which such differing interpretations would

---

[I]t is by failing to reach a real agreement with the people of Panama by trying to paper over serious deficiencies and disagreements for short-term political gain, that we could be buying ourselves a one-way ticket to another Vietnam. — Robert P. Griffin

---

create. Because it is by failing to reach a real agreement with the people of Panama by trying to paper over serious deficiencies and disagreements for short-term political gain, that we could be buying ourselves a one-way ticket to another Vietnam.

Mr. President, particularly, if we are to consider turning the canal over to Panama in the year 2000, and if the security and economic interests of the United States are to be protected, then we should not relinquish our option to negotiate for construction of a second canal, possibly a sea-level canal, in a country other than Panama.

★ ★ ★ ★

Mr. President, even though the existing canal is not obsolete, and will not be obsolete in the near future, it is necessary and important that we do look toward the day when the existing Panama Canal will no longer be adequate. The dream of a sea-level canal, a canal without locks, ought to be more than just a dream in an era when men and women are going to the moon.

It is true that studies have been made and have indicated that the least expensive place to build a second or sea-level canal would be in Panama. But I suggest that for political and other reasons, it might be very wise to construct such a second canal in another country, even though it would cost a few billion dollars more.

Furthermore, perhaps such a second canal should be built in another country under the auspices of the Organization of American States or some other arrangement of international interests.

★ ★ ★ ★

Holding open even the possibility of building a new canal outside of Panama — an option foreclosed by the proposed treaty — could provide very important and useful leverage in our relations with Panama.

After all, for the foreseeable future, Panama's economic survival is dependent on the Panama Canal. As Prof. Edwin C. Hoyt observed several years ago in the *Virginia Journal of International Law:*

If Panama is too intransigent, she may lose the [sea level] canal to one of these other countries. This would be an economic disaster for Panama.

Furthermore, if a second canal were constructed elsewhere in Latin America, Panama would be forced to keep its own tolls competitive or risk losing most of the traffic to its almost certainly more modern rival.

★ ★ ★ ★

It is my reluctant but inescapable conclusion that these treaties should not be approved by the Senate.

Any new treaty relationship built upon the ambiguities of the treaties now before us would be doomed to failure from the start. We cannot afford to approve them as they stand. To do so would be no favor either to the Panamanians or to the people of the United States.

It is argued by some that defects in the treaties can be remedied if the Senate will adopt a series of amendments. I cannot agree. Such an expedient, however attractive it may seem politically, would be inadequate and unwise. It would do both too little and too much.

If we must say "no" to these treaties — as I am now convinced we must — I believe, along with David McCullo[u]gh, that how we say "no" in this situation is very important in terms of our future relations with the people of Panama and the people of the hemisphere.

I do not favor adoption on the Senate floor of a series of substantive amendments on a take-it-or-leave-it basis. That would be an affront to the Panamanian people. Furthermore, we would run the real risk that the Panamanian ruler temporarily in power would not submit such substantive charges to a plebiscite of the Panamanian people. If this happened we would end up with a treaty relationship only with the dictator in power, but not with the people of Panama.

Accordingly, Mr. President, I believe that the appropriate course for the Senate is to withhold its "consent" to ratification of the treaties now before us — and to "advise" the President to persist in negotiations until acceptable treaties can be fashioned.

Source: *Congressional Record*, 95th Cong., 2nd sess., February 8, 1978 (Washington: GPO, 1978), 124:2724–2728.

SENATOR ROBERT C. BYRD SUPPORTS PANAMA CANAL TREATIES

APRIL 17, 1978

CROSSROADS IN HISTORY

Mr. President, we stand at a crossroads in history — not just the epic history of the Panama Canal, but the history of the U.S. Senate and the two nations which are the parties to these treaties. Approval of these treaties would be another step in America's proud history of world leadership, a proud moment for the Senate, for our country, and for Panama.

Rejection of these treaties would be contrary to our national principles and purpose, and would damage and undermine Panamanian national dignity. Today marks the thirty-seventh day of debate in the Senate on the treaties. The debate which began here on February 8, was preceded by lengthy hearings by the Committee on Foreign Relations and additional hearings by other committees.

Further, many Members of the Senate visited Panama in order to become better informed about the issues involved in the treaties.

The debate in the Senate has been one of the lengthiest and most thorough in history. In Senate consideration of treaties, only the Treaty of Versailles in 1919 and 1920 consumed more time. This debate has also been historic in that, for the first time, the Senate's proceedings have been broadcast across the Nation by national public radio.

Prior to and during the debate on the treaties, serious and legitimate concerns have been raised about their content and meaning. We have attempted to deal with these concerns through amendments to the treaties and to the resolutions of ratification. This is totally consistent with the Senate's constitutional role and our responsibility to ensure that the treaties are in the best interests of the United States.

That, in the final analysis, will be the basis for each Senator's decision — whether, in that Senator's perception, the treaties are in our best interests.

National Interest

As Benjamin Franklin wrote long ago:

There is no science, the study of which is more useful and commendable than the knowledge of the true interest of one's country.

In describing the treaties as being in our best national interests, I am talking about a time-honored concept in American foreign policy. It was Franklin, our first Ambassador and one of our earliest statesmen, who said that our foreign policy should be based on the principles of mutuality and equity.

It is a matter of determining our mutual interests with other nations and acting together to protect those interests. This is what has sometimes been referred to as enlightened self-interest. As Franklin said, "In every fair connection, each party should find its own interest."

Those are the principles upon which this treaty, and the Neutrality Treaty, are based — mutuality and equity. These are sound principles, in the best American tradition; they represent the best interests of the United States and are the best means of assuring that the Panama Canal will continue to serve the nations of the world.

Under this treaty Panama would have an increased stake in the canal and in its efficient and unimpeded operation. However, the United States would retain a high degree of control over the canal through 1999, plus defense rights thereafter, as provided under the Neutrality Treaty. Thus, these two treaties will fully protect U.S. interests for both the near and the more distant future.

There has been a tendency by some to overlook this and to overlook the fact that treaties are between sovereign powers, not between individuals. Thomas Jefferson spoke to this point in 1793 when a treaty the United States had signed with France in 1778 was questioned. That treaty had been negotiated with the French monarchy under Louis XVI. Subsequently, of course, the monarchy and Louis XVI were replaced. Jefferson said:

… The treaties between the United States and France were not treaties between the United States and Louis Capet (Louis XVI), but between the two nations of America and France; and the nations remaining in existence, though both of them have since changed their forms of government, the treaties are not annulled by these changes.

We would all do well to keep in mind Thomas Jefferson's point: Treaties are between nations. This is the case regardless of changes in the individual leadership. It should also be remembered that throughout the seventy-five years of our treaty relationship, the Panamanians, despite longstanding resentment in Panama of the 1903 treaty, have consistently honored it.

Panama

Let me turn for a moment to the Panamanians. In this lengthy and wide-ranging debate, numerous comments have been made about Panama, Panamanian history, the Panamanian people, and their government.

Panama, unlike our own richly endowed Nation, is not blessed with great natural resources. Its greatest assets are its people and its geographic location — the isthmus through which the world's two largest bodies of water have been linked.

A translated version of some of our debate has been broadcast on Panamanian radio and there has been extensive coverage in the Panamanian press. The canal is, of course, a matter of vital importance to Panama; it is the very lifeblood of that country. It is a subject about which Panamanians have felt strongly for decades. The Panamanians have taken understandable offense at some of the remarks made here, and some, I fear, have been misinterpreted or misunderstood.

I believe the Panamanians have exercised remarkable restraint, and want to commend them for maintaining their equanimity in this situation. The American people know, and I hope the people of the world understand that, in the tradition of the Senate, our debate has been free, open, and unrestrained. This is the genius of our system, which presumes that no individual, no group or party has sole access to the truth. Rather, through debate and argument, through the competition of ideas, we hope to arrive at a decision which serves the principles and the interests of this country. But when the vote is taken, when the decision has been made, we present to the world an undivided front: we speak with one voice abroad, although at home — before the time for decision — we not only tolerate but also encourage the free expression of differences.

International Implications

In addition to the intense interest in Panama, these treaties are viewed throughout Latin America as matters of great importance, and as symbolic of the United States' attitude toward its neighbors. The Senate's vote on this treaty may well determine the course of United States-Latin American relations for decades to come. Approval of these treaties is critical to our future relationships with the rapidly developing Latin American countries — countries whose destinies are closely intertwined with our own.

Furthermore, implementation of these treaties would be consistent with our role as a world leader. These treaties are evidence of wise and judicious use of power, of an attitude of compassion and cooperation, by the most powerful nation in the world.

Thus, the treaties not only serve our own world interests, but they also serve the interests of the rest of the world. A bilateral treaty, such as the one before us, attempts to reconcile the interests of both nations, as I believe this one does. However, these treaties serve the interests not only of Panama and the United States, but also of all the other nations of the world.

Let us not forget that the Panama Canal is an international canal — open to all nations. Construction of such an international canal was the goal of the original Senate resolution of 1835, requesting President Andrew Jackson to negotiate with nations of Central America for the purpose of opening "a communication between the Atlantic and Pacific Oceans, by the construction of a ship canal across the isthmus which connects North and South America, and of securing forever … the free and equal right of navigating such canal to all such nations, on the payment of such reasonable tolls as may be established."

This is the purpose of the Panama Canal. This was the motivation for that monumental effort to construct the canal. This is the purpose of these treaties: an international waterway open to peaceful transit by the vessels of all nations. And the actions taken by the Senate to improve the treaty have been with that same purpose in mind. Our actions have been directed at assuring that the canal will remain open, secure, and accessible. It is the canal, not the internal affairs of Panama, which is our concern.

These treaties are evidence of a maturing partnership, a constructive partnership, a relationship based on mutuality and equity. These treaties reflect the world of today and tomorrow — not the world of yesterday. We have an opportunity to show wisdom and foresight, to exercise forward-looking leadership. We must consider the needs of future generations.

It is a time for vision — a time for courage.

These treaties are evidence of … a relationship based on mutuality and equity. These treaties reflect the world of today and tomorrow — not the world of yesterday. We have an opportunity to show wisdom and foresight, to exercise forward-looking leadership. — Robert C. Byrd

---

No matter how long one may serve in the Senate, there are few rollcalls that have greater portent than that which will occur tomorrow. Both the short- and long-term consequences of our actions will have momentous impact. It is not an overstatement, it is not an overdramatization to say that our action tomorrow may well influence the course of world affairs for years, indeed, for generations.

We are at a crossroads. We face a critical decision. I am hopeful that the Senate will choose the road that will bring credit and honor to this body and to this country. Approval of this treaty will be a proud moment for us, for our Nation, and for Panama.

Source: *Congressional Record*, 95th Cong., 2nd sess., April 17, 1978 (Washington: GPO, 1978), 124:10245–10246.

Notes

1. J. Michael Hogan, *The Panama Canal in American Politics: Domestic Advocacy and the Evolution of Policy* (Carbondale, Ill.: Southern Illinois University Press, 1986), 176; Robert David Johnson, *Congress and the Cold War* (Cambridge, N.Y.: Cambridge University Press, 2006), 235–236; Ambler H. Moss Jr., "The Panama Treaties: How an Era Ended," *Latin American Research Review*, 1986, 21, no. 3:171.

2. *Congressional Quarterly Almanac, 1978,* (Washington, D.C.: Congressional Quarterly, 1979), 34:382; Phil Duncan, "War of Words Over the Canal," *Congressional Quarterly,* September 16, 1995, 53:2775. During the Senate debate, an amendment requiring enactment of separate legislation by both the House and Senate to dispose of U.S. property in the Canal Zone was tabled. Both the House and Senate were required to pass the laws to carry out the treaties. P.L. 96-70, 93 Stat. 452–500 (September 29, 1979).

3. Quotes are found in Marquis Childs, "McIntyre's Stand Against the Radical Right," *Washington Post,* March 14, 1978, A17; *Congressional Record,* April 17, 1978, 124:10253; Robert K. Kaiser, "What Is (and Isn't) Said in Canal Debate," *Washington Post,* April 12, 1978, A27. See also U.S. Congress, Senate Committee on Foreign Relations, *Senate Debate on the Panama Canal Treaties: A Compendium of Major Statements, Documents, Record Votes and Relevant Events,* 96th Cong., 1st sess., committee print (Washington, D.C.: GPO, 1979); U.S. Congress, Senate Committee on the Judiciary, Subcommittee on Separation of Powers, *Panama Canal Treaties*

[United States Senate debate], 1977–78, 3 vols. (Washington, D.C.: GPO, 1978–1979; George D. Moffett III, *The Limits of Victory: The Ratification of the Panama Canal Treaties* (Ithaca, N.Y.: Cornell University Press, 1985), 79–111; Hogan, *The Panama Canal in American Politics: Domestic Advocacy and the Evolution of Policy,* 190.

4. For quote see *Congressional Quarterly Almanac, 1978,* 380. See also Hogan, *The Panama Canal in American Politics: Domestic Advocacy and the Evolution of Policy,* 202–203; David N. Farnsworth and James W. McKenney, *U.S.-Panama Relations, 1903–1978: A Study in Linkage Politics* (Boulder, Colo.: Westview Press, 1983), 230–237; William J. Jorden, *Panama Odyssey* (Austin: University of Texas Press, 1984), 438–456; Moffett, *The Limits of Victory: The Ratification of the Panama Canal Treaties,* 113–137, 209–214.

5. *Congressional Record,* March 1, 1978, 124:5132–5133, 5136. See also Childs, "McIntyre's Stand Against the Radical Right," 14; Jorden, *Panama Odyssey,* 526–529.

6. Hogan, *The Panama Canal in American Politics: Domestic Advocacy and the Evolution of Policy,* 191; Johnson, *Congress and the Cold War,* 236.

7. "Treaty Concerning the Permanent Neutrality and Operation of the Panama Canal," *Congressional Record,* March 16, 1978, 124:7133–7188. See also Jorden, *Panama Odyssey,* 532–551; Walter LaFeber, *Panama Canal: The Crisis in Historical Perspective* (New York: Oxford University Press, 1989), 178–182.

8. "The Panama Canal Treaty," *Congressional Record,* April 18, 1978, 124:10476–10541). See also Hogan, *The Panama Canal in American Politics: Domestic Advocacy and the Evolution of Policy,* 195–196, 311; Ted J. Smith III and J. Michael Hogan, "Public Opinion and the Panama Canal Treaties of 1977," *Public Opinion Quarterly,* Spring 1987, 51:6–7, 28–29; LaFeber, *Panama Canal: The Crisis in Historical Perspective,* 182; Moffett, *The Limits of Victory: The Ratification of the Panama Canal Treaties,* 114.

9. Jimmy Carter, *Keeping Faith: Memoirs of a President* (New York: Bantam, 1982), 152.

Omnibus Budget Reconciliation Act of 1981 and Economic Recovery Tax Act of 1981

✳ 1981 ✳

"When Ronald Reagan steps into the White House next week," *Newsweek* wrote shortly before the Californian took the presidential oath on January 20, 1981, "he will inherit the most dangerous economic crisis since Franklin D. Roosevelt took office forty-eight years ago."[1] The observation befitted a winning candidate who campaigned against inflation, unemployment, deficits, high taxes, and debt, and promised a balanced budget. Reagan's landslide victory over incumbent president Jimmy Carter saw him carry forty-four of the fifty states and the District of Columbia. His coattails helped the Republicans gain thirty-three House and twelve Senate seats. In the Senate, a 59–41 Democratic majority was transformed into a 47–53 minority. The Democrats retained control of the House 244–191, but were a divided and dispirited group. When southern Democrats in the House were added to the Republican column, the latter constituted a conservative policy majority.

The challenge facing the incoming administration was how to gain congressional support for an agenda that called for a reduction in taxes, social programs, and government regulation of industry; a military buildup; and a balanced budget. President Reagan, who had long objected to a number of the New Deal and Great Society programs as well as the progressive income tax, personally wanted to drastically reduce taxes and limit government's role in the economy.[2]

Less than a month after his inauguration, Reagan, in a momentous budget address to Congress, outlined his "Program for Economic Recovery." It called for substantial cuts in both federal spending $225.24 billion in fiscal 1982–1984 and taxes (10 percent over three years), along with a $5 billion increase in defense appropriations. The proposed tax cuts, the linchpin of the supply-side economic theory endorsed by the administration, the White House contended, would stimulate increases in savings, productivity, and economic growth, and more than compensate for the attendant loss of revenue. With David A. Stockman, Office of Management of Budget (OMB) director, orchestrating the effort, Senate Republican leaders agreed to include all of the proposed spending cuts in one reconciliation resolution. This approach, it was hoped, would pre-

clude piecemeal changes by congressional committees and special interests groups.[3]

The two-step reconciliation process used in 1981 was established in the Congressional Budget Act (CBA) of 1974. Initially, the House and Senate Budget Committees reported concurrent resolutions on the budget that contained reconciliation instructions to fifteen House committees and thirteen Senate committees. The instructions assigned targets for cutting entitlements and authorizations for fiscal years 1982–1984 that were to be reflected in committee recommendations submitted to the budget committees. Senate debate on S. Con. Res. 9 was emotional, but outcome was never in doubt as it passed 88–10. It ordered committees to cut $36.9 billion from the fiscal 1982 budget, a figure that exceeded the instructions of the Republican-controlled Budget Committee by $500 million.[4]

When the Democratic-controlled House Budget Committee reported its instructions (H. Con. Res. 115), however, it recommended a savings of only $15.8 billion in fiscal 1982. The sharp contrast between the House and Senate versions signaled an effort by the House Democratic leadership to gain support among party colleagues, who were divided on the issue. They hoped that offering more realistic economic assumptions would highlight the difference between the president's vision on the role of government and their own.[5]

Several times prior to reporting the resolution, Budget Committee chair James R. Jones, D-Okla., tried unsuccessfully to win Stockman's support for his package. An alternative proposal — developed by committee members Phil Gramm, D-Tex., a conservative Democrat, and Rep. Delbert L. Latta, R-Ohio, the panel's ranking Republican — had the president's support but was rejected by committee. Despite an emotional plea by Speaker Thomas P. "Tip" O'Neill, D-Mass., for Democrats to "move slowly" in correcting the errors of the past, many in his party endorsed the administration-backed alternative, which passed 253–176 on May 7. The following morning the *Washington Post* described the vote in the following words: "Sixty-three Democrats joined a unanimous Republican minority in sanctioning what leaders of both parties called a historical reversal of

President Ronald Reagan's presidency opened with the proposal of his "Program for Economic Recovery." The stark differences in the House and Senate versions of the budget, however, led to months of revision and debate.
Source: Library of Congress.

course for American government, in effect a vote to dismantle or drastically cut back dozens of social welfare programs that the Democratic Party had built over the past half-century."[6]

On May 21, the House and Senate reached agreement on the budget resolution for fiscal year 1982. The resolution itself did not cut either taxes or spending, but it did set the stage for passage of the key elements of Reagan's economic program. The Economic Tax Recovery Act of 1981 (ERTA) provided for $37.7 billion in business and individual tax cuts in fiscal 1982 and $749 billion over five years (fiscal 1982–1986). The Omnibus Budget Reconciliation Act of 1981 (OBRA) cut $35.2 billion in expected fiscal 1982 spending and $130.6 billion for fiscal 1982–1984. Before OBRA was signed by the president in August, however, a House showdown over the Republican and Democratic versions provoked an unprecedented partisan battle. There was never any

doubt that the House would approve the reconciliation bill and little disagreement over switching to multiyear reconciliation. The chamber's Democrats, however, took issue with reconciling entitlements and discretionary spending programs, and they objected to certain spending cuts in the budget resolution.[7]

Once it became clear in early June that most House committees were not recommending cuts in the manner laid out in the reconciliation instructions, Stockman and Gramm hastily drafted an alternative, Gramm-Latta II. President Reagan joined the battle at a June 16 press conference, calling the Democratic reconciliation package "unconscionable," and he personally began lobbying all sixty-three Democrats who had voted with him earlier on the budget resolution. Prior to floor debate, the House rejected a rule drafted by the Rules Committee that would have forced members to vote separately on individual spending cuts instead of an up or down vote on Gramm-Latta II. Two days of frequently bitter debate followed before it passed by a mere six votes, 217–211.[8]

The decision to allow an up or down vote on Gramm-Latta II prompted Speaker O'Neill to ask whether "any time the President of the United States is interested in a piece of legislation, he merely needs to send it over?" O'Neill questioned whether his colleagues had "any regard for the process, for open hearings, discussion as to who it affects, or what it does to the economy?" "Do we have the right to legislate? Do we have the right to meet our target or can he in one package deregulate, delegislate, the things that have taken years to do?" Similarly, Representative Jones urged his colleagues "not to abandon your legislative responsibility, not to abandon looking at the substantive issues because of partisan pressures." Framing the vote quite differently, Representative Latta told the House: "It is a question of whether or not we turn the country around economically or whether we do not."[9]

In mid-July, the largest conference committee in the history of Congress began resolving the difference between Gramm-Latta II and the Senate reconciliation bill. The more than two hundred fifty conferees were drawn from some thirty congressional committees. To make the task more manageable, the conference was divided into fifty-eight subunits. Conferees from the budget committees served on all of the subunits, while the other conferees only worked on issues within their legislative jurisdiction. The largest conference in history completed its work on July 29. Two days later, the House (by voice vote) and the Senate 80–14 accepted the conference agreement. The final version of the tax bill was approved by the Senate on August 3, 67–8 and the House the following day, 282–95. President Reagan signed the reconciliation bill as well as the tax bill on August 13.[10]

REPRESENTATIVE DAVID R. OBEY OPPOSES GRAMM-LATTA II (HOUSE FISCAL 1982 OMNIBUS BUDGET RECONCILIATION)

JUNE 25, 1981

Mr. Chairman, Will Rogers said once that when two people agree on everything, one of them is unnecessary. I think that explains in large measure the concern that many members of the Democratic Party have about what is happening to this budget both in terms of substance and in terms of process.

I would like to drop all the discussion of substance for the moment and deal with what I think is fundamentally the most important question facing us on this issue, that is the question of process. It is the question of how we got where we are now.

I am pleased that the minority leader is on the floor because I have a great deal of affection for him and respect for him. I know that he has concern about the orderly processes of government.

Another philosopher said once that experience is that quality which enables us to recognize a mistake when we make it again. I believe that anyone who served here under Lyndon Johnson ought to recognize what is happening here again. I did not have that pleasure. I was not here under President Johnson. I came here on April Fool's Day of 1969. All I can do is recall what I was reading in history or in newspapers at the time and all I can do is analyze the legislation which was passed at that time. In my judgment, what Lyndon Johnson lacked more than anything else during his Presidency was constructive criticism, both within his own party and from the opposition party, effective constructive criticism.

The seeds of the Reagan landslide were planted in the early days of the Johnson administration when Congress rolled through bill after bill almost on the basis of titles, without regard to whether or not the ideas which were good translated into effective administration and effective implementation.

In short, Congress paid attention to title. It legislated on the basis of public mood and the title of the legislation in all too many instances. It did not pay sufficient attention to detail. As a result, we had programs, some of which were well intentioned, but in fact were never really worked out efficiently and, therefore, were never really structured in such a way that they could be administered effectively and the public became tired of it and therein, I believe, lay one of the seeds of the Reagan election in this last November.

What I would like to address, I suppose it is fitting that I am doing this at the close of the day when not many Members are in the Chamber, because very little attention in the House is devoted to questions of process; but I believe that the most important thing which has happened this year is something which has been related to the way we are abusing and radically altering the process by which we make budget decisions in this House.

I was reading the other day some memos which were circulated in the Democratic caucus in 1973 when the Whitten-Ullman resolution was first introduced, which was the first action which led to the eventual adoption of the Budget Control Act of 1974. It is interesting to me to note that all of the concerns that were expressed at that time about how the first resolution could be misused and abused in a way which would destroy the committee system of the House of Representatives and virtually every concern that was raised at that

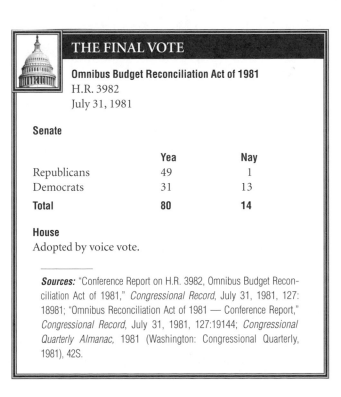

THE FINAL VOTE

Omnibus Budget Reconciliation Act of 1981
H.R. 3982
July 31, 1981

Senate

	Yea	Nay
Republicans	49	1
Democrats	31	13
Total	**80**	**14**

House
Adopted by voice vote.

Sources: "Conference Report on H.R. 3982, Omnibus Budget Reconciliation Act of 1981," *Congressional Record*, July 31, 1981, 127: 18981; "Omnibus Reconciliation Act of 1981 — Conference Report," *Congressional Record*, July 31, 1981, 127:19144; *Congressional Quarterly Almanac*, 1981 (Washington: Congressional Quarterly, 1981), 42S.

time has been proven valid by what has happened in this House in the last sixty days. What has happened is that we have gone far beyond the process that was necessary in order to achieve effective budget control.

At this point, I do not say this as a matter of criticism. I do not mean what I am about to say as personal criticism of the gentleman from Ohio. I simply want to say what I am about to say as an observation about what has happened in the last two months.

The major difference between the Jones proposal whan [*sic*] it was brought to the House floor some sixty days ago and the Obey amendment which I offered and the Gramm-Latta substitute is that the Jones proposal, and I submit the Obey amendment to the Jones proposal, both kept in mind the procedural intent of the Budget Act. Both resolutions contained reconciliation instructions for entitlement programs, for back door spending, if you will, because that is the only way in which you can effectively establish annual review over what would otherwise be runaway uncontrollable spending.

It is necessary in my judgment to deal with entitlement programs in that kind of process. The major difference between Gramm-Latta and Jones was not substance. We disagreed in the main about where $12 billion went in a $700 billion budget. Now, you figure out that percentage. It is less than 2 percent. The main difference was process. What the Gramm-Latta amendment did that the Jones and the Obey proposals did not do is to cross that line and for the first time say that we would apply the reconciliation process not only to entitlement programs, but also to the regular authorization legislation in this House. We would, therefore, be using the Gramm-Latta proposal to rewrite basic law.

I was in the Rules Committee earlier in the week and I saw member after member arguing before the Rules Committee about their version of block grants and their version of food stamp legislation. Those kinds of issues, the design of those programs, should be discussed before the Rules Committee. The Rules Committee, in spite of the fact that they represent some of the most talented people in the House, they do not have the legislative life experience to deal in great detail with those kinds of issues. The authorizing committees of this House do and the Appropriations Committee of this House does.

I ask you to keep in mind that the major strength of Congress through the years, the reason that we have remained a viable legislative body when almost any other legislative body in Western society has become nothing but a tool of the Executive is because of our ability to specialize.

It has been because of the committee system. When we lose our fealty to the orderly committee process, what we do is destroy that which has made us different than any other legislative body in the world, and that is what we have done by adopting Gramm-Latta. That is why I agree with most of what was said by the gentleman from Ohio tonight.

I believed that the product brought to us by the committee process was faulty to a great degree. The reason was because it was required by Gramm-Latta that those committees include not only budget control recommendations, but changes in basic law. That is, I think, a very dangerous precedent.

On occasion Congress has produced ideas on its own. We have had an idea here from time to time. But in the main the role of control has simply been to take the ideas presented by the President and the bureaucracy and to hang them out there in public view and to give a wide variety of opinion in this country, people from all walks of life who are affected by our actions, an opportunity to comment on what we are about to do to them before we do it to them, not afterwards.

That is what is different from the process we are using here this week.

★ ★ ★ ★

Mr. Chairman, we are not giving, because we were precluded from doing that by the timetable that was required by the Gramm-Latta amendment originally, we have been precluded from giving society an opportunity to comment on the fine print.

We represent, each of us, on an average about five hundred thousand people. We, in a sense, are their representatives in a legal case. Many of us are not lawyers but we are making law.

I submit that any lawyer who would sign a contract on behalf of his client without reading the fine print ought to be subjected to disbarment and the fact is, whichever product we would wind up supporting, be it the committee product which was produced under great duress, or be it the substitute which the gentleman from Ohio (Mr. LATTA) will offer tomorrow, either or both products will be voted on without yet any real understanding of that fine print.

The American people are not going to be affected by the general outlines of the program that we pass. They will be affected by the specifics. People will be affected in specific terms by what happens to student loans, by what happens to loan rates, by what happens to education financing, what happens to energy programs. They will be affected in specific ways, not in big ways, and we have an obligation to know what that effect will be.

I submit, and I dislike saying this, but I submit that there is not a single person in this House who really has an adequate understanding of what will be in either the gentleman's amendment tomorrow or, for that matter, what has been in the committee product. The great virtue of what was presented to us in the committee product is that it has at least been strained and sifted through the committees who know the most about it. We have not given the public an opportunity to comment on either package because the reconciliation process, as it has been abused, has prevented that from occurring.

★ ★ ★ ★

I want to make another statement, and I do not do this again to bring any approbation at all on the House. I am extremely sensitive to the fact of life that when we are forced to vote, as we are going to be forced to vote tomorrow on one or two major items, en bloc, no opportunity to change or amend, what we do is run the great risk that Congress will, down the line, be embarrassed.

★ ★ ★ ★

We all know that in documents as large as the documents which we deal with every day there is always the opportunity for somebody to slip something into a piece of legislation for the wrong reason. How much easier is it for that same kind of thing to happen when we are effectively dealing in a blind fashion with a document this large? Even with the committee product, the Budget Committee was required under the Reconciliation Act to take what was essentially a four-thousand-page document, when one takes the bill and the report which accompanied it. We were required to review that and to report it out without having a copy available at the time on the basis of one Member's description of its contents. That is what has happened to orderly process, because we have abused the reconciliation process.

I urge Members on both sides of the aisle to consider what we are doing to our obligation as an institution to make an informed choice when we abuse that process in this way. I urge my colleagues to reconsider down the line and to recognize the importance of separating out the entitlement programs from regular authorization and appropriation programs in dealing with budget control.

There is a great misconception abroad in this House that we have to have reconciliation in order to apply fiscal discipline on the authorizations. That is not so. Under the budget process, if we were right now to apply reconciliation only to entitlement programs so that they did not squeeze out discretionary spending in the budget, we would still have effective control over authorizations and appropriations because

the 302B section of the Budget Act provides that no conference report from the Appropriations Committee can go to

---

This in a sense, this reconciliation action today, is the House's Gulf of Tonkin resolution as applied to economics. — David R. Obey

---

the President if it exceeds those allocations. So we have the overall spending control.

What we should do, if we cared about orderly process, would be to exclude from reconciliation regular authorization proposals. We would keep the ceilings established by those 302B allocations but we would take the next four months to look at that fine print in that contract and what we would do is go through the regular appropriation and authorizing process and accomplish what is going to happen. We would accomplish the President's program but we would do it in a manner which we could be proud about.

This in a sense, this reconciliation action today, is the House's Gulf of Tonkin resolution as applied to economics.

Bill Fulbright spent seven years fighting the Vietnam war after he ironically had carried on the Senate floor the Gulf of Tonkin resolution, when Gaylord Nelson from Wisconsin said, "Hey, we ought to have an amendment to this thing which says that the President cannot use this resolution as authority to send troops to Vietnam." Fulbright went to the White House. The White House guaranteed him that they would never use that resolution in that way. So Fulbright himself opposed the Nelson amendment and spent the next seven years regretting his action.

I submit to you we are going to regret our actions on this legislation in the same manner.

Source: *Congressional Record*, 97th Cong., 1st sess., June 25, 1981 (Washington: GPO, 1981), 127:14182–14184.

REPRESENTATIVE DELBERT L. LATTA SUPPORTS GRAMM-LATTA II (HOUSE FISCAL 1982 OMNIBUS BUDGET RECONCILIATION)

JUNE 26, 1981

Mr. Chairman, today the House faces a historic opportunity. We will decide on the question of runaway spending, bloated deficits, and the destructive inflation and interest rates they have created.

This amendment is targeted to the mainspring of the whole Federal spending, automatic, uncontrolled, ever-increasing outlays for entitlement programs that everybody realizes are totally out of hand.

Now, Mr. Chairman, we have all heard that saying "that we cannot do anything with 75 percent of the budget because it is in entitlements," we cannot do anything about them, so we will just go ahead and increase spending year after year.

Well, now is the time to do something about the entitlement programs.

Let me say, about the time I came to the Congress we spent $14 billion per year for all entitlement programs, AFDC, social security, housing, everything.

By 1970, that had increased fivefold, to $63 billion, and then the dam broke loose. By 1980, the entitlement spending was up to $67 billion, a 423-percent increase in one decade.

If we do not act today, these automatic spending programs, food stamps, medicaid, housing, social security, you name it, will rise to $406 billion — let me repeat that: $406 billion — in the next thirty-six months. This will be an increase of $139 billion in the next three years. That is an increase of $4 billion a month.

Now, let me repeat that. This is what we are considering now, and this is what the American people are concerned about.

This will be an increase of $139 billion in the next three years, an increase of $4 billion a month. Those numbers spell just one message: More spending, more deficits, more inflation.

So the question is: Do we decide what we are going to do, or do we wait until next year? Do we say, once again, that these are entitlements, they are uncontrollable, we cannot do anything about them, and then pass the buck, without ever telling the people back home and the people of this country that this Congress created every single entitlement program and that this Congress has the duty and the responsibility either to continue them or to make adjustments when they are out of hand?

So let us not pass the buck to anybody else that we cannot do anything about entitlement programs, because we can. We put them in place, and we can change them when the occasion demands it. And I say to the Members that the occasion is now.

I would say we waited, actually, too long. I would say the taxpayer is tired of waiting. I would say the time to get started is here, right now, by voting for our amendment to the Jones bill.

Now, let us look at eight specific entitlement reform programs in this package. In contrast to the Jones bill, these provisions achieve real savings by making permanent reforms in our overgrown system of entitlement spending. We would be eliminating the unearned minimum benefit add-on. And let me stress that once again, because we have heard a lot about it and we have heard very little about what is in the committee package but, hopefully, during the next two hours that they have on the other side, we will find something of what is in the committee package. But we would be eliminating the unearned-minimum benefit add-on from the social security system, which will save $465 million in fiscal year 1982 and nearly $1 billion annually by 1984. And everybody knows that next year this social security system is going to go broke unless we do something about it.

Phasing out of the unearned social security benefits for adult students — adult students — will save an additional $220 million in fiscal year 1982 and more than $590 million in 1984.

By adopting a carefully crafted package of food stamp program reforms designed by the House Agriculture Committee minority members will save $1.8 billion in fiscal year 1982, with increased savings each year thereafter.

By refocusing child nutrition assistance on low-income children, we will save $550 million in fiscal year 1982, while preserving free school lunches for the Nation's needy youngsters.

So do not go around saying, "Well, they are taking the food away from the needy." They are not doing it at all. We are not proposing it. Free lunches remain intact. But the people who can pay for their lunches, those in the higher income brackets, will be asked by the taxpayer of lower means to pick up the tab for feeding their children.

Moderating of section eight housing programs and adjusting rent subsidy rates will achieve $1.3 billion in outlay savings over the next three years. At the same time, it will withdraw more than $9.9 billion in budget authority from the program's long-term spending dream.

Now, what are we talking about here?

I remarked about Jack Anderson's column a few weeks back. He was reporting to the American people how foolish we have been with the taxpayers' money in this program by pointing out that in New York City the taxpayers — get this — the taxpayers of this country were picking up about $1,800 a month in subsidized housing rent while the individual paying the bill was paying $200.

Can you justify that? I cannot, I cannot. And that poor individual back in my district who goes to work every day, making $4, $5, $6 an hour, he is asking why he is paying taxes for a program that you fellows in Congress put in place to subsidize $1,800 a month rent in New York City. I cannot justify it, and that program needs adjusting, and adjusting now.

We talk about adjusting the eligibility for guaranteed student loans to reflect the true educational need, and it will save $1.3 billion more than the committee bill over the next three years by restricting loans to the highest income families. Now, what is wrong with that? You know, we had a good program here for a long time on guaranteed student loans. It had an income cap, but we said, "Oh my, we have got to do something great. We are going to take the income cap off and we are going to let everybody in on the gravy train. Even the millionaires' kids can get those guaranteed student loans — courtesy taxpayers' expense."

And do they need the money? No, they do not need the money. They do not need the money. They put it in CD's, buy a new car, while that little taxpayer out in my district and your district making $4 and $5 and $6 an hour is paying income taxes to subsidize that rich student's education. I say that has gone too far.

★ ★ ★ ★

In recent weeks we have heard much weeping and wailing from the proponents of the uncontrolled entitlement spending that controlling entitlements is just too hard, that too much pain will be visited on the poor and the downtrodden. Yet, the Members of this House know in their hearts this is simply not true. The types of entitlement reforms proposed in this amendment will still leave in place a commonsense system of generous support to those who are truly in need of assistance, the sort of income security programs that the Congress designed when these programs began.

This amendment does not destroy basic income protections. Instead, it only cuts the abuses, and let me stress that once again. It only cuts the abuses that have crept into the Nation's entitlement system in the last two decades of uncontrolled entitlement spending.

Oh, it would be nice, it would be nice if we could do all of this, that is, if we could afford it. It would be nice if we could afford it, but we cannot afford it. It would be nice if we could do this for everybody, let everybody in on the gravy train, but we cannot afford it.

Inflation is eating us up. The incomes of poor people, and especially our senior citizens, are being eaten away by inflation. They cannot keep up. Income taxes keep increasing. You cannot keep up. Interest rates are out of sight. Why? Because the Federal Government must go out into the money market every week to finance this huge Federal debt.

Now, that does not make much sense, and until we have the nerve to stand up and do something about it we are not going to correct it.

★ ★ ★ ★

The amendment does more than just save money. It finally gives Members a chance to vote for the sort of welfare reforms we have been promising our constituents for years.

★ ★ ★ ★

In all, this amendment represents a major step toward bringing the Federal's massive system of uncontrollable entitlements under some control. It does not resort to wishful thinking or accounting gimmicks. It makes the fundamental program changes necessary to actually achieve the savings claimed. At the same time the changes represent a careful restructuring of the entitlement programs toward those most

> *In all, this amendment represents a major step toward bringing the Federal's massive system of uncontrollable entitlements under some control. It does not resort to wishful thinking or accounting gimmicks. It makes the fundamental program changes necessary to actually achieve the savings claimed.* —Delbert L. Latta

in need, and this certainly cannot be termed as a meat-ax approach to any type of social welfare spending.

Mr. Chairman, the amendment offers the House its first opportunity for years to vote for real entitlement reform, and I would certainly hope that the House will adopt the amendment.

★ ★ ★ ★

This is a very, very important issue.... It is a question of whether or not we turn the country around economically or whether we do not.

★ ★ ★ ★

Let me also say that this is a critical issue. The President of the United States is interested in it. We had on our side our ranking members, our leadership on the committees went down title by title and explained what was in our bill. We had no explanation as to what is in this Democrat package put out by the full committee and it is more comprehensive, goes into greater detail, and I will bet half of the membership has not even looked at the *Congressional Record* telling what Mr. PANETTA himself says the cuts are in your bill, in that committee package, and you are ready to vote on it.

I say that we need a little more light on what the committee has done to America in this package, and we have not gotten any light on this from the majority side.

My budget colleagues did not hold any hearings on it, and they do not know what is in it, and they said in the Budget Committee all we do is put it in a bundle, tie a string around it, and send it to the Rules Committee.

Source: *Congressional Record,* 97th Cong., 1st sess., June 26, 1981 (Washington: GPO, 1981), 127:14555–14557, 14680.

Notes

1. Harry Anderson, Rich Thomas, and Pamela Lynn Abraham, "The U.S. Economy in Crisis," *Newsweek,* January 19, 1981, 97:30.

2. Joseph White and Aaron Wildavsky, *The Deficit and the Public Interest: The Search for Responsible Budgeting in the 1980s* (Berkeley: University of California Press, 1989), 73–74.

3. *Guide to Congress,* 6th ed., 2 vols. (Washington, D.C.: CQ Press, 2000), 1:173.

4. Gail Gregg, "Senate Orders $36.9 Billion in Budget Cuts," *Congressional Quarterly Weekly Report,* April 4, 1981, 39:602–603; Howard E. Shuman, *Politics and the Budget: The Struggle Between the President and the Congress,* 3rd ed. (Englewood Hills, N.J.: Prentice Hall, 1992), 260–261.

5. *Congressional Quarterly Almanac, 1981* (Washington, D.C.: Congressional Quarterly), 37:257; Steven E. Schier, *A Decade of Deficits: Congressional Thought and Fiscal Action* (Albany: State University of New York Press, 1992), 67–68; Shuman, *Politics and the Budget: The Struggle Between the President and the Congress,* 261–262; Dale Tate, "House Provides President a Victory on the 1982 Budget," *Congressional Quarterly Weekly Report,* May 9, 1981, 39:783–785; Irwin B. Arieff, "Budget Fight Shows O'Neill's Fragile Grasp," *Congressional Quarterly Weekly Report,* May 9, 1981, 39:786; White, *The Deficit and the Public Interest: The Search for Reasonable Budgeting in the 1980s,* 123–125.

6. Quotes are found in "First Concurrent Resolution on the Budget Fiscal Year 1982," *Congressional Record,* May 7, 1981, 127:9016; Helen Dewar, "Reagan's Budget Plan Wins Easily in House," *Washington Post,* May 8, 1981, A1. See also White, *The Deficit and the Public Interest: The Search for Reasonable Budgeting in the 1980s,* 124–132.

7. White, *The Deficit and the Public Interest: The Search for Reasonable Budgeting in the 1980s,* 138–141. See also *Congressional Quarterly Almanac, 1981* (Washington, D.C.: Congressional Quarterly, 1982), 261–264.

8. U.S. President (Reagan), *Public Papers of the President, 1981* (Washington, D.C.: GPO, 1982), 519; Dale Tate with Andy Plattner, "House Ratifies Savings Plan in Stunning Reagan Victory," *Congressional Quarterly Weekly Report,* June 27, 1981, 39:1127–1129; "Omnibus Budget Reconciliation Act of 1981," *Congressional Record,* June 26, 1981, 127:14681–14682.

9. "Providing for the Consideration of H.R. 3982, Omnibus Budget Reconciliation Act of 1981," *Congressional Record,* June 25, 1981, 127:14080; "Omnibus Budget Reconciliation Act of 1981," *Congressional Record,* June 26, 1981, 127:14677, 14680.

10. "Conference Report on H.R. 3982, Omnibus Budget Reconciliation Act of 1981," *Congressional Record,* July 31, 1981, 127:18981; "Omnibus Reconciliation Act of 1981—Conference Report," *Congressional Record,* July 31, 1981, 127:19144; "Conference Report on H.R. 4242, Economic Recovery Tax Act of 1981," *Congressional Record,* August 3, 1981, 127:19329; "Economic Recovery Tax Act of 1981," *Congressional Record,* August 4, 1981, 127:19538; P.L. 97-34, 95 Stat. 172–356 (August 13, 1981); P.L. 97-35, 95 Stat. 357–933 (August 13, 1981). See also Robert A. Keith, "Budget Reconciliation in 1981," *Public Budgeting & Finance,* (Winter 1981), 1:43–44; Dale Tate, "Reagan Economic Plan Nears Enactment: Reconciliation Spending Cut Bill Sent to Reagan," *Congressional Quarterly Weekly Report,* August 1, 1981, 39:1371, 1377; P.L. 97-34, 95 Stat. 172-356 (August 31, 1981); P.L 97-35, 95 Stat. 357-933 (August 13, 1981).

Supreme Court Nomination of Robert H. Bork

✳ 1987 ✳

President Ronald Reagan's June 1987 nomination of Robert H. Bork to succeed retiring Supreme Court justice Lewis F. Powell Jr., Henry J. Abraham observed, "triggered one of the most protracted, arguably nastiest, political confirmation battle's in the Court's more than two hundred-year history." In naming Bork, Reagan stressed that the U.S. Appeals Court judge had outstanding professional and scholarly qualifications, and a number of qualified observers portrayed Bork as the most laudable Supreme Court nominee since the 1939 selection of Felix Frankfurter. Yet, within an hour of Bork's nomination, Sen. Edward M. Kennedy D-Mass., took the floor of the Senate to denounce the man who fired special Watergate prosecutor Archibald Cox while solicitor general. "He stands for an extremist view of the Constitution," Kennedy declared. "Robert Bork's America is a land in which women would be forced into back-alley abortions, blacks would sit at segregated lunch counters, rogue police could break down citizens' doors in midnight raids, schoolchildren could not be taught about evolution, writers and artists could be censored at the whim of government."[1]

Immediately, an intense political battle ensued between liberals and conservatives because Justice Powell's retirement left the Court's membership ideologically balanced. Conservatives saw the nomination as the culmination of the Reagan revolution, and they believed Bork, who had long criticized the Court's decision in *Roe v. Wade*, would advocate their cherished values forcefully. By the time Bork confirmation hearings began in the Senate Caucus Room on the third floor of the Russell Building on September 15, the country had already been exposed to two and a half months of impassioned debate about the man.[2]

Bork's conservative political and legal views — particularly those relating to the constitutional right to privacy and the First Amendment — and his often pungent manner of expressing them — prompted vigorous opposition and an unprecedented effort to build coalitions that could derail the nomination. At stake, opponents argued, were decades of rulings that broke down the barriers of racial discrimination in schools, housing, and employment; gave women the right to an abortion; and guaranteed the separation of church and state. A critical factor in an effort to kill the nomination was the Senate Judiciary Committee's decision to delay Bork's confirmation hearings until after the August recess, allowing the opposition time to mount an extremely effective campaign.[3]

During his more than thirty hours before the committee, Bork did little to ease public concerns or those of the Senate, and occasionally exacerbated apprehensions. Those watching witnessed an unusually penetrating debate over legal philosophy as Bork responded to often rigorous and periodically hostile questioning from opposing senators. The questions explored some of the most important legal issues governing American society — those concerning the right to privacy, the equal protection clause of the Constitution, First Amendment guarantees, and due process of law. While Bork missed opportunities for an anxious public to embrace his reasoning, he did modify a number of his long held views. There was, he said, a huge difference between academic theorizing and judicial responsibility. His judicial philosophy was neither liberal nor conservative, but rather based on a fair and full interpretation of the Constitution. He "believed in a right to privacy," "believed the equal protection clause of the Constitution protected blacks, other minorities, and women," and "supported broad protections for speech," but he had serious concerns with Supreme Court rulings on those issues. Firing Watergate special prosecutor Cox, Bork felt, was appropriate.[4]

Another fifty-seven hours of testimony by one hundred twelve witnesses over an eight-day period followed. Although typically most of the testimony at a confirmation hearing is favorable, in this instance nearly half of the witnesses opposed Bork. Public opinion polls and media advertising played an unprecedented role in the Bork confirmation process. Early polls showed he was beatable, which helped opponents to focus on the key issues to emphasize in advertisements, with the media, and when lobbying senators and they demonstrated the feasibility of expanding the Senate's traditional role in Supreme Court confirmations to include legal views as well as a nominee's background and qualifications. The anti-Bork advertising campaign was not a decisive factor, but it was important.[5]

On October 6, the Judiciary Committee voted 9–5 against confirming Bork, and most of his supporters expected him to withdraw from the process, realizing that a full vote in the

President Ronald Reagan's 1987 nomination of Robert H. Bork for Supreme Court justice sparked a long and ultimately unsuccessful confirmation battle.

Source: Associated Press.

Senate would also go against their man. Bork, however, announced that he "harbored no illusion" about his prospects of success, but felt "[t]here should be a full debate and final Senate decision." If he withdrew, it would signal that "public campaigns of distortion," like the one being waged against him, "would be mounted against future nominees" as well.[6]

The Senate floor debate was in Bork's opinion, "a non-debate," because hardly a vote on either side had not been announced. Still, the twenty-three hours of often-heated exchanges among senators are worthy of attention. Three questions dominated the debate: (1) whether Judge Bork's judicial philosophy was within a broad range of acceptable legal thought; (2) whether the Senate's role in the appointment confirmation process should be interpreted narrowly or broadly; and (3) whether Judge Bork's nomination had been considered fairly. Supporters emphasized Bork's superb professional qualifications and integrity, and they contended his judicial philosophy was misunderstood. They also urged

a limited role for the Senate in the confirmation process. Predictably, opponents took exactly the opposite stance on both issues. Exchanges on the fairness of the confirmation proceedings proved to be the most acrimonious.[7]

Sen. William L. Armstrong, R-Colo., contended that Bork had "been subjected to the worst inquisition, smear, and distortion campaign aimed at any judge in American history," and he accused special interest groups of using misleading advertisements to engage "white collar McCarthyism." Sen. Gordon J. Humphrey, R-N.H., characterized as "villainy" Senator Kennedy's earlier statement that in Judge Bork's America women would be forced into back-alley abortions and blacks would be made to sit at segregated lunch counters. Sen. John Danforth, R-Mo., whose criticism was generally low-key and free of rancor, expressed concern about the consequences of requiring a nominee to make promises in order to be confirmed and felt the confirmation process had been grossly unfair to Bork.[8]

Using language similar to that he first used in June, Senator Kennedy said that in "choosing Robert Bork, President Reagan selected a nominee who is unique in his fulminating opposition to fundamental constitutional principles as they are broadly understood in our society." Judiciary Committee chairman Joseph R. Biden, D-Del., concluded the floor debate with the following observation: "The writings and testimony of Judge Bork show him at odds with" the tradition and history of "Supreme court jurisprudence that has recognized fundamental principles of liberty." At the conclusion of Biden's October 23 remarks, one of the nation's most intense Senate confirmation battles concluded with the Senate decisively rejecting the Bork nomination, 58–42. It was the largest margin of defeat for a Supreme Court nominee in history.[9] If the Republicans had retained their Senate majority in the 1996 congressional elections, Bork might have been confirmed. A different result also might well have occurred if Reagan, who was nearing the end of his second term, had not been weakened by the Iran-Contra scandal and economic concerns that would soon prompt a Wall Street crash.

SENATOR EDWARD M. KENNEDY OPPOSES THE SUPREME COURT NOMINATION OF ROBERT H. BORK

OCTOBER 21, 1987

Mr. President, it is no secret that I oppose the nomination of Judge Bork to the Supreme Court. I stated my opposition the day the nomination was announced — and I'm proud of it.

Although I strongly oppose Judge Bork, I have often supported conservative Supreme Court nominees by conservative Republican Presidents. I voted for the nominations of Chief Justice Burger, Justice Blackmun, and Justice Powell by President Nixon. I voted for the nomination of Justice Stevens by President Ford. And I voted for the nominations of Justice O'Connor and Justice Scalia by President Reagan. In fact, President Reagan has named over three hundred judges to the Federal bench during the past seven years, and I have supported all but eight.

But from the beginning, it was clear that the nomination of Judge Bork was more than the usual nomination — which is why it has attracted more than the usual controversy and attention. Virtually everyone, no matter where they are on the issue, recognizes that the Supreme Court is at a turning point, and that whoever fills this vacancy may play a large role in setting the Court's direction for a decade or even longer to come. Rarely have we had such a combination of circumstance. The Supreme Court is closely divided — and the President has consciously sought to bend it to his will. The Justice who resigned defied any ideological category and he held the decisive balance on many critical issues — and the Justice who was nominated tilted so consistently toward one narrow ideological point of view.

No one disputes the President's right to try to force that tilt on the Supreme Court — and no one should dispute the right of the Senate to try to stop him. That's what advice and consent means in the Constitution. That was the original intent of the Founding Fathers, as that is the meaning of the constitutional role of the Senate today.

At the outset, the advocates of the nomination implicitly conceded that they had a hard case to make. They tried to discredit Judge Bork's opposition, on the foolish ground that all the Senate can or should do on a nomination is read the resume and FBI report — and if the nominee is smart enough, and has stayed out of trouble, the Senate is compelled to confirm him. Ideology shouldn't count, they said, and often it hasn't. But what is sauce for the goose is sauce for the gander. President Reagan obviously took Robert Bork's ideology into account in making the nomination, and the Senate has every right to take it into account in acting on the nomination.

★ ★ ★ ★

In choosing Robert Bork, President Reagan selected a nominee who is unique in his fulminating opposition to fundamental constitutional principles as they are broadly understood in our society. He has expressed that opposition time and again in a long line of attacks on landmark Supreme Court decisions protecting civil rights, the rights of women, the right to privacy, and other individual rights and liberties. Judge Bork may be President Reagan's ideal ideological choice for the Supreme Court, but that ideology is not acceptable to Congress and the country, and it is not acceptable in a Justice of the Nation's highest court.

In analyzing the record of Judge Bork's long professional career, and in his testimony before the Senate Judiciary Committee, a number of themes have emerged:

- Judge Bork is antagonistic to the role of the law and the courts in fundamental areas such as ensuring racial justice, protecting the rights of women, and preserving the right of privacy for individuals against oppressive intrusions by the Government.
- Judge Bork is a true believer in concentrated power, whether it is big government in the form of unrestrained executive power, or big business in the form of corporations virtually unrestrained by antitrust laws and health and safety regulation.
- Judge Bork is not only an enemy of the individual in confrontations with the Government, but he is equally an enemy of Congress in confrontations with the President or when the will of Congress is in conflict with his ideology.
- Judge Bork has little respect for precedent. His habit of intemperate statements — some made this year, on the very eve of his nomination — suggests how eager Judge Bork is to rewrite the meaning of the Constitution. His numerous confirmation conversions, implying a newfound respect for precedent, are hardly reassuring.
- Judge Bork's hostility toward individuals is nowhere clearer than in his attitude toward civil rights. People of

great courage in this country endured great risks over the past three decades in the struggle against race discrimination in America. In the 1960's, while we sought to end segregated lunch counters and "Whites Only" want ads, Robert Bork stridently opposed legislation to end racial discrimination in public accommodations and employment.

Nor can Judge Bork's intemperate opposition be passed off as the understandable aberrations of a provocative professor confounded by the swiftly moving events of a quarter century ago. In 1964, a Senator or a scholar did not have to be a liberal to weigh the issue and judge it rightly. The Civil Rights Act of that year was an historic product of mainstream America, Republican as well as Democrat. It was overwhelmingly endorsed by constitutional experts and swiftly and unanimously sustained by the Supreme Court. And Judge Bork's mentor and colleague at Yale, one of the most respected advocates of conservative legal philosophy and judicial restraint, Alexander Bickel, was a forceful voice in favor of Federal action against discrimination, but Robert Bork disagreed — he said that the historic public accommodations legislation was based on a principle of "unsurpassed ugliness" — when most Americans thought that phrase better described Jim Crow.

It took nine long years — and the pressure of his nomination to be solicitor general — for Mr. Bork to recant his opposition to that landmark measure. But that convenient retraction belies his consistent assault against other Supreme Court decisions mandating racial equality before the law.

He rejected the Supreme Court's unanimous 1948 decision outlawing court enforcement of racially restrictive clauses in deeds for the sale of property.

When voting rights were at issue, he condemned Supreme Court decisions enshrining the principle of one man, one vote, striking down poll taxes, and upholding the ban on literacy tests and other devices employed to deny the right to vote.

From the purchase of a home to the ballot box, to the job site, to the indignity of "whites only" signs in public places, to the schools of the Nation's Capital, Robert Bork has made a career of opposing simple justice.... — Edward M. Kennedy

---

At the Judiciary Committee hearings, he even indicated he could find no constitutional support for the Supreme Court's 1954 decision banning segregated schools in the District of Columbia.

From the purchase of a home to the ballot box, to the job site, to the indignity of "whites only" signs in public places, to the schools of the Nation's Capital, Robert Bork has made a career of opposing simple justice, and he does not deserve a new career on the Supreme Court of the United States.

Judge Bork has been just as wrong on the rights of women. Three weeks before his nomination, he repeated his extremist view that "the equal protection clause probably should have been kept to things like race and ethnicity" — thereby reading out of the Constitution all protection against sex discrimination.

Under the pressure of these confirmation hearings, Judge Bork retreated from that indefensible position; but he rejected the notion that more vigorous scrutiny should be applied to sex discrimination. Instead, he would decide on a case-by-case basis whether sex discrimination is reasonable. But that is the very approach under which courts upheld sex discrimination in a long line of cases extending into the 1960's, before the current stricter standard of review was adopted. As in the case of civil rights, when the issue is equal rights from women, the jurisprudence of Judge Bork is an invitation to plow up settled ground and return to the injustices of the past.

In fact, Judge Bork has set himself at odds in other areas with Supreme Court decisions hardly doubted by anyone else — and broadly accepted as basic to constitutional rights.

Legal scholars differ about the degree to which the Constitution protects a general right to privacy, but few if any espouse the extreme position of Robert Bork that there is no such right to privacy at all.

★ ★ ★ ★

Robert Bork's Constitution preserves precious little freedom for the individual against government interference with fundamentally personal human activities. Real judicial conservatives like John Marshall Harlan and Lewis Powell rejected the Bork view — and it is one of the most important reasons why the Senate should now reject Judge Bork.

Equally disturbing is his roll-back-the-clock record on free speech. It is true that he authored one strong opinion, upholding Evans and Novak against a libel suit by a Marxist professor. But a single first amendment flower does not make a constitutional spring. And it must be remembered that the real threat to a free press comes not from individuals, but from an all-powerful government.

★ ★ ★ ★

In the realm of political speech, Judge Bork persists in his criticism of the landmark opinions of Justices Holmes and Brandeis establishing the clear and present danger test before speech can be restricted.

★ ★ ★ ★

On the bench, Judge Bork has been quick to sacrifice the free speech of individuals to the preferences of the President. He dissented from the decision limiting the Government's ability to exclude controversial speakers from the United States — a decision affirmed this week by a divided Supreme Court. He has also been a persistent adversary of freedom-of-information claims. Justice Brandeis wrote that sunlight is the best disinfectant of arbitrary government — but Judge Bork leans toward secrecy and suppression.

★ ★ ★ ★

If Robert Bork were on the Supreme Court, a vast body of fundamental Supreme Court decisions would be placed in jeopardy.

Yet another persuasive rationale for rejecting this nomination is Judge Bork's bias for concentrated power. The Bork apologists have attempted to transform his role in the Watergate scandal from obedient lackey of a current President to battling savior of the Department of Justice and staunch defender of the Watergate investigation. They say, in effect, that Robert Bork only did his duty when he fired Archibald Cox and precipitated the infamous Saturday Night Massacre of October 1973; they say that he kept the trains running on time at the Department of Justice, and that he was vigilant to ensure the integrity of the Watergate investigation.

But the only Court ever to examine the issue ruled that Robert Bork broke the law when he obeyed the President and fired Archibald Cox. Rather than doing his duty, he was a dutiful apparatchik of President Richard Nixon in his desperate bid to keep the Watergate coverup from unraveling.

★ ★ ★ ★

Judge Bork's role in the Saturday Night Massacre is the leading example of his profoundly troubling belief in virtually unrestrained Presidential power, but it is not the only example. He maintained in 1973 that the President had the inherent constitutional authority to dismiss Archibald Cox from his position as Watergate special prosecutor — despite legally binding regulations.

★ ★ ★ ★

In the world according to Judge Bork, the checks and balances carefully structured in the Constitution are in disarray — he believes it is unconstitutional for Congress to take action to prevent a corrupt executive branch official from investigating himself.

The Bork view of unbounded Presidential power does not stop at Watergate's edge. In 1971, he expressed doubt that Congress could limit the scope of an undeclared war, and suggested that Congress could not even constitutionally exercise its power of the purse to forbid the invasion of Cambodia.

★ ★ ★ ★

It is bad enough that Judge Bork believes that the Constitution grants the President such vast and unrestrained authority. Even worse, he regards it as largely unreviewable. Given the chance, he would drastically restrict access to the courts by anyone, including Members of Congress, to challenge the constitutionality of Presidential action.

★ ★ ★ ★

No person nominated to the Supreme Court in this century — or the last — has demonstrated a belief in so broad and unrestricted a view of Presidential power, even when it is exercised illegally. Nothing could be further from the original intent of the Founding Fathers — the last thing they intended at Philadelphia in 1787 was to create a President with the powers of George III.

Finally, the distressing pattern of Judge Bork's jurisprudence becomes complete when we examine his conception of antitrust — the field in which he has written most extensively. In the private as well as the public sector, he decisively favors concentrated power.

★ ★ ★ ★

The Senate and House of Representatives may not have the expertise of Robert Bork on antitrust, but we do have the constitutional power to write the antitrust laws — and we do not intend to cede that power to Robert Bork.

★ ★ ★ ★

At similar moments in the past, when the issue has been the future of American justice and the fate of the Supreme Court as the ultimate guardian of that justice, Senators have risen above party. In 1937, a Democratic Senate defeated President Franklin Roosevelt's attempt to pack the Supreme Court. And, just seven years earlier, a Republican Senate defeated President Herbert Hoover's nomination to the Supreme Court of the now-forgotten John J. Parker, who had expressed bias against blacks and working men and women. During that debate, the great Republican Senator George Norris addressed the issue in words that speak to us today:

> When we are passing on a judge … we ought not only to know whether he is a good lawyer, not only whether he is honest … but we ought to know how he approaches these great questions of human liberty.

That is the standard by which Robert Bork must be measured — the standard by which any nominee for the Supreme Court should be judged, and the standard which the American people have always set for our highest court. And by that standard, Robert Bork's record does not paint the portrait of a man who should have the last word on what justice means in America.

Source: *Congressional Record*, 100th Cong., 1st sess., October 21, 1987 (Washington: GPO, 1987), 133:28695–28698.

SENATOR WILLIAM L. ARMSTRONG SUPPORTS THE SUPREME COURT NOMINATION OF ROBERT H. BORK

OCTOBER 21, 1987

Mr. President, one hundred five or one hundred ten days ago President Reagan submitted the name of Robert Bork to be a Justice of the Supreme Court and here we are, three and one half months later, finally getting down to the debate on the floor of the Senate on whether or not this man, who Mr. Reagan believes is the best qualified person to serve on the U.S. Supreme Court, should, in fact, be confirmed by the U.S. Senate.

The debate began five or six hours ago. The Chamber is already empty, the gallery is half-empty, the press has gone home and everybody assumes it is all over. Indeed, the distinguished Democratic leader suggested that this whole process of discussing, debating, weighing, sifting the qualifications of this nominee here on the floor of the Senate was in essence irrelevant.

I believe his suggestion, and I am not quoting directly but it is a fair and accurate paraphrase I think, his suggestion was that Judge Bork ought to withdraw his name in view of the fact that more than half of the Members of the Senate had already announced their opposition to his confirmation; that it would be convenient if Judge Bork just pulled his name down or if President Reagan took his nomination back and started over. I think he made some observation to the effect that this would put everybody out of their agony.

I would like to suggest, Mr. President, it would put everybody out of their agony if three or four Senators who had previously announced their intention to vote against Judge Bork would change their minds or take a walk or take a vacation; or if all the Senators would come back to the Chamber and begin to consider seriously issues which need to be addressed.

A number of our colleagues, those who are members of the Judiciary Committee, have really gone through an exercise on this and I compliment them for their patience and their stewardship. I disagree with the outcome of the committee vote, but at least they took the time and trouble to seriously consider the issue. For most of us, however, that debate has only begun today and I am sorry that most of my colleagues were not here to listen with the growing sense of admiration that I felt for the Senator from Iowa for his thoughtful and scholarly statement, a statement which addresses in detail and in an exemplary manner, the real issues in this nomination and confirmation.

I wondered, as I listened to the statement of the Senator from Iowa, whether or not at this point it makes any difference since 53–54 Members of the Senate have said, "We are against him. We are going to vote him down."

Maybe we should all fold up and go home. Maybe the distinguished Democratic leader was correct, that this is an exercise in futility.

Mr. President, I do not believe that. I do not believe it is over until it is over. Every Senator has had the experience, I would expect, of winning a battle which somebody, the experts, their campaign managers, their wives, their families, said that they were going to lose. Maybe Senators have even had the experience of winning battles after they themselves thought it was already a lost cause.

I would not be surprised, Mr. President, if every Senator has had the experience somewhere along the line of fighting for a cause which in the end did not prevail, but nonetheless went home thinking it was a fight worth making.

It is in that spirit, believing that there is still a chance, though I am under no illusions, to use a phrase Judge Bork has used, I am under no illusions about the likely outcome. But I think it is a case that deserves to be made, a battle that deserves to be fought, a cause that is worth championing.

I am not referring just to the issue of confirming or denying confirmation to Judge Bork. I am referring to the issue of the honor and integrity of the U.S. Senate.

★ ★ ★ ★

The growing sense in this Chamber and throughout the country [is] that Judge Bork has been the subject of a savage, unfair, vicious, personal attack.

Because of the seriousness of this matter, Mr. President, I intend to address it in a dispassionate manner. I am going to at least attempt to avoid the temptation of arm waving or extreme or florid rhetoric, and I urge other Senators to do so as well.

Mr. President, I want to say with every ounce of earnestness that I can bring to bear on this subject that what is at stake here is not just the confirmation of Judge Bork, but, as I said a moment ago, the integrity and honor of this process, the reputation of the U.S. Senate. I fully believe that not only will Senators render a verdict upon Judge Bork but upon ourselves, and the country, the people we are sworn to serve will render a verdict upon us as well.

A few days ago, the chairman of the Judiciary Committee made a point which I think deserves to be a starting point in this debate. That is that Senators do not control the action, the words, the advertisements, the television commercials of those outside this Chamber who are in favor of or opposed to the nomination and confirmation of Robert Bork.

There is, unfortunately, a great deal of evidence to the contrary to be found in the public record.

★ ★ ★ ★

What emerges from the public record is a skillful, highly organized, nationwide campaign to influence, some might say manipulate, public opinion.

The question that Senators ought to ask themselves, since there has been an effort to disavow, to disclaim, this relationship between Senators and the outside interest groups, the question we ought to start to ask, the threshold issue, is this: Is this wrong? Is there something morally reprehensible or even unusual about Senators working with outside interest groups? The answer is of course not.

★ ★ ★ ★

Mr. President, as I think about this outside campaign, there are three issues which concern me very much. First of all, that this campaign has been characterized by the press perhaps unfairly, though I see no evidence that it is unfair, as a campaign of fear and political terrorism designed to do three things: First, to blacken the reputation of a distinguished jurist.

★ ★ ★ ★

Our colleague from Massachusetts a couple of hours ago made the point that he thought it was just remarkable how little personal attack there had been on Judge Bork. Mr. President, that may be the view of some Senators, but it is not my view and it is certainly not the view of the *New York Post*, which wrote this in an editorial headlined "The Lies About Robert Bork," and I quote:

> Over the last several weeks Robert Bork has been the victim of one of the most extraordinary character assassination campaigns in recent history.

Some Senators may think it remarkable there had been so little personal attack against Judge Bork. That is not the view of the *Wall Street Journal*, which on October 4 wrote the following:

> Whether or not Judge Bork is confirmed, this shabby treatment of the Nation's most distinguished legal scholar and jurist will not soon be forgotten. Both conservatives and liberals who hold dear the ideals of rational discourse and honest scholarship will be passionate in their outrage, and that passion is likely to have lasting intellectual and political effects.

★ ★ ★ ★

The *Chattanooga News Free Press*, October 1, under the headline, "Bork Hearing and Verdict," asked this question: "Why the controversy?"

It is because in the hearings and out he has been subjected to the worst inquisition, smear, and distortion campaign aimed at any judge in American history. Not only Judge Bork but the principle of government by law is under radical attack by smear, according to this newspaper in Chattanooga.

★ ★ ★ ★

Mr. President, this is the first point that I want to make. Among those who favor and those who are opposed in many cases to the Bork confirmation, there is a very widely and deeply held view that he has been the subject of an unfair, unprecedented, vicious, personal smear attack. Some Senators may think what has happened in the last one hundred five days is remarkable for its lack of personal attack. I think the thoughtful judgment of people who have watched it, who have not been members of the Judiciary Committee but who have just been other Senators or who have been observers at home or have written newspaper editorials is overwhelmingly to the contrary.

Mr. President, the second point I want to raise tonight is this: The campaign against Judge Bork has been untruthful and misleading. It would be bad enough if all of these nasty, vicious things had been said about him and they were more or less true. Of course, if they were true, it would be a great tragedy for the President of the United States to submit the nomination of a person who is of the sort of character as he has been described but the fact of the matter is there is real doubt as to the truthfulness of much of what has been said about Judge Bork.

★ ★ ★ ★

Mr. President, under those circumstances, is it any wonder that thoughtful people, like one writer in the *Washington Post*, have expressed concern about the way this matter has been handled?

One of them referred to the sort of twaddle — which I find to be an entertaining word. It is not something that comes up every day, in every conversation. He referred to the sort of twaddle which Adlai Stevenson used to call "white-collar McCarthyism." I think that is exactly what it is.

★ ★ ★ ★

Mr. President, this brings me to the third issue, which deeply concerns me, and I think is of concern to thoughtful people outside this Chamber; and that is that in this way we have permitted the process to become so highly polarized that we really threaten the integrity of the whole judicial system.

I do not want to overstate my argument. I do not think the country will rise or fall on whether Robert Bork joins the Supreme Court. I do not believe that. This is a great, resilient country with a great deal of strength. But when we blatantly politicize an appointment to the highest court in the land, it raises the ugly possibility that, in the future, judges will be selected for standards of electability rather than legal reasoning, precisely the point made earlier this evening by our distinguished colleague from Utah.

Is it more important, I ask, that we have on the Court outstanding scholars or those whose appearance is pleasing on television? Is it more important that we have men and women who have made a great contribution to the advance of legal thought or those who have the ability to mount, or cause to be mounted, a nationwide political campaign?

Is it more important that we have great scholars and jurists who will faithfully, in a highly focused and precise way, interpret the Constitution, or is it important that we have people whose views we agree with?

★ ★ ★ ★

Is it more important to me, as a citizen and as a Senator, to have a person of outstanding legal reasoning and ability, or is it better to have somebody whose views I share? That is the essence of whether we think the judiciary should be a political office, ultimately subject to popular will through a public opinion poll, through the kind of campaign we have seen mounted against Judge Bork. Or is it more important that the judiciary be the branch which is not, at least in the short-run,

Is it more important that we have men and women who have made a great contribution to the advance of legal thought or those who have the ability to mount, or cause to be mounted, a nationwide political campaign?

— William L. Armstrong

responsive to the public will? This is a very dangerous thing I am saying, or a[t] least thinking about saying.

Source: *Congressional Record,* 100th Cong., 1st sess., October 21, 1987 (Washington: GPO, 1987), 133:28708–28714.

Notes

1. Quotes are found in Henry J. Abraham, *Justices, Presidents, and Senators: A History of the U.S. Supreme Court Appointments from Washington to Clinton,* rev. ed. (Lanham, Md.: Rowman and Littlefield, 1999), 267, 297; "Nomination of Robert Bork," *Congressional Record,* July 1, 1987, 133:18518–18519.

2. Norman Vieira and Leonard Gross, *Supreme Court Appointments: Judge Bork and the Politicization of Senate Confirmations* (Carbondale: Southern Illinois University Press, 1998), 22, 67, 69.

3. For discussions of the anti-Bork coalitions, see Vieira, *Supreme Court Appointments: Judge Bork and the Politicization of Senate Confirmations,* 27–32; Ethan Bronner, *Battle for Justice: How the Bork Nomination Shook America* (New York: W.W. Norton, 1989), 145–187; Michael Pertschuk and Wendy Schaetzel, *The People Rising: The Campaign Against the Bork Nomination* (New York: Thunder's Mouth Press, 1989).

4. Vieira, *Supreme Court Appointments: Judge Bork and the Politicization of Senate Confirmations,* 69, 158; Nadine Cohodas, "Bork's Grade Uncertain After Four-Day Seminar," *Congressional Quarterly Weekly Report,* September 19, 1987, 45:2223–2227; Bronner, *Battle for Justice: How the Bork Nomination Shook America,* 241. For the entire hearing record, see U.S. Congress, Senate Committee on the Judiciary, *Nomination of Robert H. Bork to Be Associate Justice of the Supreme Court of the United States,* 100th Cong., 1st sess., hearings, 5 parts, September 15–19, 21–23, 25, 28–30, 1987 (Washington, D.C.: GPO, 1989).

5. Vieira, *Supreme Court Appointments: Judge Bork and the Politicization of Senate Confirmations,* 138, 151–159.

6. Robert H. Bork, *The Tempting of America: The Political Seduction of the Law* (New York: Free Press, 1990), 314. See also U.S. Congress, Senate Committee on the Judiciary, *Nomination of Robert H. Bork to Be Associate Justice of the Supreme Court of the United States,* 100th Cong., 1st sess., Exec. Rept. 7 (Washington, D.C.: GPO, 1987).

7. Bork, *The Tempting of America: The Political Seduction of the Law,* 315. See also Vieira, *Supreme Court Appointments: Judge Bork and the Politicization of Senate Confirmations,* 175.

8. Quotes are found in "Supreme Court of the United States," *Congressional Record,* October 21, 1987, 133:28711, 28713; ibid., October 22, 1987, 28910. See also ibid., October 23, 1987, 29049–29053.

9. Quotes are found in "Supreme Court of the United States," *Congressional Record,* October 21, 1987, 133:28695; ibid., October 23, 1987, 133:29121. See also Nadine Cohodas, "Senate Debates, Then Dispatches Bork," 42–58, *Congressional Quarterly Weekly Report,* October 24, 1987, 45:2600–2603; Linda Greenhouse, "Bork's Nomination Is Rejected," 58–42; "Reagan 'Saddened,'" *New York Times,* October 24, 1987, 1, 10. For Senate vote, see "Supreme Court of the United States," *Congressional Record,* October 23, 1987, 133:29121–29122.

North American Free Trade Agreement

✹ 1993 ✹

During much of 1992, the administration of George H. W. Bush engaged in negotiations with Mexico and Canada to create the world's largest free-trade area. The five-volume, two-thousand-page North American Free Trade Agreement (NAFTA), which was officially signed on December 17, called for the gradual elimination of tariffs and other trade barriers among the three countries. To become effective, the accord still had to be ratified by the legislatures of the three countries. In the United States, the implications of free trade with Canada aroused little public or congressional concern, but the prospect of extending it to Mexico ignited a domestic debate whose intensity was likened to that surrounding the Smoot-Hawley Tariff Act of 1930.[1]

As soon as the agreement was reached in August 1992, President Bush pushed Democratic presidential challenger Bill Clinton to take a stand on the accord. Clinton responded by endorsing NAFTA in a major speech emphasizing the text should not be renegotiated, but he insisted that side agreements needed to be negotiated to address inadequacies in three areas — the environment, labor, and the threat of sudden import surges from Mexico. The speech solved an immediate campaign need but left the door open for NAFTA opponents to pressure Clinton after he won the presidency in November to withdraw his support if satisfactory side agreements could not be reached. Initially, the Clinton administration's position on NAFTA was ambiguous. While the side agreements were being negotiated, the White House made little effort to assure that congressional Democrats remained neutral. This fueled doubts about where Clinton actually stood on NAFTA, and it allowed NAFTA opponents to rally support for the agreement's rejection both in Congress and throughout the country.

Opponents included businessman H. Ross Perot, conservative Republican Pat Buchanan, liberal crusader Ralph Nader, organized labor, a number of environmental groups, and associations representing industries that would be dramatically affected by NAFTA. Their arguments focused on three major concerns: jobs, the environment, and immigration. In 1992, Perot was the most visible NAFTA opponent and a self-financed third-party presidential candidate. The following year he gave frequent speeches on the widely circulated book he coauthored entitled, *Save Your Job, Save Our Country: Why NAFTA Must Be Stopped — Now!* NAFTA, Perot claimed, would result in the loss of at least one-third of U.S. manufacturing jobs. At the same time, organized labor, which considered low-wage Mexican workers a serious threat, began lobbying Democratic friends in Congress to dissuade the president from pressing for NAFTA. The success of labor's efforts prompted Clinton's budget director, former representative Leon Panetta, to proclaim "NAFTA 'dead in the water'" that spring. Environmentalists worried that NAFTA would: (1) increase trade with Mexico, where enforcement of environmental laws was lax; (2) lead to further environmental deterioration, especially along the American-Mexican border; and (3) prompt U.S. manufacturers to relocate south of the border to circumvent more restrictive U.S. environmental standards. Proponents contended that NAFTA would significantly reduce the number of Mexican immigrants (both legal and illegal) entering the United States and result in an expansion of the Mexican economy. Opponents argued that despite recent rapid economic growth in Mexico, the flow of immigration had not been appreciably reduced.[2]

In 1993, most congressional Democrats favored free trade, but many felt a commitment to listen to the protectionist demands of their constituents. In the House, where the main NAFTA battle was fought, Speaker Thomas Foley, D-Wash., was supportive, but majority leader Richard A. Gephardt, D-Mo., opposed the accord and majority whip David E. Bonior, D-Mich., led the opposition. Given the divergent positions of the Democratic leadership, NAFTA would only be ratified if it had considerable support from Republicans and was endorsed by a substantial number of Democrats as well. Even then, it was not clear whether minority whip Newt Gingrich, R-Ga., a rising Republican force, would go along.[3]

In August, the side agreements President Clinton sought were completed. The first two created commissions composed of Cabinet-level representatives from the three nations charged with ensuring the enforcement of labor and environmental laws. The third established an early warning system to detect disproportionate increases in imports that might threaten a domestic industry. The results satisfied most

President Bill Clinton signs the North American Free Trade Agreement, as former presidents and current political leaders from the House and Senate look on. Economic, environmental, and immigration concerns comprised issues for debate before the agreement passed Congress.
Source: Associated Press.

mainstream environmental organizations, but labor remained strongly opposed. Not until after Labor Day did the White House finally embark on an earnest campaign to win votes for NAFTA. At the time, congressional mail was overwhelmingly against the agreement. The goal was to turn American public opinion around by November, before Congress adjourned. Clinton kicked off the fight with a stirring White House speech. Former presidents Gerald R. Ford, Jimmy Carter, and George H.W. Bush also spoke at the pro-NAFTA ceremony. Clinton emphasized how global changes had revolutionized the American marketplace and that the debate about NAFTA was a "debate about whether we will embrace these changes and create the jobs of tomorrow, or try to resist these changes, hoping we can preserve the economic structures of yesterday."[4]

Since Democratic leaders Gephardt and Bonior would not help, the central role for rallying support among House Democrats fell to Rep. Robert T. Matsui, D-Calif., an assistant majority whip, and Rep. William B. Richardson, D-N.Mex.

Among Republicans, minority whip Gingrich was the most effective. As the White House lobbied House members most likely to ultimate support NAFTA, it was accused of "buying votes" through different deals. The reality was while the characterization was accurate, most of the members being "bought" needed a reason to justify supporting the agreement and extracting concessions from the administration permitted uncommitted members to vote their consciences. Ratification was assured when President Clinton authorized Vice President Al Gore to accept an invitation to debate Perot on CNN's popular *Larry King Live,* and Gore dominated the encounter.[5]

In eleven hours of intense House floor debate preceding the final vote of November 17, more than half of the chamber made floor statements, which spoke to the considerable interest of their constituents. Those who opposed NAFTA, Representative Bonior told his colleagues, stood "with the people who can't cut deals when they are a few dollars short. To them NAFTA isn't some economic theory. It's real life." It was "an insult to the working families of this country." For Rep. Lee H. Hamilton, D-Ind., however, NAFTA "presented a choice between two fundamentally different views of the world, two visions of America's future. Will the United States seek to expand its political and economic influence, or will we withdraw and disengage? Do we resist or embrace change? That is why the world is watching." He reasoned that the United States would be "better off with NAFTA than without it." Rep. Robert H. Michel, R-Ill., provided a lighter moment when he characterized NAFTA foes Perot, Buchanan, and Nader as the "Groucho, Chico, and Harpo of NAFTA opposition." Many expected the final House vote to be very close. The fact that NAFTA was ratified by a comfortable 234–200 vote was somewhat of a surprise. In the Senate, whose members were less effected by labor, the vote three days later was 61–38. President Ronald Reagan signed the NAFTA Implementation Act on December 8, 1993.[6]

REPRESENTATIVE LEE H. HAMILTON SUPPORTS NORTH AMERICAN FREE TRADE AGREEMENT (NAFTA)

NOVEMBER 17, 1993

Mr. Chairman, the Members of this House face today an important and difficult vote — as important and difficult as they will ever cast. We often flatter ourselves — mistakenly — that all the world watches what we do. This time the world really is watching.

The stakes in this vote are enormous. So is our responsibility. The political passions run high. But it is my judgment that most of us will vote on the basis of what we think is best for the country.

What's at stake? Jobs, growth, and exports; United States leadership in the world; the ability of the President to negotiate trade agreements; the success of the GATT talks; our relations with Mexico; and Latin America's hopes for closer economic ties with the United States.

THE CLIMATE

The debate over NAFTA has become an epic battle. NAFTA has become a symbol of something larger than itself; it is much more than a trade agreement. We are at a great turning point.

All of us recognize the fears and anxieties among American workers, and sympathize with them. They worry, legitimately, about their jobs, their wages, and their security. They see NAFTA as a threat.

NAFTA symbolizes the enormous changes coursing through our international economy. Tougher competition. Stagnant wages. Fewer blue collar jobs. Declining military spending. A shift in opportunities from unskilled to skilled jobs.

NAFTA presents a choice between two fundamentally different views of the world, two visions of America's future.

Will the United States seek to expand its political and economic influence around the world, or will we withdraw and disengage? Do we embrace or resist change? That is why the world is watching.

The Test For NAFTA

The test to apply to NAFTA is a simple one: Will NAFTA make things better or worse for the United States?

Will NAFTA help those Americans who are hurting?
Will NAFTA improve the North American environment?
Will NAFTA promote political reform in Mexico?
Will NAFTA make for a stronger, more prosperous America?

My Position In Brief

I am convinced we will be better off with NAFTA than without it. Nearly every problem we face gets worse if NAFTA is defeated, and becomes easier to solve if NAFTA passes.

NAFTA passes the test.

WHY I SUPPORT IT: THE DETAILS

Economy

First. The economic arguments. Economically, NAFTA will have a small but positive impact. Some jobs will be lost, probably low-skilled ones, and we must help those who lose their jobs. But the net result of NAFTA will be job gains, not job losses. All serious studies reach this conclusion.

Opponents argue NAFTA will entice American companies to go to Mexico. But neither logic nor experience support this

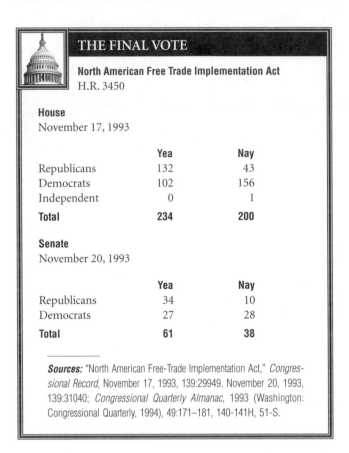

argument. A United States firm in search of low-wage Mexican labor can leave now, with no restrictions. But if we pass NAFTA, Mexico's tariffs, which are two and one half times as high as our own, will come down. Nontariff barriers will be wiped out. There will be less incentive for American firms to move to Mexico. NAFTA levels a playing field now sharply tilted in Mexico's favor.

By approving NAFTA, we give up a little; we get quite a lot. I do not know how a wealthy country like the United States can grow wealthier and create more jobs unless there is growth through trade.

Our work force already can produce as much as this country will buy. To create and maintain new manufacturing jobs, we need access to foreign markets. The United States, to prosper, must not only open up trade with Mexico, but with the world.

Side Agreements

NAFTA's side agreements are not perfect but, on balance, they are valuable. They give us the means to promote improved environmental protection in Mexico. Without NAFTA, we have no such leverage. The status quo, which is unacceptable, will continue.

Through NAFTA, we are creating financing mechanisms to help pay for border environmental cleanup. Without NAFTA, the border environment becomes more lethal.

The labor side agreement will keep Mexico moving forward in enforcing its labor laws and standards. Without NAFTA, we have no leverage, and the deplorable conditions will simply continue.

Defeating NAFTA will not curb pollution, or alleviate the exploitation of labor. Enacting NAFTA will do both.

Foreign Policy

NAFTA comes at a crucial moment for U.S. foreign policy. Decisions will be made in the coming weeks, not only on NAFTA, but at the APEC summit, and in the GATT talks. These critical events will define United State's trade relationships with Latin America, Europe, and Asia for years to come. They will shape our global economic future. How we respond, in turn, will shape our world.

Passing NAFTA will show we are engaged and standing by our commitment to open markets. NAFTA confirms our historic role in promoting free trade. Make no mistake: NAFTA's defeat will define our foreign policy as isolationist and protectionist.

The debate so far has been framed mostly in terms of jobs. But NAFTA has become one of the most important foreign policy decisions of the decade. We should pass NAFTA because important American foreign policy interests are at stake.

NAFTA will promote closer cooperation with Mexico on issues Americans care about, such as illegal drugs and immigration. These are problems we cannot solve on our own.

NAFTA will stimulate economic and political reform in Mexico and, over time, foster a more prosperous Mexico, a politically stable Mexico. This is a vital U.S. national interest.

NAFTA is a turning point in our relations with Latin America. It will help consolidate political and economic reforms already underway in Latin America, a region that could become a huge export market for the United States.

NAFTA will promote progress in global trade talks, by reminding our key trading partners that we have alternative markets close to home.

Consequences of Rejection

We also face serious consequences if NAFTA is rejected.

If NAFTA fails, our relations with Mexico and Latin America will be seriously damaged.

If NAFTA fails, the President's ability to maneuver in the international arena — whether the forum is GATT, APEC, or NATO — will be crippled.

If NAFTA fails, our leverage in other important negotiations will be undercut. If we turn our back on free trade with Mexico, how will we persuade Germany, Japan, France, and others to make politically difficult concessions in the GATT talks?

If GATT fails, global trade expansion, underway since World War II, will be at risk, and so will U.S. jobs. If NAFTA fails, we have no meaningful response to the regional trade strategies of Europe and Japan.

If NAFTA fails, a President will be wounded, and our commitment to free markets and the liberal world trade system undermined.

Flaws In Opponents' Arguments

NAFTA is not a perfect agreement, but its opponents make the classic mistake. They are making the best the enemy of the good. They have many complaints about NAFTA. But we cannot solve every problem between the United States and Mexico in a single trade agreement.

"Not this NAFTA," they say. "We can negotiate a better one that does more for the environment, more for Mexican workers, and more to bring full democracy to Mexico."

Those who await a better NAFTA will be waiting a long time. The truth is, if not this NAFTA, then no NAFTA — at least for years to come.

NAFTA's opponents are also wrong to view trade as a zero sum game. If Mexico gains, they say, we lose. They see only so much output to be produced, a finite supply of capital to be invested. They believe that if NAFTA creates economic growth in Mexico, it will come at our expense.

History proves the reverse: When trade expands, both parties gain. Market economies that engage in free trade grow richer together — not at each other's expense. Trade is a positive sum game.

NAFTA's opponents are pessimistic about America's economic strength. As one worker put it to me: "The center of our concern is fear — fear that we cannot compete."

If you listen to NAFTA's opponents, our negotiators were outsmarted. Our core industries can survive only with protection and subsidies. The United States is in inevitable economic decline and must close its borders.

NAFTA's opponents paint a distorted picture of the world's strongest economy.

NAFTA Is An Opportunity

NAFTA is an opportunity for America.

NAFTA is an opportunity for growth, not only for the United States, but for Mexico and, eventually, all of Latin America.

Put aside the statistical games. Despite all the studies that conclude that NAFTA's gains exceed its losses, no one can predict future economic trends with certainty. There will be losers, but that is no reason to defeat NAFTA.

A wider market and increased competition will benefit all three economies. NAFTA builds on the open trading system that has served us well since World War II. It offers better jobs and higher incomes, and it will promote democracy and political pluralism and stability in Mexico.

Conclusion

This vote today is among the most important votes any of us will ever cast. Our responsibility is to do the right thing, what we think is best for the country. Our decision comes down to a fundamental choice. NAFTA's opponents offer a pessimistic vision of America's prospects, a vision whose message is: We cannot compete. We cannot lead. Let us withdraw, isolate ourselves, and protect our markets.

NAFTA's supporters, along with President Clinton, Vice President GORE, and all the living former Presidents and Nobel Prize-winning economists, offer a different vision. Our message is: We can compete. We will open our markets. We must grow. We will not disengage. We will lead.

Our message is: We can compete. We will open our markets. We must grow. We will not disengage. We will lead. — Lee H. Hamilton

---

If NAFTA fails, we lose. We lose jobs and exports. We lose progress toward a GATT agreement, and we lose credibility and stature in the world.

If we pass NAFTA, we gain. We gain more jobs, a healthier economy, better relations with Mexico and Latin America, momentum toward a GATT agreement, and leadership in the hemisphere and in the world.

Source: *Congressional Record*, 103rd Cong., 1st sess., November 17, 1993 (Washington: GPO, 1993), 139:29843–29844.

REPRESENTATIVE DAVID E. BONIOR OPPOSES NORTH AMERICAN FREE TRADE AGREEMENT (NAFTA)

NOVEMBER 17, 1993

Mr. Chairman, tonight, this House of Representatives will have a chance to earn its name.

We alone were founded to be the voice of the people.

Never in my memory have I seen so many forces arrayed against those of us who oppose the agreement.

Pundits have derided us.

Editorial boards have railed against us.

The Fortune 500 has opened its corporate coffers to campaign against us.

The Government of Mexico has spent $30 million to lobby us.

All because we have dared to stand up and say this NAFTA is a bad deal.

It will cost jobs.

It will drive down our standard of living.

It will lock in place a Mexican system that exploits its own people and denies them the most basic political and economic rights.

Mr. Chairman, we are not alone tonight.

The working people who stand against this treaty don't have degrees from Harvard.

They don't study economic models.

And most of them have never heard of Adam Smith.

But they know when the deck is stacked against them.

They know it is not fair to ask American workers to compete against Mexican workers who earn $1 an hour.

That is not fair trade. That is not free trade.

We stand here tonight with the people who can't cut deals when they are a few dollars short.

To them, NAFTA isn't some economic theory.

It's real life.

When jobs are lost, these are the people who have to sell their homes, pull their kids out of school, and look for new work.

Those of us who take these concerns seriously have been called fearmongers, afraid to take risks, with no vision of the future.

That is an insult to the working families of this country.

These are the people who show their faith in this country every day.

They take risks every day that people who make their fortunes in the stock market would never understand.

They know we live in a global economy.

They know we need new markets.

They know we need free trade with Mexico.

But they also know that the work of America is still done by people who pack a lunch, punch a clock, and pour their heart and soul into every pay check.

And we cannot afford to leave them behind.

Tonight, we are their voices. And we must stand with them.

We stand tonight with auto workers in the Midwest, who can compete with any worker in the world, but ask: How can we compete if we don't have jobs?

We stand with the aerospace workers in California, who have seen jobs leave for Tijuana, and demand to know: why will we pay higher taxes to send our jobs to Mexico?

We stand tonight with church leaders, who have documented torture, corruption, and human rights abuses in Mexico, and ask us tonight: why does this treaty do nothing to stop that?

We stand with the workers in the *maquiladoras*, who hoped that when American companies moved to Mexico, they would have the opportunity to lift their families out of poverty, but instead find themselves mired in a river of toxins and when they try to raise their voices in protest, their own Government silences them.

We are their voices tonight.

We are not alone.

For standing with us in this Chamber tonight are all the Americans who came before us, who had the courage to fight against the odds and against the powers that be for a better future and a better life.

The men and women who struggled in sweatshops for a dime a day, who one day found the strength to stand up and say enough.

The farmers who faced drought and depression and foreclosure, who could have thrown it all away but found the courage to say never.

The farmworkers who saw children struggling twelve hours a day to work our harvests of plenty, who had the courage to stand up and say no more.

The men and women who crossed the bridge at Selma, who stood firm in the face of dogs, and hoses, and nightsticks. And when they were told that this was not the time to fight for justice responded we shall not be moved.

Those are the people who stand with us tonight.

Their voices echo throughout this Chamber.

We must not turn our backs on all they fought for.

We must not turn our backs on all that was earned through the toil and the tears and the courage of our parents and grandparents.

We stand here tonight with the people who can't cut deals when they are a few dollars short. To them, NAFTA isn't some economic theory. It's real life. — David E. Bonior

---

We must move forward.

This vote is about more than money and markets.

It is about more than tariffs and free trade.

It is about basic values.

It is about who we are.

And what we stand for as a people.

It's about the dignity of work.

It's about respect for human rights.

It's about democracy.

Mr. Chairman, if we don't stand up for working people in this country, who is going to?

If we don't insist that Mexico let its people earn a decent wage, who will?

If we don't stand up for democracy and human rights in our trade agreements, then what does this country stand for?

We didn't fight the cold war just so we could exploit new markets.

We did it for something larger than ourselves.

We did it to advance the cause of freedom.

And that's what this vote is all about.

We have come too far and sacrificed too much in this country to turn the clock back now.

This NAFTA is not the best we can do.

We can do better.

I urge my colleagues;

Vote for the Future.

Vote for our Jobs.

Vote for human rights and democracy.

Say no to this NAFTA.

Source: *Congressional Record*, 103rd Cong., 1st sess., November 17, 1993 (Washington: GPO, 1993), 139:29936–29937.

Notes

1. Stephen D. Cohen, Robert A. Blecker, and Peter D. Whitney, *Fundamentals of U.S. Foreign Trade Policy: Economics, Politics, Laws, and Issues,* 2nd ed. (Boulder, Colo.: Westview Press, 2003), 287; I. M. Destler, *American Trade Politics,* 4th ed. (Washington, D.C.: Institute for International Economics, 2005), 193. For the varying views of proponents and opponents see Cohen, *Fundamentals of U.S. Foreign Trade Policy,* 288–296; Don R. Haven, *NAFTA — How the Day Was Won* (Washington, D.C.: Industrial College of the Armed Forces, National Defense University, Executive Research Project S14, 1994), 6–21; Zheya Gai, *The Politics of NAFTA: The Decision-Making of the Undecided Members in the United States House of Representatives* (Ph.D. diss., University of Pittsburgh, 1997), 89–94.

2. Destler, *American Trade Politics,* 200–201; Leo H. Kahane, "Congressional Voting Patterns on NAFTA: An Empirical Analysis," *American Journal of Economics and Sociology,* October 1996, 55:396–397.

3. Destler, *American Trade Politics,* 201.

4. U.S. Presidents (Clinton), *Public Papers of the Presidents: William J. Clinton, 1993,* 2 vols (Washington, D.C.: GPO, 1994), II:1486. See also Maxwell A. Cameron and Brian W. Tomlin, *The Making of NAFTA: How the Deal Was Done* (Ithaca, N.Y.: Cornell University Press, 2000), 186–200; Destler, *American Trade Politics,* 202–203, Frederick W. Mayer, *Interpreting NAFTA: The Science and Art of Political Analysis* (New York: Columbia University Press, 1998), 165–216, 273–282.

5. Destler, *American Trade Politics,* 205; Phil Duncan, "Perot Gores His Own Ox in Debate," *Congressional Quarterly Weekly Report,* November 13, 1993, 45:3105; William Safire, "Gore Flattens Perot," *New York Times,* November 11, 1993, A27. For other discussions of the administration's wide-ranging campaign for yes votes on NAFTA, see Cohen, *Fundamentals of U.S. Foreign Trade Policy,* 296–297; Gai, *The Politics of NAFTA: The Decision-Making of the Undecided Members in the United States House of Representatives,* 100–101; Haven, *NAFTA — How the Day Was Won,* 24–33; Mayer, *Interpreting NAFTA: The Science and Art of Political Analysis,* 281–319; Eric M. Uslaner, "Let the Chips Fall Where They May? Executive and Constituency Influences on Congressional Voting on NAFTA," *Legislative Studies Quarterly,* August 1998, 23:347–371.

6. "North American Free Trade Agreement," *Congressional Record,* November 17, 1993, 139:29843, 29936, 29949; "North American Free Trade Agreement" *Congressional Record,* November 20, 1993, 31040; P.L. 103–182, 107 Stat. 2057–2225 (December 8, 1993). See also Cameron, *The Making of NAFTA: How the Deal Was Done,* 203–204; David S. Cloud, "Decisive Vote Brings Down Trade Walls with Mexico," *Congressional Quarterly Weekly Report,* November 20, 1993, 51:3257; Gai, *The Politics of NAFTA: The Decision-Making of the Undecided Members in the United States House of Representatives,* 188–208; Jon Healey and Thomas H. Moore, "Clinton Forms New Coalition to Win NAFTA's Approval," *Congressional Quarterly Weekly Report,* November 20, 1993, 51:3181–3183; Kahane, "Congressional Voting Patterns on NAFTA: An Empirical Analysis," 396; Edward S. Kaplan, *American Trade Policy, 1923–1995* (Westport, Conn.: Greenwood Press, 1995), 150–151; Robert E. Baldwin and Christopher S. Magee, *Congressional Trade Votes: From NAFTA Approval to Fast Track Defeat* (Washington, D.C.: Institute for International Economics, February 2000), 7–9; Mayer, *Interpreting NAFTA: The Science and Art of Political Analysis,* 311–315.

Line-Item Veto
✴ 1996 ✴

Between 1876 and 1996, more than two hundred proposals were introduced in Congress to amend the Constitution and give the president the authority to veto a "line-item" provision within a larger piece of legislation. By far the most common of these initiatives granted the president the power to disapprove items in appropriation bills. During the nineteenth and twentieth centuries, presidents, despite a lack of statutory authority, intentionally chose to carry out certain provisions in legislation while ignoring others on several occasions. The idea of granting the president item-veto power was first offered in the 1840s and first codified in the Confederate Constitution of 1861, which gave President Jefferson Davis the power to veto parts of appropriation bills. Following the Civil War, a number of states adopted a variation of this concept, a trend that continued through 1996, by which time forty-three of the fifty states had some form of line-item veto.

Action was not taken on the idea nearly as quickly at the federal level. Despite requests from seven different presidents, beginning with Ulysses S. Grant in 1873, and a number of lengthy and often heated exchanges on the subject, prior to 1996 on only three occasions did either a congressional committee or chamber of Congress actually vote on a line-item veto proposal. In 1884, the Senate Judiciary Committee reported a line-item veto amendment proposal but no further action was taken. More than a half-century passed before the House passed a bill giving the president power to reduce or eliminate appropriations subject to congressional disapproval within sixty days. The Senate took no action on the 1938 measure. More recently, in 1992 and 1993, the Senate rejected measures designed to give the president enhanced recession power. During the One hundred-two and One hundred-three Congresses 1991–1994, the House approved three different enhanced recession measures, but the Senate took no action. In 1995, the House passed what was called an "item-veto" bill, but it simply enhanced the president's power to rescind funds. Later that year, the Senate debated two recession proposals, but those bills were eventually withdrawn.[1]

Not until April 9, 1996, with the passage of the Line Item Veto Act, was the president finally given the item-veto authority. The act took effect on January 1, 1997. The act permitted the president to cancel in whole: (1) any dollar amount of discretionary budget authority, (2) any item of direct spending, and (3) certain limited tax benefits. In exercising this authority, the president had to determine such cancellations would: (1) reduce the federal budget deficit, (2) not impair any essential government functions, and (3) not harm the national interest. Congress was given thirty calendar days (only days when both the House and Senate are in session count), after receipt of a special message, to consider a disapproval bill under expedited procedures.[2]

Interestingly, many of the institutional issues that dominated the debate on the Line-Item Veto Act prior to its enactment were the same as those voiced during the preceding sixty years. Proponents contended that it would "reduce extravagance in public expenditures," "discourage 'pork-barrel' appropriations," "curb 'log-rolling,'" "restore to the President his veto power," and "expedite completion of the legislative program." Conversely, others reasoned that it would "lessen the responsibility of Congress," "increase the influence of the Executive whose powers have already been much expanded," "destroy the system of checks and balances established by the Constitution," "violate the principle of separation of powers embodied in the Constitution," and "defeat the legislative intent of Congress."[3]

Additionally, the Constitution, opponents argued, required the president to approve or reject bills in their entirety. The power to make laws was an exclusive prerogative of Congress, and a line-item veto would grant too much power to the president. It would not have a profound effect on federal spending, they said, because it would not be applicable to "entitlement programs" (such as Social Security) that make up more than half of the federal budget. Those programs could only be reduced by changing the laws mandating those programs. Federal appropriation bills, unlike those of many states, critics pointed out, are not itemized. Use of the line-item veto at the state level had not appreciably affected overall spending levels and often was used as partisan means for the political gains of governors and other politicians.[4]

The item-veto, proponents contended, would help the president to control spending by deleting excessive and unwise spending provisions inserted in funding measures, and it

President Bill Clinton vetos parts of a budget and tax-cutting law in 1997 in the first use of a line-item veto. After all the compromise needed to pass the Line-Item Veto Act, the Supreme Court struck it down a year later.

Source: Associated Press.

would give chief executives more opportunities to promote their budget priorities and bring about economy and efficiency. Use of the line-item veto at the state level, they reasoned, had shown it to be a useful tool in controlling spending. Attempting to mitigate constitutional concerns, advocates stressed that presidents throughout American history had declined on occasion to carry out congressionally approved spending.[5]

In 1993, three years prior to the act's passage, Sen. Robert C. Byrd, D-W.Va., the most passionate opponent, delivered a series of fourteen floor speeches on the line-item veto. Its adoption, Byrd argued, would "give rise to unwarranted expectations and possibly raise serious constitutional questions involving separation of powers, checks and balances, and control of the national purse." Subsequently, he stressed that the "survival of the American constitutional system, the foundation upon which the superstructure of the Republic rests, finds its firmest support in the continued preservation of the delicate mechanism of checks and balances, separation of powers, and the control of the purse, solemnly instituted by the Founding Fathers." During final consideration, Byrd suggested the "act should be more appropriately labeled 'The President Always Wins Bill.' From now on, the heavy hand of the President will be used to slap down Congressional opposition wherever it may exist."[6]

Supporters tended to view the act as a powerful weapon in the effort to reduce the deficit, a perception reflected in the assessment of Sen. John McCain, R-Ariz. McCain emphasized that the "line-item veto is not a means to encourage Presidential abuse, but a means to end congressional abuse. It will give the President appropriate power to help control spending and reduce the deficit. To anyone who thinks that Congress is fully capable of policing national fiscal affairs, I simply bring to the Senate's attention the $3.7 trillion public debt as irrefutable proof of our inability."[7]

Final congressional action on the Line-Item Veto Act culminated a twelve-year effort that began when President Ronald Reagan asked for the line-item veto in his third State of the Union address in 1984. The successful drive for enactment began a decade later, in September 1994, when Republican candidates for the House signed their party's "Contract with America." The first of the ten planks of the contract called for permanent, line-item veto authority for the president. The following February, the House passed a line-item veto bill. Six weeks later, the Senate passed a distinctly different version.

After almost an entire year in conference, House and Senate conferees finally worked out a compromise acceptable to both chambers. Following a brief one-day debate, the Senate adopted the conference report on March 27, 1996, 69–31. The next day, the House followed suit by "using a particularly convoluted process." To secure passage, the House "leadership attached the bill to a measure raising the ceiling on federal debt H.R. 3136," which made it "more palatable to conservatives." Debate on H.R. 3136 was governed by a rule that kept the two measures attached until the Senate officially notified the House that it had passed the line-item veto. "At that point, the line-item veto language was dropped from the debt-limit bill and considered as having passed the House as a stand-alone conference report. The House passed the rule H Res. 391 on March 28, 232–177." President Bill Clinton signed the bill on April 9, 1996.[8]

A little more than two years after President Bill Clinton signed the Line-Item Veto Act, the Supreme Court, in *Clinton v. City of New York* (1998), struck down the act as unconstitutional because it violated the procedures for enacting legislation set out in the Presentment Clause of the Constitution Article I, Section 7. The Court explained that under the Presentment Clause, legislation that passes both Houses of Congress must either be entirely approved (i.e., signed) or rejected (i.e., vetoed) by the president. The Court held that by canceling only selected portions of the bills at issue, under authority granted him by the Act, the President in effect "amended" the laws before him. Such discretion, the Court concluded, violated the "finely wrought" legislative procedures of Article I as envisioned by the Framers.[9]

SENATOR ROBERT C. BYRD OPPOSES THE LINE-ITEM VETO

MARCH 27, 1996

Mr. President, "I am no orator, as Brutus is. But as you know me all: a plain blunt man … for I have neither wit, nor words, nor worth, action, nor utterance, nor the power of speech to stir men's blood. I just speak right on. I tell you that which you yourselves do know. . . ."

★ ★ ★ ★

The Senate, you mark my words, is on the verge of making a colossal mistake, a mistake which we will come to regret but with which we will have to live until January 1 of the year 2005, at the very least. We are about to adopt a conference report which will upset the constitutional system of checks and balances and separation of powers, a system that was handed down to us by the Constitutional Framers two hundred-eight years ago, a system which has served the country well during these two centuries, a system that our children and grandchildren are entitled to have passed on to them as it was handed down to us.

And as I comprehend the appalling consequences — they may not become evident immediately, but in due time they will be seen for what they are — as I comprehend the appalling consequences of the decision that will, unfortunately, likely have been rendered ere we hear "the trailing garments of the Night sweep through these marble halls," I think of what Thomas Babington Macaulay, noted English author and statesman, wrote in a letter to Henry S. Randall, an American friend, on May 23, 1857:

> Either some Caesar or Napoleon will seize the reins of government with a strong hand; or your republic will be as fearfully plundered and laid waste by barbarians in the Twentieth century as the Roman Empire was in the Fifth — with this difference … that your Huns and Vandals will have been engendered within your own country by your own institutions.

The Senate is about to adopt a conference report, Mr. President, which Madison and the other Constitutional Framers and early leaders would have absolutely abhorred, and in adopting the report we will be bartering away our children's birthright for a mess of political pottage.

The control of the purse is the foundation of our constitutional system of checks and balances of powers among the three departments of government. The Framers were very careful to place that control over the purse in the hands of the legislative branch. There were reasons therefor.

The control over the purse is the ultimate power to be exercised by the legislative branch to check the executive. The Romans knew this, and for hundreds of years, the Roman Senate had complete control over the public purse. Once it gave up its control of the purse strings, it gave up its power to check the executive. We saw that when it willingly and knowingly ceded its powers to Julius Caesar in the year 44 B.C. Caesar did not seize power, the Senate handed power over to Caesar and he became a dictator. History tells us this, and history will not be denied.

The same thing happened when Octavianus, later given the title of Augustus in the Roman Senate, when in 27 B.C. the Senate capitulated and yielded its powers to Augustus, willingly desiring to shift from its own shoulders responsibilities of government. When it gave to him the complete control of the purse, it gave away its power to check the executive.

Anyone who is familiar with the history of the English nation knows that our British forebears struggled for centuries to wrest the control of the purse from tyrannical monarchs and place it in the hands of the elected representatives of the people in Parliament. Perhaps it would be useful for us to review briefly the history of the British Parliament's struggle to gain control of the purse strings, particularly in view of the fact that the Constitutional Framers in 1787 were very much aware of the history of British institutions, and were undoubtedly influenced in considerable measure by that history and by the experiences of Englishmen in the constitutional struggle over the power of the purse.

Cicero said that "one should be acquainted with the history of the events of past ages. To be ignorant of what occurred before you were born is to remain always a child. For what is the worth of human life, unless it is woven into the life of our ancestors by the records of history?"

To better understand how our own legislative branch came to be vested with the power over the purse, it seems to me that one should examine not only the roots of the taxing and spending power but also the seed and the soil from which the roots sprang and the climate in which the tree of Anglo-American liberty grew into its full flowering, because only by understanding the historical background of the constitutional liberties which we Americans so dearly prize can we fully appreciate that the legislative control of the purse is the central pillar — the central pillar — upon which the constitutional temple of checks and balances and separation of

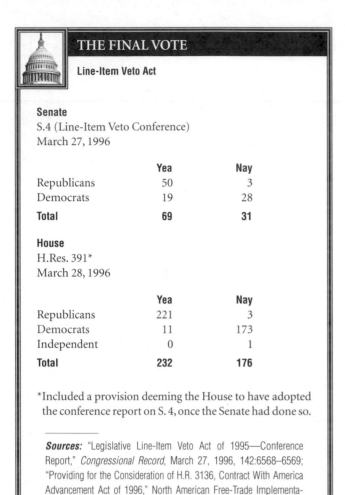

THE FINAL VOTE

Line-Item Veto Act

Senate
S.4 (Line-Item Veto Conference)
March 27, 1996

	Yea	Nay
Republicans	50	3
Democrats	19	28
Total	**69**	**31**

House
H.Res. 391*
March 28, 1996

	Yea	Nay
Republicans	221	3
Democrats	11	173
Independent	0	1
Total	**232**	**176**

*Included a provision deeming the House to have adopted the conference report on S. 4, once the Senate had done so.

Sources: "Legislative Line-Item Veto Act of 1995—Conference Report," *Congressional Record*, March 27, 1996, 142:6568–6569; "Providing for the Consideration of H.R. 3136, Contract With America Advancement Act of 1996," North American Free-Trade Implementation Act," *Congressional Record*, March 28, 1996, 42:6887–6888; *Congressional Quarterly Almanac*, 1996 (Washington: Congressional Quarterly, 1997), 52:2-28-2-32, H34-H35, S.12.

Notwithstanding William Ewart Gladstone's observation that the American Constitution "is the most wonderful work ever struck off at a given time by the brain and purpose of man," — although there is some question with regard to that quotation — the Constitution was, in fact, not wholly an original creation of the Framers who met in Philadelphia in 1787. It "does not stand in historical isolation, free of antecedents," as one historian has noted, but "rests upon very old principles — principles laboriously worked out by long ages of constitutional struggle." The fact is, Gladstone himself, contrary to his quote taken out of context, recognized the Constitution's evolutionary development.

British subjects outnumbered all other immigrants to the colonies under British dominion. The forces of political correctness are trying to change American history these days, but it cannot be changed. The very first sentence of Muzzey's history, which I studied in 1928, 1929, and 1930 — the very first sentence — says: "America is the child of Europe." America is the child of Europe, political correctness notwithstanding.

They brought with them — those early settlers from England — the English language, the common law of England, and the traditions of British customs, rights, and liberties. The British system of constitutional government, safeguarded by a House of Commons elected by the people, was well established when the first colonial charters were granted to Virginia and New England. It was a system that had developed through centuries of struggle, during which many of the liberties and rights of Englishmen were concessions wrung — sometimes at the point of the sword — from kings originally seized of all authority and who ruled as by divine right.

The Constitutional Framers were well aware of the ancient landmarks of the unwritten English constitution. Moreover, they were all intimately acquainted with the early colonial governments and the new state constitutions which had been lately established following the Declaration of Independence and which had been copied to some degree from the English model, with adaptations appropriate to republican principles and local conditions.

★ ★ ★ ★

The Declaration of Independence explicitly names, as one of the reasons justifying separation from England, that of her "imposing taxes on us without our consent."

There is, then, a certain historic fitness in the fact that first among the powers of Congress enumerated in Article I, Section 8, of the Constitution is the power "to lay and collect taxes." The power to appropriate monies is also vested by Article I solely in the legislative branch — nowhere else; not downtown, not at the other end of Pennsylvania Avenue, but here in the legislative branch.

Mr. President, we have all perhaps been subject to the notion that the Federal Constitution with its built-in systems of checks and balances, was an isolated and innovative new

powers rests, and that if the pillar is shaken, the temple will fall. It is as central to the fundamental liberty of the American people as is the principle of habeas corpus, although its genesis and raison d'etre are not generally well understood. Therefore, before focusing on the power over the purse as the central strand in the whole cloth of Anglo-American liberty, we should engage in a kaleidoscopic viewing of the larger mosaic as it was spun on the loom of time.

Congress' control over the public purse has had a long and troubled history. Its beginnings are embedded in the English experience, stretching backward into the middle ages and beyond. It did not have its genesis at the Constitutional Convention, as some may think, but, rather, like so many other elements contained in the American Constitution, it was largely the product of our early experience under colonial and State governments and with roots extending backward through hundreds of years of British history predating the earliest settlements in the New World.

instrument of government which sprang into existence — sprang into existence — during three months of meetings behind closed doors in Philadelphia, and that it solely was the product of the genius of the Framers who gathered there

---

The Senate is about to adopt a conference report, Mr. President, which Madison and the other Constitutional Framers ... would have absolutely abhorred, and in adopting the report we will be bartering away our children's birthright for a mess of political pottage. — Robert C. Byrd

---

behind closed doors to labor to make it come about. However, as I have also said heretofore, American constitutional history can only be fully understood and appreciated by looking into the institutions, events, and experiences of the past out of which the organic document of our nation evolved and took unto itself a life and soul of its own.

★ ★ ★ ★

The U.S. Constitution was, in many ways, the product of many centuries — many centuries — and it was not so much a new and untried experiment as it was a charter of government based to some extent on the British archetype, as well as on State and colonial models which had themselves been influenced by the British example and by the political theories of Montesquieu and others, who believed that political freedom could be maintained only by separating the executive, legislative, and judicial powers of government, which powers, when divided, would check and balance one another, thus preventing tyranny by any one man, as had been the case in France.

Moreover, unlike the British Constitution, which, as I say, was, generally, an unwritten constitution consisting of written charters, common law principles and rules, and petitions and statutes of Parliament, the American Constitution was a single, written document that was ratified by the people in conventions called for the purpose.

In a real sense, therefore, the U.S. Constitution was an instrument of government that was the result of growth and experience and not manufacture, and its successful ratification was, in considerable measure, due to the respect of the people for its roots deep in the past. The mainspring of the constitutional system of separation of powers and delicate checks and balances was the power over the purse, vested — where? Here in the legislative branch. That power guaranteed the independence and the freedom and the liberties of the people.

★ ★ ★ ★

[T]he founders of this republic left no doubt as to what branch of the government had control over the purse strings. The Executive was not given any control over the purse strings, with the single exception of the right of the President to veto, in its entirety, a bill — any bill — and in this case a bill making appropriations.

There was little discussion of the Presidential veto at the convention, as a reading of the convention notes will show. There was absolutely no discussion whatsoever with reference to a line item veto or any such modification thereof as we are now contemplating. Henry Clay, one of the greatest Senators of all time, in a Senate Floor speech on January 24, 1842, referred to the veto as "this miserable despotic veto power of the President of the United States." That is what he thought of a Presidential veto. It is not hard to imagine what Henry Clay would think of this conference report that is before the Senate today.

It is ludicrous — nay, it is tragic — that we are about to substitute our own judgment for that of the Framers with respect to the control of the purse and the need to check the Executive. Yet, that is precisely what we are about to do here today. We are about to succumb, for political reasons only, to the mania which has taken hold of some in this and the other body to put that most political of political inventions, the so-called "Contract with America" into law.

★ ★ ★ ★

This so-called Line-Item Veto Act should be more appropriately labeled "The President Always Wins Bill." From now on, the heavy hand of the President will be used to slap down Congressional opposition wherever it may exist. Yet, I have no doubt that this measure will pass. Political expediency will be the order of the day, for we are like Nebuchadnezzar, dethroned, bereft of reason, and eating grass like an ox.

"O, that my tongue were in the thunder's mouth! Then with a passion would I shake the world."

The efforts of those who oppose this surrender of power to the President may be likened to the last stand of General George Armstrong Custer, who with two hundred of his followers, were wiped out by the Indians at the Battle of the Little Big Horn, in Montana, in 1876, but I see this as the Battle of the "Big Giveaway," and I do not propose to go along.

As a matter of fact, I do not believe that it is within the capability of Congress to give away such a basic Constitutional power as the control over the purse strings, because that is the fundamental pillar upon which rests the Constitutional system of checks and balances.

★ ★ ★ ★

It is difficult to imagine why this body would want to deal such a painful blow, not only to itself, but to the basic structure of our constitutional form of government and to the interests of the people we represent.

Whether the President is a Democrat or a Republican is not my concern. Whether one party or another is in power in the Congress is not my concern here. My concern is with unnecessarily upsetting the balance of powers as laid out in the Constitution, and this conference report simply gives away much of the congressional control over the purse strings to a President.

★ ★ ★ ★

Supporters of the item veto bill claim that it gives the President an essential tool in deleting "wasteful" federal projects

and activities. Let us not deceive ourselves or the voters. There is not the slightest basis in our political history for believing that Presidents are peculiarly endowed by nature to oppose federal spending. Presidents like to spend money. They like proposing expensive new projects and programs, and they like to wield power, especially over the Members of the legislative branch.

Source: Congressional Record, 104th Cong., 2nd sess., March 27, 1996 (Washington: GPO, 1996), 142:6504–6508, 6511, 6513.

SENATOR JOHN McCAIN FAVORS THE LINE-ITEM VETO

MARCH 27, 1996

Mr. President, one year ago, the Senate began consideration of S. 4, legislation to give the President line-item veto authority. Ten years before that, I began my fight in the Senate to give the President this authority, and one hundred twenty years before that Representative Charles Faulkner of West Virginia introduced the first line-item veto bill. Hopefully, a one hundred twenty-year battle may soon be won.

★ ★ ★ ★

Mr. President; the power to line-item veto is not new. Every President from Jefferson to Nixon used a similar power. The line-item veto power they exercised ensured that the checks and balances between the congressional and executive branch remained in balance. In 1974, in reaction to the Presidential abuses, the Congress stripped the President of this power. Unfortunately, since that time, the Congress has abused its ability to dictate how money be spent. This bill would restore the checks and balances envisioned by the Founding Fathers.

Further, unlike impoundment power where the President could use appropriated money to fund his priorities over the objections of the Congress, this bill contains a lockbox provision as I have described. Any money line-item vetoed under this bill could be used only for deficit reduction. Mr. President, many have characterized this legislation as a dangerous ploy, not as a true budgetary reform. This is not accurate and does not take into account the greater picture of the dangers presented by our out-of-control budget process. The real danger is what has happened to the administration of the American Government. Unnecessary and wasteful spending

is threatening our national security and consuming resources that could better be spent on tax cuts, deficit reduction, or health care. I do not make the charge that wasteful spending threatens our national security without a great deal of consideration. After last year's defense appropriations bill, it is unfortunately clear how dangerous this kind of spending can be to our national security. It should now be clear how urgent the need for a line-item veto is.

At a time when thousands of men and women who volunteered to serve their country have to leave military service because of changing priorities and declining defense budgets, we nonetheless are able to find money for billions of dollars of unnecessary spending in the defense appropriation bill. At a time when we need to restructure our forces and manpower to meet our post-cold war military needs, we have squandered billions on pointless projects with no military value.

Mr. President, every Congressman or Senator wants to get projects for his or her district. Everyone wants not only their fair share of the Federal pie for their States, they want more. Therein lies the problem. It is an institutional problem. I am not a saint. But we are trying to make a difference. I am not here to cast aspersions on other Senators who secured an unnecessary project for their States. I am not here to start a partisan fight.

Congress created the problem and its Congress' responsibility to fix it. It is a Congress that has piled up a $5 trillion debt. It is a Congress that is responsible for over a $200 billion deficit this year. It is a Congress that has miserably failed the American people. It is an institution that desperately needs reform.

Anyone who feels that the system does not need reform need only examine the trend in the level of our public debt. As I stated in my analysis of the most recent budget plans, the deficit has continued to balloon and spending continues to increase. In 1960, the Federal debt held by the public was $236.8 billion. In 1970, it was $283.2 billion. In 1980, it was $709.3 billion. In 1990, it was $3.2 trillion, and it is expected to surpass $5 trillion this year.

My colleagues may ask: Why is the line-item veto so important? Because a President with a line-item veto could help stop this waste. Because a President with a line-item veto could play an active role in ensuring that valuable taxpayer dollars are spent effectively to meet our national security needs, our infrastructure needs, and other social needs without pointless pork barrel spending. And the President can no longer say, "I didn't like having to spend billions on a wasteful project but it was part of a larger bill I just couldn't say no to." Under a line-item veto, no one can hide.

According to a recent General Accounting Office study, $70 billion could have been saved between 1984 and 1989, if the President had a line-item veto.

It is important because it can help reduce the deficit. It can change the way Washington operates. Mr. President, we cannot turn a blind eye to unnecessary spending when we cannot meet the needs of our service men and women. We cannot tolerate waste when Americans all over this country are experiencing economic hardship and uncertainty.

The American public deserves better than business as usual. As their elected representatives we are duty bound to end the practice of wasteful and unnecessary spending.

The line-item veto is not a means to encourage Presidential abuse, but a means to end congressional abuse. It will give the President appropriate power to help control spending and reduce the deficit. To anyone who thinks that Congress is fully capable of policing national fiscal affairs, I simply bring to the Senate's attention the $3.7 trillion public debt as irrefutable proof of our inability.

Mr. President, a determined President will not be able to balance the budget with the line-item veto. But a determined President could make substantial progress toward that goal.

I submit that had the President been able to exercise line-item veto authority over the past ten years the fiscal condition of our Nation would not be nearly as severe as it is today.

With that in mind, I hope the Senate would consider the following quote by a prescient figure in the Scottish Enlightenment, Alexander Tytler. He stated:

> A democracy cannot exist as a permanent form of government. It can exist only until a majority of voters discover that they can vote themselves, largesse out of the public treasury. From that moment on, the majority always votes for the candidate who promises them the most benefit from the public treasury, with the result being that democracy always collapses over a loose fiscal policy.

If our debt surpasses our output, I fear that our democracy may one day collapse over loose fiscal policy.

Today is a historic day. A one hundred twenty-year battle is coming to a close. The line-item may soon be a reality.

★ ★ ★ ★

Madam President, the support of my colleagues for the line-item veto have made this long, difficult contest worthwhile and an honor to have been involved in, but even greater honor is derived from the quality of the opposition to this legislation. And every Senator is aware that the quality of that opposition is directly proportional to the quality of one Senator in particular, the estimable Senator from West Virginia, Senator BYRD.

Madam President, I would like to indulge a moment of common weakness of politicians. I wish to quote myself. I wish to quote from remarks I made one year ago when we first passed the line-item veto. I said at that time that "Senator BYRD distinguished our debate, as he has distinguished so many of our previous debates," as he has distinguished today's debate, "with his passion and his eloquence, his wisdom and his deep abiding patriotism. Although my colleagues might believe I have eagerly sought opportunities to contend with Senator BYRD, that was, to use a sports colloquialism, only my game face. I assure you I have approached each encounter with trepidation. Senator BYRD is a very formidable man."

Madam President, I stand by that tribute today. If there is a Member of this body who loves his country more, who reveres the Constitution more, or who defends the Congress more effectively, I have not had the honor of his or her acquaintance. Should we proponents of the line-item veto prevail, I will take little pride in overcoming Senator BYRD'S impressive opposition but only renewed respect for the honor of this body as personified by its ablest defender, Senator ROBERT BYRD.

Senator BYRD has solemnly adjured the Senate to refrain from unwittingly violating the Constitution. As I said, his love for that noble document is profound and worthy of a devoted public servant. I, too, love the Constitution, although I cannot equal the Senator's ability to express that love.

Like Senator BYRD, my regard for the Constitution encompasses more than my appreciation for its genius and for the wisdom of its authors. It is for the ideas it protects, for the Nation born of those ideas that I would ransom my life to defend the Constitution of the United States.

It is to help preserve the notion that Government derived from the consent of the governed is as sound as it is just that I have advocated this small shift in authority from one branch of our Government to another. I do not think the change to be as precipitous as its opponents fear. Even with the line-item veto authority, the President could ill-afford to disregard the will of Congress. Should he abuse his authority, Congress could and would compel the redress of that abuse.

Even with the line-item veto authority, the President could ill-afford to disregard the will of Congress. Should he abuse his authority, Congress could and would compel the redress of that abuse. — John McCain

---

I contend that granting the President this authority is necessary given the gravity of our fiscal problems and the inadequacy of Congress' past efforts to remedy those problems. I do not believe that the line-item veto will empower the President to cure Government's insolvency on its own. Indeed, that burden is and it will always remain Congress' responsibility. The amounts of money that may be spared through the application of the line-item veto are significant but certainly not significant enough to remedy the Federal budget deficit.

But granting the President this authority is, I believe, a necessary first step toward improving certain of our own practices, improvements that must be made for serious redress of our fiscal problems. The Senator from West Virginia reveres, as do I, the custom of the Senate, but I am sure he would agree that all human institutions, just as all human beings, must fall short of perfection.

For some years now, the Congress has failed to exercise its power of the purse with as much care as we should have. Blame should not be unfairly apportioned to one side of the aisle or the other. All have shared in our failures. Nor has Congress' imperfections proved us to be inferior to other branches of Government. This is not what the proponents contend.

What we contend is that the President is less encumbered by the political pressures affecting the spending decisions of Members of Congress whose constituencies are more narrowly defined than his. Thus, the President could take a sterner view of public expenditures which serve the interests of only a few which cannot be reasonably argued as worth the expense given our current financial difficulties. In anticipation of a veto and the attendant public attention to the vetoed line-item appropriation, Members should prove more able to resist the attractions of unnecessary spending and thus begin the overdue reform of our spending practices. It is not an indictment of Congress nor any of its Members to note that this very human institution can stand a little reform now and then.

Madam President, I urge my colleagues to support the line-item veto conference report and show the American people that, for their sake, we are prepared to relinquish a little of our own power.

I am very pleased to be here on this incredibly historic occasion.

Source: *Congressional Record,* 104th Cong., 2nd sess., March 27, 1996 (Washington: GPO, 1996), 142:6500–6502, 6568.

Notes

1. U.S. Congress, House Committee on Rules, *Item Veto: State Experience and Its Application to the Federal Situation,* Comm. Print., 99th Cong., 2nd sess., (Washington, D.C.: GPO, 1986), 1–51, 201–231, 265–268; U.S. Congress, House Committee on the Budget, *The Line-Item Veto: An Appraisal,* Comm. Print, 98th Cong., 2nd sess., (Washington, D.C.: GPO, 1984), 11–12; Louis Fisher, *Constitutional Conflicts Between Congress and the President,* 4th ed. (Lawrence: University Press of Kansas, 1997), 132–140; Robert J. Spitzer, *The Presidential Veto: Touchstone of the American Presidency* (Albany: State University of New York Press, 1988), 126–129.

2. P.L. 104-130, 110 Stat. 1200–1212 (April 9, 1996). See also U.S. Congress Committee of Conference, *Line Item Veto Act,* 104th Cong., 2nd sess., H. Rept. 104-491 (Washington, D.C.: GPO, 1996).

3. Quotes are found in Vernon L. Wilkinson, "Federal Legislation: The Item Veto in the American Constitutional System," *Georgetown Law Journal,* November 1936, 25:112–113, 115–116, 118, 121–122, 124–125, 127. See also Jasmine Farrier, *Passing the Buck: Congress, the Budget, and Deficits* (Lexington: University Press of Kentucky, 2004), 177–189.

4. *Guide to Congress,* 5th ed., 2 vols. (Washington, D.C.: CQ Press, 2000), 1:530; Michael Nelson, ed. *Guide to the Presidency,* 2nd ed., 2 vols. (Washington, D.C.: CQ Press, 1996), 1:561; Louis Fisher and Neal Devins, "How Successfully Can the States' Item Veto Be Transferred to the President?" *Georgetown Law Journal,* October 1986, 75:182–197; Spitzer, *The Presidential Veto: Touchstone of the American Presidency,* 134–138; Ronald C. Moe, *Prospects for the Item Veto at the Federal Level: Lessons from the States* (Washington, D.C.: National Academy of Public Administration, 1988).

5. *Guide to Congress,* 5th ed., 2 vols. (Washington, D.C.: CQ Press, 2000), 1:530; Nelson, *Guide to the Presidency,* 2nd ed., 2 vols., 1:561.

6. "Line Item Veto," *Congressional Record,* May 5, 1993, 139: 9260; "Line Item Veto XIV," *Congressional Record,* October 18, 1993, 139:24910; "Legislative Line-Item Veto Act of 1995 — Conference Report," *Congressional Record,* March 27, 1996, 142:6508.

7. "Legislative Line-Item Veto Act of 1995 — Conference Report," 6502.

8. *Congressional Quarterly Almanac, 1996* (Washington, D.C.: Congressional Quarterly, 1997), 2-282–32; Andrew Taylor, "Congress Hands President a Budgetary Scalpel," *Congressional Quarterly,* March 30, 1996, 54:864–867; "Legislative Line Item Veto Act of 1995 — Conference Report," *Congressional Record,* March 27, 1996, 142:6568–6569; "Providing for Consideration of H.R. 3136, Contract with America Advancement Act of 1996," *Congressional Record,* March 28, 1996, 142:6873–6888; P.L. 104-130, 110 Stat. 1200–1212 (April 9, 1996).

9. *Clinton v. City of New York,* 524 U.S. 417 (1998).

Iraq War Resolution

✷ 2002 ✷

A shocked and stunned America watched on the morning of September 11, 2001, as the worst terrorist attack in U.S. history destroyed the Twin Towers of the World Trade Center in New York City, left a gaping hole in the Pentagon outside of Washington, D.C., and resulted in a plane crash in a field in Pennsylvania. Like December 7, 1941, the day Japan attacked Pearl Harbor, it is a day that will live in infamy. In the immediate aftermath, political partisanship in Washington, D.C., quickly gave way as Congress joined with President George W. Bush in focusing on a response to the attacks. On September 14, the Senate 98–0 and the House, 420–1 passed a joint resolution S.J. Res. 23 authorizing the president to "use all necessary and appropriate force against those nations, organizations, or persons he determines planned, authorized, committed, or aided the terrorist attacks ... or harbored such organizations or persons." The president signed the legislation on September 18.[1]

Later that week, President Bush told a joint session of Congress that U.S. intelligence had connected the September 11 attacks to "a collection of loosely affiliated terrorist organizations known as Al Qaeda," led by Osama bin Laden, which were supported by the Taliban regime in Afghanistan. The president continued by demanding that the Taliban: (1) turn over to U.S. authorities all Al Qaeda and terrorists hiding in Afghanistan, (2) release all unjustly imprisoned foreign nationals, including American citizens, and (3) allow U.S. forces access to terrorist training camps. On October 7, after the Taliban rejected his demands, President Bush told a nationwide television audience that U.S. forces had begun strikes against Al Qaeda terrorist training camps and Taliban military installations in Afghanistan.[2] Although American forces experienced a quick military victory against the Taliban regime in Afghanistan, bin Laden alluded capture.

Immediately following September 11, bin Laden became America's most prominent enemy. By the end the year, however, news coverage of bin Laden began to wane as his trail grew cold, and it continued to decline. Interestingly, coverage of America's old nemesis, Saddam Hussein of Iraq, remained relatively constant. As early as December 2001, reports said that the State Department and the Pentagon were planning how to drive Hussein from power, but there was no recommendation to attack Iraq. A month later, President Bush in his State of the Union Address declared that the "war on terror" had only begun, and Iraq, Iran, North Korea, and "their terrorist allies constitute an axis of evil, arming to threaten the peace of the world.... History has called America and her allies to action, and it is both our responsibility and our privilege to fight freedom's fight." Now administration officials began to talk more openly about Iraq's hostility toward America and action that might be necessary, as did the president, several members of Congress, and the media. By April, Hussein had become President Bush's main rhetorical enemy, and the president began using the term "war on terrorism" with increased frequency.[3]

During the summer and fall of 2002, the Bush administration set the stage for a possible invasion of Iraq. Since the 1991 Gulf War, the president argued, previous attempts to constrain Hussein — inspections, economic sanctions, no-fly zones, and limited military strikes — had proven ineffectual. It was, Bush insisted, time to act. Only the credible threat of war would force Hussein to destroy his arsenal of weapons of mass destruction that threatened Middle East stability and terminate his relationships with Al Qaeda and other terrorist organizations.[4]

On September 12, 2002, one year and a day after the terrorist attacks, the president told the United Nations General Assembly:

> We must choose between a world of fear and a world of progress. We cannot stand by and do nothing while dangers gather. We must stand up for our security and for the permanent rights and the hopes of mankind. By heritage and by choice, the United States of America will make that stand. And, delegates to the United Nations, you have the power to make that stand as well.[5]

Although there was no credible evidence that Hussein was responsible for the terrorist attacks of 2001, that doubt was not a major obstacle to the administration in moving forward on Iraq. On September 19, President Bush announced he was sending Congress suggested language for authorization to use force against Iraq, and looked "forward to a good, constructive debate." A week later, Sen. Tom Daschle, D-S.D., and Sen. Trent Lott, R-Miss., introduced S.J. Res. 45, which was based on the president's proposal. Over the next ten days, negotiations between the White House and congressional leaders resulted in several adjustments in language. When Senate minority leader Daschle sought still additional concessions, the president stunned Democrats by striking a compromise with House minority leader Richard A. Gephardt, D-Mo. The compromise authorized the president "to use the Armed Forces of the United States as he determines to be necessary and appropriate to defend the national security of the United States against the continuing threat posed by Iraq." In return, Gephardt received language requiring a presidential ruling that "further diplomatic or other peaceful means alone would no longer protect the national security of the United States."[6]

President Bush announced the compromise in a Rose Garden ceremony on October 2. Later that day, Sen. Joseph Lieberman, D-Conn., and several other senators introduced the revised resolution S.J. Res. 46 in the Senate, and Speaker Dennis Hastert, R-Ill., minority leader Gephardt, and one hundred thirty-six cosponsors introduced an identical bill H.J. Res. 114 in the House.[7] While there was overwhelming bipartisan congressional support for the president's request, the ensuing debate lasted three days in the House and five in the Senate. Several members of Congress considered an endorsement of the nation's first preemptive strike against a sovereign nation problematic because there was no proof that Iraq posed an imminent chemical, biological, or nuclear threat; or that there was any direct connection between Iraq and the September 11 terrorist attacks. Waiting, supporters countered, would only allow Hussein time to increase his strength.

Most congressional Republicans supported the president, endorsing both his prerogative to define the nature of the problem and the course of corrective action. "Each day that goes by," Sen. John McCain, R-Ariz., stressed, Hussein "becomes more dangerous, his capabilities become better, and, in the case of nuclear weapons, it is not a question of

In March 2003, members of the House of Representatives voted on legislation pledging congressional support to U.S. military forces serving in Operation Iraqi Freedom. Though Congress voted in October 2002 to authorize the use of force in Iraq, debate continues over the conflict.
Source: Associated Press.

whether, it is a question of when." Sen. Mitch McConnell, R-Ky., emphasized that the president was giving the United Nations and the international community one final chance to disarm Hussein through diplomatic means. "The President has made it clear that if reason fails, force will prevail." McConnell said he was "reminded of President Franklin Roosevelt's insights into Nazi Germany and Adolf Hitler: 'No man can tame a tiger into a kitten by stroking it. There can be no appeasement with ruthlessness. There can be no reasoning with an incendiary bomb.'"[8]

A supportive but cautious Sen. Chuck Hagel, R-Neb., told his Senate colleagues that "[i]n authorizing the use of force against Iraq, we are at the beginning of a road that has no clear end." "While I cannot predict the future," he said, "I believe that what we decide in this Chamber this week will influence America's security and role in the world for the coming decades. It will serve as the framework, both intentionally and unintentionally, for the future. It will set in motion a series of actions and events that we cannot now understand or control."[9]

The Democrats in Congress were more divided on the resolution. Some were willing to grant President Bush broad latitude to decide whether and when to invade Iraq. Among that group were those who felt before going to war the president needed to issue a formal determination that diplomatic alternatives had been exhausted, and, after military action commenced, he needed to regularly consult with Congress. Others were willing to endorse military action, but sought to place limits on its scope, to extract a clear commitment to first exhaust all diplomatic options, to force the president to secure a U.N. Security Council resolution backing military action, and/or to have the president issue a formal determination to go to war. Still others strongly opposed military action and raised numerous concerns, ranging from lack of evidence that Iraq posed an imminent threat to the United States to Congress's supposed abrogation of its constitutional war-making responsibilities.

Sen. Robert C. Byrd, D-W.Va., pleaded with the Senate, in the words of one writer, "to flex its constitutional muscle and stop the march toward war." The day before the Senate voted, Byrd reminded his colleagues of what was at stake. "This is a fateful decision," he said, "It involves the treasure of this country. It involves the blood of our fighting men and women." Particularly potent was the admonition of Sen. Patrick J. Leahy, D-Vt., that "declaring war is the single most important responsibility given to Congress. Unfortunately, at times like this, it is a responsibility Congress has often shirked. Too often Congress has abdicated its responsibility and deferred to the executive branch on such matters. It should not. It should pause and read the Constitution."[10]

On the evening of October 7, three days prior to the House and Senate votes, President Bush gave a major speech in Cincinnati, Ohio in which he defended the resolution and laid out the case for war. "Saddam Hussein is harboring terrorists and the instruments of terror, the instruments of mass death and destruction," he declared, and the United States could no longer stand by and watch. Only the credible threat of military action, the argument ran, could force Hussein to immediately reveal and destroy all of his weapons programs and stockpiles, and then terminate his relationships with terrorists.[11]

Despite numerous floor challenges offered during the House and Senate debate, the outcome indicated overwhelming and bipartisan support for the president's request. On October 10, the House voted 296–133 in favor of the "Authorization for Use of Military Force Against Iraq Resolution of 2002," granting the president authority to "use the Armed Forces of the United States as he determines to be necessary and appropriate in order to: (1) defend the national security of the United States against the continuing threat posed by Iraq; and (2) enforce all relevant United Nations Security Council resolutions regarding Iraq." Shortly after

---

THE FINAL VOTE

Authorization for Use of Military Force Against Iraq Resolution of 2002
H.J. Res. 114

House
October 10, 2002

	Yea	Nay
Republicans	215	6
Democrats	81	126
Independent	0	1
Total	**232**	**133**

Senate
October 11, 2002*

	Yea	Nay
Republicans	48	1
Democrats	29	21
Independent		1
Total	**77**	**22**

*Senate session and the *Congressional Record* date is October 10, but the vote took place after midnight.

Sources: "Authorization for Use of Military Force Against Iraq Resolution of 2002," *Congressional Record*, October 10, 2002, 148:20277, 20490; *Congressional Quarterly Almanac Plus, 2002* (Washington: Congressional Quarterly, 2003), 58:9-3-9-6, H142-H143, S-48.

midnight, the Senate followed suit, 77–23. On October 16, the president signed the authorization into law.[12]

Near the end of the congressional debate on the Iraq War Resolution, David Firestone of the *New York Times* described the floor exchanges as having "little passion" despite what was at stake. "Democrats and Republicans" alike, he wrote, "took the floor to repeat, with little variation, the precise arguments for invasion that President Bush" had made. "A few dissenters struggled to raise their voices above the consensus but were reduced to unsuccessfully pleading for floor time."[13] Over ensuing years, those congressional dissenters were not only vindicated in the eyes of a majority of Americans but also in the eyes of many of their colleagues.

In March 2003, American forces, a smaller force from Great Britain, and token forces from several other nations quickly overran Iraq and toppled the regime of Saddam Hussein. During the course of the invasion, American forces suffered fewer than two hundred deaths, and in May 2003 the president proclaimed "mission accomplished." Stabilizing post-Hussein Iraq, however, proved far more challenging.

After more than half a decade of postwar occupation in Iraq, American troops still were trying to suppress a military insurgency, to establish order, and rebuild the nation's infrastructure. By mid-2008, more than four thousand American soldiers had been killed in Iraq, and another thirty thousand had been wounded. The total budgetary and economic cost of the war to the United States, it is estimated, could turn out to be as much as "$3 trillion, with the cost to the rest of the world perhaps doubling that number again."[14]

After more than five years, with no apparent end to American involvement in Iraq, each request for additional funding prompted increasingly lengthy and contentious congressional debates, which befits a conflict now perceived by many as a mistake. In the 2006 midterm election, widespread disenchantment with the war and the erroneous information offered to support the invasion contributed to the Republican Party losing control of both the House and the Senate for the first time in twelve years. In 2008, presidential and congressional candidates faced the ongoing issue of how to deal with the lingering effects of the 2002 Iraq War Resolution.

SENATOR PATRICK J. LEAHY OPPOSES THE IRAQ WAR RESOLUTION

OCTOBER 9, 2002

The opportunity and responsibility to have this debate is one of the cornerstones on which this institution, and indeed this country is built. Some have suggested that expressing misgivings or asking questions about the President's plan to attack Iraq is somehow unpatriotic. Others have tried to make it an election year issue on bumper stickers or in TV advertisements.

These attempts are misguided. They are beneath the people who make these attempts and they are beneath the issue. This is an issue of war. An issue of war should be openly debated. That is a great freedom of this Nation. We fought a revolution to have such debates.

As I and others have said over and over, declaring war is the single most important responsibility given to Congress. Unfortunately, at times like this, it is a responsibility Congress has often shirked. Too often, Congress has abdicated its responsibility and deferred to the executive branch on such matters. It should not. It should pause and read the Constitution.

In the Senate, we have a duty to the Constitution, to our consciences, and to the American people, especially our men and women in uniform, to ask questions, to discuss the benefits, the risks, the costs, to have a thorough debate and then vote to declare war or not. This body, the Senate, is supposed to be the conscience of the Nation. We should fulfill this great responsibility.

In my twenty-eight years in the Senate, I can think of many instances when we asked questions and took the time to study the facts. It led to significant improvements in what we have done here.

I can also remember times when Senators in both parties wished they had taken more time to carefully consider the issues before them, to ask the hard questions, or make changes to the legislation, despite the sometimes overwhelming public pressure to pass the first bill that came along.

I know following the Constitution is not always politically expedient or popular. The Constitution was not designed to be politically expedient, but following the Constitution is the right course to take. It is what we are sworn to do, and there is no question that having this debate, which really began some months ago, has helped move the administration in the right direction.

Today, we are considering a resolution offered by Senator LIEBERMAN to authorize the use of force. Article I of the Constitution gives the Congress the sole power to declare war. But instead of exercising this responsibility and voting up or down on a declaration of war, what have we done? We have chosen to delegate this authority and this burden to the executive branch.

This resolution, like others before it, does not declare anything. It tells the President: Why don't you decide; we are not going to.

★ ★ ★ ★

Mr. President, there is no dispute that Saddam Hussein is a menace to his people and to Iraq's neighbors. He is a tyrant and the world would be far better without him.

Saddam Hussein has also made no secret of his hatred of the United States, and should he acquire a nuclear weapon and the means to deliver it, he would pose a grave threat to the lives of all Americans, as well as to our closest allies.

The question is not whether Saddam Hussein should be disarmed; it is how imminent is this threat and how should we deal with it?

Do we go it alone, as some in the administration are eager to do because they see Iraq as their first opportunity to apply the President's strategy of preemptive military force?

Do we do that, potentially jeopardizing the support of those nations we need to combat terrorism and further antagonizing Muslim populations who already deeply resent our policies in the Middle East?

Or, do we work with other nations to disarm Saddam, using force if other options fail?

The resolution now before the Senate leaves the door open to act alone, even absent an imminent threat. It surrenders to the President authority which the Constitution explicitly reserves for the Congress.

And as I said two weeks ago, it is premature. I have never believed, nor do I think that any Senator believes, that U.S. foreign policy should be hostage to any nation, nor to the United Nations. Ultimately, we must do what we believe is right and necessary to protect our security, whenever it is called for. But going to war alone is rarely the answer.

On Monday night, the President spoke about working with the United Nations. He said:

> To actually work, any new inspections, sanctions, or enforcement mechanisms will have to be very different. America wants the U.N. to be an effective organization that helps keep the peace. That is why we are urging the Security Council to adopt a new resolution setting out tough, immediate requirements.

I could not agree more. The President is right. The status quo is unacceptable. Past U.N. resolutions have not worked. Saddam Hussein and other Iraqi officials have lied to the world over and over and over. As the President points out, an effort is underway in the U.N. Security Council — led by the United States — to adopt a strong resolution requiring unconditional, unimpeded access for U.N. weapons inspectors, backed up with force if necessary.

That effort is making steady progress. There is wide acceptance that a new resolution is necessary before the inspectors can return to Iraq, and this has put pressure on the other nations, especially Russia and France, to support our position.

If successful, it could achieve the goal of disarming Saddam without putting thousands of American and innocent Iraqi lives at risk or spending tens of billions, or hundreds of billions, of dollars at a time when the U.S. economy is weakening, the Federal deficit is growing, and the retirement savings of America's senior citizens have been decimated.

Diplomacy is often tedious. It does not usually make the headlines or the evening news. We certainly know about past diplomatic failures. But history has shown over and over that diplomatic pressure can not only protect our national interests, it can also enhance the effectiveness of military force when force becomes necessary.

The negotiations are at a sensitive stage. By authorizing the use of force today, the Congress will be saying that irrespective of what the Security Council does, we have already decided to go our own way.

★ ★ ★ ★

Many respected and knowledgeable people — former senior military officers and diplomats among them — have expressed strong reservations about this resolution. They agree that if there is credible evidence that Saddam Hussein is planning to use weapons of mass destruction against the United States or one of our allies, the American people and the Congress would overwhelmingly support the use of American military power to stop him. But they have not seen that evidence, and neither have I.

We have heard a lot of bellicose rhetoric, but what are the facts? I am not asking for 100 percent proof, but the administration is asking Congress to make a decision to go to war based on conflicting statements, angry assertions, and assumption based on speculation. This is not the way a great nation goes to war.

The administration has also been vague, evasive and contradictory about its plans. Speaking here in Washington, the President and his advisors continue to say this issue is about disarming Saddam Hussein; that he has made no decision to use force.

But the President paints a different picture when he is on the campaign trail, where he often talks about regime change. The Vice President said on national television that "The President's made it clear that the goal of the United States is regime change. He said that on many occasions."

★ ★ ★ ★

This resolution permits the President to take whatever military action he wants, whenever he wants, for as long as he wants. It is a blank check.

We have the best trained, best equipped Armed Forces in the world, and I know they can defeat Iraq. I hope, as we all do, that if force is used the Iraqi military surrenders quickly.

This resolution permits the President to take whatever military action he wants, whenever he wants, for as long as he wants. It is a blank check. — Patrick J. Leahy

---

But if we have learned anything from history, it is that wars are unpredictable. They can trigger consequences that none of us would intend or expect. Is it fair to the American people, who have become accustomed to wars waged from thirty thousand feet lasting a few weeks with few casualties, that we not discuss what else could happen? We could be involved in urban warfare where large numbers of our troops are killed.

And what of the critical issue of rebuilding a post-Saddam Iraq, about which the Administration has said virtually nothing? It is one thing to topple a regime, but it is equally important, and sometimes far more difficult, to rebuild a country to prevent it from becoming engulfed by factional fighting.

If these nations cannot successfully rebuild, then they will once again become havens for terrorists. To ensure that does not happen, do we foresee basing thousands of U.S. troops in Iraq after the war, and if so, for how many years? How many billions of dollars will we spend?

Are the American people prepared to spend what it will take to rebuild Iraq even when the administration is not budgeting the money that is needed to rebuild Afghanistan, having promised to do so? Do we spend hundreds of billions in Iraq, as the President's Economic Adviser suggested, while not providing at home for homeland defense, drought aid for farmers, education for our young people, and other domestic priorities?

Who is going to replace Saddam Hussein? The leading coalition of opposition groups, the Iraqi National Congress, is divided, has questionable support among the Iraqi people, and has made little headway in overthrowing Saddam. While Iraq has a strong civil society, in the chaos of a post-Saddam Iraq another dictator could rise to the top or the country could splinter along ethnic or religious lines.

These are the questions the American people are asking and these are the issues we should be debating. They are difficult issues of war and peace, but the administration, and the proponents of this resolution, would rather leave them for another day. They say: vote now! and let the President decide. Don't give the U.N. time to do its job. Don't worry that the resolution is a blank check.

I can count the votes. The Senate will pass this resolution. They will give the President the authority he needs to send United States troops to Iraq. But before the President takes that step, I hope he will consider the questions that have been asked. I hope he considers the concerns raised by former generals, senior diplomats, and intelligence officials in testimony before Congress. I hope he listens to concerns raised privately by some of our military officers. Above all, I hope he will listen to the American people who are urging him to proceed cautiously and not to act alone.

Notwithstanding whatever disagreements there may be on our policy toward Iraq, if a decision is made to send troops into battle, there is no question that every Member of Congress will unite behind our President and our Armed Forces.

But that time has not yet come. Based on what I know today, I believe in order to solve this problem without potentially creating more terrorists and more enemies, we have to act deliberately and not precipitously. The way the United States responds to the threat posed by Iraq is going to have consequences for our country and for the world for years to come.

Authorizing a U.S. attack to overthrow another government while negotiations at the United Nations are ongoing, and before we exhaust other options, could damage our standing in the world as a country that recognizes the importance of international solutions. I am afraid that it would be what the world expects of a superpower that seems increasingly disdainful of international opinion or cooperation and collective diplomacy, a superpower that seems more and more inclined to "go it alone."

What a dramatic shift from a year ago, when the world was united in its expressions of sympathy toward the United States. A year ago, the world would have welcomed the opportunity to work with us on a wide agenda of common problems.

I remember the emotion I felt when I saw "The Star Spangled Banner" sung by crowds of people outside Buckingham Palace in London. The leading French newspaper, *Le Monde*, declared, "We are all Americans." China's Jiang Zemin was one of the first world leaders to call Washington and express sympathy after September 11.

Why squander the goodwill we had in the world? Why squander this unity? If September 11 taught us anything, it is that protecting our security involves much more than military might. It involves cooperation with other nations to break up terrorist rings, dry up the sources of funding, and address the conditions of ignorance and despair that create breeding grounds for terrorists. We are far more likely to achieve these goals by working with other nations than by going it alone.

I am optimistic that the Administration's efforts at the U.N. will succeed and that the Security Council will adopt a strong resolution. If Saddam Hussein refuses to comply, then force may be justified, and it may be required.

But we are a great nation, with a wide range of resources available to us and with the goodwill of most of the world. Let us proceed deliberately, moving as close to our goal as we can by working with our allies and the United Nations, rather than writing a blank check that is premature, and which would continue the trend of abdicating our constitutional authority and our responsibility.

★ ★ ★ ★

I am not suggesting the administration is trying to mislead the Congress about the situation in Iraq, as Congress was misled on the Tonkin Gulf resolution. I am not comparing a possible war in Iraq to the Vietnam war. They are very different countries, with different histories, and with different military capabilities. But the key words in the resolution we are considering today are remarkably similar to the infamous resolution of thirty-eight years ago which so many Senators and so many millions of Americans came to regret.

Let us not make that mistake again. Let us not pass a Tonkin Gulf resolution. Let us not set the history of our great country this way. Let us not make the mistake we made once before.

Source: *Congressional Record*, 107th Cong., 2nd sess., October 9, 2002 (Washington: GPO, 2002), 148:19681–19683.

SENATOR CHUCK HAGEL SUPPORTS THE IRAQ WAR RESOLUTION

OCTOBER 9, 2002

Madam President, the Senate is, by design, a deliberative institution. Over this past week, we have witnessed thoughtful debate and commentary on how to meet the challenge of Saddam Hussein's Iraq. Ours is not an academic exercise; debate informs our decision whether to authorize the President to use force if necessary to enforce U.N. Security Council resolutions dealing with Iraqi disarmament.

There are no easy answers in Iraq. The decision to commit our troops to war is the most difficult decision Members of Congress make. Each course of action we consider in Iraq leads us into imperfect, dangerous, and unknown situations. But we cannot avoid decision on Iraq. The President cannot avoid decision on Iraq. The risks of inaction are too high. We are elected to solve problems, not just debate them. The time has come to chart a new course in Iraq and in the Middle East.

History informs our debate and our decisions. We know tyranny cannot be appeased. We also know our power and influence are enhanced by both a nobility of purpose and the support of allies and institutions that reinforce an international commitment to peace and prosperity. We know war has its own dynamic, that it favors neither ideology, nor democracy, nor tyranny, that men and women die, and that nations and individuals who know war are never again the same.

President Bush has rightly brought the case against Iraq back before the United Nations. Our problems with Iraq, as well as terrorism and the worldwide proliferation of weapons of mass destruction, are not America's alone. Israel, Iran, Turkey, Saudi Arabia, Kuwait, Iraq's own Kurdish population, and other nations and peoples are on the front lines of Saddam Hussein's ambitions for weapons of mass death.

The United Nations, with American leadership, must act decisively to end Saddam Hussein's decade-long violations of U.N. Security Council resolutions. America's best case for the possible use of force against Iraq rests with the American and international commitment to enforcing Iraq's disarmament. The diplomatic process is not easy, and we face the competing interests and demands of Russia, France, China, and others, whose interests in Iraq may not always be the same as ours. A regional and international coalition is essential for creating the political environment that will be required for any action we take in Iraq, and especially for how we sustain a democratic transition in a post-Saddam Iraq. We cannot do it alone.

America — including the Congress — and the world, must speak with one voice about Iraqi disarmament, as it must continue to do so in the war on terrorism.

Because the stakes are so high, America must be careful with her rhetoric and mindful of how others perceive her intentions. Actions in Iraq must come in the context of an American-led, multilateral approach to disarmament, not as the first case for a new American doctrine involving the preemptive use of force. America's challenge in this new century will be to strengthen its relationships around the world while leading the world in our war on terrorism, for it is the success of the first challenge that will determine the success of the second. We should not mistake our foreign policy priorities for ideology in a rush to proclaim a new doctrine in world affairs. America must understand it cannot alone win a war against terrorism. It will require allies, friends, and partners.

American leadership in the world will be further defined by our actions in Iraq and the Middle East. What begins in Iraq will not end in Iraq. There will be other "Iraqs." There will be continued acts of terrorism, proliferating powers, and regional conflicts. If we do it right and lead through the U.N., in concert with our allies, we can set a new standard for American leadership and international cooperation. The perception of American power is power, and how our power is perceived can either magnify or diminish our influence in the world. The Senate has a constitutional responsibility and an institutional obligation in this effort.

Federalist Paper No. 63 specifically notes the responsibilities of the Senate in foreign affairs as follows:

> An attention to the judgment of other nations is important to every government for two reasons: The one is that independently of the merits of any particular plan or measure, it is desirable, on various accounts, that it should appear to other nations as the offspring of a wise and honorable policy; the second is that, in doubtful cases, particularly where the national councils may be warped by some strong passion or momentary interest, the presumed or known opinion of the impartial world may be the best guide that can always be followed. What has not America lost by her want of character with foreign nations and how many errors and follies would she not have avoided, if the justice and propriety of her measures had, in every instance, been previously tried by the light in which they would probably appear to the unbiased part of mankind?

Remarkable words. The resolution before us today should be tried in that same light as the *Federalist Papers* points out. The original resolution proposed by the Bush administration, S.J. Res. 45, would have been a setback for this institution. It did not reflect the best democratic traditions of either Congressional-Executive relations, or the conduct of American foreign policy.

S.J. Res. 46, sponsored by Senators LIEBERMAN, WARNER, MCCAIN, and BAYH, is a far more responsible and accountable document than the one we started with three weeks ago. I congratulate my colleagues, especially Senators LUGAR, BIDEN, and DASCHLE, and the four sponsors of this resolution, for their efforts and leadership in getting it to this point.

S.J. Res. 46 narrows the authorization for the use of force to all relevant U.N. resolutions regarding Iraq, and to defend-

ing our national interests against the threats posed by Iraq. It includes support for U.S. diplomatic efforts at the U.N.; a requirement that, before taking action, the President formally determines that diplomatic or other peaceful means will not be adequate in meeting our objectives; reference to the war powers resolution requirements; and periodic reports to Congress that include those actions described in the section of the Iraq Liberation Act of 1998 regarding assistance and support for Iraq upon replacement of Saddam Hussein. This resolution recognizes Congress as a coequal partner in dealing with the threat from Saddam Hussein's Iraq.

If disarmament in Iraq requires the use of force, we need to consider carefully the implications and consequences of our actions. The future of Iraq after Saddam Hussein is also an open question. Some of my colleagues and some American analysts now speak authoritatively of Sunnis, Shiites, and Kurds in Iraq, and how Iraq can be a test case for democracy in the Arab world.

How many of us really know and understand much about Iraq, the country, the history, the people, the role in the Arab world? I approach the issue of post-Saddam Iraq and the future of democracy and stability in the Middle East with more caution, realism, and a bit more humility. While the people of the Arab world need no education from America about Saddam's record of deceit, aggression, and brutality, and while many of them may respect and desire the freedoms the American model offers, imposing democracy through force in Iraq is a roll of the dice. A democratic effort cannot be maintained without building durable Iraqi political institutions and developing a regional and international commitment to Iraq's reconstruction. No small task.

To succeed, our commitment must extend beyond the day after to the months and years after Saddam is gone. The American people must be told of this long-term commitment, risk, and costs of this undertaking.

We should not be seduced by the expectations of "dancing in the streets" after Saddam's regime has fallen, the kites, the candy, and cheering crowds we expect to greet our troops, but instead, focus on the great challenges ahead, the commitment and resources that will be needed to ensure a democratic transition in Iraq and a more stable and peaceful Middle East. We should spend more time debating the cost and extent of this commitment, the risks we may face in military engagement with Iraq, the implications of the precedent of United States military action for regime change, and the likely character and challenges of a post-Saddam Iraq. We have heard precious little from the President, his team, as well as from this Congress, with a few notable exceptions, about these most difficult and critical questions.

We need only look to Afghanistan where the Afghan people joyously welcomed our liberation force but, months later, a fragile transition government grapples with rebuilding a fractured political culture, economy, and country.

However, Iraq, because of its resources, geography, capabilities, history, and people, offers even more complications and greater peril and, yes, greater opportunities and greater promise. This is the vast unknown, the heavy burden that lies ahead.

The Senate should not cast a vote in the hopes of putting Iraq behind us so we can get back to our campaigns or move on to other issues next year. The decision to possibly commit a nation to war cannot and should not ever be considered in the context of either party loyalty or campaign politics. I regret that this vote will take place under the cloud and pressure of elections next month. Some are already using the Iraq issue to gain advantage in political campaigns. It might have been better for our vote to have been delayed until after the elections, as it was in 1990. Authorizing the use of force against Iraq or any country for any purpose should always be weighed on its own merits, not with an eye on the politics of the vote or campaign TV spots. War is too serious, the human price too high, and the implications unforeseen.

While I cannot predict the future, I believe that what we decide in this Chamber this week will influence America's security and role in the world for the coming decades. It will serve as the framework, both intentionally and unintentionally, for the future. It will set in motion a series of actions and events that we cannot now understand or control.

In authorizing the use of force against Iraq, we are at the beginning of a road that has no clear end. The votes in Congress this week are votes for an intensification of engagement with Iraq and the Middle East, a world of which we know very little and whose destiny will now be directly tied to ours.

America cannot trade a new focus on Iraq for a lesser effort in the Israeli-Palestinian conflict. The bloodshed between Israel and the Palestinians continues, and the dan-

---

In authorizing the use of force against Iraq, we are at the beginning of a road that has no clear end. The votes in Congress this week are votes for an intensification of engagement with Iraq and the Middle East, a world of which we know very little and whose destiny will now be directly tied to ours. — Chuck Hagel

---

ger mounts. Stability in Afghanistan is not assured. We must carry through with our commitment. Stability in this region depends on it. America's credibility is at stake, and long-term stability in central and South Asia hangs in the balance.

We must also continue to pay close attention to North Korea where there is no guesswork about nuclear weapons. There on the Korean peninsula reside nuclear weapons, ballistic missiles, and thirty-seven thousand American troops.

Despite setting the right course for disarmament in Iraq, the administration has yet to define an end game in Iraq or explain the extent of the American commitment if regime change is required, or describe how our actions in Iraq might affect our other many interests and commitments around the world.

I share the hope of a better world without Saddam Hussein, but we do not really know if our intervention in Iraq will lead to democracy in either Iraq or elsewhere in the Arab world. America has continued to take on large, complicated, and expensive responsibilities that will place heavy burdens on all of us over the next generation. It may well be necessary, but Americans should understand the extent of this burden and what may be required to pay for it and support it in both American blood and trade.

As the Congress votes on this resolution, we must understand that we have not put Iraqi issues behind us. This is just the beginning. The risks should not be understated, miscast, or misunderstood. Ours is a path of both peril and opportunity with many detours and no shortcuts.

We in the Congress are men and women of many parts. For me, it is the present-day Senator, the former soldier, or concerned father who guides my judgment and ultimate vote? It is pieces of all, for I am pieces of all. The responsibilities of each lead me to support the Lieberman-McCain-Warner-Bayh resolution, for which I will vote.

In the end, each of us who has the high honor of holding public office has the burden and privilege of decision and responsibilities. It is a sacred trust we share with the public. We will be held accountable for our actions, as it must be.

Source: *Congressional Record*, 107th Cong., 2nd sess., October 9, 2002 (Washington: GPO, 2002), 148:19705–19707.

Notes

1. *Congressional Record*, September 14, 2001, 147:17045, 17156; P.L. 107-40, 115 Stat. 224–225 (September 18, 2001).

2. U.S. President (George W. Bush), *Public Papers of the Presidents of the United States: George W. Bush, 2001*, 2 vols. (Washington, D.C.: GPO, 2003), 2:1140–1141, 1201, 1211–1212.

3. *Public Papers of the Presidents of the United States: George W. Bush, 2002*, 2 vols. (Washington, D.C.: GPO, 2005), 1:131–132. See also Scott L. Athaus and Devon M. Largio, "When Osama Became Saddam: Origins and Consequences of the Change in America's Public Enemy #1," *PS: Political Science and Politics*, October 2004, 37:795–797; Devon M. Largio, "Uncovering the Rationales for War on Iraq: The Words of the Bush Administration, Congress, and the Media from September 12, 2001 to October 11, 2002," BA thesis, Political Science Department, College of Liberal Arts, University of Illinois, Urbana-Champaign, 2004, 21–22, 46–91; F. Ugboaja Ohaegbulam, *A Culture of Deference: Congress, the President, and the Course of the U.S.-Led Invasion and Occupation of Iraq* (New York: Peter Lang, 2007), 175–177.

4. William G. Howell and Jon C. Pevehouse, *While Dangers Gather: Congressional Checks on Presidential War Powers* (Princeton, N.J.: Princeton University Press, 2007), 167–168; Ron Huisken, *The Road to War in Iraq* (Canberra, Australia: Strategic and Defense Studies Center, Australian National University, 2003), 11–15.

5. *Public Papers of the Presidents of the United States: George W. Bush, 2002*, 2:1576.

6. *Public Papers of the Presidents of the United States: George W. Bush, 2002*, 2:1618; S.J. Res. 45, 107th Cong., 2nd sess.; H.J. Res. 114, 107th Cong., 2nd sess. See also Louis Fisher, "Deciding on War Against Iraq: Institutional Failures," *Political Science Quarterly*, Fall 2003, 118:397–398, 403; Miles A. Pomper, "Senate Democrats in Disarray After Gephardt's Deal on Iraq," *CQ Weekly*, October 5, 2002, 60:2606–2610.

7. *Public Papers of the Presidents of the United States: George W. Bush, 2002*, 2: 1707–1708; S.J. Res. 46, 107th Cong., 2nd sess.; H.J. Res. 114, 107th Cong., 2nd sess.

8. *Congressional Record*, October 9, 2002, 148:19699; October 10, 2002, 148:20476.

9. *Congressional Record*, October 9, 2002, 148:19706.

10. Mary Dalrymple, "Byrd's Beloved Chamber Deaf to His Pleas for Delayed Vote," *CQ Weekly*, October 12, 2002, 60:2674; *Congressional Record*, October 9, 2002, 148:19694, 19681. See also Louis Fisher, "Legislative-Executive Relations and U.S. Policy Toward Iraq," in *Presidential Policies and the Road to the Second Iraq War: From Forty One to Forty Three*, ed. John Davis (Aldershot, England: Ashgate, 2006), 80–83.

11. *Public Papers of the Presidents of the United States: George W. Bush, 2002*, 2:1753.

12. *Congressional Record*, October 10, 2002, 148:20215–20277, 20377–20490; P.L. 107-243, 116 Stat. 1498-1502 (October 16, 2002). See also Gebe Martinez, "Concerns Linger for Lawmakers Following Difficult Vote for War," *CQ Weekly*, October 12, 2002, 60:2671–2673, 2675, 2677–2678.

13. David Firestone, "The Nays Won't Have It; The Ayes Talk Anyway," *New York Times*, October 9, 2002, A14.

14. Joseph E. Stiglitz and Linda J. Bilmes, *The Three Trillion Dollar War: The True Cost of the Iraq Conflict* (New York: W.W. Norton, 2008), x. Department of Defense statistics on soldiers killed and wounded in Iraq were found at http://siadapp.dmdc.osd.mil/personnel/CASUALTY/castop.htm.

Selected Bibliography

General

Bacon, Donald C., Roger H. Davidson, and Morton Keller, eds. *The Encyclopedia of the United States Congress.* 4 vols. New York: Simon and Schuster, 1995.

Baskerville, Barnet. *The People's Voice: The Orator in American Society.* Lexington, Ky.: University Press of Kentucky, 1979.

Byrd, Robert C. *The Senate, 1789–1989.* 4 vols. Edited by Mary Sharon Hall. Vol. 3. Classic Speeches, 1830–1993. Washington, D.C.: GPO, 1988–1994.

Castel, Albert, and Scott L. Gibson. *The Yeas and the Nays: Key Congressional Decisions, 1774–1945.* Kalamazoo, Mich.: New Issues Press, Institute of Public Affairs, Western Michigan University, 1975.

Congress and the Nation, 1945–2004. 11 vols. Washington, D.C.: Congressional Quarterly, 1965–2006.

Congressional Quarterly Almanac, 1945–2005. 61 vols. Washington, D.C.: Congressional Quarterly, 1948–2006.

Dictionary of American History. Rev. ed. 8 vols. New York: Charles Scribner's Sons, 1976–1978.

Grimes, Alan P. *Democracy and the Amendments to the Constitution.* Lexington, Mass.: Lexington Books, 1978.

Grossman, Richard L., ed. *Bold Voices: Great Debaters and Dissenters Speak Out in Congress at Crucial Moments in American History.* Garden City, N.Y.: Doubleday, 1960.

Guide to Congress. 6th ed. 2 vols. Washington, D.C.: CQ Press, 2008.

Haynes, George Henry. *The Senate of the United States: Its History and Practice.* 2 vols. Boston: Houghton Mifflin, 1938.

Holland, DeWitte, ed. *America in Controversy: History of American Public Address.* Dubuque, Iowa: William C. Brown, 1973.

Johnston, Alexander. *Masterpieces of American Eloquence.* New York: G. P. Putnam's Sons, 1890.

Josephy, Alvin M., Jr. *On the Hill: A History of the American Congress.* New York: Simon and Schuster, 1979.

Miller, Marion Mills, ed. *Great Debates in American History: From the Debates in the British Parliament on the Colonial Stamp Act (1764–1765) to the Debates in Congress at the Close of the Taft Administration (1912–1913).* 14 vols. Metuchen, N.J.: Mint-Print, Corp., 1970.

Oliver, Robert T. *History of Public Speaking in America.* Boston: Allyn and Bacon, 1965.

Oliver, Robert T., and Eugene E. White, eds. *Selected Speeches from American History.* Boston: Allyn and Bacon, 1966.

Reid, Ronald F., ed. *American Rhetorical Discourse.* 2nd ed. Prospect Heights, Ill.: Waveland Press, 1995.

Reid, Ronald F., ed. *Three Centuries of American Rhetorical Discourse: An Anthology and a Review.* Prospect Heights, Ill.: Waveland Press, 1988.

Remini, Robert V. *The House: The History of the House of Representatives.* New York: Smithsonian Books in Association with HarperCollins, 2006.

Smock, Raymond W., ed. *Landmark Documents on the U.S. Congress.* Washington, D.C.: Congressional Quarterly, 1999.

Stathis, Stephen W. *Landmark Legislation, 1774–2002: Major U.S. Acts and Treaties.* Washington, D.C.: CQ Press, 2003.

U.S. Congress. *Annals of Congress: Debates and Proceedings in the Congress of the United States.* 42 vols. Washington, D.C.: Gales and Seaton, 1834–1856. (1789, 1st Cong.–1824, 18th Cong., 1st sess.)

U.S. Congress. *Congressional Globe.* 46 vols. Washington, D.C.: Blair and Rives, 1834–1873. (1833, 23rd Cong.–1873, 42nd Cong.)

U.S. Congress. *Congressional Record.* Washington, D.C.: GPO, 1874–Present. (1873, 43rd Cong.–Present)

U.S. Congress. *Register of Debates in Congress.* 13 vols. Washington, D.C.: Gales and Seaton, 1825–1837. (1824, 18th Cong., 2nd sess.–1837, 24th Cong.)

U.S. Continental Congress. *Journals of the Continental Congress, 1774–1789,* 34 vols., edited by Worthington Chauncey Ford, Gaillard Hunt, John C. Fitzpatrick, and Roscoe R. Hill. Washington, D.C.: GPO, 1904–1937.

United States Statutes at Large, Vols. 1–17 (Boston: Little, Brown, and Company, 1845–1873), Vols. 18–122 (Washington: GPO, 1875–2008).

Wrage, Ernest J., and Barnet Baskerville, eds. *American Forum: Speeches on Historic Issues, 1788–1900.* New York: Harper, 1960.

Wrage, Ernest J., and Barnet Baskerville. *Contemporary Forum: American Speeches on Twentieth-Century Issues.* New York: Harper, 1962.

Zelizer, Julian E., ed. *The American Congress: The Building of Democracy.* Boston: Houghton Mifflin, 2004.

Introduction

Adams, Charles Francis ed. *The Works of John Adams, Second President of the United States.* 10 vols. Boston: Charles C. Little and James Brown, 1850–1865.

Baskerville, Barnet. *The People's Voice: The Orator in American Society.* Lexington, Ky.: University Press of Kentucky, 1979.

Bessette, Joseph M. "Is Congress a Deliberative Body?" In *The United States Congress: Proceedings of the Thomas P. O'Neill, Jr., Symposium on the U.S. Congress, Boston College, January 30–31, 1981,* edited by Dennis Hale. Boston: Boston College, 1982.

Bessette, Joseph M. *The Mild Voice of Reason: Deliberative Democracy and American National Government.* Chicago: University of Chicago Press, 1994.

Boorstin, Daniel J. *The Americans: The National Experience.* New York: Random House, 1965.

Byrd, Robert C. *The Senate 1789–1989.* 4 vols. Washington, D.C.: GPO, 1988–1993.

Celebrated Speeches of Chatham, Burke, and Erskine. Philadelphia: E. C. and Biddle, 1852.

Clark, Champ. "Is Congressional Oratory a Lost Art?" *The Century Magazine* 81 (December 1910): 307–310.

Commager, Henry Steele. "Congressional Debate and the Course of Events." *Scholastic* 38 (March 17, 1941): 10, 16.

Connor, George E., and Bruce I. Oppenheimer. "Deliberation: An Untimed Value in a Timed Game." In *Congress Reconsidered,* 5th ed., edited by Lawrence C. Dodd and Bruce I. Oppenheimer. Washington, D.C.: CQ Press, 1993.

Dawes, Henry L. "Has Oratory Declined." *The Forum* 18 (October 1894): 146–160.

Galloway, George B. *The Legislative Process in Congress.* New York: Crowell, 1953.

Garay, Ronald. "Broadcasting of Congressional Proceedings." In *The Encyclopedia of the United States Congress,* 4 vols., edited by Donald C. Bacon, Roger H. Davidson, and Morton Keller. New York: Simon and Schuster, 1995.

Garay, Ronald. *Congressional Television: A Legislative History.* Westport, Conn.: Greenwood Press, 1984.

Garfield, James A. "A Century of Congress." *The Atlantic Monthly* 40 (July 1877): 49–64.

Gross, Bertram Myron. *The Legislative Struggle: A Study in Social Combat.* New York: McGraw-Hill, 1953.

Grossman, Richard L., ed. *Bold Voices.* Garden City, N.Y.: Doubleday, 1960.

Hamilton, Alexander, James Madison, and John Jay. *The Federalist,* edited by Benjamin Fletcher Wright. Cambridge, Mass.: Belknap Press of Harvard University Press, 1966.

Historical Statistics of the United States: Colonial Times to 1970. 2 vols. Washington, D.C.: U.S. Bureau of Census, 1975.

Hopkins, Bruce. "The Decline of the Congressional Art." *American Bar Association Journal* 53 (May 1967): 480–484.

Lippman, Walter. "The Indispensable Opposition." *The Atlantic Monthly* 164 (August 1939): 186–190.

Lucas, Stephen E. "Debate and Oratory." In *The Encyclopedia of the United States Congress,* 10 vols., edited by Donald C. Bacon, Roger H. Davidson, and Morton Keller. (New York: Simon and Schuster, 1995): 2:609–610.

McConachie, Lauros G. *Congressional Committees.* New York: Crowell, 1898.

Montross, Lynn. *The Reluctant Rebels: The Story of the Continental Congress, 1774–1789.* New York: Harper, 1950.

Rossiter, Clinton. *1787, The Grand Convention.* New York: Macmillan, 1966.

Sheckels, Theodore F. *When Congress Debates: A Bakhtinian Paradigm.* Westport, Conn.: Praeger, 2000.

Smith, Steven S. *Call to Order: Floor Politics in the House and Senate.* Washington, D.C.: Brookings Institution, 1989.

Smyth, Albert Henry, ed. *The Writings of Benjamin Franklin.* 10 vols. New York: Macmillan, 1905–1907.

"Speech-Making in Congress." *Scribner's Magazine* 7 (January 1874): 294–301.

"The Standard of Congressional Oratory." *Werner's Magazine* 19 (March 1897): 250–251.

Zwirn, Jerrold. "Congressional Debate." *Government Publications Review* 8 (1981): 175–183.

Declaration of Independence (1776)

Adams, Charles F., ed. *Correspondence between John Adams and Mercy Warren.* New York: Arno Press, 1972.

Adams, Charles Francis, ed. *The Works of John Adams, Second President of the United States.* 10 vols. Boston: Little, Brown, 1851–1865.

Becker, Carl Lotus. *The Declaration of Independence.* Cambridge: Harvard University Press, 1922.

Boyd, Julian P. *The Declaration of Independence.* Washington, D.C.: Library of Congress, 1943.

Burnett, Edmund Cody. *The Continental Congress.* New York: Macmillan, 1941.

Ferris, Robert G., and Richard E. Morris. *The Signers of the Declaration of Independence.* Flagstaff, Ariz: Interpretive Publications, 2001.

Fitzpatrick, John C., ed. *The Writings of George Washington.* 39 vols. Washington, D.C.: GPO, 1931–1944.

Ford, Paul Leicester, ed. *The Writings of Thomas Jefferson.* 10 vols. New York: G. P. Putnam's Sons, 1898.

Ford, Worthington Chauncey, Gaillard Hunt, John C. Fitzpatrick, and Roscoe R. Hill, eds. *Journals of the Continental Congress, 1774–1789.* 34 vols. Washington, D.C.: GPO, 1904–1937.

Grigsby, Hugh Blair. *The Virginia Convention of 1776.* Richmond, Va: J. W. Randolph, 1855.

Hawke, David Freeman. "Declaration of Independence." In *Dictionary of American History,* 8 vols. New York: Charles Scribner's Sons, 1976–1978.

Hazelton, John H. *The Declaration of Independence: Its History.* New York: Dodd, Mead, 1906.

Hunt, Gaillard, ed. *The Writings of James Madison.* 9 vols. New York G. P. Putnam's Sons, 1900–1910.

Jillson, Calvin, and Rick K. Wilson. *Congressional Dynamics: Structure, Coordination, and Choice in the First Congress, 1774–1789.* Stanford, Calif.: Stanford University Press, 1994.

"John Dickinson's Notes for a Speech in Congress." In *Letters of Delegates to Congress, 1774–1789,* 26 vols., edited by Paul Smith, Gerard W. Gawalt, Rosemary Fry Plakas, and Eugene R. Sheridan. Washington, D.C.: Library of Congress, 1976–2000.

John Hancock to Certain States, July 6, 1776." In *Letters of Delegates to Congress, 1774–1789,* 26 vols., edited by Paul Smith, Gerard W. Gawalt, Rosemary Fry Plakas, and Eugene R. Sheridan. Washington, D.C.: Library of Congress, 1976–2000.

Kuklick, Bruce K., ed. *Political Writings/Thomas Paine*. Cambridge, UK: Cambridge University Press, 2000.

Montross, Lynn. *The Reluctant Rebels: The Story of the Continental Congress, 1774–1789*. New York: Harper and Brothers, 1970.

Mullett, Charles F. "Common Sense." In *Dictionary of American History*, 8 vols. New York: Charles Scribner's Sons, 1976–1978.

"Notes of Mr. Jefferson's Conversation 1824 at Monticello." In *The Papers of Daniel Webster: Correspondence*, 14 vols., edited by Charles M. Wiltse. Hanover, N.H.: Published for Dartmouth College by the University Press of New England, 1974–1989.

Paine, Thomas. *Common Sense*. New York: Barnes and Noble Books, 1995.

Powell, John H. "Speech of John Dickinson Opposing the Declaration of Independence, 1 July, 1776." *Pennsylvania Magazine of History and Biography* 65 (October 1941): 458–481.

"Thomas Jefferson's Notes of Proceedings in Congress." In *Letters of Delegates to Congress, 1774–1789*, 26 vols., edited by Paul Smith, Gerard W. Gawalt, Rosemary Fry Plakas, and Eugene R. Sheridan. Washington, D.C.: Library of Congress, 1976–2000.

Articles of Confederation (1777)

Boyd, Julian P., et al., eds. *The Papers of Thomas Jefferson*. 34 vols. Princeton, N.J.: Princeton University Press, 1950.

Burnett, Edmund Cody. *The Continental Congress*. New York: W. W. Norton, 1964.

Ford, Worthington Chauncey, Gaillard Hunt, John C. Fitzpatrick, and Roscoe R. Hill, eds. *Journals of the Continental Congress, 1774–1789*. 34 vols. Washington, D.C.: GPO, 1904–1937.

Greene, Jack P. "The Background of the Articles of Confederation." *Publius: The Journal of Federalism* 12 (Fall 1982): 15–44.

Jensen, Merrill. *The Articles of Confederation*. Madison, Wisc.: University of Wisconsin Press, 1948.

Jensen, Merrill. *The New Nation: A History of the United States During the Confederation, 1781–1789*. New York: Alfred A. Knopf, 1967.

Jillson, Calvin, and Rick K. Wilson. *Congressional Dynamics: Structure, Coordination, and Choice in the First Congress, 1774–1789*. Stanford, Calif.: Stanford University Press, 1994.

Levy, Leonard W. "Articles of Confederation." In *Encyclopedia of the American Constitution*, 2nd ed. 6 vols., edited by Leonard W. Levy, Kenneth L. Karst, and Adam Winkler. New York: Macmillan Reference USA, 2000.

McDonald, Forrest. *E Pluribus Unum: The Formation of the American Republic, 1776–1790*. Indianapolis, Ind.: Liberty Press, 1979.

Montross, Lynn. *The Reluctant Rebels: The Story of the Continental Congress, 1774–1789*. New York: Harper and Brothers, 1950.

Smith, Paul H., Gerard W. Gawalt, Rosemary Fry Plakas, and Eugene R. Sheridan, eds. *Letters of Delegates to Congress, 1774–1789*. 26 vols. Vols. 4 and 8. Washington, D.C.: Library of Congress, 1976–2000.

Northwest Ordinance (1781)

Allen, Michael. *The Confederation Congress and the Creation of the American Trans–Application Settlement Policy 1783–1787*. Lewiston, N.Y.: Edwin Mellen Press, 2006.

Berkhofer, Robert F., Jr. "Jefferson, the Ordinance of 1874, and the Origin of the American Territorial System." *William and Mary Quarterly*, 3rd series 29 (April 1972): 231–262.

Bestor, Arthur. "Constitutionalism and the Settlement of the West: The Attainment of Consensus, 1754–1784." In *The American Territorial System*, edited by John Porter Bloom. (Athens: Ohio University Press, 1973): 13–61.

Boyd, Julian P., et al., ed., *The Papers of Thomas Jefferson*. 34 vols. Princeton, N.J.: Princeton University Press, 1950.

Burnett, Edmund C., ed. *Letters of Members of the Continental Congress*. 8 vols. (Washington, D.C.: Carnegie Institution of Washington, 1921–1936): 8:359–360.

Catton, Bruce, and William B. Catton, *The Bold and Magnificent Dream: America's Founding Years, 1492–1815*. Garden City, N.Y.: Doubleday, 1978.

Duffey, Denis P. "The Northwest Ordinance as a Constitutional Document." *Columbia Law Review* 95 (May 1995): 929–968.

Eblen, Jack E. "Origins of the United States Colonial System: The Ordinance of 1787." *Wisconsin Magazine of History* (Summer 1968): 294–314.

Eblen, Jack Ericson. *The First and Second United States Empires: Governors and Territorial Government, 1784–1912*. Pittsburgh: University of Pittsburgh Press, 1968.

Ford, Worthington Chauncey, Gaillard Hunt, John C. Fitzpatrick, and Roscoe R. Hill, eds. *Journals of the Continental Congress, 1774–1789*, 34 vols. (Washington, D.C.: GPO, 1904–1937): 32.334–343.

Henderson, James. *Party Politics in the Continental Congress*. New York: McGraw-Hill, 1974.

Horsman, Reginald. "The Northwest Ordinance and the Shaping of the Nation." *Milwaukee History* 11 (Spring–Summer 1988): 2–16.

McCormick, Richard P. "The 'Ordinance' of 1784?" *William and Mary Quarterly*, 3rd series 50 (January 1993): 112–122.

Merriam, John M. "The Legislative History of the Ordinance of 1787." *Proceedings of the American Antiquarian Society* 5 (April 25, 1888): 303–342.

Onuf, Peter S. "For the Common Benefit: The Northwest Ordinance." *Timeline* 5 (April–May 1988): 2–13.

Onuf, Peter S. *Statehood and Union: A History of the Northwest Ordinance*. Bloomington: Indiana University Press, 1987.

Quaife, Milo M. "The Significance of the Ordinance of 1787." *Journal of the Illinois State Historical Society* 30 (January 1938): 415–428.

Rapport, Leonard. "Discussion of Sources." In *The American Territorial System*, edited by John Porter Bloom. (Athens: Ohio University Press, 1973): 56–57.

Roosevelt, Franklin D. "The President Hails the One Hundred and Fiftieth Anniversary of the Ordinance of 1787. April 30, 1935." In *The Public Papers and Addresses of Franklin D. Roosevelt*, 13 vols., compiled by Samuel I. Rosenman. Vol. 4 (1935), 125. (New York: Random House, 1938–1950).

Roosevelt, Theodore. *The Works of Theodore Roosevelt*, 20 vols. Vol. 9, 218. (New York: Charles Scribner's Sons, 1926).

Shriver, Phillip R. "Freedom's Proving Ground: The Heritage of the Northwest Ordinance." *Wisconsin Magazine of History* 72 (Winter 1988–1989): 126–131.

Smith, Paul H., Gerard W. Gawalt, Rosemary Fry Plakas, and Eugene R. Sheridan, eds. *Letters of Delegates to Congress, 1774–1789*. 26 vols. Vols. 23–24. (Washington, D.C.: Library of Congress, 1976–2000).

Sutton, Robert M. "The Northwest Ordinance: A Bicentennial Souvenir." *Illinois Historical Journal* 81 (Spring 1988): 13–24.

Webster, Daniel. "First Speech on Foot's Resolution." In *The Writings and Speeches of Daniel Webster*. 18 vols. Vol. 5, 262–263. (Boston: Little, Brown, 1903).

Bill of Rights (1789)

Bowling, Kenneth R. "'A Tub to the Whale': The Founding Fathers and the Adoption of the Bill of Rights." *Journal of the Early American Republic* 8 (Fall 1988): 223–251.

Brant, Irving. *The Bill of Rights: Its Origin and Meaning*. Indianapolis: Bobbs-Merrill, 1965.

Fitzpatrick, John C., ed. *The Writings of George Washington from the Original Manuscript Sources, 1745–1799*. 39 vols. Vol. 30. (Washington, D.C.: GPO, 1931–1944).

Leibiger, Stuart. "James Madison and the Amendments to the Constitution, 1787–1789: 'Parchment Barriers.'" *Journal of Southern History* 59 (August 1993): 441–468.

Levy, Leonard W. "Bill of Rights (United States)." In *Encyclopedia of the American Constitution*, 6 vols., 2nd ed., edited by Leonard W. Levy and Kenneth L. Karst. Vol. 1, 113–116. (New York: Macmillan, 2000).

Levy, Leonard W. *Origins of the Bill of Rights*. New Haven, Conn: Yale University Press, 1999.

Rutland, Robert A., et al., eds. *The Papers of James Madison*, 17 vols. Vol. 11. (Charlottesville, Va.: University Press of Virginia, 1962–1991).

Rutland, Robert Allen. *The Birth of the Bill of Rights, 1776–1791*. Bicentennial ed. Boston: Northeastern University Press, 1991.

Schwartz, Bernard. *The Great Rights of Mankind: A History of the American Bill of Rights*. New York: Oxford University Press, 1977.

Schwartz, Bernard, ed. *The Bill of Rights: A Documentary History*. 2 vols. New York: Chelsea House, 1977.

U.S. Congress. Senate. *The Constitution of the United States of America: Analysis and Interpretation*, 108th Cong., 2nd sess., S. Doc. 108–17. Washington, D.C.: GPO, 2004.

Veit, Helen E., Kenneth R. Bowling, and Charlene Bangs Bickford, eds. *Creating the Bill of Rights: The Documentary Record from the First Federal Congress*. Baltimore: Johns Hopkins University Press, 1991.

Judiciary Act of 1789

Goebel, Julius, Jr. *Antecedents and Beginnings to 1801. History of the Supreme Court of the United States*, Vol. 1. New York: Macmillan, 1971.

Marcus, Maeva, and Natalie Wexler. "The Judiciary Act of 1789: Political Compromise or Constitutional Interpretation?" In *Origins of the Federal Judiciary: Essays on the Judiciary Act of 1789*, edited by Maeva Marcus. (New York: Oxford University Press, 1992): 13–39.

Presser, Stephen B. "Judiciary Act of 1789." In *Dictionary of American History*, 10 vols., 3rd ed., edited by Stanley I. Kutler. Vol. 4, 498–499. (New York: Oxford University Press, 2003).

Ritz, Wilfred J. *Rewriting the Judiciary Act of 1789: Exposing Myths, Challenging Premises, and Using New Experiences*. Edited by Wythe Holt and L. H. LaRue. Norman: University of Oklahoma Press, 1990.

U.S. Congress. Senate. *Journal of the First Session of the Senate of the United States*. Washington, D.C.: Gales and Seaton, 1820.

Warren, Charles. "New Light on the History of the Judiciary Act of 1789." *Harvard Law Review*, 37 (November 1923): 49–132.

Jay Treaty (1794–1796)

Bemis, Samuel Flagg. *Jay's Treaty: A Study in Commerce and Diplomacy*. Westport, Conn.: Greenwood Press, 1975.

Bowman, Albert Hall. *The Struggle for Neutrality: Franco-American Diplomacy During the Federalist Era*. Knoxville, Tenn.: University of Tennessee Press, 1974.

Castel, Albert, and Scott L. Gibson. *The Yeas and the Nays: Key Congressional Decisions. 1774–1945*. Kalamazoo, Mich.: New Issues Press, Institute of Public Affairs, Western Michigan University, 1975.

Combs, Jerald A. *The Jay Treaty: Political Background of the Founding Fathers*. Berkeley, Calif.: University of California Press, 1970.

DeConde, Alexander. *Entangled Alliances: Politics and Diplomacy Under George Washington*. Durham, N.C.: Duke University Press, 1958.

Fitzpatrick, John C., ed. *The Writings of George Washington from the Original Manuscript Sources, 1745–1799*. 39 vols. Washington, D.C.: GPO, 1931–1944.

Perkins, Bradford. *The First Rapprochement: England and the United States, 1795–1805*. Philadelphia: University of Pennsylvania Press, 1955.

Reuter, Frank T. *Trials and Triumphs: George Washington's Foreign Policy*. Fort Worth, Tex.: Texas Christian University Press, 1983.

Sharp, James Roger. *American Politics in the Early Republic: The New Nation in Crisis*. New Haven, Conn: Yale University Press, 1993.

War of 1812 (1811–1812)

Barlow, William Ray. "Congress During the War of 1812." Ph.D. diss., Ohio State University, 1961.

Bell, Rudolph M. "Mr. Madison's War and Long-Term Congressional Voting Behavior." *William and Mary Quarterly*, 3rd series 36 (July 1979): 373–395.

Brown, Roger H. *The Republic in Peril: 1812*. New York: Columbia University Press, 1964.

Buel, Richard, Jr. *America on the Brink: How the Political Struggle Over the War of 1812 Almost Destroyed the Young Republic*. New York: Palgrave Macmillan, 2005.

Gribbin, William. *The Churches Militant: The War of 1812 and American Religion*. New Haven, Conn: Yale University Press, 1973.

Hartzenbuehler, Ronald L. *Congress Declares War: Rhetoric, Leadership, and Partisanship in the Early Republic*. Kent, Ohio: Kent State University Press, 1983.

Hartzenbuehler, Ronald L. "Party Unity and the Decision for War in the House of Representatives, 1812." *William and Mary Quarterly,* 3rd series 29 (July 1972): 376–390.

Hickey, Donald R. *The War of 1812: A Forgotten Conflict.* Urbana, Ill.: University of Illinois Press, 1989.

Hickey, Donald R. *The War of 1812: A Short History.* Urbana, Ill.: University of Illinois Press, 1995.

Horsman, Reginald. *The Causes of the War of 1812.* Philadelphia: University of Pennsylvania Press, 1962.

Horsman, Reginald. *The War of 1812.* New York: Knopf, 1969.

Johnson, Leland R. "The Suspense Was Hell: The Senate Vote for War in 1812." *Indiana Magazine of History* 65 (1969): 247–269.

Morison, Samuel Eliot. "Dissent in the War of 1812." In *Dissent in Three American Wars,* edited by Samuel Eliot Morison, Frederick Merk, and Frank Freidel. Cambridge, Mass.: Harvard University Press, 1970.

Stagg, J. C. A. *Mr. Madison's War: Politics, Diplomacy, and Warfare in the Early American Republic, 1783–1830.* Princeton, N.J.: Princeton University Press, 1983.

Taylor, George Rogers. *The War of 1812: Past Justifications and Present Interpretations.* Boston: D.C. Heath, 1963.

Missouri Compromise (1819–1821)

Brush, Edward Hale. *Rufus King and His Times.* New York: Nicholas L. Brown, 1926.

Castel, Albert, and Scott L. Gibson. *The Yeas and the Nays: Key Congressional Decisions, 1774–1945.* Kalamazoo, Mich.: New Issues Press, Institute of Public Affairs, Western Michigan University, 1975.

Dangerfield, George. *The Awakening of American Nationalism, 1815–1828.* New York: Harper and Row, 1965.

Fehrenbacher, Don E. *Sectional Crisis and Southern Constitutionalism.* Baton Rouge, La.: Louisiana State University Press, 1995.

Freehling, William W. *The Road to Disunion.* 2 vols. New York: Oxford University Press, 1990.

Moore, Glover. *The Missouri Controversy, 1819–1821.* Lexington, Ky.: University of Kentucky Press, 1953.

Pinkney, William. *The Life of William Pinkney.* New York: D. Appleton, 1853.

Webster–Hayne Debate (1830)

Bartlett, Irving H. *Daniel Webster.* New York: W. W. Norton, 1978.

Belz, Herman, ed. *The Webster–Hayne Debate on the Nature of the Union: Selected Documents.* Indianapolis, Ind.: Liberty Fund, 2000.

Curtis, George M., III, and James J. Thompson, Jr., eds. *The Southern Essays of Richard M. Weaver.* Indianapolis, Ind.: Liberty Press, 1987.

Freehling, William W., ed. *The Nullification Era: A Documentary Record.* New York: Harper and Row, 1967.

Green, Fletcher M. "Webster–Hayne Debate." In *Dictionary of American History,* 8 vols., rev. ed. Vol. 7, 434–435. (New York: Charles Scribner's Sons, 1976).

Grossman, Richard L., ed. *Bold Voices: Great Debaters and Dissenters Speak Out in Congress at Crucial Moments in American History.* Garden City, N.Y.: Doubleday, 1960.

Jervey, Theodore D. *Robert Y. Hayne and His Times.* New York: Macmillan, 1909.

Peterson, Merrill D. *The Great Triumvirate: Webster, Clay, and Calhoun.* New York: Oxford University Press, 1987.

Remini, Robert V. *Daniel Webster: The Man and His Time.* New York: W. W. Norton, 1997.

Smith, Craig R. *Daniel Webster and the Oratory of Civil Religion.* Columbia University of Missouri Press, Mo., 2005.

Wilson, Woodrow. *Division and Reunion, 1829–1909.* New York: Longmans, Green, 1912.

Veto of the Second Bank of the United States (1832)

Benton, Thomas Hart. *Thirty Years' View: Or, a History of the Working of the American Government for Thirty Years, from 1820 to 1850.* 2 vols. New York: D. Appleton, 1863.

Catterall, Ralph C. H. *The Second Bank of the United States.* Chicago: University of Chicago Press, 1960.

Chambers, William Nisbet. *Old Bullion Benton, Senator From the New West: Thomas Hart Benton, 1782–1858.* Boston: Little Brown, 1956.

Cole, Donald B. *The Presidency of Andrew Jackson.* Lawrence, Kans.: University Press of Kansas, 1993.

Hammond, Bray. *Banks and Politics in America, from the Revolution to the Civil War.* Princeton, N.J.: Princeton University Press, 1957.

Kaplan, Edward S. *The Bank of the United States and the American Economy.* Westport, Conn.: Greenwood Press, 1999.

McFaul, John. *The Politics of Jacksonian Finance.* Ithaca, N.Y.: Cornell University Press, 1972.

Myers, Margaret G. *A Financial History of the United States.* New York: Columbia University Press, 1970.

Poore, Benjamin Perley. *Perley's Reminiscences of Sixty Years in the National Metropolis.* 2 vols. Philadelphia: Hubbard Brothers, 1886.

Remini, Robert V. *Andrew Jackson and the Bank War: A Study in the Growth of Presidential Power.* New York: W. W. Norton., 1967.

Remini, Robert V. *Andrew Jackson and the Course of American Freedom, 1822–1832.* New York: Harper and Row, 1981.

Remini, Robert V. *Henry Clay: Statesman for the Union.* New York: W. W. Norton, 1991.

Remini, Robert V. *The Life of Andrew Jackson.* New York: Harper and Row, 1988.

Richardson, James D. comp. *A Compilation of the Messages and Papers of the Presidents.* 20 vols. Vol. 3. (New York: Bureau of National Literature, 1897–1927).

Schweikart, Larry. "Jackson Ideology, Currency Control, and 'Central' Banking: A Reappraisal," *The Historian: A Journal of History* 51 (November 1988): 78–102.

Smith, Walter Buckingham. *Economic Aspects of the Second Bank of the United States.* New York: Greenwood Press, 1969.

Force Bill (1832–1833)

Cole, Donald B. *The Presidency of Andrew Jackson.* Lawrence, Kans.: University of Kansas Press, 1993.

Ellis, Richard E. *The Union at Risk: Jacksonian Democracy, States' Rights and the Nullification Crisis.* New York: Oxford University Press, 1987.

Forsythe, Dall W. *Taxation and Political Change in the Young Nation, 1781–1833.* New York: Columbia University Press, 1977.

Freehling, William W. *Prelude to Civil War: The Nullification Controversy in South Carolina, 1816–1836.* New York: Oxford University Press, 1992.

Hopkins, James F., et al., eds. *The Papers of Henry Clay.* 11 vols. Lexington, Ky.: University of Kentucky Press, 1959–1992.

Massachusetts General Court. Committee on the Library. *State Papers on Nullification.* Boston: Dutton and Wentworth, Printers to the State, 1834.

Peterson, Merrill D. *Olive Branch and Sword—The Compromise of 1833.* Baton Rouge, La.: Louisiana State University Press, 1982.

Richardson, James P. *A Compilation of Messages and Papers of the Presidents.* 20 vols. Vol. 3. (New York: Bureau of National Literature, 1897–1927).

Censure of President Andrew Jackson (1833–1834)

Benton, Thomas Hart. *Thirty Years' View: Or a History of the Working of the American Government for Thirty Years, from 1820 to 1850.* 2 vols. New York: D. Appleton, 1863.

Brinkley, Alan. *American History: A Survey.* 11th ed. Boston: McGraw-Hill, 2003.

Cole, Donald B. *A Jackson Man: Amos Kendall and the Rise of American Democracy.* Baton Rouge: Louisiana State University Press, 2004.

Cole, Donald B. *The Presidency of Andrew Jackson: A Study in the Growth of Presidential Power.* Lawrence, Kans.: University of Kansas Press, 1993.

Colton, Calvin. *Life and Times of Henry Clay.* 2 vols. New York: A. S. Barnes, 1846.

Petersen, Merrill D. *The Great Triumvirate: Webster, Clay, and Calhoun.* New York: Oxford University Press, 1987.

Poore, Benjamin Perley. *Perley's Reminiscences of Sixty Years in the National Metropolis.* 2 vols. Philadelphia: Hubbard Brothers, 1886.

Remini, Robert V. *Andrew Jackson and the Bank War.* New York: W. W. Norton, 1967.

Remini, Robert V. *The Life of Andrew Jackson.* New York: Harper and Row, 1988.

Taylor, George Rogers. *Jackson Versus Biddle: The Struggle Over the Second Bank of the United States.* Boston: D.C. Heath, 1949.

Wise, Henry A. *Seven Decades of the Union.* Philadelphia: J.B. Lippincott, 1881.

House Gag Rule (1836–1844)

Adams, Charles Francis. ed. *Memoirs of John Quincy Adams.* 12 vols. Philadelphia: J.B. Lippincott, 1874–1877.

Clark, Bennett Champ. *John Quincy Adams: "Old Man Eloquent."* Boston: Little, Brown, 1932.

Dumond, Dwight Lowell. *Antislavery: The Crusade for Freedom in America.* Ann Arbor, Mich.: University of Michigan Press, 1961.

Frederick, David C. "John Quincy Adams, Slavery, and the Disappearance of the Right of Petition." *Law and History Review* 9 (Spring 1991): 113–153.

Kollen, Richard P. "The House Gag Rule Debate: The Wedge Dividing North and South." *Magazine of History* 12 (Summer 1998): 55–63.

Ludlum, Robert P. "The Antislavery 'Gag Rule': History and Argument." *Journal of Negro History* 26 (April 1941): 203–243.

Miller, William Lee. *Arguing About Slavery: The Great Battle in the United States Congress.* New York: Knopf, 1996.

Rable, George C. "Slavery Politics, and the South: The Gag Rule as a Case Study." *Capitol Studies* 3 (Fall 1975): 69–87.

Richards, Leonard L. *The Life and Times of Congressman John Quincy Adams.* New York: Oxford University Press, 1986.

Wyly–Jones, Susan. "The Antiabolitionist Panic: Slavery, Abolition, and Politics in the South, 1835–1844." Ph.D. diss., Harvard University, April 2000.

Wilmot Proviso (1846–1847)

Campbell, Ronald B. *Gone to Texas: A History of the Lone Star State.* New York: Oxford University Press, 2003.

Castel, Albert, and Scott L. Gibson. *The Yeas and the Nays: Key Congressional Decisions 1774–1945.* Kalamazoo, Mich.: New Issues Press, Institute of Public Affairs, Western Michigan University, 1975.

Fehrenbacher, Don E. *Sectional Crisis and Southern Constitutionalism.* Baton Rouge: Louisiana State University Press, 1995.

Foner, Eric. "The Wilmot Proviso Revisited." *Journal of American History* 56 (September 1969): 262–279.

Haynes, Sam W. *James K. Polk and the Expansionist Impulse.* New York: Longman, 1997.

Holt, Michael F. *The Political Crisis of the 1850s.* New York: Wiley, 1978.

Moore, John L., Jon P. Preimesberger, and David R. Tarr, eds. *Congressional Quarterly's Guide to U.S. Elections.* 4th ed., 2 vols. Washington, D.C.: CQ Press, 2001.

Morrison, Chaplain W. *Democratic Politics and Sectionalism: The Wilmot Proviso Controversy.* Chapel Hill, N.C.: University of North Carolina Press, 1967.

Pletcher, David M. *The Diplomacy of Annexation: Texas, Oregon, and the Mexican War.* Columbia: University of Missouri Press, 1973.

Rayback, Joseph G. *Free Soil: The Election of 1848.* Lexington, Ky.: University Press of Kentucky, 1970.

Richardson, James D., comp. *A Compilation of Messages and Papers of the Presidents.* 20 vols. Vol. 5. (New York: Bureau of National Literature, 1897–1927).

Smith, Justin H. *The Annexation of Texas.* New York: Baker and Taylor, 1911.

Compromise of 1850

Bauer, K. Jack. *Zachary Taylor: Soldier, Planter, Statesman of the Old Southwest.* Baton Rouge, La.: Louisiana State University Press, 1985.

Dyer, Brainerd. *Zachary Taylor.* New York: Barnes and Noble, 1967.

Freehling, William W. *The Road to Disunion.* New York: Oxford University Press, 1990.

Hamilton, Holman. *Prologue to Conflict: The Crisis and Compromise of 1850.* Lexington, Kans.: University of Kansas Press, 1964.

Holt, Michael F. *The Political Crisis of the 1850s.* New York: Wiley, 1978.

Johannsen, Robert W. *Stephen A. Douglas.* New York: Oxford University Press, 1973.

Petersen, Merrill D. *The Great Triumvirate: Webster, Clay, and Calhoun.* New York: Oxford University Press, 1987.

Potter, David M. *The Impending Crisis, 1848–1861.* New York: Harper and Row, 1976.

Remini, Robert V. *Henry Clay: Statesman for the Union.* New York: W. W. Norton, 1991.

Richardson, James D. comp. *A Compilation of Messages and Paper of the Presidents.* 20 vols. Vol. 6. (New York: Bureau of National Literature, 1897–1925).

Rozwenc, Edwin C. *The Compromise of 1850.* Boston: D. C. Heath, 1957.

Smith, Elbert B. *The Presidencies of Zachary Taylor & Millard Fillmore.* Lawrence, Kans.: University Press of Kansas, 1988.

Waugh, John C. *On the Brink of War: The Compromise of 1850 and How It Changed the Course of American History.* Wilmington, Del.: Scholarly Resources, 2003.

Wiltse, Charles M., and Michael J. Birkner, eds., *The Papers of Daniel Webster,* 7 vols. Vol. 7 (Hanover, N.H.: University Press of New England, 1986).

Kansas–Nebraska Act (1854)

Blue, Frederick J. *Salmon P. Chase: A Life in Politics.* Kent, Ohio: Kent State University Press, 1987.

Brinkley, Alan. *American History: A Survey.* 11th ed. Boston: McGraw-Hill, 2003.

Capers, Gerald M. *Stephen A. Douglas: Defender of the Union.* Edited by Oscar Handlin. Boston: Little, Brown, 1959.

Etcheson, Nicole. *Bleeding Kansas: Contested Liberty in the Civil War Era.* Lawrence, Kans.: University of Kansas Press, 2004.

Holt, Michael F. *The Political Crisis of the 1850s.* New York: Wiley, 1978.

Johannsen, Robert W., ed. *The Letters of Stephen A. Douglas.* Urbana, Ill.: University of Illinois Press, 1961.

Johannsen, Robert W. *Stephen A. Douglas.* New York: Oxford University Press, 1973.

Nichols, Roy F. "The Kansas–Nebraska Act: A Century of Historiography." *Mississippi Valley Historical Review* 43 (September 1956): 187–212.

Niven, John. *Salmon P. Chase: A Biography.* New York: Oxford University Press, 1995.

Potter, David Morris. *The Impending Crisis, 1848–1861.* New York: Harper and Row, 1976.

Rawley, James A. *Race and Politics: "Bleeding Kansas" and the Coming of the Civil War.* Philadelphia: Lippincott, 1969.

Ray, P. Orman. *The Repeal of the Missouri Compromise, Its Origin and Authorship.* Cleveland, Ohio: Arthur H. Clark, 1909.

Russell, Robert R. "The Issues in the Congressional Struggle Over the Kansas-Nebraska Bill, 1854." *Journal of Southern History* 29 (May 1963): 187–210.

Pacific Railroad Act (1862)

Ambrose, Stephen E. *Nothing Like It in the World: The Men Who Built the Transcontinental Railroad, 1863–1869.* New York: Simon and Schuster, 2000.

Daggett, Stuart. *Chapters on the History of the Southern Pacific.* New York, A. M. Kelley, 1966.

Davis, John P. *The Union Pacific Railway: A Study in Railway Politics, History, and Economics.* Chicago: S. C. Griggs, 1894.

Dufwa, Thamar Emelia. *Transcontinental Railroad Legislation, 1835–1862.* New York: Arno Press, 1981.

Farnham, Wallace D. "The Pacific Railroad Act of 1862." *Nebraska History* 43 (September 1962): 141–167.

Fogel, Robert William. *The Pacific Railroad: A Case in Premature Enterprise.* Baltimore: Johns Hopkins Press, 1960.

Haney, Lewis Henry. *A Congressional History of Railways in the United States.* 2 vols. Madison, Wisc.: Democrat Printing Co., 1910.

Jones, Helen Hinckley. *Rails from the West: A Biography of Theodore D. Judah.* San Marino, Calif.: Golden West Books, 1969.

Huneke, William F. *The Heavy Hand: The Government and the Union Pacific, 1862–1898.* New York: Garland, 1985.

Klein, Maury. *Union Pacific: Birth of a Railroad, 1862–1893.* 2 vols. New York: Doubleday, 1987.

Milnarich, Rhoda F. "The Public Career of Aaron Augustus Sargent." M.A. thesis, Texas Western College, May 1961.

Russel, Robert R. *Improvement of Communication With the Pacific Coast as an Issue in American Politics, 1783–1864.* Cedar Rapids, Iowa: Torch Press, 1948.

Wheat, Carl I. "A Sketch of the Life of Theodore D. Judah." *California Historical Society Quarterly* 4 (September 1925): 218–271.

Williams, John Hoyt. *A Great and Shining Road: The Epic Story of the Transcontinental Railroad.* New York: Time Books, 1988.

Homestead Act (1862)

Bronstein, Jamie L. *Land Reform and Working–Class Experience in Britain and the United States, 1800–1862.* Stanford, Calif.: Stanford University Press, 1999.

Deverell, William. "The American West." In Julian E. Zelizer, ed. *The American Congress: The Building of Democracy.* (Boston: Houghton Mifflin Company, 2004): 268–283.

Froner, Eric. *Free Soil, Free Labor, Free Men: The Ideology of the Republican Party Before the Civil War.* Oxford: Oxford University Press, 1995.

Gates, Paul W. *Free Homesteads for All Americans: The Homestead Act of 1862.* Washington, D.C.: Civil War Centennial Commission, 1962.

Gates, Paul W. *History of Public Land Law Development.* Washington, D.C.: Wm. W. Gaunt and Sons, 1987.

Hibbard, Benjamin Horace. *A History of the Public Land Policies.* New York: P. Smith, 1939.

Robbins, Roy M. *Our Landed Heritage: The Public Domain, 1776–1936*. Princeton, N.J.: Princeton University Press, 1942.

Sanborn, John Bell. "Some Political Aspects of Homestead Legislation." *American Historical Review* 6 (October 1900): 19–37.

Stephenson, George M. *The Political History of the Public Lands, from 1840 to 1862: From Pre–Emption to Homestead*. New York: Russell and Russell, 1917.

U.S. Department of Interior. Bureau of Land Management. *Public Land Statistics, 2006*. Washington, D.C.: Bureau of Land Management, April 2007.

Zahler, Helene Sara. *Eastern Workingmen and National Land Policy, 1829–1862*. New York: Columbia University Press, 1941.

Fourteenth Amendment (1866–1868)

Belz, Herman. *Reconstructing the Union: Theory and Practice During the Civil War*. Ithaca, N.Y.: Cornell University Press, 1969.

Donald, David Herbert, Jean H. Baker, and Michael F. Holt. *The Civil War and Reconstruction*. New York: W. W. Norton, 2001.

Flack, Horace Edgar. *The Adoption of the Fourteenth Amendment*. Baltimore: Johns Hopkins University Press, 1908.

Grimes, Alan P. *Democracy and the Amendments to the Constitution*. Lexington, Mass.: Lexington Books, 1978.

James, Joseph B. *The Framing of the Fourteenth Amendment*. Urbana, Ill.: University of Illinois Press, 1956.

James, Joseph B. "Southern Reaction to the Proposal of the Fourteenth Amendment." *Journal of Southern History* 22 (November 1956): 477–497.

Nelson, William E. *The Fourteenth Amendment: From Political Principle to Judicial Doctrine*. Cambridge, Mass.: Harvard University Press, 1988.

Randall, J. G., and David Donald. *The Civil War and Reconstruction*. Boston: D. C. Heath, 1961.

Richardson, James D., comp. *Compilation of Messages and Papers of the Presidents*, 20 vols. Vol. 8. (New York: Bureau of National Literature, 1897–1927).

Sneed, Joseph T. *Footprints on the Rocks of the Mountain: An Account of the Enactment of the Fourteenth Amendment*. San Francisco: TYSAM Press, 1997.

Wang, Xi. *The Trial of Democracy: Black Suffrage and Northern Republicans, 1860–1910*. Athens, Ga.: University of Georgia Press, 1997.

Impeachment of President Andrew Johnson (1868)

Benedict, Michael Les. *The Impeachment and Trial of Andrew Johnson*. New York: Norton, 1973.

Dewitt, David Miller. *The Impeachment and Trial of Andrew Johnson, Seventeenth President of the United States: A History*. Madison, Wisc.: State Historical Society of Wisconsin, 1967.

Hearn, Chester G. *The Impeachment of Andrew Johnson*. Jefferson, N.C.: McFarland, 2000.

Horowitz, Robert F. *The Great Impeacher: A Political Biography of James M. Ashley*. New York: Brooklyn College Press, 1979.

The Impeachment and Trial of Andrew Johnson, President of the United States: The Complete Record of the Impeachment in the House of Representatives, the Preliminary Proceedings in the Senate, the Articles of Impeachment, and the Full Proceedings in the Court of Impeachment of the Senate of the United States. New York: Dover Publications, 1974.

McKitrick, Eric L. "Afterthought: Why Impeachment." In *Andrew Johnson: A Profile*, edited by Eric L. McKitrick. New York: Hill and Wang, 1969.

Milton, George Fort. *The Age of Hate*. New York: Coward–McCann, 1930.

Myers v. United States, 272 U.S. 164 (1926).

Rehnquist, William H. *Grand Inquests: The Historic Impeachments of Justice Samuel Chase and President Andrew Johnson*. New York: Morrow, 1992.

Richardson, James D., comp. *Compilation of Messages and Papers of the Presidents*, 20 vols. Vol. 8. (New York: Bureau of National Literature, 1897–1927).

Ross, Edmund G. *History of the Impeachment of Andrew Johnson, President of the United States, by the House of Representatives, and His Trial by the Senate for High Crimes and Misdemeanors in Office, 1868*. New York: B. Franklin, 1965.

Stryker, Lloyd Paul. *Andrew Johnson: A Study in Courage*. New York: Macmillan, 1936.

Supplement of *Congressional Globe Containing the Proceedings of the Senate Sitting for the Trial of Andrew Johnson, President of the United States*. Washington, D.C.: F. & J. Rives and G. A. Bailey, 1868.

Thomas, Lately. *The First President Johnson: The Three Lives of the Seventeenth President of the United States of America*. New York: Morrow, 1968.

White, Leonard. *The Republican Era, 1869–1901: A Study in Administrative History*. New York: Macmillan, 1958.

Winston, Robert W. *Andrew Johnson: Plebeian and Patriot*. New York: H. Holt, 1928.

Fifteenth Amendment (1869)

Braxton, A. Caperton. *The Fifteenth Amendment: An Account of Its Enactment*. Lynchburg, Va: J. P. Bell, 1933.

Gillette, William. "Fifteenth Amendment (Framing and Ratification)." In *Encyclopedia of the American Constitution*, 6 vols., edited by Leonard W. Levy, Kenneth L. Karst, and Adam Winkler. (New York: Macmillan, 2000): 3:1039–1041.

Gillette, William. "Fifteenth Amendment." In *The Encyclopedia of the United States Congress*, 4 vols., edited by Donald C. Bacon, Roger H. Davidson, and Morton Keller. (New York: Simon and Schuster, 1995): 2:831–833.

Gillette, William. *Retreat from Reconstruction, 1869–1879*. Baton Rouge, La.: Louisiana State University Press, 1979.

Gillette, William. *The Right to Vote: Politics and the Passage of the Fifteenth Amendment*. Baltimore: Johns Hopkins Press, 1969.

Grimes, Alan P. *Democracy and the Amendments to the Constitution*. Lexington, Mass.: Lexington Books, 1978.

Keyssar, Alexander. *The Right to Vote: The Contested History of Democracy in the United States*. New York: Basic Books, 2000.

Maltz, Earl M. *Civil Rights, The Constitution, and Congress, 1863–1869.* Lawrence, Kans.: University Press of Kansas, 1990.

Mathews, John Mabry. *Legislative and Judicial History of the Fifteenth Amendment.* Union, N.J.: Lawbook Exchange, 2001.

Wang, Xi. *The Trial of Democracy: Black Suffrage and Northern Republicans, 1860–1910.* Athens: University of Georgia Press, 1997.

Wood, Forrest G. *Black Scare: The Racist Response to Emancipation and Reconstruction.* Berkeley: University of California Press, 1968

Civil Rights Act of 1875

Bradley, Bert. "Negro Speakers in Congress: 1869–1875." *The Southern Speech Journal* 18 (May 1953): 216–225.

Civil Rights Cases, 109 U.S. 3 (1883).

Donald, David. *Charles Sumner and the Rights of Man.* New York: Knopf, 1970.

Ezell, John S. "The Civil Rights Act of 1875," *Mid–America: An Historical Review* 50 (October 1968): 251–271.

Foner, Eric. *Reconstruction: America's Unfinished Revolution, 1863–1877.* New York: Harper and Row, 1988.

Franklin, John Hope. "The Enforcement of the Civil Rights Act of 1875." *Prologue: The Journal of the National Archives* 6 (Winter 1974): 225–235.

Gillette, William. *Retreat from Reconstruction, 1869–1879.* Baton Rouge, La.: Louisiana State University Press, 1979.

Hoeveler, J. David. "Reconstruction and the Federal Courts: The Civil Rights Act of 1875." *The Historian* 31 (August 1969): 604–617.

Johnston, Richard Malcolm, and William Hand Browne. *Life of Alexander H. Stephens.* Philadelphia: J. B. Lippincott, 1878.

Kelly, Alfred H. "The Congressional Controversy Over School Segregation, 1867–1875." *American Historical Review* 64 (April 1959): 537–563.

Lamson, Peggy. *The Glorious Failure: Black Congressman Robert Brown Elliott and the Reconstruction in South Carolina.* New York: W. W. Norton, 1973.

McPherson, James M. "Abolitionists and the Civil Rights Act of 1875." *Journal of American History* 52 (December 1965): 493–510.

Scaturro, Frank J. *The Supreme Court's Retreat from Reconstruction: A Distortion of Constitutional Jurisprudence.* Westport, Conn.: Greenwood Press, 2000.

Slaughter–House Cases, 83 U.S. 36 (1873).

Wilson, Kirt H. *The Reconstruction Desegregation Debate: The Politics of Equality and the Rhetoric of Place, 1870–1875.* East Lansing, Mich.: Michigan State University Press, 2002.

Wyatt–Brown, Bertram. "The Civil Rights Act of 1875." *Western Political Quarterly* 18 (December 1965): 763–775.

Compromise of 1877

Benedict, Michael Les. "Southern Democrats in the Crisis of 1876–1877: A Reconsideration of Reunion and Reaction." *Journal of Southern History* 46 (November 1980): 489–524.

Haworth, Paul Leland. *The Hayes–Tilden Disputed Presidential Election of 1876.* New York: Russell and Russell, 1966.

Morris, Roy, Jr. *Fraud of the Century: Rutherford B. Hayes, Samuel Tilden, and the Stolen Election of 1876.* New York: Simon and Schuster, 2003.

Nagle, John Copeland. "How Not to Count Votes." *Columbia Law Review* 104 (October 2004): 1732–1763.

Peskin, Alan. "Was There a Compromise of 1877?" *Journal of American History* 60 (June 1973): 63–75.

Polakoff, Keith Ian. *The Politics of Inertia: The Election of 1876 and the End of Reconstruction.* Baton Rouge, La.: Louisiana State University Press, 1973.

Rehnquist, William H. *Centennial Crisis: The Disputed Election of 1876.* New York: Knopf, 2004.

U.S. Congress. House. *Counting the Electoral Vote,* report to accompany H.R. 4454. H. Rept. 108, 44th Cong., 2nd sess. Washington, D.C.: GPO, 1877.

U.S. Electoral Commission (1877). *Proceedings of the Electoral Commission and of the Two Houses of Congress in Joint Meeting Relative to the Count of the Electoral Votes Cast December 6, 1876, for the Presidential Term Commencing March 4, 1877.* Washington, D.C.: GPO, 1877.

Welch, Richard E., Jr. *George Frisbie Hoar and the Half-Breed Republicans.* Cambridge, Mass.: Harvard University Press, 1971.

Woodward, C. Vann. *Reunion and Reaction: The Compromise of 1877 and the End of Reconstruction.* Boston: Little, Brown, 1966.

Reed's Rules (1890)

Binder, Sarah A. *Minority Rights, Majority Rule.* Cambridge, N.Y.: Cambridge University Press, 1997.

Chamberlain, Daniel H. "'Counting the Quorum': Or Speaker Reed's Change of Rules." *New Englander* 53 (December 1890): 510–525.

Fuller, Hubert Bruce. *Speakers of the House.* Boston: Little, Brown, 1909.

McCall, Samuel W. *Thomas B. Reed.* Boston: Houghton Mifflin, 1914.

Mooney, Booth. *Mr. Speaker: Four Men Who Shaped the United States House of Representatives.* Chicago: Follett, 1964.

Peters, Ronald M., Jr. *The American Speakership: The Office in Historical Perspective.* Baltimore: Johns Hopkins University Press, 1990.

Reed, Thomas B. "Limitations of the Speakership." *North American Review* 150 (March 1890): 382–390.

Reed, Thomas B. "Obstruction in the National House." *North American Review* 149 (October 1889): 421–428.

Reed, Thomas B. "Rules of the House of Representatives." *Century Magazine* 37 (March 1889): 792–795.

Robinson, William A. *Thomas B. Reed: Parliamentarian.* New York: Dodd, Mead, 1930.

"Speaker Reed's Error." *The Nation* 51 (July 17, 1890): 44–45.

Strahan, Randall. "Reed's Rules." In *The Encyclopedia of the United States Congress,* 4 vols., edited by Roger C. Bacon, Roger H. Davidson, and Morton Keller. (New York: Simon and Schuster, 1995): 3:1691.

X. M. C. "Speaker Reed's Error." *North American Review* 151 (July 1890): 90–111.

Revenue Act of 1894

"A Fling Wedge." *New York World,* January 31, 1894, 7.

Brinen, Joshua. "Sixteenth Amendment." In *Constitutional Amendments, 1789 to the Present,* edited by Kris E. Palmer. Detroit: Gale, 2000: 381–398.

Grimes, Alan P. *Democracy and the Amendments to the Constitution.* Lexington, Mass.: Lexington Books, 1978.

Holmes, George K. "The Concentration of Wealth," *Political Science Quarterly* 8 (December 1893): 589–600.

Joseph, Richard J. *The Origins of the American Income Tax.* Syracuse, N.Y.: Syracuse University Press, 2004.

Kyvig, David E. "Can the Constitution Be Amended? The Battle Over the Income Tax, 1895–1913." *Prologue: The Journal of the National Archives* 20 (Fall 1988): 189–195.

Long, Joseph R. "Tinkering with the Constitution," *Yale Law Journal* 24 (May 1915): 373–589.

Martin, Ralph G. *Jennie: The Life of Lady Randolph Churchill.* 2 vols. New York: New American Library, 1971.

Ratner, Sidney. *American Taxation: Its History as a Social Force in Democracy.* New York: W. W. Norton, 1942.

Ratner, Sidney. *New Light on the History of Great Fortunes: American Millionaires of 1892 and 1902.* New York: Augustus M. Kelley, 1953.

Stanley, Robert. *Dimensions of Law in the Service of Order: Origins of the Federal Income Tax, 1861–1913.* New York: Oxford University Press, 1993.

Weisman, Steven R. *The Great Tax Wars: Lincoln to Wilson, the Fierce Battles Over Money and Power That Transformed the Nation.* New York: Simon and Schuster, 2002.

Treaty of Paris and American Policy Regarding the Philippines (1898; 1899–1901)

Beisner, Robert L. *Twelve Against Empire: The Anti-Imperialists, 1898–1900.* New York: McGraw-Hill, 1968.

Coletta, Paolo E. "Bryan, McKinley, and the Treaty of Paris." *Pacific Historical Review* 26 (May 1957): 131–146.

Coletta, Paolo E. "The Peace Negotiations and the Treaty of Paris." In *Threshold to American Internationalism: Essays on the Foreign Policies of William McKinley,* edited by Paolo E. Coletta. (New York: Exposition Press, 1970): 157–175.

Hofstadter, Richard. "Manifest Destiny and the Philippines." In *America in Crisis,* edited by Daniel Aaron. (Hamden, Conn.: Archon Books, 1971): 186–200, 355–356..

Musicant, Ivan. *Empire by Default: The Spanish-American War and the Dawn of the American Century.* New York: Henry Holt, 1998.

Pratt, Julius W. *Expansionists of 1898: The Acquisition of Hawaii and the Spanish Islands.* New York: Peter Smith, 1951.

Pomeroy, William J. *American Neo-Colonialism: Its Emergence in the Philippines and Asia.* New York: International Publishers, 1970.

Smock, Raymond W., ed. *Landmark Documents on the U.S. Congress.* Washington, D.C.: Congressional Quarterly, 1999.

Tompkins, E. Berkeley. *Anti-Imperialism in the United States: The Great Debate, 1890–1920.* Philadelphia: University of Pennsylvania Press, 1970.

Trask, David F. *The War with Spain in 1898.* New York: Macmillan, 1981.

House Revolt against Speaker Cannon (1910)

Atkinson, C. R., and C. A. Beard. "The Syndication of the Speakership." *Political Science Quarterly* 26 (September 1911): 381–414.

Atkinson, Charles R. *The Committee on Rules, and the Overthrow of Speaker Cannon.* Ph.D. diss., Columbia University, 1911.

Baker, John D. "The Character of the Congressional Revolution of 1910." *Journal of American History* 60 (December 1973): 679–691.

Bolles, Blair. *Tyrant from Illinois: Uncle Joe Cannon's Experiment with Personal Power.* New York: W. W. Norton, 1951.

Cheney, Richard B., and Lynne V. Cheney. *Kings of the Hill: Power and Personality in the House of Representatives.* New York: Simon and Schuster, 1996.

Hechler, Kenneth William. *Insurgency: Personalities and Politics of the Taft Era.* New York: Columbia University Press, 1940.

Holt, James. *Congressional Insurgents and the Party System, 1909–1916.* Cambridge, Mass.: Harvard University Press, 1967.

Jones, Charles O. "Joseph G. Cannon and Howard W. Smith: An Essay on the Limits of Leadership in the House of Representatives." *Journal of Politics* 30 (August 1968): 617–646.

Lowitt, Richard. *George W. Norris: The Making of a Progressive, 1861–1912.* Syracuse, N.Y.: Syracuse University Press, 1963.

Morrison, Geoffrey. "Champ Clark and the Rules Revolution of 1910." *Capitol Studies* 2 (Winter 1974): 43–56.

Peters, Ronald M., Jr. *The American Speakership: The Office in Historical Perspective.* Baltimore: Johns Hopkins University Press, 1997.

Rager, Scott William. "Uncle Joe Cannon: The Brakeman of the House of Representatives, 1903–1911." In *Masters of the House: Congressional Leadership Over Two Centuries,* edited by Roger H. Davidson, Susan Webb Hammond, and Raymond W. Smock. (Boulder, Colo.: Westview Press, 1998): 63–89.

Seventeenth Amendment (1913)

Ames, Herman. *The Proposed Amendments to the Constitution of the United States.* New York: Burt Franklin, 1970.

Bernstein, R. B. Seventeenth Amendment." In *Constitutional Amendments: 1789 to the Present,* edited by Kris E. Palmer. Detroit: Gale, 2000: 399–417.

Buenker, John D. "The Urban Political Machine and the Seventeenth Amendment." *Journal of American History* 56 (September 1969): 305–322.

Grimes, Alan P. *Democracy and the Amendments to the Constitution.* Lexington, Mass.: Lexington Books, 1978.

Hall, Wallace Worthy. "The History and Effect of the Seventeenth Amendment." Ph.D. diss., University of California, Berkeley, 1936.

Haynes, George H. *The Senate of the United States: Its History and Practice.* 2 vols. Boston: Houghton Mifflin, 1938.

Haynes, George H. *The Election of Senators.* New York: Henry Holt, 1906.

Hoebeke, C. H. *The Road to Mass Democracy: Original Intent and the Seventeenth Amendment.* New Brunswick, N.J.: Transaction Publishers, 1995.

Johnson, Donald Bruce, comp. *National Party Platforms.* Rev. ed. 2 vols. (Urbana, Ill.: University of Illinois Press, 1978).

Mazzaferro, Jean Elizabeth. "Bicameralism, Federalism, and Passage of the Seventeenth Amendment." Ph.D. diss., Claremont Graduate University, 2004.

Musmanno, Michael Angelo. *Proposed Amendments to the Constitution: A Monograph on the Resolutions Introduced in Congress Proposing Amendments to the Constitution of the United States of America.* Westport, Conn.: Greenwood Press, 1976.

Rossum, Ralph A. *Federalism, the Supreme Court, and the Seventeenth Amendment: The Irony of Constitutional Democracy.* Lanham, Md.: Lexington Books, 2001.

Schmieder, Morris L. "House Joint Resolution 39: The Seventeenth Amendment to the Constitution." M.A. thesis, University of Texas at El Paso, 1961.

U.S. Congress. Senate. *Proposed Amendments to the Constitution of the United States Introduced in Congress from December 4, 1889, to July 2, 1926.* S. Doc. 93, 69th Cong., 1st sess. Washington, D.C.: GPO, 1926.

Federal Reserve Act (1913)

Andrew, A. Piatt. "The Problem Before the National Monetary Commission." *Annals of the American Academy of Political and Social Science* 36 (November 1910): 1–13.

Broz, J. Lawrence. *The International Origins of the Federal Reserve System.* Ithaca, N.Y.: Cornell University Press, 1997.

Friedman, Milton, and Anna Jacobson Schwartz. *A Monetary History of the United States, 1867–1960.* Princeton, N.J.: Princeton University Press, 1963.

Laughlin, J. Laurence. *The Federal Reserve Act: Its Origin and Problems.* New York: Macmillan, 1933.

Lucas, Richard B. *Charles August Lindbergh, Sr.: A Case Study of Congressional Insurgency, 1906–1912.* Uppsala, Sweden: Richard B. Lucas, 1974.

McCulley, Richard T. *Banks and Politics During the Progressive Era: The Origins of the Federal Reserve System, 1897–1913.* New York: Garland, 1992.

Stephenson, Nathaniel Wright. *Nelson W. Aldrich: A Leader in American Politics.* New York: Charles Scribner's Sons, 1930.

Timberlake, Richard H. *Monetary Policy in the United States: An Intellectual and Institutional History.* Chicago: University of Chicago Press, 1993.

Timberlake, Richard H., Jr. *The Origins of Central Banking in the United States.* Cambridge, Mass.: Harvard University Press, 1978.

U.S. Congress. House Committee on Rules. *House Resolution No. 314.* Hearings, 62nd Cong., 2nd sess., December 15, 1911. Washington, D.C.: GPO, 1911.

U.S. Congress. House. *Report of the Committee Appointed Pursuant to House Resolutions 429 and 504 to Investigate the Concentration of Control of Money and Credit.* H. Rept. 1593, 62nd Cong., 3rd sess. Washington, D.C.: GPO, 1913.

U.S. Congress. House Subcommittee of the Committee on Banking and Currency. *Money Trust Investigations.* 3 vols. Hearings, 62nd Cong., 2nd and 3rd sess. Washington, D.C.: GPO, 1913.

U.S. Congress. Joint Economic Committee. *The Federal Reserve System.* J. Comm. Print., 94th Cong., 2nd sess. Washington, D.C.: GPO, 1976.

U.S. Congress. Senate. *Suggested Plan for Monetary Legislation Submitted to the National Monetary Commission by Hon. Nelson W. Aldrich.* S. Doc. 784, 61st Cong., 3rd sess. Washington, D.C.: GPO, 1911.

Weston, N. A. "The Studies of the Monetary Commission." *Annals of the American Academy of Political and Social Science* 49 (January 1922): 17–26.

Wicker, Elmus. *The Great Debate on Banking Reform: Nelson Aldrich and the Origins of the Fed.* Columbus: Ohio State University Press, 2005.

Willis, H. Parker. "The Federal Reserve Act in Congress." *Annals of the American Academy of Political and Social Science* 99 (January 1922): 36–49.

Eighteenth Amendment (1917)

Bernstein, Richard B. "Eighteenth Amendment." In *Constitutional Amendments: 1789 to the Present,* edited by Kris E. Palmer. Detroit: Gale, 2000: 119–427.

Castel, Albert, and Scott L. Gibson. *The Yeas and the Nays: Key Congressional Decisions 1774–1945.* Kalamazoo, Mich.: New Issues Press, Institute of Public Affairs, Western Michigan University, 1975.

Grimes, Alan P. *Democracy and the Amendments to the Constitution.* Lexington, Mass.: Lexington Books, 1978.

Hamm, Richard F. *Shaping the Eighteenth Amendment: Temperance Reform, Legal Culture, and the Polity, 1880–1920.* Chapel Hill, N.C.: University of North Carolina Press, 1995.

Kyvig, David E. *Explicit and Authentic Acts: Amending the U.S. Constitution, 1776–1995.* Lawrence, Kans.: University Press of Kansas, 1996.

Kyvig, David E. *Repealing National Prohibition.* Kent, Ohio: Kent State University Press, 2000.

Pegram, Thomas R. *Battling Demon Rum: The Struggle for a Dry America, 1800–1933.* Chicago: Ivan R. Dee, 1998.

Pegram, Thomas R. "Prohibition." In *The American Congress: The Building of Democracy,* edited by Julian E. Zelizer. (Boston: Houghton Mifflin, 2004): 411–427.

Timberlake, James H. *Prohibition and the Progressive Movement, 1900–1920.* Cambridge, Mass.: Harvard University Press, 1963.

U.S. President (Hoover). *Public Papers of the Presidents of the United States, Herbert Hoover, 1929.* Washington, D.C.: GPO, 1974.

Vile, John R. *Encyclopedia of Constitutional Amendments, Proposed Amendments, and Amending Issues, 1789–1995.* Santa Barbara, Calif.: ABC-CLIO, 1996.

Nineteenth Amendment (Women's Suffrage) (1919)

Flexner, Eleanor and Ellen Fitzpatrick. *Century of Struggle: The Woman's Rights Movement in the United States.* Cambridge, Mass.: Belknap Press of Harvard University Press, 1996.

Grimes, Alan P. *Democracy and the Amendments to the Constitution.* Lexington, Mass.: Lexington Books, 1978.

Harper, Ida Husted, ed. *The History of Woman Suffrage.* 6 vols. New York: Fowler and Wells, 1881–1922.

Keyssar, Alexander. *The Right to Vote: The Contested History of Democracy in the United States.* New York: Basic Books, 2000.

Kyvig, David E. *Explicit and Authentic Acts: Amending the U.S. Constitution, 1776–1995.* Lawrence, Kans.: University Press of Kansas, 1996.

Link, Arthur S., et al., eds. *The Papers of Woodrow Wilson.* 69 vols. Princeton, N.J.: Princeton University Press, 1966–1994.

Scarbough, Mary Hertz. "Nineteenth Amendment." In *Constitutional Amendments: 1789 to the Present,* edited by Kris E. Palmer. (Detroit: Gale, 2000): 429–447.

Sims, Anastatia. "Armageddon in Tennessee: The Final Battle Over the Nineteenth Amendment." In *One Woman, One Vote: Rediscovering the Woman Suffrage Movement,* edited by Marjorie Spruill Wheeler. (Troutdale, Ore.: NewSage Press, 1995): 332–352.

Stanton, Elizabeth Cady, Susan B. Anthony, Matilda Joslyn Gage, and Ida Husted Harper. *History of Woman Suffrage.* 6 vols. New York, Fowler and Wells, 1881–1922.

"Wilson Backs Amendment for Woman Suffrage." *New York Times* (January 10, 1918): 1, 3.

League of Nations (1919)

Ambrosius, Lloyd E. *Woodrow Wilson and the American Diplomatic Tradition: The Treaty Fight in Perspective.* Cambridge: Cambridge University Press, 1987.

Bailey, Thomas A. "Woodrow Wilson Wouldn't Yield," *American Heritage* 8 (June 1957): 20–25, 105–106.

Capet, Antoine. "Versailles, Treaty of." In *Dictionary of American History,* 3rd ed., 10 vols., edited by Stanley I. Kutler. (New York: Charles Scribner's Sons, 2003): 8:315–316.

Margulies, Herbert F. *The Mild Reservationists and the League of Nations Controversy in the Senate.* Columbia: University of Missouri Press, 1989.

Margulies, Herbert F. "The Moderates in the League of Nations Battle: An Overlooked Faction." *The Historian* 60 (Winter 1998): 273–287.

Ripley, Thomas W. *Gilbert Hitchcock of Nebraska—Wilson's Floor Leader in the Fight for the Versailles Treaty.* Lewiston, N.Y.: Edwin Mellen Press, 1998.

Smock, Raymond W., ed. *Landmark Documents on the U.S. Congress.* Washington, D.C.: Congressional Quarterly, 1999.

Stone, Ralph. *The Irreconcilables: The Fight Against the League of Nations.* Lexington, Ky.: University Press of Kentucky, 1970.

U.S. Congress. Senate Committee on Foreign Relations. *Treaty of Peace with Germany.* Hearings, 66th Cong., 1st sess., S. Doc. 106. Washington, D.C.: GPO, 1919.

U.S. Congress. Senate. *Treaty of Peace with Germany: Report of the Conference Between Members of the Senate Committee on Foreign Relations and the President of the United States at the White House, Tuesday, August 19, 1919.* S. Doc. 76, 66th Cong., 1st sess. Washington, D.C.: GPO, 1919.

Walworth, Arthur. *Woodrow Wilson,* 3rd ed. New York: W. W. Norton, 1978.

Wimer, Kurt. "The League of Nations: A Victim of Executive–Legislative Rivalry." *The Lock Haven Bulletin.* Series 1, no. 2 (1960): 1–12.

Wimer, Kurt. "Senator Hitchcock and the League of Nations." *Nebraska History* 44 (September 1963): 189–204.

Smoot–Hawley Tariff (1930)

Bordo, Michael D., Claudia Goldin, and Eugene N. White. *The Defining Moment: The Great Depression and the American Economy in the Twentieth Century.* Chicago: University of Chicago Press, 1998.

Callahan, Coleen M., Judith A. McDonald, and Anthony Partick O'Brien. "Who Voted for Smoot-Hawley?" *Journal of Economic History* 54 (September 1994): 683–690.

Eckes, Alfred E., Jr. *Opening America's Market: U.S. Foreign Policy Since 1776.* Chapel Hill, N.C.: University of North Carolina Press, 1995.

Eichengreen, Barry. "The Political Economy of the Smoot-Hawley Tariff." *Research in Economic History* 12 (1989): 1–43.

Irwin, Douglas A. "From Smoot-Hawley to Reciprocal Trade Agreements: Changing the Course of U.S. Trade Policy in the 1930s." In *The Defining Moment: The Great Depression and the American Economy in the Twentieth Century,* edited by Michael D. Bordo, Claudia Goldin, and Eugene N. White. (Chicago: University of Chicago Press, 1998): 325–352.

Irwin, Douglas A. "The Smoot-Hawley Tariff: A Quantitative Analysis." *The Review of Economics and Statistics* 80 (May 1998): 326–334.

Irwin, Douglas, and Randall S. Kroszner. "Log-Rolling and Economic Interests in the Passage of the Smoot-Hawley Tariff." *Carnegie—Rochester Conference Series on Public Policy* 45 (1966): 173–200.

Jones, Joseph M., Jr. *Tariff Retaliation: Repercussions of the Smoot-Hawley Bill.* Philadelphia: University of Pennsylvania Press, 1934.

Macmahon, Arthur W. "Second Session of the Seventy–First Congress, December 2, 1929, to July 3, 1930; Special Session of the Senate, July 7–21." *American Political Science Review* 24 (November 1930): 913–946.

Ossian, Lisa L. "Hawley-Smoot Tariff (Tariff of 1930)." In *Encyclopedia of Tariffs and Trade in U.S. History,* 3 vols. edited by Cynthia Clark Northrup and Elaine C. Prange Turney. Vol. 1, 183–184. (Westport, Conn.: Greenwood Press, 2003).

Pastor, Robert. *Congress and the Politics of U.S. Foreign Economic Policy, 1929–1976.* Berkeley: University of California Press, 1980.

Schattschneider, E. E. *Politics, Pressures and the Tariff: A Study of Free Private Enterprise in Pressure Politics, as Shown in the 1929–1930 Revision of the Tariff.* New York: Prentice-Hall, 1935.

Scroggs, William O. A "Revolt Against the Tariff," *North American Review* 230 (July 1930): 18–24.

Steiner, Gilbert Y. *The Congressional Conference Committee: Seventieth to Eightieth Congress.* Urbana: University of Illinois Press, 1951.

Taussig, F. W. *The Tariff History of the United States.* New York: G. P. Putnam's Sons, 1931.

U.S. President (Hoover). *Public Papers of the Presidents of the United States, Herbert Hoover, 1929.* Washington, D.C.: GPO, 1974.

Supreme Court Nomination of John J. Parker (1930)

Burris, William C. *Duty and the Law: Judge John J. Parker and the Constitution.* Bessemer, Ala.: Colonial Press, 1987.

Burris, William C. *The Senate Rejects a Judge: A Study of the John J. Parker Case.* Chapel Hill: University of North Carolina, Dept. of Political Science, 1962.

"Committee, 10 to 6, Rejects Parker." *New York Times* (April 22, 1930): 1, 23.

Fish, Peter Graham. "*Red Jacket* Revisited: The Case That Unraveled John J. Parker's Supreme Court Appointment." *Law and History Review* 5 (Spring 1987): 51–104.

Goings, Kenneth W. "The NAACP Comes of Age: The Defeat of Judge John J. Parker." Bloomington: Indiana University Press, 1990.

Hine, Darlene Clark. "The NAACP and the Supreme Court: Walter F. White and the Defeat of Judge John J. Parker, 1930." *Negro History Bulletin* 40 (September–October 1977): 753–757.

"John J. Parker: Senior Circuit Judge: Fourth Circuit." *American Bar Association Journal* 32 (December 1946): 856–859, 901–903.

Maltese, John Anthony. *The Selling of Supreme Court Nominees.* Baltimore: Johns Hopkins University Press, 1995.

U.S. Congress. Senate. Subcommittee of the Committee on Judiciary. *Confirmation of Hon. John J. Parker to be an Associate Justice of the Supreme Court of the United States.* Hearings, 71st Cong., 2nd sess., April 5, 1930. Washington, D.C.: GPO, 1930.

Watson, Richard L., Jr. "The Defeat of Judge Parker: A Study in Pressure Groups and Politics," *Mississippi Valley Historical Review* 50 (September 1953): 213–234.

"Yellow Dog" *Contract: Menace to American Liberties.* Washington, D.C.: American Federation of Labor, 1930.

Roosevelt's Court-Packing Plan (1937)

Alsop, Joseph, and Turner Cartledge. *The 168 Days.* Garden City, N.Y.: Doubleday, Doran, 1938.

Baker, Leonard. *Back to Back: The Duel Between FDR and the Supreme Court.* New York: Macmillan, 1967.

Cope, Alfred Haines and Fred Krinsky, eds. *Franklin D. Roosevelt and the Supreme Court.* Rev. ed. Lexington, Mass.: D.C. Heath, 1969.

Kernell, Samuel. *Going Public: New Strategies of Presidential Leadership.* 3rd ed. Washington, D.C.: Congressional Quarterly, 1997.

Leuchtenburg, William E. "The Origins of Franklin D. Roosevelt's 'Court–Packing' Plan." *The Supreme Court Review* (1966): 347–400.

Leuchtenburg, William E. "Franklin D. Roosevelt's Supreme Court 'Packing' Plan." In *Essays on the New Deal by Wilmon H. Droze, George Wolfskill, and William E. Leuchtenburg,* edited by Harold M. Hollingsworth and William F. Holmes. (Austin, Tex.: Published for the University of Texas at Arlington by the University of Texas Press, 1969): 69–115.

Maney, Patrick. "The Forgotten New Deal Congress." In *The American Congress: The Building of Democracy,* edited by Julian E. Zelizer. (Boston: Houghton Mifflin, 2004): 446–471.

McKenna, Marian C. *Franklin Roosevelt and the Great Constitutional War: The Court-Packing Crisis of 1937.* New York: Fordham University Press, 2002.

Rosenman, Samuel I., comp. *The Public Papers and Addresses of Franklin D. Roosevelt.* 13 vols. Vol. 6–7, 1937–1938. New York: Russell and Russell, 1938–1950.

"The Supreme Court Controversy." *The Congressional Digest* (March 1937): 66–77.

U.S. Congress. Senate. Committee on the Judiciary. *Reorganization of the Federal Judiciary.* 6 pts. Hearings on S. 1392, 75th Cong., 1st sess. Washington, D.C.: GPO, 1937.

U.S. Congress. Senate Committee on the Judiciary. *Reorganization of the Federal Judiciary.* S. Rept. 711, 75th Cong., 1st sess. Washington, D.C.: GPO, 1937.

Fair Labor Standards Act (1938)

Bernstein, Irving. *A Caring Society: The New Deal, the Worker, and the Great Depression.* Boston: Houghton Mifflin, 1985.

Douglas, Paul H., and Joseph Hackman. "The Fair Labor Standards Act of 1938 I." *Political Science Quarterly* 53 (December 1938): 491–515.

Forsythe, John S. "Legislative History of the Fair Labor Standards Act." *Law and Contemporary Problems* 6 (Summer 1939): 464–490.

Grossman, Jonathan. "Fair Labor Standards Act of 1938: Maximum Struggle for Minimum Wage." *Monthly Labor Review* 101 (June 1978): 22–30.

Patterson, James G. *Congressional Conservatism and the New Deal: The Growth of the Conservative Coalition in Congress, 1933–1939.* Lexington, Ky.: University of Kentucky Press, 1967.

Paulsen, George E. *A Living Wage for the Forgotten Man: The Quest for Fair Labor Standards 1933–1941.* Selinsgrove, Pa.: Susquehanna University Press, 1996.

Rosenman, Samuel I., comp. *The Public Papers and Addresses of Franklin D. Roosevelt.* 13 vols. New York: Russell and Russell, 1938–1950.

Samuel, Howard D. "Troubled Passage: The Labor Movement and the Fair Labor Standards Act." *Monthly Labor Review* 123 (December 2000): 32–37.

Whittaker, William G. *The Fair Labor Standards Act: Analysis of Economic Issues in the Debates of 1937–1938.* Washington, D.C.: Congressional Research Service, October 10, 1989.

Burke–Wadsworth Bill (Selective Training and Service Act of 1940)

Chambers, John Whiteclay, II. *Draftees or Volunteers: A Documentary History of the Debate Over Military Conscription in the United States, 1787–1973.* New York: Garland, 1975.

Clifford, J. Garry, and Samuel R. Spencer Jr. *The First Peacetime Draft.* Lawrence, Kans.: University Press of Kansas, 1986.

Flynn, George Q. *The Draft, 1940–1973.* Lawrence, Kans.: University Press of Kansas, 1993.

Gallup, George H. *The Gallup Poll: Public Opinion, 1935–1971.* 3 vols. New York: Random House, 1972.

O'Sullivan, John. *From Voluntarism to Conscription.* New York: Garland, 1982.

Rosenman, Samuel I., comp. *The Public Papers and Addresses of Franklin D. Roosevelt.* 13 vols. Vol. 9, 1940. New York: Russell and Russell, 1938–1950.

U.S. Congress. House. Committee on Military Affairs. *Compulsory Military Training and Service.* H. Rept. 10132. 76th Cong., 3rd sess. Washington, D.C.: GPO, 1940.

U.S. Congress. Senate. Committee on Military Affairs. *Compulsory Military Training and Service.* Hearings on S. 4164, 76th Cong., 3rd sess., July 3, 5, 10–12, 1940. Washington, D.C.: GPO, 1940.

U.S. Congress. Senate. Committee on Military Affairs. *Compulsory Military Training and Service.* S. Rept. 2002, 76th Cong., 3rd sess. Washington, D.C.: GPO, 1940.

Lend-Lease Act (1941)

Churchill, Winston S. *The Second World War.* 6 vols. Vol. 2, *Their Finest Hour.* Boston: Houghton Mifflin, 1948–1953.

Cole, Wayne S. *Roosevelt & the Isolationists.* Lincoln, Neb.: University of Nebraska Press, 1983.

Dobson, Alan P. *U.S. Wartime Aid to Britain, 1940–1946.* New York: St. Martin's Press, 1896.

Goodhart, Philip. *Fifty Ships That Saved the World: The Foundation of the Anglo-American Alliance.* London: Heinemann, 1965.

Kimball, Warren F. *The Most Unsordid Act: Lend-Lease, 1939–1941.* Baltimore: Johns Hopkins Press, 1969.

Langer, William L., and S. Everett Gleason. *The Challenge to Isolation, 1937–1940.* New York: Harper and Brothers, 1952.

Langer, William L., and S. Everett Gleason. *The Undeclared War, 1940–1941.* New York: Harper and Brothers, 1953.

Rosenman, Samuel I., comp. *The Public Papers and Addresses of Franklin D. Roosevelt.* 13 vols. Vols. 8–9, 1939–1940. New York, Russell and Russell, 1938–1950.

U.S. Congress. House. Committee on Military Affairs. *Selective Compulsory Military Training and Service.* Hearings on H.R. 10132, 76th Cong., 3rd sess., July 10, 11, 24–26, 30–31, August 2, 12–14, 1940. Washington, D.C.: GPO, 1940.

Atomic Energy Act of 1946

Hewlett, Richard G., and Oscar E. Anderson. *A History of the United States Atomic Energy Commission.* 2 vols. University Park: Pennsylvania State University Press, 1962.

Miller, Byron S. "A Law Is Passed—The Atomic Energy Act of 1946." *University of Chicago Law Review* 15 (Summer 1948): 799–821.

Polsby, Nelson W. *Political Innovation in America: The Politics of Policy Initiation.* New Haven, Conn.: Yale University Press, 1984.

Truman, Harry S. *Memoirs.* 2 vols. Garden City, N.Y.: Doubleday, 1955–56.

U.S. Congress. House. Committee on Military Affairs. *Atomic Energy.* Hearings on H.R. 4280, 79th Cong., 1st sess., October 9, 1945. Washington, D.C.: GPO, 1945.

"What Congress Is Doing to Solve the Problem of Atomic Energy Control." *Congressional Digest* 25 (May 1946): 131–148.

McCarthyism (1950–1954)

Byrd, Robert C. *The Senate 1789–1989: Classic Speeches, 1830–1993.* Washington, D.C.: GPO, 1994.

Congress and the Nation, 1945–1964. Washington, D.C.: Congressional Quarterly Service, 1965.

Elving, Ronald D. "McCarthy and the Climate of Fear." In *Congress and the Great Issues: 1945–1995,* edited by Ronald D. Elving. (Washington, D.C.: Congressional Quarterly, 1996): 27–44.

Griffith, Robert. *The Politics of Fear: Joseph McCarthy and the Senate.* 2nd ed. Amherst, Mass.: University of Massachusetts Press, 1987.

Merry, Robert W. "McCarthy's Self-Destruction." In *Congress and the Great Issues: 1945–1995,* edited by Ronald D. Elving. Washington, D.C.: Congressional Quarterly, 1996.

Oshinsky, David M. *A Conspiracy So Immense: The World of Joe McCarthy.* New York: Free Press, 1983.

Reeves, Thomas C. *The Life and Times of Joe McCarthy.* Lanham, Md.: Madison Books, 1997.

Ritchie, Donald A. "McCarthyism in Congress: Investigating Communism." In *The American Congress: The Building of Democracy,* edited by Julian E. Zelizer. (Boston: Houghton Mifflin, 2004): 515–528.

Smith, Margaret Chase. *Declaration of Conscience.* New York: Doubleday, 1972.

"Text of McCarthy Reply." *New York Times,* July 18, 1950, 16.

U.S. Congress. Senate. Committee on Foreign Relations. *State Department Employee Loyalty Investigation.* S. Rept. 2108, 81st Cong., 2nd sess. Washington, D.C.: GPO, 1950.

U.S. Congress. Senate. Committee on Governmental Affairs. *Executive Sessions of the Senate Permanent Subcommittee on Investigations of the Committee on Government Operations. Vol. 5. Eighty-Third Congress, Second Session, 1954, Made Public January 2003.* S. Prt. 107–84, 107th Cong., 2nd sess. Washington, D.C.: GPO, 2003.

U.S. Congress. Senate, Committee on Government Operations, Special Subcommittee on Investigations, *Special Senate Investigations on Charges and Counter-Charges Involving: Secretary of the Army Robert T. Stevens, John G. Adams, H. Struve Hensel, and Senator Joe McCarthy, Roy M. Cohn, and Francis P. Carr.* Hearings, 83rd Cong., 2nd sess., June 9, 1954. Washington, D.C.: GPO, 1954.

White, William S. "Red Charges by M'Carthy Ruled False." *New York Times,* July 18, 1950, 1, 17.

"Great Debate" of 1951

Carpenter, Ted Galen. "United States' NATO Policy at the Crossroads: The 'Great Debate' of 1950–51." *International History Review* 8 (August 1986): 389–415.

Congressional Quarterly Almanac, 1951. Washington, D.C.: Congressional Quarterly, 1952.

Exon, Karen Hunt. "'Fortress America': The U.S. Senate and the Great Debate of 1950–1951." Ph.D. diss., University of Kansas, 1990.

Fisher, Louis. "The Korean War: On What Legal Basis Did Truman Act." *American Journal of International Law* 89 (January 1995): 21–39.

Hoover, Herbert. "Our National Policies in This Crisis (December 20, 1950)." *Vital Speeches of the Day* 17 (January 1, 1951): 165–167.

Kaufman, Burton I. *The Korean War: Challenges in Crisis, Credibility, and Command.* 2nd ed. New York: McGraw-Hill, 1997.

Kennedy, Joseph P. "'Present Policy Is Politically and Morally Bankrupt' (December 12, 1950)." *Vital Speeches of the Day* 17 (January 1, 1951): 170–173.

Kepley, David R. *The Collapse of the Middle Way: Senate Republicans and the Bipartisan Foreign Policy, 1948–1952.* New York: Greenwood Press, 1988.

Kepley, David R. "The Senate and the Great Debate of 1951." *Prologue: Journal of the National Archives* 14 (Winter 1982): 213–226.

Turner, Robert F. "Truman, Korea, and the Constitution: Debunking the 'Imperial President' Myth." *Harvard Journal of Law and Public Policy* 19 (Winter 1996): 563–583.

U.S. Congress. Senate. Committee on Foreign Relations and Senate Committee on Armed Services. *Assignment of Ground Forces to Duty in the European Area. Hearings on S. Con. Res. 8, February 1, 1951.* Washington, D.C.: GPO, 1951.

U.S. President (Truman). *Public Papers of the Presidents of the United States, Harry S. Truman 1951* (Washington, D.C.: GPO, 1965).

Williams, Phil. *The Senate and U.S. Troops in Europe.* New York: St. Martin's Press, 1985.

Civil Rights Act of 1964

Brauer, Carl M. *John F. Kennedy and the Second Reconstruction.* New York: Columbia University Press, 1977.

Congressional Quarterly Almanac, 1964. Washington, D.C.: Congressional Quarterly Service, 1965.

Graham, Hugh Davis. *The Civil Rights Era: Origins and Development of National Policy, 1960–1972.* New York: Oxford University Press, 1990.

Loevy, Robert D. *To End All Segregation: The Politics of the Passage of the Civil Rights Act of 1964.* Lanham, Md.: University Press of America, 1990.

Mann, Robert. *The Walls of Jericho: Lyndon Johnson, Hubert Humphrey, Richard Russell, and the Struggle for Civil Rights.* New York: Harcourt Brace, 1996.

U.S. President (Kennedy). *Public Papers of the Presidents of the United States, John F. Kennedy, 1963* (Washington, D.C.: GPO, 1964).

Whalen, Charles, and Barbara Whalen. *The Longest Debate: A Legislative History of the 1964 Civil Rights Act.* Cabin John, Md.: Seven Locks Press, 1985.

Medicare and Medicaid (1965)

Berkowitz, Edward D. *America's Welfare State: From Roosevelt to Reagan.* Baltimore: Johns Hopkins University Press, 1991.

Campion, Frank D. *The AMA and U.S. Health Policy Since 1940.* Chicago: University of Chicago Press, 1984.

Congress and the Nation. Vol. II 1965–1968. Washington, D.C.: Congressional Quarterly Service, 1969.

Corning, Peter A. *The Evolution of Medicare: From Idea to Law.* Washington, D.C.: U.S. Social Security Administration, Office of Research and Statistics, 1969.

David, Sheri I. *With Dignity: The Search for Medicare and Medicaid.* Westport, Conn.: Greenwood Press, 1985.

Editorial. "Double Defeat." *New York Times,* October 3, 1964, 28.

Funigiello, Philip J. *Chronic Politics: Health Care Security from FDR to George W. Bush.* Lawrence, Kans.: University Press of Kansas, 2005.

Marmor, Theodore R. *The Politics of Medicare.* 2nd ed. New York: Aldine de Gruyter, 2000.

"The 'Medicare' Controversy in the Current Congress." *Congressional Digest* 44 (March 1965): 65–96.

U.S. President (Lyndon Johnson). *Public Papers of the Presidents: Lyndon B. Johnson, 1965.* 2 vols. Washington, D.C.: GPO, 1966.

Zelizer, Julian E. *Taxing America: Wilbur D. Mills, Congress, and the State, 1945–1975.* N.Y.: Cambridge University Press, 1998.

Voting Rights Act of 1965

Broder, David S. "Johnson's Charge Stirs G.O.P. Wrath." *New York Times,* July 13, 1965, 22.

Congressional Quarterly Almanac, 1965. Washington, D.C.: Congressional Quarterly Service, 1966.

Duscha, Julius. "LBJ Called Laggard on Rights Issue." *Washington Post,* July 13, 1965, A1.

Garrow, David J. *Protest at Selma: Martin Luther King, and the Voting Rights Act of 1965.* New Haven, Conn.: Yale University Press, 1978.

Kotz, Nick. *Judgment Days: Lyndon Baines Johnson, Martin Luther King Jr., and the Laws That Changed America.* Boston: Houghton Mifflin, 2005.

Lawson, Stephen F. *Black Ballots: Voting Rights in the South, 1944–1969.* New York: Columbia University Press, 1976.

South Carolina v. Katzenbach, Attorney General, 383 U.S. 324 (1966).

Tuck, Stephen. "Making the Voting Rights Act." In *The Voting Rights Act: Securing the Ballot,* edited by Richard M. Valelly. Washington, D.C.: CQ Press, 2006.

U.S. President (Lyndon Johnson). *Public Papers of the Presidents of the United States, Lyndon Johnson, 1965.* 2 vols. Washington, D.C.: GPO, 1966.

Washington, James Melvin, ed. *A Testament of Hope: The Essential Writings of Martin Luther King, Jr.* San Francisco: Harper and Row, 1986.

War Powers Resolution of 1973

Congressional Quarterly Almanac, 1973. Washington, D.C.: Congressional Quarterly, 1974.

Fisher, Louis. *Constitutional Conflicts Between Congress and the President.* 4th ed. Lawrence, Kans.: University Press of Kansas, 1997.

Fisher, Louis. *Presidential War Power.* 2nd ed. Lawrence, Kans.: University Press of Kansas, 2004.

Fisher, Louis. "War Power." In *The American Congress: The Building of Democracy,* edited by Julian E. Zelizer. (Boston: Houghton Mifflin, 2004): 687–701.

U.S. Congress. Conference Committees. *War Powers.* Conference report to accompany H.J. Res. 542, 93rd Cong., 1st sess., H. Rept. 93–547. Washington, D.C.: GPO, 1973.

U.S. Congress. House. Committee on Foreign Affairs. Subcommittee on National Security Policy and Scientific Developments. *War Powers.* Hearings, 93rd Cong., 1st sess., March 7, 8, 13, 14, 20, 1973. Washington, D.C.: GPO, 1973.

U.S. Congress. House Committee on Foreign Affairs. *War Powers Resolution of 1973.* Report to accompany H.J. Res. 542, 93rd Cong., 1st sess., H. Rept. 93–287. Washington, D.C.: GPO, 1973.

U.S. Congress. Senate. Committee on Foreign Relations. *War Powers Legislation, 1973.* Hearings on S. 440, 93rd Cong., 1st sess., April 11–12, 1973. Washington, D.C.: GPO, 1973.

U.S. Congress. Senate. Committee on Foreign Relations. *War Powers.* S. Rept. 220, 93rd Cong., 1st sess. Washington, D.C.: GPO, 1973.

U.S. President (Nixon). *Public Papers of the Presidents of the United States, Richard M. Nixon, 1973.* Washington, D.C.: GPO, 1975.

Impeachment of President Richard M. Nixon (1974)

Bernstein, Carl, and Bob Woodward. *All the Presidents Men.* New York: Simon and Schuster, 1974.

Emery, Fred. *Watergate: The Corruption of American Politics and the Fall of Richard Nixon.* New York: Times Books, 1994.

Kutler, Stanley I. *The Wars of Watergate: The Last Crisis of Richard Nixon.* New York: Knopf, 1990.

Nixon v. Sirica, 487 F. 2d 700 (D.C. Cir. 1973).

Schudson, Michael. *Watergate in American Memory: How We Remember, Forget, and Reconstruct the Past.* New York: Basic Books, 1992.

U.S. Congress. House. Committee on the Judiciary. *Debate on Articles of Impeachment.* Hearings, 93rd Cong., 2nd sess., July 24, 25, 26, 27, 29, and 30, 1974. Washington, D.C.: GPO, 1974.

U.S. Congress. House. Committee on the Judiciary. *Impeachment of Richard M. Nixon. President of the United States.* H. Rept. 93–1305, 93rd Cong., 2nd sess. Washington, D.C.: GPO, August 20, 1974.

U.S. Congress. Senate. Select Committee on Presidential Campaign Activities. *Presidential Campaign Activities of 1972, Senate Resolution 60: Watergate and Related Activities.* Hearings, 93rd Cong., 2nd sess., 26 vols. Washington, D.C.: GPO, 1973–74.

U.S. President (Nixon). *Public Papers of the Presidents of the United States, Richard M. Nixon, 1974* Washington, D.C.: GPO, 1975.

United States v. Nixon, 418 U.S. 683, 713 (1974).

Watergate: Chronology of a Crisis. Washington, D.C.: Congressional Quarterly, 1975.

Panama Canal Treaties (1978)

Carter, Jimmy. *Keeping Faith: Memoirs of a President.* New York: Bantam, 1982.

Childs, Marquis. "McIntyre's Stand Against the Radical Right." *Washington Post,* March 14, 1978, A17.

Congressional Quarterly Almanac, 1978. Washington, D.C.: Congressional Quarterly, 1979.

Duncan, Phil. "War of Words over the Canal." *Congressional Quarterly* 53 (September 16, 1995): 2775.

Farnsworth, David N., and James W. McKenney. *U.S.-Panama Relations, 1903–1978: A Study in Linkage Politics.* Boulder, Colo.: Westview Press, 1983.

Furlong, William L., and Margaret E. Scranton. *The Dynamics of Foreign Policymaking: The President, the Congress, and the Panama Canal Treaties.* Boulder, Colo.: Westview Press, 1984.

Hogan, Michael. *The Panama Canal in American Politics: Domestic Advocacy and the Evolution of Policy.* Carbondale, Ill.: Southern Illinois University Press, 1986.

Hollihan, Thomas Andrew. "The Public Controversy over the Panama Canal Treaties: A Fantasy Theme Analysis of Foreign Policy Dramas." Ph.D. diss., University of Nebraska-Lincoln, 1978.

Johnson, Robert David. *Congress and the Cold War.* New York: Cambridge University Press, 2006.

Jorden, William J. *Panama Odyssey.* Austin: University of Texas Press, 1984.

Kaiser, Robert K. "What Is (and Isn't) Said in Canal Debate." *Washington Post,* April 12, 1978, A27.

LaFeber, Walter. *Panama Canal: The Crisis in Historical Perspective.* New York: Oxford University Press, 1989.

Moffett, George D., III. *The Limits of Victory: The Ratification of the Panama Canal Treaties.* Ithaca, N.Y.: Cornell University Press, 1985.

Moss, Ambler H., Jr. "Review: The Panama Treaties: How an Era Ended." *Latin American Research Review* 21 (1986): 171–178.

Smith, Ted J., III, and J. Michael Hogan, "Public Opinion and the Panama Canal Treaties of 1977," *Public Opinion Quarterly* 51 (Spring 1987): 5–30.

U.S. Congress. Senate. Committee on Foreign Relations. *Senate Debate on the Panama Canal Treaties: A Compendium of Major Statements, Documents, Record Votes and Relevant Events.* Comm. print, 96th Cong., 1st sess. Washington, D.C.: GPO, 1979.

U.S. Congress. Senate Committee on the Judiciary. Subcommittee on Separation of Powers. *Panama Canal Treaties [United States Senate Debate], 1977–78,* 3 vols. Washington, D.C.: GPO, 1978–1979.

Omnibus Budget Reconciliation Act of 1981 and Economic Recovery Tax Act of 1981

Anderson, Harry, Rich Thomas, amd Pamela Lynn Abraham. "The U.S. Economy in Crisis." *Newsweek,* 97 (January 19, 1981): 30–34.

Arieff, Irwin B. "Budget Fight Shows O'Neill's Fragile Grasp." *Congressional Quarterly Weekly Report,* May 9, 1981, 786.

Congressional Quarterly Almanac 1981. Washington, D.C.: Congressional Quarterly, 1982.

Dewar, Helen. "Reagan's Budget Plan Wins Easily in House." *Washington Post,* May 8, 1981, A1, A3.

Fessler, Pamela. "Reagan Economic Plan Nears Enactment: Tax Cut Passed by Solid Margin in House, Senate." *Congressional Quarterly Weekly Report,* August 1, 1981, 1371, 1374–1376.

Gregg, Gail. "Senate Orders $36.9 Billion in Budget Cuts." *Congressional Quarterly Weekly Report,* April 4, 1981, 602–603.

Guide to Congress. 6th ed. 2 vols. Washington, D.C.: CQ Press, 2000.

Hartman, Robert W. "Congress and Budget-Making." *Political Science Quarterly* 97 (Fall 1982): 381–402.

Jacob, Charles E. "Reaganomics: The Revolution in American Political Economy." *Law and Contemporary Problems* 48 (Autumn 1985): 7–30.

Keith, Robert A. "Budget Reconciliation in 1981." *Public Budgeting and Finance* 1 (Winter 1981): 37–47.

Leloup, Lance T. "After the Blitz: Reagan and the U.S. Congressional Budget Process." *Legislative Studies Quarterly* 7 (August 1982): 321–339.

Schier, Steven E. *A Decade of Deficits: Congressional Thought and Fiscal Action.* Albany, N.Y.: State University of New York Press, 1992.

Shuman, Howard E. *Politics and the Budget: The Struggle Between the President and the Congress.* 3rd ed. Englewood Hills, N.J.: Prentice Hall, 1992.

Tate, Dale. "House Provides President a Victory on the 1982 Budget." *Congressional Quarterly Weekly Report,* May 9, 1981, 783–785.

Tate, Dale. "Reagan Economic Plan Nears Enactment: Reconciliation Spending Cut Bill Sent to Reagan." *Congressional Quarterly Weekly Report,* August 1, 1981, 1371, 1377.

Tate, Dale, with Andy Plattner. "House Ratifies Savings Plan in Stunning Reagan Victory." *Congressional Quarterly Weekly Report,* June 27, 1981, 1127–1129.

U.S. President (Reagan). *Public Papers of the President, Ronald Reagan, 1981.* Washington, D.C.: GPO, 1982.

White, Joseph, and Aaron Wildavsky. *The Deficit and the Public Interest: The Search for Responsible Budgeting in the 1980s.* Berkeley: University of California Press, 1989.

Witte, John F. *The Politics and Development of the Federal Income Tax.* Madison, Wisc.: University of Wisconsin Press, 1985.

Supreme Court Nomination of Robert H. Bork (1987)

Abraham, Henry J. *Justices, Presidents, and Senators: A History of the U.S. Supreme Court Appointments from Washington to Clinton.* Rev. ed. Lanham, Md.: Rowman and Littlefield, 1999.

Bork, Robert H. *The Tempting of America: The Political Seduction of the Law.* New York: Free Press, 1990.

Bronner, Ethan. *Battle for Justice: How the Bork Nomination Shook America.* New York: W. W. Norton, 1989.

Cohodas, Nadine. "Bork's Grade Uncertain After Four–Day Seminar." *Congressional Quarterly Weekly Report,* September 19, 1987, 2223–2227.

Cohodas, Nadine. "Senate Debates, Then Dispatches Bork, 42–58." *Congressional Quarterly Weekly Report,* October 24, 1987, 2600–2603.

Greenhouse, Linda. "Bork's Nomination Is Rejected, 58–42; Reagan 'Saddened.'" *New York Times,* October 24, 1987, 1, 10.

Pertschuk, Michael, and Wendy Schaetzel. *The People Rising: The Campaign Against the Bork Nomination.* New York: Thunder's Mouth Press, 1989.

U.S. Congress. Senate. Committee on the Judiciary. *Nomination of Robert H. Bork to Be Associate Justice of the Supreme Court of the United States.* Exec. Rept. 7, 100th Cong., 1st sess. Washington, D.C.: GPO, 1987.

U.S. Congress. Senate. Committee on the Judiciary. *Nomination of Robert H. Bork to Be Associate Justice of the Supreme Court of the United States.* Hearings, 100th Cong., 1st sess., 5 parts, September 15–19, 21–23, 25, 28–30, 1987. Washington, D.C.: GPO, 1989.

Vieira, Norman, and Leonard Gross. *Supreme Court Appointments: Judge Bork and the Politicization of Senate Confirmations.* Carbondale, Ill.: Southern Illinois University Press, 1998.

North American Free Trade Agreement (1933)

Baldwin, Robert E., and Christopher S. Magee. *Congressional Trade Votes: From NAFTA Approval to Fast-Track Defeat.* Washington, D.C.: Institute for International Economics, 2000.

Cameron, Maxwell A., and Brian W. Tomlin. *The Making of NAFTA: How the Deal Was Done.* Ithaca, N.Y.: Cornell University Press, 2000.

Cloud, David S. "Decisive Vote Brings Down Trade Walls with Mexico." *Congressional Quarterly Weekly Report,* November 20, 1993, 3174–3185.

Cohen, Stephen D., Robert A. Blecker, and Peter D. Whitney. *Fundamentals of U.S. Foreign Trade Policy: Economics, Politics, Laws, and Issues,* 2nd ed. Boulder, Colo.: Westview Press, 2003.

Destler, I. M. *American Trade Politics.* 4th ed. Washington, D.C.: Institute for International Economics, 2005.

Dewhirst, Robert E. *Rites of Passage: Congress Makes Laws.* Upper Saddle River, N.J.: Prentice Hall, 1997.

Duncan, Phil. "Perot Gores His Own Ox in Debate." *Congressional Quarterly Weekly Report,* November 13, 1993, 3105.

Gai, Zheya. *The Politics of NAFTA: The Decision-Making of the Undecided Members in the U.S. House of Representatives.* Ph.D. diss., University of Pittsburgh, 1997.

Haven, Don R. *NAFTA—How the Day Was Won.* Washington, D.C.: Industrial College of the Armed Forces, National Defense University, Executive Research Project S14, 1994.

Healey, Jon, and Thomas H. Moore, "Clinton Forms New Coalition to Win NAFTA's Approval." *Congressional Quarterly Weekly Report,* November 20, 1993, 3181–3183.

Kahane, Leo H. "Congressional Voting Patterns on NAFTA: An Empirical Analysis." *American Journal of Economics and Sociology* 55 (October 1966): 395–409.

Kaplan, Edwards S. *American Trade Policy, 1923–1995.* Westport, Conn.: Greenwood Press, 1995.

Mayer, Frederick W. *Interpreting NAFTA: The Science and Art of Political Analysis.* New York: Columbia University Press, 1998.

Safire, William. "Gore Flattens Perot." *New York Times,* November 11, 1993, A27.

U.S. Presidents (Clinton). *Public Papers of the Presidents: William J. Clinton, 1993.* 2 vols. Washington, D.C.: GPO, 1994.

Uslaner, Eric M. "Let the Chits Fall Where They May? Executive and Constituency Influences on Congressional Voting on NAFTA." *Legislative Studies Quarterly* 23 (August 1998): 347–371.

Line-Item Veto (1996)

Clinton v. City of New York, 524 U.S. 417 (1998).

Congressional Quarterly Almanac, 1996. Washington, D.C.: Congressional Quarterly, 1997.

Farrier, Jasmine. *Passing the Buck: Congress, the Budget, and Deficits.* Lexington, Ky.: University Press of Kentucky, 2004.

Fisher, Louis. *Constitutional Conflicts Between Congress and the President.* 4th ed. Lawrence, Kans.: University Press of Kansas, 1997.

Fisher, Louis, and Neal Devins. "How Successfully Can the States' Item Veto Be Transferred to the President?" *Georgetown Law Journal* 75 (October 1986): 159–197.

Guide to Congress. 5th ed. 2 vols. Washington, D.C.: CQ Press, 2000.

Moe, Ronald C. *Prospects for the Item Veto at the Federal Level: Lessons from the States.* Washington, D.C.: National Academy of Public Administration, 1988.

Nelson, Michael, ed. *Guide to the Presidency.* 2nd ed., 2 vols. Washington, D.C.: CQ Press, 1996.

Spitzer, Robert J. *The Presidential Veto: Touchstone of the American Presidency.* Albany, N.Y.: State University of New York Press, 1988.

Taylor, Andrew. "Congress Hands President a Budgetary Scalpel." *Congressional Quarterly* 54 (March 30, 1996): 864–867.

U.S. Congress. Committee of Conference. *Line Item Veto Act.* H. Rept. 104–491 104th Cong., 2nd sess. Washington, D.C.: GPO, 1996.

U.S. Congress. House. Committee on the Budget. *The Line-Item Veto: An Appraisal.* Comm. Print, 98th Cong., 2nd sess. Washington, D.C.: GPO, 1984.

U.S. Congress. House. Committee on Rules. *Item Veto: State Experience and Its Application to the Federal Situation.* Comm. Print., 99th Cong., 2nd sess. Washington, D.C.: GPO, 1986.

Wilkinson, Vernon L. "Federal Legislation: The Item Veto in the American Constitutional System." *Georgetown Law Journal* 25 (November 1936): 106–133.

Iraq War Resolution (2002)

Athaus, Scott L., and Devon M. Largio. "When Osama Became Saddam: Origins and Consequences of the Change in America's Public Enemy #1." *PS: Political Science and Politics* 37 (October 2004): 795–799.

Byrd, Robert C. *Losing America: Confronting a Reckless and Arrogant Presidency.* New York: W. W. Norton, 2004.

Dalrymple, Mary. "Byrd's Beloved Chamber Deaf to His Pleas for Delayed Vote." *CQ Weekly,* October 12, 2002, 2674.

Department of Defense statistics on soldiers killed and wounded in Iraq. http://siadapp.dmdc.osd.mil/personnel/CASUALTY/castop.htm.

Firestone, David. "The Nays Won't Have It; The Ayes Talk Anyway." *New York Times,* October 9, 2002, A14.

Fisher, Louis. "Deciding on War Against Iraq: Institutional Failures." *Political Science Quarterly* 118 (Fall 2003): 389–410.

Fisher, Louis. "Legislative-Executive Relations and U.S. Policy Toward Iraq." In *Presidential Policies and the Road to the Second Iraq War: From Forty One to Forty Three,* edited by John Davis. (Aldershot, England: Ashgate, 2006): 62–91.

Fisher, Louis. "The Way We Go to War: The Iraq War Resolution." In *Considering the Bush Presidency,* edited by Gary L. Gregg II and Mark J. Rozell. (New York: Oxford University Press, 2004): 107–124.

Howell, William G., and Jon C. Pevehouse. *While Dangers Gather: Congressional Checks on Presidential War Powers.* Princeton, N.J.: Princeton University Press, 2007.

Huisken, Ron. *The Road to War in Iraq.* Canberra, Australia: Strategic and Defense Studies Center, Australian National University, 2003.

Largio, Devon M. "Uncovering the Rationales for War on Iraq: The Words of the Bush Administration, Congress, and the Media from September 12, 2001 to October 11, 2002." BA thesis, Political Science Department, College of Liberal Arts, University of Illinois, Urbana-Champaign, 2004.

Martinez, Gebe. "Concerns Linger for Lawmakers Following Difficult Vote for War." *CQ Weekly,* October 12, 2002, 2671–2673, 2675, 2677–2678.

Ohaegbulam, F. Ugboaja. *A Culture of Deference: Congress, the President, and the Course of the U.S.-Led Invasion and Occupation of Iraq.* New York: Peter Lang, 2007.

Pomper, Miles A. "Senate Democrats in Disarray After Gephardt's Deal on Iraq," *CQ Weekly,* October 5, 2002, 2606–2610.

Stiglitz, Joseph E., and Linda J. Bilmes. *The Three Trillion Dollar War: The True Cost of the Iraq Conflict.* New York: W. W. Norton, 2008.

U.S. President (George W. Bush). *Public Papers of the Presidents of the United States: George W. Bush, 2001.* 2 vols. Washington, D.C.: GPO, 2003.

U.S. President (George W. Bush). *Public Papers of the Presidents of the United States: George W. Bush, 2002.* 2 vols. Washington, D.C.: GPO, 2005.

Index